J
S
G

Date Due

MAY 27 1992	MAR 1 9 1995		
	MAR 19 1995		
OCT 3 0 1992	4-8-95		
	JUL 1 0 1995		
NOV 2 0 1992			
	JUL 2 7 2000		
NOV 1 6 1993	MAY 1 6 2006		
APR 2 0 1994			
May 12 1994			
OCT 1 8 1994			

BRODART, INC.   Cat. No. 23 233   Printed in U.S.A.

GOVERNING AMERICA

an introduction

GOVERNING

Under the General Editorship of
James David Barber
Duke University

AMERICA

an introduction

ROBERT SHERRILL

with

James David Barber
Duke University

Benjamin I. Page
University of Wisconsin, Madison

Virginia W. Joyner

HARCOURT BRACE JOVANOVICH, INC.
New York / San Diego / Chicago / San Francisco / Atlanta

GOVERNING AMERICA an introduction

ROBERT SHERRILL

with James David Barber   Benjamin I. Page   Virginia W. Joyner

Acknowledgments and Copyrights appear on pages 617–19, which constitute a continuation of the copyright page.

Cover photo: Dennis Brack, Black Star (Joint session of Congress, April 1975)

ISBN: 0-15-529629-9

Library of Congress Catalog Card Number: 77-88905

Printed in the United States of America

PREFACE

When Jimmy Carter made his first cross-country trip as President of the United States, he stopped off in Detroit for a round-table discussion of urban policy. A black panelist named Courtney Matthews said, "My question to you is, what is a twenty-year-old man to do when he wants to work and he wants to help his family and he wants to get a job in a city where there are no jobs for minority youth at all?"

Carter replied, "That is a good, tough question. I can't tell you I have the answer. . . . It's going to be a long, tough proposition."

Politicians may specialize in non-answers like that. But the author and consultants who turned out *Governing America* believe that good, tough political questions—especially when voiced by young people who may be taking the measure of their government for the first time—deserve a fuller, more sensitive, and essentially more respectful response. Politics may be extremely complicated at times, but we are inclined to think that young adults with questions about the hurdles in their future are perfectly capable of understanding explanations that deal with such things as budget priorities, the push and pull of interest groups, city-federal relations, congressional bottlenecks, and long-standing biases that are only now being thrashed out with much success in the courts. We have assumed that every reader of this book has a vital interest in the political processes that affect his or her future and is willing to engage seriously in a long-term discussion of what really goes on in government.

Governing, as every day's newspaper attests, is more pothole than road: a new President takes office determined immediately to cut the defense budget, reduce arms sales abroad, reform the tax system, shape up the welfare system, and establish the first national energy program—and he discovers that it is difficult to make even the one relatively minor and mostly symbolic change, reducing the size of the White House staff. The Environmental Protection Agency finds that one of the worst polluters is the federal government itself. Thirty-one years after Congress passed a law making full employment the official policy of the government, it passes *another* law making full employment the official policy of the government, and Washington politicians see no irony in the repetition. The drive for equality floods back upon itself in a panicky confrontation with reverse discrimination.

Complications everywhere. But nothing in government or politics is so complicated, we feel, that it can escape common-sense analysis and practical, even earthy, explanation. We have tried to offer these analyses and explanations in ways that anyone, novice or veteran, will enjoy and remember with pleasure.

Pleasure is, we like to think, one of the certain results of this book. *Governing America* is unabashedly aimed at helping to produce a generation of political enthusiasts—to turn students into savvy, sinewy-minded political participants. To this end, we have given careful attention to the history of American government and to its institutions, but we never permit the reader to get far away from contemporary and specific political occurrences and personalities. The substantive issues and scholarly references are covered, and covered thoroughly, but not at the sacrifice of vital, timely illustrations. Politics is more than a set of rules and institutions. It is people and politicians who manipulate, sacrifice, cajole, decide, interpret, and sometimes lie. We have attempted to convey a feeling for the realities of government—the sounds and smells and textures of its operation, from the lonely discourse of the filibusterer, to the bucket-shop atmosphere of the campaign finance office, to the judge wrapped in contemplation of a convict's handwritten appeal.

Governing America is not a radical text. It venerates the foundations of American government. Still, this book will doubtless provoke considerable disagreement and even occasional outrage among both liberals and conservatives (and sometimes both at once). Any political discussion that failed to arouse those sentiments from time to time would hardly be worth participating in. It will also leave the reader, we hope, with (1) at least a gruff affection for those adventurous souls who have tried, and are still trying, to govern America, (2) a more intelligent tolerance for the demands of the special interests and the electorate, and (3) a restless eagerness to start taking part in the political system.

Several times in the above paragraphs I have used the word *we.* That is not an editorial *we,* but a very literal *we.* I wrote *Governing America,* but I was also the amanuensis to a group of scholars. In some respects, writing this book was like running for political office for the first time. I was, so to speak, the candidate—mine is the name in the largest type. But like most political candidates—at least like those not running in a safe district, and the textbook market hardly equates with a safe district—I was to a great extent dependent on my advisers, the consultants whose advice I usually took to heart and heeded (at times happily). For a dozen years I had been covering politics in Washington for newspapers and magazines and trade-book publishers (and earlier I had covered state politics in Texas and Florida), but now I was seeking to please a different electorate, and I needed expert guidance. I received it abundantly from James David Barber, Benjamin I. Page, and Virginia W. Joyner, and from a number of reviewers who commented on the manuscript in early stages. This book has profited from the helpful criticism of: W. Lance Bennett, University of Washington; Jonathan Casper, Stanford University; David J. Danelski, Cornell University; Irwin Gertzog, Allegheny College; Alexander George, Stanford University; Louis W. Koenig, New York University; Robert Lekachman, Lehman College of the City University of New York; Robert Lineberry, Northwestern University; Grant McConnell, University of California, Santa Cruz; Alpheus Mason, Princeton University; Gary Orfield, University of Illinois, Urbana; Judith Parris, Congressional Research Service, Library of Congress; Jeffrey Pressman, late of the Massachusetts Institute of Technology; Thomas Scism, Eastern Illinois University; David Truman, Mount Holyoke College.

Robert Sherrill

CONTENTS

2 THE CONSTITUTION　28

3 CIVIL LIBERTIES　58

4 CIVIL RIGHTS 90

5 INTEREST GROUPS 122

6 PUBLIC OPINION AND POLITICAL INFORMATION   160

9 THE PRESIDENCY   274

10 CONGRESS   322

11 THE COURTS   374

12 BUREAUCRACY AND THE BUREAUCRATS   410

13 FEDERALISM AND STATE AND LOCAL GOVERNMENT 454

GOVERNING AMERICA

an introduction

To make a government requires no great prudence.
Settle the seat of power, teach obedience, and the work is done.
To give freedom is still more easy. It is not necessary to guide;
it only requires to let go the rein. But to form a free government,
that is, to temper together these opposite elements of liberty
and restraint in one consistent work, requires much thought,
deep reflection, a sagacious, powerful, and combining mind.

Edmund Burke

1
THE ART OF GOVERNING

Americans do not really like government. Our history indicates that we feel a natural antipathy toward it. We go through life being assured by teachers and politicians and newspaper editors that "we, the people" run things. But instinctively we know that that is not the whole truth. Our lives are shaped by "government," a foreign and often invisible abstraction surrounded by a sea of politics.

Polls regularly show that many of us do not know the names of our legislators. They operate apart from our thoughts, and, when they pass laws that intrude on our lives, we consider them to be just that—intruders. When they conscript us for military service in wars against nations that we can hardly find on the map, we wonder what gave our leaders the idea we wanted them to be angry on our behalf. When they multiply our taxes, we wonder where the money is going, and we are rarely given a satisfactory explana-

tion. We also wonder why taxes almost always go up, almost never down.

If we itemize our lives to see if we can find the blessings of government, we will find that there are some blessings—of a sort: a postal service that seems always on the verge of breakdown; highway commissions whose roads become more clogged the more they are widened and lengthened and propagated; police who seem unable to stymie crime, much less to reduce it; a court system that is as inconsistent as it is self-indulgently slow; schools that go on turning us out according to an increasingly faded and tattered pattern. These parts of government do not work very well, but we appreciate them because they at least seem to be trying to help us; most parts of government never contribute anything to our lives, so far as we are aware.

We would like our government to think of us as individuals. But apparently it does not. If it thinks of us at all, it is as numbers. If you have a job, the government thinks of you as a Social Security number. If you earn enough to pay taxes, it thinks of you as a Social Security number *and* an Internal Revenue Service account number. If you travel abroad, you will be thought of as a passport number.

If you complain to the bureaucracy, you will likely receive a form-letter reply. If you appeal to your elected servants, you will probably receive a form letter signed by a machine. If you write to the President and express yourself in strong enough terms about some highly controversial subject, your letter may be sent to the Federal Bureau of Investigation, and the federal police may start a file on you, complete with the inevitable number on the jacket.

That is a bleak and pessimistic picture of a citizen's relationship, or potential relationship, to his or her government. But in its hostility it is certainly an accurate portrayal of how most people in the United States *feel* about their rulers. Shortly before President Jimmy Carter took office, pollster Louis Harris surveyed a cross-sample of the American people to see what national mood the new administration was facing. He found that 58 percent felt disenchanted with or alienated from the people running the government. By a 55- to 38-percent majority, they felt that "people running the country don't really care what happens to you." By a 78- to 18-percent majority, they believed that "the rich get richer and the poor get poorer." By a 57- to 37-percent majority, they felt that "what you think doesn't count much anymore." By a 55- to 38-percent majority, they felt that "most people with power try to take advantage of you." By a 63- to 28-percent majority, they felt that "the people in Washington, D.C., are out of touch with the rest of the country."[1]

That is the voice of the majority, and the feeling it expresses was not new in 1977. (See Table 6-2.) If one gives it respectful weight, one will have to conclude that United States democracy is not working at peak performance. Perhaps our government does work better than any other existing government and much better today than it did a hundred years ago, but

[1]Harris poll, released January 3, 1977.

one must still wonder why it cannot do even better.

THE PROBLEMS ARE CLEAR

Since most people in this nation fear the consequences of pollution, poverty, and crime and since the means for getting rid of most pollution and poverty and much crime are well within reach, why do these evils still engulf us?

Since most Americans would prefer to be ruled by honest politicians and since they have the electoral machinery to get rid of the bad and elevate the good, how do so many politicians get by with operating in a shady, or even crooked, fashion?

Since most Americans believe that government concerns itself with the needs of Big Business more than with the needs of the ordinary person, while ordinary people make up the great bulk of the electorate, why haven't they forced the government to change its perspective?

Since hundreds of thousands of Americans died in wars against fascist countries in the recent past, why does the public allow the government today to support, through trade, aid, and agreements, so many authoritarian regimes around the world?

Federal lands—those presumably owned by the people—contain most of the energy resources of the United States, and yet these resources have passed into the hands of corporations that waste them, exploit them carelessly, and sell them back to the people at grossly inflated prices. Why have the people been unable to prevent this?

Corporations engage in many illegal activities—price fixing, consumer deception, forbidden political contributions, bribery, distribution of tainted foods and dangerous drugs, violations of safety and environmental laws— but they are rarely punished. Such punishment as they do receive is so trivial, considering the enormity of their crime and their ability to absorb the punishment, that one wonders why laws are written. Is this the justice of democracy?

Each year the federal government spends about $25 million to encourage the production of tobacco and to promote its sale and use; and yet

THE LEFT HAND AND THE RIGHT HAND

Herblock
© 1977 *The Washington Post*

the Secretary of Health, Education and Welfare estimates that the health costs to the federal government resulting from smoking total about $11.5 billion. Is that a rational use of tax dollars—spending millions to guarantee the loss of billions?[2]

The defense budget sometimes seems to have no relationship to real threat or to humane priorities. As of 1976, the United States had at least 25,000 nuclear warheads in stock, and the power of the weakest of these was three times the power of the atomic bomb that leveled Hiroshima; no more than 10 or 20 would be needed to reduce the Soviet Union to its preindustrial economy. And yet more and more appropria-

tions for nuclear weapons are pumped into the budget, in defiance of the precept handed down by former General of the Army and President Dwight D. Eisenhower:

> Every gun that is made, every warship launched, every rocket fired, signifies, in the final sense, a theft from those who hunger and are not fed, those who are cold and are not clothed. This world in arms is not spending money alone. It is spending the sweat of its laborers, the genius of its scientists, the hopes of its children.[3]

While surveys show that 70 percent of black preschool children in the South and 30 percent of white preschool children in the North are

---

[2]*Congressional Record*, S13726, August 6, 1976.

[3]*Defense Monitor* V, no. 9 (December 1976).

anemic, the Pentagon spends well over $100 billion a year and claims that it cannot cut a penny.[4] Are arms the only protection we need?

The list of questions goes on and on. Hardly a day passes that newspapers do not reveal another example of questionable government action. And usually, to the eye of common sense, the troubles seem to stem from ignoring an obvious solution. Surely everyone can agree on what constitutes pollution, poverty, repression, crime, greed, hunger, conflict of interest, and so forth. And if everyone agrees on the definition of the problems, why is it so difficult to agree on the method for solving them? We are an intelligent nation, a very rich nation, a kindly nation. Why the seeming paralysis, the lack of focus? What gets in our way?

THE SEARCH
FOR IMPERFECT SOLUTIONS

There are many answers to these questions. Some of them can be traced to the divisions of authority in government and to a woeful lack of communication between the electorate and its rulers (topics touched on in other parts of this book). The principal obstacles to solving our problems are these: (1) the power exerted by special interests; (2) technical difficulties inherent in some problems; (3) the structural features of our social and economic system that sacrifice public good for private advantage; and (4) unreconciled interests and opinions that impede the formation of consensus and compromise, which are essential ingredients in a democracy.

These are the boulders in the road. Here and in the remainder of this book we shall attempt to see how the nation gets around them and moves more or less intact through crises large and small, within and without. We shall discuss the basic map, the Constitution (Chapter 2), with which we try to guide ourselves through the increasingly complex maze of a growing nation. We shall discuss what are probably the greatest advances made under the Constitution to date (usually after unconscionable delays)—in civil

liberties (Chapter 3) and civil rights (Chapter 4). We shall discuss the competition and cooperation between the major institutions of government growing out of the Constitution and its supplementary statutes: the Presidency (Chapter 9), the Congress (Chapter 10), the courts (Chapter 11), and the bureaucracy (Chapter 12). We shall discuss those two rough forces that wear the barnacles off the ship of state: public opinion and the media (Chapter 6). We shall discuss the economics of politics and of society (Chapter 15), which is the subject least understood and yet closest to the heart of all Americans, for polls consistently show that what the electorate is primarily interested in getting from government is security and a decent style of life. We shall discuss political parties and the elective process (Chapters 7 and 8), government at state and local levels (Chapter 13), and the relationships of the United States with other nations (Chapter 14). Finally, we shall turn to the topic of national planning (Chapter 16), to consider the possible benefits of thinking ahead—and the perils of not doing so.

Throughout the book, from first to last, we shall keep coming back to the basic ingredient of politics: pressure. First of all, pressure from the people, individually and in groups (Chapter 5). From corporations, labor organizations, religious organizations, environmental protection organizations, militaristic organizations, right- and left-wing organizations. And from the most effective genre: big spending organizations.

The problems of politics arise, quite simply, when people disagree, which is all the time, and when their differences are brought before less-than-godlike politicians and judges and bureaucrats to be most imperfectly reconciled. In short, in talking about politics in the chapters to follow we will be proving what Lord John Morley once said of life: it is one continuous choice between second best. That is politics in a nutshell. It is less than perfect because it is run by human beings who happen to be politicians. One student of the fray has correctly concluded, ''politics is politicians: there is no way to understand it without understanding them.''[5] That is one of the pri-

---

[4]*Ten State Nutrition Survey* (Atlanta: Southern Regional Council, 1974).

[5]James David Barber, ''Strategies for Understanding Politicians,'' *American Journal of Political Science,* Spring 1974, pp. 443–67.

mary goals of this book: to understand politicians. Learning about systems, rules, and precedents is important, but not nearly so important as getting a feel for the way fallible human beings interrelate, how they react to each other in political conflict, how they sometimes manage to control the worst in themselves and exploit the best, how the human relationship sometimes breaks down, and how it is sometimes patched up again.

Consensus and Compromise

One of the principal ways of solving our problems in spite of the obstacles is a process that goes to the very root of democracy: consensus and compromise. The former is unobtainable without the latter.

Consensus is the step beyond majority rule; it is what makes majority rule work. While majority rule is simply a head count, consensus is the general feeling about whether laws passed by the majority are worth obeying.

> Consensus as a process of constitutional morality does not insist that everyone unanimously agree at once to every jot and tittle of a particular decision being proposed. Differences of opinion may persist. But it seeks a condition where the differences can be worked out, thought out, compromised out—all in order to broaden the base of consent and understanding. Only so can the majority decision be emancipated from the dangers inherent in the principle that 50 percent plus a fraction of one percent of the representatives voting constitute a "legalizing" rulemaking majority. Only so can there be formed a much larger majority of many concurrent interests, all joined in support of the decision reached.[6]

In a utopia, there is no need for compromise. Utopias are dreamed up on the assumption that all social problems can be overcome by one perfect solution.[7] In democracies, citizens are never so lucky as to share the vision of one perfect solution. One citizen's obvious answer to an obvious problem is often not the same obvious answer that has occurred to his or her neighbor—or at least the two will often part company when they get down to particulars.

It is obvious that the remedy for poverty is money. But how is the money to be placed in the hands of those who need it? By a guaranteed income? By welfare? By government-concocted jobs—even jobs for mothers whose small children would be placed in federally subsidized nurseries?

It is obvious that crime can be cut sharply by imprisoning felons. But where do you put them? The prisons are already overflowing; inmates are forced to sleep on floors, in shower rooms, and on ledges above toilets, and three people in cells built for one is not uncommon.[8] Should the crowded prisons be further crowded? Should the crowding be eased by spending the necessary billions of dollars? How much are you willing to be taxed to build human warehouses?

There are no obvious answers to the really tough political questions. They can be coped with only through compromise—balancing one evil against another, one good against another, one expense against another.

Democracy and Imperfection

Compromise has a dirty reputation, which is understandable, because it signifies something *calculatingly* less than either side considers acceptable. But in a democracy there is no way to avoid it.

People form armies and fight under the seamless banner of absolutes; but they can live together peacefully only when they are willing to hoist a patched flag of compromises. When Americans were working themselves into a lather to fight King George III and the redcoats, they spoke of taking up arms in obedience to God's law. They made the whole crisis sound like a divinely ordained either/or situation. There was no middle ground. Their cause was right and blessed, that of King George was cursed and wrong.

Once it was independent, the new nation had to go about its business with less cocksureness—or, rather, it had to establish a pit in which

---

[6]Sidney Hyman, *The Politics of Consensus* (New York: Random House, 1968), p. 41.

[7]For more on this, see Robert E. Lane, *Political Ideology: Why the American Common Man Believes What He Does* (New York: Free Press, 1962).

[8]*Corrections Magazine*, April 19, 1976.

opposing sure cocks could settle their differences with less than total victory to either. E. E. Schattschneider has written:

> Democracy is a system for the resolution of conflict, not for vengeance. Simple black-white notions of right and wrong do not fit into democratic politics. Political controversies result from the fact that the issues are complex, and men may properly have differences of opinion about them. The most terrible of all over-simplifications is the notion that politics is a contest between good people and bad people. Democracy is based on a profound insight into human nature, the realization that all men are sinful, all are imperfect, all are prejudiced, and none knows the whole truth. That is why we need liberty and why we have an obligation to hear all men. . . . Democracy is a political system for people who are not too sure that they are right.[9]

That is an accurate description of the *outcome* of democracy, but it is not quite an accurate description of its ingredients. Indeed, one of the privileges of living in a democracy—amply exercised by most of us—is that we take sides, and each side is positive that it has the right answer and the other not only is in error, but probably has been bought off by the "interests." Democracy in *process* is full of participants brimming over with passionate convictions and quirky intolerance. Democracy in *outcome* is something else again—much more rational, much more restrained, and also much less exciting and less satisfying to the adversaries, for they have all had to give up more than they wanted to.

In short, there is an element of surrender in democracy that sticks in the craw of Americans, who as a nation detest surrender.[10] In it there is an element of the biblical thought, "he who would gain his life must lose it." T. V. Smith, political philosopher and briefly a Congressman, put it this way:

> Compromise is the process whereby each party to a conflict gives up something dear, but not invaluable, in order to get something which is truly invaluable. In the very nature of the case compromise is a sacrifice exacted particularly of "good" men, a sacrifice which their very goodness requires but renders odious. . . . Equally honest men, with causes equally sincere, meet in such manner that neither of them can permit the other to have its way without loss of face and impairment of self-respect. That's politics, as met and practiced in the context of legislature or Congress.
>
> Such a case will but recall to our democratic minds a double fact: the fact, first, that there is no other way of settling such issues as justly as by compromise; the fact, second, that such settlement requires the presence of a third party. Such settlement is politics; such a third party is the politician.[11]

So there we have it, like it or not: in a nation of 210 million persons of varied interests, there are usually sharp disagreements over what the obvious answers are to the obvious problems. The politician is, as Smith says, the lightning rod that draws the various bolts of opinion safely into the ground. It is not an inspiring process, and we are lucky when the legislation that results from it rises somewhat higher than the lowest common denominator of individual consciences. But before being too harshly critical of the politicians for the often disappointing results, put yourself in their shoes. It can be done very easily with the following sample situations (one of which will involve judges, who are, though they don't like to be portrayed as such, politicians, too.) These examples will show that few of the problems facing the nation today are simple and that to deal with them one must bridge great chasms between varying demands, varying opinions, and varying interests.

PROBLEM 1: GUNS

The United States is the most violent civilized nation in the world, a fact and a reputation traced largely to its love affair with guns. Nobody

---

[9]E. E. Schattschneider, *Two Hundred Million Americans in Search of Government* (New York: Holt, Rinehart & Winston, 1969), p. 52.

[10]Lincoln best summed up the notion of government as an endless series of surrenders, pointing out that on every question one side or the other must yield ". . . or the government must cease. There is no other alternative; for continuing the government is acquiescence on one side or the other."

[11]T. V. Smith, *The Ethics of Compromise and the Art of Containment* (Boston: Beacon Press, Starr King Press, 1956), pp. 42–62.

knows how many guns are owned by Americans. Estimates range from 90 million to 200 million and up—the latter figure means one gun per man, woman, and child in the country.[12]

Background

Myths and legends arising from our political and frontier origins often assigned almost as much credit to guns as to the people behind them—for winning the Revolution or for winning the West. Deringer, Thompson, Sharps, Remington, Smith and Wesson, Gatling, Colt, Winchester, Browning, Savage—the names of the famous gun manufacturers are almost as well known to history buffs as the names Washington, Jefferson, Adams, and Roosevelt. We have made gun violence a part of our national philosophy: "God made men, but Colonel Colt made them equal." If our gunmen were violent enough, we tended to romanticize their lives—to envision Billy the Kid, for example, not as a cowardly punk who usually shot his victims in the back, which in fact he did, but as the victim of fate. Wyatt Earp is the hero of a dozen films as the officer who cleaned up Dodge City, when in fact he and his sidekick, Bat Masterson, spent most of their time making extra money as card

sharks and procurers and were generally known as "The Fighting Pimps."[13]

Violence being our heritage, Americans have tended to view the instruments of violence—and especially the gun—almost as patriotic icons: those sacred instruments that cut down the redcoats and the redskins and the rustlers and the revenooers. In some sections of the country a .22 rifle is still considered a natural gift to a boy on the threshold of manhood: machismo. Millions of people in the United States would not be without a pistol in the nightstand even though they've never shot a gun in their lives. Many ranchers would not think of owning a pickup that wasn't equipped with a rifle rack on the back window. Hunting is a billion-dollar business that could not do without its rifles and shotguns. Crime is, of course, a multibillion-dollar business that could not function without guns.[14]

Congress has been reluctant to change the pattern. Only twice has it voted gun-control laws. In the 1930s, after big-city gangs had used sawed-off shotguns and submachine guns to intimidate police and terrorize whole neighborhoods, Congress outlawed those two weapons. And in 1968, after President John F. Kennedy, Martin Luther King, Jr., and Senator Robert F.

[12]"The Ownership of the Means of Destruction: Weapons in the United States," *Social Problems* 23, no. 1 (October 1975).

[13]Robert Sherrill, *The Saturday Night Special* (New York: David McKay Co., Charterhouse Books, 1973), p. 248.

[14]*Gun Control* (Washington, D.C.: American Enterprise Institute, 1976).

Kennedy had been assassinated, Congress restricted the shipment of some guns by mail and the importation of some guns—but otherwise it left the gun market as free and loose as ever.

Meanwhile, the slaughter continued. To illustrate the extent of it: between 1966 and 1972, the ripest years of the Vietnam war, 44,000 American servicemen were killed; at home during the same years, 55,000 Americans were murdered with handguns.[15] In 1974, Detroit, with a population of 1.4 million, had 801 murders, while England and Wales, Australia, and Sweden, with a combined population of 75.8 million had about 750 murders total.[16]

The most unsocial gun is, of course, the handgun—the pistol and the revolver. The handgun is almost never used for hunting animals; it has no real purpose but to shoot people. Criminals favor it because it is concealable. There are 40 million or so privately owned handguns in this country today. Of the million violent crimes committed in a typical year, about one-third are committed with handguns. Police statistics for 1974 show that handguns were used in about 11,000 murders, 10,000 suicides, 145,000 robberies, and 100,000 aggravated assaults.

The Problem Comes to You

You are a member of the House Judiciary Committee, which has before it a bill that would ban the importation, manufacture, sale, or distribution of new concealable handguns. The bill has already passed the Senate, and it will probably pass the full House if it can get out of your committee. The other members are evenly divided, sixteen to sixteen. Your vote will decide the issue.

Most big-city mayors and most police chiefs are pressuring you to vote for passage. Many public-opinion polls have shown that urban Americans heavily favor banning handguns. This side argues that 40 million handguns in circulation is bad enough and should not be augmented by another 2 million handguns hot off the assembly line each year. They also argue

that restricting the sale of the handgun will not interfere with the sporting industry and that if handguns are harder to obtain, violent crimes will be reduced—it being difficult to rob a bank with a vial of poison or a knife or a baseball bat.

Those opposed to control—and they are by far the better organized and more vocal group— argue that guns don't kill people, *people* kill people. They argue that criminals will always be able to find guns somewhere, even if they are banned, and that this legislation will only make it more difficult for decent people in the United States to arm themselves for defense against criminals. They argue that the antigun movement is based on hysteria—that, as Schattschneider has pointed out, "the odds against being murdered are very great. On the average an ordinary American might expect to live 23,000 years before he is murdered."[17] And if you eliminate the in-family murders and stick just to murder by strangers—the kind of murder that frightens Americans the most—the odds rise to one in 40,000 years, which is about as big a risk as one would have of choking to death on food.[18]

Gun-control opponents also argue—from a specious historical perspective, to be sure—that the Second Amendment to the Constitution guarantees the right to gun ownership. ("A well regulated Militia, being necessary to the security of a free State, the right of the people to keep and bear Arms shall not be infringed.") And they argue that the cities' inability to control their criminals is no reason to interfere with the gun pleasures of people in other parts of the country. The more rabid extremists argue that it is all a plot by the communists to disarm United States citizens so that they won't be able to resist tyranny. These arguments are most expertly packaged by the National Rifle Association, one of the most powerful lobbies in Washington. (See Chapter 5.)

It is an extremely passionate issue, and no matter which way you vote you will make many

---

[15]*New Yorker,* July 26, 1976.

[16]*Washington Post,* January 12, 1975.

[17]Schattschneider, *Two Hundred Million Americans in Search of a Government,* p. 20.

[18]Maggie Scarf, "The Anatomy of Fear," *New York Times,* June 16, 1974.

permanent enemies. Remember: your vote will decide the immediate future of handgun ownership in this country. What will it be?[19]

PROBLEM 2: SOCIAL SECURITY

Although all major industrial nations today have programs safeguarding the economic welfare of individuals and families, these programs are of relatively recent origin. Until the second half of the nineteenth century, economic survival—let alone "security"—was generally a matter of every man for himself. Germany, in the 1880s, was the first nation to provide government programs of health insurance and old-age pensions. Most European countries had followed suit long before the United States adopted a social security program in the 1930s.

Background

Throughout the 1920s, efforts were made to persuade Congress to pass legislation that would provide support for old people, for widows, and for disabled persons. The Republican Presidents of that decade opposed it because they believed that people should, by thrift, make arrangements for their own emergencies and retirement. Business lobbies, which advocated "volunteer pensions," encouraged Republicans to stand firm in this attitude even after the crash of Wall Street in 1929 and the ensuing depression that swept the United States.

In 1929, about 6 million families lived in the direst poverty. There was no use talking to them about thrift; they had virtually nothing to live on, much less to put in the bank. Fifty-nine percent of all United States families earned less than $2,000 each; these families could, on the average, save only 1.4 percent of their annual income. (By contrast, a family earning $5,000 in those days saved 17 percent of its income, and a family earning between $50,000 and $100,000 could put

President Roosevelt signs the Social Security Act

aside 44 percent.) Eighty percent of the families in the United States held only 2 percent of the savings. They had no margin of income for emergency, nothing to fall back on when they got too old to work.

When President Franklin D. Roosevelt advocated the Social Security Act of 1935 and the Democratic-controlled Congress passed it (to take effect in 1937), business groups denounced it as a step toward slavery. It was also denounced as a "cruel hoax."[20] Most working-class people hailed it as a godsend.

---

[19]In 1976 this very choice was given to a member of the House Judiciary Committee, and he voted against banning handguns. The vote was seventeen to sixteen, and so the measure died.

[20]Wilbur Cohen, "From Dream to Reality," *Lithopinion*, no. 19 (Fall 1970), 73–77.

And it was a godsend. It was a tremendous success—of sorts. The first mailing of Social Security checks went to 3,682 Americans, and the combined monthly payments totalled $75,844. Forty years later, some 32 million men, women, and children were receiving monthly checks worth $6.5 billion in old age, survivors, and disability benefits.[21] The Social Security check is the only income many of these people have. They would be helpless without it.

Now this largess has fallen on difficult times. Social Security payments come from the Social Security Trust Fund, which is the accumulation of deductions from workers' pay (matched by obligatory contributions from employers). The fund began suffering heavy deficits in 1975 during an era of high unemployment, and its trustees warned that it may be exhausted within a few years. Part of the problem is that in periods of high unemployment less is put into the Trust Fund than is paid out of it. But the major long-term cause of the fund's depletion is that people are living longer and the birth rate is fluctuating. During the war years of the 1940s, the birth rate began going up, and it continued to go up in the relatively prosperous 1950s, peaking around 1957, when the fertility rate for women in the United States (that is, the number of babies born to the average woman in her lifetime) hit 3.7. The large number of people born during the baby boom began moving into the work force during the 1960s and 1970s, and their contributions to Social Security helped offset the fund's decline that had resulted from unemployment. But there is trouble ahead, for the birth rate began to drop sharply in the late 1960s, down to a fertility rate of 1.9, and demographers predict that it will stay there for quite a while.

Beginning about 2010, when the baby boom crop begins retiring, the Social Security burden will be greatly enlarged. At the same time, the number of people entering the work force and helping to support this large number of retirees will decline because of the prevailing low fertility rate.

Thus, whereas there were twelve working taxpayers for every Social Security retiree in 1950, the ratio fell to four to one in 1960 and three to one in 1975. By the time those of you reading this book are ready to receive Social Security, there will be fewer than two workers to support each retiree.[22]

The Problem Comes to You

You are on the Social Security Subcommittee of the House Ways and Means Committee. What remedies would you offer? Here are several possibilities, but each has its defects:

• Raise the Social Security tax rate. It is already too great a burden to middle- and low-income workers, some of whom pay more in Social Security taxes than in income taxes. In 1950, the maximum Social Security payroll tax was $45 a year. In 1975 it was $841. Furthermore, it is a regressive tax, applied only to earnings up to $16,500 (as of 1977) a year. Thus, the head of a family with earnings of only $5,000 a year paid nearly $300 in Social Security taxes while paying only about $100 in income taxes. But a millionaire escaped paying Social Security taxes on all income after the first $16,500.

• Raise the taxable income to, say, $25,000. This would make it less regressive and would help bolster the Social Security treasury at once; but, in the long haul, inflation and the growing ranks of retirees would eat away the advantage.

• Bolster the Social Security treasure with money from general revenue taxes. This would solve everything financially, but it would be disastrous in its effect on the character of the program—which was established as a reward for enforced thrift and as a *supplementary* income.

• Put a freeze on benefits. As of 1975, the *average* Social Security benefit was $186 per month for a retired individual and $310 for a couple. That was far below the official poverty level, and nearly 30 percent of the aged single persons and 13 percent of elderly couples have *no other* income but Social Security. About 25 percent of all people in this country above the age of sixty-five live in poverty. Refusing to let

---

[21]*New York Times*, March 7, 1976.

[22]See J. W. Van Gorkom, *Social Security—The Long-Term Deficit* (Washington, D.C.: American Enterprise Institute, 1976); Hobart Rowen, *Washington Post*, June 6, 1976; *Congressional Record*, S12515, July 14, 1975; Edward Cowan, "One Way or the Other, Social Security Will Need Help," *New York Times*, March 7, 1976.

Social Security benefits rise with the cost of living, for this group and for millions of others who have some small income besides Social Security, would be tantamount to condemning them to living without sufficient heat, clothing, or food.

You must try to avoid loading the wage earner with too great a burden, but you must also bear in mind as a practical political consideration that nearly 30 percent of the voters of your district are aged fifty-five and over and are either retired or are nearing retirement, and 65 percent of the people in the fifty-five-and-up age group go to the polls—they are by far the most enthusiastic electorate that we have.[23]

PROBLEM 3: ILLEGAL IMMIGRANTS

Everyone in this country but the Indians is an immigrant or the descendant of immigrants. Traditionally we have been proud of that. For almost one hundred years after its founding, the United States had no federal laws governing the admission of aliens. The door stood open.

Background

The first regulation of immigration came in 1875, when Congress passed a law preventing the entry of prostitutes and convicts—apparently fearful that we were about to be overrun by members of those professions. In 1882, Congress decided that further immigration by Chinese laborers should be barred; they had been invaluable in the building of the railroads, but now that need was ended. Over the next twenty-five years, other laws were passed barring physical "defectives," persons of low intellect, anarchists, paupers, and other aliens of unappealing characteristics.

But then, in 1917, Congress really started getting down to business by excluding most Asians and by requiring immigrants to be able to read and write (though not necessarily in Eng-

lish). Then, in 1921 on a temporary basis, and in 1924 on a permanent basis, Congress set up quotas, limiting immigration to a specific number each year of persons from favored countries in the Eastern Hemisphere (there was no limit to the number of immigrants from Western Hemisphere countries as yet). This "national origin" quota was liberalized in 1952, but the new law still favored migrants from northwestern Europe and discouraged immigration by Asians and blacks. In 1965, the national origins principle was eliminated altogether; a ceiling of 170,000 a year was placed on Eastern Hemisphere immigrants, and, for the first time, a ceiling was also placed on Western Hemisphere immigrants, at 120,000.

This did not stop the flood of Western Hemisphere immigrants; it simply made many of them illegal. Now the Immigration and Naturalization Service (INS) catches and deports between 800,000 and 1 million illegal aliens every year, and experts estimate that at least three to five times that many get through the INS net and take up residence here. Some of them come on tourist visas or student visas and simply never return home again. Some are smuggled across the Mexican border. Some go from the Dominican Republic to Puerto Rico and pretend to be natives of that commonwealth, which would make them United States citizens; from Puerto Rico they simply hop a plane for the United States. Some buy fraudulent passports. Some officials believe there are twice as many illegal as legal immigrants coming in each year. Some warn that the increase in illegals is greater than the natural increase of our own population.

Nobody knows how many illegal aliens are in this country; estimates range from 2 million to 12 million. The INS puts the figure at about 8 million. Most come from Latin America, especially Mexico—which supplies an estimated three-fourths of the total. Like all migrants of all races before them, they come looking for work. And they find it. Some find employment as bookkeepers, accountants, or skilled laborers at $20,000 a year or more; but most do not fare so well. The INS estimates that more than half the illegal aliens earn more than $2.50 an hour, which seems a princely sum to aliens coming—as most do—from countries in which per capita

[23]Report of the Democratic Study Group of the House of Representatives, July 25, 1974.

income ranges from $100 to $900 a year, where unemployment constantly stays between 20 percent and 30 percent of the labor force, and where the chance for work is steadily decreasing because of a birth rate that doubles the population every twenty-five to thirty-five years.

Not only do the illegal aliens take approximately a million jobs from United States citizens, but they have other adverse effects. They save their money and send it home faithfully, which may be admirable as a family consideration, but hurts the United States economy by draining more than $1 billion a year from it (according to a House subcommittee on immigration). The INS claims that the illegal aliens evade at least $115 million each year in taxes, which must be made up by United States citizens, and are collecting welfare, receiving medical care, getting unemployment compensation, sending their children to public schools, receiving federal housing loans, and even receiving fraudulent Social Security payments at a total cost to taxpayers of about $13 million a year.

The Problem Comes to You

You are Attorney General. Since the Department of Justice has jurisdiction over the INS, you are on the spot. Organized labor is demanding that you beef up the INS force to keep out these people who are taking jobs away from United States citizens. The Treasury Department is angered by the outflow of dollars and the cheating on taxes, and it joins labor in demanding a blockade that works, and so do law-enforcement agencies, which contend the illegals are raising the crime rate. It's obvious that if the INS is going to do the job at all, it is going to have to have more manpower. As of 1976, it had only three hundred guards on the four-thousand-mile Canadian border and, more to the point, only about seventeen hundred agents along the two-thousand-mile Mexican border, where the United States has clearly lost control of the situation. But more manpower would not shut the faucet entirely; even if two-thirds of the illegal horde were turned back, at least 1 million would still get into this country each year. "You could put 10 divisions of Marines along the Mexican border and not seal it," says Leonel J. Castillo, INS Commissioner.[24]

The get-tough advocates also urge you to seek legislation making it a crime for employers to hire illegal aliens, with stiff fines for violators. Polls show that Americans, by a ratio of six to one, favor this course of action.[25] And many urge legislation that would throw illegals in jail (a costly solution), not merely return them to their homelands (from which most turn around and try again).

You are caught in a cross fire. Mexico, a very important ally, warns against a get-tough policy. Mexico's population is soaring—twenty-five years ago it had a population of 25 million, today its population is 62 million and climbing fast—and Mexico tacitly encourages migration to the United States, illegal or otherwise, as a safety valve. Half of Mexico's population is under fifteen years of age, and the job prospects for that group—always the last to be employed—are dim indeed. Unemployment for the population in general regularly hovers around 30 percent.

Some humanitarians argue that the emphasis should not be on trying to turn back the illegal immigrants but on helping Mexico raise its economic standards so high that there will be jobs at home. They also urge the United States to delicately pressure Mexico into controlling its birth rate, perhaps with a trade-off of economic aid.

The State Department, trying to maintain cordial relations with all Latin American countries, is also urging you not to get too tough. Agribusiness and some factory and restaurant owners also favor leniency, for much of their labor comes across the border at night. For that matter, many wealthy people (including some of

Washington, D.C.'s, top officials) would hate to see you chase the illegals home because their maids are in that group.[26]

Which side do you intend to offend?

PROBLEM 4: HEALTH

Health care costs seem to be spiraling out of control (consumers spent 50 percent more for health in 1974 than in 1970). Although most people in the United States are covered by some form of private health insurance, many fear that their coverage is not sufficient for major health crises. Since the 1960s, polls have shown that most Americans would favor a government-guaranteed health insurance program to cover all citizens. But there are several crucial obstacles to such a program.

Background

Prior to the enactment of the Medicare and Medicaid programs in 1966, the federal government's activities in the health field were confined to regulating drugs (Pure Food and Drug Act), the distribution of funds to build and modernize hospitals (Hill-Burton Act), and various programs supporting medical education and medical research.

For half a century, the American Medical Association (AMA) had successfully fought off any federal program for assisting the elderly sick and the impoverished sick. The juggernaut of the heavily Democratic Congress coupled with the buccaneering Presidency of Lyndon B. Johnson made it clear to the AMA in the mid-1960s, however, that it was about to lose the war. So it switched tactics. It concentrated—successfully—on influencing the language of the legislation. At

---

[24]Quoted in the *New York Times,* April 24, 1977.

[25]Gallup poll, released April 24, 1977.

[26]Information for this section comes from "Smugglers, Illicit Documents, Etc.," U.S. General Accounting Office Report, Washington, D.C., August 30, 1976; *Proposals to Prohibit Employment of Illegal Aliens* (Washington, D.C.: American Enterprise Institute, 1975); "Million Illegal Aliens in Metropolitan Area," *New York Times,* December 19, 1974; *Washington Post,* August 17, 1975, August 11, 1976; "Can We Stop the Invasion of Illegal Aliens?" *Parade,* February 29, 1976; *U.S. News and World Report,* April 25, 1977.

the insistence of the AMA, the Medicare and Medicaid legislation was written in such a way that it gives the government very little control over the billions of tax dollars that flow through these programs and into the pockets of the hospitals and the doctors. It created an open season on federally subsidized hospital bills. They soared.

The Federation of American Scientists explained the phenomenon:

> The effect of these two programs was to stimulate an extraordinary inflation in health costs. The reason was simple enough. The old and the poor constituted an enormous pool of previously unfinanced health care needs. Once their needs began to be financed, demand for health care jumped still farther ahead of supply. For those who provided health services, these programs were a bonanza. The doctors were committed only to "reasonable" charges. They were released from worrying about what and whether these patients could pay. Naturally, their charges rose. [The hospitals began sticking it to the government even more emphatically.] *Net* income per patient day rose from $1.50 to $2.50 from 1965–1971 for non-profit hospitals. For profit hospitals net income rose from $2.00 to over $6.00![27]

And in the next five years the pace picked up, at an inflationary rate even higher than the runaway inflation in the economy as a whole. In fiscal 1976, Americans spent $139 billion on doctors, hospitals, and drugs, which was $17 billion more than they had spent the year before, which represented 11.4 percent of total household income. The cost of the "average stay" in the hospital, not counting doctor bills or other costs, was about twelve hundred dollars—for 7.8 days. The same room that cost $130 in 1976 had cost $53 in 1967. Doctors' fees had doubled.[28]

On top of the inflated costs, there was outright fraud. Estimates of the fraud ran as high as $3 billion a year under the Medicaid program alone. A Senate investigation concluded that some 10,000 doctors participated in the fraud. (Fraud or not, more than 2,500 doctors, dentists, pharmacies, and medical laboratories grossed more than $100,000 each from Medicaid in 1975.) Some nursing home officials billed Medicaid for minks, art, liquor, and hi-fi sets. A female investigator for the Senate was told by a Los Angeles clinic that her urine sample was normal—even though it was not urine at all, but a soap and cleaner combination she had concocted in the rest room. At other clinics, Senate investigators were given X-rays without film plates in the machines or were given chest and foot X-rays with dental X-ray equipment. On the basis of four-minute examinations, perfectly healthy Senate investigators were told they had asthma and chest spasms. When they complained of having colds, they were tested for heart trouble, tuberculosis, allergies, glaucoma, and brain disorders. Some crooked doctors got rich; very few were punished. One nursing home operator who bilked the Medicaid program of $2.5 million served only four months in federal prison. [29]

As a result of inflation and corruption and bad management (while some hospitals are critically overcrowded, there is also an excess of 100,000 hospital beds[30]), Medicare and Medicaid patients were not getting the service that the government was paying for. At the same time, medical costs in general had been pushed so high that unless a person was old or poor or had a good private medical insurance policy, he or she was in danger of going bankrupt if that person or anyone in his or her family got very sick. Premiums on private health insurance policies had risen so much that even giant corporations were beginning to quiver. General Motors complained that it paid more to Blue Cross/Blue Shield than it did to the United States Steel Corporation, the major supplier of metal for its cars. These policy payments were passed on to GM auto buyers—raising the price of each car by $175. The big three auto companies—who pay for health premiums as part of a union agreement—spent more than $1 billion in 1975, or an

---

[27]Federation of American Scientists Public Interest Report, April 1974.

[28]Sources: Council on Wage and Price Stability, March 19, 1976; Health Insurance Institute report released to the *Chicago Sun-Times* March 5, 1976; Report of the Democratic Study Group of the House of Representatives, July 18, 1974.

[29]Sources: *New York Times*, September 5, 1976, September 17, 1976; *Washington Post*, July 29, 1976, November 9, 1976, November 18, 1976, August 30, 1976.

[30]*Congressional Record*, S13577, August 5, 1976.

average of about eighteen hundred dollars per employee, for medical insurance. All this was passed along in such a way as to contribute significantly to the inflation in the general economy.

Ironically, while spending more for health than any other nation in the world, we weren't getting healthier. As of 1974, the United States ranked fifteenth among nations in infant mortality, twelfth in maternal mortality (while in 1950, the United States had the lowest maternal mortality rate), twenty-seventh in life expectancy for men (twenty of the twenty-five countries in Europe had lower male mortality rates), twelfth in life expectancy for women (a drop from seventh two years earlier), and sixteenth in the death rate for middle-aged men. And those were national averages; for persons at the bottom of the economic scale, the situation was far worse.[31]

The Problem Comes to You

You are Secretary of Health, Education and Welfare, and the President has promised to follow your recommendations.

In particular, the President wants your recommendations on legislation under consideration in Congress that would extend federal health coverage to every man, woman, and child of every economic status. The program favored by Congress would be funded by a special tax, levied according to income, and money would also come from the general treasury. It would add at least another $80 billion to the federal budget—and that could be expected to rise sharply in the years ahead, just as Medicare and Medicaid did.

If you like that idea in general, would you favor permitting the hospitals and doctors to go on charging whatever they thought was "reasonable," or would you impose a strict price list above which they could not go—so much for removing tonsils, so much for taking out a gall bladder, and so on?

What if many doctors and hospitals refused to participate in the program at those prices and said they would cater only to private-fund patients instead? Would you attempt to force them into the program?

Some people have suggested that a federal medical program should extend to the average citizen only for "catastrophic protection"—protection against having one's medical bills exceed a fixed amount. In other words, the average person, who is not covered by an exceptionally generous health policy, would be financially wiped out if he or she had to spend three months in the hospital. But that person might be able to afford a maximum of, say, two thousand dollars if the government paid the rest.

An argument for a variant of the catastrophic plan comes from Reo M. Christenson:

> There is no pressing reason why this affluent, essentially middle-class nation needs a national insurance plan to cover the typical medical bills of the average family or the family with the above-average income. Although normal medical bills may be painful, they are not beyond the capacity of these groups to pay. What *is* needed is adequate coverage for lower-income groups, help with unusually heavy medical costs for the middle-income family and an end to catastrophic medical bills for almost everyone.
>
> Heads of families and other adults now submit an income tax statement to Washington each year. Suppose each person or family were to receive an annual check from the Internal Revenue Service for medical expenses which exceed 10 percent of their income for the preceding year. (The percentage could be reduced for low-income families.)[32]

The American Medical Association, on the other hand, proposes that a person simply receive tax credits to offset premiums paid for private health insurance and that federal insurance be skipped altogether for everyone not covered under Medicare and Medicaid. But 20 percent of the people have neither federal nor private coverage at present. What if a tax credit didn't persuade them to take out a policy?

Whatever program you decide on will be open to some degree of abuse along the lines already uncovered. How would you police the industry to reduce the fraud and overcharges? What punishments would you suggest?

---

[31]Report of the Democratic Study Group of the House of Representatives, July 18, 1974.

[32]Quoted in the *Washington Post,* May 16, 1976.

In setting up this program, you will be under intense pressure and attack from those who believe strictly in free-enterprise medicine on the one hand, and those who believe in 100 percent socialized medicine on the other, and from everyone in between. Where on the scale between free enterprise and socialism do you intend to stop? How do you intend to do so? And why?

PROBLEM 5: HOUSING

Home ownership is a central part of the American dream, and every census shows that more citizens are reaching that goal. Only 36 percent of nonfarm residences were owner-occupied in 1900, but 62 percent were owner-occupied in 1974.[33] What's happening to those people who can't afford to own and can barely afford to rent?

Background

When Congress passed the Federal Housing Act of 1949, it declared its purpose was to supply a "decent home" for every person in the United States. Presumably the emphasis was to be on assisting people at the lower end of the economic scale, for the act was divided into two major efforts: (1) "urban renewal" and (2) the building of public, low-rent housing.

The plan for urban renewal called for the federal government to put up two-thirds of the money and the cities, one-third. This money was to be used to buy old, deteriorated neighborhoods (whether the residents wanted to sell or not), to tear down the houses and apartments that were there, and then to sell the land to real estate developers for the construction of bigger, spiffier apartments and office buildings.

The alleged purpose was to rid cities of terribly blighted areas and to replace them with good housing and with office space that would attract business and industry into the city and thereby bolster the job supply.

But the program was widely abused and exploited; it ended up not helping the residents of the area but making real estate developers rich. In New York, Boston, Philadelphia, and a number of other major cities, the urban renewal funds were used not just to get rid of rat-infested slums but to destroy whole neighborhoods where contented, proud, tightly knit ethnic groups lived in homes that were old but still very serviceable and comfortable. After the homes were wiped out, the city sold the land cheap to developers who were friends of city officials (one plot in New York City was bought with $41 million of government money and resold for $20 million to private investors and developers).

Many in Congress who had fought for passage of the Housing Act thought the new homes and apartments built in renewed areas would be priced to attract low-income people. It rarely worked out that way. Most apartments built with urban renewal subsidies were posh affairs with high rents. The hundreds of thousands of families displaced by urban renewal had no choice but to crowd into other areas of the city that were already crowded, and often less desirable.[34]

As for the part of the Housing Act that authorized the building of low-rent public housing, it was also a disastrous failure, but in a different way. The congestion of city slums runs from three hundred to seven hundred persons an acre. This is a concentration not only of bodies but of problems, fears, anxieties, and vices. It would obviously be sensible to break up this kind of congestion. But the cities built their federally subsidized public housing projects right in the middle of the slum areas or jammed them alongside railroad tracks or squeezed them into warehouse districts on land nobody else had any use for. No space was left for parks or for playgrounds. Schools and stores were usually beyond walking distance. The buildings themselves were cheaply constructed and thereby guaranteed to become instant slums; they were to be inhabited by poor people who had no experience in keeping up property. Because city offi-

---

[33]*Statistical Abstract of the United States: 1973* (Washington, D.C.: U.S. Bureau of the Census, 1973), p. 743.

[34]Leonard Downie, Jr., *Mortgage on America* (New York: Praeger Publishers, 1974), pp. 60–66.

A concentration not only of bodies, but of problems, fears, anxieties, and vices

cials didn't want to waste land on them, the public housing projects were often high-rises. "There was nothing wrong with these buildings," as Lewis Mumford correctly judged, "except that, humanly speaking, they stink."[35] They often did literally stink. Children found they could not get from their sidewalk games to their seventh-floor apartment in time, so they would use the halls and elevators as toilets; winos found the privacy of the elevators useful for the same purpose; robbers and rapists found the isolation of the hallways perfect for their avocations. Sunlight, air, the policing eyes of neighbors, the reassuring touch of the earth (many of these people had come from rural areas), the neighborliness of stores—all were missing.

The pinnacle of the urban renewal failure was reached in St. Louis at the infamous Pruitt-Igoe towers. Completed in 1955 at a cost of $100 million, the thirty-three eleven-story towers were built in dense rows right in the middle of an ocean of slums, and they housed 10,000 people. Within fifteen years the buildings had become such a haven for cutthroats and dope addicts and had become so run-down that four-fifths of the apartments were abandoned; shortly thereafter the government admitted, as one official put it, that "this development has been a complete and colossal failure from a social, moral and economic standpoint"—and the $100 million monstrosity was demolished.[36]

In short, the urban renewal projects—sometimes known as "Negro removal" projects, though they might also have been called "Italian-American" or "Polish-American" removal projects—were misused to destroy functional neighborhoods for the sake of real estate promoters. And the public housing projects, because they were for poor people, were built as cheaply as possible, designed like prisons, and placed in neighborhoods that breed crime. As a result of these failures, there are today fewer low-priced houses and low-rent apartments in our urban centers than at any time in history.

---

[35]Lewis Mumford, *The Urban Prospect* (New York: Harcourt Brace Jovanovich, 1968), p. 184.

[36]Downie, *Mortgage on America*, p. 57.

The Problem Comes to You

You are Secretary of the Department of Housing and Urban Development (HUD), and the President has told you to give top priority to providing homes for the urban poor. How would you go about it—without breaking the federal budget?

• Would you offer federally guaranteed, low-interest mortgage loans to low-income families so that they could buy their own homes? It sounds like a good idea. But it was tried recently, with disastrous results.

For many years the Federal Housing Administration (FHA) had refused to guarantee mortgage loans for inner-city residents because the FHA considered them too great a financial risk. In the late 1960s, Congress ordered HUD (parent of FHA) to reverse that policy and to start approving mortgages in the older, declining urban areas. That is, savings and loan institutions and banks would make the mortgage loans at, say, 9 percent interest. The government would pay 7 percent of that; the low-income buyer would pay the other 2 percent. If the low-income buyer defaulted, the government would pay off the mortgage and take ownership of the house. So, as with all government-guaranteed loans, the lenders ran no risk at all.

Crooked lenders and real estate profiteers immediately began to milk the program in collusion with HUD officials. They approved mortgages on homes that were about to fall down and that were priced at several times their true value. The low-income buyers of the rickety property couldn't afford to make the needed repairs, and, when the homes became uninhabitable, these people simply moved out and disappeared. The mortgage holders quickly foreclosed, and, by 1975, HUD was the unhappy owner of 166,000 often worthless homes. The real estate agents came out of the mess with enormous profits; the poor buyers, with a loss of some money and bad credit records; and HUD (or the United States taxpayers), with 166,000 houses it didn't know what to do with. While the agency tried, usually futilely, to resell the homes, many were stripped and burned by vandals, making the neighborhoods look like bombed-out war zones. About five hundred realtors and HUD officials were convicted of swindling the government out of millions of dollars. But that kind of justice just scratched the surface of the crime against society, and, in any event, it did nothing to help the worn-out neighborhoods or the people who still needed homes.

• Would you give low-rent public housing another try? Public housing was never given a fair chance. If it were built in good neighborhoods, if the apartments had balconies, air conditioning, attractive grounds, and, perhaps, a swimming pool, if low-income people were given the incentive to maintain their apartments, if enough janitors and police were hired to watch over them, it might work.

But if you try to build public housing in nice neighborhoods, especially in the suburbs, the other property owners will fight you with passion, for an influx of poor people would drive down property values.

Judging from past experience, whatever you try, you will be faced with these obstacles: banks and savings and loan companies won't give mortgages to inner-city residents unless they are virtually forced to do so and unless they are assured of rich profits by the government; builders will not participate in your programs unless a ridiculous amount of profiteering is permitted (in New York City, some housing projects cost $30,000 *a room*), and middle-class and upper-class property owners will not want you to subsidize low-cost housing in their neighborhoods.

How do you intend to cope with these antagonists? If you wish to retain your cabinet post, you may not be permitted to throw up your hands, like HUD Secretary Carla A. Hills of the Ford administration did, and say that "home ownership for the poor is probably an unrealistic goal in today's economy."[37]

PROBLEM 6: AFFIRMATIVE ACTION

When politicians and judges finally tell members of oppressed groups, "The burden of past biases has been lifted from your back, go out and compete as equals," is that comforting assurance really enough to give them an equal chance?

Background

After the United States Supreme Court and Congress firmly established that schools and employers could not discriminate against anyone because of race, it became clear that the rulings and statutes were not going to change things quickly for members of minority races. Absence of discrimination would allow them to move toward equality of opportunity, but a full transition would take many years.

For blacks and Chicanos, the catch-up pace would be especially slow. In terms of this generation and perhaps the next, improvement in opportunity for them would be scanty unless something drastic were done to change the pattern that had been set by many generations of low income and inferior schooling.

How to break the pattern? Federal officials decided that since an absence of discrimination wouldn't do it quickly, universities and businesses with federal contracts would have to follow a policy of "affirmative action," which was to be applied to women as well as to racial minorities. By affirmative action, the government meant that the universities and businesses receiving federal funds should not wait passively for a qualified member of a minority group or a woman to come along and bowl them over with his or her abilities; they should actively seek out minority members and women and enroll them or hire them—based on preliminary tests—even if they aren't as qualified as white male applicants. To prove that they were obeying the affirmative action edict, universities and businesses were expected to be able to show that they had enrolled or hired a certain percentage of blacks, Chicanos, and women—in other words, they had a quota to fill.[38]

---

[37]Quoted in the *Washington Post*, September 13, 1975.

[38]The federal government was hardly in a position to give sermons to private business. As of 1977, women (who make up 51 percent of the population) comprised 35 percent of the federal work force but held only three-tenths of 1 percent of the supergrade positions; blacks (11 percent of the population) comprised 29 percent of the federal work force and held 3.9 percent of the supergrade positions. (Data from Barbara Blum of the White House Staff, December 29, 1976.)

Advocates of affirmative action pointed out that graduate-school enrollments were overwhelmingly white and that 90 percent of the jobs paying $15,000 a year or more in this country were held by white males.[39]

The affirmative action edict created an historic clash between two beloved liberal ideals: (1) everything must be done for minorities and for women to make up for centuries of neglect and (2) everyone should be judged strictly on his or her merits and not on the basis of race or sex. Affirmative action seemed to create an automatic conflict between those two ideals.

As a result, two very important cases went to court. The first arose in 1971 when the University of Washington Law School turned down the application of Marco DeFunis, Jr., a white, a member of Phi Beta Kappa, and a graduate magna cum laude of the University of Washington's undergraduate college.

The selection procedure was set up like this: all white applicants whose grades and test scores fell below a certain line were almost automatically rejected. Those scoring above the line—and DeFunis was above—then competed for places in the class. The applications from blacks and other minorities were handled separately. No matter how low their scores, they were still considered for admission. They competed among themselves, not with the white applicants' scores. Of the 275 applicants the school accepted, 74 had lower test scores than DeFunis, and 36 of these were blacks or Chicanos. Even if none of the 36 minority members had been admitted, DeFunis still might not have made it. However, if DeFunis had been black or Chicano, he would have been admitted. This, everyone acknowledged.

In other words, he had not exactly been turned down because he was white, but because he was *not* black or brown; either way, he had lost out because of his race. So he went to court, charging reverse discrimination. The trial court ruled in his favor; the Washington State Supreme Court ruled against him, saying that the equal protection guarantees of the Fourteenth

Amendment do not require a university to be "color-blind" and that "the state has an overriding interest in promoting integration of public education." So DeFunis took his case to the United States Supreme Court.

The next case arose in 1974 when Allan Bakke, a thirty-four-year-old civil engineer, was rejected by the University of California School of Medicine at Davis. Of the one hundred places available at the medical school each year, the University of California set aside sixteen to be filled by minority students. Bakke, who is white, tested out as better qualified than most of the Chicano, black, and American Indian applicants who received special treatment for the sixteen slots. He went to court, charging reverse discrimination, and the California Supreme Court upheld him by a vote of six to one, ruling that the university's medical school acceptance program was guided strictly by racial criteria and that such "a quota becomes no less offensive when it serves to exclude a racial majority."

The Problem Comes to You

You are on the United States Supreme Court when these cases arrive. The other eight justices are evenly split, four to four, on whether these cases represent reverse discrimination of an unconstitutional sort. The outcome of the decision is up to you. Whichever way you vote, you will be looked on as having betrayed the underdog; women's groups and black organizations favor affirmative action, while Jewish groups are against any system that makes race or religion a part of the admission or rejection process (as recently as forty years ago, Jewish-Americans were admitted to many universities only on a quota basis). You hear arguments pro and con of the following sort. The argument for affirmative action is aptly made by Herbert J. Gans:

> . . . when race and sex have been used for over a century as criteria for not hiring people, it is hypocritical to argue that they should not be used as criteria for hiring because this would be "reverse discrimination." In terms of equality of results, this simply means the continuation of the traditional discrimination, albeit for a different reason.

---

[39]Herbert J. Gans, *More Equality* (New York: Pantheon Books, 1973), p. 72.

To be sure, if faculty with poorer credentials are hired or students with a poorer educational background are admitted to a university, "standards" will decline. The new faculty may teach at lower levels of abstraction, and the new students may sometimes be unable to comprehend what the incumbent faculty is teaching; and insofar as the newcomers can affect the teaching program or the intellectual climate, the levels of both will be lowered, at least from the perspective of the incumbents. But for the newcomers, who will have a chance to teach and learn at higher intellectual levels than before, the standards will be raised, and the real issue is whose perspectives are to be favored.[40]

The argument against affirmative action is neatly capsuled by Richard Posner:

> If affirmative action means affording preferences or benefits to people on the basis of racial identity or sex or national origin, then I think it is a form of discrimination and an evil practice.
>
> I don't think the way to fight the discrimination that we don't like is with more discrimination. One of the reasons why we have a problem of discrimination in this country is a habit of thinking about people in terms of types. You look at a person and what you see is a type—a black or a Jew or an Armenian; you don't see an individual. And when you begin ascribing characteristics to all individuals on the basis of this one element that the person has, you are prejudiced, you are bigoted.
>
> Affirmative action, or reverse discrimination, is just an extension of this stereotypical thinking. Once again you are looking not at the individual but at his type. If a person can prove that he or she has some percentage of Negro ancestry, or the right number of chromosomes to be a woman, or what have you, that person is automatically entitled to some benefits: preferential admission, a better job, and so on. That is discriminatory thinking. The individual disappears behind his type. To reinforce stereotypical thinking in the name of fighting discrimination seems to me to be wrong and foolish.[41]

How would you vote?

---

[40]Gans, pp. 72–73.

[41]Richard Posner, *Affirmative Action: The Answer to Discrimination?* (Washington, D.C.: American Enterprise Institute, 1975), pp. 5–6.

PROBLEM 7: POLLUTION

In 1962, Rachel L. Carson's *Silent Spring* was published. The book warned of what might happen if the spread of pesticides went unchecked; its main target was DDT. The book, a landmark, was followed by other exposés. The public became aware of an incredible array of industrial chemicals and pollutants that threaten the life cycles of plants, fish, and animals—including human beings.

Background

Ten years after *Silent Spring* was published, Congress banned the sale or use of DDT in this country. But by then it had become evident that DDT was just a piece of the problem. A survey by the Bureau of Water Hygiene in 1970 revealed that 41 percent of the nation's water supply systems were delivering water ranging from "inferior" down to "potentially dangerous."[42] Much of the poison in the drinking water came from industrial dumping and from farm drainage. At least once a year, 30 million acres of farmland are sprayed with some kind of pesticide and fertilizer; millions of acres of residential lawns and gardens get the same treatment; millions of acres of forest are sprayed for protection from insects; and, along mile after mile of highway, the shoulders are sprayed to kill weeds. Then come the rains, and shortly thereafter all these toxic chemicals are in our waterways, heading for the home faucet.[43]

The farmers said they had to have pesticides, so every time the Environmental Protection Agency (EPA) banned one pesticide as too dangerous, the pesticide industry cranked out a deadlier one. After DDT, aldrin was banned, then dieldrin, so the farmers turned en masse to toxaphene. Seventy-six million pounds of toxaphene were being strewn over the landscape every year. Then scientists made a chilling dis-

---

[42]Melvin I. Urofsky, ed. *Perspectives on Urban America* (New York: Doubleday & Co., Anchor Press, 1973), pp. 174–75.

[43]Benjamin H. Alexander, "Will Man Survive His Polluted Environment?" *The Review* (Chicago State University), October 1976, p. 4.

covery: fish living in waters polluted with toxaphene were suffering skeletal deformities, including broken backs, and they were reproducing at 30 percent below the normal rate.[44] Since World War II, more than a billion pounds of toxaphene have gone into the United States environment.

From 1966 through 1975, the Allied Chemical Corporation and one of its subcontractors dumped the pesticide Kepone into the James River in central Virginia. Kepone can cause cancer and nerve disease. When state and federal officials finally got around to stopping this pollution, Kepone had contaminated the waters of the James River, the Chesapeake Bay, and some areas of the Atlantic Ocean so thoroughly that the pesticide was found in fish as far north as Rhode Island. At least seventy persons who worked in the Kepone manufacturing plant suffered a variety of ailments, including paralysis.

In 1976, several workers at the Velsicol Chemical Corporation plant in Bayport, Texas, were discovered to be suffering from disorders of the central nervous system. Velsicol manufactures a nerve-destroying pesticide named leptophos. Leptophos, like two other pesticides manufactured by Velsicol, chlordane and heptachlor, was banned in this country by the EPA as suspected cancer-causing agents. So Velsicol shipped its wares overseas to many countries. In Egypt, an estimated twelve hundred water buffalo died after becoming paralyzed in the hindquarters; leptophos, which was being used in Egypt for the first time, was suspected as the cause. Velsicol also made large sales of leptophos to Mexico, where the pesticide was used on tomatoes that were later sold to the United States.[45]

---

[44]Abigail Trafford Brett, "Fish: Man's Early Warning System," *Washington Post*, September 14, 1975.

[45]*Washington Post*, December 9, 1976. Velsicol has had a fascinating history in the pesticide wars. According to the *Washington Post* (December 14, 1976), it tried to prevent the publication of Rachel L. Carson's *Silent Spring* by warning her publisher that "sinister influences" were attempting to stop the use of pesticides "so that our supply of food will be reduced" in relation to that of the communist countries.

Perhaps the most famous chemical pollutant of the 1960s and 1970s (aside from DDT) was the poisonous industrial chemical known as PCB (polychlorinated biphenyls), a colorless and tasteless compound with a thousand industrial uses in insulators, sealers, heat transfer fluids, inks, paints, lubricants, and plastics. In use since 1929, it did not make the Ten Most Feared list until the 1960s. Nursing infants of rhesus monkeys were fed PCBs experimentally and were found to develop serious diseases, brain and nervous disorders, and stunted growth; some died. Then it was discovered that human mothers' milk in ten states contained what some federal investigators described as "worrisome" amounts of PCBs. Other studies linked PCBs to liver cancer—which is always fatal. In 1971, the only manufacturer of PCB in this country, the Monsanto Company, voluntarily stopped selling the chemicals to "several thousand" customers, but millions of pounds of imported PCBs continued to pour into the country. Even if the chemical were no longer made or sold, it would still be a massive problem for generations; an estimated 750 million pounds are in use, and another 450 million pounds are distributed in landfills, water, soil, and air.[46]

Speaking of the air, how clean is it? Each day 250,000 tons of pollutants pour into the skies above the United States—from motor vehicles alone. That does not include the 72,000 tons of industrial pollutants, the 70,000 tons of pollutants from power plants, the 25,000 tons from space heating, or the 16,000 tons from refuse disposal. In New York City, autos and trucks contribute 97 percent of all carbon monoxide that is in the air. Other cities are not far behind in auto filth. The National Academy of Sciences estimates that as many as four thousand persons may die each year because of air pollution from cars and as many as 4 million illness-related days off per year could be caused by auto air pollution in urban areas.[47]

The Problem Comes to You

You are the President. Your predecessor had this to say on the problem:

> I cherish the outdoors and I stand with those who fight to preserve what is best in our environment. But as President, I can never lose sight of another insistent aspect of our environment—the economic needs of the American people. I pursue the goal of clean air and pure water but I must also pursue the objective of maximum jobs and continued economic progress. Unemployment is as real and as sickening a blight as any pollutant that threatens this nation.[48]

It was a slick political balancing act, but what did he mean? You can't get by with such vagaries—*you* will have to cope with specifics. Take the famous example of the Reserve Mining Company, which, in 1977, was spewing 60,000 tons of taconite waste a day into Lake Superior. If you use federal law to close down the mining company, 3,100 employees—virtually the whole town of Silver Bay, Minnesota—will be out of work. On the other hand, if you let Reserve Mining continue to pollute the lake, you may further endanger the health of the 150,000 people in five communities who take their drinking water from the lake.

Your choice, at bottom, is between health and jobs. You, of course, will try to steer a middle path in such a way as to preserve both. Reserve Mining will probably promise to clean up its mess—in time. Most polluting corporations promise to do so, but they always ask for time, and they usually ask for federal financial help. Reserve Mining has been dumping dangerous waste into the lake for two decades. How much more time do you think the company deserves? And now who should pay for its mess, if Reserve Mining refuses to?[49]

Moving up from that microcosm, you will see that the same problem applies on a massive scale. The pesticide industry is a $2.6-billion-a-year business ($7 billion globally). Some powerful corporations are involved: Dow, Eli Lilly,

---

[46]Sources: *Washington Post*, August 28, 1976, September 12, 1976; *Wall Street Journal*, October 10, 1975.

[47]Sources: Benjamin H. Alexander, "Will Man Survive His Polluted Environment?"; *New York Times*, May 16, 1975; United Press International, September 5, 1974.

[48]Gerald R. Ford, White House release, July 3, 1975.

[49]*Environment Midwest* (Region V, U.S. Environmental Protection Agency Publication), May 1974.

Du Pont, Shell, Monsanto, and Chevron, to name only a few. To what extent do you dare dislocate that industry by challenging its safety and health standards? Your concern, as the leader of the world's most powerful nation, must also embrace weaker nations that depend on us. Will you permit the Agency for International Development to continue subsidizing our pesticide industry to send millions of pounds of its produce overseas? State Department officials say that pesticides, which can increase farmers' yields by an average of 40 percent, are vital to poor nations. But is it worth risking the lives of chemical workers in Texas and New Jersey so that farmers in Egypt and Pakistan can produce abundant crops and themselves avoid death from starvation?

Your science advisers tell you that from 60 to 90 percent of all cancers are linked to exposure to chemical and other human-produced environmental factors and that cancer costs the United States over $15 billion annually. They tell you that of the more than 200,000 infants born with physical or mental damage each year, about 40,000 (or 20 percent) are suffering from defects attributed to drugs, radiation, and chemicals. But your economic advisers warn that if you try to suddenly shut off the chemical toxins that are squirted from cans, exhausted from cars and trucks, spewed from smokestacks, plowed into farmland, and pumped into food and water, you will paralyze our national economy—which already is suffering from high unemployment and stagnant investment.

What do you do?

ARE THERE ANY ANSWERS?

The decisions that you, as a hypothetical politician, might make if really faced with problems of the kind just presented would be much easier to arrive at, and much more just, if the pressures on you were exerted by equals, or at least by reasonably near-equals. Sometimes this in fact is the case, as in affirmative action versus reverse discrimination. But, in many situations, it is a case of massively structured elements of society threatening to squeeze individuals and small groups out of an effective role in politics. This is probably the most important problem facing the people of the United States today: how to keep the individual from getting trampled on by big labor, big lobby, big network, big foundation, big newspaper, big trust, big bank—by Big Business in general; how to guarantee that the shrill piping of the individual will be heard above the roar of the avalanche of big money. Government by compromise cannot be restored until Americans face up to the dangerous imbalance of wealth, power, and influence, which makes compromise increasingly difficult, if not impossible, to achieve.

Summary

1. Many Americans dislike government. They feel alienated from its leaders and removed from the lawmaking process, which shapes their lives.

2. This sense of a lack of control over what government does, as well as the feeling of an inability to deal with major problems, stems from a number of factors: the division of government authority, the lack of communication between the electorate and its leaders, the features of a social and economic system that favor private advantage over public good, the technical difficulties inherent in some problems, the power of certain special interest groups, and unreconciled interests and opinions.

3. The basic ingredient of politics is pressure. When people disagree, they bring their differences to the politician and they press for a solution. The politician acts as the third party in helping to settle disputed issues. To understand politics, then, is to understand something of what kind of people politicians are.

4. The basic way to resolve disputes in a democracy is by the process of consensus and compromise.

5. Consensus is the general feeling that the laws passed by the ruling majority are worth obeying—it is what makes majority rule work.

6. The consensus is formed by compromise; the opposing sides each give in a little in order to reach an agreement. Democracy allows for the unrestrained expression of opinions, but it also calls for a restrained resolution of conflicts.

7. Some problems that need resolution by consensus and compromise are gun control, social security reform, illegal immigration, health care, housing for the poor, discrimination, and pollution.

8. In settling unreconciled differences, there is a danger that the politician will consult only the opinions of the wealthy and the massively structured elements of society—such as Big Business and Big Labor. The individual and the small, unorganized, or underfinanced group tend to be shut out of the process of consensus and compromise.

Additional Reading

Alexis de Tocqueville's *Democracy in America,* ed. Phillips Bradley, trans. Henry Reeve, 2 Vols. (New York: Random House, Vintage Books, 1954), is an insightful analysis of the virtues and problems of the United States democracy as seen by a foreign visitor in the early nineteenth century; it remains fresh and interesting today. Similar themes concerning the theory and practice of majority rule and minority rights are pursued in Robert A. Dahl, *A Preface to Democratic Theory* (Chicago: University of Chicago Press, 1956). A less cheerful account of the American political order is given in Grant McConnell's *Private Power and American Democracy* (New York: Random House, Vintage Books, 1970), which argues that special interest groups dominate policy making.

Some of the specific issues of this chapter are discussed in Robert Sherrill, *The Saturday Night Special* (New York: David McKay Co., Charterhouse Books, 1973); Ralph Nader and Kate Blackwell, *You and Your Pension* (New York: Viking Press, Grossman Publishers, 1972); *American Medical Avarice* (New York: Abelard-Schuman, 1975) and *Unfit for Human Consumption* (Englewood Cliffs, N.J.: Prentice-Hall, 1971), both by Ruth H. Harmer; Theodore R. Marmor, *The Politics of Medicare* (Chicago: Aldine Publishing Co., 1973); Daniel Schorr, *Don't Get Sick in America* (Nashville, Aurora Publishers, 1970); Henry J. Aaron, *Shelter and Subsidies: Who Benefits from Federal Housing Policies* (Washington, D.C.: Brookings Institution, 1972); Leonard Downie, Jr., *Mortgage on America: Slums, Suburbs, and New Towns in the United States and Europe,* new ed. (New York: Praeger Publishers, 1974); Lewis Mumford, *The Urban Prospect* (New York: Harcourt Brace Jovanovich, 1969); Herbert J. Gans, *More Equality* (New York: Pantheon Books, 1973); Rachel Carson, *Silent Spring* (Boston: Houghton Mifflin Co., 1962); Barry Commoner, *The Closing Circle: Nature, Man, and Technology* (New York: Random House, Alfred A. Knopf, 1971); John C. Esposito, *Vanishing Air: The Report on Air Pollution,* Ralph Nader's Study Group Reports (New York: Viking Press, Grossman Publishers, 1970); Frank Graham, Jr., *Since Silent Spring* (Boston: Houghton Mifflin Co., 1970); Gene Marine, *America the Raped: The Engineering Mentality and the Devastation of a Continent* (New York: Simon & Schuster, 1969); Morton Mintz and Jerry S. Cohen, *Power, Inc.* (New York: Viking Press, 1976); Ralph Nader and Mark J. Green, *Corporate Power in America* (New York: Viking Press, Grossman Publishers, 1973); and David Zwick and Marcy Benstock, *Water Wasteland: The Report on Water Pollution,* Ralph Nader's Study Group Reports (New York: Viking Press, Grossman Publishers, 1970).

2
THE CONSTITUTION

Law! What do I care about the law! Haint I got the power?

Cornelius Vanderbilt

Laws are of several kinds and qualities. Some state broad, general principles, and some compel or forbid specific actions. The Constitution is the fundamental law of principle in this country. It contains about six thousand words—about one-third the length of this chapter. Something so refreshingly brief could not possibly give detailed guidance for the operation of the government and the conduct of individual lives. That is done by federal, state, and local statutes that run to millions of complex and questionable pages.

Nowhere in the United States Constitution, for example, does it say that blacks shall be served in public restaurants, whether or not the white proprietors want to serve them—one of the violent issues of the early 1960s. The Constitution does say, however, that Congress has the power to regulate interstate commerce. By some stretch of the imagination, eating in restaurants is considered part of interstate commerce. Con-

gress therefore had the blessing of the Constitution when it passed the Civil Rights Act of 1964, which, among other things, desegregated lunch counters. The general had given birth to the specific.

So it must be kept in mind that constitutional law has many dimensions. There is the written law of broad precepts and the written law of specific applications. Engrained in these laws, and adding to them, are interpretations that society has made as the result of its past experiences and its ideals for the future. Constitutional law, in effect, is a society's vision of what it is and what it wants to be. The written Constitution is just the beginning of this vision.

Most of the laws that an individual or a corporation encounters each day—marriage laws, criminal laws, mortgage laws, health and safety laws, bankruptcy laws, libel laws, and so forth—seem to have only the loosest ties to the Constitution. They flow from many sources:

Congress, state legislatures, county commissioners, city councils, and bureaucratic administrations. Behind this great reservoir of diverse laws, nevertheless, stands the Constitution. And ultimately, in every case, there is the possibility of its being brought into play.

If you are charged with murder, you will be tried in a state court, not a federal court, because murder is not a federal crime and there is no constitutional question involved. If the police prepared their case against you by tapping your phone, however, or if they failed to inform you of your right to keep silent and to obtain a lawyer, then the case begins to relate to the Constitution itself, with its guarantees of protection against unfair government actions. Issues of this sort may take a murder case, a prostitution case, or even a simple trespassing case right up to the United States Supreme Court.

There are, in short, two levels of law: constitutional law, which can be made and unmade only by the people (an extremely laborious procedure), and statutory law, which can be made and unmade by legislators and administrators as well as by the people. There are no bounds to the potential of constitutional law, but statutory law must stay strictly within the boundaries set by the Constitution itself.

Any effective national constitution must be at once inflexible in principle and flexible in application. For civilized peoples have a morality built around certain timeless principles, but those principles can be applied differently as times change. When Franklin D. Roosevelt praised Oliver Wendell Holmes for his "capacity to mold ancient principles to present needs," he paid an indirect tribute to the United States Constitution as much as a direct tribute to the great Supreme Court justice.

Change, when it comes, is a process of slow and painstaking deliberation. There are no sudden lurches in constitutional law; one of its central characteristics is stability. Even statutory law is relatively constant. When it isn't, it quickly earns the contempt of the citizenry. The statutes of the Internal Revenue Code are in constant flux, and for that reason—aside from the fact that any change in those statutes usually means more money out of one's pocket—they are generally despised, a dangerous response in a republic.

Despite obvious lapses of morality in statutory law and even graver lapses in the administration of all law, United States citizens still have an awesome faith in their Constitution, an unflinching conviction in the face of evidence all around them to the contrary that it has achieved the miracle of law: fair play. Legends are absolutely necessary for the healthy and happy functioning of a government, and the legend of fairness to all was never better enunciated than by the Supreme Court in the famous case *Ex parte Milligan* (1866):

> The Constitution is a law for rulers and people, equally in war and in peace, and covers with the shield of its protection all classes of men at all times and under all circumstances.[1]

Considering the circumstances, any document that stirs such imaginative devotion and faith probably deserves all that it receives. The Constitution at least deserves our close attention, for it stands at the very center of our politics, holding it together, and its roots are in the foundation of the government. The establishment of this government in the eighteenth century can be, for convenience' sake, divided into two periods: one of rebellion and experimentation, followed by one of conservatism and codification.

In the first period, attention was focused on cutting the ties with England and getting the feel of independence. The second period was given over to cooling the rebellious blood, cancelling out many of the democratic notions that had given momentum to the rebellion, reestablishing the preeminence of property rights, centralizing power, and getting the plan down on paper.

The first period was dominated by the glorious rhetoric of the Revolution, the second by coolheaded managers. The first period was inspired by the spirit of Thomas Jefferson, who sometimes believed in the people (and sometimes didn't); the second belonged to the spirit of Alexander Hamilton, who believed only in an elite and almost never in the sovereignty of the people. Fortunately, neither spirit totally dominated the Constitution that has come down to

---

[1] *Ex parte Milligan,* 4 Wall. 2 (1866).

Faith of Our Founders

In the beginning was the Constitution; and the Constitution was with the Founding Fathers; and the Constitution was the Founding Fathers.

This, without much exaggeration and with most of its connotations, describes the relation between the American attitudes toward history and toward the Constitution. The Constitution, like the era from which it came, is an object of almost religious adoration. There have been times, particularly during crises such as the Progressive Era and the Great Depression, when serious and loyal citizens, criticizing the Constitution as archaic and unworkable under modern conditions, have proposed drastic revision. But these exceptions have been small and futile. Change, perhaps, but a new Constitution, no.

America has been a nation of Constitution-worshippers almost from the beginning. "The laws and the Constitution of our government," declared a state judge in a charge to the jury in 1791, "ought to be regarded with reverence. Man must have an idol. And our political idol ought to be our Constitution and laws. They, like the ark of the convenant among the Jews, ought to be sacred from all profane touch." The same thought has continued to the present. "Founding Fathers" itself is a phrase that in both expression and orthography connotes a sacredness. Led by the charismatic figure of George Washington, this group has exercised a constitutional control comparable to that of ancestral spirits in a primitive society. An historian writing about that era has said: "The first function of the founders of nations, after founding itself, is to devise a set of true falsehoods about origins—a mythology—that will make it desirable for nationals to continue to live under common authority, and, indeed, make it impossible for them to entertain contrary thoughts." One of the most important of these "true falsehoods" is the accepted story of the chaos and uselessness of the Confederation period. With the Founding Fathers, particularly Washington, providing a spiritual and physical link between the two heroic points, Revolution and Constitution, it has been relatively easy virtually to expunge the Articles of Confederation from historical memory as out of keeping with a sanctified era. The Constitution has been accorded the status of the original, as well as the true, faith and fundamental law.

From Charles A. Miller, *The Supreme Court and the Uses of History* (Cambridge, Mass.: Harvard University Press, 1969), pp. 181–82.

us. Their influence was tempered by the traditions, experiences, and philosophies of past centuries.

PRE-REVOLUTIONARY THEORY AND EXPERIENCE

Neither phase of America's founding was entirely spontaneous. The rights that the colonists fought for and institutionalized had long been recognized and upheld as ideals. The goal of the Founders, unlike the goal of later revolutionary leaders in other countries, was not to displace or destroy the ruling element of the past but to balance it with others. In fact, in not being a sharp break with the past, the American Revolution may have been the most revolutionary by being the least revolutionary of revolutions.

"In 1776 the American Revolution was already centuries old," writes Stephen J. Tonsor. "Indeed the Revolution was waged in the name of a conservative appeal to rights won and cherished—rights the American colonists believed to have been usurped and violated." The spokesman for their cause appealed "to political conservation and the hard-won but immemorial rights of free men."[2] Robert A. Nisbet makes the same point: "The essence . . . was a war of restitution

[2]Stephen J. Tonsor, in the Introduction to *America's Continuing Revolution* (Washington, D.C.: American Enterprise Institute, 1973–75), p. ix.

[of traditionally English political rights] and liberation, not revolution; the outcome, one set of
political governors replaced another."[3] Key
phrases that are proudly associated with the
formation of this government—"consent of the
governed," "rule of law," "limited powers"—
were, in fact, borrowed.

Out of the past, several major intellectual
tributaries poured into the thinking of the American Revolution. Of the writers, perhaps the
most important were Thomas Hobbes (1588–
1679), John Locke (1632–1704), and Baron de
Montesquieu (1689–1755). As Saul Padover has
pointed out, what Locke, Hobbes, and Montesquieu "had in common—and what appealed to
the Americans of the Eighteenth Century—was a
rational approach to politics. They rejected political mysticism and the long-established idea that
government was divinely ordained."[4] If there
was a divinity involved, to them it was in human
rationality itself, and in its best products—
including government.

The most important of the three writers—not
because he was especially profound or original,
but because his writings had the happy accident
of being influential—was Locke. He believed, as
did others, that human beings possess certain
rights that precede government. (Hobbes, on the
other hand, believed that man's rights came into
existence only after he entered into a social contract with the government, to which he surrendered certain liberties in exchange for certain
rights: tit for tat.) Said Locke, "The state of
nature has a law to govern it, which obliges
everyone: and reason, which is that law, teaches
all mankind, who will but consult it, that being
all equal and independent, no one ought to harm
another in his life, health, liberty or possession."[5]

Locke often grouped life, liberty, and property in this way, nearly a century before the
American Revolution. Considering the popularity of his writings, it is hardly surprising to find
echoes of them in colonial declarations (the declaration of the Massachusetts Council in 1773,
for example, stated that "life, liberty, and property" were "natural rights") before Jefferson had
gotten around to incorporating "Life, Liberty
and the pursuit of Happiness" into the Declaration of Independence.

Exit Fear, Enter Liberty

It is difficult to believe that such elementary
concerns as life, liberty, and property were for
centuries at the very heart of political debate. For
here, in the third quarter of the relatively comfortable and almost luxuriously democratic
twentieth century, the governmental machinery
is working fairly well for us. But it has only been
five hundred years—just two and a half times as
long as this young government has been
around—since the Western world began to
emerge from the dark melancholy and chaos that
had lain across Europe since the sixth century.
There were so many threats to life and property
that law and order held top priority. People were
glad to give total allegience to the ruler who
could offer the most security. The human hunger
for social unity, for warmth in the association of
community and state, was intense. If that kind of
unity could be spun around a king, divinity was
happily conceded to him. And things were still
that way when this continent was discovered.

By the time the Pilgrims landed at Plymouth
Rock in 1620, Europe had made social progress.
People could afford the luxury of questioning
their governments, and they had begun to do so.
No longer so hungry and fearful as their ancestors in the Middle Ages, they had become prom-
isingly cocky. Less enchanted with the idea of
divine kings or slavish obedience to court or
church, they wanted a piece of the governmental
action. No one was seriously suggesting anything remotely like a popular government yet,
but at least it was being proposed that the people
were part of the formula that made a king's
power. And a natural law and natural rights—
meaning the restrictions and opportunities that
came from nature itself and transcended the
edicts of kings—were being recognized. Even
today politicians and judges sometimes refer to

---

[3]Robert A. Nisbet, "The Social Impact of the Revolution" in
America's Continuing Revolution, p. 73.

[4]Saul Padover, ed., *To Secure These Blessings: The Great Debates
of the Constitutional Convention of 1787* (Millwood, N.Y.: Kraus
Reprint Co., 1962), p. 24.

[5]John Locke, *Two Treatises of Government*, ed. Peter Laslett
(New York: Cambridge University Press, 1960).

natural rights and natural laws, although they probably do so more for rhetorical effect than out of the devout conviction of the American revolutionists. But the notions held a central place in all theories questioning the power of the crown, down to the American Revolution and beyond.

John Adams spoke of "rights antecedent to all earthly government, rights that cannot be repealed or restrained by human laws—rights derived from the great Legislator of the universe."[6] Alexander Hamilton, resorting to more vivid prose than usual, wrote, in 1774, that the "sacred rights of mankind . . . are written, as with a sunbeam, in the whole volume of human nature, by the hand of divinity itself, and can never be erased or obscured by mortal power."[7] In the Declaration of Independence, Thomas Jefferson spoke of "the law of nature and of nature's God" and the "unalienable rights" with which, he said, "the Creator endowed all men."

Rebellious Religious Minorities

Another important source of America's revolutionary thought were certain Protestant sects. Almost always in the minority, they stressed the rights of minorities. Because they flourished apart from and in opposition to the Anglican church, the established state religion, they stressed the right to revolt against the worldly monarch if *they* judged his actions contrary to the commands of God.

John Knox (1505–72), one of the founders of Presbyterianism, was especially hot for the right to rebel. The stress was on individualism. Everyone, in this fervent Protestant movement, would be his or her own pope. With the printing of the Bible in the common tongue, one could go straight to holy writ for guidance, and to hell with priestly intermediaries.

Inevitably, the rebellion of the Calvinists and the Presbyterians gave birth to religious intellectuals who rebelled against all sects and against all

authority. They were not exactly anarchists, but they were anarchists in their particular contexts. John Milton (1608–74) was a political pamphleteer as well as a poet. His arguments—for freedom of expression (*Areopagitica*), in favor of killing tyrants if necessary and replacing them with popular sovereignty (*Tenure of Kings and Magistrates*), and on behalf of a free commonwealth (*The Ready and Easy Way*)—were permanently implanted in the minds of English opinion-shapers more than a hundred years before the English in America decided to revolt. Milton's arguments actually became part of practical politics. They were an important part of the Puritan revolution that overthrew and beheaded King Charles I in 1649, establishing the Commonwealth under Oliver Cromwell.

Some of the most important theory supporting the American Revolution goes back at least another half a century before Milton, to the tracts of the French religious wars. They argued two of the most important premises of the American Revolution: (1) the contract theory, that governments are not imposed but are set up by agreement between ruler and ruled; and (2) the *right* of any given people to representative government.[8]

Common-Law Roots of the Revolution

New governments, however, are not constructed from theories. They are an extension of actual experience. "Experience must be our only guide," warned John Dickinson (1732–1808), an important conservative. "Reason may mislead us."[9] Theory seeps into experience over many years, but it is experience itself that counts.

A central part of the English experience was the common law, most particularly as it had been courageously expounded by Sir Edward Coke, chief justice of the King's Bench in the early 1600s. It was Coke's opinion that every law-abiding Englishman was constitutionally guar-

[6]John Adams, *Life and Works* (Boston: Little, Brown and Co., 1850–56), 3:448–64.

[7]Alexander Hamilton, *Works*, ed. Henry C. Lodge (New York: G. P. Putnam's Sons, 1885–86), 1:108.

[8]Charles M. Wiltse, *The Jeffersonian Tradition in American Democracy* (New York: Hill & Wang, 1960), pp. 8–9.

[9]Quoted in Hannah Arendt, *On Revolution* (New York: Viking Press, 1963), p. 168.

anteed trial by his peers and due process of the law as protection from a royal threat to his life, liberty, and property. Coke backed his conviction with edicts from the bench that often offended the king and put his own neck in jeopardy. Common law drew this provision from the Magna Carta of 1215: "No free man shall be taken, imprisoned, disseised [dispossessed of his land], outlawed, banished, or in any way destroyed, nor will We proceed against or prosecute him, except by the lawful judgment of his peers and by the law of the land."[10]

In 1354, during the reign of King Edward III, other statutes confirming and strengthening the Magna Carta were passed by Parliament. The most important guaranteed that "None shall be condemned without trial." Also, that "no Man, of what Estate or Condition that he be, shall be put out of Land or Tenement, nor taken, nor imprisoned, nor disinherited, nor put to death, without being brought to Answer by due Process of Law."[11]

In the seventeenth century—the century just preceding the American Revolution, remember—great contests were waged between royal prerogatives and the English common law. The common law won, permanently. The king was put in his place, beneath the British constitution. With the enactment of the Bill of Rights of 1689, that constitution asserted that every Englishman's "ancient rights and liberties" must henceforth be protected in this way: the crown would not be allowed to suspend laws; the crown would not be allowed to impose taxation without grant from Parliament; the crown would not be permitted to interfere with freedom of speech on the floor of Parliament; the crown would not be permitted to impose excessive bail, or excessive fines, or unusual punishment.[12]

Being English, the American colonists believed these rights and protections to be theirs, by long tradition. This makes it easier to understand why the first United States Congress saw no pressing need to write our Bill of Rights into the Constitution. Many members looked upon such rights as already in effect, a carryover from British common law.

Community Experience, the Crucial Ingredient

To the colonists, their social contract with the king was rather vague. They had lived in the New World, an ocean away, for generations. What they cared about was the compact they had with each other and with the town councils for living together from day to day according to accepted standards of permissible conduct. It was at the heart of their very existence from the beginning. Even before setting to work at Plymouth, the Pilgrims had sat down in the cabin of the *Mayflower* and drafted the celebrated Mayflower Compact. It was a community agreement binding them into a "civil body politic," promising to make "just and equal laws." The majesty of the court and the weight of the scepter must already have seemed a long way off. Other colonial compacts followed, and Hannah Arendt catches the spirit and the worth of them:

> The unique and all-decisive distinction between the settlements of North America and all other colonial enterprises was that only the British emigrants had insisted, from the very beginning, that they constitute themselves into "civil bodies politic." These bodies, moreover, were not conceived as governments, strictly speaking; they did not imply rule and the division of the people into rulers and ruled. The best proof of this is the simple fact that the people thus constituted could remain, for more than a hundred and fifty years, the royal subjects of the government of England. These new bodies politic really were "political societies," and their great importance for the future lay in the formation of a political realm *that enjoyed power and was entitled to claim rights without possessing or claiming sovereignty.*[13]

So the general populace of the colonies had the luxury of being subjects of a ruler who was largely a symbol, a fiction. They were thus free to build a communal life based on reciprocity and industry and local standards of merit and a kind

---

[10]See Arthur L. Goodhart, *Law of the Land* (Charlottesville, Va.: University of Virginia Press, 1966).

[11]Goodhart, p. 38.

[12]Goodhart, pp. 49–50.

[13]Arendt, *On Revolution*, p. 167 (emphasis added).

of presumed equality.[14] In short, a practical democracy existed in America long before the theorists wrote it into the federal Constitution.

THE ERA OF REBELLION

Although the freedoms of the typical colonist were not abridged much, if at all, by the crown,[15] the profits of manufacturers, large farmers, and rich landholders were another story. America's number one export, tobacco, was among the American commodities required by British regulation to reach the world by way of Britain. When America began exporting iron, British iron-makers got Parliament to forbid the colonists to build any new factories. Furthermore, the colonists were virtually obliged to buy some commodities from Britain that they could have obtained cheaper on the world market. America had one of the world's finest shipbuilding industries, an iron industry that was already turning out one-seventh of the world's crude iron, a fast-developing textile industry, and a corner on such products as cotton and tobacco. Americans of property felt, with good reason, that they could multiply their riches if they controlled their politics.

The Practical Side of the "Glorious Rhetoric"

The colonial merchants and landholders, having decided that they could do better in a

country independent of England (a country where *they* would control the rule-making machinery of commerce and taxation), set about recruiting the general populace, who would do the fighting, through a campaign of propaganda that portrayed British rule as the worst of tyrannies. It wasn't.

To be sure, the American colonies were subject to taxation without representation in the British Parliament. So, today, are United States citizens living in the Virgin Islands, Puerto Rico, and the District of Columbia taxed without voting representation in Congress (and so were the citizens of Alaska and Hawaii until the 1950s).

Furthermore, even if the British government did tax without representation, it was quite sensitive to American reactions. When Parliament passed the Stamp Act on March 22, 1765, delegates from nine colonies resolved to embargo all British goods on which the Stamp Act tax was imposed. Four and a half months after it went into effect, Parliament repealed it. In 1767 Parliament laid a tax on tea, glass, paints, lead, and paper. The colonists protested, and there were confrontations with British troops. In one clash, the troops fired on a Boston crowd and killed five people. They did so in the same foolishly high-handed manner with which United States troops shot and killed four unarmed citizens at Kent State University in 1970 at a rally protesting the United States' invasion of Cambodia. British officials were much more contrite about their troops' misconduct than United States officials were nearly two hundred years later. Thirty-four days after the Boston Massacre the taxes were repealed, but the illegal assault on Cambodia continued for three years.

On May 10, 1773, Parliament passed the Tea Act, giving a subsidy to the East India Company, which was in danger of going bankrupt. This gave the company a commercial advantage over American tea merchants—in the same way that this era's federal subsidies to the airlines, to the bankrupt Penn Central and other railroads, and to the giant trucking companies prevent the growth of smaller, competing transportation firms. These subsidies are taken right out of the taxpayers' pockets, just as the subsidies to the East India Company were taken out of the colonists' pockets, without their direct approval.

---

[14]Arendt, p. 169.

[15]In May 1776, the Continental Congress urged all colonies to establish "such government as shall best conduce to the happiness and safety of their constituents." Significantly, Connecticut and Rhode Island simply changed a few words in their seventeenth-century charters—declaring that their power came from the people and not from the king—and called them constitutions. When New Hampshire had trouble coming up with a constitution that all could agree on, it asked John Adams of Massachusetts for advice. He responded by urging them to adopt "a plan resembling the government under which we were born. Kings we never had among us. Nobles we never had. But governors and councils we have always had as well as representatives. A legislature in three branches ought to be preserved, and independent judges." Clearly, life under the British crown had not been so bad. (*Time,* special 1776 issue, vol. 105, no. 20, p. 34.)

Boston, 1767; Kent State University, 1970

In short, if King George III and the British Parliament were tyrannical, they were not greatly more so than their counterparts in this country today. All governments are unfair to some people, and all governments are guilty of bullying from time to time. Those characteristics are intrinsic to government.

To arouse the populace to risk their lives in war against superior armies—or what many feared would be superior armies—the Founders had to exaggerate the contrast between the actual government of George III and Parliament and the possible government of the new nation. The easiest way to achieve the proper outrage was to pretend that America's problems were caused not by Parliament but directly and solely by the king. It is difficult to imagine a true tyranny coming from a collection of many rational men. Ogres are almost always singular. Parliaments and congresses may sometimes be despised, but they are not easy to hate. Hatred was required, so the Founders concentrated on the king. The Declaration of Independence focused on the throne, and its twenty-seven specific charges justifying the Revolution were aimed at "the present King of Great Britain." Parliament was not mentioned, an absurd omission at best.

The first draft of the Declaration of Independence was written by Jefferson between June 11 and 28, 1776. He allowed John Adams and Benjamin Franklin to read it, and they made a few suggestions. Then members of the Continental Congress changed it here and there before unanimously approving it on July 4, 1776. It was not the official Declaration of Independence. That Declaration, or resolution—that the colonies "are, and of Right ought to be, FREE AND INDEPENDENT STATES"—was introduced by Richard Henry Lee of Virginia and finally passed twelve to zero on July 2, with New York abstaining. The passage of Lee's resolution marked the first time in history that a legislature gave legitimate standing to a revolution.

Lee's resolution was for legitimatizing; Jefferson's was for propagandizing at home and abroad. Congress wanted to mobilize world opinion. As Jefferson said fifty years later, the object was "to place before mankind the common sense of the subject, in terms so plain and

firm as to command their assent, and to justify ourselves in the independent stand we are compelled to take."[16]

A Declaration of Glittering Generalities

The terms were anything but plain. They were florid and filigreed, like most of Jefferson's writing.[17] They inspired Massachusetts Senator Rufus Choate's apt description in the last century, "the glittering and sounding generalities of the Declaration of Independence."[18]

Many of the charges in the Declaration were sober and well founded; others were downright trivial. Some, if taken seriously, would make us think twice today. "He has erected a multitude of New Offices, and sent hither swarms of Officers to harrass our People, and eat out their substance," huffs the Declaration of Independence. Like the multitude of nosy bureaucrats the American people are asked to support and tolerate today? "He has kept among us, in times of peace, Standing Armies without the Consent of

---

[16]Quoted in Lally Weymouth, ed., *Thomas Jefferson: The Man, His World, His Influence* (New York: G. P. Putnam's Sons, 1974), p. 180. Many colonial newspapers printed the Declaration. Washington had it read to all his troops, to convince them, presumably, that the cause was worth fighting for. State legislatures endorsed the Declaration. Abroad, it was reprinted widely and received with the usual division of opinion. (Spain did not permit its publication.) Predictably, the British press in general was cool or hostile, scorning the Declaration's egalitarian theme as hypocritical, and of course most of Britain's ruling class agreed with King George III that the colonies were acting like "ungrateful children." On the other hand, the Declaration did evoke some sympathetic and even some supportive comments in Parliament. Also predictably, France, which welcomed Britain's discomfort, generally had high praise for the Declaration.

[17]Jefferson wrote business correspondence requesting payment of bad debts for his law practice as though he were writing another Declaration of Independence. Garry Wills reports that when Jefferson and five other men, including Patrick Henry, formed a league to collect delinquent legal fees from their clients, the compact ended with this ringing promise: "for the invariable Observance of which we mutually plight our Honor to each other." The concluding sentence in the Declaration of Independence is, "And for the support of this declaration . . . we mutally pledge to each other our lives, our fortunes & our sacred honour." ("Prolegomena to a Reading of the Declaration," in Weymouth, p. 70.)

[18]Quoted by Garry Wills, in Weymouth, pp. 69–70.

Drafting the Declaration of Independence

our legislatures," says the Declaration of Independence with indignation. Like the federal troops stationed in Little Rock during the racial turmoil of the 1950s, without the consent of the state legislature?

The Declaration of Independence was very down on George III because "He has affected to render the Military independent of and superior to the Civil Power," a complaint that some reasonable citizens have made about recent Presidents. One of the grievances that Jefferson wrote into the original draft of the Declaration was that George III had abetted the slave trade and thus

was guilty of waging "cruel war against human nature itself and violating its most sacred rights of life and liberty." The Continental Congress knocked that out. It was a curious charge for Jefferson to make inasmuch as (1) a decision of the Court of King's Bench in favor of a runaway slave in 1772 had virtually ended slavery in England; (2) the demands of the Southern *colonies* had caused the Continental Army to end its policy of freeing any runaway slave who signed up for army service; and (3) Jefferson himself was, and would continue to be, a slaveholder— so were George Washington and Patrick Henry

("Give me liberty or give me death!" must have sounded queer to the blacks he owned).

The Nice Side of Hypocrisy

Hypocrisy was one of the building blocks of the new government. But hypocrisy is a building block in any government. If the colonial experience proved anything, it was that men who demand freedom for themselves when they are subjects are not so keen on freedom for others when they are in control. The Puritans, whose influence was heavy in the new government, were like that. As Clinton Rossiter has put it:

Radicals in England, men with contempt for established order and with detailed blueprints for a new one, they became—thanks to a bracing ocean voyage—conservatives in America, men whose blueprints were now the foundation of an order established to their liking.

And when the Puritans' New World order was challenged, they quickly denounced their challengers as "phanatick Opinionists" and "sowers of sedition."[19]

Within limits, hypocrisy is not necessarily an evil element. Revolutionists must believe in the purity of their cause; new governments must believe they are acting from the noblest of motivations. State of mind is everything. Just as Jefferson thought it necessary, in the Declaration of Independence, to describe a muddled and ineffective monarch in satanic terms:

He is at this Time transporting large Armies of foreign Mercenaries to compleat the works of death, desolation and tyranny, already begun

with circumstances of Cruelty and perfidy scarcely parallelled in the most barbarous ages, and totally unworthy the Head of a civilized nation . . .

he also thought it necessary to ascribe the most saintly motives to the revolutionaries: "We hold these truths to be self-evident"—

- That all men are created equal
- That they are endowed with "unalienable" rights
- That these rights include life, liberty, and the pursuit of happiness
- That it is to secure these rights that government is instituted among men
- That governments so instituted derive their just powers from the consent of the governed
- That when a form of government becomes destructive of these ends, men may alter or abolish it
- That men have the right, then, to institute new governments designed to effect their safety and happiness

The difference between pre-Revolutionary propaganda and post-Revolution management can be seen in the fact that of these seven supposedly "self-evident" truths, five were either ignored or played down or opposed when it came to writing the Constitution.

For Jefferson to talk of governments deriving their just powers from the consent of the governed in colonial days was a joke. Jefferson's home state of Virginia, for example, was the richest of the colonies and was run by about one hundred families. Although they went through the formality of passing laws in the legislature, which they ran with an iron fist, those families imposed their will on the masses of Virginians with far more tyranny than bumptious George III could ever have hoped to exercise. Not only did they run Virginia, they looted it:

Between 1743 and 1760 the Virginia Council [run by the one hundred families] granted forty-three tracts amounting to more than three million acres to groups of elite "realtors"—the Loyal Land Company, the Ohio Land Company, the Greenbrier Company—the associates of which were the leading families of Virginia. Attempts by the crown to control this orgy of acquisition were

---

[19]Clinton Rossiter, *Conservatism in America: The Thankless Persuasion* (New York: Random House, Vintage Books, 1962), p. 99. Something similar was seen at the time of the Revolution. Americans who piously complained that George III was depriving them of life, liberty, and property were depriving their neighbors of liberty and property, and sometimes life, for no crime except being loyal to the established government. The Loyalists, Americans who could not, in good conscience, turn against their king, were abused by the revolutionists—"patriots" by our lights today, but traitors by the standards of the British government then. Loyalists suffered censorship of the press and of speech, unreasonable search and seizure, and cruel and unusual punishment. Some were hanged; some were stripped naked, their bodies covered with scalding tar and feathers, and the feathers lighted. More than 100,000 Loyalists fled to Canada to escape such terrorism, committed in the pursuit of happiness.

resented, the resentment mounting into what one historian calls a "pre-Revolutionary revolt." . . .[20]

When the delegates to the Continental Congress of 1776 came together, John Adams wrote to a friend that the idea of forming a truly republican government seemed "abhorrent to the inclinations of the barons of the South, and the proprietary interests of the middle colonies, as well as to that avarice of land which has made upon this continent so many votaries of Mammon that I sometimes dread the consequences."[21] He was being unfairly harsh toward the South; barons with similar inclinations lived in the North also. There were awesome class distinctions in colonial America. The landed gentry sometimes controlled estates that medieval barons would have envied. The Van Rensselaer manor on the Hudson measured some twenty-four miles by twenty miles; the Fairfax estate in Virginia contained 6 million acres. The people who controlled these estates were—and would remain—royalty in every way but title. They had as little in common with most of the population—the tenant farmers, artisans, mechanics, small freeholders, laborers, indentured servants, and slaves—as Nelson A. Rockefeller has with an Exxon service-station attendant. Whatever Jefferson may have meant by all men being created equal, he certainly could not have meant an equal chance to control the economy or, through it, the politics of America.

Men like George Washington and John Adams wished the so-called revolution to carry America no further than mere separation from England.[22] General Washington called the New England troops under his command "an exceedingly dirty and nasty people."[23] His estimation of the common people was no loftier after he became our first President. As for Adams, our second President, his view of equality was probably not much different from that of George III, judging from such statements as these:

> A physical inequality, an intellectual inequality, of the most serious kind is established unchangeably by the Author of nature; *and society has a right to establish any other inequalities it may judge necessary for its good.*

> God Almighty has decreed in the creation of human nature an eternal aristocracy among men. The world is, always has been, and ever will be governed by it.[24]

Similar opinions were held by the overwhelming majority of the leadership, if indeed there were any exceptions. To such men, the rebellion of 1776 was anything but a glorious revolution to establish the dominion of the proletariat by seizing all machinery of production and placing it in the people's hands. Few men of influence in that era would have disagreed with Adams's heated defense of property rights:

> The moment the idea is admitted into society, that property is not as sacred as the laws of God, and that there is not a force of law and public justice to protect it, anarchy and tyranny commence.[25]

Out of such notions it is extremely difficult to weave a revolutionary flag that will stir the people's hearts. If the leaders of the colonies wanted a revolution, they would have to make their speeches accordingly. Thus, the enormous fighting value of the Declaration of Independence cannot be overemphasized. It was an appeal to the growing popular spirit of nationalism.

Nothing happens in politics solely as the result of logic. Laws are not passed simply because they should be passed. If they were, laws against child labor, for example, would have been passed generations earlier. Laws are seldom passed even when circumstances seem to say they *must* be passed. Otherwise, slavery would have been handled in the legislature rather than on the battlefield. Laws are passed—and constitutions are written and rebellions are

---

[20]Howard Mumford Jones, *O Strange New World: American Culture: The Formative Years* (New York: Viking Press, 1964), p. 158.

[21]Quoted in Jones, p. 59.

[22]Rossiter, *Conservatism in America*, p. 102.

[23]*Time*, special 1776 issue, p. 34.

---

[24]Quoted in Rossiter, *Conservatism in America*, p. 112 (emphasis added).

[25]Quoted in Rossiter, p. 114.

launched—because opinion shapers (politicians, journalists, corporate managers) decide it is time for them to be passed and then carefully manipulate the minds of a sufficient majority of the public to support and accept them. Rationalization, conviction, education, propaganda, experience, and the interpretation of experience are all used to the desired end. Then things fall into place.

To the gentlemen who sat around the coffee-houses of Philadelphia and New York and Boston working up a passion about the Revolution, phrases like "natural rights" and "unalienable rights" and "natural law" set exactly the mood that they needed—just as expressions like "national security" and "American way of life" have been used, sometimes sincerely and sometimes calculatedly, to create other moods and launch other movements in the twentieth century.

THE ERA OF EXPERIMENTATION

At the same time that the Continental Congress was approving its resolution to cut away from England, it was also putting together a plan for the operation of the new government. This plan, The Articles of Confederation and Perpetual Union, was ratified by the last of the thirteen states, not without a considerable amount of debate and complaint, on March 1, 1781, seven months before the end of the Revolutionary War.

The Articles of Confederation

History has reserved glamour for the Constitution, which came into existence years later and is the oldest written constitution in effect in the world. But the Articles have their own grandeur, even though they were a failure. They were the Western world's first written constitution, and what a first that was. The prospect of their leaders starting from scratch and putting into writing any guarantees they chose electrified the imagination of Americans. They knew

> . . . that all previous nations had been compelled to accept their constitutions from some conqueror or some supreme lawgiver or had found themselves entrapped by a form of government molded by accident, caprice, or violence. They knew—and they told themselves repeatedly—that they were "the first people whom heaven has favoured with an opportunity of deliberating upon, and choosing the forms of government under which they should live."[26]

Anything seemed possible. As Thomas Paine wrote at the time, "The answer to the question, can America be happy under a government of her own, is short and simple, viz. as happy as she pleases; she hath a blank sheet to write upon."[27]

Where the Articles Failed

The first writing on the blank sheet was done by men who were opposed to a strong central government—the same men, that is, who had been the most sanguine leaders of the rebellion. They were later known as the anti-Federalists.

It is commonly said that the Articles allowed the states too much autonomy, permitting them to operate too independently of each other, and did not establish a tightly knit nation with a strong central government. Such criticisms are justified. Under the Articles, Congress was a one-house outfit deriving its powers not from the people but from the state legislatures. It could not levy taxes, regulate commerce, or really influence the citizens except through the state governments. It was especially difficult in wartime, under the Articles, to raise troops and cash. Legislation had to be passed by at least two-thirds of the members of Congress; amendments to the Articles had to be approved by all thirteen state legislatures. There was no executive authority. The Confederation of states was virtually a body without a head. It has been accurately described as "a league of friendship entered into by sovereign states."[28]

Unfortunately, the friendship often cooled. There was considerable bickering between the

---

[26]Gordon S. Wood, *The Creation of the American Republic, 1776–1787* (Chapel Hill, N.C.: University of North Carolina Press, 1970), p. 127.

[27]Quoted in Wood, p. 125.

[28]C. Herman Pritchett, *The American Constitutional System,* 3rd ed. (New York: McGraw-Hill, 1971), p. 4.

states and far too much commercial wrangling. New York would stick Massachusetts with a burdensome tariff on incoming oysters; Massachusetts would retaliate with an excruciating tariff on New York's two-penny nails. And in all that commercial knife-play, the central government was helpless to intervene.

Symbolic of the central government's helplessness was the absence of any president or federal court system. The Articles, in their overwhelming capitulation to state pride, had made no provision for either.

Strengths of the Articles

Whatever the shortcomings of the Confederation, it served its immediate purpose. In fact, under the Articles, a great deal was accomplished by the states that assisted the drafters of the Constitution in 1787. It is unlikely that the Constitution would have shown so much imaginative boldness had the states not been encouraged to try their own hands at writing state constitutions in the more freewheeling era of the Articles.

"Many important constitutional principles," notes Bernard Schwartz, "have first been developed in the states and then been adapted for use in federal law. This was true of the very concept of a written constitution and bill of rights. Twelve states had written constitutions, and eight of them had bills of rights before the federal Constitution and the first ten amendments were written."[29]

Having enjoyed this period of sovereignty, the states were wisely reluctant to surrender more than was necessary when it came time to write a constitution creating a federation of states under a stronger central government. In fact, the Tenth Amendment in the Bill of Rights assures that "powers not delegated to the United States by the Constitution, nor prohibited by it to the States, are reserved to the States respectively, or to the people."

Under that vague clause—the states' rights clause—much evil was later committed. Several

state governments insisted that the Tenth Amendment permitted them to abuse some of their residents in local style. But this clause also accomplished much good, for it left the states with ample room to experiment in social programs and legal concepts. "It is one of the happy incidents of the federal system," said Justice Louis D. Brandeis, "that a single state may, if its citizens choose, serve as a laboratory; and try novel social and economic experiments without risk to the rest of the country."[30] Some of our most humane and progressive ideas have been tried first at the state level before being adopted by the federal government.

If nothing else, the Articles of Confederation were of enormous value during this era of experimentation in showing how the government should *not* be set up. They demonstrated that, much as the colonists had come to hate the king as a symbol, a reasonably strong central government was useful in maintaining intranational peace and developing international respect. The Articles were not a stupid document; they were far from it. But circumstances conspired against them, and they were allowed to expire quietly—not even given the dignity of formal repeal and bureaucratic burial, but simply allowed to slip into disuse, ignored at the last.

Hard Times for the Articles

The Confederation did not have a fair chance. Coping with just the normal problems of a new nation would have been a heavy enough burden. But to that normal burden was added a war and a postwar depression. When times are good, people would just as soon forget their government; when times are lousy, they look to it for remedies and are quick to lose patience.

In 1786 the Confederation was heavily in debt because it had no taxing power. There was confusion in commerce because of a lack of uniform currency (each state could print its own) and because of tariff rivalries between states. And there was the depression, one element of which was a tight money supply. Debtors demanded that the state governments print more money—

---

[29]Bernard Schwartz, *The American Heritage History of the Law in America* (New York: American Heritage Publishing Co., 1974), p. 60.

[30]Quoted in Schwartz, pp. 59–60.

creating an artificial inflation—so that it would be easier for them to get their hands on the money they needed to pay their debts. But money that is just cranked off the printing press has a hard time holding its value; the merchants of New England, where money was most heavily circulated, began scorning it as funny money. Some refused to accept it. Nevertheless, debtors went on insisting that the legislatures produce more. In Rhode Island, the legislature went along. When the Massachusetts legislature refused, outraged farmers in the western part of the state mobilized under Daniel Shays and began invading courtrooms and disrupting bankruptcy cases.

This spirited continuation of the Revolutionary mood in the winter of 1786–87 struck terror into the hearts of the moneyed class everywhere. The plain people of America taking up arms to make politicians do their bidding? Horrors! At that juncture the Continental Congress, usually moribund, came to life and raised an army to crush Shays' Rebellion. The Massachusetts legislature, which had been sluggish about helping the busted farmers, showed remarkable speed in putting down this minor uprising of desperate citizens who had, in what they thought was the best American tradition, taken matters into their own hands.

As a rebellion it was of no consequence. But the Federalists interpreted it as proof that a powerful central government was needed that could act swiftly and overwhelmingly to protect the propertied interests against a citizenry that took the idea of participatory democracy too seriously.

Also, international traders were becoming nervous. When other nations get the idea that a government is unreliable, that it is unstable and giddy, they are inclined to take their trade elsewhere. Foreign relations are worth money. So the leaders of the United States' commerce were understandably concerned when they saw that their country's reputation had not improved much since the new Confederation was established in 1781. In that year Josiah Tucker, dean of Gloucester in England, had prophesied:

As to the future grandeur of America and its being a rising empire under one head, whether repub-lican or monarchical, it is one of the idlest and most visionary notions that ever was conceived even by writers of romance. . . . They never can be united into one compact empire under any species of government whatever, a disunited people till the end of time, suspicious and distrustful of each other, they will be divided and sub-divided into little commonwealths or principalities.[31]

The general mood of the electorate as a whole, not only the elite, was shifting toward welcoming the concept of a stronger central government, of more law and order, more security, and more direction. In hard economic times, that is usually the response.

THE ERA OF CONSERVATISM AND CODIFICATION

The idea of committing one's destiny to a central government that was far removed both physically and technically from most of the citizens must have seemed to promise as little democracy in those days as it does today. However, the state legislatures that functioned under the Articles of Confederation were generally as crude and ineffective as state legislatures are today. They were in themselves no great recommendation for continuing life under the Articles. And so the groundwork was laid for the writing of the Constitution.

Money Interests Take Over

A desire to work out a smoother agreement for interstate commerce led to a rump convention of politicians in Annapolis in 1786, but nothing much came of it except a resolve to hold another convention in Philadelphia in May 1787.

The Philadelphia convention, which lasted from May 25 to September 17, was attended by fifty-five delegates, including some of the biggest names of the day: George Washington, Benjamin Franklin, Alexander Hamilton, and

---

[31]Josiah Tucker, *Cui Bono,* quoted in Goodhart, *Law of the Land,* p. 61.

Eighteenth-century painting of a colonial plantation

James Madison. Notably missing was Thomas Jefferson, on diplomatic duty in France. Patrick Henry, the firebrand of the Revolution, stayed away with the candid explanation that he "smelt a rat." Most of the good old democrats of the king-baiting days were absent.

In their place were a group of neo-Tories, many of whom were motivated by something besides patriotic altruism. There were owners of government securities who were worried about not getting paid; land speculators who wanted the Indians pushed back by force; manufacturers who wanted high, uniform tariffs; and financiers and creditors who were eager to check what they considered to be "radical" state legislation.

Arthur N. Holcombe estimates that "two-thirds of the delegates were wealthy landowners or merchants or professional men connected with the families of wealthy landowners and merchants and largely dependent upon these classes for clients and professional success."[32] In nine of the states represented at the convention, men of the upper crust were definitely in the majority. The one-third of the delegates who were not economic aristocrats were mostly lawyers—a group whose outlook is not ordinarily sympathetic to people with no money.[33]

Charles Beard has counted pocketbooks and found that of the fifty-five convention members, forty held public securities, fourteen were land speculators, eleven were in manufacturing or merchandising or shipping, and fifteen were

[32]Arthur N. Holcombe, *Our More Perfect Union* (Cambridge, Mass.: Harvard University Press, 1967), p. 25.

[33]Forrest McDonald has a different count: thirty-four lawyers, eighteen farmers (sixteen large-scale), fifteen with mercantile interests (including eight of the lawyers). But this adds up to the same well-heeled character. (*We the People: The Economic Origins of the Constitution,* Chicago: University of Chicago Press, 1976, pp. 86–87.)

slaveholders. He holds that these "personalty" interests were allied against and overrode small farming and debtor interests in the writing of the Constitution.

From these points of view, the convention would seem to have been rigged against the poor farmer (there were few poor city-dwellers in those days, because not many people lived in cities), the frontiersman, and the poor tradesman. The only large group of delegates who would be considered "middle class" were the lawyers, mentioned above.

If not rigged against that group, at least the convention appears to have been most concerned with the needs of the well-established, moneyed interests. A simple reading of the Constitution would support that conclusion. Historians, however, to whom nothing is simple, have continued to pore over the economic pedigrees of the convention members and have produced a number of variations on the same theme. Some people balk at such a strict economic interpretation of the Constitution as Beard's. According to Robert Brown, nearly all Americans living in 1787 had some property to protect and therefore something to gain from the new government.[34]

Whatever view one takes of the framers' motives, one can easily point to the specific economic provisions they built into the document. Most were common-sense rules and were in no way evidence of a class conspiracy. Among the powers granted to Congress in Article I, Section 8 were the power to regulate foreign commerce and the power to levy uniform duties (thus allowing for protective tariffs on foreign imports competing with domestic goods), the power to regulate interstate commerce (thereby ending interstate tariff rivalries), the power to coin money and regulate its value (thereby preventing states from permitting inflation to aid debtors), and the power to provide a militia to put down insurrections and invasions. Article IV, Section 4, guarantees that the national government will protect each state from invasion and (on application of state legislature) against domestic violence.

All debts contracted under the Confederation were made valid under the Constitution (Article VI). Payment of debts was protected by Article I, Section 10, which provided that no state could make "any thing but gold and silver Coin a Tender in Payment of Debts." To make sure that businessmen had all the stability they needed, Section 10 restricted the states from passing any law "impairing the Obligation of Contracts."[35] That section also prohibited states from levying duties on imports or exports. Article IV, Section 2, charged states to return persons "held to Service or Labour" who had escaped from another state. The Fifth Amendment provided that no person will be deprived of life, liberty, *or property* without due process of law and that private property may not be taken for public use without just compensation.

Limited Democracy

The framers were concerned lest the masses control the government, so they were careful to limit the idea of popular sovereignty. The only office for which popular election was even provided in the original Constitution was that of delegate to the House of Representatives. Senators were to be chosen by the state legislatures (Article I, Section 3). Only in 1913, with the Seventeenth Amendment, was popular election of the Senate prescribed by the Constitution, although a number of states had already taken this step on their own. The President was to be elected by a unique system removed from the electorate—the electoral college, whose members were to be chosen as the legislature of a state might direct (Article II, Section 1).

---

[34]Robert Brown, *Charles Beard and the Constitution* (New York: W. W. Norton & Co., 1965), pp. 21, 197.

[35]On the very first occasion that that portion of the Constitution was tested, the Supreme Court ruled in such a way as to be a lesson for all posterity. The details of the case are revealing: in 1795 the Georgia legislature sold 35 million acres of highly desirable land to four companies for only $500,000. Then it was discovered that the land companies had bribed every member of the legislature but one. Georgians were so outraged at this swindle that they forced a newly elected legislature to repeal the sale. But the land companies refused to give back the land, went right on selling it, and appealed the case to the Supreme Court, where John Marshall, the first great Chief Justice (1801–35), handed down the opinion that even business contracts based on crookedness were sacred. (Samuel J. Konefsky, *John Marshall and Alexander Hamilton*, New York: Macmillan, 1967, pp. 122ff.) The United States was clearly on its way.

FIGURE 2-1 THE FEDERAL GOVERNMENT: DIVISION OF POWERS, CHECKS AND BALANCES

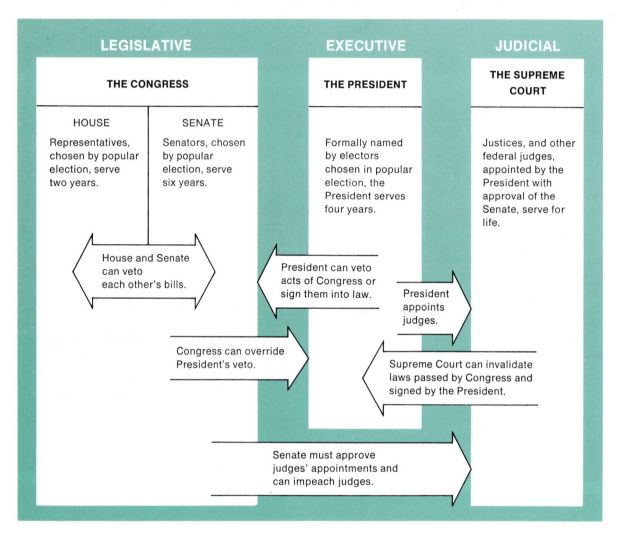

The Constitution omits any reference to property ownership as a qualification for voting. That decision was left to the individual states. Many of the delegates favored some restriction, but they could not agree on its exact definition. Moreover, if the Constitution had specified a more (or less) restrictive suffrage than certain of the states, ratification might have been in jeopardy in those states.[36] It was safest to sidestep the issue.

Of course, the framers did nothing to adjust the limited suffrage within each of the states. State constitutions varied as to voter qualifications, but the franchise generally excluded the propertyless, women, and slaves. It was not until 1870 that the Constitution established the right of blacks to vote (Fifteenth Amendment) and not until 1920 that the vote for women was made constitutional (Nineteenth Amendment).

There were notable spokesmen at the convention who made no bones about wanting to make sure that the rabble didn't dominate the

[36]Brown, *Charles Beard and the Constitution*, pp. 105–06.

new government. Perhaps the most candid of the group was Gouverneur Morris, who proposed that the Senate be set up in such a way as to check whatever power might be found in the popular branch (the branch of the "masses") of the national legislature. Membership in the Senate, he said, should be limited to those with "great personal property," so that the attitude of the Senate as a whole would be a "love to lord it through pride." With relish, he described the ideal Senate: "The rich will strive to establish their dominion and enslave the rest. They always did. They always will." It was a spirit, he felt, that was much needed to balance any counternotions of democracy. Hamilton, too, saw an eternal class struggle between "the few and the many. The first are the rich and the well-born, the other the mass of the people," with each side willing to oppress the other if given the opportunity. He was especially eager that one branch of Congress be a fortress of the rich.[37]

Calvinist doctrine—which was very influential in America—equated material blessings with civil and spiritual stature. One who had great wealth must be a favorite of God; the belief was a perfect foundation for American-style capitalism. Its grasping and greedy nature was not, however, a perfect foundation for humanitarianism. It pointed to an elite: those who had the most deserved the most because God obviously loved them the most; those who had the most should receive special deference. Men of substance, whatever their religious backgrounds, generally agreed that people with property had a greater stake in the community, would consequently be better citizens, and therefore deserved more protection and deserved more participation in community affairs than those without property.

This may fall somewhat short of the kind of equality that we would like to think the Founders had in mind when they endorsed the assertion that "all men are created equal." For all their rhetoric, and the sincerity that went with it, the drafters of the Constitution were, first of all and preeminently, practical men. The great revolutionaries of 1776 had preferred the optimistic

---

[37]Quoted in Holcombe, *Our More Perfect Union*, p. 24.

philosophy of Locke, who believed that man was the product of his environment and could improve. The great leaders of the Constitutional Convention, though influenced by Locke in many ways, were more inclined toward the philosophy of Hobbes, the perfect pessimist, who believed that man was basically a rotter.

Divided Powers, Checks and Balances

One of the miracles of the Constitutional Convention was that the social contract that emerged from it was reasonably evenhanded in its protection of all levels of society. Given the economic makeup of the convention, a sizable majority might have sided with Hamilton and Morris against the masses. In fact, they did, but not at all in an oppressive fashion. If, as is true, the Constitution provided more protections for property rights than for human rights, we—with the advantage of an extra two hundred years' experience in living together—must temper our modern judgments by remembering that the distinction between property rights and personal rights was not so sharp then as it is today. Or, to put it another way, the two rights then seemed more closely allied. By refusing to even seriously consider guaranteeing a place in the democratic process for nonpropertied citizens, much less guaranteeing universal suffrage, the framers believed they were acting with wise circumspection toward the depravity of the masses, which they felt was often evidenced in ignorance and sloth. But they also recognized the depravities of their *own* classes (perhaps the most profound sign of their democratic attitude was their acknowledgment of depravity in *all* classes) and made provisions for circumscribing them, too.

In this lies another of the remarkable characteristics of the American Revolution. In a very real sense, it was an intraclass revolution. Free of class hatred, or almost free of it, the American Revolution's lasting beauty stemmed from what Robert A. Nisbet has called its "moderateness of spirit . . . the absence of the kind of passion, zeal, and millennialist conviction that in other countries produced terror and left a heritage of bitterness lasting to the present day."[38] All subsequent major revolutions of the nineteenth and twentieth centuries were led by men of peasant or, at best, bourgeois background—Robespierre, Stalin, Lenin, Mao, Castro—whereas the preponderance of the leaders of the American Revolution were aristocrats.

The revolutionists of other countries tore down the upper class and established rules of government that would suppress, in varying degrees, their chosen enemies, the aristocrats. In America the task was much more difficult—the leaders of the Revolution had to set rules to control themselves and their own class, as well as the masses. This they attempted to do in a variety of ways that have remained central to our government. For one, they hoped that conflicting interest groups would hold each other in check. This idea of checks and balances was perhaps the one touch of pure genius in our revolution. It was almost a religion with the Founders.

First, constitutional powers were divided by the framers among three branches—legislative, executive, and judicial—to prevent the accumulation of all powers in one hand—"the very definition of tyranny" according to Madison. The experience of the "headless" Confederation had at least demonstrated that some good can result from the dispersal of authority. The framers divided powers between the central government and the state governments according to the concept of federalism. Broad but restricted powers were given to the federal government; those powers not delegated to it, nor prohibited to the states (Article I, Section 10), were reserved for the states (Tenth Amendment).

Even with separation of powers, the framers were still concerned that one element might dominate, so they provided each branch with the means to check the powers of the others. The federal judiciary could declare acts of Congress unconstitutional[39] and had the independence of lifetime tenure (Article III, Section 1), but a federal judge had to be nominated by the President and approved by the Senate (Article II, Section 2) and was subject to removal by impeachment in Congress (Article II, Section 4). The President was given potent (if sometimes vague) authority, especially in appointive powers and duties as commander in chief (Article II, Section 2) and in veto power over legislation (Article I, Section 7). But Congress could restrain the President to some extent by the power to override presidential vetoes with a two-thirds vote, by its control of the budget, by the Senate's veto power over presidential appointments and treaties, and by the threat of impeachment (Article I, Sections 2, 3, and 7).

Special provisions were needed to ensure that the legislature would not dominate the government. There would have to be two houses, almost jealous rivals. The will of the masses (as represented by the popularly elected House of Representatives) would be checked by what was expected to be a conservative upper house, the Senate. Chosen by state legislatures, the Senate would thereby also operate as a voice for state interests.

The question of state representation in Congress caused one of the most bitter disputes of the convention. A one-state-one-vote proposal ran into immediate problems. Virginia, which had a population of 800,000, saw no reason why a state such as Delaware, which had fewer than 50,000 citizens, should have equal voting power in Congress. Other large states shared Virginia's view. They were especially concerned lest the Constitution give the less populated states equal say in the levying of taxes. On the other hand, the less populated states were not about to submit their sovereignty solely to the whims of states with superior head counts. The compromise: in the Senate, all states would be equally represented—two legislators each—but in the House, population would be the basis of representation. Furthermore, taxes would be determined strictly according to population, all tax bills originating in the House (Article I, Sections 2, 3, and 7). (To drive the matter home, even the slaves would be counted—not at full value, of course, but at a generous three-fifths of a human being each—and Indians and indentured ser-

---

[38]Nisbet, "The Social Impact of the Revolution," p. 88.

[39]This power of judicial review is not specifically stated in the Constitution, but was inferred by Chief Justice John Marshall In *Marbury v. Madison.* (See Chapter 11.)

FIGURE 2-2   AMENDMENT OF THE CONSTITUTION

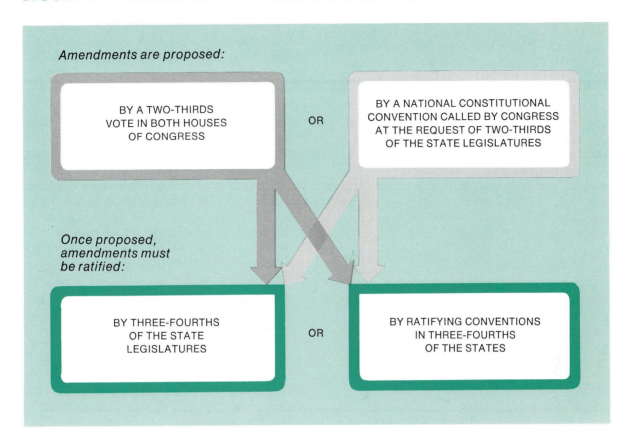

Amendments are proposed:

| BY A TWO-THIRDS VOTE IN BOTH HOUSES OF CONGRESS | OR | BY A NATIONAL CONSTITUTIONAL CONVENTION CALLED BY CONGRESS AT THE REQUEST OF TWO-THIRDS OF THE STATE LEGISLATURES |

Once proposed, amendments must be ratified:

| BY THREE-FOURTHS OF THE STATE LEGISLATURES | OR | BY RATIFYING CONVENTIONS IN THREE-FOURTHS OF THE STATES |

vants would also be counted for determining a state's representation in the House.)

Different terms of office were provided for the President and for members of the House and the Senate. That way it would not be possible for one faction to overturn the government completely in a single election. The President would serve a four-year term,[40] representatives in the House would serve two years, and senators six years. In addition, only one-third of the senators would stand for election at any one time (Article I, Section 3). The President could not at the same time be a member of the House or Senate.

Amendment of the Constitution was made a complex and lengthy process. An amendment can be proposed in two ways: by a two-thirds vote in each house of Congress or by a convention called by a vote of two-thirds of the state legislatures. The proposed amendment must then be ratified by three-fourths of the state legislatures or by ratifying conventions in three-fourths of the states (Article V).

In referring to this system of checks and balances, John Adams said:

The great art of lawgiving consists in balancing the poor against the rich in the legislature, and in constituting the legislative a perfect balance against the executive power, at the same time that no individual or party can become its rival. The essence of a free government consists in an effectual control of rivalries. The executive and the legislative powers are natural rivals; and if each has not an effectual control over the other, the weaker will ever be the lamb in the paws of the

---

[40]The four-year tenure of the President is of anti-Federalist length; some delegates suggested terms of as long as twenty years. (Padover, *To Secure These Blessings*, p. 335.)

wolf. The nation which will not adopt an equilibrium of power must adopt a despotism.[41]

The framers did adopt an equilibrium of power. But if an equilibrium is a halfway posture, one must still decide halfway between what and what. Most historians would agree with Saul Padover that the Constitution is a compromise between pure democracy and authoritarianism,[42] and most would place the point of balance, as Clinton Rossiter does, at a medium height: the Constitution is something to celebrate not only because its best qualities are remarkably good, but also because its bad qualities are not irremediable—"a triumph for conservatism, not reaction."[43] It failed to outlaw some injustices to which we are more sensitive today; however, it did not explicitly support these injustices. The original Constitution left the states free to continue placing whites over blacks and men over women and the propertied over the nonpropertied in the hierarchy of citizenship, but it did not establish an unbreakable economic stratification, and it did not establish an official ruling class.

The Conservatism of Slow Motion

The conservatism of the Constitution was in making the machinery of change so difficult to activate and so slow to move.

The typical citizen sails in a very small boat. He must adjust his sails constantly; he must take account of every sizable wave. His life is in the immediate. He thinks of today; perhaps he thinks of next month; next year is almost too distant to plan.

This typical citizen would probably prefer (at least until he saw its results) to have a government that he could manipulate swiftly to meet his constantly shifting, oscillating fortunes. He wants a government he can get hold of, one that will respond to his pressures with the same urgency with which he responds to the outside pressures in his life. In short, most people would

like a government that can easily change direction.

What kind of governmental machinery would that be? It would have a legislature with one body, not two; there would, consequently, be no wrangling between bodies and no need to compromise between contradictory bills that issued from two bodies. This populist machinery would force politicians to stand for election annually; the voters would have virtually constant opportunity to get rid of officials who didn't respond to their whim of the moment. Furthermore, the President would have no veto over a legislative act. This populist government would offer a Constitution that could be easily amended—perhaps simply by placing the proposed amendment (proposed, say, by getting the signature of 1 percent of the population) on the annual ballot, with a simple majority sufficient for adoption. And the judiciary would be elected, not appointed—certainly not appointed for life.

But business, since its prosperity depends on long-range planning, must have a stable government, a government where change comes slowly and painstakingly, if at all. Businesses—whether they deal in black slaves or in plastics—cannot invest smartly unless their contracts are protected and their investments are secure from some future confiscatory taxation. They love stability. Which is why the businessmen of this country have always been the greatest admirers of the United States Constitution. (When the South seceded from the Union, its wealthy planters adopted a Constitution very much like the one they abandoned.)

The Constitution is a citadel of the status quo. It mandates a government of so many effective checks and balances that, in fact, it is brought to a standstill sometimes when confronted with complex and controversial issues.

The Ratification Battle

One might suppose that with all the compromises woven into the Constitution it would have been swiftly ratified by the states. Instead, they moved slowly to accept it. Especially in the passionate quarrel over whether the Constitution should favor centralized or decentralized

---

[41]Quoted in Rebecca Grumer, ed., *American Nationalism, 1783–1830* (New York: G. P. Putnam's Sons, 1970), p. 65.

[42]Padover, *To Secure These Blessings,* p. 32.

[43]Rossiter, *Conservatism in America,* p. 104.

government—that is, whether the dominant power should rest with the federal government or with the states—each side had given away more than it wanted to. It took two and a half years before the thirteenth state finally consented to the new government. Having seen trouble ahead, the framers provided in Article VII that only nine states need ratify the Constitution to establish the new government, and this was accomplished by June of 1788. Expediency, not principle, won. "Ratification," as Arthur N. Holcombe has written, "was a triumph of temporizing leadership, enlightened opportunism, and a sound spirit of moderation in politics"—the kind of middle-level flight that would be the best our national politics has ever been able to boast.[44]

The ratification debate was hot. Naturally, since any good debate involves name calling and sloganeering, the opposing sides had labels: the Federalists supported the Constitution as written; the anti-Federalists opposed it. The public must have been somewhat turned off by both sides, as so often happens in politics, for each side had its obvious defects and its less obvious virtues. If the Federalists were dominated by gentlemen who today would be categorized as fat cats, the anti-Federalists were too heavily influenced (though not dominated) by men who were as suspicious of learning and graciousness as they were of wealth. If the Federalists were sometimes superciliously concerned about "the tyranny of the majority," the anti-Federalists often seemed almost paranoid on the subject of aristocracy. If the Federalists sometimes seemed too coldblooded about the majesty of property, the anti-Federalists sometimes seemed too starry-eyed and romantic about the source of human virtues. Jefferson, for example, believed that farmers were the chosen people of God and warned that if the "mobs of great cities" should ever dominate, the country was doomed. That warning might have made him sound like just the man to lead the country in the eighteenth century, when the population was 95 percent rural, but it hardly inspires confidence in his advice in the twentieth century.

The anti-Federalists charged a frame-up. They said that the convention delegates had gone far beyond their instructions, had deliberated in secret, and had produced a document—not surprisingly—that sabotaged the independence of the states and failed to adequately protect the liberty of individuals. Nothing would do, said the anti-Federalists, but to call a second convention for revising the Articles in a less drastic and a more honest manner. The anti-Federalist arguments were best presented in a series of articles by Richard Henry Lee, called *Letters of the Federal Farmer to the Republican*. In this, another of the propaganda battles that marked the founding of the nation, the anti-Federalists were the underdogs because they simply didn't have as much access to the press as the Federalists had.

To these charges—that they were rogues—the Federalists naturally responded with indignation and self-righteousness. They were only trying to save the nation, they said. To them the choice seemed perfectly clear: adopt the Constitution and so preserve security and the union, or reject it and invite chaos and disunion. The Federalist arguments reached the nation through a series of brilliant essays published in the New York newspapers under the name of "Publius," pseudonym for Alexander Hamilton, James Madison, and John Jay. In book form these essays are known as *The Federalist Papers*, and they are still considered to be the classic defense for the Constitution.

The debate for the most part did little to stir the electorate. The framers had provided that the ratifying convention in each state be popularly elected, but it is estimated that only a small percentage of the 80 to 85 percent of adult men who were eligible to vote did so. Robert Brown concludes that "the Constitution was adopted with a great show of indifference."[45]

As a general rule, though not in every instance, support for the Constitution came most readily from the small states. All the large states except Pennsylvania debated long and hard before ratifying, and the votes were all close.[46] It

---

[44]Holcombe, *Our More Perfect Union*, p. 23.

[45]Brown, *Charles Beard and the Constitution*, p. 170.

[46]Holcombe, *Our More Perfect Union*, p. 23.

was simply a matter of experience. As Forrest McDonald points out, "those states that had done well on their own [that is, operating under the freewheeling Articles of Confederation] were inclined to desire to continue on their own, and those that found it difficult to survive independently were inclined to desire to cast their several lots with the general government."[47] The small states had found survival the roughest.

The first state to ratify was Delaware. Within three months of the close of the Philadelphia convention, four others—Pennsylvania, New Jersey, Georgia, and Connecticut—had ratified. Massachusetts, a key state, was next. Its margin of approval was slim: 187 to 168. John Hancock's support was crucial, and it may have been won by a hint from the Federalists that George Washington's Vice President would certainly be a New Englander. Maryland, South Carolina, and New Hampshire, the seventh, eighth, and ninth states, ratified by June 1788.

The security of the new union, however, would not be assured without the approval of two large states—Virginia and New York. James Madison led the Federalist forces in the Virginia convention against Richard Henry Lee. Aided by a letter from Washington urging ratification, Madison was able to carry the day. New York, influenced by Hamilton, soon followed suit. North Carolina rejected the Constitution in one convention and then ratified it in a second several months after the new government had been in operation. Rhode Island, after refusing seven times to even call a convention, finally did ratify in 1790, after several towns had threatened to secede otherwise.

The Federalists had won, but the anti-Federalists were able to eke out one not-so-small victory—the promise of the Federalists that passage of a bill of rights would be one of the first items on the agenda of the new government.

Afterthought: The Bill of Rights

To win the support of democrats—democrats with a small *d*, who feared that the centralization of power would encroach mightily on their individual liberties—the ten original amendments, now known as the Bill of Rights, were added to the Constitution by the first Congress in 1789. They were ratified in 1791. To most Americans, these are the most valuable jewels in the box. They are the specifically enumerated freedoms and safeguards that go into the Flag Day orations: freedom of speech; freedom of the press; freedom of religion; the right to bear arms; prohibition against unreasonable searches and seizures; safeguards against government seizure of private property; guarantees of felony indictments only by grand jury; safeguards against being forced to testify against oneself; the right to speedy trial; the right to confront adversary witnesses; prohibition against excessive bail, excessive fines, or cruel punishment.

Oddly enough, the amendments were passed with little enthusiasm and over considerable opposition. James Madison was the prime mover of the congressional debate and is sometimes called, with the usual hyperbole of history, "the father of the Bill of Rights." And Madison himself was lukewarm toward these amendments until he saw them as a route to popular support for his House candidacy.

When Madison, who did not have a loud voice or an aggressive demeanor, tried to interrupt debate in the House to ask consideration for his amendments, he was brushed aside time and again. The House was much more concerned with debating import and tonnage duties than with considering guarantees of fundamental rights, and at one point a fellow member chastised Madison with the remark that even if he did think the subject of rights deserving of attention, the other members "will surely not neglect the more important business which is now unfinished before them." It was also argued that Madison's amendments would "take up more time than the House can now spare."[48]

Such indifference to what is today considered the very heart of the Constitution may seem callous, or even stupid. But actually there were good reasons why delegates to the Constitutional Convention had adjourned without adopting a bill of rights and why members of the

---

[47]McDonald, *We the People*, p. 416.

[48]Quoted in Schwartz, *The American Heritage History of The Law in America*, p. 47.

first Congress were not at all eager to make up for the deficiency. In the first place, the document that emerged from the Constitutional Convention did indeed protect many individual rights from abuse by arbitrary government. Some argued, reasonably, that the entire Constitution was a charter of rights and liberties.

Defenders of the original Constitution pointed out that already the main body of the document:

- Forbade the government from suspending the writ of habeas corpus except in cases of invasion or rebellion (Article I, Section 9)
- Prohibited bills of attainder (the enactment of laws punishing particular persons without judicial trial) and *ex post facto* laws (Article I, Sections 9 and 10)
- Required that persons charged with crimes against the United States be tried by juries in the states where the crimes were allegedly committed (Article III, Section 2)
- Set strict limits on the definition, trial, and punishment of treason (Article III, Section 3)
- Prohibited religious tests as a prerequisite for officeholding (Article VI)
- Guaranteed that a citizen of any state would be free to travel and trade throughout the nation without any restrictions except those that each state set on its own citizens (Article IV, Section 2)

If these protections were not enough, weren't the declarations of rights written into many of the state constitutions sufficient? Another popular argument against adding a bill of rights was that the listing of rights would be dangerous, for it would imply that the rights *not* listed could be ignored or denied by the government.

But perhaps the greatest obstacle in Madison's path as he pushed for passage was the general feeling that the declaration of rights in the state constitutions had little more value than sermons and that the same would be true of any declaration of rights in the federal Constitution. Such declarations were looked upon as educational, as admonitory, as virtuous precepts that helped set the tone of society—but not as law. This judgment was understandable. The Virginia bill of rights, for example, stated that excessive bail "ought not" to be required. The Pennsylvania and North Carolina bills of rights stated that standing armies "ought not" to be supported in times of peace.[49] The states' "should nots" and "ought nots" were cautions, not prohibitions, and therefore they could not carry the weight of law.

Madison countered these arguments adroitly. He pointed out, correctly, that the states were not dependable on this point because not all had bills of rights and that the bills of rights that did exist varied from state to state. Some, indeed, were so defective that they took away rights rather than protected them. As for the argument that the proposed amendments to the Constitution would carry no more weight than the states' bills of rights, he responded that this could be easily prevented by replacing the precautionary "should" and "ought" with the mandatory "shall." This new language, he said, would supply the courts with renewed determination to "resist every encroachment [by the legislatures and the executive] upon rights *expressly stipulated. . . .*"[50]

The argument appealed to the anti-Federalists, especially when the amendments were written in such a way as to curtail only the power of the central government, without restricting the states at all. Many Federalists were willing to go along with Madison because they saw the amendments (as indeed did Madison himself at first) as safeguarding the ruling minority against the whims of the masses.[51]

Thus, from both sides, Madison, one of the most persuasive of the Founders, drew enough reluctant support from the first Congress to

---

[49]Alexander Hamilton, James Madison, and John Jay, *The Federalist Papers*, ed. Clinton Rossiter (New York: Times Mirror Co., New American Library, 1961), p. 159.

[50]Quoted in Irving Brant, *The Bill of Rights* (Indianapolis: Bobbs-Merrill Co., 1965), pp. 49–50 (emphasis added).

[51]Madison's way of putting it was, "Although it may be generally true . . . that the danger of oppression lies in the interested majorities of the people rather than in usurped acts of the Government, yet there may be occasions on which the evil may spring from the latter source; and on such, a bill of rights will be a good ground for an appeal to the sense of the community." (Quoted in Holcombe, *Our More Perfect Union*, p. 286.)

win passage of twelve proposed constitutional amendments. Of these, ten were ratified by the states.

The Other Amendments

That the Constitution is hard to amend can be proved by simple arithmetic: since the Bill of Rights was ratified in 1791, only sixteen changes have been made in the Constitution. Three of these amendments (the Fourteenth, in 1868; the Fifteenth, in 1870; and the Twenty-fourth, in 1964) elaborated on rights that many people thought were already in the Constitution. The only other amendments that significantly changed the ingredients of politics in this country were the Thirteenth (1865), abolishing slavery; the Nineteenth (1920), giving the vote to women; and the Sixteenth (1913), which introduced the income tax. Of these, only one—the income tax amendment—was a direct move to lift up the economic underdog by reducing the wealth of the economic upper dog. A review of the torturous ordeal the nation had to go through to bring it about shows how successful the drafters of the Constitution had been in erecting a bulwark against democrats.

During the Civil War, a graduated income tax (5 percent on incomes up to five thousand dollars and 10 percent above that) was passed by Congress and approved by the Supreme Court. But pressure from the wealthy class to repeal the act became so intense that Congress did so in 1872. Eventually the growth of government activities—especially its military buildup—forced Congress to return to the income tax font in 1894. In an appeal to the Supreme Court in 1895 (Pollock v. Farmers Loan and Trust Company), opponents of the income tax argued that it was "communistic in its purposes and tendencies," and that people who supported it were "a tyrannical majority who want to punish men who are rich and confiscate their property."[52] The Supreme Court, which was overwhelmingly probusiness in those days, agreed that the income tax was part of "a war of the poor against the rich; a war constantly growing in intensity and bitterness."[53] Clearly the real basis for the decision was economic politics, but the official reason given by the majority of the Court was that the tax was unconstitutional.

To allow the income tax to be levied, the Constitution would have to be changed. There was no question that a majority of the voters—an overwhelming majority in the South and West—favored the tax, but it took eighteen years of constant agitation after the Supreme Court ruling of 1895 to get the income tax into the Constitution.

AN ALL-AMERICAN DOCUMENT

American members of a secret parachute operation that dropped behind Japanese lines in Indochina in 1945 found that one of the Indochinese political leaders, Ho Chi Minh, was so certain of his country's future that he was preparing to write its declaration of independence. He asked the covert American visitors if they happened to have a copy of Jefferson's handiwork; they didn't. But apparently Ho obtained one, for when the declaration of independence of the Democratic Republic of Vietnam was published in 1945, the first sentence contained the words, "All men are created equal."[54]

The United States' experience has been a guide and an inspiration to novice nations everywhere. None has duplicated our success, and the reason may be that each people's experiences and backgrounds are different, not to be borrowed. What are natural rights in the world of the Magna Carta and the Constitution may not be natural in Vietnam or Ethiopia, or at least not yet.

Which is certainly not to say that the product of the English-American experience is perfect, not by a long shot. The tone of the Constitution, for example, might be more useful in today's United States of America if the British colonies

---

[52]John C. Chommie, *The Internal Revenue Service* (New York: Praeger Publishers, 1974), p. 12.

[53]Quoted in Sidney H. Asch, *The Supreme Court and Its Great Justices* (New York: Arco Publishing Co., 1972), p. 81.

[54]*Smithsonian Magazine*, July 1975, pp. 30–35.

had not been so healthy and prosperous. It was a land, as Hannah Arendt has reminded us, of some poverty but no misery (except among the blacks, who were ignored anyway). Her criticism may be justified:

> Since there were no sufferings around them that could have aroused their passions, no overwhelmingly urgent needs that would have tempted them to submit to necessity, no pity to lead them astray from reason, the men of the American Revolution remained men of action from beginning to end, from the Declaration of Independence to the framing of the Constitution. Their sound realism was never put to the test of compassion. . . . This lack of experience gives their theories, even if they are sound, an air of lightheartedness, a certain weightlessness, which may well put into jeopardy their durability.[55]

Somewhere in the second two hundred years Arendt may turn out to be right. But if the constitutional structure does fail, it will more likely be the result of how the Constitution is used, rather than the result of defects in the document itself. Much of the compassion that Arendt desired can be wrung from the present constitutional provisions. If the Fourteenth Amendment, which was added to the Constitution to help open the door of citizenship to black people, was for many years perverted to protect corporate plunder instead, that was not the fault of the Constitution, but of the judges who interpreted it. If some of the most pernicious kinds of child labor were permitted in this country and all congressional efforts to end it were ruled unconstitutional until the 1930s, that was not the fault of the Constitution itself, but of a majority of the Supreme Court justices, who decided to interpret it that way. When, from time to time in the past two hundred years, congressional and executive department efforts to end price fixing, false advertising, and similar assaults on the consumer were ruled unconstitutional by the Supreme Court, it was the Court and not the Constitution that spoke harmfully.[56]

To be more exact, the harmful use of the Constitution in these instances was achieved not simply by the Court, but by the special interests who nominated, and the majority of the voters who elected, Presidents callous enough to appoint justices who would come up with decisions adverse to the public interest.

In that respect, the Constitution is a kind of natural element—like fire or water. It is up to the user to decide whether the results are constructive or harmful; the document itself is neutral. Its great virtue is that it gives us freedom to be ourselves. If good people interpret it, and good people enforce it, then the effect will probably be good. Otherwise not.

And when it is not, the Constitution still has aided us by saving for our use the rudiments by which it all began—the embers, if not the flame, of civil disobedience. "It is not," said Edmund Burke, in trying to make the government of King George III understand how the American experiment began, "what a lawyer tells me I *may* do; but what humanity, reason, and justice tell me I ought to do."[57]

Most United States citizens still agree with that; conscience still takes precedence over the written law when the issue stirs them up.[58] They are law-abiding so long as they agree with the law, and when a passionate minority disagrees with it, the law is in trouble. "What is above all important is consent—not presumed theoretical consent but a continuous actual one, born of continual responsiveness," writes Alexander M. Bickel. "There is a popular sovereignty, and there are votes in which majorities or pluralities prevail. But that is not nearly all, for majorities are in large part fictions. They exist only on

---

[55]Arendt, *On Revolution*, pp. 90–91.

[56]Asch, *The Supreme Court and Its Great Justices*, pp. 86–97.

[57]Quoted in Alexander M. Bickel, *The Morality of Consent* (New Haven, Conn.: Yale University Press, 1975), p. 103.

[58]Sometimes this attitude prevails even deep within the establishment created by the written law. Writes Bickel: "The assault upon the legal order by moral imperatives was not only or perhaps even most effectively an assault from outside . . . it came as well from within, in the Supreme Court headed for fifteen years by Earl Warren. When a lawyer stood before him arguing his side of a case on the basis of some legal doctrine or other, or making a procedural point, or contending that the Constitution allocated competence over a given issue to another branch of government than the Supreme Court or to the states rather than to the federal government, the chief justice would shake him off saying, 'Yes, yes, yes, but is it *right*? Is it *good*?' " (Bickel, p. 120.)

election day and they can be registered on very few issues."[59]

Living in a constitutional democracy has to mean more than making decisions by the ballot or taking cases to court. We can give or withhold our support on election day, but usually we have only the vaguest of notions what our vote will, or could, mean. We vote for people we know only in a shadowy way; we rarely have an opportunity to vote on issues. Living in a constitutional environment has at least an equally significant meaning between elections. We can give our support to, or withhold it from, laws. We can try to change the government or alter its course by

every means short of armed rebellion. Even for committing civil disobedience, we can be reasonably sure that the government will not punish us beyond our endurance, and we can also be reasonably sure that a sufficient amount of civil disobedience (witness the civil rights movement) will force law itself to give ground. Pressure groups and public opinion brought about our separation from England; pressure groups and public opinion shaped our Constitution; pressure groups and public opinion brought about certain interpretations and reinterpretations of the Constitution, and certain additions to it. The Constitution is the firmest law we have, but even it is subject to weathering by the public mind in motion.

---

[59]Bickel, p. 100.

Summary

1. The Constitution is the fundamental law of principle for the nation. It sets up the framework of our government.

2. Important influences on the Founders were: (1) the writings of philosophers who argued for the natural rights of man and for a rational approach to government, (2) the example of religious minorities that declared their right to rebel against a monarch, (3) the rights provided by English common law, and (4) the day-to-day social compacts made among the colonists.

3. There were two distinct periods in the establishing of the nation. During the first, the colonists broke away from England and experimented with forming their own government. The second period, during which the Constitution was written, was a time when cooler tempers and a spirit of compromise prevailed.

4. The break with England was promoted by colonists with commercial interests, who objected to British interference in colonial industry.

5. The Declaration of Independence was written primarily as propaganda to rouse the populace to revolution.

6. The first government of the independent nation was established by the Articles of Confederation. The Articles gave a great deal of power to the individual states and did not provide for a central executive authority.

7. The chaos created by the thirteen nearly sovereign states pointed to a need for a stronger central government. Representatives of the states agreed to meet in Philadelphia in 1787 to write a new constitution.

8. The delegates to the Constitutional Convention were predominantly of the upper class, propertied, and conservative. Provisions in the Constitution reflect their concern with protecting property and limiting the democracy of the masses.

9. The framers of the Constitution proposed to control the governing class's influence by separating powers and instituting a system of checks and balances. Power was divided among three branches of government—legislative, executive, and judicial—and each branch was given the means to check the others, so that no one branch would be dominant. Power was also divided between the federal government and the state governments.

10. Ratification of the Constitution was supported by the Federalists, who wanted a strong central government, and opposed by the anti-Federalists, who wanted more power for the states and a guarantee of individual liberties. In order to win support, the Federalists agreed to pass a Bill of Rights in the first Congress.

11. The Bill of Rights (1789–90), which establishes individual liberties, contains the first ten amendments to the Constitution. There have been only sixteen more amendments since the Bill of Rights.

12. The Constitution is a flexible document that can be interpreted according to the needs of the times and the motives of the users.

Additional Reading

The Constitution of the United States is reprinted at the end of this book; it is also available in several paperback editions. Edward S. Corwin's *The Constitution and What It Means Today,* rev. 13th suppl. ed., ed. Harold W. Chase and Craig R. Ducat (Princeton, N.J.: Princeton University Press, 1974), is a brief guide to the Constitution as interpreted by the Supreme Court. The classic discussion of constitutional provisions, written to support ratification, is Alexander Hamilton, James Madison, and John Jay, *The Federalist Papers,* ed. Clinton Rossiter (New York: Times Mirror Co., New American Library, 1961).

Max Farrand's *The Framing of the Constitution of the United States* (New Haven, Conn.: Yale University Press, 1913) gives a blow-by-blow account of the Constitutional Convention. Charles A. Beard, in *An Economic Interpretation of the Constitution of the United States* (New York: Macmillan, 1935), argues that the convention delegates had selfish economic motives. Some of Beard's interpretations and evidence is challenged in Robert E. Brown's *Charles Beard and the Constitution* (New York: W.W. Norton & Co., 1965) and in Forrest McDonald's *We the People: The Economic Origins of the Constitution* (Chicago: University of Chicago Press, 1976).

The colonial background of the United States and the ideas underlying the Constitution are treated in Daniel J. Boorstin, *The Americans: The Colonial Experience* (New York: Random House, Vintage Books, 1958), and in Clinton Rossiter, *Seedtime of the Republic* (New York: Harcourt Brace Jovanovich, 1953). Seymour Martin Lipset, *The First New Nation: The United States in Historical and Comparative Perspective* (New York: Doubleday & Co., 1963) gives a sociological interpretation of the emergence of American political ideas and institutions, comparing them with those of developing countries today.

Robert G. McCloskey's *The American Supreme Court* (Chicago: University of Chicago Press, 1960) is a fast moving history of the Court's evolving interpretations of the Constitution.

3
CIVIL LIBERTIES

*They that can give up essential liberty to obtain
a little temporary safety deserve neither liberty nor safety.*

Benjamin Franklin

High officials in government have a tendency to drift into self-righteousness, especially when their positions make them feel immune from public inspection and public judgment. It's as if those entrusted with great power believe they were somehow blessed with a special wisdom about what is right for America. This conceit is most dramatically lodged in the White House, but it can also be found in some of the more sacrosanct corners of the bureaucracy, notably the Federal Bureau of Investigation and the Central Intelligence Agency.

In the White House, President Richard M. Nixon set up a "dirty tricks" squad, a group of people willing and able to commit burglaries in order to gather evidence against his political enemies. He also made a list of his political enemies and used the Internal Revenue Service to hound them.[1] When the cabinet officer in charge of the IRS, Secretary of the Treasury George P. Shultz, protested this illegal action, Nixon threatened to fire him if he didn't keep quiet.

Carried away by hyperthyroid concepts of patriotism, the FBI and the CIA have sometimes decided they were above the law. They have tapped phones, opened private mail, and burglarized homes and offices, all with the highest motives and the most dangerously undemocratic results. The fault was only partly theirs. Congress and Presidents have delegated awesome

---

[1]*Washington Post,* July 19, 1974.

Freedom Where It Counts

The Supreme Court is not supreme. We are deceived by its regal appearance, its weighty volumes of reports, its exalted position in the scholarly mind and the public imagination. In the academy constitutional experts make meticulous studies of Supreme Court decisions, political scientists invent complex formulas to predict the votes of justices, and students are led to believe they can determine the state of civil liberties by reading the Constitution and the *U.S. Reports*.

But we are looking in the wrong place to assess the liberties of American citizens. And this error leads us to a false notion of what to do to make ourselves more free.

Both the source and the solution of our civil liberties problems are in the situations of every day: where we live, where we work, where we go to school, where we spend most of our hours. Our actual freedom is determined not by the Constitution or the Court, but by the power the policeman has over us on the street or that of the local judge behind him; by the authority of our employers; by the power of teachers, principals, university presidents, and boards of trustees if we are students; by parents if we are children; by children if we are old; by the welfare bureaucracy if we are poor; by prison guards if we are in jail; by landlords if we are tenants; by the medical profession or hospital administration if we are physically or mentally ill.

Freedom and justice are local things, at hand, immediate. They are determined by power and money, whose authority over our daily lives is much less ambiguous than decisions of the Supreme Court. Whatever claim we Americans can make to liberty on the national level—by citing elections, court decisions, the Bill of Rights—on the local level we live at different times of the day in different feudal fiefdoms where our subordination is clear.

Over the last four years my students, checking formal constitutional rights against the realities of everyday life in the Boston area, found these formal rights meaningless. If they had confined themselves to the classroom they might have concluded that a whole string of Supreme Court decisions, from *Lowell v. Griffin* (1938) to *Flower v. U.S.* (1972), have given us all the right to distribute literature to our fellow citizens; they discovered instead that on the street it is the police who decide if that right exists. The Supreme Court is far away and cannot help at that moment when the policeman says "Get going!" (or something more pungent).

A few years ago in Lynn, Massachusetts, young radicals distributing leaflets in front of a high school were arrested for "promoting anarchy" (an old but still useful Massachusetts statute). In Harvard Square a young man with one arm in a cast was selling copies of a communist newspaper. He was chased by police, beaten, and charged with assault and battery (he spat on the policeman, the latter testified; two eyewitnesses saw no spitting). It doesn't matter that eventually the young people in the first case were acquitted and the newspaper seller was found guilty; all were deprived of freedom of expression at the time they sought it.

From Howard Zinn, *The Civil Liberties Review,* Fall 1973, pp. 186, 187.

powers to these agencies and then failed to provide the kind of supervision that is obligatory for the proper functioning of a republic.

The FBI in Peace . . .   For ten years, while organized crime seemed to prosper without hindrance, the FBI spent much of its time harassing the Socialist Workers party—an insignificant political organization—by trying to get members fired from their jobs, leaking information about their sex lives to the press, and urging local police to hound them with petty prosecutions.[2] By order of Director J. Edgar Hoover, the FBI kept files on the personal lives of at least thirty members of Congress and all recent Presidents.[3]

[2] *New York Times,* March 18, 1975. An idea of the FBI's priorities can be found in its budget for fiscal 1976: more than $7 million for political spies and less than half that amount for informants used against organized crime. (*New York Times,* April 29, 1976.)

[3] *Washington Post,* January 19, 1975.

J. Edgar Hoover

President John F. Kennedy's sex life received special attention. FBI wiretaps were placed on the telephones of such people as boxer Muhammad Ali and newspaper columnist Joseph Kraft in the name of national security.[4] The illegal wiretapping of the telephones of "political enemies" and newspaper reporters began at least as early as the Kennedy administration, and it was continued enthusiastically through the next two administrations. When an FBI tap on the telephone of former Defense Secretary Clark M. Clifford disclosed that he was preparing a magazine article critical of the Vietnam war, Hoover passed the information along to President Nixon so that he could take counterpropaganda measures.[5]

[4]*Washington Post*, March 21, 1974.

[5]*Wall Street Journal*, July 19, 1974.

Over a period of fifteen years, the FBI undertook many covert actions under a counterintelligence program, which was called Cointelpro, aimed at disrupting radical and right-wing political groups. A Senate Select Committee on Intelligence report described the actions as "designed to break up marriages, terminate funding or employment and encourage gang warfare between violent rival groups," and cited "violations of both federal and state statutes prohibiting mail fraud, wire fraud, incitement to violence, sending obscene material through the mail, and extortion." Over a period of twenty years, the FBI investigated nearly a million "subversive" and "extremist" matters and compiled files on half a million Americans.[6]

For several years the FBI kept Martin Luther King, Jr., under surveillance in an effort to discredit him and undermine the civil rights movement, which Hoover felt was heavily infiltrated with communists. Fifteen bugs placed in various hotel rooms used by King produced twenty reels of tape on his personal activities, including what Hoover considered to be evidence that the black leader was carrying on with women. Later Hoover played a recording of the eavesdroppings for visiting newspaper editors. He sent a tape recording, anonymously, to Mrs. King.[7]

Sheer Nosiness Despite administration assurances "that no American citizen can be wiretapped any place in the world without the approval of the Attorney General of the United States," the American Civil Liberties Union discovered that actually twenty agencies of the government were having a field day wiretapping just about anybody they wanted to.[8]

Wiretaps were not the only kind of intrusion. At the request of various bureaucrats, the United States Postal Service read thousands of citizens' mail. Of the 8,586 "mail covers" in one two-year period, only 544 were for alleged "national security" purposes; the rest were the result of sheer nosiness.[9] United States narcotics agents broke into dozens of homes and tore up furniture looking for drugs—only to discover they were at the wrong address.[10]

The CIA at Home Although legally prohibited by the 1947 National Security Act from engaging in any domestic police work or any internal security functions, the Central Intelligence Agency, from 1967 to 1973, collected index files on 300,000 —and full dossiers on 7,200—United States citizens.[11] Even President Nixon was spied on. The CIA helped train police officers, and it lent equipment to police departments for the purpose of spying on civil rights and antiwar groups.[12] For twenty years the CIA intercepted and read mail from citizens of this country— some 250,000 first-class letters.[13] For ten years that agency hired Cuban exiles living in this country to spy and keep secret files on United States citizens the CIA didn't like and to picket and harass the embassies of countries the CIA was "at war" with.[14] All these activities were illegal, but no CIA official was fired or even reprimanded for taking part in them.

The Army at Home For at least five years, the United States Army maintained a political spy network made up of fifteen hundred plainclothes agents, working out of three hundred offices and scores of bases from coast to coast. They kept computer tapes, dossiers, card files, and microfilm records not only on such underground outfits as the Minutemen and the Weathermen—both notoriously prone to violence—but also on such groups as the Southern Christian Leadership Conference and the National Association for the Advancement of Colored People. They maintained files not only on such individuals as Gus Hall of the Communist party and Robert Shelton of the Ku Klux Klan but also on Brigadier General Hugh Hester and Rear Admiral Arnold True (both outspoken critics of

---

[6] *New York Times,* April 29, 1976.

[7] Robert Sherrill, paper delivered at the Conference on FBI, Princeton University, Princeton, N.J., October 29, 1971. See also the *New York Times,* March 9, 1975, April 29, 1976.

[8] American Civil Liberties Union release of deposition, quoted in the *Washington Post,* April 7, 1975.

[9] *Washington Star,* April 5, 1975.

[10] *Congressional Record,* S10885, June 19, 1974.

[11] *New York Times,* April 29, 1976.

[12] *Washington Post,* March 13, 1975.

[13] *New York Times,* April 29, 1976.

[14] *New York Times,* January 4, 1975.

the Vietnam war), Georgia State Representative Julian Bond, actress Jane Fonda, and folk singers Pete Seeger and Arlo Guthrie. Disguised as hippies, army spies infiltrated antiwar groups; disguised as reporters, they sat among delegates at the Democratic and Republican national conventions.[15] Army spies also conducted widespread surveillance of United States citizens living in Europe, including a group called Democrats for McGovern, which had adopted the Bill of Rights as their constitution.[16]

A Safe City—for Automobiles On May Day, 1971, Washington police—under White House instructions—made mass arrests during an antiwar protest. They arrested many protesters, to be sure, but they also arrested just plain citizens walking down the sidewalk on their way to work. Before the arrest orgy was over, police had stuffed 13,400 persons into makeshift jails. Many were held for sixteen hours or longer without bail, without food, without being allowed to contact an attorney, without adequate (or in some instances any) restroom facilities. It was the largest mass arrest in United States history, and it was also the largest mass violation of constitutional rights in our history (with perhaps the exception of the internment of Japanese-American citizens in World War II). At least three constitutional articles had been shattered.

Administration officials congratulated themselves on a job well done. The federal workday, as it is sometimes called, had not been disrupted. But others were not so pleased. Their discontent was voiced by Senator Edward M. Kennedy: "The object was to enable [Attorney General] John Mitchell to say at 10 A.M. on Monday morning that he had made the city safe for automobiles. Of course the city may have been safe for cars at the time, but it was a very unsafe place for citizens."[17] Later, officials admitted that most of the arrests were illegal. A court agreed, awarding damages for false arrest.

A HIGHER LAW?

These are only a few examples of government's potential for oppressiveness, of its willingness to break the law, of its callousness toward the very people who pay for its support. Unchecked, government tends to look for ways to put citizens at a disadvantage, to become their master rather than their servant. Unchecked, it begins to look for ways to invade privacy, to cut corners in the courtroom, to peel off a layer of constitutional protection "for the good of the country" or for "law and order."

The key word is *unchecked.* The Senate committee report on intelligence noted that the abusive acts stretching over six presidential administrations and four decades were not just acts of a "few willful men," but were the result of "excessive" growth of executive power unchecked by Congress. From Franklin D. Roosevelt on, Presidents requested reports on "subversives" or "rightists" or "agitators" or just plain political opponents, delegating broad authority without giving precise standards for conducting the investigations. The general assumption seemed to be that a government agency would never break the law. So the agencies developed their own standards. William C. Sullivan, who headed the FBI's Domestic Intelligence Division, said, "Never once did I hear anybody, including myself, raise the question: 'Is this course of action which we have agreed upon lawful, is it ethical or moral?' We never gave any thought to this line of reasoning, because we were just naturally pragmatic." According to the Senate committee report, the general attitude among FBI personnel was that "the nation's intelligence needs were governed by a higher law." One FBI supervisor said, "It was my assumption that what we were doing was justified by what we had to do. . . the greater good, the national security."[18] The pious excuses given for the government's illegal actions—"national security," "anticommunism," "internal security," or the like—only made them that much more dangerous. The "father-knows-best" syndrome has preceded the establishment of every police state.

[15]Christopher H. Pyle, "Military Intelligence Overkill," in *Uncle Sam Is Watching You: Highlights from the Hearings of the Senate Subcommittee on Constitutional Rights* (Washington, D.C.: Public Affairs Press, 1971), pp. 74–75.

[16]*Congressional Record,* S11949, July 9, 1974.

[17]Quoted in *Newsweek,* May 17, 1971.

[18]Quoted in the *New York Times,* April 29, 1976.

WHAT THE CONSTITUTION SAYS

A citizen's bulwark against an overbearing government is known generically as that person's *civil liberties.* Civil rights provide the means by which a person can, with luck, be assured of equal protection under the laws with all other citizens. That is, civil rights (if effectively applied) guarantee that there will not be one group of first-class citizens and another group of second- or third-class citizens—the difference arising from generic characteristics. Civil liberties provide citizens with the means of staving off an oppressive government, whether in the form of the police or in the form of a President who thinks the Presidency carries a mandate to act above the law. Civil liberties are based on the assumption that any government will become oppressive if it gets the chance.

There is interdependence between civil rights and civil liberties. It is no great achievement to give a black person and a white person equal justice if the quality of justice that both receive is second-rate. It does the poor very little good to be guaranteed the same legal safeguards as the rich if those safeguards cost more than the poor can afford.

The principal and perpetual font of our civil liberties is the Bill of Rights and the Fourteenth Amendment. Their sources lie far back in English history. As we have seen in the preceding chapter, as early as 1215 Englishmen took note of the propensity for abuse by government. The nobles who drew up the Magna Carta declared that the king's power was not absolute, that he was bound by law, and that Englishmen had fundamental rights—such as the right not to be taxed without consent, the right to due process of law, and the right to a fair trial. The Petition of Right (1628) and the Bill of Rights (1689) also confirmed the "true, ancient, and indubitable rights and liberties of the people." In the second of his *Two Treatises of Government* (1690), John Locke held that government was necessary only to enforce the natural law, to control those who were lawless, and to protect the basic rights of a people. If the government overstepped the boundary of its purpose, then the people had the right to rebel against it and create a new government.

The American colonists were steeped in this heritage, and most of the early state constitutions included bills of rights modeled on the English lines. The framers of the Constitution itself seem to have been more concerned with protecting property than with protecting the personal rights of individuals. George Mason, a Virginia delegate to the Constitutional Convention, was so unhappy with the original Constitution's failure to discourage slavery and encourage more individual freedom that he refused to sign it. Under pressure from such libertarians, and also persuaded by the experience of the states, the authors of the Constitution finally offered the Bill of Rights amendments, explaining that "in order to prevent misconstruction or abuse of its [the federal government's] powers" they were tacking on "further declaratory and restrictive clauses," which would arouse more "public confidence in the government."

The goal, then, was *restriction.* Of the ten amendments in the Bill of Rights, eight are couched in negative terms: "Congress shall make no law . . .," "the right of the people . . . shall not be infringed . . .," "no person shall be held . . .," and so forth. All eight of these sternly negative prohibitions protect the rights of individual citizens. In addition, there is one positive admonition, the Sixth Amendment, which details the procedure to be followed when an individual is brought to trial.

The Tenth Amendment is the only article in the Bill of Rights that protects the rights of an entity larger than the individual—the state. This amendment further inhibited the growth of the powers of the central government, but the twentieth century has seen a steady erosion of its provision that "the powers not delegated to the United States by the Constitution; nor prohibited by it to the States, are reserved to the States respectively, or to the people." The federal government has, gradually and with the increasing assistance of the courts, come to make all business its business. This is a condition for which the states can largely blame their own conduct; for too long officials in many states interpreted their basic right under the Tenth Amendment as the right to do nothing in the face of pressing injustices and inequities that they could have corrected. And so, in the name of justice, the federal government stepped in. This trend, in which some liberty may be lost for the sake of benevolence, poses some dangers; but the peril has been balanced by a blessing. Whereas the Bill of Rights' protections of the individual used to apply only to the actions of the federal government, today most of them apply to *all* levels of government. Bigness and overbearingness used to be thought of as characteristics only of the central powers, which is what the Bill of Rights was originally aimed at cutting down. The shapers of the Constitution could not have foreseen the monstrous size to which state governments and municipalities can grow. The gradual expansion of the Bill of Rights to all levels of government, through the Fourteenth Amendment (1868), is within the spirit of December 15, 1791, the day the Bill of Rights became effective.

But for a very long while, the Supreme Court refused to recognize such an extension of the Bill of Rights. Significantly, when the Court decided to budge from that position, it was to protect property rights, not personal rights: in 1897, it loosened up just enough to rule that the Fifth Amendment's explicit guarantee against the taking of private property without just compensation is included in the due process clause of the Fourteenth Amendment and is therefore applicable to the states.[19] Not until 1925 did the Supreme Court manage to work up enough vitality to admit that even such basic liberties as freedom of the press and of speech must also be protected by the states.[20] This, 134 years after passage of the Bill of Rights and 57 years after passage of the Fourteenth Amendment, was the first major breakthrough.

Even so, as late as 1937 the Court was willing to let a man be tried twice for the same capital offense (he was sentenced to death the second time around), despite guarantees to the contrary in the Fifth Amendment.[21] In 1947, the Court was still flatly saying that the "due process clause of the Fourteenth Amendment . . . does not draw all the rights of the federal Bill of Rights under its protection,"[22] and as late as 1961 it was at least implying that any similarity between the Fourteenth Amendment due process guarantees and the Bill of Rights was coincidental.[23] Since 1964, the Court has accelerated the pace by which it selectively incorporates the provisions of the Bill of Rights into the Fourteenth Amendment until today nearly all the requirements set forth in the Bill of Rights apply to the states.

What, exactly, does the Bill of Rights say to the government? It is this: your citizens can write and say anything they want to say, and you can't shut them up. Your citizens can worship anything or anybody they want to worship, or not worship anything at all, and there's nothing you can do about it. You can't go barging into homes and offices at whim, taking whatever you want to take with the excuse that it is "evidence"; you've got to keep your hands off citizens and their property unless you can show an awfully good reason for thinking they are lawbreakers. You can't take a person's life or liberty or property without allowing him or her some defense against your efforts in a court of law. If you have anything against a citizen, take the matter to court and make it snappy, and let other citizens decide whether your charges are worth listening to. Furthermore, until a person is proven guilty, there's no reason why he or she shouldn't be allowed freedom; and if that person is proven guilty, you can't punish him or her more harshly than the crime deserves.

Probably no major nation of modern times has had a higher standard of government-citizen relationship than that, and perhaps none has come closer to living up to its high standard. But that is not to say we haven't from time to time fallen stupidly and shamefully short of the mark, sometimes on an *ad hoc* basis and sometimes as a matter of long-term national policy.

[19]*Chicago, Burlington Railroad v. Chicago,* 166 U.S. 226 (1897). This ruling overturned *Barron v. Baltimore,* 7 Pet. 243 (1833), an important decision handed down by Chief Justice John Marshall. He had held that a federal court suit, brought by a citizen of Baltimore who had been deprived of property by the city without just compensation, was not proper, since the Fifth Amendment (and, thereby, the whole Bill of Rights) was not applicable to states or their local governments.

[20]*Gitlow v. New York,* 268 U.S. 652 (1925).

[21]*Palko v. Connecticut,* 302 U.S. 319 (1937).

[22]*Adamson v. California,* 322 U.S. 46 (1947).

[23]*Cohen v. Hurley,* 366 U.S. 117 (1961).

FREEDOM OF EXPRESSION

The First Amendment states that "Congress shall make no law respecting an establishment of religion, or prohibiting the free exercise thereof; or abridging the freedom of speech, or of the press; or the right of the people peaceably to assemble, and to petition the Government for a redress of grievances."

Free Conscience

Modern America has been so loose about religion that the guarantee of religious freedom and of a nonstate religion has grown rusty from disuse. But there was good reason for its being put in the Constitution, and it still serves a good purpose occasionally.

Religious Tolerance or Religious Influence? The notion that the American colonists were marvelously tolerant in matters of religion is a pleasant myth. True believers in that day were as scornful of other religions as true believers are today. Another part of the myth is that the colonists one and all despised the notion of a state religion. That could hardly have been the case, since most of the settlers were English and most were members, and comfortably so, of the Anglican church—the Church of England—a state religion. Moreover, some of the non-Anglicans, notably the Puritans of the Massachusetts colony, used their state's machinery to try to force everyone into their orthodoxy. Tolerance wasn't exactly rampant in the original colonies.

By the time the Constitution was written, it was plain that there was so much religious diversity that each sect would fare better if all agreed not to try to be dominant via the government. As an example of the kind of virtue that grows out of multiple vices (a hallmark of democratic evolution), these suspicious and sometimes warring sects of colonial times came to a permanent truce in the strict constitutional separation of church and state. There has never been a moment's danger that any one sect could come even close to successfully breaking the truce. On the other hand, the pious folks of many sects have sometimes teamed up successfully to make God seem officially in league with the state (as when they inserted the words "under God" in the Pledge of Allegiance), whether atheists liked the idea or not. Perhaps no great harm has resulted from such antics, but it is worth pointing out that they go against the spirit of the Constitutional Convention itself, where, as Richard Morgan has written: "Under Washington's chairmanship there were no invocations, and when Benjamin Franklin (himself no orthodox Christian) moved that the meeting pray for divine guidance, he was defeated."[24]

Conscientious Objections: An Example For the most part, the issue of religious freedom as processed through the Supreme Court this century has, in an evolutionary fashion, strengthened the First Amendment as a whole. The evolution is perhaps most clearly seen in the Court's increasingly vague interpretation of what constitutes "religious belief."

When the United States entered World War I, a military draft was set up. Congress allowed exemption from service only to those men who were members of a "well-recognized sect or organization" that believed in pacifism. Quakers, Amish, and Adventists were obviously exempt. Members of other recognized churches, such as Baptists, who were pacifists even though pacifism was not an essential doctrine of their churches, had a harder time getting out. In any event, the general rule was that one could be exempt only if he based his stand on belief in God, church membership, and religious upbringing. In World War II, exemptions were again limited to those who "by reason of religious training and belief" would not go to war. God had had to whisper in their ear, but church membership was dropped as a criterion. After the war, Congress, in 1948, legislated that "exemption extends to anyone, who, because of religious training and belief, and belief in his relation to a Supreme Being, is conscientiously opposed" to being a part of the armed services.

The role of God in getting an exemption was not seriously challenged until the Vietnam war. Then, in 1965, Daniel Seeger told his draft board that he wasn't sure whether he believed in a

---

[24]Richard Morgan, *The Supreme Court and Religion* (New York: Free Press, 1972), p. 21.

"Religious freedom is my immediate goal, but my long-range plan is to go into real estate."

Supreme Being and that he wasn't basing his claim for an exemption on religious training. Instead, he based it on his personal estimate of the immorality of war. Seeger took his case to the Supreme Court, where his lawyer argued that when Congress showed favoritism toward those who believed in a Supreme Being over those who didn't, it was violating the First Amendment's prohibition against the establishment of a state religion. The Court ducked the question of the constitutionality of the law and instead resolved the case, in Seeger's favor, by offering a substitute route to exemption via "a sincere and meaningful belief which occupies in the life of the possessor a place parallel to that filled by the God of those admittedly qualifying for the exemption. . . ."[25]

But America's youth was not through straining the Court's creativity. In 1970, Elliott Ashton Welsh II appealed his draft case to the justices. He based his claim for an exemption on readings not in the Bible or in theology or ethics but "in the fields of history and sociology." The Court ruled his claim justified. Nationally, the result was a flood of new appeals for exemption. One Chicago draft board simply closed down, explaining that the Welsh case had left it so confused it couldn't pass judgment between those who really opposed military service and those who only claimed they did.

The attitude of the Court had changed radically since World War I. Conscience—any sincere, deeply felt belief—had been made equal to organized religion as a guide, and a belief in God was no longer necessary at all. The Court's rising evaluation of the individual conscience bodes well, if continued, for all First Amendment rights. For, as Justice William O. Douglas has said, "conscience and belief are the main ingredients of the First Amendment rights. They are the bedrock of free speech as well as religion."[26]

Religious Freedom Advances Free Speech

As written originally and presented by James Madison, the guarantees of religious freedom and freedom of the press and of speech were in separate articles; later he was instrumental in blending the two articles into one. At first glance this might appear a strange combination, but Madison, like Justice Douglas, saw the tight correlation between the two. In his original version of the religion article, Madison had concluded with the words "nor shall the full and equal rights of conscience be in any manner, or on any pretext, abridged." It is clear that he saw expressions of conscience and speech and press

to be too nearly allied to be put in separate articles.[27]

The interplay between freedom of speech and freedom of religion and the crucial assistance that advocates of the latter have given to strengthening the former, is dramatically illustrated in the Jehovah's Witnesses cases of the 1930s and 1940s.

The Jehovah's Witnesses—or the Watch Tower Bible and Tract Society, as it is sometimes called—is one of the fastest growing fundamentalist churches in the United States today. It has, after a fashion, been accepted. But in the 1930s, only sixty years after the sect was founded in Pittsburgh, it was still looked upon as a far-out group. Many people felt that the Witnesses had strange ideas and tried to spread them too enthusiastically; for they would swarm over a neighborhood, punching doorbells and waylaying people on street corners, proselytizing with a vengeance.

Certainly they were not meek. When the Witnesses were arrested for distributing their leaflets or selling their tracts without city permits, they went to court; when they ran into municipal statutes forbidding them to make door-to-door visits, they went back to court. They fought their cases all the way to the Supreme Court, claiming that these restrictive statutes interfered with their religion. The Supreme Court upheld them every time. More to the point, it supported them not only on the grounds that the Witnesses had a right to practice their religion but also that they had the right to disseminate their ideas: they were given protection under the free speech clause as much as under the religion clause of the First Amendment.[28]

Pressure from the Witnesses expanded free speech in another way. Their children refused to salute the flag at school because they felt that this was worshiping graven images, an act forbidden by the Bible. At that time, we were on the eve of entering World War II. Richard Morgan

---

[25] *United States v. Seeger*, 380 U.S. 163, 176 (1965).

[26] *Gillette v. United States* and *Negre v. Larsen*, 401 U.S. 437 (1971).

[27] See Irving Brant, *The Bill of Rights* (Indianapolis: Bobbs-Merrill Co., 1965), p. 226.

[28] See *Lovell v. City of Griffin*, 303 U.S. 444 (1936); *Cantwell v. Connecticut*, 310 U.S. 296 (1940); *Jones v. Opelika*, 319 U.S. 103 (1943); *Murdock v. Pennsylvania*, 319 U.S. 105 (1943); *Martin v. Struthers*, 319 U.S. 141 (1943).

describes the situation: "War clouds were gathering; dictatorships were on the march; there was the natural upsurge of patriotic feelings. And while Witnesses were being jailed and fined for passing out leaflets in the streets, they were occasionally tarred and feathered because their children refused to take part in school flag-salute exercises."[29]

In the Minersville School District of Pennsylvania, an area that was predominantly Roman Catholic, Jehovah's Witnesses' children who refused to salute were expelled. They took their fight to the Supreme Court, which, in 1940, ruled against them.[30] The Court concluded that making the school children *perform* this simple act did not interfere with their *thinking* anything they wanted to think or believe.

The most effective opinion handed down in the case, however, was one in dissent, by Justice Harlan Fiske Stone. He argued that requiring a student to recite words that he or she did not believe was the height of governmental coercion. And three years later, in another Witnesses case (*West Virginia State Board of Education v. Barnette*), a Supreme Court with an altered membership switched to Stone's viewpoint, ruling that nobody—whether refusing on religious grounds or for some other reason—could be compelled to salute the flag.[31] What had started out being debated on religious grounds wound up, as so often happens, being decided on the broader grounds of secular freedom and advancing it.

Does *No Law* Really Mean *No Law*?

Irving Brant writes:

Strangely enough, the greatest uncertainty about the meaning of the [Bill of Rights] has developed where the wording seems most clear and definite: in the command that "Congress shall make no law . . . abridging the freedom of speech, or of the press." These were the protections most vociferously demanded by the people. Nobody in Congress challenged them and they were approved [at the Constitutional Convention] without discussion.[32]

For generations, Englishmen who wrote and said things that offended the government had been subjected to whippings, imprisonment, fines, or even physical mutilation. The Americans obviously wanted to get away from that. But how far away? Debate has centered around this question: did the framers of the Constitution really mean *no law,* or did they mean *no harsh and unreasonable law*? And if they meant the latter, what kind of restrictions did they think were okay? Does Congress have the constitutional right to outlaw speech and writings that advocate the overthrow of the government? Does Congress have the right to punish people who write and distribute pornographic material? Should the government be allowed to punish its critics? How much freedom is *freedom*? These dilemmas have plagued us from the beginning of the government, and they continue to plague us today.

Dissent in Wartime: Clear and Present Danger
Some constitutional analysts maintain that the framers intended the First Amendment to deal only with *prior* restraint—that is, the attempt to suppress expression before it is spoken or published—not with subsequent punishment of those who spoke or published. They point out that less than eight years after the Bill of Rights supposedly went into effect, Congress passed the Sedition Act of 1798. At that time, the country was engaged in an undeclared war with France, and intrigue was running high. Anyone who said or wrote anything defamatory about a member of Congress, about the President, about the government in general, or about its policies could be imprisoned for up to five years and fined up to five thousand dollars, which was a small fortune in those days.

Not many federal lawmakers stood up against this grave loss of liberty. In the Senate, the law was passed by a vote of sixteen to six (the vote being taken, ironically enough, on July 4), and the House waited only ten days before following with a vote of forty-seven to thirty-seven. The public performed better. Congress-

---

[29] Morgan, *The Supreme Court and Religion,* p. 68.

[30] *Minersville School District v. Gobitis,* 310 U.S. 596 (1940).

[31] *West Virginia State Board of Education v. Barnette,* 319 U.S. 624 (1943).

[32] Brant, *The Bill of Rights,* p. 224.

Daniel Ellsberg, former Pentagon official, the man who leaked the Pentagon Papers to the press

was not until World War I that the federal government again really lost all perspective in this regard. There was something about the hysterically pious patriotism of that war that drove United States officials into a frenzy such as has not been seen since. Under the Espionage Act, more than two thousand persons were prosecuted for saying or writing things that panicky officials considered to be aimed at disrupting the war effort. Indeed, many of them were exactly that. But weren't such statements protected by the First Amendment? The Supreme Court said No, and said it repeatedly.

The most famous case was *Schenck v. United States*. A number of pacifists were convicted of trying to cause insubordination in the armed services and trying to obstruct the recruiting and enlistment service. Actually, the circulars they distributed hadn't been successful at all. The government had not been endangered by their effort, but it was true that they had tried. For this they were convicted and sent to prison, and the Supreme Court upheld their conviction. Justice Oliver Wendell Holmes spoke for the Court on that occasion, and the most famous part of his judgment was:

> We admit that in many places and in ordinary times the defendants in saying all that was said in the circular would have been within their constitutional rights. But the character of every act depends upon the circumstances in which it is done. . . . The most stringent protection of free speech would not protect a man in falsely shouting fire in a theatre and causing a panic. It does not even protect a man from an injunction against uttering words that have all the effect of force. . . . The question in every case is whether the words used are used in such circumstances and are of such a nature as to create a clear and present danger that they will bring about the substantive evils that Congress has a right to prevent. It is a question of proximity and degree.[34]

An unsettling measure of the constant peril hanging over free speech can be found in the fact that Justice Holmes's ruling was then, and still is, considered progressive. By the standards of the day, it was considered quite permissive of the

man Matthew Lyon of Vermont was the first to be convicted under the Sedition Act—for denouncing President Adams's "unbounded thirst for ridiculous pomp, foolish adulation, and selfish avarice"; the people of Vermont reelected him while he was still in prison and the public raised twice his one-thousand-dollar fine.[33] Other political enemies of the Federalist administration, including newspaper editors, were imprisoned before the act expired in 1801. Far from ruling the law unconstitutional, the Supreme Court had steadfastly upheld it and encouraged its use.

Free speech and free press were nullified at the whim of the government during the Civil War in the name of national security. After that it

[33] Brant, p. 273.

[34] *Schenck v. United States*, 249 U.S. 47 (1919).

Court to allow the public dissemination of all speech and writings that did not present a "clear and present danger" to the functioning of the government. But look at it from the other direction. Holmes's standard *does* permit government to outlaw any speech and writings that *are* considered immediately dangerous—and leaves it up to nine politically appointed justices to decide what constitutes a clear and present danger. Even in the hands of enlightened justices, that is a sharp limitation indeed on the First Amendment. Nevertheless, it was several years before the Court loosened up enough to make even Holmes's stringent interpretation its standard measure for freedom of expression.

During the Vietnam war, the government attempted to suppress dissenters by harassment, infiltration of their ranks by federal undercover agents, falsified records, and contrived indictments that cost the defendants time, money, and, perhaps, reputation. But only on one notable occasion—perhaps because it was an undeclared and highly unpopular war—did the government hazard a direct assault on the press with the full force of the Justice Department. In 1971, a number of major newspapers, led by the *New York Times*, published secret documents from Department of Defense files—generically known as the "Pentagon Papers"—which revealed in embarrassing detail how the Kennedy and Johnson administrations had often misled the people into accepting further United States commitments in Southeast Asia. The Nixon administration attempted to block publication of the papers with a court order, arguing that their publication would do "grave and irreparable" damage to the national interest. The Supreme Court refused to go along with the idea of pre-publication censorship, but its support of the press was reluctant, and there were veiled threats that the press might go too far someday. Only two of the justices—Hugo L. Black and William O. Douglas, as usual—flatly opposed censorship of any sort and under any conditions. The final showdown between press and government obviously still lies in the future.

The Communist Threat: Hypothetical Danger It is not only in time of war that free speech and other civil liberties are subject to government abuse. It can also occur in ideologically turbulent periods in peacetime. From the late 1930s to the early 1960s, a subject of government concern was the patriotism of United States citizens, particularly those who were members of or associated with the Communist party.

Congress's pursuit of suspected communists in this country was launched legislatively in 1940 with the passage of the Smith Act. This act made it a federal offense to knowingly advocate the violent overthrow of the government or to organize a group that advocates the violent overthrow of the government or to conspire to advocate or organize. The Smith Act was ignored during World War II, possibly because Russia was our ally at the moment and diplomacy called for the suppression of our natural anticommunistic instincts. But with the end of World War II, we immediately entered the cold war. Now Russia was our chief enemy, and the Smith Act was brought into service.

Eugene Dennis, General Secretary of the Communist Party U.S.A., and ten others were, in 1948, convicted of violating the act. The only evidence against them, which they acknowledged readily enough, was that they believed and parroted the doctrines of Karl Marx. But the home-grown communists insisted, as grounds for their defense, that their belief was a long way from being a clear and present danger to the government of the United States. To be sure, they believed that all capitalistic governments were doomed to violent overthrow sooner or later, and they believed that when this happened communism would step into the breach. But, they argued, a few thousand communists, poorly organized and wretchedly financed, believing and praying and urging others to prepare for such a thing to happen, were a far cry from an actual threat to the government.

When measured against Holmes's clear-and-present-danger test, it was obvious that what they said was true. So the Supreme Court changed the rules. No longer would clear and present danger be the measure. Now a vague and distantly hypothetical danger would be sufficient. Chief Justice Frederick M. Vinson, speaking for a majority of the Court, declared:

> The argument that there is no need for Government to concern itself, for Government is strong, it possesses ample powers to put down a rebellion, it

may defeat the revolution with ease, needs no answer. For that is not the question. Certainly an attempt to overthrow the Government by force, even though doomed from the outset because of inadequate numbers or power of the revolutionists, is a sufficient evil for Congress to prevent. The damage which such attempts create both physically and politically to a nation makes it impossible to measure the validity in terms of the probability of success or the immediacy of a successful attempt.[35]

To be sure, the harassment of the Smith Act (a number of communists were prosecuted successfully) eventually faded away, as did the use of similar legislation, but it was not as a result of any especially courageous defense of the First Amendment on the part of the Supreme Court. In 1961, the Court (having changed personnel considerably since the Vinson era) finally ruled in *Scales v. United States* that simply being a "nominal" or "passive" member, not an "active" member, of an organization advocating the overthrow of the government was not a criminal offense.[36] But by that time the ruling had very little practical significance. The Communist Party U.S.A. had lost so many members as to be virtually defunct, and nobody but the FBI paid it much attention.

The most questionable activity of Congress during this time was its indulgence of special committees that investigated "un-American activities." It was done, of course, in the name of national security. Several members of Congress—notably Richard M. Nixon, Joseph McCarthy, Martin Dies, and James O. Eastland—became nationally renowned as the chairmen of these committees. Some critics, a small minority, denounced the investigations as shameful witch hunts, unworthy of a democratic nation; but the great majority of the American people and the press acclaimed the committees as the frontline defense against "godless communism."

The committees were, all agreed, quite ruthless in their techniques. They would sometimes seize private files—steal them, it could be argued—without proper search warrants. They often used hearsay testimony, rumors, false and doctored documents, private correspondence, confidential files of the government, wiretapped conversations, and perjured witnesses to blacken the reputations of "subversive persons"—a loose category meaning anyone from a bomb-throwing Trotskyite to a liberal social worker (and including a lopsided number of artists, authors, screenwriters, and actors; creative people were just naturally suspect). Persons called before the investigating committees were almost never allowed to know who their accusers were, much less to confront them. These were not trials in the strict sense of the word, but a person who did not answer all the questions could be—and some were—charged with contempt of Congress and packed off to jail. Despite this real peril, hostile witnesses were never allowed even the most rudimentary due process of law.

The Supreme Court, under Chief Justice Earl Warren, whittled away at the McCarthyist techniques by using technical points to restrain the committees—for example, questions had to be relevant, the Fifth Amendment could be used, cases had to be cited. Yet in the 1950s, when the investigating committees were most vigorous in harassing American citizens, only once, despite many appeals, did the Supreme Court rule against the congressional action as a violation of free expression, due process, or privacy.[37] In fact, rarely in its history has the Supreme Court invalidated either congressional legislation or congressional investigation as an abridgment of free speech.[38]

The moral that keeps surfacing is that under normal conditions the Bill of Rights is only of theoretical value. It is rarely called upon to protect the freedom of a speaker at a Rotary Club meeting who damns the welfare system or the freedom of a newspaper that editorializes against an increase in the national debt ceiling. Very seldom does that kind of expression provoke police action. It's the person on the fringe of orthodoxy who must often lean on the Bill of

---

[35] *Dennis v. United States,* 341 U.S. 494 (1951).

[36] *Scales v. United States,* 367 U.S. 203 (1961).

[37] *Watkins v. United States,* 354 U.S. 178 (1957).

[38] Telford Taylor, *Grand Inquest: The Story of Congressional Investigations* (New York: Ballantine Books, 1961), p. 161.

COMMUNIST PARTY ORGANIZATION U.S.A—FEB. 9, 1950

Senator Joseph McCarthy makes his case for the communist threat

Rights, and it remains only a cold, theoretical comfort unless it is supported by the court system all the way to the top. In periods of stress, when the tide of national emotions is running high against the dissenter and the oddball and the critic, the practical effect of the Bill of Rights is put to the gravest test, and regrettably it is in just such moments that the Supreme Court and the lower courts most often fail to stand firm and to give substance to the Constitution.[39]

---

[39] Even assuming that the exercise of free speech is guaranteed, there still remains the problem of whose speech is loudest. In refuting John Stuart Mill's argument that truth comes out of the "collision of adverse opinions"—in a kind of marketplace of ideas—some critics have pointed out that the competition of ideas is frequently unequal. How can truth emerge when the news media are controlled by huge corporations, when government officials lie and cover up, and when they either withhold information or feed it selectively to the public and the press?

The Tribulations of "Dirty" Free Speech

Although the Constitution does not say, "Congress shall make no law abridging the freedom of *clean* speech or of the *clean* press," society and the courts have generally acted as though it does say just that. Until very recent times, speech and press that middle America viewed as "dirty" (obscene, lewd, smutty, risqué, naughty—the editorial shadings are endless) got virtually no protection from the First Amendment. Even today, it gets only halfhearted and vague protection. The judge who would defend the right of a communist to advocate the overthrow of capitalism will rarely step forward eagerly to defend the free expression of ribald stories illustrated with naughty photographs. For most of our history, the lower courts auto-

" 'Adult' means 'dirty.' "

Drawing by William Hamilton
© 1973 The New Yorker Magazine, Inc.

matically supported state and municipal statutes aimed at curbing pornography, and the Supreme Court simply nodded silently or looked the other way.

Obscenity and the First Amendment   Getting a law that prohibits the circulation of obscene printed material is easy enough to do. The torture begins when the courts try to decide on a *definition* of obscenity. "To come to grips with the question of obscenity," said Judge Curtis Bok, "is like coming to grips with a greased pig.'"[40] The nineteenth century's most famous and most influential interpretation of the word *obscenity* was made by Sir Alexander Cockburn of Great Britain in 1868 in *Hicklin v. Regina.* Our conservative judiciary adopted *Hicklin,* and not until

the 1930s did they begin to concede that, though they were by then well-covered with grease, the pig had gotten away.

The most important part of Cockburn's opinion, which influenced both sides of the Atlantic for a long time, reads: "The test of obscenity is this, whether the tendency of the matter charged as obscenity is to deprave and corrupt those whose minds are open to such immoral influences, and into whose hands a publication of this sort may fall." Susceptibility and availability were the key tests.

But these were extremely vague definitions, suitable perhaps for the moral certitude of the Victorian era, but hardly for the sophistication of the twentieth century. Couldn't the nation's highest tribunal come up with fresh criteria?

In 1957, for the first time in its history, the United States Supreme Court ruled directly on the constitutionality of obscenity laws relating to printed material. This was the famous *Roth v. United States* decision. On July 20, 1955, Samuel Roth, a very minor author and marginal book dealer, was convicted of peddling obscene literature through the mails and was sentenced to five years. The Supreme Court upheld his conviction, explicitly ruling that obscenity is not covered by the First Amendment.

> The First Amendment is not meant to cover every utterance. All ideas having even the slightest redeeming social importance—unorthodox ideas, controversial ideas, even ideas hateful to the prevailing climate of opinion—have the full protection of the guarantees, unless excludable because they encroach upon the limited area of more important interests. But implicit in the history of the First Amendment is the rejection of obscenity as utterly without redeeming social importance.[41]

That still left the Court with the problem of defining obscenity. This is the yardstick offered in *Roth*: "Whether to the average person, applying contemporary community standards, the dominant theme of the material, taken as a whole, appeals to prurient interest," which is to say, "having a tendency to excite lustful thoughts." The material didn't have to actually provoke a man to pinch a woman; if it made him

[40] Quoted in Paul Blanshard, *The Right to Read: The Battle Against Censorship* (Boston: Beacon Press, 1955), p. 148.

[41] *Roth v. United States,* 354 U.S. 476 (1957).

daydream lewdly, that was enough to rate it obscene.

Though libertarians denounced it as a prissy standard, it was much more liberal than the *Hicklin* test. Under *Hicklin*, isolated passages were focused on; under *Roth*, the material had to be judged "as a whole." Under *Hicklin*, the test was the effect on the most susceptible individuals; under *Roth*, the measure was the impact on "the average person."

In 1966, the Court again loosened the standards—in *Memoirs v. Attorney General of Massachusetts*—ruling that something could be judged obscene only if it met *all three* tests: (1) it had to offend the community as a whole, by which the Court meant the nation, not a village; (2) its basic theme had to appeal to base instinct; and (3) the work had to be useless ("utterly without redeeming features").[42]

As a result of *Roth* and *Memoirs*, works of literature such as James Joyce's *Ulysses*, D. H. Lawrence's *Lady Chatterley's Lover*, and Edmund Wilson's *Memoirs of Hecate County*—all of which had had their troubles with censorship—were freed of harassment. On the other hand, the loosening of the standards resulted in a great increase in the flesh-flash industry. *Playboy* and *Penthouse* magazines sprinted to see which could be first with the most explicit details of anatomy. "Adult" bookstores proliferated in city and hamlet. Sighs of passion were bringing in billions of dollars. Chief Justice Warren E. Burger, decrying this "crass commercial exploitation of sex," mustered a majority (five to four) in June 1973 (*Miller v. California*) to tighten the standards.[43] Henceforth, said the Court, it would be local tastes, not national, that would determine what constituted obscenity. The broad measure would no longer be absence of "redeeming social importance," but lack of "serious literary, artistic, political or scientific value." In 1977, the publisher of *Hustler* magazine, an especially raunchy production, was sentenced to prison for offending the community standards of Indianapolis, but this seemed unlikely either to develop into a cele-

brated First Amendment case or to discourage the publishers of racy magazines.

Clearly, the obscenity fight is far from over. The Court, with the best of intentions, has handed down rulings that can only be applied in muddled, confused ways. Periodically the obscenity standard will have to be tinkered with, like a dirty carburetor, to allow the nation to run smoothly for a few more miles.

Why Does Obscenity Matter? The history of the obscenity issue is important, not because obscenity plays a large part in the United States' life, but because it dramatically illustrates the difficulties that arise when legislative bodies and the courts try to adjust constitutional absolutes to practical, everyday life. "Congress shall make no law . . . abridging the freedom of speech, or of the press." That's an absolute. But the establishment would not live with it. First the Supreme Court decided that the absoluteness of that mandate must be modified if free speech resulted in harmful actions or if there was a clear and present danger that such would be the result of free speech. The emphasis was on action. One could talk or write about overturning the government with impunity. But when the talking and writing seemed likely to result in an attempt to *do* it, then the government, said the Court, had the constitutional right to protect itself by stepping in and suppressing speech and press.

But what about the spreading of ideas that do not lead to harmful action—or that cannot be proved to lead to any action at all? Are *they* protected by the First Amendment? If so, then why isn't obscenity protected? If obscenity were tried as a clear and present danger, it probably would not be found guilty. No Supreme Court decision on obscenity has ever been based on the assumption that the offensive material led to overt, antisocial sexual misconduct—rape, exposure, child abuse—or that it probably would. The question of action has never entered into it. The question has always been whether the material stirred dirty *thoughts*, whether it implanted filthy *ideas*. This is an extremely treacherous swamp, and it is not surprising that the Court has constantly sunk to the hips in trying to traverse it.

The motivation of the Court cannot be faulted, however. It has tried to give fair play to

---

[42] *Memoirs v. Attorney General of Massachusetts*, 383 U.S. 413 (1966).

[43] *Miller v. California*, 93 S.Ct. 2607 (1973).

all segments of society, including that large segment—perhaps a majority—that worried about adult bookstores lowering property values of certain neighborhoods and about the lowering of juvenile morality by exposure to spicy books and magazines. This segment of the population feels victimized by an "excess" of freedom of speech and press.

The Court's response, however, was for many years misdirected and futile. Reasonable restrictions can be achieved by striking in a different direction. As Paul Freund suggested in 1975, the Court could get the job done by confining its treatment of obscenity "to public displays, on the analogy of public nuisance; to distribution to juveniles, as an adjunct to parental control, and to zoning restrictions for theaters and bookstores specializing in this form of popular culture."[44] To force flesh magazines to be peddled in a more circumspect manner and to force adult bookstores and X-rated movie houses

to do their business only in neighborhoods suitable to their wares does not require a lessening of freedom of speech and press.

In 1976 the Supreme Court took this step: in *Young, Mayor of Detroit et al. v. American Mini Theaters Inc. et al.*, the Court ruled (five to four) that Detroit does not have the right to ban all X-rated theaters and adult bookstores but it does have the right to limit their location to the city's skid row and also to prohibit a heavy concentration of this kind of theater or store (no two establishments of the sort could be nearer than one thousand feet to each other).[45] Thus, the Court seemed to be saying that some kinds of expression may be more heavily regulated than others, even though they are still protected by the overriding imperative of the First Amendment.

[44] Quoted in the *Washington Post*, May 1, 1975.

[45] *Young, Mayor of Detroit et al. v. American Mini Theaters Inc. et al.*, 427 U.S. 50 (1976).

Fairly applied, the ruling would seem to be one that even the late Justice Hugo L. Black might have supported. Black voted to strike down every obscenity law. At the same time, however, he insisted that freedom of speech, press, and peaceful assembly applied only in those places where people have a legal right to be (not on other people's property or on reasonably restricted public property) and that nobody has the freedom to inflict ideas on people who do not want to see or hear them.[46]

FREEDOM FROM SNOOPING

The rest of our armory of civil liberties is stocked with freedoms from governmental invasion of privacy, from kangaroo courts, and from loaded justice. These are the civil liberties that, with a great deal of luck, will allow even a lawbreaker to maintain the dignity due every citizen.

Illegal Searches

The Fourth Amendment protects us—our physical bodies as well as our homes and offices—from "unreasonable searches" and from raids on our property unless the raiding officers can show the court that there is "probable cause" to believe—not just to guess wildly—that the place contains evidence that we are guilty of a specific crime and that they should therefore be given a warrant to search.

The protection is not ironclad and absolute. The legislatures and the courts have ruled that where life and property are at stake, the rights of the individual must be balanced by the rights of the community. Where common sense and reasonable evidence suggest that a crime has been committed and that delay to seek a search warrant would virtually guarantee the criminal's escape, the normal safeguards of individual freedom may be temporarily laid aside to protect the community. This was the Court's conclusion in *Warden v. Hayden* (1967). After being told that an armed robber had just entered a particular house, the police went crashing in, without a search warrant, and they were rewarded with discovery of a weapon and incriminating material that they used to convict the suspect. The Supreme Court said the police had stretched the Constitution only a reasonable amount, for:

> the Fourth Amendment does not require police officers to delay in the course of an investigation if to do so would gravely endanger their lives or the lives of others. Speed here was essential, and only a thorough search of the house for persons and weapons could have insured that Hayden was the only man present and that the police had control of all weapons which could be used against them or to effect an escape.[47]

There is much confusion about the right of police to stop and frisk citizens on the street. The courts have generally held that a police officer does not need a warrant to frisk someone he or she has just arrested—but there is no clear-cut definition of what constitutes "arrest."

The rule of "exigent circumstances" justifies some warrantless searches, and it has been used, and challenged, under some bizarre terms. While Willie Schmerber was being treated in a hospital after an automobile accident, the police ordered the doctors to take a blood sample. The sample showed that Schmerber had been driving while drunk, and the evidence was used to convict him. Schmerber said he hadn't consented to the blood-taking and therefore the police had, in effect, conducted a warrantless raid on his body in violation of the Fourth Amendment. But a five-man majority of the Supreme Court turned him down in *Schmerber v. California* (1966), upholding the police action on the grounds that time was of the essence; if police had dillydallied long enough to get a court order, the proof of drunkenness might have been eliminated from the body.[48] However, courts have found that it was a violation of the due process clause of the Fourteenth Amendment for police to use a stomach pump on a suspect without his permission, and to remove a

[46] Walter F. Murphy and C. Herman Pritchett, *Courts, Judges and Politics*, 2nd ed. (New York: Random House, 1974), p. 682.

[47] *Warren v. Hayden*, 387 U.S. 294 (1967).

[48] *Schmerber v. California*, 384 U.S. 757 (1966).

bullet from beneath the skin of another suspect.

Perhaps the most remarkable aspect of the constitutional guarantees against illegal searches is that it took more than a century for the Supreme Court to get around to allowing them to have practical impact. It was hardly comforting to abused citizens that the police raids were illegal if the material seized in the raids could still be used against them. Not until 1914 did the Supreme Court forbid federal courts to accept evidence obtained in violation of the Fourth Amendment.[49] This still left state courts—where, by far, the bulk of criminal cases wind up—free to use illegal evidence. Not until the case of *Mapp v. Ohio* in 1961,[50] and then only by a bare five-to-four majority, did the Supreme Court formally declare that illegally seized evidence had to be excluded from state trials too.

Electronic Snooping

Equally sluggish was the Supreme Court's response to the intrusion of, and the seizing of evidence by, electronic devices such as wiretaps and bugs. The Supreme Court ruled in 1928 (*Olmstead v. United States*) that the Fourth Amendment covered only the searching and seizure of *physical* property—papers and documents and guns and drugs and that sort of thing.[51] Ralph Olmstead was a highly successful bootlegger operating in and around Seattle in the Prohibition era. Federal Treasury agents tapped his telephone, and, after accumulating more than seven hundred pages of transcribed telephone conversations full of details about his operation, they arrested him. Olmstead was convicted, despite the fact that a Washington state law made wiretapping a misdemeanor. The United States Supreme Court, by a five-to-four vote, upheld the conviction—gingerly sidestepping their own 1914 decision against the use of illegally seized evidence. Chief

Justice William Howard Taft, writing for the majority, argued that *that* wasn't the kind of illegal evidence the Court had had in mind:

> The Amendment does not forbid what was done here. There was no searching. There was no seizure. The evidence was secured by the use of the sense of hearing and that only. There was no entry of the houses or offices of the defendants. . . .

Having thus determined that the Fourth Amendment proscribed the use of hands and feet and eyes, but not the use of ears, in the gathering of illegal evidence, Taft went on to suggest that if people really desired privacy they would not commit their voice to a wire that extended beyond the boundaries of their homes or offices.

> With the invention of the telephone fifty years ago and its application for the purpose of extending communications, one can talk with another at a far distant place. The language of the Amendment cannot be extended and expanded to include telephone wires reaching to the whole world from the defendant's house or office. The intervening wires are not part of his house or office any more than are the highways along which they are stretched. . . .

So much for the Fourth Amendment in the age of science.

After that, federal, state, and local police went on such a wiretapping spree that Congress, in 1934, tried to impose some restraints. In the Federal Communications Act of that year it decreed, "No person not being authorized by the sender shall intercept any communication and divulge or publish the existence, contents, substance, purport, effect, or meaning of such intercepted communication to any person. . . ."

Law-enforcement officials responded by either ignoring the law entirely or arguing that it contained a loophole. The law didn't prevent their listening in; it only prohibited their listening in *and divulging* what they heard to a third party. Furthermore, one federal official could divulge wiretap material to another federal official, because, since they both worked for the same government, they were really one and the same person.

In 1937 the Supreme Court ruled (*Nardone v. United States*) that in fact the Federal Communi-

---

[49] *Weeks v. United States,* 232 U.S. 383 (1914).

[50] *Mapp v. Ohio,* 367 U.S. 643 (1961).

[51] *Olmstead v. United States,* 277 U.S. 438 (1928).

cations Act of 1934 did apply to federal officials as much as to private persons.[52] Nevertheless, federal officials (to say nothing of state and local law-enforcement officials) went right on violating the law and, in fact, did so with the approval and specific instructions of President Franklin D. Roosevelt in 1940 and President Harry S Truman in 1946.

Finally, in the face of widespread and notorious electronic surveillance by dozens of government agencies, the Supreme Court, in 1967, by a six-to-three majority, overturned *Olmstead v. United States*—ending an interlude of thirty-nine years—and ruled that wiretapping and bugging came under the proscriptions of the Fourth Amendment. The Supreme Court's first ruling to this effect was in *Berger v. New York* (1967).[53] It was followed the same year by the more celebrated *Katz v. United States*.[54] Katz was a gambler who transmitted betting information from a telephone booth in Los Angeles to his colleagues in Boston and Miami, and the FBI had tuned into his conversations with an electronic listening device. Justice Potter Stewart had the pleasure of bringing the Court up to date with the ruling that "the Fourth Amendment protects people—and not simply 'areas'—against unreasonable searches and seizures." A person in a telephone booth had a right to expect privacy and "the fact that the electronic device . . . did not happen to penetrate the wall of the booth can have no constitutional significance."[55] The next year the Court ruled that warrantless wiretap evidence had to be excluded from state trials as well as federal.

Unwilling to let this expansion of freedom go by unchallenged, Congress moved in 1968 to authorize wiretapping and eavesdropping for the first time, in ways that make it very easy to get around the Fourth Amendment.[56] It autho-

rized these measures through the Omnibus Crime Control and Safe Streets Act.

In any event, the recent disclosures of government eavesdroppings and buggings, detailed at the beginning of this chapter, indicate that little attention is being paid to the law. In the first five years after passage of the Safe Streets Act, the government listened in on 1,623,000 phone conversations involving 120,000 persons.[57]

As technology has become more sophisticated, the abuses seem to have increased also. Now there are sensitive listening devices that can pick up conversations in open air several hundred yards away; telephone conversations can be intercepted via microwave; and tiny mikes can be concealed just about anywhere—on walls and coat lapels, in phones and flowerpots.

Law-enforcement officials today enjoy instant access to gigantic data banks that supply information on citizens. In 1974, the Subcommittee on Constitutional Rights, headed by Senator Sam J. Ervin, Jr., released a landmark study showing that there were 858 federal data banks containing over 1.2 billion records on individuals. Over 86 percent of these files are computerized. Various data banks hold information on citizens' employment records, medical problems, driving habits, criminal histories, financial dealings, military service, and other sensitive subjects. *At least 29 data-bank files concentrate on derogatory information. In more than 42 percent of the cases, citizens are not notified that such records about them are being kept. And only 16 percent of all these data banks have been expressly authorized by law.* The United States is apparently well down the pike

---

[52]*Nardone v. United States*, 302 U.S. 379 (1937).

[53]*Berger v. United States*, 388 U.S. 41 (1967).

[54]*Katz v. United States*, 389 U.S. 347 (1967).

[55]Some legal scholars feel that now that public phone booths have been covered by the privacy law, the Supreme Court may someday go on and protect public toilets—a favorite hunting ground for police.

[56]One exemption to the law permits the President to wiretap and eavesdrop at will, so long as it has been determined that it is in the interest of "national security"—a catchall phrase that every recent President has used to describe just about any eventuality. Another exception to the coverage of the law, as Stephen Gillers explains in *Getting Justice: The Rights of People* (New York: Times Mirror Co., New American Library, 1973, pp. 91–92), "allows complete invasion of conversational privacy if done with the consent of at least one party to a conversation, no matter how many other parties there may be." That's a loophole that the Justice Department should be able to move through four abreast.

[57]Gaylord Nelson, "How to Stop Snooping," *Progressive*, August 1973, pp. 14–16.

toward what Arthur R. Miller calls "the computerized dossier society."[58]

It is probably realistic to conclude with Hethro K. Liberman that

> given the history of the government to date, the luminous statement of then U. S. Assistant Attorney General William H. Rehnquist (now a Supreme Court justice) in 1971 that "self-discipline on the part of the executive branch will provide an answer to virtually all of the legitimate complaints against excesses of information gathering" is not merely ludicrous but indicative of the very mentality Rehnquist was supposed to be countering.
>
> If self-discipline would do it, we would not only not need law but we would not need a government to administer it—nor would any complaints be "legitimate." Mr. Rehnquist neglected to point out that unlike private citizens, agents of the government need rarely fear that the law will be enforced against them.[59]

THE SLOW EVOLUTION OF PROCEDURAL RIGHTS

The Fifth, Sixth, Seventh, and Eighth Amendments contain procedural rights—the rules by which the federal government must conduct itself before, during, and after a trial. These rules were largely incorporated in the due process clause of the Fourteenth Amendment, and so eventually applied to the states, too. Their value is quickly learned by any citizen who runs afoul of the law.[60] These amendments guarantee, among other things, the right to keep silent, the right to a lawyer, the right to a jury, the right to fair bail, and the right to equitable punishment. It was these rights Justice Felix Frankfurter had in mind when he remarked, "The history of liberty is largely the history of the observance of procedural safeguards."[61]

If Frankfurter was correct, then the history of liberty in the United States has been spotty indeed. For the bulk of our nation's life, the procedural safeguards have been applied to only a small percentage of criminal cases. The "due process" clause of the Fifth Amendment ("No person shall . . . be deprived of life, liberty, or property, without due process of law") supplements all the other procedural rights; it brings them together in a bundle and presents them to citizens as something they can, theoretically, be sure of receiving if they have to go to court. But for the first seventy-seven years, this due process guarantee, along with the Bill of Rights itself, applied only to the *federal* courts, where only a small fraction of the criminal cases were tried. By far the largest number were in state courts, which could ignore the Bill of Rights' procedural guarantees with impunity, and often did. Even after the Fourteenth Amendment supposedly applied these rights to state and local government in 1868, the Supreme Court ruled against its use time after time, as noted earlier in this chapter.

In 1964, a bare majority of the Court took a big step in the other direction in *Malloy v. Hogan*. Malloy, a gambler, had refused to answer questions put to him by the Superior Court of Hartford County, Connecticut, claiming that the Fifth Amendment protected him from being required to give self-incriminating evidence. Connecticut said its version of due process didn't protect against self-incrimination. Malloy took his case to the Supreme Court, where Justice William J. Brennan, speaking for the majority, said "the Fourteenth Amendment secures against state invasion the same privilege that the Fifth Amendment guarantees against federal infringement. . . . The Court has rejected the notion that the Fourteenth Amendment applies to the states only a 'watered-down subjective version of the individual guarantees of the Bill of Rights. . . .' "[62]

---

[58] Arthur R. Miller, *The Assault on Privacy: Computers, Data Banks, and Dossiers* (Ann Arbor, Mich.: University of Michigan Press, 1971), p. 39.

[59] Hethro K. Liberman, *How the Government Breaks the Law* (Briarcliff Manor, N.Y.: Stein & Day Publishers, 1972), p. 93.

[60] Research done in 1967 indicates that 58 percent of white urban males and 90 percent of nonwhite urban males will be arrested at some time during their lives. (Arthur B. Shostak, *Modern Social Welfare Reforms: Solving Today's Social Problems*, New York: Macmillan, 1974, p. 282.)

[61] *McNabb v. United States,* 318 U.S. 332 (1943).

[62] *Malloy v. Hogan,* 378 U.S. 1 (1964).

Eight of the Scottsboro Boys in prison

The Right to a Lawyer

Perhaps the most dramatic and impressive step toward extending the Bill of Rights to all state procedures was the guaranteeing of legal counsel. Certainly it was the most highly publicized development.

At the time the Bill of Rights was adopted, the Sixth Amendment's guarantee that "the accused shall enjoy . . . the Assistance of Counsel for his defence," really applied only to those who could afford legal counsel. While that interpretation of the meaning was challenged intermittently during the next 140 years as laying too heavy a commercial taint on liberty, the Supreme Court never directly considered the question of whether counsel was *necessary to a fair trial* until 1931, in the notorious Scottsboro Boys case.

Nine black boys riding a freight train through Alabama got into a fight with some white boys and threw them off the train. Also aboard the train were two white women, who weren't thrown off. Later the women told an Alabama sheriff that they had been raped by the blacks—rape was a capital offense. Of the nine blacks—all tried together without services of an attorney—only one, a thirteen-year-old, escaped the death sentence. The trial had lasted one day.

National outrage at what appeared to be kangaroo justice followed the case all the way to the Supreme Court, where Justice George Sutherland, a staunch conservative, wrote the

Court's indignant opinion. The Court acknowledged for the first time that a proper defense could not be built by persons ignorant of the law. Wrote Sutherland:

> Even the intelligent and educated layman has small and sometimes no skill in the science of law. If charged with crime, he is incapable, generally, of determining for himself whether the indictment is good or bad. He is unfamiliar with the rules of evidence. Left without the aid of counsel he may be put on trial without a proper charge, and convicted upon incompetent evidence, or evidence irrelevant to the issue or otherwise inadmissible. He lacks both the skill and knowledge adequately to prepare his defense, even though he have a perfect one. He requires the guiding hand of counsel at every step in the proceedings against him. Without it, though he be not guilty, he faces the danger of conviction because he does not know how to establish his innocence. If that be true of men of intelligence, how much more true it is of the ignorant and illiterate, or those of feeble intellect.

After that superb summation of the general handicap, Sutherland applied it to the particular case, where it was multiplied by

> . . . the ignorance and illiteracy of the defendants, their youth, the circumstances of public hostility, the imprisonment and the close surveillance of the defendants by the military forces, the fact that their friends and families were all in other states and communication with them necessarily difficult, and above all that they stood in deadly peril of their lives. . . .

It was an impossible situation, and the Court decided that henceforth,

> where the defendant is unable to employ counsel, and is incapable adequately of making his own defense because of ignorance, feeble-mindedness, illiteracy, or the like it is the duty of the court, whether requested or not, to assign counsel for him as a necessary requisite of due process of law. . . . In a case such as this, whatever may be the rule in other cases, the right to have counsel appointed, when necessary, is a logical corollary from the constitutional right to be heard by counsel.[63]

Although this served as an eloquent denunciation of Alabama's racism, the ruling itself was cautious and narrow. In federal courts, indigent defendants in capital cases already were receiving free lawyers. The Scottsboro ruling merely extended the same protection to state courts in capital cases, but only if the defendants were of low mental competence and impoverished—and it gave no protection at all to indigents charged with other types of felonies.

Six years later, in *Johnson v. Zerbst*,[64] the Court extended free legal services to indigents in all federal cases, capital or not. Twenty-four years after that, this right was extended to indigents in noncapital cases in state courts. The change came about, as discussed in Chapter 11, on an appeal from Clarence Earl Gideon, age fifty-one, who had acted as his own lawyer and had been sentenced to five years for burglarizing a poolroom. He had asked the Florida judge to provide him with a lawyer and had been refused.

If justice is not complete without a lawyer in court, why not require a lawyer at an earlier stage? After all, the case is put together long before it gets to court. In two other famous cases of the 1960s the Supreme Court agreed and expanded pretrial protections, first in *Escobedo v. Illinois* (1964) and then in *Miranda v. Arizona* (1966).[65]

Danny Escobedo was taken into custody on January 30, 1960. Shortly afterward his attorney arrived at Chicago police headquarters and asked to see him. He was told that Escobedo didn't want to see him, although in fact the defendant had repeatedly asked for his lawyer and would continue to ask for him until 1 A.M., January 31. By that time, Escobedo had made incriminating statements to the police, and these statements were used in his trial and helped to convict him. The Supreme Court ruled that when police questioning has moved from simple inquiry to the "accusatory" stage and when the defendant has asked for his or her attorney and has not been pointedly told that he or she has a constitutional right to remain silent, then to deny the use of an attorney is a violation of the Sixth Amendment.

---

[63]*Powell v. Alabama*, 287 U.S. 45 (1932).

[64]*Johnson v. Zerbst*, 304 U.S. 458 (1938).

[65]*Escobedo v. Illinois*, 378 U.S. 478 (1964); *Miranda v. Arizona*, 384 U.S. 436 (1966).

Ernesto A. Miranda, twenty-three years old, described by some as "mentally troubled," was arrested in 1963 after an eighteen-year-old girl accused him of kidnapping and rape. After two hours of intensive interrogation by police, Miranda confessed. The Supreme Court decided he hadn't had a fair shake, for when a person has actually been taken into custody by police, the questioning that ensues takes on a coercive effect because of the pressures of the situation.

Describing what it considered to be a typical police interrogation, the Court wrote:

> When normal procedures fail to produce the needed result, the police may resort to deceptive stratagems such as giving false legal advice. It is important to keep the subject off balance, for example, by trading on his insecurity about himself or his surroundings. The police then persuade, trick, or cajole him out of exercising his constitutional rights.
>
> Even without employing brutality, the "third degree" or the specific stratagems described above, the very fact of custodial interrogation exacts a heavy toll on individual liberty and trades on the weakness of individuals. . . .

In such an environment, a person who could afford to hire a lawyer to come and give advice and comfort would certainly do so. Therefore, said the Court, a person who could not hire a lawyer was being denied equal justice. It ruled that before interrogation began, defendants should be informed of their constitutional rights to remain silent, they should be informed that anything they said could be used against them, and they should be informed of their right to counsel. Anyone asking for a lawyer, including an indigent, should be supplied one before questioning resumed.

Needless to say, such decisions were not received with grace or good spirits by law-enforcement officers. There was resistance at every level, and a whittling away of the intent of the Court's rulings. Frequently, police simply ignored the *Miranda* ruling. Prosecutors were equally rebellious, even at the highest level.

By 1971, the United States Supreme Court—Chief Justice Warren having been replaced by Burger—was ready to do some trimming itself. It ruled that cross-examination of the defendant in a trial could be based on a confession obtained after police gave an inadequate warning of the suspect's right to counsel. In 1975 the Court carried the exception a step further, ruling that anything suspects said after they asked for a lawyer but before the lawyer arrived could be used against them. And in 1977, the Court ruled that people have to be told what their rights are only after they are "in custody." Thus, while not overturning *Miranda* officially, the Court had significantly diluted its effectiveness. Apparently the ruling meant that once again, as in pre-*Miranda* days, police would be free to question suspects without advising them of their rights, as long as they had not been officially placed under arrest.

If these swift slippages seem a bit startling, one should remember that law and order has always been a popular political issue, especially so in the socially disturbed mid-twentieth century, and that, as Stephen Gillers has pointed out, "since law is ultimately a result of political forces, the evolution of 'due process of law' necessarily reflects the nation's political development."[66] Evolution is never one smooth movement; there are always momentary relapses. But the momentum of the 1960s is probably too great to be stopped.[67]

---

[66] Gillers, *Getting Justice*, p. 24.

[67] No reputable group is likely to even challenge the most important recent reform, the *Gideon* decision. (See Chapter 11.) After an uneasy reception, Americans have become quite proud of it. As James F. Simon recounts, "When the Gideon ruling was announced in 1963, many lawyers fretted that the Court's mandate would simply overwhelm the legal profession and the courts. Where would lawyers be found to represent the 350,000 felony defendants every year? And even if bar associations could supply the lawyers, could the courts possibly cope with the sure-to-increase caseloads of contested suits? . . ." But "right to counsel for the poor as well as the rich was such an elemental concept of justice that there was very little room for debate. For that reason, the Warren Court's ruling was one of its most popular among lawyers and laymen alike. Just as important as the concept of justice embodied in *Gideon* . . . was the fact that the legal profession soon found it could meet the new demands of *Gideon*. In a word, *Gideon* worked." (James F. Simon, *In His Own Image: The Supreme Court in Nixon's America*, New York: David McKay Co., 1973, pp. 254–55.) Noting this popularity, the Burger court topped *Gideon* by ruling that Jon Richard Argersinger was improperly convicted of carrying a concealed weapon and sentenced to three months in the Leon County, Florida, jail because he—like Gideon, being poor—hadn't been able to afford a lawyer. So the Burger Court ruled that no person could be jailed even for a petty offense unless he had been furnished free legal counsel or waived the right. Would deprivation of income—like a traffic offense for a taxi driver—be covered next?

Unequal Means, Unequal Justice?

At its best, procedural due process is still far from being an actuality. Inequality of income still makes for inequality of justice, since lawyers obviously are reluctant to set up shop in the poor sections of town. Robert B. McKay puts the problem in perspective:

> I know that in New York City, where I work with the Legal Aid Society, there is about one lawyer for every 10,000 poor persons on the civil side, whereas the total lawyer population in the city is about one to 250 persons. Lawyers in New York are almost entirely serving those who can afford to pay some relatively handsome fees.[68]

But the inequality of justice does not afflict only indigent citizens. Indeed, in some respects the middle-income citizen is now discriminated against the most. Theodore J. St. Antoine, dean of the University of Michigan Law School, computed that at least 140 million Americans have inadequate access to legal services; they don't earn enough to be able to afford an attorney's time, and they aren't poor enough to avail themselves of assistance from public defenders or legal aid societies.[69]

People of average means can be wiped out financially even if they prove they shouldn't have been hauled into court in the first place. Many court reformers have suggested that when society is unsuccessful in pressing charges it should be willing, perhaps at the discretion of the judge and jury, to recompense defendants for their legal costs. Otherwise, they may wind up proved innocent but punished more than if they had foregone the luxury of an attorney, been found guilty, and been made to pay a small fine.

Nor has society even begun to figure out how to lift the low-income or indigent defendant into anything resembling a dignified round of justice. Consider what justice looks like today to the person who hasn't got much. Call him Barney. Barney was arrested for entering a residential garage and stealing a wrench. Barney habitually has trouble when he gets drunk, which is often. He is charged with first-degree burglary, and the judge sets bail at one thousand dollars pending trial. Barney doesn't have one thousand dollars; he doesn't even have the one hundred dollars a bail bondsman would require, so he must go to jail until his day in court arrives. He had a job at a filling station, but since he won't be paid while he's in jail his family will have to go on welfare.

Jails are for poor people like Barney. More than half the people in United States jails—52 percent, according to the 1970 National Jail Census—are pretrial detainees, held for trial because they can't pay bail. Although they are still legally innocent, they are prisoners in the most degrading institutions in the criminal justice system. Homosexual rape is commonplace in United States jails; so is overcrowding, by 100 percent, with as many as four inmates in a six-by-nine-foot cell.[70] Eighty-six percent of our more than four thousand jails (actually nobody knows just how many jails there are, possibly because society would rather forget them) have no recreational facilities, 90 percent of them have no educational facilities, more than half have no medical facilities, and one-fourth have no visiting facilities.[71]

The Eighth Amendment of the Bill of Rights guarantees that "excessive bail shall not be required," but if a person is broke or nearly so—as most of the inhabitants of jails are—*any* bail is excessive. To this person, $1,000 bail is more excessive than the $1.5 million bail Patricia Hearst had to pay while awaiting trial. Actually, most of the pretrial detainees are not vicious (most of the 150,000 in jail on any given day were arrested for victimless crimes—drunkenness, prostitution, gambling) and could be released safely without bail, but this would end the quarter-of-a-billion-dollar business enjoyed by the insurance companies who back the local bondsmen.[72]

So Barney waits. The lawyer appointed by the court is not going to make much from this

---

[68]Robert B. McKay, "How Just Is Our Justice?" *Barrister Magazine*, Winter 1977, p. 15.

[69]*Congressional Record* S13589, August 5, 1976.

[70]Ronald Goldfarb, *Jails: The Ultimate Ghetto* (New York: Doubleday & Co., 1975), p. 7.

[71]Goldfarb, p. 308.

[72]Goldfarb, p. 36.

case, so he isn't interested. He keeps asking the court for delays while he handles better paying cases. And the district attorney, who is swamped with work, asks for delays, too. This is tremendously costly to the taxpayer. One Puerto Rican man had his case postponed fifty-five times while he sat in New York's "Tombs" prison for nearly two years. It cost the city $16,000 just to supply him food, a place to stay, and somebody to watch over him. The annual cost of United States city and county jails is $148 million.[73]

Barney never gets a trial. Relatively few defendants do. If everyone charged with a crime asked for and received jury trial, the court system would break down immediately. There aren't enough judges, courtrooms, or time. So defending attorneys and prosecutors usually make deals: if the defendant will plead guilty to a lesser charge, the prosecutor will drop the tougher charge and ask the judge to go light.

> Many guilty pleas submitted in American courts are not free acts of the accused: they are gained by psychological coercion through threat of severe punishment. . . . Considered practically, lesser included offenses are inserted in criminal codes to encourage defendants charged with serious crimes to buy relief with a plea of guilty to a knocked down charge.

> A man in jail awaiting trial is stuck, punished by each day of delay. His suffering is used by prosecutors to pressure him into pleading guilty. Statistical studies have shown that the detained defendant is more likely to plead guilty as the time spent in jail awaiting trial increases. If he stays in jail for six months or a year, which is not unusual, a judge is likely to sentence him to "time served" if he pleads guilty to a minor crime. . . . He goes home free. But if he insists on his right to be tried, he lies in jail until the prosecutor and court find time to try him.[74]

Psychological coercion, the long wait in jail, and the threat of a five-year sentence if he goes to trial for burglary easily persuade Barney to plead

---

[73]Task Force Report, Presidential Committee on Law Enforcement (1967), p. 5.

[74]Arthur Rosett and Donald R. Cressey, *Justice By Consent: Plea Bargains in the American Courthouse* (Philadelphia: J. B. Lippincott Co., 1976), pp. 22, 29–30.

guilty to the lesser charge of unlawful entry. That agreed on, he is run through the courtroom as if he were on a high-speed assembly line. In some of our shabby courtrooms, cases are shoveled through at the rate of three hundred a day or more. Prostitutes and drunks are sometimes handled in batches of thirty or forty, all being "heard" and sentenced simultaneously.[75]

For the wealthy defendant, justice is something else—it is almost clean and orderly enough to seem constitutional. When one can afford to pay a top-flight lawyer like Edward Bennett Williams $250,000 for defense, one doubtless gets the glow of patriotism. But to the typical defendant who can't afford much of a lawyer or any lawyer at all and who can't make bail or can't afford law's inevitable delays, the promises of 1791 still come through rather indistinctly.

A CONSENSUS ON LIBERTIES?

It is tempting to set up absolute standards for our civil liberties so we can say "this is good, this is not; this is constitutional, this is not." If it were possible to say such things with absolute firmness we would, among other blessings, be relieved of a great burden of lawyers, who sometimes seem to exist solely for the purpose of making our lives more complicated: lawyers who get elected to legislatures and write statutes, lawyers who get elected or appointed to prosecutory offices and enforce those statutes, lawyers who line up at the courthouse door to hire themselves out to citizens who feel that someone has trod on their liberties. Wherever there is legal confusion, lawyers thrive.

And there is a woeful amount of confusion surrounding our civil liberties. Regarding most of them, there is no public consensus. In many cases it is not clear what the writers of the Constitution themselves meant. Some of the liberties conflict with other liberties. One court often disagrees with another court; one era disagrees with another era; one community disagrees with another community.

The whole emphasis of civil liberties has changed within the past fifty years. "Merely to repeat the 1922 statement of a federal judge 'that of the three fundamental principles which underlie government, and for which government exists, the protection of life, liberty, and property, the chief of these is property' is to show how far out of line such a statement is with the present-day legal scale of values."[76]

It was once considered a civil liberties truism that people could do just about anything they wanted with their own property without government interference. No more. Nowadays the government's concept of civil liberties often legally requires owners and operators to use their property in a way that is convenient, aesthetically pleasing, and altogether safe for society, and it says that to do otherwise is a violation of some individuals' civil rights. Property rights have, in some instances, been made subordinate to personal rights.

The right to privacy is so wholeheartedly assumed to be a good thing by most citizens that it comes almost as a surprise to learn that in fact the Constitution does not explicitly mention any such right. However, as Justice Harry Andrew Blackmun has written, the Court has for many years "recognized that a right of personal privacy, or a guarantee of certain areas or zones of privacy, does exist under the Constitution," under a variety of Amendments, including the First, Fourth, Fifth, Ninth, and Fourteenth.[77]

With such an umbrella of amendments guarding privacy, there would seem to be little grounds for disputing it. Nevertheless, the proper *scope* of the concept is disputable. For example, all sorts of intimate and social reasons dictate the right of a woman to decide for herself whether she should have an abortion: would the birth hurt her physically? Would it hurt her mentally? Is she financially capable of taking care of the child? Would other members of the family resent the new child? Would she be liable to suffer the stigma of being an unwed mother? Et cetera. Speaking to this situation, Justice Black-

---

[75] "Justice on Trial," *Newsweek*, March 8, 1971.

[76] Bernard Schwartz, *The American Heritage History of the Law in America* (New York: American Heritage Publishing Co., 1974), pp. 237–38.

[77] Murphy and Pritchett, *Courts, Judges and Politics*, p. 485.

mun, writing for the Supreme Court's majority, acknowledged with significant reservations: "We therefore conclude that the right of personal privacy includes the abortion decision, but that this right is not unqualified and must be considered against important state interests in regulation."[78] So, at some point the mother's right to privacy must be weighed against the unborn child's right to life—a right that is guaranteed by the Constitution. The problem is: when does the fetus become a "person"—a person who is therefore covered by the Constitution? The Constitution does not define "person" in so many words. The courts have held that until the end of the first trimester of prenatal life the fetus is less than a person, but that is the subject of considerable debate.

---

[78] Quoted in Murphy and Pritchett, p. 486.

The First Amendment right of freedom of the press is another liberty that has come into conflict with other rights, particularly the Sixth Amendment right to a fair trial. Some people feel that pretrial publicity endangers a defendant's right to a fair trial; they argue in favor of letting the judge impose a "gag rule"—a kind of prior censorship on what the press might publish about the trial.

The right to freedom of speech has a wide consensus in its favor, but not as an absolute standard. It is easy to see the danger in allowing someone to falsely yell "fire" in a crowded theater. But what about the speaker who calls on his or her fellow citizens to overthrow the government? The reason there was not a storm of public protest against McCarthyism in the 1950s was that there just was not a public consensus on the limits of free speech.

At some point the mother's right to privacy must be weighed against the unborn child's right to life—a right that is guaranteed by the Constitution

Society is equally ambiguous about restrictions on illegal searches. Many people might go along with tapping the wires of a Soviet agent or of a Mafia chief for reasons of national security and protection from crime, but public opinion would be divided on whether to bug the phone of a Marxist history professor or listen in on the calls of a journalist critical of the government.

No matter how enlightened a Supreme Court may be, nor how circumspect legislation may be, there will be no guarantee of protection unless there is a public consensus on liberties. The Supreme Court cannot enforce its decisions. It is the police officer, the local prosecutor, the lower-court judge, and so on, who apply the rules, and they are impelled by the vigor and quality of public opinion. As Alexander Hamilton said in regard to liberty of the press, "Its security, whatever fine declaration may be inserted in any constitution respecting it, must altogether depend on public opinion, and on the general spirit of the people and of the government."

Summary

1. Unchecked, government has a tendency to become oppressive—as can be seen in recent abuses of power by the FBI, the CIA, the army, and the White House.

2. Civil liberties are a citizen's protection against an oppressive government. The Bill of Rights and the Fourteenth Amendment together are the font of these liberties.

3. The Bill of Rights protects citizens from abuses by the *federal* government. The Fourteenth Amendment extends the protection of individual liberties to all levels of government. After many years of resistance by the Supreme Court, today nearly all the protections of the Bill of Rights have been applied to the states.

4. The First Amendment guarantees freedom of expression—in religion, speech, and the press. Court cases dealing with matters of conscience have shown a strong connection between freedom of religion and freedoms of speech and the press.

5. Freedom of speech and of the press is to be abridged by "no law," but there is dispute about what that means—no law at all, or no unreasonable law? Many laws have abridged these freedoms by various degrees—from the Sedition Act of 1798 to the Smith Act of 1940.

6. The obscenity issue—the question of free "dirty" speech and press—illustrates the difficulty of applying absolute principles to everyday life. Court rulings in the last few decades have fluctuated between permissiveness and restrictiveness.

7. The Fourth Amendment protects citizens from illegal searches. Even so, for a long time evidence found in illegal searches was allowed in courts. In 1914, such evidence was disallowed in federal courts, and in 1961 it was disallowed in state courts. In 1967, using the Fourth Amendment, the Supreme Court ruled that evidence gained by electronic devices was illegal.

8. The Fifth, Sixth, Seventh, and Eighth Amendments enumerate procedural rights—the rules that the federal government must abide by before, during, and after a trial. The "due process" clause of the Fourteenth Amendment extends these rules to the states, but the Supreme Court did not give its backing to the extension until the 1960s. In recent decades, a major step forward in procedural rights was the establishing of legal counsel as a necessity for a fair trial.

9. Equal justice is hampered by the fact that not all defendants have equal means. Poor people cannot afford to hire the first-rate lawyers that rich people retain. Middle-income defendants also suffer, for they do not qualify for free legal aid, so they must sink their savings into lawyers' fees.

10. There is no consensus on liberties. Sometimes it is not clear what the framers meant, and some liberties conflict with others. Moreover, courts disagree, eras disagree, and communities disagree on the scope and intent of Constitutional protections. Without a public consensus on a liberty, it is impossible to guarantee its protection.

Additional Reading

John Stuart Mill, *On Liberty,* ed. David Spitz (New York: W. W. Norton & Co., 1975), is an eloquent defense of individual rights, particularly free speech. Henry David Thoreau, *Walden: On the Duty of Civil Disobedience,* ed. Norman H. Pearson (New York: Holt, Rinehart & Winston, 1948), upholds the right to dissent from authority.

Henry J. Abraham, *Freedom and the Court: Civil Rights and Liberties in the United States,* 2nd ed. (New York: Oxford University Press, 1972), gives a detailed examination of how the Supreme Court has protected individual rights and liberties. Robert G. McCloskey's *The Modern Supreme Court* (Cambridge, Mass.: Harvard University Press, 1972), and Samuel Krislov's *The Supreme Court and Political Freedom* (New York: Free Press, 1968) cover similar ground.

Anthony Lewis, *Gideon's Trumpet* (New York: Random House, 1964) is a lively, engrossing account of how the case of one accused criminal led to a broadening of constitutional rights.

The best early history of the FBI, to the eve of the McCarthy era, is Max Lowenthal's *The Federal Bureau of Investigation,* first published in 1950 (Westport, Conn.: Greenwood Press, 1971); Walter Winchell called it "vicious." Humorous insight into the operation of the FBI and the quirks of its famous director, J. Edgar Hoover, are given by former FBI agent Joseph L. Schott in *No Left Turns: The FBI in Peace and War* (New York: Praeger Publishers, 1975). Ovid Demaris interviewed many officials both inside and outside the FBI to put together *The Director: An Oral Biography of J. Edgar Hoover* (New York: Harper's Magazine Press, 1975).

David Wise and Thomas B. Ross, *The Invisible Government* (New York: Random House, 1964), is the first important history of the CIA and the most readable.

4
CIVIL RIGHTS

You know how prejudice works: one does not win over it by running up against it. Accommodations are necessary. Necessary above all are patience and time.

Talleyrand

The Constitution, as amended, is supposed to protect every citizen from gross exploitation, from unfair competition, from irrational discrimination, and from being cheated out of opportunities that belong to the general populace. That protection is what we mean when we talk about civil rights. It is also what we mean when we talk of equality before the law.

We are all familiar with the ground rules. If a person's pursuit of happiness is made more difficult by arbitrary hurdles raised on account of his or her race, sex, or national origin, that person's civil rights are being violated. Everyone is supposed to have the same chance at the pie in this country, and if people fail to get their share it should be as a result of their own stupidity or bad luck or poor planning, not as a result of their happening to be the "wrong" sex or the "wrong" race. Socialists, housewives, and black sharecroppers are entitled to the same chance for happiness as white, middle-class, Republican Rotarians—subject to the vagaries of educational and employment opportunities.

This ideal of equality of treatment is not a new notion. It is explicitly set forth in the Declaration of Independence: "We hold these truths to be self-evident, that all men are created equal, that they are endowed by their Creator with certain unalienable Rights, that among these are Life, Liberty and the pursuit of Happiness." The doctrine of equality was stated constitutionally for the first time in the Fourteenth Amendment (1868): "No state shall make or enforce any law which shall . . . deny to any person within its jurisdiction the equal protection of the laws." This amendment lent constitutional validity to the civil rights legislation passed by Congress in 1866, which gave blacks the status of citizens, with "full and equal benefit of all laws."

All subsequent civil rights legislation has been grounded in the requirement that equal protection under the laws shall be guaranteed to all. The Civil Rights Act of 1875 outlawed social discrimination by individuals. The next civil rights legislation, passed eighty-two years later in 1957, created a permanent commission on civil rights to investigate discrimination and disfranchisement. In 1960, an act was passed that provided for protection of a black voter's access to the polls. In 1964, the comprehensive Civil Rights Act committed federal government agencies and resources to providing equal protection under the laws in order to combat a wide range of political, social, and economic discrimination.

EQUAL RIGHTS FOR BLACK AMERICANS

Only within the last decade has the theory of equality even come close to reality. The progress of that decade and the promise that it holds for the future, however, is sufficiently broad and deep to make one wonder why it was so late in coming. The answer is the same one that applies to every aspect of the law: it is only as strong as the willingness of the politicians and courts to enforce, and the people to accept, what is said on paper. Nowhere has this been made more tragically clear than in the efforts of black people to gain full protection under the Constitution.

From Slavery to Emancipation

The earliest recorded shipment of slaves to America was in 1619, at Jamestown. Nobody knows how many African slaves were brought during the next two centuries. Estimates range from 5 million to 100 million.[1] The human cargo was so harshly treated in passage that probably 15 percent died en route. Once in the hands of their masters, they were treated both carefully and brutally—driven hard, but kept in reasonably good repair, for they were valuable. They were so valuable, in fact, that some planters gave up agriculture and turned to the operation of slave-breeding farms.[2] The economy of the entire South was built on slavery and land, land and slavery; from 13,000 bales in 1790, cotton

production rose at a fantastic rate until, on the eve of the Civil War, the South was producing 5 million bales a year. To the South, or at least to its wealthier inhabitants (of the South's free population of 1.5 million families in 1860, only one-quarter were slave owners, and half of the slave owners held fewer than five slaves each), the blacks were considered as indispensable as is today's automobile assembly line. They were the means of production.

In the North, blacks were objects of indifference because they had no high economic value (except to the Yankee slave-trading captains, of course). Indeed, many northerners looked on their slaves as a burden and readily welcomed laws to free them. In the last two decades of the eighteenth century, Pennsylvania, Massachusetts, Connecticut, Rhode Island, New York, and New Jersey enacted laws of gradual emancipation. Even Virginia and North Carolina passed laws encouraging emancipation.[3] And, in 1787, the Northwest Ordinance prohibited slavery in any states created out of the Northwest Territory.

"In that same year," note August Meier and Elliott Rudwick, with suitable irony, "the Constitution was written. From the point of view of American Negroes, the Constitution, coming at the close of an era of distinct improvement in their status, must be regarded as a retrogressive document."[4] The Constitution treated blacks as partial human beings and partial property—which gave the South a double advantage. The Constitution offered the masters full protection of their property rights in slaves but gave slaves no protection from their masters. Furthermore, it

---

[1] Gilbert Osofsky, *The Burden of Race: A Documentary History of Negro-White Relations in America* (New York: Harper & Row, Publishers, 1967), p. 6.

[2] August Meier and Elliott Rudwick, *From Plantation to Ghetto*, rev. and enl. ed. (New York: Hill & Wang, 1970), p. 56.

[3] Some of the leading planters urged an end to the slave trade simply because they were afraid for their lives. Many blacks did not take their subjection placidly, and there were numerous slave revolts. (Richard Howard, *Black Cargo*, New York: G. P. Putnam's Sons, 1972, p. 62.) A ruling by a North Carolina judge, in 1852, indicated that the fearful white establishment would not tolerate the "insolence" of "a look, the pointing of a finger, a refusal or neglect to step out of the way when a white person is seen to approach. Each of such acts violates the rules of propriety, and if tolerated, would destroy the subordination, upon which our social system rests." (Quoted in Herbert Aptheker, *American Negro Slave Revolts*, New York: International Publishers Co., New World Paperbacks, 1943, p. 55.)

[4] Meier and Rudwick, *From Plantation to Ghetto*, p. 51

endorsed the continuation of the slave trade and prohibited Congress from interfering with it until 1808. It required states to support slavery by returning any runaway slaves to their masters. So far as blacks in America were concerned, the Constitution was a total disaster.[5]

To be sure, some of the Revolutionary spokesmen, including Thomas Paine, pleaded eloquently for an end to slavery. But George Washington was the richest slave owner among the revolutionists, and there were enough others who were unwilling to surrender their rich black property that the Constitution became a formula for racial oppression. The unwillingness of the Founders to suppress the slaveholders' greed in favor of the national harmony that would have been derived from a totally free population was, without question, a most costly error. What resulted was a national curse, a fratricidal bitterness that divided the people and disrupted every important aspect of our social and economic life.

The fault lies with both North and South. The South was crueler and more unrelenting in its determination to exploit the blacks, but the North had no desire to give them real equality. Gordon S. Wood writes,

> In 1800 in many states of the North, free Negroes possessed the right to vote (often as a result of the general extension of the franchise that took place during the Revolution), and they exercized it in some areas with particular effectiveness. But in subsequent years, as the electorate continued to expand through changes in the law and the mobilization of new voters, the blacks found themselves being squeezed out. There is perhaps no greater irony in the democratization of American politics in the first half of the nineteenth century than the fact that as the white man gained the vote the black man lost it. During the heyday of Jacksonian democracy white populist majorities in state after state in the North moved to eliminate the remaining property restrictions on white voters while at

the same time concocting new restrictions to take away the franchise from Negro voters who had in some cases exercised it for decades. No state admitted to the union after 1819 allowed blacks to vote. By 1840, 93 percent of northern free Negroes lived in states which completely or practically excluded them from the suffrage and hence from participation in politics.[6]

For many in the North, mere disfranchisement of the free blacks was not enough. They would have preferred to expel them from the country bodily, and some prominent whites organized the American Colonization Society, in 1816, with the intent of transporting free blacks to Africa. The society argued that the blacks "are a dangerous and useless part of the community."[7]

Whatever hope there might have been for solving the slavery question peacefully was destroyed by the Supreme Court's ruling on March 6, 1857, in the case known as *Dred Scott v. Sanford*. Dred Scott was a slave who had been taken by his master into a free state, where they lived for five years before moving back into a slave state. Scott's original owner died, and he had several other masters before he became the ward of an abolitionist, a Missouri businessman named Henry Blow. Scott's actual owner, John F. A. Sanford, was also ardently against slavery. With Sanford's approval, Blow instituted a lawsuit against him to free Scott. The issue: did a black man who moved to a free state become permanently free, or did his status depend always on the laws of the state in which he lived?

Scott lost in the Missouri courts and appealed to the Supreme Court. Chief Justice Roger B. Taney, speaking for a majority of the members, ruled that Scott had no right to sue in federal court because he wasn't a citizen, nor could he ever become a citizen *because the Constitution did not contemplate the possibility of black citi-*

---

[5]In *The Federalist Papers*, Number 42, Madison gets pretty touchy in his defensiveness. He said that those persons who argue that constitutional perpetuation of the slave trade until 1808 is "a criminal toleration of an illicit practice" deserve no answer. They are, he said, simply being unreasonable. (Alexander Hamilton, James Madison, and John Jay, *The Federalist Papers*, ed. Clinton Rossiter, New York: Times Mirror Co., New American Library, 1961, pp. 266–67.)

[6]Gordon S. Wood, "The Political Integration of the Disenfranchised," in *America's Continuing Revolution* (Washington, D.C.: American Enterprise Institute, 1973–75), pp. 111–12.

[7]Herbert Aptheker, ed., *A Documentary History of the Negro People in the United States*, 5th ed. (Secaucus, N.J.: Citadel Press, 1968), 1:71.

zenship. He ruled further that no matter how long a black lived in a free state, he did not thereby become a free man.[8] There was a crucial third element in Taney's ruling to the effect that "the act of Congress which prohibited a citizen from holding and owning property of this kind in the territory of the United States north of the line therein mentioned, is not warranted by the Constitution, and is therefore void." Taney was speaking of the Missouri Compromise of 1820, in which it was agreed by Congress that slavery in the territories—that is, those areas in the process of being settled—should be restricted by a border on a line with the southern border of Missouri. Congress said future states coming into the Union below that line could have slavery, those above it could not. This, to Taney, was an unconstitutional interference with property rights. This was the first time since *Marbury v. Madison* (1803) that the Supreme Court had thrown out a congressional law as being unconstitutional.

The *Dred Scott* ruling virtually guaranteed war between the North and the South. The issue of slavery was not predominantly a difference of morality between the two sections, but rather a contest of economics and political power. North and South, each determined to lay its imprint on the territories to the west, used slavery, or non-slavery, as the most convenient battle cry.

It was to preserve the Union, not to free the slaves, that President Abraham Lincoln took the nation to war. In the 1850s, he had consistently taken the position that gradual emancipation, not sudden freedom, was the best course for the blacks; he opposed the expansion of slavery but did not oppose its continuing where it already existed. After the outbreak of the war, Horace Greeley upbraided Lincoln for not taking a more forceful position against slavery. To this Lincoln replied,

> My paramount object in this struggle is to save the Union. . . . If I could save the Union without freeing any slave, I would do it; and if I could save it by freeing all the slaves, I would do it; and if I could save it by freeing some and leaving others alone, I would also do that. What I do about slavery and the coloured race, I do because I believe it helps to save the Union; and what I forbear, I forbear because I do not believe it would help to save the Union.[9]

For the first two years of the war the North refused to accept black volunteers as soldiers, and, when blacks were taken into the armed forces, they were paid far less than whites. A white chaplain received one hundred dollars a month, a black chaplain seven dollars a month; a white hospital steward was paid thirty dollars, a black steward seven dollars; a white sergeant major earned twenty-one dollars, a black sergeant major seven dollars; and so on. Blacks were, in every respect, viewed by the North as second-class soldiers.[10]

As political pressure from abolitionists increased during the war, Lincoln felt impelled to announce the Emancipation Proclamation in 1862. The odd thing about the proclamation is that it freed slaves only in the rebelling states where his decree would have no effect; slavery in areas under Union jurisdiction was not affected. It was a matter of tactics: create havoc behind the enemy lines, but don't disrupt the friendly or occupied states. Nevertheless, the Emancipation Proclamation represented an important change in the war's aims—from simply a united nation to a united nation without slaves—and it spelled the ultimate doom of the system of slavery.

[8]The effect of the Court's ruling was shattering. Only two days before the decision was rendered, President James Buchanan, in his inaugural address, had assured the nation that the slavery question "is a judicial question, which legitimately belongs to the Supreme Court of the United States, before whom it is now pending, and will, it is understood, be speedily and finally settled." But the antislavery forces were not about to accept as final a ruling that (1) blacks could not be citizens and (2) Congress had no power to set the limits of slaveholding in the territories. At the very least, it was clear, a constitutional amendment would be necessary to dislodge the Court's ruling. As it turned out, it took three constitutional amendments—the Thirteenth, Fourteenth, and Fifteenth—and a civil war. (See Bernard Schwartz, *The American Heritage History of the Law in America*, New York: American Heritage Publishing Co., 1974, pp. 70–71.)

[9]Quoted in Lord Longford, *Abraham Lincoln* (New York: G. P. Putnam's Sons, 1975), pp. 69, 220.

[10]Dudley Taylor Cornish, "The Sable Arm: Negro Troops in the Union Army, 1861–1865," in William M. Chace and Peter Collier, eds., *Justice Denied: The Black Man in White America* (New York: Harcourt Brace Jovanovich, 1970), p. 148.

The Era of Reconstruction

The Union victory ushered in the dozen or so years of Reconstruction, when the North undertook to "punish" (or "reconstruct") the South, draw it back into the Union, and provide for the freedom of black slaves. There was animosity and disagreement on ends and means, not only between North and South, but between President and Congress and among members of Congress. What emerged, on paper at least, were three important amendments affecting civil rights.

The Thirteenth Amendment, ratified on December 18, 1865, outlawed slavery and involuntary servitude. The Fourteenth Amendment, which went into effect on July 28, 1868, conferred citizenship on the blacks and made civil rights a federal matter by requiring that the states toe the constitutional line:

> No State shall make or enforce any law which shall abridge the privileges or immunities of citizens of the United States; nor shall any State deprive any person of life, liberty, or property, without due process of law; nor deny to any person within its jurisdiction the equal protection of the laws.

Henceforth, whatever rights, privileges, protections, and liberties were accorded to white people would—theoretically, at least—be accorded to people of all colors. For the first time, the Constitution forced the states to recognize the Bill of Rights as applicable to their affairs, too. The states would have to give their citizens the same guarantees of speedy trial, trial by impartial jury, and all the other protections of the first ten amendments. Previously, the Bill of Rights had been binding on the federal government alone. One intent of the Fourteenth Amendment, obviously, was to make sure that the defeated southern states did not take indirect revenge on the blacks. The Fifteenth Amendment, which entered the Constitution two years later, on March 30, 1870, prohibited the states from interfering with the voting rights of any citizen "on account of race, color, or previous condition of servitude."

All three amendments were vital to the blacks' civil rights, of course, but the great Fourteenth Amendment was depended on the most. Unfortunately its strength, as well as the strength of the Fifteenth Amendment, was debilitated by the failure of the Supreme Court, Congress, and the general public to lend the support that was necessary.

When the slaves were freed, virtually all were illiterate, all were propertyless, and few had any skills except as field hands. They were in a perfect condition to be exploited by their former masters, who wasted no time. Southern state governments, by passing restrictive laws called "black codes," managed to keep a large part of the black population in a tightly controlled, propertyless, serflike state.[11]

In an effort to assist the blacks through their turbulent transitional period and to protect them from exploitation, the federal government established the Freedmen's Bureau, which set up schools for blacks and in other ways gave guidance to the new citizens. Also, the federal government quartered army troops throughout the South to guarantee that the blacks would not be abused and would be permitted to vote. But the task of reconstruction was enormous, and northern politicians grew weary of it. They had never felt much affection for the blacks—indeed many, including Lincoln himself, had seriously considered the best solution to be shipping them to other countries. A long, drawn-out, and costly program of bringing the ex-slaves into the economic and social mainstream held little attraction for them.

When we speak of northern politicians in this context, we are speaking primarily of Republicans, for they dominated the federal government at the time. And when we speak of the Republican party, we are speaking of bankers, manufacturers, shippers, and merchants, for they controlled the party.[12] They were much more interested in exploiting the South and dominating it commercially than they were in

---

[11]Alvin M. Josephy, Jr., *The American Heritage History of the Congress of the United States* (New York: American Heritage Publishing Co. and McGraw-Hill, 1975), p. 239.

[12]See Lawrence Goodwyn, *Democratic Promise: The Populist Movement in America* (New York: Oxford University Press, 1976), p. 7.

Former slaves listening to a Freedmen's Bureau representative

uplifting the blacks or in building a postwar party in the South based on black suffrage.

The Era of Jim Crow

The second subjugation of the blacks, and the revival of southern segregationist power, was the result of betrayal by the blacks' northern "saviors" at the end of reconstruction. The betrayal took on an official stamp in 1877, only thirteen years after the Union victory. Democrat Samuel J. Tilden of New York and Republican Rutherford B. Hayes of Ohio each claimed victory in the presidential election. The election had been so grossly corrupt that it was impossible to tell who had won, and the method worked out by Congress for determining the winner obviously pointed to a vicious national schism. The South, where power was again almost totally in the hands of the whites, had gone solidly for Tilden. Angry Democrats, in the North and in the South, threatened to march on Washington if their candidate was not sworn in. The Hayes faction, after a wholesale rigging of the ballot boxes in South Carolina, Florida, and Louisiana, claimed those states. An honest and fair outcome was impossible.

So the blacks were sacrificed to achieve interparty and intersectional peace. Hayes was given the Presidency, in return for which massive federal sums were pumped into the South to help rebuild it, the army was withdrawn from the South, and federal officials shut their eyes to the following actions of southern legislatures to complete the disfranchisement and second subjugation of the blacks through legal racism, known as Jim Crow.[13]

Black Disfranchisement in the South　At first, white southerners had used violence to keep blacks away from the ballot boxes. When some were courageous enough to vote despite physical threats, their ballots were either destroyed or counteracted by phony ballots backing the opposition candidates. Finally the southern legislatures turned to "legal" means, with Mississippi (1890) and South Carolina (1895) leading the way; then, between 1898 and 1908, came Louisiana, North Carolina, Alabama, Virginia, Oklahoma, and Georgia. They all changed their constitutions in some way to exclude blacks from

---

[13]Josephy, *The American Heritage History of the Congress of the United States*, p. 264.

the electorate—either by poll taxes or by literacy or property qualifications. Since the literacy tests, even tolerantly applied, would have excluded many poor whites as well, the new constitutions usually provided an escape hatch—the so-called grandfather's clause—waiving the literacy test for anyone whose forebears had voted in 1860.

Florida, Arkansas, and Texas did not change their constitutions to exclude blacks, but they did raise the poll tax and devise other barriers to their participation in elections.[14] Furthermore, all southern states, between 1898 and 1915, passed laws restricting the vote in primary elections to white persons. Since in the solidly Democratic South elections were determined in the primaries, not in the general elections, this meant, in effect, that, even if all other restrictive devices failed, blacks would not be permitted to participate at any meaningful level of politics.

Although all these actions were legal in the sense that they were laws passed by representatives of the people, they were all clearly in violation of the Constitution. And yet throughout this period the Supreme Court approved the disfranchisement of the blacks, either overtly or tacitly, by refusing to hear their appeals.

Southerners justified the disfranchisement of the blacks as the only way to restore honesty to government. It is quite true that, during Reconstruction, state government in Dixie had been bothered by considerable corruption. But corruption was not exactly a strange element in southern politics before or since Reconstruction, and, in any event, the blacks could hardly be blamed for much of it. At no time during Reconstruction did the blacks control any southern state. Only in South Carolina did they hold a majority of even one house of the legislature, and only Mississippi sent a black to the United States Senate. A majority of the key offices in all southern states remained in the hands of the whites, even during the years when Union army troops stood in the capitol doorways.[15]

From the moment the Fourteenth Amendment took effect, it was clear that simply forbidding the states to make laws discriminating against blacks would not be enough to achieve equal treatment. What about private actions that kept them out of inns, streetcars, and theaters? In 1875, Congress passed the Civil Rights Act, which was aimed at outlawing private discrimination too. But in the civil rights cases of 1883, the Supreme Court severely limited the scope of the Civil Rights Act. It held that the Fourteenth Amendment protected against discrimination by the states but not by individuals, for the amendment says: "No *state* shall . . ." Public opinion generally went along with this interpretation.

Plessy v. Ferguson In 1896, the national mood was such as to receive placidly and with approval one of the most troublesome and pernicious rulings of the Supreme Court—*Plessy v. Ferguson*.[16] Under the guise of equality and fairness, that decision sanctioned a continuation of legal racism in the United States for another half century and more. This was a period during which the United States was reaching out in the world and dealing lusty blows of imperialism to "the lesser breeds," as they were considered—the dusky-skinned inhabitants of Cuba, Mexico, and the Philippines. So it is hardly surprising that our own black citizens came in for some of the same.

In 1892, Homer Plessy, a Louisianan who was one-eighth black, bought a train ticket in New Orleans and took a seat in the car reserved for whites. The conductor insisted that he ride in the nonwhite car, in accordance with a Louisiana law that separated the races in transit. Plessy sued, claiming that his rights under the Fourteenth Amendment's equal protection provision had been violated. Four years later the Supreme Court ruled against Plessy, saying that segregation did not equate with inequality. "Laws permitting, and even requiring their separation in places where they are liable to be brought into contact do not necessarily imply the inferiority of either race to the other," and if blacks felt that being forced to sit at the back of the bus, to eat in the kitchen at public restaurants, or to sit in the peanut gallery at theaters was racially discriminatory, said the Court, in effect, this reaction on

---

[14]Meier and Rudwick, *From Plantation to Ghetto*, p. 178.

[15]Meier and Rudwick, p. 170.

[16]*Plessy v. Ferguson*, 163 U.S. 537 (1896).

their part did not prove the acts to *be* discriminatory, but only proved that the blacks were thin-skinned.

It was not a unanimous decision. John Marshall Harlan, the Court's only southerner and a former Kentucky slave owner himself, issued a dissent that shamed his colleagues:

> We boast of the freedom enjoyed by our people above all other peoples. But it is difficult to reconcile that boast with a state of law which, practically, puts the brand of servitude and degradation upon a large class of our fellow citizens, our equals before the law. The thin disguise of "equal" accommodations . . . will not mislead anyone, nor atone for the wrong this day done.

He was right, of course, but it would be many years before a majority of the Court would agree with his position. In the meantime, *Plessy v. Ferguson* had established the infamous "separate-but-equal" doctrine that would keep blacks separate, all right, but they would be enjoying a social condition in no way equal to that of whites. The Court had supplied the foundation for the building of Jim Crow. The separate-but-equal black schools would often have no libraries and no shop equipment; the textbooks used by blacks would be castoffs from white schools. The separate-but-equal restrooms for blacks in public places would often be one toilet for both men and women. And the separate-but-equal hospital wards were often nonexistent. In World War I and even in World War II, it was virtually impossible for a black man to win a commission in the navy or the air force, and commissions in the army were made available only as a way to maintain Jim Crow rules from top to bottom.

The Use and Nonuse of the Fourteenth Amendment

It is no exaggeration to say that for the last fifteen years of the nineteenth century and for most of the first fifty years of this century the Supreme Court disregarded the clear intent of the Fourteenth Amendment, which was to protect blacks. Instead, by one of the strangest twists of interpretation, the Court encouraged the use of that amendment to protect big business excesses from government regulation and restraint. Property, not people, got the Court's attention.[17]

A similar attitude of hostility or indifference to blacks was evident in the White House for much of that time. President Theodore Roosevelt spoke understandingly of the southerners' stunning record of lynching blacks (about 100 a year during the 1880s and 1890s, peaking with 235 in 1892)—almost always ostensibly for "raping white women."[18] President William Howard Taft favored ballot restrictions for blacks and opposed higher education for them. President Woodrow Wilson increased segregation in the federal government and, to make that easier, appointed no blacks to office.[19] Under that leadership and style, the United States passed through World War I—which was identified as the war "to make the world safe for democracy."

The 1920s saw a flowering of black pride and significant black achievements in the arts; it was the decade of the "Harlem Renaissance," when the black poet, musician, and dramatist became faddish. But the vast majority of blacks saw no improvement whatsoever in their economic, legal, or political status.

The ice began to break, slowly, in the 1930s. Loyal to the party that had freed them, blacks had traditionally voted Republican. But after receiving 80 percent of their votes in 1928, Republican President Herbert C. Hoover scorned them. The blacks responded accordingly. In the 1932 presidential election, 50 percent of the blacks went for Democrat Franklin D. Roosevelt. In 1936 they went for FDR by a very large majority. By now the Democrats were aware that the black vote in the big northern cities could be crucial; indeed, it could be decisive in sixteen

---

[17]Laws requiring corporations to provide certain safety standards for their employees, proscribing child labor, protecting women laborers, regulating hours of labor, guaranteeing minimum wages, and suppressing fraudulent marketing were repeatedly killed by the courts, including the Supreme Court, as infringements upon the liberties guaranteed by the Fourteenth Amendment. It was legal Darwinism—survival of the toughest and most unscrupulous corporations—and the courts saw no reason to interfere.

[18]See Meier and Rudwick, *From Plantation to Ghetto*, p. 192.

[19]Meier and Rudwick, pp. 186, 192–93.

states with 278 electoral votes. In 1940, blacks were mentioned for the first time in the Democratic party platform, which promised to uphold due process and equal protection of the law. The election of 1944 proved how wise the Democrats had been to court the blacks: if Roosevelt had received no larger a percentage of black votes than had his Democratic predecessors, the Republican candidate, Thomas E. Dewey, would have turned him out of the White House. And again, in 1948, if the blacks had voted for Dewey instead of for Harry S Truman, Dewey would have won.[20]

Roosevelt and Truman showed their gratitude, but timidly. Roosevelt's greatest show of thanks was appointing more liberal judges to the Supreme Court, which in 1944 outlawed the all-white primary—the first big breakthrough for

---

[20]Pat Watters and Reese Cleghorn, *Climbing Jacob's Ladder: The Arrival of Negroes in Southern Politics* (New York: Harcourt Brace Jovanovich, 1967), p. 11.

Black voters' line for a Georgia primary election in 1946

southern blacks since Reconstruction. With this incentive, blacks thronged to the polls in such numbers that not even corrupt registrars could turn them all away. The registration of blacks in the South rose from 250,000 in 1940 to 1,008,614 in 1952. But the surge was short-lived, soon subsided, and did not pick up again for another decade.

There were other signs, too, that the Supreme Court was beginning to see blacks as authentic citizens—proving once again that the Court reads election returns. From the mid-1930s to the mid-1950s it handed down significant decisions based on the equal protection clause. *Norris v. Alabama* (1935) outlawed the systematic exclusion of blacks from juries.[21] *Gaines v. Canada* (1938) provided for equal (though not desegregated) advantages in higher education.[22] *Smith v. Allwright* (1944) outlawed the all-white primary.[23] *Morgan v. Virginia* (1946) outlawed segregation in interstate travel.[24] *Shelley v. Kraemer* and *Hurd v. Hodge* (1948) outlawed restrictive covenants that made it impossible for blacks to buy houses.[25] *Sweatt v. Painter* (1950) ordered white law schools to open their doors to blacks.[26]

Desegregation: The *Brown* Decision

In 1954, the Supreme Court handed down the *Brown v. Board of Education* ruling.[27] It was the first important decision under Chief Justice Earl Warren and probably the most important action of the Supreme Court in this century. Although its narrow purpose was to overturn the separate-but-equal doctrine of *Plessy* as applied to schools, it also activated a whole series of other court rulings, congressional acts, and executive mandates that revived the meaning of equality not only in education but in political activities and in respect to the rights of criminal defendants.

At the time of the *Brown* decision, seventeen states and the District of Columbia forbade black children to go to public schools with white children. It was a time of oppression in the South, where blacks could not vote (or very few could vote) and could not use public facilities without the stigma of segregation. That was the reality that confronted the Supreme Court—not merely private prejudice, but a pervasive inequality from top to bottom, imposed by the force of law. *Brown* was the first major blow aimed at chipping away the crust of quasi slavery. The Court ruled that separate schools were "inherently" unequal.

For all practical purposes the Court's rulings—including even the famous and supposedly potent *Brown* ruling—had little impact immediately. In the states where they mattered, the white power structure simply ignored them or gave them only the amount of attention necessary to meet the barest letter of the law. Public opinion did not demand reform action, nor did the federal government.

As the 1960s opened, more than 90 percent of the schools that were segregated at the time of the *Brown* ruling were still totally segregated; many of the others had only a token number of blacks. In 1963, in one hundred black belt counties—which collectively contain one-third of all blacks of voting age in the eleven southern states—only 8.3 percent, or 55,000 people out of about 668,000, had access to the ballot. Federal funds appropriated in 1958 and doled out to six southern states to support public higher education was distributed as shown in Table 4-1.

The same indifference was shown by the federal government in enforcing fair distribution of funds for elementary schooling, health, welfare, and housing. In 1960, only 4.3 percent of the federal farm housing loans went to blacks—the group most in need of such loans. In Florida, Georgia, and Tennessee, not a single farm ownership loan was made to a black.[28] Burke Marshall, Assistant United States Attorney General

---

[21]*Norris v. Alabama,* 294 U.S. 587 (1935).

[22]*Missouri ex rel. Gaines v. Canada,* 305 U.S. 337 (1938).

[23]*Smith v. Allwright,* 321 U.S. 649 (1944).

[24]*Morgan v. Virginia,* 328 U.S. 373 (1946).

[25]*Shelley v. Kraemer,* 334 U.S. 1 (1948); *Hurd v. Hodge,* 334 U.S. 24 (1948).

[26]*Sweatt v. Painter,* 339 U.S. 629 (1950).

[27]*Brown v. Board of Education,* 347 U.S. 483 (1954).

---

[28]Herbert Aptheker, *Soul of the Republic: The Negro Today* (New York: Marzani & Munsell, 1964), p. 95.

TABLE 4-1

DISTRIBUTION OF FEDERAL FUNDS FOR HIGHER EDUCATION, 1958

STATE	PER STUDENT	
	WHITE	BLACK
Alabama	$144.10	$13.11
Florida	156.00	15.30
Georgia	185.70	14.37
Louisiana	110.97	5.83
Mississippi	250.41	19.22
South Carolina	169.71	28.82

SOURCE: Herbert Aptheker, *Soul of the Republic: The Negro Today* (New York: Marzani de Munsell, 1964), p. 95.

for Civil Rights, explained part of the problem in a lecture at Columbia University:

> The [segregated] system has been protected thus far, since the mid-1870s, by nonrecognition of federally guaranteed rights. This has not necessarily meant massive resistance in the sense of outright defiance of federal authority, although we have had that, but it does mean an open failure to comply with unquestioned standards of federal law until forced to do so. There is no parallel to be found in law enforcement. It is as if no taxpayer sent in a return until he personally was sued by the federal government, or no corporation respected the Sherman Act until an injunction was issued against it. The crisis is more deplorable, of course, because it is not private persons, individual or corporate, who are failing to comply with laws, but the states themselves, and the instrumentalities of state law.[29]

Southern politicians in Washington encouraged the resistance. The "Southern Manifesto," written in 1956 and signed by most members of Congress from the Deep South, urged state governments to "resist forced integration by any lawful means"—which, in practice, meant just about any means short of a declaration of war.

Clearly, Supreme Court rulings, hobbled by stubborn state governments and a lethargic fed-

[29]Burke Marshall, *Federalism and Civil Rights* (New York: Columbia University Press, 1964), pp. 7–8.

eral government, were not going to be enough to bring the Constitution and federal statutes into proper focus for black citizens unless additional pressure was brought to bear. Resistance from the southern populace and from southern officials had simply cancelled out the law. At best, southern blacks were met with indifference; at worst—and not uncommonly—they were met with lynchings, castrations, arson, bombings, and mob violence of every sort.

The Civil Rights Movement

Black people would have to try some method other than legislation and litigation to obtain justice. Thus was born "the movement." One of its earliest and most dramatic steps began on December 1, 1955, when Rosa Parks, a black seamstress, boarded a bus in downtown Montgomery, Alabama, and took a seat in the section reserved for whites. All the seats in the black section were occupied. The bus driver ordered her to move back to the black section anyway, but Rosa Parks's feet were tired, and she didn't relish the thought of standing. So she stayed where she was. For that, she was arrested. Led by Reverend Martin Luther King, Jr., in his first major role in the civil rights movement, the blacks of the city responded. They boycotted the Montgomery bus system for a year and maintained so much unity that they won. It was the first mass action by southern blacks. Another milestone was passed on February 1, 1960, when four freshmen at Agricultural and Technical College—a black school—in Greensboro, North Carolina, took seats at a downtown F. W. Woolworth Company lunch counter. For an hour they sat, denied service and taking insults, until the manager closed the lunch counter. Howard Zinn, a historian and participant in the movement, writes:

> It is hard to overestimate the electrical effect of that first sit-in in Greensboro, as the news reached the nation on television screens, over radios, in newspapers . . . . In a matter of days, the idea leaped to other cities in North Carolina. During the next two weeks sit-ins spread to fifteen cities in five Southern states. Within the following year, over 50,000 people—most were Negroes, some were white—had participated in one kind of demonstration or another in a hundred cities, and over 3,600 demonstrators spent time in jail.[30]

The moral commitment of blacks to getting their share of constitutional rights was arousing considerable sympathy among nonsouthern politicians in Washington and among their constituents. But they were probably also moved, to some degree, by fear of this new force in the United States, for, by 1963, blacks were beginning to sound a tougher and more belligerent note. At the 1963 March on Washington, attended by a quarter of a million persons, John Lewis, leader of the Student Nonviolent Coordinating Committee (SNCC), spoke passionately of a black revolution:

> To those who have said, "Be Patient and Wait," we must say that "Patience is a dirty and nasty word." We cannot be patient, we do not want to be free gradually, we want our freedom, and we want it now. . . . The revolution is a serious one. Mr. Kennedy is trying to take the revolution out of the street and put it in the courts. Listen, Mr. Kennedy, listen Mr. Congressman, listen fellow citizens, the black masses are on the march for jobs and freedom, and we must say to the politicians that there won't be a "cooling-off" period.[31]

---

[30]Quoted in Chace and Collier, eds., *Justice Denied*, p. 332.

[31]Quoted in Chace and Collier, eds., pp. 358–59.

Four years later, after black riots had racked some cities during the most sustained spasm of civil disorder in our history, it had become commonplace to hear even moderates such as John Conyers, Jr., a black congressman from Detroit, say,

> This thing is becoming two armed camps, but it's a risk black people are willing to take. Look, we started the whole civil rights business with two presidents who both told Martin Luther King we can't get a civil rights bill—it's impossible. But the pressure of events made it possible. Confrontation is both inevitable and creative. There's nobody who can call in anybody and turn it off.[32]

The revolution that SNCC leader Lewis foresaw never really developed, and, ultimately, the political parties Lewis disdained brought about the Civil Rights Act of 1964 and the Voting Rights Act of 1965. The Civil Rights Act provided for enforcement of the right to vote, outlawed discrimination in places of public accommodation, forbade discrimination in federally funded programs, and established an Equal Employment Opportunity Commission to monitor discriminatory practices in employment. The Voting Rights Act suspended literacy tests in all states and counties where less than 50 percent of the voting-age population were registered on November 1, 1964, provided for federal examiners to register persons in these areas, and called for court action against the enforcement of poll taxes. (An amendment in 1970 eliminated literacy tests for voting and abolished residency requirements of more than thirty days for national elections.)

Subsequent Supreme Court rulings supported those acts, reviving the innate vitality, at last, of the Fourteenth and Fifteenth Amendments. But it was an emotional blitz—the "creative confrontation" Conyers mentioned—more than logic and reason and a love for law that got these things going.

The Status of Blacks Today

In recent years the complexion of the southern school system has become mixed to a

---

[32]Quoted in *Newsweek*, November 20, 1967, p. 35.

dramatic degree. In the mid-1960s, hardly 1 percent of the black children in the eleven Confederate states were in school with whites; by the mid-1970s, nearly 50 percent were in predominantly white schools.[33] By contrast (because of de facto segregation established many years ago along neighborhood lines), only 28 percent of the blacks in northern and western states attended white schools. Nationally, more than 90 percent of the 2.5 million black pupils had at least some white classmates. For those who prefer to call the glass half empty rather than half full, it could also be said that two-thirds of them were, in the mid-1970s, still in schools in which blacks formed a majority, and nearly 40 percent were attending classes that were virtually all black.

In both North and South, the large urban areas, with their "racially isolated" central-city schools, posed the great problem. One of the most dramatic examples of the difficulty is in Detroit, where more than 90 percent of the blacks live in the central part of the city—a concentration that results in 50 percent of the black students going to schools that are more than 98 percent black. Similar concentrations with similar results, are found in Baltimore, Cleveland, New York, Chicago, and Washington, D.C. As the black concentration intensifies in the cities, whites panic and move to the suburbs—making the de facto segregation of the cities all the worse. (See Table 4-2.) By the mid-1970s, nine of the twelve largest, and fourteen of the twenty largest, cities had majority black enrollments in their schools, and the proportion of black students to white students was steadily rising. In its February 1977 report, the United States Commission on Civil Rights unhappily observed:

> To a very great extent the remaining problems of segregation by race and national origin in public schools are problems that exist in big cities. While nationally . . . two out of every five black children attend intensely segregated schools [that is, 90 to 100 percent minority enrollment], in the 26 largest cities of the United States almost three of every four black pupils are assigned to such schools. . . .
>
> In the wake of two great migrations—the movement of black people from the rural South to big cities throughout the country and of whites from central cities to the suburbs—the racial composition of these school systems has changed dramatically from predominantly white to predominantly black.[34]

Efforts to ease the intensity of de facto segregation by busing students from one school to another were resulting in great opposition from many white parents.

Voting rights statutes were applied with such effectiveness that, in the ten years following the Voting Rights Act of 1965, the number of blacks registered in Dixie jumped from less than 1.5 million to 3.5 million; as of mid-1976, there were 3,979 elected black officials in the nation, which more than tripled the number since 1969, and 57 percent of the black officeholders (2,300) were in the sixteen states of the South. Nationally, the number of black mayors had jumped from 0 to 152 (including 11 black women). Nevertheless, blacks continued to account for less than 1 percent of the more than 522,000 elected officials in the nation.[35]

The civil rights laws and edicts of recent years have indeed written a more optimistic scenario for minorities, but what of economic reality? "Democracy," as Maury Maverick once pointed out, "is liberty plus economic security. We Americans want to pray, think as we please—and eat regular."[36] Have recent laws helped blacks to eat more regular?

Job discrimination, though still deep and wide, is now more subtle. And it has begun to be uprooted in a timid and inefficient way through such federal agencies as the Equal Employment Opportunity Commission, which was created by the 1964 Civil Rights Act. Ten years after that act, the steel industry, for example, finally

---

[33]Unfortunately, blacks were being taken into the mixture so rapidly in the South that some whites were panicking and fleeing. Of the 20,000 white students still living within Atlanta's city limits, 10,000 were going to private schools in 1975. Faced with the disturbing probability that the flight of whites would resegregate many previously desegregated schools, even civil rights lawyers were beginning to soften their insistence on following the law to its ultimate. (*New York Times*, June 29, 1975.)

[34]*Congressional Record*, S10898–99, June 28, 1977.

[35]Joint Center for Political Studies, Washington, D.C., press release, August 2, 1976.

[36]Quoted in John W. Gardner and Francesca Gardner Reese, *Know or Listen to Those Who Know* (New York: W. W. Norton & Co., 1975), p. 223.

TABLE 4-2   **MINORITY CONCENTRATION IN CITY SCHOOLS, 1972**

MAJOR URBAN SCHOOL DISTRICTS	PERCENTAGE MINORITY	PERCENTAGE CHANGE IN WHITE ENROLLMENT 1967–72
New York City	67.0	−5.0
Los Angeles	39.8	−12.0
Chicago	70.4	−23.0
Philadelphia	62.2	−6.0
Detroit	81.4	−30.0
Houston	65.8	−21.0
Baltimore	75.5	−38.0
Dallas	54.9	−21.0
District of Columbia	96.3	−40.0
Cleveland	62.2	−13.0
San Diego	33.7	−10.0
Milwaukee	40.2	−19.0
Memphis	71.2	−15.0
New Orleans	80.8	−39.0
Boston	49.3	−16.0
Indianapolis	45.7	−25.0
St. Louis	72.2	−27.0
San Francisco	51.1	−25.0
San Antonio	52.3	−13.0
Kansas City	68.0	−27.0

SOURCE: *Congressional Record*, S10898, June 28, 1977.

agreed to pay millions of dollars to minorities it had discriminated against in the past and promised not to discriminate against them in the future.[37] But the pace of job desegregation is slow everywhere, and nowhere slower than in the federal government itself. Among nine-hundred professional jobs on Senate staffs in 1975, only twenty-eight were held by blacks. And, typical of the bureaucracy, minorities made up only 5 percent of the work force of the National Aeronautics and Space Administration (NASA).[38] Nor was the federal government exerting all its pressure to bring about job equality on the outside.

Ten years after an executive order was issued prohibiting discrimination by federal contrac-

tors, the Labor Department still did not have a means for evaluating progress in the employment of blacks or women. The executive order of 1965 prohibited discrimination on the basis of race, sex, or national origin and required companies holding federal contracts to submit an "affirmative action" plan for hiring and upgrading minority workers. In 1975, one-fifth of the "affirmative action" plans approved by the Pentagon for its contractors did not meet federal guidelines. Seventy percent of the plans approved by the General Services Administration, which is the housekeeping agency of the federal government, fell short of the guidelines and, moreover, lacked sufficient safeguards to bring about job equality.[39]

---

[37]*New York Times*, April 14, 1974.

[38]*Washington Post*, March 31, 1974, November 21, 1974.

[39]Report of the U.S. General Accounting Office, Washington, D.C., released May 4, 1975.

In the mid-1960s, only 2 percent of southern black families were earning $15,000 or more a year. But, in 1974, 13 percent of them were in that bracket.[40] Such statistics are impressive only when viewed independently of the whole economy. Progress was not good compared to that of white males. The United States Commission on Civil Rights noted in 1975 that "despite laws, executive orders and regulations committed to equal employment and despite some gains in recent years," the economic improvement of minority-group men and white women had been "marginal." The only real advance was by black women, whose median income had become almost equal to that of white women; but this advance was made possible only because the income of white women had "increasingly dropped behind the income of all men." While 2.5 million blacks "moved out of poverty between 1959 and 1973, more than 13 million whites also moved out of poverty during this same period." The unemployment rate for non-whites, double that of whites, had remained virtually unchanged since 1954. It was still true for most blacks, as Kenneth Clark pointed out, that whites viewed them as a blight and that, as a result, their lives were blighted.[41]

Thus it was clear that in employment, in education, and in housing the struggle for equality would have to continue, though on a different plateau. After two decades of court decisions, legislative battles, mass demonstrations, and a few riots, the laws of the land had been made colorblind. Discrimination based on race was officially outlawed. But now new questions, more subtle and perhaps even more difficult, have arisen. Is it enough to simply stop discriminating, or would past wrongs have to be righted in some other way? Would additional favoritism have to be shown blacks for a while in order to balance the scales? If so, how would it be accomplished? As one observer put it, the central questions come down to this:

---

[40]*New York Times*, January 9, 1977.

[41]Kenneth Clark, "The Negro and The Urban Crisis," in Kermit Gordon, ed. *Agenda for the Nation* (Washington, D.C.: Brookings Institution, 1968), pp. 131–33.

TABLE 4-3

DISCRIMINATION AND INEQUALITY OF OPPORTUNITY, 1973

STATUS	WHITE	BLACK
Income		
Median income of families	$12,595	$7,596
Percentage of persons in poverty	9.9	26.6
Percentage of families with incomes of $10,000 or more	63.9	35.0
Education		
Median years of school completed by men 25 years or older	12.3	10.6
Percentage of persons 25–29 years old who have completed high school	75.5	64.7
Percentage of persons 25–34 years old who are college graduates	19.0	8.3
Unemployment rates (percentage)		
Adult men	2.9	5.9
Adult women	4.3	8.5
Teenagers	12.6	31.4

SOURCE: Paul A. Samuelson, *Economics*, 10th ed. (New York: McGraw-Hill, 1976), p. 95. Data from U.S. Bureau of the Census; U.S. Bureau of Labor Statistics.

To what extent must white Americans be inconvenienced and even themselves discriminated against so that blacks can have a better chance at good schools, good jobs and good housing? . . .

Specifically, should white children, who never practiced discrimination themselves, be transported to schools out of their neighborhoods so that black children, whose parents were forced to attend inferior segregated schools, can get a better education?

Should black workers, who lack job seniority because of decades of discrimination, be given promotions over whites, who worked hard over the years to build up their seniority?

Should colleges and universities give black applicants preference over whites in order to create a generation of black doctors, lawyers, teachers and other professionals?

Should public housing projects be constructed in white suburbs so that blacks can afford to live near the booming job market outside the central cities?[42]

Congress, state legislatures, the courts, and the chief executives of federal and state governments are already struggling to arrive at answers—none of which, it is almost certain, will be satisfactory to either side.[43] That's what happens when rights are long delayed: they leave a vacuum that fills with enormously complex social tangles, which take generations to straighten out.

---

[42]David E. Rosenbaum, "A New Rights Drive Perplexes Nation," *New York Times*, July 3, 1977.

[43]If the questions are confusing, so are some of the answers. Consider the groping of the Supreme Court: in March 1976, the Court, by a vote of five to three, ruled that victims of hiring discrimination are entitled to seniority dating from the employer's refusal to hire them because of race or sex discrimination (*Franks v. Bowman Transportation Company*, 424 U.S. 747). The Court said that in cases of proved job bias, the victims should be advanced over workers hired after the date they were denied employment—even if this resulted in "arguably innocent" fellow workers being laid off.
Was the Court scrapping the principle of union seniority to make amends for past discrimination? Not at all, for in June 1977, the same Court, voting seven to two, upheld seniority systems that perpetuate past employment discrimination against minority races and women (*T.I.M.E.-D.C. Inc. v. United States*, 431 U.S.). The Court said that although the seniority system under dispute allocated "the choicest jobs, the greatest protection against layoffs, and other advantages" to the oldest employees—all white, all male—the seniority system itself was not unlawful. In short, the employment system had discriminated against minority races and women but the seniority system hadn't.

EQUAL RIGHTS FOR WOMEN

Despite the many legal and social restrictions placed on their lives, women, in the early years of this nation, especially on the frontier, were considered the valuable allies of men because of their work in the fields and in "cottage industries"—spinning, weaving, cloth making, candle making, and so forth. The merchant's wife was often essentially his business partner. On the frontier, the woman who could use a rifle coolly while under fire, who could swing an ax to clear a trail, who could help build a mud or log home was not unusual and was admired for her rugged talents. In the higher strata of early American society, women were encouraged to show themselves in salons as the equal of men in wit, conversation, and counsel.

But with the approach of the industrial age, with the passing of the frontier and the leveling of society, women became increasingly restricted to the home and to their own company. J. C. Furnas writes:

The Pawtucket girl whom Samuel Slater married in the 1790's came of a textile family and knew the business well enough to invent a new way to double-twist cotton thread that made her people's fortune. In the 1830s the typical shipowner's or silversmith's wife was much less familiar with the family business than her grandmother had been. The shop or countinghouse was no longer on the property but downtown, whither husband daily repaired early, not returning until midafternoon dinner.[44]

The Domesticity of Women

By the 1830s, most women's lives had become rather inflexible; they were prisoners of custom, encased and bound by English common law and by the fervent quasi religion of Family Life, of which they were high priestess, whether they liked it or not.

English common law, which America had adapted on this point with few modifying statutes, gave the husband almost total control over

---

[44]J. C. Furnas, *The Americans: A Social History of the United States, 1587–1914* (New York: G. P. Putnam's Sons, 1969), p. 486.

his wife and over her property. Legally, the wife stood in court on a par with a minor child or an idiot. Where the law was concerned, she spoke through her husband.

Growth and instability in the United States—movement to the frontier and to the cities; the shifting of employment from farm to factory; the increasing diversity of church sects; the spread of education and, through it, the increased questioning of old standards—made more intense the need for the home as a dependable place of stability, organized around the wife-mother and operated by an unvarying code.[45]

If a woman were unable to find a husband, she was relegated to the pitiable (or so it was thought) category of "spinster" and was usually limited to one of the traditional spinster jobs: teacher, librarian, nurse, or clerk. Most professions excluded women. In 1872, upholding an Illinois statute barring women from practicing law, the United States Supreme Court said, "Man is, or should be, woman's protector and defender. The natural and proper timidity and delicacy which belongs to the female sex evidently unfits it for many of the occupations of civil life."[46] Well into this century many colleges and universities would not accept women, at least at the undergraduate level. For those who did not want to move directly into the role of housewife or into the spinster trades, there were special women's colleges and finishing schools to prepare them to be "ladies."

But, ultimately, a woman's success or failure was measured by whether or not she married, had children, and fitted into the home hierarchy. It was an important role for a woman to play. But it was also restrictive, subordinating, and, in some ways, spiritually debilitating. She became not so much a person as a formula. The "good wife" was equated not only with fertility but with housekeeping skills; the "virtuous" woman was the woman who ran an efficient home. Not only husbands supported this viewpoint; so did

the commercial world, which strongly favored a class of people who did nothing but manage and promote consumption (as well as produce more consumers). John Kenneth Galbraith writes:

> The conversion of women into a crypto-servant class was an economic accomplishment of the first importance. Menially employed servants were available only to a minority of the pre-industrial population; the servant-wife is available, democratically, to almost the entire present male population. Were the workers so employed subject to pecuniary compensation, they would be by far the largest single category in the labor force. The value of the services of housewives has been calculated, somewhat impressionistically, at roughly one-fourth of total Gross National Product. The average housewife has been estimated (at 1970 wage rates for equivalent employments) to do about $257 worth of work a week or some $13,364 a year. If it were not for this service, all forms of household consumption would be limited by the time required to manage such consumption—to select, transport, prepare, repair, maintain, clean, service, store, protect and otherwise perform the tasks that are associated with the consumption of goods. The servant role of women is critical for the expansion of consumption in the modern economy.[47]

Under the guise of protecting and respecting woman, the commercial male world further isolated her and depleted her efforts to take part in shaping reality. The image they promoted was epitomized in the 1880s and '90s by the mythical Gibson girl, the goddesslike, voluptuous creation of artist Charles Dana Gibson. Women paid a heavy price for this involuntary elevation to the pedestal. They were the prisoners of a special code of morality. Men could smoke in public, but for women it was considered bad taste;[48] most public bars were off-limits to women; men could have mistresses with only mild public censure, but women could have lovers only at the sacrifice of their reputations. To have a child out of wedlock was, as a breach of society's rules, worse than prostitution.

---

[45]See Sheila M. Rothman, "Rights v. Needs: American Attitudes Toward Women, Children and Family," in Irving Kristol and Paul H. Weaver, eds. *The Americans: 1976* (Lexington, Mass.: D. C. Heath & Co., Lexington Books, 1976).

[46]*American Heritage*, February 1975.

[47]John Kenneth Galbraith, *Economics and the Public Purpose* (Boston: Houghton Mifflin Co., 1973), p. 33.

[48]One cigarette manufacturer used an advertisement showing a beautiful woman imploring a cigarette-smoking man, "Blow some my way." It was in bad taste for her to smoke her own, but okay to breathe used smoke.

Having isolated women from business and banished them to a never-never land of romantic morality, it was easy enough for men to insist also that women not bother their delicate brains or sully their gentle hands with the grubby strategy and levers of politics.

The Struggle for Suffrage

Naturally, some women rebelled against their ersatz status and against their loss of freedom and sought the right to vote. The first political victories for women came in the Far West, where social codes were less rigid and the pioneer woman was respected for her indomitability. She had survived mud, snow, dust storms, Indians, disease, wild animals, and her own menfolk, so it was natural to presume that she might also survive politics.

Wyoming's was the first government in the world to give women the right to vote and to hold office. William H. Bright introduced a women's suffrage bill into the territorial Wyoming legislature in 1869. A native of Virginia, Bright did not like the idea of blacks voting, but he was convinced that if the Fourteenth and Fifteenth Amendments legally entitled them to vote then women ought to have the same right. Thus, he was not so much in favor of women's rights as he was piqued by the new rights of blacks. The law was passed, also for reasons having nothing directly to do with the issue. The legislators thought the whole thing was a big joke, and they voted for it amidst an outpouring of low wisecracks and frontier humor. Moreover, they hoped that the law would entice more women to move West; the 1870 census showed 1,049 females and 6,107 males.[49] With the vote, women also got the right to sit on juries. But

apparently the politicians thought women took their court duty too seriously; after 1871 they were relieved of it, and their exclusion continued until 1950.

All of the early states that gave women the right to vote were in the West, but even there progress was slow. By 1896 only Wyoming, Utah, Colorado, and Idaho had been so daring. The state of Washington surrendered to the suffrage movement in 1911, and California and Oregon ran up the white flag in 1912.

One is justified in using the language of war, for in many respects and in many locations the struggle for suffrage did sometimes become a war between the sexes. Women of stalwart physical and psychological courage led the movement. Abigail Scott Duniway, one of the great crusaders, was sometimes pelted with eggs and fruit by audiences in Oregon, Washington, and Idaho.

In the East, women organized under the leadership of Elizabeth Cady Stanton, Lucretia Mott, Susan B. Anthony (the most famous of all), Anna Howard Shaw, Carrie Chapman Catt, Olympia Brown, Lucy Burns, Alice Paul, and Inez Milholland. There were a number of organizations, but most of them grew out of, or combined with, each other: the National Woman Suffrage Association and the American Woman Suffrage Association, both organized in 1869; the National American Woman Suffrage Association, a combining of the earlier two, founded in 1890; and the National Woman's Party, established in 1916. The women often broke the law, sometimes provoked violence, and sometimes resorted to violence in order to attract attention to their cause. If they had not done so, the male-dominated establishment would simply have politely ignored them. (President Woodrow Wilson did, doffing his hat as he passed through their picket lines around the White House; finally, when he began to fear that their protest might hurt wartime morale, he caved in and grudgingly supported their cause.)

The suffragettes perfected the modern propaganda strategy of courting arrest to make headlines. When police ordered them not to demonstrate or parade, they demonstrated and paraded; when city officials refused permits for rallies, they rallied anyway; sometimes they and

---

[49]The Wyoming women moved into politics so enthusiastically that in the 1870 election—their first time to participate—they sent several Republicans to the previously all-Democratic legislature. This outraged the Democratic lawmakers, and, in the 1871 session, they passed a bill repealing women's suffrage and then tried to bribe the Republican governor into signing it. He vetoed it instead, and the Republicans in the legislature were just barely strong enough to uphold the veto. From this shaky and unenthusiastic beginning, Wyoming today claims the title of "The Equality State." (From Lynne Cheney, "It All Began in Wyoming," *American Heritage*, April 1973, p. 62.)

their followers—both factory women and upper-crust ladies—threw stones and cursed police, which was shocking enough at the turn of the century to get them hauled off to jail. These techniques had been used successfully in England by Emmeline, Christabel, and Sylvia Pankhurst, the widow and daughters of a top official of the British Labour Party. Several American women apprenticed with the Pankhursts and returned to this country to spread the techniques of protest cum imprisonment. One was Alice Paul, who was arrested outside the White House on October 20, 1917, and sentenced to seven months in the District of Columbia jail. In an effort by the government to discredit her, she was confined in the psychopathic ward. When she launched a hunger strike, jail officials force-fed her through the nose. Such physical suffering by the leaders of the movement was not uncommon. Inez Milholland—who led many a suffragette parade sitting astride a black horse—worked such long hours for the movement that in 1916, in the middle of a speech, she collapsed and died. She was twenty-eight.

Finally the male politicians capitulated. The Nineteenth Amendment, giving women the right to vote, passed Congress in 1919 and was ratified by the states in 1920. The United States was far from being the first nation to enfranchise its women. New Zealand had done so in 1893, Australia in 1902, Finland in 1906, Norway in 1913, and Russia in 1917. In 1918, Britain had given the vote to married women, women householders, and women university graduates aged thirty and over. (Not until 1928 did Britain put aside the notion that only by maturity, marriage, and a college education could women equal callow or senile male dolts.)

There was little logic to the male resistance in the United States (or elsewhere). Two of the strongest sources of opposition to women's suffrage came from big-city political bosses, who felt that women might launch a reform sweep of their machines, and from the liquor interests, who feared that women were genetically opposed to demon rum and would vote solidly for prohibition. As it turned out, these fears were as nonsensical as most other arguments. National prohibition was voted into the Constitution (Eighteenth Amendment) *before* women got the

Alice Paul, suffragette

vote nationally. And after women were enfranchised, big-city machine politics perked right along as if nothing had happened.

Political Impact of the Vote

For the first fifty years, the enfranchisement of women had, in most respects, only a moderate impact on their lives and on the life of the nation.

Political offices remained almost totally occupied by men.[50] In the first two centuries of this nation's existence, only ninety-five women served in Congress, and thirty-seven of these rode to office on their husbands' shirttails—succeeding them as widows or, as in the case of a Kentucky wife, getting elected to office when her ex-Congressman husband went to prison (for bootlegging).

The first woman to be elected to the United States Senate was Hattie Wyatt Caraway of Arkansas. Her husband had been a senator; when he died in 1931, the governor of Arkansas appointed her to fill out the term. Although she was elected again in 1938, her career was thoroughly undistinguished. The first woman to be elected to the United States House of Representatives was the great Jeannette Rankin. Montana sent her to Washington in 1917, three years before the Nineteenth Amendment was ratified. A vigorous fighter for the suffrage amendment, the eight-hour day for women, tax-law reform, legislation protecting children, and prohibition, Rankin stands highest in history as an apostle of peace. She was the only member of Congress to vote against United States' entry into both world wars.

Other women of outstanding character have served in Congress. Edith S. Green of Oregon was a powerful member of the House Education and Labor Committee until her retirement in 1975. Margaret Chase Smith of Maine served in the House from 1940 to 1949, then moved up to the Senate, where she served until 1973—the only woman in the upper chamber. As fearless as she was stubborn, Senator Smith was the first Republican to dare attack the greatest demagogue of our era, Senator Joseph McCarthy. On several other notable occasions she also defied her party by her stand on both issues and appointees.

The late 1960s and the 1970s produced a wave of strong-willed, strong-voiced, influential women in Congress—including ardent feminist Bella S. Abzug, presidential candidate Shirley Chisholm (the first black woman elected to Congress), Elizabeth Holtman (the youngest woman ever elected to the House), and, effective foe of the military-industrial complex, Patricia Schroeder of Colorado.[51] One can, in fact, see the late 1960s as the beginning of the modern feminist movement, in which women worked together to upgrade their place in politics and their role in economic policy making and money getting.

The Modern Feminist Movement: Political Assault

Women were slow to put women into political offices for two reasons: (1) they could only vote for people on the ballot, and, since the nominating machinery was in the hands of men, men got on the ballot and (2) for many years after they got the right to vote, they remained unsure of their own abilities and were happy to lean on the strong political arms of men—in the words of today's militant feminists, they were "niggerized."

In the late 1960s, the mood changed. Women achieved a new unity of purpose, and they made their assault on the status quo at a time when the ramparts had been weakened by the black civil rights movement and the antiwar movement of college youths. Old standards were already beginning to crumble. The women just kept the process going.

There had been a time when they would have agreed with New Orleans Mayor Moon Landrieu, that "women do the lickin' and the stickin' "—filling the role of behind-the-political-scenes drones who sealed the envelopes, ran the mimeograph machines, made the telephone calls, and brewed the coffee—"while men plan the strategy." But no more. Party reforms opened up the 1972 presidential conventions to participation by women in unprecedented num-

---

[50]When women did succeed in politics at the state or local level prior to the 1960s, it was usually considered to be the result of a fluke—as indeed it sometimes was. James Edward ("Pa") Ferguson, Governor of Texas, was impeached for a variety of crookedness. So he twice successfully managed the gubernatorial campaigns of "Ma" Ferguson. The Texas State Historical Association's supposedly complete *Handbook of Texas*, 1952 edition, devotes three columns to the career of Pa, but nothing apart for Ma.

[51]See Joint Committee on Arrangements for the Commemoration of the Bicentennial, "Women in Congress," House Report, 94-1732, Ninety-fourth Congress, Second Session, 1976.

"Welcome aboard. This is your captain, Margaret Williamson, speaking."

bers, and they went home panting for more power. More importantly, many women had already decided that they were going to work for female candidates instead of male candidates.

The election of 1974 was the New Woman's great watershed. In state legislatures, women won 587 seats (compared to 305 in 1969). Connecticut elected the first woman ever to become a governor in her own right, Ella T. Grasso. North Carolina named the first woman supreme court chief justice in history, Susie Sharp. Californians chose the first woman mayor to reign over a city of more than half a million people, Janet Gray Hayes, in San Jose. Of the women running for office in Colorado, 62 percent won their elections, compared with 48 percent of the men. Mary Anne Krupsak, with the campaign slogan "She's not just one of the boys," was elected lieutenant governor in New York. And Boston elected an avowed lesbian to the state house of representatives.

The South contributed a couple of other firsts the next year, when both Mississippi and Kentucky elected women lieutenant governors for

the first time. And in Phoenix, Margaret Hance—without the political-machine endorsement that for thirty years had been considered mandatory—was elected mayor with 55 percent of the vote in an eight-way race.

But the dramatic advances of 1974 did not continue in 1976. For the moment, women were on a plateau. In fact, their number dropped by one in the House of Representatives (from nineteen to eighteen) when Bella Abzug retired to try for a Senate seat. The male-dominated nominating machinery continued to turn women down as candidates. Fredi Wechsler of the nonpartisan National Women's Political Caucus complained that women are usually nominated only if it looks like there is no chance to whip the male incumbent.[52] Women also had cause to complain about their role at the national conventions. At the Democratic convention, women made up only 30 percent of the delegates, com-

---

[52]James M. Perry, "The New Congress," in *Collier's Yearbook 1977* (New York: Macmillan Educational Corporation, 1977).

pared to 40 percent in 1972; at the Republican convention, they held 28 percent of the seats, compared to 30 percent in 1972.

Still, in organizational ability, rhetoric, sense of theater, grasp of issues, TV image, and all the other vagaries and intangibles, women, when given the chance, were showing themselves at least the equals of male candidates. But they still had a long way to go before they held a share of the offices equal to their share of the vote (51 percent).

Economic Assault: The ERA

Women's next cause was to upgrade their place in economic policy making and money getting. To that end they worked for passage of the Equal Rights Amendment (ERA) to the Constitution. This effort had begun in 1923, just three years after passage of the voting rights amendment. Leaders of the feminist movement were quick to see that mere voting rights were not enough. Men's attitude toward women remained essentially unchanged, and women remained in a subordinate, sometimes slavish, position. In many states, women were still unable to buy property without their husbands' written consent, were barred from receiving credit unless their husbands were willing to cosign, and generally had inferior legal status. Although women were among the most militant and fearless participants in the labor movement, they held few labor union policy-making positions and customarily received less pay than men for doing the same work. The legal, medical, and other lucrative professions were extremely difficult for women to break into, because professional schools shunned their applications. Many state laws discriminated between the sexes.

That's the way it was in 1920, and that was still the way it was fifty years later. Whether in private or public employment, women were clearly getting second-class treatment. In 1970, male high-school graduates were earning a yearly average of $9,100; women high-school graduates averaged $5,280. Male college graduates averaged $13,320 a year, women college graduates, $7,930. In other words, a woman who spent four years in college could hope to make about $1,200 a year less than a man with a high

school education. The atmosphere creating this situation went right up to the top of government. Every President since Franklin D. Roosevelt had talked a good line, but prior to 1977 only two women had been appointed to cabinets: Frances Perkins, Secretary of Labor (1933 to 1945) under FDR, and Oveta Culp Hobby, Secretary of Health, Education and Welfare (1953 to 1955) under Dwight D. Eisenhower.

If discrimination against women existed, why wasn't it in violation of the Fourteenth Amendment, which states that "No state shall . . . deny to any person within its jurisdiction the equal protection of the laws"? On the face of it, one would have supposed that this did outlaw discrimination against women, as well as against all other citizens. But the Fourteenth Amendment was of no use to women, because the United States Supreme Court repeatedly stated that they were not covered by it. The Court had admitted that women were persons and that women were citizens; nevertheless, it simply would not extend all rights of citizenry to them.

Something else was needed, something so clearly stated that not even the Supreme Court could be blind to its meaning. Thus was born the proposed Equal Rights Amendment, which declared: "Equality of rights under the law shall not be denied or abridged by the United States or by any State on account of sex."

That was simple enough. It was also basic enough. Certainly it contained not even a whiff of revolution. But for nearly two generations, Congress would not seriously entertain the notion. Chairman Emanuel Celler, ruler of the House Judiciary Committee, through which the amendment would ordinarily have had to pass, would not even give the bill a hearing for twenty years. When Representative Martha W. Griffiths of Michigan (in Congress from 1955 to 1975) introduced an equal rights bill and asked him to let the committee consider it, Celler just laughed at her. He liked to joke about the problem: "There is as much difference between a male and a female as between a horse chestnut and a chestnut horse—and as the French say, *Vive le difference.*"[53]

---

[53]*Congressional Record*, H7949, August 10, 1970.

The Women's Caucus

There is not much wrong with America that couldn't be cured if the majority of the population (women) was fairly represented in Congress. Also, with a woman in the White House, the country might avoid war, if for no other reason than that women are seldom afflicted with machismo, the most dangerous vice of male Presidents.

The belief that women officeholders tend, more than men, to oppose a belligerent foreign policy and extravagant military spending is borne out by a study of the 1975 voting records of women members of Congress, the first such analysis ever made. There are now 19 women in the House, and they voted unanimously against U.S. involvement in the Angolan war, including the five women Republicans who had the courage to go against the policy of their own party leader.

Large majorities of the 19 women also opposed the leaders of both major parties in voting against the costly new B-1 bomber. They balked at providing arms or security aid to the Chilean military dictatorship; they supported a ban on using U.S. funds to plan assassinations or to influence foreign elections.

All but two of the group voted to override President Ford's vetoes of a bill controlling strip-mining and legislation creating a public works jobs program. A majority of the women of both parties had voting records more liberal than their party leaders.

Despite this independence, the women's bloc—the best and biggest in history—is still not as effective as the Congressional Black Caucus with its 17 members. While the women representatives are intelligent and diligent, they are not tightly organized like the Black Caucus, which, by working closely together, has achieved notable clout.

The women members are also handicapped by lack of seniority and committee chairmanships, but what they need most is leadership of their own. There are more than 6 million more women of voting age than men, yet after 56 years of suffrage and a decade of Women's Lib, their political status shows little improvement.

There used to be two women in the Senate; there are none now. The 19 House total is only two more than it was 30 years ago. . . . And there is still no woman on the Supreme Court. A complete count of all the elected women officials in the entire nation shows them holding fewer than 5 per cent of the offices.

It is difficult to understand this political standstill, for in other fields the female work force has grown from 16.6 million in 1947 to 37 million in 1975. Moreover, all the polls show the climate for women in politics is now more favorable than ever before.

The latest Gallup survey reports 7 out of 10 Americans believe the nation would be governed as well or better if more women held political office. Further, 73 per cent now say they would vote for a woman for President. Four years ago it was 66 per cent, and in 1937 only 31 per cent. . . .

From Clayton Fritchey, *Los Angeles Times*, April 24, 1976.

So she outfoxed and outfought him. The hardest method of getting a bill out of committee is to solicit enough names on a discharge petition. This is a direct slap at the committee's chairperson, for it is a way of saying that he or she does not know how to run his or her affairs. Since members of Congress are afraid of chairpersons and don't like to insult them, they don't like to sign discharge petitions. Only a handful of such petitions have succeeded in the last generation. Griffiths' was one of them. In the summer of 1970, when it became clear that her juggernaut could not be stopped, Celler surrendered, announcing that he would hold hearings on the amendment. But Griffiths, feeling she deserved some vengeance after years of waiting, went ahead and filed her petition—and flattened Celler, both in committee and in debate on the floor, where the bill passed 346 to 15.

The Senate added its approval to the equal rights bill after a two-year delay that was caused by uneasiness among some ordinarily strong prorights groups. Several prominent women's organizations—the National Council of Jewish Women and the National Council of Catholic Women, for example—actively opposed the ERA for fear it would upset a whole body of law dealing with complex personal and family relationships: divorce, child custody, military service, age of consent, and so forth. Some labor organizations feared that the amendment would kill laws they had fought for to protect women on the job.[54] Having cleared Congress, the proposed amendment began the rounds of the state legislatures for final approval before being added to the Constitution. As of 1977, thirty-five states had approved it. Thirty-eight are needed.

Assuming equal rights wins, will it mean for women, in the condescending slogan of a cigarette company, "You've come a long way baby"? Not at all. It will only mean that women in the United States, after more than two hundred years, have finally come legally as far as, but no farther than, males of all colors. Even without the protection of the ERA, women have begun to make strides in improving their economic status. But they still lag far behind. In 1975, they were still holding few of the top jobs in government and private business, and their median income was just over half the median income of men. On the nation's Bicentennial birthday, it was embarrassingly true that no industrialized country in the world had a smaller percentage of women doctors, women lawyers, women engineers, women physicists, women lawmakers, and women justices than the United States. That, eventually, may be reversed; most professional schools—not out of the goodness of their hearts, but under intense pressure—are taking special pains to find space for women. And, for whatever it's worth, women are now admitted to all military academies and trained for combat.

The women's rights issue is not an easy one to settle. For instance, what does it mean to "discriminate" against a woman in a case where sex differences may actually be relevant? Perhaps the best way to handle those cases is to specify the characteristics required rather than to make a flat distinction by sex. A more difficult problem is the accumulated effect of traditional family roles. Women in Western society have been the homemakers and child raisers. Now the woman has been freed from many of the ties of home by education, modern technology, the birth control pill, disposable diapers, and the rest, but society has not yet adjusted itself to this fact. Only slowly is it becoming apparent that the woman and the man can change roles, and that the woman doesn't have to be a housewife or mother. Meanwhile, the woman who aspires to a career in business often has to deal with her own feelings of guilt, resentment by competing males, and the need to prove her ability beyond what would normally be required of a man.

THE RIGHTS OF OTHER MINORITIES

Blacks and women make up the large bulk of those whose rights have been neglected or abused. But there are many other groups in the United States who have been discriminated against. Among them are Indians, Mexican-Americans, and Puerto Ricans.

American Indian Rights

It was not until 1924 that an American Indian was even considered a United States citizen. For most of the nineteenth century, the United States dealt with the Indian tribes as sovereign nations and made (and broke) treaties ending wars and reserving land for the tribes. With the Dawes Act of 1887, the federal government attempted to break down the tribal structure by parceling reservation land out to individual Indians. The Indian Reorganization Act of 1934 put a stop to this practice. In the 1950s, Congress attempted to end the policy of federal trustee-

---

[54]Both sides did agree on one thing: the Supreme Court was to blame. It had consistently failed to give women even the same share of the Fourteenth Amendment that it had, slowly and grudgingly, given blacks and other minorities. In 1938, the Supreme Court forced the admission of a black to the University of Missouri Law School, but, in 1960, it refused the same protection to three women who applied to all-male Texas Agricultural and Mechanical College. (*Congressional Record*, H7953, August 10, 1970.)

Not until 1975 did the Court come around to ruling that states could not keep women off juries and that women must be on a jury to insure a "fair cross-section of the community"—thus reversing a 1961 ruling of the Court. A thirteen-year delay in changing its mind on such an elementary concept was not likely to persuade women that full equality could be obtained via the courtroom.

Armed American Indians at Wounded Knee, 1973

ship of the Indians, but, in the face of a strong Indian resistance to losing federal protection, did not enforce this policy.

In general, the Constitution's "guarantees" have never given the American Indian a full life, much liberty, or much protection of property. Traditionally, the Indian equated life, liberty, and property with one thing, land: land to roam over, land to hunt on, land to cultivate.

But white people were remarkably adept at taking land from the Indians. At first the technique was to persuade the Indians to accept large reservations in exchange for giving up their vast aboriginally owned lands. As part of the exchange, the government signed treaties promising that the Indians would have ownership of the reservation lands "forever." Having pushed virtually all Indians onto large reservations by the 1880s, the government—with the encouragement of cattle barons, timber companies, railroads, and other commercial interests desiring to exploit the West—set about whittling down the size of the reservations, explaining that it had been too generous and that the Indians didn't need so much land.

> Between the years 1887 and 1966 the Indian land base has decreased from 138 million acres to 55 million acres. Indian land remains the subject of continual and unrelenting expropriation—most frequently in the name of progress. Indian land is cheaper, easier and less dangerous politically to take. So it is taken. Construction engineers, road builders and dam erectors have an uncanny knack for discovering that the only feasible and economical way to do what must be done will, unfortunately, necessitate taking the Indian's land.[55]

After being shunted onto shrinking, inhospitable, and usually unproductive reservations, the Indians were further neglected and cheated by government officials, with the result that in 1977 their condition was accurately described in

---

[55]Edgar S. Cahn, ed., *Our Brother's Keeper: The Indian in White America* (Cleveland: World Publishing Co., 1969), p. 69.

Cesar Chavez, head of the United Farm Workers, speaks in California against child labor

In the last decade, many Indians have taken their complaints to the public, sometimes in spectacular ways. In 1972, hundreds of Indians arrived in Washington on what they called "The Trail of Broken Treaties." They occupied the offices of the Bureau of Indian Affairs for six days in a dramatic protest against broken promises of Richard M. Nixon's administration. In early 1973, in perhaps their most calculated protest, the militant wing of the American Indian Movement seized the town of Wounded Knee in South Dakota, where the famous massacre of Sioux Indians had taken place in 1890. After seventy days of highly publicized news coverage, the militants surrendered to United States marshals under the terms of a peace agreement.

These protest demonstrations were unsuccessful in recruiting much support. They appeared to the public as outbursts of anger without focus, as vandalism for the sake of vandalism. The specific reforms sought by the Indians were unclear. In any event, the demonstrations brought no significant improvement in government-Indian relationships.

The one bright spot has been in the Indian Claims Commission, established in 1946 by the Indian Claims Commission Act. The Commission was scheduled to die in September 1978 and its work to be taken over by the United States Court of Claims. Thanks to the Commission, through 1977 Indians had received more than $800 million for lands they lost, and a number of large claims were still to be adjudicated.

this way by Margaret Hunter Pierce of the United States Indian Claims Commission:

> Of all minorities, Indians suffer from the greatest poverty, the lowest life expectancy, the worst education, the highest suicide rate, the highest percentage of alcoholism, and, for most, a sense of frustration that is nearly unbearable. They exert practically no political pressure on federal or local governments, and their attempts at self-help are limited by their lack of education and the built-in impotence of the one bureau of the federal government that has the most to do with how they live their lives—the Bureau of Indian Affairs, a relatively minor division in the large Department of the Interior.[56]

Although some employees of the Bureau of Indian Affairs are sensitive to Indian needs, the bureau as a whole has been notoriously callous and unresponsive. It has even participated in cheating the Indians.

Hispanic Rights

Just over 11 million people in the United States, about 5.3 percent of the population, are Americans of Spanish-speaking origin. They experience many of the same forms of discrimination—in education, employment, and housing—that blacks do, but the Hispanic-Americans are a little better off economically. Their median income in 1975 was $9,551, compared to $8,779 for blacks (and $14,268 for whites).

Mexican-Americans (Chicanos) have formed an independent political party, the La Raza Unida party, in an attempt to promote their cultural identity and develop their own political candidates. According to Chicano leader Albert

[56]"The Work of the Indian Claims Commission," *American Bar Association Journal* 63 (February 1977): 227.

Gurule, the Hispanics must "cut the umbilical cord from the gringo."[57] But the Chicanos have yet to bridge the gap between their people who live in the cities and those who live in rural areas.

Rural Mexican-Americans, who form the large mass of migrant farm workers in the western United States, have long struggled just to maintain a subsistence standard of living. Constantly on the move to follow the harvest, they have often been exploited by the growers, both in pay and in living and working conditions. Under the leadership of Cesar Chavez, some migrant farm workers have unionized in recent years. Aided by a nationwide boycott of non-union lettuce and grapes, they have forced the growers to upgrade pay and working and living conditions.

Most of the 1.7 million Puerto Ricans in the continental United States inhabit the poorest sections of eastern seaboard cities, such as New York, Philadelphia, and Newark, New Jersey. Puerto Rico was annexed by the United States during the Spanish-American War, and now it exists in that political nether world called a *commonwealth*—neither an independent nation nor a full-fledged member of the federal state system. American citizenship was conferred on Puerto Ricans in 1917, and, for many years, there was heavy migration from the island to the mainland by Puerto Ricans looking for a way out of poverty. Usually, the trip resulted simply in the exchange of one kind of poverty for another. More than half the Puerto Ricans on the mainland live in New York City, and their economic condition there, as in the thirty other cities with Puerto Rican populations of five thousand or more, is worse than that of other Hispanics and most other ethnic groups. Their unemployment rate is twice the national unemployment rate. One-fourth of the Puerto Rican families in New York City depend on welfare to some extent.[58] In many cases, the Puerto Ricans encounter not only discrimination by whites, but also hostility from blacks, whose jobs may be lost to Puerto Ricans willing to work for less pay.

THE ANATOMY OF CIVIL RIGHTS

More than half of the inhabitants of the United States have been effectively barred from enjoying the fruits of citizenship for most of the first two hundred years of this nation's life. Laws that would have made their lives happier and more prosperous were long delayed; once passed, they were often ignored.

The reasons, of course, are varied and complex. But one of the principal reasons is this: bias usually prevails over logic and justice if there is a conflict. White males wrote the Constitution, and white males have written all constitutional amendments, and white males have controlled every legislature and Congress since the nation began, and white males have run the Justice Department, and white males have sat on virtually every federal or state judicial bench that ever existed. They have created the government in their own image. And, since they have had the power to judge their creation, naturally they have found it good and have hated to change it. They have defended their creation with arguments of natural superiority: the white person is superior to the black (or brown or red), the male superior to the female.

The Role of Stereotypes

Toward the nonwhite, the white person (male or female) has generally felt contempt, the kind of contempt that feeds on extravagant stereotypes. The stereotype of the black has been: lazy, of low intellect, immoral, shiftless, animalistic. Alexis de Tocqueville, commenting on what he believed would be a permanent schism between whites and blacks, stated:

> You may set the Negro free, but you cannot make him otherwise than an alien to the [white man]. Nor is this all; we scarcely acknowledge the common features of humanity in this stranger whom slavery has brought among us. His physiognomy is to our eyes hideous, his understanding weak, his tastes low; and we are almost inclined to look upon him as a being intermediate between man and the brutes.[59]

[57]*New York Times*, November 29, 1971.

[58]David Vidal, "Dream Still Eludes Mainland Puerto Ricans," *New York Times*, September 11, 1977.

[59]Alexis de Tocqueville, *Democracy in America*, ed. Phillips Bradley, trans. Henry Reeve. 2 Vols. (New York: Random House, Vintage Books, 1945), pp. 370–72.

Strong words, those. But they do not exaggerate in the slightest the attitude of many, if not in fact most, white people of his day. Many educated and otherwise balanced people, including the great democrat Thomas Jefferson, looked on blacks as not only inferior in station but inferior in fact.

The opinion survives. More than once since World War II, Senator James O. Eastland of Mississippi voiced the opinion that "the mental level of those people [blacks] renders them incapable of suffrage." Former Mississippi Governor Ross R. Barnett received great local support for his prosegregation statement in 1959, "The Negro is different because God made him different to punish him. His forehead slants back. His nose is different. His lips are different, and his color sure is different. . . . We will not drink from the cup of genocide."[60]

One of the most popular tracts in the South during the 1950s—popular not merely with the Ku Klux Klan, but among many community leaders, businessmen, and preachers—was *Black Monday* (named for the day the Supreme Court integrated schools), written by Judge Tom P. Brady of Mississippi, who had once taught sociology at the University of Mississippi. The pamphlet's premise was that "the men of the South . . . were largely responsible for [the] miracle" of persuading blacks to "lay aside cannibalism" and be "introduced to God." He praised southern whites for being so generous as to give the black "a language" and "a moral standard . . . he could never have created for himself and which he does not now appreciate. His soul was quickened." And yet, wrote Judge Brady, all of this was "a veneer . . . superficial," and it would take many generations to change the black, whom he likened to a chimpanzee.[61]

To be sure, one was more likely to hear such extravagantly derogatory remarks uttered in last-ditch Dixie outposts, but even as late as 1975, the sophisticated Senator J. William Ful-

bright of Arkansas—a Rhodes scholar, former university president, and the Chairman of the Senate Foreign Relations Committee—was saying that blacks had not had "adequate preparation" for equality and that he was "not sure" they should have been given the right to vote. He also said that blacks needed more "education and health care" to overcome certain defects before they were allowed to mix with white students.[62]

This kind of disparagement has naturally made it extremely difficult for black people to obtain a full and practical expression of civil rights. It has subjected them also to special cruelty. Although blacks represent only about 11 percent of the population, 54.6 percent of the persons executed for crime since 1930 (when accurate statistical records on the death penalty were first kept) have been black. Ninety percent of the men executed for rape were blacks; no white has been executed for raping a black woman; and all persons executed for burglary were black.[63] The unofficial brutality has been worse, and it has been protected by an indifferent white male system of justice.

In contrast to the black experience, the mistreatment of women has been almost benign—a sort of kindly neglect. But it, too, was caused by an inability to make men treat them as persons rather than as stereotypes.

The male-manufactured image of woman was a strange mixture of things: clinging vine, henpecker, gossiper, sex object. She was viewed as flighty, scatterbrained, and weak. Men indulged her with condescending nicknames: broad,[64] skirt, bimbo, doll, dame. The female's chief role in World War II was as a pinup. In peacetime, too, the emphasis was always on body, not brain. In movie roles she was a dancer, vamp, housewife, or trollop (just as the black for many years was always maid, handyman, comic

---

[60]Quoted in Robert Sherrill, *Gothic Politics in the Deep South* (New York: Viking Press, Grossman Publishers, 1968), pp. 74, 211.

[61]Quoted in Osofsky, *The Burden of Race*, pp. 482–83.

[62]Sources: Personal interview with J. William Fulbright, July 1974; Associated Press, May 30, 1975.

[63]Elinor L. Horwitz, *Capital Punishment U. S. A.* (Philadelphia, J. B. Lippincott Co., 1973), pp. 282–83.

[64]When Congresswoman Martha Griffiths looked for an equal rights bill she had left with the House Judiciary Committee, she found that it had been filed under B for "Broads."

chauffeur, or tap dancer); rarely was there a female role that portrayed wisdom or courage. The man always rescued the woman, never she him; she was always the gold digger, he was always the dug; she drove him to drink, rarely he her. These were the standards in movies, jokes, and fiction.

The other minorities suffer from stereotypes too. Until recently, almost every western turned out by Hollywood portrayed Indians as savage, animalistic, and untrustworthy—a menace to white pioneer women and the implacable foe of the good guys in the United States Cavalry. Such films can be seen weekly on late-night television. Chicanos and Puerto Ricans are lumped together in the stereotype of the happy-go-lucky, dimwitted Hispanic.

Laws and High Emotions

One of the great hurdles that civil rights laws have had to contend with is the fact that they were passed only in moments of high emotion. The legislation served as a tranquilizer—and then was ignored when emotions had cooled down. Most of the basic laws relating to civil *liberties*, on the other hand, have been in the Constitution since its beginning. They were the product of sober contemplation and were consciously written for the ages. In contrast, most of our civil rights laws have usually been passed, or enunciated, in explosive times.

Lincoln made his Emancipation Proclamation at the height of the Civil War. The Thirteenth, Fourteenth, and Fifteenth Amendments were passed during a period when North and South still hated each other and when the North was eager to force laws on the South that would embarrass and humiliate it. The Nineteenth Amendment rode in on a wave of postwar egalitarian fervor (and because the feminists were disturbing the peace). In 1941, Franklin D. Roosevelt issued his famous Executive Order 8802, setting up a Fair Employment Practices Commission—because we were moving into World War II and he needed blacks in the war industries (and also because A. Philip Randolph threatened to march on Washington with 100,000 blacks if Roosevelt didn't help them find jobs). The Civil Rights Act of 1964 and the Voting Rights Act of

1965 were passed with a number of other major reform acts as a kind of tribute to the assassinated President John F. Kennedy (and in response to a multitude of violent racial acts in the South and the mammoth peaceful marches led by civil rights leaders). The proposed Twenty-seventh Amendment for women's rights also winged through Congress during an emotional period, when women were high on their own potential, forming their own organizations, and demonstrating.

Laws passed at a passionate crest may be very good laws, but they almost always suffer when the passion is depleted. As blacks and women have learned all too well, there is always the letdown. One feminist leader found the analogy in her own life: "I've been married to a liberal and to a Marxist, and neither one carried out the garbage." Just so in our nation's life: after the honeymoon of passing high-minded laws, the government often neglects to carry out its promises. Historically, in the bright light of the morning after, it has gone back to its stereotypes.

The Moral

There is only one way to make sure that the carrying out of the law does not depend on whim and does not depend on whether white males *like* blacks, females, Indians, and Chicanos. That way is through the ballot. And for those minorities with enough voting power, this is one time when it is more effective to begin right at the top: in presidential, senatorial, and congressional races, or at least in those races where true party competition exists and where a determined, unified minority can provide the deciding margin.

Blacks have now registered in such numbers and have become so politically sophisticated in bargaining and women have become such efficient organizers that they each have the strength in a presidential race to negotiate for top policy positions as a payoff. Politicians, whether they *like* it or not, have been forced to pay at least symbolic tribute to black power and female power, and nowhere more so than at the top.

Jimmy Carter could not have won the Presidency in 1976 without the support of the Old Confederacy states. If he had had to rely on the white folks of that region, he would never have made it. White southerners gave him only 45 percent of their votes, but the blacks everywhere in the country went for Carter by margins of up to nine to one.

Carter paid off: he appointed a black woman Secretary of Housing and Urban Development; a black man, Secretary of the Army; a black man, ambassador to the United Nations. In fact, of his first three hundred top appointments, thirty-two were blacks.[65] Although only 13 percent of the appointments at that level were women, at the cabinet level there was a real breakthrough: the all-male tradition stretching back twenty-two years was broken with the appointment of not only one, but *two* women—Patricia Harris, Secretary of Housing and Urban Development, and Juanita Kreps, Secretary of Commerce.

Carter, a southerner, professed to want blacks at the highest level of government, and women, too. But whether he wanted them or not was beside the point. The point was that political realities—namely the vote—had obliged him to appoint them. The white male government was being forced to dilute itself.

---

[65]United Press International, June 19, 1977.

Summary

1. Civil rights assume the equality of citizens before the law. A person's race, sex, national origin, or creed should not subject him or her to unfair treatment.

2. The Fourteenth Amendment gives constitutional validity to citizens' claims to civil rights. But no one's rights are assured until they are accepted by the general populace and enforced by the courts.

3. Black Americans have had a long struggle to secure their civil rights. From the beginning, the Constitution implicitly endorsed slavery, and the Supreme Court's *Dred Scott* decision in 1857 held that the Constitution did not contemplate citizenship for blacks.

4. The Civil War did not begin in 1861 as a fight to free the slaves, but as an economic and political struggle between North and South. It was Lincoln's Emancipation Proclamation of 1862 that set the goal of ending slavery.

5. Three important amendments were passed after the Civil War: the Thirteenth (1865), outlawing slavery; the Fourteenth (1868), giving citizenship to blacks and requiring states to protect the civil rights and liberties of their citizens; and the Fifteenth (1870), giving blacks the right to vote.

6. These amendments were not enforced. After a brief era of Reconstruction, the South entered the era of Jim Crow, when legal means (such as the rewriting of state constitutions) were used to restrict the rights of blacks.

7. The Supreme Court helped uphold Jim Crow by such decisions as *Plessy v. Ferguson* (1896), which ruled that segregation did not equate with inequality. For many years the Court used the Fourteenth Amendment to protect business, not blacks.

8. A more liberal Court began using the Fourteenth Amendment to rule in favor of blacks in the 1930s and '40s, culminating in 1954 with *Brown v. Board of Education*. *Brown* ruled that separate schools were inherently unequal; it set in motion liberalization in other areas as well.

9. During the civil rights movement of the 1950s and '60s, blacks put pressure on the government by means of confrontation tactics—boycotts, sit-ins, marches. These helped to bring about passage of the Civil Rights Act of 1964 and the Voting Rights Act of 1965.

10. Today blacks still encounter job discrimination, segregation, and economic set-backs, but they are stronger at the polls, and a number of black officials have been elected.

11. The women's civil rights struggle began with the battle for suffrage, which led to the passage of the Nineteenth Amendment in 1919. The women's rights movement today is pressing for more political gains and for a larger share of economic benefits.

12. The Equal Rights Amendment, guaranteeing equal protection for women under the law, was passed by Congress in 1972, but as of 1977 was bogged down in the ratification process.

13. Other minorities in need of protection of their civil rights are American Indians and Puerto Ricans, Chicanos, and other Hispanic-Americans.

14. The progress of civil rights is hampered by prevailing stereotypes of women and minorities that reinforce the biases of white males and by the fact that government officials tend to neglect civil rights laws once the passion that brought them into being has subsided.

Additional Reading

Stanley M. Elkins, *Slavery: A Problem in American Institutional and Intellectual Life,* 3rd ed. (Chicago: University of Chicago Press, 1976), analyzes the causes and consequences of black slavery in America. The treatment of blacks in the United States up to World War II is discussed by Gunnar Myrdal in *An American Dilemma: The Negro Problem and Modern Democracy* (New York: Harper & Row, Publishers, 1962), and by John Hope Franklin in *From Slavery to Freedom: A History of American Negroes,* 4th ed. (New York: Random House, Alfred A. Knopf, 1974).

Slavery and discrimination are analyzed from a personal point of view by Eldridge Cleaver in *Soul on Ice* (New York: Dell Publishing Co., 1968), and by William H. Grier and Price M. Cobbs in *Black Rage* (New York: Basic Books, 1968). The *New York Times* eds., *Report of the National Advisory Commission on Civil Disorders* (New York: E. P. Dutton & Co., 1968) is an official study of the ghetto riots of the mid-1960s, with recommendations for federal remedies.

Anthony Lewis, with the staff of the *New York Times, Portrait of a Decade: the Second American Revolution* (New York: Random House, 1964) tells the story of the civil rights movement of the 1950s and early 1960s. The Supreme Court cases that have expanded civil rights are analyzed in Henry J. Abraham's *Freedom and the Court: Civil Rights and Liberties in the United States,* 2nd ed. (New York: Oxford University Press, 1972), and in other readings suggested for Chapters 2 and 3.

The plight of American Indians is discussed in Dee Brown's *Bury My Heart at Wounded Knee: An Indian History of the American West* (New York: Holt, Rinehart & Winston, 1971) and that of Hispanic Americans in Oscar Lewis's *La Vida: A Puerto Rican Family in the Culture of Poverty—San Juan and New York* (New York: Random House, 1966).

General readings about women and the women's movement can be found in Jo Freeman, *Women: A Feminist Perspective* (Palo Alto, Calif.: Mayfield Publishing Co., 1975); Jane Jacquette, ed., *Women in Politics* (New York: John Wiley & Sons, 1974); Marianne Githens and Jewell Prestage, eds., *A Portrait of Marginality* (New York: David McKay Co., 1977)—which contains valuable material on black women as well as general readings on women; Susan Tolchin and Martin Tolchin, *Clout: Woman Power and Politics* (New York: Coward, McCann, & Geoghegan, 1974).

Politics is a strife of interests masquerading as a contest of principles, the conduct of public affairs for private advantage.

Ambrose Bierce

5
INTEREST GROUPS

Times were hard for Pan American Airways in 1974, and it wanted the government to increase the taxpayers' subsidies. Congress was balking at the idea. One of the foremost balkers was Senator William Proxmire, Chairman of the Senate Banking Committee. That position made his a potent voice in the debate. Pan American's officials wanted to get Proxmire's ear and try to persuade him to change his position, but he said he was too busy to sit down with them.

Now everyone in Washington, including Pan Am's officials, knew that Proxmire, a physical-fitness fanatic, jogged from his home to the Capitol and back every day. So they decided that if he wouldn't sit down with them, they would jog with him—which is what they assigned one of their pilots, outfitted in shorts and track shoes, to do. He ran along beside Proxmire (who wasn't too happy with the companionship) for several miles each day, for several days, and explained Pan American's position.

That's pressure politics.

In the early 1970s, when oil and gas prices shot upward to alarming heights, the public began thinking sullen thoughts about the petroleum industry. Big Oil was suspected of conspiring with the Middle East nations to create artificial shortages. A Senate investigating team accused the nation's ten largest oil companies of deliberately slowing down refinery output. The General Accounting Office estimated that the oil companies profited by as much as $2 billion by cheating on federal regulations. The Federal Trade Commission accused the eight largest oil companies of conspiring to monopolize the gasoline market. As a result of this mood, legislation to break up the oil industry into more controllable pieces received heavy support in the Senate in 1975.

Fighting back, the major oil companies set up a special lobbying task force in Washington, staffed by high-priced lawyers and publicists, and began cranking out a flood of propaganda. Congress was swamped with it; so were newspaper editorial offices. Oil lobbyists swarmed over Capitol Hill. Other oil lobbyists were meeting with civic groups and unions across the nation, carrying the message that the government should keep its hands off the industry. As of 1976, it was costing an estimated $100 million a year.

That's really pressure politics.

A PROFILE OF PRESSURE POLITICS

Pressure politics is usually a group activity, and the participating groups come in all sizes and motivations. They spring from every economic level and are called by a variety of titles: lobbies, special interest groups, selfish interest groups.

Kinds of Lobbies, and Their Budgets

The oldest term used in the United States for pressure groups is *lobbies*—a name derived from the fact that for many years the main arena for their activity was in the hallways, or lobbies, just off the legislative chambers. This position allowed lobbyists to buttonhole the legislators as they came and went. They are still there, still buttonholing, still cajoling and pleading. Because of the unethical conduct of many of its practitioners down through the years, "lobbying" conveys a somewhat disreputable meaning. Recent disclosures of multimillion-dollar payoffs by giant corporations to politicians both in this country and abroad have further damaged the reputation of pressure groups. And yet, at the same time that scandals are lowering the public's

opinion of lobbyists, the number plying their trade in Washington[1] and the amount of money they are plying it with continue to soar, undeterred. In the 1971–72 session, 374 lobbyists registered with Congress for the first time; in 1974–75, nearly 1,000 joined the fray. And their reported spending jumped from $6.1 million in 1972 to more than $10 million in 1974. Emphasize the word *reported*. *Actual* expenditures by lobbyists, according to congressional studies, probably exceed $1 billion annually.

Some lobbies aim at improving an economic position, some at furthering an ideology or policy, and some at both. The Democratic Study Group, made up of House Democratic liberals, broadly categorizes the special interest groups it encounters as "education," "labor," "senior citizens,"[2] "rural/farm," "women," "consumer," "liberal," "environment," "business," and "conservative." Two of the important categories it leaves out are the domestic ethnic/race lobbies and the foreign lobbies.

Of the ethnic/race lobbies, the two most significant are the black, best known for the pioneering work of the National Association for the Advancement of Colored People, and the Jewish. Of these two, by far the more powerful is the Jewish lobby, which is also part of the foreign lobby because of its interest not only in legislation affecting the lives of Jews in this country but also—especially in recent years—in United States foreign policy affecting the security of Israel. Most powerful of the Jewish lobbying groups are the American Israel Public Affairs Committee (AIPAC), B'nai B'rith, the American

---

[1] When people think of lobbyists, they usually think of Washington lobbyists. But that is missing what may be the larger part of the picture. Lobbying in state legislatures is just as prevalent, just as influential in shaping laws that affect the average person's cost of living and life style, and just as successful in defending the position of the moneyed interests.

[2] Science has helped create one of the newer strong lobbies: old people. In 1900, only 4 percent of the United States population was over the age of sixty-five. Today 10 percent of the population is sixty-five or older, and by the middle of the next century, if medicine and the food supply hold out, it will be 25 percent. One-fourth of the nation's elderly live below the poverty line. They intend to fight for more government assistance through such organizations as the National Association of Retired Persons (7.7 million members), the National Council of Senior Citizens (3 million members), and the Gray Panthers.

Jewish Committee, and the American Jewish Congress. In their book on the foreign lobby, Russell Warren Howe and Sarah Hays Trott reported: "Today, the AIPAC bulldozer commands three quarters of the vote in the Senate, well over half the vote in the House, and two thirds of the whole foreign-aid bill—for less than one thousandth of the world's population."[3] There are several reasons for the Jewish lobby's success; one of the most notable is money. According to a *Congressional Quarterly* estimate, Jews make at least half of the large contributions to Democratic campaigns and at least 40 percent of the contributions to Republican campaigns.[4]

Other foreign lobbying groups heavily concentrated in Washington are set up to win profitable concessions from the government for the buying and selling of rice, wheat, oil, sugar, and other key commodities. Many billions of dollars ride on the outcome of these negotiations, which invariably are carried on in secret between the foreign agents, our bureaucrats, and our members of Congress. Rumors of payoffs and a wide variety of corruption have always plagued the foreign lobby.

Public versus Private Interests

Every lobby is motivated by selfish interests in the sense that it wants something that is not wanted by everyone and is probably intensely opposed by some. Selfish interests, however discreditable they might be in a perfect world, are the electricity that makes the democratic motor run. "The role of the people in the political system," E. E. Schattschneider has commented, "is determined largely by the conflict system, for it is conflict that involves the people in politics and the nature of conflict determines the nature of the public involvement."[5] The Sierra Club wants to preserve the redwood forests for future

generations to enjoy; the giant lumber companies want to cut down the redwoods for patio furniture and profits. One group wants to increase school busing in order to improve the educational opportunities of black children; another group wants to eliminate forced busing in order to preserve the personality of neighborhood schools. One group wants to outlaw strip mining in order to protect the forests, the topsoil, and the rivers; another group wants to vastly increase strip mining in order to make the United States independent of foreign energy sources and to make a profit.

Because there are so many conflicts of that sort, it has become popular to differentiate between "private interest" groups and "public interest" groups. The difference between them is essentially the difference between private property and public property. It has to do with exclusive motives versus nonexclusive motives.[6] The lumber companies that want to cut down the redwood trees and sell them are clearly motivated by the desire to make money for a few. On the other hand, the groups that are motivated by the desire to save the redwoods as a national monument are not trying to benefit anyone in particular. As far as they are concerned, the lumberman and his family are just as welcome as anyone else to sit under the redwoods and have a picnic.

In judging pressure politics, this is a useful distinction only so long as it is understood that one class of interests is just as well-meaning as the other. It is probably safe to say that not one executive of any of the major lumbering corporations would tell you, "I want to cut down the redwood trees so that future generations will not know what those magnificent trees that have lived a thousand years really look like, or know what it feels like just to stand in their presence. I want this generation to be the last to have those pleasures." On the contrary, the lumber executives will express their motivations on just as high a plane as the environmentalists; they will explain that by cutting down the trees they are exercising the muscles of the American free enterprise system, that they are giving people jobs,

[3]Russell Warren Howe and Sarah Hays Trott, *The Power Peddlers: How Lobbyists Mold America's Foreign Policy* (New York: Doubleday & Co., 1977), p. 190.

[4]Howe and Trott, p. 193.

[5]E. E. Schattschneider, *The Semisovereign People: A Realist's View of Democracy in America* (New York: Holt, Rinehart & Winston, Dryden Press, 1975), p. 129.

[6]Schattschneider, p. 26.

that they are supplying needed wood to build homes and patios and are thereby improving the American standard of living.

Likewise, the manufacturers' lobbies that fight antipollution laws never do so because they favor pollution, but because they want to defend the capitalist system against government interference. To them, that is an almost sacred motivation. And when the United States Chamber of Commerce opposes consumer protection laws, it is not because it wants to see consumers swindled but because it feels that business has a right to be left alone.

Pressure politics can be judged sensibly only by its results, not by its motivations.

CLASHING INTERESTS AND THE PUBLIC GOOD

The seemingly incurable headaches that come with pressure politics were anticipated by the men who set up this government two hundred years ago, though it would have been impossible for them to even imagine the diversity of pressure politics that exists today. The smartest summation of what lay ahead came from James Madison in *The Federalist Papers*, Number 10.

First he laid down his definition of a pressure group, or faction:

> By a faction I understand a number of citizens, whether amounting to a majority or minority of the whole, who are united and actuated by some common impulse of passion, or of interest, adverse to the rights of other citizens, or to the permanent and aggregate interests of the community.

Humankind has such a bottomless zeal for feuding and fussing that just about any excuse for creating a faction will do, said Madison,

> but the most common and durable source of factions has been the various and unequal distribution of property. Those who hold and those who are without property have ever formed distinct interests in society. Those who are creditors, and those who are debtors, fall under a like discrimination. A landed interest, a manufacturing interest, a mercantile interest, a moneyed interest, with many lesser interests, grow up of necessity in civi-

lized nations, and divide them into different classes, actuated by different sentiments and views. The regulation of these various and interfering interests forms the principal task of modern legislation and involves the spirit of party and faction in the necessary and ordinary operations of government.[7]

That analysis still holds. And nothing has happened to lessen the correctness of Madison's fatalism, when he said that the only ways to avoid factions are (1) to make everyone think the same way and have the same passions, which is impossible, or (2) to destroy the liberty that is necessary for the existence of factions, a remedy "worse than the disease." So we are left only with the hope that the people we put in government can cope with the problem. Even there, Madison responds with a kind of wry pessimism that is near to humor: "It is in vain to say that enlightened statesmen will be able to adjust these clashing interests and render them all subservient to the public good. Enlightened statesmen will not always be at the helm."[8]

The Right to Petition

Justification for the existence of active special interest groups is to be found in the First Amendment, but, like almost all other guaranteed rights in the Constitution, it has a venerable historical lineage.

In the English-speaking world, it began to take shape in the Magna Carta of 1215, that marvelous progenitor of our Constitution. Chapter 61 says, in part, that if a worthy Englishman feels the king or the king's judges or any of the king's officers have violated the provisions of the Magna Carta, the offended gentleman can complain to four barons, and these "four barons shall repair to us, or our justiciary, if we are out of the realm, and laying open the grievance, shall petition to have it redressed without delay."

Ultimately some of the ancient language found its way into our First Amendment—"Congress shall make no law respecting an

---

[7] Alexander Hamilton, James Madison, and John Jay, *The Federalist Papers*, ed. Clinton Rossiter (New York: Times Mirror Co., New American Library, 1961), pp. 78–79.

[8] Hamilton, Madison, and Jay, pp. 78, 80.

establishment of religion, or prohibiting the free exercise thereof; or abridging the freedom of speech, or of the press; or the right of the people peaceably to assemble, and to petition the Government for a redress of grievances.''

Resistance from Government

Like most of the freedoms guaranteed by the Bill of Rights, freedom to assemble to petition the government, or even simply to petition by writing, has turned out to be considerably less than an absolute freedom.

In the early 1830s, the movement to abolish slavery began to pick up momentum. A torrent of petitions flooded Congress. The lawmakers got fed up with the public's enthusiasm for the subject, and, in 1840, the House adopted as a standing rule: "That no petition, memorial, resolution, or other paper praying the abolition of slavery in the District of Columbia, or any State or Territories of the United States in which it now exists, shall be received by this House, or entertained in any way whatever."[9]

So much for the right to petition, circa 1840. Several years later the law was repealed, but not before Congress's willingness to suspend certain freedoms on an *ad hoc* basis was made clear. That position was restated in 1918 when citizens were jailed for petitioning Congress to repeal the espionage and sedition laws and to end the military draft.[10]

Those who have made personal appearances in Washington to present their grievances have sometimes fared just as poorly, and, for some of them, their failure has been more dramatic than the tossing of a paper into a wastebasket. In 1894, Jacob Sechler Coxey of Ohio organized armies of unemployed persons to march on Washington—peacefully and without arms—and present petitions for assistance. Their leaders were arrested for trespassing on public property (the Capitol grounds). In 1932, one of the worst years of the Great Depression, unemployed veterans of World War I marched on Washington and peti-

tioned Congress to pass bonus legislation. They, too, assembled peacefully, but the government responded by calling out troops, which dispersed the veterans with bullets and tear gas and burned their camps.

Notice that these examples of heavy-handed suppression involved the petitions of groups advocating more freedom for the powerless or more money for the poor. The government very rarely jails or tear-gases those who petition for more liberties for the powerful and more wealth for the wealthy.

WHO ORGANIZES? AND WHO ORGANIZES BEST?

There is some disagreement among scholars as to just how much organizing Americans do.[11] But they all like to quote Alexis de Tocqueville on this point. When he toured America in the 1830s, he observed that "Americans of all ages, all conditions, and all dispositions constantly form associations. They have not only commercial and manufacturing companies, in which all take part, but associations of a thousand other kinds, religious, moral, serious, futile, general or restricted, enormous or diminutive." He concluded that is was just as well that they had the

---

[9]Edward S. Corwin, ed., *The Constitution of the United States: Analysis and Interpretation,* rev. ed. (Washington, D.C.: U.S. Government Printing Office, 1964), p. 915.

[10]Report of the Attorney General, 48 (1918).

[11]Sidney Verba and Norman Nie, for example, found these percentages in a sample reporting (they count membership in a labor union as belonging to an organization): 62 percent said they belong to an organization; 39 percent said they belong to more than one organization; 40 percent said they were active in organizations; 31 percent said they belong to an organization in which politics are discussed; 44 percent said they belong to an organization active in community affairs. (*Participation in America: Political Democracy and Social Equality,* New York: Harper & Row, Publishers, 1972, p. 176.)

On the other hand, Schattschneider reports: "A study made by Ira Reid of a Philadelphia area showed that in a sample of 963 persons, 85 percent belonged to no civic or charitable organization and 74 percent belonged to no occupational, business or professional associations, while another Philadelphia study of 1,154 women showed that 55 percent belonged to no association of any kind. A *Fortune* farm poll taken some years ago found that 70.5 percent of farmers belonged to no agricultural organizations. A similar conclusion was reached by two Gallup polls showing that perhaps no more than one-third of the farmers of the country belonged to farm organizations while another *Fortune* poll showed that 86.8 percent of the low-income farmers belonged to no farm organizations." (*The Semisovereign People,* p. 33.)

urge to organize into political associations, for

> among democratic nations . . . all the citizens are
> independent and feeble; they can do hardly any-
> thing by themselves, and none of them can oblige
> his fellow men to lend him their assistance. They
> all, therefore, become powerless if they do not
> learn voluntarily to help one another. . . . A people
> among whom individuals lost the power of
> achieving great things single-handed, without
> acquiring the means of producing them by united
> exertions, would soon relapse into barbarism.[12]

Organizational pressure is most often engaged in by middle-income and upper-income citizens—the people with the time and money to spare for such activities. Apparently, low-income citizens either are not sophisticated enough to realize that they could improve their position through the use of organized pressure groups, or they expend so much of themselves simply staying alive and making ends meet that they do not have the required surplus energy or time to get together with their peers for an organized effort. In any event, organized interest groups are definitely biased in favor of the upper crust.[13]

This, of course, does not mean the poor and the underprivileged do not have pressure groups that represent their interests. There are even a few—such as Cesar Chavez's United Farm Workers' union—that draw strength from people at the lower economic level and work solely for their benefit. That kind of pressure group is rare, however. More often the poor must depend upon the largess of organizations whose members are well-off—such as the American Federation of Labor-Congress of Industrial Organizations (AFL-CIO), the National Catholic Welfare Board, and the National Council of Jewish Women, all of which take a vigorous and constant interest in legislation promoting antipoverty programs and fair labor policies. But when the poor and the unorganized must borrow their pressure from others, the results, as

Abraham Holtzman has pointed out, are "unpredictable, haphazard, and uncertain."[14] The organized group is apt to sacrifice the interests of the "adopted" unorganized mass if its own internal unity or advantage is threatened. And the politician knows that the unorganized tend not to vote or to exert pressure on the government.

Scholars disagree over the inequality of pressure. David B. Truman believes that all interests are organized actually or potentially (that is, Americans are at least inbred with the impulse and power to organize, given the right motives) and that their competing interests offset one another so that no one group has disproportionate power. For example, if one group has organized to win legislation banning pets from public housing, then a competing group—dog lovers, cat lovers, anteater lovers, or what you will—has the potential of joining together to counteract such an attempt. Truman's is a benign view of the pressure group system: potential groups will organize whenever special interests get out of line, and, moreover, the mere fear that potential groups will organize tends to keep the organized interests in line.[15]

Mancur Olson, Jr., views the system differently. He does not believe that a lobby will be voluntarily formed by a large number of individuals with a common interest. "Unless the number of individuals in a group is quite small, or unless there is a coercion or some other special device to make individuals act in their common interest, *rational, self-interested individuals will not act to achieve their common or group interests.*"[16] Small groups succeed in organizing for a common good because group agreement is more readily attained among a few members and each member will get a substantial share of the total gain. In large groups, there is much less incentive to participate, since the contribution of any one individual will be imperceptible and the share of the collective benefit will be small (and,

[12]Alexis de Tocqueville, *Democracy in America,* ed. Phillips Bradley, trans. Henry Reeve, 2 vols. (New York: Random House, Vintage Books, 1954), 2: 114–16.

[13]See Schattschneider, *The Semisovereign People,* and Abraham Holtzman, *Interest Groups and Lobbying* (New York: Macmillan, 1966), p. 6

[14]Holtzman, p. 7.

[15]David B. Truman, *The Governmental Process: Political Interests and Public Opinion* (New York: Random House, Alfred A. Knopf, 1951).

[16]Mancur Olson, Jr., *The Logic of Collective Action: Public Goods and the Theory of Groups,* rev. ed. (Cambridge, Mass.: Harvard University Press, 1971), p. 2.

in any case, will be the same for all, regardless of the degree of participation).

To succeed as a lobby, a large group must be disciplined: it must keep its members in line by using both punishment and reward. Labor unions, for example, use such means of coercion as compulsory membership (union shop) and picket lines and such positive inducements as insurance and welfare benefits, guaranteed seniority rights, handling of grievances, and recreational programs. Otherwise, it is unlikely, in Olson's view, that laborers would voluntarily organize to work for common interests. State bar associations also use coercive means; it is required by law that practicing lawyers belong to their state bar association. An organization may have subtle forms of coercion. The American Medical Association is so powerful that it can pose an economic threat to recalcitrant members. But the positive inducements of the AMA are strong too—malpractice defense, access to technical publications, and educational conventions.

Olson's point is that the powerful lobbies are the by-products of discipline and services to members that only a large organized group can attain. That leaves many large unorganized groups that are unable to function as pressure groups through a voluntary effort alone—such as migrant farm workers, white-collar workers, taxpayers, consumers, and peacemakers. As Olson notes, "the groups that have no lobbies and exert no pressure, are among the largest groups in the nation and they have some of the most vital common interests."[17]

So one bias in the interest-group system favors those groups that are tightly organized or that are able to "buy off" the participation of their members. Another bias in the system favors middle- and high-income citizens, for they are the people with the time and the money to spare for organizational pressure.

Who Rules within Groups?

Early in this century, the Swiss sociologist Robert Michels made a study of European social democratic parties and found that an "iron law

of oligarchy" operated within the parties. That is, there was a great distinction between the elitist leaders of an organization and those being led. This law also operates within private organizations in the United States. As Grant McConnell points out, organization requires leadership; not only do members need leaders, they often "crave" them. "The leaders control not merely by virtue of their superior abilities and the submissive tendencies of the masses, but also by an array of simple but crucial devices. The list of members, the files, the organization press—the apparatus of organization—are all in the leaders' hands."[18]

The leaders, moreover, are often "professionals," and may not even have come out of the organizations' ranks. Their time and efforts are spent exclusively on organizational activities. McConnell notes that these leaders have little in common with members in terms of activities, status, or interests. They tend to be conservative and have all the advantage in the inevitable conflicts between leaders and led.

The oligarchic elite is fostered by apathy and inertia within an organization's membership. Also, as mentioned earlier, many members join, not for political benefits, but for unrelated professional services, such as subscriptions to technical periodicals or charter air flights. Their affiliation helps to build a power base for the leaders, but they may be genuinely indifferent about how that power is used. For the member who does care and who wants to replace or redirect the leadership, there is little recourse; the internal organization is characterized by many undemocratic features. Rarely are there countervailing groups *within* an organization to protect members from overbearing leadership. (The Typographical Union, with formal internal parties, is a notable exception.) And competition between parallel associations is rare; a monopoly in fields of interest is generally maintained and respected. Leadership within corporate associations is usually self-perpetuating. Union leaders are elected, but most union business is conducted outside the annual convention of members.

[17]Olson, p. 165.

[18]Grant McConnell, *Private Power and American Democracy* (New York: Random House, Vintage Books, 1970), p. 122.

Lobbying Leviathans

Some of today's lobbies are so massive and so intricate that there is really no sure way to determine their membership and their alliances. Foremost among them is the military-industrial lobby, a monstrous tower of Babel with so many decks and corridors and buttresses that it is almost impossible to describe it as a whole. One part of the lobby is made up of forty-one private, military-oriented, tax-exempt organizations with a combined membership of more than 6 million—with some overlap—and combined annual operating budgets of nearly $36 million.[19] Many of these groups keep registered lobbyists in Washington. Others do their pressuring via waves of mail and telegrams. At the first sign of a serious move to cut the defense budget, these organizations begin to bombard Congress with counteropinions.[20]

Almost as impressive as the military-industrial lobby, and even more complicated, is the highway lobby—the "highwaymen" or "road gang," as it is called by its detractors. The highway lobby is one of the broadest based of all pressure groups. Automobile, oil, rubber, construction, asphalt, and limestone industries; car dealers and renters, bus lines and trucking concerns that depend on the highways; banks and advertising agencies with clients in the companies involved; the American Automobile Association and other organizations of motorists; state and local officials who want the federal government to pay for more and better highways in their areas—all these and many more forces make up the highway lobby. Its power is evident from the sea of asphalt and concrete that has rolled across the nation since World War II. The 42,500-mile interstate highway system, the most massive public works program in the nation's history, will cost more than $100 billion by the time it is finished.

The highway lobby has been able to virtually dictate its own terms for doing business with the government. One of its most spectacular successes was in commandeering a special part of federal revenues—the taxes on gasoline, tires, and other "highway-related" items—and persuading Congress to place this money in a special trust fund that, until recent years, was spent entirely on building more highways, whether they were needed or not. Recently, the lobby grudgingly permitted a trickle from this fund to be used for constructing urban transit systems.

Why does the highway lobby succeed? Simply because, as one House member explained, "Highways are the best single pork barrel there is. It's a lot nicer to cut a ribbon on a new highway than it is to cut one on a poverty program or a school for the disadvantaged."[21]

Doctors were among the first big nonindustrial groups to band together politically. A tidal wave of lobbying from the late 1940s through the early 1960s prevented enactment of a national health insurance program. In its last futile effort to stop Medicare, the AMA, from 1962 through 1965, spent at least $850,000 in Washington and probably another $3 million at the state and local levels.[22] Although the legislation was eventually passed, the AMA lobbying effort must certainly be considered a success; it blocked passage for a generation despite the fact that polls showed the public constantly in favor of a national health insurance program, at least for the elderly and needy.

One of the most determined lobbies in Washington is the National Rifle Association. It is the voice of the multimillion-dollar sporting-arms industry (hunting rifles, shotguns, handguns). Dollar for dollar, the NRA is probably the most effective lobby in Washington. Its assets hardly put it in the same league with the oil lobby, and for a crash campaign it cannot gather the kind of slush fund the AMA raised to fight Medicare. But among grass-roots lobbying organizations that specialize in letter-writing campaigns, the

---

[19]These organizations include the Air Force Association, the American Legion, the Association of the United States Army, the Non-Commissioned Officers of the United States of America, the Retired Officers Association, the U. S. Naval Institute, the Veterans of Foreign Wars, the American Security Council, the Aerospace Industries Association, the Electronic Industries Association, the Air Force Sergeants Association, the Fleet Reserve Association, the Marine Corps League, the National Guard Association of the United States, and the Naval Reserve Association.

[20]*Congressional Record*, S2049, February 21, 1973.

[21]Quoted in the *New York Times*, April 2, 1972.

[22]George Thayer, *Who Shakes the Money Tree?* (New York: Simon & Schuster, 1974), pp. 211–12.

National Rifle Association is in a class by itself. Its officials have boasted that they can get their million-plus members to hit Congress with at least half a million letters on seventy-two hours' notice. This is probably an exaggeration; at least it has never been done. But at the height of the Vietnam war, Senator Edward M. Kennedy of Massachusetts said he was regularly getting more mail on the pending gun-control legislation than on the war.

What makes letters from the gun lobby so impressive is their passion. Legislators who propose gun-control laws can depend on occasionally receiving letters threatening their lives. More commonplace is the kind of friendly letter received by a procontrol politician with an Italian name:

> You dirty wop. You should go back to your Italy and Mafia. How did you get in this country anyway? I bet you are the type who has no gun in his house to protect himself and would let any housebreaker come in and help himself to anything, even your wife, and then you would pray for a humble spirit to bear it. God help America with such as you in office. Were your parents ever married?[23]

Politicians have thick skins, but when hundreds of letters like that come pouring into their offices, it makes them think twice. Anyway, for whatever reason, the NRA and its allies have so intimidated Congress that although President John F. Kennedy, Senator Robert F. Kennedy, and Martin Luther King, Jr., have been killed, Senator John C. Stennis seriously wounded, and Governor George C. Wallace permanently crippled—all from gunfire—no truly effective gun-control law has yet emerged from Congress.

HOW PRESSURE POLITICS WORKS

How do business lobbyists influence politicians? Let's start by acknowledging some of the most flamboyant methods.

---

[23]Robert Sherrill, *The Saturday Night Special* (New York: David McKay Co., Charterhouse Books, 1973), p. 196.

The Money Passers

When John Dowdy, a Texas Democrat, was in the House of Representatives, he was given $25,000 in cash, nicely packed in a briefcase, by a man who was interested in preventing a Maryland construction firm from being indicted for fraud. Dowdy promised to do what he could to help. A federal court, in 1971, found Dowdy guilty of taking a bribe and of conspiracy and perjury. The court of appeals, in a highly controversial decision, overturned the bribery and conspiracy convictions, but Dowdy still went off to jail for perjury.

Before Senator Daniel B. Brewster of Maryland left the United States Senate in 1968, he took a $4,500 payoff from a lobbyist for a Chicago-based mail-order firm. After a long and involved court battle, Brewster pleaded no contest to the federal charge and was fined but not imprisoned.[24]

Some politicians can't resist temptation; some can. Congressman Henry B. Gonzalez, a Democrat from Texas and a member of the House Banking and Currency Committee, was offered $14,000-worth of free stock in a San Antonio bank. It was an obvious bribe, and Gonzalez threw the banker out of his office.

Outright bribe offers are probably relatively uncommon. Plenty of cash still changes hands, but if one can judge from the number of politicians actually caught taking payoffs, virtually gone are the crude old days when a lobbyist would come right out and say, "If you will do what I ask, Mr. or Ms. Congressperson, I will pay you X dollars." The money passers still get the job done, for many politicians have their hands out, but the transfer is subtler. Much of it is done by way of campaign contributions. (Also see Chapter 8.)

Special interest groups gave a record $22.6 million to candidates for Congress in 1976, nearly double their 1974 contributions. (See Figure 5-1.) The most dramatic increase came from corporate and business trade association political committees—$7.1 million, almost 300 percent more than they had given only two years

---

[24]*Washington Post,* June 26, 1975.

FIGURE 5-1 CAMPAIGN CONTRIBUTIONS OF SPECIAL INTEREST GROUPS TO MEMBERS OF KEY CONGRESSIONAL COMMITTEES, 1976

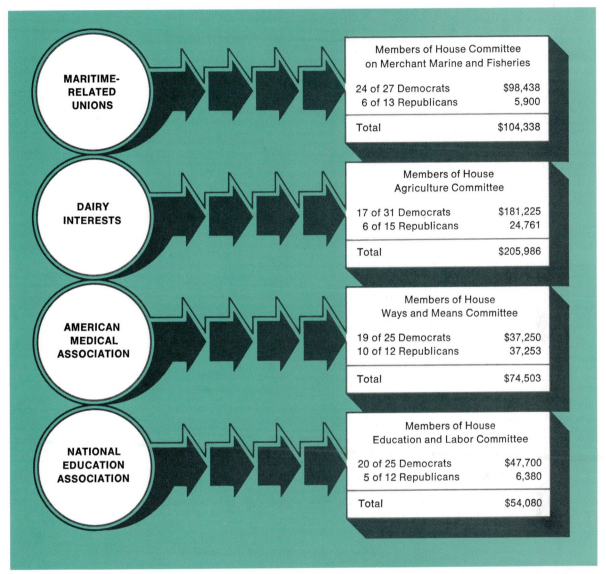

MARITIME-RELATED UNIONS	Members of House Committee on Merchant Marine and Fisheries
	24 of 27 Democrats — $98,438
	6 of 13 Republicans — 5,900
	Total — $104,338
DAIRY INTERESTS	Members of House Agriculture Committee
	17 of 31 Democrats — $181,225
	6 of 15 Republicans — 24,761
	Total — $205,986
AMERICAN MEDICAL ASSOCIATION	Members of House Ways and Means Committee
	19 of 25 Democrats — $37,250
	10 of 12 Republicans — 37,253
	Total — $74,503
NATIONAL EDUCATION ASSOCIATION	Members of House Education and Labor Committee
	20 of 25 Democrats — $47,700
	5 of 12 Republicans — 6,380
	Total — $54,080

SOURCE: Adapted from Common Cause, "Report to the American People on the Financing of Congressional Election Campaigns," May 1977, p. 8.

earlier. Labor unions, however, gave even more —$8.2 million.[25] The expected swap-off was obvious. The fourteen major committee chairmen who largely controlled the Senate, for example, received nearly $900,000 in campaign contributions from special interest groups, which was about 20 percent of all the money they received. Some senators were inundated with this kind of money; Senator Harrison A. Williams, Jr., of New Jersey, head of the Labor Committee, received 47 percent of his campaign budget from such sources.[26]

---

[25]Common Cause release, February 15, 1977.

[26]*New York Times*, January 15, 1977.

To what extent do the special interests "buy" the politicians in this way? Answers Fred Wertheimer, chief lobbyist for Common Cause:

> People understand that when they get and when they accept large contributions, those people are going to be back looking for things to be done. When money plays a too powerful role in the way in which elected leaders reach their decisions, then you've got a distortion of the process that is basically corrupting. What is happening ultimately is the whole system is being, in effect, purchased.[27]

Were Minnesota Mining and Manufacturing Company (3M) officials trying to buy the system when they secretly and illegally funneled nearly $500,000 to political candidates?[28] Or was Ashland Oil Company, when it secretly and illegally gave $50,000 to the campaign of Congressman Wilbur D. Mills of Arkansas, then Chairman of the House Ways and Means Committee?[29] Or was Armand Hammer, Chairman of Occidental Petroleum Corporation, when he unlawfully gave $54,000 to the 1972 Nixon reelection campaign?[30] Or was Gulf Oil Corporation, when it gave millions of dollars illegally; or Firestone Tire and Rubber Company, when it illegally contributed $330,000 to politicians?[31] Or were they, and the dozens of other corporations caught passing money, only trying to make friends around the political campfires of Washington?

One of the more transparent ways for a lobbying group to obtain the key to a federal politician's heart is with a "lecture fee." Senator James G. Abourezk of South Dakota, one of the most outspoken pro-Arab politicians in Washington, reportedly picked up $49,425 in lecture fees in 1973 for addressing Arab-American groups. He received $10,000 for one address—a record.[32] The average lecture fee runs about $2,000. The Seafarers International Union, for example, likes to hear political speeches very much. One year it invited twenty-two members of Congress and four senators to speak for money at its special luncheons. Not unexpectedly, the most popular invited speakers were members of the House Merchant Marine Subcommittee.[33]

Favors Large and Small

On a balmy day in April 1972, a team of *New York Times* reporters went to the National Airport outside Washington to observe the comings and goings of government officials and members of Congress. Federal laws forbid all public officials —elected and appointed—to accept gifts from any source that might raise a conflict of interest. What the reporters saw that day—and what they could have seen just about any other day— raised questions about whether or not that law was very widely respected. There went Senator Robert J. Dole of Kansas, then the Republican National Chairman, winging away to a dinner engagement in a plane owned by Clayton Enterprises, a company that operates a motel chain. And there went Senator Robert Taft, Jr., Republican of Ohio, off to a dinner in a plane owned by the Nevele Country Club. And there went Secretary of Commerce Peter G. Peterson, flying free to Chicago in a Lockheed Jetstar owned by a subsidiary of Standard Oil of Indiana. The reporters learned that this kind of freebie was a daily occurrence and in the past had included free trips for members of Congress and bureaucratic officials aboard planes owned by Tenneco, the big Texas oil and land conglomerate; the Southern Railway Company; the Lockheed Aircraft Corporation; and the United States Steel Corporation, to name just a few of the generous companies.

Lobbyists are also often thoughtful enough to pick up the hotel, bar, and dining room tabs for vagrant politicians. And then, too, there are the smaller items: theater tickets, imported liquor, French perfume, birthday cakes, and even free Kleenex for secretaries. Occasionally, lobbyists, unable to think up appropriate gifts for the politicians who have everything, simply send along credit cards.[34]

---

[27]Quoted in the *Washington Star*, February 1, 1977.

[28]*Washington Post*, January 1, 1975.

[29]*New York Times*, August 9, 1975.

[30]*Wall Street Journal*, March 5, 1976.

[31]*Washington Post*, June 8, 1976.

[32]Howe and Trott, *The Power Peddlers*, p. 243.

---

[33]Jack Anderson, "How to Bribe a Congressman," *Parade*, May 6, 1973.

[34]Anderson, "How to Bribe a Congressman."

Drawing by Weber; © 1975 The New Yorker Magazine, Inc.

Social Pleasures

Washington can be a lonely, small town after the workday has ended, and members of Congress, all of them away from their real homes, appreciate the soft touch of friendship and the soft flow of booze on such occasions. Parties and dinners are available every night, with lobbyists picking up the tab. Female companionship on these occasions is always accessible, but that is so commonplace in Washington—where the female population is much larger than the male—that it would be unfair to exactly accuse the lobbyists of serving as providers of flesh. Occasionally, friendly lobbyists will rent a pied-à-terre in their own name so that politicians they want to impress will have someplace to meet their mistresses.[35]

The lobby also provides escapes from the pressures of Washington. Northrop Aircraft has, for years, been host to hundreds of bureaucrats and members of Congress at its swanky hunting camp on the Maryland shore near Washington. "It was done in the spirit of maintaining a close relationship," Northrop's chief executive acknowledged, but he denied that Northrop was trying to buy anyone. "After all," he pointed out, "they provided their own ammunition."[36]

Southern Railway hosted former Agriculture Secretary Earl L. Butz at its country resort (golf course, swimming pool, bird hunting, six lakes, lodge, and so forth) north of Charleston, South Carolina. Southern Railway was, in 1976, transporting about 40 percent of the dollar value of farm products in the South. The Agriculture Department actively participates in rail rate cases before the Interstate Commerce Commission.[37]

The foreign lobby is always whisking members of Congress and their spouses, sweethearts, and aides off on exotic vacations. Does it get results? The South African Foundation, a privately financed public relations firm, gave Ed Fuelner, staff director of the House Republican Study Committee, a ten-day trip to South Africa. When the House was ready to take up an anti-South African resolution, a lobbyist for the South African Information Department delivered to Fuelner a fact sheet opposing the resolution. Fuelner gave a copy of the fact sheet to Representative Philip M. Crane, Illinois Republican, who (with his wife and five aides) had also been given a subsidized trip to South Africa. Equipped with the fact sheet, Crane spoke against the resolution—but, of course, did not tell his colleagues the source of his speech. The resolution was defeated by twenty-three votes. Ten of the members of Congress who voted against it had received subsidized trips to South Africa during the previous twenty-two months.[38]

---

[35]Charles B. Lipsen (former Washington lobbyist for the National Cable Television Association), "Power Brokers," *Penthouse*, March 1977, p. 71.

[36]Quoted in the *New York Times*, June 11, 1975.

[37]*Washington Post*, March 6, 1976.

[38]Walter Pincus, "South African Lobby," *Washington Post*, January 29, 1977.

The Buddy System

The most successful kind of personal lobbying is that which requires no pressure, except the pressure of a handshake or a chummy arm around the shoulder. A lobbyist is, naturally, most potent when dealing with old pals. The lobbyist works hard to get his or her "friend" elected—through campaign contributions and campaign work—and then works with that person in Washington, preparing and pushing forward favorable legislation. The lobbyist usually does not even need to cajole the legislator; he or she just has to *interpret* a client's position and plant the necessary information. So legislators who claim they do not feel "pressured" aren't lying; through the cozy system, they are simply doing friendly things for groups they wanted to help anyway.

Naturally, lobbyists who have served in Congress or in the bureaucracy, or who have been lobbying around Washington so long that they are looked upon as part of the gang, are at a distinct advantage in this system. That's why former members of Congress are so thick in the galaxy of lobbying stars. Among the dozens of congressional has-beens who returned to the cloakrooms of the Capitol to lean on their old comrades are Andrew J. Biemiller, chief lobbyist for organized labor; Frank N. Ikard, head of the oil lobby; Craig Hosmer, lobbyist for the atomic industry; William E. Minshall, a defense industry lobbyist; J. William Fulbright, lobbyist for Arabian interests. Every lame-duck season another flock swoops in, soliciting clients, as ex-Representative Roger H. Zion, Republican from Indiana, did. He sent out letters to businesses and industries he thought could use his services, pointing out: "Since I will continue to be in the Congressional prayer breakfast group, in the House gym, the members' dining room and on the House floor, I will maintain contact with my good friends who affect legislation."[39]

Lobbyists who have a chummy relationship with the White House are, of course, in a hallowed position. Lobbyists all over Washington must have envied three of their colleagues when they picked up the *New York Times* on March 24, 1975, and read:

---

[39]Quoted in *Parade*, March 21, 1976.

After the session [with his economic advisers at the White House], the President drove to the Burning Tree Club in Bethesda, Md., for a round of golf with William Whyte, vice president and Washington lobbyist for the United States Steel Corp., Rod Markley, a Ford Motor Co. vice president and lobbyist, and Jack Mills, a vice president and lobbyist for the Tobacco Institute.

Two days before he became President, Gerald R. Ford listed steel lobbyist Whyte as an adviser. Because the most effective lobbyists play down their power lest the public and their competitors take fright, however, Whyte discounted his role as adviser, claiming instead to be only Ford's "friend and golfing companion. . . . I would be very careful not to bend his ear on specific matters. He uses me as a sounding board to get my views, but I don't urge my views on him." At that level of lobbying, "urging" is considered bad taste.[40] Dropping a casual remark about tax credits or import quotas, while teeing up for the ninth hole, will often do the trick.

The Information Connection

The most important gift the lobbies have to give is information. Politicians like to look smart and sound smart. But some topics are so subtle and some are so complex that the legislator's personal education and experience don't equip him or her to handle them.

Questions of great complexity come flooding over Congress every day. They are questions that experts cannot agree on—there are good arguments on both sides. For example, highly educated people who have made careers trying

---

[40]*New York Times*, November 17, 1974.

FLORIDA HOME BUILDERS ASSOCIATION

Tallahassee, Florida

October 10, 1974

Honorable John Sparkman
Chairman, Committee on Banking, Housing, and Urban Affairs
United States Senate
Washington, D.C.

Dear Mr. Chairman:

For and on behalf of the Florida Home Builders Association, I am pleased to respond to your request of September 30, 1974 for our views with respect to S. 3658 and S. 4047 now under consideration by your Subcommittee on Housing and Urban Affairs.

On behalf of the 5,800 member firms of the Florida Home Builders Association I thank you for your consideration of the attached statement.

Sincerely,

FLORIDA HOME BUILDERS ASSOCIATION

Hunter W. Wolcott
Governmental Affairs Committee

to understand the proper marketing of oil or wheat have widely varied theories on import quotas or price supports. And if they cannot agree—if tax experts can't agree on taxation policies, if immigration authorities can't agree on immigration policies—how can the legislator be expected to come up with the wisest answer all on his or her own?

Practically speaking, the legislators probably shouldn't be expected to come up with it, until they have received plenty of advice. And much of this advice will come from all sorts of lobbies. The very fact that they are prejudiced makes pressure groups valuable as easily interpreted touchstones. Legislators know, long before they get to Washington, which organizations come closest to reflecting their personal philosophies and which come closest to reflecting the sentiments of their constituents. So when those organizations recommend certain votes, the legislators can be reasonably sure the recommendations are not alien to their own career positions—that is, they know that some lobbies have biases similar to their own.

That may sound like the legislators are rubber stamps for their friendly lobbies. Quite often they are. Some people estimate that probably half the bills introduced in Congress are written at least in part by lobbyists.[41] And lobbyists are equally prolific as speechwriters. When Senator John G. Tower of Texas, for example, wants to make a speech urging the deregulation of oil prices, he may ring up the American Petroleum Institute and ask his friend Frank N. Ikard to send over a speech he can read on the Senate floor. (That is, assuming the API hasn't anticipated his wishes and already sent the speech over.) Or when Senator George S. McGovern of South Dakota wants to take the "proper" position on the price of wheat, he—or, rather, his staff—will get in touch with, say, the National Farmers Union and find out what position McGovern should take and what argument he should make for taking that position. In any debate on a tough question, most of the major speeches in Congress have probably been written in large part by the appropriate lobbies.

These are not situations where the lobbies "persuade" the politicians; the politicians already knew generally where they stood ideologically and theoretically. But in turning to the lobbies to do their thinking for them at such moments, the politicians become naturally bound much tighter to the lobbies. This practice puts the lobbyist in a position to say to the politician, "Did I steer you wrong last time? Of course not. Now listen to me on this. . . ."

Getting Them at the Grass Roots

One of the most effective ways for the lobbies to influence Washington politics is by going to the grass roots—the real people out there in the nation—and stirring *them* up to bring pressures on Congress. If a gun-control bill were being debated in the Senate and a member who had been against the measure announced that he or she was thinking of changing his or her position, the announcement would immediately trigger action at the headquarters of the National Rifle Association. An IBM 370 computer, programmed with the names of five hundred key persons in the senator's home state, would begin churning out telegrams to them. The telegrams would not have to tell them what to do. The five hundred folks back home would start assaulting the senator's office with telephone calls, telegrams, and letters demanding that he or she stay in line.[42]

Faced with tougher auto emission controls from a pending bill, General Motors, Ford, Chrysler, and American Motors spent an estimated $800,000 advertising in nearly all of the daily newspapers. The ads warned that the legislation would raise the price of autos, and they closed with a call to arms: "Let your U.S. Senators and Representatives know your choice."[43]

The first rule of lobbyists working at the grass roots of society is to get some of the grass in their hair so that they will appear to be just plain folks, like the people next door. Thus, the AFL-CIO Industrial Union Department distributed a prop-

[41]James Deakin, *The Lobbyists* (Washington, D.C.: Public Affairs Press, 1966), p. 74.

[42]John Fialka, "Capital Lobbying: Grass Roots Is the Vogue," *Washington Star*, December 18, 1975.

[43]Fialka, "Capital Lobbying."

THE WEST WASN'T WON
WITH A REGISTERED GUN!

264

aganda brochure entitled "The All Union Family," in which its mythical family was said to live at "99 Shady Lane, Anytown, U.S.A." and the members of the family were identified as "Mr. and Mrs. John Q. America and their two wonderful kids."[44]

When the energy crisis developed in the early 1970s, the major oil companies launched a grassroots campaign to quiet public suspicions that they were responsible and to convince Ameri-

[44]L. Harmon Ziegler and G. Wayne Peak, *Interest Groups in American Society,* 2nd ed. (Englewood Cliffs, N.J.: Prentice-Hall, 1972), p. 115.

cans that they had the public's welfare at heart. In Texaco television commercials, men dressed up like oil field roughnecks—just plain hard-workin' folks with denim shirts and hard hats, big muscles and chapped hands—came before the camera and declared that they were trying their darnedest to find new sources of oil, but that the hunt cost a heap of extra money. The appeal was touching, and ended with the assurance, "We're working to keep your trust." It was all very neighborly, and doubtless most Americans who looked at the sunburned fellows with the Texaco patches on their pockets forgot that

"YOU SEE, ALL THE CARS THAT MEET HIGHER STANDARDS ARE MADE BY WITCHES AND MUNCHKINS"

CLEANER AND MORE EFFICIENT AUTOS WOULD MEAN UNEMPLOYMENT

From Herblock,
© 1977 *The Washington Post*

they were actually speaking for a global corporation that takes in $25 billion a year[45] and whose executives earn $250,000 a year and up.

When spiraling food prices outrage shoppers during periods of inflation, the agribusiness giants lay down a heavy barrage of grass-roots propaganda. The higher prices are only fair play for the family farmer toiling out there in the fields to feed America, they say. Actually, the family farmer no longer dominates the United States' food-producing industry; indeed, the family farmer is dying out—or, rather, is fast being driven out by corporate "farmers," such as Boe-

ing, Purex, General Foods, Coca-Cola, Safeway, Greyhound, and Ling-Temco-Vought. Giant corporations today either farm directly on land that they own or contract with smaller farmers to produce 55 percent of the fresh vegetables, 88 percent of the processed vegetables, 92 percent of the chickens, and 47 percent of the citrus fruit grown in this country. Tenneco, the $6-billion-oil-and-pipeline conglomerate, has become the United States' biggest farmer, and it is well on its way to dominating the fresh vegetable and fruit market.[46] But when Tenneco lays down

---

[45]*Fortune*, May 1975.

[46]Jim Hightower, *Eat Your Heart Out: Food Profiteering in America* (New York: Crown Publishers, 1975), pp. 130, 163, 166.

its grass-roots lobbying line for higher food prices, the consumers will probably get the idea they are listening to just a lil' ol' jolly green hayseed, ho ho ho, in bib overalls.

MONEY IS THE ROOT OF MOST LOBBYING

If there seems to be a recurrent theme of money in this discussion of pressure politics, it is because big money is almost an essential ingredient of effective lobbying—and *some* money is an absolute essential. Money has many uses.

The clashing of selfish interests, which occurs constantly, sets in motion other activities crucial to political campaigning, elections, court fights, and the structuring and operation of government. Each side wants passionately to win, but winning is not a matter of flipping a coin; it is, more than anything else, a matter of *collecting* coins—and collecting paper money, lots of it. Lobbying also means spending what is sometimes more important than money—human energy. Victory in a clash between competing interests will depend on which side can collect enough money and recruit enough campaign workers to elect legislators who favor their point of view or defeat legislators who favor the opposite point of view. Victory can also mean collecting enough money for a national propaganda campaign or for one of the most expensive exercises of all—fighting an issue through the courts after legislation is passed.

Having a lot of money available often seems to distort and twist the minds of lobbyists. When a lobbyist for the United Mine Workers' union was asked if it was a healthy situation for Representative John H. Dent of Pennsylvania, Chairman of the Labor Subcommittee of the House Education and Labor Committee, to be so blindly pro-UMW, the lobbyist snapped: "If you don't like it, go get your own Congressman."[47] Most big money lobbyists do think in terms of "getting" a member of Congress, preferably a chairperson, of buying him or her, or of drowning him or her in obligations—in short, of somehow making the legislator a captive of a special inter-

est group. That is a long way from simply trying to persuade a member of Congress to see a particular side of an issue.

The Exception: Citizen Lobbies

The typical citizen does not have this kind of clout. Nor is it easy for a group of citizens to band together in a lobbying group. Yet necessity, in recent years, has seen a flowering of that very thing: citizen lobby groups, consumer groups, environmental groups, civil rights groups. They do not bribe; they do not hand out credit cards; they do not wine and dine. But they have shown themselves to be solid friends and dangerous foes at election time, for they have learned how to get out the vote—the magic wand of democracy. The ability to swing large blocs of votes is almost worth all the riches of the old-time lobbies in terms of making politicians listen. For many years, Wayne N. Aspinall, Colorado Democrat, was Chairman of the House Interior Committee, in which position he helped the big lumbering companies, cattle barons, and mining companies loot the public lands of the West. Conservationists, he said, were "a lunatic fringe." By 1972, the conservationists had banded together into such a potent lobby that they persuaded the people of Aspinall's district to throw him out of office. Because he would not listen to reason in Washington, the conservationist lobby sent him home to listen to the wind in the Colorado spruce. And ever since then, other politicians around Washington have been much more polite to the conservationists.

Despite relatively meager budgets, other public interest groups, too, manage to hold their own in Washington encounters. The reason for their success, when they have it, is probably the same as for any lobby: intensity and persistence. As *New York Times* reporter David E. Rosenbaum put it: "Their [the public interest lobbies'] strength lies in their willingness to master a subject and then wear out shoe leather and reams of Xerox paper to get their point across."[48] Also, they have scores of local affiliates, full of loyal and enthusiastic missionaries who are willing to

---

[47] Personal interview with a UMW lobbyist, March 1974.

[48] *New York Times*, September 12, 1976.

Ralph Nader

work without pay to generate grass-roots pressure on Congress. Their very poverty and their indifference to personal gain has a propaganda potency that cannot be bought. "Ralph Nader's great strength," Congressman Benjamin S. Rosenthal once pointed out, "is his public acceptability. When he comes in here, he comes with clean hands. The business lobbyists come to feather their own nests."[49]

Like other consumer lobbyists, but to a unique degree, Nader has a genius for developing working friendships with the working press (in contrast, say, to the President of Humble Oil). Nearly every reporter in Washington with muckraking aspirations has been slipped an exclusive story by Nader or his staff about drug frauds or auto cheats or monopoly chiseling. Thereby Nader wins their allegiance. In this way, he gets literally millions of dollars in free publicity for his causes. His business adversaries often claim that he exploits the press unfairly, but in lobbying—as in love and war—nothing is unfair, not even clean hands and a pure heart.

[49]Quoted in the *Washington Post*, July 5, 1974.

Big Business, Big Clout

Despite random victories by public interest pressure groups, there is still a dangerous imbalance of power in favor of the private groups—dangerous in the sense that it is difficult for all sides to get a fair hearing.

Most of the lobbies in Washington are in the employ of business, and when anyone speaks of "business interests" in Washington, it is safe to assume, without further identification, that they mean Big Business, for Big Business controls the three main business lobbying organizations—the United States Chamber of Commerce, the National Association of Manufacturers,[50] and the Business Roundtable.[51]

Like labor's chief lobby, the AFL-CIO, these business lobbies are highly undemocratic—a tiny minority runs the show. But that, considering the concentration of power at the top of the business-industrial pyramid, is to be expected. A glance at the top of that pyramid will give some indication of what kind of pressure can be developed on behalf of business interests by a relatively small group of executives.

Eight institutions, including six banks, appear to control, or at least dominate, most of the nation's giant corporations through stock holdings, according to a study by the Senate Government Operations Committee.[52] Stepping down one level of the pyramid, we find that the two hundred largest corporations control more than 58 percent of all manufacturing assets and that the top five hundred corporations control well over 75 percent.[53] Most of the oil industry is controlled by seven corporations; the auto industry

[50]Olson, *The Logic of Collective Action*, pp. 146–47.

[51]The Business Roundtable is the newest and most elite of the business lobbies. As of 1976, the group counted among its 158 corporate members 63 of the nation's top 100 industrial companies. Its success is due to its technique of sending corporate officials themselves—rather than hired lobbyists—to meet with members of Congress privately. (See Steven Rattner, "Big Industry Gun Aims at the Hill," *New York Times*, March 7, 1976.)

[52]Senate Subcommittee on Intergovernmental Relations and Budgeting, Management, and Expenditures of the Committee on Government Operations, *Disclosure of Corporate Ownership*, December 27, 1973 (released January 1974).

[53]John Mitchell quoted in Jerry S. Cohen and Morton Mintz, *America Inc.* (New York: Dell Publishing Co., 1973), p. 16.

Elephants among the Chickens

Corporate power in the political process is a reality. You don't have to believe that, somewhere, there are twelve bankers, politicians, and corporate executives who meet once a week to decide the future of America—there aren't—to see that General Motors has more to say about federal air pollution standards than you or I or even millions like us do. . . . The individual citizen is the basic unit of our political system. Only he or she can vote, hold public office, or influence legislation—the latter, at least in theory. Unions, farm organizations, and environmental groups are membership organizations, made up of citizens, each of whom have political rights to be exercised separately or jointly. Corporations, on the other hand, are entirely different structures, chartered by the government to serve certain public purposes, and generally organized to make profits for their owners. Only their owners are citizens, with political rights. In his book, *The Corporation Takeover,* Professor Andrew Hacker refers to the familiar pluralist model of democracy, which is a

> society composed of a multiplicity of groups and a citizen body actively engaged in the associational life. . . . Were groups such as the American Medical Association, the United Automobile Workers, the National Association for the Advancement of Colored People, and the American Legion the only participants in the struggle for political and economic preferment then the sociology of democracy would continue as an effective theory. For in cases like these it may still be assumed, in spite of tendencies toward bureaucratization, that the power of these associations is simply an extension of the individual interests and wills of their constituent members.
>
> But when General Electric, American Telephone and Telegraph, and Standard Oil of New Jersey enter the pluralist arena we have elephants dancing among the chickens. For corporate institutions are not voluntary associations with individuals as members but rather associations of assets, and no theory yet propounded has declared that machines are entitled to a voice in the democratic process. . . .

From Fred R. Harris, "Politics of Corporate Power," in Ralph Nader and Mark J. Green, eds., *Corporate Power in America* (New York: Viking Press, Grossman Publishers, 1973), pp. 26, 37–38.

is totally controlled by four, and most of the steel industry is controlled by four or five corporations. Pick any major industry and put it to the test—four firms or fewer will be found to dominate it. The concentration of lobbying power that can be built on the foundation of this concentration of assets is awesome. These corporations are, in a way, the economic equivalent of nations. General Motors employs about as many people (800,000) as work for the federal government in Washington, D.C., and its environs. GM's sales *dropped* $4 billion in 1974, and it *still* had a total income greater than the gross national product of fourteen or fifteen nations.[54]

The Big Business influence in government is so well established that it has become not merely accepted but sought after. Former President Dwight D. Eisenhower, for example, often talked of the desirability of business-government "partnerships." Former President John F. Kennedy, though considered a liberal, sometimes went out of his way to prove that he could show a more conservative bias in favor of business than Eisenhower did.[55] The impotence of the recent "liberal" administrations, those since Franklin D. Roosevelt's time in office, in significantly checking the business lobby—or even in offering a strategy for checking it can be easily understood; their economic advisers are weak on strategy. John Kenneth Galbraith, one of the economic gurus of the liberal camp, actually

[54]See *Fortune,* May 1975.

[55]Kennedy's tax proposals were almost identical to proposals made by the United States Chamber of Commerce. C. Douglas Dillon, a Wall Street broker whom Kennedy made his Secretary of the Treasury, said, "I don't think there had been a President in a long time who had basically done as much for business." (Quoted in Robert Sherrill, *The Last Kennedy,* New York: Dell Publishing Co., Dial Press, 1976, p. 23; see also Bernard D. Nossiter, *The Mythmakers,* Boston: Houghton Mifflin Co., 1964.)

believes that "private economic power is held in check by the countervailing power of those who are subject to it. The first begets the second."[56]

It is a rather naive conception of "countervailing" lobbies to suggest, for example, that the multibillion-dollar agribusiness industry, by mistreating migrant workers, begets labor movements among the field hands, movements that thereafter keep the agribusiness giants "in check." Of course, things aren't that way in reality. Cesar Chavez's lettuce-and-grape-picking lobby is not ever likely to be a match for the kind of concentrated agribusiness persuasion described by Jim Hightower as being clustered in concentric waves around the seats of government:

> Within eight blocks of the White House there are 14 Washington offices of food corporations and three Washington offices of trade associations that represent food corporations. Other food firms have locations throughout the Nation's Capital, but just these seventeen offices account for well over $100 billion worth of food power—more than a tenth of this country's total Gross National Product.[57]

Hightower points out that representatives of some of the major food companies—such as Ralston Purina, Del Monte, and Safeway—were invited to appear at congressional hearings dealing with the issue of monopoly power as a factor in rising food prices. But they declined the invitation. That did not mean, however, that they were disinterested. It simply meant that they preferred to do their talking quietly, in private. Several of the food executives had breakfast with the subcommittee chairman one morning during the hearings. Hightower comments that

> There would be no request at breakfast to lay off the industry, nor any hundred-dollar bills slipped under the chairman's toast. It simply would be an opportunity for big business to make its position known directly, personally, comfortably, and off the public record. Business enjoys that opportunity day in and day out.[58]

---

[56]John Kenneth Galbraith, *American Capitalism* (Boston: Houghton Mifflin Co., 1956), p. 118.

[57]Hightower, *Eat Your Heart Out*, p. 212.

[58]Hightower, p. 212.

Superlawyers and Influence Peddlers

The most certain key to success in Washington pressure politics is surely not in knowing how to bribe a crooked politician—probably not many are so crooked that they can be bribed—but in knowing the right lawyer with the right contacts and in having the money to afford him or her. The money is the thing that separates the big boys from the little, the giant corporations from Mr. John Q. Public, as cartoonists like to label us. "The problem," as former Federal Communications Commissioner Nicholas Johnson once said sadly, "is not that you can buy a Congressman for $10,000, but can buy a Washington lawyer for $100,000."[59] They are indeed for sale, and the legal flesh market is not only respectable, but very hoity-toity.

Most of the great Washington law firms trace their beginnings no farther back than the 1930s. In places like New York and Boston, it is not uncommon for the same family names to have been on the door since the early nineteenth century. Not in Washington. To the legal fraternity, it was, until recent years, a sparsely settled frontier. But just as tavern maids, loan sharks, merchants, and preachers follow pioneers, lawyers follow the path of a spreading government. More government means more money passed around. It also means more regulations, and that means more special interests will be nearby to see that the regulations are aimed in the right direction (or misdirection) and that they get their share of the money. It simply is one of the physical laws of government, that where government abounds, countergovernment (or outside special interests) will also abound.

So it is natural that the greatest proliferation of Washington lobbyists and influence peddlers has occurred since the 1930s. They are the offspring of the New Deal, the Fair Deal, the New Frontier, and the Great Society—which is to say, they are largely the response to the Democratic administrations from 1933 to 1968 (with eight years out for Republicans between 1953 and 1960). Democrats have been the most

---

[59]Quoted in Mark J. Green, *The Other Government: The Unseen Power of Washington Lawyers* (New York: Viking Press, Grossman Publishers, 1975), p. 3.

The Superlawyers

The Washington Lawyer in recent decades has stepped beyond the attorney's traditional role as legal representative. The Washington Lawyer accepts government as an existential fact and tries to direct what it does to the benefit of his corporate clients. The Washington Lawyer affects public policy when it is being shaped in the Congress and the regulatory agencies and in the executive departments, either as a proponent of original ideas or in reaction to those from elsewhere. He is a markedly more sophisticated man than knee-jerk conservatives of the 1930s, for he recognizes the government as a source of subsidies, as a partner in legalized price fixing, as a deterrent to competition. The lawyer's historic role was that of advising clients how to *comply* with the law. The Washington Lawyer's present role is that of advising clients how to *make* laws, and to make the most of them.

From Joseph C. Goulden, *The Superlawyers: The Small and Powerful World of the Great Washington Law Firms* (New York: Weybright & Talley, 1972), p. 6.

Modern products, from nuclear plants to flammable pajamas, can inflict damage far more severe than could their antecedents of fifty years ago. If, as a Covington & Burling partner acknowledged, a lawyer should report to the authorities a client who promised to murder someone tomorrow, what does a lawyer do with a pharmaceutical client whose dangerous drug can also "murder" or pain thousands of people tomorrow, albeit invisibly and at a distance from the client?

The ultimate issue, then, is not classic, money-under-the-table corruption by lawyers. As one walks through the handsome and elegant offices of a Washington law firm, there is hardly the odor of corruption. Instead, many of the best graduates of the best law schools represent the largest corporations in the country—corporations that are not your fly-by-night operations. But, as C. S. Lewis suggested in *The Screwtape Letters*, the greatest offences can be "conceived or ordered—moved, seconded, carried and minuted—in clean, carpeted, warmed and well-lighted offices, by quiet men with white collars and cut fingernails and smooth-shaven cheeks who do not need to raise their voices."

What can be done about a one-sided process in which giant companies hire Washington law firms to rationalize all client misbehavior regardless of the public cost?

From Mark J. Green, *The Other Government: The Unseen Power of Washington Lawyers* (New York: Viking Press, Grossman Publishers, 1975), pp. 284–85.

A sea of lawyers retained by the defendants—twenty-nine oil companies—in a single antitrust suit

"I'd like to present Mr. Bilkins. Mr. Bilkins is not a lawyer."

Drawing by Richter; © 1976 The New Yorker Magazine, Inc.

enthusiastic about Big Government being the answer to social problems. Most of the regulatory agencies and the administrative agencies that overflow in Washington today were set up during those decades, and the big Washington law firms were organized in response to the need of corporations to deal with the many new rules and regulations.

Corporations would be very foolish if they did not seek the representation of wily law firms, for, as Mark J. Green has pointed out, the agencies

> have substantial authority to help or hurt the nation's 1.5 million corporations. They can dispense great wealth via licenses, subsidies, contracts, and approved rate schedules, or can limit great wealth by tax, antitrust, and regulatory

standards. The big six regulatory commissions (the FCC, the SEC, the CAB, the ICC, the Federal Power Commission [FPC], the Federal Maritime Commission [FMC], have direct authority over some $120 billion of commerce. The Pentagon contracts out $40 billion in weapons contracts annually. The banking industry can do little without approval from the Federal Reserve Board, the comptroller of the currency, or the Federal Deposit Insurance Corporation. The Internal Revenue Service and the Environmental Protection Agency have the ability to make any manufacturing firm in the country miserable.

Unsurprisingly, corporations, through their Washington counsel, try to turn these enterprises to their advantage.[60]

---

[60]Green, p. 6.

For doing a good job of it, the Washington attorneys are well paid. Half-million-dollar lobbying fees from one corporation for a single year's labor are not unusual. That's what Braniff Airways, for example, paid the law firm Arnold and Porter in 1973. With that kind of money floating around, the lure of the Washington law firms is mighty. Fifteen thousand lawyers call the nation's capital their home. A couple of years after he left the United States Senate to go into law practice in Washington, George A. Smathers of Florida exclaimed joyfully to a reporter, "I've found the pastures outside are a lot greener than I had reasoned. A fellow with my background can make more money in thirty days out here than he can in fifteen years as a Senator."[61] One of the key characteristics of the successful lawyer-lobbyists is that they know their way around government. More often than not, they learned it by having once been top officials. No small part of Arnold and Porter's rich success can be traced to the fact that of the firm's forty-four partners, fourteen previously held important federal posts in which they made the kind of lasting friendships that continued to pay off after they left government. Paul A. Porter, for example, was in and out of government thirteen times between 1932 and 1962.[62]

Probably the most famous of all Washington lawyers over the past quarter of a century has been Clark M. Clifford of the firm Clifford, Warnke, Glass, McIlwain and Finney. Clifford was a close adviser to every Democratic President since Harry S Truman, winding up, briefly, as Secretary of Defense in 1968. Each of Clifford's partners also worked in the upper echelons of the bureaucracy and/or in top staff positions on Capitol Hill before joining his firm. Exactly how does Clifford see his work? He explained to a *Fortune* magazine reporter, "That [lobbying] is not the kind of work we do. We run a law office here, with a background of experience in the general practice of law, topped off by an intimate knowledge of how the government operates."[63]

That is a euphemism for lobbying that any big-time lobbyist would love. In Clifford's case, it means he rarely does anything so crass as to directly approach a member of the House or the Senate. Instead, he tells his corporate clients how to plan their strategy in the courts and in Congress. And, in addition, he "keeps in touch" with his old friends around Washington—old friends that included Presidents Kennedy and Johnson, who frequently called on Clifford for what they insisted was free advice, although in fact no Washington lawyer gives any advice that does not have a price tag on it somewhere. (Hoping to pass this interchange off as a joke, Kennedy once quipped, "All he asked in return was that we advertise his law firm on the backs of one-dollar bills.")[64]

CONTROLS ON LOBBY INFLUENCE

Plainly, the lobby is a part of government. But it is a part that largely operates outside the law. It is a key influence in the promotion of candidates and in their election; it helps write our legislation; it frequently determines the outcome of congressional voting and of bureaucratic enforcement—and yet it is not accountable to the public.

This is a scary situation. Democracy is by nature a disorganized, undisciplined, and largely amateurish operation. Wealthy or intensely organized subgroups can subvert it unless they are properly controlled. Many efforts have been made to control the lobby, but all have failed. Only once, in 1946, have such efforts resulted in a law.

Looking back, one finds that the threat of the lobby has been recognized for well over a century—which makes it all the more remarkable that so little has been done to lessen the threat. It was in the 1850s that the value of manufactured goods first exceeded that of farm products. Business and manufacturing associations proliferated and became powerful, and they sent their representatives to Washington in such swarms that James Buchanan wrote to Franklin

---

[61]Quoted by Joseph C. Goulden, *The Superlawyers: The Small and Powerful World of the Great Washington Law Firms* (New York: Weybright & Talley, 1972), p. 339.

[62]*National Journal*, January 8, 1972, p. 50.

[63]Quoted in Deakin, *The Lobbyists*, p. 172.

[64]Quoted in Goulden, *The Superlawyers*, p. 70.

Pierce: "The host of contractors, speculators, stock-jobbers, and lobby members which haunt the halls of Congress, all desirous . . . to get their arm into the public treasury, are sufficient to alarm every friend of his country. Their progress must be arrested."[65]

But it wasn't. Indeed, they continued to thrive, for the moral climate of the nation's legislatures, including its federal legislature, was not the highest. United States senators were, in those days, elected by state legislatures, which meant that their election was often purchased and that they came to Washington virtually owned by the special interests that had engineered their success. Secondly, most legislative committee activity, in those days, was done behind closed doors, and shady deals could be completed without the public's being aware of what was going on. Votes were routinely purchased by lobbyists. In that atmosphere, the highest morality sometimes seemed to belong to those legislators who, having been bought, stayed bought.

"In the 20 years between 1865 and 1885," writes James Deakin, "the concept of government by all the people, so movingly reaffirmed by Abraham Lincoln, almost went into eclipse. Special interest pressure and corruption in government mounted to dizzying heights. Popular democracy was threatened as never before in this country."[66]

Around the turn of the century, the character of lobbying slowly began to change. Muckraking reporters zeroed in on the corruption of the legislatures. After 1913, all senators were elected by the populace, which made them somewhat less responsive to moneyed interests and somewhat more cautious about offending the average voter. Big Business, threatened as never before by the public's antitrust and antibigness sentiments, began for the first time to realize the benefits of good public relations. As a result of all these influences, lobbying became somewhat more discreet.

Although more respectable, the lobby did not change much in its imbalance. It was still overwhelmingly dominated by Big Business. In 1912, when Woodrow Wilson was first running for the Presidency, he made this comment repeatedly as a way to stir up the electorate to support him as a "man of the people":

> The masters of the government of the United States are the combined capitalists and manufacturers of the United States. . . . Suppose you go to Washington. You will always find that while you are politely listened to, the men really consulted are the big men who have the biggest stake—the big bankers, the big manufacturers, the big masters of commerce, the heads of railroad corporations, and of steamship corporations. . . . Every time it has come to a critical question, these gentlemen have been yielded to and their demands treated as the demands that should be followed as a matter of course. The government of the United States is a foster child of the special interests.[67]

Faithful to his instincts, Wilson was no sooner sworn into office than he ordered the lobbyists out of town. The order was singularly ignored.

In 1935, the lobby was still so thick with heavy-handed high-pressure fellows that Senator Hugo L. Black, later to become one of the great justices of the Supreme Court, made a radio speech in which he warned that the American people had better take heed of the fact that lobbying "has reached such a position of power that it threatens the government itself. Its size, its power, its capacity for evil; its greed, trickery, deception and fraud condemn it to the death it deserves."[68]

However, the legislation Black introduced to control the lobby fell far short of a death sentence. A staunch advocate of freedom of speech,

---

[65]Congressional Quarterly Service, *Congress and the Nation* (Washington, D.C.: Congressional Quarterly, 1965), p. 1547.

[66]Deakin, *The Lobbyists*, p. 67. In the 1870s, the railroads formed the first giant industrial lobby. Collis Huntington, President of the Central Pacific and the Southern Pacific, had the typical railroad baron's attitude. He put all politicians in three categories: the clean, the commercial, and the communists. A "clean" politician was one who would vote for the railroads and do their bidding without having to be paid. A commercial politician would vote for the railroads, but only in return for some favor. A communist was a politician who would not do as the railroads demanded, for money or for any other inducement. (David J. Rothman, *Politics and Power: The United States Senate 1869–1901*, New York: Atheneum Publishers, 1969, pp. 195–96.)

[67]Deakin, *The Lobbyists*, p. 74.

[68]Quoted in Deakin, p. 76.

Lobby Reform: A Problem of Momentum

Lawmakers' zeal for lobby reform appears to be waning at a time when lobbyists' assaults on Congress have rarely been heavier:

- Trial lawyers opposing no-fault car insurance legislation have amassed $400,000 to help re-elect their congressional allies.

- Oil and gas interests helped contribute more than $200,000 in campaign funds to Rep. Robert C. Krueger (D) of Texas while he led the congressional fight to deregulate natural gas prices.

- A now-resigned lobbyist for Gulf Oil Corporation is accused of channeling illegal political contributions from a $10.3 million secret fund to 25 senators and at least six representatives.

- The wife of a senior Republican on the Senate Foreign Relations Committee, Jacob K. Javits of New York, resigned under pressure from her $67,000-a-year job promoting Iran's national airlines.

But most such influence on the nation's laws goes undisclosed under the sieve-like 1946 lobby law, which reveals only about 1 percent of lobbying expenditures and a fraction of the 5,000 to 10,000 Washington lobbyists.

From Peter C. Stuart, "Congressional Lobbying Reform Bill Lies Dormant," *Christian Science Monitor*, February 27, 1976, p. 5.

Black did not want to do anything that would disrupt the channels of communication even between deceitful people and their elected representatives. So he proposed merely that all lobbyists be required to register and to disclose the source of their income. The bill did not pass.

The 1946 Lobby Act

Finally, in 1946, Congress did something about the lobby: not much, but something. It passed the Federal Regulation of Lobbying Act, a kind of crippled chicken that in no way restricted the activities of pressure groups operating in Washington. Its impact can be measured by the fact that, in 1953, the Justice Department disbanded its lobbying enforcement unit as a waste of time, brains, and money. As of 1977, the 1946 law was still the only control in force.

The law defines a lobbyist as a person or an organization that receives money for trying to influence the passage or the defeat of legislation and whose "principal purpose" is to influence the creation and existence of legislation. Any person or organization fitting that description is required to register with the Secretary of the Senate or with the Clerk of the House, to report how much money is received from what sources, and to report how much is spent on lobbying. But no official is assigned to examine and evaluate these reports for accuracy.

The phrase "principal purpose" left quite a loophole. Many, if not most, of the best lobbyists in town claim that their "principal purpose" is not to lobby—and so they don't register; or, if they do register, they put down only a fraction of the money they earn and spend each year, claiming that the rest is for "legal advice," "education," or "research."[69]

Other exceptions to the coverage of the law make it a mockery.

---

[69] The National Association of Manufacturers, the nation's most powerful business association, has an annual budget of $6 million. Much of that is spent on lobbying, but for many years the NAM did not register as a lobby. This so infuriated Common Cause, the self-designated citizens' lobby, that it took the NAM to court in 1975 to force it to register.

More Exceptions than Applications

In 1953, the Supreme Court ruled that the Federal Regulation of Lobbying Act applies only to "lobbying in its commonly accepted sense—to direct communications with members of Congress on pending or proposed federal legislation," but not to indirect lobbying by "attempts to saturate the thinking of the community."[70] In other words, this exempted grass-roots lobbying—pressures exerted and propaganda spread among the populace to influence Congress indirectly—the method by which much lobbying is done. Nor does the law apply to lobbying done in the executive branch of the government or to lobbying done in the bureaucracy, a crucial omission.

The importance of the bureaucracy to the business lobby is seen in the fact that New York is no longer the favorite headquarters for professional and trade groups. Washington is. More than one thousand such organizations, from the American Public Health Association to the Onion Packers Council and the National Frozen Pizza Institute, now have representatives in the federal capital. They employ 50,000 people—making trade associations the fourth largest industry in Washington. They are there, says James P. Low, President of the American Society of Association Executives, "to combat the harassment brought on by federal laws. . . . Ninety percent of the associations in the United States have government relations programs [meaning they have contracts or some other profit-making arrangement with Washington], so they almost have to be here to guard their industries."[71] One way they guard their industries is to lobby constantly with the bureaucracy for a more favorable interpretation of regulations.

THE MORE THEY FIGHT, THE CLOSER THEY GET

It must not be presumed that pressure politics is made up of unbridgeable differences, hatreds, eternal feuds, and the like. As a matter of fact, the most effective lobbyists come to respect, even as they oppose, each other. Schattschneider notes accurately:

> The most powerful instrument for the control of conflict is conflict itself. A generation ago E. A. Ross, a distinguished American sociologist, pointed out that conflicts tend to interfere with each other and that the very multiplicity of cleavages in a modern community tends to temper the severity of social antagonisms.[72]

Over an extended period of time, opposing interest groups tend to take on each other's coloration. Nowhere has this developed more dramatically than in the case of the two most influential special interest groups, ostensibly "opponents"—Big Business and Big Labor.

Traditionally, our capitalistic society has been the battleground for an unceasing war between the wage earner and the boss, between the worker and the owner. The tradition was built up over so many decades that it is now presumed to be still alive, whereas, in fact, the war has been reduced to only an occasional skirmish. The reason for this cease-fire is not that greed and exploitation have been banished from the marketplace, but that *organized* labor—which Olson has called, with few to dispute him "probably the most important single type of pressure-group organization"[73]—has won enough concessions from Big Business to feel friendly toward it. Big Business, in turn, has found the hierarchy of organized labor easier and more profitable to swing deals with than a mob of unhappy, unorganized workers. Here is how success can change a lobby's viewpoint and character.

"Don't Mourn. Organize!"

Wages and working conditions have been important political issues since the United States really began to gear up for the industrial revolution in the 1850s. Workers immediately began agitating for a ten-hour workday (at that time most laborers worked twelve to fourteen hours) and safer and cleaner working conditions. Children and women in textile mills and men in coal

---

[70]*United States v. Rumely*, 345 U.S. 41, 47 (1953).

[71]Quoted in the *New York Times*, June 8, 1975.

[72]Schattschneider, *The Semisovereign People*, p. 67.

[73]Olson, *The Logic of Collective Action*, p. 135.

mines were customarily worked from sunrise to sunset. Seamen were notoriously abused. New immigrants, unable to speak the language and therefore especially vulnerable, were frequently cheated by their employers. Morever, all workers were at the mercy of the boom-bust cycles that continued well into this century. After the panic of 1873, thousands of businesses went bust, and millions of workers lost their jobs. *Harper's Weekly* reported that during the winter of 1873, 900 persons in New York City alone died of starvation, 3,000 infants were abandoned on doorsteps, and more than 11,000 boys were left homeless. It was commonplace for men and women to live in the parks or in hallways.[74]

The working class was well aware of how it could improve its condition. Samuel Gompers, the first President of the American Federation of Labor, said, in 1891:

> On every hand we find . . . combination on the part of those who own or control wealth, and using

their possessions to crush out the liberties, to stifle the voice, and pervert the rights of the toiling masses. . . . The combinations can only be successfully met and coped with by a compact and thorough organization of wage workers.[75]

Organization. That was the key. In 1915, Joe Hill, one of the famous men of the radical labor movement, was convicted (with trumped-up evidence, many believe) of killing a Salt Lake City grocer and was executed by a five-man firing squad. The day before he died, he wrote to another leader of the International Workers of the World (better known as the Wobblies): "Goodbye Bill. I die like a true blue rebel. Don't waste any time mourning. Organize!"[76]

The workers did keep organizing and reorganizing, sometimes in political-action parties (such as the Workingmen's party); sometimes strictly for collective bargaining, to raise pay and improve working conditions; sometimes for a bit of both politics and pay, with some long-range economic ideology thrown in. A truly national

---

[74]In M. B. Schnapper, *American Labor: A Pictorial Social History* (Washington, D.C.: Public Affairs Press, 1972), p. 93.

[75]Quoted in Schnapper, p. 225.

[76]Quoted in Schnapper, p. 377.

Strike riot in Bayonne, New Jersey, July 1915

labor organization was slow in developing. The Noble and Holy Order of the Knights of Labor reached an awesome membership of 750,000 in 1886—and then swiftly declined. In that same year was born the American Federation of Labor, fashioned around six of the leading craft unions.

FDR and a Boost for Labor

The craft unions had little to offer the newer generation of industrial workers—the miners, the steelworkers, the mill workers, the railroad workers—and they were the most brutally exploited. If industrial workers complained as a group, they would commonly be set upon physically by federal troops, state guardsmen, local police, and professional goons. In the textile workers' strike in Lawrence, Massachusetts, in 1912, pickets approached the gates of the mill in subfreezing weather; they were hit by streams of ice water trained on them from fire hoses on adjoining roofs. When the strikers retaliated by hurling back pieces of ice, thirty-six were arrested and sentenced to a year in prison. In 1917, Arizona mine strikers were loaded into railway cattle cars, hauled miles into the desert, and thrown out, without food or water. In 1929, textile workers in Gastonia, North Carolina, went on strike; strikebreakers hired by the company shot and killed six and wounded twenty-five. A general strike encompassing almost the entire textile industry broke out in 1934; troops were called in, and fourteen workers were killed, either by bullets or in bayonet charges. In 1937, 150 South Chicago police attacked an impromptu parade of Republic Steel Company strikers and their families, killed ten, and injured one hundred.

Although the AFL had about 5 million members after World War I, its membership dropped 40 percent over the next decade.[77] Workers were disinclined to join unions partly because they didn't enjoy getting their heads bashed in on the picket line and partly because, in the prosperity of the 1920s, they did not feel the need to organize.[78] The Great Depression of the 1930s changed that thinking. The workers were

desperate, and in their desperation they once again began to unite in a massive surge. Violent opposition to unions continued into the mid-1930s, but it was becoming obvious that business was waging a losing battle.

The administration of President Franklin D. Roosevelt, which came to power in March 1933, was unshakably prolabor. With the encouragement of labor, Congress, in 1935, passed the National Labor Relations Act (usually known as the Wagner Act, because its author was Senator Robert F. Wagner). It was by far the most significant labor law ever enacted in the United States. The Wagner Act guaranteed workers "the right to self-organization, to form, join, or assist labor organizations, to bargain collectively through representatives of their own choosing, and to engage in concerted activities for the purpose of collective bargaining or other mutual aid or protection." The act also set up the National Labor Relations Board (NLRB), composed of labor and employer representatives, which was supposed to settle disputes arising from union organizing and collective bargaining.

Although many employers tried to ignore the Wagner Act and the NLRB, they had to capitulate when, in 1937, the Supreme Court ruled that the Wagner Act was both constitutional and just. In the very year of this Supreme Court ruling, union membership jumped 55 percent.[79] The phenomenal growth during the mid-1930s was also attributable to the fact that, in 1935, a group of AFL union executives, disgruntled because they felt the AFL was not giving enough attention to organizing by industry rather than by craft, broke away and formed the Congress of Industrial Organizations, which swept through the mining, steel, textile, and auto industries, gathering millions of members.

Today about one-quarter of the nation's work force is organized—about 25 million persons. But growth is slow, or declining. Nonunion workers are not rushing to sign up. The appeal of organized labor has diminished sharply. Big Labor has become so tightly structured, so undemocratic, and so narrow of vision that it is debatable how much attention even union members give their top officials.[80]

[77]McConnell, *Private Power and American Democracy*, p. 300.

[78]Paul A. Samuelson, *Economics*, 10th ed. (New York: McGraw-Hill, 1976), p. 137.

[79]Olson, *The Logic of Collective Action*, p. 79.

[80]Olson, p. 135.

Business and Labor Bury the Hatchet

By the 1950s, Big Business and Big Labor had discovered that, far from being enemies, they could get along with each other very nicely. Indeed, they came to depend on one another. The increasingly noncompetitive character of Big Business and the rigid hierarchy of Big Labor created an atmosphere of stability and status quo that both sides enjoyed. "Radicals" became as unwelcome to the bureaucracy of Big Labor as they were to Big Business's board of directors.

The AFL-CIO, for example, like its business counterpart, was a fanatical supporter of the cold war policy, and it was an equally fanatical supporter of the Vietnam war. War-protesting college students were sometimes beaten up by hard hats. Gone was the old spirit that opposed colonialism and the exploitation of helpless and unorganized peoples anywhere in the world. As for minority races at home, many unions made a policy of excluding them. Gone was the spirit that in 1896 saw farmers and factory hands nearly put William Jennings Bryan in the White House as a protest against Big Business's throttlehold on the economy. By the 1970s, many of Big Labor's leaders had so comfortably adapted to the system that they scoffed at any "populist" candidate as unrealistic and urged the rank and file to vote Republican or for George C. Wallace rather than support a liberal Democrat. Jimmy Carter, who gave off some musk of populism in his 1976 campaign, received AFL-CIO President George Meany's support late and only after it became clear that Carter would probably win.

Today, the AFL-CIO lobby operates out of a $4 million building just across the park from the White House and just around the corner from the United States Chamber of Commerce. Within an easy walk from the Capitol, the Teamsters' union pulls its strings from a building as grand as most government temples. And why not? The union is rolling in dough. As of 1977, Teamster President Frank Fitzsimmons was receiving $156,250 a year in salary (a bit more than three-fourths the salary of the President of the United States). His attitude toward the rank and file was summed up in a statement made at the 1976 Teamsters' convention: "To those who say it is time to reform this organization and it's time the officers stopped selling out the members of this organization, I say to them, 'Go to hell.'"[81] The Teamsters' convention was held in Las Vegas, Nevada, where the union reportedly has a $210 million stake in gambling casinos and hotels. Teamster officials get about in their own fleet of limousines and their own jet planes. At union headquarters, they dine on the creations of their own French chef.[82]

The Teamsters' union is exceptionally flamboyant, and its officials are the highest paid; but its defects are, to a lesser extent, those of organized labor as a whole. Only a Teamster president would be so candid as to say: "Unions are big business. Why should truck drivers and bottle-washers be allowed to make big decisions affecting union policy? Would any corporation allow it?"[83] But the same undemocratic spirit pervades most big unions. Teamster officials may indulge more than any others in patsy relationships with industry officials, but the same questionable chumminess is found elsewhere. Edward Sadlowski, the rebel United Steelworkers official, was right on target when he said of other top officials in the Steelworkers' union: "Most of these sons of bitches would rather go have a Martini with the chairman of U. S. Steel" than talk to rank-and-file members.[84] AFL-CIO President Meany always seemed very comfortable playing golf with the fat cats at the exclusive Burning Tree Country Club. One would never have guessed that he once was a plumber.

Labor's leaders have come a long way since the day Joe Hill faced a firing squad. Their viewpoint and their goals have changed drastically. No longer do they want to raise the condition of all workers and make the nation more humane; now they seek mainly to solidify their position in the major industries, most of which long ago succumbed to the notion of the closed shop (an agreement between management and labor that requires workers to belong to the union). Labor leaders seek to secure their own power by making unions a more integral part

---

[81]Quoted in the *New York Times*. June 23, 1976.

[82]*Washington Post*, June 20, 1976.

[83]Dave Beck, Teamsters' President until 1957, when he went to jail for tax evasion, quoted in the *Washington Post*, June 20, 1974.

[84]*Newsweek*, May 10, 1976.

TABLE 5-1

UNION MEMBERSHIP IN MAJOR INDUSTRIES, 1975

INDUSTRY	NUMBER OF WORKERS	PRINCIPAL UNIONS
Representative major contracts	Total covered in contracts at left	
Petroleum refining (6 contracts)	25,000	Oil, chemical, atomic workers
Rail (master contract)	462,000	Locomotive Engineers, Maintenance of Way Employees, Railway Signalmen, United Transportation Union
Retail trade (food) (4 contracts)	86,000	Retail Clerks
Lumber (2 contracts)	43,000	Carpenters, Woodworkers
Construction (many local contracts)	750,000	Local building-trades unions
U.S. Postal Service (master contract)	605,000	American Postal Workers, Letter Carriers, Mail Handlers, Rural Letter Carriers
Apparel (3 contracts)	18,000	Amalgamated Clothing Workers, Garment Workers (ILGWU)
Apparel (1 contract)	103,000	Garment Workers (ILGWU)
Trucking (master contract)	450,000	Teamsters
Rubber (4 contracts)	68,000	Rubber Workers
Electrical equipment (2 contracts)	162,000	Electrical Workers (IUE), Electrical Workers (UE)
Auto (3 contracts)	705,000	United Auto Workers
Farm machinery (2 contracts)	59,000	United Auto Workers

SOURCE: Irwin Ross, "How to Tell When the Unions Will Be Tough," *Fortune*, July 1975, pp. 100–03, 151–56.

of the corporate economy. They are like pilot fish, perfectly happy to live off the shark. Typical of this trend was the Steelworkers' agreement not to strike for a given number of years in return for greater job security, and their further willingness to negotiate for a "lifetime employment" plan in return for further cooperation with management.[85] Such a plan would ultimately put labor officials and company officials on the same side of the bargaining table. It is not fate that does it, but the attitude of flesh-and-blood officials, grown fat and corrupt by

[85]*Wall Street Journal*, February 11, 1977.

wealth and power, like W. A. ("Tony") Boyle, former President of the United Mine Workers and later a resident of a federal penitentiary. During the years Boyle was head of the UMW, he did virtually nothing to force mine owners to make working conditions safer. Asked by a *Fortune* reporter why he took a hands-off attitude toward such a crucial issue, Boyle replied, "The UMWA will not abridge the rights of the mine operators in running the mines. We follow the judgment of the coal operators, right or wrong." *Fortune* accurately concluded that "the aims, interests and policies of the union and the companies [had become] inextricably intertwined. . . ."[86]

There is no question that the AFL-CIO has the best-trained lobby in Washington. Seven of its lobbyists meet every Monday morning with forty legislative representatives from member unions to map that week's lobbying assault on Capital Hill and the bureaucracy.[87] But the goals of the national labor lobby are as often probusiness as prolabor. With rare exceptions in recent years, unions have joined employers in asking Congress to give business relief from taxes and government regulations. The railroad brotherhoods have urged Congress to lend badly managed railroads more funds. Steelworkers have joined industry in demanding tariffs or quotas on steel imports. Auto workers' unions have supported car manufacturers in pleading for a delay of the emission-control deadlines. In turn, Big Business capitulates to most of Big Labor's wage demands, knowing that these can be passed along to the general (and largely unorganized) public in higher costs.

In short, if Big Labor has learned to sympathize with billion-dollar corporations, perhaps it is because Big Labor has become enormously rich. Its treasuries and pension funds themselves contain billions of dollars. Increasingly, Big Labor has forgotten what life is like at the bottom. It is no longer the underdog, and it is often noticeably unenthusiastic about pressuring government on behalf of the underdog. Noted B. J. Widick, a long-time observer of the labor movement,

To be sure, on paper and in legislative proposals before Congress, unions argue for social welfare programs, but the undeniable fact is that last spring [1975] . . . labor's most intense lobbying was spent on helping major industries like the auto industry. Social programs [aimed at helping the unemployed and unorganized poor, who make up one-fourth of the population] were pushed to the so-called "back burner."[88]

Join Forces for Jobs and Profit

Big Business and Big Labor, though still going through the ritual of being "enemy" pressure groups, quickly join forces when any outside pressure group, for whatever lofty motives, threatens to interfere with an established profit-and-pay pattern. They seem especially willing to join forces to fight environmentalists. In 1971, the Delaware legislature banned further development of heavy industry along the coastline to prevent fouling of the beaches and sea. Fighting the bill (but losing), and then seeking its repeal, were industrialists and Big Labor.[89]

These strange bedfellows merged classically in the "bottle and can battle." Since the late 1960s, environmentalists had been trying, with little success, to pass city, state, and federal legislation prohibiting throwaways and requiring deposits on soft-drink and beer containers. Groups favoring the legislation argued that the national energy waste attributable to throwaway beverage containers was equal to 10 million tons of coal per year, that consumers in the United States were paying 30 percent more for beverages in throwaway containers than in returnable-refillable glass bottles, and that a ban on throwaways would vastly reduce litter, for more than 60 billion no-deposit beverage containers are thrown away each year. Oregon, where the first state law requiring deposits was passed in 1972, reported that the switch from nonreturnable containers was saving the state $657,000 annually in litter collection.

Industry and labor, however, opposed the legislation. Their alliance, tight and powerful,

---

[86] Quoted in Thomas O'Hanlon, "Anarchy Threatens the Kingdom of Coal," *Fortune*, January 1971.

[87] *Washington Post*, June 29, 1975.

[88] *Nation*, September 6, 1975.

[89] Betty D. Hawkins, "Cities and the Environmental Crisis," in Melvin I. Urofsky, ed., *Perspectives on Urban America* (New York: Doubleday & Co., Anchor Press, 1973), p. 182.

included the United Steelworkers, the Glass Bottle Blowers Association, the National Soft Drink Association, and the U.S. Brewers Association. They feared the loss of profits and jobs. Because they had superior lobbying tactics and more money, the labor and industry alliance won. Between 1970 and 1975 there were seven state and local referendums on deposit legislation, and the Big Business-Big Labor team won them all. A typical encounter occurred in Dade County, Florida. Forty civic groups, led by the environmentalists, raised a total of $1,741 for propaganda to get voters to back the referendum. The opposition raised more than $180,000 —cleverly solicited in the name of the "Dade Consumer Information Committee"—and splurged it on everything from airplanes dragging streamers to signs on supermarket pushcarts. The environmentalists didn't have a chance.[90]

When special interests that have been at odds for a long time come to terms, adjust contentedly to each other's strengths, and settle into a pragmatic armistice, then some spectators of the political process suspect that either one side or the other has sold out or turned spineless. That, of course, is always a possibility. But an interest group does not take a lifetime vow to pursue one course, no matter how circumstances may change. Any intelligent interest group is constantly reappraising its position in the light of new developments. If, for example, labor seems unusually chummy with industry, considering their historical animosities, perhaps it is not entirely that labor's leaders have grown fat and slothful. Perhaps they recognize that the incredibly complex interrelatedness of society today has made the militancy of labor circa 1930 as antiquated as the greed of industry circa 1900.

Everywhere—in finance, industry, labor, politics, religion, professional sports, education, and sex—new relationships are developing so swiftly that those involved are sometimes uncertain where exactly their legitimate interests lie. If, in the midst of chaos, they need comfort, let it come with this realization: As vital as selfish conflicts are to the strength of a democracy, there is something even more important. Schattschneider describes it in this way:

> The diet on which the American leviathan feeds is something more than a jungle of disparate special interests. In the literature of democratic theory the body of common agreement found in the community is known as the "consensus" without which it is believed that no democratic system can survive. The reality of the common interest is suggested by demonstrated capacity of the community to survive. There must be something that holds people together.[91]

---

[90]*Washington Post,* June 30, 1975; July 1, 1975. Environmentalists themselves have shown a willingness to make strange alliances for profit. In 1975, a *Los Angeles Times* reporter discovered that, for instance: the Audubon Society leased part of its largest wildlife sanctuary to Cities Service for oil and gas exploitation and was earning about $300,000 a year from that partnership; the Sierra Club owned stocks and bonds in the Exxon Corporation—holder of 25 percent interest in the Alaska pipeline—as well as stock interests in strip-mining firms, pulp-mill operations, and utility companies, all sinners in the eyes of environmentalists. In pressure politics, even the bitterest enemies turn out to be economic Siamese twins, joined at the buck. (*Congressional Record,* E4180, July 28, 1975.)

[91]Schattschneider, *The Semisovereign People,* p. 23.

Summary

1. Pressure politics is the attempt to influence legislation at various levels of government on behalf of large and small factions of citizens who are motivated by special interests—interests not shared by the nation as a whole.

2. The political activities of special interest groups are justified constitutionally by the First Amendment's guarantee of the right "to petition the Government for a redress of grievances."

3. Pressure groups, or lobbies, come in all sizes and motivations. Important categories of interests are: education, labor, senior citizens, rural and farm, women, consumers, liberal, environmental, business, conservative, and ethnic and race.

4. Lobbying began as an informal "buttonholing" of legislators in the hallways of Congress, but has grown into a mammoth industry employing thousands of lobbyists who spend an estimated $1 billion every year.

5. The distinction between pressure groups representing private interests and those representing public interests rests on the difference between exclusive and nonexclusive benefits, not on any judgment of the worthiness of the groups' motives. Pressure politics can be judged sensibly only by its results in a democracy.

6. Interest groups are more likely to be successful if they are tightly organized and if they are able to coerce or buy their members' participation in some way. Such organizations are generally led by a small elite of professionals, who maintain their control more or less permanently.

7. Among the largest, most complicated lobbies are the military-industrial lobby, the highway lobby, the American Medical Association, and the National Rifle Association.

8. Lobbying performs a service to legislators and bureaucrats in providing contacts with citizens. Lobbyists commonly do the legislators' homework for them by researching complex questions, and, in addition, they provide a whole range of favors and other compensations. Lobbyists undertake vast propaganda campaigns to win the backing of the general populace (grass-roots support).

9. Money is essential to successful lobbying—for recruiting campaign workers, for propaganda, and for educational programs. Lobbies lacking in money must compensate for it with more intense human effort and persistence, the strong point of the public interest groups.

10. With the proliferation of regulatory and administrative agencies and the resulting flood of intricate rules and statutes, the right lawyer has become an important key to success in pressure politics. Interest groups pay about $300 million a year to Washington law firms.

11. Lobbyists with contacts in high places are particularly effective. The right friends, the right publicity, and government-agency experience are valuable assets to a lobbyist.

12. Lobbying has gone through periods of more or less overt corruption. To control it, the Federal Regulation of Lobbying Act was passed in 1946. It requires lobbies to register with Congress and to report how much money they receive and spend, but contains so many loopholes that it is virtually useless. For example, it does not regulate grass-roots lobbying or lobbying of the executive branch or the bureaucracy.

13. The most successful of the opposing lobbies eventually come to resemble and complement each other. The best example of this is the merging of the interests of Big Business and Big Labor over the past century.

Additional Reading

James Madison, in *The Federalist Papers,* Number 10 (Alexander Hamilton, James Madison, and John Jay; ed., Clinton Rossiter; New York: Times Mirror Co., New American Library, 1961) argues that the interplay of diverse interests is the best protection against tyranny by any particular faction. A similar theme of balancing interests runs through pluralist group theories, such as David B. Truman's *The Governmental Process: Political Interests and Public Opinion* (New York: Random House, Alfred A. Knopf, 1951).

A quite different argument, that American politics is dominated by certain special interest groups—especially those of Big Business—can be found in C. Wright Mills, *The Power Elite* (New York: Oxford University Press, 1956); E. E. Schattschneider, *The Semisovereign People: A Realist's View of Democracy in America* (New York: Holt, Rinehart & Winston, Dryden Press, 1975); Grant McConnell, *Private Power and American Democracy* (New York: Random House, Vintage Books, 1970); Murray Edelman, *The Symbolic Uses of Politics* (Urbana, Ill.: The University of Illinois Press, 1967); and Theodore J. Lowi, *The End of Liberalism* (New York: W. W. Norton & Co., 1969).

The structure and workings of organized interests are analyzed in Truman, *The Governmental Process,* and in James Q. Wilson, *Political Organizations* (New York: Basic Books, 1973). L. Harmon Ziegler and G. Wayne Peak, *Interest Groups in American Society,* 2nd ed. (Englewood Cliffs, N.J.: Prentice-Hall, 1972), and the Congressional Quarterly Service, *The Washington Lobby,* 2nd ed. (Washington, D.C., 1974) describe the most active groups; particular groups are also analyzed from time to time in the *National Journal.*

Mancur Olson, Jr., *The Logic of Collective Action: Public Goods and the Theory of Groups,* rev. ed. (Cambridge, Mass.: Harvard University Press, 1971), offers a theory of how and why groups form, contending that some interests are left unrepresented.

The only way that democracy can be made bearable is by developing and cherishing a class of men sufficiently honest and disinterested to challenge the prevailing quacks. No such class has ever appeared in strength in the United States. Thus the business of harassing the quacks devolves upon the newspapers. When they fail in their duty, which is usually, we are at the quacks' mercy.

H. L. Mencken

6

PUBLIC OPINION AND POLITICAL INFORMATION

More than anything else, governing and being governed in a democracy is a process of communication. The public is constantly trying to tell the politicians and bureaucrats what is on its mind, and the politicians and bureaucrats are constantly trying to find out how they can please the electorate and stay in office. They are also constantly trying to sell the public on what they think it *should* want (which usually means what the government is willing to supply). In short, in a democracy, public opinion—what the people think and what they feel—matters. If the people are ill-informed or misinformed, if they are angry or viciously prejudiced, if they are compassionate and tolerant, it will be imprinted on the way the government operates.

It is important, then, to know something about the shape of American public opinion. How is it formed? How does it change? What are its major dimensions? How is it measured? Is it informed? Where does the information come from? And how reliable is it? These are some of the questions that this chapter will try to answer. Along the way, it will become clear that, although there are many imperfections and biases in the system of providing it, the information available to citizens is more plentiful and more accurate than ever before.

THE SHAPING
OF AMERICAN PUBLIC OPINION

Political attitudes are constructed partly from reason, but in larger part from emotions. They evolve from an interplay of propaganda, persuasion, reason, and information. Political opinions begin at home, where children usually learn to love their country and respect its leader. As Robert E. Lane and David O. Sears point out, this positive, uncritical view is based not on information but on emotional grounds.[1] As children grow to identify with various groups—religious, ethnic, racial, and so forth—they learn some partisan opinions, generally those of their parents. It is from our families that we first learn to identify with a particular party.

Children acquire a positive view of government in their early school years. Then a big spurt of political education takes place between grades seven and nine, when they learn how government applies to the community in addition to themselves.[2] Exposed to more information and different viewpoints, high-school students start to have opinions of their own that may differ from their parents'. According to Lane and Sears, education generally makes a person more tolerant of other ideas, more in favor of civil liberties and civil rights, less authoritarian and prejudiced, and more aware of his or her own political effectiveness and participation—in all, education makes one a more political being.[3] As students expand their circle of acquaintances, they tend to identify themselves with a particular class and caste—a peer group from which the individual hopes to obtain recognition and approval. The influence of the peer group is powerful; it may reinforce the old family and school viewpoints—or it may encourage a rebellious attitude toward the politics of parents and teachers.

In other words, adults are politically influenced by the social group they move in. They may begin to experience a conflict between their ideologies and their party labels—for example, if they move into a higher class but still retain the social-welfare ideology of the lower class. But as people settle into their life styles, their opinions become more and more congenial with those of others in their social environment.

There is, of course, not "one" public opinion; there is a great range of opinion on just about any issue. There are, however, subjects of general agreement among Americans—issues on which a majority may coincide, even though there will be extremes at both ends. By pulling together what appear to be "typical" attitudes, one can fairly say that most Americans favor domestic social welfare programs, such as aid to education, unemployment compensation, and social security, but feel uneasy about welfare and guaranteed income. (Figure 6-1 shows poll results indicating that public support of the national welfare system depends upon the program.) Americans are not racist in the sense that they hate or despise persons of minority races, but they are made nervous and irritable, mostly for social-class reasons, when confronted with forced housing integration and school busing. They develop a tolerance for civil rights, over a period of time, but have considerable distaste for demonstrations, even peaceful ones. They strongly support "law and order," including harsh treatment of blue-collar criminals, but they are strangely tolerant of big corporations that rob them "legally." They abhor foreign military action almost anywhere, but loudly applaud it when it has been successful.[4]

The average United States citizen has strong opinions about government performance, particularly in the economic sphere, and about the personality of leaders, preferring them strong, warm, and decisive. There can be little doubt that most Americans support capitalism, free enterprise, individual initiative, and "representative" government with two-party elections and oppose any schemes to redistribute wealth by radical means like really soaking the rich or nationalizing production.

---

[1]"Information follows evaluation, rather than preceding it, in the course of the child's development." (Robert E. Lane and David O. Sears, *Public Opinion*, Englewood Cliffs, N. J.: Prentice-Hall, 1964, p. 19.)

[2]Robert S. Erikson and Norman R. Luttbeg, *American Public Opinion: Its Origins, Content and Impact* (New York: John Wiley & Sons, 1973), p. 129.

[3]Lane and Sears, *Public Opinion*, p. 26.

[4]Erikson and Luttbeg, *American Public Opinion*, pp. 41–54.

FIGURE 6-1 AMERICANS' ATTITUDES TOWARD WELFARE, 1977

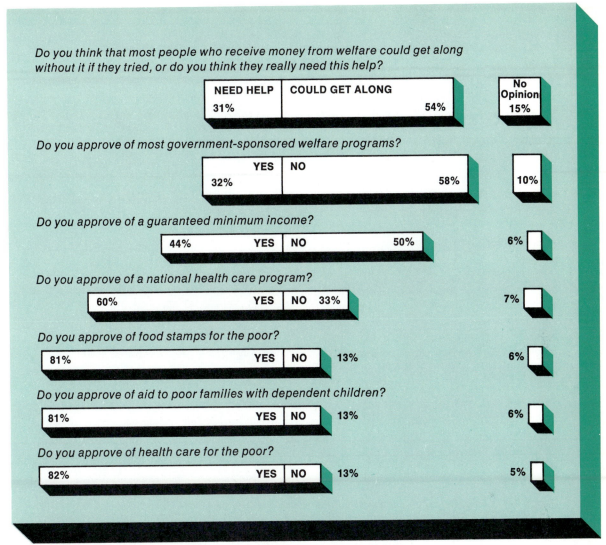

Do you think that most people who receive money from welfare could get along without it if they tried, or do you think they really need this help?

NEED HELP	COULD GET ALONG		No Opinion
31%		54%	15%

Do you approve of most government-sponsored welfare programs?

	YES	NO	
32%		58%	10%

Do you approve of a guaranteed minimum income?

YES	NO	
44%	50%	6%

Do you approve of a national health care program?

YES	NO	
60%	33%	7%

Do you approve of food stamps for the poor?

YES	NO	
81%	13%	6%

Do you approve of aid to poor families with dependent children?

YES	NO	
81%	13%	6%

Do you approve of health care for the poor?

YES	NO	
82%	13%	5%

SOURCE: New York Times CBS News Poll, *New York Times*, August 3, 1977.

In spite of these broad areas of accord, all is not harmony in the United States. In recent years, there has been an enormous increase in public expressions of cynicism, distrust, and distaste for politicians as a result of Vietnam and Watergate. Politicians and bureaucrats cannot afford to ignore these popular mutterings. One would think that men and women smart enough to be elected and appointed to top government positions would know that. But success some-

times breeds arrogance. For a long time, politicians and bureaucrats ignored the people's increasing complaints about Big Government, even though disenchantment was clearly written in the polls. (See Tables 6-1 and 6-2.) By the mid-1970s, the public had become so testy about federal officials' indifference and waste that the politicians and bureaucrats felt threatened; they began to assume a very low profile and sound more modest. Ironically, the leading presidential

TABLE 6-1

DECLINE OF POPULAR TRUST IN GOVERNMENT: SURVEY RESPONSES, 1964–1970   (percentage)

Q. How much of the time do you think you can *trust* the government in Washington to do what is right—*just about always, most of the time,* or *only some of the time?*

RESPONSE	1964	1966	1968	1970
Always	14.0	17.0	7.5	6.4
Most of the time	62.0	48.0	53.4	47.1
Only some of the time*	22.0	31.0	37.0	44.2
Don't know	2.0	4.0†	2.1	2.3

Q. Would you say the government is pretty much run by a *few big interests* looking out for themselves or that it is run for the *benefit of all* the people?

RESPONSE	1964	1966	1968	1970
For benefit of all	64.0	53.0	51.8	40.6
Few big interests*	29.0	34.0	39.2	49.6
Other; depends; both checked	4.0	6.0	4.6	5.0
Don't know	3.0	7.0	4.3	4.8

Q. Do you think that people in the government waste *a lot* of the money we pay in taxes, waste *some* of it, or *don't waste very much of it?*‡

RESPONSE	1964	1966	1968	1970
Not much	6.5		4.2	3.7
Some	44.5		33.1	26.1
A lot*	46.3		57.4	68.7
Don't know; not ascertained	2.7		5.3	1.5

Q. Do you feel that almost all of the people running the government are smart people who usually *know what they are doing* or do you think that quite a few of them *don't seem to know what they are doing?*‡

RESPONSE	1964	1966	1968	1970
Know what they're doing	68.2		56.2	51.2
Don't know what they're doing*	27.4		36.1	44.1
Other; depends	1.9		1.8	2.3
Don't know; not ascertained	2.5		5.9	2.4

*Indicates response interpreted as *cynical.*
†Includes 1 percent coded *it depends.*
‡These items were not included in the 1966 election study interview schedule.

SOURCE: Arthur H. Miller, "Political Issues and Trust in Government: 1964–1970," *American Political Science Review* 68 (September 1974): 953. The data were compiled by the University of Michigan Survey Research Center.

TABLE 6-2

HARRIS POLL RESULTS ON CYNICISM, 1966–1973
(percentage)

	1971	1973
Q. Do you agree or disagree with the statement that "most men go into public office to help others?"		
A. Agree	80	38

	1966	1968	1971	1972	1973
Q. Do you tend to feel or not tend to feel that:					
—the rich get richer and the poor get poorer?					
A. Yes	45	54	62	68	76
—what you think doesn't count much anymore?					
A. Yes	37	42	44	53	61
—people running the country don't really care what happens to you?					
A. Yes	26	36	41	50	55

SOURCE: *Washington Post*, December 9, 1973.

candidates of both parties in 1976 tried to outdo each other at sounding antigovernment.

Public opinion can force such a change, superficially at least. That is why politicians, who have found that the easiest way to live comfortably is to blow with the public wind, are constantly testing the currents with public-opinion polls. The sensitivity of politicians to these polls reached its apogee in President Lyndon B. Johnson, who usually had a half-dozen polls in his pocket and referred to them with remarks like, "The Negro costs me fifteen points in the polls and Vietnam costs me twenty."[5]

[5]Kenneth O'Donnell, "LBJ and the Kennedys," *Life*, August 7, 1970.

MEASURING PUBLIC OPINION

The science of public-opinion sampling is relatively new. The best-known polls, conducted by the American Institute of Public Opinion (called the Gallup poll after its founder, the pioneer pollster George H. Gallup), did not come into existence until 1935. The second-best-known polls are conducted by Louis Harris, who entered the business of public-opinion research in 1947, when he joined Elmo Roper, another early pollster. Harris set up his own firm in 1956, and he became a syndicated columnist-pollster in 1963.

From the beginning, polls and pollsters have had a mixed reception. In 1935, a bill was introduced in Congress to stop the "vicious practice" of taking opinion surveys.[6] Now opinion surveying is thoroughly respected—and probably too much trusted. Some people rate it as a science, but there are persuasive critics who take a contrary view. Michael Wheeler writes:

> Pollsters have been able to insulate themselves from criticism by constructing a barricade of statistical and scientific jargon. "Cross-tabulation," "area random sampling," "flow-coding"—their language sounds so technical, so formidable that most of us are intimidated into believing that we are not qualified to judge whether public opinion polling is a legitimate science.
>
> To the same end, many pollsters affect the same pretensions assumed by faith healers, astrologers, and other quacks: it is *Dr.* Gallup's American *Institute* of Public Opinion in *Princeton*, New Jersey. New polling firms spring up right and left, and each one seems to be called Survey Research Associates or some such name which conjures up images of white-jacketed computer technicians poring over print-outs.
>
> If polling is a science, however, it is at best a crude one. . . .[7]

Wheeler cites a number of polls in which the interviewees were hassled and their responses were changed or, in a few instances, falsified.

Another potent critic of opinion polling, Seymour Martin Lipset, joins Wheeler and others in arguing that most important issues cannot be boiled down to a simple yes or no answer, that there are too many variables and that the public's response is too complex for snappy packaging in polls. Lipset points out that over a four-month period, three of the most reputable polling organizations—Gallup, Harris, and Yankelovich—got responses of 66 percent, 45 percent, 31 percent, 28 percent, 16 percent, and 54 percent in favor of "sending or selling arms and/or troops to aid Israel." How could a government build its foreign policy around such wildly erratic responses? To make things all the more confused, midway through all this polling, another Harris survey found the public *opposed* to "sell-

ing military equipment to [all] nations" by 53 percent to 35 percent.[8] "Most issues are quite complicated and require a number of questions to explore the nature of the views held," Lipset reminds us. "Many questions asked of people deal with matters of little concern to them; they often know little and care less, yet they answer the questions."[9]

Despite justified criticism, however, polling is thriving. A thousand commercial concerns, plus government agencies, universities, and newspapers are pursuing the public in quest of its opinions on everything from deodorants to detente.

How to Construct a Useful Poll

Above all, a successful poll must be a representative cross-sectional sampling. To achieve this characteristic, pollsters painstakingly select their samples at random. "Random" selection is anything but accidental selection; it is random only in the sense that the pollster does not base the selection on anything but numbers. To make a national poll, for example, a pollster may send interviewers to 1 out of every 100 political districts and into 1 out of every 150 homes in that district, where they will interview every third person in the household. Pollsters do not worry about the geography, about the financial status of the districts and the homes they go to, or about the race or professional or educational background of those who are interviewed—those things will take care of themselves, so long as they stick to the numerical randomness that they decided on at the beginning of the poll. The end result is that every adult in the nation has had the same chance of being selected, which is the kind of precise randomness that gives modern polling an uncanny accuracy.

It is uncanny—at least it is to laymen—because to conduct a national poll that will have a good chance of being accurate within three percentage points, an expert pollster need interview only about fifteen hundred persons. That's the size sampling that the typical Gallup poll deals

[6]Daniel J. Boorstin, *The Decline of Radicalism: Reflections on America Today* (New York: Random House, 1969), p. 113.

[7]Michael Wheeler, *Lies, Damn Lies and Statistics* (New York: Liveright, 1976).

[8]Seymour Martin Lipset, "The Wavering Polls," *Public Interest* 43 (Spring 1976): 80.

[9]Lipset, p. 87.

with. It has been found that adding another hundred or another thousand persons does not improve the accuracy much. Gallup has explained the principle of random sampling in this way: "When a housewife wants to taste the quality of the soup she is making she tastes only a teaspoonful or two. She knows that if the soup is thoroughly stirred, one teaspoonful is enough to tell her whether she has the right mixture of ingredients."[10]

The key is mixture, not quantity. The most celebrated (and embarrassing) proof of this point occurred in 1936. The *Literary Digest* mailed over 10 million sample post-card ballots to voters and received 2,376,523 responses—an enormous poll, from which the *Digest* predicted the 1936 national election. It underestimated the vote for Franklin D. Roosevelt by 19.3 percent and actually predicted that Roosevelt's opponent, Alfred M. Landon, would win! That still stands as the biggest goof ever committed by a supposedly reputable poll. How did the *Digest* go wrong? It got the names from telephone directories and lists of people who owned automobiles. 1936 was the very pit of the Great Depression, and the people who could afford telephones and who owned automobiles were generally at the upper end of the economic scale. Thus, the poll did not represent a true cross section of the electorate. It was not built on random selection; it was built on economic selection. Consequently, it failed miserably—so miserably, in fact, that the public laughed the *Digest* out of existence.[11]

Aside from being a random selection, a poll, to be accurate, must be conducted at the right time. It must not be conducted while the public is still making up its mind; enough time must be allowed for opinion to settle in.

The Tet Offensive in February and March 1968, was one of the most brutal engagements of the Vietnam war. The enemy poured into South Vietnam, and our troops paid a terrible price in holding them off. Ultimately, the slaughter of the Tet Offensive started a majority of the public thinking seriously about getting the United States out of Vietnam. But a Gallup poll taken right after the offensive began seemed to indicate that, in fact, the public wanted to plunge in deeper. Two experts in opinion sampling, Charles W. Roll, Jr., and Albert H. Cantril, cite that Gallup poll as evidence that there is great danger in "rushing ahead with a survey before opinion has begun to jell in a stabilized way. A public official would have been seriously misled had he allowed the February poll results to guide him in any way."[12] Table 6-3 shows the "jelling" of opinion on Vietnam.

Of course, pollsters cannot wait for public opinion to settle when they are testing it during political campaigns. In such periods, the public mind is in a constant boil; and taking a survey of it is like trying to read the fine print on a map while driving over a bumpy road. A Gallup poll of Republicans and independents in October 1975 showed Gerald R. Ford leading Ronald Reagan 48 percent to 25 percent; a month later, Gallup found Reagan leading Ford 40 to 32 percent; shortly thereafter, the roller coaster reversed itself again.[13]

A poll must also be narrowly focused to be of any guidance. During the Vietnam war it was not enough to ask people if they were hawks or doves. Many supposed hawks were hawks only for all-out war; if the United States was only going to wage a limited war, then they saw no reason for being in Vietnam at all and favored withdrawing. In short, if offered only a limited war, they were doves.

The wording of a question has a crucial effect on the results of a poll. Milton Rosenberg, Sidney Verba, and Philip E. Converse make this point:

Many of the people whom the pollster questions do not have very well-formed and deeply held opinions on the matters about which a pollster is

---

[10]George H. Gallup, *The Sophisticated Poll Watcher's Guide* (Princeton, N.J.: Princeton Opinion Press, 1972), p. 46.

[11]Gallup, pp. 64–65. Not that Gallup and his cross-section experts are always right. They predicted that Thomas E. Dewey, the Republican presidential nominee, would win in 1948; instead, Harry S Truman won. But that was an extremely tight race, and pollsters do not pretend surgical precision.

[12]Charles W. Roll, Jr., and Albert H. Cantril, *Polls: Their Use and Misuse in Politics* (New York: Basic Books, 1972), p. 118.

[13]*New York Times*, December 12, 1975.

TABLE 6-3

TREND ON HAWK-DOVE IDENTIFICATION, 1967–1968

DATES OF INTERVIEWING	PERCENTAGE OF PEOPLE DESCRIBING THEMSELVES AS:		
	HAWK	DOVE	NO OPINION
December 9–13, 1967	52	35	13
Tet Offensive (January 31–March 31)			
February 3–7, 1968	61	23	16
March 16–20, 1968	41	42	17
October 1968	44	42	14
End of All Bombing of North Vietnam			
Mid-November 1968	31	55	14

SOURCE: Charles W. Roll, Jr., and Albert H. Cantril, *Polls: Their Use and Misuse in Politics* (New York: Basic Books, 1972).

asking. They are likely to be responding to a question to which they have not given much or any previous thought. What this means is that the wording of the question makes a big difference in how they reply. It also means that the answers that any individual gives can possibly change from day to day. If an individual has not given serious thought to a question, his answer is likely to be offhand. If the pollsters were to come back the next day, a somewhat different answer would be obtained. . . . If a question is asked in which negative symbols are associated with withdrawal from the war, people sound quite "hawkish" in their responses. Thus, people reject "defeat," "Communist take-overs," and "the loss of American credibility." On the other hand, if negative symbols are associated with a pro-war position, the American public will sound "dovish." They reject "killings," "continuing the war," and "domestic costs." Turning the matter upside down, we see the same thing. If positive symbols are associated with the war, the American public sounds "hawkish." They support "American prestige," "defense of democracy," and "support for our soldiers in Vietnam." On the other hand, if positive symbols are associated with "dovish" positions, the people sound "dovish." They come out in support of "peace," "worrying about our own problems before we worry about the problems of other people," and "saving American lives."

Thus it is possible, even in the same poll, to have the American public sounding like hawks and doves at the same time. . . .[14]

Interpreting Polls

There are two different kinds of interpreters of polls. One is the political pollster who interprets from a short-term, practical perspective during campaigns. For example, the pollster wants to know how the candidate's chances are looking in, say, Massachusetts. What issues that are important to the voter should his or her candidate be stressing? (See Chapter 8.) The

[14]Milton Rosenberg, Sidney Verba, and Philip E. Converse, *Vietnam and the Silent Majority: The Dove's Guide* (Gloucester, Mass.: Peter Smith, n.d.), quoted in Lipset, "The Wavering Polls," p. 85.

other kind of interpreter examines opinion polls from an academic or theoretical point of view to ascertain trends and shifts, to knock down old theories, or to construct new ones, for example. This kind of interpreter looks at citizen consciousness and the political system from a long-term perspective.

Public opinion is not always easy to figure out, no matter who's doing the interpreting. It speaks clearly only when approached in the right way. L. L. L. Golden accurately diagnoses the problem:

> Not even the best opinion pollsters know what the public is thinking at certain times, and pollsters are the first to admit that many people polled do not reveal their innermost thoughts. In addition, what the public thinks in a hypothetical case will not always be the same as in a real situation.[15]

Pollsters have shown this many times. One of the first famous illustrations was developed by the Gallup poll in 1940. A cross section of Americans was first asked, "Do you believe in freedom of speech?" Ninety-seven percent answered Yes. Only 1 percent answered No. (Two percent answered that they didn't know.) But then the 97 percent who had said they believed in freedom of speech were asked, "Do you believe in it to the extent of allowing fascists and communists to hold meetings and express their views in this community?" Suddenly their belief melted. Only 22 percent said Yes (and only 4 percent said they felt *strongly* that such groups should be allowed to hold meetings). Seventy percent said No (and 48 percent felt *strongly* that communists and fascists should be denied free speech).[16]

In the late 1950s, a sample of voters of Ann Arbor, Michigan, and Tallahassee, Florida, were asked if they agreed with these statements: "Democracy is the best form of government." "Public officials should be chosen by majority vote." "Every citizen should have an equal chance to influence government policy." "People in the minority should be free to win majority support for their opinions." These pretty Fourth-of-July-style declarations were very popular; between 95 and 98 percent of all the voters polled said they heartily believed in them.

But when the pollsters got down to specifics, the results changed dramatically. About four-fifths of the voters polled in the two cities said they also approved of the statement, "In a city referendum deciding on a tax-supported undertaking, only taxpayers should be allowed to vote." About a third were opposed to permitting an antireligion speech to be given in their city. And two-fifths of the Tallahassee voters and one-fifth of the Ann Arbor voters went along with the statement, "A Negro should not be allowed to run for mayor of this city."[17]

What do such contradictions indicate? For one thing, they mean that people think on two levels—the ideal and the practical. In an ideal situation, all things being equal, they believe in freedom of speech; but when freedom of speech intrudes upon their lives in such a way that they are made uneasy or fearful, then they are willing to curtail their principles for practical comfort. For that reason, political leaders know that public-opinion polls cannot always be taken at face value. The problem is to guess what they really mean if they don't mean what they seem to be saying.

Conflicting responses might also be simply a reflection of the political environment. For twenty years, American leaders lectured their fellow citizens about free speech while at the same time they were denying that right to "communists" through passage of such repressive legislation as the Smith Act.[18]

HOW INFORMED IS THE PUBLIC?

Polls are like computers: they are accurate only if the right material is fed into them. And public opinion is ultimately useful to the democratic process only if it is well-informed. If the public doesn't understand what is going on in the

---

[15]L. L. L. Golden, *Only by Public Consent* (New York: Hawthorne Books, 1968), p. 4.

[16]Hadley Cantril and Mildred Strunk, eds., *Public Opinion, 1935–1946* (Princeton, N.J.: Princeton University Press, 1951), p. 245.

[17]James W. Prothro and Charles M. Grigg, "Fundamental Principles of Democracy: Bases of Agreement and Disagreement," *Journal of Politics* 22 (May 1960): 276–94.

[18]See the section on The Communist Threat in Chapter 3.

"Your opinions are every bit as salty as his, dear, but Truman was, after all, the President, while you're more or less just a crank."

nation and in the world, it can hardly be expected to give an educated guess as to how national and world problems should be solved.

Pollsters and analysts point to signs that the public is pretty dumb. Roll and Cantril report that in one of the larger eastern industrial states, where one might expect that matters pertaining to union contracts would be common talk, only one person in five knew the correct meaning of the right-to-work law.[19] Seymour Martin Lipset comments:

> A study of attitudes toward the John Birch Society in the 1960's found that when those with opinions

about the organization were also asked whether they thought it was a leftist or rightist group, one third of them described the Birch society as leftist! . . . What is one to make of the fact that, in a 1974 survey, over a third of those who said they preferred George Wallace to Richard Nixon or George McGovern agreed with the item, "I would not vote for a right-winger"?[20]

Pollster Louis Harris told a Senate committee that although 89 percent of people could correctly name their own state governors, only 59 percent could name one United States senator from their state, only 39 percent could name both senators, and only 46 percent really knew who

---

[19]Roll and Cantril, *Polls*, pp. 129–31.

[20]Lipset, "The Wavering Polls," p. 87.

their member of the House was. Harris concluded that people might know even less about the details of legislation or foreign policy.[21] Senator Harrison A. Williams, Jr., of New Jersey, having served without distinction for twenty-two years in Congress, discovered in a preelection poll, in 1976, that only 13 percent of his constituents had ever heard of him. Nevertheless, he was reelected easily.

The National Assessment of Educational Progress showed that only 44 percent of Americans between the ages of twenty-six and thirty-five knew how to use a ballot, and only 60 percent knew how presidential candidates are nominated.[22] It also found that, although they were within a year of being eligible to vote, 47 percent of the country's seventeen-year-olds did not know the basic fact that each state has two United States senators. One of every eight seventeen-year-olds believed that the President is not required to obey the law, and one of every two believed that the President can appoint members of Congress.[23]

Polls that do not take the public's basic political ignorance into consideration can ask some pretty stupid questions and result in some pretty useless responses. In early 1977, for example, a Harris poll asked this question: "As you know, in the new Congress, new leadership is taking over. In the House of Representatives, the new Speaker will be Rep. Thomas P. (Tip) O'Neill. What kind of a job do you think Speaker O'Neill will do—excellent, pretty good, only fair or poor?" In a nation where less than half the electorate can name their own representatives in Congress, how many people can be expected ever to have heard of "Tip" O'Neill—and what possible significance can there be in the fact that 42 percent thought that he would do a good job?[24]

The typing of the voter as contentedly uninformed had its scholarly beginnings in the 1950s in a famous study entitled *The American Voter,* by Angus Campbell, Philip E. Converse, Warren E. Miller, and Donald E. Stokes. These four authors studied the American electorate as seen in the 1956 presidential election, supplemented by a study of the 1952 presidential election, and the 1958 congressional election. The cross-sectional portrait they drew was of a voter who took little interest in politics, knew virtually nothing about the major issues of the day, had only token loyalty (if any) to a political party, and was vastly unaware of what elected officials were doing, or not doing. Their summation:

> We have, then, the portrait of an electorate almost wholly without detailed information about decision making in government. A substantial portion of the public is able to respond in a discrete manner to issues that *might* be the subject of legislative or administrative action. Yet it knows little about what government has done on these issues or what the parties propose to do. It is almost completely unable to judge the rationality of government actions.[25]

Admittedly, to some extent the stereotype of the ignorant voter is justified, just as the stereotype of the ignorant politician is justified. Considering the awesome responsibilities placed on both voters and elected officials, the preparaton both undergo is usually unforgivably haphazard and casual. But the stereotype should be put in perspective. When the public is either fuzzy on important social issues or downright ignorant of them, it is usually for one of several very good reasons. One reason, the least defensible, is that voters are ignorant by their own choice. Although they are not nearly so happily stupid as politicians and some political scientists have thought them to be,[26] voters do typically prefer to avoid the hard choices and unpleasant reali-

---

[21]Louis Harris, in testimony before the Senate Subcommittee on Intergovernmental Relations, 1973.

[22]*Parade,* January 27, 1974. In 1975, with the nation's Bicentennial celebration already underway, a Gallup poll showed that 28 percent of the public could not identify what important event occurred in this country in 1776. (*New York Times,* November 30, 1975.)

[23]New York Times News Service, January 2, 1977.

[24]Harris poll, released January 10, 1977.

---

[25]Angus Campbell, Philip E. Converse, Warren E. Miller, and Donald E. Stokes, *The American Voter: An Abridgement* (New York: John Wiley & Sons, 1964), p. 543.

[26]An attitude perfectly illustrated by the reelection pitch of Senator Joseph M. Montoya, Democrat of New Mexico: "We've heard a lot of rhetoric in this campaign. The people want to get back to Kojak and the football games. At least I'm looking forward to that myself." (Quoted in the *New York Times,* October 23, 1976.) Montoya lost.

ties of politics. In July 1974, for example, only one month before Nixon resigned to avoid being impeached, a Harris poll discovered that most voters felt that the press had given too much attention to uncovering details of the most corrupt and dangerous administration in the nation's history. Too much truth was beginning to make the voters nervous.[27]

A more reasonable cause for the public's political ignorance is that many voters lack a conviction that their participation and their votes really matter. Preoccupied with more immediate needs (like earning a living), few people have the time or motivation to take part in politics simply out of a sense of civic duty or for the fun of it. Most people who do take part are motivated by selfish interests. They give money to candidates, learn about the issues, take time to vote, and so forth, because they feel that by doing so they can improve the tone and economy of their lives. Before taking part, they study the odds. They ask themselves: What reward do I stand to receive if I invest X amount of time and money in politics? The less reward they see, the less they will invest. If they don't think their vote will count for much one way or the other, or if they feel that the system is rigged against the average person, they will not be inclined to read up on the candidates and to cast an informed vote. Some students of political behavior would agree with Anthony Downs that,

> In general, it is irrational to be politically well-informed because the low returns from data simply do not justify their cost in time and other scarce resources. Therefore many voters do not bother to discover their true views before voting, and most citizens are not well enough informed to influence directly the formulation of those policies that affect them.[28]

Another reason the public does not trouble to inform itself may be that there are not any issues that it is greatly concerned with. Take this study as an example:

> When Samuel Stouffer, at the height of the McCarthy era [1950–54] asked a sample of the American public about what it was that worried them, he

found that most people responded with concerns from their personal and daily lives: their jobs, their families, their health. Relatively few (about 15 percent) mentioned things that could be thought of as involving the public issues of the day, and almost no one (about 1 percent) mentioned domestic communism. . . . In retrospect the result seems obvious. Of course people are likely to worry about job, family, and health, but at the time it seemed somewhat surprising. The issue of loyalty and security dominated the media and dominated the conversations of those with deep concern for politics—journalists, scholars, government officials. It would have been perfectly reasonable to expect, extrapolating from the media attention and from the dominant concerns of the most politically sophisticated and concerned citizens, that the average American did indeed check for communists under his bed each night.[29]

Such studies were both accurate and misleading. It is quite true that, in the 1950s, most American voters were not excited about the editorial-page issues of the day. But not many exciting issues were being kicked around the political field then. Except for the question of domestic subversives—which the general public can surely be excused for ignoring, since many of the political elite considered it a phony issue—the years from 1953 to 1961, the years of Dwight D. Eisenhower's administration, were relatively barren of significant quarrels. It was a decade that asked few questions and offered no answers. Its characteristic posture, as Stephen Whitfield accurately recollects, "was rigid, as though, in the atmosphere of the Cold War, Americans staked out a claim as God's frozen people."[30] The great social issues that were to come along in the 1960s were dormant; southern barons ran Congress, and Ike was on the golf course. The attitude of the electorate in general was exemplified in the political life of Edward M. Kennedy, who, from 1953 to 1960, could have voted on 16 occasions but in fact voted only three times—when his brother was on the ballot.[31]

---

[27]*Washington Post,* July 7, 1974.

[28]Anthony Downs, *An Economic Theory of Democracy* (New York: Harper & Row, Publishers, 1957), p. 259.

[29]Norman H. Nie, Sidney Verba, and John R. Petrocik, *The Changing American Voter* (Cambridge, Mass.: Harvard University Press, 1976), p. 15*n.*

[30]Quoted in Robert Sherrill, *The Last Kennedy* (New York: Dell Publishing Co., Dial Press, 1976), pp. 26–27.

[31]Sherrill, *The Last Kennedy,* p. 19.

Then came a dramatic change. The electorate of the 1960s and 1970s became much more alert to issues. For one thing, voters were getting a better education. For another, the press was doing a better job of delineating the issues. But the essential fact was simply that now there was something to get excited about. A number of very passionate issues suddenly confronted the nation, demanding resolution: racial confrontation, corruption in the FBI and the CIA, corruption in Congress and in the White House, the Vietnam war, and a potpourri of social concerns broadly defined as crime in the streets, the drug problem, the environmental problem, and the welfare problem.

Although the percentage of Americans who turned out to vote did not significantly change, the fervency and style of the participants certainly did. Young people began to turn away from the easy voting patterns of their parents. Party labels began to come unstuck. Among voters under thirty, in the 1970s independents outnumbered those identified with both parties. And among voters of all ages, jumping the party traces became commonplace. Democrat George S. McGovern was hurt by this trend in 1972, when 44 percent of his party's voters voted against him in the presidential election.[32]

One conclusion is plain: when important problems are presented clearly and often enough to cut through the smog of everyday life, the electorate—or a good portion of it—will respond with sufficient enthusiasm to pump up the old democratic hopes once again. What sometimes has passed for voter stupidity, or lethargy, was more likely the result of failure on the part of political leaders and press to present the problems adequately—as we will see below.

MAJOR SOURCES OF POLITICAL INFORMATION

Two kinds of information flow out of Washington, D.C.—free-enterprise information and tax-bought information. That is, there is the information prepared by the press, and there is the information prepared by the government. The press is selling news that will supposedly help the public to understand how the government really operates. The government is selling a point of view that it hopes will make the taxpayers support the way it is conducting itself. The stereotypical judgment of these two types of information is that the press is intent on serving the public with facts, and the government is intent on serving (or protecting) itself with propaganda. But that good guys/bad guys picture must be dispelled from the very outset.

The Media: Big Business

The activities of the media, however beneficial, must be seen as the product of a big business. The press lords of the United States— Arthur Hays Sulzberger, Katharine Graham, John S. Knight, William Randolph Hearst, Jr., and their peers—have at least one eye on the cash register at all times. Network officials at NBC, ABC, and CBS are in television for money. News is just another commodity, and not the most popular commodity at that.

The Networks To be sure, TV news is put out in an extremely costly package. The CBS Washington bureau, for example, spends more than $7 million a year on twenty-one reporters and eight camera crews, but they treat their viewers to no more than eight minutes of Washington "news" every night (out of twenty-three minutes of national news). All networks schedule about the same amount. In other words, as one group of surveyors put it generously, "the typical 30-minute network news show would take no more than one page of the *New York Times* if it were set into print."[33] When a network devotes only eight minutes to the President, Congress, the Supreme Court, and the bureaucracy, obviously it is not really interested in disseminating the news. It is primarily interested in selling advertising time. News is just a minor pause between the quiz shows and the police dramas.

The commercial preoccupation of the local TV stations is even more intense. A study conducted

---

[32]Richard W. Boyd, "Electoral Trends in Postwar Politics," in James David Barber, ed., *Choosing the President* (Englewood Cliffs, N.J.: Prentice-Hall, 1974), p. 184.

[33]Erikson and Luttbeg, *American Public Opinion*, p. 147.

Two Crises in Modern Consciousness

The first great crisis in modern consciousness in the West came with the invention and spread of printing. The knowledge of the few became the knowledge of the many, with the effect, as Carlyle observed, of "disbanding hired armies, and cashiering most kings and senates, and creating a whole new democratic world." The vistas of the past were opened. The accumulated knowledge of science was put within the reach of everyman. The language of the marketplace became the raw material of enduring literature. The debates and acts of legislatures could be known by all. The peccadillos and the crimes of rulers could be spread abroad. The products of craftsmen and factories, of artists and authors and composers, could be advertised. Millions of unfurnished minds would now be furnished, others would be refurnished.

The crisis of our time, the next great crisis of human consciousness, has come with television. The act, or rather the non-act, of television viewing now consumes more of our citizens' and our children's waking hours than is spent reading or eating, and almost as many hours as are spent sleeping. This is revolution. This has revised our American vocabulary, and now governs our times of rising and of eating and of retiring, the hours set for public events, the schedule of our daily lives. Television has become the authenticating experience. We can no longer say, with Oscar Wilde, that Life imitates Art, for now Life imitates Television. . . .

The impact of television has been strikingly similar to the historic impact of printing. Even in this, television's first half-century, we have seen its power to disband armies, to cashier presidents, to create a whole new democratic world—democratic in ways never before imagined, even in America. Of course, none of us is so simple-minded as to believe that one cause explains any historical event. But we cannot ignore the fact that the first era when television became a universal, engrossing American experience, the first era when Americans everywhere could witness in living color the sit-ins, the civil rights marches, was also the era of a civil rights revolution, of the popularization of protests on an unprecedented scale, of a new era for minority power, of a newly potent public intervention in foreign policy, of a new, more publicized meaning to the constitutional rights of petition, of the removal of an American President. The Vietnam War was the first American war which was a television experience. Watergate was the first national political scandal which was a television experience. The college-student protests of the '60's were the first non-sporting college events to become television experiences.

While the book democratized knowledge, television has democratized experience. Our television experience is vivid and explicit, it is ungraded and undemanding. People who would never have read lengthy accounts of civil rights organizers or of wars in Southeast Asia or of Washington political intrigue have had all these brought vividly, instantly, repeatedly, effortlessly, willy-nilly, into their very own living rooms and bedrooms.

From Daniel J. Boorstin, in a speech at the dedication of the National Humanities Center, North Carolina Research Triangle Park, reprinted in the *Congressional Record*, E3095, May 18, 1977.

by the American Association of University Women in 1974 disclosed that after commercials, weather reports, and sports, the typical half-hour newscast had only sixteen and a half minutes left for news items—Washington, national, state, and local. The study indicated that an average of fourteen stories were covered in the sixteen-and-a-half-minute period, along with "billboards" for what's coming next and third-rate vaudeville repartee between the reporters.[34] Moreover, fearful of politicians and timorous in all matters that might jeopardize their government-granted licenses, TV stations and the TV networks, who are very sensitive to their outlet stations' feelings, studiously avoid seeming

---

[34]*Washington Star*, March 5, 1975.

Television and Politics

Years of contact with station operators, documenting their crises and deeds in both small and large cities, have taught me that most of the men who control the country's electronic media bend to two things: money and political power. They will carry programs against their principles if they are profitable, and they will sell out their last vestige of First Amendment freedom to any politician who would give them a sense of permanence as licensees. They are pushovers for a government that would seek absolute rule. . . .

Big broadcasting has always had its lines out to the federal government. Largely through the connections of certain company officers, NBC was well wired to the Kennedy Administration, CBS was very thick with Lyndon Johnson, and ABC was closest of the networks to Richard Nixon. Nor were Presidents above making use of their network contacts. . . .

News was sometimes "adjusted," compromised, and even censored to please a President. It was probably no coincidence that all three networks declined live coverage of the huge Vietnam Moratorium demonstration in the capital on November 15, 1969, knowing as they did that the President wished it to be ignored, but at the request of the White House all three networks carried some part of the "Honor America Day" patriotic festivities in Washington on July 4. Similarly, on October 31, ABC cut away from the field during the half-time show of its regional telecast of the Buffalo-Holy Cross football game when the State University of Buffalo marching band staged an extravaganza titled "Give Peace a Chance," which was critical of the war in Vietnam, racism, and pollution. But several weeks later it broadcast the half-time show at the Army-Navy college football game, which honored those who took part in the American raid on a prisoner-of-war camp near Hanoi and featured Admiral Thomas H. Moorer, chairman of the Joint Chiefs of Staff. Roone Arledge, president of ABC Sports, explained that the pro-peace show in Buffalo was blacked out because it was political in nature. Apparently, the network did not consider the pro-war show to be out of line as a partisan comment.

From Les Brown, *Televi$ion: The Business Behind the Box* (New York: Harcourt Brace Jovanovich, 1971), pp. 220–21.

"political" in any sense. Therefore, they give controversial political topics only the lightest brush.[35]

The standard industry reply to criticism of the news is that the public gets what it wants. If TV viewers don't want a lot of news, they won't get it. No one is going to sponsor an unwanted product; that's just the way free enterprise works. This brings up the question of who should decide what we hear and view. Should it be the market or the marketers? Or should it be some public interest group? Should news and entertainment for the whole nation be determined only by those rich enough to sponsor the

broadcast? Would a tax-supported (but politically independent) network be more likely than a commercial network to report on what the special interest groups are up to in Washington? (The proposal should not be discarded simply because the existing Public Broadcasting System has done so little in this regard. PBS has existed in chaos and near-anarchy most of its life and can be considered a "network" in only the loosest sense. Furthermore, it has been forced to exist on a mish-mash of funding—part governmental, part corporate, and part poor-mouth solicitation. There is no reason why a public network should be any less generously funded or less efficiently organized than a commercial network.)

At issue here is simply the question of what the people deserve versus what they get. Theoretically at least, the public, not the broadcasters,

---

[35]The Federal Communications Commission does not directly regulate content of programs, but station self-discipline is fostered by the FCC's ability to refuse to renew a station's license.

owns the airwaves. Through the largess of the government, a broadcaster is licensed to operate over a particular channel on behalf of the public. This is quite a gift, for there is a very limited number of channels to be given out. So, logically, the public should have a strong voice in determining the programs offered. But who exactly *is* "the public"? And should its wishes be determined by the principle of majority rule, as in political elections? Is the majority to be determined by the popularity of certain hair sprays and detergents and denture glues offered by the sponsors of the TV shows? The fact is that, at the present time, the broadcasters do not know what the public wants, and they make no significant effort to find out. The industry instead relies primarily on random telephone polls, which are interested mainly in finding out which *existing* programs people are watching. This whole problem might be no more than an interesting social phenomenon, except for one thing: television is where a large group of Americans get their information about the government and about politicians. (See Figure 6-2 and Table 6-4.)

FIGURE 6–2   AUDIENCES REACHED BY LEADING NEWS MEDIA

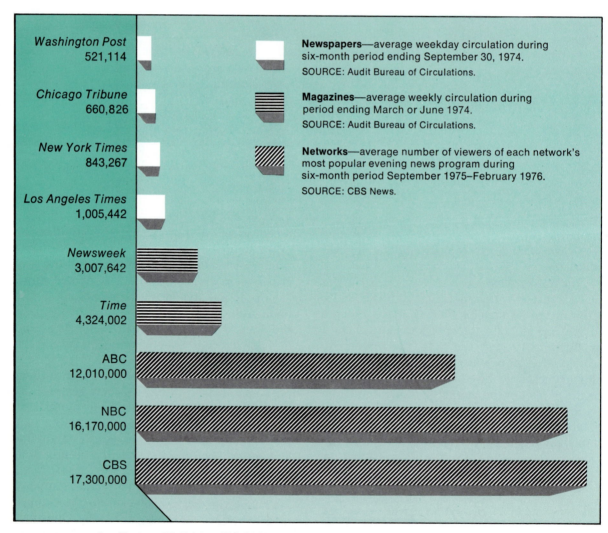

SOURCES: *Ayer Directory of Publications* (Philadelphia: Ayer Press, 1975) and CBS News.

TABLE 6-4

PUBLIC ATTITUDES TOWARD NEWS MEDIA, 1959–1976

MOST BELIEVABLE	1959	1971	1976
Television	29%	49%	43%
Newspapers	32	20	21
Other media	22	19	18
Don't know, no answer	17	12	18

SOURCES: 1959 and 1971: "An Extended View of Public Attitudes toward Television and Other Mass Media 1959–1971," a report by the Roper Organization to the Television Information Office; 1976: NBC poll reported in the *Washington Post,* January 9, 1976.

There is some ground, of course, for being skeptical of self-serving polls taken by TV networks. Some scholars feel that the importance of television in shaping public opinion is considerably overrated. One such scholar is Thomas E. Patterson, who wrote a book with Robert D. McClure called *The Unseeing Eye: The Myth of Television Power in National Politics.*[36] Asked if he thought people were conscious of the quality of the coverage they get from television, he answered:

No, I don't think so. It's quite unconscious and a lot of people say that they get most of their information from television even though they are not regular viewers of television. Television seems to have a magical hold on people and you ask people to compare channels of communication and they're likely to point at television as the most important and most influential on them. But there are some indications that it has less impact on them than they'd like to think. You ask a lot of people after they watch a television newscast to recall stories from it, describe it; a good number of them cannot recall a single story that they saw. This is not true of a newspaper reader who is more likely to recall something and more likely to give an accurate description of it.[37]

Nevertheless, television is the primary conduit by which politicians try to reach the public during campaigns. These efforts are usually nothing but flashy, superficial attempts to achieve name recognition. Neither during nor between campaigns does television offer even an offhand treatment of important local or national issues confronting the political representatives. An unusual effort was made in 1960 and in 1976 to raise presidential campaigning to the level of the issues via "debates" between the two major candidates. But it was amply demonstrated in 1976 that, even when the debates are conducted with the best of intentions, the medium itself restricts them to very mediocre and frustrating results. President Gerald R. Ford and challenger James E. Carter conducted three nationally televised ninety-minute debates in Philadelphia, San Francisco, and Williamsburg, Virginia, under the sponsorship of the League of Women Voters. Polls indicated that Ford won the first, Carter the second, and that they split the third. But in a real sense neither man won any, for the polls also showed that the debates did not change many people's opinions.

How could they—barring a demonstration of tongue-tied incompetence by one of the candidates? The format was impossible. Some of the long, involved questions, asked by a panel of reporters and editors, took up nearly as much time as the candidates' answers. Questions about some crucial issues—such as the need to

[36]Thomas E. Patterson and Robert D. McClure, *The Unseeing Eye: The Myth of Television Power in National Politics* (New York: G. P. Putnam's Sons, 1976).

[37]Quoted in the *Washington Star,* August 4, 1976.

reduce United States troops overseas—were never asked, so they were never answered. Other key issues, such as the proliferation of nuclear weapons, received only cursory treatment. A murky, disquieting air of vagueness hung over the programs; there was no precision, no forthrightness, no clarity—but how could there be when each debater was given a maximum of only three minutes (allowing about the number of words that can be put on two double-spaced typewritten pages) to talk about his position on an issue as complicated as strategic-arms agreements?

Under the best of conditions, television hardly offers broad intellectual horizons for the politically sophisticated. Broadcasters have improved a great deal since the days when one network refused to let writer-producer Rod Serling mention Hitler's gas ovens because a gas company sponsored the show,[38] but their courage is still so cramped by the profit motive that they aim primarily for programs that may not satisfy but at least do not arouse much conflict. They shun diversity of opinion to avoid offending advertisers.

Avoiding Dissent   When Kenneth A. Cox was head of the Federal Communications Commission, he acknowledged that

> a good many people . . . point out that our advertiser-supported privately owned system tends to produce a great volume of rather similar programs designed to attract the maximum possible audiences, but that it does not work nearly so well in developing public affairs, religious, instructional, or even more serious entertainment programming. They say that their tastes and interests are not represented proportionally in the programming beamed to the public.

If this group had cause to complain, said Cox, it was because the TV scene is overwhelmingly dominated by three national commercial networks. "If none of them is impressed by a program idea, it dies. The program executives of the three networks have similar backgrounds, interests, and objectives. . . ." Paramount among their objectives is moneymaking. Programs presenting "dissenting" viewpoints don't attract advertisers, so "off-beat programming often falls victim to the policy of avoiding trouble and lying low."[39] And yet, *by law*, broadcasters are supposed to find a place in their programs for dissenting viewpoints, for argument—for the kind of intellectual tension that sharpens the public's awareness of, and interest in, crucial issues.

If Texaco floods the airwaves with commercials saying that drilling for oil is good for the ecology, shouldn't somebody be allowed to argue that drilling for oil often spoils the environment? If Mogen David and Wild Irish Rose buy air time to persuade the public that drinking wine is fun, shouldn't somebody get time to warn that drinking can lead to alcoholism? Questions such as these forced the government long ago to face the problem of divvying up air time fairly in a pluralistic society. As is typical when the government sets out to regulate powerful commercial interests, the reform results were more form than substance.

In 1943, the Supreme Court held that the Federal Communications Commission is responsible for regulating broadcast content; the FCC defined that responsibility as the Fairness Doctrine. Under the Fairness Doctrine, a station is supposed to notify a person against whom it broadcasts a personal attack and offer free time so that he or she can make a rebuttal. The doctrine also requires that a station make time available for conflicting views on issues of public importance. This, however, does not necessarily mean giving free time for rebuttal or even allowing an equal amount of purchased time. It simply means that the presentation of a viewpoint should not be totally one-sided. The ratio of time allowed to opposing sides may be 15 to 1, but at least there should be that 1.

But the FCC ignores most appeals for time to present opposing opinions. It rarely uses the doctrine to intrude on the operation of the networks or of the individual stations. And when it does intrude, it usually does so much too late to be of any practical service. In 1976, for example, environmentalists in California attempted to

---

[38]*Washington Post*, June 29, 1975.

[39]Kenneth A. Cox, in a speech at Oregon State University, Corvallis, Oregon, May 16, 1969.

stop the expansion of the nuclear power industry; the issue was put on the ballot as a referendum. Atomic industrialists flooded the TV stations with pronuclear ads. Environmentalists often found that they could not even buy time to respond. They appealed to the FCC; six months after the election was over (the environmentalists lost the election, by the way) the FCC was still "studying" the case. The time lag is typical.

One of the FCC's worst performances was its failure to police the operation of a TV station in Jackson, Mississippi, in the late 1950s and early 1960s. The station was guilty of the most flagrant racial and religious discrimination. It would cut off network civil rights broadcasts with signs reading "Sorry, cable trouble."[40] Many blacks and some whites appealed to the FCC for fair play. The FCC did nothing, so the petitioners went to federal court, and the court took away the station's license.

In 1976, the FCC delivered an extraordinary ruling that, for a change, supported the spirit of its statutory mandate. It ordered radio station WHAR-AM in Clarksburg, West Virginia, to devote a reasonable percentage of broadcasting time to the strip-mining issue. Strip mining was, in fact, the most controversial topic in West Virginia, and the station had neatly avoided discussing it by ignoring *both* sides. The FCC declared that certain issues may be of such magnitude in a local community that it would be an unreasonable exercise of editorial judgment to ignore them. Never before had the FCC been brave enough to apply the "affirmative obligation" section of the Fairness Doctrine in this way to supercede the news judgment of a licensee. The industry shuddered.[41]

Broadcasters feel that they should not be subjected to that kind of regulation and punishment. They do not object when advertisers censor programs (which happens quite often), but when the FCC, acting on behalf of the general public, overcomes its normal timidity and demands that the broadcasters promote free speech by offering some time to all sides of a controversial issue, they noisily complain that their First Amendment rights are being violated. Many, probably most, of the owners of radio and TV franchises argue that they should be ruled only by free enterprise. In the words of John J. Koporra, Vice President for News for Metromedia, at a House hearing in 1968: "There's a very orderly procedure for taking care of a bad broadcaster in the capitalistic system. That is, he will go broke, and be forced to sell. A bad broadcaster will not survive."[42]

That's a cute theory, but there is no record of any group of local advertisers in Mississippi ever forcing a station out of business for performing in a racist fashion or of any group of Texas advertisers refusing to do business with a local station because it would not give air time to an anti-oil program. Parochial business groups are, as a rule, even less broadminded than national and international ones, and they have a powerful influence on the format of local television stations. The local stations, in turn, have a powerful influence on what the three major networks offer—the local affiliates don't have to take what the networks offer, and if they think a program is too "liberal" or too "controversial" they very often don't. Every refusal costs the networks money, so they bend to the normal conservative wind of the local affiliates.

The Press The quest for profits also shapes the flow of printed news, although the results are not so dramatically dollar-bound. Compared to television's coverage, newspapers are well named. Still, no major newspaper gives more than 40 percent of its space to nonadvertising material, and this 40 percent includes comics, crossword puzzles, astrology charts, letters to the editor, editorials, columns, and—yes—the news. Some newspapers give no more than 20 percent of their "news" space to news.

Newspapers are loathe to open their pages to a diversity of opinion. And they have found support in the Supreme Court for their position. It came about as the result of a case originating in

[40]*Congressional Record*, S21585, December 16, 1974.

[41]Reporters Committee for Freedom of the Press, *Press Censorship Newsletter*, no. x (September/October 1976): 113.

[42]Quoted in the debate at the Fiftieth Anniversary Convention of the National Association of Broadcasters, Las Vegas, Nevada, November 20, 1974, cited in the *Congressional Record*, S21583, December 16, 1974.

Florida. Pat Tornillo, a 1972 candidate for the Florida legislature, was criticized by the *Miami Herald* in two editorials. Tornillo invoked Florida's long-forgotten 1913 criminal law that provided that "if any newspaper . . . assails the character of any candidate for nomination or election . . . or otherwise attacks his official record, such newspaper shall upon request . . . immediately publish free of cost any reply he may make in as conspicuous a place and in the same kind of type" as the original article. The *Herald* refused to submit to the law, claiming that the First Amendment made newspapers immune from government instructions as to what they must print. Tornillo went to court. He was upheld by the Florida Supreme Court, but in 1974 the U.S. Supreme Court struck down the Florida law as unconstitutional.[43] Many applauded the decision as another victory for the First Amendment's guarantee that Congress (and, by later extension, government at any level) "shall make no law . . . abridging the freedom . . . of the press. . . ." But in another way, the case, whatever its outcome, can be seen as a sad defeat for the intent of the Constitution. When any person, politician or other, feels compelled to go to court to get a fair shake in the local press, the channels of communication have obviously become constipated.[44]

Monopoly helps crowd out diversity of opinion. In only 64 of the 1,547 cities with daily newspapers is there competition; monopoly ownership controls the press in the other 1,483 cities. Furthermore, in many cities the television stations are owned by newspapers, or vice versa. The increasing narrowness of the industry is written in statistics. In 1920, there were 700 cities with competing newspapers.[45] In 1910, 100 million people in the United States were served by 2,400 newspapers. Sixty-five years later, the population had doubled, and the number of newspapers had dropped by one-fourth. "What you have in a one-paper town," press critic A. J. Liebling pointed out, "is a privately owned public utility that is constitutionally exempt from public regulation. . . ."[46] Efforts in Congress to end the monopolistic and anticompetitive practices in the news business have been bitterly opposed by both the TV networks and the major newspaper corporations.

The monopolistic character of the newspaper industry is heightened further by the fact that so many of the dailies are owned by chains. Three out of five of the nation's 1,756 daily newspapers were under chain ownership (about 170 companies involved) in 1977, and the trend was growing. Seven years earlier, only about half the dailies had been under chain ownership. The industry cannibalism—big papers buying up smaller ones, big chains buying up smaller ones—resulted in great concentration of ownership: as of 1977, the twelve largest chains were distributing 38 percent of the 61 million newspapers in the United States each day. Each paper in the Hearst, Gannett, Newhouse, or Times Mirror chain was not automatically like every other, but there was not much editorial variety. Homogenized opinion was the rule. Says Everette Dennis: "I don't think they can avoid being affected by the thinking of the editorial flagship paper."[47] And usually the "thinking" of the flagship paper, where the publisher of the chain holds court, is concentrated on making money and defending a system that allows the freedom of the press to be enormously profitable, for profits were the purpose of the expansion in the first place. Samuel I. Newhouse, the biggest of the newspaper-chain industrialists, did not pay $305 million for the Booth newspapers in 1976 just for the fun of it.

---

[43]*Miami Herald Publishing Company v. Tornillo*, 418 U.S. 241 (1974).

[44]A few, very few, newspapers responded to this victory in the proper spirit of remedy via voluntary fair play. The *Charleston* (West Virginia) *Gazette*, for example, immediately incorporated into its policy a guarantee that persons whose judgments and conduct are questioned by editorials may respond at reasonable length and that the responses would be displayed as prominently as the newspaper's own comment on the same subject. But the *Gazette* and its owner-publisher, W. E. Chilton III, are rare birds in the jungle of journalism.

[45]*Nation*, May 14, 1977.

[46]Charles B. Seib, *Washington Post*, November 19, 1976.

[47]Everette Dennis, *New York Times*, February 15, 1977.

The Press and Its Myths

Over these 200 years the American press has performed some great public services and some outrageous public disservices. But we have created about our industry a web of myth designed to create false impressions about the way we are. And, sadly, we have come to believe the myth.

Come National Newspaper Week, editors and publishers like me will go before civic clubs and college forums brandishing the First Amendment, wrapping ourselves in the American flag and declaiming in ringing tones how downright upright we are in serving the public interest. We recite a litany of saintly qualities which we insist are inherently ours: We serve the public interest; we represent "the people"; we are objective, above all else. And there is a new claim: We provide the public access to our columns.

But I will tell you this. As a reporter, I can't ever recall sitting down at a typewriter and thinking, as I drafted a story, that I was the voice of the people. I think such an attitude by a reporter is presumptuous and by an editor or publisher is dangerous. Reporters must never be allowed to use that crutch to replace credibility. . . .

When we boast of our "objectivity," we deal in semantics. There is little pure objectivity in the American press. If reporters are industrious and probing and honest in gathering facts, then their *subjective* judgments may be vital to the news story. Indeed, in the most crucial work we do—reporting on areas of societal controversy and conflict—the reporter's subjectivity, not his objectivity—and by that I mean his or her sense of facts developed, his or her conclusions, indeed his or her trained instincts—may make the difference in the reader's comprehension of issues. . . .

What about the question of providing the public access to the columns of a newspaper? The Supreme Court in the Tornillo case ruled that we cannot be required to give access. Let's tell the truth. At most, we provide minimal access to our pages. We say, "write us a letter" or "do us a guest column" or "we have an ombudsman, call him," or "we have a press council." That isn't the sort of access special interest groups want; it isn't the access minority groups want.

The truth is, they don't have access and we are going to give them damned little because we don't think they are entitled to it—and maybe just because we don't want to. . . .

Having made all my criticisms, I still find the press today better than ever. Its people are more aware, better educated, more alert, more committed, more dedicated, more selfless than when I came into the business almost 30 years ago.

The press has survived one economic threat after another in the last quarter century—shifting advertising markets, a decline in the number of hometown dailies, the loss of advertising revenues to television.

And yet after two centuries, we continue to live with myths. We should finally face up to the truth about ourselves. For, our economic viability notwithstanding, we may find that the truth is all that will keep us free another hundred years.

From John Siegenthaler, "The Press and Its Myths," *Washington Post*, June 12, 1977.

The thirteen leading publicly owned newspaper firms in fiscal 1976 had an average income of $25.7 million *after* taxes—an *increase* of 35.8 percent over the average net income for 1975.[48] If there are few Thomas Paines among today's press lords, perhaps that is because Paine operated at a somewhat lower economic level.

One of Samuel Newhouse's managing editors said of him, "Sam never pretended to be a public benefactor. He doesn't claim to be with the people. He's a capitalist."[49] All publishers are capitalists. As a group, they reserve their

[48]*Washington Post*, August 3, 1977.

[49]International Typographical Union, "Federal Responsibility for a Free and Competitive Press," Washington, D.C., 1967, p. 69.

"Stick to local papers and you won't get so depressed."

passions for developing more efficient ways to make money. The American Newspaper Publishers Association spends more than $500,000 a year for research, but little of the research is for uncovering ways to improve editorial content. Most goes for figuring out better methods of printing or bookkeeping.[50]

Financially healthy newspapers are often the best ones, editorially. But concern for profits in the board room rubbing against concern for news in the newsroom can result in a schizophrenic quality—a fitful inconsistency. Reporters must answer to editors who must answer to publisher-owners—who ultimately set the tone and direction of the news-gathering organization. To be sure, some publishers—those who feel that selling news is a higher calling than, say, selling shoes—may encourage wide latitude and aggressiveness in reporting specific stories, even stories that embarrass their business friends, but few publishers are so open-minded as to permit their own newspapers to challenge the very

---

[50]Lester Markel, *What You Don't Know Can Hurt You: Study in Public Opinion and Public Emotion* (Washington, D.C.: Public Affairs Press, 1972), p. 196.

system and social structure of which they are an important part.

When oil and gas prices quadrupled in the early 1970s, only a few newspapers assigned investigative reporters to follow up rumors that the major oil companies were engaging in profiteering schemes based on phony shortages. For the most part, newspapers simply parroted a "crisis" line handed out by the petroleum companies (major advertisers). Little coverage was given to congressional hearings on the energy problem. "We've been dismayed," said one senator. "When you start debating an issue like this, nobody in the press seems to know or care what you're talking about."[51] The banking, housing, agricultural, and other industries crucial to everyday life are covered only spasmodically by the press, and the stories usually land on the financial page—which is not exactly the page most people turn to first. When tax legislation is under debate in Congress—legislation that usually winds up favoring the rich special interests and gouging the ordinary taxpayer—it gets virtually no coverage at all. The corruption of politics gets front-page attention fairly often, but the corruption of industry and Big Business rarely does. Few newspapers ever convey the idea that capitalism as presently practiced may have some serious defects.

The most important role of journalism is setting the agenda for national attention. Only those problems that are deemed "newsworthy" have a chance of getting solved. Not until journalists decided to make racial discrimination the big news story of the early 1960s did major legislation to relieve the problem get passed in Congress. Consumer and environmental problems—dangerous pesticides, cancer-causing food additives, unsafe autos, filthy rivers—plagued the public for many years without a political hand being raised to correct the situation. The reason: virtually nobody was writing on those problems. Then, in the 1960s, filth and poison in daily life became an "in" news topic. A score of remedial laws resulted. Politicians, like

the public in general, measure the boundaries of life to an unsettling degree by what they read in the newspaper and hear on the six o'clock news. Until a problem is emphasized in those formats, it often does not receive sufficient recognition to trigger the momentum of political reform.

This is why the concentration of ownership in the press is so dangerous. And, of course, the danger is much more acute in the TV networks because they reach so many millions. Kevin P. Phillips sums it up quite accurately:

> Here are these three operations [networks] that have this incredible power to beam into our living rooms the political agenda for the nation; they choose the people who say in the morning or the evening who is good and who is bad, what happened in the world, what you are to think about, what the agenda is. . . . The people . . . who sit up in New York behind whole corridors of power, ten to twelve offices removed from any place the public could possibly penetrate without an official pass, just like the Pentagon. These are the people that are calling the shots.[52]

Government Information Peddling

If the media are something less than pure in their dissemination of information, the government is far more than merely a propagandist, although it is certainly that, too. Call the government's product what you will; it is costly. And it is often illegal.

Since 1913, the federal law has laid down this prohibition: "Appropriated funds may not be used to pay a publicity expert unless specifically appropriated for that purpose."[53] In 1967, however, the Associated Press estimated that the federal government was spending $400 million for public information and public relations—hiring people to supply information to newspaper and TV reporters, to engage in community relations, and to prepare films, speeches, publication exhibits, and advertisements for federal agencies. Barely disguised among the govern-

---

[51] Quoted in "Whatever Happened to the Natural Gas Crisis?" *Columbia Journalism Review*, March/April 1976.

[52] Kevin P. Phillips, in William Ruckelshaus, et al. *Freedom of the Press* (Washington, D.C.: American Enterprise Institute, 1976), p. 61.

[53] U.S. Code, Section 3107.

ment's information specialists are scores of the proscribed publicity experts—nobody knows for sure how many. They are easily identified by their total commitment to making their bosses and their corners of government seem much more important than they are and glossing over defects. Their job is to puff, to aggrandize, and basically to con the public. Congress seldom does anything so bald as to appropriate money specifically for "publicity," and the publicity experts on the payroll are never specifically identified as such, but they exist and flourish nonetheless.[54]

Whether true information specialists or publicity hacks, this costly, mixed brigade does its work with heavyweight budgets and the best of equipment. The government has about $1-billion-worth of motion picture, television, and radio equipment and plants to project its image, and its "audio-visual" activities cost $500 million a year (since 1960, the government has produced twenty-two films on how to brush your teeth). In a typical year, the government spends $110 million on advertising, which makes it the nation's tenth largest advertiser, ranked right up there with Colgate-Palmolive and R. J. Reynolds. One result of this advertising expenditure is that you probably feel quite at home with such phrases as "Take Stock in America" (United States Savings Bonds), "Don't Be Fuelish," (Federal Energy Administration), and "Remember—Only *You* Can Prevent Forest Fires" (United States Forest Service).[55]

At best, much of what emerges from the government's publicity machine is nothing but pep talks; at worst, it is illegal lobbying for, or misleading promotion of, a bureaucratic program. Most of the information disbursed by the government, however, is not only defensible, but highly practical and even, in our complex economy, downright necessary. As one former senator, a bitter enemy of the propaganda side of government, acknowledged:

Such information ranges from the daily weather forecast to the monthly Consumer Price Index to the decennial census. The influence of this information on daily living, public attitudes, economic developments, and political decisions is as wide-ranging as the subjects themselves.

Although a Weather Bureau forecast of rain may only bring out umbrellas and raincoats, a hurricane warning can mobilize the resources of an entire region. A Coast and Geodetic Survey chart of the Chesapeake Bay may keep a weekend sailor from running aground, but it also guides a laden tanker to port. The Agricultural Research Service's booklet *Removing Stains from Fabrics* may be a housewife's boon, but the Department of Agriculture's crop report can influence the whole farm economy. The price index compiled and published by the Bureau of Labor Statistics affects the wage rates of millions of workers and national economic policy as well. A shift in population found through the census can change a state's representation in Congress.[56]

In addition, the government serves as its own muckraking reporter. Most of the news stories revealing dirty work on the part of politicians and bureaucrats originate *not* with the press, but with investigators on the public payroll. They dig it up, and the press takes it to the public. Although the press must be given credit for relentlessly uncovering the Watergate scandals in its early stages and forcing Congress finally to enter into the hunt for White House corruption, it should not be forgotten that the crucial evidence—the existence of the White House tapes—came about as the result of the work of Senate investigators. Without the damning evidence of the tapes, President Richard M. Nixon would doubtless have survived the scandal. Likewise, it was a Senate investigation that uncovered multimillion-dollar briberies involving United States corporations and foreign governments; it was a Senate investigation that uncovered monopolistic collusion among oil companies to create an artificial shortage of oil and natural gas. It was the House Banking Committee and the Senate Committee on Government Operations that produced monumental studies to show the dangerous interlocking directorships and stock ownership between banks and

---

[54]"All together, federal expenditures on telling and showing the taxpayers are more than double the combined costs of news gathering by the two major U.S. wire services, the three major television networks, and the ten largest American newspapers." (Wilbur Schramm and William Rivers, *Responsibility in Mass Communications*, rev. ed. New York: Harper & Row, Publishers, 1969, p. 97.)

[55]John J. Fialka, *Washington Star*, April 12–15, 1976.

[56]J. William Fulbright, *The Pentagon Propaganda Machine* (New York: Liveright, 1970), p. 18.

other industries. It was a Senate investigation that first revealed the scope of the Teamsters' corruption. It is investigators in both houses of Congress—not in the press—who regularly turn up the truly stunning examples of defense profiteering. It is investigators in such agencies as the Federal Trade Commission and the Food and Drug Administration who publicize data on shoddy and dangerous products and swindling business practices.

Without this assistance the press would be lost, for it covers regulatory agencies and the Pentagon in an almost casual fashion; only a couple of dozen newspapers ever send reporters to the Pentagon, and only two newspapers, the *New York Times* and the *Washington Post*, assign as many as two reporters to that department—though it absorbs a fourth of our budget. For guidance to the closets where the skeletons are, the press is heavily dependent on the many members of the bureaucracy and the federal legislature who are basically honest and who feel that the public deserves to be told even the bad news about its government.

GOVERNMENT AND PRESS: BOTH FRIENDS AND FOES

Though they often do work together with an openness and a constructiveness that is found in no other nation in the world, our government and our press are just naturally enemies. This is the one direct legacy that the American press enjoys from its colonial ancestors. Antagonism toward government was, after all, the one great contribution of the press to the American Revolution; in that respect the Revolution lives on.

The reasons for this animosity are obvious. First of all, part of the business of the press is, to put it bluntly, to embarrass fools and catch rascals, and the government, in every era, is unfortunately infiltrated by a great many of both, who do all that they can to frustrate their pursuers. Second, it is much more comfortable, even for honest and efficient members of government, to work without members of the press peering over their shoulders and kibitzing. There were times when even Thomas Jefferson, a great defender of a free press, was stung by what he considered its

"licentiousness and lying" and admitted he would be overjoyed to see some of his journalistic detractors prosecuted.[57]

How to Frustrate a Reporter

The government's antagonism is usually revealed not in personally attacking members of the press, but merely in trying to frustrate it. There are a number of very effective ways to achieve this. The most obvious one is simply to lie. When Arthur Sylvester was Assistant Secretary of Defense for Public Affairs in the early 1960s, he gained some fame with his candor. On one occasion, he advised a group of United States reporters in Saigon, "Look, if you think any American official is going to tell the truth, then you're stupid."[58] Sylvester was exaggerating to make a point. Officials do sometimes tell the truth, but they often don't tell all of it, or they shade it, or they mangle it. Sylvester's moral was that any reporter or any other citizen who takes an official's word without challenging it is indeed stupid.

With disheartening frequency, Americans have been reminded in recent years that their government is only too willing to lie to them. In 1965, for example, President Johnson hastily assembled the White House press corps to announce that he had just received a telephone call from Ambassador W. Tapley Bennett, Jr., in the Dominican Republic. He warned, said Johnson, that unless the President sent marines there, "American blood will run in the streets." Even as they discussed this hysterical situation, said Johnson, Bennett was hiding under his desk while bullets whizzed through the embassy's windows. Alas, it was all a lie. Johnson was just making it up to excuse his foreign policy in that part of the globe.[59]

The Vietnam war provided many more examples of governmental lying. Presidents Kennedy, Johnson, and Nixon all found it necessary

---

[57] Vermont Royster, in a lecture at Stanford University, Stanford, California, June 1974.

[58] Quoted by Morely Safer, "TV Coverage of the War," *Dateline*, April 1966.

[59] Dale Minor, *The Information War* (New York: Hawthorne Books, 1970), p. 76.

to fabricate incidents, conceal actions, or fail to keep their word in Southeast Asia. As part of the government's cover-up of illegal activities in Cambodia, Secretary of State William P. Rogers told the Senate Foreign Relations Committee, in April 1970, that "Cambodia is one country where we can say with complete assurance that our hands are clean and our hearts are pure." Actually, the United States was drenching Cambodia with bombs, delivered in thousands of secret B-52 air raids. Top Pentagon officials falsified records to make it appear that the raids were conducted over South Vietnam.[60]

Another obvious method of frustrating reporters is to avoid them. Some government officials do this the easy way, by taking three-hour lunches and leaving at noon on Fridays. Some avoid them by issuing belligerent edicts. One recent chairman of the Federal Trade Commission selected ten reporters he would talk to and banned all others.[61] The White House has, from time to time, refused to issue press passes or release news material to reporters it considered unfair or politically dangerous.[62] Given a President of inflamed ego, any bad publicity, however inconsequential, may result in the banning of a reporter. Charles P. Gorry, an Associated Press photographer, snapped a picture of President Lyndon Johnson picking up his two beagles by the ears in 1964. Many dog lovers across the country were outraged, and, when their protests flooded into the White House, Johnson reacted by banning Gorry from the White House for a week.[63] When reporters disclosed that the United States Agency for International Development was covering up massive swindling in Laos, USAID retaliated by ordering its employees not to talk to reporters.[64] Nobody in government *has* to grant interviews to reporters.

Next to refusing to talk, officials can achieve almost as effective a blackout by throwing up physical hurdles. In 1976, the chairman of the Securities and Exchange Commission barred reporters from free and unrestricted movement in the SEC headquarters; he banished the press room to the first floor (his office was on the eighth floor, and the press room had been nearby) and ordered that reporters be "marshalled" to interviews (that is, accompanied by official monitors) and "marshalled" back to their press room again, to prevent their roaming and snooping. This order was handed down after several corporations complained to the chairman that SEC officials had leaked evidence of corporate crookedness and bribery.[65]

Since most news stories depend on timeliness for their survival, officials need not refuse to give information—they can simply dawdle long enough to let the story die. Lloyd Norman, a veteran *Newsweek* reporter at the Pentagon, explains how reporters can be victimized by contrived delays:

> Right after Daniel Ellsberg leaked the Pentagon Papers, I was told to find out how many other serious leaks had occurred at the Pentagon in recent years. I needed the information that week. Well, a week passed and Pentagon officials said they were having trouble putting the information together. Then two weeks passed. I told them, "Don't you guys know, by God, who in your organization has committed serious violations of security? I'm not talking about the piddling stuff where somebody forgets to lock his safe. I mean serious stuff, where somebody has taken documents out and given them to somebody."[66]

But Norman's wrath was fruitless. Pentagon officials calmly explained that they were still "researching" his question. They never refused to give him the information; they just went on researching until Norman quit asking—and the Pentagon had won. It happens in every agency, all the time.

The Freedom of Information Act

In 1966, Congress passed a Freedom of Information Act that was supposed to make it possible for the press and the public to obtain govern-

---

[60]*New York Times,* July 29, 1973.

[61]Reporters Committee for Freedom of the Press, *Press Censorship Newsletter,* no. vi (1974): 19.

[62]*Press Censorship Newsletter,* no vii (1975): 44–45.

[63]*Washington Post,* September 17, 1976.

[64]*Washington Star,* January 16, 1974.

[65]Associated Press, April 29, 1976.

[66]Personal interview with Lloyd Norman, April 1972.

ment documents more easily. It applied to just about everything except documents in nine exempt categories, including those relating to private matters (income tax, for example), those relating to trade secrets, and those that might imperil the nation's security. As is often the case with the first round of reform legislation, however, the FOI Act was written in such a cumbersome fashion that it was virtually useless. Nearly every department and agency in the federal government opposed passage of the act, and afterward they did everything within their power to frustrate its application. If an investigator didn't like being rebuffed, he or she had to go to court to get the FOI Act of 1966 enforced. This was enormously expensive and time consuming.

In 1974, Congress tried again. It passed an amended FOI Act, which survived a veto from President Ford. The chief improvement of the new act was that it set a time limit for delivery of the information. In general, an agency could legally take no more than ten days to make requested information available or give its reasons for refusing, with twenty additional working days allowed to decide on appeals. In the first six months, the law resulted in the release of a Pentagon report on Vietnam atrocities by United States forces, documents revealing FBI spying (often illegally) on citizens for political reasons, FBI documents on some of the famous espionage cases of the early 1950s, records of illegal campaign contributions, and one page of the FBI phone book. The new FOI Act was grudgingly obeyed by many agencies, but it inspired other agencies to think up ways to frustrate it. The FBI, the CIA, and the Internal Revenue Service continued to flout the ten-day time-release requirements. The FBI got nine months behind in filling requests for data. The CIA began charging discouragingly expensive "search fees" for producing material that was at its fingertips. The Justice Department and the National Security Agency sometimes denied the existence of documents that were later unearthed by other agencies.

As of mid-1976, there were about five hundred lawsuits pending that related to the FOI Act's application. While businesses and law firms found the FOI Act useful in prying information from the government, reporters who could not afford delays and expensive fees found it of limited help. (In 1976, two-thirds of all FOI requests to the Federal Trade Commission came from business executives and lawyers, and only 5.3 percent from the press.) Reporters, knowing they will run into bureaucratic stalling tactics, simply don't try to use the law when speed is crucial. "I haven't had a newsman fighting a deadline ask a question yet," said Quinlan Shea, head of the Justice Department's Freedom of Information Appeals Unit.[67]

But when investigative reporters are in a position to wait it out and defeat the government's delaying tactics, the payoff is sometimes very impressive. In 1975, for example, the *Washington Post* and the *New York Times* asked the Energy Research and Development Administration and the Nuclear Regulatory Commission to supply their joint estimates of how much nuclear material had been lost or stolen from government-subsidized laboratories and factories during the past thirty years. The request was made under the FOI Act. Then the newspapers sat back and waited, and waited. Two years later, in August 1977, the government finally admitted the startling truth: it had lost—somehow, but it wasn't sure how—more than eight thousand pounds of nuclear material, enough to make five hundred Hiroshima-sized atomic bombs.[68]

The worth of the FOI Act was weakened in June 1975, when the Supreme Court ruled that the act permits federal officials to withhold confidential information if there is a law allowing nondisclosure "in the interest of the public." That ruling gave government officials the right to cite numerous broadly worded laws—nearly one hundred of them—to maintain secrecy at their own discretion. And, as history has constantly demonstrated, public officials are apt to think that secrecy is "in the public interest" when they want to cover their own tracks.

One of the most glaring deficiencies of the Freedom of Information Act was calculatingly built into it by Congress in exempting itself from the law. Thus, despite its many merits, the FOI

---

[67] Quoted in the *Washington Post*, July 27, 1976.

[68] *New York Times*, August 5, 1977.

Act underscored the enduring fact that a government's candor depends mainly on good faith, not on coercive laws.

Self-censorship in the Press

If the press does not tell all the news that's fit to print, it often has only itself to blame—not the government. The strength of the press is sorely weakened by the most natural of human passions: friendship. Publishers get chummy with Presidents, editors have cocktails with senators and cabinet members, reporters drink beer with their sources, and pretty soon the press has lost some of its objectivity, has drawn in its stinger a bit, has decided "just this once" to cover up some indiscretion committed by those friendly fellows they socialize with.

Stephen Hess had been an aide to Presidents Eisenhower and Nixon. In 1974 he wrote:

> The general impression around the country at this time is that the press and the President are locked in deadly combat. This may be true, but if so, it is atypical of the usual state of affairs that exists between government officials and the media. To someone viewing us from a distance, it is much more likely to appear that government officials and reporters are allies in an elaborate and unwritten system of back-scratching based on mutual convenience. . . .
>
> In Washington, journalist and government leader are contained in the same social class. They call each other by their first names, drink together after hours, and comfortably commingle as part of one world. You can also find the kind of reporter here who claims to know more about what is going on than he is willing to write for his paper. When pressed, he may say that he does not write a given article because he knows that his paper would not print it.[69]

The more likely truth is that the reporter has simply succumbed to the timid and unsavory code of chummy self-censorship that the Washington press corps follows to keep in good with government allies.

James Reston, one of the *New York Times*'s top columnists and editors, censored himself voluntarily from disclosing information he had ob-

tained on the notorious U-2 espionage flights. Reston could have shown that President Eisenhower was lying, but he withheld the information to keep from embarrassing the President. The *Times* also censored itself from revealing the preparations that were underway for the disastrous invasion at the Bay of Pigs in Cuba—and that had as much to do with the friendship of the *Times* editors with President Kennedy as it had to do with national security. Indeed, the "national security" excuse has recruited many reporters and editors into collusive silence. There was a period, in the 1950s, when the press seemed ready to do just about anything the CIA wanted it to do, and the CIA's Deputy Director at the time is said to have boasted that he could play news media executives "like a mighty Wurlitzer."[70] The CIA is still sometimes able to play them at least like a small accordian. For more than a year, CIA Director William E. Colby successfully kept a lid on the story about the secret salvaging of a Russian submarine that had sunk in the Pacific. During that year the *New York Times*, the *Washington Post*, NBC, ABC, *Newsweek*, and the *Washington Star* all learned about the salvage job—its enormous expense and its failure. But Colby persuaded them all, on the grounds of "national security," to keep quiet. Not until the spring of 1975 did the press finally tell the story—after columnist Jack Anderson broke the silence. For weeks thereafter, the editors were sheepishly explaining why they bowed to Colby when, as it turned out, the revelations did not damage national security at all.[71]

Friendship can also lead to unequal news coverage. When it was alleged that Congressman Wayne Hays of Ohio had put his mistress on his staff at taxpayers' expense (total cost: $36,000), newspapers kept it on the front page for days and the TV networks gave the running account of Hays's sexual adventures priority even over presidential-primary news. Perhaps a major reason for this emphasis was that Hays, aside from being one of the most powerful people in Congress, was also one of the most despised. Many of his colleagues and most mem-

---

[69]Quoted in the *Washington Post*, July 31, 1974.

[70]Quoted in the *New York Times*, July 20, 1976.

[71]*Time*, March 31, 1975.

bers of the press considered him an obnoxious bully. Doubtless they delighted in embarrassing him. At least, one cannot suppose that the press was motivated strictly by outrage over an elected official's use of public money for private pleasures. If that were the case, reporters would not have ignored the sexual peccadilloes of President Kennedy, which allegedly included affairs with a Mafia moll, with actresses Jayne Mansfield and Marilyn Monroe, and with two secretaries who, according to *Time* magazine, "displayed few secretarial skills" and "usually were assigned quarters near the President and were assigned the code-names 'Fiddle' and 'Faddle' by the Secret Service."[72] Many of the same newspapers that sounded so shocked by the Hays affairs and kept the congressman on their front pages for days knew about the Kennedy escapades at the time they were happening, but covered them up and wrote not a line about them until years after Kennedy was dead. One explanation is that the President—any President—gets kid-glove treatment from the press when it comes to his private life. But another likely explanation is that Kennedy, unlike Hays, was highly popular with the press; he was a personal friend of some of the reporters and editors who participated in the cover-up.

A similar comparison can be made of the way the press (whose top management and owners were heavily Republican) treated Democrat Harry S Truman with the way it treated Republican Dwight D. Eisenhower over the acceptance of questionable gifts. When Truman was given a deep freezer, editorial writers across the country made it seem that his soul had been purchased. But when his successor, Eisenhower, received hundreds of thousands of dollars worth of gifts from oil executives, the press was strangely indifferent.[73] To the editorial writers of that era, morality was shaped by stereotypes rather than by fair play: Truman was the epitome of the machine politicos who liked to govern from a circle of cigar-smoking cronies, while Ike was the preeminent father image and heroic soldier rolled into one. The stereotypes resulted in a gross imbalance in the treatment given the two Presidents.

There are other unsettling relationships between the press and the people they are supposed to be covering. To fully understand what appears in the newspaper, one must sometimes know a great deal about the private affairs of certain reporters and columnists—and this knowledge is usually not available to the general reading public. For example, when Nelson A. Rockefeller was being investigated by the Senate prior to his confirmation as Vice President, certain of his loans were bitterly criticized. But Tom Braden, whose column is syndicated in about fifty newspapers, rose to Rockefeller's defense. The people who read Braden's columns defending Rockefeller might have liked to know that Braden had, once upon a time, received more than $100,000 in loans from him to finance the purchase of a newspaper.[74] At the Senate confirmation hearings, it was also discovered that Rockefeller had subsidized the publication of a scurrilous book about his 1970 gubernatorial opponent, Arthur J. Goldberg. Columnist William F. Buckley, Jr., defended this expenditure. What Buckley neglected to tell his readers was that he was chairman of the firm that published the book for Rockefeller.[75]

Some of the press's self-censorship and lack of diversity can be traced to plain laziness, to an unwillingness to buck friendly political sources, to peevish envy of successful colleagues, to a devotion to journalistic "stylishness" (a cultural preference for the going thing), and to philosophical uncertainty and anxiety that induces it to move with extreme caution.

When the Watergate burglary took place, almost the entire national press corps in Washington and an even higher percentage of the press in the hinterland dismissed it as an event of no consequence—or, worse, as a story that the *Washington Post* was blowing all out of proportion in order to hurt President Nixon unfairly in the approaching presidential campaign. While

---

[72]Quoted in United Press International, December 22, 1975.

[73]David A. Frier, *Conflict of Interest in the Eisenhower Administration* (Baltimore: Pelican Books, 1970), pp. 208–10.

[74]*New York Times*, October 13, 1974.

[75]Charles B. Seib, *Washington Post*, January 2, 1975.

big name reporters like columnist Joseph Kraft, reluctant to offend the White House, insisted that "President Nixon and John Mitchell couldn't have been involved [in Watergate] because they are too honorable and high-minded, too sensitive to the requirements of decency, fair play, and law,"[76] two young metropolitan reporters—Bob Woodward and Carl Bernstein of the *Washington Post*—went right on digging to the bottom of the biggest story of the century. They were fortunately unencumbered by social ties with the White House, the FBI, and the CIA sources.

Why didn't the stunning series of Woodward-Bernstein exposés have a substantial effect on the presidential campaign? J. Anthony Lukas explains:

It didn't—primarily because the White House had largely isolated the *Post*. With few exceptions—Sandy Smith of *Time* magazine; Jack Nelson and Ron Ostrow of the *Los Angeles Times*; and, sporadically, *The New York Times, Newsday, Newsweek*—the major institutions of the American press did not support their embattled colleague with any solid investigative reporting that summer and fall. Most newspapers dismissed the Watergate burglary as a joke; their favorite word for it that fall was "caper." Ben Bagdikian, writing later in the *Columbia Journalism Review,* reported that of the 433 reporters in the 16 largest newspaper bureaus in Washington, fewer than 15 reporters were assigned full time to the Watergate story. The average Washington bureau had no one on the story full time. . . . And most newspapers, magazines, and television networks devoted relatively little attention to Watergate in the months before the election.

In part, this was what Russell Baker of *The New York Times* has called "the tendency . . . . to hope that the story will go away because it makes you

[76] Quoted in J. Anthony Lukas, *Nightmare: A Narrative History of Watergate* (New York: Viking Press, 1976), p. 276.

look bad for missing it." But this was not just a missed story, it was a dangerous story, a story sure to arouse the ire of the Biggest News Source of Them All. The press shied away from it in large part because the administration's three-year campaign of intimidation had succeeded—beyond its wildest expectations. The television networks in particular—because of the great powers of the Federal Communications Commission and the persistent writ-rattling of the White House Office of Telecommunications Policy—feared a head-on confrontation with the President. . . . And when news generated by the *Post* or *Times* did percolate into the heartland, it was often disregarded simply because it came from sources that [vice president] Agnew and Nixon had effectively discredited. (As usual, most newspapers around the country supported the Republican candidate for President— but this time, by an even larger margin. According to a poll by Editor & Publisher, 753 daily papers endorsed Nixon, while only 56 endorsed McGovern.)[77]

The ingrown, almost incestuous atmosphere in which the press operates also explains some of its timidity. Reporters (and editors and publishers) quickly develop a herd instinct; they go after the same stories, cover them the same way, interpret the government's actions in the same light, swallow the same excuses, believe the same rumors, and pat each other on the back for the mutual limitations of "responsible journalism"—by which most of them mean not taking risks, not going after the hard ones, not "embarrassing the profession" by upsetting the establishment. There's a clubby, lazy, selfish reason why reporters covering the same beat are content to follow the pack: if one of them should break away and dig up a hard-hitting story on his or her own, others would be obliged to get out and do some extra work, too.

News versus Government Use of the Press

Investigative reporters like Woodward and Bernstein have become folk heroes of a sort. They deserve their adulation, no doubt. But the melancholy truth is that virtually all major stories are uncovered only because somebody in government *wants* them uncovered.

Most of the big headlines in Washington begin with a leak—the passing of a news item from official to reporter. Sometimes the leaker is a federal employee who is tired of seeing the public pushed around; sometimes it is a federal employee who wants to get even with the boss or with a colleague; sometimes it is an official who wants to put the reporter in his or her debt. In any case, the leaker uses the press as a tool. If these motivating passions of public-spiritedness, revenge, self-righteousness, and crafty self-interest did not burn in the hearts of bureaucrats and politicians, the press would be hard up for stories. (The most mysterious and renowned leaker in recent Washington history is "Deep Throat," Woodward and Bernstein's source. Deep Throat's identity has yet to be revealed.)

The public does benefit from such monumental leaks as the "Pentagon Papers." These secret documents showed, in precise detail, how the Kennedy and Johnson administrations had led the nation, often by deceit, into the hopeless Vietnam war. The Pentagon Papers were given to the *New York Times* by an ex-Pentagon official, Daniel Ellsberg. The *Times* received a Pulitzer Prize for this story; indeed, it did a great deal of work and spent an estimated $100,000 filtering the voluminous documents through the minds of expert journalists so that the story was clear to the general public. The fact remains, however, that the *Times* did not dig up the story. It was *handed* the story in one great big beautiful package, and that is how it usually happens.

On the negative side, some reporters, hungry for "scoops," allow themselves to be conduits for leaks that may be unethical or inaccurate. When President Nixon wanted to undercut George C. Wallace, a potential rival in the 1972 campaign, he and his staff decided to leak confidential tax data relating to Wallace's brother. They unloaded it through Jack Anderson's column, the most potent in the business because it is carried in nine hundred newspapers.[78] And George McGovern's ill-fated 1972 campaign fell apart on

---

[77]Lukas, pp. 274–75.

[78]Clark R. Mollenhoff, *Game Plan for Disaster* (New York: W. W. Norton & Co., 1976), pp. 90–91.

the launch pad when it was uncovered publicly that his running mate, Senator Thomas F. Eagleton, had once received psychotherapy in a hospital. Completing the picture of a disastrous running mate was a column by Anderson in which Anderson claimed to have "located photostats of half a dozen arrests [of Eagleton] for drunken and reckless driving." This was not true. Anderson had been victimized by someone who wanted to use him as a political hatchet man.[79]

Any President hates people within his administration who leak information. But all Presidents love to use the leak device for their own purposes. When the press was getting news out of the State Department that he didn't want it to get, Lyndon Johnson upbraided a group of startled officials in that agency by shouting, "You're just a bunch of goddamned puppy dogs, running from one fire hydrant to the next." But Johnson himself was constantly whispering self-serving tidbits into the ears of favored reporters. Carl T. Rowan, who is now a syndicated columnist, but was, in the early 1960s, head of the United States Information Service, recalls that when Johnson was still Vice President he arrived in Vietnam furious with officials there for passing secrets to reporters. But—

> About an hour later I stumbled upon a cluster of U. S. newsmen in a frantic huddle on a Saigon sidewalk. I peeked inside and there was Lyndon Johnson, reading to them from a "top secret" cable that he had just received from Kennedy.
>
> Johnson was doing what Kennedy, Richard Nixon, Henry Kissinger and 1,000 other top officials here have done. He was engaged in a self-serving leak. . . .
>
> I remember how gumshoes once stumbled all over the State Department trying to find out who leaked to Peter Lisagor [Washington bureau chief, *Chicago Daily News*] and the late Marguerite Higgins [of the *New York Herald-Tribune*] the content of a conversation between President Kennedy and Soviet Foreign Minister Andrei Gromyko. I had leaked it—on private and specific instructions from President Kennedy.[80]

THE WHITE HOUSE AND THE PRESS

The willingness of the press to butter up officials and the willingness of officials to bully and lie to the press are epitomized in the executive department. If the President does not wish to answer questions, he does not answer questions. If he wants to make a statement to the entire nation, he has only to lift an eyebrow; the networks surrender prime time and the newspapers turn over the front page to even his most vacuous remarks. When the President wants to censor the network news, the networks turn to marshmallow. For example, John Kennedy, eager to court the friendship of Big Business, was afraid that taped interviews of his economic adviser Walter Heller and his Commerce Secretary Luther H. Hodges would sound too critical of the steel industry. Early on the day the interviews were to be aired, a Kennedy aide telephoned network officials and said magisterially: "I am calling for the President. He would like the interviews dropped from the program." Network officials argued, but in the end they gave in.[81] They almost always do.

Plans for manipulating the press begin long before Presidents reach Washington. Indeed, that's one way they get there. In 1972, Governor Jimmy Carter received a seventy-two-page memo from his executive secretary outlining the steps by which he would be able to seize the Democratic nomination and then the Presidency. Among the admonitions: "It is necessary that we begin immediately to generate favorable stories and comments in the national press. Stories in the *New York Times* and *Washington Post* don't just happen, but have to be carefully planned and planted." Carter was urged to find ways to write flattering notes to columnists and "spend an evening or leisurely weekend with" the media heavyweights.[82]

Some print journalists who cover the White House have permitted Presidents to edit their copy and make changes. Some newspaper editors—while professing objectivity in their editorial pages—have secretly helped write campaign

[79]Timothy Crouse, *The Boys on the Bus* (New York: Random House, 1973), p. 332.

[80]Carl T. Rowan, *Washington Star*, March 19, 1976.

[81]*New York Times*, July 1, 1975.

[82]*Newsweek*, May 10, 1976.

One President's Way to Good Press

Lyndon B. Johnson was probably not at all exceptional in his attitude toward the press. His confidante, Doris Kearns, says of him:

> Johnson regarded members of the press as similar to the membership of any other interest group. And he acted on the assumption—congenial to his natural traits and conduct—that he could find a way to bargain with them for good coverage and favorable stories. "Reporters are puppets," Johnson said. "They simply respond to the pull of the most powerful strings. Every reporter has a constituency in mind when he writes his stories. Sometimes it is simply his editor or his publisher, but often it is some political group he wants to please or some intellectual society he wants to court. The point is, there is always someone. Every story is always slanted to win the favor of someone who sits somewhere higher up. There is no such thing as an objective news story. And if you don't control the strings to that private story, you'll never get good coverage no matter how many great things you do for the masses of the people. There's only one sure way of getting favorable stories from the reporters and that is to keep their daily bread—the information, the stories, the plans, and the details they need for their work—in your own hands, so that you can give it out when and to whom you want. Even then nothing's guaranteed, but at least you've got the chance to bargain."*

*Doris Kearns, *Lyndon Johnson and the American Dream* (New York: Harper & Row, Publishers, 1976), pp. 246–47.

speeches for Presidents and for presidential candidates. Publishers love to play kingmaker. Arthur Hays Sulzberger, publisher of the *New York Times,* contributed speeches and counseling to Eisenhower's campaign.[83] Philip Graham, the late publisher of the *Washington Post,* participated backstage in persuading Lyndon Johnson to accept the vice-presidential place on the Kennedy ticket. Publishers and editors are slow to criticize those they help put in office.

To some Presidents, the press is a villain under any conditions. This was certainly the case with Richard Nixon, who feared and hated journalists so much that those feelings apparently made him a bit unbalanced mentally. William Safire, a Nixon speech writer, has said that Nixon "took everything critical as a personal blast at him; when he read a byline, the writer came to life in his mind, grinning evilly at him."[84] Not surprisingly, when the Nixon crowd

put together an Enemies List of persons whom they considered too critical of the President and who were therefore to be harassed by the IRS and the FBI, a number of reporters were high on the list. At one point, some members of the Nixon group became so enraged at Jack Anderson that they tentatively contemplated poisoning him.[85] After Anderson published information based on classified documents, the CIA assigned sixteen agents to spy on him around the clock in an effort to discover the sources of his material.[86] Nixon officials also ordered the wiretapping of telephones in an attempt to discover news sources, but this sort of spying was nothing new.

The White House Press Conference

The President does not have to hold press conferences. There is no law that says he must meet with reporters at all. And yet the presiden-

[83] Bill Lawrence, *Six Presidents, Too Many Wars* (New York: Saturday Review Press, 1972), pp. 185, 197.

[84] See William Safire, *Before the Fall: An Inside View of the Pre-Watergate White House* (New York: Doubleday & Co., 1975), p. 345.

[85] Sources: Associated Press, November 2, 1973; Jack Anderson, June 15, 1975, July 2, 1976.

[86] *Washington Post,* May 4, 1977.

tial press conference has become so entrenched that it is hard to realize that this is strictly a twentieth-century innovation. Before Woodrow Wilson, Presidents talked only to the few reporters they wanted to talk to, and these audiences were rare. Wilson came into office in 1913 promising that he would submit to "pitiless publicity," but like many presidential vows, that one withered and died when he found the press more pitiless than he had bargained for. The next three Presidents—Warren G. Harding, Calvin Coolidge, and Herbert C. Hoover—stifled the press by answering only questions submitted in writing.

Nearly two decades elapsed before Franklin D. Roosevelt revived the press conference. During his long administration, it was brought to near perfection. Roosevelt did away with the inhibiting requirement that all questions be written. He usually had two press conferences a week, which he clearly enjoyed, and he conducted them as though they were lively conversations with the public, with the press serving merely as an intermediary. To be sure, FDR's calculated bonhomie covered up more than it revealed. He too played the press—and through it, the public—in a self-serving fashion. But he did establish the character of the modern presidential press conference.

The next great leap forward occurred in the administration of Eisenhower, who permitted the conferences to be televised—after they were edited by the President's staff. (The first presidential TV press conference was shown on January 19, 1955.) Ike's successor, John Kennedy, took the final step of permitting the news conference to be telecast live, running the risk of accidental gaffs but winning points for spontaneity. President Johnson had a total of 125 press conferences in five years, the frequency declining steadily as his distaste for the press increased. Nixon, who hated the press and was convinced that the feeling was mutual, held only 37 conferences in five and a half years—fewer than any other President in forty years.

Generally, a press conference is a sort of unrehearsed opera buffa in which there is only one prima donna, the President, surrounded by a sea of spear carriers, the reporters. Under the blinding TV lights, the President sweats and grins, or glowers, as he gestures for one newsperson after another to rise and ask a totally expected question. One reason the questions fail to take the President by surprise is that his press secretary has planted many of them with cooperative reporters. Almost never do the press conferences produce startling news. Their primary purpose seems to be to show the public that the man they voted into office is still alive and mentally functioning.

White House Spokesman Conferences

Equally spotty as a significant news source are press briefings, which are conducted almost daily by the President's press secretary. These are not televised for the public, which is therefore deprived of witnessing one of the less attractive government-press interplays. The *Wall Street Journal*, in 1975, accurately described the White House press room atmosphere in which these briefings take place:

Most mornings find 50 or 60 high-powered people milling around in two adjoining rooms—a million or so dollars worth of talent just . . . waiting. They are White House correspondents and, like everybody else, they are waiting for Press Secretary Ron Nessen and his daily press briefing—an institution that may be the most bizarre happening of all. . . .

The daily question-and-answer session isn't nearly as well-known as the presidential news conference. The White House hardly ever allows it to appear on television. . . . Mr. Nessen doesn't enjoy conducting the briefing, and reporters don't enjoy going to it. It has its own arcane rules and, almost like some small village, it has its village notables and its village idiots. And yet, day in and day out, this curious institution may well be the single most important determinant of the news most Americans will get about their President and his policies. . . .

A typical briefing is a standing-room-only crowd of reporters trying to browbeat, wheedle and cajole increments of information out of a press secretary who evades, quibbles and obfuscates. A briefing is Ron Nessen, as part of a job that pays $42,500 a year, informing reporters that Gerald Ford will play golf on Saturday, had an English muffin for breakfast, is building a swimming pool or met with a beauty queen. A briefing is reporter Sarah McClendon heatedly telling Mr. Nessen

Planned Spontaneity

President John F. Kennedy was a master of the press conference, but what he made seem easy was actually the result of rigorous training behind the scenes. Louis W. Koenig reconstructs the drama of the preparation:

> On the afternoon before the conference, the President's press secretary, Pierre Salinger, summoned the information chiefs of the executive departments to his White House office to share their experiences of the past week with press inquiries. On the day of the news conference Salinger, with his sundry notes, breakfasted with the President. Also partaking of the meal were Secretary of State Dean Rusk; Walter Heller, chairman of the Council of Economic Advisers; Theodore Sorensen, the President's counsel; McGeorge Bundy, assistant for national security affairs; and Myer Feldman, deputy counsel. The breakfast group canvassed the news questions that occurred to them and supplied Kennedy with data for answers.*

*Louis W. Koenig, *The Chief Executive,* 3rd ed. (New York: Harcourt Brace Jovanovich, 1975) p. 106.

that "the whole United States" demands an answer to a question she had just asked.[87]

Some presidential press secretaries are apologists (Johnson's Billy Don Moyers), some are oily and slippery (Nixon's Ron Ziegler), some are squidlike experts at throwing out great inky clouds to obscure the issues (Johnson's George Christian)—but all lie. At a 1976 conference of White House press secretaries who served in three administrations, all agreed that they had lied (though they claimed it was usually "accidentally," as a result of inaccurate information) to White House reporters.[88] Only one press secretary in history, Ford's Jerald F. terHorst, has had the integrity to resign when he discovered that his boss had given him false information to feed the press.

Of all modern press secretaries, Eisenhower's James C. Hagerty was probably the closest to a genius at manipulating the press for the advantage of his boss. Patrick Anderson explains:

> From where Hagerty sat, the key fact about Eisenhower as President was that—because of his illnesses, because of his vacations, because of his restricted concept of the presidency—he was not making much news. It became Hagerty's job to fill the void with manufactured news. He did this in several ways. He perfected a newsmaking device that came to be called "woodworking"—from Hagerty's good-humored line, "Boy, I sure had to dig into the woodwork for that one." Woodworking was the art of uncovering minor announcements—cost-of-living statistics, grants-in-aid, planned conferences, etc.—and having them made by the President, on slow days at the White House, instead of by the agencies involved. Over the years, the effect of Hagerty's woodworking was to give the casual newspaper reader an impression of ceaseless activity by the President. . . .
>
> Another of Hagerty's techniques was called "blanketing"—manufacturing a favorable story to draw attention away from an unfavorable one. For example, in 1955, Sherman Adams [Ike's top aide] ordered Secretary of the Air Force Harold Talbott to resign because of an apparent conflict of interest. With this unsavory affair about to hit the front pages, Hagerty summoned five scientists to the White House to make a timely announcement of plans for America's first earth satellite. As a result, although Talbott's resignation was carried under a one-column headline on the New York Times' front page, it was "blanketed" by the satellite story's five-column headline, half-page picture, and two related stories.[89]

The Hagerty techniques have been imitated, with varying success, by all subsequent press secretaries.

CAN WE KNOW THE WHOLE STORY?

There is simply no way to know how much information the public should have that it is not getting, either because of governmental secrecy or through press failure. This much is clear: (1) Of the great flood of governmental activity behind the scenes, only a trickle gets into the press. (2) The pressures and collusion that go into the writing of legislation and that go into the enforcement or nonenforcement of laws are rarely reported—the press seldom tells us exactly who ends up benefiting and who ends up losing as a result of actions taken by government. Only in a few of the most dramatic cases (such as President Nixon's raising the milk price as a political payoff) is the veil lifted. Most interest-group victories are never mentioned, only felt by the public, which is left to wonder what unseen forces are making life poorer, dirtier, and less free. (3) Government officials will not voluntarily confess their misconduct, their nonperformance of duty, or their bias on behalf of special interests. Special interests will not step forward willingly and give an account of their heavy-handed, and sometimes illegal, manipulation of the government. If the public learns about these things, it will only be because the press forces them into the open.

---

[87] *Wall Street Journal*, June 13, 1975.

[88] Associated Press, April 24, 1976.

[89] Patrick Anderson, *The Presidents' Men: White House Assistants of Franklin D. Roosevelt, Harry S Truman, Dwight D. Eisenhower, John F. Kennedy, and Lyndon B. Johnson* (New York: Doubleday & Co., 1968), pp. 182–84.

Doomed to Be Diddled . . .

It is obvious that the above formula results in an extremely costly situation. "The longer I live the more I am convinced," wrote H. L. Mencken, "that the common people are doomed to be diddled forever."[90] That does not mean they like being diddled or that they would not exert themselves to prevent the diddling if they only knew how. To the extent that television, the printed press, and the government itself fail to educate people—fail to speak to them with candor, fail to come clean—the government is robbed of the guidance it needs from the weight of public opinion. Proof of this can be found in the worst failures of government in recent years—the tragedy of Vietnam and Cambodia, the disgrace of Watergate, the lawless meddling of the CIA and the FBI. All these things were the product of governmental secrecy. They would not have happened if the public had not been excluded from the decision-making process.

No other war in this century has divided the nation so harshly or cost the nation so much in self-respect as the Vietnam conflict. Would we have entered it if the decision had been put to a straw vote of the people? Myth has it that the rank and file of the people are much more volatile than their leaders, much more apt to take up arms for the sake of jingoism, much more likely to go off half-cocked, to leap into foolish wars. Polls, however, have shown that this is not true; they have shown, in fact, that the public, without the benefit of inside information and with only its instincts to guide it, is less impetuous and just as thoughtful as its leaders when it comes to thinking about going to war.

Some people have suggested that the major decisions of the country might best be made via an electronic referendum, an arrangement whereby the question of the day—Shall the federal government raise income taxes 2 percent?—is flashed on the TV screen and voters respond by punching a Yes or No button. Such proposals rather lose sight of the concept of representative government. And they also ignore the fact, as James Bryce pointed out long ago, that even

when public opinion can wisely determine ends, "it is less fit to examine the select means to those ends."[91] There will always be a place in our lives, if not in our hearts, for politicians and bureaucrats. Even so, the polls show that an educated public's opinion is a governmental energy source that has only begun to be tapped.

. . . But Getting More Facts than Ever

Whatever communication failures can be blamed on the government and on the press, the fact remains that the United States government is more candid and open, and the press is freer, than at any time in our history. And all signs point to a continuation of this trend. In one respect, and perhaps only one, freedom of the press is not so great today as when the nation was founded. When the Constitution was written, the press collectively presented a broad range of opinions because entry into publishing was inexpensive. A true marketplace of ideas existed, and there was relatively easy access to the channels of communication. That condition no longer prevails. If politicians don't like what the *New York Times* prints about them and the *Times* won't open its pages for rebuttal, what can the politicians do about it—buy their own newspapers? They are of course perfectly free to do so, and conceivably they could make some kind of effort at competing with the *Times* if they were ready to risk a minimum of $35 million, which is what the *New York Post* sold for in 1977. If they don't like the treatment they receive from the TV networks, they might as well shrug it off; no mortal can launch another network. The vast sum of money involved in any significant entry into the publishing world these days gives an ironic meaning to the phrase "free press." Freedom of the press is first of all a privilege available to those who can pay for it, and second a theoretical right protecting that privilege. "Freedom of the press," in the words of A. J. Liebling, "belongs to the man who owns one." And since freedom of the press is, strictly speaking, the luxury of the rich, the press must be considered

---

[90] Quoted in *American Heritage*, April 1977.

[91] Quoted in Gallup, *The Sophisticated Poll Watcher's Guide*, p. 8.

"And that's the opinion of Herman Fletcher. This
is Herman Fletcher, signing off."

"the weak slat under the bed of democracy."[92] The dangers of this situation have been recognized for a long time. In 1947, the report of the Commission on Freedom of the Press warned, "Protection against government is now not enough to guarantee that a man who has something to say shall have a chance to say it. The ownership and managers of the press determine which persons, which facts, which versions of the facts and which ideas shall reach the public. . . ."[93]

At the same time, it must be acknowledged that the monopoly and near-monopoly press of today seems far more concerned with bringing significant information to the public than did the highly competitive press of, say, fifty years ago. As mentioned earlier, the civil rights revolution of the 1960s could not have taken place without faithful coverage—one might almost say promo-

[92] Quoted in Charles B. Seib, *Washington Post,* November 19, 1976.

[93] Quoted in the *Washington Post,* November 19, 1976.

tion—by the major newspapers. The same intense attention, with the same progressive results, was given to consumer affairs and environmental affairs, which are topics that the press would scarcely have noticed a generation ago. The most significant sign that the press has grown up is to be found in the quality of its reporters. The trend is to hire experts—reporters with law degrees to cover the courts, reporters with science degrees to cover consumer and environmental and other science-related fields, reporters with degrees in political science to cover the legislature. The result, of course, is that the public is treated to news of greater depth and accuracy than ever before.[94]

This is a description of the advances made by the best newspapers—still a discouragingly small minority. Most newspapers continue to give cursory coverage to major activities, or no coverage at all. Each day, in newsrooms across the country, editors throw away news stories to save space and money. And the worst of it is the public doesn't rise up in outrage. As *New York Times* editor A. M. Rosenthal correctly observed,

> The consumer who would raise hell if he were short-changed at the supermarket or who found himself buying watered milk says nothing and does nothing to try to persuade the local editor or publisher or broadcaster that he does want to know what is going on in the world or the country even when there is not a disaster or crisis taking place.[95]

Whatever sophistication the press has achieved would be frustrated if, at the same time, there was not a much more expansive and free atmosphere within which to operate. In this respect especially we have come far since the early days of the nation. When the Founders (who, by the way, wrote the Constitution in secret session—something they would not likely get away with today) guaranteed that "Congress shall make no law . . . abridging the freedom of speech, or of the press," that was in fact all they meant—*Congress* would make no such laws. That left the state governments free to throttle speech and press, and some tried to.

Even after passage of the Fourteenth Amendment (1868) and the numerous court decisions supporting it, the notion of a free press remains elusive. Periodically it has been challenged. During the Civil War, President Lincoln arrested the publishers of the *New York World* and the *Journal of Commerce* for what seemed to him seditious libel. Theodore Roosevelt, a peacetime President, wanted to have the *New York World* and the *Indianapolis News* prosecuted for "a string of infamous libels." Today, an effort of that sort on the part of a President or a member of Congress would probably evoke ridicule; the courts have ruled that newspapers can report virtually anything and everything about politicians without peril of litigation, so long as no malice is involved.[96]

With the approach of World War II, President Franklin D. Roosevelt decided that the press should start taking orders like good little troopers. When the *New York Post* scheduled publication of an eighteen-part series on German espionage in the United States, Roosevelt brought suit to restrain it. Regrettably, the *Post's* publisher backed down before going to court.[97] In 1971, the Nixon administration attempted to prevent publication of the Pentagon Papers. The government claimed—as usual when it wants to keep something quiet—that publication would cause "irreparable injury to the defense interests of the United States." The Supreme Court handed down a decision that freed the press to publish those particular documents, but it left in confusion the question of whether the government has the right to impose prior restraint.[98]

---

[94] Television is an exception to this maturity. It is still trying to grow up. "One study of network news coverage over a two-month period in 1969 found that only 1 percent of the news items dealt with the topics of population and birth control, world hunger, pollution, and conservation. By contrast, over three times as much news about accidents was broadcast over this time period." (Erikson and Luttbeg, *American Public Opinion*, pp. 147–48.)

[95] Quoted in Morton Mintz and Jerry S. Cohen, *Power, Inc.* (New York: Viking Press, 1976), p. 337.

[96] *The New York Times Company v. Sullivan*, 376 U.S. 254, 285 (1964).

[97] James Russell Wiggins, "The First 200 Years—Reflections of a Veteran Editor," *Overseas Press Club Journal*, 1976, p. 37.

[98] *The New York Times Company v. United States*, 403 U.S. 713 (1971).

The struggle over disclosure will continue, and the press cannot always depend on the public for support. After the publication of the Pentagon Papers, a Gallup Poll found that 48 percent of the people disapproved of the government's action in trying to prevent the publication and 33 percent approved. At the same time, 57 percent said that the greatest danger in the confrontation was that of harm to the nation's security, and only 34 percent saw a greater danger in reduction of freedom of the press. Adding to the confusion was a third question in the poll: "Do you think the press is too quick to print classified information whether or not it might hurt the nation's security?" To this, 56 percent said Yes, 28 percent No, and 16 percent had no opinion.[99] Clearly, in a clash between press and government, the general public tends toward the flag.

The conflict, obviously, will be permanent. The best reporters take considerable pleasure in the battle and, as is their style, make it sound like a holy war. Perhaps it is. Swashbuckling, Pulitzer Prize–winning columnist Jack Anderson speaks for this sort:

> Muckrakers, from Ida Tarbell to Ralph Nader, have typically believed in the decency of the average person once the foot is off his neck; in the proper response of society, if it knows the truth; in the workability, indeed the genius, of the American political and economic system, so long as its malefactors and malfunctions are regularly exposed. . . .
>
> The proposed cure is always the same: to open the books, to let in the light of public disclosure. Muckraking, because it essentially believes in the American society, believes that the truth will make us free.[100]

---

[99]*Newsweek*, July 5, 1971.

[100]Quoted in Wiggins, "The First 200 Years," p. 37.

Summary

1. Public opinion is shaped first by an individual's family, then by his or her education and peers, and finally by his or her social and economic group.

2. Americans have differing opinions on most issues, but there are some areas of general agreement, such as law and order, peace, and the free-enterprise system. Politicians keep tabs on what the public thinks by means of public-opinion polls.

3. Polls are useful only if they are constructed properly. The sample must be representative and selected randomly; opinion on an issue must have had time to jell; and the questions should be narrowly focused and clearly worded.

4. Polls may be interpreted for short-term purposes, as in political campaigns, or for long-term uses, as in noting trends.

5. Recent polls show that the public is not well-informed on political matters. This may be because (1) the public prefers to avoid hard choices and political realities; (2) people are more concerned with other things, like making a living; (3) the results of voting seem too insignificant compared to the costs of getting informed; (4) the prevailing political issues are not of interest to the general public; and (5) not enough concrete information reaches the public.

6. The major sources of political information are the government and the media. Neither is an infallible source.

7. The media are tied up with Big Business: the TV networks are owned by large corporations, and the local broadcasting stations and newspapers are being bought up by chains. The media depend on corporate advertising for income, so their news is, in effect, "subsidized." Instances of corporate misconduct tend not to be covered by the media.

8. The Fairness Doctrine requires broadcasters to make time available for conflicting views on public issues, but the Federal Communications Commission rarely invokes it.

9. Since politicians pay attention to what the media emphasize, it is the media that set the political agenda for the nation.

10. The government sells itself in much of the information it gives out. But it also supplies practical information—like the daily weather forecast—and it conducts important investigations.

11. The media's ability to expose government's foibles makes the media and the government natural enemies. Government officials tend to frustrate the work of reporters by lying, concealing, avoiding, impeding, and delaying. The Freedom of Information Act was meant to provide easier public access to government documents, but it is difficult to invoke and is packed with exemptions.

12. Reporters are susceptible to self-censorship as a result of friendships with government officials, considerations of national security, laziness, excess caution and timidity, ground rules set by the publisher, and the herd instinct of the press.

13. The press is used by government officials who purposely leak certain stories. The President uses the press to get his views across to the public and build his image.

14. A great deal of governmental activity, particulary behind-the-scenes pressure by interest groups, goes unreported. The public cannot be expected to provide guidance through the weight of its opinion if it is not fully informed.

15. In spite of imperfections and biases in the system of disseminating information, the press is freer, government is more open, and more information of an accurate nature is getting out now than ever before.

Additional Reading

Robert E. Lane and David O. Sears, *Public Opinion* (Englewood Cliffs, N.J.: Prentice-Hall, 1964), is a lucid, brief introduction to the way Americans think politically. Robert S. Erikson and Norman R. Luttbeg, *American Public Opinion: Its Origins, Content and Impact* (New York: John Wiley & Sons, 1973), summarizes a wealth of information from opinion surveys. Robert E. Lane's *Political Ideology: Why the American Common Man Believes What He Does* (New York: Free Press, 1967) is based on in-depth interviews with fifteen men; it explores the psychology of opinions.

A comprehensive source on poll results is George H. Gallup's three volume *The Gallup Poll, 1935–1971* (New York: Random House, 1972), supplemented by the monthly *Gallup Opinion Index;* it should be read in the light of Gallup's *The Sophisticated Poll Watcher's Guide* (Princeton, N.J.: Princeton Opinion Press, 1973).

David Wise, *The Politics of Lying, Government Deception, Secrecy, and Power* (New York: Random House, 1973), documents the history of government secrecy and deception, especially in foreign policy. Bob Woodward and Carl Bernstein, *All the President's Men* (New York: Simon & Shuster, 1974), tells of the authors' pursuit of the Watergate story and shows that the press can sometimes penetrate official misinformation.

A theoretical statement of the causes and consequences of limited political information is the latter part of Anthony Downs, *An Economic Theory of Democracy* (New York: Harper & Row, Publishers, 1957).

7
POLITICAL PARTIES

No America without democracy, no democracy without politics, no politics without parties, no parties without compromises and moderation . . .

At the time of this nation's founding, many of its leaders were embarrassed by the very thought of a political party. They feared that parties (or factions) would lead to endless bickering and to the exploitation of public passions. They were, as it turned out, altogether correct about that. But they were totally wrong to think that politics could *avoid* parties and still be meaningful for all the people in the United States, not just the elite class to which the Founders belonged.

Fortunately, antiparty elitism was squelched almost from the beginning, and for these two centuries United States citizens have been joining together in political parties to bicker and exploit passions and enjoy the fruits thereof. The parties—some important, some trivial—have been myriad. Voters in 1976, for instance, were offered a choice of candidates not only from the Democratic party and the Republican party, but from the American party, the Independent Freedom party, the Libertarian party, the Communist Party of the United States of America, the Committee for a Constitutional Presidency, the Socialist Worker's party, the Prohibition party, the People's party, the American Independent party, the Socialist Labor party, and the United States Labor party.

The Democratic party is this nation's oldest political organization, dating from 1792. It has supplied us with seventeen Presidents, beginning with Thomas Jefferson. The Republican party that has come down to the present day (there had been an *earlier* Republican party) was organized in 1854, at a time of increased sectionalism and states'-rightism; its emphasis was on nationalism. Its strongest adherents were the opponents of slavery, and its first winning presidential candidate, in 1860, was Abraham Lincoln. There have been fourteen Republican Presidents since then. These two major parties—the Democratic and Republican—have dominated our politics.

ORIGIN AND DEVELOPMENT OF THE MAJOR PARTIES

A political party can be defined as a group engaged in the business of electing public officials and organizing government. There is also some accuracy in Felix Frankfurter's definition of political parties as "organized appetite." People support a party because they want to get something out of it. But the selfish motivations that permeate a political party are different from those that permeate an interest group. Most people support a particular party with the hope that by doing so they can in some *general* way reshape their lives along happier lines. But this is a forever-receding goal that cannot be reached by making a few specific changes. The ideals that people hope to strengthen by supporting a political party are as often the product of neighborhood moods, submerged class biases, half-forgotten experiences, and family habits as they are of formally stated goals. Consequently, party leaders must base their appeal for support on a potpourri of broad aims; they must make party membership more inclusive and party policy more general than those of interest groups.

Parties often begin in legislatures, where factions form around legislative issues. One faction discovers the advantage of meeting privately and presenting a united front to work its will on a few particular issues. This tactic spreads to other issues, and the faction grows and develops some degree of formal organization. In order to protect its interests against this group, a second faction coalesces. Each group then finds it profitable to reach out to the electorate and organize the voters so that as many allies as possible will be elected to the legislature.[1]

This is just about what happened in the early United States. To be sure, there were some signs of incipient parties in the debates between the Federalists and the anti-Federalists at the time the Constitution was ratified. But parties really got going only in 1790–91, in the United States Congress, when members lined up on one side or the other, for or against the programs of George Washington's administration.

Federalists and Republicans

Alexander Hamilton, Secretary of the Treasury, was the guiding force behind Washington's legislative program. He was pushing legislation to assume Revolutionary War debts of the states and to fund debts of the Confederation (that is, to pay back at face value the nearly worthless paper held by investors and speculators), to create a Bank of the United States, and to impose tariffs and excise taxes. All of these measures were "conservative" in today's parlance. They were designed to build a strong central government and to promote trade and commerce.

The members of Congress representing Yankee (New York and New England) bankers, merchants, and traders who backed the Washington-Hamilton program gradually came to be known as the Federalists and organized themselves to get their bills passed. In reaction, James Madison and then Thomas Jefferson organized an opposing coalition to represent the ("liberal") interests of farmers, frontiersmen, laborers, and debtors, mainly in the central and southern states. This coalition was first known as the Republican party and later known as the Democratic-Republican party; it was the ancestor of today's Democratic party.[2]

Almost as soon as the parties organized in Congress, they began to establish committees of correspondence and other ties with voters in the

[1]E. E. Schattschneider, *Party Government* (New York: Holt, Rinehart & Winston, 1942), Chapter 3.

[2]William Nisbet Chambers, *Political Parties in a New Nation: The American Experience 1776–1809* (New York: Oxford University Press, 1963).

states and localities. By 1800, the Republicans had a broad grass-roots organization that helped elect Jefferson President. The Federalists were totally defeated and, in fact, stopped trying for the Presidency after 1816. The Republicans stayed in power until 1828 with Presidents Jefferson, Madison, James Monroe, and John Quincy Adams. During most of this period, the congressional party caucus was king; it organized the legislative program and even picked the party's candidate for President.

Democrats and Whigs

In the 1820s, however, the Republican party suffered a decline; President Monroe, in particular, paid little attention to party, and the Republicans began to divide into factions. President Adams followed policies that looked a lot like Hamilton's, including the support of internal improvements (road and canals). Andrew Jackson, the Tennessee war hero, and Martin Van Buren of New York built a new coalition of small farmers, frontiersmen, and working people: the Democratic party. Jackson, after a narrow defeat in 1824, won the Presidency in 1828. His election inaugurated an era characterized by what became known as Jacksonian democracy when, for the first time, large numbers of citizens got involved in politics. Also for the first time, most of the electoral college—and therefore the President—was chosen by popular vote.

Those who favored states' rights, internal improvements, and the Bank of the United States opposed Jackson and organized into the Whig party. It was not a harmonious group, for it included southern advocates of states' rights and northern advocates of a strong central government, incorporating plantation owners, manufacturers, commercial interests, and bankers. By emphasizing what they opposed rather than what they stood for, the Whigs managed to elect two Presidents before 1860.

Both party coalitions were too fragile to cope very well with the issue of slavery that divided North and South in the 1850s. The Whig party simply disintegrated, while the Democrats maintained a precarious national constituency by taking the slavery issue out of national politics as much as possible and making it a matter for the territories to decide.

The New Republican Party

A new party emerged in 1854 to protest slavery's extension into the territories. It brought together northern Whigs, a sprinkling of northern Democrats, antislavery crusaders, and a variety of other crusaders, ranging from those advocating restrictive immigration to prohibitionists. The group organized as the Republican party. In its second presidential contest in 1860, that party managed to elect its candidate—Abraham Lincoln.

The Republicans became the party of the Union and as such reaped the benefits of the Union's victory in the Civil War. Republican supporters after the war included northern industrial and financial interests, workers, midwestern farmers, and the newest citizens—the blacks. The Democrats maintained their southern base and added to it the support of northern urban political machines. Both of these Democratic elements were more concerned with local and regional issues than with national ones, but they kept up the pretense of a two-party system while the Republicans dominated national politics for more than fifty years. Until 1912, the only Democratic President during that half-century was Grover Cleveland; he was elected twice—in 1884 and 1892.

During this time, neither party differed very much on principles; both were essentially conservative. Most elections turned on personalities rather than issues. The western farmers, who were feeling squeezed out by the attention and resources given to industrialization in the latter half of the century, turned to another party—the Populist. In 1896, the Democrats appropriated the spirit of populism with its candidate, William Jennings Bryan. But Bryan lost overwhelmingly to William McKinley, leaving the Democrats a minority party for more than three decades.

Twentieth-Century Alignments

When Theodore Roosevelt tried to introduce some progressivism into the Republican party in the early 1900s, the party split into conservative and progressive factions, enabling Democrat Woodrow Wilson to win the Presidency in 1912.

NATIONAL REPUBLICAN CHART

PRESIDENTIAL CAMPAIGN, 1860

After World War I, the nation chose to return to the "safe" leadership of the Republicans. But during the 1920s, while the Republicans were serving the interests of Big Business, the Democrats added to their ranks growing numbers of the ethnic groups, Catholics, and the industrial working class—especially with the 1928 candidacy of urban Catholic Alfred E. Smith. The Great Depression solidified a new coalition for the Democrats—white southerners, city bosses, farmers, immigrants, labor, and blacks; this coalition elected Franklin D. Roosevelt four times. The Democrats presided for two decades, until the 1950s, '60s, and '70s brought about a dilution of the New Deal coalition.

Weakened though the New Deal party alignment may be, even today it defines the social and economic differences between the parties. Blacks, who had remained faithful to the party of Lincoln (the Republicans) from the Civil War through the 1920s, were finally dislodged by the Depression and by 1936 began to vote heavily Democratic. This tendency, dampened somewhat in the 1950s, was reinforced by the civil rights struggles of the 1960s so that blacks are now the most overwhelmingly Democratic group in the United States. As mentioned in Chapter 4, Jimmy Carter, in 1976, won only a minority of the white votes; heavy support by blacks put him into the White House.[3]

Similarly, the commitment of Jews who joined the Democrats during the Depression was reinforced by the Roosevelt-led war against Hitler, and they remain heavily Democratic today. Catholics, union members, and working-class voters have sometimes strayed from the Democratic fold in recent years (issues of life style and law and order led many of them to vote for Richard M. Nixon, George C. Wallace, and Gerald R. Ford), but labor-union money and manpower are still crucial to the Democrats. It is in the white South, where voters have resisted civil rights, that the Democrats' New Deal coalition has lost the most support. Many presidential votes went to Dixiecrat J. Strom Thurmond in 1948, to Dwight D. Eisenhower in 1952 and 1956, and then to Nixon, Barry M. Goldwater, Wallace, and Nixon again. Although Jimmy Carter brought the South back to the Democrats, Ford's 45 percent of the Dixie vote showed that the Republicans still have a substantial base of support in that region, at least for presidential contests.

The Republican party in the South is still capable of electing members of Congress and governors, but there are signs that its strength has reached a temporary plateau, sloping slightly downward. In 1974, Republican seats in the eleven states of the Old Confederacy (Alabama, Arkansas, Florida, Georgia, Louisiana, Mississippi, North Carolina, South Carolina, Tennesee, Texas, and Virginia) dropped 30 percent in state legislatures and 20 percent in Congress; and in 1976, Republicans lost another 8 percent in the state legislatures, which put them back to where they were a decade earlier, with only 10 percent of all legislative seats in that region. Further evidence of Republican insecurity in the South, political writer Jack Bass has pointed out, can be found in the fact that, since the early 1960s, "only two of their candidates have been elected to any statewide office below that of governor—a public service commissioner in Florida in 1972 and a lieutenant governor in Virginia in 1973."[4]

The failure of the Republicans to capitalize on the splintering of the old New Deal alliances in the South can be traced to several causes: (1) they consciously rejected black support; this strategy was enunciated by Senator Barry Goldwater in 1961: "We're not going to get the Negro vote as a bloc in 1964 and 1968, so we ought to go hunting where the ducks are";[5] (2) southern Republican-

---

[3]If President Gerald R. Ford had received even 13 percent of the black vote—as Nixon had in 1972—he probably would have returned to the White House. But, in effect, the Republicans wrote off the black vote, virtually conceding it to the Democrats, and Ford paid the penalty. After the election, Ford's vice-presidential running mate, Senator Robert J. Dole, admitted that the Republican party's future depended on mending fences with the blacks: "We're not going to win many elections if the other side gets 95 percent of the black vote." (Quoted in the *Washington Post*, December 14, 1976.)

---

[4]Jack Bass, "Southern Republicans: Their Plight Is Getting Worse," *Washington Post*, July 12, 1977.

[5]Quoted in Bass, "Southern Republicans."

ism is uniquely rigid in its adherence to a right-wing ideology, showing little hospitality for moderates; and (3) President Nixon preferred to support powerful southern Democrats in Congress who could help pass his programs rather than offend them by building a Republican opposition to their incumbency. Some leaders of the southern wing of the Republican party are now trying to revive their movement by courting black voters and by taking a slightly more moderate position on social issues.

Thus, there is strong continuity in the makeup of the parties, but, from time to time, major changes do occur. In the last century or so there have been three such changes, or *realignments*. The first, around 1860, was the breakup of the Democratic party over slavery and the rise of the Republicans in the North. The second, around 1896, was the takeover of the Democrats by the William Jennings Bryan–wing (western, agrarian, anti-industrial) and the rise of the Republicans as the party of the industrial United States. Finally, from 1928 through 1936, there was the forging of the New Deal Democratic coalition.[6] The current strains within the Democratic majority suggest that a new realignment may be imminent or under way. Or, as will be seen later in this chapter, there may be a *de*alignment, in which both parties lose favor and no clear regrouping emerges.

PARTY ORGANIZATION

Loose Structure, Loose Controls

Political parties in some countries—and even some minor parties in the United States—are tightly organized, with official membership lists, required dues, and a hierarchy of officials who carry out the orders of those at the top. Not so with the major parties in this country. The Republican and the Democratic parties are loose coalitions of voters, party workers, and elected officials, who are in rough agreement about ideology and in definite agreement about wanting to get and hold power. Anybody who wants to be a Republican or a Democrat can become one simply by adopting the label. There are, for the most part, no duties or obligations. Party officials can try to give orders, and sometimes do try, but there is no assurance that anybody will obey.

Each main segment—elected officials, party workers, and voters—of both party coalitions has its own characteristics. In one sense, the top party positions are those of the elected officials. Certainly the President of the United States is the leader of his own party; he and his subordinates in the executive branch of government form a powerful element of the party.

The parties are also important in Congress. They are the basis of organizing the leadership, selecting committee members, and the like. The majority party—even if it has a majority of only one member in the entire house—controls a majority of the seats on every committee and, most importantly, controls the chair of every committee. Also, party lines often determine how members vote. (See Chapter 8.) There has been some decline in party-line voting over the years, but it is still true that on many bills in the House and in the Senate a majority of Republicans votes against a majority of Democrats. This is especially true on the issues that have divided the parties since the New Deal: social welfare spending programs, labor relations, and the regulation of business.[7]

But it would be a mistake to think that the parties in Congress are highly disciplined, unified groups. In fact, when they vote together it is more a matter of shared convictions than one of central control. The Speaker of the House and the majority leader of the Senate have some resources, including a voice in committee assignments and in the scheduling of matters for consideration. But, at best, these are only bargaining chips that can be used to help persuade fellow partisans to go along. Nothing can compel them. Even legislative wizards like Sam Ray-

---

[6]See Walter Dean Burnham, *Critical Elections and the Mainsprings of American Politics* (New York: W. W. Norton & Co., 1970) and James L. Sundquist, *Dynamics of the Party System: Alignment and Realignment of Political Parties in the United States* (Washington, D.C.: Brookings Institution, 1973).

[7]Julius Turner, *Party and Constituency: Pressures on Congress*, rev. ed. by Edward V. Schneier, Jr. (Baltimore: Johns Hopkins University Press, 1970).

burn and Lyndon B. Johnson were limited in working their will. Within the Democratic party, in particular, many southern representatives frequently defect and vote in a conservative coalition with the Republicans.

Nor do a President and his fellow partisans in Congress always agree. It is in their interest to present something of a common front and to come up with a record that will please the voters, but quite often they go off in different directions. And when they do, it is far from certain that the President will prevail, as Jimmy Carter found in 1977 when he tangled with Congress over a series of popular water projects he wanted to cancel.

Much the same is true of elected officials in the legislative and executive branches of state and local governments. Each is elected from a different constituency, usually has an independent campaign organization, and feels responsible to his or her supporters and constituents, not to other officials who happen to share a party label. There is no guarantee that a Republican governor of New York, for example, will agree with a Republican President of the United States or with a Republican governor of Georgia—or even with a Republican majority in the New York legislature. And if they disagree, there is no central authority to enforce harmony.

National and Local Levels

At the national level each party does have a formal structure of party workers, with nominal leaders, the national committee, and its chairperson. The committee members are elected from all the states and meet two or three times a year. The chairperson of the party that is in the White House is hand-picked by the President; the out-party's chairperson is picked by the losing presidential candidate or (if he loses too badly) by the national committee. Each national committee has a large staff, headquartered in Washington, that coordinates fund-raising activities and provides advice and information for party candidates throughout the country.

Any impression that the national party officials are very powerful within the party, however, would be misleading. It is true that the headlines and magazine profiles are reserved for the national party committees and their chairpersons. On the Democratic side, such figures included Lawrence O'Brien, confidante of several Presidents, and Robert S. Strauss, the rich Texas lawyer who once described his job of Democratic National Committee Chairman as "a little like makin' love to a gorilla. You don't quit when you're tired—you quit when the gorilla's tired"; on the Republican side, there have been much less colorful chaps, like George Bush, the Houston millionaire who, after leaving his party's chair, became head of the Central Intelligence Agency. The national officials may get the headlines, but they don't have the organizational clout of the men and women who run party affairs at the state and local levels.

The national party committee means very little at lower levels. On the national level, the party has only two main purposes—to elect Presidents and to organize Congress. The state and local nominations and campaigns are quite separate from the national effort, and these are managed by party organizations at the state, county, ward, and precinct levels. Because of this multiplicity of organization—dictated by the federal form of government (see Chapter 13)—the parties are decentralized, loose, and disjointed. Whatever control exists is from the bottom up, from the grass roots, where the rules for getting on the ballot and for selecting delegates to state and national conventions are made. The arrangement has been described accurately by James J. Kilpatrick:

> Structurally, we do not have (as in England) two national parties; we have conglomerations of state parties whose delegates swim upstream every four years to spawn a candidate and a platform. Traditionally, we always have resisted the notion of absolute party loyalty, party discipline, expulsion from the party, and all the rest.[8]

This is a somewhat anarchistic situation. Allowing the fifty state party organizations to decide how candidates can get on the ballot and how delegates to the national conventions are chosen has led to chaos (a side effect of democracy, which will be discussed in the next Chapter). Nevertheless, the system does have virtues.

---

[8] *Washington Star*, December 27, 1975.

The lack of discipline and the variegated opinions that shoot upward from everywhere demanding responses from the top give the two major parties their lasting power by making them, in a roundabout way, the voice of the people rather than the voice of a tightly organized national hierarchy.[9]

The chief honchos on the state and local levels—the state party chairpersons, the county chairpersons, the ward leaders, and the precinct captains—are generally thought of as the party regulars, the professionals who see their party's candidates through from campaign to campaign. They are less concerned with being on the right side of issues than with fielding a candidate who can win. These party regulars are often involved in politics for material incentives—for party salaries or, more often, for patronage jobs in local government, ranging from trash collector to clerk or assistant city attorney. Sometimes party organization on this level is hierarchical, with a chain of command by which county leaders can activate a whole army of precinct workers who get voters registered, pass out literature, and help supporters get to the polls.

There is another brand of party activist, the purist, who surfaces commonly on a one-time basis in election contests to push a candidate committed to a particular cause or ideology. Purists want their candidates to be elected, but do not choose them solely on electability.[10] Some nominating contests, including, occasionally, those at the national party conventions, are struggles between party regulars and party purists.

The Rank and File

Below the party workers, of whatever type, are the parties' rank and file—those ordinary citizens who choose to identify with one party or another. Most United States citizens name a party when asked: "Generally speaking, do you consider yourself a Republican, a Democrat, an Independent, or what?" (This question is regularly included on sample surveys by the Center for Political Studies at the University of Michigan.) About two-thirds consider themselves either Republican or Democrat, even during the current period of growing independence.

As noted earlier, nothing really binds these people to their party—they pay no dues and have no obligations. But voters are surprisingly loyal to their parties. They tend to adopt the same party identification as their parents, and they tend to keep it through most of their lives—without change—usually voting for the party's candidates. This loyalty is sometimes seen as a mere habit, a rather rigid and mechanical response to the political world. But actually it can help people vote sensibly. The parties usually differ in predictable ways, and, over the years, a voter can build up an acquaintance with what the parties do when in power. This knowledge may be much more reliable than the candidate's campaign promises in any particular election. In fact, with ambiguous rhetoric and a bewildering variety of complicated issues, it may be very hard for voters to figure out exactly what candidates stand for. Reliance on party labels can be a perfectly rational response to the high cost of getting good political information.

Of course it makes sense to vote party only if the parties line up in opposition to each other on issues of importance to the voters and only if the voters feel much closer to one party than to the other on those issues. This was definitely true in the 1930s and '40s and even in the 1950s when both parties and voters were heavily concerned with the social welfare issues of the New Deal. But in the 1960s and '70s, new issues like race relations, the Vietnam war, and legalization of marijuana and abortion came into prominence and cut across the old party cleavages. Many voters could not find agreement with their opinions in either party, and so party loyalties declined. These are matters that will be discussed in Chapter 8 as well as later in this chapter. For the moment, the important point is that when it comes to rank-and-file voters, the parties are even less structured and less organized than are the loose coalitions of officials and party workers at the top.

---

[9]See Morton Grodzins, "The Federal System," in *Goals for Americans: Report of the President's Commission on National Goals* (Englewood Cliffs, N.J.: Prentice-Hall, 1960), pp. 271–76.

[10]James Q. Wilson, *The Amateur Democrat: Club Politics in Three Cities* (Chicago: University of Chicago Press, 1962).

*"I guess I'm a conservative, if you mean do I
put up a lot of jams and jellies."*

The Machine: An Exception

One important exception to the no-discipline generalization in party politics has been the urban political machine. Its crucial element is party discipline. The machine is typically dominated by a party boss (commonly the mayor), who has handpicked his loyal ward and precinct leaders and kept them loyal by liberally bestowing benefits and payroll jobs. They, in return, supply the votes within each precinct. Minor officials, like precinct captains, are vitally important because they are the ones who develop the personal relationships with the voters that win elections. Usually those who vote for the machine are those of the lower-income groups, especially immigrants, who welcome the friendship, advice, and protection extended by machine officials.

In the past, almost every large city had its party boss and its machine politics. Today the old party bosses, like Chicago's Richard Daley, are dying off, and so are the urban machines. There are a number of reasons for this—the growth of Civil Service jobs has eliminated some sources of patronage; the increase in federal welfare benefits has decreased the value of machine inducements to precinct voters; immigration has declined, and immigrant groups formerly susceptible to the overtures of precinct captains have begun to assimilate and find their own way in city life. And steady criticism of the corruption of party machines has led to intraparty reform. Political influence in the cities has shifted into a more decentralized and competitive pattern. Today, only a few areas, including Philadelphia and parts of New York City, still operate in a disciplined party-machine style.

PARTY IDEOLOGY

One reason parties in the United States are notoriously undisciplined is that they are not ideologically narrow or simple. They are broad, diverse, complex, and filled with internal tensions. This is especially true of the two major parties, and these characteristics largely account for the major parties' moderation. E. E. Schattschneider explains:

> A large party must be supported by a great variety of interests sufficiently tolerant of each other to collaborate, held together by compromise and concession, and the discovery of certain common interests, and so on, and bearing in mind the fact that a major party has only one competitor and that party managers *need not meet every demand made by every interest.* To make extreme concessions to one interest at the expense of the others is likely to be fatal to the alignment of interests that make up the constituency of a major party.[11]

Little Choice on the Surface

The need to appeal to a broad spectrum of interests sometimes makes the two parties sound very similar or, at least, equally vague. This is especially true when a campaign is burdened by what politicians call no-win issues—such as whether or not abortion should be legalized. On issues like that, any position a candidate takes will cost heavily in votes. When faced with such questions, both parties' candidates will try desperately to fuzz over their positions so that it is hard to tell the candidates apart.

Even on issues that are not no-win, the rhetoric of opposing presidential candidates often offers the voter very little choice. Both candidates will invariably promise high employment, low inflation, vigorous efforts to balance the budget, more attention to the needs of middle America, resistance to the evil selfishness of the special interests, and development of the most powerful military machine in the world.

Anthony Downs takes note of what happens when two parties forage in each other's territories for voters:

> In the middle of the scale, where most voters are massed, each party scatters its policies on both sides of the mid point. It attempts to make each voter in this area feel that it is centered right at his position. Naturally, this causes an enormous overlapping of moderate policies.[12]

Some political scientists see the overlapping aspects of the two major parties—the "depoliticizing" of the parties—as part of an insidious plan by the masters of capitalism to keep the people calm and easy to control. Alan Wolfe outlines this theory:

> A capitalist class that found competition intolerable in the economic sphere was no less inclined to view it with disdain in the party sphere. . . . The politicizing character of party systems began to disintegrate as capitalist elites no longer found it to their advantage. . . . Twentieth-century experience with parties is a history of depoliticization. . . . U.S. parties demonstrate by their behavior that they would rather nominate colorless candidates sure to bore the citizenry rather than dynamic ones who **might** stir up real political sentiment. In an insightful, if sloppily argued, book, Walter Karp makes this clear: "The whole purpose of party organizations at every political level is to sift out, sidetrack and eliminate men of independent political ambition, men whom the party cannot trust. . . . Anything that stirs up the electorate, anything that rouses their interest in politics, is harmful to party organization. . . ."
>
> The importance of depoliticized parties to late capitalism cannot be overestimated, since an active state requires a passive citizenry, and the party system, by default, becomes the best available means for ensuring that passivity . . . a lack of excitement is exactly what late capitalist parties are supposed to encourage.[13]

---

[11]Schattschneider, *Party Government*, p. 85.

[12]Anthony Downs, *An Economic Theory of Democracy* (New York: Harper & Row, Publishers, 1957), p. 135.

[13]Alan Wolfe, *The Limits of Legitimacy: Political Contradictions of Contemporary Capitalism* (New York: Free Press, 1977), pp. 306–07.

Barry Goldwater: Too much choice?

The cautious duplication between the two major candidates arouses contempt in the hearts of third-party candidates. George Wallace—nominally a Democrat, but seemingly most at home as the American Independent party candidate in 1968—sounded their theme when he said "there isn't a dime's worth of difference" between the major party opponents.

Nevertheless, the general lack of success of third parties makes it clear that being too different—even if the difference is built on worthy ideas—is courting disaster. Barry Goldwater's 1964 Republican presidential theme was "A Choice, Not An Echo," and he did indeed give the voters a very dramatic choice. It was so dramatic (he wanted to sell off the Tennessee Valley Authority, for example) that he fright-ened them away. When a candidate indicates that he or she is going to be unbendingly faithful to an ideology, whatever the consequences, voters tend to run for shelter. Goldwater won only six states—his home state of Arizona and five in the Deep South. Eight years later, George S. McGovern, the Democratic presidential candidate who was passionately antimilitary, gave the voters anything but an echo of his opponent, President Nixon. With the defense budget steadily rising under Nixon, McGovern proposed cutting the military budget by $50 billion (most politicians would consider themselves courageous if they proposed cutting it by $5 billion, which was, in fact, Jimmy Carter's proposal in 1976). McGovern seemed too different to many voters. Doubts about his competence

"Well, sir, my position on strip-mining stands four-square in the mainstream of those sterling qualities that made our great land true-blue in adherence to principle and untarnished in its concern for all. Next question, please."

Drawing by Herb Brammeier, Jr.
© 1974 Audubon Society

(fed by his choice of Thomas F. Eagleton as running mate and his subsequent change of plans under pressure) and his stands on issues caused him to lose in all states except Massachusetts and in the District of Columbia.

The lesson written on the political gravestones of such men as Goldwater and McGovern has inspired most candidates to play it cautious and cool, to go for the middle ground and to try

not to be intellectually different (at least outwardly, during the campaign), and only be distinguishable in personality. Knowing that they will get most of the members of their party this way, they reach for the independent voters with a gentle hand and a soothing voice, so as not to frighten them away. It is, after all, these voters who determine the outcome. And since both major party candidates usually solicit the mainstream independent voter in much the same way, it is sometimes difficult to tell them apart.

More than a Dime's Worth of Difference

In fact, as most people in the United States know by the time they reach voting age, this sameness of the major parties is only on the surface. Actually, the two parties are at heart quite different. The difference is acknowledged when Republican candidates invariably accuse Democrats of wanting to spend the nation into the poorhouse and when Democratic candidates accuse Republicans of being stodgy and heartless. Both sides are referring to social programs, which, since the early 1930s, have been the hallmark of the national Democratic approach to government: more money for welfare, housing, employment, and retirement benefits. Democrats as a group have been more willing, Republicans as a group less willing, to initiate new social service programs and to give generous support to old programs. Likewise, Democrats have been more willing and Republicans less willing to permit the federal government to regulate corporate and individual lives.

The ideological coloration of the two parties is more consistently maintained by the parties' leaders than by the rank and file—through issue-lean years and issue-fat years. Rather clear differences show up in the opinions of Republican and Democratic party activists and also in party platforms;[14] in roll-call votes in Congress; and in the policies that Republican and Democratic

---

[14] For further discussion on how the Democratic and Republican platforms differ, see Gerald M. Pomper, *Elections in America: Control and Influence in Democratic Politics* (New York: Dodd, Mead & Co., 1968), Chapters 7, 8.

Presidents and congressional majorities pursue.[15] The strongest feelings are at the top, not at the bottom. But again, this was truer in the 1950s than it is today. The ideological schism of the electorate is widening; the rank and file tend to split more sharply now than they did twenty years ago, as studies conducted in the two periods have shown.

In the late 1950s, a national field study of political beliefs and affiliations was conducted among party leaders and followers. The results showed that the leaders of the two parties differed widely on issues, but the followers differed very little. On some issues—like public ownership of natural resources, enforcement of integration, foreign aid, and defense spending—the rank and file of the two parties could hardly be told apart. There were some differences on issues more related to the New Deal conflicts—regulation of public utilities, social security, and the minimum wage, for example—but even here Republicans and Democrats differed by only 10 to 15 percent. (See Table 7-1.) However, in 1972, Gerald M. Pomper published a study relating party identification to policy beliefs as of 1968. (See Figure 7-1.) It showed that the differences

[15]Sources: Turner, *Party and Constituency*; James L. Sundquist, *Politics and Policy: The Eisenhower, Kennedy and Johnson Years* (Washington, D.C.: Brookings Institution, 1968).

TABLE 7-1

COMPARISON OF PARTY LEADERS AND FOLLOWERS ON ISSUES IN THE 1950s

ISSUES	LEADERS		FOLLOWERS	
	DEM.	REP.	DEM.	REP.
Public ownership of natural resources				
Percentage favoring increase	57.5	12.9	35.3	31.1
Percentage favoring decrease	18.6	51.9	15.0	19.9
Enforcement of integration				
Percentage favoring increase	43.8	25.5	41.9	40.8
Percentage favoring decrease	26.6	31.7	27.4	23.6
Foreign aid				
Percentage favoring increase	17.8	7.6	10.1	10.1
Percentage favoring decrease	51.0	61.7	58.6	57.3
Defense spending				
Percentage favoring increase	20.7	13.6	50.5	45.7
Percentage favoring decrease	34.4	33.6	16.4	15.4
Regulation of public utilities				
Percentage favoring increase	59.0	17.9	39.3	26.0
Percentage favoring decrease	6.4	17.6	11.1	12.0
Social security benefits				
Percentage favoring increase	60.0	22.5	69.4	57.0
Percentage favoring decrease	3.9	13.1	3.0	3.8
Minimum wage				
Percentage favoring increase	50.0	15.5	59.0	43.5
Percentage favoring decrease	4.7	12.5	2.9	5.0

SOURCE: Herbert McClosky, Paul J. Hoffmann, and Rosemary O'Hara, "Issue Conflict and Consensus among Party Leaders and Followers," *American Political Science Review* 54 (June 1960): 406–27.

FIGURE 7-1   PARTY IDENTIFICATION AND POLICY BELIEFS, 1968

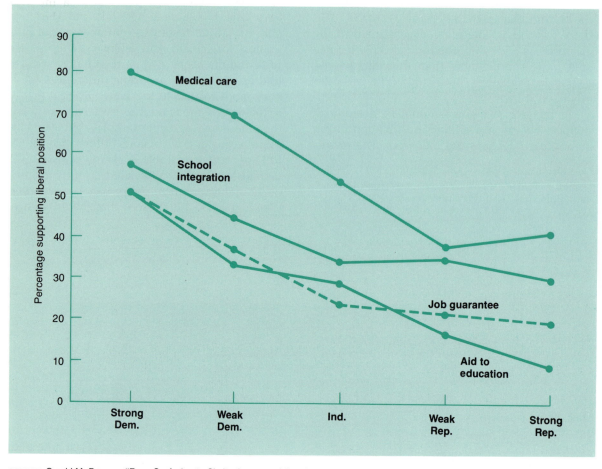

SOURCE: Gerald M. Pomper, "From Confusion to Clarity: Issues and American Voters, 1956–1968,"
American Political Science Review 66 (June 1972): 417.

between the two parties' followers were becoming clearer.[16]

A heating up of ideological tempers and an enthusiasm for issues—if not carried to a fanatical degree—are very healthy for party politics. As Douglas Hallett, a former Nixon White House aide, has pointed out,

> Major political parties do not ordinarily die because of their views. Historically, political parties which have lost public favor, the Whigs in this country and the Liberals in England, have done so

because they have lost track of the need for any views—because they have become, as the Whigs were called, the "Stupid Party."[17]

Within the heart of every powerful political party is the vision of an ideal nation, and the power of the party is in direct proportion to the attractiveness and clarity of that vision. That is why the Republican party, the so-called Grand Old Party (GOP), is in trouble today. Republicans, as Irving Kristol has pointed out,

> are the party of "practical" men, uninterested in large ideas or in a precise elaboration of the relation

[16]Gerald M. Pomper, "From Confusion to Clarity: Issues and American Voters, 1956–1968," *American Political Science Review* 66 (June 1972): 415–28.

[17]Quoted in the *Wall Street Journal*, January 3, 1975.

of means to ends. Being so excessively "practical," they soon find themselves the prisoners of circumstances—they become political managers entirely, with no sense of political entrepreneurship. . . .

Since the end of World War II, the Republican Party and the Democratic Party have occupied the White House for the same number of years, but no one thinks of these as Republican years. . . . The conservatives and the Republican Party just do not seem to be part of the history of the country in this century in the way in which the Democratic Party so clearly is.[18]

The President's Partisan Imprint

The most successful Republican President since World War II went out of his way to play down partisanship. The political allegiance of Dwight Eisenhower (President from 1953 to 1961) was so fuzzy that no less a Democrat than Hubert H. Humphrey tried to drum up support for him at the 1948 Democratic convention. Humphrey thought that if Ike wasn't a Democrat, at least he wasn't a Republican either. And, actually, Humphrey wasn't so far wrong.[19]

As a President, Ike was notoriously cold to the idea of assuming the role of party leader. His close friend and adviser Arthur Larson has written that Eisenhower found party patronage "nauseating" and that "partisan political effect was not only at the bottom of the list—indeed, it did not exist as a motive at all." He was not at all bothered by having to work with a Democratic-controlled Congress. When it was suggested that he might want to try to get some more Republicans elected, he replied, "Frankly, I don't care too much about the Congressional elections."[20] Another aide remembered that Eisenhower "never lost his view of himself as standing apart from politics generally and from his own party in particular."[21]

Some nonpartisan behavior by Republican Presidents reflects the problem of a minority party: there isn't much use boasting about the Republican party label in elections when only about one-quarter of the people consider themselves Republicans. Nor would it make sense to be a purist and seek only Republican votes in Congress when the Democrats have had congressional majorities almost without a break since 1932.[22] Eisenhower, Nixon, and Ford were happy to pick up the support of Democratic members of Congress (mostly southerners) any time they could.

By contrast, recent Democratic Presidents have gone out of their way to flaunt their partisanship, to revel in the fact that they were card-carrying members of the "whiskey-drinkin', poker-playin', hiya-honey Democrats," as some of their critics characterized them.[23] Any serious candidate for the Democratic presidential nomination is expected to mention as a litany, and pay homage to, the names of Franklin Roosevelt, Harry S Truman, and John F. Kennedy (Lyndon Johnson is of too recent and smudged memory to be included yet in the pantheon). These are guardian spirits of the campaign trail, and they are always identified as *Democrats*. Republican candidates rarely evoke the memory of Eisenhower, much less Nixon, nor do they try to bring their party to life as an ongoing programmatic stream.

The character of the modern Democratic party was shaped in the 1930s and 1940s by President Roosevelt, whose administration lasted twenty years (counting, as one must, the Truman administration as being an extension of the FDR era). Since this was a time first of economic crisis, and later of military crisis, Roosevelt had leeway in imprinting a centralized welfare philosophy on the government, and he took advantage of that. During his administration, such measures as farm subsidies, favorable labor organizing laws, urban subsidies, and pension plans were enacted. Roosevelt thus won the

---

[18]Quoted in the *Wall Street Journal,* May 14, 1976.

[19]Penn Kimball, *Bobby Kennedy and the New Politics* (Englewood Cliffs, N.J.: Prentice-Hall, 1968), p. 47.

[20]Quoted in James David Barber, *The Presidential Character: Predicting Performance in the White House* (Englewood Cliffs, N.J.: Prentice-Hall, 1972), p. 157.

[21]Quoted in Barber, p. 160.

[22]The only exceptions were 1947–48 and 1953–54.

[23]This description of the Democrats entered into the political folk language after being widely and popularly used by the Republicans during the Truman administration.

support of a coalition of forces that became identified with the Democratic party. They included left-wing intellectuals, city-dwelling ethnic groups, blacks, farmers, city bosses, and southerners.

In the 1950s and 1960s, that New Deal coalition began gradually to splinter and break away, and, by the 1970s, the southerners, the city-dwelling ethnic groups, the farmers, and even labor had proved in several elections that their votes were up for grabs. However, this did not signify an estrangement from the broad Democratic precepts. Indeed, these blocs had begun to show a willingness to vote for the individual rather than for the party only because, throughout all the years since FDR, the Republican party had indicated a basic willingness to perpetuate the changes made during the Roosevelt administration. In 1960, Clinton Rossiter wrote:

> The Democrats have held the whip hand for the better part of a generation; and, despite the dissensions in their own team, they have used their superior power and sense of purpose to move us at a pretty fast clip—fast, in any case, for American tastes—along the road to Big Government with Big Responsibilities. The Republicans have been forced by political considerations, the march of events, and the more progressive members of their own team to abandon their original posture of obdurate opposition to this trend and to follow the Democrats at a safe distance. The Democrats have been resting for some years now, partly through choice and partly through circumstance, and the Republicans seem to have caught up all along the line. They vote dutifully and almost as enthusiastically as the Democrats for appropriations to keep the Social Security Administration and our delegation to the United Nations in business, and they are supported in their votes by a majority of those in the ranks. . . .
>
> The Republicans only "seem" to have caught up, however, and when the next lunge forward at home or abroad is taken by the Democrats, as it must be taken sooner or later, they will (and, as conservatives, should) drop back again to the distance of that safe city block. . . . The Republicans have been traveling the same road as the Democrats, but they are ten or fifteen years behind and have not enjoyed the trip nearly as much. They did not plan to take it in the first place, and besides they have had to swallow a lot of dust—an occupational hazard with which men who prefer to be conservatives must learn to live.[24]

Since Rossiter wrote that, the Democrats and the Republicans have held the White House about the same length of time. In domestic affairs, the Democrats once again stole the show, making the "lunge forward" that Rossiter had predicted. With a great outburst of imaginative and sometimes hasty legislation in the Kennedy and Johnson years, the Democrats stepped forward with programs so ambitious as to seem aimed at trying to solve all civil rights, poverty, environmental, and health problems. Dozens of agencies were formed; hundreds of programs were launched; billions of dollars were spent. In short, as in the 1930s and 1940s, the Democrats had hustled us another furlong down the road to Bigger Government with Bigger Responsibilities.

That was done during the first eight years after Rossiter's appraisal. The second eight years, however, saw Republicans in the White House; and, for six of those years, it was a very powerful Republican, who used his positive and negative powers so adroitly that many observers feared that Congress (under Democratic control) was being dangerously overshadowed by the Presidency. Nevertheless, once again the Republican administration did little more than trim back the weaker Kennedy-Johnson programs and discredit the shoddily constructed ones. It did *not* print upon the national consciousness a philosophy of its own. There was no significant thriftiness, no significant reduction in the size and responsibilities of the federal government, no real alternatives offered for meeting the civil rights, poverty, and environmental problems. Quite the contrary: the budget and the national debt soared as never before, the size and complexity of government soared right along with the budget, and most of the Kennedy-Johnson solutions stayed on the statute books.

That is why the Republican party has largely lost its character. Today it is not identified by

---

[24]Clinton Rossiter, *Parties and Politics in America* (New York: Times Mirror Co., New American Library, 1964), pp. 134–35.

Drawing by Ed Arno
© 1975 The New Yorker Magazine, Inc.

*"And so I say ask not for whom the bell tolls.
It tolls for moderate Republicanism."*

creative achievements that are peculiarly its own; it has become more and more identified as simply the "other" party. Besides the lack of a positive alternative (except for the unfortunate Goldwater experiment of 1964), the Republicans, in the 1970s, were saddled with Watergate and the sour legacy of the Nixon administration. Moreover, throughout this historical period, voters who had been brought up in the Republican period of the 1920s and earlier and who stayed loyal to the party throughout their lifetime gradually died off and were replaced by young voters who absorbed the Democratic values of their day.

So it is not surprising that, while the Democrats have held fairly steady in partisan strength in the past half of the century, the Republicans have dropped sharply. The percentage of voters who identify themselves as Democrats has only once gone above 52 percent (1964) and only once gone below 42 percent (1974). As for the Republicans, their share has dropped almost yearly from 43 percent in 1920 to 18 percent in 1976.[25]

A count of officeholders shows why some people are despondent about the future of the GOP. In 1976, the Republicans controlled both houses of only 4 state legislatures and held only 13 of 50 governorships, 38 of 100 Senate seats, and 145 of 435 seats in the House of Representatives. Moreover, most Republican governors and

---

[25]Richard C. Wade, *New York Times Book Review*, July 11, 1976.

United States senators in the 9 largest states were considered liberal by Republican standards—which would seem to indicate less a Republican victory than a repudiation of the party's cornerstone ideology.

Republican leaders are trying for a comeback by building—or trying to build—a new image. They are quite aware that most voters view the Republican party as quaint at best, hollow and meaningless at worst. House GOP leader John Rhodes reminded his party's executive committee in 1977, "If we're going to get a story across, we've first got to have a story to tell." What would the story be? GOP National Chairman William Brock says the new GOP story must sound "pro-people":

> We've got to quit sounding like a bunch of accountants talking about how we'll balance the budget because our proposals will cost less. We've got to talk about potholes in the roads, street lights, bus schedules, the impact of unemployment and the effect of inflation on people with fixed incomes.[26]

In other words, Republicans of Brock's persuasion believe the best chance for a comeback is to sound more like Democrats. Their strategy also includes trying to double their support among blacks—which would bring it up to roughly 20 percent of the black electorate.

THE TWO-PARTY SYSTEM

Despite the gloomy talk about the Republican party's decline, there is no imminent prospect of its death. It has too many things propping it up, including the same forces that have given us a two-party system during most of this nation's history.

Why Two Parties?

The question Why two parties? is really two questions: Why more than one party? and Why not more than two? The first question is easy to answer. No matter who has power, there are always discontented minorities who want something different; and so long as there is freedom of political action, the strongest minorities will organize and contest elections. In fact, any time a party gets much larger than 51 percent, there will be some people in it who wonder whether the goodies aren't being spread too thin: why not split off and join with the minority to form a bare majority so that everyone in the new majority can get a larger share of what there is to be had?[27] Big parties topple of their own weight; there is always an incentive for losers to form an opposing party. Even though there have been long periods of dominance by a single party in the United States, only seldom has there been no significant competing party.[28]

Why there are only two parties is a harder question to answer—and a traditional puzzle of political science—since the United States seems so unusual in this respect. Some say that just naturally there have always been two main factions in the United States, beginning with the Federalists and the anti-Federalists and continuing to the present day. Some say we don't have the sharp, multiple divisions of European countries, with their clerical and anticlerical, agrarian and urban, working-class and middle-class factions all finding expression in political parties. This argument ignores the fact that there are plenty of lines of division in the United States, and, indeed, parties have been organized around different cleavages at different times: North versus South, East versus West, farmers versus commercial and industrial workers, and so on. Why doesn't each faction have a party?

A more convincing answer has to do with particular institutional arrangements that make life hard for third parties. Most United States officials are elected on a plurality vote, winner-take-all basis. A minority party might win 20 or 30 percent of the vote in every single congressional district and yet elect no members of Con-

[26] James R. Rickenson, "Times Have Been Hard for GOP and May Get Worse," *Washington Star*, April 13, 1977.

[27] This is the central idea of the "minimal winning coalition." See William H. Riker, *The Theory of Political Coalitions* (New Haven, Conn.: Yale University Press, 1962).

[28] The chief exception is the unopposed rule of Jefferson's Republican party at the beginning of the nineteenth century.

gress at all and thus have no part in the national legislature. (The proportional representation system used by many countries would give this party 20 or 30 percent of the seats and a chance to enter a governing coalition.) Moreover, having a *unitary executive*—a single governor or President who controls the state or federal executive branch—means that only one party at a time plays a part in the executive branch, and a party without a good chance at electing a President is largely shut out of government. (Again, the cabinet governments of many countries give minority parties a voice in the executive branch when they form coalition governments.) There are also many state and local laws written to support the two-party system as it exists today. These laws are weighted against the easy formation of new parties. The federal campaign financing laws also serve to bolster the two major parties and to inhibit the development of ambitious third parties.[29]

The Foreign-Policy Factor

These arguments apply to the two-party system in general, but there is also a crucial reason why the Republican party in particular will continue to be important, at least at the presidential level. That reason is the electorate's deep desire for peace. The United States has, in recent years, developed something of a reputation for warmongering, but this should not be blamed on the voters. When they had their say at the ballot box, it was usually in favor of moderation and peace in foreign affairs, which accounts for the Republican successes in presidential races. Only once since 1944 (the exceptional election of 1964, when Lyndon Johnson ran against a Republican candidate who was identified as an extrem-

ist), has the Democratic party managed to get an absolute majority of the votes in a presidential election. Candidates with a Republican label have achieved this three times during the same period: 1952, 1956, and 1972. (In the other presidential years, neither party won 50 percent of the vote.)

Since World War II, the voters of this country appear to have chosen their Presidents first of all by the standard of their seeming ability to provide leadership, preferably peaceful leadership, in world affairs. They do prefer the generosity of Democratic Congresses for domestic programs, but they will happily take a President of either major party label so long as he measures up to their foreign-policy standards. This was the reason for Eisenhower's great popularity in 1952 and 1956; his image was that of a man capable of waging war but whose first impulses were toward peace. He extricated the United States—sloppily, but still he did extricate us—from the Korean War; he was a man that Americans were proud to have representing them at summit conferences with the Russians; and yet he was cool in a crisis, not quick to threaten or bluster. And he usually requested *less* money for the defense budget than Congress gave him.

The hairbreadth division of votes in the Kennedy-Nixon election of 1960 is probably attributable to the fact that the two men offered little choice in foreign affairs: both seemed erratically militaristic and were quick to use abrasive cold war clichés. The voters perceived a sharp difference in the foreign policies of the two candidates in 1964, however, which resulted in a landslide endorsement (61 percent) of Johnson over Goldwater. Recalls pollster Louis Harris,

A substantial 60 percent late in the campaign in October [1964] said the most important issues for the next president to handle were international: foreign aid, Cuba, the Cold War with Russia, and Vietnam. It may seem ironic in retrospect, but the biggest areas of Johnson superiority to Goldwater could be found in his "ability to keep the U. S. out of war" (70 percent to 30 percent), to "handle a sudden world crisis" (68 percent to 32 percent), to "work for peace in the world" (68 percent to 32 percent), to "give leadership to the free world" (66 percent to 34 percent), and to "handle Khrushchev" (63 percent to 37 percent). Goldwater had

---

[29]When Eugene McCarthy ran as a third-party presidential candidate in 1976, he found all sorts of obstacles. California, for example, wouldn't let him on the ballot until he had presented a petition of 99,284 names; he fell 15,000 short. Fifteen states tried to keep him off the ballot simply because he was an independent candidate, and he had to enlist the help of the Supreme Court to change their minds. Some states, however, are fairly loose about it. New Jersey requires only 800 signatures to get on the ballot, and Oklahoma makes it a strictly cash transaction: a two-hundred-dollar filing fee per elector. (*New York Times Magazine*, October 24, 1976.)

frightened the voters by his talk about using atomic weapons to defoliate the jungles of Vietnam. The most effective Johnson TV commercial that fall, banned after one showing, simply had a little girl picking petals of a flower to a countdown in the background, and when it reached zero, an atom bomb mushroom cloud went up behind her. A better than 2 to 1 majority of the voters felt Goldwater "would act before thinking things through." The issue that shadowed the 1964 campaign was which candidate the voters trusted to have his finger on the button that could set off the bomb.[30]

In 1968, Humphrey and Nixon sounded very much like intellectual twins in their positions on Vietnam and other foreign-policy affairs.[31] Nixon was elected by a very narrow margin that might just as easily have gone the other way a few days later. But his reelection in 1972 was overwhelming; he won 60.7 percent of the vote, partly because there was no Wallace to sap his support, but also because he had begun to wind down the Vietnam war and had recently made dramatic overtures to end the old animosities with Communist China as well as to relax tensions between the United States and the Soviet Union. Although his opponent, George McGovern, ran as the peace candidate, Nixon had projected himself as a peace President (or relatively so, as recent Presidents had gone), and voters were more impressed by performance than by promises.

Thus it is plain that a presidential candidate bearing a Republican label will be seriously considered for election, despite the general weakness of that person's party, if the candidate offers a superior prospect in foreign affairs.

[30]Louis Harris, *The Anguish of Change* (New York: W. W. Norton & Co., 1973), pp. 250–51.

[31]"Taken as a whole, the Vietnam positions of both candidates amounted to advocacy of war as usual, with a rather gradual de-escalation of American effort if and when certain conditions were met. Members of the public were entirely justified in seeing Nixon and Humphrey as standing close together near the center of the Vietnam policy scale, far from the extremes of immediate withdrawal or escalation for complete military victory. One major explanation for the absence of Vietnam-policy voting, therefore, is not that the public failed to perceive reality, but that in reality there was little difference between the candidates." (Benjamin I. Page and Richard A. Brody, "Policy Voting and the Electoral Process: The Vietnam War Issue," *American Political Science Review* 66, 1972: 985.)

A Plague on Both Houses

The popularity of the Republican party in foreign affairs and the popularity of the Democratic party in domestic affairs has, however, not enabled either party to kindle lasting enthusiasm among the voters. As the electorate has become more issue oriented and more intimately concerned with social problems, it also has become more disenchanted and impatient with politicians of both parties. One result of the disenchantment has been an increase in the number of voters content to stay outside organized politics. As figures cited earlier indicate, the decline in the Republican party's strength has *not* been accompanied by a rise in the strength of the Democratic party. It has meant, instead, a swelling of the ranks of "independent" voters, unlabeled but nevertheless quite often firmly ideological. During the 1960s, the proportion of voters calling themselves independents rose from 20 to 30 percent—the highest in thirty-five years of polling. Accompanying this was the highest incidence of ticket-splitting in the country's history. (On one day in 1968, voters of Arkansas, normally Democratic, gave majorities to American Independent George Wallace for President, Republican Winthrop Rockefeller for governor, and Democrat J. William Fulbright for senator.)

Many in this unlabeled area of the electorate believe that neither party answers their needs. Or, to state it more exactly, they believe that both parties are deficient.[32]

[32]In 1975, Market Opinion Research of Detroit found, in a nationwide survey based on two thousand personal interviews, that only 27 percent of those surveyed thought Republicans were competent, compared with 30 percent who thought they were incompetent and 43 percent who had no opinion. In contrast, 44 percent regarded the Democrats as competent, 13 percent thought them incompetent, and 43 percent had no opinion. Only 25 percent thought the GOP trustworthy, compared with 38 percent who thought the party untrustworthy and 37 percent who had no opinion. The Democratic figures were 45 percent trustworthy, 13 percent untrustworthy, and 42 percent no opinion. Since they failed to get a majority vote of confidence, Democrats could take pride only in being viewed as the lesser of two evils.

Surveying at the same time, pollster Paul Newman of Los Angeles reported that when voters were asked to name one thing they liked about the Republican party, two-thirds could not find anything to mention. But 40 percent of the voters also said they could not find a single good thing to say about the Democratic party. (*Washington Post*, January 25, 1975.)

The roots of this discontent are not hard to discern: first the Democrats' foreign policy brought us the Vietnam war, and their domestic reign was characterized by urban riots, rapid inflation, and growing bureaucracy; then, in the Republican years, the United States had to face Watergate, the energy crisis, and stagflation. The series of shocks cast doubt on both parties' performance. But, in addition—as we have seen earlier in this chapter—the *differences* between the parties on some of the most pressing issues of the day no longer seemed so relevant.

The independents' disillusionment with the present two-party system has been heightened by the fact that, for the fourteen years between 1953 and 1976, it created a government that was schizophrenic, with the Republicans holding the White House while the Democrats controlled Congress. Many solutions to important problems were stalled by the resulting friction.

The growing weakness of one of the major parties, plus the general disenchantment with both parties, plus the semistalemate that has resulted from long periods when different parties have held the White House and Congress, have prompted some political scientists and politicians to view pessimistically the future of the two-party system.[33] We cannot be sure where the parties are heading. The movement of blacks into the Democratic party and white southerners into the Republican party suggests a possible realignment along liberal-conservative lines in which the parties would differ substantially on life-style issues as well as on civil rights and the New Deal social welfare issues. But another possibility is a dealignment, with the parties muddling through about as they are and with a low degree of voter loyalty and a high level of cynicism and defection.

The Role of Third Parties

Disillusionment with the two major parties is not likely to lead to a viable third-party alternative. As mentioned earlier, all the laws and structural arrangements that prop up the two parties discourage the formation and success of others.

In the past, third (and fourth) parties have sprung up when ideas that the two major parties considered too radical or inflammatory to handle or too parochial to appeal to a wide range of voters have had currency. The third party's role has been to bring out ideas and express tension. Some of these third-party movements have been highly influential. The Populist party, following the oratorical banner of William Jennings Bryan, was able to force some of its prolabor, profarmer, proinflation, anti–Big Business ideas on the Democratic party. Theodore Roosevelt's Progressive party took enough votes away from William Howard Taft and the Republican party to put Woodrow Wilson in the White House. Henry A. Wallace's Progressive party frightened the Democrats into taking a much firmer civil rights position. George Wallace's amazingly strong third party, the American Independent party, won nearly 10 million votes in 1968 and forced on the consciousness of the political establishment an anti-Washington theme that was picked up and made a central issue in the major-party campaigns of 1976.

Nevertheless, the objective in politics is not simply to frighten the opposition, but to win office, and no third party has established itself with electoral success in running for the Presidency.[34] (See Table 7-2.) Locally, and occasionally on the state level, a third party can win the votes of a plurality. James L. Buckley of New York, for example, was elected to the United States Senate on the Conservative ticket in 1970 (but not reelected).

HOW WELL DO PARTIES WORK?

Parties serve many functions, some better than others. Ideally they should recruit the best candidates for office, clarify alternatives, conciliate

---

[33]See Samuel Lubell, *The Future While It Happened* (New York: W. W. Norton & Co., 1973), p. 44. Especially gloomy about the future of the parties, and fearful of the consequences of their disappearance, is Walter Dean Burnham. See "The End of American Party Politics," *Transaction* 7 (December 1969).

[34]A quibble: some say the Republican party when it elected Lincoln in 1860 was a third party. In any event, since the Civil War, third parties have polled more than 10 percent of the vote in only four elections—those of 1892, 1912, 1924, and 1968.

TABLE 7-2

MINOR PARTIES IN PRESIDENTIAL ELECTIONS, 1880–1976*

YEAR	PARTY	CANDIDATE	PERCENTAGE OF POPULAR VOTE
1880	Greenback-Labor	James B. Weaver	3.4
1888	Prohibition	Clinton B. Fisk	2.2
1892	People's (Populist)	James B. Weaver	8.5
	Prohibition	John Bidwell	2.2
1904	Socialist	Eugene V. Debs	3.0
1908	Socialist	Eugene V. Debs	2.8
1912	Progressive (Bull Moose)	Theodore Roosevelt	27.4
	Socialist	Eugene V. Debs	6.0
1916	Socialist	A. L. Benson	3.2
1920	Socialist	Eugene V. Debs	3.4
1924	Progressive	Robert M. La Follette	16.6
1932	Socialist	Norman Thomas	2.2
1948	States' Rights (Dixiecrat)	J. Strom Thurmond	2.4
	Progressive	Henry A. Wallace	2.4
1968	American Independent	George C. Wallace	13.5

*Only parties polling 2 percent or more of the popular vote are listed. No minor party received 2 percent in 1976 or 1972.

SOURCES: Data from Donald B. Cole, *Handbook of American History* (New York: Harcourt Brace Jovanovich, 1968), pp. 304–05; from *Historical Statistics of the United States: Colonial Times to 1957* (Washington, D.C.: U.S. Government Printing Office, 1961), pp. 682–83; and from the U.S. Department of Justice.

differences, unify the electorate, staff the government, and link the public with the governing elite, as well as joining one branch of the governing elite with another. But there is disagreement over the extent to which parties can, or should, or do engage in these activities.

The one unchallenged role of parties is in nominating candidates. Indeed, some people feel that presiding over the nominating process is the only official function that can properly be assigned to the parties. But that is no small role; it may be the most important institutional role in the democratic process. After all, elections depend on having candidates for the people to vote for, and the only way to have meaningful candidates is to have a limited number of candidates on the ballot, nominated in an orderly and prearranged procedure (as described in Chapter 8) and offered to the electorate with a label that gives some indication of what they stand for or don't stand for.

To avoid chaos, something similar to the present party machineries has to exist—that is, there has to be means for selecting a supply of candidates who are both electable and of reasonably high intelligence and character. Sometimes they fail dismally in one or the other of these criteria, or in both. As Donald R. Matthews points out, the Republicans in 1964 and the Democrats in 1972 nominated candidates "who were virtually certain losers." Making McGovern's 1972 loss all the more certain was the discovery, a few days after his nomination, that the Democratic vice-presidential candidate, Eagleton, had a record of emotional instability and psychiatric treatment. On the other side, the 1972 nominations produced Republican presidential and vice-presidential nominees who were certain winners but whose crooked activities caused them both to be forced to resign from office after being reelected.[35]

The 1976 nominees were not the sort to make voters sing. The Republicans decided on Gerald Ford, a party hack for twenty-six years who would never have been considered as a potential occupant of the White House if he hadn't already been there (handpicked by Nixon as his successor), and the Democrats chose the former governor of one of the poorest and least progressive states in the union, James Earl Carter, Jr. Their contest was conducted at such an uninspiring level that sometimes it seemed that the most important questions were (1) whether or not Carter, a Baptist deacon, should have given an interview to *Playboy* magazine, (2) whether or not Ford had taken money illegally during at least one of his congressional races, (3) whether or not Carter should have called former President Johnson a liar and cheat, and (4) whether or not Ford should have shown more haste in firing his Secretary of Agriculture, Earl L. Butz, for telling a joke that was both vulgar and racist. The electorate wasn't offered much to go on.

Once the candidate is elected, the party label becomes less important. Because of the decentralized, undisciplined character of the party system, there is no way to hold an elected official accountable to the party platform. A voter cannot vote for a party and be assured that its candidate will deliver what has been promised.

One claim often made for parties, with some foundation, is that they help organize politics for those on the bottom of society, who would otherwise be confused and apathetic and perhaps unrepresented. In the United States, the Democratic party does this, to some extent, for poor and working-class people,[36] but not nearly to the extent of the radical and labor parties of Europe. In any event, this role is limited by the inequalities of wealth and resources in society.

No matter what the structure or ideology of the two parties is, they both tend to serve a political elite, a group that has the resources and the desire to act politically. In our society, that means people who have money to stoke the party coffers—especially Big Business and Big Labor. As a result, the parties are responsive to their wishes to a greater extent than to those of, say, the poor and uneducated and unorganized.

The way the parties are organized, the backers they attract, the way the electoral system reinforces a two-party system—all these factors have the effect of maintaining the status quo, stifling dissent, and keeping genuinely revolutionary ideas off the agenda. Still, nothing has yet been devised that can take the place of parties—that can provide the means of selecting candidates and permitting the orderly transfer of power that parties can accomplish. And as the following chapter makes clear, there is an increasing democratization going on within the parties, so that more and more United States citizens are having a share in party decisions.

---

[35]For more of Matthews's pessimism, see his "Presidential Nominations: Process and Outcomes," in James David Barber, ed., *Choosing the President* (Englewood Cliffs, N.J.: Prentice-Hall, 1974), pp. 35ff.

[36]In recent decades, the Republican party has given little attention to winning support from the lower economic class by developing programs to improve its condition. The result has been a serious alienation of a large voting bloc made up not simply of the dirt poor, but of many nonwealthy. Naturally, this bothers some Republicans. Nixon aide Jeb Stuart Magruder writes in his book *An American Life: One Man's Road to Watergate*, "One idea we sometimes kicked around in the White House was changing the name of the Republican Party. We felt that in the minds of too many average Americans 'Republican Party' meant the party of the rich and privileged. One way to attract Middle Americans to our cause might be by offering what seemed to be a new party. The title that most attracted us was Conservative Party . . . but nothing ever came of it." (New York: Atheneum Publishers, 1974, p. 140.) Notice that the ambition of the Nixonites was to appeal to *middle Americans,* not poor Americans. They had written off the poor, dismissed the poor as generically Democratic. Elsewhere Magruder explained, "We didn't spend time on the disadvantaged for the simple reason that there were no votes there." (*Harper's,* October 1973.) In point of fact, more poor people vote Republican than Magruder realized.

Summary

1. A political party is a group engaged in electing public officials and organizing government. There have been many parties in America, but only two have dominated politics at any one time.

2. The two major parties today—the Democratic and the Republican—have controlled national politics for more than a century; they have shown strong continuity, although there have been major realignments from time to time.

3. Party organizations—consisting of voters, party workers, and elected officials—are generally loose and undisciplined. Party organization exists at every level—precinct, ward, county, state, and national—but there is more influence from the bottom up than from the national hierarchy down. The one exception to undisciplined party structure is the urban political machine.

4. There are two kinds of party workers—the "regulars," who make a profession of politics, and the "purists," who generally enter politics on a one-time basis, in order to elect a particular candidate.

5. Voters who identify with one party tend to be loyal to it; the party helps them to orient themselves politically.

6. Because a major party must attract and hold a wide variety of interests, each one tends to hug the middle ground. On some issues it is hard to distinguish one party from the other.

7. Parties do differ in ideology, however. This shows up in the views of party activists, in party platforms, in roll call votes in Congress, and in policies pursued by Republican and Democratic Presidents.

8. Democratic Presidents have left a greater partisan imprint than Republican Presidents, partly because the Democratic party has been the majority party for a number of years and because it has led in social and economic innovations. In electoral contests, however, the electorate's preference for Republican leadership in foreign affairs somewhat offsets the decline in their registered voters.

9. The fact that there have always been only two major parties may be attributable to (1) a natural division into two political factions from the time of the ratification of the Constitution, (2) institutional arrangements, such as single-member election districts and the plurality vote, and (3) state election laws that bolster the two-party system.

10. Recently the electorate has shown signs of disenchantment with both parties. There may be a realignment of the parties along liberal/conservative lines or, perhaps, a dealignment, which would be reflected in low party loyalty and a high rate of defection from organized parties.

11. Third parties serve the function of expressing ideas too inflammatory or parochial for the major parties to handle, but third parties have had a notable lack of success in national electoral contests.

12. Parties have performed well in nominating candidates and providing for an orderly transfer of power. But parties don't always offer clear alternatives, nor can they hold elected officials accountable to party platforms. Moreover, both parties tend to serve an elite—those special interests who fill the party coffers.

Additional Reading

V. O. Key, Jr., *Politics, Parties, and Pressure Groups,* 5th ed. (New York: Thomas Y. Crowell Co., 1964); and Frank J. Sorauf, *Party Politics in America,* 2nd ed. (Boston: Little, Brown and Co., 1972), are general treatments of the organization and activity of political parties in the United States.

The history of the parties is given in William N. Chambers, *Political Parties in a New Nation: The American Experience, 1776–1809* (New York: Oxford University Press, 1963); William N. Chambers and Walter Dean Burnham, eds., *The American Party Systems,* 2nd rev. ed. (New York: Oxford University Press, 1975); James L. Sundquist, *Dynamics of the Party System: Alignment and Realignment of Political Parties in the United States* (Washington, D.C.: Brookings Institution, 1973); Wilfred E. Binkley, *American Political Parties: Their Natural History,* 4th rev. ed. (New York: Random House, Alfred, A. Knopf, 1963); and Everett Carl Ladd, Jr., *American Political Parties* (New York: W. W. Norton & Co., 1970).

Samuel J. Eldersveld's *Political Parties: A Behavioral Analysis* (Skokie, Ill.: Rand McNally & Co., 1964) is a detailed study of the attitudes and behavior of local party workers. Herbert McClosky, Paul J. Hoffman, and Rosemary O'Hara, "Issue Conflict and Consensus among Party Leaders and Followers" *(American Political Science Review* 54, June 1960: 406–27), contrasts the opinions of party elites with those of the rank and file. William L. Riordon's *Plunkitt of Tammany Hall* (New York: E. P. Dutton & Co., n.d.), a fascinating account of "honest graft," illustrates the workings of a political machine.

E. E. Schattschneider, *Party Government* (New York: Holt, Rinehart & Winston, 1942), gives a concise analysis of American parties and argues for a more "responsible," centralized party system; Austin Ranney, *The Doctrine of Responsible Party Government: Its Origins and Present State* (Urbana, Ill.: University of Illinois Press, 1962), analyzes and critiques the doctrine.

Anthony Downs, *An Economic Theory of Democracy* (New York: Harper & Row, Publishers, 1957), views parties as unified teams competing for votes and derives a number of theoretical predictions about voters and politicians.

In 1956, I heard Adlai Stevenson make a very impassioned and beautiful speech, after which an overzealous reporter jumped up in the back of the room and said, "Governor Stevenson, if every right-minded person in the country votes for you, you'll be President of the United States." And Stevenson's remark was, "I'm sorry. That's not enough. I need a majority."

Russell Hemenway

The people have spoken—the bastards.

Morris K. Udall

8
CAMPAIGNS, VOTING, AND ELECTIONS

As Adlai Stevenson and Mo Udall found out, it is not easy to get elected in America, particularly to the Presidency. It requires stamina, ambition, patience, political know-how, persuasion, and money. Stevenson, who won the Democratic nomination twice, and Udall, who ran unsuccessfully for the nomination in twenty-two state primaries in 1976, had all those attributes. What they obviously did not have enough of was charisma—that indefinable and priceless quality that makes a candidate attractive to the public.

There are three types of candidate that generally make it over the hurdles to win the nomination for President. The first is the good party man, who has worked his way up through party activism and elective office (often in the Senate). Gerald R. Ford, Hubert H. Humphrey, Richard M. Nixon, and Lyndon B. Johnson fit into this category. Then there is the insurgent candidate. This type wraps up the nomination by working the state party meetings (caucuses), conventions, and primaries with the help of a faction of party activists. George S. McGovern, Barry M. Goldwater, and James E. Carter made it that way. The third type is the outside hero—like Dwight D. Eisenhower and Ulysses S. Grant. Celebrated soldiers are especially apt at parlaying the outside hero's role, because their popularity transcends political party lines.

Whoever emerges on top of the heap when the last vote is counted in November has come a long way, usually starting two years earlier on the road to nomination—building recognition, entering primaries, working caucuses, passing inspection at the national convention. Then comes a two- or three-month grind of constant campaigning[1]—making as many personal appearances as possible, grabbing air time, meeting contributors, answering questions from the press, and, above all, avoiding blunders. If that formula is put together successfully, it will perform political miracles. It did for Jimmy Carter. When he appeared on the TV show "What's My Line?" in 1973, the panelists could not guess his name even after being told he was governor of Georgia. Three years later he was elected President.

In this chapter, we will examine how electoral politics looks both to the candidate and to the voter.

THE ROAD TO NOMINATION

In the evolution of the presidential nominating process there has been a trend toward more democratic selection of delegates to the national conventions, at which the candidates are chosen. Originally, the voter had nothing directly to do with nominations. Presidential candidates, in the early years of the nineteenth century, were nominated by congressional caucuses. This was unsatisfactory to politicians outside Congress, particularly those in state governments, and they forced the establishment of national party conventions, at which they could have a share in the nominating power. Together, these politicians made up the nominating claques that have been celebrated in the legends about the "smoke-filled rooms." Party insiders picked their man. The public was excluded.

Needless to say, reform politicians and the general public began pounding on the door, demanding more democracy, and in recent years changes have been made. The reforms have been especially visible in those states where party caucuses are the first cog in the machinery that determines party nominations. This machinery consists first of meetings at the ward or precinct level to select delegates to the state conventions, where candidates for state office are nominated and the delegates to the national conventions are chosen. Until the 1970s, this internal party system—passing the nominating power up from precinct to state convention to national convention—was the method by which most presidential delegates were chosen. It was a method that was firmly controlled by party professionals. But reform insurgents have achieved, beginning with the 1972 election, a greater role for ordinary rank-and-file members in the nominating and delegate-selecting process. Even so, this system is not the most fulsome example of direct democracy, for only the party faithful have the stomach—and the necessary sense of involvement and partisan ambition—to attend the dull caucuses and conventions. This is why the caucus system has sharply lost favor in recent years and why the direct primary—the second type of reform—has become so popular.[2]

A primary election is an intraparty fight; a general election is interparty. That is, a primary is a party's elimination round. It is a way of thinning the ranks of contestants for the party's nominations. Primaries for state and local offices in which no one candidate wins a majority of the votes may call for a runoff election between the two top contestants. The winner of the runoff will then be the party's nominee for that particular office in the general election. A presidential primary consists of a state-wide election in which party voters choose delegates to the national party convention. Presidential primaries are also elimination contests, for candidates who hope to swing the nomination at the national convention had better show up with plenty of state delegates behind them. About 80 percent of the convention delegates are now chosen in primaries.

---

[1] Unless the candidate is a popular incumbent President, in which case the best campaign is no campaign but sticking close to the White House and pretending to be aloof from the grubbiness of politics.

[2] In 1910, Oregon conceived the first presidential primary, and, fanned by Robert M. La Follette's Progressives in Wisconsin, it began to sweep the country like a prairie fire. Within six years, twenty-six states had adopted the primary system. But the popularity of the primary died down as swiftly as it had flared up. There were only seventeen state primaries in 1968. Then their popularity swelled again. The 1972 election saw twenty-three primaries, and, in 1976, there were thirty.

The Majority

Majority rule rested on a democratic faith. This was a faith in the long-run prudence and wisdom of the greater number of voters. It translated into domestic politics Voltaire's assertion that "God is on the side of the big battalions." "In God we trust." Our political system, then, like others, has historically rested on belief that the right to govern derives from some higher power.

The higher mystery, in our representative government, has been embodied in the sacrament of the ballot box. There the Many become the One. On Election Day, the separate wills of millions of citizens become a single, clear "mandate." "*Vox populi, vox dei*"—the voice of the people is the voice of God—simply expresses "the divinity that doth hedge a majority."

The weaknesses and indecisions and selfishnesses of all the individual voters become purified and transformed. Behind this quasi-religious belief in the divine right of the majority, and giving it some reality in the commonsense world, was a simple fact. The majority really *was* a mystery. The single voice of the majority as it issued from thousands of ballot boxes could be heard loud and clear. But who could be sure of what it would say? Who could be sure of which particular voices had entered its resonance?

By a series of steps, now nearly forgotten, our voting system was changed to preserve, deepen, and keep sacred this mystery of the majority. Originally, most states actually did not have the secret ballot: voters stood up before neighbors and announced their preference, which was then marked on a public scoreboard. Only gradually did the secrecy of each citizen's vote come to be protected. At first, each party printed its own "ticket" (commonly a different color from that of the other parties), but spectators could still see a voter's preference by the color of his voting paper.

The campaign for the secret (or so-called "Australian") ballot began in earnest in the 1880s. What was probably our first secret-ballot law was enacted by Kentucky on February 24, 1888. Other states followed. Reformers argued that there could be no true democracy without the secret ballot. For secrecy reduced incentives to bribery and intimidation, made it impossible for corrupt politicians to be sure they were getting the votes they were willing to pay for, and so purified the voice of the majority.

The democratic paradox, which itself became an article of faith, was that majority rule really worked only so long as it could *not* be known precisely who was in the majority. This was the Mystery of the Majority. Of course, the elections themselves produced some voting statistics—on wards, congressional districts, or states—from which shrewd politicians could draw their own conclusions. But these official statistics were always wholesale and geographic. The Mystery of the Majority remained a mystery, which an enlarging and mobile electorate and a secret ballot only made more impenetrable.

From Daniel J. Boorstin, *The Decline of Radicalism: Reflections on America Today* (New York: Random House, 1969), pp. 110–11.

Some hard-nosed professionals are filled with nostalgia for the old days, when more sober party regulars picked the candidates.[3] But for this moment in history, at least, there is little chance of going back to such an arrangement. Not many political professionals are so bold as to even mention the possibility. The more common sentiment is aptly summed up by Austin Ranney:

[3] See Burns W. Roper, "Distorting the Voice of the People," *Columbia Journalism Review*, November/December 1975.

No American who wishes to be taken seriously dares to argue right out in public that our presidential nominees should be chosen by a few party bosses making secret deals in air-conditioned (no longer smoke-filled) rooms. To be sure, such nominees as Thomas Jefferson, James Madison, James Monroe, Henry Clay, Abraham Lincoln, Grover Cleveland, and Woodrow Wilson were chosen that way. But then so too were William Henry Harrison, Zachary Taylor, Franklin Pierce, James Buchanan, and Warren Harding; so the bosses-and-deals method is not guaranteed to produce or prevent a nominee of top quality, and in any case it runs sharply counter to the *Zeitgeist* of the 1970s.

That *Zeitgeist* requires us all to affirm that the nomination should be made by, or at least be in accordance with, the wishes of a much larger group—the "party members," the "rank and file," or simply "the people."[4]

In short, the people increasingly have come to relish making their own mistakes, without the advice of professionals, who, after all, have not exactly produced a shining record of nominations.

More Democratic, More Confusing

The proliferation of democracy both in the caucus states and in the primary states has been accompanied by a high degree of confusion. Not only does each of the fifty states have its own rules for putting candidates on the ballot and selecting delegates to the national convention, but the two parties have different rules nationally, and different rules in each state as well. In some states, for example, Republicans operate by the winner-take-all principle; the Democrats have outlawed that method, and they now divvy up the delegates in proportion to each candidate's share of the votes. Most of the primaries—both Republican and Democratic—result in the election of delegates committed to voting for a particular candidate at the national convention. Some delegates who run in the primaries, how-

ever, are uncommitted. And in a few states, the primaries are known as "beauty contests"; their results are only advisory, because the delegates are not bound by the voters' preference.

To add to the confusion, in some states, such as New Hampshire, the list of names on the ballot is composed of candidates who have met filing requirements. In some other states, such as Massachusetts, the Secretary of State decides which candidates will be on the ballot, and anyone who wants to be *removed* must file a statement of noncandidacy. In still other states, such as Oregon, once the Secretary of State has put a candidate's name on the ballot there is no way to get it off. (At least that's the way it was in 1976; the rules change like quicksilver from election to election.)

If you find the rules confusing, you are not alone; the candidates do, too. George C. Wallace placed second in popular votes in Wisconsin in 1972, but he got not a single delegate. Hubert Humphrey placed third in Wisconsin and got 13 delegates. Why the difference? Wallace had failed to file a proper delegate slate according to Wisconsin's rules. In Pennsylvania, Wallace finished second but won only 2 delegates; McGovern, who finished third, got 37, and Muskie, who finished fourth, got 29. Once again, Wallace had fumbled the rules.

As in most complicated games, the master of the rules has a great advantage. Sometimes it seems that knowledge of the rules can be used to cheat the spirit of the process. Consider the McGovern nomination in 1972. In January of that year, a Gallup poll that surveyed Democrats' choices for the nomination produced these results (in percentage):

Edmund S. Muskie	89
Hubert H. Humphrey	29
Eugene McCarthy	8
John V. Lindsay	7
Henry M. Jackson	3
George S. McGovern	3
Samuel W. Yorty	2
Shirley Chisholm	2
Vance Hartke	under 1
No preference	7

Edward M. Kennedy had ranked second in the poll, but said he would not be a candidate.

[4]Austin Ranney, "Changing the Rules of the Nominating Game," in James David Barber, ed., *Choosing the President* (Englewood Cliffs, N.J.: Prentice-Hall, 1974), p. 75. The yearning for intensified democratization of the nominating process pushed the Democrats to decide, before the 1972 convention, that women, blacks, and young people should be guaranteed a quota of delegates roughly equivalent to their proportion of the general population—51 percent women, 11 percent blacks, and 27 percent between the ages of eighteen and thirty. But quotas have always stuck in the craw of most Americans, and, before the 1976 nomination, the Democrats had considerably modified this requirement. After all, if it was undemocratic to exclude certain people because of biological characteristics, it was also undemocratic to assume that people of certain biological characteristics could be fairly represented only by their own kind. The Republicans, who had never been troubled about the question of egalitarian representation at the national convention, had passed up the quota experiment.

Clearly, McGovern was not popular at that stage; he was even seen as an insignificant candidate. And yet, six months later he walked into the national convention hall in Miami with the Democratic nomination virtually sewn up. How did he manage it?

The Caucuses

McGovern's nomination can't be explained simply by the delegates he had amassed in twenty-three primaries. To be sure, these comprised two-thirds of the delegate strength he took to the Miami convention, and they were obtained by brilliant organizing and against great odds. But those delegates would not have been enough to protect him from the Democratic party leaders who disliked him because he was a maverick and (they thought) a radical. If he had gone to the convention with only his primary delegates, he would not have been in a strong enough position to win the nomination on the first ballot, and the party regulars would have had the time to organize and defeat him on the second ballot.

The margin of delegate strength that allowed him to win on the first ballot had come from the largely unpublicized nonprimary states—where the delegate fights were conducted in local party caucuses and in state party conventions. In these, McGovern had won 364 of a possible 1,009 delegates, compared with fewer than 100 delegates for either of his closest rivals—the odds-on favorites of the Democratic regulars, Humphrey and Muskie. McGovern had made his move before the other candidates were wise to what he was up to. As early as the fall of 1970—two years before the election—McGovern's workers were quietly moving in to fill the vacuum at the precinct level, a vacuum created by normal voter lethargy. Throughout 1971, polls showed that no more than 5 percent of the Democrats wanted him for their nominee.[5] Most candidates would have interpreted that as a sign to get out of the race. To McGovern it was a sign he could win. He knew that no more than 5 or 6 percent of the party's voters show up for caucuses. So long as

they were *his* 5 or 6 percent (even 3 or 4 percent was enough for majority control), he could take the caucuses.

The key to McGovern's success in both primaries and caucuses was intense, even fanatical, organization[6] and a willingness to be unorthodox. Many of McGovern's workers were young people who opposed the war in Vietnam. In one district, a McGovern campaign manager spoke at local high schools and got students to help

---

[6]The embodiment of this intense organizational drive was Gene Pokorny, then twenty-five years old, McGovern's Middle West regional coordinator. Pokorny's timeless advice: "Organization is a very simple thing. All politics is is names. Get their names and telephone numbers and put them on 3 × 5 cards. The guts of politics is on 3 × 5 cards." Muskie and Humphrey had all the big endorsements from labor leaders and party bosses, but McGovern had the little cards. (Robert Sherrill, "Primaries and Conventions," *Collier's Yearbook, 1972*, New York: Macmillan Educational Corporation, 1973, p. 13.)

Presidential candidate McGovern has a cafeteria lunch at Dartmouth College

---

[5]*New York Times*, June 11, 1972.

turn out young voters for the precinct meetings. A teacher at a school for juvenile delinquents on probation gave his eighteen-year-old students credit for participating in precinct meetings. Members of two communes helped ring door-bells and solicit pro-McGovern voters to turn out for the precinct delegate voting. The result: McGovern swept the caucuses in that district. His workers showed similar imagination in hundreds of precincts. It was perfectly legitimate; it may even have been an admirably enthusiastic participation in government. But the result was the nomination of a candidate who did not reflect the cross-sectional sentiment of his party, to say nothing of the cross-sectional sentiment of voters in general. And the further result was, of course, a disastrous defeat in the general election.

The Primaries

If caucuses can be won with an insignificant fraction of the voters, primaries—in which three-fourths of the delegates to both Democratic and Republican conventions are chosen—are not much more representative. In 1976, for example, only about one-fifth of the eligible voters cast primary ballots. Jimmy Carter won eighteen of the twenty-nine primaries he ran in (he failed to enter only one, West Virginia's)—far more than any candidate had ever before won. But the number of votes he needed to attain that remarkable record puts a dismal light on it: of the 150 million Americans eligible to vote, about 60 million call themselves Democrats. Of these, only 16 million voted in the Democratic primaries and only 6.2 million, or 39 percent, voted for Carter. So an impressive majority—61 percent—of the relatively small number of Democrats who cared enough to vote in the 1976 primaries would have preferred a nominee other than the winner.

Some political observers believe that the primaries (as well as the reformed caucuses) are weighted in favor of the "outsiders"—the politicians who wouldn't have a prayer of a chance if their fate was left to party leaders. Neither McGovern, in 1972, nor Carter, in 1976, would have stood much chance of receiving the Democratic nomination if the choice had been left to the people who make up that vaguely felt, inde-

finable thing called the Democratic establishment. Some of the people who bother to vote in the primaries, however, pay little attention to what the establishment in either party asks of them. Those people often use the primaries to cast "rebellion" votes—not for candidates they expect to win in November, but for candidates, like George Wallace, Eugene McCarthy, and Ronald Reagan, who reflect their own feelings of unhappiness or who represent minority factions.

Moreover, if there are, say, three moderates splitting the center-to-right vote, it is entirely possible for a very liberal Democrat to walk off with a plurality in enough primaries to secure the nomination, although in the general election—as McGovern proved—the candidate would be incapable of enticing the mainstream of his party, much less the independents.[7] In a situation like that, the accumulation of delegates cannot be equated with an expression of party popularity or an expression of party philosophy.

The most obvious defect in the primaries is that they last so awfully long. A candidate who enters all of them—and very few candidates have done that—will have his or her first test in the snows of New Hampshire and wind up the road show under the summer sun of California. It is not a process but an ordeal. Though drawn out over several months, the primaries demand such a packed schedule that the candidate cannot possibly spend more than three or four days in most states. A normal campaigning day may include a breakfast speech in Florida, a lunch meeting with backers in Illinois, and a fund-raising dinner in North Carolina—all in prepara-

---

[7]Something similar *could* happen on the Republican side, but in practice the Republicans usually do not flood the primary tickets with candidates the way Democrats do; they postpone their donnybrooks until the national convention itself. The nearest thing to a McGovern-type fiasco in the Republican party in recent years was Barry M. Goldwater's nomination in 1964. His strength, like McGovern's, came from intensely devoted, hard-working followers at the grass roots, and his victory at the convention came, like McGovern's, from splitting the majority into warring factions so that his minority could win. The moderate Republicans—divided among supporters of Richard M. Nixon, George W. Romney, Nelson A. Rockefeller, and William W. Scranton—failed to unify, and red-hot conservative Goldwater walked off with the prize. His defeat in the general election was only slightly less crushing than McGovern's loss eight years later.

tion for primaries grouped within a two-week period.

That sort of mad scrambling goes on steadily from late February to early June. It leaves both the candidates and the general public feeling that they have been subjected to politics by roulette rather than politics of reason. It leaves all sides wondering, "What if." What if Ronald Reagan had been able to campaign one more day in New Hampshire, where a switch of only 794 votes would have given him a priceless victory over Gerald Ford? Instead, he had felt compelled to race off to start campaigning in Florida. What if he had had time to campaign even one day in Wisconsin's winner-take-all election, where he got 44 percent of the votes without campaigning at all? Campaigning against a sitting President, with all the tremendous advantages that incumbency gave Ford, Reagan had still won ten of the twenty-two Grand Old Party (GOP) primaries and, at the Kansas City convention, had only 111 fewer delegates than Ford. What if he had had the time and money (his campaign was virtually flat broke for most of April) to enter the Pennsylvania, New Jersey, New York, or Ohio primaries, instead of passing them by? To be sure, politics is always full of "what ifs," but those arising from the present primary system seem especially arbitrary, especially surrealistic, especially the product of a jerry-built procedure.

Just about everyone agrees that having dozens of primaries scattered over several months of the year makes no sense at all. But as with most needed reforms, there is diversity of opinion as to the best method for streamlining the present system.

Some people have proposed one national primary, wiping out state boundaries. President Woodrow Wilson first proposed this plan. It is unlikely to be adopted. Its many critics argue that one primary would favor the candidate who was already well-known, whereas multiple primaries allow underdogs to develop "popularity momentum." They also argue that, with only one primary, several moderate candidates might split up the votes of the centrist majority in such a way as to allow an extremist candidate to walk away with a winning plurality.

Another proposal is to establish a series of five or six primaries, held two weeks apart from late March to mid-June, to be conducted by region. Congressman Morris Udall of Arizona, who ran himself ragged in the 1976 primaries, has proposed a plan whereby the states would continue to hold their own primaries, but there would be a limited number of dates—say, three or four—on which all of the states could call for a vote.[8]

The Power of the Poll

For at least a generation, opinion polls have had the power to shape the outcome, as well as the conduct, of political campaigns. They have even had a powerfully persuasive effect on who gets into a race and who stays out. In 1968, Governor George W. Romney decided to quit the Republican presidential contest before the first primary because polls showed that Nixon would subject him to an embarrassing defeat. It may only have been a coincidence, but President Johnson's announcement that he would not seek reelection in 1968 came on the very day that a Gallup poll reported Johnson's popularity at an all-time low.

Polls used by a candidate to guide himself or herself can be useful; and if they are harmful, they harm nobody but the candidate. On the other hand, polls published by the media that estimate the current strength of candidates and the probable outcome of races are looked on with some suspicion. How useful are they to the general public? Indeed, how dangerous can they be to the conduct of a fair campaign? Does the publication of polls persuade some of the electorate to "go with an apparent winner," thus making it even more difficult for the trailing candidate to catch up?

Lester Markel, a former editor of the *New York Times*, believes polls do more harm than good:

> Usually there is little social purpose served by election soundings; now and then, it is true, they may act as warnings that renewed efforts are needed to defeat an undesirable candidate. In general, though, it can be said that the electorate can well wait until the returns are in to find out

[8]A good discussion of these various plans can be found in William R. Keech and Donald R. Matthews, *The Party's Choice* (Washington, D.C.: Brookings Institution, 1976).

How to Choose a Candidate

Everyone seems to have ideas on how to improve the presidential campaign contests. James Reston, an executive at the *New York Times,* has come up with a wry list of suggestions for picking candidates.

- All candidates should be subjected to a rigorous physical and psychological examination before the nominating conventions. Anybody with minor psychological hangups should be accepted in order to assure that *somebody* is available, but congenital liars, twisters, and obvious nuts should be rejected before the primary elections begin.

- Eliminate the Politics of Bribery. Anybody who promises "a generation of peace" or a prosperous world without war or inflation should be hooted out of town.

- All candidates should have a valid driver's license.

- No man married to a ninny who adores her spouse and tells him he's always right should even be considered.

- Let each state propose at least one nonpolitician for the job. Politics may be too serious to be left to the politicians alone.

- Indict George Gallup and Lou Harris for running popularity polls and obstructing individual judgment and common sense.

- Make both parties pick their Vice-Presidential candidates at least fifteen minutes before they're shoved out on the convention stage.

- Forget about "charisma" and look for a few straight characters who simply know the difference between right and wrong and yes and no.

- Amend the Constitution to get rid of any President who obviously loses the confidence of the people before his four years are up.

- Look for somebody who has read a book.

- Eliminate any man who is obviously running for the Presidency but says he's not and won't even think about it for another year or two.

- Have the newspapers publish the texts of the average extemporaneous speeches made by candidates on the stump so that the people can know just how bad they really are.

- Concentrate on the men who are coming instead of the men who are going.

- Get all candidates, in advance, to define "executive privilege" and "national security," and check their income taxes.

- Keep book on their lies and deceptions during the campaign.

- Make all candidates and White House aides read the Constitution before they swear to uphold it.

- Don't look at the candidates, listen to them and think about them.*

*James Reston, *New York Times,* January 27, 1974.

who are the victors; that the delay can inconvenience only the gamblers; that there is always the danger that polls may bring about a "bandwagon vote" (a desire to be on the winning side) and that a bad showing in the polls may make it difficult for a candidate to raise money.[9]

George H. Gallup argues that there is no such thing as a bandwagon effect.

> Surveys show that voters are not inclined to jump on bandwagons. In past Presidential elections, support for the candidate leading in early September test elections has closely matched his vote in the November election, despite the continuous publication of polls showing him in the lead. Richard Nixon's support in an early September test election in 1972 was 64 percent; his vote in the election was 61.8 percent. Nixon's support in early September, 1968, was 43 percent; his vote in the election that year was 43.5 percent. In 1964, Lyndon Johnson's support in an early September test election was 62 percent; his vote in November was 61.3 percent. And the examples can be carried back to the mid-thirties, when scientific polling was first undertaken.[10]

Perhaps Gallup is right, but the experience of President Harry S Truman, when he was running for reelection in 1948, would indicate that even when polls do not create an unfair bandwagon effect, they may result in unjustified hardships. All major polls showed that Truman would lose to Republican candidate Thomas E. Dewey. Most newspaper columnists thought so, too; but the columnists, after all, were just guessing, and the polls were looked on as being almost scientific, so they carried much more weight. On September 9, 1948, Elmo Roper, a respected pollster, reported that Dewey was leading Truman 44 percent to 31 percent. Such an overwhelming lead, said Roper, was irreversible, and he would conduct no more polls in the campaign. The announcement had a chilling effect on the Truman campaign in that it cut off two things that no campaign can run without: money and credit. Who wants to back a guaranteed loser? Sometimes Truman couldn't be sure he would have money to pay for a radio broadcast until the very last minute before he went on the air, and the networks were insisting on payment in advance, because they didn't want to be left with bills unpaid by a defeated candidate. At one point, it was reported that his campaign train could not leave Oklahoma because of a shortage of funds to pay the railroad.[11]

Political sociologist Seymour Martin Lipset believes that this also happened to Humphrey's campaign in 1972.

> Hubert Humphrey was greatly disadvantaged in the decisive California primary by published surveys which showed him farther behind McGovern than the actual results suggested he had been. The highly reputable California Poll reported four days before the June primary that McGovern was ahead of Humphrey by 20 percent (46 percent to 25 percent), but just a few days later McGovern won by only five percent.[12] At the time, Humphrey's California campaign manager credited this poll with determining the outcome of the 1972 election, by cutting off campaign contributions: "It was just like turning off the water tap with one flick of the wrist. If it had been more accurate, we would have raised more money, spent more money and we would have won. If we had won California, there are a lot of people who say we would have won the nomination and won the election."[13]

Distortion by the Media

The potential effect of polls depends entirely on how they are publicized and stressed by the media. If newspaper and TV reporters use polls with moderation and caution, there is little chance that they will result in distortions and unfair campaigns. But if the reporters drag in the polls as hoopla to create a circus atmosphere, to rate and classify and reject candidates out of hand, then of course the polls can indeed be

[9]Lester Markel, *What You Don't Know Can Hurt You: Study in Public Opinion and Public Emotion* (Washington, D.C.: Public Affairs Press, 1972), p. 15.

[10]George H. Gallup, quoted in *Family Weekly*, January 4, 1976.

[11]Joseph C. Goulden, *The Best Years* (New York: Atheneum Publishers, 1976).

[12]It should be pointed out, however, that opinions were known to be volatile at that time, and the poll was taken previous to televised debates in which McGovern made a poor showing.

[13]Seymour Martin Lipset, *The Wavering Polls* (Washington, D.C.: American Enterprise Institute, 1976), p. 72.

damaging. But it is the press's fault, not the pollsters'.

The press also can distort news by creating false expectations about a "front-runner." Here is an oversimplified description of how the development of false expectations can destroy fairness in the primaries:

Throughout the months before the first presidential primary, the press cranks out stories about the front-runner. These are rather meaningless stories that serve little purpose but to allow the reporters to mark time until the real campaigning gets under way. Actually, there is no such animal as a front-runner until all the candidates have been lined up and tested in three or four primaries. Throughout 1971, for example, Senator Edmund Muskie, who had been the Democratic vice-presidential nominee in 1968, was hailed by the press as the party's front-runner. The press enshrined him in the ballyhoo of a "sure-thing" candidate, and party leaders, carried away by what they were reading in the newspapers, called him a sure thing, too.

Timothy Crouse, a reporter for *Rolling Stone*, wrote the following account:

> At the beginning of the campaign, that was the wisdom of the screening committee of national political journalists. . . . If there was a consensus, it was simply because all the national political reporters lived in Washington, saw the same people, used the same sources, belonged to the same background groups, and swore by the same omens. They arrived at their answers just as independently as a class of honest seventh graders using the same geometry text—they did not have to cheat off each other to come up with the same answer. All signs pointed to Ed Muskie as the easy winner, and as the wisdom of the national political men began to filter down through the campaign reporters and the networks to the people, victory began to seem assured for the Senator from Maine.[14]

Crouse's description of the Washington press, generally accurate, was wrong on that last point. "The people" didn't necessarily, at that early date, think of Muskie as the ultimate winner. But at least Muskie's name, through constant repeti-

tion by the press, was one that many people recognized; so when pollsters came around in February 1972, 60 percent of the people surveyed said they thought he would win the New Hampshire primary, which was to be held in March. According to this survey, Senator George McGovern, who had received little press attention, would run a weak second, with 25 percent of the vote.[15]

The way these polls were played up by the press became a burden to Muskie and an asset to McGovern. Muskie kept insisting that he would be *lucky* to win 50 percent of the vote, but nobody would listen to him. The polls had raised the press's and the public's expectations to an unrealistic level. Muskie wouldn't be thought of as a winner if he won only a plurality; he had to win *big*, by at least a majority, or he would be in deep trouble. "McGovern's people kept the idea firmly planted," and "the press took exactly the story line most favorable to McGovern: a distant underdog, surging, who in order to win could safely lose, so long as Muskie—with ten candidates in the field—was kept under 50 percent."[16]

Sure enough, Muskie won 46 percent of the New Hampshire vote, and the press clucked and said it was a "poor" showing; McGovern, who lost with 37 percent of the vote (a 9 percentage-point spread that would have been termed a horrible defeat in a general election) was said to have done "well." The victor was made out to be a loser because he had failed to live up to inflated expectations, and the loser was made out to be a winner because he hadn't failed as much as the press had anticipated. Muskie was now in serious trouble. The press talked of his "disappointment," of his "problem"—an unrealistic ap-

---

[14]Timothy Crouse, *The Boys on the Bus* (New York: Random House, 1973), p. 44.

[15]One thing that makes the early polls so misleading is that they are inevitably tied to the New Hampshire primary, whose importance is grossly distorted by the press. Having just come through a dull and uneventful political winter, the press always pounces on the first presidential primary and reports its every detail, as though it were a microcosm of the nation itself. This is nonsense; New Hampshire has less than 4 percent of the nation's population, and it is a highly atypical 4 percent. As columnist James J. Kilpatrick has pointed out sarcastically and accurately: "By any yardsticks of population, race, religion, age, education, occupation and political affiliation, New Hampshire has no national meaning." (*Washington Star*, December 6, 1975.)

[16]Michael Novak, *Choosing Our King: Powerful Symbols in Presidential Politics* (New York: Macmillan, 1974), pp. 176–77.

"Quick, Marjorie! They're about to announce the winners of the November elections."

praisal, but it became a part of reality simply because the press made it so. One thing led to another. It became increasingly difficult for Muskie to raise funds. Without funds, he was forced to cut back on his effort, which led to a poorer showing in other primaries, which further increased the difficulty of fund raising, and so on, and on. By May, the front-runner of February was politically dead.[17]

---

[17]Candidates dread the defeat-breeds-defeat syndrome, and for good reason. For example, in 1976, Carter's bandwagon might have been stopped if Udall had won in Michigan. He lost by only one-tenth of 1 percentage point. A shift of a thousand votes away from Carter would have given Udall the victory. After the election, a CBS-*New York Times* poll discovered that 10 percent of all the people voting for Carter in Michigan had actually preferred Udall but didn't want to waste their vote on a "loser." And, indeed, Udall had been a loser in previous primaries, but sometimes (in Wisconsin, for example) by no more than 1 percentage point. In primaries, only a few hundred votes here and there can mean the difference between a winning and a losing image. Considering the fact that presidential primaries, having multiple candidates, almost always deal in pluralities rather than in majorities, voting for the "winner" is a foolish response on the public's part, but it is a very permanent and potent foolishness.

The moral to the story is that polls in themselves are not often harmful, but they can be harmful if used by the media to create hallucinations. The problem rests basically with the dangerous notion, endemic to newspaper and TV political reporters, that they must make everything sound dramatic—dramatically powerful, dramatically cynical, dramatically corrupt, dramatically inevitable, or dramatically something else. The truth is that the best of politics is pretty dull stuff. It's almost impossible to make national health insurance sound exciting, or farm subsidies sound thrilling, or Social Security sound sexy. But issues of this sort are the core of a nation's life, and they should be the things that the press emphasizes and insists that candidates address themselves to. Instead, the press usually goes for the splashy item.

To continue with Muskie as our laboratory example, little press coverage was given to his position on issues in the New Hampshire primary of 1972. The one thing that was written about interminably was the episode in which

Muskie stood on the steps of the *Manchester* (New Hampshire) *Union-Leader* and denounced its publisher, William Loeb, for having made some unkind remarks about the senator's wife. It was the kind of biting cold day that might bring tears even to the eyes of a happy man, so it's not surprising that, for one reason or another, there were tears in Muskie's eyes—or so some reporters thought—when he stood there unhappily denouncing Loeb. For weeks thereafter they wrote of the "tearful" Muskie, until the image he had cultivated over the years—of the calm, carefully controlled, unemotional Yankee—was thoroughly shattered and replaced by the image of an emotionally unstable person. Some people claim that the press did the public a great service by seizing on this symbolic episode and depicting the "true" Muskie, for it was well-known by Washington insiders that Muskie was a quick-tempered fellow of mercurial moods.[18] Others contend that, in resorting to tears, Muskie was only showing a natural emotion that other politicians have also shown (Nixon has cried at least four times in public) but without having their tears so unfairly magnified. Whoever is right in this instance, the fact remains that, given a choice between a dramatic but possibly irrelevant episode and a crucial but dull issue, the press will focus on the former every time.

Malcolm MacDougall, one of President Ford's publicists, noted in 1976: "To get an issue-oriented speech on the network news was almost impossible . . . all you get is the goofs."[19] To be sure, one hears such complaints mainly from the losers, but they are none the less accurate. And when the press runs out of goofs, it falls back on what Thomas E. Patterson calls the "horse race" aspect of campaigns. Patterson monitored news coverage of the 1976 campaign and found that the press has an

> increasing tendency to report the election primarily as a competition to be won or lost, and only secondarily as a conflict over issues and national leadership. This tendency . . . contributed to an electorate which was largely uninformed about the issues, confused about the candidates, vulnerable

to trivial episodes and uncertain about the election's meaning.

What received the heaviest press coverage in 1976? It was, for lack of a better term, the "horse race"—the candidates' strategies for wooing voters, their sources of support, their comings and goings on the campaign trail and their prospects for victory or defeat.

In the early phases of the campaign, when journalists had to cover 30 primaries, two conventions and more than a half dozen serious candidates, these horse-race topics dominated every news medium. The range of emphasis was from a low of 57 percent for the evening newscasts of ABC, CBS and NBC to a high of 64 percent for Time and Newsweek. . . .

The press can never give voters what many of them really want, which is the "truth" about the candidates. As Walter Lippmann noted five decades ago, the truth and the news are seldom the same. Any final assessment of a Carter or a Ford is not one that can be made solely on the facts. It will depend on the values used to judge the facts. It will not be truth. It will be a political opinion. But the press could give the voters more facts, so that their opinions will be informed. If they chose to do so, reporters could place more emphasis on what the candidates are saying on the issues, on their public records, on their qualifications, and so on. The horse race does not have to occupy 50 percent or more of the news space.[20]

For the Survivors, on to the Conventions

Those candidates who have managed to survive the primaries and come through with a negotiable number of delegates will next seek their destiny at the national party conventions. These are happenings to which about three thousand or so delegates and twice that many reporters come to hear speeches heavily laden with what John Kenneth Galbraith once described as "platitudes launched like spaceships—all in hopeless pursuit of a thought." If it is the national convention of the party that is out of power, there will be endless speeches calling for "revitalization of national leadership." If it is

---

[18]Novak, *Choosing Our King,* p. 169.

[19]Quoted in the Associated Press, November 14, 1976.

[20]Thomas E. Patterson, *Washington Post,* December 5, 1976.

FIGURE 8-1 PRESS COVERAGE OF THE PRESIDENTIAL CAMPAIGN, 1976*
(percentage)

	Network Evening News		Los Angeles Times		Erie (Pa.) Times		Time / Newsweek	
The Horse Race								
Winning and losing		16		17		25		19
Strategy, logistics, and support	62	22	51	19	57	18	55	28
Appearances and crowds		24		15		14		8
The Substance								
Candidates' issue positions		10		13		6		9
Candidates' characteristics and backgrounds	24	6	30	7	24	7	31	13
Issue-related (for example, party platforms)		8		10		11		9
The Rest								
Campaign events calendar		2		4		6		3
	14		19		19		14	
Miscellaneous (for example, election procedures)		12		15		13		11

*Based on a year-long study conducted by Thomas E. Patterson under a grant from the Markle Foundation. A panel of 1,100 voters in Los Angeles and Erie, Pa.—cities chosen because they differ greatly in their range of news media—were interviewed seven times during the 1976 campaign to learn what they thought about the election and to discover what part their exposure to the media was playing in their reactions. In addition, election coverage throughout the campaign was monitored and analyzed for content: television network newscasts in both cities, Time, Newsweek, the Los Angeles Times and the Erie Times. . . . Figures based on a random selection of at least 20 per cent of the coverage by each news source. Figures include opinion and analysis as well as regular news reports.

SOURCE: Thomas E. Patterson, *Washington Post*, December 5, 1976.

the convention of the party that is occupying the White House, there will be endless speeches calling for the "continued pursuit of our national purpose." Most speakers will counsel the delegates, "let us go forth," and so on, as if it were possible to do anything else.

It's mostly ritualistic rhetoric, and the person who is supposed to top all the others in this high pursuit is the keynote speaker. He or she is supposed to set the tone for the convention, but setting a tone amidst all that cacophony is very difficult.

In recent decades the convention's decision-making burden has been lightened a great deal, since most of the decisions are made by a direct vote of the electorate in primaries or by preconvention caucuses. Not since the Democratic convention of 1952 has the nominating procedure had to go beyond one roll call. For the most part, the conventions' function is merely to ratify what the party bosses (where they still have power) and the voters in the primaries and caucuses have already decided. There are exceptions, of course; the 1976 Republican convention was one. President Ford and his challenger, Ronald Reagan, came to the convention almost neck and neck—Ford presumably had 1,180 delegate commitments to Reagan's 1,069. But the situation was still slightly fluid; if Reagan had been able to turn around just 56 votes, he would have won the nomination. In a close race like that, conventions still have meaning as a place for brokering delegates, a place for buying their support with favors or promises of favors—although, to be sure, such things are done subtly, for it is against federal law to either offer or seek material gain in return for a vote. But the close convention is the exception. Incumbent Presidents usually get at least 75 percent of the vote on the first convention ballot if they are seeking reelection. And the nomination is usually wrapped up before the convention, even when an incumbent is not involved.

Does that mean national conventions have become almost useless? The answer depends on what one is willing to settle for. They do provide a forum to write the party platform—which is of minor significance—and party rules and to kick off the campaign. Edward S. Corwin sees the convention as serving the purpose of a high-level symbol: "The national convention is the periodic reminder of the party's entity. It dramatizes and climaxes the procedures by which a party sustains the consciousness of its nationwide character and mission."[21] One must read such a description with some cynicism, for, in fact, the "character and mission" of a national party convention often seem to be determined by those people called demonstration chairpersons, who arrange for the distribution of balloons, confetti, beach balls, frisbees, placards, and clacking noisemakers and who arrange cheering sections and "spontaneous" marches,

all of which play no small part in the nominating process.

The word *spontaneous* deserves those quotation marks. There is a great deal of noise but very little spontaneity at national conventions. At the 1972 Republican convention, a script of the convention fell accidentally into the hands of the press. The script instructed speakers when to smile, when to gesture, when to nod, when to accept "spontaneous" hosannas from the throng. It orchestrated everything right down to the split second—even to instructing one speaker when he was to be interrupted in mid-sentence by a "spontaneous" demonstration. President Nixon was to be renominated, according to the script, at 10:33—and that would be followed immediately by a "ten-minute spontaneous demonstration with balloons."[22]

If that kind of packaged hokum seems offensive, one should understand that *all* modern conventions have been arranged as TV spectaculars. Thousands of reporters are on hand for every convention, but the show is really aimed at the propaganda-elite squads, the TV network commentators and producers. Everything is scheduled for their convenience, for they are the means to the largest possible audience, the TV viewers.

Presidential candidates who try to pretend that that isn't the case, who play it straight and let the convention unroll at whatever clumsy pace fate dictates, will discover that they have done so at their peril. George McGovern was such a candidate in 1972. *He* wasn't going to force delegates to conform to a tight schedule; *he* wasn't going to silence any politician who wanted to seize the microphone and drone on for hours, making seconding speeches and ideological harangues. It was free speech and an open convention all the way. As a result of that easy-going attitude, McGovern wound up making his acceptance speech at 2:30 in the morning (eastern standard time). He had failed to crack the whip over the windbags of partisan politics, and he paid for his kindness by being deprived of some priceless limelight. To most TV viewers, he might as well not have been at the convention.

[21]Edward S. Corwin, *The President: Office and Powers 1787–1957* (New York: New York University Press, 4th rev. ed. 1957), p. 20.

[22]Crouse, *The Boys on the Bus,* p. 165.

Learning from the dramatic mistakes of the two previous conventions, Democratic National Committee Chairman Robert S. Strauss set about to make "his" convention in 1976 a profitable showpiece. He knew that there were two absolute necessities: (1) maintaining the *appearance* of decorum and (2) slanting everything toward the national TV audience. Failure to do this in 1968 and in 1972 had been disastrous for the Democrats. Before the Chicago convention in 1968, Hubert Humphrey was trailing Richard Nixon by 6 percentage points in the polls. After the riots in the streets and the intraparty feuding within range of the TV cameras, Humphrey came out of the convention trailing Nixon by 15 points. McGovern went into the 1972 convention trailing Nixon by 12 points. After his inept and chaotic handling of the convention ritual, he left trailing by 23 points.[23]

At the 1972 Democratic convention, the chairman had spent a total of four hours banging his gavel for order. He got none, and he had, with all his banging, simply conveyed to the millions of people watching on television that he was presiding over bedlam. In 1976, Chairman Strauss was prepared. He ordered that, no matter how much chaos was occurring on the floor, the gavel would be banged on no more than three occasions during each session, and never for more than one minute at a time. There was as much chaos as ever, but to the TV audience it seemed like less—and that was the audience Strauss was playing to. As Congresswoman Barbara C. Jordan prepared to mount the steps to make the keynote speech, Strauss counselled her: "Barbara, there'll be no one out in the hall listening to you. Forget them. Let them talk to each other. You're talking to millions of people on television."[24] The attitude paid off. Carter had come into the convention 13 percentage points ahead of Ford, and he left it leading by a stunning 39 points.

There is, in short, a circus air about national party conventions, although the show is not nearly so gaudy and hilarious and melodramatic as it used to be. In 1924, for example, a real circus had preceded the Democratic convention in Madison Square Garden. Though seven tons of chemicals had been used to clean the air, much of the stink remained to further oppress the delegates who sat there through two sweaty weeks and 103 bitter roll calls before selecting their nominee.[25]

Those were the un-air-conditioned days. H. L. Mencken, who covered the hellish 1932 Democratic convention in Chicago, during which two delegates died of heat exhaustion, writes of how "the sun began to shine down through the gallery windows, and presently the floor was a furnace again, and the delegates got out their foul handkerchiefs and resumed their weary mopping and panting."[26] But in these air-conditioned days, some other excuse must be sought for the conduct and the results.

The delegates to national party conventions may sometimes act like drunken sailors, but in fact they represent the upper stratum of American society. In 1976, only 6 percent of the Democratic delegates and 2 percent of the Republican delegates earned less than $10,000 a year, compared to 44 percent of the general public; 43 percent of the Democratic delegates and 55 percent of the Republican delegates earned $30,000 a year or more, compared to 7 percent of the general public; 61 percent of the Democratic delegates and 65 percent of the Republican delegates had a college degree, compared to only 8 percent of the general public.[27]

For better or worse, the voice of national political conventions is not the voice of the common citizen. Nor is it always the voice of the average party member. Herbert McClosky and several other scholars used the delegates to the 1956 party conventions as a representative cross section of the party leadership and compared their ideological responses to questions on national issues with those of a representative sample of

---

[23]Richard Reeves, *Convention* (New York: Harcourt Brace Jovanovich, 1977), p. 220.

[24]Reeves, pp. 36–37, 75.

[25]See Robert K. Murray, *The 103rd Ballot: The Democrats and the Disaster in Madison Square Garden* (New York: Harper & Row, Publishers, 1976).

[26]H. L. Mencken, *Vintage Mencken*, ed. Alistair Cooke (New York: Random House, 1955), p. 209.

[27]Sources: *Washington Post*, July 11, 1976, August 15, 1976.

the party rank and file. They found very little consensus between Republican followers and Republican leaders. The leaders tended to be more conservative. The conflicts between Democratic followers and leaders were found to be less severe, but the leaders were generally more "progressive" than the followers.

No comparable study has been made in the intervening years, and perhaps the gap between leaders and followers in both parties is not so great as it was then. But to the extent that there is this division, there is a risk that the party elite will choose a candidate whose views are either more conservative (for the Republicans) or more progressive (for the Democrats) than the electorate would like. In any event, so long as there are intraparty gaps between purists and pragmatists, there will be strong tension at the national conventions between those wishing to nominate someone who would win votes and those wishing to nominate someone who would be on the "right" side of the issues—as happened with the Goldwater nomination in 1964 and the McGovern nomination in 1972.

THE CAMPAIGN
FOR GENERAL ELECTION

Packaging and Selling

Neither of the parties' nominees would think of venturing forth alone to harvest the votes. Each candidate's staff is extensive, and they operate like storm troopers. The most important staff members are the campaign manager, who gives overall supervision; the chief fund-raiser, who knows the best mailing lists to use to solicit money (one doesn't use a *New Republic* mailing list to raise funds for a conservative candidate); the advance man, who travels ahead of the candidate to schedule the stops, get help in drumming up crowds, and make appointments to meet local big shots; the press manager, who keeps the members of the press entourage happy, keeps them supplied with coffee and with the candidate's speeches, tries to prevent them from seeing the candidate's darker side,

and helps them find lodgings and typewriters when the candidate is on the road; and above all, the pollsters.

As mentioned earlier, public-opinion polls have become a common tool of most serious candidates who are running for major offices. During campaigns, candidates either employ pollsters on an *ad hoc* basis or keep them on the payroll full time. The reason is obvious: there is no better way to find out what the voters want and what they think of a particular candidate than to go out and ask them. Polling the public and then arranging the candidate's stance accordingly, via mass media, is a central part of what has been called "the new politics." Some critics have denounced this as slick and superficial—packaging candidates and selling them like soap. Practitioners of the art, such as political consultant Walter DeVries, argue that the critics must have something against the real world, in which voters want to be heard and politicians—if interested in being elected—want to listen. DeVries says,

> I find nothing Machiavellian about asking what problems bother people or asking what they think ought to be done about these problems. Once I find that out, I don't think it Machiavellian to find the best media to inform people what the candidate intends to do or not do about these problems, or why he is better able to handle them than his opponent.[28]

Pollsters are worthless unless they are objective. If they try to feed their political clients what the clients want to hear, they are worse than worthless; they are dangerous. The quality of objectivity in good pollsters allows them, like mercenary soldiers, to work for either side. In 1960, pollster Louis Harris did extensive surveying for Democrat John Kennedy in Kennedy's drive for the White House; in 1971, Harris worked for Republican Nixon's Domestic Council when Nixon was revving up for the 1972 campaign.

[28]Walter DeVries, "Taking the Voter's Pulse," in Ray E. Hiebert, ed., *The Political Image Merchants: Strategies in the New Politics* (Washington, D.C.: Acropolis Books, 1971), pp. 63–64.

Presidential candidates in televised debates; above: Carter and Ford, 1976; below: Kennedy and Nixon, 1960

Another aspect of packaging the candidate is the media blitz. The candidates prefer to play to the TV cameras instead of the printed press. Using an example out of the 1976 GOP primaries, CBS commentator Roger Mudd gave an easy explanation, while acknowledging that his medium was distorting the picture:

> Reagan had spent 3 hours and 5 minutes talking to not more than 2,000 people in the flesh. He took no new positions, he broke no new ground; but that night on Los Angeles' three early evening newscasts, he was seen by an audience of 1,071,000 people for 5 minutes and 51 seconds. And that night on the three network newscasts, he was seen for 4 minutes and 4 seconds by 37 million people.[29]

The role of television in a political campaign is both grossly overrated and underrated. It is overrated in importance as the conveyor of "image" politics. During the 1972 campaign, Thomas E. Patterson and Robert D. McClure conducted one of the first systematic studies of the impact of television on voters; they analyzed the content of every televised political commercial and every week-night evening network newscast and conducted two thousand hour-long interviews with voters. Their conclusion:

> The myth is that "images," more than either issues or parties, win votes. As one-time Nixon assistant Raymond Price has put it, "It's not what's there that counts, it's what's projected." As one-time Humphrey aide Joseph Napolitan put it, "It's not what you say, it's how you say it." In McLuhan's phrase, the medium *is* the message. None of this is so.[30]

They found that if the voter likes or agrees politically with what the candidate is saying, this equates with a good TV impression. But if the voter disagrees, the candidate comes across negatively regardless of how polished a performer he or she is or how good he or she looks.

The myth of the potency of TV imagery in presidential campaigns goes back to the first Kennedy-Nixon debate in 1960. Kennedy arrived in time to go through a dry run in his hotel room, with aides tossing anticipated questions at him. He was well-tanned and rested. Nixon, by contrast, arrived late, had no time to bone up on questions, was exhausted, had lost twenty pounds during a recent illness, and looked pale and drawn. When Nixon learned that Kennedy had not put on any heavy TV makeup, he refused to have more than a light touch-up—with the result that his perpetual five o'clock shadow made him look thuggish. Nixon lost that election by only a hairsbreadth, and the accepted wisdom has been that his haggard appearance on that first televised debate cost him the difference.

But, in fact, as Michael J. Robinson has pointed out, "The 1960 debates—even the first debate—moved very few voters from one side to the other. Remarkably, Richard Nixon dropped only *one* percentage point in the Gallup Poll the week after the first debate."[31] Nevertheless, the myth persisted, and nobody believed it more than Nixon himself; and as a result he poured many millions into packaging himself for television in 1968 and 1972.

Scholars recently have decided that much money is wasted on this sort of thing. Voters buy soap for one reason; they buy politicians for another. They did not give Nixon an overwhelming vote in 1972 because he had transformed his image into prettiness and smoothness—in fact, his TV image was still stiff, perspiring, corny, and shifty-eyed. He was elected primarily on issues. Some of the most successful politicians of this era—Lyndon Johnson and Hubert Humphrey being outstanding examples—had awful TV styles: Johnson that of a conniving hayseed, Humphrey that of a blabbermouth. They won votes on issues.[32]

Breaking the TV habit is difficult. Politicians don't like to take the risk. In the last ten days of his presidential campaign, Gerald Ford spent $400,000 a day on TV advertising. Even so, some

[29]Quoted in the *New York Times,* June 8, 1976.

[30]Thomas E. Patterson and Robert D. McClure, *The Unseeing Eye: The Myth of Television Power in National Politics* (New York: G. P. Putnam's Sons, 1976).

[31]Michael J. Robinson, "The Potential of Presidential Debates," reprinted from the *Wall Street Journal* in the *Washington Post,* September 11, 1976.

[32]See Herbert E. Alexander, "Communications and Politics: The Media and the Message," *Law and Contemporary Problems* (Duke University), Spring 1969.

practical political strategists have joined the doubting scholars in seeing things differently. John P. Sears, manager of the brilliant campaign that nearly dumped Ford and won the GOP nomination for Ronald Reagan in 1976, says, "If we had any guts, we would admit that television advertising does virtually no good and we'd never buy another minute of it."[33]

However, television can have a tremendous impact in a negative way—by neglecting to pass substantive stuff to the electorate, feeding them fluff and puffery instead. Patterson and McClure found in their in-depth study of the 1972 election that

> in place of serious matters, ABC, CBS, and NBC substitute the trivia of political campaigning that makes for flashy pictures—hecklers, crowds, motorcades, balloons, rallies, and pompom girls. . . . A classic example: one noon during October in New York City, in ample time for evening newscast coverage, McGovern stated important policy positions on crime, prison reform, gun control and the courts. Two networks completely ignored the address, covering instead a McGovern motorcade in Boston later that day. He was pictured in crowd scenes. Indeed, 60 percent of all campaign stories showed one candidate or the other hustling through crowds.[34]

Knowing that dramatic irrelevancies are the meat that TV newscasters feed on in campaign years, politicians and their strategists are quick to exploit this appetite. Their advance men search out the friendliest neighborhoods to guarantee that the TV cameras catch the largest turnouts of partisans eager to "press the flesh" in what Michael Novak has called "the ritual of connectedness," a ritual by which candidates, by moving physically among the crowds, try to say in effect: " 'Here I am among you. Drawing

vitality from you. You make me godlike. My power flows from you.' "[35]

When John Kennedy was running for President in 1960, he arrived late at the Detroit airport. By the time his plane landed, the crowd had become an impatient mob, and, as he descended the plane's stairway, the waiting people surged through the rickety snow fence that had been put up to hold them back. Network newscasters played it big. Jerry Bruno, Kennedy's advance man, recalls:

> It looked so good on film that from then on we made sure the crowds surged over Kennedy. I'd have two men holding a rope by an airport or along a motorcade. Then, at the right moment, they'd just drop the rope and the crowd would rush Kennedy. We made it a standard part of every Kennedy campaign stop.[36]

Ethnic Appeal

When the parties' nominees set out to win votes, the effort is anything but abstract. They have precise groups of voters in mind.

One group—the largest, in fact—is made up of WASPs—white Anglo-Saxon Protestants. It is a group that thinks very highly of itself, and understandably, for it has been the favored group through most of our history. As Peter Schrag has pointed out,

> For 150 years the politicians, the writers, the poets, the social theorists, the men who articulated and analyzed American ideas, who governed our institutions, who embodied what we seemed to be, or hoped to be—nearly all of them were WASP. Hawthorne and Melville, Twain and Howells, Veblen and Beard, Holmes and Story, Adams (John, Brooks, Henry) and Lodge, James and Dewey, Lester Frank Ward and John Fiske, Bryan and Wilson, Henry George and Edward Bellamy and nearly every other major American statesman, writer and scholar. . . . Of all the major figures discussed by Commager in The American Mind, not one is a Jew, a Catholic or a Negro. The American

[33]John P. Sears, " 'Give 'em hell, Jerry!' " New York Times Magazine, September 19, 1976.

[34]Patterson and McClure, The Unseeing Eye. The TV rule is that action is three times more useful than thought—even if the action is phony. One evening's network news during the 1976 campaign showed President Ford as he climbed onto the deck chair of a Mississippi steamboat, held onto a flagpole, and waved toward the bank of the river. What the millions watching those TV newscasts didn't know was that Ford was waving at nothing. There were no people on the bank of the river.

[35]Novak, Choosing Our King, p. 173.

[36]Quoted in David Chagall, "How People Vote," Family Weekly, October 19, 1975.

LBJ (far left) in the midst of well-wishers during the 1964 campaign

mind was the WASP mind. And America was a WASP preserve. . . .[37]

Not until 1960 did WASP America dare to entrust the White House to an Irish-Catholic. It was hailed as a great breakthrough.

No national politician can hope to succeed without finding favor with the WASPs. But it can also be said that no national politician can hope to succeed without finding some favor with the last people off the boat. About 65 million Americans are in the "ethnic" category.[38] This includes hyphenated Americans—Italian-Americans, Polish-Americans, Irish-Americans, and so forth—as well as black and Spanish-speaking Americans (both of whom sometimes prefer the hyphen also: Afro-Americans and Hispanic-Americans). These groups have persisted so stubbornly as a state of mind, as well as in physical fact, that the nation's leaders have quit trying to make them become 100 percent homogenized Americans and have instead begun courting them in their hyphenated and ethnic reality.

It hasn't been that way for long. Theodore Roosevelt once laid down the gauntlet:

> We welcome the German or the Irishman who becomes an American. We have no use for the German or the Irishman who remains such. We have no room for any people who do not act and vote simply as Americans, and as nothing else. . . . If [the immigrant] tries to retain his old language, in a few generations it becomes a barbarous jargon; if he retains his old customs and ways of life, in a few generations he becomes an uncouth boor. . . .[39]

Perhaps the reason he considered them uncouth boors was that they did not all vote Republican. They had walked off the boat to be welcomed by the Democratic big-city machines and to be shunned by the Protestant Yankee establishment to which Teddy Roosevelt belonged.

[37]Peter Schrag, *The Decline of the Wasp* (New York: Simon & Schuster, 1973), pp. 19–20.

[38]Reserving the word *ethnic* for non-WASPs indicates that WASPs have dominated everything in this country, including its language. Using *ethnic* in that way implies a kind of second-class otherness. Actually, everyone in this country belongs to an ethnic group. The two broadest categories are most easily broken down along religious lines: Protestant ethnics—those families originated mainly in England, Protestant Ireland, Germany, and Scandinavia—make up 56 percent of the national population. Catholic ethnics—mainly from Ireland, Germany, Italy, and Poland—make up 26 percent of the national population. Jews make up about 2 percent of the population; blacks about 11 percent, and Hispanic-Americans about 5 percent.

[39]Quoted in Schrag, *The Decline of the Wasp*, p. 20.

The biggest of all immigration waves, from 1890 to 1920, was largely from southern and eastern Europe. By 1920, Italians and Jews accounted for 40 percent of New York City's population, and other northeastern cities were similarly influenced, though not to such a great extent.[40]

The cornerstone ethnic groups (Italians, Irish, Germans, Poles, Slavs, and Jews) forced a sharp change in the character of the Democratic party. Well into the 1920s, the Democratic party was predominantly shaped by Protestantism, prohibitionism, and the agrarian mind of the South. But by 1920, half the nation's populace was living in big cities, and, as the percentage climbed sharply in the next ten years, the Democrats wisely began to woo the city vote. After a period of hesitation (the Jewish vote went to the Republican presidential candidates in 1920 and 1928, for example), the ethnic blocs moved solidly into the Democratic ranks, helped along by the Democratic candidacy of Alfred E. Smith, a Catholic, in 1928, and by the onset of the Depression during the Republican administration of Herbert Hoover. By the time of Franklin Roosevelt's election in 1932, the urban ethnic blocs had become the Democrats' most dependable vote.

But their loyalties, for a variety of reasons, are no longer so certain or so overwhelming, and on rare occasions they have been broken. In 1968, Nixon carried New York's Italians—the first time in recent decades that a Republican presidential nominee had carried any of the six major ethnic groups in any state. In general, however, the slippage has been less dramatic. The big city Jews, Italians, Slavs, and Irish are still mostly Democratic, but it has been correctly pointed out that "the difference between winning by four to one and winning by two to one is all too critical to a candidate in a closely contested election"—and most of the major industrial states are closely contested. These are the states where most presidential elections are decided, often by less than 4 percentage points.[41]

No ethnic bloc has greater potential than the blacks, as they have shown when organized and motivated to vote. Blacks claim credit, perhaps with justification, for the surprise election of Harry Truman in 1948, for John Kennedy's wafer-thin margin of victory in 1960,[42] and for Jimmy Carter's edge in 1976.

Everyone seems to agree with the blacks' own appraisal of their role in the Carter victory, though there are differences in the measure of their support. A CBS News poll estimated that 82 percent of the black votes went to Carter. A study done by the Joint Center for Political Studies concluded that Carter won 94 percent of the black votes. More important was the way the black votes were clustered. In Ohio, where Carter won by only 7,586 votes, he received 285,000 votes from blacks. With the help of 135,000 black votes in Mississippi, Carter edged past Ford by 11,537 votes. In Pennsylvania, Carter received 298,000 votes from blacks—more than 90 percent—and defeated Ford by 123,372 votes. In Texas, where Carter's margin was 207,334, he won 295,000 black votes. The Joint Center for Political Studies estimated that in at least seven states the black vote provided Carter with his winning margin.[43]

Postelection analyses by Republicans concurred. Malcolm MacDougall, one of Ford's advertising experts, said, "Blacks were . . . written off [by the GOP]. Writing off the blacks was the most significant thing in the election. It was a terrible mistake, a total disaster."[44] Predicting the future by what happened in 1976, Ford's vice-presidential running mate, Senator Robert Dole, acknowledged, "We're not going to win many elections if the other side gets 95 percent of the black vote."[45] Ford had won 52 percent of the white vote.

Republican presidential candidates, in recent years, have made little effort to win the support of black voters; they have failed to support substantive programs that would benefit blacks or make symbolic gestures of sympathy. In the 1976 campaign, the GOP spent only about $200,000 in direct appeals for black support. Ford had made

[40]Kevin P. Phillips, *The Emerging Republican Majority* (New Rochelle, N.Y.: Arlington House, 1969), p. 54.

[41]Mark R. Levy and Michael S. Kramer, *The Ethnic Factor: How America's Minorities Decide* (New York: Simon & Schuster, 1972), pp. 15, 19, 209.

[42]Hanes Walton, Jr., *Black Politics: A Theoretical and Structural Analysis* (Philadelphia: J. B. Lippincott Co., 1972), p. 164.

[43]Associated Press, November 11, 1976.

[44]Quoted in the Associated Press, November 14, 1976.

[45]Quoted in the *Washington Post*, December 14, 1976.

some important black appointments during his truncated administration, and he had also given significant help to minority businesses, but neither he nor his campaign aides played up this record.

Democrats, on the other hand, have carefully nourished the black vote by both symbol and substance. Kennedy, for example, once placed a phone call to help get black leader Martin Luther King, Jr., out of jail. Democratic administrations have funneled money for jobs and social services into black neighborhoods and have passed the only significant voting rights and civil rights acts of this century. Blacks have consistently repaid them at the polls with 90 percent and upwards of their vote.

In areas where the black population is at loggerheads with other ethnic populations, candidates will of course shape their pitch with an awareness of which groups not only have the most potential votes but also are most likely to actually cast a ballot (United States Census Bureau surveys show that black voter-turnouts are consistently about a dozen points below the white turnouts). At the same time, they will try not to write off any group. The result is campaigning that involves a very delicate sort of diplomacy. In 1976, for example, Democratic contender Jimmy Carter, campaigning in the North, said he favored maintaining the "ethnic purity" of neighborhoods. But when black leaders denounced that as a racist remark, he hurriedly scheduled a series of speeches to black church congregations on one of his favorite themes, the politics of brotherhood.

Regional Appeal: A Dramatic Shift to the Sun

In recent years, the electoral omnipotence of the northern industrial states has begun to fade, and some political scientists believe that the future lies with the South and the Southwest. Throughout the nation's history, the shifting of the population toward new frontiers has changed the center of political power. The present shift is toward the sun, and the shifters are largely the kind of people who get involved in politics because they have the time and because they have a better-than-average income to pro-

tect at the ballot box. They are, says Kevin P. Phillips,

> a super-slice of the rootless, socially mobile group known as the American middle class. Most of them have risen to such status only in the last generation, and their elected officials predictably embody a popular political impulse which deplores further social (minority group) upheaval and favors a consolidation of the last thirty years' gains. Increasingly important throughout the nation, this new middle-class group is most powerful in the Sun Belt. Its politics are bound to cast a lengthening national shadow.[46]

He supports his prediction with the chart of sample states shown in Table 8-1.

This thesis is supported by Kirkpatrick Sale, who points out that "the Southern Rim, running through the South and Southwest to California, has gained electoral votes with every succeeding census, rising from 161 votes in 1948 to 184 in 1972, while the Northeast has declined in votes from 235 to 218." By Sales's count, the Sun Belt now accounts for 68 percent of the 270 electoral votes necessary to win an election, and the percentage is certain to grow. The Sun Belt has supplied six of the last eight presidential nominees of the two major parties (Carter, Johnson, Goldwater, and Nixon three times), the most important third-party nominee (Wallace), and much of the national party leadership.[47]

The Sun Belt has also influenced the North through irritation. Responding to hardships in the South, millions of blacks have migrated to northern urban centers. The racial tensions that have arisen from the resulting change in neighborhoods have caused the North to become somewhat "southernized." Forty percent of New York's Italians, for example, are living in the same neighborhoods their parents lived in; they love their Little Italy, and they are among the most ardent foes of black encroachment. As Table 8-2 shows, many northern city-dwellers welcomed the only slightly disguised racist campaign of Wallace in 1968.

---

[46]Phillips, *The Emerging Republican Majority,* p. 437.

[47]Kirkpatrick Sale, *Power Shift: The Rise of the Southern Rim and Its Challenge to the Eastern Establishment* (New York: Random House, 1975) pp. 89–90.

TABLE 8-1

THE ELECTORAL VOTE BY SECTIONS, 1928–1976

STATE	1928	1932	1948	1956	1964	1976
Maine	6	5	5	5	4	4
Massachusetts	18	17	16	16	14	14
New York	45	47	45	43	41	41
Pennsylvania	38	36	35	32	29	27
Northeastern group total	107	105	101	96	88	86
Arizona	3	3	4	4	5	6
Texas	20	23	23	24	25	26
Florida	6	7	8	10	14	17
California	13	23	25	32	40	45
Sun Belt group total	42	56	60	70	84	94

SOURCES: Kevin P. Phillips, *The Emerging Republican Majority* (New Rochelle, N.Y.: Arlington House, 1969), p. 436; *The World Almanac* (New York: Newspaper Enterprise Association, 1977).

TABLE 8-2

IN THE SOUTHERN IMAGE: WALLACE VOTE IN NORTHERN WHITE PRECINCTS, 1968

CITY	PERCENTAGE OF PRECINCTS GIVING WALLACE 15 PERCENT OR MORE OF THE VOTE
Gary	78
Cleveland	71
Newark	65
Baltimore	55
Columbus	48
Pittsburgh	45
Akron	44
Cincinnati	43
Indianapolis	42
Flint	41
Detroit	35

SOURCE: Samuel Lubell, *The Hidden Crisis in American Politics* (New York: W. W. Norton & Co., 1970), p. 90.

The Cost of Campaigns

When George Washington was running for the Virginia House of Burgesses from Fairfax County in 1757, he is said to have warmed constituents to his cause by treating them to twenty-eight gallons of rum, fifty gallons of rum punch, thirty-four gallons of wine, forty-six gallons of beer, and two gallons of cider royal. Considering the era and the scope of his campaign, that liquor supply represented a considerable expenditure of money, for Washington's district contained only 391 voters. It came to a quart and a half per person—a ratio that might still win an election.

When he ran for President, Washington spent virtually nothing. But, then, he had virtually no opposition. If he had truly wanted the job and had had stiff opposition, even the great Washington would have had to dig into his jeans for another supply of rum, and he was a good enough politician to know it. Most political happenings don't just magically happen; somehow, somewhere, money is involved. (Later in the chapter, some of the more undemocratic effects of this truism are explored.) Table 8-3 shows the growth of spending by national-level political committees, primarily on presidential elections, up to 1972. The number of people voting in national elections climbed from 15 million in 1912 to 78 million in 1972, but the campaign cost per vote remained pretty stable until the 1950s. The outlay per vote was about $0.19 in 1912; in 1952 it was still about $0.19. But by 1968 it had shot up to $0.60 per vote, and in 1972 it soared to $1.28 per vote. The total cost of elective and party politics in 1968 at all levels—federal, state, and local— was about $300 million, an increase of 50 percent over 1964. In 1972, the total expenditure at all levels of politics was an estimated $600 million. A candidate for congressional office may end up spending $500,000, and a candidate for the United States Senate can spend $2 or $3 million.

In any discussion of big-spending politics, the impression is that money is invincible. But it isn't quite. Sometimes luck plays an enormous part. And, sometimes, it turns out that no amount of money can make up for lack of simple popularity. Examples of this can be found in almost any campaign year. In 1964, for example, Nelson A. Rockefeller spent about $3 million out of his own pocket in a futile effort to win the Republican presidential nomination. He spent

TABLE 8-3

NATIONAL POLITICAL-COMMITTEE SPENDING, 1912–1972 (in millions)

YEAR	SPENDING	YEAR	SPENDING
1912	$ 2.9	1944	$ 7.7
1916	4.7	1948	7.8
1920	6.9	1952	11.6
1924	6.4	1956	12.9
1928	11.6	1960	19.9
1932	5.1	1964	24.8
1936	14.1	1968	44.2
1940	7.8	1972	100

SOURCE: Herbert Alexander, *Money In Politics*. (Washington, D.C.: Public Affairs Press 1972), p. 79.

$250,000 in New Hampshire alone, and so did Barry Goldwater (though not out of his own pocket). Yet the man who walked away with the New Hampshire primary was Henry Cabot Lodge, Jr., who spent only $20,000 in that state and whose campaign workers were so broke they sometimes depended on Rockefeller's free campaign buffets for meals.

Another example of the occasional impotence of money was seen in 1976, when New York's Senator James L. Buckley, despite the overwhelming advantage of incumbency (which can be translated into dollars) and despite the fact that he spent twice as much, lost his seat to colorful Daniel Patrick Moynihan.

The upward swing of presidential-election costs was not only brought to a halt, it was reversed in 1976 with the imposition of a new law that provided each candidate with about $21.8 million from the public treasury for use in the campaign. To obtain this funding, the candidates had to refrain from accepting *direct* supplemental contributions from private sources.[48] Some campaign workers complained that the $21.8 million federal budget was much too restrictive. They said they could not begin to set up the kind of machinery that was necessary to do the job right. Both Carter and Ford were strikingly short of campaign paraphernalia and hoopla, and this may have had a depressing effect on voter turnout.[49] In general, however, the presidential campaign of 1976 was hailed as refreshingly clean. Special interest money carried only moderate weight for the first time in recent history. The success of the public funding in restoring the electorate's morale made it seem certain that sooner or later congressional races would also be publicly financed.

Campaign costs have risen so dramatically in the last couple of decades because the strategies and accouterments of the modern campaign are costly. Recent campaigns have been based, to an overwhelming extent, on media advertisements—in the newspapers, on television, over the radio. A couple of minutes of prime time on national television might cost $50,000 or more, depending on the popularity of the program the political ad interrupted. During the 1976 presidential primaries, Democratic candidate Mo Udall tried to stretch his dollars by buying on the outer fringe of prime time—getting five-minute spots at 10:55 P.M. for $12,000.[50] That was considered a bargain. Other practices, especially air travel, have sharply increased campaign costs. As Herbert Alexander points out:

> Chartered campaign jets require not only flight crews but radio and telephone operators to keep in touch with headquarters. Replete with equipment like duplicating machines, they are in effect jet-offices. Every speech, every activity requires planning by the candidate, his campaign manager, his headquarters, advisors, advance men, research team, speech writers, publicity men, communication specialists, cleanup men. On the travelling staff of Senator Kennedy in 1960 were a speech professor to teach the candidate voice control, a psychologist to evaluate the size, composition,

[48]Actually, Carter spent nearly $35 million to win the Presidency (which can be compared to the $60 million Nixon spent in 1972). That's about $0.80 a vote. In addition to the $21.8 million in the general election, Carter spent about $13.2 million in primaries—roughly one-fourth of which came from the public treasury. The rest was collected in private donations, none larger than $1,000 (the highest the law allowed), before he won the nomination in mid-July. After that he could no longer accept private money. But the law did allow organizations to spend money on their own. Thus, labor unions spent more than $1 million to urge their members to vote for Jimmy Carter. Corporations, like the unions, are forbidden to contribute directly to the candidates; they spent a total of only $28,200 to promote the reelection of President Ford. (*Time,* January 30, 1977.)

[49]Trivia—bumper stickers, buttons, and so forth—may be of questionable educational value, but they are important for alerting voters to the fact that there is an election on and

getting them thinking about what is in their interest. Nixon's trivia budget for 1968 added up to $1.4 million:

Buttons (20,500,000)	$300,000
Bumper stickers (9,000,000)	300,000
Balloons (560,000)	70,000
Posters and placards (400,000)	70,000
Straw skimmers (28,000)	70,000
Brochures (30,000); speeches and position papers (3,500,000)	500,000
Paper dresses (12,000)	40,000
Jewelry	50,000
TOTAL	$1,400,000

(Herbert E. Alexander, *Money in Politics,* Washington, D.C.: Public Affairs Press, 1972, p. 84.)

[50]Personal interview with the office staff of Congressman Morris K. Udall, April 1977.

and reactions of campaign crowds, an official photographer, and a two-man stenographic team to transcribe every public word of the candidate so that transcripts were available to reporters within minutes after a speech. . . .

The cloud of helicopters moving the candidate and his aides may tend to overshadow the groundwork below but both entail considerable expenditures. Rallies and parades are not spontaneous demonstrations of affection for the candidate but well-planned affairs with a large investment in public relations, telephone calls, buses, and other means for summoning crowds.[51]

THE VOTE

The mad scramble for support is over, all the promises have been made and remade, all the special interest groups wooed, all the babies have been kissed and the shopkeepers' hands shaken. Now it's up to the voters. Will they turn out? And if so, in what mood?

Who Votes?

The eternal mystery of the voter's frame of mind has become more intense as the electorate itself has become more diversified. When the nation was founded, blacks, women, Indians, and most nonpropertied men had no voice in elections (fewer than 800,000 of the 4 million citizens were qualified to vote).[52] Blacks, women, and Indians gained their franchise only after protracted court fights and physical demonstrations in the streets. For the most part, they have been welcomed at the voting booth only recently. They have been the victims of racial and sexual bias. But to no small degree they have also been victimized by the practical impulse of the power elite, who want to remain masters of their political environment. If voters are all of one kind, of one race, of one economic stratum, they are more manipulatable and more predictable. This makes for a much more comfortable atmos-

phere for the power elite, and it is doubtless one key reason why the Founders, gentlemen all, wanted to keep those unpredictable women and the unpredictable riffraff out of the political process. It was a motivation that lasted into this century.

When the Civil War and the Fifteenth Amendment to the Constitution gave black males the right to vote, the white establishment in the South declared that they were being run over by barbarism. When the immigration floodgates filled the northern cities, the genteel establishment declared that the American way of life was in peril. The establishment, in both the North and South, complained that the new voters were being manipulated by demagogues. Piously explaining that they were only interested in preventing fraud at the ballot box, legislatures, toward the end of the nineteenth century, brought into existence all sorts of laws to make voting more difficult for people of deprived background. Far more than fear of fraud was involved; the elite was fighting to protect its position from the nonelite. And it was a highly successful move.

In the 1880s and 1890s, southern states systematically disenfranchised their black voters and many poor whites as well. In less than twenty years (1884–1904) the participation rate in Arkansas dropped from over two-thirds to just over one-third. Mississippi's rate fell from almost 80 percent in 1876 to less than 17 percent in 1900. Texas dropped fifty points, from 80 percent in 1884 to 30 percent twenty years later. But South Carolina outdid all other states. Participation plunged from 83.7 percent in 1880 to 43 percent in 1884 to 18 percent in 1900. . . .

Northern turn-of-the-century legislatures also enacted laws designed to reduce the franchise. Fears that the growing numbers of immigrants would fall under the sway of corrupt political party machines spurred the enactment of voter-registration laws, longer residency requirements, more poll taxes and literacy tests. The mobility of prospective voters was an open invitation to fraud, and registration was viewed as a way to restrict and detect fradulent voting. Almost half of the northern states wrote authority for registration requirements into their constitutions between 1876 and 1912. Many of the others already had voter registration or enacted it without explicit constitu-

---

[51]Alexander, *Money in Politics,* p. 80.

[52]George Thayer, *Who Shakes the Money Tree?* (New York: Simon & Schuster, 1974), p. 24.

"Election day is dawning, and I'm still undecided."

tional authority as "necessary and proper" for fraud-free elections.[53]

But the twentieth century has been moving, slowly at first and rapidly in recent years, in the other direction—toward opening the path to the polls and extending suffrage to groups that never had it. In 1920, women were brought into the national electorate via the Nineteenth Amendment to the Constitution; in 1965, as mentioned earlier, federal laws were enacted to restore blacks' voting rights by assisting registration and removing unconstitutional voting requirements; and in 1972, the Twenty-sixth Amendment gave persons over the age of eighteen the right to vote. At the same time, many states were liberalizing electoral laws and removing obstacles to voting. And yet, ironically, it has been during this most recent period of liberalized voter assistance that the turnout of voters (by percentage) has dropped most sharply. From 1920 to 1960, the turnout trend was upward, climbing from 43.4 percent to 63.1 percent, and since then it has been downward.[54]

Black turnout at the polls in both 1964 and 1968 was relatively heavy. Since then, however,

[53]Kevin P. Phillips and Paul H. Blackman, *Electoral Reform and Voter Participation* (Washington, D.C.: American Enterprise Institute, 1975), pp. 7–8.

[54]Richard W. Boyd, "Electoral Trends in Postwar Politics," in Barber, ed., *Choosing the President,* pp. 181–83.

the black turnout has fallen off sharply, which means it is returning to its customary secondary stratum—lower than white turnout.[55] In 1972, for example, 64.5 percent of the whites said that they had voted, compared to 52.1 percent of the blacks. (Both figures may be high, because people don't like to admit that they didn't vote.) For congressional races, the turnout is worse, but the margin is about the same. In 1974, 46.3 percent of whites and 33.8 percent of blacks voted.[56]

New voters apparently are slow to get involved. In 1974, four out of five persons between the ages of eighteen and twenty-one—the group that had just been given the vote—stayed away from the polls.[57] The most faithful participators are middle-aged people, affluent white people, college graduates, and farmers, or any combination of those.[58] The least likely to vote are young people, the uneducated, and those with low incomes.[59]

Some people don't vote because they are disenchanted with the candidates. Some people don't meet a state's residency requirements. Some are sick or out of town on election day. Some may simply be discouraged by long lines at the polling place. For whatever reason, no more than 55 percent of the electorate has turned out in the last two presidential elections.

The 53 percent turnout in 1976 was the lowest since 1948. Almost 70 million people of the 150 million of voting age did not vote. Jimmy Carter won with the support of only 27 percent of the eligible citizens. Although the number of potential voters had risen by some 10 million in the previous four years, only 2.3 million more voted. What was happening? A study done by the nonpartisan Committee for the Study of the American Electorate concluded that people who

had once been active in politics were dropping out. The CSAE estimated that some 15 million Americans had dropped out of the electoral process in the past eight years. "What is occurring," said Curtis B. Gans, codirector of the study, "is a trend for which the term apathy is too mild a word. There are substantial numbers of Americans who are disenchanted with the political process, disgusted with their leaders, and disillusioned by the failure of government of both political parties to meet their needs."[60] That was probably as good a guess as any, and it was supported by a Philips-Sindlinger poll taken in the fall of 1974, which showed that 55 percent of the people hoped they would be offered a viable alternative to the two major-party candidates in 1976.[61] They weren't.

A few months after he took office, President Carter proposed legislation that could dramatically increase voter turnout. His proposal would allow every qualified voter, regardless of whether he or she was registered, to vote in federal elections by simply going to the polls on election day and showing proof of identity and place of residence. The plan has the support of the committee chairpersons responsible for processing the legislation. One of them, Senator Howard W. Cannon, estimates the plan could boost voter turnout by 10 percent. Four states that already use this system (Maine, Minnesota, North Dakota, and Wisconsin) ranked in the top five states in voter turnout in 1976.

How Does the Voter Decide?

For those who identify with a party (and almost two-thirds of the adults in the United States do), the party tie is the most crucial element in the voting decision. Studies have shown that more than 70 percent of the party identifiers vote for the presidential candidate of their party. For some, party voting is simply a habit; for those who haven't the time or the resources to equip themselves with information on a candidate, party identification provides a shortcut to a voting decision. An individual's

---

[55] However, blacks in the upper-income level turn out more than whites.

[56] Phillips and Blackman, *Electoral Reform and Voter Participation*, p. 45.

[57] Associated Press, January 27, 1975.

[58] Phillips and Blackman, *Electoral Reform and Voter Participation*, p. 73.

[59] Sidney Verba and Norman H. Nie, *Participation in America: Political Democracy and Social Equality* (New York: Harper & Row Publishers, 1972).

[60] Quoted in the *Washington Star*, November 19, 1976.

[61] *Nation*, August 30, 1975.

FIGURE 8-2

DECLINING MEMBERSHIP IN THE REPUBLICAN PARTY, 1944–1977

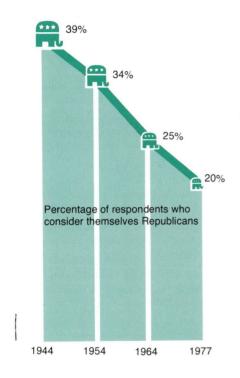

39%

34%

25%

20%

Percentage of respondents who consider themselves Republicans

1944   1954   1964   1977

SOURCES: Gallup poll; *New York Times*, August 21, 1977.

vote can be predicted more accurately by party affiliation than by any other personal characteristic, such as race, religion, or social class. Moreover, it is usually a better predictor than the individual's attitudes on any of the political issues of the day.[62]

If party identification is so crucial in voting, why don't the Democrats win all the time? After all, a survey in 1977 showed that 49 percent of the voters identified themselves as Democrats and only 20 percent claimed to be Republicans.[63] In the preceding chapter, we saw that Republicans tend to get elected as President when there is a

strong desire on the part of the electorate for a peaceful foreign-policy leadership. This is one of a number of *short-term forces* that each election brings with it and that affects the outcome.

One of the most important of the short-term forces is the candidate's personality. Eisenhower's image was so attractive to people in both parties and to independents that he overwhelmed his Democratic opponent in 1952 and 1956. Of course, it works both ways; if a candidate's good imagery can successfully inflate a party beyond its normal boundaries, bad imagery can shrink those boundaries on a short-term basis. The Goldwater image in 1964, for example, was so negative that the Republicans lost 7 percent (6 million voters) of their normal party strength.[64]

Another short-term force is government performance. When the Depression hit during Herbert Hoover's Presidency, the Republican government was booted out of office. When the Korean and Vietnam wars dragged on too long under Democratic administrations, the Democrats were evicted. Ford's lack of leadership in handling a sluggish economy led to his departure from office in 1976. In general, it is government's performance—that is, how effective it is in dealing with issues—more than its ideological stands on the issues that concerns voters. But American voters are just beginning to be issue-oriented, and the candidates themselves don't always offer a clear stand.

Having made a case for the influence of imagery and issues, it is necessary to reemphasize, however, that partisanship is still much more important, either on a short-term or long-term basis. Imagery and issues may provide

[62]There are, however, great difficulties in assessing the relative importance of party and issues.

[63]Gallup poll, August 1977.

[64]At this distance in time, it is hard to believe that Goldwater, an easygoing fellow with a solid core of common sense and a good sense of humor, could have aroused such intense dislike. He was denounced by many Democratic leaders as a dangerous fanatic. George Meany and Martin Luther King, Jr., said they saw "signs of Hitlerism" in Goldwater's campaign. Senator J. William Fulbright declared that "Goldwater Republicanism is the closest thing in American politics to an equivalent of Russian Stalinism." Columnist James Reston warned Goldwater that he seemed to be following a course laid down by the "extremist tyrants of history." That kind of talk bubbles up in campaigns, such as in 1964's, fueled by intense ideologies. (Quoted in William F. Buckley, Jr., column of October 17, 1973.)

the margin of support that swings an election, but the basic influence is still party loyalty. A study of the voting in the 1968 election, when the Vietnam war was the most headlined story of the day and presumably on everybody's mind, found that party identification had "fifty times the net impact of the Vietnam issue."[65] This was helped by the fact that the candidates did not differ greatly in their stands on the issue.

It is plain, as Nelson W. Polsby and Aaron B. Wildavsky put it, that:

> People go to the polls and vote for many reasons not directly connected with issues. They may vote on the basis of party identification alone. Party habits may be joined with a general feeling that Democrats are better for the common citizen or that Republicans will keep us safe—feelings too diffuse to tell us much about specific issues. Some people may vote on the basis of a candidate's personality, or his "image." Others follow a friend's recommendation. Still others may be thinking about policy issues but may be all wrong in their perception of where the candidates stand. It would be difficult to distinguish the votes of these people from the votes of those who know, care, and differentiate among the candidates on the basis of issues. We do know, however, that issue-oriented persons are usually in the minority, while those who cast their ballots with other things in mind are generally in the majority.[66]

As the quotes and data from the "experts" should make abundantly clear, there are no real experts on the subject of why Americans vote as they do. The motives of the electorate are highly mixed, and the origin of their motives range from gut instincts to intellectual analysis.

Who Really Elects the President?

It's that November morning after election day. The race has been run, the votes have been counted, the *assumed* winner has been announced. But the emphasis must continue to be on *assumed* until the votes have officially been translated into electoral-college votes and tabulated by Congress the following January. The real electors are the members of the electoral college, a ceremonial organization that, except on the rarest of occasions, rubber-stamps the will of the people.

The electoral college is a weird vestige of the nation's early history. The nation's Founders were, in general, leery of the masses. They feared—and, as history has shown, with good reason—that the masses would sometimes be deceived by charlatans and wicked fellows who wanted office only to abuse it. The masses were presumed to be easily misled, easily duped. As George Mason, a delegate to the 1787 Constitutional Convention, put it, "It would be as natural to refer the choice of a proper character for Chief Magistrate [President] to the people as it would to refer a trial of colours to a blind man." So they decided that each state would be allowed only to "appoint, in such Manner as the Legislature thereof may direct, a Number of . . . Electors [who] shall meet in their respective States, and vote" for some fit person as President, the precautionary rationale being, as Alexander Hamilton put it in *The Federalist Paper*, Number 69, "Talents for low intrigue, and the little arts of popularity, may alone suffice to elevate a man to the first honors in a single state; but it will require other talents and a different kind of merit to establish him in the confidence of the whole union. . . ." John Jay, who agreed wholeheartedly with this manner of electing the President, also pointed out the advantage that it would safeguard against "party zeal."[67] So the framers wrote into the Constitution, in Article II, provisions that they thought would guarantee choice by a cool-headed elite. The provisions, as amended, are as follows:

When voters cast their ballots for a presidential candidate, they really are casting them for an electoral slate. Each party in each state offers its own slate of electoral candidates. Members of

---

[65] Richard A. Brody, Benjamin I. Page, Sidney Verba, and Jerome Laulicht, "Vietnam, the Urban Crisis, and the 1968 Presidential Election: A Preliminary Analysis," paper delivered at the American Sociological Association meetings in San Francisco, September 1969.

[66] Nelson W. Polsby and Aaron B. Wildavsky, *Presidential Elections: Strategies of American Electoral Politics*, 4th ed. (New York: Charles Scribner's Sons, 1976), p. 274.

[67] Alexander Hamilton, James Madison, and John Jay, *The Federalist Papers*, Numbers 64, 69, ed. Clinton Rossiter (New York: Times Mirror Co., New American Library, 1961).

the slate representing the winning candidate in the state come together a couple of weeks after the November election, and they cast ballots for a presidential candidate. Almost inevitably every member of the electoral slate votes for his or her party's nominee. Usually the electors have sworn that they will do so; occasionally they have remained "unpledged." In other words, a person on the Republican slate will be unfaithful if he or she votes for, say, the Libertarian candidate. That sort of waywardness has happened rarely; in fact, of the 17,000 electors since 1789, only 7 have gone astray.

Furthermore, it is a winner-take-all situation. If the Democratic candidate wins 53 percent of a state's popular votes, he doesn't get just 53 percent of that state's electoral votes. He gets *all* of them.

The electoral results in each state are sent to Washington, where the ghostly electoral college "meets" in January. It meets only in the sense that the House and Senate count the votes of the various states' electoral slates, and thereby a President is offically chosen. If there is a tie in electoral votes, the choice of who will be President is left to the House.

Why continue to go through this hocus-pocus? Why not simply tally up the popular vote and let it go at that? Because the Constitution mandates the electoral-college route, and Congress has not yet agreed to change it. As long as it exists, there is the possibility—a faint possibility, but, still, always there—that the electoral-college system will frustrate the popular will. The last time it did so was in 1888, when Benjamin Harrison, with 95,096 fewer popular votes, defeated Grover Cleveland in the electoral count 233 to 168. In this century there have been five elections in which tiny shifts in the popular vote in a handful of states would have elected a candidate who lost the popular vote. In 1976 a shift of 9,245 votes in Ohio and Hawaii from Carter to Ford would have elected Ford, even though Carter had a plurality of 1.7 million votes nationwide.

In 1916, the contest between Woodrow Wilson and Charles Evans Hughes finally hinged on California's 13 electoral votes.

> Excluding California, the electoral count stood at 264 for Wilson, 254 for Hughes. Whichever man won California would be President. An agonizing delay in the vote count now occurred, and it was not until several days later that the California vote was finally tallied and Wilson found to be the victor. But Wilson had carried California by only 3,806 votes out of almost a million cast in the state. A shift of less than one-fifth of one percent of the California vote would have elected Hughes, despite Wilson's national popular vote plurality of well over half a million votes.[68]

In 1948, Harry Truman won by more than 2 million popular votes, but a shift of only 12,487 votes in California and Ohio would have given Thomas Dewey a tie in electoral votes, and the contest would have gone to the House of Representatives. In 1960, in one of the closest elections in history, a shift of only 4,480 votes from Kennedy to Nixon in Illinois (a state notoriously capable of shifting votes even after they have been cast) and a shift of only 4,491 votes in Missouri would have thrown the decision into the House.

One might hastily conclude that if this had happened the results would have been the same—Kennedy would have become President—because the House of Representatives was heavily Democratic. But the constitutional rules for the tallying give each state's delegation one vote—fifty votes for the whole House. In 1960, the breakdown of the fifty votes went like this: twenty-three delegations controlled by Democrats from northern and border states, who would probably have voted for Kennedy; seventeen delegations controlled by Republicans, who would have voted for Nixon; the balance of power lay with the six nominally Democratic delegations from the Deep South and the four delegations split evenly between the parties. What would have been the outcome of the bargaining? It's anybody's guess. Among the darker suggestions is Tom Wicker's: "Kennedy might have become President only at the price of Senator James O. Eastland for Attorney General, or some other arrangement as grotesque."[69] Eastland is a notorious racist.

---

[68]Neal R. Peirce, *The People's President: The Electoral College in American History and the Direct-Vote Alternative* (New York: Simon & Schuster, 1968), p. 95.

[69]Quoted in Peirce, p. 10.

In a famous moment of triumph, President Truman displays a premature headline on election day, 1948

As a result of these close calls, the electoral college may be slated for reform. President Carter has submitted a proposal to Congress asking for a constitutional amendment to abolish the electoral college and allow for direct popular election of the President and Vice President. If it clears Congress, such a proposal seems likely to be approved by the required three-fourths of the states. Polls show that nearly 80 percent of Americans endorse the plan.

THE WORKINGS
OF ELECTORAL DEMOCRACY

To what extent can elections be said to produce an authentic choice of the people? Isn't it possible that the elaborate nominating process and the pious efforts to get out the vote often have nothing to do with satisfying the wishes of the people? No group knows better than the electorate itself how true was the observation of V. O. Key, Jr., that it

> can be mischievous error to assume, because a candidate wins, that a majority of the electorate shares his views on public questions, approves his past actions, or has specific expectations about his future conduct. Nor does victory establish that the candidate's campaign strategy, his image, his television style, or his fearless stand against cancer and polio turned the trick. The election returns establish only that the winner attracted a majority of the votes—assuming the existence of a modicum of rectitude in election administration. They tell us precious little about why the plurality was his.

For a glaringly obvious reason, electoral victory cannot be regarded as necessarily a popular ratification of a candidate's outlook. The voice of the people is but an echo chamber. The output of an echo chamber bears an inevitable and invariable relation to the input. As candidates and parties clamor for attention and vie for popular support, the people's verdict can be no more than a selective reflection from among the alternatives and outlooks presented to them. Even the most discriminating popular judgment can reflect only ambiguity, uncertainty, or even foolishness if those are the qualities of the input into the echo chamber. A candidate may win despite his tactics and appeals rather than because of them. If the people can choose only from among rascals, they are certain to choose a rascal.[70]

Some undemocratic features of the electoral process appear to defy solution—such as the overrepresentation of the well-to-do. Those who most genuinely need the benefits only a government can confer—the poor, the uneducated, the minorities—do not control the ballot. Election results are determined by those who participate in the selection of candidates, who work for them, and who vote for them; and, typically, they are of the middle or upper class and are politically savvy and secure—and intent on preserving their security.

The greater the interest and involvement one has in an election, the more likely one is to vote. This is what gives an upper-class bias to voting—those who are better off and better educated vote because they have an economic stake in the ballot and have access to political information.

Their electoral participation is one explanation for overrepresentation of those who are well off; their money is another. Money is the great unequalizer.

Money and Politics

It's not good manners to put a price tag on democracy, but it has to be done. It takes money to catch the voter's eye. In a way, loosely speaking, every political office has always been bought. But things have improved. It used to be that some offices were bought outright. Until

1913, United States senators were elected by state legislatures, and state legislatures often proved very susceptible to bribery. Simon Cameron, who gave to political lore the precept "An honest politician is one who, when he is bought, stays bought," bribed the Pennsylvania legislature four times to elect and reelect him to the United States Senate. Pennsylvania was a notable breeding ground for political scoundrels of this type. Boies Penrose successfully bought a Senate seat from the legislature for $500,000, defeating John Wanamaker, who had mistakenly been told that the legislature could be had for $400,000.[71] We have come a long way toward political righteousness since that golden age of boodle, or at least we have learned to travel a more subtle path of corruption. When politicians' integrity is strangled to any degree, that is corruption of a sort. When, against their better instincts, they give undue weight to the wishes of the special interests who contributed the most to their campaign treasuries, they may not have exactly sold out, but they have certainly been compromised.

How does a candidate who is not publicly financed—as the presidential candidates now are—avoid the big contributors? Only with great difficulty, if at all. It is pleasant to think of campaigns being run on five-dollar contributions from clerks and storekeepers who have no axes to grind, but a campaign for a state-wide or nation-wide office is a gargantuan operation that defies a return to simplicity.

A United States senator from California serves the largest constituency ever represented by a legislator in the history of the world. More than 21 million people look to him or her for assistance. When the California senator goes to the 21 million people for their electoral support, the senator must have a big voice to reach into all the crannies of their existence, and big campaign voices are bought with big money; in California this means several million dollars. Of course, the money *could* be accumulated in small amounts, but the reality of successful solicitation to date has meant that most money has come in big

---

[70]V. O. Key, Jr., and Milton C. Cummings, Jr., *The Responsible Electorate: Rationality in Presidential Voting, 1936–1960* (Cambridge, Mass.: Harvard University Press, 1966), pp. 2–3.

[71]Thayer, *Who Shakes the Money Tree?*, pp. 44–46.

hunks.[72] The result of the big money is predictable, and California Senator Alan Cranston spells it out:

> The effect of large contributions on the victorious candidate is sometimes blatant but usually subtle. He knows his victory was won in part by the generosity of those individuals who made large donations. He knows who they are; he remembers their names and the names of their companies.
>
> If he is an honest man, he will not let big contributors determine how he is going to vote. But even the honest public official finds that he must give to the big donor's concerns his time and attention, his sympathetic ear, his willingness to intervene when he can do so legitimately.
>
> The officeholder recognizes that while some big givers contribute solely for the sake of good government and a belief in the candidate and his principles, they are a minority. He knows that the majority expect their contributions will at least give them access to him. And access, at the least, means ability to drop in anytime for an informal visit or to present their views before the officeholder acts on an issue.
>
> A busy public official can see only a limited number of people in any one day. But he must always do his best to fit a major contributor into his schedule. That may squeeze out someone else who has as much—perhaps more—to say; it is utterly unfair, but inescapable under present conditions.[73]

Since politicians must have money to run for office, and since they will naturally be supported by people who expect them to be sympathetic with their way of life, what's so suspicious about campaign contributions? Nothing is suspicious, unless the gift of money seems to be in anticipation of, or in payment for, a *specific* action on the part of the politician. Or, to put it another way, a campaign contribution seems to take on the aura of bribery or payoff when there is some question as to whether the government official would have done what he or she did if the money hadn't been in mind.

Were the following just campaign contributions—or were they bribery?

- In 1968, then–Secretary of State Dean Rusk overruled his legal adviser and refused to approve extradition to Canada of a former Seafarer International Union official charged with perjury there. Shortly afterward, the Seafarers contributed $100,000 to the Democratic campaign fund.[74]

- Senator Harrison A. Williams, Jr., a New Jersey Democrat, was preparing legislation to tighten the regulation of the securities industry. Williams allowed his legislation to be amended in such a way as to weaken it. To show appreciation, the Securities Industry Association, the American Bankers Association, and various individual members of both organizations contributed $34,600 to Williams's reelection fund. Was Ralph Nader fair in calling it "institutionalized bribery"? Was a New Jersey newspaper fair to editorialize that it smacked of "what used to be called a shakedown"?[75]

- On March 12, 1971, Agriculture Secretary Clifford M. Hardin decided not to permit milk prices to be raised. On March 23, representatives of the dairy industry met with President Nixon and reminded him that they had pledged $2 million to his reelection fund. Nixon decided to overrule his Secretary of Agriculture, and, after the dairy industry privately reaffirmed their $2 million promise, he raised milk prices.[76]

- Both the companies and the unions of the maritime industry serve as constant examples of questionable dealings of this kind. It is one of the most heavily subsidized industries—receiving

---

[72]When Florida's Governor Reubin Askew decided to run a "people's campaign" in 1974, he voluntarily imposed a one-hundred-dollar ceiling on contributions. Here was an opportunity for the voters who had been complaining about big contributors buying politicians to get into the game themselves and show that small contributors, if encouraged, would do the job. Well, it didn't work out that way. Of the state's 3.5 million registered voters, fewer than nine thousand—one-fourth of 1 percent—chipped in to the governor's campaign. If he hadn't been the incumbent and just naturally a vote-getter, it might have been a tragic experiment for him. Former Florida State Senator Louis A. de la Parte justifiably groused: "You can put 1,000 average voters in a room and say, 'How many of you have ever contributed to a campaign, any campaign?' and not one of them will have contributed. Then you ought to be able to ask them: 'Then where in the hell do you think the money came from?'" (Quoted in Herbert E. Alexander, *Campaign Money: Reform Reality in the States,* New York: Free Press, 1976, pp. 314–15.)

[73]Alan Cranston, "How to Cure the Corruption," *Nation,* September 17, 1973.

[74]Thayer, *Who Shakes the Money Tree?,* p. 106.

[75]*New York Times,* June 22, 1975.

[76]*Chicago Tribune,* May 12, 1974.

Why Business Supports Republicans

Campaign financing is not always based on logic. If it were, business would be much more generous to Democrats than to Republicans.

During the Eisenhower years there were three recessions, and, as a result of those hard times, the average annual rate of business failures was twice as high as during the Truman years. When the Democrats took over the White House again, the economy picked up. After eight years of the Kennedy-Johnson administrations, business failures had finally been cut back to the lowest rate since Truman's time. Then came Nixon, and the rate of failures began climbing again. Nor did the giant firms escape the trend. In 1970, more companies on *Fortune*'s top 500 list lost money than in any comparable period since *Fortune* began collecting the data in the mid-1950s.

A Citibank historical summary shows that the profit rate—which is the most important test of business health—was higher, often much higher, under recent Democratic Presidents than under Republican Presidents. So one might expect business, big and small, to favor the Democratic candidates overwhelmingly and lavish most of its political money on their campaigns. But that doesn't happen. The Democrats do receive large contributions from business, of course, but Republican presidential candidates usually receive *five to six times more.*

Why? Sociologist R. D. Corwin and economist Lois Gray believe it is because—strange as it may seem—people, even business executives, sometimes rate psychological comfort higher than profits.

> Some values associated with Republicanism transcend economics, and these may be attractive, even compelling, to businessmen. They see the Republican party as *their* party—and perhaps, to some extent, as their party, right or wrong. Republican rhetoric—dramatizing and approving the vital role of business in American life—is reassuring. These are sounds to which businessmen have been conditioned to respond. Eventually, with Pavlovian logic, the phrase becomes the reward.
>
> Rewards beyond the rhetorical are associated with Republican ascendancy. Businessmen are honored by pronouncement and appointment, recognition and prestige. When a Republican is President, businessmen are intimately tied into the highest levels of government—they feel at home; they can, as it were, take their shoes off in the White House.
>
> In the minds of many businessmen, moreover, the presence of the Republicans in office entails a major additional benefit—the absence of the Democrats. For one thing, since many regulatory agencies were established during Democratic administrations, businessmen feel that Democrats are more rigorous in their regulatory activity. With a Republican administration businessmen have a sense of relief, of freedom from governmental restraint and harassment. This feeling of liberty is of great importance to them—it is the pivotal point of their value system and essential to their self-image.*

Fortune, July 1971, p. 128

tax advantages and direct subsidies each year worth an estimated $1 billion—and the maritime folks like to show their gratitude. In 1973, both houses of Congress passed a bill to require that a greater portion of the nation's oil imports be shipped in United States tankers operated by United States crews. This would have increased the cost of the oil, for United States maritime salaries are higher than those paid in most countries. It would have also increased the direct load on the taxpayer: of a typical tanker crewman's pay of $13,800 a year, $10,350 comes from federal subsidies.[77] Nevertheless, Congress passed the bill, and maritime unions promptly paid $333,000 to the legislators who had been friendly. Of the 266 members of Congress who voted for the bill, 126 received donations. But of the 136 who voted against it, only three received union money.[78] In the Senate, the bill had been

[77]*Washington Post,* August 23, 1974.

[78]Associated Press, September 16, 1974.

introduced by Senator Daniel K. Inouye of Hawaii, who then received $10,000 from the maritime unions for his 1974 campaign—even though he had no opposition either in the primary or in the general election.[79] Was the money a gesture of political loyalty, or was it a payoff?

• The same can be asked of the $350,000 that the oil industry paid to eight members of the Senate Finance Committee before the committee reviewed the industry's tax breaks.[80]

• In 1974, H. Ross Perot, the millionaire Texas businessman, gave $55,000 to twelve members of the House Ways and Means Committee—all but one of the contributions were made *after* the members had been elected. In 1975, the House Ways and Means Committee voted a tax break worth $15 million to Perot, the largest individual tax favoritism ever given.[81]

• During the 1974 elections, one hundred members of Congress, who voted against a bill to tighten real estate tax shelter loopholes, received $100,000 from the real estate lobby. Was the pressure group paying for services rendered, or was it simply interested in the democratic process?[82]

• Almost every election year scandals break forth to show that campaign contributions are one of the most obvious devices used by lobbyists to gain advantage. But sometimes the contributions are used piggyback fashion—they are used by an ally of the giver rather than directly by the giver. When Earl L. Butz was Secretary of Agriculture, he bragged about his method of influencing members of Congress: "Find the Congressman's financial angel. That is the way I worked to beat a bill raising price supports 25 percent. I called up one chap and started to explain the bill. He said, 'Hell, don't bother. I'll just tell the Congressman I don't want it.' He did and that was it."[83]

• Walter H. Annenberg, media and railroad magnate, gave $254,000 to Nixon's campaigns and wound up as ambassador to Great Britain. Ruth L. Farkas, the wife of a wealthy department store owner, gave $300,000 to the Republican campaign and was appointed ambassador to Luxembourg. Would it be fair to suggest that such appointments were purchased?[84]

• In 1960 John ("Jake the Barber") Factor, a rich reformed mobster, gave $20,000 to Kennedy's campaign. It was his first recorded campaign contribution. Two years later, Factor received a presidential pardon for a 1943 mail-fraud conviction.[85]

• Two senators who voted for national no-fault auto insurance in 1974 voted against it in 1976. After they cast their negative votes, a trial lawyers' political campaign committee gave each of them five thousand dollars. No-fault insurance takes much of the cream out of trial lawyers' business.[86]

In most cases there is no way to prove that campaign contributions have the effect of bribery on policy making, but the coincidences are all too common. Bribery is not the only concern, however. There is another dangerous consequence of financing by special interests: money can put candidates into office who simply *agree* with the money givers and who are perfectly honest in acting in accord with their interests. This, like the obtaining of "access," introduces a conservative bias into the electoral system, for money interests are nearly always conservative ones.

The Winding Road to Reform of Campaign Financing

The politicians in Washington, like those in state government, have been very shy about reforming campaign financing. The history of reform is brief and, for the most part, ugly.

The first attempt to control money in politics was the 1867 congressional law forbidding politicians to assess federal employees for campaign contributions. The law was routinely violated; federal employees did not escape forced contributions until the Civil Service Reform Act of

[79]*New York Times,* September 14, 1975.

[80]*Christian Science Monitor,* October 8, 1975.

[81]Dow Jones News Service, November 7, 1975.

[82]Common Cause release, December 10, 1975.

[83]Quoted in the *Nation,* October 26, 1974.

[84]*Congressional Record,* E3344, May 21, 1973.

[85]*Fortune,* March 1970.

[86]*Washington Post,* August 30, 1976.

1883.[87] In 1907, Congress passed legislation forbidding banks and corporations from contributing to the election of federal officials. In 1944, under the Smith-Connally Act, and in 1947, under the Taft-Hartley Act, the prohibition was extended to labor unions. These laws were ignored. In 1939 and 1940, Congress passed the Hatch Act, forbidding federal employees below the highest level from participating in campaigns on behalf of a candidate. The law also set a five-thousand-dollar limit on individual gifts to a federal candidate. This law was consistently violated, and the violators were almost never punished.

The best known of the early laws was the Federal Corrupt Practices Act, passed in 1925, ostensibly to bring campaign contributions out in the open and blunt the influence of the big money interests. The law, which incorporated most of the restrictions of the earlier laws, was so riddled with loopholes that more than half the money spent on campaigns went unreported, and the money that was reported was listed as having come from phony committees (Wyoming Bell-Ringers for Nixon, Brooklyn Trumpeters for Javits, and so forth). Unions and corporations continued to get around the law by using the names of individual members or simply by slipping money under the table and ignoring the law. It was illegal for politicians to receive such money, but no politician ever went to jail for doing so.[88] Only once in fifty years did a labor official go to jail for breaking the law that had been, in fact, smashed into a thousand pieces every election. Because of the loopholes in this act, each campaign year scores of candidates for Congress were able to legally file reports indicating they received no money and spent no money on their campaigns.[89]

But Americans have clearly been embarrassed by the corruption of their politics. Over the years there has been a steady demand for honesty in campaign financing. Politicians, being the beneficiaries of the corruption, generally resisted these demands. Finally, however, the public outcry became so great that, in 1971, Congress passed the Federal Election Campaign Act, the first serious reform to the federal elections laws, and, in 1974, it added several additional amendments to further improve the reforms.

The three major features of the 1971 law and its 1974 amendments mandate disclosure of money sources, set limits on campaign contributions and spending, and offer public financing for presidential races. Originally, the law had set limits on the amount of his or her own funds a candidate could spend. Subsequently, the Supreme Court ruled that, in an era of mass communications, restricting the amount of money candidates could spend to present their political message is the same as restricting free speech itself, which would violate the First Amendment. It was official recognition of the old saying, "money talks." So the Court compromised: it permitted a limit on the amount of money individuals or groups could give *directly* to the candidate, for it considered these outside contributions only loosely related to free speech but closely related to the corruption the law was trying to end. However, it permitted candidates to spend any amount of their own *personal* money,[90] and it permitted individuals and groups to spend any amount of money for the election of a candidate so long as they spent the money themselves and didn't give more than the ceiling amount directly to the candidate. Also, the Court ruled that if a candidate received public financing, he or she must accept a ceiling on the amount of private money spent.[91]

In presidential primaries, each candidate is permitted to spend no more than $10 million. There are matching public funds of up to $4.5 million

[87] Alexander, *Money in Politics*, p. 199.

[88] Dozens of members of both the House and the Senate received illegal campaign contributions from Gulf Oil Corporation, for example, but all of them bluffed it out, and nothing happened to them. Except one. Congressman James R. Jones, Democrat from Oklahoma, pleaded guilty to failure to report the money he received from Gulf. He could have been fined one thousand dollars and put in jail for a year; instead, he was fined two hundred dollars.

[89] Report of the Democratic Study Group of the House of Representatives, November 1971.

[90] Which legitimatized the strategy of such politicians as the late Kennedy brothers, the Rockefellers, and H. John Heinz III, the pickle heir, all of whom spent millions of family dollars in quest of office.

[91] Alexander, *Campaign Money*, pp. 5–6.

Public Campaign Financing

Common Cause, a national public affairs lobbying organization, has been one of the loudest voices in opposition to the traditional system of privately financed political campaigns. It summarizes its argument in support of public-financed campaigns in this way:

> In studying the corrupting role of big money in politics and how it works to destroy a competitive political system, we see the following:
>
> • INCUMBENTS—Those in office stay in office. More than 90 percent of all incumbents who ran for re-election during the last decade, won. In 1976 they were given $3 of special interest money for every $1 given to challengers. One group—the dairy interests—favored incumbents over challengers by more than 7 to 1.
>
> • COMPETITION—Because of the difficulty in raising money to run against an incumbent, competition often fails to develop. In the last election, 51 House seats went unopposed by major party candidates—nearly 11 percent of the total House of Representatives. Thus, voters in those 51 districts had virtually no choice.
>
> • WOMEN AND MINORITIES—Women and minority candidates have historically had trouble raising enough money to run an effective and competitive political campaign. Blacks, who make up 12 percent of the U.S. population, make up only 4 percent of the House with 16 members. The situation for women is even worse. They make up 51.3 percent of the population but are represented by only 18 women in the 435 member House of Representatives. Among the 100 Senators, there is only one black and there are no women.
>
> • WEALTHY CANDIDATES—Because a Supreme Court ruling prohibits restrictions on the amount of personal money a candidate can use—unless there is public financing—any wealthy candidate is assured of the means to spend as much as he or she feels is necessary to win victory at the polls, and thus has an enormous advantage. For example: H. John Heinz III in 1976 spent more than $2.5 million of his own money—double what his opponent was able to raise—to become a U.S. Senator from Pennsylvania.
>
> • POWER IN CONGRESS—Special interests put their money where it counts—those who hold power through chairmanships or key committee assignments in Congress. For example: in 1976 two-thirds of the campaign expenditures of 15 major House committee chairmen came from special interest groups, according to the New York Times.
>
> • CUMULATIVE EFFECT—Contributions have a block building effect in obligating the candidate. It works this way: If you are a legislator and have played the game right, you can count on the same help next time around. And, when it comes time to vote on an issue, you remember your indebtedness for past support along with your hopes for future financial help.

Common Cause, "Report to the American People on the Financing of Congressional Election Campaigns," May 1977.

per candidate; but to qualify for these matching funds a candidate must first raise $100,000 in amounts of at least $5,000 in each of twenty states or more. No one political party may receive more than 45 percent of the total amount of federal money available for the primaries, and no single candidate may receive more than 25 percent of the total money available. Under this system, third-party candidates can qualify for federal matching money. *In the general presiden-*tial election campaign, a candidate may choose to accept either private financing or public financing but may not mix the two. Major-party candidates automatically qualify for full public funding—at a maximum of $21.8 million each. Minor-party candidates are, in effect, shut out of the public funding.

Congress, which wrote and passed the law, was much less restrictive on itself than it was on presidential candidates. Congressional candidates can still go forth freely into the clubrooms and union halls of the special interests to collect money.[92] Indeed, by writing a law that chased contributors out of the presidential counting-houses, Congress effectively made them more available to their own campaigns. And that's the way it turned out. In the 1976 congressional elections, special interest groups lavished a record-breaking amount of money, $22.6 million, into the House and Senate campaigns—about double what they had invested in 1974.[93]

But the new law has achieved two notable reforms. First of all, it has made the fattest fat cats virtually extinct in the presidential election. Take W. Clement Stone, for example. He had been the champion political contributor of all time, having personally given $5.3 million in federal elections between 1968 and 1972.[94] In 1976, he gave only a few thousand dollars. The law prohibits an individual from giving more than $1,000 for each federal primary, runoff, and general election (whether presidential or congressional) and limits a person's aggregate contribution to all federal candidates annually to $25,000. That spells curtains for the fattest fat cats unless and until they find ways to spend unlimited funds on behalf of a candidate without giving the funds directly to the candidate.

The second major achievement of the new campaign law is in the area of disclosure. Instead of having the freedom to finance themselves through a thousand campaign committees, which makes it impossible for the public to find out how much money candidates have received and from whom, each candidate is required to establish one central campaign committee through which all contributions and expenditures must be reported. Candidates are required to file full reports of collections and expenditures with the Federal Election Commission ten days before and thirty days after every election. Contributors are forbidden to make contributions in somebody else's name. The law requires any organization that spends any money or commits any act for the purpose of influencing any election to file reports as a political committee.

As with all new laws, the reforms of 1971 and 1974 spread some confusion and chaos and put a chill on campaign activities. For example, according to Gallup polls, there are more than 6 million volunteer workers in a typical presidential election year, but in 1976 many who wanted to work for candidates were turned away either because the candidates' headquarters didn't know whether volunteer work counted as a contribution and was therefore illegal or because there were no bumper stickers and buttons for the volunteers to pass out. Some of the unhappy experiences of the 1976 election are certain to result in changes in the law. And it remains to be seen whether the unrestricted spending that is allowed individuals as long as it doesn't go directly to the candidates will cause the new law to have relatively little impact. But even as it stands, it is a major step toward the sunlight.

The states have also been busy with reform. Thirty-one states, as of 1976, had enacted campaign expenditure limits, and twenty-three had set limits to contributions from individuals and groups. Eleven states offered some form of direct public support; eleven others gave state income tax deductions for political donations. Between 1972 and 1976 all but one state—North Dakota—passed laws to restrict the flow of pressure money, and the secrecy surrounding it, in their elections.[95]

Incumbency: An Unfair Advantage?

The efforts to reform campaign-spending laws seldom address themselves to what everybody acknowledges is one of the great, imbedded injustices of politics—the advantage of incumbency.

At the presidential level, the advantage is especially awesome. In fourteen contests involving incumbent Presidents, only Grover Cleveland, William Howard Taft, Herbert Hoover,

[92]In 1974, of the seventy-five most senior members of Congress, who command all the committee chairs and most of the leadership positions and are in a position to barter with special interests, only twelve voted for public financing on the congressional level.

[93]Common Cause "Report to the American People on the Financing of Congressional Election Campaigns," May 1977.

[94]Joseph P. Albright, "The Price of Purity," *New York Times Magazine,* September 1, 1974.

[95]Sources: John W. Gardner, in Foreword to Alexander, *Campaign Money,* p. vii; Alexander, p. 8.

and Gerald Ford managed to blow it, and they were the victims of highly unusual circumstances—Cleveland won the popular election but fell victim to the electoral college, Taft was the victim of a splintered party, Hoover the victim of the principle that depressions are very depressing indeed, and Ford the victim of Watergate and a heavy recession.[96] The rate of reelection among state legislators and United States members of Congress is 90 percent and up; among United States senators it is 80 percent and up.[97]

It is not really known why seats have become increasingly safe. But one reason might be the law of political physics, which says money runs most easily in the direction of proved winners. Since people who are in office have, as statistics show, an overwhelmingly excellent chance of staying there, campaign contributors with special interests to protect prefer giving to incumbents.[98] In 1974, for example, Senate Republican incumbents received an average of $594,477, and Senate Democratic incumbents received an average of $631,475, compared to $281,634 for Republican and $384,512 for Democratic challengers.[99]

At the state legislative level, incumbents usually hit an even more generous jackpot. In Florida in 1974, for example, of the 66 incumbent legislators in contested races, 53 won. The 53 winners had received as much campaign money as their 188 opponents. A *Miami Herald* study found that $0.71 of every campaign dollar given to the winners came from special interest groups; lobbyists preferred incumbents because, by bowing to the wishes of the special interest

groups in the past, they had proved that they were "reliable."[100]

In the days before public financing, the President had unequalled power to raise campaign funds through threat and promise. The coercive operation that enabled Nixon to raise $60 million for his reelection campaign was successful because many big business executives viewed the alternatives in the same perspective as George A. Spater, Chairman of the Board of American Airlines (who gave $100,000): "There were two aspects: would you get something if you gave it, or would you be prevented from getting something if you didn't give it?"[101]

For the members of Congress, seniority works the same kind of magic. As long as the big moneyed interests know that a senator with seniority is likely to continue chairing an important committee, no matter how doddering he is and no matter how much his colleagues despise him, that senator is going to get the financial support of the special interests who stand to benefit from the work of his committee.

Senator Jennings Randolph of West Virginia got so much money for his campaign in 1972 that he couldn't spend it all. His Republican opponent raised so little that she had to sink $32,000 of her own money into the race. Seniority had made Randolph Chairman of the Public Works Committee years ago. If he had been defeated, Senator Edmund Muskie would have inherited the committee. Industrialists who feared antipollution legislation that Muskie might push if he were chairman of the committee scrambled to give Randolph money; so did shippers who used the thousands of miles of rivers and canals (toll free) that are supervised by the Public Works Committee. Most of Randolph's money came from outside his home state.

The incumbent President enjoys a great manipulative advantage over the airwaves in pushing his candidacy. His opponent must either pay for air time or rely on the chance that he or she will say or do something that the networks will squeeze into a few seconds on the evening news.

[96]The incumbent President's chances of getting his party's support for reelection are virtually guaranteed. Only one sitting President has ever been denied renomination when he wanted it. That was Franklin Pierce; but, again, Pierce was an oddity. Ralph Waldo Emerson was really not far off the mark when he said that Pierce's "miserable administration admits of but one excuse, imbecility." (Quoted in David Epstein, "Remembering Franklin Pierce (Which Few People Do)," *Washington Post,* November 17, 1970.)

[97]Sources: Gardner, in Foreword to Alexander, *Campaign Money,* p. viii; Americans for Democratic Action report, August 25, 1975.

[98]It's somewhat of a vicious circle—because the incumbents can get money easily, they win all the more easily.

[99]Common Cause release, August 11, 1976.

[100]William Mansfield, "Florida: The Power of Incumbency," in Alexander, *Campaign Money,* pp. 55–57.

[101]Sale, *Power Shift,* p. 232.

When it comes to getting free air time in this way, the challenger is at the mercy of the network news programmers. Not so the President. What he does or says is automatically news and automatically gets priceless air time. When he walks in the rose garden, calls a press conference, goes to the opera, or speaks to the Lions Club in Peoria, he does so with the assurance that reporters from all the networks will accompany him and keep his visage and message before the public. In the second of his debates with challenger Jimmy Carter, President Ford made several errors of fact. His image was damaged. To fight back, Ford called a press conference, leisurely explained away the errors he had made, and denounced Carter in bitter terms. It was, strictly speaking, a political news conference, not a "presidential" news conference, but it was covered by all networks and by a full compliment of the pencil press. The President had one-upped his opponent, for Carter had no comparable access to the networks, unless he wanted to pay for the time.[102]

Incumbent members of Congress are also lavishly supplied with perquisites of the same sort. In 1975, the Americans for Democratic Action estimated that a member of the House of Representatives receives benefits and special privileges that give him or her, on the average, a $500,000-plus election year advantage over nonincumbent candidates, including $121,000 for travel and communication.[103]

Every year, members of Congress send out more than $43 million in free mail. That's the equivalent of $80,000 a year per member of Congress. Flooding the constituency year after year at that rate keeps the incumbent's name out front in a way that would sorely strain a challenger's budget, were he or she to attempt to compete. In addition, the member of Congress gets to provide constituents with freebies at government expense—everything from a short pamphlet entitled "Controlling Clover Mites Around the Home" to a ninety-seven-page softcover, "Your Child from 1 to 6," to "Making Pickles and Relishes at Home." By the time members of Congress get through scattering those great pieces of literature over their districts, they're well on their way to reelection. And don't forget the free TV documentaries and radio tapes they are permitted to cut at the Capitol, at taxpayers' expense, and which they send to the TV and radio stations back home.

Of course, it is good democracy to help federal politicians keep the home folks informed. But at what point do they stop "informing" the home folks and start twisting their arms to reelect them? It's not an easy question to answer. Several courts have recently ruled that such things as "questionnaires" sent out by members of Congress to their constituents were in fact campaign literature and should not be allowed the free postage that traditionally is given a representative's mail.

If elections are to be fair, something will have to be done to balance this advantage. Perhaps an incumbent's primary and general election opponents should be given several free mailings of campaign literature to get their names before the public; perhaps they should also be given free radio and TV time well in advance of the election. Throughout the election year, the incumbent should certainly not have any tax-paid opportunities that his or her challengers do not have.

No Sure Solutions

Campaign politics is clearly marred by tainted money, by laws and customs that favor the "ins," and by laws that create confusion and exhaustion for participants at all levels. But the money is much cleaner today than it was at the turn of the century, and Congress has made some conscientious efforts to instill more sanity into campaign laws.

It must be remembered that electoral politics is not an exact science. There are no sure solutions. A few questions will illustrate.

• Are there drawbacks to public financing? Very likely. Some politicians argue, with consid-

---

[102] A reasonable approach to the problem of free media time was laid out by Newton N. Minow, John Bartlow Martin, and Lee M. Mitchell in *Presidential Television: A Twentieth Century Fund Report*: "The national committee of the opposition party should be given by law an automatic right of response to any presidential radio or television appearance made during the ten months preceding a presidential election or within the ninety days preceding a congressional election in nonpresidential years." (New York: Basic Books, 1973.)

[103] Americans for Democratic Action report, August 25, 1975.

erable logic, that giving public money to candidates weakens the party system by making the candidates less dependent on the parties. After all, parties have traditionally been not only the machinery for recruiting and nominating candidates, but also, by passing the hat through private parlors and board rooms, the candidates' most dependable source of money. Whether or not the weakening of the parties in this way is a risk worth taking (or an advantage worth seeking) is something that must be measured carefully in the years just ahead.[104] But not all politicians fear the decline, or even the death, of party politics as it operates in some states today. And they are cool to the idea of parties as a money source. This feeling is especially likely to be found in the heart of the younger politicians, some of whom seem to feel that they succeeded *despite,* not because of, the entrenched party establishment. Senator Joseph R. Biden, Jr., who was elected in 1972 at the age of thirty, claims that he received virtually no financial support from the Democratic organization in Delaware. In a number of speeches, he has stated his belief that only public financing of all federal elections can save the two-party system, by eliminating the taint of special interest domination. His argument is that, at the present time, the small contributor feels that the Democratic party "belongs" to Big Labor and the Republican party "belongs" to Big Business, so why contribute anything? Why participate in a partisan way? Why identify with either party?[105]

• As for the turnout, *is* it too small? How small is too small? *Should* greater participation at the polls be encouraged? In 1974, only 36.1 percent of the voting-age population bothered to vote in the congressional elections—the first time since 1946 that less than 40 percent turned out. Some observers become very pessimistic as a result of statistics like that. But who's to say that the outcome would have been different if stay-at-

homes had voted? And wasn't their absence perhaps a typically eloquent American statement on the candidates?

As mentioned earlier, four out of five United States citizens between the ages of eighteen and twenty-one stayed away from the ballot box in 1974. Having come of political age in the middle of Watergate and at the embarrassing end of the Vietnam war, perhaps their nonvoting demonstrated a political sensitivity. In Australia, everyone of voting age must vote or be fined. But Australian voters are permitted to cast a blank ballot, signifying their opinion of all the offered candidates. Perhaps staying away from the polls is the United States equivalent of the blank ballot.

In 1976, pollster Peter D. Hart found that 82 percent of the surveyed American nonvoters agreed at least partially that "sometimes government and politics seem so complicated that a person like me can't really understand what's going on." If that was an honest response, isn't it possible that the nation is better governed by their staying away from the ballot box? Also in 1976, several communities tried a new experiment: allowing the inmates of homes for the mentally retarded to vote. Just how far should democracy be stretched?[106]

• Are we, as some contend, sitting on an "electoral time bomb"?[107] Perhaps. But perhaps the bomb, if it went off, would only sputter rather than explode. Let us listen to the anguished complaint of that intrepid foe of the electoral college, Neal R. Peirce:

> The record shows that three times in U.S. history (1824, 1876, 1888) the popular vote loser was elevated to the presidency, and that four times in this century (1916, 1948, 1960 and 1968) miniscule shifts in the popular vote in a handful of states would have frustrated the popular will again.[108]

Would that have been so bad? In 1824, with none of the four candidates winning a majority of the

[104]Richard T. Stout, ed., *Money/Politics: Report of Citizens Research Foundation Conference,* no. 24 (Princeton, N.J.: Citizens Research Foundation, 1974), p. 33.

[105]Another argument against panic in the face of party decline can be found in Everett Carll Ladd, Jr., and Charles D. Hadley, *Transformations of the American Party System: Political Coalitions from the New Deal to the 1970s* (New York: W. W. Norton & Co., 1975), p. 337.

[106]Sources: *Washington Star,* September 21, 1976; Associated Press, October 11, 1976.

[107]See TRB, "The Constitution's Electoral Time Bomb," *Washington Star,* October 9, 1976.

[108]Neal R. Peirce, "Perils of an Electoral College Misfire," *Washington Post,* October 12, 1976.

electoral-college votes, the election was thrown into the House, which picked John Quincy Adams—certainly among our better Presidents. As for the four elections of this century—1916, 1948, 1960, and 1968—that Peirce says came close to going to the other candidate through a tilt in the electoral college, is it not fair to take some hindsight comfort in seeing that if the popular will had been thwarted in those elections the United States just might have avoided participating in World War I, the Korean War, the Vietnam war, and Watergate?

There is no guarantee that the popular-vote winner will be the *better* President. Those who favor electing the President by popular vote argue, however, that legitimacy is best served by being certain that the candidate who wins even just one more popular vote than the opponent is elevated to the Presidency and that if this did not occur there would be a feeling of oddity or quirkiness about the political system. It is a sound argument.

But there are equally sound arguments on the other side, in favor of the electoral college. The electoral-college results magnify the popular will rather than diminish it—or at least they have almost always done so. In 1976, for example, Carter beat Ford 40,291,626 to 38,563,089—a margin of 2.2 percentage points of the total. Hardly a landslide. But in the electoral college, Carter won 297 to Ford's 241—a better than 9-percent margin. In 1972, Nixon took 60.7 percent of the popular vote to McGovern's 23.2 percent. But in the electoral college, Nixon almost wiped McGovern out—520 to 17. In 1968, Nixon's margin of victory over Humphrey was very narrow, 43.4 percent to 42.7 percent of the popular vote. But in the electoral college, Nixon moved up to a comfortable 303 votes to Humphrey's 191.

It could be reasonably argued that by the electoral college's magnification of the winner's popular victory, the winner goes into office with the additional psychological strength that a President needs to carry out his programs.

There are other sound arguments for retaining the electoral college. Among the more persuasive is that a system of popular election might dilute the black vote and all the other minority constituencies to the point that they would be-

come inconsequential elements. Although blacks make up only about 11 percent of the electorate, they are, as Eddie N. Williams, President of the Joint Center for Political Studies, has pointed out, "strategically concentrated in the metropolitan areas of key states with large numbers of electoral votes; and historically, they have tended to vote as a bloc. This strategic concentration has been especially important, and it is this factor that would be lost" if the electoral college were done away with and the blacks' 11 percentage points were mixed with the stew of fifty states.[109] The great majority of the nation's 6 million Jews live in New York City and its environs. They have an enormous impact on the politics of New York state (which has a population of slightly more than 18 million) and, naturally, on the disposition of New York's forty-one electoral votes—second only to California's forty-five—as an electoral bloc. The Jewish vote is, under the present electoral-college system, obviously very important. But if it is submerged in the general popular vote, it will lose its clout. For good or ill, the electoral-college system forces the two major parties to pay particular attention to the voice of certain clustered minorities.

[109]*Washington Post,* April 14, 1977.

Summary

1. Three types of candidates generally make it over the electoral hurdles to the Presidency: the good party politician, the insurgent, and the outside hero.

2. Recently, the process of selecting delegates to the national conventions has been democratized. State party caucuses have been opened to the participation of rank-and-file members, not just the party regulars. Many states have instituted direct primaries to choose delegates.

3. States and state party organizations vary in their rules and requirements for selecting delegates. Knowing the rules and building support at local levels are often keys to success.

4. The media can distort campaigns by publicizing polls, by creating false expectations for a "front runner," and by blowing up trivial issues and ignoring important ones.

5. National party conventions are geared to the TV audience as a means of kicking off the nominee's campaign. The delegates do little more than ratify the choice of the state caucuses and primaries, except when a race between nominees is very close.

6. In a general-election campaign, the nominees make use of extensive campaign staffs and saturate the media with ads. But the power of TV imagery may be a myth, since there is some evidence that voters are more concerned with what a candidate says than with his or her "image."

7. Candidates must direct their appeals to various ethnic groups, such as WASPs, Jews, blacks, and Italians. They must also pay attention to regional differences; today, electoral power is centered in the Sun Belt.

8. Until public financing for presidential contests went into effect in 1976, the costs of national campaigns skyrocketed each election year, mostly as a result of increasing use of media advertising, polling, air travel, and large campaign staffs. Some congressional races are still costly, but most are within reason.

9. For many years, large segments of the United States' population—including women and blacks—were unable to vote. After those groups were enfranchised, states continued to restrict voting through various electoral laws. Only recently have such laws been dropped or eased.

10. The electorate has increased, but voter turnout is in a downward trend. Among those least likely to vote are the young, the uneducated, and the poor. Because those who are well-off tend to use the ballot most, there is an upper-class bias to voting.

11. People tend to vote according to their party ties and according to various short-term forces associated with an election—such as the personalities of the candidates, the performance of the incumbent, and current issues. But the motives of the electorate are mixed, and there is no one formula to explain how a voter decides.

12. Voters in the presidential election actually elect slates of electors chosen by the state parties. These electors are the members of the electoral college, and they cast their votes to "elect" the President. Because this system can elect a candidate who has lost the popular vote, reformers have called for direct popular election to replace the electoral college.

13. Money has an unequalizing effect on the electoral process. Those who make big contributions to campaigns have easier access to politicians than do small contributors or those who don't contribute at all. A campaign finance reform act was passed in 1971 (and amended in 1974) in an attempt to dilute the strength of well-financed special interests.

14. Incumbency gives an unfair advantage to candidates running for reelection, because incumbents get more campaign contributions than challengers, and their activities are more publicized.

Additional Reading

Useful overviews are Herbert B. Asher, *Presidential Elections and American Politics: Voters, Candidates, and Campaigns since 1952* (Homewood, Ill.: Dorsey Press, 1976); Nelson W. Polsby and Aaron B. Wildavsky, *Presidential Elections: Strategies of American Electoral Politics,* 4th ed. (New York: Charles Scribner's Sons, 1976); and James David Barber, ed., *Choosing the President* (Englewood Cliffs, N.J.: Prentice-Hall, 1974).

Joe McGinniss's, *The Selling of the President, 1968* (New York: Trident Press, 1968) is an intriguing behind-the-scenes account of Nixon's TV image making. Stanley Kelley, Jr., *Professional Public Relations and Political Power* (Baltimore: Johns Hopkins University Press, 1966), tells of media campaigns by Eisenhower and others in the 1950s. Theodore H. White's *Making of the President* series (New York: Atheneum Publishers, 1961, 1965, 1969, 1973), especially the 1961 volume dealing with the Kennedy-Nixon race, offers colorful descriptions of the political maneuvering involved in nominations and elections.

The role of money in elections is discussed in the old but still important book by Alexander Heard, *The Costs of Democracy* (Chapel Hill, N.C.: University of North Carolina Press, 1967); in periodic reports by Herbert Alexander and the Citizens Research Foundation; and in *Dollar Politics: The Issue of Campaign Spending* (Washington, D.C.: Congressional Quarterly Service, 1972, 1974).

The standard work on voting behavior, which emphasizes the importance of party identification, is Angus Campbell, Philip E. Converse, Warren E. Miller, and Donald E. Stokes, *The American Voter: An Abridgement* (New York: John Wiley & Sons, 1964); it has been updated in Norman H. Nie, Sidney Verba and John R. Petrocik, *The Changing American Voter* (Cambridge, Mass.: Harvard University Press, 1976). Bernard Berelson et al., *Voting: A Study of Opinion Formation in a Presidential Campaign* (Chicago: University of Chicago Press, 1954), a pioneering study of the 1948 election, emphasizes sociological factors.

Sidney Verba and Norman H. Nie, *Participation in America: Political Democracy and Social Equality* (New York: Harper & Row, Publishers, 1972), discusses who takes part in politics and who doesn't.

Walter Dean Burnham, *Critical Elections and the Mainsprings of American Politics* (New York: W. W. Norton & Co., 1971), analyzes historical realignments and argues that party loyalties are eroding.

Some of the best work on voting has appeared in articles, including several reprinted in Angus Campbell et al., eds., *Elections and the Political Order* (New York: John Wiley & Sons, 1966). Others are Philip E. Converse, "The Nature of Belief Systems in the Mass Public," in David E. Apter, ed., *Ideology and Discontent* (New York: Free Press, 1964); and Donald E. Stokes, "Some Dynamic Elements in Contests for the Presidency," *American Political Science Review* (March 1966).

9

THE PRESIDENCY

Whether a man is burdened by power or enjoys power;
whether he is trapped by responsibility or made free by it;
whether he is moved by other people and outer forces
or moves them—that is the essence of leadership.

Henry L. Stimson

How the President should perform has been debated for two hundred years, and it will be debated as long as there is a United States of America. Should the President be the omnipotent guide, the handyman of Congress, or something middling? The Presidency is, a great historian once said, the "dark continent" of our government—explored many times but still terra incognita. No two scholars, no two politicians can agree on its correct boundaries.

The Constitution itself is typically vague on the matter. Originally the framers wanted the powers of government centered in Congress, the lawmaking body, and they specified in some detail how Congress should do its work. The President's powers were outlined in almost cryptic terms, specifying little more than his responsibility for the conduct of foreign relations, his duties as commander in chief of the armed forces, and his vague obligation to see that the laws are "faithfully executed." Of course these powers evolved into something much more expansive and complicated than could have been foreseen.

The President derives his guidance and powers from Article II of the Constitution. It is, as Edward S. Corwin has noted,

the most loosely drawn chapter of the Constitution. To those who think that a constitution ought to settle everything beforehand it should be a nightmare; by the same token, to those who think that constitution makers ought to leave considerable leeway for the future play of political forces, it should be a vision realized.[1]

At the time of its founding, ours was the only government established on the principle of separation of powers, with three distinct branches—the executive, legislative, and judicial—checking and balancing each other from their autonomous centers. That's the way it is in theory; that's what we have been brought up to believe is the arrangement. But, in practice, the operation of the government clearly shows a gross imbalance in this tripodal structure. It also clearly shows that the powers are not in fact very separate.

Article II of the Constitution states that "the executive Power shall be vested in a President." That seems simple enough. But the President's powers do not stop at the executive boundary. His veto power gives him a strong hand in the legislature. His appointive powers can be used to shape the federal judiciary and the executive agencies that have immense quasi-judicial influence over the life of the nation.[2] Under the Articles of Confederation, the responsibility of foreign relations rested solely with Congress; as practiced with the blessing of the Constitution today, foreign relations are the special domain of the President. Through his constitutional role as commander in chief of the armed services, as head of his political party, and as the only federal politician (except for the Vice President, of course) elected by the nation as a whole, the President also has available a multilevered apparatus for creating pressure and propaganda that

is not available to either the legislature or the judiciary. It is the kind of power that Assistant Secretary of State William P. Bundy had in mind when he wrote President Lyndon B. Johnson a memo on November 5, 1964, suggesting that if Johnson wanted to whip up support for heavier participation in Vietnam, then a "strong presidential noise to prepare a climate for an action statement [a quasi declaration of war] is probably indicated."[3]

In short, there is a separation of powers, but the separation is not clean and absolute, and the three branches are not equal in strength. The weight is significantly on the side of the Presidency. The Constitution has increasingly been construed to favor the Presidency, and both Congress and the Supreme Court have ceded some of their power to it, either formally or tacitly, on key occasions.

GROWTH OF THE PRESIDENCY

When George Washington assumed office as President, the United States was a country of 3 million farmers, merchants, and tradesmen.

---

[1]Edward S. Corwin, *The President: Office and Powers: 1787–1957*, 4th rev. ed. (New York: New York University Press, 1957), pp. 3–4. Occasionally a President will openly state that he is not guided by the Constitution so much as by his own feelings or intuition or conscience—whatever that means. "The Constitution is the supreme law of our land and it governs our actions as citizens," said President Gerald R. Ford, but he then added, "Only the laws of God, which govern our consciences, are superior to it." (Quoted in *Newsweek*, February 5, 1975.) But who's to say what the laws of God are? Or the laws of conscience? It is a position that anarchists adhere to, and revolutionists, and seems to give no clear idea what that particular conservative Republican President had in mind as to the constitutional limits of action. Metaphysics seems to afflict every President at some time in his career.

[2]Another "judicial" power in the presidential arsenal is the power to pardon convicts and ex-convicts and thus restore their civil rights (and, in the case of convicts, their freedom). Ordinarily this is an insignificant power in the scheme of things, and it is considered a no-win power, because the President is much more likely to be criticized than praised for exercising it. Ordinarily, pardons are given to insignificant ex-cons—bartenders, for example—who can't go back to their regular line of work without one.

But, in recent years, a more ominous aura has come to the pardon power. There was considerable concern, for example, when President Richard M. Nixon, without explanation and without publicity, commuted the sentence and released from prison Angelo ("Gyp") DeCarlo, a high-ranking member of a New Jersey Mafia family, who was known to have ordered several gangland executions. (*Washington Post*, April 2, 1973.) A year earlier, Nixon had been criticized for commuting the sentence of former Teamster boss James R. Hoffa. Some felt it was done to get support from the powerful union in the 1972 election. The power to pardon fell into further disrepute when President Ford, after indicating that he would not pardon former President Nixon, did pardon him, on September 8, 1974, of all crimes he had committed while in office.

[3]Office of Congressman Les Aspin, press release, October 31, 1973.

Their domestic concerns were on a small enough scale that Congress could deal with them without much imaginative leadership on the part of the President. As for foreign affairs, what the President did or didn't do in that realm left most of the population untouched. The President was given adequate independence and authority to carry out his constitutional duty, but that was thought to be a modest enterprise. Since then, the character of the office has changed radically. It started as a nonpolitical and moderately powerful office. Today the person who occupies that office automatically becomes a highly political figure, an active policy maker, a charismatic symbol of leadership (even though he actually may not be much of a leader), and the nominal boss of a huge bureaucracy. Every act of the President in domestic or foreign affairs is followed with intense interest by most people of voting age.

Historical Forces and Figures

In the course of nearly two centuries, strong forces and events have tested and shaped some of the Presidents of the United States. Those willing to use their powers have had them greatly increased. International wars and foreign trade wrenched the nation out of its isolation and imposed new responsibilities on the President as a world leader. Industrialization and large-scale immigration turned a simple society into one so complex that the federal government became increasingly involved in its regulation and welfare. In making laws to meet the growing needs of the nation, Congress granted more and more powers to the President, including, in 1921, the power to prepare the budget.

To be sure, most of our thirty-eight Presidents have been rather lethargic, willing to maintain the office in quiet dignity and friendly ineptitude.[4] Their ranks were filled with the likes of William Howard Taft, who took a pinched,

legalistic view of his job, claiming that he could do nothing that he was not specifically empowered to do by the Constitution.[5] In jest, but with considerable accuracy about his own administration, Taft said, "I have come to the conclusion that the major part of the work of a President is to increase the gate receipts of expositions and fairs and bring tourists into the town."[6] Preeminent among this genre was Calvin Coolidge, who did not permit the burdens of office to shorten his eleven-hour sleep each night or his afternoon nap. When asked how he stayed fit, Coolidge replied, "By avoiding the big problems."[7] Such Presidents usually served in periods of little stress, however. Their lack of energy harmonized with the times and was probably a blessing.

Other Presidents, activists, left their mark on the office. Thomas Jefferson made a political forum of the Presidency. He took strong charge of his Democratic-Republican party and used it to control Congress. The Presidents who immediately followed him, however, were inept as political leaders and forfeited some of their powers to Congress. Andrew Jackson, in 1833, lost no time in wresting control of the government again and reasserting the independence and authority of the Presidency. He made the Presidency, not Congress, the seat of popular power; indeed, he was the first President elected by the people instead of by state legislators. And he was a major influence in democratizing the office of President.

Abraham Lincoln was the first President to proclaim "emergency powers," which has become a favorite means of aggrandizing presidential power. During the Civil War, Lincoln justified the breaking of fundamental laws (including suspension of habeas corpus) on the grounds that only thus could he prevent the government from falling to pieces. According to Clinton Rossiter, "Lincoln raised the Presidency to a position of constitutional and moral ascendancy that left

---

[4]Corwin believes that "not more than one in three has contributed to the development of its [the office's] powers; under other incumbents things have either stood still or gone backward." (*The President*, p. 30).

[5]William Howard Taft, *The President and His Powers* (New York: Columbia University Press, 1967), p. 139.

[6]Quoted in *Parade*, September 7, 1975.

[7]Quoted in James David Barber, *The Presidential Character: Predicting Performance in the White House* (Englewood Cliffs, N.J.: Prentice-Hall, 1972), p. 147.

no doubt where the burden of crisis government in this country would thereafter rest."[8]

The next strong President was Theodore Roosevelt, who first took office in 1901. Roosevelt's attitude was that, under the Constitution, he was subject only to the people—not to Congress and not to the Supreme Court—and that in the name of serving the people he could do anything that the Constitution "does not explicitly forbid him" from doing.[9] Roosevelt popularized the office of the President by publicizing it and glorying in what he called its "bully pulpit."

In 1908, four years before he was elected President, Woodrow Wilson noted that

> the President can never again be the mere domestic figure he has been throughout so large a part of our history. The nation has risen to the first rank in power and resources. . . . [The President] must stand always at the front of our affairs, and the office will be as big and influential as the man who occupies it.[10]

World War I tested whether Wilson, as President, could be more than a "mere domestic figure." Working with Congress, Wilson consolidated an extraordinary hold on the United States wartime economy. After the war, he strained his resources as President in a vain attempt to persuade the United States to join with other countries in the League of Nations.

It was Franklin D. Roosevelt who created the modern Presidency.

> Only Washington, who made the office, and Jackson, who remade it, did more than he to raise it to its present condition of strength, dignity, and independence. . . . The press conference, the Executive Office, the right to reorganize the administration, and the powers to protect industrial and financial peace are all parts of Roosevelt's legacy to the modern Presidency.[11]

President Wilson returns from the Versailles peace conference, 1919

Efforts to cope with the Great Depression of the 1930s, followed by the national management of the war effort in the 1940s, resulted in a vast expansion of the executive department; some of the agencies were temporary, but most were permanent.

Most recent Presidents, with the notable exceptions of Dwight D. Eisenhower and Gerald R. Ford, seem to have felt that they were neglecting their duty unless they were at least giving the appearance of constant action, as if the people would feel cheated if their President allowed a day to pass without making some momentous decision. Actually, Eisenhower, the least active of recent Presidents, was also the most popular. But the moral of his popularity seems to have been lost on most of the Presidents who fol-

[8]Clinton Rossiter, *The American Presidency*, rev. ed. (New York: Harcourt Brace Jovanovich, 1960), p. 101.

[9]Theodore Roosevelt, *The Autobiography of Theodore Roosevelt* (New York: Charles Scribner's Sons, 1958), p. 197.

[10]Quoted in Rossiter, *The American Presidency*, p. 85.

[11]Rossiter, p. 151.

lowed. Lyndon Johnson, for example, was convinced that the deliberative President, the cautious and thoughtful President, would be a disappointment. He once said,

> What the Americans like is action, drama, and a clear conclusion. They don't like "measured" anything. They want all things to be settled, one way or the other. If I went to Hanoi to make peace, my popularity polls would immediately go up 10 percent—*and* they would do exactly the same if I bombed Peking.[12]

Modern Use of Emergency Powers

Recent Presidents have inflated their office by exploiting crises, real or pretended. Presidents declare the beginnings of emergencies by proclamation; it's as simple as that. But they very seldom declare an *end* to emergencies. In this way their power grows.

Immediately after he was inaugurated in 1933, President Roosevelt proclaimed an emergency to deal with the economic catastrophies of the times. On December 16, 1950, President Harry S Truman declared an emergency associated with "recent events in Korea and elsewhere." On March 23, 1970, President Richard M. Nixon, confronted with a postal strike, invoked emergency provisions permitting the Secretary of Defense to call up to a million ready reservists to active duty. And on August 15, 1971, Nixon declared a national emergency in regard to the decline in the United States balance of payments—surely one of the weirdest "emergencies" ever imagined.

The four Roosevelt-Truman-Nixon "emergencies" were still in effect in 1972. Congress, in its glacial way, had finally begun to sense that the presidential use of emergency powers should perhaps be checked and modified. So it established the Senate Committee on National Emergencies and Delegated Emergency Powers to root around in the statute books and see just what singular powers were available to the President. With the aid of a computer, the committee identified and compiled 470 special statutes that could be invoked by the President during a declared national emergency. "Taken together," announced Senator Frank Church, cochairman of the committee, "these hundreds of statutes clothe the President with virtually unlimited power with which he can affect the lives of American citizens in a host of all-encompassing ways. This vast range of powers constitutes enough authority to permit one-man rule. . . ."[13]

In September 1976, Congress passed, and President Ford signed (in private, without the usual fanfare that goes with bill signing), the National Emergencies Act. It declared that in two years—1978—the Roosevelt-Truman-Nixon emergencies would end. The act also required that presidentially declared emergencies be subject to congressional review at least every six months and that they would automatically terminate after one year unless the President expressly called for an extension. It is doubtful that the act will greatly discourage future Presidents from finding an emergency whenever they want to find one, thereby obtaining extraordinary powers.

Where does a President get the idea he can declare an emergency? The Constitution says little or nothing about emergencies, and what it does say clearly suggests that dealing with emergencies should be left to Congress. Article II, Section 3 provides that the President can "on extraordinary Occasions convene both Houses," presumably to ask the legislators to give him guidance and authority to take action.

But the modern declarations of emergency have been made with the plain intent of acting autonomously. Unchallenged by Congress, these emergency proclamations have automatically triggered a hodgepodge of "emergency" clauses in about five hundred existing statutes—statutes cluttered with permissive language like "national economic or other emergency," "hostilities imminent or threat of hostilities," "state of public peril or disaster," "internal security emergency," "public exigency," and so forth. During the emergencies, the Presidents have done

---

[12]Quoted in Emmett John Hughes, *The Living Presidency* (New York: Coward, McCann & Geoghegan, 1973), p. 290.

[13]Quoted in an American Bar Association press release, February 17, 1977.

Chicago Tribune cartoon by Carey Orr
Photo from the Chicago Historical Society

pretty much as they pleased, excusing their actions with one law or another. One critical observer noted,

> There was always an economic emergency, a state of war, or a Korean emergency to fall back upon. And if these were not suitable to invoke the necessary powers, one could always whip up public opinion by referring to outside threats and get Congress to do one's bidding. For those really far-out matters, which the public might not stomach under any conditions, such as bombing of neutral Cambodia, or fixing elections abroad, there was respectively, either injunctions of secrecy or the Directorate of Plans in CIA. Thus an illusion of

compliance with law could be maintained either through subterfuge or by reshaping the law to provide enormous powers. The primacy of rule through law was maintained but not tested. . . .[14]

An adroit Chief Executive can use a crisis to arouse public opinion in such a way as to strengthen his hand. This was neatly demonstrated by President Truman in 1948 in resurrecting the Selective Service Act, which enabled

[14]Federation of Atomic Scientists, *Public Interest Report* 26, no. 10 (December 1973).

the government to draft citizens into military service. The draft was used as an emergency measure in the Civil War, in World War I, and in World War II. After each conflict, it was allowed to die a natural death. But Truman and the military hierarchy wanted to resurrect and perpetuate the draft, so on March 17, 1948, the President went to Congress with an emergency message. He asked for reinstatement of selective service because, he said, the Soviet army was on the move. This phony war scare, based on false information supplied by the Pentagon, mysteriously disappeared as soon as Congress had done Truman's bidding and brought into existence the nation's first peacetime draft—a draft that would survive for a generation.[15]

As for negative evidence of the power of crisis, one need only look at the later defeats of Franklin Roosevelt. After 1938, when it became plain that somehow the American people would survive the Depression, Roosevelt had no more domestic crises to use as a lever on Congress. The conservatives in the federal legislature were able to regroup so successfully that, as Aaron B. Wildavsky has pointed out, Roosevelt did not get another piece of significant domestic legislation through Congress.[16]

The Aura of the Office Today

With the increase in power have come the symbols and trappings of power. Presidents are isolated from everyday heartaches, swaddled in flattery, pampered, and spoiled. President Wilson's most intimate adviser once wrote to him, "I do not put it too strongly when I say you are the one hope left in this torn and distracted world. Without your leadership, God alone knows how long we will wander in the darkness."[17] Every President will be told repeatedly that he is absolutely essential. Although a President may be fortunate enough to have a few friends who

stubbornly go on calling him Lyndon or Dick or Jerry or Jimmy, most old friends who once called him by his first name are suddenly embarrassed to address him by anything but his title, and in awe-stricken tones. Pierre Salinger, Kennedy's press aide, said, "I never heard anyone address John Kennedy as anything other than Mr. President or Sir."[18]

The semblance of regality, the ermine atmosphere, is also created in material ways. George Washington was paid $25,000 a year ($2,000 a year less than Richard Nixon's secretary received as a retirement pension); neither he nor any President before 1906 received any expense money; they even had to buy their own food. On Thomas Jefferson's inauguration day, he stayed in a boarding house, returned to those modest quarters on foot after the ceremony only to find that the landlord had not saved him anything for supper, and went to bed hungry. When President Franklin Pierce arrived at the White House to take up residence in 1853, he found it in such a mess that he slept the first night on the floor. President Abraham Lincoln shined his own shoes. And George Washington made a three-month trip through the Deep South, accompanied only by a man to handle the horses and a valet; he was not accompanied by guards, advisers, aides, secretaries, publicity people, or speech writers. He stayed at common inns.[19]

Times have changed. The President now receives a salary of $200,000, plus a $50,000 personal expense allowance. Taxpayers give him $1,372,000 for household maintenance expenses and $9,767,000 for staff salaries and then throw in an extra $1.5 million slush fund in case he runs short.[20] Actually, the President freeloads an awful lot; the State Department and the Defense Department pick up many of his banquet and travel expenses.

George Washington's White House staff was usually limited to two men. Sometimes when his secretary was on vacation Washington penned his own letters. Jefferson's White House staff, in

---

[15]Information on the contrivance of the scare can be found in John M. Swomley, Jr., *The Military Establishment* (Boston: Beacon Press, 1964).

[16]Aaron B. Wildavsky, "The Two Presidencies," *Trans-Action* 4, no. 2 (December 1966): 230–43.

[17]Quoted in Barber, *The Presidential Character,* p. 62.

[18]Quoted in the *Washington Post,* May 31, 1974.

[19]Sources: *Washington Post,* November 27, 1970; *Parade,* December 15, 1974; *Time,* August 4, 1973.

[20]*Fortune,* October 1973.

1801, consisted of one messenger and a part-time secretary; Ulysses S. Grant, though the government had expanded greatly in the intervening seventy-five years, still had an executive staff of only six. Woodrow Wilson, serving in the White House during the first global war, got by with a staff of seven. FDR, before World War II, ran the Executive Office with thirty-seven employees.

In 1976, the White House staff exceeded six hundred, including half a dozen speech writers

Just Plain Jerry

Ford's first three appointments as President were a full-time personal photographer, a new press secretary, and a chief speech writer. He knew the central role and top priority of ballyhoo just as his predecessors had—and as his successor does. But Ford was confronted with a unique problem. His main selling point to the American people was not that he was smart or had ever shown leadership, but that he looked and acted like a "regular fellow." His ballyhoo was directed at preserving that image. Vic Gold, once a press aide for Vice President Spiro T. Agnew, recalled in a book written during President Gerald Ford's administration:

> The new President's flacks are fond of pointing out that their boss, unlike his PR-conscious predecessor, doesn't even wear makeup at televised news conferences. Encouraged by a favorable press, they promote this image of Just Plain Jerry, the uncosmetized President; despite the fact that Ford, far from eliminating or even curtailing the massive public relations superstructure created by Nixon, is rapidly expanding it. Measured in terms of paid flacks per carpeted square inch, this will be the most image-conscious White House in history. . . .
>
> So we have Just Plain Jerry. If he did not exist, he would have to have been invented. It is an image that the media, as much as the new President's retained imagectomists, seem eager to sell to the public. Just what central casting ordered for a post-Nixon White House scenaria: A Middle American ex-football player, with a Brueghel-peasant look and manner. . . . What the American people need, *want*, is the image of a President with an unassuming, *uncontrived* life- and work-style. This is the image the media seek to project in their coverage of the White House. And they will do it, if necessary, by contrivance.*

*Vic Gold, *PR as in President* (New York: Doubleday & Co., 1977), pp. 35–36.

and forty-one press aides. There were also some image makers, hired because it is apparently believed that in this age of television people would rebel at being led by a President who did not know how to wear pancake makeup, read cue cards, and make one-line jokes.[21] The household functions are handled by seventy-five butlers, twenty-one gardeners, and a vast assortment of maids, cooks, caretakers, maintenance workers, and other flunkies, who watch over the 132 rooms of the White House and the business conducted therein. Of Nixon's courtiers, there was one whose job was to walk beside the President and tell him in advance whether to turn right or left at a corner or how many steps were in a stairway, so that he would not stumble.

When the President travels, he can call on five Boeing 707s, sixteen helicopters, and eleven Lockheed Jetstars. His basic vehicle, Air Force I, cost $7.4 million, and an additional $1.7 million was spent to make the cabin more comfy.[22] At the White House, he is protected by a wall of one hundred Secret Service agents and three hundred uniformed White House police; on the road, dozens of Secret Service agents go with him, as do innumerable aides.[23]

No longer do Presidents have to buy their own groceries, of course, and the menus they sometimes select at taxpayers' expense are quite impressive. At one of President Ford's dinners, the menu was fresh lobster flown in that day from Maine, bibb lettuce sprinkled with chrysanthemum leaves, prime ribs of beef, braised Belgian endive, hearts of celery, artichoke bottoms, zucchini stuffed with imported mushrooms, Chinese peapods, Belgian carrots, tomatoes provencale, and rosette potatoes. For dessert,

[21]Every President of modern times has hired a specialist to advise him on how to wear makeup and/or dye his hair and how to project the right appearance on television. Some have also hired gag writers. Ford, for example, paid $40,000 a year to the same joke-smith once employed by Jack Paar and Red Skelton, plus $40,000 to a personal TV director. (Richard Reeves, *A Ford, Not a Lincoln*, New York: Harcourt Brace Jovanovich, 1975.)

[22]*New York Times*, September 23, 1973.

[23]*Fortune*, October 1973.

It Pays to Be an Ex-President

When Gerald R. Ford moved into the White House on Aug. 9, 1974, he was practically broke. He had even had to borrow $10,000 the previous year to meet family expenses. Today, however, he is well on his way to being a millionaire.

Did he make his money while in office? No. Rather, he is going to get rich because he *was* in office.

The American taxpayer is already paying him $96,500 a year in pensions [counting his pension for time served in Congress, too] and footing an estimated $600,000-a-year bill for permanent private office and staff, jet transportation when he wants it, a chauffeured limousine, Secret Service protection, postage stamps (including those for Christmas cards) and other benefits. But all of this is not enough for Jerry Ford. Commercially speaking, there is no hotter property just now than the former President of the United States. Skillfully packaged and merchandised, Ford—and his family—stand to make as much as $3 million within the next few years alone.

The greening of Jerry Ford and the former First Family is not unique. All recent ex-Presidents have experienced it to some degree and our other living ex-President, Richard Nixon, is still at it. . . .

Still, a question nags: To what extent should a past President enhance his personal wealth by trading on the fact that he was the nation's Chief Executive? The argument that all Ford's predecessors seem to have done it in one fashion or another does not necessarily make it right or good for the country. . . .

Of his many ventures, Ford insisted that "as long as they are constructive, I will do them. The money side is for my agent to work out, and if the money comes, fine." Then he fell back to the Maginot Line of defense used by all past Presidents and government bigwigs whenever the question is raised about converting experiences in public office into private gain. "That is what the free enterprise system is all about," Ford declared.

Well, yes and no. One expects the Nixons, the Deans, the Colsons and others to look upon their years as public servants as a lode ready for mining. We may even cluck our tongues while rushing to the book stores to buy the latest works of those who turn government memoranda into private memoirs for handsome profits.

On the other hand, many of us expected honest, decent Jerry Ford to set a higher standard for ex-Presidents than has been the case in the past. All this huckstering and hustling and merchandising of the presidency—with Ford's eager assent—robs the office of something fine and decent. . . .

Until 1958, there was no presidential pension. Unless he was already wealthy, a former President had to scrounge around as best he could. For the first five years of his retirement, Harry Truman had little choice but to market his memoirs in order to make ends meet. Even so, he stoutly refused high-paying job offers from private industry and other opportunities to trade on his position as a former President. Why did he resist?

"They were not interested in hiring Harry Truman, the person," he told daughter Margaret. "It was the former President of the United States they wanted. I could never lend myself to any transaction, however respectable, that would commercialize on the prestige and dignity of the office of the presidency."

Harry Truman was one of Ford's heroes when he moved into the White House in 1974. It's a pity that Truman didn't remain a model when Ford left office this past January. That "nice guy" image of Jerry Ford is getting harder and harder to see behind the pile of money on his Palm Springs doorstep.

From Jerald F. terHorst, *Free Enterprise*, July/August 1977.

---

there was an ice bombe with chocolate topping, plus fresh strawberries flown from California and petits fours. There were two wines and a champagne.[24]

---

[24]*Washington Post*, February 16, 1975.

The President can always retreat to more relaxed surroundings at Camp David, the 180-acre playpen near Washington that taxpayers have supplied him with. There he can romp and play at a heated free-form swimming pool, a bowling alley, archery and skeet ranges, pool table, tennis courts, pitch-and-putt golf green, movie theater, or on the miles of nature trails. It costs $640,000 to operate Camp David each year.[25] Almost every President had a nice home before he reached the White House, and if he prefers to retreat to his old house occasionally, it too will be spruced up and made more comfortable at the taxpayers' expense. President Nixon spent an estimated $17 million of public money to improve and maintain his private homes in Florida and California.[26]

It used to be that when a President's term ended he was poorer than before and had to find employment—sometimes not very nice work— to stay alive. Thomas Jefferson left office $20,000 in debt and considered declaring bankruptcy; Andrew Jackson stayed solvent only through the contributions of friends; Woodrow Wilson lived on his wife's income in retirement; and Calvin Coolidge wrote a newspaper column for income.

No longer do retired Presidents face poverty or even lean years. The presidential pension is $63,000 a year, with automatic cost-of-living increases. A retired President also gets a cool million dollars, a "transitional" fund, to ease his way back into the nonpresidential world; it helps him to surface slowly so that he will not get psychological bends. He also receives $96,000 a year for life to run and staff an office. Even Nixon, who resigned in total disgrace and one jump ahead of the sheriff, was given a $75,000 federal pension (the extra money came from his congressional pension). The taxpayers, moreover, paid the $300,000 cost of his legal defense.[27] (This was rather ironic, since, in 1971, Nixon had vetoed legislation creating the Federal Legal Services Corporation, which was to aid people too poor to afford a lawyer in civil cases.)

Presidents often get so used to the perquisites supplied by the people of the United States that they begin to think they actually *own* not only the trappings of the Presidency, but everything else in the public domain. Lyndon Johnson, after delivering a speech at a military base, started walking toward what he thought was the plane he had come in; he was stopped by a young airman who said, "Mr. President, *your* plane is over *there.*" Johnson responded, "Son, all of them—the ones over here and the ones over there—are *my* planes."[28] Nixon went him one better by actually giving away a $2 million helicopter to Egyptian President Anwar el-Sadat as a thank-you gift, like a five-dollar potted plant, without any authorization for the gift from Congress.

Although the expansion of the Presidency was accompanied by a great many complaints from citizens who believed that the executive branch was overflowing the mold built by the Founders, no great alarm was voiced until the early 1970s. After ten years of the Vietnam war (an undeclared war that was manufactured by three Presidents, not by Congress) and then the Watergate scandals in which an extraordinary list of illegal actions was charged to the Nixon administration, it was generally felt that the constitutional checks on presidential power were not working so well. In fact, many students of the Presidency believed that the office had become an uncontrollable monster.

So far as is known, no United States President has ever harbored delusions of monarchy;[29] none has given concrete evidence of wanting to be even a part-time dictator. And yet, things *have* changed radically in the last forty years or so to make the President more remote from the people, more isolated and guarded from the infor-

[25]*Washington Post,* October 16, 1973.

[26]*New York Times,* September 3, 1974.

[27]Clayton Fritchey, syndicated column, April 15, 1974.

[28]Joseph A. Califano, Jr., *A Presidential Nation* (New York: W. W. Norton & Co., 1975), p. 227.

[29]Richard N. Goodwin, a speech writer for Presidents Kennedy and Johnson, would disagree mildly on this point. He has written, "Every modern President, with the possible exception of Eisenhower, has had occasional fantasies of benevolent tyranny and sincerely believed that the welfare of the country would be improved if he could run things as he wished without the interference of Congress, courts, press and public opinion. Most of them have expressed such sentiments to intimates. They were restrained from exercising such power, not by abstract convictions about the nature of democracy, but by institutions, laws, traditions, and centers of private power within the society." (*Washington Post,* March 17, 1974.) However, this is no more heinous a charge than to say that most of us have at one time or another dreamed of robbing a bank of a billion dollars and fleeing to the supposed happiness of a South Sea island and were only dissuaded by thoughts of armed police in pursuit. For whatever reason, almost all of us, like almost all Presidents, obey the law.

mal restraints of public opinion and the formal restraints of the judiciary and Congress, and more absolute in his administration of the Executive Office. The reality of presidential power, together with its monarchial symbols, began to be spoken of as the Imperial Presidency, and to be feared as such. Where would it end? How aloof would the "sovereign"—as Nixon called the occupant of the White House[30]—become from his presumed subjects? Would future Presidents feel that they could commit crimes with impunity—would they act on the belief, as

30*Washington Star,* March 16, 1976.

President Carter and his wife Rosalynn walk home from the inauguration

Nixon put it, that "when a President does it, that means that it is not illegal"?[31] These were dark concerns that ran through the nation's political psyche in 1976 and contributed to the election of James Earl Carter, Jr., the peanut farmer from Georgia. One of Carter's most appealing traits was that he seemed determined to maintain his ties with the grass roots and to resist the temptation to become kingly.

No sooner was he sworn into office at the Capitol inaugural ceremony than he began deflating the imperial style. Instead of riding back to the White House in an armor-plated limousine, Carter and his wife climbed out of the car and walked the length of Pennsylvania Avenue, hand in hand. Within a few days he began trimming the White House perquisites: he ordered that the two presidential yachts be sold; he reduced the motor pool by 40 percent and ended the practice of giving staff big shots chauffeur service from their homes to work; he ordered White House aides to use military aircraft as rarely as possible and instead to fly commercially, tourist class; he ordered three hundred TV sets and about two hundred AM-FM radios removed from the White House.

Before Carter's administration, a presidential entrance at a major social event was always accompanied by the marine band playing "Ruffles and Flourishes" and "Hail to the Chief," not to mention several salvos from a column of trumpeteers. Carter ended most of that. In his first TV address to the nation as President, he wore a cardigan sweater. At his first cabinet meeting—a hastily convened emergency session and therefore understandably less formal—he wore no tie. He warned the press that, whether they liked it or not, he would try to lead the life of a normal man: "I'm not going to relinquish my right to go to the zoo with my daughter, to the opera with my wife or to pick up arrowheads on my farm without prior notice to the press."[32] He taught Sunday school at a Baptist church in Washington, just as he had in Plains, Georgia. Shortly after taking office, he opened his personal telephone line to the public and, over a two-hour

period, took forty-two calls from citizens in twenty-five states. The implied message: The President was an available neighbor.

For taking these steps to reduce pomp, some critics charged that Carter was merely symbol-minded, earning popular support by cheap and insignificant actions. They were nearly right on one count, but totally wrong on the other. A confidential memo surfaced in May 1977 showing that Carter was most certainly symbol-minded; his advisers had put together a calculated strategy to persuade the public that he had a bold, new approach. As one of his key advisers, Patrick Caddell, reminded his boss: "Too many good people have been defeated because they tried to substitute substance for style. They forgot to give the public the kind of visible signals that it needs to understand what is happening."[33] But for critics to call Carter's symbolic actions cheap and insignificant was a woeful misjudgment. Every action a President takes is weighted with significance. Actions that *in themselves* are of no great importance assume considerable importance at a time when the public is looking for signs by which to interpret the President's administration; for this reason, even the seemingly trivial actions of new Presidents are subjected to especially intense magnification and scrutiny by the public. Knowing that he was being watched for signs of his intent, Carter realized it was quite necessary to reduce the regal trappings of office and to assume an attitude of openness and quasi modesty if he was to be credited with sincerity in his early admonitions to government employees: "Remember that we're nobody's boss, we're servants."[34] Whether or not Carter is able to restore some of the Jacksonian spirit and character to the Presidency, the fact is that the fundamental awesome power of the office remains with him.

Morally obscene and politically obnoxious as presidential luxury may be, especially considering that it is supported by taxes, those are not

[31]TV interview with David Frost, May 19, 1977.

[32]Quoted in the *Washington Post*, February 18, 1977.

[33]"The Scenario: Most of Carter's Early Moves Charted in 1976 Caddell Memo," *Washington Post*, May 4, 1977.

[34]Quoted in the *New York Times*, February 13, 1977.

its most troubling aspects. The main worry is that such luxury and power will give the President a dangerously big head. It happened to Johnson and to Nixon, with appalling results for the nation; but it didn't happen to Ford (whose head, to all outward appearances, swelled only moderately), and so far it doesn't seem to be happening to Jimmy Carter. Indeed, if one were to put together a conglomerate "norm" of the thirty-nine men who have filled the office of the Presidency, the profile that would emerge would show that Johnson and Nixon exploited their powers so far beyond the average that they became virtual caricatures. They stand in history not as accurate samples of the presidential norm but as warnings of the mutations that can occur. One can reasonably conclude that delusions of personal grandeur are not *automatically* the result of moving into the White House but are, instead, the offshoot of a basic character condition.

THE PRESIDENT
AS COMMANDER IN CHIEF

The President's predominant role in military crises is written into the Constitution. In 1832, South Carolina's legislature, already itching to secede from the Union, took umbrage at a federal tariff act and refused to obey it. The legislature furthermore summoned volunteers to repel whatever federal troops might show up to enforce the act. The governor of Virginia, aroused to sympathy, announced that any federal troops marching from Washington to South Carolina would proceed only over his dead body. President Andrew Jackson is said to have replied,

> If it becomes necessary for the United States troops to go to South Carolina, I, as Commander-in-Chief of the army, will be at their head. I will march them by the shortest route. They may pass through Virginia. But if the Governor makes it necessary to pass over his dead body, it will be found that I have previously taken off both ears.[35]

Nowhere in the Constitution does it say that Presidents have the right to remove governors' ears. In fact, it does not even say that Presidents have the right to use troops against a state. But, as President Jackson pointed out, the Constitution "forms a government, not a league"[36]—and a government governs by governing (which sometimes means by force), not merely by soliciting cooperation and approval. Therefore, if necessary: off with the ears.

The story may only be a legend, but, if so, it is a useful one, for it colorfully illustrates one of the mysterious fountains of the Chief Executive's perpetual strength. It is the fountain of *ad hoc* necessity (or presumed necessity). This is particularly true in his role as international spokesman for the nation, as commander in chief of the armed forces, and as those two duties overlap in foreign affairs. This power has been heightened in recent decades because the immediacy of foreign threats sometimes makes quick action the only safe response—or at least the only effective response.

The Constitution gives the war-making power to Congress. But the Constitution was written in an age when the waging of war was done by one government against another government, not by one nation against another. When the United States went to war against England in 1812, it did so with a very limited army of mercenaries and recruits, and there was no national commitment—no coordination of all industrial forces, no national draft encompassing all able-bodied men. Furthermore, the steps leading the United States into war in those days were at a different pace and in a different style. The President went before Congress and presented reasons why he considered the government of the opposing nation to be made up of rascals and why he thought they should be punished by being deprived of some of their property. And then Congress, after due deliberation, decided that his argument made good sense and gave approval for the government to raise an army and go forth to fight. That done, the rest of the nation—if it had paid much attention to the proceedings at all—would slump back

[35]Quoted in Leon A. Harris, *The Fine Art of Political Wit* (New York: E. P. Dutton & Co., 1964), pp. 63–64.

[36]Quoted in Hughes, *The Living Presidency*, p. 211.

into its normal routine of life, while the government's knights (who were *not* looked upon as "our boys," but as mercenary soldiers) took care of the belligerencies. The rest of the nation might be interested in the news floating back from the front, but it did not feel much involved.

That all changed in 1861 with the Civil War. This was the country's first total war, and the way Lincoln exercised his power as commander in chief made him our first wartime presidential "dictator." Another dramatic change in the scale of commitment came with World War I, which prompted a national draft. The press volunteered (though not always openly) to propagandize for the war and to censure criticism of it. Industrialists gladly turned over their plants to the war effort (and to war profits), and many volunteered as dollar-a-year men, to serve in Washington as advisers for industrial mobilization and perhaps also as lobbyists when the defense contracts were handed out. Women volunteered as Red Cross nurses. Some college professors volunteered to spy on their colleagues and ferret out the "disloyal."

The national spirit of involvement in World War I was increased during World War II. Before 1941, Lucky Strike cigarettes were marketed in a green package. But for some reason the armed forces needed that green dye, so the cigarette packages had to do without. The manufacturers of Lucky Strike thereafter proudly advertised, "Lucky Strike green has gone to war." That's the way people felt about everything, and not always just because it was a good sales pitch. Gasoline was rationed; meat was rationed; pants lost their cuffs, and the material went into uniforms. Everything went to war, and no one, anywhere in the country, was untouched by it. War was no longer simply an act of the government performed by its specially recruited army and navy; war became a national blow delivered by the muscle and sinew of the whole population and its economy.

It might be argued that this shift in the scope of war should have tied the war-making power even more tightly to Congress. With war affecting more people more profoundly, shouldn't the decision to go to war be made in the most republican fashion, just as the Constitution—and logic—has always dictated? Ironically with modern war came influences that would frustrate both the Constitution and logic. When intercontinental bombers can strike within a matter of hours, when intercontinental ballistic missiles can strike within a matter of minutes, can the nation afford the luxury of congressional debate over what to do? The answer to that lies in a little black bag carried by an army officer who accompanies the President wherever he goes. In that black bag is the code by which the President can order a nuclear counterattack. He does not need to get permission from Congress. He can act on his own, and he can act instantly. The concept of modern war is based on reflex, not on reflection, and the President's reflexes are the most crucial. President Nixon once remarked to two members of Congress visiting him in the White House, "I can go in my office and pick up the phone and 70 million Russians can be killed in 20 minutes."[37]

As long as the United States was successful in war, Congress was comfortable leaving the decisions largely, or totally, in the hands of the commander in chief. In only five of its eleven wars had the belligerencies been formally declared by Congress—the War of 1812, the Mexican War, the Spanish-American War, World War I, and World War II. Congress had not declared war before the government embarked on the other six conflicts (the naval war with France, 1798–1800; the first Barbary War, 1801–05; the second Barbary War, 1815; the Mexican-American belligerencies, stretching between 1914 and 1917; the Korean War, 1950–53; and the Vietnam war, 1961–75). More significantly, the Presidents had not even *asked* for a declaration of war. They simply went ahead and started war on their own hook.

A modern contrivance for getting around the constitutional provision for congressional approval of war has been the congressional resolution—a kind of blank check that the President can fill in at whim. This gimmick was introduced by President Eisenhower in 1955, when he and his advisers wrote, and Congress approved, a resolution authorizing him "to employ the Armed Forces of the United States as he deems

---

[37]Quoted in the *Los Angeles Times*, February 10, 1976.

necessary for the specific purpose of securing and protecting Formosa and the Pescadores against armed attack." This was in response to Communist China's belligerent mutterings.[38] Eisenhower again pulled the resolution trick, with Congress's approval, in the 1956 Middle East crisis.

President Johnson, apparently in imitation of Eisenhower, in 1964 wrote and got congressional approval of the infamous Tonkin Gulf Resolution[39] authorizing him to take "all necessary measures" to "repel any armed attack" against United States forces and "to prevent further aggression" in Vietnam. The interpretation of this vague wording was left up to the President. Thus, as the result of what originally seemed to be an insignificant and questionably authentic naval engagement off the coast of Vietnam, Johnson (and, four years later, Nixon) was allowed to expand the United States' "peacekeeping" efforts in Vietnam until we had more than half a million troops in that country, suffered 55,000 deaths, spent $150 billion on the longest war in our history, finally pulled out in defeat, and had endured a domestic trauma more divisive than any since the Civil War.

All of that arose not from a congressionally declared war, as provided for by the Constitution, but from one carte blanche resolution. If the United States had, despite the cost in lives and money, won the war, Congress probably would have decided that the making of presidential wars—with or without an accompanying congressional resolution of approval—was still right and proper, even if it did take liberties with the Constitution. But when it became apparent that the presidential war in Vietnam was going to be a total disaster, Congress decided—a bit late—that the Tonkin Gulf Resolution had been ill-conceived and that the President's war-making powers had been abused.

In 1973, Congress passed the War Powers Act. It provided that the President could undertake emergency military action without a declaration of war, but that within forty-eight hours after committing the armed forces to combat abroad he must give Congress a report in writing on what he was up to. Unless Congress approved the action, he must end the combat within sixty days. The deadline could be extended for another month if the extension were needed to guarantee the safe withdrawal of the troops. This law did more to bolster the ego of Congress than to lessen the power of the President. History has shown repeatedly that once "our boys" are engaged in a war, whether formally declared or not, Congress rushes forward in a yahoo fashion, without hesitation, to support them with funds, arms, and propaganda. There is very little cool balancing of alternatives at such moments.[40]

Louis W. Koenig is justifiably doubtful about the War Power Act's ability to do what Congress hoped it would do:

> Precisely how Congress, as a practical matter, could reverse Presidential commitment of the armed forces strains one's imagination. Worst of all, despite the appearance of limiting the President, the law may actually enlarge the Executive's war-making capacity to extremes that even the most bellicose Presidents would never dream of. For the War Powers Act can be read as a blank-check empowerment of the Chief Executive to fight anywhere, for whatever cause, subject only to a sixty- to ninety-day time limit, indefinitely renewable.[41]

---

[38]Louis W. Koenig, *The Chief Executive*, 3rd ed. (New York: Harcourt Brace Jovanovich, 1975), pp. 217–18.

[39]On August 4, 1964, the United States destroyer *Maddox* was allegedly fired on by North Vietnamese PT boats in the Gulf of Tonkin. The next night, the *Maddox* and the destroyer *Turner Joy* were again allegedly fired on, although some experts doubt it. Evidence indicates the strong possibility that the destroyers provoked the attack, if, in fact, the second attack ever occurred. In any event, the only reported damage to the *Maddox* was a broken searchlight. But President Johnson used the incident as an excuse to pull the resolution out of his pocket and send it to Capitol Hill. (See Joseph Goulden, *Truth is the First Casualty*, Skokie, Ill.: Rand McNally & Co., 1969.)

[40]Wildavsky, "The Two Presidencies."

[41]Koenig, *The Chief Executive*, p. 220. Perhaps the best suggestion for cooling a President's war powers came from Eugene McCarthy: "It might be a good idea to plough under the rose garden [on the White House grounds] and replace it with a patch of humble squash and cabbages. Presidents seem to find it easy to declare war, or near-war, while standing in the rose garden. A President in a cabbage patch might have a better perspective on his role in history. . . ." (In a speech before the National Press Club, Washington, D.C., June 3, 1976.)

The War Powers

In 1848, Congressman Abraham Lincoln addressed himself to the question of presidential war powers:

> Allow the President to invade a neighboring nation, whenever he shall deem it necessary to repel an invasion, and you will allow him to do so whenever he may choose to say he deems it necessary for such purpose—and you allow him to make war at his pleasure. Study to see if you can fix any limit to his power in this respect. . . . If today he should choose to say he thinks it necessary to invade Canada to prevent the British from invading us, how could you stop him? You may say to him, I see no probability of the British invading us but he will say to you be silent: I see it if you don't.*

*Quoted in W. Stuart Darling and D. Craig Mense,
"The War Powers Flop," *Washington Post,* March 6, 1977.

Chairman Mao Tse-tung
of the People's Republic of China
shakes hands with President Nixon

THE PRESIDENT
AS CHIEF DIPLOMAT

The President's role in foreign affairs (more fully developed in Chapter 14) was neatly summed up by President Truman: "I make American foreign policy."[42] Since the power to make foreign policy is largely determined by the power to wage war and since Congress and the cautions that accompany atomic science have, for all practical purposes, transferred the war-making power to the President, it is only a natural consequence that the making of foreign policy is largely the President's, too. Other factors also contribute to this authority in foreign policy. The President alone has immediate access to all the conduits of intelligence—the Central Intelligence Agency, the National Security Agency, the Federal Bureau of Investigation, and the armed forces intelligence units. The President is in a position to take quick action when needed; unlike Congress, he is in "continuous session." And he has authority over the embassies and consulates abroad.

Reality, in addition to ego, prompts the President to see himself as the key to peace and war. One of the White House tapes uncovered during the Watergate scandal carries this exchange between Nixon and his aide, John D. Ehrlichman:

> NIXON: . . . what the hell, it is a little melodramatic, but it is totally true that what happens in this office in these next four years will probably determine whether there is a chance—and it's never been done—that you could have some sort of uneasy peace for the next 25 years.
>
> EHRLICHMAN: Uh huh.
>
> NIXON: And that's my—whatever legacy we have, hell, it isn't going to be in getting a cesspool for Winnetka, it is going to be there [in foreign policy].
>
> EHRLICHMAN: Yep, yep.[43]

Yep, yep, indeed. The President knew what he was talking about. And because peace/war rests largely on his shoulders, a President may sometimes act as if he were under the illusion that he should not, and could not, share the

---

[42]Quoted in Rossiter, *The American Presidency*, p. 27.

[43]Quoted in the *Wall Street Journal*, April 6, 1974.

burden a bit. He keeps to himself. He negotiates as secretly as possible. He does not consult as many people in Congress or in the State Department or in other friendly governments as common sense might dictate. When Nixon culminated negotiations to reopen relations with the People's Republic of China after twenty-two years, he did so without informing any of our allies what he was about to do. They were caught completely unprepared for this momentous development. Nixon did not even take into his confidence the chief Far Eastern diplomats, such as ambassador to Japan Armin H. Meyer, who first heard of the diplomatic turnabout on the radio.[44] Nixon did not even inform his own Vice President what was happening. Asked if he had done so, Nixon replied in an incredulous tone: "Agnew? Oh, of course not."[45] For twelve months in 1974 and 1975, Nixon's diplomatic czar, Henry A. Kissinger, held secret talks with Cuban officials—secret even from the State Department official charged with monitoring and coordinating U.S. policy toward Cuba.[46]

A centerpiece of Jimmy Carter's campaign was the promise to bring to an end the Nixon-Kissinger era of diplomatic secrecy. In his first foreign-policy statement as a candidate, he said, "We must never again keep secret the evolution of our foreign policy from Congress and the American people. They should never again be misled about our options, our commitments, our progress or our failures."[47] But when he became President, Carter discovered that open diplomacy is much more pleasant as an ideal than as a practice. (President Wilson, who called for open negotiations between nations in 1917, had made the same discovery.) Open diplomacy can make foreign officials lose their candor, can result in open confrontations (and thereby create a much uneasier world), and can frustrate the gentle coaxing that sensitive negotiations require.

Presidents who desire secrecy in foreign affairs can utilize their power to make executive agreements after secretly negotiating with foreign countries. While the Constitution requires that a treaty be approved by a two-thirds vote of the Senate, executive agreements need only be submitted to the Senate as notification of what has occurred. Executive agreements are just as binding as treaties; they are *faits accomplis* of the sort that make presidential hearts sing. And they have become increasingly popular as a way to bypass consultation with Congress. During the first fifty years of the nation's existence under the Constitution, Presidents entered into at least twenty-seven international agreements without obtaining the consent of the Senate under the treaty procedure. During the last thirty years, Presidents have made more than five thousand executive agreements covering everything from trade to military bases. Some four thousand are now in force.[48]

In 1972, Senator Clifford P. Case of New Jersey tried to bring the Senate back into the picture by offering a bill that would require the President to tell Congress within sixty days of any new executive agreement he makes with a foreign country. Case's proposals went on to suggest that an agreement deemed by a President to be too sensitive to publish would be transmitted to the two foreign relations committees under an injunction of secrecy, which only the President could lift. The trouble with that proposal was plain enough: it made Congress a helpless party to presidential secrecy. A President could sidestep a quarrel simply by telling Congress confidentially about the new agreement he wanted to conceal.

Out of the executive drive for secrecy in foreign affairs has arisen the theory that the President has the right to withhold from Congress information about anything even remotely related to national security. Ever since George Washington refused, in 1786, to give Congress his records relating to the negotiation of the Jay Treaty,[49] Presidents have occasionally balked at

[44]See Armin H. Meyer, *Assignment Tokyo: An Ambassador's Journal* (Indianapolis: Bobbs-Merrill Co., 1975).

[45]Quoted in the *Wall Street Journal*, May 31, 1974.

[46]Don Oberdorfer, "Moscow Mission Illustrates Dangers of Public Diplomacy," *Washington Post*, April 1, 1977.

[47]Statement issued while in Tokyo for a Trilateral Commission meeting, May 1975.

[48]*Congressional Record*, S10871, June 11, 1973.

[49]Corwin, *The President*, p. 182.

supplying information. They have even gone so far as to claim a constitutional basis for their refusal. They call it *executive privilege*, a term first used in 1953. The Supreme Court has failed to speak clearly on the question, but some noted constitutional scholars argue that this "right" is a myth.[50]

Recent Presidents have conducted a personal style of diplomacy known as *summit* diplomacy, beginning with FDR's wartime strategy sessions with Allied heads of state. Eisenhower had a famous series of summit talks with Soviet Premier Nikita S. Khrushchev in Geneva. Among the numerous summits of the Kennedy and Johnson years was the famous meeting between LBJ and Soviet Premier Aleksei N. Kosygin at, of all places, Glassboro State College in New Jersey. Nixon carried summit diplomacy to its farthest perimeters by traveling to mainland China to meet with Mao Tse-tung and Chou En-lai. He also met with Soviet Premier Leonid I. Brezhnev both here and in the Soviet Union and held numerous talks with European and Middle Eastern heads of state. Carter had hardly settled into the White House before he was huddling with the chief executives of Mexico, Canada, and major western European nations.

Despite differences in *style,* post–World War II Presidents have tended to pursue a similar *type* of foreign policy. It is based, to a large extent, on support of "free" dictatorships, protection of United States business abroad, and cold war strategy. This consistency is due partly to the fact that policy, once set in motion, is hard to turn aside, as Johnson and Nixon discovered in the course of the war in Southeast Asia. Some policies simply take on a momentum of their own. (See Chapter 14.) Another reason for the similarity in policy is that Presidents are all subject to the same pressures during their ascent to office—the interest groups of business and labor, the capitalist ideology, the public concern with

"freedom" and "godless communism." These are strong influences on anyone who makes it to the top of the political heap, because they are essentially the forces that put him there.

THE PRESIDENT AS CHIEF ADMINISTRATOR

The President is the point on a human pyramid. Below him are his Vice President, his personal staff, his cabinet, and that seething mass of bodies collectively known as the executive branch. (See also Chapter 12.) The President derives a great deal of power from the fact that he is responsible for administering this huge bureaucracy and that he can call upon it for advice, information, and action on executive proposals. But the task of administration is not without its obstacles. The fact that an official is a member of the executive branch does not necessarily mean that the President has the power to command that official. Agency administrators are responsible not only to the President, but also to Congress, their clients, their staffs, and themselves. They have their own statutory base and administer their own rules. Assuming that a President can even ascertain what a particular agency is doing, he must engage in a certain give and take to induce the administrators to follow his own course of action. It is not like dealing with the White House staff, over which the President has virtually complete control.

Presidents tend to exaggerate their helplessness in dealing with the bureaucracy, although, to be sure, they do have their problems. Lyndon Johnson wailed his frustration with the bureaucracy: "Power? The only power I got is nuclear—and I can't use that." Even Harry Truman complained about being helpless in the face of the bureaucracy. Here was the man who ordered the dropping of the first atomic bomb, seized the steel mills under his emergency powers, lectured the Russian ambassador as he would a schoolboy, and became famous as "Give 'em Hell Harry" because of his feud with Congress; but the bureaucracy forced him to admit, "About the biggest power the President has, and I've said this before, is the power to persuade

[50]Raoul Berger, for example, has written: "A limited power of secrecy was given to Congress, not to the President. No word about 'executive privilege' or 'confidentiality' is to be found either in the Constitution or its history. . . .

"James Wilson, second only to James Madison as an architect of the Constitution, . . . assured the Pennsylvania Ratification Convention that 'not a single privilege is annexed' to the President. . . .' " (*New York Times,* July 8, 1974.)

people to do what they ought to do without having to be persuaded."[51] One oft told John F. Kennedy story is about the gentleman who proposed a splendid new method for operating a federal program. "That's a good idea," said Kennedy. "Now let's see if we can get the government to accept it." Presidential literature is replete with such anecdotes, plaintively reminding the electorate that its most powerful politician does not control, but merely negotiates with, "the government," whether it be the bureaucracy or Congress.

Executive Reorganization

Aside from its independence, the bureaucracy's main characteristics—as every activist President since Theodore Roosevelt has complained—are inertia and inefficiency. Every recent activist President has made efforts, some major and some not so major, to reshape the bureaucracy and force it to be more responsive. In 1967, Johnson wanted simply to merge the departments of Labor and Commerce; he proposed it in his State of the Union message, and the ensuing flak was such that he just dropped the subject.

In 1971, Nixon disclosed his own version of the presidential dream. Officially designated Part 6 of the "New American Revolution," as enunciated in his State of the Union address, President Nixon's major goal was to cut the number of cabinet posts from twelve to eight and to reshuffle the parts of the departments according to their "missions." With the departments of State, Treasury, Defense, and Justice left untouched (and the Post Office Department already transmogrified into a government corporation), this left seven to go into four. Agriculture, Labor, Commerce, Housing and Urban Development, Transportation, Interior, and Health, Education and Welfare all would, at least in title, disappear. In their place would have been established the departments of Natural Resources, Human Resources, Economic Affairs, and Community Development.

The plan was the conclusion of a two-year commission study, the latest of a half-dozen formal efforts to diagnose the ills of bureaucracy since World War II. Each reform group vowed that if its suggestions were followed, there would be, in addition to more efficiency, billions of dollars in savings. None of their plans were carried out, since the promises could never overpower the fearsome opponents of reorganization, who mostly fall into these three categories: business groups that have a comfortable relationship with the bureaucracy as it is now and see no profit in changing; the entrenched bureaucrats, who fear the loss of rank, salary, or status; and congressional committees that fear a shaking up of the bureaucracy would disturb old alliances from which the committees draw power.

Another source of opposition—largely undefined, unorganized, and even unspoken, but potent nevertheless—is the basic American suspicion of the person at the top. The President may *say* he wants to make government more efficient, but what are his *real* intentions? Does he want to reorganize simply to seize more power, and what does he mean to do with it after he has seized it? Such underlying fears (not necessarily foolish) support whatever other reasons Congress may have for frustrating presidential plans to change the bureaucracy.

Nixon's plan for reorganization may have been inspired, but it never had a chance. A member of the Senate Government Operations Committee, through which the reorganization legislation had to pass, summarized the problem: "The restructuring plan is logical from a management point of view. But it does not seem to be drafted with much attention to politics."[52] When President Ford came forth with his plan to reorganize the regulatory agencies, he faced the same imbedded opposition.

Since the President is expected to be the chief administrator, it is strange that any President who has tried to make significant changes in the administrative machinery has been damned as a suspicious meddler, if not as a downright tyrant.

[51]Merle Miller, *Plain Speaking: An Oral Biography of Harry S Truman* (New York: G. P. Putnam's Sons, 1973), p. 4.

[52]Quoted by Robert Sherrill, *New York Times*, March 28, 1971.

FIGURE 9-1 REORGANIZATION OF THE EXECUTIVE OFFICE PROPOSED BY PRESIDENT CARTER, 1977

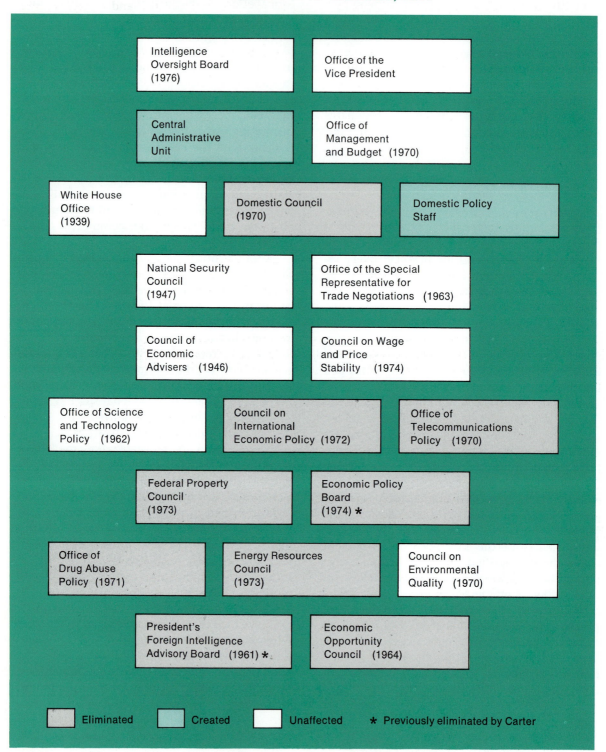

SOURCE: Office of Management and Budget; *New York Times*, July 16, 1977.

In two hundred years, few Presidents have succeeded in reorganizing the executive department. The most crucial need for reorganization came with the government's efforts in the early 1930s to keep the economy from literally falling apart. Because of bank failures, fearsomely high unemployment, some actual starvation, mass evictions, and thousands of bankruptcies, Roosevelt's New Deal administration, equipped with emergency powers, set up so many agencies and bureaus to cope with the problems that the executive branch and the bureaucracy became chaotic and wasteful. In a matter of three or four years, the government had grown to twice its normal size. Nothing like this explosion had ever before occurred; something had to be done to give it some order.

Roosevelt appointed a commission to recommend a reorganization of the executive branch. Legislation was prepared and submitted to Congress in 1938, but by this time the old FDR magic was on the wane; Roosevelt could no longer get anything he wanted from Congress. Members of Congress who wanted to restrict executive authority (a wish that beats perpetually in many congressional breasts) or who wanted to protect pet bureaus from being placed under new management or who wanted to embarrass the Democratic administration united to kill the bill. They did so largely by launching a propaganda campaign implying that Roosevelt hoped to become a dictator. So loud became these charges that Roosevelt—in perhaps the strangest denial ever forced from a President—actually went so far as to publicly state, "I have no inclination to be a dictator; I have none of the qualifications which would make me a successful dictator."[53]

Having humbled the President in 1938, Congress passed a drastically modified Reorganization Law in 1939. It permitted the President to shuffle and restructure agencies, subject to congressional veto by a majority vote. With this law, FDR brought the Executive Office of the President into existence. Some political scientists believe that the establishment of the Executive Office was the most important single step taken in recent decades toward the institutionalization of the Presidency.[54] Figure 9-1 shows the make-up of the Executive Office and a streamlining plan proposed to Congress by President Carter in July 1977.

Since 1939, the Executive Office has come to include (among other agencies) the Council of Economic Advisers, which helps the President decide on monetary and fiscal policies; the National Security Council (a controversial adjunct of which is the Central Intelligence Agency), the highest circle of military and foreign affairs strategists; and the Office of Management and Budget, which gives the President budgetary control over the bureaucracy.

Fiscal Management

The constitutional powers to raise and spend money rest with Congress. These are powers that Congress is understandably very jealous of. They are often thought to be powers that can help hold the President in check; after all, he can't very well continue with some wild scheme—or some wise scheme—if Congress doesn't give him the money.

But, in fact, Congress does not often try to use its money powers in this way, because it is a clumsy way to check the President. Congress has the authority over whether money will be spent on a program, but it does not try to exercise a close watch over precisely how the money is spent, or how fast or how wisely. It watches these things only in a general way, complaining and demanding from a distance. In this area, Congress is to the President as a husband is to a housewife—he may have the power to say how much she will spend on groceries, but she is the one who decides at what store to shop, which brands to buy, and how to cook the food. In effect, the housewife role is that of the Office of Management and Budget (OMB), which, in recent years, has taken on vast administrative responsibilities for the President.

The OMB can wield enormous power over the bureaucracy because, in representing the President, it reviews all appropriations legis-

---

[53]Quoted in Richard Polenberg, *Reorganizing Roosevelt's Government: The Controversy over Executive Reorganization, 1936–1939* (Cambridge, Mass.: Harvard University Press, 1966), p. 159.

[54]See James McGregor Burns, *Presidential Government: The Crucible Leadership* (Boston: Houghton Mifflin Co., 1966), p. 73.

lation that the departments and agencies submit to Congress. If the OMB doesn't like the requests, it changes them. Then, after Congress has passed the legislation, OMB takes a second look and makes recommendations as to whether or not the President should veto the measure. Furthermore, the OMB sets up committees to advise the government on what policies it should be carrying out, and how. Somebody in OMB watches every major piece of legislation that passes through Congress and watches every program in operation to see how the bureaucracy is doing its work. If the OMB disapproves of the way things are going, it will recommend to the President—who usually takes its advice—that more muscle should be put here or that something should be choked back there. A House of Representatives' study acknowledged in 1973, "Next to the President, the director of OMB is the most powerful person in the executive branch."[55]

The thing that makes the OMB so potent in money matters, compared to Congress, is that the OMB has the computers and the staff to put together information on everything that is happening in government, down to the most minute detail. Although in recent years Congress has tried to develop budgetary savvy of its own by establishing its own budget committees, it still has nothing comparable to OMB's information-gathering systems. Where the making of the budget is concerned, the President is still king of the hill. Senator Edmund S. Muskie of Maine, Chairman of the Senate Budget Committee, has conceded: "In the long run, Congress reacts to the country's reaction to the President. The whole budget process [in Congress] is a reaction."[56]

The President has other devices that he can use to control bureaucratic expenditures and to outfox Congress. One is called *reprogramming*. This is a shifting of funds by the executive branch *within* an appropriation account. The executive branch has the ability to move money from one program to another—say, from testing of an aircraft to its actual production or from a con-

gressionally approved procurement program to one that does not have approval. The effect is simply to bypass both houses of Congress. In 1966, Defense Secretary Robert S. McNamara began spending on his electronic battlefield, known as the McNamara Line, by reprogramming money that Congress had appropriated for other purposes. The project cost the taxpayers more than $2 billion before being temporarily abandoned, and it was not generally known about by Congress, much less approved. A member of the Senate Armed Services Committee first learned of the McNamara Line by reading about it in a magazine several years later.[57]

One of the most controversial techniques of fiscal control a President uses is the *impoundment* of funds. Impoundment can mean holding money and refusing to spend it, even though Congress has ordered it spent on a particular program, or it can mean simply postponing the expenditure. The President's right to disobey congressional spending instructions in this way has been debated for a long time. But whatever "right" the President may or may not have, he has the power to do it—to a point short of impeachment. As Truman once remarked in an impoundment battle, "If the President doesn't feel like the money should be spent, I don't think he can be forced to spend it. How would you go about making him spend it?"[58]

Of course, sometimes impoundment has congressional approval. This is the common-

[55]Quoted in Milton Viorst, *Washington Star,* May 31, 1973.

[56]Quoted by Jack W. Germond, "Congress and Carter: Who's in Charge?" *New York Times Magazine,* January 30, 1977, p. 22.

[57]See Louis Fisher, *Presidential Spending Power* (Princeton, N.J.: Princeton University Press, 1975). For more on the electronic battlefield, or automated battlefield—a concept that has again become very popular with the Pentagon—see James W. Canan, *The Superwarriors: The Fantastic World of Pentagon Superweapons* (New York: Weybright & Talley, 1975), especially pp. 267–305; and Phil Stanford, "The Automated Battlefield," *New York Times Magazine,* February 23, 1975. A quick feeling for the electronic battlefield can be obtained from Stanford's article: "Battery-operated sensors, dropped behind enemy lines, able to detect the vibrations of marching troops or trucks on the move, sensitive to metal, heat, sound, even the smell of urine. Drones circling high above the battlefield, relaying the signals broadcast by the sensors to a distant control center—Igloo White [as it was called in Vietnam]—where giant computers analyzed the data and presented probable targets to military technicians in attendance. Fighter-bombers piloted by their own computers. Bombs dropped by computer."

[58]Quoted in the *Congressional Record,* S1166, February 4, 1974.

sense, or good management, type of impound-ment, for example, when there is no longer a need for the money. Congress once gave Jefferson $50,000 to buy gunboats, in case he needed them to fight the French on the Mississippi River. But when the Louisiana Purchase created a peaceful atmosphere in which the gunboats seemed unlikely to be used, Jefferson set aside the $50,000. After World War II, Truman temporarily delayed spending money appropriated by Congress for building veterans' hospitals. He wanted to wait until the veterans came home and settled down, so that he would know where the hospitals would be most useful. In instances such as those, Congress credits the President with good management rather than recalcitrant stinginess.[59]

President Nixon, on the other hand, explaining that he wanted to stifle inflation, impounded money appropriated by Congress for many programs—such as highway construction, hospital construction, and water-pollution control. He aroused the fury of the Democratic-controlled Congress and was frequently taken to court (once he was sued by fourteen Senate Democratic chairmen), where he usually lost. But Nixon, unperturbed by these losses, simply cut back somewhere else. In 1974, Nixon had been weakened by Watergate, and Congress saw its chance. It resoundingly passed a new budget law to take effect in 1976 protecting its appropriations against impoundment. Nixon, realizing he had reached veto impotency, grudgingly signed the bill. Congress's protection is not absolute, however, and Nixon's signing did not mean that the Presidency had retreated even a step in the continuing war over the control of money.

The Vice President

Historically, the office of the Vice President has been the butt of jokes. It has been denigrated as useless. Even in the first Senate, when the titles of the various officials were being determined, it was proposed, probably only half in jest, that the Vice President be called His Superfluous Excellency.[60]

At the Constitutional Convention, some people felt that there was no need for a Vice Presidency, and there are political scientists today who hold that view. The Constitution makes it very clear that "the executive Power shall be vested in a President"—that the executive powers are not to be shared. The framers decided to establish the office of Vice President, however, to give the President a constitutional heir, to provide someone to preside over the Senate who was not beholden to any one state, and also to allow for a deciding vote in case of a tie on the Senate floor.

At first the assumption was that the office of the Vice Presidency would be simply a consolation prize, to be given to the presidential candidate who had won the second highest number of votes in the electoral college (Article II, Section 1). The candidates for President and Vice President did not originally run as a party ticket. Electors were not even permitted by the Constitution to designate their choice of President and Vice President. They were instructed only to cast votes for two persons, with the stipulation that "one at least shall not be an inhabitant of the same State with themselves." This allowed electors to vote for a favorite son of their home state, as it was supposed many would do, but at the same time encouraged them to cast at least one vote for a politician of national stature. It was presumed that the latter votes would produce a suitable President and that the runner-up would be a suitable Vice President, also of national reputation.

The original constitutional formula was critically deficient in that it failed to foresee the rise of party politics. It left open the possibility of the election of a President of one party and a Vice President of another party. In 1796, John Adams, a Federalist, was elected President, and Thomas Jefferson, a Republican, was elected Vice President. Firmly committed to different political views, Adams and Jefferson were anything but a harmonious team.

An even more serious deadlock of ambitions occurred in 1800. Although both candidates ran

[59]Louis Fisher, "Impoundment of Funds: Uses and Abuses," reprinted in the *Congressional Record*, S1162, February 4, 1974.

[60]Corwin, *The President*, p. 60.

as Republicans, neither Jefferson nor Aaron Burr received a majority of the electoral vote. As the Constitution provided, the House of Representatives decided the outcome. Actually, Burr had never hoped to be more than Vice President, but since the Constitution forbade the electors to say which of their votes they meant for President and which for Vice President, he went into the House race on an equal footing with Jefferson. He then decided to make a try for the top office. By doing so, he momentarily split his own party, came close to sparking an armed conflict, and did much to damage the office of Vice President. Jefferson won the House vote and became President, but of course he had as little as possible to do with Vice President Burr. Thus the long eclipse of the Vice Presidency began. The only positive result of the 1800 confrontation was that it brought about the Twelfth Amendment to the Constitution, which provides that electors must cast one vote designated specifically for the President and one designated for the Vice President.[61]

As originally conceived by the Founders, the Vice President's duties left him, as Clinton Rossiter has noted, "suspended in a constitutional limbo between executive and legislature, and in a political limbo between obscurity and glory."[62] He can be saved from that limbo and given real stature only if the President wills it, and, until recent years, the President has not. Presidents have left their Vice Presidents suspended, thereby wasting potentially useful public servants. In the past, the Vice President was generally ignored even in times of crisis. During the last year and a half of his administration, Woodrow Wilson, though gravely ill and incapacitated for weeks—to the extent that his wife was sometimes President by proxy—did not (except briefly, just before the inauguration of his successor) exchange one word with Vice President Thomas R. Marshall, much less pass on to him any of the duties of the presidential office.[63]

When Franklin Roosevelt died, Vice President Harry Truman took over in almost total ignorance of what the Presidency was all about. He had been excluded from most important decision-making duties and did not even know the full extent of FDR's illness. Truman moved to rescue future Vice Presidents from that condition. Beginning with his administration, the Vice President has been a statutory member of the National Security Council, where the most secret and the most important national policies, especially in periods of crisis, are made. Under Truman's successor, Dwight Eisenhower, the Vice Presidency took a giant leap forward. For the first time in history, the Vice President was empowered to preside over the cabinet and the National Security Council in the President's absence (as when Eisenhower was hospitalized with a heart attack). Eisenhower and all subsequent Presidents have used their Vice Presidents to fill important speaking engagements at home that previously would have been filled only by the President, and they have sent them on fact-finding missions to foreign nations. Eisenhower used Richard Nixon to set the tone of campaign politics (Nixon, the tough guy, allowed Ike to play the nice-guy role), and, when Nixon became President, he gave the same campaign role to his Vice President, Spiro Agnew.

In President Carter's administration, the Vice President's office was moved into the White House for the first time. Carter promised that Vice President Walter F. Mondale would receive exactly the same briefings he does and would have an important voice in the making of administration policy. This, of course, did not mean that the Vice President would be anything but very subordinate. Shortly after returning from his first round-the-world trip as the White House emissary to foreign governments, Mondale outlined for news reporters a program of other activities he hoped to embark on, adding, with a note of realism, "If Jimmy lets me."

The presidential candidate's choice of running mate usually results from political bargaining and/or the strategy called "balancing the ticket," either for geography or style or political philosophy. John Kennedy, who was considered a northern liberal, chose Lyndon Johnson for the balance of a southern moderate-conservative;

---

[61]For more on this, see Donald Young, *American Roulette: The History and Dilemma of the Vice-Presidency* (New York: Holt, Rinehart & Winston, 1972).

[62]Rossiter, *The American Presidency*, p. 136.

[63]Young, *American Roulette*, p. 143.

Carter, a southern moderate-conservative who was looked on with some suspicion by organized labor, chose as his running mate Senator Mondale, a northern liberal with a perfect prolabor record; and so forth. Republicans have generally paid less attention to balancing for philosophy (preferring to have conservatives on both sides of the ticket) than to achieving a geographical balance.

Aides and Advisers

Traditionally, the President's official advisers and coadministrators have been cabinet members. The cabinet includes the heads of the executive departments:

1. Secretary of State
2. Secretary of the Treasury
3. Secretary of Commerce
4. Secretary of the Interior
5. Secretary of Agriculture
6. Secretary of Defense
7. Secretary of Labor
8. Secretary of Housing and Urban Development
9. Secretary of Health, Education and Welfare
10. Secretary of Transportation
11. Attorney General
12. Secretary of Energy

Although these have been his formal advisers in the operation of the executive branch, the actual participation of cabinet members has varied widely over the years. The cabinet functions only as actively as a President wishes. The Constitution does not use the term *cabinet* and does not recognize the cabinet as a legal body. Former President William Howard Taft put this group in its proper perspective by noting that

> while the Constitution refers to the head of a department and authorizes the President to make him an adviser as to matters in his own department, it contains no suggestion of a meeting of all the department heads, in consultation over general governmental matters. The Cabinet is a mere creation of the President's will. It is an extra-statutory and extra-constitutional body. It exists only by custom. If the President desired to dispense with it, he could do so.[64]

Despite the absence of the word *cabinet*, it is clear that the Founders, far from intending to belittle these departmental heads, meant them to serve as a check on the President.[65] During some of the early administrations, Presidents did appoint to their cabinets men who had been their principal rivals for the nomination, and these men did operate to some degree as weights on the presidential balloon. James L. Sundquist writes:

> Prominent members of the Senate were commonly appointed, along with political leaders from the major states. Men like Clay and Calhoun, Webster and Seward, Sherman and Bryan sat in presidential cabinets because they had independent power bases that demanded, or deserved, recognition.[66]

These men not only were armed with a strong degree of independent judgment and independent political power, but were valued for it.

Eisenhower valued independence—and insisted on it—among his cabinet, and, to a limited extent, so does Carter. When Secretary of Defense Charles E. Wilson pestered him once too often over details, Eisenhower growled: "Look here, Charlie, I want *you* to run Defense. We *both* can't run it, and I *won't* run it. I was elected to worry about a lot of things other than the day-to-day operation of a department."[67]

One of President John Tyler's vetoes, in 1841, so outraged his cabinet that, except for the Secretary of State, it resigned en masse. That was a rare show of independence.[68] More usually, the tradition has been for each President to appoint departmental heads who are characterized by loyalty to him and his goals and who will await a presidential signal before acting. This is true even when a President appoints a cabinet officer from the opposite party, which is not unusual. Defense Secretary McNamara was a Republican, for example, but he was totally loyal to the Democratic administrations of Kennedy and Johnson.

---

[64]Taft, *The President and His Powers*, pp. 29–30.

[65]Allan L. Damon, "The Cabinet," *American Heritage*, April 1976, p. 51.

[66]*Brookings Bulletin* 10, no. 4, (1973): 9.

[67]Quoted in Barber, *The Presidential Character*, p. 163.

[68]Joseph Nathan Kane, *Facts About the Presidents* (New York: Charter Publications, 1976), p. 121.

A Carter cabinet meeting in early 1977. At table, clockwise: Cyrus Vance, Secretary of State; President Carter; Harold Brown, Secretary of Defense; Juanita Kreps, Secretary of Commerce; Michael Blumenthal, Secretary of the Treasury; Bert Lance, Director of the Office of Management and Budget; Cecil Andrus, Secretary of the Interior; James Schlesinger, Secretary of Energy; Patricia Roberts Harris, Secretary of Housing and Urban Development

When Nixon took office he promised an "open" administration with "direct lines of communication" between him and cabinet officers,[69] but members of the cabinet quickly learned that it would be very difficult to get the President's ear and that their first duty was obedience. In the words of Nixon's chief adviser on domestic policy, John Ehrlichman, "When he says jump they [should] only ask how high."[70] After he took office, Nixon vowed, "I don't want a Cabinet of 'yes men.'"[71] But when his cabinet members disagreed with him, he fired them. When one of his aides suggested that Treasury Secretary George P. Shultz might object to using the Internal Revenue Service illegally, Nixon responded,

> I don't want George Shultz to ever raise the question because it would put me in the position of having to throw him out of the office. He didn't get Secretary of the Treasury because he has nice blue eyes. It was a goddam favor to him to get that job.[72]

Nixon's attitude toward, and use of, the cabinet was nicely defined by a *Fortune* writer in this way:

> No President before Richard Nixon ever took quite so literally Vice President Charles Dawes's remark that "the members of the Cabinet are a President's natural enemies."
>
> As an avowedly conservative President, Nixon's aim was to turn the direction of government away

[69]Arthur M. Schlesinger, Jr., *The Imperial Presidency* (Boston: Houghton-Mifflin Co., 1973), p. 220.

[70]Quoted in the *New York Times,* October 12, 1975.

[71]Quoted in the *New York Times,* March 15, 1974.

[72]Quoted in the *Washington Post,* July 27, 1974.

from what he considered a bankrupt and discredited liberalism. Since this meant discontinuing old programs that had powerful constituencies, it required no dark, paranoid urges to imagine that he would find opposition not only in a Congress dominated by liberal Democrats but within the executive branch as well. One of Nixon's elaborate precautions was to have his Cabinet officers report through a management system that looked less like an organization chart than a Jackson Pollock painting. Another was to make sure that no one stayed put long enough to develop the illusion of independence. Along the way, this Administration established an all-time record for Cabinet turnover, with thirty-one appointments in five years. Franklin D. Roosevelt made only twenty-five appointments in more than three terms.[73]

Nixon was, as James Reston once said, "the most prolific Cabinet-maker since Chippendale."[74]

One should not judge Nixon's use of the cabinet too harshly, however. Because he left office in disgrace, pundits have tended to judge all his actions as suspect. Actually, he had every right under the Constitution to ignore the cabinet and to fire department heads as often as he wanted. A President is charged with running an extremely complex piece of machinery, and he has great latitude in how he does it.

Nor was Nixon's determination to have the loyalty of his cabinet any different from that of recent Democratic Presidents. Johnson was perfectly happy to adopt the carryover Kennedy cabinet as his own—so long as they saw things his way. But when, in 1968, Defense Secretary McNamara decided that some radical alterations should be made in the conduct of the Vietnam war, Johnson confided to a friendly senator that "McNamara has gone dovish on me," and shortly thereafter McNamara was dumped from the cabinet.[75] When Brock Adams was a member of the House of Representatives from Seattle, home of the Boeing Aircraft Company, he was gung-ho to build a supersonic transport plane (SST). But as soon as he became Secretary of Transportation in the Carter administration, he announced that he had changed his mind. He now agreed with President Carter that the SST was "a very noisy airplane" and should not be built.[76] Adams was simply adjusting to the reality described by Joseph A. Califano, Jr., a Johnson aide and Carter's Secretary of Health, Education and Welfare: "The demand for loyalty is the paramount characteristic of every presidential personality."[77] Loyalty has as much to do with institutional needs as with personality needs though. Having the full weight of the executive responsibilities on his shoulders alone, the President must have full control over "those officers who are to aid him in the execution of the laws," as Andrew Jackson explained after firing his Secretary of the Treasury in 1815.[78]

At least since Jackson, who assembled the first Kitchen Cabinet—a group of friends he felt surer of than he felt about his official cabinet—many Presidents have relied more strongly on a few of their top White House staff members than on their department heads.

And if the President requires loyalty from his cabinet, he needs it even more intensely from his staff, whom he sometimes looks upon as almost a physical extension of his political self. Califano describes the feeling:

> The congenial reflection of a president's demand for loyalty is his need to feel politically and personally comfortable with the men around him, particularly those on the White House staff. It is no surprise that John Kennedy placed so many 'Irish mafia' on his staff . . . or that his staff was so crowded with Roman Catholics. It was natural for him to reserve his greatest confidences for his brother, Robert, whose loyalty was total and unwavering. Similarly, it is no accident that Lyndon Johnson brought so many Texans to the White House. . . . So, too, the staff of Richard M. Nixon reflected his California instincts and ambitions. . . . Men like this are essential for a president. They are intimately close to him; they have shared many of his experiences; they satisfy his need for personal loyalty.[79]

---

[73]*Fortune,* January 1974.

[74]*New York Times,* March 15, 1974.

[75]Alfred Steinberg, *Sam Johnson's Boy* (New York: Macmillan, 1968), p. 832.

[76]*Washington Star,* February 18, 1977.

[77]Califano, *A Presidential Nation,* p. 244.

[78]Quoted in Corwin, *The President,* p. 83.

[79]Califano, *A Presidential Nation,* p. 190.

Carter followed suit, surrounding himself with Georgians, some of whom had been with him since he first ran for governor of Georgia in 1966.

The presidential staff

> is counted and called upon to perform functions of infinite variety: to save time, to gather data, to verify rumor, to screen visitors, to answer mail, to prepare messages, to draft speeches, to schedule trips, to prod departments, to coax Congress, to court journalists, to recommend appointments, to summarize news, to smother scandal, to baffle opponents, to cheer followers—all in all, to keep the President and the world beyond the White House gates on speaking terms both cordial and trustful.[80]

The dangerously biased attitude of Presidents toward their pals was made evident in the first real crisis of President Carter's administration, when Bert Lance, Director of the Office of Management and Budget, was accused of having operated his bank in Georgia in a highly questionable fashion. Lance was one of Carter's best friends and one of his oldest political backers. In a press conference at the time Lance resigned from government, Carter admitted that he had done nothing to check out the rumors and allegations concerning Lance's business practices. He said, "I don't know the details of Bert's financial dealings back home. I don't have the time, nor the inclination to learn them. All I know about it is what I have had a chance to read in the news media." He didn't have "the time, nor the inclination" to find out about the morality of the man who headed perhaps the most important office in the bureaucracy? Such willing blindness to their cronies' defects has been characteristic of many Presidents.

A number of modern Presidents have consulted one person who seemed to the outside world a mysterious and almost frightening wielder of power in the name of the President. Wilson had his Colonel Edward M. House, Eisenhower his Sherman Adams, FDR his Harry L. Hopkins, Nixon his Henry Kissinger (or, if one prefers, his H. R. Haldeman). Each of these men had the total confidence of the President. Each

also had immediate access to the President and the power to block the access of others.

Groupthink in Policy Making

Aides who truly have their President's welfare and reputation at heart can exploit their position of trust in such a way as to strengthen the President and protect the nation; but to serve in this way the aides must have moral courage and a disregard for their own careers. They must be willing to give the President tough advice even if it makes him angry. Califano puts it correctly:

> Presidents need men [and women] around them who bleed when they are cut. That kind of dedication can be essential to extracting from [them] the utmost their talents can produce to deal with seemingly intractable public problems. . . . But if a presidential personality demands a knee-jerk loyalty that suffocates debate and inhibits public policy options from reaching his desk, then it has merely reflected his own insecurity and has badly served his interests and those of the people. . . . The president holds loyalty in its most productive perspective when he perceives loyalty rendered by aides who argue with him, press him with new ideas, and help him to face unpalatable realities.[81]

In the Carter administration, such debates have sometimes occurred, with impunity and even encouragement, right in the President's own home and with full publicity. On July 15, 1977, nearly forty women and three men, all Carter appointees or their aides, met in the White House to express "anger, outrage and disappointment" with the President's opposition to Medicaid financing for elective abortions. They prepared a memo for Carter, hoping to change his position. Among the dissenters were some of the highest-ranking people in the Carter administration: Margaret Costanza, for example, the top-ranking woman on the White House staff; Carol T. Foreman, Assistant Secretary of Agriculture for Food and Consumer affairs; Barbara Babcock, Assistant Attorney General for the Civil Division; Patricia Wald, Assistant Attorney General for Legislative Affairs, and Patricia Der-

---

[80]Hughes, *The Living Presidency*, p. 139.

[81]Califano, *A Presidential Nation*, pp. 191–92.

ian, State Department Coordinator for Human Rights and Humanitarian Affairs. Such organized and outspoken opposition within the Johnson and Nixon administrations would have been unheard of.[82]

But the interplay between a President, his cabinet, and his aides is often a vicious circle. By his demands of loyalty, he helps to create faulty aides, and they in turn give the kind of distorted, servile assistance that hurts the Presidency. George E. Reedy, Jr., Lyndon Johnson's aide, has noted:

> It is certain that whatever neurotic drives a president takes with him into the White House will be fostered and enhanced during his tenancy. He lives in a world that is the delight of the immature personality—a universe in which every temper tantrum is met by instant gratification of the desire which caused the tantrum. Nobody is going to say "no" to his little demands, and the "no's" that are said to the big demands come in the most diplomatic and tactful forms.[83]

Hugh W. Sloan, Jr., said of his two years in the Nixon White House, "There was no independent sense of morality there . . . . If you worked for someone, he was God, and whatever the orders were, you did it . . . . It was all so narrow, so closed . . . . There emerged some kind of separate morality about things."[84] Of course the top god in the pantheon was the President himself.

In that kind of environment, one created by the President and in turn created for the President, the judgment and advice of his underlings cannot be very reliable. Although many high members of the Johnson administration acknowledged—*after* the administration had come to an end—that the Vietnam war, conducted for five years by Johnson, had been both impractical and evil, not one member of the White House staff, not one member of the cabinet, not one high bureaucrat quit in protest to Johnson's expansion of the war during those five years. What

guidance did he get from the people around him?

All too often the result of a policy decision reached by a President and his group of advisers is a national fiasco, particularly in the foreign policy area. Irving L. Janis has made a study of a number of such policy-making disasters and identified the problem as *groupthink*—a mode of thinking that results from group pressures.[85] People do things in groups that they would never do as individuals. They tend to seek unanimity at the cost of realistically appraising other alternatives; disagreement is avoided because it might cause the group to dissolve. Also, there is a feeling that the President is not "helped" by an atmosphere of dissent. The more cohesive the group and the more the members depend on each other for support in dealing with the stresses of decision making, the more likely groupthink is to occur.

Some of the symptoms of groupthink that Janis identifies are (1) an illusion of invulnerability shared by the members, which encourages risk taking, (2) collective rationalization to discount warnings against a policy decision, (3) a belief in the group's inherent morality, (4) suppression of personal doubts and doubts of others, and (5) a shared illusion of unanimity. The classic groupthink-induced fiasco was the Bay of Pigs plan adopted by President Kennedy and his advisers in 1961, which led to the abortive invasion of Cuba by Cuban exiles with United States support. The group considered only two plans, failed to examine the chosen plan for flaws, failed to reconsider the other option when those flaws became known, failed to consult with a wide range of experts, ignored contradictory information brought to their attention, and did not provide proper contingency plans.

Janis suggests some obvious remedies for groupthink in the White House: The President should encourage criticism and airing of doubts and should emphasize that he will accept criticism of his own judgments. He should give an impartial presentation of the problem and not state his own preferences at the outset. Inde-

---

[82]Associated Press in the *Baltimore Sun,* July 17, 1977.

[83]George E. Reedy, Jr., *Twilight of the Presidency* (New York: Times Mirror Co., New American Library, 1971), pp. 174–75.

[84]Quoted in the *New York Times,* May 18, 1973.

[85]Irving L. Janis, *Victims of Groupthink* (Boston: Houghton Mifflin Co., 1972). See also Alan C. Elms, *Personality in Politics* (New York: Harcourt Brace Jovanovich, 1976).

President Johnson greets Congress members after delivering his last State of the Union message, 1969

pendent study groups should also be set up to consider solutions. Group members should get feedback on the problem at hand from trusted associates. Experts should be invited to group meetings and encouraged to challenge views of the members. One member should be appointed as a devil's advocate at every meeting. After a course of action has been settled on, a "second-chance" meeting should be held to air all residual doubts.

THE PRESIDENT AS LEGISLATIVE LEADER

The Constitution does not contain many specific provisions for presidential legislative initiative.

It calls for the President to give a State of the Union message to Congress "from time to time," allows him to recommend measures he deems "necessary and expedient," and permits him to call Congress into special session (but does not allow him to dismiss Congress). Over the years, however, Presidents have greatly extended their power over the legislative branch through calculated use of their veto power, executive privilege, and impoundment of funds; through the fact that Congress itself has delegated legislative powers to the President in such areas as executive reorganization, tariff control, wage and price control, and emergency energy policy; and through leadership in submitting specific legislation drawn up and lobbied for by the executive branch.

The President usually sets forth his major proposals for congressional action in the State of the Union address. These proposals deal with substantive issues of the day, like energy needs, civil rights, welfare reform, and arms control. Their success, and that of others spelled out in written messages, depends a lot on the President's political prestige (was he elected by a landslide or just by a narrow margin?), on whether the Congress is in the hands of his party or the opposing party, and on his own forcefulness and persuasiveness. Recent Presidents have had varying degrees of success. Generally, activist Democratic Presidents have been more effective legislative leaders than passive Republican Presidents.

Perhaps the most successful legislative leader among Presidents was FDR. It was through him that the New Deal legislation emerged—including such carryovers today as social security, the Tennessee Valley Authority, the Federal Housing Administration, and the Securities and Exchange Commission. Of course, some of these ground-breaking measures had been formulated in earlier administrations, but it was under Roosevelt that they were finally made law. Truman, also a Democratic President, espoused many progressive ideas, such as a national health insurance plan and civil rights reform, but he governed at a time when the United States was preoccupied with internal security, cold war tactics, and the Korean War; the timing was not right for pushing social legislation.

Eisenhower, a Republican, presided over eight years of relative peace when an active President might have accomplished some far-reaching domestic policy. But Eisenhower's administration was a cautious one, committed to fiscal orthodoxy and minimal government interference. Most of the social reforms that were debated in the 1950s had to wait for fulfillment until the Democratic administrations of Kennedy and Johnson. For instance, Eisenhower, in his first three years, asked for no civil rights legislation and resisted proposals for it. In 1957, while he cautiously endorsed a civil rights bill, he indicated his skepticism that hearts and minds could be changed through legislation. When Kennedy became President in 1961, although committed to civil rights legislation, he deferred action until he thought the time was favorable. A bipartisan civil rights bill had just reached the Rules Committee when he was shot in November 1963. A few days later, President Johnson cited the civil rights bill as an immediate task and lobbied hard for its passage in 1964. Johnson used the momentum he had generated to press for a voting rights law, too, and even addressed an extraordinary evening session of Congress. That bill passed in five months.

Another example of Democratic presidential action is the poverty program. Eisenhower had never sent any message to Congress on poverty as such (only on matters dealing with unemployment or social security). Kennedy, in 1962, asked his staff for a report on the poverty problem in the United States. In the spring of 1963 he decided on a broad war on poverty instead of continuing a piecemeal approach. After Kennedy's assassination, President Johnson ordered "full speed ahead" on the poverty program and won its passage in Congress.

It's the same story in education. In his State of the Union address of 1953, Eisenhower asked for "prompt effective help" for the nation's schools, but neglected to follow this up with a bill or message. He eventually called a White House conference on education and supported bills for aid to school construction, but he had accomplished very little before JFK assumed office. Kennedy put all aid-to-education proposals in one omnibus bill so that the various educational organizations would pull together instead of fighting each other for pet bills. LBJ expanded the education bill and won its passage. Other objectives toward which the Kennedy and Johnson administrations led the way were medical care for the aged and environmental programs. James L. Sundquist notes that

President Eisenhower may have flirted, in moments of weariness, with the Whig notion that the legislative branch should legislate and the executive branch should execute . . . but to John Kennedy and Lyndon Johnson the Whig conception of a "weak presidency" had not even fleeting charm. Both explicitly believed in a strong presidency, and both consciously used the vast resources of the office to establish the president firmly in his role of legislative leadership.[86]

The Republican Nixon and Ford administrations were not noted for generating domestic legislation. Nixon was preoccupied with the Vietnam war in his first term and with Watergate for most of the two years of his second term. In his first term, Nixon had proposed a far-reaching welfare reform bill, but lost interest in it and did not urge it in his second term.

Tactics of Persuasion

When a President has an idea for a program he wants enacted into law, he has a relatively easy time getting the legislation drafted in his executive branch. The proposal may pass through many hands and many stages—various agencies involved make suggestions, experts are consulted, and committees are formed to refine the ideas and draft the bill, which is then submitted to the President for approval. The President has the final word before the legislation is submitted to Congress. It is at this point that the President faces his most difficult task—convincing Congress of the program's merits. In his position, he has a whole bag of tricks he can use to persuade the legislators. He can persuade by flattery and favors. An invitation to a White House dinner, a trip on his personal plane, a round of golf, a flattering mention at a presidential press conference, a telephone call of congratulations or condolence, or the expansion of a water project—and the man in the White House has put somebody in debt to him. An auto company president who gets invited to the President's daughter's wedding is going to be much more willing to hold the line on prices when the President asks it as a personal favor. A senator whose wife's funeral is attended by the President is going to be much more receptive to the President's programs. (Lyndon Johnson was always rushing off to attend somebody's funeral.)

Of recent Presidents, Johnson was the greatest master of persuasion. His tactics ranged from flattery, to appeals, to pity, to threats. Johnson wanted a rent subsidy bill passed. Among those who opposed it was Representative Thomas P. ("Tip") O'Neill, Jr., of Massachusetts, ordinarily a strong supporter of any Democratic program. When Johnson found out that O'Neill was going to vote against the bill, he got him on the phone and, as O'Neill recalls,

> He thanked me all over the place for the fine things I had said about him in a speech I had made in my home district and for all the help I'd given him in the past. Then he got to the point. He said it would be damned embarrassing for him to lose this one, and didn't I know what problems he had without this thing falling flat. Well, hell, what do you say to the President of the United States?
>
> I told him I'd sleep on it. Then the next morning I said to myself, I've always been a party man, and if he really needs me, of course I'll go along, even if the bill wasn't set up exactly the way I wanted it. Probably I took a half-dozen guys with me. We won in the crunch by six votes—208 to 202. Now, I wouldn't have voted for it except for his call. He made me feel a little guilty and cheap for letting him down.[87]

Although the *formal* lobbying of Congress by the executive branch is illegal, it flourishes openly under six hundred "legislative liaison" officials from virtually every agency, including a dozen from the White House itself. Counting salaries and office expenses, the executive branch's lobbying effort probably costs the taxpayer well over a million dollars a year. "The foremost lobbying organization in this country," Senate majority leader Robert C. Byrd has said, "is not the National Association of Manufacturers, the AFL-CIO, the Chamber of Commerce or the veterans' lobby. It is the White House and federal executive branch, hands down."[88]

These lobbyists make sure everyone knows what the White House position is; they find senators and representatives to offer amendments in committee or on the floor at the right time or to stall when necessary; they remind members of Congress when their vote is crucial and that they shouldn't be absent; they maintain

---

[86]James L. Sundquist, *Politics and Policy: The Eisenhower, Kennedy and Johnson Years* (Washington, D.C.: Brookings Institution, 1968), p. 489.

[87]Quoted in Steinberg, *Sam Johnson's Boy*, p. 711.

[88]Quoted in the *Washington Post*, May 12, 1974.

liaison between different members backing the White House position; and they write speeches for members of Congress, usually in praise of the President and his program.

And when it appears that the vote will be close (it is the White House lobby's duty to know this), the President's persuaders have been known to send air force planes to bring senators back from hunting in the wilds of Wisconsin or from basking on the beaches of the Bahamas in time for the roll call.

Sometimes the President will use the bureaucracy to lobby in a very high-handed fashion. In 1973, for example, Nixon wanted to kill the antipoverty agency known as the Office of Economic Opportunity (OEO). Congress was inundated with speeches demanding the agency's death. Were the members writing their own speeches? No, the speeches were being written for them, under orders from the White House, by a political speech-writing shop *set up in the OEO itself.* It was an incongruous situation. Officials on the OEO payroll were writing speeches that opened, for example, "Mr. Speaker, over the last several months we have heard the passionate pleas of those who wish to prolong the massive inefficiency, waste and bureaucratic nightmare of the Office of Economic Opportunity. . . ."[89]

By far the most effective lobbying is done by the President himself. This was where Lyndon Johnson's personal-contact technique paid off— gripping a senator's knee as he leaned into his face and loosed a verbal torrent of cajolery, scorn, pleas, humor, threats, or flattery, all carefully tailored to the personal susceptibilities of the senator at hand and all delivered at point-blank range with Johnson's impressive physical bulk at its most intimidating. Johnson had great confidence that he would win this game, for he considered many members of Congress stupid tacticians. He would frequently say of them that they "wouldn't be able to get the Lord's Prayer through Congress on Sunday morning."[90] But he never told *them* that; in fact, he dug as deep as necessary to unearth some hint of precious metal in their character that he could praise—so long as they went along with him.

As a rule, members of Congress actually *prefer* to be dominated by the President and do what pleases him. They *like* to give in and be cooperative—but they feel cheated unless the President puts out a little effort first. Senator Hubert H. Humphrey tells the difference between two Presidents in this regard:

> Now Johnson used to rob the Senate, but when he wanted to take something from you, he'd invite you to lunch. He'd put his arms around you and talk to you while he picked your pocket. You'd go away thinking you'd contributed something, and you'd at least feel consulted. But Nixon stuck you up in the night. You didn't even see him. It was like rape without any personal contact. I mean, the Senators are used to being had, but not to being ignored. That drives them mad. Under Nixon, you would find out about program cuts on cheap departmental press releases.[91]

And, of course, a President will often sweeten his persuasive powers by engaging in some soft bribery—helping a member of Congress get a dam for his district, for example, or, as Franklin Roosevelt once did, pardoning a couple of murderers who are dear to the heart of a powerful southern senator.[92]

A President's powers of persuasion with Congress also rest, to a great extent, on taking pains so that members do not vigorously dislike him. They may not actually *like* him, but, so long as they don't dislike him, the prestige of the Presidency itself, in spite of the man's personality, may see him through. President Wilson's failure to get the League of Nations treaty adopted by the Senate stemmed as much from the real hatred several powerful senators felt for Wilson as it did from their philosophical differences with him.

Franklin Roosevelt, the first Democrat in the White House after Wilson, was determined to avoid his Democratic predecessor's personality failure. He intended to make even his political enemies give him some personal amity, however grudging, for as long as possible. Following this strategy to its unprincipled but practical end,

---

[89]Quoted in the *Washington Star*, June 11, 1973.

[90]Quoted in Califano, *A Presidential Nation.*

[91]*Congressional Record*, S13198, July 12, 1973.

[92]Harold L. Ickes, *The Secret Diary of Harold L. Ickes,* 3 vols. (New York: Da Capo Press, 1974).

FDR refused to back antilynching legislation in 1934, even though his wife wanted him to fight for it, and, presumably, FDR himself favored it. When Walter White, secretary of the National Association for the Advancement of Colored People, came to him and asked for support, Roosevelt turned him down with the explanation:

> I did not choose the tools with which I must work. Had I been permitted to choose them I would have selected quite different ones. But I've got to get legislation passed by Congress to save America. Southerners, by reason of the seniority rule in Congress, are chairman or occupy strategic places on most of the Senate and House committees. If I come out for the anti-lynching bill now, they will block every bill I ask Congress to pass to keep America from collapsing. I just can't take that risk.[93]

Vetoes

Even if persuasion, favors, threats, and all else fail to give a President his way with Congress, he still has the means to prevent that which he does *not* want. He can always resort to one of the great powers bestowed on him by the Constitution—the power of the veto. When legislation has passed both houses of Congress, it is sent to the President for his signature. If he does sign it, the legislation becomes law. If he does not sign the bill but lets it lie dormant for ten days, it will also become law, by default. But he can try to kill the legislation by sending it back to Congress with an explanation of why he opposes it. This rejection is called the *veto*—a Latin term meaning "I forbid." Once the President has taken this action, the legislation can be revived and passed into law only by a two-thirds vote in both houses.[94]

On controversial legislation, there is all the difference in the world between needing a majority vote and needing a two-thirds vote. Indeed, as Nixon, in a moment of pique, was quoted as saying, "I don't need Congress—all I need is one-third of one house to have my way."[95] That was almost correct. To be precise, a President needs the support of one-third plus one vote in either house to prevent Congress from overriding his veto.

So long as a President remains at least moderately popular, the odds are heavily in his favor that the veto will be sustained in Congress. This is true even when Congress is dominated by the opposite party. Even President Ford, who came to the White House with a zero mandate from the public, was able to maintain his vetoes 80 percent of the time, despite the fact that he was a flagrant user of the power—he resorted to it sixty-six times in two and a half years, compared to Nixon's forty-two vetoes in five and a half years. The scoreboard between the beginning of 1929 and the end of 1976 is shown in Table 9-1.

A President who wants inaction is well served by the veto power, but, of course, an activist (especially a liberal) President cannot count on getting anything done that way. Occasionally, the threat of a veto can be used as a means for getting something else passed, but, in

---

[93]Quoted in Frank Friedel, *F. D. R. and the South* (Baton Rouge, La.: Louisiana State University Press, 1965), p. 86. Roosevelt's willingness to do extravagant things to win votes sometimes aroused cynicism. H. L. Mencken said of him: "If he became convinced tomorrow that coming out for cannibalism would get him the votes he so sorely needs, he would begin fattening a missionary in the White House backyard come Wednesday." ("Three Years of Dr. Roosevelt," *American Mercury*, March 1936.)

Roosevelt's ability to win amiable respect even from his political enemies was epitomized by William Allen White's editorial comment to FDR: "We who hate your gaudy guts salute you." (Baltimore Sun Magazine, September 18, 1977, p. 31.)

[94]The President can also exercise the "pocket veto," though the opportunities for this are much rarer. The Constitution says, "If any Bill shall not be returned by the President within ten Days (Sundays excepted) after it shall have been presented to him, the Same shall be a Law, in like Manner as if he had signed it, *unless the Congress by their Adjournment prevent its Return*, in which Case it shall not be a Law" [emphasis added]. In other words, if, at some time during the ten days that the President has to sign or reject a bill, Congress leaves town, then the President only has to stick the bill in his pocket and go his way and wait for the ten days to elapse; at the end of that time, the bill is dead. The pocket veto has been used only a few dozen times, including Nixon's constitutionally questionable use during *recesses* of Congress (as opposed to adjournments).

[95]Quoted in *Newsweek*, January 21, 1974.

TABLE 9-1

PRESENTIAL VETOES, 1929–1976

PRESIDENT	YEARS	VETOES	VETOES OVERRIDDEN	PERCENTAGE OVERRIDDEN
Ford	2.5	66	12	18.1
Nixon	5.5	42	6	14.3
Johnson	5	30	0	0
Kennedy	3	21	0	0
Eisenhower	8	181	2	1.1
Truman	8	250	12	4.8
Roosevelt	12	635	9	1.4
Hoover	4	37	3	8.1

SOURCES: *Statistical Abstract of the United States: 1977* (Washington, D.C.: U.S. Bureau of the Census, 1977), p. 461; *The World Almanac and Book of Facts* (New York: Newspaper Enterprise Association, 1977), p. 949.

general, there is a conservative bias in the veto power.

THE PRESIDENT AS NATIONAL LEADER

The President is the only politician (aside from his running mate) who is elected from the nation as a whole and is expected to speak for all the people of the United States. He is thus a symbol of unity, and, as that symbol, he can "fix national goals, alter national morale, and raise national standards" in a way that no other public official can.[96]

A voice in opposition to the President has to be formidable to be heard. According to Rossiter,

The President who senses the popular mood and spots new tides even before they start to run, who practices shrewd economy in his appearances as spokesman for the nation, who is conscious of his unique power to compel discussion on his own terms, and who talks the language of Christian morality and the American tradition, can shout down any other voice or chorus of voices in the land.

Even when a President has been forced to meet a popular antagonist—as President Truman had to confront General Douglas MacArthur in 1951—"in the end . . . the battle was no Armageddon, . . . it was a frustrating skirmish fought between grossly ill-matched forces."[97]

The President is also national leader of his *party*, a fact that may diminish somewhat his role as symbol of national unity but is a necessary extension of his political position. As party leader the President chooses the national party chairperson, participates in fund-raising affairs, maintains a partisan stance in his legislative opinions, and distributes jobs to loyal party supporters. A President who neglects his duties as party leader may forfeit some of his political base and jeopardize his reelection prospects. And a President who relies more on his personal organization than on the party organization, as

[96]Richard F. Fenno, Jr., *The President's Cabinet* (Cambridge, Mass.: Harvard University Press, 1959).

[97]Rossiter, *The American Presidency*, pp. 32–33.

Nixon did in 1972, can cause tensions within the party and weaken its structure from the top down to local organizations.

Even though there have been times in recent years when polls showed that the public had less confidence in the President than in the local trash collector,[98] in the long run it is more accurate to say, as Russell Baker said,

> Americans tend to like the President and dislike the people who oppose him. The President is one of those universally revered modern American institutions like Mother, Friday night, the flag, burgers, progress, and plenty of free parking which everybody assumes that all decent, right-thinking citizens approve of and support. Other countries have the cult of personality; we have the cult of the Presidency. "I may not like the man or anything he does," we say, "but I respect the office."[99]

Once a person is sworn into the Presidency, he is transformed in the public's eyes. One of the most glamorous of recent Presidents was John Kennedy, the youngest and certainly the handsomest fellow to live in the White House in this century. But the public did not always view him as it today views the memory of him. Penn Kimball writes:

> It is sometimes difficult to remember now that the enormous popularity of the Kennedy name came some time after he had won the Presidency by the merest eyelash. Polling data from the 1960 campaign show that Kennedy then had less appeal among women than did Richard M. Nixon. The President's youth was a fact that he actually sought to submerge all during his long, hard fight for the nomination. His legendary style and grace were so invisible in the 1950s that delegates to the Connecticut state Democratic convention walked out on his keynote address. Reporters once

groaned when assigned to cover the beautiful but dull Jacqueline. . . .[100]

The Presidency transformed Kennedy and his wife into something a bit extrahuman, and when Kennedy was assassinated the public's grief was much deeper than it would have been for the death of another celebrity. In the President's death they felt a diminution of the nation that he represented. Writes Fred I. Greenstein,

> The response to a presidential death is so profound that for many people it entails somatic symptoms. The National Opinion Research Center survey of public reaction to President Kennedy's death found, for example, that 43 percent of a national sample of adults experienced loss of appetite during the four days following the President's assassination, 48 percent reported insomnia, 25 percent headaches, 68 percent general feelings of nervousness and tenseness, and substantial numbers of people reported such anxiety symptoms as "rapid heart beats" (26 percent) and perspiring (17 percent). . . . The *main* immediate stimulus for this flood of spontaneous feeling does not seem to have been the violent circumstances of the President's death, nor does the feeling seem to have been a result of John F. Kennedy's personal characteristics—his youth, his appealing manner and so forth. Rather, it is that *the President* has died. The historical record suggests that comparable public responses have followed each of the presidential deaths in office since Lincoln—Roosevelt, McKinley, Garfield and even Harding. Further, nothing like this emotional outpouring ensues following the deaths of other figures in public life, including ex-Presidents.[101]

The public and the press give great latitude to the private life of a President. Gaucherie, misconduct, or questionable associates that would damage the reputation of an ordinary mortal tend to be overlooked for the President. Given the slightest opportunity, the press is inclined to write lush rhapsodies about him, in terms that could turn a mortal's head. John Hersey, reporting for the *New York Times* on a week spent with President Ford, seemed to feel that being in the

[98]A Harris poll of December 9, 1973, showed that 52 percent of the people responding had "a great deal" of confidence in their local trash collector, but only 18 percent expressed that much confidence in the White House. Nevertheless, that does not alter any President's basic appeal—an appeal that even reaches overseas. A 1972 Gallup poll in Great Britain discovered that among admired leaders, Nixon tied Prince Philip for first—ahead of Britain's own prime minister. (*Washington Post*, March 3, 1974.)

[99]Russell Baker, "Nobody Here But Us Presidents," *New York Times*, August 15, 1972.

[100]Penn Kimball, *Bobby Kennedy and the New Politics* (Englewood Cliffs, N.J.: Prentice-Hall, 1968), pp. 32–33.

[101]Fred I. Greenstein, "Popular Images of the President," *American Journal of Psychiatry* 122 (1965): 523–29.

President Kennedy gives his inaugural address, 1961

Oval Office with the President was like being in the presence of divinity:

> This room is an egg of light. I have seen that each person who comes into it is lit up in two senses: bathed in brightness and a bit high. . . . There are also dazzling parabolas of power here; authority seems to be diffused as an aspect of the artificial light in the room, and each person who comes into this heady glow seems to be rendered ever so slightly tipsy in it and by it . . . even the President's closest friends and even the President himself, sitting in a bundle of light behind the desk of the chief, seem to me to take on a barely perceptible extra shine in the ambiguous radiant energy that fills this room.[102]

Louis XIV of France could hardly have had a more adulatory scribe at hand.

It is that hyped-up feeling of pursuing a mandated mission (plus their egos) that makes some Presidents furious when they are stymied or opposed in their efforts. How dare Senator X

---

[102]John Hersey, "President," *New York Times Magazine*, April 20, 1975.

Truman on Wiretapping

The only President of the postwar era who, everyone seems to agree, did not use the FBI for political ends was Harry S Truman, who despised FBI Director J. Edgar Hoover. Harry Vaughan, one of Truman's closest aides, recalls:

> When we went in, the FBI had about a dozen phone taps on various people in Washington, and they used to give me a report on the phone conversations. For example, they had one on Tommy Corcoran, you know, Tommy the Cork, who was sort of a lawyer here who was on Roosevelt's kitchen cabinet. He's a big wheeler-dealer, and for some reason Roosevelt was a little suspicious of him and had the FBI put a tap on him. When these reports started coming in, I said, "What the hell is this?" And they said "This is a wiretap on so-and-so," and I said, "Who ordered it?" and they said, "Oh, that's been going on for six months, three months," or what have you. I told the President, "I'm getting these reports. I read them over and it's the most dull, deadly stuff—Mrs. Corcoran calls up the grocer and orders this, she calls her hairdresser." "Well, I don't give a goddamn whether Mrs. Corcoran gets her hair fixed or don't get her hair fixed," Harry [Truman] told me. "What the hell is that crap?" I said, "That's a wiretap." He said, "Cut them all off. Tell the FBI we haven't got any time for that kind of shit."*

*Ovid Demaris, *The Director: An Oral Biography of J. Edgar Hoover* (New York: Harper's Magazine Press, 1975), p. 109.

refuse to support the President's program? How dare some corporate or union executive come around complaining and interfering with the way the President is operating? Hyperactive Presidents quickly develop the "how dare they" attitude. Johnson had it. He didn't take criticism kindly, and he was frank to admit it.

Nixon became so angry with his opponents that he privately vowed (as revealed in the Watergate tapes),

> They are asking for it and they are going to get it. We have not used the power in this first four years. . . . We have never used it. We have not used the [Federal] Bureau [of Investigation] and we have not used the Justice Department but things are going to change now.[103]

"The power" in this instance was a generic term that included all the awesome police and harassment powers available to the President through misuse of the Federal Bureau of Investigation, the Central Intelligence Agency, the Internal Revenue Service, the federal grand jury system, the Securities and Exchange Commission, and the press. (See Chapter 3.) But as the scandals of the Nixon administration began to surface in 1973–74, a greater expose followed close behind—namely, the discovery that most modern Presidents had abused their executive agency powers to "get even" with and embarrass political enemies. As far back as Franklin Roosevelt, congressional investigators discovered, the FBI had been misused to spy on journalists, dissenting politicians, civil rights leaders, and organizations opposed to prevailing national policy.

PRESIDENTIAL SELECTION AND REMOVAL

With some exaggeration but also some truth, Arthur S. Miller has complained,

> All too often in this century the people's choice for President has become the people's curse. At least four, perhaps six or even seven or eight, Twentieth Century Chief Executives should have left office before they did. Four completely lost the confidence of Americans in their ability to govern and

[103]Tape of a conversation with John W. Dean III and H. R. Haldeman, September 15, 1972, *Submission of Recorded Presidential Conversations to the Committee on the Judiciary of the House of Representatives by President Richard Nixon* (Washington, D.C.: U.S. Government Printing Office, April 30, 1974, pp. 55–75).

govern well: Herbert Hoover, Harry Truman, Lyndon Johnson, and Richard Nixon. Woodrow Wilson was physically incompetent for many months during his second term, as was Franklin Roosevelt during the last year of his life. The possible eighth was Dwight Eisenhower after his two illnesses.[104]

Whether or not all of those Presidents qualified as "the people's curse," some certainly did. One need only recall "those fearful years when a bewildered, panic-stricken President [Hoover] sat frozen in the White House for almost four years while a despairing people, helpless to remove him, fell prey to mass unemployment, bankruptcy, despair and suicide."[105] Hoover was not a bad man or a stupid man or a venal man. But he was devastatingly ineffectual in that office.

Presidents, like anyone, can panic, can break or freeze in crisis. When President Kennedy and his top advisers were trying to decide what to do about the threat of Soviet missiles in Cuba—Go to atomic war? Give in? Compromise by offering to take our missiles out of Turkey if they would take theirs out of Cuba?—some of the President's men clearly began to break under the burden of decision making (a burden that would have been lightened if it had been spread, say, over the congressional foreign relations committees) and to show signs of becoming mentally unhinged.[106] If that can happen at the aide level, it is all the more likely to happen to the President, in whom the power to press that atomic button rests.

There is some evidence—though shaky by scientific standards—that the President's mind must undergo far more stress than the ordinary citizens. Insurance actuarial tables show that of deceased Presidents who served during this century, only two, Hoover and Truman, survived their life expectancy at inauguration by a wide margin, whereas six (not counting the assassi-

nated Kennedy) had considerably shorter lives than they could have expected had they not served in the White House.[107]

Reading the agenda for a presidential day, a person may wonder where the stress comes from. Often the President is scheduled to do no more than, say, meet with a group of advisers on some pending bill and then have his picture taken with the Easter Seal poster girl or listen to the complaints of some Minnesota dairymen. Many, if not most, presidential days seem to be filled with quite ordinary activities. Where does the stress come from? To a great extent it can be traced simply to the officeholder's perception of his job, which of course varies from President to President; if the President *feels* he is under pressure, working hard, facing one crisis after another, then the stress is there, whether or not his perception is accurate. Calvin Coolidge was a President of legendary inactivity; but he *felt* very busy, and he complained of the work load.

But there are also long periods, during wars, economic upheavals, or personal tribulations, when the sledgehammering effects of mental stress must reach what can only be called "presidential proportions." In the months of the unfolding of the Watergate scandal, and especially in the closing weeks when it became evident that he would be driven from office, Nixon's mental condition deteriorated noticeably. In their book *The Final Days*, Bob Woodward and Carl Bernstein report that as early as December 1973 (Nixon did not leave office until August 1974), Senator Barry M. Goldwater, after meeting with the President, was prompted to ask one of Nixon's aides, "Is the President off his rocker?" He was told, "No. He was drunk." Secretary of the Treasury William E. Simon is reported to have "often found the President dazed." His frequent drunkenness continued. In October, Secretary of State Kissinger was reported to

---

[104]Quoted in the *Congressional Record*, H7158, July 21, 1975.

[105]Clayton Fritchey, syndicated column, August 17, 1974.

[106]Robert F. Kennedy, *Thirteen Days: A Memoir of the Cuban Missile Crisis,* ed. Richard Neustadt and Graham Allison (New York: W. W. Norton & Co., 1969), p. 31.

[107]Based on Metropolitan Life Insurance Company, *Statistical Bulletin,* April 1969. Those who lived beyond normal life expectancy were William Howard Taft, by .8 years; Herbert C. Hoover, 16.7 years; Dwight D. Eisenhower, 1.4 years; Harry S Truman, 11 years. Those who lived less than normal life expectancy were Theodore Roosevelt, by 8.8 years; Woodrow Wilson, 6.2 years; Warren G. Harding, 15.6 years; Calvin Coolidge, 12 years; Franklin D. Roosevelt, 9.6 years; John F. Kennedy, 25.7 years; Lyndon B. Johnson, 9 years.

have said, "Sometimes I get worried. The President is like a madman." Columnist Joseph Alsop, a confidant of Kissinger and of Nixon's aide, Alexander Haig, ultimately concluded, on the basis of what he heard from his friends, that Nixon was "ninety-nine percent nutty as a fruitcake." In the closing weeks of Nixon's ordeal, write Woodward and Bernstein, the President's son-in-law Edward Cox "was worried about the President's mental health. The President was not sleeping, and he had been drinking. The man couldn't take it much longer, Cox said. The President had been acting irrationally." He broke into tears and spoke of suicide. Cox (who later denied it) is quoted as saying he had seen the President walking the halls at night, "talking to pictures of former Presidents—giving speeches and talking to the pictures on the wall."[108]

It is quite possible that the world lived for some time under the threat of a United States President who was mentally deranged and who could, at whim, have pressed the wrong button. Officials at the Pentagon are reported to have been sufficiently concerned about the possibility of irregular orders coming from the White House that they kept unusually close control over all lines of command during the last days of the Nixon administration.[109]

The possibility of a presidential mental breakdown is always there. If there is sufficient warning, statutory provisions exist for relieving the President of his duties. But in practice the statutes may not give sufficient protection, for the truth is that the Presidency so intimidates most officials that, as Johnson aide George Reedy, claimed with some exaggeration, "No one is going to act to interfere with the presidential exercise of authority unless the president drools in public or announces on television that he is Alexander the Great. And even in these extreme cases, action would be taken hesitantly indeed."[110]

---

[108]Bob Woodward and Carl Bernstein, *The Final Days* (New York: Simon & Schuster, 1976), pp. 104, 191, 199, 230, 395.

[109]*New York Times*, August 24, 1974.

[110]Reedy, *Twilight of the Presidency*, p. 168.

How to Remove a President

The Constitution allows for removal through resignation (used by one President, Richard Nixon). Or it can be done through exercise of the Twenty-fifth Amendment, which says that if the Vice President and a majority of the cabinet find the President to be incapacitated, then the Vice President, for a period, shall become Acting President. Or it can be done through the process of impeachment: The Constitution provides (Article II, Section 4) that the "President, Vice President and all civil Officers of the United States, shall be removed from Office on Impeachment for, and Conviction of, Treason, Bribery, or other high Crimes and Misdemeanors."

The vagueness of this passage is emphasized by all scholars. The Constitution throws no light on what constitutes "other high Crimes and Misdemeanors." Although the prevailing assumption is that "Misdemeanors" in impeachment cases refer to crimes connected with the conduct of office, that leaves much in limbo. Gaddis Smith has pointed out that

> authorities disagree over whether or not the adjective "high" in the constitutional clause modifies misdemeanors as well as crimes. If it does, no one knows what a "high misdemeanor" is. . . . Depending on which remarks one quotes from the debates in 1787 [at the Constitutional Convention], it is possible to prove almost anything.[111]

---

[111]Gaddis Smith, "The American Way of Impeachment," *New York Times Magazine*, May 27, 1973.

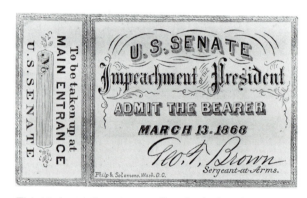

Ticket to impeachment proceedings for Andrew Johnson

America is in trouble today not because her people have failed, but because her leaders have failed. And what America needs are leaders to match the greatness of her people.

Richard M. Nixon, accepting the Republican presidential nomination,
Miami Beach, August 8, 1968.

The looseness of the language allows it to mean anything to anybody and sometimes different things to the same person.[112]

Such considerations are really academic. The impeachment process has been used only twelve times in the nation's history to try to get rid of federal officials, first in 1797 and most recently in 1936. But most of these efforts have been directed at judges, not at elected politicians; four of the accused were convicted and removed from office. Only once, in 1868, was a President subjected to impeachment by the House and trial by the Senate.[113] This was Andrew Johnson, Lincoln's Vice President and successor. Johnson's "crime" was defying the Tenure of Office Act by removing an official appointed with the advice and consent of the Senate before the Senate had approved that official's successor. Johnson said that the law passed by Congress was unconstitutional (he was right) and ignored it.[114] So he was put to trial, but survived by a margin of one vote.

---

[112]When Gerald Ford was a member of Congress, he led an unsuccessful impeachment effort against Supreme Court Justice William O. Douglas, during which effort Ford argued that "an impeachable offense is whatever a majority of the House of Representatives considers it to be at a given moment in history; conviction results from whatever offense or offenses two-thirds of the other body considers to be sufficiently serious to require removal of the accused from office." (Quoted in "President Ford: The Man and His Record," *Congressional Quarterly Special Report,* August 1974, p. 57.) At that time—1970—his reading of the Constitution was that if the House and Senate didn't like the number of martinis a President drank before supper or didn't like his jokes, they could throw him out of office. But only four years later, when Ford was Vice President in an administration headed by a President in serious trouble, Ford changed his interpretation: now, he said, a President could only be impeached for really indictable crimes—perjury, theft, bribery, and the like.

---

[113]The House acts like a grand jury, in impeaching (or indicting) the officer; the Senate then sits as a jury, to either convict or acquit.

[114]The real issue behind the impeachment proceedings was the conflict between Congress and the President over Reconstruction policy.

Not until the administration of Nixon did Congress again seriously consider impeaching a President, and then it moved with extreme reluctance and only after many felonies and subversions of statutory law had been traced to the White House. If a Democratic Congress was that hesitant to move against a Republican President so plainly guilty of having violated the law (a guilt that President Ford said Nixon conceded by accepting his subsequent pardon), then it is clear that the impeachment process has little appeal to Congress.

The timid performance of Congress in the Nixon matter immediately raised calls for some new method of disposing of criminal or useless Presidents. A number of alternatives were proposed, including recall elections, comparable to those in some state and local jurisdictions, and votes of "no confidence," such as the British Parliament can use to topple a government.[115] No measure stirred widespread enthusiasm, however, and the need for a more efficient method of getting rid of Presidents seems likely to be ignored until the next crisis. United States citizens will probably have to get used to the idea that the ballot is the only sure way of changing Presidents.

How to Pick a President

If the right person is chosen for the job, the need to remove him probably won't arise. There may be no way to guarantee that the nuts and misfits won't become President, but we can predict roughly what kind of aberrations we might expect from our presidential candidates, and we can vote accordingly.[116]

The Presidents who have served this country fall into four general categories that can be called active-positive, active-negative, passive-positive, and passive-negative. They are rated active or passive according to how much zest and energy they brought to the office. They are rated positive or negative according to how they felt about their job, how much enjoyment they derived from it, and how they felt about themselves.

The active-positive type enjoys using power. He has well-defined personal goals, and he is flexible and adaptable as he moves toward them. Franklin Roosevelt, Harry Truman, John Kennedy, and Jimmy Carter are active-positive types.

The active-negative President desires power but, unlike the active-positive President, does not derive pleasure from using it and is twisted with guilt when he makes a mistake. Worst of all, he can't laugh at himself. The active-negative President is compulsively active, is motivated by anxiety, and has difficulty controlling his more aggressive emotions. When faced with a crisis, he becomes extremely rigid and unable to adapt to changing circumstances. Presidents of this type are prone to tyranny and duplicity when they see that the tide of opinion is running against them. They overreact and see themselves as destiny's children. In this group are Woodrow Wilson, Herbert Hoover, Lyndon Johnson, and Richard Nixon.

Wilson could have won ratification of the League of Nations treaty by adjusting to a few fairly reasonable compromises that were suggested by his friends as well as by his enemies in the Senate, but he refused to budge because he was convinced that he was following "the hand of God who led us into this way." And when the Senate drubbed him, Wilson still saw himself right up there beside the Almighty: "I have seen fools resist Providence before and I have seen their destruction." Similarly, in their own crises, Hoover and Johnson and Nixon inflexibly followed their noses to disaster.

The active-negative President also feels constantly called upon to defend his policies as though they were his manhood. Just as Johnson swore he would "never tuck tail and run" in Vietnam, Nixon explained his escalation of the bombing in 1972 by saying, "When they jump on you, you've got to hit back." And when one of his plans goes sour, or his wishes are frustrated by his opponents, the active-negative President takes it as a personal insult. After his nominee to the Supreme Court, Judge G. Harrold Carswell, failed to win approval, Nixon damned his opponents as "vicious," "malicious," and full of "hypocrisy."

---

[115]National Academy of Public Administration, *Report to the Senate Select Watergate Committee,* March 20, 1974.

[116]The remainder of this chapter follows closely the theory and supportive data found in James David Barber's *The Presidential Character.*

The active-negative Presidents have had peculiar ideas about their relationship to the public and to the press. They are highly suspicious. "You know very well," Nixon once said, "that whether you are on page 1 or page 30 depends on whether they fear you." Each had up-down emotions. One day Johnson would boast that the people "cling to my hands like I was Jesus Christ walking in their midst," and the next day he would ask mournfully, "Why don't people like me?" With the exception of the one really embarrassing defeat in 1962, when he failed in his try to become governor of California, Nixon had always had lucky breaks and success as a politician (the narrowness of his defeat by Kennedy in 1960 can hardly be considered a terrible failure). Still, he thought that "my political career has been one of very sharp ups and downs."

In short, although the active-negative President can bring memorable leadership to the White House, he is an unbalanced leader and can develop a national tragedy out of his personal tragedy. Conceivably that risk could be worth taking, but only if the alternative were a do-nothing President at a time when the nation's problems demanded that something be done.

The passive-positive President is cheerful and tail-waggingly eager to be liked. The risk from this President is that he will fail to take corrective actions for fear of hurting somebody's feelings, with the result that the government could collapse from corruption. Warren G. Harding was of this type. One can say of the passive-positives as a class what a friend said to Harding: "Warren, it's a good thing you weren't born a gal because you'd be in a family way all the time. You can't say No."

And, finally, there is the passive-negative type—who doesn't enjoy power, doesn't enjoy politics, doesn't like the natural controversies of public life, doesn't like having to cope with details or remember all those names and bills and budgets. They are motivated only by a painful sense of duty. Dwight Eisenhower and Calvin Coolidge were this type.

How does one predict which category a candidate will fall into when he gets to the White House? One searches through the candidate's early history. Find out what the child and the young man were like and you will have valuable insight into what the President will be like. A single candid comment from a politician's mother about his childhood is worth a ton of campaign speeches. Mama Johnson once reminisced about Lyndon: "We always did feel that Lyndon was tryin' too hard to *prove* something." It was a golden clue.

The primary rule (for those who want to play this game of selection) is look to character first. And look for it early. By the time people reach adulthood, they will have revealed their proto-political orientations. They will have shown whether they actively make their environment or are passively made by it. Secondly, they will have demonstrated how they feel about the experience of shaping or being shaped—whether they considered it a burden or a pleasure.

Keeping that rule in mind, let's test it briefly in the lives of our active-negatives—Wilson, Hoover, Johnson, and Nixon—for they are the ones who had the most tempestuous administrations. Those four men shaped their environment, but only after the roughest beginnings. Wilson was made to feel that he was a dunce because he didn't learn the alphabet until he was nine years old, didn't learn to read efficiently until he was eleven, was kept out of school until he was nearly twelve, and then earned grades well below average. The searing bitterness of those days stayed with him even after he was a university president and then President of the United States. Hoover was extremely introspective; an orphan by the age of nine and thereafter passed around among his uncles, he had a childhood that was mostly hard work and not much love. Johnson was caught as a youth between a blowhard father and a domineering mother, who tried to smother him with love; he was a shiftless teenager, a fruit tramp, a road-gang bum. Nixon's father was an overbearing, cantankerous loser, always fighting poverty and seldom winning; his mother was a patient drudge who worked sixteen-hour days to keep the family store open and baked as many as fifty pies in the morning. She taught son Richard that it was not nice to display emotions. Each of these four really hit his stride in college, even to the point—at least with Wilson and Johnson—that they held a heavy hand over their classmates. But each of the four was convinced that it was not brains but work and willpower that put a man on top, not grace but drudgery, not good fortune but stubborn persistence.

Out of these backgrounds, the four men came to politics, and ultimately to the White House, still trying to free themselves from an inner sense of inadequacy, trying to make up for something, to salvage through leadership some lost or damaged part of himself. And, as Mama Johnson said of her boy, each tried too hard. The price to the nation for their excessive effort was heavy indeed. Could it have been foreseen? By careful analysis, quite possibly. At least all the clues were there, to be ferreted out by the voters, before they went to the polls.

Summary

1. The power of the Presidency has grown because there is no agreement on what its exact boundaries are, because Congress has ceded more and more powers to the President as society has become more complex, and because strong Presidents have exploited their use of power, especially their emergency powers.

2. In recent years, the trappings of power—cars, planes, salary, fringe benefits, staff, and so forth—have created almost an Imperial Presidency. In 1976, Jimmy Carter won a great deal of public support by promising to deflate the imperial style.

3. As commander in chief, the President has the power to wage wars. Presidents have also gradually usurped Congress's power to declare war by making use of congressional resolutions giving them carte blanche in military crises.

4. In their role as chief diplomat, Presidents have tended to favor secret negotiation, and they have consulted with Congress as little as possible. They make executive agreements more often than treaties, since the former don't require approval of the Senate. Most Presidents follow a similar type of foreign policy, although their styles may differ.

5. The President is responsible for administering the bureaucracy. He controls its fiscal affairs through the Office of Management and Budget, but otherwise his control rests on his powers of persuasion, since he cannot command agency administrators. Presidential attempts to reorganize bureaucracy have run up against allied interests in business, the bureaucracy, and congressional committees.

6. The President has more control over his aides, his advisers, and the Vice President than over the bureaucracy. The Vice President used to be ignored by Presidents, but recently the office has been upgraded and brought further into the governing circle.

7. The President's formal advisers are his cabinet members, who may be given a great deal of leeway or kept on a short leash. The White House staff includes many of the President's unofficial advisers.

8. In their decision-making sessions, Presidents and their staffs and advisers are sometimes subject to groupthink, the tendency to ignore alternatives and avoid disagreement in a desire to reach unanimous decisions.

9. Activist Democratic Presidents have proved to be stronger legislative leaders than passive Republican Presidents. Presidential legislative leadership is exercised through tactics of persuasion, to get bills passed, and through the veto, to prevent the passage of legislation.

10. As national leader, the President sets national goals and commands the respect and attention of the nation. Some Presidents have violated the trust of the people by abusing their powers.

11. A President may be removed by resignation, impeachment, or use of the Twenty-Fifth Amendment.

12. Presidents tend to fall into one of four categories—active-positive, active-negative, passive-positive, and passive-negative. By looking at the formation of character in a candidate's early history, it is possible to predict what kind of a President he or she would make.

Additional Reading

Louis W. Koenig, *The Chief Executive,* 3rd ed. (1975), and Clinton Rossiter, *The American Presidency,* rev. ed. (1960)—both published in New York by Harcourt Brace Jovanovich—are useful overviews. Richard E. Neustadt's *Presidential Power* (New York: John Wiley & Sons, 1960), based on the experience of working with several Presidents, is an excellent blend of concrete description and theoretical insight. Edward S. Corwin, *The President, Office and Powers* (New York: New York University Press, 1957), offers a comprehensive analysis of the legal powers of the Presidency, which needs only limited amendment in the light of recent events such as those chronicled in Arthur M. Schlesinger, Jr., *The Imperial Presidency* (Boston: Houghton Mifflin Co., 1973).

A highly readable argument on the importance of the President's personality, with abundant anecdotes, is James David Barber's *Presidential Character: Predicting Performance in the White House,* 2nd ed. (Englewood Cliffs, N.J.: Prentice-Hall, 1977). Alexander L. George and Juliette L. George, *Woodrow Wilson and Colonel House: A Personality Study* (New York: Dover Publications, 1964), gives an elegant analysis of Wilson's personality and its consequences for American foreign policy. Garry Wills's *Nixon Agonistes: The Crises of the Selfmade Man* (New York: Times Mirror Co., New American Library, 1971) remains a perceptive analysis of Richard Nixon's character and its relation to Americans' values. Doris Kearns's *Lyndon Johnson and the American Dream* (New York: Harper & Row, Publishers, 1976) is based on a close personal relationship with the President.

Much of the best material on the Presidency appears in historical and journalistic accounts of particular Presidents, including James MacGregor Burns, *Roosevelt: The Lion and the Fox* (New York: Harcourt Brace Jovanovich, 1956); Theodore C. Sorensen, *Kennedy* (New York: Harper & Row, Publishers, 1965); Arthur M. Schlesinger, *A Thousand Days: John F. Kennedy in the White House* (Boston: Houghton Mifflin Co., 1965); George E. Reedy, Jr., *The Twilight of the Presidency* (New York: Times Mirror Co., New American Library, 1970), on the Lyndon B. Johnson years; Rowland Evans, Jr., and Robert D. Novak, *Nixon in the White House: The Frustrations of Power* (New York: Random House, 1972); and Theodore H. White, *Breach of Faith: The Fall of Nixon* (New York: Atheneum Publishers, 1975). All such accounts should be read with awareness of the authors' point of view, however. Even greater skepticism must be applied to the autobiographies of Presidents, such as Lyndon B. Johnson's *The Vantage Point: Perspectives of the Presidency, 1963–69* (New York: Popular Library, 1972). A unique source is the White House version of the Nixon tapes, *The White House Transcripts: The Full Text of the "Submission of Recorded Presidential Conversations to the Committee on the Judiciary of the House of Representatives by President Richard Nixon"* (New York: Viking Press, 1974); there are some important differences in the official version of the House Judiciary Committee, which is available as a government document.

Patrick Anderson, *The Presidents' Men* (New York: Doubleday & Co., 1968), and Richard F. Fenno, Jr., *The President's Cabinet* (Cambridge, Mass.: Harvard University Press, 1959), analyze the President's staff and cabinet.

There is one thing better than good government and that is government in which all the people have a part.

Walter Hines Page

10 CONGRESS

Whether the Constitution made the President equal to Congress or subservient to it is an age-old debate. Nobody has ever suggested that the Constitution made the President superior to Congress. When one speaks of a strong Presidency, it implies that a President has achieved superiority over Congress through his peculiar force of character, by exploiting circumstances, and by stretching the law beyond its normal bounds, not by following the clear formula of power as set down in the Constitution. In recent decades, our government has tended toward strong presidencies. But this trend does not alter the fact that the predominant notion during the formative years of our nation (as James Monroe acknowledged in his 1822 inaugural address) was that Congress was by far the most important branch.[1]

Perhaps we need not be bound by the original intent, but Congress at least deserves the extra respect due seniority, for it was the first branch in existence. It was there to count the electoral votes for the first President and to help Washington organize his administration; it brought the federal court system into being.

The public sees Presidents as individuals, not as parts of a continuing institution. Congress, however, is viewed as a human stream. Its glory is not in personality but in numbers, and its membership is sufficiently large to make it seem to *be* the voice of the people. Angry with the President in 1867, Thaddeus Stevens, the tough congressman from Pennsylvania, declared with the kind of fury that the legislative body loves, "He and his minions shall learn that this is not a government of kings and satraps, but a government of the people, and that Congress is the people."[2]

With allowances for rhetorical license, Stevens spoke roughly the truth. But, in fact, the

---

[1] Ernest S. Griffith and Francis R. Valeo, *Congress: Its Contemporary Role*, 5th ed. (New York: New York University Press, 1975), p. 5.

[2] Quoted in Alvin M. Josephy, Jr., *The American Heritage History of Congress of the United States* (New York: American Heritage Publishing Co. and McGraw-Hill, 1975), p. 6.

designers of the Constitution had had difficulty determining just how much "the people" should be able to govern through Congress (or any other way). Only a few radicals, like Thomas Paine, would have been willing to risk the establishment of a true democracy, with the people making governmental decisions directly. That idea was dismissed by most of the new nation's leaders as wildly unrealistic.

The problem was that the Founders had little notion of how a mass society should function. They did not think of "mass armies." They did not know about "masses of workers." They were not familiar with "mass production" or the "mass media." Nor had they considered "mass suffrage" or the "mass political party. . . . The techniques of organizing, disciplining, and directing the large scale institutions of modern society were strange to the early leaders."[3]

Indeed, as we have seen in Chapter 2, the writing of the Constitution and the structuring of our government were partly determined by fear of the masses. James Otis had warned at the time of the Revolution, "When the pot boils, the scum will rise." At most, a republican, representative government would be allowed; a unicameral (one-house) legislature could not be permitted, because that would probably mean an imbalance of representation. If the general electorate alone determined the membership of a unicameral legislature, who would represent the propertied class, the aristocratic class, the class then conceived of as producing the "natural" leaders? For them a second—balancing—house in the legislature would have to be established.

The myth in those days was that wealthy people were wise and common people were honest and good. The best government, therefore, as John Adams insisted, was an "exact balance" of the aristocratic and the democratic.[4] And so the Senate was established to be a check on the populist House of Representatives. Members of the Senate would not be subjected to the popular vote, as representatives were.[5] Senators would be appointed by the state legislatures, an arrangement that was not ended nationwide until the Seventeenth Amendment was added to the Constitution in 1913. Only in this century has the popular vote ruled both houses. The Founders' concept of balance has been preserved, however: as the Senate became more democratized—through urbanization and industrialization as well as through the Seventeenth Amendment—the House became more conservative, as a result of increasing tenure, professionalization of a House career, specialization in committee subject matter, and the narrow base of its constituencies (making them more susceptible to special interest pressure).

Congress today, as we shall see, is a jumble of anachronisms, inefficiencies, inflamed ambitions, and petrified creeds. It operates sometimes in an atmosphere of chaos, sometimes in a vacuum. Seldom do things run smoothly for Congress. Its motivations are a hodgepodge of conflicting interests; greed and paranoia are always niggling at its elbow. At the same time, by whatever mysterious chemistry can account for it, Congress is also the greatest democratic institution available.

Many of Congress's virtues are the same as its defects. Its bungling, its inefficiency, its standpattism are often just what the country needs at a particular moment to escape greater evils. And if nothing else, Congress—not the Presidency and not the Supreme Court—has, by its example, freed humankind everywhere from fear of the "undisciplined masses."

THE HUMAN SIDE OF CONGRESS

Congress is the public writ large. It has all society's virtues and vices, exaggerated. Any session of Congress contains a majority of conscientious civil servants, brilliant lawmakers, ingenious tacticians, and patriots—real or pretended; but it

---

[3] Alfred de Grazia, "Toward a New Model of Congress," in Alfred de Grazia, ed., *Congress: The First Branch of Government* (Washington, D.C.: American Enterprise Institute, 1966), p. 2.

[4] Gordon S. Wood, *The Creation of the American Republic, 1776–1787* (Chapel Hill, N.C.: University of North Carolina Press, 1970), pp. 197–98.

[5] Even the popular vote for the House wasn't so very popular—originally, no women, blacks, or people without property could vote.

will also invariably contain enough nuts, buffoons (like the senator from Virginia who called a press conference to deny he was the dumbest man in Congress), demagogues, and outright rogues to sink the ship of state.

Even in their most pontifical and egotistical moments, the 535 very human beings who comprise Congress are never allowed to presume that they have been touched with divinity—an air that, by contrast, often seems to envelop the White House. Senators and representatives, being looked on as just people, are viewed as fairer targets for gossip than Presidents. Indeed, the public is shocked at the thought of a boozing chief executive (like Lyndon B. Johnson, roaring off across the prairie, tossing beer cans out the car window), but it accepts drunken members of Congress as a commonplace spectacle. It averts its eyes when the press cautiously and after long delay discloses that a President may have been a sexual cutup (passing over Johnson's affairs almost entirely and not writing about John F. Kennedy's until he had been dead twelve years), but the sexual exploits of members of Congress receive contemporary and detailed discussion.

Members of Congress operate at a level most people can understand, as when Senator Ralph W. Yarborough, begging the Senate to save the Big Thicket Forest of Texas from further destruction, burst into a series of whistling imitations of the birds that live in that area. And he was at that level again when he and Senator J. Strom Thurmond, arguing outside a committee room, suddenly wrestled into a heap on the corridor floor. And when Congressman Henry B. Gonzalez socked Congressman Ed Foreman for calling him a "pinko," that, too, was at the marvelously populist pitch that seems to be denied, perhaps unfortunately, to Presidents and chief justices.[6] A century or so ago, violence and threats of violence were not uncommon in either house, thanks largely to the southern influence. Senator Henry S. Foote of Mississippi would, if provoked, wrestle another senator in the aisles or challenge him to a duel or threaten to hang him "to the highest tree in Mississippi" if he ever tried to pass through Foote's homeland.[7]

Members of the federal legislature can occasionally see themselves as many others see them—windy, ineffective, and somewhat comical. Asked how he liked serving in Washington, freshman Senator Edward Zorinsky of Nebraska replied that he would rather be in Omaha, where "the den mother of a Cub Scout pack" could solve problems better than his Senate colleagues. "During the energy crisis, I saw senator after senator rise to their feet and give speeches about how sympathetic they are to people who are cold, that are out of jobs because they had to shut industries and businesses down. That same time could have been spent evolving a far-reaching energy policy, because that's what would resolve the situation, not sympathy."[8] He received more than six thousand letters in praise of his candor. Congressman Dewey Short of Missouri, angered by his colleagues, denounced them publicly as "that supine, subservient, soporific, supercilious, pusillanimous body of nitwits."[9] What President these days would appraise himself and his predecessors in the Presidency with such bouncy candor? When Congresswoman Edith Green of Oregon, then the House's foremost expert in higher education, announced her retirement in 1974, she explained that "in my judgment, the job . . . of the congressman is just too big. None of us can do it well."[10] One would not likely catch a President in a moment of such insightful modesty.

In short, the defects of Congress are real and cannot be dismissed; but they are *our* defects, too, and they are the product of those federal politicians whom we can reach out and touch. As House Speaker Carl Albert liked to say,

> People don't really vote for a President [that is, their direct vote is only for electors]. They sure

---

[6]Actually, in the nation's robust youth, there was at least one President, Andrew Jackson, who just might have done something of that sort. It was Jackson, after all, who said, "I have only two regrets: that I have not shot Henry Clay or hanged John C. Calhoun."

[7]Josephy, *The American Heritage History of Congress of the United States,* p. 208.

[8]Quoted in the Associated Press, March 17, 1977.

[9]Quoted in Warren Weaver, Jr., *Both Your Houses: The Truth About Congress* (New York: Praeger Publishers, 1972), p. 30.

[10]Quoted in the *Washington Post,* February 16, 1974.

don't vote for admirals, generals, or judges. They do vote for the members of Congress, and that's why Congress is the most important branch of our government, because it's the only branch that the people themselves created and keep re-creating over and over again. This is where the people can and literally do, when they get enough of being abused and misgoverned and mistreated, this is where they can rise up and throw the rascals out.[11]

Not Just Ordinary Folks

Just because members of Congress can sometimes be earthy does not mean they are plain folks. The late House majority leader Hale Boggs once described Congress as "a collection of ordinary men dealing with extraordinary problems."[12] He would have been much more accurate if he had said Congress is an extraordinary collection of men and women dealing with ordinary problems—raising money from the world's most compliant taxpayers and spending it on armies, roads, schools, and subsidies to all sorts of special interests. The problems confronting Congress are no different in kind, though considerably different in scope, from the problems facing the governments of Transylvania or Borneo.

It is an extraordinary collection of men and women *not* because among them there are former professional football, basketball, and baseball stars, former professional boxers, former Olympic gold-medal winners, and former astronauts and professional singers—although Congress does indeed include members with these colorful backgrounds. It is an extraordinary group because, for one thing, its members are so highly concentrated in a few professions; more than half of them are lawyers. It has been estimated that one out of every thousand lawyers in the United States is in Congress. The remainder of the 535 members of the House and Senate come, in a descending scale of numbers, from business, education,

agriculture, journalism, and a scattering of other professions, including those mentioned above.[13] Whether a group with that high a concentration of lawyers is safe to lead the country is debatable, but it is certainly in no way an "ordinary" group.

About 60 percent of the members have upper-class occupational backgrounds, compared to 15 percent of the national population. Only about 1 percent of the members were actually blue-color workers before being elected to Congress. Furthermore, while more than half the population at large is comprised of women and 11 percent of blacks, in 1977 there were, among the 535 members, only seventeen women and sixteen blacks; the Senate had one black, and no women.

The Senate is especially atypical in its wealth. In 1976, at least twenty-one senators were millionaires; four were worth between half a million and a million dollars; eighteen were worth between $250,000 and $500,000; thirty were worth between $50,000 and $250,000; only five were known to be worth under $50,000, and the wealth of the twenty-two others could not be figured out accurately from public records.[14] This ratio of 21 percent millionaires is about the same today as it was in 1902, when a compilation by the *World Almanac* found eighteen millionaires among the ninety senators then in office. Indeed, since the founding of the republic, the Senate has been considered a rich man's club.[15]

In short, Congress is very much an elite group. Does that mean it is unable to feel the

---

[11]Personal interviews, October and November 1973.

[12]Quoted in Jim Wright, *You and Your Congressman* (New York: Coward, McCann & Geoghegan, 1972), p. 23.

[13]Wright, p. 24.

[14]Data compiled by Ralph Nader's Citizens Action Group, quoted in Lloyd Shearer, "The Richest Men in the U.S. Senate," *Parade*, May 23, 1976.

[15]*New York Times*, December 25, 1975. Perhaps that's why senators, as a group, have acted in a more genteel manner than representatives, especially in the early days. Writing home to London in 1853, Frederick Lehmann reported, "The arrangements in the Senate are the same, only the room looks quieter; there is not the same number of members, not the same bustle, not the same talking, and last (though in America never least) there is less spitting." (*Memoirs of Half a Century: A Record of Friendships*, Part II, ed. R. C. Lehmann, London, 1908, pp. 275–77.)

needs of the broad public?—unable to know what it means to skimp on food, to worry about hospital bills, to give up even small luxuries to pay for necessities? If one looks at certain individual politicians, it is plain that riches don't necessarily blunt sympathy for the less privileged. One of the richest members of Congress is Senator Edward M. Kennedy; he has also been a leader in pushing for legislation to help middle-income and poor people. The same can be said for several other millionaires, but, broadly speaking, it seems reasonable to suppose that the upper-crust background of its members has shaped Congress's work and attitude significantly.

It requires a real effort to keep, or achieve, the common touch. Few members make the effort. But one who did was Congressman Edward P. Beard, Democrat of Rhode Island, who was a house painter before he was elected to Congress in 1974; he carried a paintbrush in his breast pocket to remind himself of his unpretentious origins. Congressman Thomas R. Harkin, Democrat of Iowa, also elected to Congress in 1974, spent holidays working as a mailman, a riveter, and a nurse's aide, because "you can't really represent people unless you know what they're going through in their daily lives." [16]

Junkets and Other Benefits

One characteristic of today's members is that they don't stay in Washington if they can find an excuse to leave town. It usually doesn't take much of an excuse. When Wright Patman was Chairman of the House Banking Committee and floor manager for a crucial bill aimed at controlling prices and wages, he suddenly announced that debate would have to be interrupted for four days so that he could go home to Texarkana to be enshrined as a thirty-third-degree Mason.[17] Some absences are almost automatic. Often it is impossible to hold committee hearings or floor action on Mondays or Fridays because so many

members, known collectively as the Tuesday-to-Thursday Club, are out of town.

Members ended the last half of the Ninety-third Congress in 1974 in typical style. Having failed to cope with pending legislation relating to trade, tax reform, pension reform, budget reform, the critical fuel shortage, the worst inflation in two decades, and campaign spending frauds, what did members do? They took a one-month vacation. And when they returned after Christmas, they worked two weeks and then took *another* vacation, the House for six days and the Senate for ten days. And how did Congress face its problems during the first year of the Ninety-fourth session? With six ten-day holidays, a month's vacation in the summer, and early adjournment for Christmas.

The standard explanation for leaving town when there's still work to be done in Washington was given by Senate majority leader Robert C. Byrd: "The basic theory behind the recesses is to give members a chance to get back home and listen to their people and talk with their people—otherwise you lose touch and don't know what the public wants."[18]

That sounds good, except that during any typical year about half the members of Congress will take tax-paid trips overseas, not home, at a cost exceeding $2 million. The overseas trips are supposed to be educational—educational for members of Congress and for their colleagues, who receive a report on the junkets. (Members do not call the trips junkets. They prefer to call them "briefings," "inspection tours," "defense analysis missions," "intergovernmental seminars," "exchange visits," and "study projects.")

King of this generation's junketeers was Congressman Wayne L. Hays, who ended twenty-seven years of service to his country in 1976. In the previous ten years he had made about fifty recorded trips abroad at taxpayers' expense. His usual excuse for going was that he wanted to "inspect" United States diplomatic facilities. He inspected the United States embassy in London—his favorite world capital—twenty-eight times. Many others have tried to copy Hays's

---

[16]*Christian Science Monitor,* March 25, 1975.

[17]*Newsweek,* December 20, 1971.

[18]Quoted in the *Washington Post,* May 23, 1975.

style—taking along their wives, pals, and women friends, hiring chauffeur-driven limousines to ferry them to the world's gay places for their official inspections. Hundreds of congressional inspections have been given the Taj Mahal, the Sphinx, the chauteau regions of the Loire, the Swiss lake country, and the costliest eateries and hotels that can be found in any friendly nation. A dozen members of Congress and their wives (who said they went along for "protocol" reasons) got away from the January chill in Washington for an inspection trip of the South Pacific. The bill came to $100,000 and covered the price of opera tickets, caviar, Alaskan king crab, lobster, and many cases of liquor. The purpose of the trip: to "monitor U.S. diplomatic relations with Pacific nations." A dozen senators and their wives had made that junket the previous month.

What does the taxpayer get in return? Usually a perfunctory report that could have been written—and sometimes is—by a staff researcher who never left the Capitol ("——— is a mountainous country with an average rainfall of nineteen inches. . . ."). Sometimes the taxpayer doesn't even get that much. Former Speaker Albert of Oklahoma, after completing a $124,000 junket to four countries (including $9,100 for such things as tips to dancers), did not turn in a report because—as one of his aides explained—that would have been an "additional" expense to taxpayers and "My God! you know how people today don't want to spend money!"[19]

The most remarkable thing about the institutional junketing of Congress is that its practitioners believe they have fooled everyone. They actually seem to be puzzled that the public would respond cynically when, say, Congressman Olin E. Teague, Democrat of Texas, explained that, strictly in the line of duty as Chairman of the House Veterans Affairs Committee, he was going to take a free trip to England, Belgium, Luxembourg, Italy, and France to "look into the condition of military cemeteries."[20] It's all done with a very straight face.

[19]Scripps-Howard, September 19, 1976.

[20]*Washington Post,* November 18, 1972.

The Finest Federal Politicians Money and Fringe Benefits Can Buy

Considering the financial squeeze that most citizens must endure, our federal politicians—who set their own pay and perquisites—do quite well for themselves. The presiding officers in the House and the Senate are paid $75,000 a year, majority and minority leaders, $65,000, and members of the House and Senate, $57,500. (Retirement pay for members ranges up to about $40,000.) This puts members of Congress in the top 1 percentile of national income. In addition, some of their rewards include free doctor's care, cut-rate hospitalization, cut-rate insurance, and 33 (for House members) to 40 (for Senators) tax-paid trips home each year, plus at least a $2,250 travel allowance, a $6,500 stationary allowance, unlimited mailing, $6,000 for phone calls (plus unlimited phone use between 5 P.M. and 9 A.M.), free flowers, free picture framing, free access to swimming pools and gyms, free research assistance, a staff allowance of between $244,000 and $900,000 a year (the latter for big-state senators), an office allowance for the home district, and cut-rate, tax-free meals in the Capitol's posh dining rooms.

That isn't all. The special interests, both private and public, pour a thousand lovely remembrances from their cornucopia upon our lawmakers. For instance, the world's most exclusive airline—officially known as the Eighty-ninth Military Airlift Wing of the United States Air Force—stands ready to serve the more notable members of Congress. This is a fleet of twenty-three plush aircraft, which cost the taxpayers about $6 million a year to operate. At a moment's notice, around the clock, these planes will take important members of Congress to a football game at West Point or to a fish fry down in Mississippi.

The total cost of operating the legislative branch comes to something over $1 billion—about $1.7 million per member of Congress. Nobody is sure of the exact amount, but, after all, it's only taxpayers' money.

So posh is the life of our federal politicians that they are inclined to get an inflated idea of their own worth. "The minute a guy becomes a member of Congress, there's free parking, special elevators . . .," says a staff member. "Every time he sits down, there's a pretty girl putting a cup of coffee in front of him. Pretty soon they start taking things for granted, and start thinking they're special, and not bound by the rules that govern everyone else."[21] They aren't. While traveling to and from work or while at work, they are immune from all but felony charges. When Congress passed the Freedom of Information Act, requiring most parts of the government to open its books to the public, it exempted itself. It also exempted itself from civil rights laws. Members of Congress who discriminate against employees because of race or sex cannot be sued. They have also exempted themselves from the spirit of civil rights laws. Many statutes have come out of Congress in recent years promoting the integration of schools. But as of the 1976–77 school year, only two members of Congress—Congressman Ronald V. Dellums, a black ultra-liberal from California, and Congressman John W. Jenrette, Jr., a white conservative from South Carolina—were sending their children to the District of Columbia's almost wholly black schools. Other members either sent their children to private schools, or they lived in the suburbs where their kids could go to mostly white schools.[22]

Congressional Ethics

Congress is sensitive to appearances. Conscious of its roguish members and the bad press they generate, Congress tries periodically, but at very long intervals, to achieve a higher standard of operating morality.

Former Congressman Brooks Hays of Arkansas may have been correct when he said of the official morality of members of Congress: "Their standards are about what you would find among 535 bank presidents, or 535 presidents of Rotary Clubs, or 535 stewards in the Methodist Church,

or 535 deacons of the Baptist Church."[23] It is an analogy that, if not examined too closely, may give some comfort. And, judging strictly by how many members of Congress have been convicted of serious crimes—less than two dozen this century—it would certainly seem that they are at least as honorable as their constituents. Nevertheless, in recent years there has been an unusual rash of criminal indictments (see Table 10-1), near indictments, and reports of questionable income and favors involving members of Congress—so much so that congressional morality is once again the cause of public ridicule. Charges have included tax evasion, bribery, perjury, mail fraud, and the acceptance of illegal gratuities.

The Constitution gives Congress the authority to control and punish its members. Members can also be punished in regular court, like anybody else; but the only way a member can be kicked out of Congress or censured for his or her conduct as a member is by the actions of colleagues. Censuring is only a kind of embarrassment—the accused member must stand in the well at the front of the chamber and listen to the presiding officer read the formal denunciation of conduct. Even this trivial punishment is rarely administered.

Hoping to improve their reputation, both House and Senate established ethics committees, the Senate in 1966 and the House in 1968. The ethics committees were supposedly going to assure that errant members would be swiftly punished. To that end, codes of conduct were written. The House rules were much stricter than those of the Senate, not only prohibiting members from accepting gifts of "substantial value" (meaning, loosely, those having more than a fifty-dollar value) from anyone having a direct interest in legislation before Congress and prohibiting the diversion of campaign funds for personal use, but also laying down the broad admonition that a member "shall conduct himself at all times in a manner which shall reflect

---

[21]Quoted in the *New York Times,* January 30, 1977.

[22]*Washington Post,* December 7, 1976.

[23]Personal interview, May 17, 1970. Which is something like what the Pirate King said in *The Pirates of Penzance:* "I don't think much of our profession, but, contrasted with respectability, it is comparatively honest."

TABLE 10-1

A ROSTER OF INDICTED MEMBERS OF CONGRESS

The following members of Congress and congressional aides have been indicted on criminal charges since 1968. Only Jones and Hansen were still in Congress as of 1977.

NAME	CHARGE	DISPOSITION
Rep. Cornelius E. Gallagher (Democrat, N.J.)	Tax evasion 1972	Pleaded guilty; served 17 months of 2-year prison sentence.
Rep. Frank J. Brasco (Democrat, N.Y.)	Bribery 1973	Convicted; served 3-month prison sentence.
Rep. John Dowdy (Democrat, Tex.)	Perjury 1971	Convicted; served 6-month prison sentence.
Rep. Bertram L. Podell (Democrat, N.Y.)	Conspiracy—conflict of interest 1973	Pleaded guilty; served 6-month prison sentence.
Rep. Andrew J. Hinshaw (Republican, Calif.)	Bribery 1975	Convicted; on appeal.
Rep. Irving J. Whalley (Republican, Pa.)	Mail fraud—obstruction of justice 1973	Pleaded guilty; placed on probation.
Rep. George V. Hansen (Republican, Idaho)	Campaign violations 1974	Pleaded guilty; served 2-month prison sentence.
Rep. Angelo D. Roncallo (Republican, N.Y.)	Extortion-conspiracy 1974	Acquitted.
Rep. James R. Jones (Democrat, Okla.)	Campaign violation 1975	Pleaded guilty; fined $200.
Rep. Henry Helstoski (Democrat, N.J.)	Extortion 1976	Awaiting trial.
Rep. James F. Hastings (Republican, N.Y.)	Mail fraud—filing false statements 1976	Convicted; awaiting sentencing.
Rep. Martin McKneally (Republican, N.Y.)	Failure to file income tax returns 1970	Pleaded guilty; placed on probation, fined $5,000.
Sen. Daniel B. Brewster (Democrat, Md.)	Accepting illegal gratuity 1969	Pleaded no contest; fined $10,000.
Sen. Edward J. Gurney (Republican, Fla.)	Perjury 1974	Acquitted.
Martin Sweig Congressional aide	Perjury 1970 Bribery-conspiracy 1971	Convicted of all charges; served 1 year of 3-year sentence, paroled.
Robert T. Carson Congressional aide	Conspiracy-bribery, perjury 1971	Convicted; sentenced to 18 months in prison, fined $5,000.

SOURCE: *New York Times*, January 30, 1977.

"You can't legislate morality, thank heaven."

creditably on the House of Representatives.'' The Senate's code of conduct primarily dealt with prohibitions against accepting illegal campaign funds or bilking campaign treasuries for personal expenditures.

In 1967, the Senate, after an investigation by its Ethics Committee, voted the censure of Senator Thomas J. Dodd of Connecticut for misusing political funds and for billing Congress twice for public and private travel expenses. After that, all was quiet. Dozens of members were known to have taken campaign contributions from corporations and labor unions (such contributions are illegal), but the Senate Ethics Committee did nothing about it. Some senators were known to have taken thousands of dollars from companies while pushing legislation to help them. Was this corruption? The Ethics Committee didn't try to find out.

The House Ethics Committee was equally moribund. For eight years it did nothing, although it had plenty of opportunity to act. On

July 23, 1974, a dairy lobbyist pleaded guilty to giving illegal corporate contributions to six members of Congress, including Congressman Wilbur D. Mills, then Chairman of the House Ways and Means Committee. On March 12, 1975, the Securities and Exchange Commission charged Gulf Oil with giving illegal contributions to at least four House members. On September 26, 1975, Phillips Petroleum Company admitted that it gave illegal funds to eighteen members of the House. At various times in the early 1970s, numerous defense contractors and labor unions were alleged to have given illegal money to members of Congress. Between 1968 and 1976, eight members were found guilty in civil courts of having committed crimes ranging from soliciting prostitutes to taking kickbacks, and at least three others were under indictment during this period. None was censured.

Not until 1976 did the Ethics Committee move against a member, and then it acted only under intense pressure from public interest groups outside Congress. It recommended that one of the old bulls of the House, Congressman Robert L. F. Sikes, Democrat of Florida, receive a reprimand—a much lighter scolding than a censure—for misusing his power over a period of years to help pass legislation in which he had a financial interest. He was also removed from a subcommittee chair. This was only the second time in fifty-five years that a House member was punished.

In 1977 Congress tried again. Spurred by public criticism of recent hefty pay raises (29 percent) and a new wave of lobby payoff scandals, both the House and Senate voted new codes of ethics. Both codes limited outside earned income to 15 percent of members' base salary (but put no limit on income from stocks, bonds, or property transactions—an exemption that favored the richer members), ended lame-duck travel at public expense, prohibited members from accepting gifts worth more than one hundred dollars, and required fuller financial disclosure. The codes were accepted by the members of Congress with the kind of reluctance expressed by Senate majority leader Byrd—"I think it's absurd that the Senate has to demean itself by enacting a new code"—and by Senator John Stennis, who warned that a tough ethics code would "scare away" members with "broad experience."[24]

Still, before throwing stones at the politicians, one should ask if they tolerate mischief any more easily than does the public. In 1976, about forty members of the House who were running for reelection went into their campaigns carrying the taint of scandals from sexual exploits, disorderly boozing in public, or questionable financial dealings. But voters defeated only three of them. As for Congressman Sikes, the voters of north Florida—doubtless influenced by the fact that he had brought $500 million worth of defense contracts into his district and apparently convinced that jobs should take precedence over morality—returned him to Congress with an overwhelming majority. Congressman Hays received similar tolerance back home in Ohio. After it was disclosed that he had been keeping a mistress on the federal payroll, he won the Democratic primary handily, and all signs pointed to his victory in the general election; he dropped out voluntarily. In 1974, after Congressman Mills had been televised cavorting on a Boston stage with stripper Fanne Foxe and after his other escapades with the Argentine Firecracker had been headlined around the world, the voters of the second district of Arkansas reelected him.

We may also ask if the public does not, by its self-centered and often immorally selfish demands on members of Congress, create an atmosphere in which shady conduct is accepted as a logical adjunct to winning votes. Many members complain that their constituents do not allow them to follow their conscience. As one congressional aide described the dilemma:

> Their constituents don't judge them on how well they supervise the Department of Interior, but only on the number of land-reclamation projects they get for their state. . . . That's the thing that permeates this place. There are pressures from back home that say "get everything you can for the state," whether it's good or not, whether they deserve it or not. What sort of ethics do you expect when they're voting hundreds of millions of dollars like that day after day?[25]

---

[24]*Washington Post*, April 1, 1977, February 1, 1977.

[25]*New York Times*, January 30, 1977.

THE MACHINERY OF CONGRESS

Contrary to a rather common romantic assumption, the firm hand of authority is not fatal to democracy. Nowhere is the need for a sensible degree of firm direction more evident than in Congress. As Senator Hubert H. Humphrey once put it, "You can't run this Congress on the basis of mutual admiration, affection and being nice guys. We have 535 prima donnas up here and unless somebody takes charge, we're just going to wander around and get in trouble."[26]

Party Influence

The "somebodies" who take charge are determined along party lines. Partisanship is the supreme power in Congress. It provides discipline, organization, guidance, fellowship, and cohesion. Members of the same party usually hang out together; they socialize together. The veteran members "look after" the younger; they give tips on how to cut corners, how to save time, and how to save face. It should not be supposed, however, that party membership plays a constant, conclusive role in determining how members vote. Party leaders, though they doubtless wish they could, aren't able to call signals like a football quarterback and expect members to vote accordingly. Too many other influences—ideologies, lobbying pressures, personalities—are competing with partisanship. As a result, the two parties do not operate strictly as opposites, but, in fact, cooperate in the shaping and passage of legislation—as the 1976 session shows. With a Republican in the White House and a two-to-one Democratic majority in Congress, most of the legislation that passed bore the mark and the approval of bipartisanship.

Nearly two-thirds (63 percent) of the recorded votes found a majority of Democrats and Republicans voting together, especially in the areas of defense spending and energy. Of 661 roll-call votes in the House, 424 (64 percent) were bipartisan; in the Senate, there were 432 bipartisan votes (63 percent).[27] The willingness to

ignore party lines on votes is much more common among Democrats than among Republicans. The reason is simple: although the Democratic party is programmatically liberal, many Democratic members are conservatives; the Republican party is programmatically conservative, and very few Republican members swerve even slightly from that philosophy.

For most of this century, the core of Democratic conservatism in Congress has been the southern membership. Until recently, there were about sixty or seventy southern Democrats in the House and a dozen in the Senate who properly should have belonged to the most conservative wing of the Republican party. They gave virtually no allegiance to the national Democratic party. They called themselves Democrats only because it was necessary to be a Democrat in the then one-party South and because wearing that title hoisted them up the seniority ladder in Congress. For many years, they were enormously powerful as obstructionists, but their grip on Congress began to weaken in the 1960s. The rebirth of the southern wing of the Republican party reduced their support on the right, and the rebirth of the black electorate demanded concessions to the left. The tyrannical drawl of the South is no longer so loud, or taken so seriously, in the halls of Congress as it once was.

The influence of political parties is most evident in congressional organization, usually originating in party caucuses. The caucus is a coming together of everyone bearing the same party label to approve or disapprove committee assignments, elect the leadership, and thrash out party policies.

At the beginning of a new session, each party in the House of Representatives offers a nominee for Speaker, and the full House chooses between the two. This is merely a technical concession to the spirit of intraparty democracy; actually the majority party always wins. The losing nominee then serves as the floor leader for the minority party.

In addition to electing a speaker, the majority party in the House elects a floor leader. Each party also elects an assistant floor leader, called a "whip," who is assisted by a dozen regional whips. The Senate goes through a similar rou-

---

[26]Quoted in the *Washington Post,* June 8, 1975.

[27]*Congressional Quarterly Weekly Report,* October 30, 1976, p. 3099, November 13, 1976, p. 3178.

...aders except for the office of ... es not exist in the Senate.

... keep members informed as ...lls are coming up for debate ... are all about; they try to build ...tion to bills; and they try to get ... parties to be on hand for votes.

...nt, they try to determine how ...eir side will have, for it is very embarrassing ...or the leadership to predict incorrectly the outcome of a vote.

Negative powers are widely dispersed through both the House and Senate. Chairpersons can stall; committees and subcommittees can mangle legislation and sit on it for months on end; senators can filibuster; members of both houses can crush legislation under a load of extraneous and frivolous amendments. But the positive powers, as Nelson W. Polsby has pointed out, "the power and the responsibility to get things done—especially big things—is predominantly in the hands of party leaders."[28]

When the President is of the same party, the need is for party leaders who will serve as conduits for executive programs, who are technicians rather than innovators. Senator Gary W. Hart characterized a Senate Democratic leader during a Democratic administration as "a hollow log in which both sides leave messages."[29]

The Speaker of the House

The Speaker holds the highest office of any person in Congress—House or Senate. Although he is supposed to give a fair shake to members of both parties in that he must give members of the opposition party ample time to be heard on the floor, the Speaker cannot escape the constant reminder that he is armed and outfitted by his own party and owes it for the privilege of sitting in the chair.

In two hundred years, four Speakers stand out above all others. Henry Clay, who came to the post in 1811 and held it for six terms without serious opposition, was the first master of the chair's powers. His theory for success: "Decide, decide promptly, and never give your reasons for the decision. The House will sustain your decisions, but there will always be men to cavil and quarrel about your reasons."[30] That tone of haughtiness is characteristic of all the great Speakers.

The next great Speaker did not come for another sixty-five years. He was Thomas B. Reed of Maine, a towering figure, physically and mentally, who demanded and got obedience. He was so egotistical that he finally quit the House rather than deal with President William McKinley, whom Reed considered his inferior. Fearless and outspoken to the point of rudeness, he often treated colleagues as children or half-wits, but he got by with such treatment because he was a parliamentary genius.[31]

The pinnacle of power came with the Speakership of Joseph G. Cannon of Illinois, who took the chair in 1903. For a time he became a virtual dictator within the House and certainly a coequal to the President. He had the power to appoint committee chairmen, make committee assignments for all members, and assign bills to the committees of his choice; he was Chairman of the Rules Committee (which decides which bills will be allowed to come up on the House floor for vote); and, finally, he had the power to recognize members during debate. Cannon welded these powers together into a chain with which he held the House virtually a prisoner to his will. Members obeyed him, or they had absolutely no say in the operation of the House.

> . . . the career of an individual Representative could be made or broken by the committee assignments he received. Every two years, the Speaker assigned whom he pleased to whatever committee he pleased, and he designated as well the chairman. . . . This power . . . gave him, of course, great power to discipline members of the House. At times, the Speaker even refused to

---

[28] Nelson W. Polsby, *Congress and the Presidency*, 3rd ed. (Englewood Cliffs, N.J.: Prentice-Hall, 1976), p. 95.

[29] Quoted in the *International Herald Tribune*, January 6, 1977.

[30] Quoted in Josephy, *The American Heritage History of Congress of the United States*, p. 149.

[31] Richard Bolling, *Power in the House: A History of the Leadership in the House of Representatives* (New York: E. P. Dutton & Co., 1968), p. 55.

name any members to any committees until the House approved an important bill he wanted passed.[32]

While the importance of individual members diminished, the importance of the House as a whole increased. Because a majority of the members of the House transferred their personal power and prestige to the Speaker, Cannon in turn gave the House a cohesion and a dominance in government that it would not otherwise have had and which it would not have again after he was dethroned. He spoke for the House as a whole. Once a Democrat asked Cannon if he thought a certain bill could be passed. "Oh, this House could pass an elephant if the gentleman in charge of it could catch the Speaker's eye," Cannon replied.[33]

Such extravagant influence, intrinsically alien to the American political character, could not last. Cannon became intolerable. In the spring of 1910, a revolt of House members stripped him of his key powers: no longer would he be allowed to appoint committee chairmen or preside over the Rules Committee. With that stroke, autocracy was not cut out of the House, it was merely shredded. The autocracy of the Speaker was scattered and conferred instead on the committee chairmen—whose lesser tyrannies were made increasingly intolerable in the years ahead by the seniority system.

The model of the modern Speaker is generally conceded to have been Sam Rayburn, Democrat of Texas, who served in that capacity from 1940 to 1961, relinquishing the gavel only when Republicans held a majority membership in 1947–49 and 1953–55. Rayburn was a short man with a large bald head full of political dicta, the most famous of which was, "If you want to get along in the House, go along." It was a saying that came to be hated by reformers, for it seemed to sum up all the reasons why the status quo could not be budged. Rayburn was very much a defender of the status quo, for that's where he got his acceptance from the committee chairmen

and party leaders of the House. In those days, there was much stricter adherence to tradition than there is today.

Rayburn was Speaker for so many years and was held in such esteem by the House members that, during the last years of his life, it is said he could often dominate the debate by simply giving a scowl from the chair at the right moment. In his later years, when he was a crotchety guru, an institution in his own right, he could wield the gavel like a minor czar. But he was best known for backroom persuasion, which was made legendary by his so-called "Board of Education" meetings, held in a secret room of the Capitol, where late each afternoon he met with congressional leaders to drink and plot the next day's maneuvers. He often claimed there was no way to describe the instincts that a Speaker develops: "You can't really say how you lead. You feel your way, receptive to those rolling waves of sentiment. And if a man can't see and hear and feel, why then, of course, he's lost."[34]

Aside from that rather mystical approach to leadership, there are a number of practical approaches. First of all, any effective Speaker tries to get as many members in his debt as possible. He will help members—especially the younger ones—get promising committee assignments; he will help members get their bills assigned to sympathetic committees; he will go into members' districts at election time and make exaggerated speeches on their behalf ("No member in the history of the Fisheries and Hatcheries Subcommittee has done so much to protect minnows as your Congressman McGurk.").

Second, an effective Speaker knows when to call in his chits. He never reminds members of their debts to him unless he has to—and he knows when he has to because an effective Speaker is a master of nose-counting. On any important bill, he will know ahead of time (with the help of the majority leader and the whip), within three or four votes, what the probable outcome will be. If it is going to be a tight count and the legislation is important to the party, he

---

[32] Neil MacNeil, *Forge of Democracy: The House of Representatives* (New York: David McKay Co., 1963), p. 125.

[33] Quoted in Richard Bolling, *House Out of Order* (New York: E. P. Dutton & Co., 1966), p. 32.

[34] Quoted in MacNeil, *Forge of Democracy*, p. 75.

Speaker of the House "Tip" O'Neill addresses the opening of Congress

will go out and call in his chits to make certain of passage.

In recent years, however, Speakers have been confronted by a much more difficult and complex job of juggling the membership to achieve majority votes. No modern Speaker can fairly be compared to Rayburn, because when Rayburn came to power at least half the members of the House were from agricultural districts; their interests were simple, and similar. Farmers stick together; urbanites don't. Today not more than fifty members of the House depend on the farm vote for their election; the others represent a galaxy of highly diversified interests—ethnic, union, white collar, core city, suburban, age blocs. Today's Speaker must try to pull his fol-

lowing from all of them. He must, in short, draw his support from conflicting groups without getting a reputation for hypocrisy.

Also, the House membership is getting younger. Nearly half the members have been there less than nine years. The newcomers are increasingly less tolerant of institutional gods; they want legislative results. After conferring with a group of freshmen members who were angry because they felt he wasn't giving enough leadership, Carl Albert (Speaker from 1971 to 1977) snapped, "They don't want a Speaker, they want a bouncer. I don't twist arms, I shake hands."[35]

---

[35] Quoted in the *Washington Post,* June 19, 1975.

Albert's successor, Speaker Thomas P. ("Tip") O'Neill, Jr., of Massachusetts, though he much prefers the role of accommodator, is occasionally willing to twist arms to get action. O'Neill has established a more aggressive relationship with the White House, as indicated by the photo on his office wall showing him forcefully gesturing over a luncheon table at President Carter, who sits raptly drinking in the advice. Across the top of the picture Carter has written, "Thanks for another political lesson." If O'Neill, who was elevated to the job in 1977, proves to be one of history's forceful Speakers, as some anticipate, considerable credit must go to the fact that, unlike most of his predecessors this century, he is able to dominate the Rules Committee—which controls legislative traffic in the House; and it's very difficult to get a bill to the floor by any other route.

After the revolt against Cannon in 1910, authority to appoint members to the Rules Committee was taken from the Speaker and given to the Committee on Committees, whose membership was identical with the Democratic membership of the Ways and Means Committee. It was dominated by conservatives, particularly southern ones. Consequently, the Rules Committee was known for several generations as the graveyard of good legislation. Typical of that era was the reign of Congressman Howard W. Smith, a flinty conservative from Virginia who became chairman in 1955. Smith, and a majority of the committee, disliked progressive, urban-oriented legislation. To block transit to the floor of such legislation, Smith would simply disappear, usually to his Virginia farm "to see if the rainstorm hurt my hay." Until he returned, the Rules Committee couldn't be called into session. When the offending legislation was withdrawn or when it was too late in the session to pass it, he would return.[36]

Speaker Albert, through deals and dickering, began getting members appointed to the Rules Committee who were more in tune with the national Democratic programs. But his influence with the committee was mainly diplomatic. O'Neill's influence is much greater. He is the first speaker of modern times to have appointive powers over the Rules Committee. He is much less likely than most recent speakers to be crushed by a legislative logjam.

The Senate Majority Leader

There is no Speaker in the Senate, either in title or power. The Vice President presides over the Senate when he wants to, but he usually doesn't want to. It is a boring job. Usually he turns the task over to whichever senator is handy and has nothing better to do than perch on the vice presidential chair. (The Constitution does provide for a President *pro tempore*, who is supposed to preside in the Vice President's absence; he is elected by his fellow senators but has no formal power.) The only significant role played by the Vice President in Senate affairs is on those rare occasions when the members have stalemated in a tie vote. Then the Vice President is permitted to cast the tie-breaking ballot. Unlike the Speaker, the Vice President does very little lobbying for legislation.

Nearest the Speaker in power is the Senate majority leader. In his hands largely rests the fate of the President's program in the Senate. Before bringing an important administration bill to the floor for debate and action, the Senate majority leader may talk to every member of his party. (No similar amount of persuasion is exerted on—and no similar degree of responsibility rests with—any one person in the House. On that side of the Capitol, the effort to persuade and orchestrate support will come as much from White House lobbyists as from the party leadership itself.) There have been only three powerful Senate majority leaders in this century: Nelson W. Aldrich of Rhode Island, who held the job briefly (1908–09) and who had sole power to name all members of the standing committees—an institutional power that was short-lived; Joseph T. Robinson of Arkansas (1928–37), whose power came from the steady accumulation of personal influence during fourteen years as party floor leader; and Lyndon B. Johnson (1955–60).

In Johnson's time, the Senate establishment was still very much alive—"The Club," as the inner circle of mostly southerner old-timers was

[36]MacNeil, *Forge of Democracy,* pp. 103–04.

called—and Johnson was a master of using the establishment's muscle to bring the majority of the Senate into line. But he also had other keen devices. For one thing, he manipulated the seniority system. He did not hold the dictatorial control over committee assignments that Aldrich had held, but as Chairman of the Democratic Steering Committee, which made committee assignments, Johnson was able to have his say in most cases.

Members who voted as Johnson wanted them to vote were rewarded with good committee assignments. Members who rebelled against his leadership were banished to Siberia committees. Johnson put Senator J. Allen Frear, Jr., a Delaware mediocrity, on both the Finance Committee and the Banking and Currency Committee, where Frear could watch out for the interests of E. I. Du Pont de Nemours and other powerful moneyed interests of his home state; this was a reward for voting or changing his vote at the wave of Johnson's hand, even though it made him look like a lackey. On the other hand, Senator Paul H. Douglas of Illinois, one of the most public-spirited politicians of his generation and by any measure the most brilliant economist in Congress, had to wait eight years to get on the Finance Committee—after five others who came to the Senate in the same year he did—1948— went ahead of him. Coincidentally, all five believed in tax breaks for the oil companies; Douglas did not.[37]

Aside from using committee assignments for reward and punishment, Johnson was also adept at using them to buy allies. In 1954, Senator Wayne Morse of Oregon—a liberal—said: "Johnson has the most reactionary record in the Senate. Look at his voting record. If he should ever have a liberal idea, he would have a brain hemorrhage." Then Johnson put Morse on the Foreign Relations Committee, a position that Morse heartily desired and appreciated. Thereupon Morse changed his tune: "During the past year, I have been the beneficiary of one kindness after another from Lyndon Johnson. I consider

him not only a great statesman but a good man."[38]

But equally important in Johnson's aggrandizement of the majority leadership was his person-to-person technique, the famous "Johnson Treatment" (also noted in Chapter 9). Russell Baker of the *New York Times* described the treatment this way:

> It was a form of hypnosis by movement which seemed to leave the victim pliantly comatose. He might saunter up to his man and begin by seizing his lapels. Then the big hands would start, flashing around the fellow's ears and the Leader would lean into him, nose to nose, talking constantly, pounding fist into palm, kneading the victim's elbows, bobbing and weaving, withdrawing abruptly, then thrusting his face just as abruptly against the gentleman's own, forcing him to retreat in mental disarray.[39]

Johnson was succeeded by Senator Mike Mansfield of Montana, a gray personality, an indifferent and vacillating spokesman for the party. He knew nothing about how to make threats, stroke egos, flatter, coax, or appeal to partisanship or patriotism. He didn't consider that his business. Asked why so many of the Nixon-Ford vetoes could not be overridden by a Democratic-controlled Congress, Mansfield cheerfully replied, "Majorities without discipline are not majorities." He hastened to add that he would never attempt to exert discipline, "because the sense of independence each Senator has is very important. I don't know what reforms are needed, and I'm certainly not the one to get them through. That will be a matter of decades."[40] A good majority leader would never put off for the decades what he might accomplish

---

[37]Rowland Evans and Robert Novak, *Lyndon B. Johnson: The Exercise of Power* (New York: Times Mirror Co., New American Library, 1966), p. 101.

[38]Quoted in Alfred Steinberg, *Sam Johnson's Boy* (New York: Macmillan, 1968), p. 410.

[39]Quoted in Steinberg, p. 455. Other observers, especially Republicans, were not so admiring of the Johnson technique, nor so awed by its accomplishments. Senator George D. Aiken, a Vermont Republican, called Johnson "a strong-fingered man without finesse. . . . Lyndon would go around and try to change votes by pounding his forefinger into your chest and yelling at you, 'You better vote the other way.' If you got in bad with him, he punished you by never calling your bills off the Calendar." (Quoted in Steinberg, p. 456.)

[40]Quoted in the *Washington Post,* June 8, 1975.

this session. Under Mansfield, the Senate fell into a kind of genial anarchy. It was probably inevitable, however, for already the Senate establishment was beginning to decline—old age and changing times taking their toll—and Mansfield no longer had the power base that Johnson had in his day.

Mansfield's successor, Senator Robert Byrd of West Virginia, is a popular majority leader with his colleagues because he built his power base strictly by the quid pro quo technique, doing favors to develop followers. Donald R. Matthews describes the ways a majority leader could develop popularity:

> Does a senator want an office overlooking the Mall? Is he looking for an administrative assistant? Does he need to be out of town when an important roll call vote is likely to be taken? Does he desire a seat on the Foreign Relations Committee? Wish to make a four-hour speech next Thursday? . . . Does he need to get his pet bill passed in order to stand a chance for re-election? Or does he want to know what S. 123 would *really* do to his constituents? The leader can be of at least some help, and often of very great assistance, in grappling with questions of this sort. As a result, the leader is in an excellent position to know every member's problems, ambitions, and idiosyncracies. If the leader makes a firm commitment to be of aid, a senator can count on his battling to keep his word—and reminding the senator of the favor if it should ever be necessary to do so! [41]

The Committee Chairpersons

The importance of committee chairpersons depends upon the importance of their committees,[42] how firmly and adroitly they draw support from a majority of the members, and how good they are at guessing what bills will pass in the chamber.

Over the years there have been, occasionally, tyrannical chairmen, such as Charles Campbell, Chairman of the House Rules Committee from 1919 to 1928, who told his colleagues: "You can go to hell. It makes no difference what a majority of you decide. If it meets with my disapproval it shall not be done. I am the committee; in me reposes absolute obstructive power."[43] Today, the tyrannical chairman is no longer tolerated. Still, there are degrees of power; some chairmen dominate their committees by sheer intellect and will power, some dominate by default, and some fail to dominate in any significant way—and their committees drift.

The late Congressman Carl Vinson and the late Senator Richard B. Russell, both of Georgia and each for many years Chairman of his house's armed services committee, for example, had legendary power. They dominated the work of their committees, but this was no special credit to their own abilities. They were powerful because they embodied the majority sentiment on those committees, and, although they saw that massive amounts of defense money were spent in Georgia, they also saw that that their loyal supporters on the committee were liberally rewarded with defense contracts for their home states. The Vinson-Russell power was awesome only because it was solidly based on the committee majority's promilitary and proboondoggle bias.

Occasionally, power is drawn to chairmen because they are the acknowledged masters of the subject matter that comes before their committees. This kind of overpowering specialization is often found among House chairmen simply because they do not, like their Senate counterparts, disperse their time and attention among so many committees. But even on the Senate side, some chairmen have dominated through mastery of their subjects and through hard work. Senator Russell B. Long, for example, can manipulate the Finance Committee because he has studied the legislation that comes before it with more care than anyone else. Sen-

[41] Donald R. Matthews, *U.S. Senators and Their World* (New York: Random House, Vintage Books, 1960), p. 127.

[42] Some chairpersons forget that their power resides not in themselves, but in their positions. It is a dangerous thing to forget, as Congressman Wilbur D. Mills found out. When reporters asked Mills, who was Chairman of the Ways and Means Committee, if he didn't think his much-headlined escapade with a burlesque queen might be endangering his career, Mills replied: "This won't hurt me . . . nothing can hurt me." He found out he was wrong. He was forced out of his chairmanship. Devoid of position, he was also devoid of power. Stunned and baffled by his fall, Mills spent the rest of his career sitting around the House lobby, working crossword puzzles.

[43] Quoted in Bolling, *House Out of Order*, p. 39.

"Now, Baxter, you've got to get over these naive feelings of being discriminated against by your committee chairman. I'm sitting on a lot of bills—not just yours."

Drawing by Ed Fisher. Reprinted by permission of the Chicago Tribune-New York Daily News Syndicate.

ator Warren G. Magnuson, Chairman of the Appropriations Committee's Subcommittee on Health, Education and Welfare, held awesome control over the many billions of dollars processed through the panel because he took the time to master the details. Senator Norris Cotton, once the ranking Republican on that subcommittee, explained: "The other subcommittee members have too many obligations to get involved in all the details of the HEW appropriations. So Maggie [Magnuson] and I sit there day after day for months going over each item. The rest of the subcommittee will generally go along with our decisions."[44]

Seniority is the traditional ticket to the top. Once assigned to committees, members are never removed unless they want to be. Instead, they climb the long seniority ladder to the chair (unless, of course, they have aroused a great deal of opposition on the way up).

Recently, the seniority system in the House has been rocked by rebellions that resulted in the overthrow of a few chairmen.[45] Nevertheless, as a rule, the way a member becomes chairperson is

---

[44]Quoted in Gerald R. Rosen, "What Maggie Wants, Maggie Gets," *Dun's Review,* April 1972.

[45]In 1973, House Democrats adopted a plan whereby the whole Democratic caucus would vote for chairpersons by secret ballot; the nominees were to be supplied by a Steering and Policy Committee. As a result of this new system, in 1975 three southern chairpersons were replaced by younger liberals from the North.

by becoming the senior member of the majority party on the committee. This is especially true in the Senate, where only five times in the last 125 years have senior members been refused chairs.[46]

Those members of Congress who like to have their history neatly packaged say the seniority system was adopted by the Senate in 1846 and by the House in 1910.[47] Actually, the seniority system grew up in an uneven and evolutionary way. But those dates do figure prominently into that evolution. Before 1846, committee chairmen and committee members were chosen by secret ballot in the Senate; in 1846, both parties agreed to nominate committee chairmen and committee members in caucus, with the nominations routinely ratified by the Senate as a whole. The new method served the purpose of allowing party leaders tighter control over members. The leaders used the new system to introduce seniority as the basic method for selection. Since the Senate leaders usually had the most seniority, this put them in a good position; but it also gave them a method for organizing the committees to avoid even fiercer than ordinary feuding between northerners and southerners. They could excuse their choices by saying that seniority had taken the matter out of their hands. But as a matter of fact, the system had a built-in partiality, and, in 1859, a northern Democrat had good reason to complain that seniority "has operated to give to Senators from slave-holding states the chairmanship of every single committee that controls the public business of this government. There is not one exception."[48] The seniority system was submerged during the radical Republican domination of the Senate in the first decade after the Civil War, but, by the mid-1870s, it began to reemerge, and, by the 1890s, the selection of chairmen by seniority in the Senate was an ironclad rule.[49]

It would have been fruitless to have a seniority system in the House during most of the nineteenth century, for the turnover of the membership was great. When Henry Clay entered the House in 1811, the average tenure was only four years. Seniority meant nothing. The power levers were held by young men. Clay himself was only thirty-four when elected Speaker; the chairmen of committees at that time were no older.[50] From 1861 to 1881, every newly convened House had a majority of members serving their first terms. The voters in many congressional districts deliberately "passed around" the job in Washington, looking on it as a plum that should not be enjoyed by just one person. Gradually that attitude changed. And so did the House's attitude toward experience. The House, as an institution, developed the concept of seniority long before it was formalized. Toward the end of the nineteenth century there came to be a general feeling that the longer a member served on a committee, the more of an expert he became in its area of jurisdiction and the more he deserved to stay on that committee and be given increasing responsibilities. It was only a small mental step from that to the conclusion that the most senior majority party member of a committee had the *right* to its chair. Notwithstanding the evolution of this concept, the Speaker had a free hand in making committee assignments until the revolt against Speaker Cannon in 1910.

Many consider seniority to be probably the most deadening policy extant; it destroys the spirit of young, ambitious members by paying tribute to longevity, while ignoring the virtues of the mind and conscience. In short, it rewards members for simply staying alive long enough.[51]

---

[46]See Mark J. Green et al., *Who Runs Congress,* rev. ed. (New York: Bantam Books, 1972), p. 59.

[47]Wright Patman, *Our American Government and How It Works,* rev. ed. (New York: Barnes & Noble Books, 1974), p. 95.

[48]Quoted in *Congress and the Nation: 1946–1964* (Washington, D.C.: Congressional Quarterly Service, 1965), p. 1412.

[49]David J. Rothman, *Politics and Power: The United States Senate 1869–1901* (Cambridge, Mass.: Harvard University Press, 1966), p. 51.

[50]Sven Groennings and Jonathan P. Hawley, eds., *To Be a Congressman: The Promise and the Power* (Washington, D.C.: Acropolis Books, 1973), p. 125.

[51]Young members frequently become terribly impatient and critical of the way seniority protects the high priests of Congress. A typical outburst came from Congressman Anthony Toby Moffett of Connecticut: "Every day you can go into the Democratic cloak room [members' lounge], and maybe the Republican cloak room, too, and they'll be sitting there glassy-eyed watching 'Search for Tomorrow' or 'As the World Turns.' There's no way an industry could survive if it worked like the United States Congress. There's absolutely no way with that kind of tenure. It's literally tenure. They're like university professors, in a sense, because there is no way these people get removed." (Quoted in the *Washington Star,* October 29, 1975.)

The wait to rise to the top is staggering. Computer simulations predict that the average congressman who was newly elected in November, 1972, will have to wait forty-one years to chair the House Appropriations Committee. Or thirty-nine years to lead Armed Services, 37 years for Banking and Currency, 39 years for Public Works, or 38 years for Ways and Means. He or she will be 78 when enthroned on Rules, 76 on Appropriations. If you elect a new congressman today and are patient enough to wait until the year 2013, you, too, can enjoy the benefits of the seniority system. Unless, of course, you aren't around by then.[52]

For many years, the seniority system has contributed to the imbalance of regional power in Congress. Members who come from the safest states and districts—safest in the sense that they would rarely, if ever, receive any opposition from the other party in their election contests—naturally have the best chances to rise to the top, and for a long time the safest seats were in the South. As late as the Ninety-third Congress (1973–74), half of the standing committee (and all of the important ones) were chaired by southerners—an overwhelmingly lopsided regional influence over the nation's laws.

Moreover, with one exception, none of the southerners chairing important committees in either house was born, reared, or lived in a major urban area. The great majority of them had rural or small-town backgrounds; they were tuned to the agricultural and small merchant way of life. The problems of sidewalk crime, crowded slums, overloaded sewage systems, and all the other complex ailments of big-city life were things with which they had had no personal experience. They were nineteenth-century people leading a twentieth-century legislature.

Since 1974, the lineup of chairmen has suddenly begun to change radically, as a result of death, retirement, and defeat at the polls. More and more safe seats are being held by northern liberals and urban representatives at the same time as more and more southern seats have shifted hands, so that committees may in the future be led by politicians who reflect different regional and ideological balance.

The Committee System

There are twenty-two standing committees in the House, fifteen standing committees in the Senate, seven major joint committees (on which members of both houses serve), and more than two hundred subcommittees spreading out like a giant web beneath these. Standing committees are permanent panels that write and approve legislation; joint committees and select committees (the latter established to handle *ad hoc* problems, ranging from development of the Outer Continental Shelf to management of the House beauty shop) can only recommend solutions that *may* lead to legislation.

Congress's three major duties—legislation and appropriation, oversight, and investigation—are mostly handled in committees. (Much oversight is carried out by the government operations committees of both houses. Their duty is to see if programs passed by Congress are being developed by the executive branch as they should be.) The real work is done at the committee level; floor debate is simply a matter of the final threshing.

The First Congress (1789–91) not only could have easily read all 268 of the bills that it handled, it could almost have memorized them. These days, a typical Congress (in a two-year session) is likely to handle upwards of 20,000 bills. Some of these are essentially duplicates, of course, but, in any event, there are so many that they cannot be coped with, much less dealt with comprehendingly, except by proxy. That is, they are parcelled out to committees. Every committee—both in the Senate and the House—has supposedly developed its own expertise, which it usually subdivides into a number of specialized subcommittees.

By passing a bill, a committee, in effect, recommends its passage by the full House or Senate.[53] If the committee's recommendations are

---

[52]Green et al., *Who Runs Congress*, p. 62.

[53]Donald R. Matthews did a study of the Eighty-fourth Congress and found that if a proposal was supported by 80 percent or more of the committee members, it passed in the full house every time (thirty-five out of thirty-five); if 60 to 79 percent of a committee supported a proposal, it would pass 90 percent of the time; but if only 50 to 60 percent supported it—that is, if half or nearly half the committee opposed it—it would pass only 56 percent of the time. (Matthews, *U.S. Senators and Their World*, p. 170.)

rejected, it is not because members of the House or Senate know more about the legislation than the committee members, but only because a majority of the full chamber differs from the committee's majority in ideological persuasion or because the lobbies opposing the legislation have done their work well.

Which is not, however, to say that the committees always know what they are doing. On an appropriations committee, a taxation committee, or an armed services committee, the legislators cannot possibly absorb intelligently all the material they receive. They can only make intelligent suppositions and instinctive appraisals based on their overall knowledge of government and on their experience with past legislation.

The more candid members of these committees admit that they indulge in high-level guesswork. When the tax legislation emerged from the Senate Finance Committee in 1976, it was 1,536 pages long, thicker than a city telephone directory. Tax bills have become so massive, the procedures under which they are written are so haphazard, and the safeguards surrounding the process are so few and ineffective that no one, not even members of the committees responsible for studying the tax bills, knows what is in them.

An appropriations committee may have no more than four staff members attempting to analyze the Pentagon's $100 billion budget—a budget that was compiled by hundreds of experts (experts at hiding information as well as at divulging it). And since the committee (as well as members at large) depends on those four staff persons, all votes will be cast from a basic ignorance. This is why defense appropriations bills just breeze through, often with no more than one or two members raising any substantive questions during floor debate. It takes a certain amount of expertise and information to enable members to ask questions, and they seldom have enough of either.[54]

Members of the armed services committees have been known to vote approval for the production of weapons they were hearing about for the first time and about which they knew noth-

ing.[55] On the House Armed Services Committee, members are allowed only five minutes to cross-examine Pentagon witnesses. Five minutes is hardly enough time to ask a complicated question, much less get an answer.

Arnold R. Weber, who served as Associate Director of the Office of Management and Budget under President Nixon, speaks pitifully of the imbalance in the expertise battle between the executive and legislative branches:

> [Congress is] outgunned, outmanned and outmemoed almost consistently. This applies at the appropriations level and in many instances at the authorization committee level as well. I remember, without much satisfaction, going up to the Labor-HEW Subcommittee of the House Appropriations Committee with my phalanx of 15 budget experts and behind them 200 more down on M Street, to be confronted with three staff people assisting Chairman Flood. It was no contest.[56]

In view of how much work is done in committee, it matters a great deal to members what committees they get assigned to. In each chamber, there is a committee that makes the assignments.[57] Regional bias, economic bias, ideological preferences, district interests, expertise, just plain seniority, good fellowship—all sorts of elements go into the chemistry of selection. Does

---

[54]*Congressional Record*, H2101, March 22, 1973.

[55]Sometimes the impossibility of keeping up with the flood of information that pours over a major committee makes members, perhaps unfairly, seem stupid. J. Ronald Fox, formerly a top official with the Pentagon, illustrates this with a vignette from a 1971 House Armed Service Committee hearing: "Under discussion was the AH-1G Cobra helicopter program. In the five years preceding 1971, this committee had authorized several hundred million dollars for the Army to purchase Cobra helicopters from Bell Aircraft Company. Well in advance of the 1971 hearings, the Army had provided the committee with several pages of pictures and descriptive material on the Cobra. During the hearings, however, one Congressman appeared confused by the budget request. After indicating that he did not understand the discussion, he finally asked, 'What is a Cobra?' " (*Arming America: How the U.S. Buys Weapons*, Cambridge, Mass.: Harvard University Press, 1974, p. 125.)

[56]Hearings of the Select Committee on Committee Organization in the House, Vol. 2, part 3 (1973): 396.

[57]Republicans are assigned by a Committee on Committees in each house. Democrats in the Senate are assigned by the Democratic Steering Committee. House Democrats, until the mid-1970s, got their assignments from Democratic members of the Ways and Means Committee; now the assignments are given by the Democratic Steering and Policy Committee.

a very popular member need to transfer to a more prestigious committee in order to win re-election? Then his or her popularity and needs may influence the assigners. Friendships made in the Capitol gym or on the cocktail circuit have their impact on the selection process. Intelligence, all other things being equal, will count; if a member is known for stupidity, no amount of after-hours charm is going to make him or her welcome on one of the tougher committees.

The assigning committee is influenced to a significant degree by the wishes of the leadership, by the wishes of the committee chairpersons, by the pressures from state delegations, and by tradition. Efforts are usually made not to disrupt the prevailing atmosphere of particular committees. For years the agriculture committees have been run overwhelmingly by members from the cotton and wheat states. Since the wide-open spaces in the United States are closely linked to the affairs of the Interior Department and its Bureau of Reclamation, members from the West have traditionally dominated the interior committees in both houses. There is considerable logic in this kind of appointment, but it also makes for committees easily dominated by special interests.[58]

These constituency-oriented committees are often geographically imbalanced, and committees that specialize in particular issues, like Education and Labor, are often ideologically imbalanced. But the committees that serve the more general interests—like Ways and Means (concerned with taxation policy) and Appropriations (concerned with funding)[59]—are carefully representative of the House as a whole. And because the House is basically conservative, these committees are basically conservative, too. Richard Fenno made a study of the House Appropriations Committee in the 1960s and concluded that it was a very stable social system, where newcomers quickly learn to temper individuality and

imaginative spending concepts to the panel's prevailing staidness.[60] But that condition began to change slightly in the mid-1970s. Previously, and for many years, the work of the Appropriations Committee was tightly controlled by the chairman and his "college of cardinals"—the nickname for the chairmen of the thirteen appropriations subcommittees. Because the crucial decisions were made in subcommittee, the chairman of the full committee assigned himself and senior members who saw eye-to-eye with him on spending matters to chair the subcommittees that handled the most sensitive and important spending bills. At the subcommittee level, the chairman and ranking minority member constituted the dominant force. They worked things out quietly together. The result was that a very small clique made the basic spending decisions for Congress. As one intimate observer described the situation in 1972:

> These subcommittees are much like small private clubs, where the initiates do not overpresume. Party lines mean very little; any division is more likely to reflect liberal-conservative or urban-rural distinctions. The senior members lay out the plan. Adjustments are made to accommodate members of middle seniority, considerably fewer for their juniors.
>
> Once this House subcommittee bill is prepared, something approaching 90 percent of the basic decisions have been reached. The full House Appropriations Committee makes few changes as each subcommittee defers to the others' autonomy and expertise; indeed, it is almost regarded as bad manners to question subcommittee decisions. In general, the full House follows this policy of respect. Floor amendments to appropriations bills are voted, and occasionally there is a pitched battle over one or more items, but relatively few changes are made altogether.[61]

But in 1973, the very next year after that was written, reformers pressed new rules on the House that altered the operation of all committees, including Appropriations. For one thing, it

[58]Groennings and Hawley, eds., *To Be a Congressman*, pp. 109–20.

[59]Here it should be made clear that committees that write legislation and those that appropriate the funds for programs are distinctly different. When Congress passes legislation for things like education, jobs, housing, environment, it is only *authorized* at that point. It is up to the appropriations committees to decide how much money the programs will have.

[60]Richard Fenno, "The House Appropriations Committee as a Political System," in Raymond E. Wolfinger, ed., *Readings in American Political Behavior*, 2nd ed. (Englewood Cliffs, N.J.: Prentice-Hall, 1976), pp. 44–45.

[61]Weaver, *Both Your Houses*, pp. 255–56.

Representative Al Ullmann (center), House Ways and Means Committee Chairman, confers with committee members during a House vote, 1977

was ruled that no House member could chair more than one subcommittee. This broke the iron grip on subcommittee power held by senior conservatives and opened the way to junior members who had never before even come close to holding power. Another new rule took away the subcommittee assignment powers from the full committee chairman and gave them to the Democratic Steering and Policy Committee and the Democratic caucus—groups that represent all Democratic members in the House. Consequently, a few more economic liberals were appointed to the Appropriations Committee. But the results have not been radical. In general the entrenched and self-perpetuating staidness that

Fenno noticed a decade earlier has continued. The triumphs of reformers were not overwhelming. They were pleased, for example, that the 1976 defense appropriations bill was debated by the full committee for one full day, instead of breezing through with a few perfunctory comments as would have happened in earlier years. That was considered quite a change—one day's discussion for a $100 billion budget.[62]

A similar self-perpetuating structure characterizes the powerful House Ways and Means

---

[62]*Inside Congress* (Washington, D.C. Congressional Quarterly Service, 1976), p. 106.

Committee, which originates all taxation policy for both houses and is also responsible in the House for allocating retirement, medical, and welfare benefits. The power of this committee is such that not only do few people leave it, but those who want to get on it usually must have some seniority in Congress. The result is that in this committee, as Gary Orfield notes, "the time lag before changes in the political parties are reflected . . . is probably the greatest in Congress."[63] For example, nearly two decades after President Harry S Truman first proposed national medical insurance, and well after the public demonstrated its desire for it, the committee managed—by a one-vote margin—to get the bill onto the floor.[64]

Even so, it should be pointed out that there is a limit to Ways and Means' autocracy. In some respects, it must be especially sensitive to House wishes, for its bills usually go onto the floor by way of a procedure known as closed rule—that is, they have to be voted either up or down; they cannot be amended. Since committee prestige depends on how successful its bills are on the floor, it is in the interest of the members of Ways and Means to draw up acceptable legislation.

The Senate committee system does not dominate the decision-making process to any comparable degree. For one thing, the aura of expertise does not hang over Senate committees as it does over House committees. Senators spread themselves much thinner and do not have the time to develop the kind of intense specialization that some House members have. The typical House member sits on only two committees— one of primary importance and one of secondary importance—and on four subcommittees. (House members who sit on either Rules, Ways and Means, or Appropriations—the most demanding committees of all—ordinarily receive no other assignment.) In the Senate, the field for a typical member is twice that broad; it is not unusual for a member of moderate seniority to sit on two committees of primary importance and two or three committees of secondary importance, as well as on half a dozen subcommittees.

The achievements of a committee depend to a great extent on the goals it sets for itself at the start of a session and the extent to which it develops unity of support for those goals among its members. Stanley Bach, an analyst for the Congressional Research Service of the Library of Congress, interviewed the members and staffs of six House and Senate committees to learn their approach to agenda-setting. He found the two extremes to be in the House Interstate and Foreign Commerce Committee and its counterpart in the Senate, the Senate Commerce Committee. The other committees fell in between. Bach's report:

> In the House Commerce Committee, power has come to reside increasingly at the *subcommittee* level, until it has reached a point where, according to top committee staff, "No attempt is made at the full committee level to define a legislative program for the committee." Each subcommittee plans its own agenda. Subcommittee staff members may meet informally with staff from the full committee and/or other subcommittees, and they occasionally do. However, there is no formal mechanism to require (or even to encourage) coordination and discussion among subcommittees, despite the fact that their jurisdictions clearly interrelate, and indeed in some cases, overlap. The general tenor of the relationships among subcommittees is one of competition rather than cooperation.
>
> In contrast, the Senate Commerce Committee undertakes a highly structured and integrated effort to define the goals of the full committee and to set its agenda for the coming session. All activities of the subcommittees are considered as part of this process. This procedure is possible because the Senate Commerce Committee operates through an integrated staff, with all staff hired by and answerable to the chairman of the full committee, despite the fact that many staffers are assigned responsibilities relating exclusively to one or more subcommittees. Because all subcommittees and the full committee rely on a single staff, all must participate in the coordinated planning effort if they are to receive staff support for their agenda items.
>
> The procedure followed by the Senate Commerce Committee is as follows: Three to four months before the start of a new session, all legis-

---

[63]Gary Orfield, *Congressional Power: Congress and Social Change* (New York: Harcourt Brace Jovanovich, 1975), p. 273.

[64]See John F. Manley, *The Politics of Finance: The House Committee on Ways and Means* (Boston: Little, Brown and Co., 1975), pp. 27–29, 36–38.

lative staff members are asked to submit proposed agendas for the new session, including new initiatives, oversight, and crucial legislation in their areas of responsibility. The full staff then meets in retreat (away from Washington, D.C.) for an intensive discussion of these staff reports. At this time, when the committee's priorities are being set, the staff may also seek the advice of outside experts who have analyzed various issues which the staff is considering or who believe the committee should take an active interest in certain "emerging" issues. The result of this process is a so-called "goals letter" which is published in report form and made available to the public. This document guides the committee in its activities for the coming session. . . .

A structured, deliberate procedure for identifying issues, setting goals, and planning the committee's agenda such as that adopted by the Senate Commerce Committee would go a long way toward putting greater direction and rationality into the activities of other congressional committees. That is not to say, however, that the recent movement toward reducing the autocratic power of full committee chairmen and encouraging more active participation in legislative activity by a wider range of members should be reversed. Rather, the Senate Commerce Committee model could be adopted by chairmen at the subcommittee level to improve planning for their subcommittee activities.[65]

Committee System Reforms

As noted earlier, the 1970s have seen dramatic changes made in Congress's committee system—for the first time in three decades. Freshmen were in revolt. Between 1975 and 1977, the House saw an influx of 159 new members, and the Senate 30. In 1976 alone, 18 freshman senators were sworn in—the highest turnover in that body in two decades. The newcomers brought with them a restless impatience with tradition—particularly tradition that was so obviously inefficient and organizationally undemocratic. The newcomers became the voice of protest in party caucuses.

Prior to 1970, the House Democrats caucused only once every two years. Now they began meeting monthly. House caucuses used to go through their organizational elections by rote; now the members took an intense interest in everything and challenged the leadership at every turn. Previously, members of Congress took for granted that some committee chairpersons would abuse their power. Now the caucus was ready to stand up to them. In January 1973, the House Democratic caucus dumped three crusty old barons—W. R. Poage of Agriculture, F. Edward Hebert of Armed Services, and Wright Patman of Banking—because a majority of the Democrats felt they had become excessively highhanded.

House newcomers, who had provided the leverage for that revolt, made no secret of their willingness to do the same thing to any other overbearing chairmen. Said House Majority Leader James C. Wright:

> The day is ended when any committee chairman can run his domain like a feudal barony, oblivious to the wishes and sensitivities of other members. All now have been put on notice that their colleagues will hold them accountable for their stewardship. The office of committee chairman must now be regarded no longer as a right but a privilege, a gift of opportunity bestowed by one's peers, and those who give also can take away.[66]

In the Senate, reform was made more cautiously. It did agree in 1975 to allow the election of committee chairpersons by secret ballot if one-fifth of the caucus so desired. But the freshmen did not only want to make those in power mind their manners, they also demanded a greater share of the power. They wanted subcommittee chairs and a louder voice in the decision-making process in committee. These demands were heard as much in the Senate as in the House.

In 1977, the Senate managed to get through some committee reform. It adopted a plan to reduce the number of Senate committees by one-fifth, the number of subcommittee assignments for the average senator by one-third, and the number of chairs accumulated by some senior members by one-half. Jurisdictions of the surviving committees were broadened, so that, for the

[65]Stanley Bach, "Policy Making in the House of Representatives," in Advisory Committee on National Growth Policy Processes to the National Commission on Supplies and Shortages, *Forging America's Future: Strategies for National Growth and Development* (Washington, D.C.: U.S. Government Printing Office, 1976), Appendix, Vol. 2.

[66]Quoted in the *New York Times*, March 20, 1977.

first time, committee descriptions and Senate rules took formal note of such concepts as transportation, energy research, environmental protection, international economic policy, consumer protection, government information, intergovernmental relations, and revenue-sharing. For example, energy issues, which formerly had been scattered over seven different committees, were combined in a new Committee on Energy and Natural Resources.[67] These changes opened chairs for junior members. Indeed nearly every one of the sixty-two Democrats wound up holding a subcommittee chair. Senators who had just been sworn in for the first time suddenly found a gavel being thrust into their hands, and they were officially part of management.

In the House, even more far-reaching changes were made. Prior to 1973, a House committee chairman generally had great leeway in naming the chairmen of his subcommittees, in assigning members to subcommittees, in giving or withholding money from subcommittees to hire staffs, and in deciding which subcommittee would handle which pieces of legislation. In short, he could send bills to subcommittees whose membership he had stacked and who would treat them the way he wanted them treated. On some committees, the subcommittees did not even have names, but merely numbers.

But, in 1973, the Democratic caucus passed the Subcommittee Bill of Rights, which freed the subcommittees of such manipulations. The Bill of Rights required that all subcommittees have fixed jurisdictions and that all legislation would be referred to subcommittees of appropriate jurisdiction within two weeks. The Bill of Rights took the assigning powers away from the committee chairperson and gave them to the committee caucus of Democratic members. Thereafter, no House member could chair more than one legislative subcommittee—thus opening up many chairs to younger members—and no member could sit on more than two of a committee's subcommittees.

Also prior to 1973, the House Ways and Means Committee had had no subcommittees at all; for sixteen years its business had been tightly orchestrated by Chairman Wilbur Mills, who dictated that all bills be handled first and last by the full committee. The Subcommittee Bill of Rights ordered all committees of more than twenty members to set up at least four subcommittees. In addition, it stipulated that committees must have written rules, and it authorized subcommittees to have their own staffs.

Had nirvana arrived? As with all changes in a mechanism as complicated as Congress, even greater democracy must receive only a cautious welcome until it has been tested. "A word of caution is in order," warns Robert L. Peabody, for if party leaders had difficulty wangling a coordinated program out of a score of powerful committee chairmen in the old days, they may discover that they are faced with even more difficulty in trying to effect party coordination from more than a hundred subcommittee chairpersons intoxicated with their new powers.[68] On the other hand, some observers warn that shaking up the old system will not sufficiently reform it unless a method is discovered for shaking it up constantly. Some have proposed that committee memberships and chairs be rotated so that members will not get cozy with the special interests that cluster around those committees whose decisions affect them directly. On this point, Roger H. Davidson argues that rotation "would ensure a steady inflow of young tigers on each committee. . . . Often, the long term veteran has lost the critical capacity or the creative edge which would allow him to bring an extra dimension of leadership to his post."[69]

Still untouched by reform, however, is one of the most pervasive problems of committee work: the abundance of it—the abundance of the information that results from it and the overwhelming task of attempting to let members (not to mention the press and public) know what is going on. The proliferation of subcommittees has compounded the problem. It is accurately

[67]David Broder, *International Herald Tribune*, February 15, 1977.

[68]Robert L. Peabody, *The Leadership Perspective* (Annals of the American Academy of Political and Social Sciences) 411 (January 1974): 139–40.

[69]Roger H. Davidson, *The Leadership Perspective* (Annals of the American Academy of Political and Social Sciences) 411 (January 1974): 58.

described by Walter Pincus: "Almost every sub-committee, to justify its existence, churns out reports or legislation which clog the mails and the floor calendar and accomplish little except to send Congress off in hundreds of different directions."[70] In the Senate, where there are fewer members to man the dike (and, therefore, the threat of flood is always imminent), a typical year—1975—saw committees and subcommittees holding 2,734 meetings to take testimony from more than eight thousand witnesses.[71] From these hearings came records and reports filling more than half a million printed pages. It was virtually impossible for a member to digest even the most important material relating to the problems he or she was personally most interested in.

Congress has yet to discover a method—perhaps some computerized digest—to bring committee data under control and disseminate it in such a way that will allow the whole body to legislate more intelligently.

Procedures on the Floor

Congress does most of its work in committees, but it gives most of its "performances" before the full House or Senate. That is the theatrical stage. Until recent years, the chambers of the House and the Senate were the scenes of some truly eloquent, and often heated, debates. To be sure, not many members became so exercised as Congressman Stephen A. Douglas, of whom John Quincy Adams wrote, "In the midst of his roaring, to save himself from choking, he stripped off and cast away his cravat, and unbuttoned his waistcoat, and had the air and aspect of a half-naked pugilist."[72] The florid style has not been popular for several generations. But modern Congresses have boasted members—senators like Wayne Morse, Everett Dirksen, Paul Douglas, Hubert Humphrey, and Edward Kennedy—who could, in their specialty fields, marshal mountains of data as deftly, and could offer

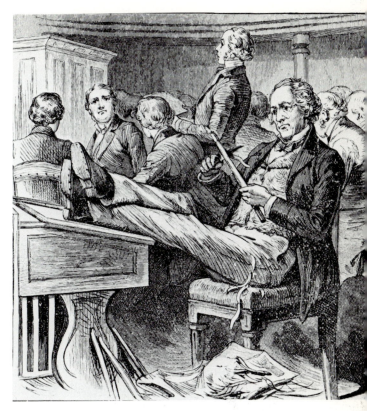

Sam Houston whittling in the Senate

it as persuasively, as any of the illustrious orators of the nineteenth century. By the 1970s, the atmosphere of the toga and the debating club was long gone, and the change was especially evident in the Senate. Nearing the end of his long career, Senator J. William Fulbright could accurately complain, "The Senate has deteriorated to a point where nobody listens to debate. . . . It is the rarest thing to have a dialogue or a debate on the floor of the Senate, as we did in the old days." Now, as David E. Rosenbaum accurately reported,

> Debates on the floor normally consist of little more than one Senator reading a prepared statement to a nearly empty chamber, or two or three Senators engaging in what is known in senatorial parlance as a 'colloquy.' . . . The cajoling and horsetrading that precede important votes take place in private conversations in the cloak rooms or in whispered huddles during quorum calls on the floor.[73]

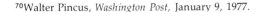

[70]Walter Pincus, *Washington Post*, January 9, 1977.

[71]*Washington Star*, December 19, 1976.

[72]Quoted in Josephy, *The American Heritage History of Congress of the United States*, p. 215.

[73]Sources: J. William Fulbright, *Progressive*, January 1973; David E. Rosenbaum, *New York Times*, January 25, 1976.

As a rule, members avoid going to the chamber if at all possible. They consider their committee work and their constituent work far more important, as indeed it usually is. But it is sometimes possible to attract great flapping flocks of federal politicians to a debate, given the right motivation. When the issue was whether or not to grant themselves a $12,500 annual pay raise, Senator James B. Allen of Alabama took the floor to oppose the proposal and observe wryly:

> The other day, when the war powers bill was being considered, there were exactly three senators on the floor discussing this extremely important matter. I recall that on many of the end-the-war amendments an attendance of four to six senators was a pretty good turnout. We have passed multibillion-dollar appropriation bills with only four or five senators on the floor. But this afternoon we have around 75 senators in attendance.[74]

Although Congress operates on an almost year-round basis, senators spend an average of only 1,200 hours on the floor each year, and Representatives only 770 hours. Many of these hours are consumed in quorum calls and roll calls, so the time remaining for debate becomes dear indeed—and it cannot be hogged. In the House, where 435 members divide the time, it must be treated with special thriftiness. Debate is limited; usually the limits for a debate are from 4 to 8 hours, with the time divided equally between the two political parties. This usually means no member gets more than 5 minutes.

In the Senate, where only one hundred members divide the time, it is treated much more generously. Any senator can speak as long as he likes, or almost. This permissiveness is sometimes abused. If a senator or minority group of senators want to prevent a bill from coming up for a vote, they can launch a marathon talk—that is, they can try to talk it to death. This is the *filibuster*. The filibuster record belongs to Senator Strom Thurmond of South Carolina, who once held the floor for twenty-four hours and eighteen minutes.

Shutting off a filibuster (called *cloture*) requires a three-fifths vote of the entire membership. Before 1975, a two-thirds vote was required, and, since it was very difficult to get that many votes for cloture, it was achieved only four times prior to 1960. Cloture was used in 1964 in the civil rights debate only after the bill had been discussed for sixty-eight consecutive days—days filled with 6 million spoken words.[75] Reformers hope to eventually change the required vote for cloture to a simple majority.

The *Congressional Record,* which costs some $7 million annually to print, is supposed to be a record of transactions on the floor of both houses, but in one respect—insofar as the *Record* conveys the impression that the "speaker" was actually on hand and actually spoke the words that are printed—a significant share of its millions of words each session is fraudulent. Sixteen secretaries, working in ten-minute shifts, constantly note what is said in the Senate and House. Within thirty minutes, their notes are transcribed and available to the members for "correction." Originally this rule was simply to allow the members to pretty-up their grammar and correct any obvious errors of fact that slipped into their speeches via a subconscious lapse. But for many years, members have abused the rule by editing out massive sections of what they said and inserting long "phantom speeches," which make it appear that they were present during a debate, when in fact they were off at a cocktail party or playing handball.

History as a mirage reached a peak of some sort on July 2, 1970, when the *Congressional Record* ran to 112 pages. The Senate had met for only eight seconds on that day, the House had convened not at all. All the speeches and debate that allegedly took place on that day were actually cranked out of congressional staff workers' typewriters and sent directly to the *Congressional Record*'s printer. A "speech" by Congressman Hale Boggs appeared in the *Record* two days after he was killed in a plane crash.[76]

The Senate, stung by years of ridicule and complaint from the press, decided late in 1977 that speeches that were inserted into the *Record* by its members but not actually spoken on the

---

[74]Quoted in *Human Events*, September 29, 1973.

---

[75]Wright, *You and Your Congressman*, p. 163.

[76]Sources: *Parade*, August 20, 1972; *Congressional Record*, H3404, April 29, 1975.

floor would be denoted by a "bullet"—a large black dot. The House, however, declined to go along with that reform, and both Senate and House continue to permit members to clean up, edit, and omit statements that had been made on the floor. Thus, while many things that didn't take place have been going into the *Record*, some fascinating things that did occur have been, and will continue to be, taken out. When Senator Abraham Ribicoff of Connecticut told Senator Jacob Javits of New York, "I don't think you have the guts" to pass a particular school integration bill, his appraisal of Javits's courage was removed before the *Record* went to the printers.[77] Senator Henry M. Jackson said to Senator Mike Gravel, "You have no honor or decency," but it

came out in the *Record*, "This is a question of honor and decency."[78]

It is Congress's own quaint kind of gentility. Emotions are masked behind ritual words—"the gentleman," or "my distinguished colleague"— that permits real loathing to pass for politeness, as in this exchange between ideological foes:

> MR. GROSS: Does the gentleman not think this is a most irregular procedure?
>
> MR. ECKHARDT: No, the gentleman does not think so. The gentleman thinks it is an excellent procedure, because otherwise we would have to take up each single amendment—75 of them—separately, but the gentleman has absolute notice of precisely what the committee will urge in the substitute, because it is identical with what the gentleman has read.

[77]Weaver, *Both Your Houses*, p. 21.

[78]*Congressional Record*, S17756 October 1, 1976.

MR. GROSS: If the gentleman will yield further, I think this is probably one of the worst exhibitions of legislative insanity. . . .[79]

There are still other occasions when things are not as they seem on the floor of the Congress. Neither the House nor the Senate is supposed to transact certain business unless an agreed-on number of members—a quorum—is present. After all, there's no use talking to an empty house. Several times during a typical day of debate, a member will raise a point of order as to whether or not a quorum is present. When that is done, the clerk must call the roll. This takes quite a bit of time. Is the quorum call always necessary? Not at all. Often it is a ploy. Many times two members will get together and say, "Let us have a quorum call so that we can go have something to eat." Sometimes one member will interrupt a speech by another member whom he does not like and demand a quorum call—thus shattering the tempo and continuity of the enemy's line of argument.[80] So, when the *Congressional Record* shows that several hundred members answered a quorum call in the House of Representatives, this does not necessarily mean they stuck around to hear the debate that followed. More often, they leave as soon as they have answered to the roll call. "It is a farce," in the judgment of former Congressman Chet Holifield. "When we have a quorum call, and 387 answer the call, say, it conveys the impression that they are here on the floor doing business,"[81] when in fact they flee back to their offices or to the congressional gymnasium or to a bar or cafe. They leave the chamber, in the description of one newspaper reporter,

> like the inside of a giant SST passenger jet making its second transatlantic crossing—following the unfortunate crash of the plane's maiden flight a week earlier. . . . As soon as the real debate began everybody left the House floor in order to allow the debaters to address an empty chamber. Voices droned lifelessly in the empty pit. It was soporific enough to put a hen to sleep. . . . By count, 35

congresspersons sat dismally still, glancing neither left nor right, staring into the void.[82]

Congressional Aides

Columnist Tom Braden, an old-time Washington-watcher, once predicted:

> Someday a U.S. congressman will vanish from this town and nobody will know it. The congressman will still deliver speeches for the Congressional Record; he will still be quoted on the evening news; his mail will be answered, his views made known, his legislation introduced and his coffee poured. But he will be gone, laughing from a gazebo on the Rhone or testing the waters off the Bahamas.
>
> It could happen . . . and the Fifth Estate [the congressional aides] is what makes such a happening quite possible. . . .[83]

Braden was making a very serious point about the power of the top members of the congressional staffs.

The old complaint attributed to Czar Nicholas I—"Not I but 10,000 clerks rule Russia"—could be adapted to this country and restated by the czars of Capitol Hill, most of whom are critically dependent on their hirelings, persons who are unknown to the general public. When Michael Pertschuk, who had been chief counsel of the Senate Commerce Committee for twelve years, was nominated to be Chairman of the Federal Trade Commission, it probably came as a surprise to newspaper readers that Pertschuk "has been accused by critics of being the person who really runs the Commerce Committee," not Commerce Committee Chairman Warren Magnuson.

Some see that kind of anonymous power as the rule rather than the exception. Senator Robert Morgan of North Carolina takes the most extreme view:

> This country is basically run by the legislative staffs of the members of the Senate and members of the House of Representatives. We ought to have the best staffs available that we can find anywhere, because they are the ones who give us advice as to

[79]*Congressional Record,* H11174, December 12, 1973.

[80]John H. Dent in the *Congressional Record,* H2732, April 9, 1974.

[81]*Congressional Record,* H2737, April 9, 1974.

[82]Tom Dowling, *Washington Star,* October 11, 1973.

[83]Tom Braden, *Washington Post,* March 20, 1976.

The Congressional Aide

There is one person who can be more threatening to a political marriage than a mistress, more of a rival to a political wife than the most doggedly devoted secretary. This person's role is symbiotic and complex—surrogate wife, alter ego, fueler of the narcissism endemic to a politician's life and zealous devotee to the one thing the politician reveres most: himself. I am referring to the male aide.

In elective politics, where personality is so exalted (principles, issues, ideas, values are all personalized and exemplified through the most popular vote getter), it is not only the President who is considered royalty. Every congressman, senator, governor, or mayor is cosseted by a staff of "handmaidens and foot rubbers," as one former senator's aide put it, whose excellence at this art reach paramedical proportions. Like satellites around a sun, they revolve, twirling, hopefully, into their own special orbits. For one who is—or wants to be—a most valued political aide, it is in his own special interest to make his boss look good; his tenure is measured by his ability to perform one or more of a variety of functions in the pursuit of that aim—from getting good press, writing the most effective speech or the best piece of legislation, offering the best political advice, running the best campaign, being an alert tactician and master organizer, on down to reinforcing the candidate on how well he's doing, brushing the dandruff off his shoulders before he makes a speech, covering and sometimes pimping for him and his sex partners.

Aides do not serve a company or a newspaper or a law firm; they serve one person and, therefore, the Hill is a more modest version of what happens in the White House. Politicians tend to be surrounded by sycophants and hangers-on; the insecurity fosters, as one political consultant said, "a lot of ass kissing." An aide, no matter how capable, often finds himself vying in a natural rivalry for his boss's time and attention. Jealousy and hostility among the staff and, often, between the aide and the wife, are the result.

"Let's face it," said one wife whose husband ran for national office, "during a campaign they actually hate the wife and the children or any person who might take him away from their twenty-four-hour goal of getting him reelected. They want to get him elected, so they can have a job." . . .

The relationship [between aides and members of Congress] has its peculiarities. More than one former aide described the union as "man-child" or "master-servant," which reminds me of a conversation in a cab I shared with two men going to the Hill. They were young and obviously trying to impress one another as much as me and the cabdriver. They discussed a couple of pending bills, as knowledgeable insiders, you understand, and then one asked the other, "What does your man do? What committees is he on?" You would have thought you were listening to two English valets. . . .

From Myra MacPherson, *The Power Lovers* (New York: G. P. Putnam's Sons, 1975). Reprinted by permission.

---

how to vote, and then we vote on their recommendations.[84]

One must be careful about exaggerating the staffs' importance in the congressional scheme of things. There are, among the 18,000 staff people working for Congress and its committees, plenty of deadheads. But the savviest are very savvy indeed, and they virtually become the members' proxies. These trusted administrative assistants, legislative assistants, press aides, staff counsels, and staff economists are there, when needed, to handle the legislation, make the deals, listen to the lobbyists, advise their bosses how to vote, keep the back-home political pipes flushed out, think up ways to get their bosses' names in print, determine what mail the members actually see and what they do not see, and determine who gets to see the members and who must settle for a conversation with a flunky. They rewrite the *Congressional Record* to make their employers sound coherent. They write the immortal speeches, the magazine articles, and the books

[84]Description of Michael Pertschuk in the *Washington Post*, February 21, 1977; Robert Morgan, *Washington Post*, June 5, 1977.

that carry their bosses' names (Senator William Proxmire once remarked, "I was reading a book the other night. . . ." and then decided that that was not quite the way to speak of a work he was supposed to have written).

How else can a senator from a major state operate? New York's Jacob Javits sits on five committees and half a dozen subcommittees. He may be confronted with four hearings in a single morning, some going on at the same time. He makes the best of an impossible situation by assigning an aide to each of the hearings to keep tabs. When Javits arrives, the staff worker greets him with a fast summary of what's been done. Javits tries to push in a question out of turn, to make the record reflect his presence, then he is off to the next meeting. Sometimes he won't attend a committee meeting at all but will depend on an aide's summary of what happened. Meanwhile, the morning mail has brought a thousand or so letters from constituents; political queries are coming in by phone from New York; and he has yet to review what he's going to say on the Senate floor. But Javits will be saved by his faithful retainers.

Members delegate not only much of their routine committee work to staff members, but also much of their more sensitive endeavors, such as investigations. The show is, once again, deceptive. Outwardly, the public sees the big-name politicians going after the crooked defense contractors, the profiteering oil companies, the unsafe drug and food concerns, the compromised bureaucrats. But, in fact, the skills and the muscle—and often the original plans—that lead to investigative success come almost entirely from the staffs. This is true on both sides of Congress, but it is especially true in the Senate, where each member's time is stretched much thinner over a multiplicity of committees. Senators are too busy working on the surface of things to stop and dig.[85]

The intimate relationship between staff members and politicians can best be explained by those who served. Listen to Stewart McClure, one of the Senate's experienced aides:

> When you see an aide mumbling something over the shoulder of his Senator at a hearing, the range of the coaching can be infinite. . . . When the staff guy leans in, he's likely to be saying, "That sure would work hell in Phoenix," or "The White House is hot for that." He's got to know the political input, what the lobbies are saying, what the constituent reaction is liable to be—as well as the content of bills.

And when the lawmakers go to the chamber to do rhetorical battle, indispensable aides will be there, too. McClure recalls the drill:

> You're sitting there on a stool beside the Senator during debate and boy, oh boy, sometimes they won't listen to you and they make an ass of themselves and you have to fix up the Record. And after you fix your Senator's mistakes, you may have to call the staff of the other Senator and say, "How about changing your guy to saying something else so my guy will make sense?" You're not supposed to correct the contents of the Record, but we do— it's better than having the wrong thing in there because the courts use it for guidance.
>
> Maybe the Senator has been to lunch with a constituent and he's come in late and he hasn't seen the bill for six months, and you have to fill him in fast. Whether he listens depends on whether he has confidence in you or wants to play god. Usually everything is moving so fast in debate, he has to trust you. You just say, "Look here" and stick the information in front of him and brief him in a phrase, and he catches on and goes boom, boom, boom.
>
> These guys are smart. They catch on fast. Maybe there aren't as many experts as there used to be— Bob Taft used to read the Treasury's report at 7 o'clock every morning, and that kind of expertise seems to be losing ground—but all of the members are smart just by osmosis. It's almost impossible not to know a lot around here.[86]

There are obvious dangers in entrusting so much of the nation's legislative life to these hidden, faceless, and (to most of the public) nameless staff members. They are, after all, not elected.

---

[85]One unique exception to that rule was Senator Frank E. Moss of Utah, who led an investigation into Medicaid abuses by dressing up in old work clothes and visiting doctors to see to what extent they gave phony examinations and needless prescriptions.

---

[86]John L. McClellan and Stewart McClure are quoted in Robert Sherrill, "How to Succeed on the Potomac: Be an Investigator," *New York Times Magazine,* October 8, 1967.

THE WORK OF CONGRESS

Members of Congress are always quick to point out that they work harder than did their legislative grandfathers. Go back half a century, around World War I, and you will find Congress meeting four or five months a year. The typical representative would receive a couple of dozen letters a week. Rarely did constituents visit their federal politicians. Today, Congress is in session ten or eleven months a year, and demands have increased proportionately. From 1970 to 1976, the number of House committee meetings doubled, while the amount of mail received by the House tripled to 42 million pieces a year, and visits from constituents more than doubled.[87]

Writing in 1960 of the changes he had seen during his lifetime in Congress, former Speaker of the House Joseph W. Martin, Jr., recalled that in the 1920s the House Foreign Affairs Committee spent an entire week debating one, and only one, topic—

> the question of authorizing a $20,000 appropriation for an international poultry show in Tulsa. This item, which was finally approved, was about the most important issue that came before the committee the whole session. From one end of a session to another Congress would scarcely have three or four issues of consequence besides appropriation bills. . . .[88]

Today so many bills come flooding out of committee that they hit the floor in a tidal wave and members vote on them in utter confusion. Sometimes the confusion is so great, in fact, that members won't know what they passed until they read about it much later—perhaps when the new law is printed in the *Congressional Record* for their education, or perhaps when newspaper reporters dig into the new laws and discover the skeletons. Some sympathy must be reserved for the legislators. How could the average member know, for example, that tucked about a third of the way inside the 1,536 page tax bill that reached the Senate floor in 1976 was an item that would have added a single, ninety-six word sentence to the Internal Revenue Code—a sentence that was designed to save the major oil companies an estimated $400 million over the next decade? Tax bills, like much other legislation, are simply so complicated that once they emerge from committee they must be taken on faith, or the legislative machine will come to a halt.[89]

And legislating is only one of several functions Congress performs. The Constitution requires members of the Senate to approve presidential appointments of ambassadors, federal justices, and cabinet officials and to approve treaties. The whole Congress exercises oversight over the executive branch by means of hearings and investigations. And by custom and electoral necessity, members of Congress spend a great deal of time serving their constituents.

Legislating: The Origin, Route, and Exit of the Typical Bill

After a bill or resolution has been drafted (usually by the executive branch or by a lobby, but sometimes by members of Congress themselves), it is formally introduced. With the exception of revenue-raising bills, which are required by the Constitution (Article I, Section 7) to begin in the House, bills can originate in either house or in both simultaneously. After a bill has been introduced, it is referred to a committee, and the chairperson of the committee refers it to a subcommittee. Then hearings are held.

The purpose of the hearings is to bring debate on the bill out in the open, recruit public enthusiasm, develop a constituency for it, and sail its ideas on a shakedown cruise to see if they have any leaks that should be plugged up. Experts and interested parties (both for and against a bill) are invited to testify. Members of the committee not only subject these witnesses to intense (and sometimes not so intense) questioning, but also make statements of their own as to what they think the legislation will do. A stenographer is always on hand to take down all statements

---

[87]*New York Times,* June 22, 1976.

[88]Joseph W. Martin, Jr., *My First Fifty Years in Politics* (New York: McGraw-Hill, 1970), p. 48.

[89]The *Congressional Record,* H7436, August 3, 1973, acknowledges ignorance. Peter Milius's story in the *Washington Post,* June 29, 1976, tells about the $400 million paragraph.

Our Busy Representatives

The House Commission on Administrative Review interviewed 154 members and concluded that most of them were having great difficulty "effectively performing their public duties." The reason: "severe fragmentation of a [House] member's time; the huge growth of work that threatens Congress' ability to effectively discharge its lawmaking, oversight and representative duties; and uneven, ineffective and inefficient distribution of labor within the House."

The world, the Commission noted, was getting too complex for the average member to cope with; the complexities arose from a growing bureaucracy, the development of "new" issues, such as environmental pollution and nuclear weapons proliferation, and more demands from the home folks. The number of committee and subcommittee meetings more than doubled, from 3,210 in 1946 to 6,975 in 1976. During the same two decades, the number of hours the House was in session almost doubled, from 937 to 1,789.

The Commission said, that the typical representative's eleven-hour day includes:

- Four hours and twenty-five minutes on the House floor or in committee or subcommittee meetings
- Forty-six minutes answering mail and signing letters
- Twenty-six minutes with constituents
- Three minutes in conference with the House leadership
- Fifty-three minutes conferring with their staffs.

Most of the remainder of the typical day is taken up with scattershot activities, except for two alarmingly brief periods: eleven minutes daily devoted to reading and twelve minutes on legislation and speech writing.

The Commission's bleak conclusion:

> Rarely do [House] members have sufficient blocks of time when they are free from the frenetic pace of the Washington "treadmill" to think about the implications of various public policies.
> No matter how conscientious a representative might be, the splintering of his/her time into so many tiny bits and pieces hampers the effective conduct of lawmaking, oversight and constituent service functions.

Consequently, the systematic oversight of federal programs has become a "near impossibility."*

*Report of the House Commission on Administrative Review, released August 27, 1977.

made by the witnesses and the committee members. Out of this comes the hearing record, which other members of Congress and their staffs can read for guidance. Without a set of hearings to give it legitimacy, a bill ordinarily has little chance of making its way to final passage. It is at the subcommittee stage that the bill is subjected to "mark-up," or drafting, sessions, in which the original bill's wording is altered.

After leaving the subcommittee, the bill moves up to the full committee for further attention. There it will run into a logjam, for each major committee has numerous subcommittees, and all these subcommittees compete for the parent committee's time and attention—each urging *its* bills as deserving priority treatment.

After the bill has been passed by the full committee (if indeed it is passed—only 10 percent of all the bills introduced make it out of committee), it is ready for debate and vote by the full house; but, to get to the floor for debate and vote, it must first be placed on the calendar of business pending. In the House, there are five calendars, for different types of bills; ordinarily getting a bill off the calendar and onto the floor means "getting a rule" for debate from the Rules Committee. If the Rules Committee sends a bill to the floor, it will do so with instructions as to whether amendments will be permitted from the floor and the amount of debate time. "Open rule" permits amendments from the floor; "closed rule" does not.

There are ways to bypass the Rules Committee. Bills from the Appropriations Committee don't need to get Rules Committee approval. And on the first and third Mondays of each month, legislation can bypass the Rules Committee simply by getting recognition from the Speaker of the House. There is one drawback: bills that reach the floor in this fashion must receive two-thirds support for passage, rather than a simple majority. The third way to bypass the Rules Committee is to get a majority of the House to sign a discharge petition, but this method runs against tradition and is rarely used.

FIGURE 10-1   HOW A BILL BECOMES A LAW

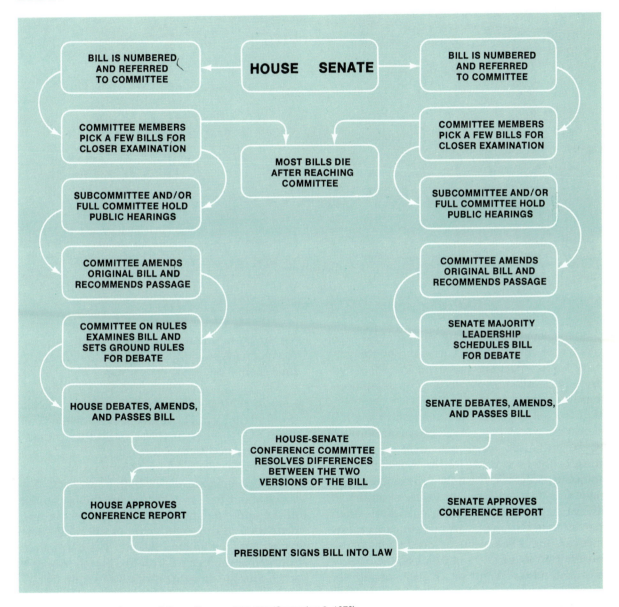

SOURCE: "The Working Congress," *House Document* 94–623 (September 9, 1976).

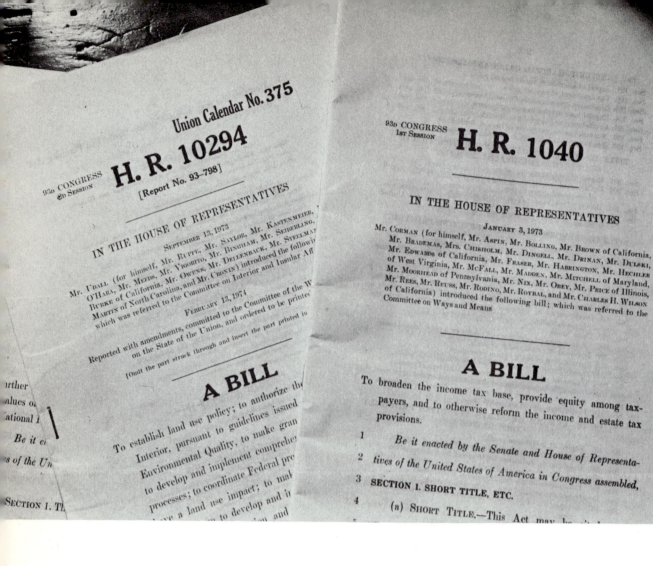

In the Senate, there is only one calendar—the calendar of bills—which is arranged by the majority leader. Bills are called up in order—but they can be called up out of order by unanimous consent.

If the bill is passed as submitted to the full membership and if the same version is approved by both houses (each bill must pass both houses), then it is ready for the President's signature. If, however, the bill has been altered by amendments in either or both houses—as almost always happens with major legislation—then the differences must be worked out in conference committee before it goes farther. One of the most important groups in Congress, the conference committee has no set chairperson, no set membership, no set meeting place, and no set schedule. "Conference committee" is, in fact, a generic name for many committees that come together each session and then dissolve, having done their work.

The conference committee is the ultimate point in the legislative process, where a small group sits around a table and decides on the final shape of legislation that has passed the House and Senate in different forms.

Although their rules for selecting conference-committee members differ, both houses actually follow about the same procedure: the presiding officer appoints the conferees on the recommendation of the chairperson of the committee having jurisdiction over the bill. The delegation from each chamber is controlled by the majority party, and the delegation votes as a unit. These rules are aimed at ensuring that the delegation will represent the attitude of the full chamber, and, in fact, it is not uncommon for a chamber to specifically instruct the delegation to be guided by the intent that was shown in debate at the time the bill was passed. Furthermore, the conference committee is not supposed to introduce new matter; it is expected to stay roughly within the bounds of the versions that came out of the two houses. These bounds are often stretched. In any event, there is no way to enforce compliance with such instructions, and the conferees can only be reprimanded by Congress's rejecting whatever compromise bill they bring back from conference. Rarely is this done.

Because committee chairpersons are so influential in the selection of the conference delegations, there are frequent complaints—sometimes justified—that they stack the delegations with conferees who reflect their biases. Usually a chairperson will select senior members, which means that, in a sense, the delegation is stacked with the encrusted attitudes that have long dominated the committee. But in recent years, chairpersons have increasingly appointed to the conference delegation the chairpersons of the subcommittees that first handled the bills, and many of these are junior members.

Until 1975, the conferees did their wheeling and dealing behind closed doors—on the theory put forth by Winston Churchill that two things, legislation and sausage, should never be made in public. But since 1975, the conference meetings have been open. Under rules agreed to in that year, members can close the meetings only by voting publicly to do so. Whether the open sessions will be totally satisfactory remains to be seen. Some people feel that, because such intense horse-trading goes on, the conferences can operate effectively only if members are allowed to operate in private. Some veteran members, such as Congressman Richard Bolling of Missouri, feel that the open meetings will be a charade—with most of the agreements reached elsewhere and by other means, after which members will come together "openly" and go through a ritual agreement. "If we have to meet in our wives' boudoirs for the tough dickering that members do not want to do in public," says Bolling, "we will."[90]

[90]*Inside Congress*, p. 109.

The version of the bill that comes out of conference is final and must be voted up or down in both houses without further alteration. If approved, the bill is sent on to the White House for the President's signature. He may sign or veto it within a period of ten days. If Congress is in session and the President does not sign the bill within ten days, it automatically becomes law. If Congress is not in session and the President doesn't sign the bill within ten days, it does not become law. This is known as the pocket veto. If the President returns the bill to Congress with a veto message, it may still become law if it is passed by a two-thirds majority in both the House and Senate.

Clearly, as the foregoing travelogue indicates, there exists in Congress a bias against passing legislation. It is far less difficult to defeat a bill than to pass one. The extremely difficult process of passing a bill requires an inordinate amount of consensus on the part of the majority of both chambers. Since Congress is made up of men and women with diverse political ideologies who must answer to a wide variety of constituents and financial backers, any important bill—which usually means any controversial bill—will succeed only after a considerable amount of compromise. Purists call this "gutting" the bill, or "watering it down," but, like it or not, that's what happens when 535 persons operate as a group.

However, there are ways to improve a bill's chances. Passing laws is not like processing citrus fruit or manufacturing automobiles. It is much more like planting and growing crops with the guidance of an almanac, wherein one gets advice on which phase of the moon to favor, which side of the hill to plant on, and what kind of manure to spread. Passing legislation takes druidic skills.

A controversial bill's chances for passage will be vastly improved if it is sent to a committee that will be sympathetic with its contents. If the author intends for his or her bill to go to a particular committee, the wording must be chosen carefully. For instance, Senator Pete V. Domenici of New Mexico was tired of the multibillion-dollar barge industry's getting to use the nation's waterways without paying any fees; it was, he felt, as if the trucking industry didn't have to pay any taxes for the upkeep of highways. So, in 1977, he introduced a bill to require the barge operators to pay for using government-built waterways. But before doing so, he thought long and hard about the wording. He knew that if he wrote the bill around the idea that there would be a "tax," the bill would be assigned to the Finance Committee, whose Chairman, Senator Long of Louisiana, detested the idea of a barge tax. The bill would die under Long. So Domenici decided to call the tax an "inland waterways charge." This would likely head the bill in the direction of the Senate Commerce Committee, which has jurisdiction over "inland waterways (except construction)." Commerce's Chairman, Senator Magnuson of Washington, did not exactly favor barge fees, but at least he was more kindly disposed toward them than was Long. So that's the way Domenici worded his bill, and it did wind up in Magnuson's committee. Even better for Domenici, the bill was also assigned to a second committee, Public Works, where the attitude toward his idea was downright friendly. His wording had at least given the bill a chance to be born.

Writing a bill "right" in this way takes no small talents. For example, in the Ninety-fourth Congress, nearly 1,000 energy-related bills and resolutions were introduced. Of these, approximately 200 were introduced in the Senate and 750 in the House. One might suppose that all energy-related bills would go to the same committee. But that isn't the case. Other factors are considered. Does the bill seem to be aimed primarily at changing the tax base? At helping rural families get heating oil and gasoline for their tractors? At coping with Middle East foreign relations? At developing offshore oil fields? At combating the monopoly tendencies of the oil companies? At the pricing of oil and gas? An "energy" bill can be written to have all sorts of characteristics—and the same is true of most bills. The energy bills of the Ninety-fourth Congress were, in the Senate alone, sent to fourteen committees and two joint committees.[91]

The crafty legislator will pace the introduction of his or her bill to catch the crest of public opinion. If feelings are running high enough, a bill may just race through without opposition. When the Arabian nations cut off oil shipments to the United States in the fall of 1973, sympathy for the Arabs' enemy, Israel, became so intense that a bill for $2.2 billion in emergency aid to Israel shot through the Senate with only one day of hearings.[92] The wise legislator (or executive or lobbyist) will also time a bill's introduction to mesh with the legislative programs of the administration and of congressional leaders, and also adjust the timing to benefit from such influences as the condition of the economy. A lobbyist who wanted higher subsidies for wheat farmers, for example, would hardly ask a politician to introduce legislation at a time when wheat prices were so high that consumers were complaining about the price of bread. George Galloway points out another obvious consideration: "A Presidential election year is usually considered a favorable time for introducing a tax-reduction bill, but a bad time for raising taxes."[93]

A legislator will generally not have too much trouble getting through a pork-barrel bill—one that distributes benefits to his or her constituency. In the friendly game of logrolling, the other legislators recognize the importance of a local project for reelection prospects, and they are sympathetic, knowing that they too will be treated well when they ask for their own pork-barrel bills.

Private bills, affecting specific individuals (such as immigration cases), generally meet with little opposition because their effect is so limited. But a legislator who sponsors a bill that is highly partisan or represents large interest groups or concerns controversial national issues runs into trouble—the other legislators may sense potential trouble from it in their districts. In these cases, the sponsoring legislator may be acting more out of symbolic than practical reasons. He or she knows the futility of passing the bill, but wants to claim credit for trying.[94]

---

[91]*Congressional Record*, S14236, July 29, 1975.

[92]*Congressional Record*, S23161, December 17, 1973.

[93]George B. Galloway, *History of the House of Representatives*, 2nd rev. ed. (New York: Thomas Y. Crowell Co., 1962), p. 163.

[94]David Mayhew, *Congress: The Electoral Connection* (New Haven, Conn.: Yale University Press, 1974), p. 119.

Congressional Investigations

Next to handling legislation, Congress's most important job is investigating. Its probing power, as Chief Justice Earl Warren wrote, is exceedingly broad.

> It encompasses inquiries concerning the administration of existing laws as well as proposed or possibly needed statutes. It includes surveys of defects in our social, economic or political system for the purpose of enabling the Congress to remedy them. It comprehends probes into departments of the federal government to expose corruption, inefficiency or waste.[95]

It has the power to investigate criminal conduct as well as stupidities. The power to pass laws carries with it, under the Constitution, the power to supervise the administration of laws and police the misapplication of laws. Every nook and cranny of government is a fair target: the executive branch, the judiciary, the bureaucracy above all, and Congress itself.[96]

Some of the most flamboyant episodes in our history have taken shape in congressional investigations—the uncovering of the Credit Mobilier scandal in the 1870s, the revelations of the Teapot Dome scandal of the 1920s, and, of course, the Watergate scandal of the 1970s. But the discovery of scandal for its own sake is seldom, if ever, the point. The most fruitful congressional investigations have led to great reform legislation. Out of the Money Trust investigations of 1912–13, which revealed the dangerous concentration of economic power, came the Federal Reserve Act of 1913, the Clayton Antitrust Act of 1914, and the Federal Trade Commission Act of 1914. As a result of the Senate Banking Committee's investigation of the stock market in 1933, Congress was moved to pass the Banking Acts of 1933 and 1935, the Securities Act of 1933, the Securities Exchange Act of 1934, and the Public Utility Holding Company Act of 1935. One of the most comprehensive investigations of the 1950s, Senator John McClellan's probe of union corruption—over two years the committee listened to 1,726 witnesses—led to the Landrum-Griffin Act, aimed at making it more difficult for crooked labor bosses to manipulate the rank and file.

Some congressional investigations have not led to new laws, but only to an awakening of the public to the existence of certain dangers. Often hearings of this sort have had the auxiliary effect of giving the involved politicians so much publicity that they became presidential candidates. Such was the result of Senator Estes Kefauver's widely headlined probe in 1950–51 of organized crime and Senator Frank Church's investigations of multinational corporations in 1974–75 and of the CIA in 1976. Previous to those investigations, neither man's name was exactly a household word.

Sometimes a probe is handled by one of Congress's standing committees; sometimes one house or the other sets up a special committee that exists only for the purpose of looking into a particular problem, as did the Watergate committee. In either case, the tools available to the investigators are the same:

Subpoena Powers Subpoenas are usually issued to force someone to testify or to supply confidential written material, or both. Senate committees had this power only on an *ad hoc* basis until the Legislative Reorganization Act of 1946 delegated the power to all standing committees. In the House, the leaders of both parties, fearing that committee chairmen—already too powerful—would become insufferable, blocked the extension of automatic subpoena powers to standing committees until 1975, by which time the chairmen were no longer considered a threat.

---

[95]*Watkins v. United States,* 354 U.S. 178 (1957).

[96]One of the most useful tools for investigation and oversight at Congress's disposal is the General Accounting Office. Although the GAO has been in existence for more than half a century, it is virtually unknown to the general public and is not well known even to many members of Congress. It does not seek notoriety; it does its work with all the gray efficiency of a bookkeeper in the back room.

The Budget and Accounting Act of 1921 gave the Comptroller General, head of the GAO, "access to and the right to examine any books, documents, papers, or records" of all federal departments and agencies. Unfortunately, for many years the GAO was unable to utilize this power to its fullest because some departments—especially the Pentagon and the State Department—would often simply refuse the GAO the records it demanded. This is still a problem. The Internal Revenue Service has also consistently refused to cooperate with the GAO. And unless Congress backs the GAO in its demands, it invariably loses in these confrontations with recalcitrant bureaucrats. Recently, Congress has shown more of an inclination to support the GAO and, equally important, to go to the GAO for investigative work, especially in sifting through crooked campaign records and in exposing Pentagon waste.

Until then, the authority in the House was delegated on a case-by-case basis.

The power is, of course, a necessity for any extensive investigation of controversial problems. To get the data it needs, Congress must often deal with people who bitterly resent intrusions and would refuse to supply information if they could legally get away with it. Some investigations are built on a great mound of subpoenas; during the probe of labor unions in 1957–59, Senator McClellan's investigators issued more than eight thousand subpoenas. Nobody is beyond the reach of a congressional subpoena—as President Nixon discovered during the Watergate probe of 1973–74.

Power to Punish Subpoenas could be disregarded safely if Congress did not have the power to cite for contempt anyone who tries to frustrate its work. A person who disobeys a lawful order to cooperate with Congress can be punished in either of two ways. After voting a contempt citation, the injured house can send its own sergeant-at-arms to arrest the obstructionist and throw him or her in jail. This is what James Hamilton calls the "self-help" method;[97] it is rarely used. The other method is for one house to vote contempt, submit the contempt citation to a federal grand jury, which, if it decides there are grounds for action, will recommend prosecution. Several people have gone to prison by this route. Three-fourths of all contempt citations voted by Congress have occurred since 1945, and most of these arose from the unwillingness of subpoenaed witnesses to give testimony during the "un-American activities" hearings of the 1950s.[98] Most of these contempt citations seemed to be aimed more at harassment than at obtaining information.

Publicity The effectiveness of congressional investigations depends, to a great degree, on the use of publicity—on manipulating the press with leaks and arousing public opinion with headlines. That may sound a bit crude, but it is, in fact, a very delicate and necessary ingredient of the investigative process, for the objective of congressional investigators is (1) to scare or shame an official or an agency into reform; (2) to spotlight the crimes or irregularities of private individuals or groups, hoping in this way to either bring about indictments or at least shame the investigatees into reform; or (3) to hustle Congress into passing corrective legislation. Publicity provides the energy of reform, and it takes careful, crafty planning to squeeze the right kind of publicity from investigations.

Walter Pincus, a newspaperman who was the Senate Foreign Relations Committee's impresario of the foreign lobbying investigations a few years ago, attributed his success to having got the committee, the witnesses, and the public to dance along together. He explained:

> You've got to choreograph the thing, not just make headlines. As investigator, you have to know what each witness is going to say. You can't let some guy say something one day, and then let another guy say something another day that cancels the previous impact. You've got to herd the public along.[99]

When successful, Congress, through its investigations, has been the conscience and the watchdog of the federal government. Its successes can be measured not only by a long list of reform legislation and bureaucratic shake-ups, but also by the cancellation or renegotiation of many billion-dollar contracts, by the indictment of more than one hundred persons and the jailing of a couple dozen (most notably, Teamster boss James R. Hoffa). As the result of congressional investigations, two cabinet officers have been bumped (Navy Secretary Fred Korth and Air Force Secretary Harold Talbott), another cabinet officer escaped felony prosecution for perjury by pleading guilty to a misdemeanor charge (Attorney General Richard G. Kleindienst), and a President has been forced to resign.

At the same time, there are strict limitations on the investigative powers of Congress. It cannot—or at least it is not supposed to—stick its nose into private affairs just for the purpose of embarrassing someone; it is not supposed to meddle and pry unless it has the legitimate

[97]James Hamilton, *The Power to Probe: A Study of Congressional Investigations* (New York: Random House, Vintage Books, 1976), p. 86.

[98]Hamilton, p. 95.

[99]Sherrill, "How to Succeed on the Potomac."

purpose of correcting a situation that adversely affects the public. And when it gets confidential information via subpoenas, it is supposed to protect that information. But Congress has frequently violated all of these legal limitations. It has sometimes acted like a meddlesome gossip, blackening reputations merely for the perverse pleasure of getting even with someone whose ideology is unpopular. And it has often leaked information that it had solemnly promised to keep confidential.

Serving Constituents

When Senator Donald W. Riegle, Jr., of Michigan was starting out in politics, as a lowly member of the House, he kept a diary. It is filled with entries such as:

> *Saturday, September 18.* As soon as I arrived in Flint, I held constituent office hours. An old woman whom we'd helped with a Social Security problem brought me a jar of homemade strawberry jam. She was frail, and her kindness penetrated all my defense mechanisms. I gave her a hug. . . .[100]

And she, no doubt, gave him her vote.

A large part of the job of a member of Congress consists of wooing constituents—meeting them, answering mail, doing favors, canvassing opinion, solving problems. These are time-consuming tasks. A recent study of the Senate found that the typical member spends only one-third of the day on the floor or in committee, with the rest of the day taken up in meetings outside the office, with mail and press relations, and with meetings with lobbyists and conferences with staff aides. Much of that adds up to what members of Congress call "constituent service."[101] House members, who are tuned even more sensitively to the home folks, spend an even greater proportion of their time performing constituent service.

House majority leader Jim Wright went back through the log of requests from his Fort Worth constituents over a period of one week and found these samples:

A small industrial firm wants to offer its products to the federal government but doesn't know which agency to deal with or the proper form in which to prepare its bids.

A disabled veteran needs hospitalization in a hurry. The nearest Veterans' Administration Hospital is overcrowded and cannot possibly admit him. Arrangements must be made to get him into another one.

A student preparing a thesis needs some information from the Library of Congress.

A local manufacturer is in trouble with the Federal Trade Commission because of an advertisement. He feels he is being discriminated against and that the FTC is treating him more harshly than it is treating his competition. He wants a top-level interview with officials.

A family is coming to Washington for a visit. Where should they stay, and what should they see?[102]

Wright estimates that about one-third of the mail to a member of Congress comes from people with requests for help or guidance in cutting through government red tape and in escaping from the web of bureaucracy.

Most of the requests can be fulfilled by interceding with some part of the federal bureaucracy. But some of the requests require the introduction of what are called "private bills," thousands of which are introduced in each session of Congress.

Each member has at least one office back home staffed with caseworkers, who try to help aggrieved constituents solve problems with the government; in their Washington offices, there are also at least four or five "skilled professionals who can play the bureaucracy like an organ— pushing the right pedals to produce the desired effects."[103]

Recent surveys have thrown a new light on congressional and public attitudes toward this service. A national poll taken by Louis Harris for the House of Representatives found that 94 percent of the voters surveyed believed that the most important function of a member of Congress was "making sure his district gets its fair

---

[100]Donald W. Riegle, Jr., and Trevor Armbrister, *O Congress* (New York: Doubleday & Co., 1972), p. 123.

[101]*Washington Star,* December 19, 1976.

[102]Wright, *You and Your Congressman,* pp. 40–41.

[103]Mayhew, *Congress,* p. 55.

share of government money and projects," and 58 percent felt that members of Congress should spend their time "helping people . . . who have personal problems with the government."

However, another survey for the House—this one by Victor J. Fisher, who interviewed 153 members individually for one and a half hours each—indicated that most members felt their constituents were a burden and that many felt their constituent work conflicted with their national responsibilities. "Strikingly, some 57 percent of those surveyed said that demands of constituents detract from their performance or ability to properly meet other obligations and duties." What other obligations and duties? "The biggest complaint here was that the time demands imposed by serving constituents impair or detract from the legislative function." Members surveyed believed, by a margin of 45 to 24 percent, that "their primary responsibility was to look after the needs and interests of the nation as a whole."[104]

Members of Congress have only themselves to blame for some of their increased constituency workload. In 1976, for example, Congress spent $60 million to send out 560 million pieces of mail to voters—newsletters, unscientific questionnaires, form-letter congratulatory messages, and giveaway items, including calendars and pamphlets—on subjects ranging from how to raise chickens to how to raise children. Indeed, Congress sent out 8 pieces of mail for every 1 it received.[105] Its mass mailings—much of them done in a blatant effort to win votes—generate a tremendous amount of mail. People who ordinarily would never give their senator or representative a passing thought receive something from Washington in the mail, suddenly realize that their federal politicians are alive, and begin bombarding them with requests.

As constituents' letters, constituents' requests for help, and constituents themselves poured into Washington in higher waves in recent years, members of Congress have reacted with desperation. In an effort to cope with the flood, they have gone on a hiring orgy. In twenty years, congressional staffs have tripled in size. As of 1977, there were more than 18,000 people working for Congress and its committees, 3,100 more than three years earlier. People have been hired so rapidly that little effort has been made to ensure that the new employees are efficiently used.[106] For the most part, the new employees are receptionists, clerks, typists, or secretaries. They act as a sea wall, protecting their bosses. Some members of Congress have personal staffs of over fifty people. It has become increasingly difficult for constituents to get through these hirelings to the person they elected.[107]

Members of Congress not only have surrounded themselves with protective cordons of office help, but they have also surrounded themselves with police—more than a thousand uniformed officers. That's as many police as are found in some cities with a population of 700,000—although, in fact, Capitol Hill and its buildings are almost totally devoid of crime, except that which the members of Congress commit. The atmosphere, anything but democratic, is described by *New York Times* columnist Russell Baker:

I go to the Capitol in search of Congress and find only policemen. The place is swarming with them. They are on steps, in doorways, outside elevators, patrolling corridors. . . . I roam through acres of cops, and at the House of Representatives I am forced to pass through a metal detector before they let me enter the press gallery.

At the public galleries, some 200 tourists are emptying pocket and purse of keys, coins, souvenirs. This is only a mite of the total-security orgy which is placing a blockade of guns between government and the governed. . . . Eventually, I am told, bulletproof glass walls may be installed between the Congressional galleries and the Senate and House, and Congress will become known as the men in the glass booths.

The effect of it, finally, is to heighten the sense of disconnection between the government and us. So many police hips bulging with firepower, so many cool appraising police eyes, give one the impression of being looked upon as a menace, of being

---

[104]*Washington Star,* February 4, 1977.

[105]Associated Press, March 28, 1977.

[106]Survey performed by Senator Harold E. Hughes, released in 1976.

[107]Sources: *Washington Post,* June 1, 1975; Charles Bartlett, *Washington Star,* May 14, 1975.

not quite safe. One hesitates about striding right through doors and gates. There is a sense of lost freedom.[108]

Influences on the Work of the Legislator

It is hardly necessary to point out that a legislator is no blank tablet—untouched, unimpressionable, and unwritten upon. Many factors influence a legislator's work and voting decisions—party officials, campaign fund-raisers and contributors, voters, congressional party leaders, interest groups, and colleagues. Bound up with all of these influences is the concern with reelection.

Political scientists don't agree on which influences are most important. In some cases their theories conflict; in other cases the evidence is poor. Perhaps it is just as well to admit that, at this point, no one knows how much influence any one factor has. Research is still going on, and important questions have yet to be answered—one question still to be answered is the extent to which the member of Congress heeds constituency opinion.

Seeking to determine what influences have shaped voting decisions, Lester Markel, a former editor of the *New York Times,* sent a questionnaire to members of Congress. He received replies from fifteen senators and ninety-four representatives; in addition, he personally interviewed seventeen senators and eleven representatives. The result of his sampling, done by parties and by geographical area:

101 of the 137 members of Congress who responded in the survey said that the most important factor was their own viewpoint; only 36 placed constituency opinion first. But these figures should be taken with large grains of salt. Most members are influenced by "grass roots" sentiment; almost all strive constantly to discover it. . . .

Significantly, 62 of the 137 members listed "personal contacts" as the single most important method of determining opinion trends in their districts; 52 listed it as second or third.

Members of Congress generally consider mail from constituents an invaluable clue to public opinion even though there are studies showing that fewer than a quarter of the voters have ever written to their representatives in Washington. Twenty members in the Congressional survey listed the mail as the most important factor in influencing their decisions; 75 others rated it second or third. . . . Senator Harry Byrd Jr. of Virginia says: "I try to see as many letters as I can, especially those that affect legislation, or give viewpoints on matters before Congress. Most Senators don't do this. I spend four hours a day reading mail. They say I'm a damn fool to spend so much time on it. But I say it's damn foolish to get out of touch with your constituents."[109]

The reason most members would consider Byrd a damn fool to spend so much time on them is that letters, though valuable as one element in a sampling of opinion, are by themselves an unbalanced survey. Many studies have shown that people who disagree with a politician's position are much more likely to write than are people who agree. Moreover, it is a highly unrepresentative group that writes—a 1965 survey showed that, in the preceding year, 4.8 percent of those earning under $5,000 a year had written, compared with 21 percent of those earning over $15,000.[110] The unrepresentative quality of the mail was uncovered in another survey, which showed that only about 15 percent of the public admits to ever having written a public official and that about 66 percent of all letters written to officials originate from about 3 percent of the public.[111] Finally, on any controversial issue, the bulk of congressional mail will be generated not by individuals, but by organizations that recruit letter-writing campaigns to push a particular view.[112]

Lewis Anthony Dexter has a theory that constituents' messages are important not for their content, but for drawing attention to an issue. In other words, messages act as triggers, not as

---

[108]Russell Baker, *New York Times Magazine,* February 15, 1976.

[109]Lester Markel, *What You Don't Know Can Hurt You: Study in Public Opinion and Public Emotion* (Washington, D.C.: Public Affairs Press, 1972), p. 129.

[110]Mayhew, *Congress,* p. 109.

[111]Philip E. Converse et al., "Electoral Myth and Reality: The 1964 Elections," *American Political Science Review* 59 (June 1965): 333.

[112]Markel, *What You Don't Know Can Hurt You,* pp. 128–29.

persuaders. "Congressmen are well attuned to grievances as an index to the sources of public alarm, rather than as specific guidance on legislative drafting. . . . The complaint is a signal to him to do something, not a command as to what to do."[113]

Most members claim they do their job according to the Burkean principle—that is, the principle laid down by Britain's most famous eighteenth-century politician, Edmund Burke, who argued that his constituents did not elect him to be their rubber stamp, but to follow his own intelligence and conscience. One hears echoes of Burke all over Capitol Hill.

"None of us was elected to be a megaphone for the loudest voices in our constituencies," said Senator George D. Aiken of Vermont.[114] "It is not my job to represent their [his district's voters'] views on any matter," said Congressman Charles E. Wiggins of California. "I am always sensitive to that and don't mean to sound callous, but I represent my best judgment on issues and they have the right to choose someone else if they don't agree."[115] Warned Congressman James F. Hastings of New York, "If you base your position on the highest stack of letters, you could be in serious, serious trouble. . . ."[116]

Special interests are another significant influence on a legislator, as we have seen in Chapter 5. Sometimes they are part of the district constituency, but, more often, they are part of the legislator's committee constituency. For example, a member who serves on the House Banking and Currency Committee will find he or she is courted by banking associations.

It is clear that congressional performance cannot be judged on the basis of single influences. It is much too complex for that. Sometimes members of Congress play Burkean trustee, sometimes they play instructed delegate of the people, sometimes responsible party legislator, sometimes interest group advocate, and sometimes the roles mix.[117] As Barbara Hinckley put it, "a senator from Texas acts at one time for the oil interests, at another for 'Texas' or the 'South,' at still another for the national interest."[118]

A legislator's vote on a particular issue is usually shaped most powerfully, says Congressman Bob Eckhardt, "by those with intense interests and long memories" and by those things that "generate campaign contributions and tend to make him feel important."[119] This is why the public is sometimes subjected to the spectacle of what appears to be split-personalities at work—eminently decent legislators occasionally bending to the wishes of avaricious lobbies and to the most immoderate element of the electorate. These legislators have concluded, after feeling out their major financial backers and the public, that only by capitulating on some money or bias issues will they be left in office and left alone to follow their consciences on other major issues.

Despite an alarming increase in gun homicides and despite many national polls showing that most Americans eagerly want Congress to pass laws controlling the sale of guns, Senator Frank Church of Idaho always votes against gun control. Church is a very progressive fellow, much more oriented to the nation and the world than he is to Idaho. So why does he vote against gun control? It's quite simple: Idahoans, avid hunters and touched still with some of the wild West spirit, love their guns and would throw him out of office if he voted to restrict gun ownership. Church puts it this way:

> Some things come along on which, for one reason or another, opinion is absolutely and wholly

[113]Lewis Anthony Dexter, "The Job of the Congressman," in Wolfinger, ed., *Readings in American Political Behavior,* 2nd ed., p. 15.

[114]*Congressional Record,* S20004, November 7, 1973.

[115]Quoted in the *New York Times,* January 18, 1974.

[116]Quoted in the *Washington Star,* January 25, 1974.

[117]For more on this, as applied to state legislatures, see Heinz Eulau et al., "The Role of the Representative: Some Empirical Observations on the Theory of Edmund Burke," *American Political Science Review* 53 (September 1959): 742–56.

[118]Barbara Hinckley, *Stability and Change in Congress* (New York: Harper & Row, Publishers, 1971), p. 38. One can also profit from Warren E. Miller and Donald E. Stokes, "Constituency Influence in Congress," *American Political Science Review* 57 (March 1963); and from Angus Campbell et al., *Elections and the Political Order* (New York: John Wiley & Sons, 1966).

[119]Bob Eckhardt and Charles L. Black, Jr., *The Tides of Power: Conversations on the American Constitution* (New Haven, Conn.: Yale University Press, 1976).

On Second Thought...

Congressional actions that seem from a distance to be the products of madness sometimes turn out, on closer inspection, to be simply the result of moneyed pressure. In 1977, one congressman launched a personal crusade against a wasteful inconsistency in the government's attitude toward tobacco. What happened to his intentions is told by Mary Russell, a reporter for the *Washington Post:*

Rep. James Johnson (R-Colo.) had come a long way, baby, with his campaign to kill federal subsidies for tobacco growers.

Since he first argued over a month ago that it is schizophrenic for the government to subsidize tobacco growers while at the same time spending money to warn against the health effects of smoking, Johnson had received what Rep. William Natcher (D-Ky.) daily called "considerable publicity." There had been dozens of news stories, network TV coverage and support from HEW Secretary Joseph A. Califano Jr.

But Monday, when it came time for Johnson to offer his farm bill amendment ending the $44 million a year in tobacco price supports, Johnson announced he wouldn't.

What caused his fire for the proposal to go up in smoke?

House members from tobacco growing states winked knowingly and said Johnson had been "beet-en down."

Johnson represents one of the largest sugar beet growing districts in the country. Sugar growers are in trouble because the bottom has fallen out of the world market and sugar that sold for 60 cents a pound a few years ago is selling for 8 to 10 cents this year, while it costs 13 cents a pound to produce. Without government support, domestic sugar growers contend, they will be driven out of business by foreign producers.

Though the tobacco state members demur at putting it in such crude terms, they told Johnson their support for a sugar subsidy depended on his dropping his crusade against tobacco subsidies.

"We sweetened the pot," Rep. Charles Rose (D-N.C.) said. "He wanted help on his sugar problem. We wanted help on tobacco. We convinced him to modify his position."

Rep. Walter Jones (D-N.C.), chairman of the tobacco subcommittee, assured Johnson he would hold hearings on tobacco supports if he lessened his opposition. Tobacco state members also agreed they would not object if Johnson offered an amendment to knock out some $24 million in foreign tobacco sales under the Food for Peace plan. . . .

Jones "had a conversation" with Horace Godfrey, a former Agriculture Department administrator from North Carolina, who now lobbies for Florida, Louisiana and Texas sugar cane growers.

Godfrey said, "I just told him (Johnson) we don't want to make the tobacco boys mad at us."

Godfrey also acknowledged he made sure the "60 to 70 sugar growers in here last week" talked to Johnson. . . .

Yesterday Johnson offered his amendment to knock out some $24 million in the sale of subsidized tobacco under the Food for Peace program. . . .

He called tobacco "cannon fodder for cancer" and said 890,000 people could be fed with the $24 million.

Natcher was enraged. "We don't produce any sugar beets in my home county," he shouted. "But the 20 states that produced tobacco marched down the aisle for the sugar bill. When sugar is in trouble my people are concerned."

Johnson's amendment was watered down to say only that food and fiber should be a priority for sales under the Food for Peace program.

That passed 259 to 151.*

*Washington Post, July 27, 1977.

formed. To oppose that opinion is to invite political defeat—immediate death. Then you must weigh its importance. Is this an issue of such importance to the country that I should take a stand and take defeat, or should I reflect the viewpoint of my constituents—recognizing the facts of life?[120]

The best of our politicians must face that kind of question every week, and all they can do is hope that they rationalize out of principle rather than out of expediency.[121]

Concern with reelection enters into every phase of legislative life. David Mayhew has developed a very plausible theory that the need (and the quest) for reelection is the dominant influence on a legislator. He characterizes the modern Congress as "an assembly of professional politicians spinning out political careers," whose pursuit requires continual reelection. While granting that legislators have other goals too—such as achieving influence in Congress and making good policy—he sees reelection as underlying everything else.

Mayhew describes three activities that every legislator finds "electorally useful." They are advertising, credit claiming, and position taking. Through advertising, the legislator's name becomes a household word among the constituents; name recognition gives incumbents a tremendous edge over challengers. Credit is claimed for any benefits obtained for the constituency (or for whatever political element of it that has put the legislator into office—labor groups, chambers of commerce, minorities, and so on). Position taking is also carefully geared to the relevant part of the electorate. In this activity, Mayhew notes, a member of Congress is "a speaker rather than a doer. The electoral requirement is not that he make pleasing things happen but that he make pleasing judgmental statements." Perhaps the most emphatic statement is a roll-call vote on a controversial issue. Although one roll-call vote may not make an impression on the electorate, the broad pattern of votes generally will, for these are monitored carefully and rated by groups like Americans for Democratic Action, Common Cause, and Americans for Constitutional Action. The legislator is not necessarily concerned with consistency in his or her position taking. For example, at one stage of a bill the member may vote for it; at another stage, against it. One congressman described how he gave a pro–Vietnam war speech to one group and later in the day gave an antiwar speech to another group: "My positions are not inconsistent. I just approach different people differently."[122]

HOW WELL DOES CONGRESS WORK?

Congress is variously charged with being inefficient, unresponsive, insensitive, inconsistent, indecisive, incompetent, and unimaginative. Critics usually focus on institutional factors—rules, structure, procedures—and there is some accuracy in that.

However, Congress, in fact, has taken some steps to improve its mode of operation—to make it more responsive and more efficient. Aside from the extensive changes in committee operations in both houses mentioned earlier in this chapter, Congress also passed (the House in 1973, the Senate in 1975) a "sunshine law" that opened committee meetings during most bill-drafting sessions. The Senate, in 1975, made the first major change in the cloture rule since 1959;

---

[120]Quoted in Markel, *What You Don't Know Can Hurt You*, p. 133.

[121]Purists should, however, bear in mind that expediency does not always control the votes even on the most emotional issue. Sometimes members *are* willing to risk their careers to step ahead (according to their conscience), to be more tolerant or more constitutional or thriftier than their constituents would want. Speaker of the House Carl Albert not only voted against, but orated eloquently against, passage of a constitutional amendment that would have permitted prayer in public schools. He considered it an abridgment of the separation of church and state. This was a dangerous position for him to take, coming from a very fundamentalist section of Oklahoma. An antiprayer vote had recently helped defeat Senator Ralph W. Yarborough of Texas, and yet, when the prayer amendment reached the House, several Texas representatives—one conservative, one moderate, and three liberals—laid their careers on the line to vote against it, as did three members from Tennessee, the center of the so-called "Bible Belt." (Wright, *You and Your Congressman*, pp. 122–23.)

[122]Mayhew, *Congress*, pp. 15, 49–77, 62, 65.

the number of votes needed to end a filibuster was lowered from two-thirds to three-fifths of the full Senate. By 1975, the once-rigid seniority system had received the first significant crack in modern times, by being made subject to the will of the caucuses in both houses.

Congress also made several important moves to improve its ability to balance presidential powers. As discussed in Chapter 9, in the Ninety-third (1973–74) session, it enacted the War Powers Resolution, requiring the President to report to Congress within forty-eight hours after committing any troops overseas and to obtain congressional approval within sixty days if he intended to keep the troops in combat; and it passed the Congressional Budget and Impoundment Control Act, which, for the first time, put Congress in a powerful position to challenge the assumptions of a President's budget. "Ever since the era of Congressional government at the close of the Civil War . . ., the flow of power had been all one way, in the direction of the President," wrote James L. Sundquist of these reforms. "In just two years, the trend of a hundred years was dramatically reversed."[123] But the changes were all in form, on paper. Output and efficiency seemed relatively unchanged.

Still, the public is probably not as concerned about whether or not Congress operates in a slick fashion as whether or not it operates in a way that gets to the heart of the nation's problems. Senator Humphrey had a splendid point to make when he declared, in his evangelical way:

> You can read the Declaration of Independence and all of the grievances therein listed and not once did our founding fathers talk about the inefficiency or the efficiency of government. They had grievances about the injustice and the inequities that were imposed upon them.
>
> You can read the Constitution of the U.S. from the Preamble to the last word and not once find the word "efficiency. . . ."
>
> Hitler was efficient and so was Bismarck. That did not give them justice and I think that what the American people want is justice. I think they want some justice in tax laws and they know they are

not getting it. I think what they want out of the Congress and the Executive is not a fight over procedure, but what you are going to do about your cities before they blow up.[124]

Congress *is* slow to respond to national problems. Usually when a big, new issue hits Congress—such as Medicare or federal aid to education—five or ten years will pass before a consensus is formed. And the legislation that it does pass has a distinctly conservative cast. Much congressional delay and resistance to change can be explained by former Senator William B. Saxbe's statement: "If you don't stick your neck out, you don't get it chopped off."[125] Necks must be extended to pass legislation redistributing income, closing tax loopholes, or desegregating urban neighborhoods.

But congressional scholar Gary Orfield believes that recent Congresses have been reflecting the public's own indecision and confusion about social change. He claims that much of the criticism of Congress has been misdirected, blaming institutional factors for a politically created situation. "Most of the time, we have the Congress we really want and the Congress we deserve. We send the same members back to Washington time after time." Orfield also believes that the inconsistency of policy directions in Congress (for example, the Judiciary Committee's creating legislation to protect rights of blacks and the Appropriations Committee's voting to starve the programs) is not unique to the legislative branch. It is exceptionally visible there because of its decentralized decision making and ineffective leadership. Other branches of the government have conflicts too, but these are usually worked out in private.[126]

The final appraisal of Congress's work should be made cautiously. Its defects are pretty obvious. Its strong points are sometimes hidden. Some criticisms aimed at Congress are based on false expectations. Some hopes for future "reformed" Congresses are based on irrelevancies.

---

[123]James L. Sundquist, *Setting National Priorities* (Washington, D.C.: Brookings Institution, 1976), p. 597.

[124]*Congressional Record*, H3061, April 19, 1973.

[125]Quoted in Mayhew, *Congress*, p. 11.

[126]Orfield, *Congressional Power*, pp. 10, 279.

One very prevalent false expectation is a Congress that competes with, or replaces, the President in setting national policies and priorities. It can't be done.

Shortly before assuming office, President Jimmy Carter stated in numerous speeches across the country,

> I respect the Congress, but the Congress is inherently incapable of leadership. Our founding fathers never thought that the Congress would lead this country. There's only one person that can speak with a clear voice to the American people, or inspire the American people to reach for greatness or excellence, or call on them to make a sacrifice, or set a standard of morality, or set out the answers to complicated questions, or correct discrimination and injustice, or provide us with the defense posture that would make us feel proud again. And that's the President.[127]

Carter may not have been correct in his interpretation of what the Founders thought, but for the rest of it, he was absolutely on target. The power that is available to Congress is as great as, or greater than, the power available to a President, but it is a different kind of power. It is not the sort of power that enables Congress to exert national leadership.

The most dramatic recent proof of this was in the Ninety-fourth Congress, which began service in January 1975. If ever it was to happen, that was the time for Congress to take over. The Nixon administration was in a shambles. Corruption had chased Nixon into exile; his successor, Gerald R. Ford, was doubly weak—being Nixon's handpicked choice and having had no public vote of confidence. The situation seemed ideally suited for a reassertion of "congressional leadership."

The new Congress came to town very cocky indeed. Nearly one-fifth the full House of 435 members were freshmen, an extraordinarily large and powerful bloc of first-termers, and they came swearing to reform the system, to "make it work." Additionally, the two-to-one Democratic majority in the House and the nearly as large majority in the Senate made the Congress seem to be veto-proof.

Nineteen months later, the Ninety-fourth Congress limped out of town, its banner in tatters. Not that it was a complete failure. It had made important reforms of the legislative and administrative process. It had worked longer, held more votes, passed more laws than any Congress in history. But out of all this had come no cohesive national policy. Its laws added up to a solar system without a sun. It had made brave promises to write a national energy program, but it produced none. It had promised tax reforms, but there was no significant amount of reform buried in the mammoth (fifteen-hundred-page) tax bill that was enacted. And when Congress did produce legislation to help the economy, President Ford vetoed it with ease and impunity. He hit the Ninety-fourth with fifty-nine vetoes, and he was overridden only twelve times, the poorest showing of congressional strength in twenty years.

The leadership failures of the Ninety-fourth were no reflections on that particular body; they were the result of natural and long-established forces, and they could have been predicted. Congress simply cannot replace the executive branch as a national policy-maker. In harness with a President who shunned activism and whose whole career had been built on obstructionism to Democratic programs, the Democratic-controlled Congress could rise no higher than its own leadership, and it was made up of people who did not think in an executive way.

The power that Congress exercises comes not from innovation, but from deliberation. Caution is its keynote, and, on balance, maybe caution is not always such a bad thing. The same forces that keep Congress from passing some good laws also prevent our being burdened with many evil laws. Many of the bills that Congress receives should *not* be passed, many are poorly thought out, many are mischievous in intent, many are of good intent but would work havoc on the population.

The unrefined, rough, and crotchety qualities of Congress are given a salvation status by Bertram Gross, who sees in the United States what he thinks could be the rough beginnings of "the Big Business-Big Government alliances that characterized the old-time Corporate States under the fascist regimes of Hitler, Mussolini and

---

[127] Quoted in David Broder, *Washington Post*, May 2, 1976.

Japan's zaibatsu-military complex." But Gross thinks we will probably be saved from that development by certain maverick elements, chief of which is Congress, "a somewhat unpredictable and uncoordinated body in which all sorts of members and committees have the habit of popping up and upsetting applecarts. . . ."[128]

Another advocate of that position is former Senator Sam J. Ervin, Jr., who offers this traditionalist argument:

> Congress is a collection of committees that come together in a chamber periodically to approve one another's action. Insofar as the legislative process is concerned, it is a system of successive cautious steps, of successive checks and rechecks and a continuous accommodation and compromise. It is not streamlined; it was never meant to be. But it has this great and overriding virtue; it tends to check tyranny.
>
> The great function of Congress is to harmonize diversity, to compromise the differences, to arrive at a solution that the nation as a whole can live with in peace. There is no shortcut to solutions of that kind. Speed is the enemy of compromise and

compromise is the very essence of our system of government.[129]

If any lesson is to be learned that should be carried forward in a reorganization of Congress, it is that rules made in haste, with the best of intentions today, may come back to haunt the nation tomorrow under opposite circumstances. Nelson W. Polsby points out,

> The experience of recent years should teach us how important it is that those responsible for the design and reorganization of political entities take a longer view. If liberals had prevailed in their eagerness to cripple the autonomy of the Supreme Court in the 1930s, or had succeeded in the 1950s in bringing Congress wholly under presidential domination, as they wanted to do, one somehow doubts that either of these branches of government would have survived in so robust a condition to take up liberal causes in later years. Conservatives, it seems to me, can profit from the same lesson.[130]

Examples of that useful precaution are easily found in all that Congress does. And in all that it does not do.

---

[128]Quoted in the Hearings of the Select Committee on Committee Organization in the House, Vol. 2, part 3 (1973): 773.

[129]Quoted in the *Washington Post,* March 11, 1973.

[130]Quoted in the Hearings of the Select Committee on Committee Organization in the House, Vol. 2, part 3 (1973): 9.

Summary

1. Congress is the voice of the people. Members of its two branches are directly elected, although until 1913 senators were chosen by state legislatures, as a means of checking the "will of the masses" in the House.

2. Members of Congress reflect society's virtues and vices, but they are not ordinary citizens; they are an elite group—members are concentrated in a few professions, and they are mainly upper class and wealthy.

3. Periodically, the houses of Congress pass codes of ethics to govern the conduct of their members. But members rarely vote to censure or expel a colleague.

4. The leadership of Congress is chosen along party lines. The Speaker of the House, although elected by the whole chamber, is the choice of the majority party; in the Senate, the majority leader, chosen by party caucus, is the nearest in power to the Speaker. Party caucuses in both houses elect minority floor leaders and whips to help mobilize votes.

5. Tyrannical committee chairpersons are no longer tolerated. Today their power primarily comes from the support they have in committee, the importance of their work, their success in passing legislation, and their knowledge of committee subject matter.

6. As a rule, seniority on a committee determines who will be chairperson. As a result of recent reforms, the seniority system is occasionally circumvented by vote of party caucus.

7. The committees do the real work of Congress. The standing committees and their subcommittees (which tend to specialize in expertise) write and approve legislation. Joint committees and select committees make recommendations for legislation.

8. The House committee system is highly organized and hierarchical; the Senate system is less dominating of the decision-making process.

9. Reforms in the committee system between 1973 and 1977 have made committee operations more democratic, dispersed power, streamlined work, and given more authority to the party caucus.

10. Members of Congress spend relatively little time on the floor of the chamber. Debates in the House are limited in time, but in the Senate they are unlimited, allowing senators to conduct filibusters, which block voting on legislation.

11. Legislative aides and staff have become increasingly important as the legislators' workload has grown.

12. The three main functions of the members of Congress are legislating, investigating and overseeing government operations, and serving constituents.

13. The legislator's work is affected by so many influences—including party officials, campaign contributors, voters, leaders in Congress, interest groups, colleagues, and his or her own conscience—that it is difficult to determine which are most important. Tied up with all these influences is the legislator's concern with reelection.

14. It is unrealistic to expect Congress to match the President in setting national policy or to be speedy and innovative in its decision making. Perhaps the value of Congress lies in its deliberation, its caution, and its ability to compromise.

Additional Reading

Nelson W. Polsby, *Congress and the Presidency*, 3rd ed. (Englewood Cliffs, N.J.: Prentice-Hall, 1976), gives a clear and concise account of how Congress is organized and how a bill becomes a law. For a critical perspective, see Mark J. Green et al., *Who Runs Congress*, rev. ed. (New York: Bantam Books, 1975). David Mayhew's *Congress: The Electoral Connection* (New Haven, Conn.: Yale University Press, 1974) is a perceptive and critical theoretical essay on how the goal of reelection affects the behavior of members of Congress.

First-hand accounts are Donald W. Riegle, Jr., and Trevor Ambrister, *O Congress* (New York: Doubleday & Co., 1972), and Clement Miller, *Member of the House: Letters of a Congressman* (New York: Charles Scribner's Sons, 1962). John W. Kingdon's *Congressmen's Voting Decisions* (New York: Harper & Row, Publishers, 1973) reports representatives' explanations of why they vote as they do. Donald R. Matthews, *U.S. Senators and Their World* (New York: Random House, Vintage Books, 1960) still provides the fullest treatment of the Senate.

Some of the best works on Congress concern the committees of the House of Representatives. Richard F. Fenno, Jr., *Congressmen in Committees* (Boston: Little, Brown and Co., 1973), compares the structure and functioning of six committees. The leading studies of particular committees are Fenno's *The Power of the Purse: Appropriations Politics in Congress* (1966) and John F. Manley's *The Politics of Finance: The House Committee on Ways and Means* (1975), both published in Boston by Little, Brown and Co. A number of interesting articles on the committees—and on other aspects of Congress—are collected in Nelson W. Polsby and Robert L. Peabody, eds., *New Perspectives on the House of Representatives* (Skokie, Ill.: Rand McNally & Co., 1963), and in Ralph K. Huitt and Robert L. Peabody, *Congress: Two Decades of Analysis* (New York: Harper & Row, Publishers, 1969).

Congressional Quarterly Weekly Report and the annual *Congressional Quarterly Almanac* offer up-to-date accounts of legislative events, voting patterns, committee membership, and the like.

Charles E. Lindblom's *The Policy-Making Process* (Englewood Cliffs, N.J.: Prentice-Hall, 1968) is a lucid introduction; and Aaron B. Wildavksky's *The Politics of the Budgetary Process,* 2nd ed. (Boston: Little, Brown and Co., 1974) describes the strategies and maneuverings involved in appropriating money for government. (See also Fenno's *Power of the Purse,* above.) James L. Sundquist, *Politics and Policy: The Eisenhower, Kennedy and Johnson Years* (Washington, D.C.: Brookings Institution, 1968), gives a comprehensive history of a decade of domestic legislation. Jeffrey L. Pressman and Aaron B. Wildavsky, *Implementation: How Great Expectations in Washington Are Dashed in Oakland, or, Why It's Amazing that Federal Programs Work At All* (Berkeley, Calif.: University of California Press, 1973), shows how there can be many a slip between a law and its effects.

There are a number of interesting accounts of particular legislation, including Theodore R. Marmor, *The Politics of Medicare* (Chicago: Aldine Publishing Co., 1973), Daniel Patrick Moynihan, *The Politics of Guaranteed Income: The Nixon Administration and the Family Assistance Plan* (New York: Random House, 1973), and John A. Ferejohn, *Pork Barrel Politics: Rivers and Harbors Legislation, 1947–1968* (Stanford, Calif.: Stanford University Press, 1974). Allan P. Sindler, ed., *Policy and Politics in America: Six Case Studies* (Boston: Little, Brown and Co., 1973), and John F. Bibby and Roger H. Davidson, *On Capitol Hill: Studies in the Legislative Process,* 2nd ed. (New York: Holt, Rinehart & Winston, 1972), describe some brief case studies.

11
THE COURTS

*Americans alone of western peoples made constitutionalism
a religion and the judiciary a religious order
and surrounded both with an aura of piety.*

Henry Steele Commager

*John, I want you to remember that a judge
is a law student who corrects his own papers.*

H. L. Mencken

The Constitution makes it all sound so simple. It says that the judicial power of the United States is vested in a Supreme Court and "in such inferior Courts as the Congress may from time to time ordain and establish." Then it gives a two-paragraph summary of the Supreme Court's jurisdiction, which is generally over cases arising from federal laws and cases arising from disputes that cross state boundaries. This was the only blueprint the new nation had; the United States began without a federal court system and without any clear idea of what such a system's duties would be. The situation was further complicated by Federalist/anti-Federalist strife. The very thought of a federal court system frightened and offended anti-Federalists. They were convinced that the federal court system, if and when it was established, would be employed as a powerful instrument to crush important defenses of states' rights that had been developed within the state court systems.

One of the great achievements of the first Congress was the writing of the Judiciary Act of 1789, which developed the third branch of government, and the winning of its acceptance. The principal authors were Senators Oliver Ellsworth of Connecticut, William Paterson of New Jersey, and Caleb Strong of Massachusetts. Their product showed the typical genius of our early politicians in that it scattered authority and at the same time bound it together.

The Judiciary Act established that the Supreme Court would consist of a chief justice and five associate justices (since 1869, the number of justices has been nine); it established a district judge in each state and required that that judge be a resident of the state; it set up three traveling circuit courts of appeal, each presided over by two Supreme Court justices and whatever district court judge was at hand. Jurisdiction was also elaborately and delicately balanced. Federal courts would have judicial review over state legislation (something not mentioned in the Constitution), but state courts would retain all the authority they had before the Constitution was adopted and would also have jurisdiction over many matters arising from federal law. In general, a state's supreme court would have the final say over appeals not relating to federal law. State courts were not demoted to a secondary role, but were made what might be called a less potent equal.

The fundamental development of the court system has occurred, however, not by edict, but by practice. Looking back on the past two hundred years of experience, certain things stand out and will be discussed more fully in this chapter. The exercise of law, we will see, has little kinship with mathematical certainties. The written two-plus-two of the legal statutes may equal four, but the interpreted statute, after being run through the head of a judge, may come out three or five—or, more likely, three-and-a-half. We will see that judges, by their interpretations, actually make law, and, consequently, we will see why it is absolutely imperative for the well-being of the nation that only the keenest minds be appointed to the court.[1] We will see the court's intellectual strengths, its political weaknesses, its undemocratic nature, its remarkable integrity.

---

[1] When one of President Richard M. Nixon's nominees to the Supreme Court was denounced as being mediocre, Senator Roman L. Hruska of Nebraska offered this defense: "Even if he were mediocre, there are a lot of mediocre judges and people and lawyers. They are entitled to a little representation, aren't they, and a little chance?" (Quoted in James F. Simon, *In His Own Image: The Supreme Court in Nixon's America* (New York: David McKay Co., 1973, p. 122.) To take the Hruska dictum seriously would be disastrous.

LAW AND ITS INTERPRETATION

Law is the understanding by which society agrees to reconcile its differences. As long as everyone is in agreement on an issue, law can be ignored. Mutually satisfied citizens never take each other to court or lobby for new legislation. That happens only when parties fall out, when neighbors disagree over rights of way, when corporations insist on using similar trademarks, when athletes want to break contracts and move to another team, when sheepmen feel that cattlemen have too much of the federal range, when people living downstream decide they are being abused by an upstream utility company's pollution. In short, it is only when one element of society feels that others have conspired to deny it a fair chance at the bonanza of life and liberty that the law is appealed to for relief.

Laws have several different origins. Some are born of custom and tradition, the hardy ancestry of common law. Some come from legislation, some from executive fiat. There is a rare genre of law that comes from the deliberation of conventions, as the United States Constitution did. Most law is obliquely shaped by the whim of judges—both brilliant judges and judges of the sort once described by California Governor Edmund G. ("Pat") Brown: "superannuated and senile and mentally ill and alcoholics."[2]

The Work of Judges

Regardless of its origin, most people tend to regard law as something majestic and pure. They think of it as a system of known rules impartially applied by a judge. They think the judges "find" their decisions in some great body of law and pull them out, uninfluenced by their own beliefs and values. Justice Louis D. Brandeis rejected this notion of the "brooding omnipresence" of law. In *Erie Railroad v. Tompkins*[3] he argued that law is simply what is laid down by an authority (in the case of *Erie,* the authority being

---

[2] Quoted in Robert Sherrill, *The Saturday Night Special* (New York: David McKay Co., Charterhouse Books, 1973), p. 232.

[3] *Erie Railroad v. Tompkins,* 304 U.S. 64 (1938).

the state of Pennsylvania). When judges lay down the law, they are influenced not only by logic, history, and custom, but also by utility, accepted standard of conduct, patterns of social welfare, and their own instincts, beliefs, and convictions. In short, the assumption that a judge only "finds" law is inaccurate; a judge also makes law. But judges are not really free to make it from whole cloth and whim. They must recognize certain patterns. As Benjamin N. Cardozo notes, the judge is "not a knight-errant roaming at will in pursuit of his own ideal of beauty or of goodness. He is to draw his inspiration from consecrated principles . . . he is to exercise a discretion informed by tradition, methodized by analogy, disciplined by system. . . ."[4] C. Herman Pritchett and Walter F. Murphy set forth a similar view:

> . . . Judges are men who are influenced in their judging by personal predilections, commitments to ethical norms and perceptions of the realities of political life. But at the same time it must never be forgotten that the freedom of the judge is limited by the institutional ethos and by the traditions of his calling.[5]

Judges cannot go out and seek cases, nor can they fabricate them. They must wait until an issue is disputed and litigated. Even then, they must ascertain that the case is within their jurisdiction before they can hear it.

The point of departure for a judge's work in deciding a case is the principle of *stare decisis,* which Cardozo says should be "at least the everyday working rule of our law."[6] *Stare decisis* (literally, "to stand by what has gone before") means deciding cases according to precedents that are applicable. Each new decision then becomes a precedent for future cases; but it does not serve as a final truth, only as a working hypothesis "continually retested in those great laboratories of the law, the courts of justice."[7]

When precedents are unavailable or do not fit, then a judge must fashion law, and that can involve policy making. But judge-made law is secondary to law made by legislators, or statutory law; and statutory law is subordinate to constitutional law. When a code of law or a statute is unambiguous, a judge has a clear command for his or her judgment. Often, however, statutes or codes need interpretation. In the case of a statute, a judge must determine what the *intention* of the legislature was and rule accordingly, even if that intention is erroneous by present-day standards. The only justification for invalidating legislation is if it is unconstitutional.

When a point of constitutional law is disputed, judges are faced with a slippery case indeed. For, as Edward H. Levi points out, "the Constitution in its general provisions embodies the conflicting ideals of the community."[8] It is a question not only of which way to interpret it, but also of how much a judge can stretch the meaning of the Constitution. As we shall see, this is a matter of some controversy, and it vitally affects the work and impact of the Supreme Court.

The Flexibility of the Constitution

The notion that the Supreme Court need only follow the Constitution—indeed, is duty bound to do no more than follow that written word—is an idea that not many people treat seriously. It is called *strict construction,* and it is a theory analogous to the belief that the Bible means just what it says, no more and no less. Strict constructionists are, in effect, legal fundamentalists.

Sam J. Ervin, Jr., whose long career saw him at various times serving as country lawyer, country judge, and United States senator from North Carolina, was, until he retired in 1974, considered to be one of the outstanding constitutional authorities in the United States Senate. Ervin was an eloquent strict constructionist. This, in brief, was his creed:

---

[4] Benjamin N. Cardozo, *The Nature of the Judicial Process* (New Haven, Conn.: Yale University Press, 1921), p. 141.

[5] Walter F. Murphy and C. Herman Pritchett, *Courts, Judges, and Politics* (New York: Random House, 1974).

[6] Cardozo, *The Nature of the Judicial Process,* p. 20.

[7] Cardozo, p. 23.

[8] Edward H. Levi, *Introduction to Legal Reasoning,* rev. ed. (Chicago: University of Chicago Press, 1962), p. 58.

We are told that the words of the Constitution automatically change their meaning from time to time without any change in phraseology being authorized by Congress and the states in the manner prescribed by Article V, and that a majority of the Supreme Court justices possess the omnipotent power to declare when these automatic changes occur, and their scope and effect. This notion is the stuff of which a judicial oligarchy is made. . . . Everyone will concede that the Constitution is written in words. If these words have no fixed meaning, they make the Constitution conform to Mark Twain's description of the dictionary. He said the dictionary has a wonderful vocabulary, but no plot.[9]

"Fixed meaning"? Do men like Ervin actually believe that the Constitution offers a solution for every governmental problem, written so clearly and precisely that its meaning is fixed for all time? In 1968, as the great activist era of the Supreme Court under Chief Justice Earl Warren was obviously coming to an end, Richard M. Nixon promised that if elected he would appoint men to the Court who would be "strict constructionists" of the Constitution, not men who would try to "modernize" it or "make new law" that could not be found in the Constitution. Did he really think his appointees would be so closely bound by the "fixed meaning" that Ervin touted?

It was a notion very pleasing to many conservatives who heard him, especially southern conservatives who had been outraged by the Warren Court's civil rights decisions. And they were pleased with Nixon's appointments to the Court. After Nixon had been in office nearly two years, it was written in the arch-conservative newspaper *Human Events* that

President Nixon has broken many of his major campaign promises to the electorate. . . . But credit must be given where credit is due. In the area of judicial appointments, the President has continued to make good his 1968 pledge that he would nominate "conservative" or "strict constructionists" to the Supreme Court.[10]

The people at *Human Events*, like other conservatives, were especially ecstatic over Nixon's appointment of William H. Rehnquist, probably the most severely conservative lawyer to be appointed to the Court in a generation. And yet, Rehnquist was not a strict constructionist at all, nor had he pretended to be. Two years before his appointment he had written in the *Harvard Law Record*: "It is no accident that the provisions of the Constitution which have been most productive of judicial law-making—the 'due process of the law' and 'equal protection of the laws' clauses—are about the vaguest and most general of any in the instrument." He saw this as no defect, however, so long as the right judges (that is, presumably, judges who agreed with him) were on the Court to interpret the Constitution's vagueness. He went on to make this point unmistakably clear:

It is high time that those critical of the present Court recognize with the late Charles Evans Hughes that for 175 years the Constitution has been what the judges say it is. If greater judicial self-restraint is desired, or a different interpretation of the phrases "due process of law" or "equal protection of the laws," then men sympathetic to such desires must sit upon the high court.[11]

One can almost sympathize with conservatives who were alarmed by the Warren Court's interpretive activities. It wasn't just the character of the decisions that bothered them; it was the overwhelming flood of decisions.

Alpheus T. Mason has pointed out that during the latter 1950s and early 1960s many conservative citizens literally thought that the Warren Court was preparing the nation for a revolution. This fearful conviction was prompted by such traumatic occasions as that

single sitting, June 17, 1957, [when] the judiciary had a field day. It upheld the right of anyone to preach the overthrow of government, so long as the preaching was limited to "abstract principle" and did not openly advocate specific action to overthrow government. It limited the power of congressional committees to make investigations and to require witnesses to testify. It denied the power of states to require witnesses to testify in

[9]Sam. J. Ervin, Jr., and Ramsey Clark, *Role of the Supreme Court: Policymaker or Adjudicator?* (Washington, D.C.: American Enterprise Institute, 1970), pp. 51–52.

[10]*Human Events*, October 30, 1970.

[11]Quoted in the *New York Times*, November 3, 1971.

This SIGN has been torn apart twice by those who would abolish our -- CONSTITUTION

THIS IS NOT A JOHN BIRCH PROJ.

Impeach!
Chief Justice
EARL WARREN

READ "NINE MEN AGAINST AMERICA"

investigations authorized by state legislatures. It restricted the power of officials to discharge government employees.[12]

All in one day. Policy-making field days like that were not unusual during the Warren era. For citizens accustomed to more cautious action from previous Courts, these seemed wildly irresponsible actions. "Revolutionary" was a label commonly attached to the Warren Court. It was often accused—as Nixon accused it—of "making laws" rather than following the law, of disregarding the Constitution, of going its own whimsical way, of basing its decisions strictly on sociology and philosophy and vague notions of humanitarianism—not on prior law, not on legal traditions, not on that term so beloved of judicial conservatives, *stare decisis*.

[12] Alpheus T. Mason, *The Supreme Court from Taft to Warren,* enl. and rev. ed. (Baton Rouge, La.: Louisiana State University Press, 1968), p. 2.

Liberties in Peril

Most of the animus built up against the Supreme Court during its libertarian periods has been grounded on opposition to specific decisions sustaining liberty, establishing equality, or upholding due process of law. . . . The difficulty is vastly increased—indeed it is hard to maintain well-established liberties—when the wrong people ask for the right remedies. Lawyers who have the courage and sense of professional duty to act as counsel for Communists, though hating their doctrine and despising their conduct, are assailed as sympathizers with the system they condemn. Judges who insist on fair procedures for persons accused of crime are described as "bleeding hearts." Courts that protect the rights of citizens . . . invite not only the scurrility of extremists but concerted attacks in Congress that put the very foundations of government in peril.

In 1958, half a dozen bills to override libertarian Court decisions or restrict the appellate power of the Supreme Court were defeated in the Senate by the skill and determination of Democratic Majority Leader Lyndon B. Johnson. In 1964, to undo the decision that outlawed "rotten boroughs" as a denial of equal protection of the laws, the House passed a bill to strip the Court of any jurisdiction in that field. The deadly aspect of all this lies in the fact that such a movement should ever reach the danger point in Congress.

Supreme Court decisions on the meaning and application of the Constitution may be right or wrong, good or bad, wise or rash. But when the power to make them is taken away by a vote in Congress, the Constitution ceases to be anything more than the gaunt skeleton of a frame of government, open to all the conflicting blasts of the winds of passion.

From Irving Brant, *The Bill of Rights*
(Indianapolis: Bobbs-Merrill Co., 1965), pp. 512–13.

To some extent the critics were right. The Warren Court repeatedly made federal policy, repeatedly made law, repeatedly shattered tradition. But to say only that is to distort the issue; the question was properly not whether the Court did these things, but, rather, whether it could avoid doing them, whether any Court in any era could avoid making law. Does such a thing as "strict construction" actually exist?

The answer—given by history and by virtually every eminent student of the Court as well as by nearly every justice who has served on the Court—is simply No. Some Courts are more creative than others, some Courts are more experimental, some are more daring. But all Supreme Courts have interpreted the Constitution; they have not simply followed it. In effect, the Constitution has always been, in every era, what a majority of the Supreme Court said it was.

How could it be otherwise? The Constitution is a relatively brief document. One can read it—and all its amendments—in less than an hour. It could not possibly include such precise language that it would cover every conceivable problem of government that might arise in a nation that has changed so dramatically in two centuries. Strict constructionists would be out of luck if they expected to find the Constitution talking about antitrust laws or child labor laws or school integration or income taxes or a thousand other major issues that might be mentioned. The language is not there.

What *is* there is wonderfully elastic language, beautifully broad generalities that can be stretched in such a way that they can cover just about any problem of government. No language in the Constitution is more elastic, for example, than that of the Fourteenth Amendment:

All persons born or naturalized in the United States, and subject to the jurisdiction thereof, are citizens of the United States and of the State wherein they reside. No State shall make or enforce any law which shall abridge the privileges or immunities of citizens of the United States; nor shall any State deprive any person of life, liberty, or property, without due process of law; nor deny to any person within its jurisdiction the equal protection of the laws.

Virtually the same guarantee of "due process" is found in the Fifth Amendment; in the Fourteenth it is merely extended to cover state actions as well as federal.

But what exactly does "due process" mean? Does it mean that every defendant must be given a lawyer, whether or not he or she can pay for counsel? Does it mean that a state can twice require a person to stand trial for a crime that puts his or her life in jeopardy? To such questions, the Court has sometimes said Yes, sometimes No. The application of due process is one of the most confusing demands on the Court. "Due process of law" is perhaps the most fluid phrase in the Constitution. Its fluidity has embroiled the Court in some great rhetorical wrestling matches. Indeed, Justices Louis D. Brandeis and Felix Frankfurter once got into such a frustrating argument over what exactly the phrase "due process" must mean that they wound up agreeing that it should be thrown out of the Constitution.

And what about the last phrase of the Fourteenth Amendment, "equal protection of the laws." Does it mean that black children should be allowed to attend the same schools as white children, or does it only mean that, so long as their schools offer equal educational opportunities, they can be segregated? And can the separate-but-equal rule also be applied to interstate transportation facilities? These, of course, are the questions that—as we have seen in Chapter 4—have torn the nation apart during the last generation. The Court answered them one way in the nineteenth century, another way in the mid–twentieth century.

If the language of the Constitution is fixed and precise, as some claim, then the justices would not have been so troubled by it and would not have shifted their position so often. The Fourteenth Amendment was ratified in 1868, and the justices who sit on the highest court in the nation are still trying to figure out how it should be applied. That's the way much of the Constitution affects them. It's their job to make imprecision *seem* precise, and to accomplish this they must depend on a great deal more than law books.

The words of the Constitution, wrote Justice Frankfurter, are

so unrestricted by their intrinsic meaning or by their history or by tradition or by prior decisions that they leave the Justice free, if indeed they do not compel him, to gather meaning not from reading the Constitution but from reading life. . . . Members of the Court are frequently admonished by their associates not to read their economic and social views into the neutral language of the Constitution. But the process of constitutional interpretation compels the translation of policy into judgment. . . .[13]

Even before he was appointed to the Court and could speak from experience, Frankfurter had already laid down his faith in the role of Supreme Court justices as "moulders of policy, rather than impersonal vehicles of revealed truth."[14]

Strict constructionists today are very fond of the memory of Justice Frankfurter because, as an early participant in the Warren Court, he was prone to take what is considered the conservative position. Yet nobody has ever made more frequent acknowledgment of the looseness and pliability of the Constitution than he. No member of the Court ever defended more eloquently the "creative" aspects of its work, which the strict constructionists damn so heartily. On one occasion he wrote:

Words like "liberty" and "property," phrases like "regulate Commerce . . . among the several States," "due process of law," "equal protection of the laws," doctrines like those of separation of powers and the non-delegability of the legislative function, are the foundation for judicial action upon the whole appalling domain of social and economic fact. But phrases like "due process of law" are, as an able judge once expressed it, of "convenient vagueness." Their ambiguity is such that the Court is compelled to put meaning into the Constitution, not to take it out. Such features of the Constitution render peculiarly appropriate a favorite quotation of John Chipman Gray: "Whoever hath an absolute authority to interpret any written or spoken law, it is he who is truly the lawgiver to all intents and purposes, and not the person who first wrote or spoke them." . . . The scope for interpreting the Constitution is relatively

---

[13] Felix Frankfurter, "The Supreme Court," *Parliamentary Affairs* 3 (1949): 68.

[14] Felix Frankfurter, "The Supreme Court and the Public," quoted in Mason, *The Supreme Court from Taft to Warren*, p. 206.

wide and the opportunity for exercising individual notions of policy correspondingly free.[15]

Frankfurter's description of the justices as cartographers who give temporary location but do not ultimately define the ever-shifting boundaries between state and national power and between freedom and authority would not be seriously challenged by many legal scholars, whatever their ideology. Frankfurter has simply described the way the Court operates. The legal scholar Philip B. Kurland, a moderate-conservative and a frequent critic of the Warren Court, takes much the same position:

> It must be made clear that the essential question is nothing so simple as whether the Court is adhering to the commands of the Constitution. For the commands of the Constitution are often written in Delphic language. Strict construction of vague language is not possible for mere mortals. That is why so many of us resort to dogma in lieu of reason to explain the "plain meaning" of abstruse phrases.[16]

All of this supports the proposition that it is impossible for the Supreme Court to be other than activist. One must add, however, that there are certainly degrees of activism and that we are now living in the most activist era the courts have ever seen.

Relaxed legal standards make it easier today than it was at any time in our history for a citizen or a group to gain standing at court—that is, to be allowed to bring suit or to challenge the constitutionality of laws or government policies. The courts have simply become more willing to throw open their doors to aggrieved citizens, and, although the Supreme Court under Chief Justice Warren Burger has made some minor efforts to narrow the opening, the doors will probably remain wide open.

Moreover, a great portion of the legal fraternity has become imbued with a new concept of the Court's obligation. Traditionally—going back to English common law and to the spirit that guided our early courts—a lawsuit was seen as a neatly packaged dispute between two parties seeking a referee; they brought their difference to court, and the judge ruled on which one was right *in that particular instance*. The implications of the ruling would affect other cases, but the purpose of the ruling was aimed at nothing broader than righting a wrong that occurred in the past. That is still the basic function of our courts—settling one particular dispute and then moving on to another particular dispute.

But our generation has seen the birth, after many decades of gestation, of what Abram Chayes calls "public law litigation."[17] Its hallmark is the class-action lawsuit. Public law litigation often involves many parties, not just two; it is not merely aimed at righting a past wrong, but at establishing a policy, setting up a program that will guarantee an end to certain kinds of injustice. Moreover, judges are not merely expected to come up with rulings; they are being looked to for what might more accurately be called "solutions." And they very often find themselves playing an intensely activist role. In recent years, federal and state judges have been administering mental-health programs and state prisons, prescribing what athletic equipment a high school should buy, and overseeing union pension funds and other supervisory nuts-and-bolts programs.[18] As of 1977, state and federal courts had stepped in and taken over, for varying lengths of time, the operation of jails in St. Louis, Baltimore, New Orleans, Toledo, New York City, Boston, Jacksonville, Knoxville, and Lubbock and Harris counties in Texas. Such actions were taken on the grounds that the inmates were being deprived of certain constitutional rights; the courts mandated not only general reforms, but specific steps, such as reduc-

---

[15] Felix Frankfurter, *Mr. Justice Holmes and the Supreme Court* (Cambridge, Mass.: Harvard University Press, Belknap Press, 1938), pp. 6–8.

[16] Philip B. Kurland, *Politics, the Constitution, and the Warren Court* (Chicago: University of Chicago Press, 1973), p. xlv.

[17] See Abram Chayes, *Harvard Law Review*, Fall 1976.

[18] The ultimate, perhaps, was reached by Judge Frank M. Johnson, Jr., of Alabama, one of the most active of federal judges, who did not stop with an order that the state's mental health facilities be generally improved, but got right down to the kind of specific orders that many consider revolutionary for a judge: "Thermostatically controlled hot water shall be provided in adequate quantities and maintained at the required temperature (110° Fahrenheit at the fixture) and for mechanical and laundry use (180° Farenheit at the equipment)." (Quoted in the *Washington Post*, July 18, 1976.)

tions in prison population and more mopping of corridors.[19] When necessary, the courts gained compliance to their orders for improving the operation of public institutions by threatening to hold recalcitrant governors, mayors, council members, wardens, and hospital administrators in contempt of court.

The long-range results of the courts' activist role can only be guessed at. It may, as it seems in the short run, turn out to be totally benevolent. But some critics believe that the wholesale intervention of the judiciary in the functions of the executive and legislative branches could result in the development of an imperial judicial oligarchy. Some observers fear that the public will come to rely excessively on judges, causing a harmful withering of the democratic branches of government. Activist judges respond that they have been forced to take the initiative because the legislative and executive arms have failed to service society's obvious needs. It is easy to sympathize with that attitude, but the fact remains that it fuzzes the outlines of law and the lines separating the branches of government. In 1958, Chief Justice Earl Warren said that the Eighth Amendment's prohibition against cruel and unusual punishment "must draw its meaning from the evolving standards of decency that mark the progress of a maturing society."[20] This pretty statement would have been more useful to other judges, however, had he gone on to explain how the "evolving standards" could be identified. Such looseness of language makes it possible for the courts to do a great deal of good, but probably at a high cost to the concept of law itself.

Thus we come to a fascinating question: if some intelligent people, such as former Senator Ervin, believe that the Constitution means what it says, no more and no less, and if one of our best justices of the past, Hugo L. Black, heatedly argued all his career that the constitutional guarantee of free speech means *absolute* free speech,

what can they possibly hope to achieve when almost the entire legal fraternity stands against them? The best answer is that extremism serves a very useful purpose in keeping pragmatists on target. One constitutional scholar puts it this way:

> If the judges tell themselves and the world that the constitutional language, as construed, does define absolutes, even if not "in imagined chemical purity" but "in the practical sense in which chemicals labelled "chemically pure" are "pure," the tendency of their judgments and those of their posterity will be affected thereby. There will be a tendency, for example, to let more speech be heard more freely in more circumstances if the First Amendment is thought of as a literal absolute than if it is conceded that the Amendment is merely an invitation to contemporary judgment.[21]

In short, even the most freewheeling interpreters of the Constitution must operate under the belief that there is a basic foundation of absolutes in that document. Although many people differ in their definition of "freedom," for example, there is a core meaning that everyone agrees on—and it is the core meaning in the key words of the Constitution that maintain the *attitude* of justice at its highest level. In this sense, a striving for strict construction has a very practical, as well as idealistic, place in the role of the Supreme Court.

THE QUALITY OF JUSTICES

It hardly need be pointed out that the Supreme Court is, and always has been, peopled by mere mortals. They have the same lusts, egos, tempers, and ambitions as other men. They are simply better at controlling themselves.[22] Supreme Court justices are influenced by a bad night's sleep and an acid stomach just as bus

[19]Martin Tolchin, "Federal State Courts: Not Since 1803 Such Expansion of Authority," New York Times News Service in the *Washington Star*, April 25, 1977.

[20]Quoted in Arthur S. Miller, "The Supreme Court: Time for Reforms," *Washington Post*, January 11, 1976.

[21]Alexander M. Bickel, *The Least Dangerous Branch: The Supreme Court at the Bar of Politics* (Indianapolis: Bobbs-Merrill Co., 1962), p. 93.

[22]Charges of failing minds and low character are so rarely aimed at Supreme Court justices that one must assume that the nation is especially lucky in those chosen to sit on the highest bench.

Judicial Tenacity

Vacancies on the supreme bench are not always the work of fate. Not every tired or disabled constitutional warrior is disposed to "bow to the inevitable" and retire promptly and unhesitatingly without regard to how his successor will vote on the crucial issues ahead. Judges have, in fact, displayed conspicuous determination and capacity to stay on pending political change—incumbency of a new President of the right political stripe. On more than one occasion, Presidents or Justices themselves have felt impelled to resort to the embarrassing task of advising a senescent judge to quit.

Though he felt his powers failing, John Marshall died in the center chair, because Jackson triumphed in the 1832 election. In 1875 Justice Samuel Miller complained bitterly of his inability to induce colleagues "who are too old [to] resign." Taft, mistaking Hoover for a "progressive," faced retirement with trepidation, and urged like-minded colleagues to hang on. Holmes, the most sophisticated of judges, acutely aware of his aging colleagues' tendency to stay on and on, had himself to be asked to step down. For five years after Franklin D. Roosevelt's election in 1932, the supreme bench, comprised of judges averaging age seventy-two plus, remained unchanged, one reason being their hope that the people would return to their senses and elect a Republican president.

From Alpheus T. Mason, *The Supreme Court from Taft to Warren,* enl. and rev. ed. (Baton Rouge, La.: Louisiana State University Press, 1968), pp. 228–29.

Eight of the "nine old men" on the Hoover-Roosevelt Court

drivers are. Some justices are witty, some aren't; some are creative, some are less so. They are subject to the demands of the flesh, and they quicken to the calls of the spirit. Justice Abe Fortas was an excellent violinist off the bench and a clever fellow on it. When one of his law clerks became too solemn about a case, Fortas chided him: "Your trouble is that you have no sense of Halloween." Justice Byron R. White, a former professional football player, likes to unwind with a fast game of basketball. A former clerk recalls coming upon White in the gym, dribbling a ball in the middle of the court. White, lost in thought and mumbling, suddenly shouted, "What if . . . ," asking a question relating to a case then before the Court. "And that question presented the key that unlocked the case," according to the clerk, "and after that he played a hell of a game."[23]

Chief Justice Burger washes his hair in beer and uses pomade to keep it brilliantly white; he is a talented painter and sculptor and a connoisseur of wines (his cellar holds about five hundred bottles).[24] His temper is not always under control; he has had several name-calling run-ins with the press. And tempers sometimes grow short in the justices' dealings with each other. Justice Frankfurter's diaries show he considered Justice Black capable of indulging in "a harangue worthy of the cheapest soap-box orator" and looked upon Justice William O. Douglas as "the most systematic exploiter of flattery I have ever encountered in my life."[25]

Supreme Court justices, like all federal judges, are appointed for life. They can be removed only by impeachment, which almost never occurs. Like all mortals, judges decline physically with age, and sometimes they decline mentally as well. But they are slow to admit it. After serving thirty-five years on the Court, Justice Douglas suffered a stroke. How damaging it was to him physically or mentally, neither

he nor his staff gave any indication. For months he was in and out of the hospital, maintaining secrecy about his condition. Partly paralyzed and restricted to a wheelchair, he still plied his way through the back halls of the Court, voting on cases when he chose, skipping votes when he chose, hanging on and on until editorial comments and the opinions of his colleagues finally forced him to surrender his seat. Because of his reluctance to concede his weakness, the work of the whole Court suffered for nearly a term.

But if the justices are just ordinary men (of perhaps extraordinary intelligence), they do like to create an aura of superiority and even of majesty. They may believe it to be their patriotic duty to create this atmosphere as a way to help implement their decisions, for they probably know that, as law professor Telford Taylor once put it, "The Court is in large part what people think it is; to labor an overworked expression, it is an 'image.'"[26]

To create this image, the justices combine pomposity with an authentic striving for self-improvement. Some display a hypersensitive concern for the trappings of office and for the surface deference due it. Lawyers who appear before the Supreme Court to deliver oral arguments have learned that some members of the bench have an overriding concern for attire. "Who is that beast who dares to come in here with a grey coat," Justice Horace Gray, a denizen of the Supreme Court around the turn of the century, was heard to mutter on one occasion. More recently, Chief Justice Burger was described as "dismayed" when an attorney showed up wearing a morning suit with a pearl gray vest instead of a dark one.

The judicial branch of government is the least democratic. In fact, it is not democratic at all. Federal judges at every level are appointed by the President (and confirmed by the Senate) for life. After that, they can, and many do, retreat into a shell that has little contact with the public. Some Supreme Court justices are regulars on the Washington cocktail circuit, but they almost never give interviews. Most members of the

---

[23] *Washington Post,* June 16, 1974.

[24] Julius Duscha, "Chief Justice Burger Asks: 'If It Doesn't Make Good Sense, How Can It Make Good Law?' " *New York Times Magazine,* October 5, 1969.

[25] Felix Frankfurter, *From the Diaries of Felix Frankfurter,* ed. Joseph P. Lash (New York: W. W. Norton & Co., 1975).

[26] Quoted in Robert Sherrill, "Earl Warren," *Lithopinion* 9, no. 4, issue 36 (Winter 1974): 15.

Court assiduously avoid—as they should—any kind of close contact with politicians that could be interpreted as showing an unsavory, partisan bias. But there have been notable exceptions to this rule. Justice Fortas was constantly running to the White House to give advice to and take suggestions from President Lyndon B. Johnson. Justice Frankfurter was a notorious busybody, running back and forth between the Court and the White House. And White House transcripts of taped conversations show that Chief Justice Burger consulted with Attorney General Richard G. Kleindienst when the search was on for the first special Watergate prosecutor in 1973.[27]

But if justices of the Supreme Court sometimes feel that it is safe to breach the proper separation of branches by talking with Presidents or with agents of Presidents, they seldom deign to speak to lesser mortals about their business, and it is absolutely unheard of for them to discuss actual cases. Their clerks are also sworn to secrecy. There is a practical reason for the secrecy that surrounds their deliberations. If, for instance, there were premature disclosure—or hints—of a Court decision regarding a major antitrust divestiture suit, it could have a harmfully galvanic impact on the stock market.

But, as Warren Weaver of the *New York Times* has pointed out, with understandable irritation, "Over the years, this insistence on maintaining absolute secrecy as to *what* the Justices decide has tended to expand automatically to cover *how* they decide, cloaking the entire operation of the Court in a kind of unnecessary and undemocratic mystery."[28] The Supreme Court building itself, across the street from the Capitol, is largely off-limits to the public,[29] and the justices' conference room is off-limits, on conference days, to even the clerk of the Court.

This secrecy does not hurt the public, however, nearly so much as it hurts the "brethren" (as the justices call each other). For it implants in

them a false sense of Olympian excellency—what one critic of the Court, Judge Jerome N. Frank, once described as "the cult of the robe," meaning that human beings who don the judicial robe think that they thereby become automatically instilled with a sagacity that is beyond other people in government. They forget, as the late Justice Robert H. Jackson once remarked, that Supreme Court justices are infallible because they are final, not final because they are infallible.[30]

THE JUDICIAL PROCESS

The Supreme Court has two kinds of jurisdiction—original and appellate. The Constitution stipulates the conditions of original jurisdiction: "Cases affecting Ambassadors, other public Ministers and Consuls, and those in which a State shall be Party." The Court exercises its appellate jurisdiction under regulations set by Congress. Some cases are appealed to the Court on the grounds that constitutional rights, rights under federal law, or treaties have been violated. Most cases are submitted as petitions for a writ of certiorari (meaning "made more certain"), which directs a lower court to send the record in the case to the Supreme Court for review. The Court considers all petitions and decides which cases to grant certiorari. Generally, only those cases that present a substantial issue in law or policy are accepted. The acceptance

> is not intended merely to give a litigant another chance, nor does it depend on the dollars involved or the private interests affected, but upon the importance of the case to a uniform and just system of federal law.[31]

Thus, the Court controls its docket and decides what it wants to hear—and not hear. Many of the

---

[27] *Washington Post,* June 13, 1974.

[28] Warren Weaver, *New York Times,* February 6, 1975.

[29] When a District of Columbia Superior Court judge made a speech on the steps outside the Supreme Court building, Chief Justice Burger became so incensed at this "trespass" that he threatened to have him arrested and thrown in jail. (*Washington Star,* March 18, 1976.)

[30] Alexander M. Bickel, *The Caseload of the Supreme Court* (Washington, D.C.: American Enterprise Institute, 1973), p. 13.

[31] Robert H. Jackson, "The Supreme Court as a Unit of Government," in Alan F. Westin, ed., *The Supreme Court: Views from Inside* (New York: W. W. Norton & Co., 1961), p. 24.

cases that are refused have legal merit, but the Court is not prepared to form an opinion on the issue. Some cases are rejected not because they are unimportant, but simply because the Court does not even have time to hear all the important cases.

The number of appeals to the Supreme Court is increasing at a startling rate. In a typical October-to-June term in 1951, 1,353 cases were filed with the Court for review. Ten years later, the number had jumped to 2,570. And by the mid-1970s, the number of cases appealed to the high court had passed 5,000. In the eight-month term, the justices will accept only about 150 cases. And even 150 cases a term strain the Court's facilities and abilities. In a single term, the justices could be called on to wrestle with profound complexities arising from quarrels about taxation, freedom of the press, obscenity, separation of powers, and antitrust legislation. They must show, or at least pretend, some expertise in economics, psychology, political science, engineering, history, semantics, and ethics. Issues that would never have come to the Court in an earlier era—such as pollution and consumer quarrels—are commonplace. To grapple with this intellectual octopus, the justices have the assistance of a meager research staff and an equally lean clerk staff.

The truth is that the judges of the highest court, like their brethren below, make many judgments in the dark. They do not know the impact of an antitrust action or a probusing action. Sometimes, recognizing the limits of their expertise, they simply sidestep complex cases. Rarely does the Supreme Court take an appeal from one of the regulatory agencies relating to, say, natural-gas pricing, or communications jurisdiction, or securities sales, or rail-rate setting, or the like. (When William Howard Taft was on the bench, he acknowledged privately that he always dodged radio questions because he didn't understand them.) In effect, they acknowledge the greater expertise of the regulatory commissioners and bow to their judgments—thereby making them the true "supreme court" in such matters. The same supremacy is usually conferred by default to the Court of Claims and the Court of Customs and Patent Appeals.

Procedures of the Court

When a case is accepted for review, the justices receive written briefs in which each side presents its arguments. Then a day is scheduled for presentation of the case by oral argument in court. The oral argument is one of the few operations of the Supreme Court open to public view. According to Anthony Lewis, sitting in on an argument gives a citizen a sense of the institution:

> The exhaustive probing of a single set of facts shows, if it is done well, how our adversary system of justice must make truth emerge from conflict. It shows also how close the questions are that the Supreme Court must answer. . . . The comments from the bench—sometimes funny, sometimes quite blunt—bring out the personalities of the justices and remind us that the Court is a collection of strong-minded individuals, much less institutionalized than the typical agency of the Executive Branch. [32]

The oral argument is important because it is a true exchange between the Court and the lawyers. Justice Frankfurter remarked that the Court was not to be regarded as "a dozing audience for the reading of soliloquies, but as a questioning body, utilizing oral argument as a means for exposing the difficulties of a case with a view to meeting them."[33] Because the oral argument is likely to be fresh in the justices' minds when they make their decision, it is often more persuasive than the written brief.

The lawyer must make his or her case in an awesome setting. Justice Harlan Fiske Stone called the Supreme Court building "almost bombastically pretentious," with its enormous columns, velvet hangings, high ceilings, and friezes carved on the walls. And yet, as Anthony Lewis has pointed out, "when an argument begins, all the trappings and ceremony seem to fade, and the scene takes on extraordinary intimacy. In the most informal way, altogether without pomp, Court and counsel converse. It is conversation—

---

[32] Anthony Lewis, *Gideon's Trumpet* (New York: Random House, Vintage Books, 1964), pp. 161–62.

[33] Quoted in Lewis, p. 162.

as direct, unpretentious and focused discussion as can be found anywhere in Washington."[34]

The Court ordinarily allows either an hour or half an hour to each side of the case. The time limit is strictly enforced. Five minutes before a lawyer's time is up, a white light flashes on; a red light means he or she must stop instantly—one lawyer was stopped on the word "if." The responsibility of arguing extremely important and difficult points of law in such a brief time puts so much stress on the attorneys—whose presentations are always interrupted by sharp, and sometimes acerbic, questioning by the justices—that some have been known to faint, and at least one attorney had a heart attack in the courtroom.

The responsibility weighs heavily on the justices, too, for, aside from the guidance of the oral arguments, they have only the written briefs and the decisions of the lower courts to go on. All in all, a case that will intimately affect the lives of 220 million Americans may not get more than half a dozen hours of each justice's attention before he must render a decision.

On the Friday of the week during which the oral arguments have been heard, the justices meet to discuss the case briefly and to make their tentative decision. By now the pressures are beginning to build. These Friday sessions begin with a handshake all around; it is a gentlemanly tradition that has lasted nearly a century. Judges value decorum above almost anything else, but occasionally tempers do surface. Frankfurter and Black, it is said, would sometimes yell at each other with such abandon that they could be heard by the guards in the hallway outside the conference room.[35]

The chief justice opens the discussion by stating the facts of the case, summarizing points of law, and suggesting ways to dispose of the case. He then asks each justice for his views and conclusions. A majority vote decides the case. If the vote is a tie, the decision of the lower court stands. If the chief justice sides with the major-ity, he assigns the writing of the opinion; if not, the senior justice among the majority assigns the writing. Each justice is free to write a dissenting opinion.

Although the chief justice's vote is but one in nine, he can use his sources of power—his prestige, his position as chairman of the conference, and his ability to assign the writing of opinions. The chief justice likes to be on the winning side, for appearance' sake if nothing else. That way, it looks like he had a persuasive hand in the outcome. Chief Justice Burger has been known (as were a number of his predecessors) to switch sides at the last minute when it became clear that he would otherwise be among the minority.[36] Often the chief justice plays an important role as "Court unifier," minimizing dissent and working up as large a majority as possible.

Psychologically, the larger the majority supporting the Court's opinion, the better. Sometimes justices will swallow their true feelings in order to bolster the *seeming* solidarity of the Court. Justice Lewis F. Powell, Jr., conceded that this was the motivation behind at least one of his votes: "In order to avoid the appearance of fragmentation of the court on the basic principles involved, I join the opinion of the court."[37] The impact of a unanimous opinion is intense because the public is naturally impressed when none of the nine strong-willed and independent men can find an excuse to go his separate way. "When unanimity can be obtained without sacrifice of conviction," said Chief Justice Charles Evans Hughes, "it strongly commends the decision to public confidence."[38] To gain this kind of impact, Chief Justice Earl Warren filibustered, wheedled, and coaxed his fellow justices into line in the landmark segregation case, *Brown v. Board of Education.* (See Chapter 4.) In May 1954, when the vote stood at eight to one, Warren told Justice Stanley F. Reed, "Stan, you're all by

[34] Harlan Fiske Stone quoted in Lewis, p. 167.

[35] Nina Totenberg, "Behind the Marble, Beneath the Robes," *New York Times Magazine*, March 16, 1975.

[36] Totenburg, "Behind the Marble, Beneath the Robes."

[37] Quoted in the *Washington Star*, March 21, 1976.

[38] Quoted by Philip B. Kurland in Leon Friedman and Fred L. Israel, *The Justices of the United States Supreme Court, 1789–1969: Their Lives and Major Opinions* (New York: R. R. Bowker Co., 1969), 4:2563–64.

yourself in this now," and argued persuasively that a unanimous decision would be in the national interest.[39]

The opinion-writing stage is a crucial one. Until the very moment that the Court's decision is made public, the justices are free to change their minds. As they hear each other thinking aloud or read each other's opinions on a case, they are frequently persuaded to change their own opinions. It is commonplace for one or several to do so while the Court's opinion is being fabricated—and what started out as a majority opinion will sometimes end up as a dissenting one.

The Court's opinion is what a majority of the nine justices decide. On that point, at least, there is a democratic quality to the Court. Unlike the often passionate tone of dissenting opinions, the majority opinion is usually dull reading—full of the dullness of consensus. Before the justice who is assigned to write the majority opinion is done with it, it has passed through the hands of all his concurring brethren, who criticize it, edit it, quibble with it, and often force it through several rewritings. This process crushes something. The sharp, cutting edges of logic and passion may have to be dispensed with. The justice who writes the Court's opinion cannot indulge his own fancies. He is, after all, writing an opinion that is a compromise, a leveling-out, a blending of a number of individual opinions—and, like all compromises, the Court's opinion will inevitably be something less than any of the concurring members considers perfect. It is not a matter of intellectual art but of intellectual craft.

A well-written majority opinion will be, above all else, instructive and easy to understand. The first duty of the justice who writes it is to explain, in unmistakable terms, the rationale by which the majority reached its decision. Clarity and completeness are prized because the reasoning behind the decision gives guidance to the judges of inferior courts and to the legal fraternity in general. The power of the Court stems, in large measure, from its success in impressing the lower courts and the bar with the clarity and precision of its thinking. So, the majority opinion is also a method for showing off professionally, strutting a bit, and demonstrating that the Supreme Court is indeed supreme because it has plenty of savvy—in short, the handing down of a crisp, compelling opinion is the very best way the Supreme Court can give leadership.

For that reason, one of the worst things the Court can do is make a ruling without explanation. For example: in 1976, the Supreme Court was asked to rule on a Virginia law relating to "crimes against nature"—specifically as the law related to homosexual relations between consenting adults in private. A three-judge United States district court had upheld, by a two-to-one vote, convictions made under the Virginia law. Similar laws existed in three dozen states. Civil libertarians argued that these laws could not be squared with recent Supreme Court rulings that birth-control measures and abortion practices were matters of constitutionally protected privacy. In any event, the legal atmosphere covering individuals' private use of their bodies was still murky. A clear statement from the Supreme Court was needed. Instead, the Court handed down a ruling consisting of only four words. Referring to the results at the appellate level, it ruled: "The judgment is affirmed."

That kind of ruling—sometimes alternating with "the appeal is dismissed"—is not uncommon. It is an abdication of power that does the lower courts and the bar a great disservice by spreading further confusion. Nobody knows for sure what such rulings mean. Do they mean that the Supreme Court literally adopts all the principles incorporated into the lower court's decision? Or does it simply mean that the high court is too busy to be bothered by thinking the problem through? Or does it mean the high court is willing to go along with the lower court's decision for a while but will probably overturn it later on? Trying to interpret skimpy decisions, says Charles Alan Wright of the University of Texas School of Law, is somewhat "like a lottery."[40]

---

[39] See Richard Kluger, *Simple Justice: The History of Brown v. Board of Education and Black America's Struggle for Equality* (New York: Random House, Alfred A. Knopf, 1976).

[40] Quoted in the *Washington Post*, April 18, 1976.

The Uses of Dissent

Every justice who disagrees with the prevailing opinion of the Court is entitled to write his dissenting opinion. These opinions are enormously useful. A dissenting opinion does not compromise; it is the opinion of just one man, and he is free to be as passionate and argumentative as he wishes. The spirit of the typical dissent is that of a prophet crying in the wilderness: he deeply regrets that his brethren on the Court who constitute a majority have gone astray; he believes that they will live to regret their decision; and he prays that either they or future courts will see the light and return to the path of rationality. In a very real sense, dissents in controversial cases are a way of appealing to public opinion, of saying to the public, "Look, my fellow justices have really missed on this one. They got carried away by the mood of the era. But if enough newspaper editors and preachers and business executives and lawyers raise hell about the Court's decision, maybe it will take the first opportunity to reverse itself." Of course, the actual wording is much more lofty and circumspect, but that was what Justice Black was really saying when he wrote in a famous dissent:

> Public opinion being what it now is, few will protest the conviction of these Communist petitioners. There is hope, however, that in calmer times, when present pressures, passions, and fears subside, this or some later Court will restore the First Amendment liberties to the high preferred place where they belong in a free society.[41]

The most moving dissents do, in fact, usually foretell the future. Dissents on the side of humanity and mercy only have to wait; sooner or later they will become the majority. This is a generalization that is true often enough to suggest that humankind really is improving. The concept of "equal justice under the law," for example, has been one of the catch phrases of government in this country for more than two hundred years, but it has come close to realization only in the last generation, spurred on to

some extent by one of the great Supreme Court dissenters, Justice Black.

In 1938, Smith Betts, forty-three years old and on relief, was charged with using a firearm to rob a country store in Maryland. When he was brought to trial he was too poor to afford an attorney, but the judge went ahead with the trial anyway because, in his opinion, there was no question about Betts's guilt and "counsel could have done little more than prolong the cross-examination without advantage."[42] Betts appealed all the way to the Supreme Court, claiming that he had been denied his rights under the Sixth Amendment. ("In all criminal prosecutions, the accused shall enjoy the right . . . to have the Assistance of Counsel for his defence.") In federal courts this was already interpreted to mean that counsel should be provided for those too poor to pay for it. But this had not been mandated by the Supreme Court for state courts, except in capital cases, such as murder and rape. The Supreme Court had required state courts to supply attorneys for paupers in such cases since *Powell v. Alabama* in 1932.[43] The Court had explained on that occasion:

> Even the intelligent and educated layman has small and sometimes no skill in the science of law. If charged with crime, he is incapable, generally, of determining for himself whether the indictment is good or bad. He is unfamiliar with the rules of evidence. Left without the aid of counsel he may be put on trial without a proper charge, and convicted upon incompetent evidence, or evidence irrelevant to the issue or otherwise inadmissible. He lacks both the skill and knowledge adequately to prepare his defense, even though he may have a perfect one. He requires the guiding hand of counsel at every step in the proceedings against him. Without it, though he be not guilty, he faces the danger of conviction because he does not know how to establish his innocence.

Too true. But if it were true of a lawyerless pauper in a trial where life was at stake, why wasn't it just as true in a trial where liberty was at stake? However obvious the common-sense an-

---

[41] *Dennis v. United States*, 341 U.S. 494 (1951).

[42] Quoted in Alan Barth, *Prophets with Honor: Great Dissents and Dissenters in the Supreme Court* (New York: Random House, Vintage Books, 1975), pp. 87–88.

[43] *Powell v. Alabama*, 287 U.S. 45 (1932).

Clarence Gideon

swer to that might be, the Supreme Court was still unwilling, in 1942 when Betts's case arrived, to extend the right of counsel in all felony cases in state courts. By six to three, they upheld his conviction.[44] Of the three dissenting opinions, Black's is the most memorable:

> A practice cannot be reconciled with "common and fundamental ideas of fairness and right" which subjects innocent men to increased dangers of conviction merely because of their poverty. Whether a man is innocent cannot be determined from a trial in which, as here, denial of counsel has made it impossible to conclude, with any satisfactory degree of certainty, that the defendant's case was adequately presented. . . . Denial to the poor of the request for counsel in proceedings based on charges of serious crime has long been regarded as shocking to the "universal sense of justice" throughout this country. . . . And most other states have shown their agreement by constitutional provisions, statutes, or established practice judicially approved, which assure that no man shall be deprived of counsel merely because of his poverty. Any other practice seems to me to defeat the promise of our democratic society to provide equal justice under the law.[45]

Most states did have such laws, but many were casual about enforcing them. Other states, as Black said, did not have the provision. Pro-

viding counsel would not be standard practice until the Supreme Court required it. Black's dissent kept the agitation going for full reform. As Alan Barth writes, "The *Betts* decision created no great stir around the country, the subtle distinction it drew being somewhat esoteric for the ordinary citizen. Among law professors and thoughtful lawyers, however, the Black dissent evoked echoes."[46] Twenty years later, in the famous *Gideon v. Wainwright* case, the Court decided to go along with Black—and, properly, Justice Black was assigned the pleasant job of writing the *Gideon* decision, which was handed down on March 18, 1963.[47]

Clarence Gideon, a wispy, middle-aged white man who sometimes earned a living as an electrician, was convicted in Panama City, Florida, of burglarizing a poolroom. Like Betts, he fought his courtroom battle without aid of an attorney because he couldn't afford one, and, when he asked the court to supply one, it had refused to do so. Gideon was convicted.

Sitting in Florida's Raiford penitentiary, he started mailing out neatly hand-printed appeals.

---

[46] Barth, p. 95.

[47] *Gideon v. Wainwright*, 372 U.S. 335 (1963).

Justice Hugo L. Black

---

[44] *Betts v. Brady*, 316 U.S. 455 (1942).

[45] Quoted in Barth, *Prophets with Honor*, p. 94.

They were rejected regularly, until his appeal reached the United States Supreme Court. Louie Wainwright was Director of the Florida prison system. Gideon considered Wainwright to be his improper keeper because he hadn't received a fair trial; the Court agreed. It ruled that a pauper facing any felony charge, not just murder or rape charges, in state court as well as in federal, should be supplied with an attorney.

This was certainly good news for Gideon —but it was good news as well for forty-five hundred of the eight thousand Florida penitentiary inmates at the time who had been convicted after pleading guilty or standing trial without the advice of an attorney. Many thousands of prisoners in other states had been similarly convicted. All could now ask for a new trial, and many did. Critics of the Court predicted that the Gideon decision would throw open the prison gates everywhere and free hordes of criminals. It didn't turn out that way. Some who gained new trials were acquitted (Gideon among them), but many were convicted a second time. Critics also warned that society could not stand the expense of supplying attorneys for all paupers facing felony charges; they called the idea the ultimate socialization of the legal profession. That fear, too, proved to be entirely farfetched. The problem has not been in finding the money, but in finding enough attorneys (and properly qualified ones) to represent the poor.

The Court would probably have changed its mind ultimately even without Black's dissent in 1942. But when such an eloquent appeal is written into the record, it cannot be ignored. It serves, in the words of Chief Justice Hughes, as an "appeal to the intelligence of a future day,"[48] and hastens the coming of that day.

THE SUPREMACY OF THE SUPREME COURT

Government is possible only when there is general agreement on who has the final word. This is as true in the judicial as in all other branches of government. The American judiciary is organized into two separate systems of courts— federal and state. For a number of years, the state courts were reluctant to concede that the Supreme Court had the last word. In 1813, for example, after the Supreme Court had reversed a decision by the Virginia Court of Appeals, the Virginia high court declared that it felt free to ignore the ruling. It argued that the federal courts and the state courts were two separate sovereignties and that, while the judges of the state courts were duty bound to obey the Constitution and other federal laws, they did not have to accept the Supreme Court's interpretation of those laws.[49] Such squabbles are almost never heard anymore, for the proper relationship of the state and federal courts, and the supremacy of the Supreme Court in that relationship, has for many years been acknowledged.

The Dual Court System

On the federal side, the Constitution established only one national court, the Supreme Court, but Congress, with the Judiciary Act of 1789, set up a system of lower federal courts. Thus, although it is very unlikely that Congress will ever change the system, the existence and jurisdiction of the lower federal courts are at its pleasure.

At the lowest level of the federal court system are the district courts—trial courts of original jurisdiction. All federal criminal cases and most federal civil cases start there. The next level of courts, the courts of appeals, have only appellate jurisdiction; they review decisions of district courts and actions of some regulatory agencies. The United States is divided into eleven circuits, each with its own court of appeals. At the top of this three-tiered system is the Supreme Court. There are four hundred district judges, ninety-seven court of appeals judges, and nine members of the Supreme Court (a number fixed by Congress). In addition, the federal system includes five specialized courts: Court of Claims, Tax Court, Customs Court, Court of Customs and Patent Appeals, and Court of Military Appeals (the "GI Supreme Court").

---

[48]Charles Evans Hughes, *The Supreme Court of the United States* (New York: Columbia University Press, 1928).

[49]*Martin v. Hunter's Lessee*, 1 Wheaton 304, 4 L. Ed. 97 (1816).

Article III of the Constitution defines the jurisdiction of the federal courts on the basis of subject matter and nature of parties involved. In the first category are all cases in law and equity arising under the Constitution, under federal law, and under treaties made by the United States and all cases of admiralty and maritime jurisdiction. In the second category are controversies to which the United States is a party—between two or more states; between a state and citizens of another state; between citizens of different states; between a state or its citizens and a foreign state or its citizens; and all cases affecting ambassadors, other public ministers, and consuls.

The *state* court system conducts most of the judicial business in the United States—most criminal cases, disputes between individuals, interpretation of state laws and constitutions. The states have many layers of courts ranging from justices of the peace, to municipal courts, to county courts, to special jurisdiction courts, to intermediate courts of appeal, to courts of appeal (or state supreme courts).

As mentioned earlier, the federal courts have supremacy over the state courts. Usually, the Supreme Court reviews state court decisions only when a case involves a federal question and after all channels of appeal have been exhausted at the state level. While most of the cases that the Supreme Court accepts on appeal from the state judiciary arise from constitutional issues, in recent decades it has become commonplace to see the shadowy thread of the Constitution running through every fabric of our lives, until the Supreme Court seems to have appellate jurisdiction over virtually all questions. Some constitutional authorities, such as Kurland, now despair "that the areas of government in which the states are sovereign have been reduced almost to nonexistence."[50]

Judicial Review

The right to review the constitutionality of state court decisions was granted to the Supreme Court by the Judiciary Act of 1789. Although this right was not established without opposition, it was a relatively easy step—a natural consequence of the union of states. Much more controversial was the Court's winning the right to review *federal* congressional legislation. One of the great ironies of history is that the Supreme Court attained this supremacy almost by accident; at the very most it was attained by default.

The Supreme Court established itself as the final word on the constitutionality of congressional or executive actions in the opinion handed down by Chief Justice John Marshall in the famous case, *Marbury v. Madison* (1803).[51]

In the lame-duck days of his administration, President John Adams appointed quite a few federal judges and justices of the peace who would be sympathetic to his Federalist party philosophy. Congress confirmed them, and Secretary of State John Marshall put the great seal of the United States on the commissions. But then Marshall goofed. He was also supposed to see to it that the commissions were *delivered*. He, however, had just been appointed chief justice of the Supreme Court by Adams, and, in the hustle-bustle of changing jobs, Marshall had neglected to deliver some of the commissions.

Naturally, the incoming President, Thomas Jefferson, had been outraged by Adams's lame-duck appointments, and when he discovered that some of the commissions had not been delivered, he was delighted. So far as he was concerned, the undelivered commissions were dead. But one of the victims of this political tug of war, William Marbury, a banker and land baron from Maryland, decided not to lose his commission without a struggle. Using the Judiciary Act, which Congress had passed seven years earlier and which gave the Supreme Court original jurisdiction in such disputes, Marbury asked the Court to order Jefferson's Secretary of State, James Madison, to issue him the sidetracked commission.

At first glance, it looked like Marshall and his fellow justices had only two choices.[52] They

---

[50] Kurland, *Politics, the Constitution, and the Warren Court*, p. 53.

[51] *Marbury v. Madison*, 1 Cr. 137 (1803).

[52] Actually, Marshall himself had only one choice if he had wanted to act ethically: he should have stepped aside for this case, since he was so personally involved in the Adams administration's actions leading up to it.

"Say—maybe he did *take it to a higher court."*

could issue the order or they could excuse themselves by saying they didn't have jurisdiction over the executive branch. If they had taken the first course of action, they would have run the risk of losing face, for what if they had ordered Jefferson and Madison to hand over the commissions and they had refused? The Court had no enforcement powers (nor does it have today), and, at that very early period in the life of the Court, it would have been folly to risk the kind of rebuff from the Chief Executive that would have set a dangerous precedent. On the other hand, to follow the second course of action—disclaiming jurisdiction—would have been an unnecessary concession of weakness that would have plagued all future Supreme Courts.

However, that may make the choices sound too dramatic. There is no historical evidence that the principals in this case felt they were participating in such high drama. To all outward appearances this was a trivial and even boring case. From the beginning of the country to the present day there have been unpleasant fusses between outgoing and incoming Presidents over appointments: the latter always feel that the former took unfair advantage of last-minute vacancies.

But, perhaps more by accident than by intent, Marshall managed to turn the case upside down and inside out in such a clever fashion that it was made into one of the most important developments in the Court's history. He neither ordered the commissions to be given nor disclaimed jurisdiction over the executive branch. He did not take issue at that level. Instead, he reached behind the President's actions, back to the action of Congress out of which the quarrel had grown, and ruled that the legislation creating the commissions was unconstitutional.

It was a very neat sidestep. It ignored Marbury's complaint. It avoided a head-on test with the President. And perhaps that is all Marshall intended to do: sidestep a quarrel. But what he also did, whether he meant to or not, was establish, for the first time, that the Supreme Court had the final say on constitutionality of federal actions. The issue here was over congressional actions, but by implication it included the President's actions, too. This made it, in the words of Alexander M. Bickel,

> the most extraordinarily powerful court of law the world has ever known. The power which distinguishes the Supreme Court of the United States is that of constitutional review of actions of the other branches of government, federal and state. Curiously enough, this power of judicial review, as it is called, does not derive from any explicit constitutional command. The authority to determine the meaning and application of a written constitution is nowhere defined or even mentioned in the document itself.[53]

The Marshall ruling does not explain *why* the Court should have the last word; it simply says it does. If either Congress or President Jefferson had challenged the Marshall Court on this ruling, the entire course of United States history might have been radically altered, although whether it would have been altered for better or for worse is a matter of guesswork. At the time, the clay of our government had not yet hardened; it could have been rather easily molded along any lines. Viewing the action from the level of the people, it's difficult to see any logical reason why the Supreme Court should assume the power to judge the actions of Congress and the President, who were, after all, elected by and responsible to the people. Wasn't that what a republic was all about? If anyone should have the power to measure congressional acts against the Constitution, why shouldn't it be the ultimate representative of the people, the President, or even the people themselves, through referendum?

Bickel, in his appraisal of this momentous event, sees merits and demerits. One major demerit is that "judicial review runs so fundamentally counter to democratic theory that in a society which in all other respects rests on that theory, judicial review cannot ultimately be effective. We pay the price of a grave inner contradiction in the basic principle of our government. . . ."[54] A second major demerit is that by passing the responsibility of the final decision to a nondemocratic body, citizens and their representatives grow lazy and slovenly.

On the merit side, Bickel feels that, because courts have "the leisure, the training and the insulation in pursuing the ends of government," they can, presumably, measure matters of principle against a more enduring standard than is generally available to the legislative and executive branches.[55] The second merit Bickel candidly calls "mystic," but it is no less important for being that—and, in fact, it very easily could be more important. If the Supreme Court has the power to invalidate actions, it must also have the power to validate them. It has, in effect, the power of secular sanctification. The supremacy of the Supreme Court, Bickel suggests, is something that humankind needs—and it achieves it, not only with such extra power as comes via the power of judicial review, but also through its stability. As Earl Warren told friends when he explained why he would prefer to sit in the center seat on the Supreme Court than in the White House, "There have been 34 Presidents, but only 13 Chief Justices."[56] Presidents come and go, but it is not uncommon for a justice to serve thirty years or more on the Court. This stability, this continuity, does give a quality that would be otherwise lacking in the transiency of democratic politics.

[53]Bickel, *The Least Dangerous Branch*, p. 1. The Court has not used its power of judicial review to alter the stream of federal legislation to any great degree. After *Marbury v. Madison*, it waited fifty years before overturning another federal statute, and in total it has not negated more than eighty or so federal laws as being unconstitutional.

[54]Bickel, p. 23.

[55]Bickel, p. 25.

[56]Quoted in Sherrill, "Earl Warren," p. 12.

But whatever benefits the people derive from the practice of judicial review by the Supreme Court, the political establishment benefits much more. Judicial review sanctifies not only the actions of government, but the very existence of government. Because of its fundamentally undemocratic nature, some people believe that the Court should be watched with special skepticism by the citizens of a democracy. It is, after all, the only branch that does not take its power directly from the people; it is a creature of the political establishment, and its first loyalty is to its creators.

Charles L. Black, Jr., contends that

> the prime and most necessary function of the Court has been that of validation, not that of invalidation. What a government of limited powers needs, at the beginning and forever, is some means of satisfying the people that it has taken all steps humanly possible to stay within its powers. This is the condition of its legitimacy, and its legitimacy, in the long run, is the condition of its life. And the Court, through its history, has acted as the legitimation of the government.[57]

Illustrating his argument, Black moves from the abstract to the specific:

> Almost everybody living under a government of limited powers, must sooner or later be subjected to some governmental action which as a matter of private opinion he regards as outside the power of government or positively forbidden to government. A man is drafted, though he finds nothing in the Constitution about being drafted. . . . A farmer is told how much wheat he can raise; he believes, and he discovers that some respectable lawyers believe with him, that the government has no more right to tell him how much wheat he can grow than it has to tell his daughter whom she can marry. A man goes to the federal penitentiary for saying what he wants to, and he paces his cell reciting . . . "Congress shall make no laws abridging the freedom of speech." . . . A businessman is told what he can ask, and must ask, for buttermilk.
>
> The danger is real enough that each of these people (and who is not of their number?) will confront the concept of governmental limitation with the reality (as he sees it) of the flagrant overstepping of actual limits, and draw the obvious conclusion as to the status of his government with respect to legitimacy.[58]

At that point, the Court steps in to smother dissent by conferring legitimacy on the government's actions.

When people begin to view their government as a bully, an interloper, or an illegitimate power, they begin to think dangerous thoughts—dangerous, that is, for the government. But the Supreme Court, because most people are willing to consider its decisions final, is able to divert their anger and maintain their allegiance. On a short-term basis, a government can be secure by being popular; but on a long-term basis, government is secure only when it and its actions are—or seem to be—legal. That's where the Supreme Court comes in.

BALANCES AND COUNTERBALANCES

Here, at first glance, seems to be a fearful institution indeed: the Court was not set up to be a "democratic" institution, but rather an imperious institution, officially unresponsive to the electorate; and the Court is not bound by the words of the Constitution either, because they are often so vague. And yet to put it that way, although strictly factual, distorts the Supreme Court's place in the government. To say such things about the Court makes it sound like an alien and unfriendly influence. And of course in recent years it sometimes has been quite the contrary, showing itself—especially during the Warren Court era—as the most compassionate part of the government and the most concerned for the populous minorities that had a hard time getting any other part of the government to listen to them. There are several reasons why the Supreme Court, even during its most insensitive and reactionary periods, has not been overbearing in the use of its power.

[57] Charles L. Black, Jr., *The People and the Court* (New York: Macmillan, 1960), p. 52.

[58] Black, pp. 42–43.

Nine Wills, Nine Egos

The Supreme Court has seldom been anything resembling a monolithic group of judges, which is a blessing, for the internal tensions and internal thought abrasions of the Court act as a brake to keep it from running away from the rest of government at an impudent gallop. Its moments of total harmony are rare, partly because of the changing personnel (a total of seventeen justices, for example, served on the Warren Court at one time or another), partly because the nine justices who make up the Supreme Court represent nine vigorously independent minds and nine well-tended egos, and partly because, in most eras of the modern Court, there has been a fairly wide representation of ideological beliefs on the high bench.

Differences among justices, as mentioned earlier, sometimes result in sedate mudslinging. In 1944, Justice Owen J. Roberts ridiculed the majority opinion in a case, saying it converted the law into a "game of chance." Two years later Justice Jackson publicly denounced Justice Black as a "stealthy assassin" of judicial proprieties.[59] Those things were said in public. Behind-the-bench conflicts can be much more bitter. Black was so outraged by an opinion written by Abe Fortas—in fact, he said that it was the worst-written First Amendment opinion he had seen in a dozen years—that he forced the Court to carry the case over to another session, by which time it was ready to reverse its opinion.[60]

Another technique for fighting the ideological war behind the bench was explained by reporter Nina Totenberg:

According to Court sources, the liberal Justices have an "unwritten agreement" to try to keep many cases out of the hands of the Court so long as the conservatives have the five-vote majority needed to carry a decision. Thus, for example, if an important First Amendment case comes up on appeal, the liberals will vote not to hear it—even if it involves what they consider a horrendous lower-court decision—for fear a conservative majority would result in a Supreme Court decision restricting First Amendment rights. It is better to save final resolution of the issue for another day and a more liberal Court, they reason.[61]

Public Opinion

Although the Supreme Court is supposedly immune to outside pressures, it is not. A Supreme Court justice does not take a monastic vow. These are not hermits we are talking about, but men of the world, who, from all appearances, feel very much in the center of the stream—a small island of relative stability, which, nevertheless, sometimes gets inundated with the passions of the day. To that extent, the Supreme Court does become, willy-nilly, a part of the "democratic" process, sometimes for ill, sometimes for good.

The most shameful and embarrassing example of the high court's being caught up in temporal passions occurred during World War II. Bowing to the hysteria that swept the nation after the Japanese attack on military installations at Pearl Harbor, Hawaii, on December 7, 1941, President Roosevelt authorized the military commanders to round up and intern some 70,000 native-born United States citizens of Japanese ancestry. We were at war with Germany and Italy at the time, but no citizens of German or Italian descent were put in detention camps. It was done only to the luckless Japanese-Americans because they "looked different," not because they were a threat—no act of espionage or sabotage was ever proved against a Japanese-American.

Here was a situation, if there was ever one, that called for relief via the cool, restraining character that the Supreme Court is supposed to possess and with which it is supposed to temper popular actions in moments of crisis. But the Court ducked the responsibility entirely. Twice it received appeals from Japanese-Americans who had been interned, and twice it refused to rule on the constitutionality of relocating and interning United States citizens for no reason except that they were unwelcome neighbors to a majority of

---

[59] Robert G. McCloskey, *The Modern Supreme Court* (Cambridge, Mass.: Harvard University Press, 1972), pp. 53–54.

[60] Totenberg, "Behind the Marble, Beneath the Robes."

[61] Totenberg, p. 60.

hysterical people. "Among nine judges who were as a group more alert to claims of individual rights than any Court in our history until then," writes Robert G. McCloskey, "only three dissented against ratifying the most extreme invasion of rights in our history."[62] Ironically, the three who stood fast for freedom did *not* include either Justice Black or Justice Douglas, who later gained reputations as libertarians in cases that took much less courage to rule on.

If the Court is sometimes swept up in the extreme patriotism that goes with war, it can also sometimes be carried away by the extreme patriotism of peacetime. For the first decade after World War II, the Red Menace was the most influential and the most bullying lobbyist in Washington or in state government. And the Supreme Court did little to keep the red scare under control. Fears aroused by catchwords like "subversives," "fellow-travelers," and "comsymps" (a popular abbreviation for "communist sympathizers") eroded the concepts of free speech and free press; the Supreme Court, during the time when Frederick M. Vinson was chief justice (1946–53), went along with the popular fears.

Public opinion not only has an influence on the substance of some Supreme Court decisions, but also on the style in which they are written. When the Court decides that it must upset some long-standing social custom or that it must push some passionate element of society back into line, it often wisely attempts to serve up its opinions in such a way as to make the fullest possible use of public opinion—if not swinging the public to its side, at least avoiding the arousal of antagonistic reactions. Justice Oliver Wendell Holmes once explained how the Court could help prevent the nation from being stirred up into warring factions:

> Now, one of the ways to prevent that is when you handle the hot social issues you never dramatize them. You handle them in such a way that you decide the particular case before you on as narrow ground as possible. You make no big talk about how this great right is being protected.

White [Chief Justice Edward Douglass White of Louisiana] and I had a technique. He wrote opinions so long no one could understand, except the result; I wrote opinions so short no one could understand, except the result. But we edged the law along.[63]

Chief Justice Warren explained how he tried to shape public opinion in his style of writing *Brown v. Board of Education* in 1954:

> I assigned myself to write the decision, for it seemed to me that something so important ought to issue over the name of the Chief Justice of the United States. In drafting it, I sought to use low-key unemotional language and to keep it short enough so that it could be published in full in every newspaper in the country. . . . I kept the text secret (it was locked in my safe) until I read it from the bench.[64]

There is every reason for the Court to lay precise strategy for getting its opinions accepted by politicians and the rest of the public. After all, the only way the Court has of even indirectly enforcing its opinions is through recruiting the public's support. An ignored opinion is a useless opinion.

Institutional Limitations

Another balance on the Supreme Court's actions is the system of institutional controls. The Court may have the power to declare legislation unconstitutional, but Congress has its means of controlling the Court. The Senate has the right to approve appointments to the bench. The House and Senate, working together, can impeach and remove justices. Congress can abolish judgeships, confer or withdraw appellate jurisdiction, cut off money for the Court's staff, deny funds to carry out decisions, enact new statutes to "correct" judicial interpretation of old law, and propose constitutional amendments to counter the effect of decisions.

Presidents, too, have their means of controlling the Court. They have the power to appoint justices (with the consent of the Senate); they

---

[62] McCloskey, *The Modern Supreme Court,* p. 49.

[63] Quoted in Carroll Kilpatrick, *Washington Post,* March 12, 1975.

[64] Quoted in Sherrill, "Earl Warren."

Legal Reasoning and Human Reasons

Why does the Supreme Court make the constitutional law that it does? Why do the justices of the Court vote as they do? The answers lie in the interaction between the values of the individual judges and the currents of the society in which they live, including the prevailing attitudes towards law, the judiciary, and the Supreme Court. The political values of the judges are also principles of adjudication. But these values are categories of belief, not of argument. While principles as vehicles explain how a decision was reached and refer to legal reasoning, principles as political values explain why a particular decision was made and refer to human reasons. Holmes declared seventy years ago that in doubtful cases which present "a conflict between two social desires" and for which precedent offers no solution "judges are called on to exercise the sovereign prerogative of choice." Cases that reach the Supreme Court are almost always such doubtful cases, and no judges exercise the sovereign prerogative of choice more than the justices of the Supreme Court.

In exercising the prerogative, Benjamin Cardozo said, a judge should give effect "not to his own scale of values, but to the scale of values revealed to him in his readings of the social mind." Yet this test may fail, and then the judge must "look within himself." When they look within, judges, like other men, find a view on the good society in America. In addition, judges, unlike most other men, hold views on the nature of the judicial function. To discover the views of judges one must go both behind the decision to the man and to the Court and forward from the opinion to the political and social impact of the case.

From Charles A. Miller, *The Supreme Court and the Uses of History*
(Cambridge, Mass.: Harvard University Press, Belknap Press, 1969), pp. 28–29.

---

may forbid administrative officials to enforce Court decisions; they can pardon anyone cited for contempt for disobeying judicial orders. And, as Justice Jackson once pointed out, dynamic Presidents are not at all timid about colliding with the Court: "Jefferson retaliated with impeachment; Jackson denied its authority; Lincoln disobeyed a writ of the Chief Justice; Theodore Roosevelt, after his Presidency, proposed a recall of judicial decisions; Wilson tried to liberalize its membership; and Franklin D. Roosevelt proposed to 'reorganize' it."[65]

Other limits on the Court are imposed by its own organization and judicial traditions. The Court cannot initiate action—a case must be started by a litigant in the lower courts, must be decided there, and must meet the jurisdictional requirements before it can reach the Supreme Court. The judicial process precludes advisory opinions—even when they are asked for—and pronouncements on abstract, contingent, or hypothetical issues. The Court's decision binds only the parties in the case at issue; an expansion of the decision's impact can be delayed or entirely frustrated by a refusal of politicians and the public to go along with the spirit of the decision and by distorting interpretations made by lower-court judges in subsequent cases. As Jackson notes,

> The Supreme Court is a tribunal of limited jurisdiction, narrow processes, and small capacity for handling mass litigation; it has no force to coerce obedience, and is subject to being stripped of jurisdiction or smothered with additional Justices any time such a disposition exists and is supported strongly enough by public opinion.[66]

Politics

Although the Supreme Court is anything but democratic, it is very much a political instrument, sensitive to political moods and even to

---

[65] Quoted by Kurland in Friedman and Israel, *Justices of the United States Supreme Court*, p. 41.

[66] Jackson, "The Supreme Court as a Unit of Government," p. 31.

political power. In this respect, some Court-watchers believe it to be woven tightly into the dominant political structure of any given era and timid about challenging the actions of the structure of which it is a part.

Robert A. Dahl points out that the Court rarely attacks the constitutionality of legislation within four years after passage (that is, it does not challenge the legislature while it may be presumed that the same majority that passed the legislation is still around). Dahl's study is likely to make one wonder if the power of judicial review has not been, so far as policing Congress is concerned, a hollow and perhaps even harmful thing. He writes:

> In the entire history of the Court there is not one case arising under the First Amendment in which the Court has held federal legislation unconstitutional. If we turn from these fundamental liberties of religion, speech, press and assembly, we do find a handful of cases—something less than ten—arising under Amendments Four to Seven in which the Court has declared acts unconstitutional that might properly be regarded as involving rather basic liberties . . . it is doubtful that the fundamental conditions of liberty in this country have been altered by more than a hair's breadth as a result of these decisions. . . .[67]

Meanwhile, the Court was frequently busy sanctifying legislation that preserved "the rights and liberties of a relatively privileged group at the expense of the rights and liberties of a submerged group: chiefly slaveholders at the expense of slaves, white people at the expense of colored people, and property holders at the expense of wage earners and other groups."[68]

The surprising thing about the Supreme Court is not that it is tinged by politics, but that it isn't totally steeped in politics. The appointment of a federal judge at any level is a political action. Nominees for the bench are picked from among lawyers who are friends of party leaders or are friends of big campaign contributors or have themselves given service and money to the Pres-

ident's party.[69] In states where the senators are of the President's party, they make the nominations. Even senators from the opposite party have the power to veto nominations, though they do not have the power to nominate. In this way political biases and social quirks of a region are perpetuated. President John F. Kennedy, wanting to stay on the good side of Senator James O. Eastland of Mississippi, Chairman of the Senate Judiciary Committee, always listened to his counsel before making appointments to the Fifth Circuit, which includes Alabama, Georgia, Florida, Texas, Louisiana, and Mississippi. Of twenty appointments Kennedy made to district judgeships in the Fifth Circuit between 1961 and 1963, five went to men who were flagrantly hostile to civil rights, and their hostility frequently showed in the way they ran their courts and in their rulings.[70]

But aside from the necessary political concessions, a President likes to have a pretty good idea of a judicial candidate's ideology. Attorney General Robert F. Kennedy (who helped his brother pick judges at every level) was told of one candidate, "He is our kind of Democrat." The administration of Dwight D. Eisenhower "proceeded cautiously" when considering a candidate with a liberal reputation.[71]

For good or ill, Presidents have always looked upon the Supreme Court as a place where, through appointments, they could carry out policies that they believed the electorate had put them in office to carry out. In Dahl's study of

---

[69] Personal preference often has little to do with a President's actions. Transcripts of White House tapes between Richard Nixon and John Ehrlichman on July 24, 1971, reveal the following conversation:
PRESIDENT: . . . Nobody follows up on a God damn thing. We've got to follow up on this thing; however, we, uh, we, uh, we had that meeting. You remember the meeting we had when I told that group of clowns we had around there. Renchburg and that group. What's his name?
EHRLICHMAN: Renchquist [sic].
PRESIDENT: Yeah, Rehnquist.
  Three months later Nixon would name William H. Rehnquist to the Supreme Court as "one of the finest legal minds in this whole country today."

[70] See Victor S. Navasky, *Kennedy Justice* (New York: Atheneum Publishers, 1970).

[71] Sheldon Goldman, "Judicial Appointments to the United States Court of Appeals," *Wisconsin Law Review*, Winter 1967, pp. 186–214.

---

[67] Robert A. Dahl, "Decision Making in a Democracy: The Role of the Supreme Court as a National Policy-Maker," *Journal of Public Law* 6 (1958): 279–95.

[68] Dahl, pp. 279–95.

the political side of the Supreme Court, he found that

> over the whole history of the Court, on the average one new justice has been appointed every twenty-two months. Thus a President can expect to appoint about two new justices during one term of office; and if this were not enough to tip the balance on a normally divided Court, he is almost certain to succeed in two terms.[72]

Does this really mean that Presidents try to "tip the balance" in favor of their party and ideology? Indeed. It started with George Washington, who named six loyal Federalists to the Court (and in those days the Court had only six members)—six men, that is, who would follow Washington's own favoritism toward a strong central government and the propertied classes. Abraham Lincoln, who seldom tried to hide his contempt for the Court, knew from intimate experience that "our judges are as honest as other men and not more so. They have, with others, the same passions for party, for power, and the privilege of their corps."[73]

That was his judgment before he became President; after he was elected, he acted on his appraisal by appointing such fellows as Salmon P. Chase, his Secretary of Treasury, to the high bench with the candid acknowledgment:

> We wish for a chief justice who will sustain what has been done in regard to emancipation and the legal tenders. We cannot ask a man what he will do, and if we should, and he should answer us, we should despise him for it. Therefore, we must take a man whose opinions are well known.[74]

Even more candid was Robert Kennedy: "You wanted someone who generally agreed with you on what role government should play in American life, what role the individual in society should have," he once explained. "You wanted . . . someone who agreed generally with your views of the country."[75]

[72] Dahl, "Decision Making in a Democracy," pp. 279–95.

[73] Quoted in Simon, *In His Own Image*, p. 10.

[74] Quoted in Simon, p. 12.

[75] Quoted in Simon, pp. 16–17.

It is not at all certain—in fact, it is rather unlikely—that many voters even consider what their presidential votes will mean in terms of Supreme Court appointments and, consequently, Supreme Court rulings. They would be wise to do so. Two justices appointed by Franklin Roosevelt were still serving on the bench five Presidents later.

The ideology of a President lives on for decades after he is gone. Long after Richard M. Nixon retired in disgrace to San Clemente, California, and Gerald R. Ford retired to the golf links at Palm Springs—and after the nation turned to Jimmy Carter, a moderate liberal—the five justices Nixon and Ford appointed, making a majority of the Court, were setting a conservative course for the nation and would doubtless continue to do so for years: the rights of defendants were being narrowed; the civil rights movement was being checked; citizen access to federal courts was being reduced; the First Amendment once again was running into a stricter interpretation of the libel laws; and Big Business was getting far more sympathy than it had received in a generation. In short, the Court was charting a course that matched the philosophy of two rejected Presidents, but it did not necessarily come even close to paralleling the philosophy of the incumbent.

Still, there was no way for Nixon and Ford to be sure that their appointees would perform as they have. Appointees are not guaranteed to be predictable moons to their presidential suns. In fact, they often swing far from the course that the President who sponsored them expected. President Kennedy's first appointment was Justice Byron White. Although Kennedy was a somewhat liberal fellow, his appointee became increasingly conservative. Ten years after Kennedy's death, as Nixon's first term came to an end, the ideological balance on the Court was almost evenly divided. The swing vote was that of Justice White. In the final weeks of the 1972 term, there were eighteen decisions that turned on five-to-four votes, with White siding with the conservative majority in all but two of the cases. The spectacle was enough to prompt columnist Clayton Fritchey to remark, "John F. Kennedy, who put White on the court, must be turning over in his grave at the satisfaction his appointee is giving Kennedy's old enemy, Richard Nixon."[76]

Many presidential appointments have gone astray in that fashion. Theodore Roosevelt appointed Oliver Wendell Holmes to the Supreme Court. Later, Justice Holmes was urged by Roosevelt to throw his vote in the *Northern Securities* case[77] the way Roosevelt wanted it thrown, but Holmes refused. Furious at what he interpreted as a "betrayal," Roosevelt declared that he could have carved a justice with more guts out of a banana.[78] President Eisenhower, a phlegmatic conservative, appointed two men to the Court, Earl Warren and William J. Brennan, Jr., whose votes were usually opposite to Ike's wishes. Eisenhower once said of Warren that appointing him was "the biggest damfool mistake I ever made."[79] President Nixon must have had the same reaction when two of his three appointees to the Supreme Court (the third abstaining) joined in the opinion that he must surrender the damning White House tapes to the House Judiciary Committee, which used them to round out the charges of impeachment to be made against him.

THE IMPACT OF THE COURT

We have seen how the Court decides, and we've seen the political, institutional, social, and human factors that influence its decisions. But what happens *after* a ruling is issued? Can the Court secure compliance? How much impact does the Court have?

A ruling's impact depends on a number of factors—the public's opinion on the issue, the attitude of lower-court judges who interpret the ruling, the disposition of law-enforcement officials, and the timing and precision of the decision. Occasionally, the Supreme Court will lead the nation in establishing policy, as it did in its decisions on desegregation, reapportionment, abortion, and rights of criminal defendants. But it is not an easy matter to establish a policy. If most people disagree with aspects of a decision, it may not be carried out, and there are some built-in factors that limit the Court's ability to assert its authority.

First of all, the Court has no way to enforce its decision. The responsibility of enforcing the law belongs to the Chief Executive, who may not try too hard if he doesn't agree with it. Second, a Court's ruling applies only to the litigants in each particular case. The only way it can apply to others is if another lawsuit is brought by interested parties in a lower court. Pritchett and Murphy note:

> Citizens undoubtedly have a moral obligation to conform their conduct to the constitutional standards announced by the Supreme Court, and perhaps a legal obligation as well. But a failure to do so does not render one subject to penalty. Not until a suit is brought and an order issued are recalcitrants under an enforceable obligation to obey a Supreme Court ruling. . . .[80]

Even then, the order will be from a lower court, and how a federal judge chooses to interpret and apply a Supreme Court decision has much to do with its impact.

There are many ways to delay or avoid complying with a ruling: "footdragging, bringing of new lawsuits, efforts to reverse the decision by legislation or constitutional amendment, threats against the tenure of the justices, proposals to eliminate some categories of federal court jurisdiction or to limit the appellate jurisdiction of the Supreme Court."[81] Or just plain ignoring the decision.

In 1948, the Supreme Court ruled (eight to one) that Vashti McCollum was right when she sued to make the Champaign, Illinois, school system stop allowing pupils time off to take religious instruction. McCollum claimed that this violated the constitutional separation of church and state by giving tacit state approval to religious teaching. The Court agreed.[82] This was

[76] Clayton Fritchey, *Washington Post*, June 30, 1973.

[77] *Northern Securities Company v. United States*, 193 U.S. 197, 396–97 (1904).

[78] From an interview with Thomas G. Corcoran, once secretary to Holmes, quoted in the *Congressional Record*, S6085, April 17, 1975.

[79] Quoted in Sherrill, "Earl Warren," p. 9.

[80] Murphy and Pritchett, *Courts, Judges, and Politics* p. 623.

[81] Murphy and Pritchett, p. 626.

[82] *McCollum v. Board of Education*, 333 U.S. 203 (1948).

The justices of the Supreme Court, 1976 (left to right): FRONT ROW—Byron R. White, William J. Brennan, Jr., Chief Justice Warren E. Burger, Potter Stewart, Thurgood Marshall; BACK ROW—William H. Rehnquist, Harry A. Blackmun, Lewis F. Powell, Jr., John Paul Stevens

an unpopular decision with large segments of the public. Many school systems simply ignored it and went right on letting their children out of secular classes to attend religion classes. The released-time programs fell off by only about 20 percent, and the drop in pupil attendance at the religion classes fell off about 10 percent.[83]

Four years later, the Court came up with a curious change of direction. It did not reverse *McCollum,* and yet, in *Zorach v. Clauson,*[84] it

ruled, six to three, that the New York City schools were not violating the Constitution when they released children during the regular school day to attend church classes. The differences in the two cases were technicalities. In *McCollum,* the religion classes were held on the school premises; in *Zorach* they were held off the school grounds. In *McCollum,* the religion classes were announced by the school; in *Zorach* they weren't. But the results were basically the same: students were released to study religion. The Court's arguments supporting the New York arrangement were exceedingly vague. Justice William Douglas wrote for the majority:

> The First Amendment does not say that in every and all respects, there shall be a separation of Church and State. . . . We are a religious people

[83] Frank J. Sorauf, "Zorach v. Clauson: The Impact of a Supreme Court Decision," *American Political Science Review* 53 (September 1959): 777–91.

[84] *Zorach v. Clauson,* 343 U.S. 306 (1952).

Distant Scenes

If the Court, at the other extreme from merely composing for the anthologies, sat merely to render *ad hoc* judgments applicable solely to the precise circumstances of a controversy immediately before it, then also it would not be the powerful institution it is, and its function would need no elaborate justification. The matrix paradox of all paradoxes concerning the Court is, as I have noted, that the Court may only decide concrete cases and may not pronounce general principles at large; but it may decide a constitutional issue only on the basis of general principle. In the performance of this function—to use a fittingly lofty phrase of Chief Justice Hughes—the Court's "mental vision embraces distant scenes." Hence, while the [1954 School Segregation] Cases immediately before the Court exemplified and concretized the issue of principle, they could not be treated as if they involved only the admission of three or four dozen children to a dozen schools. Rather, these five cases did necessarily bring into view the total situation in all the states having school districts which are organized on a segregated basis.

From Alexander M. Bickel, *The Least Dangerous Branch: The Supreme Court at the Bar of Politics* (Indianapolis: Bobbs-Merrill Co., 1962), pp. 247–48.

whose institutions presuppose a Supreme Being. . . . When the state encourages religious instruction or cooperates with religious authorities by adjusting the schedule of public events to sectarian needs, it follows the best of our traditions.

It was all very confusing. And in the confusion, the released-time advocates pushed ahead. Within one year after *Zorach,* all the losses due to *McCollum* were recouped, and thereafter released-time participation shot ahead.

What had happened? The general public, many politicians, and even some lower courts decided—perhaps out of wishful thinking—that *Zorach* had, in effect, cancelled out *McCollum* without any strictures of its own.[85] And having decided that, they simply acted as though *McCollum* didn't exist. By rendering a lukewarm and imprecise decision, the Court had allowed public opinion to overrule it.

Sometimes a Court decision is so momentous that it creates important new policy and sets off a series of related political events. But where such an important policy is concerned it may take years, and reams of rulings and legislation, to finally secure compliance. A prime example is the *Brown* decision of 1954, which desegregated schools.[86]

That decision applied to only five school districts; if other districts did not choose to comply voluntarily—and there were many—it required lawsuit and court order to compel them to do so. A lawsuit is a very expensive procedure; not many individuals or groups have the time or the finances to carry through with one. Even if the funds were available, the desegregation suit would generally be brought in a federal-district court, where the judge was likely to be close to the local situation. Judges in the southern district courts, in particular, might agree with the segregationists. No matter how the judge ruled, there were almost always appeals of the decision.

The courts of appeals, for the most part, reversed rulings that permitted delay or resistance to desegregation proposals. The Supreme Court got into the act again in 1958 when it ruled, in *Cooper v. Aaron,*[87] that there was no constitutional method to evade the *Brown* mandate. This ruling was in response to any number of tactics employed by state governors and legislators to

---

[85] Sorauf, "Zorach v. Clauson," pp. 777–91.

[86] This section is drawn from Pritchett and Murphy, *Courts, Judges, and Politics,* Chapter 19.

[87] *Cooper v. Aaron,* 358 U.S. 1 (1958).

avoid complying with *Brown*. These tactics included closing public schools, paying tuition for pupils in private schools, and even "standing in the schoolhouse door" to keep out black students, as Governor George C. Wallace did in Alabama. Another governor who actively resisted *Brown* was Orval Faubus of Arkansas. His resistance to desegregation in Little Rock forced President Eisenhower to order federal troops sent there in 1958. But even Eisenhower personally opposed the Supreme Court decision and sent the troops to maintain peace rather than to promote integration. Congress at first gave little support to the ruling. In 1956, close to one hundred members of Congress challenged its legality. As desegregation moved into the northern states, where de facto segregation was strong, "forced busing" became the issue, and Congress came under a lot of pressure to pass antibusing legislation. And there has been talk of a constitutional amendment against busing.

So, a quarter of a century after *Brown*, there is still not full compliance, and large parts of the public still oppose the ruling. But it is gradually taking hold. The South has largely come to terms with integration, and as desegregation proposals are given a chance to work in the North, there is growing public acceptance. Politicians have found it politic to uphold *Brown*. *Brown* was a major decision that radically changed the status of blacks in the United States and gave momentum to all subsequent civil rights legislation. It was clearly a case of the Supreme Court leading a reluctant nation and shaping its course.

Except with his war-making powers, not even the cleverest and most popular President can come close to shaping a nation's life with the permanency of the Court's actions. Justice Frankfurter did not exaggerate when he said that

> this tribunal is the ultimate organ—short of direct popular action—for adjusting the relationship of the individual to the separate states, of the individual to the United States, of the forty-eight states to one another, of the states to the union, and of the three departments of government to one another.[88]

---

[88] Quoted by Kurland in Friedman and Israel, *The Justices of the United States Supreme Court*, p. 58.

"EQUAL JUSTICE"

The stability of law is seen in its equal application. Society's deepest instincts demand it. Nothing creates such destructive unrest and cynicism in a community as the unequal application of law. The judiciary is aware of the dangers of unequal justice. These are evils that most judges would wholeheartedly like to see disappear from their craft. From time to time, federal judges submit to informal surveys to see if the scales of justice are balanced. The results are usually disappointing. In 1974, for example, the Federal Judicial Center submitted twenty "sample" cases to more than fifty judges of the Second United States Circuit, which includes the federal courts of New York, Connecticut, and Vermont. The examination was made up of summaries of real cases (with only the names and judgments withheld) that had already passed through the courts. The judges were asked to say what judgments they would have given. The disparities were impressive. Some typical ranges:

- The harshest judge said he would give a bank robber who was in his twenties and had had two previous convictions an eighteen-year sentence and a five-thousand-dollar fine. The most lenient judge, basing his decision on exactly the same information, said he would have given that defendant a five-year term.

- One judge said he would have imposed a ten-year sentence on a forty-year-old taxicab driver who pleaded guilty to one heroin sale. Another judge said he would have given the cabbie a one-year sentence.

- One judge said he would have sent a union official to prison for twenty years for loan-sharking and tax evasion; another judge said he would have let the man off with a three-year term.

So far apart were the judges that in sixteen of the twenty cases there was sharp disagreement over whether imprisonment was appropriate at all. Clearly, here is a situation that can easily breed contempt for the very concept of justice. In a system where going to prison for five years or going free on probation depends solely on which courtroom one's case is assigned to, defendants see themselves balanced not on the scales of right and wrong, but on the scales of good luck and bad luck.

Power Makes Its Own Immunity

Destructive cynicism is spread in the community when it becomes apparent that the punishment does not fit the crime.[89] Ideally, the law plays no favorites; ideally, justice is blind—blind, that is, to social status and bank accounts. Unfortunately, it is not and has never been. It shows favoritism in what it allows and in what it doesn't allow. The wealthy and powerful always get a better shake than the poor and the weak. Ralph Nader and Mark J. Green give an illustration:

> Last year in Federal Court in Manhattan . . . a partner in a stock brokerage firm pleaded guilty to an indictment charging him with $20 million in illegal trading with Swiss banks. He hired himself a prestigious lawyer, who described the offense in court as comparable to breaking a traffic law. Judge Irving Cooper gave the stockbroker a tongue lashing, a $30,000 fine and a suspended sentence.
>
> A few days later the same judge heard the case of an unemployed Negro shipping clerk who pleaded guilty to stealing a television set worth $100 from an interstate shipment in a bus terminal. Judge Cooper sentenced him to one year in jail.[90]

This kind of grotesque contrast is commonly acknowledged. The radical economist C. Wright Mills spelled out the formula like this: "It is better to take one dime from each of ten million people at the point of a corporation than $100,000 from each of ten banks at the point of a gun. It is also safer."[91] In one recent flurry of free enterprise, twelve oil companies forced consumers to pay an extra $165 million in fraudulent charges and were caught by the Federal Energy Administration. But nobody went to jail. Twenty-two top corporate executives were convicted of breaking federal campaign laws in 1972 by contributing crooked money to the reelection of Richard M. Nixon, but only three of the twenty-two went to jail. Would twenty-two pickpockets, caught in the act, have been treated so gently in court?

This most prized myth of the English-speaking world—that law applies alike to rich and poor, to powerful and humble—goes back to 1215 when the English barons forced the king to sign the Magna Carta, which included the statement that the king should observe the law of the land or pay the penalty for breaking it. On the continent, Roman law gave the will of the king the force of law, whereas in English jurisprudence the supreme ruler of the land was as much subject to the common law as the lowliest member of the community. Theoretically. In practice, the king, except when his rule became intolerable, conducted himself pretty much as he wanted to.

In the United States, the same has been generally true of our top politicians. When Richard Kleindienst was Attorney General of the United States in the Nixon era, he lied to a Senate committee investigating an important antitrust case. He could have been charged with perjury and sentenced to five years in jail, but he pleaded guilty to a misdemeanor and spent not one day in jail. The judge, a Republican appointee, said that Kleindienst's only crime was having "a heart that is too loyal and considerate of the feelings of others."[92] Senator Daniel B. Brewster was convicted of taking a bribe but did not go to jail. Vice President Spiro T. Agnew was convicted of taking bribes and payoffs but did not go to jail. President Richard M. Nixon committed a

[89] Fairness of punishment was also written into the Magna Carta. Chapters 20, 21, and 22 mandate that fines shall be levied according to the offense—a small fine for a small offense, and progressively heavier fines for more serious ones. (Thurman Arnold, "The Criminal Trial as Symbol of Public Morality," in A. E. Dick Howard, ed., *Criminal Justice In Our Time*, Charlottesville, Va.: University of Virginia Press, 1965, p. 139.) It should be sadly observed, however, that this only goes to show once again that writing something into law doesn't necessarily bring it about. Five hundred years later, the British were still hanging men for stealing apples, while captains of industry in Leeds and Newcastle were praised as benefactors for poisoning the populace with heavy layers of coal dust and working little children to death in mills and mines.

[90] Ralph Nader and Mark J. Green, *Corporate Power in America* (New York: Viking Press, Grossman Publishers, 1973), p. 277.

[91] C. Wright Mills, *The Power Elite* (New York: Oxford University Press, 1956), p. 95.

[92] Quoted in the *Washington Post*, June 8, 1974.

"Warrington Trently, this court has found you guilty of price-fixing,
bribing a government official, and conspiring to act in restraint of
trade. I sentence you to six months in jail, suspended. You will now
step forward for the ceremonial tapping of the wrist."

Drawing by Lorenz
© 1976 The New Yorker Magazine, Inc.

felony by covering up numerous other felonies, but he neither went to jail nor was even subjected to the embarrassment of impeachment.

Most people would probably agree that the scales of justice are weighted unfairly. If the typical American were given the opportunity, he or she would probably end the imbalance between punishments administered as the result of crimes in the street and punishment administered (if at all) as the result of crimes in the executive suite. A 1969 Harris poll showed that a manufacturer of unsafe automobiles was regarded by respondents as worse than a mugger (68 percent to 22 percent), and a business executive who illegally fixed prices was considered worse than a burglar (54 percent to 28 percent).[93] But never in the history of this country has anyone served time for making unsafe autos, and only once has someone served time for fixing prices. That sort of thing has a danger-

---

[93] Nader and Green, *Corporate Power in America*, p. 189.

ously debilitating effect on the public's attitude toward law and government.

Correcting the unequal treatment of defendants is the justice system's most pressing unfinished task. Many proposals have been made, and some adopted, for better screening of nominees for judicial and prosecutorial appointments. Many proposals have been made, but few adopted, to make it easier to impeach and disbar judges and prosecutors who are unfit or who use their powers abusively. Bar associations have begun to set sterner ethical standards for their members, but powerful special interest groups still seem to receive special treatment from the bar.

The great problem facing reform is that our Constitution and our statutes are written with intentional looseness, and Americans would probably not want it any other way. They have become accustomed to laws that provide for the full stretch of intelligent discretion—including discretion in punishments. There is a positive side to this, for only thus can laws be expanded to include mercy and to make a place for all the diversities of society. But the same stretch of discretion that allows for mercy and tolerance also allows for cruelty, for class bias, for economic bias, for judicial arrogance, for unwarranted privileges, for the exercise of judicial prejudices and prosecutorial biases, and for sloppy thinking of all sorts. With hundreds of state and federal judges, the results are mixed, and the impact on the nation's concept of justice is confused. This condition will probably prevail until all can agree on some method of making the application of law precise, unwavering, and mandatory without blunting the best instincts of the judiciary.

Summary

1. Law is what allows people to live together and reconcile their differences. Some of its sources are custom, tradition, legislation, executive fiat, and deliberation by conventions (constitutional law).

2. To a great extent, law is what judges say it is. But in their rulings, judges must abide by legal precedents (the principle of *stare decisis*) and by ethical norms and legal traditions.

3. In ruling on points of constitutional law, judges cannot simply follow the Constitution; they have to interpret its meaning because its language is so elastic and vague.

4. The Supreme Court can hear only a small percentage of the cases submitted to it. After receiving written briefs and hearing oral arguments on the cases they have accepted, nine justices decide the cases in secret deliberations. One judge is assigned to write the majority opinion; any of the dissenting judges may write a dissenting opinion.

5. The Supreme Court was established by the Constitution. The lower federal courts—the district courts, circuit courts of appeals, and the five specialized courts—were set up by the Judiciary Act of 1789.

6. Most civil and criminal cases are heard in state courts, which are comprised of a multileveled system ranging from justices of the peace to state supreme courts. A federal court can review a state court decision if the case involves a federal question and is raised properly.

7. The power of judicial review, the Supreme Court's right to review the constitutionality of federal actions (by either the executive or the legislative branches), was established in 1803 by *Marbury v. Madison.*

8. The power of the Supreme Court is kept from being overbearing by factors such as these: (1) the requirement that a majority of the justices agree on a case, (2) the weight of public opinion, (3) institutional limitations and traditions, and (4) the politics of Supreme Court appointments.

9. The Supreme Court is unable to enforce its decisions. Compliance depends on the acceptance and good will of the public and of law-enforcement officials, and on the favorable interpretation of lower-court judges.

10. Justice is not yet equal. The application of justice still depends a great deal on who the judge is and how wealthy or powerful the defendant is.

Additional Reading

Edward H. Levi's *Introduction to Legal Reasoning,* rev. ed. (Chicago: University of Chicago Press, 1962), discusses the nature of law and the legal way of thinking. Henry J. Abraham, *The Judicial Process: An Introductory Analysis of the Courts of the United States, England, and France,* 3rd rev. ed. (New York: Oxford University Press, 1975), and Herbert Jacob, *Justice in America, Courts, Lawyers, and the Judicial Process,* 2nd ed., (Boston: Little, Brown and Co., 1972), provide comprehensive analyses of the theory, the organization, and the actual workings of the United States court systems.

The role of the Supreme Court in American history and in present times is treated in two books by Robert G. McCloskey: *The American Supreme Court* (Chicago: University of Chicago Press, 1960) and *The Modern Supreme Court* (Cambridge, Mass.: Harvard University Press, 1972). Its actual effects are discussed in Theodore L. Becker and Malcolm M. Feeley, *The Impact of Supreme Court Decisions: Empirical Studies,* 2nd ed. (New York: Oxford University Press, 1973).

Ramsey Clark's *Crime in America: Its Nature, Causes, Control and Correction* (New York: Simon & Shuster, 1970) analyzes the myths and realities of crime. Jonathan D. Casper, *American Criminal Justice: The Defendant's Perspective* (Englewood Cliffs, N.J.: Prentice-Hall, 1972) explores the rights of the accused. The jury system is described and evaluated in Harry Kalven, Jr., and Hans Zeisel, *The American Jury* (Boston: Little, Brown and Co., 1966).

12
BUREAUCRACY AND THE BUREAUCRATS

The bureaucracy is the part of the federal government citizens know best. It is tangible; we encounter it daily. Bureaucracy's job is to administer all the tasks assigned it by Congress and the President, in every particular. Nearly 3 million civilian employees keep the enormous, clanking, steaming machine lumbering along. Without the bureaucracy we would have no mail, no social security checks, no passports, no protection from untested drugs or spoiled meat or unfair prices. Without the bureaucracy, our 2 million servicemen and women would not be housed, fed, armed, and maneuvered into position. Relations with other nations would be difficult to maintain; international trade would become unpredictable and even more avaricious than it is.

Critics of the bureaucracy are ambivalent. That is understandable, for in many respects it is a magnificent achievement, a stalwart and surprisingly efficient operation that has somehow managed to survive two centuries of tinkering by members of Congress and often-hyperactive Presidents. In other ways, it is a Rube Goldberg contraption that takes a thousand movements to turn one screw. The contradiction is expressed by Senator Patrick J. Leahy of Vermont:

Most federal workers are intelligent, dedicated people who do a day's work for a day's pay. Unfortunately, when you put these same people into the crazy-quilt of departments, agencies, commissions and bureaus that comprise the federal government, too often you get a radically different result: an intractable bureaucracy which in size and power is one of the most difficult-to-control creations man has ever yet devised.[1]

Along with doing its useful duties, the bureaucracy often performs in ways that seem wasteful, unnecessarily intrusive, and silly. Although many of its unwelcome practices are traceable directly to orders from the White House or Congress, the bureaucracy gets the blame—and the headlines. Consequently, the bureaucracy has come to stand for government in its most derogatory sense. It has become the symbol of the increasingly heavy burden of taxes, the symbol of governmental indifference to citizen needs, the symbol of governmental waste.

So very much money—well over $400 billion a year—is tossed around by the federal govern-

---

[1]*Congressional Record*, S21275, December 5, 1975.

ment that it is not surprising that some of it is spent foolishly. In such amounts as *four hundred billion* (400,000,000,000), dollars seem almost unreal. Some of the things they are spent on also seem unreal. Senator William Proxmire, the most vocal member of the Joint Economic Committee, watches the federal budget to uncover wasteful spending; he regularly awards a "Golden Fleece of the Month" to embarrass those who have frittered away the taxpayers' dollars. He has made his award to the National Science Foundation for spending $46,100 to study how the sight of scantily clad women affects men's driving in Chicago,[2] $84,000 to find out why people fall in love,[3] and $500,000 to determine why monkeys and men clench their jaws. The Federal Aviation Administration won the prize for spending $417,000 on indoor meteorological instruments so that FAA employees could make weather predictions without going outside to read already existing instruments.[4]

No part of the bureaucracy is eager to cease operations. The Rural Electrification Administration was set up in 1935 to help bring electricity to rural America. Ninety-nine percent of the homes in rural America now have electricity, but the REA budget and staff continue to grow. Three generations ago, Congress got the bright idea that there weren't enough sharpshooters around, so it established the National Board for the Promotion of Rifle Practice. It still exists, pumping out $365,000 a year to encourage people to shoot at targets.[5]

Left to its own devices, bureaucracy will almost invariably sidestep controversial duties and spend its time on pettiness. There are 22,000 toxic substances, some deadly, that are used by United States industry. The Occupational Safety and Health Administration is supposed to protect workers by regulating the amount of poisons that industry subjects them to. But in its first six years, OSHA published exposure limits on only seventeen substances. During the same time, it

produced twelve pages of regulations on the proper construction of portable wood ladders, and it published twenty-eight pamphlets on farm safety. One pamphlet, "Safety with Beef Cattle," tells farmers that "hazards are one of the main causes of accidents" and reminds them that if you step in wet manure, "you can have a bad fall."[6] The pamphlets cost $500,000 to produce. The National Institute on Alcohol Abuse and Alcoholism has spent millions of dollars—it has successfully cloaked exactly how many millions—over the years to try to find out if drunk fish are more aggressive than sober fish and whether young rats are more likely than adult rats to turn to alcohol to reduce anxiety.[7]

Granted, if one added up all the dopey expenditures of this sort, the total would be a rather trivial part of the federal budget. But such spending may serve as a barometer of the general thoughtlessness that goes into the bureaucratic priorities. There is a tendency in the bureaucracy—one that also afflicts Congress and the Chief Executive—to think of the money spent as "theirs," not "ours," as though taxpayers existed in one world and the government in another. This, of course, is an attitude that the public resents heartily.

VAST, IMPENETRABLE, AND WELL-PAID

Above all, the bureaucracy stands for what many citizens have come to fear and loathe the most: Bigness. It started small, even for a new country. When the federal government moved from Philadelphia to Washington in 1800, the bureaucracy consisted of about 130 clerks. At the end of John Quincy Adams's administration there were 301 government employees; the Civil War helped swell the ranks to 7,000; the coming of the twentieth century saw 26,000 employed; the New Deal multiplication of agencies jumped the payroll to 166,000 by 1940, on the eve of World War

[2]*Washington Post,* March 16, 1976.

[3]*Washington Post,* March 11, 1975.

[4]Office of Senator William Proxmire, press release, May 20, 1976.

[5]*Wall Street Journal,* April 4, 1977.

[6]*Washington Post,* February 12, 1977.

[7]Robert Sherrill, "Our Hopeless Government," *Playgirl,* October 1976, pp. 32+.

FIGURE 12-1 HEALTH, EDUCATION AND WELFARE CONGRESSIONAL COMMITTEE RELATIONSHIPS

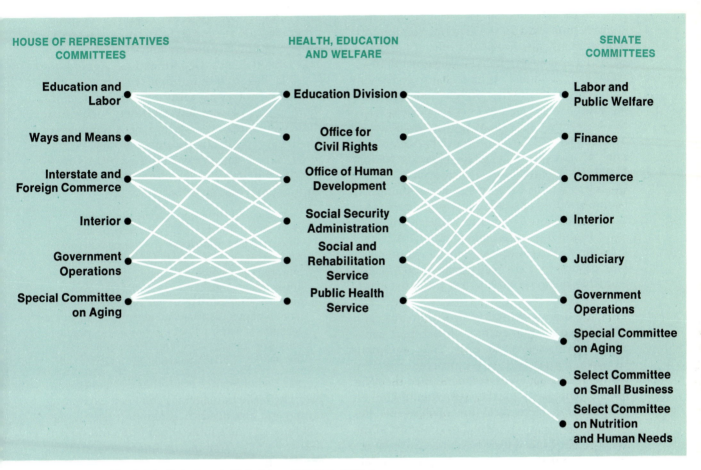

SOURCE: *Journal* (Institute for Socioeconomic Studies) 1, no. 2 (Autumn, 1976): 4.

II. That was the point of no return.[8] By war's end, the civilian employment had pushed well past 2 million.

[8]Stewart Alsop, *The Center: People and Power in Political Washington* (New York: Harper & Row, Publishers, 1968), p. 87. Wars have a permanent ballooning effect on government. After the War of 1812, and again after the Mexican War, the budget remained twice as large as before each of these wars. After the Civil War, the budget was stabilized at five times the prewar level. The Spanish-American War, a relatively petty adventure, left the postwar budget only 66 percent larger than the prewar budget. World War I left the budget permanently raised 400 percent. After World War II, the budget was 700 percent higher than the prewar budget, and it has been climbing ever since. (E. E. Schattschneider, *Two Hundred Million Americans in Search of a Government*, New York: Holt, Rinehart & Winston, 1969, p. 33.)

Today the dimensions of the bureaucracy, whether measured by bodies or paper or concrete, are stunning. It is made up of 12 cabinet departments; between 44 and 75 agencies (depending on who's counting); and between 1,175 and 1,240 advisory boards, committees, commissions, and councils (again, depending on who does the counting). Actually, nobody knows for sure what the bureaucracy consists of. Organizational charts depict it as an impenetrable cobweb. (See Figure 12-1.) When President Jimmy Carter came into office, he promised to trim and reorganize the bureaucracy (see also Figure 9-1); to do so, he of course needed a list of its parts. After three months of searching, a White House spokesman admitted, ''We were unable to obtain any single document containing a complete and current listing of government units which are part of the federal government."[9]

The *United States Government Organization Manual*, published by the General Services Administration, calls itself "the official handbook of the federal government." An eight-hundred-page book, it scarcely begins to convey the size and complexity of the United States government. The subject index is a sea of descriptive titles; strange names float to the top: Office of Space Science, Surplus Property Administration, Operation Mainstream, Perry's Victory Memorial Commission, Micronesian Claims Commission. The list seems endless. Among the twelve hundred or so advisory committees is the Condor Advisory Committee, which advises bureaucrats on the habits of that bird, the Advisory Panel on Academic Music, and many other esoteric groups that are paid between $60 million and $100 million a year to tell the bureaucrats what to think.[10]

There are so many agencies, bureaus, and whatnots in the bureaucracy, in fact, that sometimes they get lost. In early 1976, President Gerald R. Ford issued an executive order relating to intelligence activities. He mentioned the "National Commission for the Protection of Human Subjects for Biomedical and Behavioral Research." News reporters had never heard of the agency. They called the President's press secretary. He had never heard of it either. The White House staff, searching diligently, could find no mention of the commission in the *Organization Manual*, where all agencies are presumably listed. Nor was it in the telephone book. The press and the White House hunted the NCPHSBBR for two days before they found it—tucked away near the Kenwood Country Club in the suburbs of Washington, where it had been shyly drawing its pay for two years. Nobody has any idea how many other agencies may be lost, or at least out of sight.[11]

Operating with so much autonomy, not to mention chaos, bureaucratic units often duplicate each other many times over. The federal government operates about 228 different health programs, 156 income security and social service programs, and 83 different housing programs.[12] The United States Department of Agriculture (USDA) has 80,000 full-time employees—one bureaucrat for every thirty-four farmers. Since there are 33 percent fewer farmers today than there were fifteen years ago, USDA bureaucrats often have difficulty passing the day. A *Wall Street Journal* reporter visited the USDA's massive Washington headquarters and came away impressed by the spirit of limbo:

> Even a casual stroll through the department suggests something is awry. Throughout the main office building, old clocks are stopped at various hours as if time, too, had stopped. At all hours, hundreds of people mill about the corridors or linger in the large, sunny cafeteria. . . . Asked to describe a typical day in her office, the department's deputy assistant administrator for home economics, says, "I've answered the phone a couple of times this morning. That's about it. It's a normal day." She is paid $33,700 a year. . . .[13]

The Secret Service is another excellent example of how the bureaucracy can keep expanding far beyond any need. A generation ago the Secret Service was a rather humdrum and out-of-the-way agency that mostly hunted counterfeiters. It assigned a few of its idle agents, but not many, to accompany the President as bodyguards. Then came the assassination of President John F. Kennedy in 1963. Using that tragedy as an excuse for growth, the Secret Service became a veritable army. Between 1963 and 1977, the number of its agents grew from 450 to 1,650, and its budget swelled from $5.8 million to $115 million. With typical bureaucratic ambition (and the support of the agency's congressional allies), it pushed its authority into new areas. It began serving as the bodyguard not only of Presidents, Vice Presidents, and past Presidents, but of major presidential candidates. Having plenty of

[9]Sources: *Nation*, April 2, 1977; *Wall Street Journal*, April 4, 1977; *Washington Post*, May 8, 1977.

[10]*Wall Street Journal*, April 4, 1977.

[11]Sherrill, "Our Hopeless Government," pp. 32+.

[12]Rochelle Jones and Peter Woll, "The Interest Vested in Chaos," *Nation*, April 2, 1977.

[13]*Wall Street Journal*, April 13, 1977.

agents to spare, it even began bodyguarding cabinet members. Nixon's Treasury Secretary, William E. Simon, got Secret Service protection, though there was no indication he had ever been threatened by more than a lusty boo. Secretary of State Henry A. Kissinger, though the State Department was heavily staffed with its own bodyguards, was guarded intensely by the Secret Service. When he walked his dog, five agents always accompanied him.[14] On one occasion, several Secret Service agents showed up at Fenway Park in Boston wearing baseball gloves to protect Kissinger from possible foul balls.[15]

What does all this bureaucratic policing really add up to? Is it necessary? Under the guise of offering protection from psychopathic killers, has the Secret Service done much more than prevent the President and other favored politi-

cians from dealing directly and personally with the general public? Is protection there when really needed? George C. Wallace, campaigning for President in 1972, was accompanied by Secret Service agents, but they failed to prevent his being shot by a gunman not more than three steps away. In September 1975, a young woman named Lynette Alice ("Squeaky") Fromme—who had a history of violence, had twice been accused of murder, and had indirectly threatened the life of the President in a newspaper interview—stood on a curb in Sacramento, California, and pulled a gun from her purse as President Ford passed by within reach. The Secret Service is supposed to know the whereabouts of notorious would-be killers before a President travels in public. How had it allowed Fromme to get so close? Reporter Stephen Isaacs extends the puzzle:

> Despite galloping growth since 1963 . . .; despite millions spent on new technology, including a computer that maintains names of 47,000 potential

[14]*Wall Street Journal,* January 21, 1977.

[15]*Washington Star,* October 22, 1975.

disruptors or assassins of a President; despite stronger liaison with local law enforcement agencies and with the FBI on potential troublemakers—all of this could not prevent a potential assassin, gun in hand, from approaching to within two feet of a President. . . .[16]

Pomposity and Paperwork

The federal government owns more than 400,000 buildings and is spending $1 billion a year to construct more. Federal workers, as the *Wall Street Journal* has pointed out, occupy office space equivalent to that in 1,250 Empire State Buildings. The main industry within the federal walls seems to be paper work. Federal agencies issue regulations and announce programs filling 60,000 pages of fine print in the *Federal Register*

---

[16]Stephen Isaacs, *Washington Post,* September 9, 1975.

HEW Secretary Joseph Califano
displays a stream of welfare forms

each year, and every one of these regulations and programs generates a whirlwind of paper work from the beleaguered citizenry at large.[17] As of 1976, government workers, citizens, and businesses had to cope with 5,012 different types of government forms, *excluding* tax and banking forms.[18] Each week, the Department of Health, Education and Welfare (HEW) issues so many regulations that to read them all (though many are admittedly unreadable) would be the equivalent of wading through *War and Peace* twice.[19] When the Interior Department finished studying the environmental impact of a natural gas pipeline in Alaska, it had a document that was 9,570 pages long, two feet thick, weighing forty pounds.[20]

The Office of Management and Budget estimated that Americans, especially those in business, spend more than $100 billion in time or wages filling out federal report forms. For a long time, the Federal Power Commission required utility companies to supply it with the longitude and latitude of every gas meter in the country.[21] An Oregon company operating three small television stations reported that its license renewal application weighed forty-five pounds.[22] Eli Lilly and Company, a major pharmaceutical firm, was required to file 120,000 pages, including duplicate and triplicate copies, for an application to sell a drug to relieve arthritis—and the company claimed that only about 25 percent of the pages contained information important to the Federal Drug Administration's evaluation of the drug.[23] Colleges and universities, according to former HEW Secretary Forrest David Mathews, spend $2 billion annually in responding to federal requirements for data.[24]

---

[17]Sources: *Washington Star,* September 7, 1976; *Nation,* April 2, 1977.

[18]Associated Press, June 1, 1976.

[19]*Washington Post,* March 27, 1977.

[20]*Washington Post,* February 13, 1977.

[21]Jack Anderson, syndicated column, February 22, 1977.

[22]Murray L. Weidenbaum, *Government-Mandated Price Increases* (Washington, D.C., American Enterprise Institute, 1975).

[23]*New York Times,* June 21, 1976.

[24]*Washington Star,* January 11, 1977.

How to Talk Bureaucratic

When President Carter took office, he complained that federal regulations were gobbledygook and promised that he would make the bureaucracy write them "in plain English, for a change." Why was he complaining? Here are some examples of bureaucratese:

From a Veterans Administration memorandum:

My expectation is that many of the near catastrophic situations that we have experienced in the past will never reach fruition in that their harbingers will be detected and remedial action will be effectuated at a preliminary stage of the potential difficulty.

From a report issued by the Federal Council for Science and Technology:

We have found it heuristically instructive to consider two alternative hypothetical extremal approaches to the present dilemma of the multiplicity of competing media and the confusion that this introduces into the orderly communication system.

From an Environmental Protection Agency memorandum:

B. To the fullest extent possible, to make formal determinations on disclosure and releasability of documented information within ten working days, using the telephone as an instrument of informal personalized response to the maximum extent required to resolve questions or assist the requester in improving the formulation of his request.

From a Civil Service Commission personnel management evaluation report:

The base level of work supervised is defined as the grade of the highest level of nonsupervisory substantive work under the supervision of the position being evaluated, which represents a significant portion of the total substantive work of the unit in which it appears and requires of the immediate supervisor the use of technical skills of the kind typically needed for directing work at that level.

From the Federal Tax Guide Reports:

When a return becomes due during a return period following the return period during which the return was presented to the taxpayer for filing, the three-year period commences at the close of the latter period.

From a quarantine notice in the Federal Register dealing with Japanese beetles:

Regarding the area removed from regulations, the provisions of the regulations with respect to the interstate movement of regulated articles from regulated areas in quarantined States will not apply to the interstate movement of such articles from the specified counties but the provisions with respect to the interstate movement of regulated articles from nonregulated areas in the quarantined States will be applicable.

From various "Gobbledygook" columns in the *Washington Star.*

Nobody knows for sure where all the forms come from. The Office of Management and Budget admits that it cannot identify all the agencies now spewing forth forms. But we do know what happens to the forms when they are returned. They are filed away—4.5 million cubic feet of new records each year that cost $8 billion to print, shuffle, sort, and file.[25] Still, who's to say it isn't worthwhile? After all, among the eight thousand record systems scattered throughout the bureaucracy, you can find the records of soldiers who were hospitalized with trench mouth in World War I, the "behavioral performance" records of Kentucky tollbooth operators, and which air force reservists have been assigned tool kits.[26]

Overlooking no opportunity to do its thing, the government has spent millions in vain on studies to reduce the paper flood. The Paper

---

[25]J. Glenn Beall, Jr., *Congressional Record,* S2759, March 4, 1976.

[26]*Washington Post,* September 16, 1975.

Management Office, by running an annual contest, tries to encourage federal employees to cut down on paper work. Every office can nominate workers "who have contributed significantly to the efficiency or cost reduction of Federal paperwork systems." *Six* copies of each nomination must be submitted.

Paper that isn't filed away is chewed up or burned. Every day the Pentagon sends ten to fourteen tons of what it calls "secrets" through a special chewing-disposal machine.[27] At the Central Intelligence Agency headquarters, other tons—how many the CIA won't say, of course—are shredded and burned each day, and the same thing happens to an estimated twenty tons of "secrets" a day at the National Security Agency, which has a $1.2 million "classified waste destructor." It is not always efficient. Sometimes unshredded, unburned "secrets" go up the stack and blow around the neighborhood; sometimes the shredder gets so jammed that workers have to come in with jackhammers and break up the "secrets."[28]

Farming Out

The federal government employs about 5 million civilian and military persons, at an annual fringe and payroll cost (as of 1977) of $70 billion. These figures are deceptive. The number of people on the permanent payroll has not increased greatly since World War II, and government officials like to make this point in their argument that the bureaucracy is not getting out of control. But the permanent payroll is only part of the story, for a staggering amount of the bureaucracy's work is farmed out to private firms. An estimated $66 billion or so is spent each year through contracts with about 250,000 outside businesses and institutions. But that dollar figure covers the cost of "hardware" purchases and construction. What is the additional cost of outside personnel—experts, consultants, advisers, planners? Nobody knows for sure. Not even the government itself. A study by a House Gov-

ernment Operations subcommittee estimated the number of contract employees at 1.3 million—roughly 40 percent of the size of the visible civilian federal payroll. A Senate subcommittee later cautiously agreed with the House investigators' ballpark figure, but hastened to add that, in fact, the hiring was so rampant and chaotic that many of the 178 agencies involved in its own investigation were unable to say how many consultants they hired, who they were, or how much their services cost.[29]

This contractual, quasi arm of the government exists in virtual anonymity, and it is only remotely responsible to the general public. In the Department of Defense, 80,000 employees do nothing but contract with private corporations—at an annual cost of about $48 billion—to do the actual work of defense.[30] In 1977, the Justice Department, which had about 3,500 lawyers on its permanent payroll, asked Congress for $4.8 million to hire private attorneys to do part of its work. Some of the money will be used to defend government officials who engaged in illegal activities. In some agencies, the featherbedding and hiring of outsiders to do the insiders' work seems out of control. In 1976, the Energy Research and Development Administration hired the equivalent of 13 outside consultants for every agency employee.[31] "Studies" are constantly being produced by the Department of Commerce, the Department of Housing and Urban Development, the Department of Agriculture, and the Department of Interior to "prove" that certain programs should be established or continued to benefit the industries that come under the wing of those departments. In fact, many of those studies have been anonymously produced on government contract by the very corporations that will do the jobs being endorsed.

---

[29]Sources: *Washington Star*, April 4, 1977; Report of the Senate Governmental Affairs Committee's Subcommittee on Reports, Accounting and Management, issued August 7, 1977.

[30]Sources: CBS Television News Special, January 26, 1975; *Washington Post*, February 15, 1977.

[31]Sources: *New York Times*, February 4, 1977; Report of the Senate Governmental Affairs Committee's Subcommittee on Reports, Accounting and Management, issued August 7, 1977.

---

[27]CBS Television News Special, "Mr. Rooney Goes to Washington," January 26, 1975.

[28]*Washington Post*, June 3, 1975.

The Ideal Employer

In the public's psyche lurks a suspicion that federal workers are "different" and don't understand the troubles of other people. To some extent this feeling is accurate.

Although two-thirds of the federal bureaucracy is scattered over the rest of the nation, its effective heart resides in the Washington area. Civilian and military personnel, plus the many thousands of federal retirees living there, make the nation's capital virtually impervious to economic recession. While some areas of the nation were suffering from 12 percent unemployment as early as 1974 and while the national average pushed past 9 percent that year, unemployment in the Washington area did not reach 6.5 percent until mid-1975, and this was the highest it had been since the Great Depression of the 1930s. This economic stability lends an air of unreality to the capital. When the rest of the nation suffers, Washington feels little pain, so neither politicians nor bureaucrats are moved to help with the efficiency and swiftness that they might show if their living standards were affected as the rest of the nation's are.

Some observers feel that the cost of maintaining the bureaucracy is out of control. The alarmists can point to 1962 as the year of downfall. In that year, Congress passed, and the President signed, the Federal Employee Salary Act. Its goal was to bring federal salaries into line with those for comparable work in private industry, since federal salaries were then lower by ratio. But in the next ten years, while private industry's salaries were climbing less than 70 percent, federal salaries jumped 100 percent, and the average salary was 50 percent higher than in industry.[32] United States bureaucrats, like United States members of Congress, are paid 40 to 60 percent better than any comparable group in the world.[33]

The top of the federal ladder is especially bountiful. When the $36,000 career federal pay ceiling was established in 1969, fewer than 1,000 workers received it. By 1977, 20,000 were getting the maximum paycheck, and by then it had climbed to $47,500. The federal payroll is a plum tree ready for picking. Where else but in the federal bureaucracy is $30,000 a year paid to someone with the title Suggestions Award Administrator, or Fringe Benefit Specialist?[34] Other lucky employees include the 150,000 receiving both a military pension *and* a civil service paycheck—a group not so affectionately known as "double-dippers."

Are the civil servants earning their pay? Doubtless many are. But many are not even beginning to earn their money, and the sluggards know they have nothing to fear. As the *Harvard Business Review* disclosed, most pay raises are automatic rewards for simply staying alive and showing up to punch the clock; fewer than 4 percent of the white-collar workers receive *merit* raises. On the other hand, fewer than 1 percent are penalized for poor work by being denied regular longevity pay raises.[35]

Thanks to the generosity of the American taxpayers (most of whom can look forward to no more than a $300-a-month Social Security check at age sixty-five), a federal employee could, in 1975, retire on as much as $2,808 a month. Taxpayers are now supporting 1.2 million federal retirees or their survivors at a cost of more than $370 million a month.[36] Actuaries predict that by 1982 the cost of supporting federal retirees will be about $1 billion dollars a month.[37] To be sure, federal workers contribute 7 percent of their salaries to the pension fund through withholding, but the average federal retiree gets back within the first eighteen months of retirement all that he or she paid into this fund.

There are other appealing features of working for the federal government, too. About 15,000 federal workers get free or cut-rate parking space near their offices, at a cost to taxpayers of about $11 million a year. Of course, the closer to the top, the swankier things become. About 800 federal officials are chauffeured around Washington in government automobiles. Several cabinet officers have private chefs. About 500 of the Pentagon's top officials eat in five "executive dining rooms," where they can get a seven-course luncheon with dessert for the cost of the food alone—about $1.75 in mid-1975—and the mess-jacketed servers, the silverware, and the other finery cost taxpayers about $1 million a year.[38]

Titles are another thing that federal employment offers. If you can't make it to the very top of the tree and become Secretary of a cabinet department, there is still the chance to be Assistant Secretary, or Deputy Assistant Secretary, or Associate Deputy Assistant Secretary, or Special Assistant to the Assistant Secretary. The possibilities, like the titles, are endless.

The peak of taxpaid luxurious living for the cabinet was reached in the Nixon/Ford years. Whenever Secretary of State Kissinger flew abroad, another plane, carrying two bullet-proof limousines, went along. Once he decided to stop

[32]*Washington Star*, April 22, 1975.

[33]Statistics released by Congresswoman Patricia Schroeder with the observation, "Public officials think the American taxpayer is some sort of hardy deciduous tree which annually sheds its earnings into their pockets." (Press release, January 26, 1977.) Which is why there was some truth in Vice President Alben W. Barkley's joke: "A bureaucrat is a Democrat who holds a job a Republican wants." (Quoted in William Safire, *Before the Fall: An Inside View of the Pre-Watergate White House*, New York: Doubleday & Co., 1975, p. 247.)

[34]*Washington Monthly*, April 1977.

[35]Sources: *Harvard Business Review*, January 1974; Mike Causey, *Washington Post*, February 17, 1975.

[36]Robert Sherrill, "Is Anybody Out There Doing His Job?" *Playboy*, November 1974, pp. 103+.

[37]*Washington Post*, April 8, 1974.

[38]*Wall Street Journal*, February 7, 1975.

over in a French coastal resort for a thirty-six-hour visit with a friend, thus idling twenty-two aircraft crew members, thirty-four security agents, four communications experts, and his own staff—at a cost of only $400,000. Just to say hello.[39] Under the Carter administration, there are somewhat fewer Civil Service coat holders, martini mixers, and uniformed aides in evidence. Cabinet officers are sometimes seen eating in public cafeterias rather than in their private dining rooms. But the perquisites are so lavishly ladled out, even now, in Carter's administration of relative "austerity," that the life of Washington's bureaucracy is still foreign to the taxpayers who support it.

No Popularity Prizes

Unable to get at the bureaucracy with votes, the public pelts it with expressions of distaste and contempt—like the wry hyperbole of Judge Thurman Arnold, quoted at the beginning of this chapter. In his State of the Union address to Congress in 1971, President Richard M. Nixon left his prepared speech to interject, "Let's face it. Most Americans today are simply fed up with government at all levels." In 1976, candidate Jimmy Carter owed much of his popularity to the repeated promise that he would "do something" about "the horrible bureaucratic mess in Washington."[40]

That's the way people feel outside government. Inside, among nonbureaucrats, antagonisms are different but sometimes just as intense. Many people around Congress and in the White House seem to view the bureaucracy as a dragon that, for all their hacking and sticking, refuses to be slain. When Carter called the bureaucracy a "horrible mess," he was speaking as one who had not yet reached the Presidency. Having arrived, he has used more decorous and diplomatic terms, but they add up to the same thing. In almost every administration, White House officials customarily talk of their dealings with the bureaucracy as though they were engaged in outright warfare or sabotage. William Safire, one of the more candid officials in the

Nixon White House, wrote that "the government moves only when it is whipped or teased" and that the "manipulation of the bureaucracy" calls for using "the tricks of leak, threat, transfer, appointment, browbeating, and lavish praise."[41] Similar complaints are heard in liberal White Houses. After leaving the Kennedy administration, Arthur Schlesinger wrote,

> Getting the bureaucracy to accept new ideas is like carrying a double mattress up a very narrow and winding stairway. It is a terrible job, and you exhaust yourself when you try it. But once you get the mattress up it is awfully hard for anyone else to get it down.[42]

Such remarks reflect what John P. Roche, a political scientist and Lyndon B. Johnson White House adviser, correctly called "the love-hate relationship which every strong executive has with his bureaucracy."[43]

But enough quibbles and disparaging remarks. Whatever their justification, they should be weighed against this background: the bureaucracy has been, and continues to be, a reflection of the people and the people's representatives. Congress and the President created the bureaucracy, sometimes together, sometimes independently of each other. They created the cabinet departments, the independent agencies, the bureaus, the commissions—and they always did so in response to the wishes of some part of the public, some constituency.

One should bear in mind that, although the bureaucracy may be at fault for having never, in any part, committed suicide or admitted that it was superfluous, the final guilt for perpetuating redundant, wasteful, useless, and antiquated bureaucratic programs must rest with Congress and the President. The bureaucracy, in all its wonderful elements, does not multiply on its own, like amoebae. It multiplies and thrives through the generosity of Congress and the President. Powerful and influential as the bureaucracy may be, it is not impregnable. It does

[39]Washington Post, January 29, 1977.

[40]Quoted in New Republic, August 21–28, 1976, p. 15.

[41]Safire, Before the Fall, p. 247.

[42]Arthur M. Schlesinger, Jr., A Thousand Days: John F. Kennedy in the White House (Boston: Houghton Mifflin Co., 1965), p. 679.

[43]John P. Roche, "A Chronicle of Camelot," Harper's Magazine, December 1965, p. 117.

not function in a walled and armored city, repelling all intruders. It does not manufacture its own money and determine its own life—except by congressional and presidential license, mandate, or default. For members of Congress or the President to say that the bureaucracy is an omnipotent force in itself is nonsense. Any time it wants to, Congress, with the President's support, can do anything it wants to do with the bureaucracy.

Outside critics should also look inward before damning the bureaucracy. Almost every time some new program is added to the seemingly endless list of bureaucratic missions, it is added in response to the demands of some part, usually some large part, of the public. Many Americans insist that government is too big and should be cut back, at the same time urging the passage of new programs and the expansion of old ones. Some people suggest cutting the defense budget and expanding the welfare budget; some would make the cuts and additions the other way around. With democratic compromise, both budgets are expanded. The public has made it clear that this is the way it wants things to be, for the only two recent presidential candidates who urged extreme cutbacks (Barry M. Goldwater in welfare and George S. McGovern in defense) were slaughtered at the ballotbox.

Bureaucracy has been caught on the knife-edge of a changing national outlook. By simply doing what it was asked to do, it has been made to seem sinful. Such is the penalty enacted by the old tradition of thrift in American politics.[44] But bureaucracy also represents (admittedly, not always gracefully or efficiently) the new, humane standards of government that require bigness. It represents, as Norman John Powell has pointed out,

> the values of big government in advancing the public welfare by means of an enormous range of activities. "We are told," said Lyndon Johnson, "that this is the age of the oversize organization, of big business, big unions and big government.

Does the government undermine our freedom by bringing electricity to the farm, by controlling floods, or by ending bank failures? Is freedom betrayed when in 1964 we redeem in full the pledge made a century ago by the Emancipation Proclamation? The truth is—far from crushing the individual—government at its best liberates him from the enslaving forces of his environment." Government bureaucrats cannot only promote public health and further economic growth; they can even help lift the quality of life in America. An illustration is the use of the tax system as an instrument for promoting the arts by letting people take sizable deductions for purchases from their taxable income. *Time* has said that, "As a patron of the arts the U.S. Internal Revenue Service has made Lorenzo the Magnificent look like a piker."[45]

There are, obviously, good and bad aspects of the establishment, growth, and conduct of the bureaucracy. If one keeps this in mind, the cantankerous problems arising from within the maze of government will not seem so mysterious, or so overwhelming—nor will the spasmodic blessings of the bureaucracy seem so accidental.

POWERS OF THE BUREAUCRACY

Presidents and members of Congress are uneasy with the bureaucracy because it is a maverick; it does not carry the constitutional brand. The Constitution, in fact, acknowledges the probable existence of the bureaucracy only in two places: where it says the Congress will have the power "to make Rules for the Government" (Article I, Section 8), and where it says the President "may require the Opinion, in writing, of the principal Officer in each of the executive Departments" (Article II, Section 2). What did the framers intend the bureaucracy to be? How large, in what shape, and with what powers? The vision of government, in 1787, made only indirect provisions for the bureaucracy, and so the bureaucracy grew up outside the constitutional structure of checks and balances. Having established

---

[44]See Schattschneider, *Two Hundred Million Americans in Search of a Government*, p. 31. For another opinion on this point, see Daniel Patrick Moynihan, "The Third Generation and the Third Century," in *Qualities of Life: Critical Choices for Americans* (Lexington, Mass.: D. C. Heath & Co., 1976), pp. 401–64.

[45]Norman John Powell, *Responsible Public Bureaucracy in the United States* (Boston: Allyn & Bacon, 1967), p. 40.

a system wherein the judicial, legislative, and executive branches would keep each other under control, the Founders rested. Their serenity would have vanished, no doubt, had they known that the size and complexity of administration would eventually create a fourth element of government, a strange creature with a massive body but, seemingly, with no head—or a hundred heads, or one head, depending on who is looking at it. Outwardly bland and subservient, the bureaucracy is actually enormously powerful—in some peoples' view, as powerful as any of the three branches of government established by the Constitution.

For convenience, the bureaucracy is often said to be in the executive branch. However, it would be better to classify it in its own—"administrative"—branch, for bureaucracy's powers are a combination of legislative, judicial, and executive. The framers of the Constitution did not intend to separate the powers of the three branches of government absolutely; they simply hoped to balance the powers so that no one branch could operate free of sharp interferences from the other two. They were constantly reminded by the likes of James Madison that "the accumulation of all powers, legislative, executive, and judiciary, in the same hands, whether of one, a few, or many, and whether hereditary, self-appointed, or elective, may justly be pronounced the very definition of tyranny."[46] All three types of powers are lodged in the bureaucracy:

Legislative Much of the legislation passed by Congress has been drafted wholly or in part by bureaucrats, who then, of course, follow through by testifying before congressional committees on behalf of their legislation and by lobbying for its passage behind the scenes. The administrative and regulatory agencies also engage in some of their own lawmaking through the countless rules and regulations they issue—for example, decisions about what commodities and services can be offered at what prices and under what conditions. These rulings are pub-

lished in the *Federal Register,* which constitutes the bulk of federal "law" today.

Judicial In the case of an administrative ruling that is disputed, Congress has delegated to the regulatory agencies power to make judicial decisions. The courts can review these decisions, but they rarely do. Judicial reluctance to interfere in such cases contributes to the quasi-judicial functions of the bureaucracy.[47]

Executive The executive role of the bureaucracy is most obviously filled in those departments and agencies closest to the President—the cabinet departments, the Office of Budget and Management, and the other components of the Executive Office of the President.

Does the blending of the three functions make the bureaucracy, by Madison's definition, a tyranny? That would be an exaggeration. But its size, cost, influence, and power have alarmed the Presidents of recent years, and each of them has tried, without much luck, to reorganize the bureaucracy along more responsive lines. Members of Congress have compared their own impact with that of the bureaucracy and suffered shriveled egos. Republican Congressman Del Clawson of California warns:

> Only a few "horror stories" are required to persuade us that eternal vigilance is the price we must pay if we are not to relinquish the law-writing function to a swarm of eager bureaucrats. Under the guise of "implementation" they can wreak changes, build empires, soar to heights of imaginative mismanagement of the public weal undreamed of in the halls of Congress when the original legislation was written and enacted.[48]

---

[46]James Madison in Alexander Hamilton, James Madison, and John Jay, *The Federalist Papers,* No. 47, ed. Clinton Rossiter (New York: Times Mirror Co., New American Library, 1961).

[47]"Theoretically, the courts are to judge the constitutionality and legality of challenged administrative decisions that can reasonably be presumed to fall within judicial competence. . . . [but they] refuse to review most administrative decisions, simply because they do not have the time to consider the vast volume of cases that arise in the normal course of regulatory administration.

"The expansion of administrative discretion in cases involving judicial matters has resulted from the agencies' specialization, and their ability to maintain some continuity of public policy. Despite their theoretical control, the courts are unable to limit the power of administrative agencies through the device of judicial review to the extent that many consider desirable in our constitutional system." (Peter Woll, *American Bureaucracy,* New York: W. W. Norton & Co., 1963, p. 21.)

[48]*Congressional Record,* H4536, May 21, 1975.

Bureaucratic Power

It would be an absurd caricature of the American economic power structure to suggest that all economic power, and with it corresponding responsibility, is lodged in private (that is to say, non-Statist) corporations. Chiefly due to repeated political intervention, the American political State today exercises a great deal. It regulates the price of practically all forms of public transportation. It controls, through the indirect management of the banking system, both long-term and short-term interest rates. It outlaws a whole range of trade practices, such as private price-fixing agreements, arrangements not to compete in given territories, and (less successfully) abuse of financial strength permitting cut-throat price competition and price discrimination. In a newer and steadily growing range of specific situations, the State intervenes to provide or require production (as in the case of the Rural Electrification Authority) or to adjust current supply of product to current demand (as in the case of the oil and refined sugar industries). It fixes minimum wages for most of nonagricultural industry and attempts a roughly equivalent operation in farming by establishing prices for staple agricultural commodities. It assists in providing credit, which is the greatest single element in the housing industry. Were it possible to draw a map of the extent of American economic power, it would be found that a very substantial, though minority, proportion of such power was exercised by one or another instrumentality of the United States Government or, locally, by the governments of the various states.

From Adolf A. Berle, *Power without Property: A New Development in American Political Economy* (New York: Harcourt Brace Jovanovich, 1959), pp. 93–94.

And Senator James G. Abourezk, Democrat, of South Dakota said:

Last year the Congress enacted 647 public laws while approximately 6,000 administrative rules were adopted by 67 Federal agencies, departments, and bureaus. More law, in the sense of rules governing our society, is produced by the executive branch and independent agencies than is produced by the national legislature. Administrative agencies, the headless "fourth branch" of Government, have grown up virtually unsupervised. Administrative rulemaking has filled the gaps between the broad principles embodied in acts of Congress, yet this process has not been subjected to effective congressional control and direction. . . .

I believe that the procedures which permit civil servants and appointed officials to pass upon thousands of far-reaching laws that in some circumstances put the liberty or property of our citizens in jeopardy are in need of reexamination.[49]

In what follows, we will attempt the reappraisal that Senator Abourezk called for.

What is the bureaucracy, physically? What are the motivations and alliances of the bureaucrats? How do they shape politics while claiming neutrality? Where are their power bases? In what ways does the bureaucracy fall short of the ideal? Does it fall short on purpose, or accidentally? What harm does it do? If the United States is suffering from a regulatory binge, can we pull out of it without doing more harm than good? Perhaps we will come across some of the answers here.

THE GREAT DEPARTMENTS

As has already been noted, the mammoth structure of the bureaucracy as we know it today is relatively new. Although the Army, Navy, State, and Treasury departments were creatures of the eighteenth century, most of the other cabinet departments appeared far later: Interior (1849), Justice (1870), Post Office (1872), Agriculture (1889), Commerce (1913), Labor (1913), Defense (1947), Health, Education and Welfare (1953), Housing and Urban Development (1965), Transportation (1966), and Energy (1977).

---

[49]*Congressional Record*, S7587–88, May 7, 1975.

Evolution of the Cabinet

The source of the creative energy that goes into the growth of bureaucracy can be discerned in the birthdates of the cabinet departments. Westward expansion—with the resulting need for range management, forest management, and mine management—gave birth to Interior. The great outburst of industrialization and commerce emphasized the need to regulate unscrupulous and too-powerful business (Justice) and the need for tying the nation closer together (Post Office). With the westward expansion almost completed, there was obviously a need for developing farm markets in a coherent fashion and for giving a voice in government to the rural population. Thus came Agriculture. The increasing urbanization of America saw business interests passing from cutthroat laissez faire into an era of cooperation, forming trade and business organizations. Since it was obvious that government was going to be butting into business more and more in the future, business wanted to be part of government. Thus, the Commerce Department. And, in the same year, with violence over labor issues becoming increasingly common, it was obvious that something had better be done to soothe the wage earner. And so the Labor Department came into being.

Population growth, urbanization, industrialization, wars, and interdependence of the population are all written into the history of the cabinet. The formation of each of these cabinet departments was motivated by one or several interest groups that felt inadequately represented in Washington. By 1913, every major segment of society had gained a podium. The social and economic stagnation that followed is seen in the fact that no further change was made in the cabinet system for thirty-four years, and then the change was not in kind but in size— when the Army Department and the Navy Department were merged into Defense. The Defense Department obviously would continue to speak for the same groups that used to have Army and Navy to represent them, but now their voice would be more powerful because it was unified.

After 1913, there was no truly new addition to the cabinet until forty years later, when HEW was set up to speak for educators, the medical professions, welfare groups, and all the potent lobbies that had emerged from the new welfare state. The postwar building boom and urban sprawl led construction companies and land speculators to demand their special place in government, a place from which they could seize the outpouring subsidies, and so came Housing and Urban Development (HUD). The postwar explosion of shipping and travel encouraged the railroads, truckers, bus lines, airlines, highway construction companies, auto and bus manufacturers, and other allied interests to support the establishment of a cabinet office through which they could exert pressure for federal funding of transportation facilities and equipment and through which they could manipulate performance and safety regulations. (But of course they did not want the department to take over the economic regulatory and rate-setting activities of existing federal agencies, which they already had well under control.) Thus, the Department of Transportation. Then, in the 1970s, when oil and natural gas companies began exploiting real or claimed shortages and when the overseas oil producing countries quadrupled their prices, the need for a national energy policy and some semblance of cohesive supervision of energy production (previously energy responsibilities had been scattered throughout fifty bureaucratic agencies) forced the creation of the Department of Energy.

Each cabinet department is broken into offices, bureaus, and subunits, each concerned in more detail with the demands of special interest groups. The Department of Health, Education and Welfare, for example, has an Office of Consumer Affairs, an Office for Civil Rights, and an Office of Human Development (under which there are such units as the Office of Child Development and the Office of Rural Development). Under HEW's Assistant Secretary for Health is the Public Health Service, which is broken down into such units as the Center for Disease Control, the Food and Drug Administration (FDA), the National Institutes of Health, and so forth. Under the FDA is the Bureau of Foods, the Bureau of Drugs, the Bureau of Veterinary Medicine, the Bureau of Radiological Health, and so forth. The cabinet departments are splintered into Offices, the Offices are splintered into Bureaus, or Centers, and so forth. There always seems to be another *so forth* in the division of the bureaucracy.

The Independent Agencies

In addition, a major segment of the bureaucracy is made up of the independent agencies—"independent" in the sense that they operate outside the cabinet department hierarchy and supposedly (though not actually) are free of political interference from either the executive or legislative branches. Some administer broad economic or social policies. Among these agencies are the Equal Employment Opportunity Commission and the National Labor Relations Board. Some agencies, usually specified as "regulatory," set rates and dictate operating conditions for certain industries. Among these are the Federal Communications Commission, the Civil Aeronautics Board, and the Interstate Commerce Commission.

The scope and intensity and kind of regulation that comes from these independent agencies differ a great deal. Morton Mintz and Jerry S. Cohen explain some of the differences:

> Natural-monopoly regulation usually involves control of entry, exit, and mergers; regulation of rates; and the prevention of unjustified rate and service discrimination. The scope of regulation turns on the presumed or accepted need for it. For example, the basis of regulation may be health or safety, as in the case of the Food and Drug Administration, and may require powers of inspection, testing, labeling, and removal of a product from the market. Or the need may be to prevent fraud and deception in the marketplace, and regulation may take the form of cease and desist orders, as is the case with Federal Trade Commission enforcement, or full disclosure before entering the market, as is the case with Security and Exchange Commission regulation. In still other cases, regulation may be predicated on the need to promote or contract the supply of credit. In these cases, regulation may take the form of federal insurance, control of interest rates, inspection of financial books and records, and civil sanctions or criminal fines and jail sentences. [50]

[50]Morton Mintz and Jerry S. Cohen, *America Inc.* (New York: Dell Publishing Co., Dial Press, 1971), pp. 177–78.

THE PRESIDENT AND THE BUREAUCRACY

Presidents often complain that they have precious little control over the bureaucracy, but in fact they have quite a bit. The President appoints all cabinet department heads and more than two thousand other top officials. He appoints all members of the independent and regulatory agencies. In short, he has hired and can fire at will everyone with an auspicious title like Cabinet Secretary, Assistant Secretary, Deputy Secretary, Deputy Assistant Secretary, *ad infinitum*—everyone entitled to a chauffeur or a silver water pitcher.

The President can also do a considerable amount of shuffling and consolidation *within* a cabinet department. He cannot shift a program from one department to another—say, from HEW to Labor—without getting Congress's approval. But he can do independently as President Carter did shortly after taking office: Carter put the Medicare and Medicaid programs, previously operated separately, under a new Health Care Financing Administration; he gave the Social Security Administration administrative responsibility for all welfare programs; and eight student financial-assistance programs—previously divided among three offices—were consolidated into a single bureau. Since all of these programs had previously been in HEW and would remain in HEW, no congressional approval was needed. It was strictly a matter of intradepartmental personnel changes, like moving furniture around within a room. The President cannot, however, either create or abolish whole departments or independent agencies. When, for example, Carter wanted to establish the Department of Energy, he had to get Congress's approval. As part of his energy reorganization, Carter asked that the power to regulate natural-gas prices be taken away from the Federal Power Commission, an independent regulatory agency, and given to the new Energy Department. Instead, Congress shifted the FPC into the Energy Department but left it with rate-setting powers independent of the Secretary of Energy.

The President also has great *generalized* control over the bureaucracy through the Executive

" 'scuse me, sir—I was wondering if you'd care to be born again . . ."

Drawing by Oliphant; © 1977 Washington Star

Office, especially through its budget-making powers. Special attention must be paid to the Executive Office, which came into existence in the one great reorganization achieved by a President. When Franklin D. Roosevelt became President in 1933, he launched his New Deal, which was an assortment of hundreds of new programs aimed at relieving the terrible economic paralysis gripping the nation. Most of these programs had never been tried before, and they did not fit easily into the established bureaucracy. Furthermore, Roosevelt was afraid that the new programs would fail at the hands of the established bureaucracy, since most of the federal workers were holdovers from the arch-conservative Republican administrations that had preceded him. So he set up, within the bureaucracy, new units that were committed to his Democratic administration.[51]

The result was bureaucratic expansion on a scale that had never been seen before. Within a few years, Roosevelt realized that he had created a Frankenstein's monster, a bureaucracy grown so enormous and so complex that he was having a hard time finding out all he needed to know about its activities in order to operate the White House intelligently. The answer, he felt, was to expand his supervisory staff, and he asked the Congress to let him do this. Congress, though suspicious of his ambitions, gave him permission to create a little kingdom of advisers and lieutenants. On September 8, 1939, Roosevelt issued Executive Order 8248, which has been described as a "nearly unnoticed but nonetheless epoch-making event in the history of American institutions."[52] It created the modern "Presidency"—as seen apart from the President. To be exact, it created the Executive Office. Un-

---

[51]See Rexford G. Tugwell, *Roosevelt's Revolution: The First Year* (New York: Macmillan, 1977), pp. 129–30.

[52]Clinton Rossiter, *The American Presidency*, rev. ed. (New York: Harcourt Brace Jovanovich, 1960), p. 129.

der that general title are suspended the President's White House staff and, in addition, such general command lines as the Council on Wage and Price Stability, the Domestic Policy Staff, the Council of Economic Advisers, the National Security Council, and the Office of Management and Budget (OMB).

As mentioned in Chapter 9, the OMB is the nerve center of the President's organized effort to control the bureaucracy and to influence (and sometimes threaten) Congress. The OMB puts together the President's budget, which is another way of saying that it establishes, in a dollars-and-cents way, the President's and the nation's priorities. The OMB also coordinates departmental advice on legislation, keeps the President informed on programs and personnel in the government, and performs a host of other duties that go with the operation of any enormous enterprise. (See also Chapter 16.)

In an effort to control the bureaucracy through the purse, President Carter instituted "zero base budgeting." Traditionally, at budget-writing time the bureaucracy had only to make a good argument for its continued growth. The Carter plan was to force each piece of the bureaucracy first to argue that it had a good reason to exist; only then would the President consider how much, if any, budget increase it deserved.

Spoils and the Civil Service

Despite these points of control, Presidents are justified in complaining that much of the bureaucracy operates with awesome autonomy, immune to political trends and often indifferent to the immediate needs of the general public. There are several reasons for this. The first is a technical reason: the Civil Service.

Until the end of the 1820s, the bureaucracy was stable, hardly ruffled by partisan changes in the White House. But, Andrew Jackson, inaugurated in 1829, believed in the martial dictum, "to the victor belong the spoils." He filled the bureaucracy with his own people, arguing that only thus could he see that the will of the electorate that put him in office was carried out. He also believed—and history has proved how right he

was—that long experience on the job can leave the spirit encrusted and calloused. He said,

> There are perhaps few men who can for any great length of time enjoy office without being more or less under the influence of feelings unfavourable to the faithful discharge of their public duties. Their integrity may be proof against improper considerations immediately addressed to themselves, but they are apt to acquire a habit of looking with indifference upon the public interests and of tolerating conduct from which an unpracticed man would revolt.

Therefore, he said, it was a good idea to install new faces in the bureaucracy every few years. As for the argument that this would waste expertise, Jackson's reply was:

> The duties of all public offices are, or at least admit of being made, so plain and simple that men of intelligence may readily qualify themselves for their performance; and I cannot but believe that more is lost by the long continuance of men in office than is generally to be gained by their experience.[53]

Jackson's argument was, and is, persuasive up to a point. But, ultimately, reformers prevailed. When President James A. Garfield was assassinated by a man who thought he was going to get a spoils job and didn't, Congress passed the Pendleton Act of 1883 (the Civil Service Act), which set up a merit system for federal employment. The Civil Service Commission runs the system. A job candidate must meet the Civil Service prerequisites in order to be hired, and once hired, a Civil Service employee is hard to fire. Usually the employee can be discharged only if found guilty of dishonesty or for refusing to carry out assigned duties. Although the Civil Service Act did take most of the spoils out of the system, it did not eliminate incompetence, laziness, or lack of public spirit.

For that matter, the Civil Service Act did not offer absolute immunity from intrusion by Presidents who want to corrupt the system; nor are the supposedly independent regulatory agencies immune to pressure from a President who wants to feather his friends' nests. Since the primary job of the bureaucracy is to hand out

---

[53]*Encyclopaedia Britannica,* 1970 ed., s.v. "Spoils System."

money—for salaries, welfare, work grants, and purchases—and since the amount handed out each year is beyond ordinary comprehension, a crafty President will find ways to manipulate at least part of the bureaucracy into supporting his political fortune.

Despite the supposed strictness of the Civil Service's merit system, examinations, and other prerequisites to hiring, illegal favoritism still exists. If you've got pull, it makes a difference. The General Services Administration—the federal government's construction, supply, and housekeeping agency—fired a qualified employee and hired the son of a former Secretary of the Treasury, even though he was not legally eligible for the job.[54] The cousin of a Texas congressman was given a federal career job after the Chairman of the Civil Service Commission personally intervened.[55] As a matter of standing policy, some federal agencies operate a "special referral system" to give hiring preference to job applicants sponsored by politicians.[56] When there are no job openings for political favorites, job holders are sometimes pressured to quit to make room for the favorites.[57]

The misuse of the federal bureaucracy as a political cornucopia has occurred in virtually every administration, Democratic and Republican, but it reached new extremes in the Nixon administration. White House operatives set up a program to insure Nixon's reelection in 1972 by awarding millions of dollars in federal grants to key states and voting blocs; federal agencies were pressured into hiring Nixon supporters to fill career Civil Service positions; and regulatory agencies were urged to act in ways that would gain support for the Republican administration. Although a staff of the Senate Watergate investigating committee indicated that this effort to politicize the bureaucracy violated federal criminal and civil laws and may have risen "to the level of a conspiracy to interfere with the lawful functioning of government,"[58] no charges were filed, and nobody was ever prosecuted for it.

The Politics of Appointment

Any impression that the rules of the official government game are often violated is an accurate one. Whether or not the bureaucracy operates according to the book depends on the President's willingness not to interfere illegally and on important bureaucrats' determination to stick to official policy. Most especially, the smooth and independent operation of the bureaucracy depends on how well outside pressure groups can be kept under control. They seldom are.

Pressure groups not only penetrate the defenses of the bureaucracy, they virtually come into the bureaucracy and set up shop, either through friendships cultivated over many years or through the placement of their own people in the bureaucracy, or both. These same outside pressures also weaken the President's influence with the bureaucracy and prevent his being his own boss. Although, theoretically, the President has full control of at least the top of the bureaucracy through his appointive powers, even there his control is not absolute. His top appointments are often made under pressure.

A President picks his cabinet and major sub-cabinet officials to please friends and groups that helped him get elected, to concoct an image of stability and equal representation, and—most of all—to appease powerful interest groups. President Carter, for example, chose a personal friend to be Attorney General; he named women and blacks to Commerce and to Housing to fulfill campaign promises; and he picked six persons for the cabinet from previous Democratic administrations for continuity. In virtually every instance, he double-checked his appointees to see if they satisfied the wishes of the interest groups they would be dealing with. He did this not only for the cabinet, but for other units, such as the

---

[54]*Washington Post*, January 9, 1975.

[55]*St. Louis Post-Dispatch*, September 25, 1974.

[56]Sources: Report of the U.S. Civil Service Commission, Washington, D.C., October 23, 1973; Mike Causey, *Washington Post*, December 18, 1974.

[57]Letter from Gerald E. McNamara, Administrator of General Services Administration Region 8, to House Subcommittee on Manpower and Civil Service, released December 14, 1974.

---

[58]Quoted in the *Washington Post*, July 8, 1974.

Central Intelligence Agency. When he failed to do so or when he ignored the wishes of the interest groups, he got in trouble.

Having been organized and funded to perform certain duties for particular interest groups, the bureaucracy has potent allies it can appeal to when any President tries to meddle. President Carter wanted to appoint Theodore C. Sorensen, who had been a key adviser in the Kennedy White House, as Director of the Central Intelligence Agency. But Sorensen had been a conscientous objector during the Korean War, was believed to have held a grudge against the CIA for the bad advice it gave Kennedy prior to the Bay of Pigs invasion, and was thought to have a rather cavalier attitude toward secrets. So the spy establishment recruited its many friends in Congress, especially those on the Senate committee handling the CIA nomination, to put the heat on Sorensen. He was subjected to embarrassing questions, innuendoes, and cloudy accusations. It worked. Sorensen asked President Carter to withdraw his nomination. A career military man, sympathetic to the spy traditions, got the post instead, and the agency went back to business as usual. Faced with a similar frustration, President Nixon once told an aide, "Any change is resisted because bureaucrats have a vested interest in the chaos in which they exist."[59]

Career Bureaucrats

The influence of the vested interests is especially pervasive among the second-level career officials—the bureau chiefs and their assistants, who watch Presidents and cabinet members come and go while they stay on the job for thirty or forty years, doing business pretty much as always. Part of their power comes from the fact that they are, practically speaking, invisible.

Distance is the great weakener of central authority. If the President manages to keep in touch with twelve cabinet secretaries, the head of the White House staff, the Director of the OMB, the Vice President, the head of the National Security Council, and perhaps a dozen

other key personnel, he is very lucky and very industrious.[60] But that leaves dozens of other top-rank, hundreds of near-top-rank, and thousands of middle-rank personnel in a shadow world. The farther down the ladder they are, the less control the President has over them. He cannot effectively browbeat or threaten them into doing his wishes, for in truth he doesn't know they exist. So he and his immediate subordinates must rely on a kind of foreign diplomacy within the executive branch. They get what they get with a carrot, by inspiration, by negotiation, and even by barter.[61]

The President and his immediate aides are, in short, bucking an enormously ingrown establishment, peopled by career bureaucrats protected by the Civil Service system.

> For these [bureaucrats], changes in administration are not too important—unless, of course, the individual bureaucrat has close connections with, or has excited the violent antagonism of, the incoming president or his chief power-holding delegates. They consider, not wholly without reason, that they know more about the precise business of handling foreign problems or fiscal policy, operating the Internal Revenue Bureau or dealing with social security, or running the postal system or the Library of Congress than anyone else. Incoming political officeholders can only work—at least in their early period of office holding—through the machinery the bureaucracies have set up and administer. Each cabinet secretary is almost, though not quite, helpless in the hands of his inherited bureaucrats if he antagonizes them. If they seriously disagree with policies he puts forward, they do not even need to enter into public controversy. They need merely drag their feet or silently oppose by delaying, requiring further study, seeking interpretations, raising practical objections, and leaking information to opposition senators, congressmen, and press commentators. Though a bureaucracy that wants to get something done can only occasionally arrange to do it, if it desires to block action, it can hinder realization of almost any project. . . .
>
> Almost invariably the chief of a bureau, division, or section is entirely sincere in thinking that

---

[59] Safire, *Before the Fall*, p. 247.

[60] Louis C. Gawthrop, *Bureaucratic Behavior in the Executive Branch* (New York: Free Press, 1969), p. 65.

[61] Gawthrop, pp. 66–67.

*"I refuse to respond to an appointee of an official
appointed by an appointed official."*

he best serves the United States in the attitude he takes toward declared policy. Not infrequently he is right: he knows that some decision, however well intentioned, will make trouble, perhaps has failed before. Usually he really believes that he is "protecting" the president or his department head, and with him the United States, from a blunder. In any case, most men dislike having their habits disturbed, and bureaucrats perhaps more than others. So they expedite the machinery if they are in favor, and retard it if they are not, awaiting the inevitable time when the top power holders either leave office or come around to their point of view.[62]

To be sure, if the government were full of *ideal* bureaucrats, an administration would not have the problem of recalcitrance. Ideal bureaucrats, says Fritz Morstein Marx, a scholar of bureau-

cracy, perform in this way: they commit themselves to the *ad hoc* political majority, as represented by the politicians whom that majority sends to Washington, but they commit themselves to it only so long as its *ad* is *hoc*. They remain mentally pliable enough to change and change again in response to the nation's fluctuating ideologies and not resort to the hypocrisy of pretending to change when they have no intention of doing so. They are enthusiastic advisers, but they know that an adviser's position is subordinate. They know when to obey without question, and they know when to question. They do not "fall back on two-faced answers in order to get by" or resort to "the smoke-screen of busy business."[63]

---

[62]Adolf A. Berle, *Power* (Harcourt Brace Jovanovich, 1969), p. 317.

[63]Fritz Morstein Marx, "The Higher Civil Service as an Action Group in Western Political Development," in Joseph LaPalombara, ed., *Bureaucracy and Development* (Princeton, N.J.: University of Princeton Press, 1967), pp. 93–94.

CONSERVATISM AND INERTIA

Working against the ideal are a number of forces, one of the most powerful being inertia. As George J. Stigler, former President of the American Economic Association, once observed, government has two central characteristics: it cannot do anything quickly, and it never knows when to quit.[64]

If the bureaucracy were to choose a coat of arms for itself, it very likely would select an anchor and chain over rampant mothballs, with the motto *Status quo procreat status quo*. The bureaucracy does not appreciate change; it thrives on stability; it loves still air and lukewarm temperatures. Anthony Downs writes:

> Like most large organizations, bureaus have a powerful tendency to continue doing today whatever they did yesterday. The main reason for this inertia is that established processes represent an enormous previous investment in time, effort, and money. This investment constitutes a "sunk cost" of tremendous proportions. Years of effort, thousands of decisions (including mistakes), and a wide variety of experiences underlie the behavior patterns a bureau now uses. Moreover, it took a significant investment to get the bureau's many members and clients to accept and become habituated to its behavior patterns.[65]

The entrenched bureaucratic chieftains do not hold their redoubts only on their own behalf or by their own stratagems. They also protect the status quo for the sake of, and with the help of, powerful allies. First of all, the senior careerists operate in league with the chairpersons and ranking members of the congressional committees that have jurisdiction over their part of the bureaucracy. Second, they operate in league with lobbyists whose businesses are keyed to that portion of the bureaucracy.[66] These alliances between bureau chief, congressional chairperson, and lobbyist are what John W. Gardner,

looking back on his nearly three years as Secretary of HEW, identified as "the unholy trinity" that caused him so much trouble—

> Little threesomes. Fellows who have gone fishing together for years. Their wives have played bridge together. They are part of a permanent invisible Washington. Their names are not known to the general public. They rarely make the headlines. But they've seen Presidents come and go, and they determine a great deal of what actually goes through Congress.[67]

Or what is done by the bureaucracy.

A similar situation was noted by Interior Secretary Cecil D. Andrus almost as soon as he joined the Carter cabinet. He had found his department, he said, split into "little fiefdoms" and taken over by private interest groups in collusion with the other two members of the unholy trinity—

> The policy has been for the grazing interests to have their chunk here, for coal to have another chunk; lumber, mining, all with their own part of the department. This place was like a centipede with each little pair of legs scuttling off in its own direction. That's going to change now.[68]

Many cabinet officers have made the same vow, in vain.

Advisory Committees: Outside Insiders

By alliances with the giant "advisory committee" system, the unholy trinity is further protected from interference and change. Advisory committees are made up of persons whose professional ties are outside government. Mostly their ties are to Big Business and to industry. Although they are not technically part of the bureaucracy, the government pays them to give advice on how the bureaucracy should operate. As of 1977, there were about twelve hundred federal advisory commissions with over 23,000 members, thousands of staff members, and an

---

[64]*New York Times Book Review*, July 27, 1975.

[65]Anthony Downs, *Inside Bureaucracy* (Boston: Little, Brown and Co., 1967), p. 195.

[66]See Gawthrop, *Bureaucratic Behavior in the Executive Branch*.

[67]Sources: Quoted in Robert Sherrill, "Cause without a Rebel," *Playboy*, July 1972, pp. 109+; personal interview with John W. Gardner, April 1972.

[68]Quoted in the *New York Times*, February 4, 1977.

---

annual budget of between $60 million and $100 million. The taxpayer is charged for consultant fees (up to $100 a day), staff salaries, and travel allowances.[69] That, as bureaucratic expenses go, is a bargain, considering the fact that it buys some of the best corporate brains in the country. But there is a hitch. Advisory committees tend to see problems not from the perspective of broad national interests, but from that of narrow special interests. The committee that advises the Treasury Department on banking policies, for example, will typically be full of such people as the former Chairman of Bank of America. Advisory committees recommending policy for foreign oil imports are heavy with executives from multinational oil corporations. Officials from ITT and Standard Oil International and their peers serve on committees that advise the State Department on international business problems.[70]

This quasi-governmental "insider" position is strategically invaluable to the advisers. Senator Lee Metcalf, Chairman of the Subcommittee on Budgeting, Management and Expenditures, which has given this problem intense investigation, explains the payoff to the advisers:

> Legally, their function is purely as kibitzer, but in practice many have become internal lobbies—printing industry handouts in the Government Printing Office with taxpayers' money, and even influencing policies. Industry committees perform the dual function of stopping the government from finding out about corporations while at the same time helping corporations get inside information about what the government is doing. Sometimes, the same company that sits on an advisory council that obstructs or turns down a government questionnaire is precisely the company that is withholding information the government needs in order to enforce a law.[71]

Bureaucrats, who want to strengthen their own position by getting a bigger budget, exploit the advisory committees. Aaron B. Wildavsky explains:

> Get a group of people together who are professionally interested in a subject, no matter how conservative or frugal they might otherwise be, and they are certain to find additional ways in which money could be spent. . . . Advisors may be used to gather support for a program or agency in various ways. They may directly lobby with Congress or the President . . . [or they] may provide a focus of respectability and apparent disinterest to take the onus of self-seeking from the proponents of greater spending. They may work with interest groups and, indeed, may actually represent them. They may direct their attempts to the public media. . . .[72]

When editors have been leaned on by some of their full-page advertisers, they know they've been leaned on.

"These Things Get Rolling . . ."

Protecting the status quo, resisting the tremors of executive department changes, worshipping stability—these instincts are not all bad. Indeed, one of the great virtues of the bureaucracy is that it provides continuity between administrations. But when bureaucrats refuse to adjust to the changing mood and the changing needs of the electorate, when they refuse to carry out reasonable policy shifts because that would mean creating friction with their old lobbyist pals, or when they refuse to do something simply because it would result in more work and a new style of operation, then the public weal is almost bound to get inferior service. Evidence of what can result from this kind of bureaucratic inertia can be seen in the broken trees and scattered debris on a hillside near Washington's Dulles International Airport. In 1970, Trans

[69]Sources: Third Annual Report of the General Services Administration, Washington, D.C., March 1975; Wall Street Journal, April 4, 1977.

[70]Report of the Senate Government Operations Committee, released January 7, 1974. One might justifiably worry about the kind of advice they give. Senate investigators discovered that ITT offered the CIA $1 million to overthrow the left-wing Chilean government and restore a better "business atmosphere" in that country; Standard Oil officials admitted slipping millions of dollars secretly to Italian political parties that suited their business ideology. (Associated Press, May 17, 1975.)

[71]Lee Metcalf, "The Vested Oracles: How Industry Regulates Government," Washington Monthly, July 1971, p. 231.

[72]Aaron B. Wildavsky, The Politics of the Budgetary Process (Boston: Little, Brown and Co., 1964), pp. 63–84.

The Bureaucratic Mind at Work

World Airlines asked the Federal Aviation Administration to clarify its rules relating to approach altitudes. The FAA replied that it was "undertaking a study." Four years later, with the same regulations in effect and unclarified, a TWA plane crashed—after the pilot had been cleared for approach—killing all ninety-two persons aboard.[73]

When the Department of Transportation was brought into the cabinet in 1966, one of its tasks as outlined by Congress was to establish a formal national transportation policy. A decade later, no policy had been formulated; meanwhile, the highways, railroads, airlines, trucks, and buses operated in a world of growing chaos.

When Bob Bergland took over as Secretary of Agriculture in February 1977, he found two thousand employees of the USDA planning new dam projects even though the USDA already had a ten-year backlog of dams planned and awaiting construction. Bergland ordered a halt to the planning. Two months later, the USDA's Assistant Administrator for Water Resources said he hadn't heard anything about the order and that so far as he was concerned the planning would proceed at full speed.[74] In 1977, President Carter ordered thirty-four water projects cancelled, including a dam in South Carolina. Governor James B. Edwards of that state was also against construction of the dam, but he figured it would be built anyway, for "bureaucracies are such that these things get rolling and all the politicians in the world can vote against them and they still go on. It's a pretty bad reflection on government."[75]

AUTONOMY PERVERTED: FBI AND CIA

At best, the powerful heads of bureaus or agencies can defend their turf against improper political advances. At worst, they can turn their organizations into something offensive. The FBI and the CIA are the most flagrant examples of how this happens. Disclosures of the 1970s have shown that those agencies have existed for many years as little kingdoms whose rulers are intent on promoting their ideologies at the expense of constitutional protections and statutory restrictions.

In 1974 and 1975, it was discovered that the CIA had, for many years, conducted burglaries, wiretaps, mail interceptions, and other disruptive tactics *in this country* aimed at people whose politics it disapproved of. It had done these things despite the fact that the statute under

[73]*Washington Star,* February 1, 1975.

[74]*Wall Street Journal,* April 13, 1977.

[75]Quoted in the *Washington Post,* April 3, 1977.

which it operates strictly forbids all domestic activities. The aura of autonomy that hangs about the CIA is such that neither the President nor a majority of Congress ever worked up enough courage even to suggest that the shadowy lawbreakers within The Company, as it is called, should be brought to the same bar of justice that awaits ordinary citizens.[76]

However obnoxious such CIA activities are to the ideal of bureaucracy, they were not carried out against nearly so interesting a background as were the highhandedness, the illegalities, and the kingly goofs of the FBI, especially during the long reign of Director J. Edgar Hoover. After all, one side of the CIA was meant to be a dirty-works factory; it was officially established as such; its ethics were never expected to be very high. Whether or not it should play dirty domestically as well as internationally was the only real matter of debate.

But the FBI is supposed to be different. The comic strip legends said that it was highminded and the very embodiment of lawfulness. The FBI's trim, brave, unflappable gangbusters—the movies assured us for three generations—were the United States' first line of defense against the "underworld rats." That image was the result of the most successful public-relations campaign in bureaucratic history, and it was largely the doing of the bulldog-jawed Hoover. As a result of it, the FBI's budget requests sailed through Congress without challenge. As another result of it, the first action taken by Kennedy, Johnson, and Nixon on ascending to the Presidency was to assure the world that the glamorous Mr. Hoover (born in 1895) could stay on as head of the FBI despite the fact that he was past the legal retirement age for federal employees.

And then came the ugly awakening of United States citizens to what had really been going on behind the FBI's wall of autonomy. While the Mafia and other sophisticated crime syndicates went about their business relatively undisturbed, Hoover kept his agency spying on "radical" organizations that he disliked—mostly antiwar and civil rights groups that were no threat to either the public peace or the public's well-being—or on solving lesser crimes (such as auto thefts, after local police had found the stolen cars) that would jack up their success record.

Hoover's hang-up over what he called "left-wing dupes" sent FBI agents scurrying down some strange trails. They put together a dossier on a seventeen-year-old girl in Newark, New Jersey, who wrote a high-school essay on the Socialist Labor party.[77] Fearing for the minds of some Boy Scouts, FBI agents tried to drive a Newark scoutmaster out of town because his wife was a socialist.[78] In Washington, D.C., they tried to get a socialist kindergarten teacher fired lest she lead her tots into Marxism.[79]

Hoover's hatred for draft dodgers was so intense that he would sometimes assign one hundred agents to run down one draft evader. Records from FBI files indicate that the agency spent at least 40 percent of its time in political surveillance[80] and in trying to disrupt political organizations with techniques that post-Hoover Attorney General William B. Saxbe called "abhorrent in a free society."[81] But no Attorney General, though nominally his boss, ever dared talk that way about Hoover's work while he was alive. Information obtained from FBI officials after Hoover's death indicated that the Director had been downright quirky about some other things, too. He liked to put together files that could have been—even if they weren't—used for blackmail: files full of data about the private lives of important people (like Presidents and members of Congress), including their sexual and drinking habits.[82]

---

[76]When CIA horror stories, including its assassination contracts with the Mafia, began coming to light in 1975, James R. Schlesinger, former Director of the CIA, responded with the kind of complacent attitude that makes real bureaucratic reform very difficult to achieve. He said, "All bureaucracies have a tendency to stray across the line." (Press conference, Washington, D.C., January 15, 1975.)

[77]United Press International, August 30, 1974.

[78]*New York Times*, March 23, 1975.

[79]*Washington Post*, June 26, 1975.

[80]Thomas Emerson, "The FBI as Political Police," in Pat Watters and Stephan Gillers, eds., *Investigating the FBI* (New York: Doubleday & Co., 1973), pp. 239–54.

[81]Quoted in the *New York Times*, November 24, 1974.

[82]Associated Press, January 31, 1975.

CIA headquarters in Langley, Virginia

How does a fellow like J. Edgar Hoover turn his part of the bureaucracy into a private kingdom? Several factors go into the formula for his success: longevity, propaganda, fear, cronyism, control of information. But perhaps the most important factor is secrecy. Hoover operated behind a wall of secrecy: Presidents often did not know what he and his agents were up to; the outer ring of the FBI often did not know what the inner ring was doing.

An even more impenetrable crust of secrecy made the CIA inviolable. Ninety-nine percent of the members of Congress have never had the slightest idea what the CIA's budget was, or is, much less any details of its programs. The thing to bear in mind is that the CIA is just a part of the huge fraternity of secrecy in government. The nine federal intelligence agencies—including the various military intelligence units—hire an estimated 200,000 persons, spend over $6 billion a year,[83] and operate in comfortable obscurity.

THE REGULATORS

One big factor contributing to excessive bureaucratic autonomy is the kind of delegated power

---

[83]*New York Times,* June 29, 1975.

that comes from Congress. The first congressional directives to regulatory agencies were concrete and well-defined, calling mostly for proscriptive regulation. Agencies were empowered to prevent specific *sub*standard, *im*moral, *un*healthy, *un*fair activities; their purpose was, quite simply, to protect the public from being cheated and poisoned too flagrantly. But gradually, as Theodore J. Lowi points out, the regulators' target was expanded by a more general delegation of powers.[84] No longer did they aim solely at the relatively contained bull's-eye of evil-prevention. Now they were commissioned with the broad authority to do good—to decide how business should operate so that it would result in better products, larger markets, higher profits, fatter consumers, and safer competition. The circles of the target were extended to the infinity of a theoretical perfection. Such a policy, encouraged by special interests who stood to benefit by being able to define that perfection, resulted at times in dangerously unrestrained regulation. At least that is how some critics view the regulatory world; it may be an exaggerated view.

Broadly speaking, of course, almost every corner of the government is occupied by regulators and always has been. As Thomas K. McGraw has pointed out,

> Every one of the federal executive departments . . . has regulatory functions. The State Department regulates travel abroad. The Department of Health, Education and Welfare issues hundreds of rules on dozens of subjects. Defense, with its huge power of the purse, enforces equal employment opportunity among its thousands of contractors. Thus, the members of the Cabinet are among the most powerful individual regulators in America.[85]

But when we speak of the regulators, we usually mean a special group of independent agencies, some of whom regulate economic forces and some of whom regulate industrial behavior.

The independent regulatory agencies got a late start in the bureaucracy. None was founded until the nation was about a century old.[86] And there was a negative basis to their establishment, in contrast to the cabinet departments, which were set up for ordinary housekeeping and management—for example, to supervise the military; manage money and public lands; tend to the government's legal business; represent business interests, farmers, and laborers; and administer the government's social largess. The basic tone of the cabinet is positive; it is a tone that recognizes the best in the citizenry. Most of the independent regulatory agencies were established in recognition of the *undesirable* qualities in people: greed, avarice, duplicity, carelessness. They were established to protect people from the rapacious monopoly of railroads (Interstate Commerce Commission), from the harmful fluctuations of an irresponsible money market (Federal Reserve Board), from overloading the airwaves (Federal Communications Commission), from the crooks of Wall Street (Securities and Exchange Commission), from bullying employers and bullying labor unions (National Labor Relations Board), from unfair trade practices (Federal Trade Commission), from unsafe and untrustworthy airlines (Civil Aeronautics Board and Federal Aviation Administration), from oppressive rates set by energy monopolies (Federal Power Commission), and from cutthroat competition that provided cheap rates at the expense of service and dependability.

Hopeless Burdens

The independent regulatory agencies were supposed to be "big brother" government at its

---

[84]See Theodore J. Lowi, *The End of Liberalism* (New York: W. W. Norton & Co., 1969).

[85]Thomas K. McGraw, "The Controversial World of the Regulatory Agencies," *American Heritage*, April 1977, p. 41.

[86]Those that get the headlines most often are these: Interstate Commerce Commission (1887), Federal Reserve Board (1913), Federal Trade Commission (1914), Federal Power Commission (1920), Federal Communications Commission (1934), Securities and Exchange Commission (1934), National Labor Relations Board (1935), Civil Aeronautics Board (1938), Atomic Energy Commission (1946, which was superseded in 1975 by two commissions, the Nuclear Regulatory Commission and the Energy Resources and Development Agency), the Federal Aviation Administration (1958, which superseded the Civil Aeronautics Administration—which was created in 1940 after the Civil Aeronautics Authority was abolished), and the Environmental Protection Agency (1970). The Food and Drug Administration is one of the best known of the regulatory agencies, but it is not "independent"; it is a part of HEW.

best—defending the weak against the bullies on the block. The agencies' original motivation was strong; their impact from then to now has, on balance, been preponderantly benevolent. But in recent decades, there have been disquieting changes. With the growing complexity of society and its economy, the efficiency of the regulatory agencies has fallen sharply at the same time that the agencies have swollen in size (the Federal Aviation Administration, for example, has more than twice as many employees as the State Department).[87] Their reputation is clouded by red tape and unconscionable delays.[88] A heavy aura of hopelessness hangs over much of their effort, partly because the regulators sometimes lack motivation, partly because they are not given clear standards to go by, and partly because the vast job of overseeing and regulating is simply too much for them.

Most government regulators have responsibilities of overwhelming scope. In 1977, the Federal Railroad Administration had only 376 safety inspectors to stay on top of 330,000 miles of track (some segments of which were in such sorry shape that they permitted no faster travel than six miles an hour), 1.8 million freight cars and 30,000 locomotives, plus whatever few passenger cars remained at large.[89] The Office of Pipeline Safety still had only twenty-one professional staff members in 1974, although there had been 4,963 pipeline accidents between 1970 and 1973.[90] The Food and Drug Administration, similarly overwhelmed by its job, announced in late 1974 that it was going to stop trying to get rid of all "poisonous and deleterious" substances in food and instead aim at holding down to "tolerable" the levels of lead poison in evaporated milk, of mercury poison in fish, and of afla-

toxin—a cancer-producing mold—in peanuts, corn, and other grain.[91]

The Securities and Exchange Commission is another vital regulator with a seemingly hopeless burden. In 1936, when Wall Street was, by today's comparison, as simple as a mom-and-pop grocery store, the SEC had a staff of 1,800 persons. By the mid-1970s, its staff had grown by only 119 in the intervening thirty-eight years, while the job, as appraised by one reporter, had grown to this:

It means supervising the activities of about 5,000 broker-dealers and 3,500 investment advisers, regulating 1,300 investment companies, bringing enforcement actions to assure financial responsibility and fair dealing, studying 1,000 corporate reorganizations each year, obtaining full and accurate information from 10,000 corporations and watching the trading in another 10,000.[92]

Conflicts of Interest

By far the most depressing effect on the spirit and activity of regulation has come from conflicts of interest. The bureaucracy has been heavily infiltrated by officials who are alumni of the industries they are supposed to be regulating, or who anticipate being employed by them when they leave government service, or who are so incestuously allied to those industries that they cannot judge them objectively.

These regulators are not appointed by accident. Louis M. Kohlmeier, Jr., who covered the regulatory agencies for the *Wall Street Journal* for many years, tells it right:

The test of competence to which a candidate for initial appointment is subjected consists of the submission by the White House of his or her name to industry executives before sending it on to the Senate for confirmation. CAB appointees are cleared with airline executives, FPC appointees with gas and electric companies, ICC appointees with railroad officials and usually truckers, too.

Every President in recent history has run some sort of check with industry before appointing or reappointing a regulator. . . .The appointment machinery apparently works well enough, for ex-

---

[87]*Congressional Record*, H2538, April 8, 1975.

[88]In 1975, the Federal Communications Commission was forty-one years old; one of its cases, a dispute between an Albuquerque, New Mexico, radio station and a New York City radio station, had been around for thirty-three years.

[89]*Washington Star*, October 31, 1973. The count of the safety inspectors comes from the office of Congressman Fred B. Rooney, Chairman of the House Subcommittee on Transportation and Commerce, press release, July 26, 1977.

[90]*Washington Post*, April 25, 1974.

[91]*Washington Post*, December 7, 1974.

[92]Felix Belair, Jr., *New York Times*, June 30, 1975.

---

ample, to the thinking of a bank executive who said of the banking regulators: "This system works best if there's a blob in every job."[93]

Conflict of interest is so widespread in the regulatory agencies and in the overseer sections of the cabinet departments that it does not even cause comment unless it becomes rampant, as when it was discovered that fifty-eight former oil industry employees, including fourteen with authority to decide prices and policy, were holding key positions in the Federal Energy Office.[94] On another occasion, investigators for the General Accounting Office were startled to discover that nineteen Federal Power Commission officials—who helped develop data on which was based a multibillion-dollar natural-gas rate increase—illegally held stock in gas production, pipeline, and electric power companies.[95]

In 1975, the Associated Press obtained documents showing that at least 350 decision makers in the regulatory agencies once worked for the industries they were supposed to be regulating. For example, more than 100 officials in the Food and Drug Administration, who were helping to decide what drugs could be sold and what chemicals could be put in food, had once worked for drug or chemical companies. And the SEC was a haven for more than 30 top-level regulatory officials who once worked for brokerage firms and stock exchanges. The revolving door funnels in both directions. The Associated Press also found that at least 41 top agency officials had left their positions in the previous five years to take what were usually more lucrative posts with companies in those same regulated industries.[96] Federal law forbids any former federal official from participating in a matter in which he or she was involved while in government for at least one year after leaving the government. But not everyone agrees on what *participating* means.

William D. Ruckelshaus was the first Director of the Environmental Protection Agency, from 1970 to 1974. When he left that post, several other EPA officials left with him. They set up a law firm in Washington. Many of their clients were corporations—including several that manufacture cancer-causing chemicals—that were having problems with the EPA. Ruckelshaus was doing nothing unusual. Many of Washington's most powerful lawyers once worked for regulatory agencies, and, as one writer pointed out, they "continue to be part of the [agencies'] inner circle, enjoying easy access to their successors in government. Sometimes, it's as if they had never left."[97] (See also Chapter 5.)

Low Morale

In 1977, the Senate Government Operations Committee, completing a fifteen-year survey of the regulatory agencies, concluded that appointments to the agencies under Democratic and Republican administrations alike were not of a high quality and included many persons who did not even know the laws they were asked to administer. They found that a high percentage of the appointees came from the industries they were supposed to regulate, and that most commissioners were white, male lawyers. Women, minority members, and persons with backgrounds in economics, engineering, political science, accounting, or other nonlegal professions were seldom appointed. In fifteen years, out of 150 appointments to nine large regulatory commissions, only 7 were women and 4 were blacks. The result, said the senators, was that "the commissions had been heavily weighted in the direction of a single approach or a particular point of view."[98]

The result is often low morale and a feeling of intense frustration among those officials who do want to carry out their duties. The House Commerce Subcommittee on Oversight and Investi-

[93]Louis M. Kohlmeier, Jr., *The Regulators: Watchdog Agencies and the Public Interest* (New York: Harper & Row, Publishers, 1969), p. 48.

[94]Office of Congressman Benjamin S. Rosenthal, press release, March 5, 1974.

[95]Report of the U.S. General Accounting Office, Washington, D.C., September 15, 1974.

[96]Associated Press, September 7, 1975.

[97]John A. Jenkins, "Working Both Sides of the Court: The Cozy Game Between Federal Agencies and Washington Law Firms," *Student Lawyer*, February 1977.

[98]Senate Government Operations Committee release, February 10, 1977.

gation surveyed 272 career employees who left nine health, safety, and economic agencies. It found that 59, or 21.7 percent, cited frustration in carrying out their mandate as their reason for leaving.[99] But part of their frustration also stems from the laws they apply—sometimes written with the kind of sloppy imprecision that invites crookedness, sometimes grown meaningless because their social context has changed completely.

Many regulations founded on humanitarian grounds have long since had little reason to exist except for narrow profiteering. They are archaic laws, and they offend the public's common sense in ways voiced by Eileen Shanahan:

> Why should not airlines be allowed to compete freely with each other in attempts to attract new business by offering cut-rate flights? The prohibition rests on a decision by Congress that airlines would be tempted to skimp on safety devices if they got into rate wars that cut their profits. But that rationale has not really been re-examined for 40 years.
>
> Why should farmers be allowed to get together and agree to ban the sale of undersized fruit that is perfectly wholesome? This practice is an unforeseen result of a law that goes back to the days when farmers by the tens of thousands were being driven into foreclosure by low prices for their products. The extra cost to the city dweller was seen as justifiable in the interests of keeping farmers on their land, but it has not been re-examined in the light of today's domination of agriculture by large agribusiness organizations.[100]

Obviously, government regulation has increasingly lost its original purpose and direction. It might be more accurate to state that the regulatory agencies have lost what the general public *thought* was their original purpose and direction, namely the protection of the public. Numerous thoughtful scholars of government regulatory bodies have reconstructed history in such a way as to indicate that the industries supposedly regulated by the regulatory commissions actually welcomed their creation and were, in fact,

the chief authors of the legislation bringing the commissions into being—to fix prices, to reduce competition, and, generally, to run the show with the highest possible degree of independence from public interference. That is the most cynical view. But the collusion need not be prearranged. It can come about simply through the natural life cycle of regulatory agencies.

When first created by Congress, the regulatory agencies are imbued with the youthful zeal of reform. They respond enthusiastically to the public's need for protection. But as they age, they lose their muscle and avoid fighting off the pressures of the industries they are supposed to be regulating. Operating in the isolation that was meant to protect their independence, they grow remote from and indifferent to the general public, whereas they see the industry's representatives always close at hand, offering friendship and favors. At length, in full maturity and decay, they become the protectors and allies of their regulated wards rather than of the public itself.[101]

When critics are asked for an example of this life cycle, they almost always cite the Interstate Commerce Commission, the oldest of all the agencies. Long ago it proved the accuracy of Attorney General Richard Olney's prediction. In 1892, he wrote this reassuring letter to a railroad president who was afraid the then-new ICC might interfere with profiteering:

> My impression would be that looking at the matter from the railroad point of view exclusively it would not be a wise thing to undertake [that is, the abolition of the Interstate Commerce Commission] . . . . The Commission, as its functions have now been limited by the courts is, or can be made, of great use to the railroads. It satisfies the popular clamor for a government supervision of the railroads, at the same time that that supervision is almost entirely nominal. *Further, the older such a commission gets to be, the more inclined it will be found to take the business and railroad view of things. It thus becomes a sort of barrier between the railroad*

[99]Report of the House Commerce Subcommittee on Oversight and Investigation, October 22, 1976.

[100]Eileen Shanahan, *New York Times*, September 1, 1974.

[101]See M. H. Bernstein, *Regulating Business by Independent Commission* (Princeton, N.J.: Princeton University Press, 1955), pp. 74–102; Grant McConnell, *Private Power and American Democracy* (New York: Random House, Vintage Books, 1970), pp. 287–88.

A cartoon printed in 1887 shows the newly instated Interstate Commerce Commissioners preparing to tame the railroads

corporations and the people and a sort of protection against hasty and crude legislation hostile to railroad interests. . . . The part of wisdom is not to destroy the Commission, but to utilize it.[102]

The Sorry Saga of the ICC

Industry moved westward with caution in the last century. One had only to stand on a hillock in almost any county west of the Mississippi River to realize that the market here was skimpy and far-flung. Last century's politicians felt it their duty to settle the West and Middle

West as rapidly as possible. The obvious solution lay with the railroads; if they moved into the open spaces, population would follow. So the railroads were enticed to spread out, and they were enticed in a very generous style. The usual method was to give them every other section of land bordering their tracks. The total giveaway of federal land came to about 130 million acres, some of which had been designated Indian territory by previous treaties. When tribes tried to oppose these takeovers, they were, of course, driven away by United States troops. The railroads would sell this "checkerboard" land to settlers, who in turn would produce farm goods to send to market on the railroads.[103]

---

[102]Quoted in Walter Adams, "The Antitrust Alternative," in Ralph Nader and Mark J. Green, eds., *Corporate Power in America* (New York: Viking Press, Grossman Publishers, 1973), p. 132 (emphasis added).

---

[103]See Kohlmeier, *The Regulators*.

In those days, there were no interstate truck lines, so the trains had a monopoly. Moreover, the big lines either bought up the little lines or killed them with cutthroat prices. By the end of the 1880s, seven large groups dominated the nation's railroad systems.[104] Farmers were at their mercy, as were all long-distance shippers and travelers who could not use the waterways. It cost as much to send wheat by rail from the Dakotas to Chicago as by ship from Chicago to Liverpool, England.

Finally, Congress decided that the vicious monopoly it had helped create should be controlled. So, in 1887, it established the Interstate Commerce Commission and instructed it to keep freight and passenger rates low. The ICC was given authority to set maximum rates. It was made an independent agency, with no direct supervision from the cabinet. With the authority to decide on the fairness of rates, the authority to enforce rate schedules, and the authority to issue all sorts of safety and operational edicts, the ICC had the powers of the courts and the executive and legislative branches rolled into one. (This would be the pattern for other independent agencies, too.)

The railroads responded in typical fashion. If they could not squeeze an unconscionable rate from the hide of the farmers, they would squeeze it out of their own hides. They let their equipment run down—rails, roadbeds, engines; everything was allowed to go to pot in the name of profit. Dee Brown writes:

> By the time the nation entered World War I, the railroads and their equipment were in such dilapidated condition that the government had to put them under federal control, rebuilding and restocking at government expense in order to meet the transportation needs of the war. This was the second, third and fourth time that the American people had paid for some of these railroads. . . .[105]

After the war, Congress decided to modernize the ICC with the Transportation Act of 1920, which no longer mandated the ICC to keep fares as low as possible, but allowed rates to be set in such a way as to give the rail lines a "fair return"—meaning, about 6 percent on investment.[106] The ICC could now set *minimum* rates. The act also called on the ICC to establish a nationwide plan of consolidation. Congress hoped that with fewer railroads, those surviving would be healthier and more efficient.

By 1935, the national network of highways had spawned a trucking industry that was biting deeply into the railroad's market. So Congress, instead of freeing the railroads to operate competitively, brought the trucks under ICC control to squelch interindustry competition. By 1940, the merger plan for railroads and the formula of setting rates according to percent of investment had proved to be unworkable. Now the directive from Congress was simply to "foster sound economic conditions."

In effect, this congressional mandate allowed the carriers to set their own rates—with antitrust immunity—after which the ICC would go through the formality of approving them. That's the regulatory sham that exists today. Although, theoretically, the ICC reviews all rates, in fact it reviews less than 1 percent. The others are rubber-stamped.

Thus, by World War II, the ICC compass had swung 180 degrees from where it started, and it remained stuck in that new position: away from the protection of the consumer and toward a rigged market for industry. The ICC no longer hopes to achieve the lowest reasonable rates for the shipper and rider, but now hopes to achieve the highest practical profits for the carrier. After 1940, the ICC took as its goal the limitation of "both price competition and the number of new competitors in the industries it regulates. It attempts to keep rates and revenues reasonably high and to allocate the available business among the railroads, truck, barge and bus lines it regulates."[107]

That is just about as far from free enterprise as you can get. It is a description of government-regulated monopolies; or, to use a phrase that most of the people who run these companies

---

[104]Robert H. Wiebe, *The Search for Order: 1877–1920* (New York: Hill & Wang, 1967), p. 186.

[105]Dee Brown, *Hear That Lonesome Whistle Blow: Railroads in the West* (New York: Holt, Rinehart & Winston, 1977).

[106]Kohlmeier, *The Regulators*, p. 147.

[107]Kohlmeier, p. 150.

would shudder at, it is neo-socialism. To escape antitrust laws, to escape the risks of competition, to escape the risks of natural supply-and-demand laws, the transportation industries have surrendered their "freedom" to government regulators in return for guaranteed markets and guaranteed profits. And yet, the swap has obviously failed. By the mid-1970s, the railroads were competitively comatose. Eight railroads in the Northeast and Middle West, including the Penn Central, the nation's largest, were bankrupt and operating only by the largess of massive federal subsidies.[108] Rail service was so wretched that, in one sixteen-month period, officials of Amtrak—the national rail passenger service—kept their free rail passes in their pockets and spent $778,000 for air travel.[109]

The ICC has become infamous for turning aside innovative services proposed by regulated companies, requiring mountains of paperwork, propping up inefficient firms with artificially high rates, preventing the entry of promising new carriers into interstate business, and dragging out the hearings and protest processes so long that justice is denied. Typical of the ICC in action: in 1961, the Southern Railway Company, one of the nation's few efficient lines, combined with Reynolds Metal to produce a freight car that would carry twice as much grain and that could be loaded and unloaded much faster than the standard car. With this, Southern proposed lowering its rates up to 66 percent. But the rail line's competitors—barge and truck as well as rail—persuaded the ICC to step in and block the move. Only after a four-year fight that went all the way to the Supreme Court did Southern force the ICC to back down and allow the public to benefit from the lower rates.[110]

It is also typical of the ICC that for many years it has restricted competition between truck lines in such a way that many trucks, after making a delivery, were forced to return empty. In 1976, a haphazard and incomplete study by the ICC showed that at least 20 percent of the trucks on the interstate highway system were empty.

Many experts believe the percentage is much higher—all written into wasted gasoline and higher shipping rates.[111] By such rigid, hidebound tactics, the government's regulation of the surface transportation industry not only wipes out any hope for improved service, but also costs consumers between $4 billion and $9 billion a year.[112]

How total the collapse of the ideal. In 1887, as Grant McConnell has summarized, "the ICC was designed to bring monopoly power under popular control; it was intended to be expert; and it was built to be free of 'politics.' "[113] It wound up just the opposite of all those things. And, ironically, this greatest failure of the regulatory commissions was the model for those that followed.

Criticizing the Critics

When Lewis A. Engman had been Chairman of the Federal Trade Commission long enough to become incautiously honest, he gave a group of businessmen his candid estimate of how one of the great hopes of the Progressive era—government regulation of Big Business and Big Industry—had failed:

> Though most government regulation was enacted under the guise of protecting the consumer from abuse, much of today's regulatory machinery does little more than shelter producers from the normal competitive consequences of lassitude and inefficiency. In some cases, the world has changed, reducing the original threat of abuse. In other cases, the regulatory machinery has simply become perverted. In still other cases, the machinery was a mistake from the start. In any case, the consumer, for whatever presumed abuse he is being spared, is paying plenty in the form of government sanctioned price fixing.[114]

The only thing unusual about Engman's comments is that they come from a key regulator.

[108]Congressional Record, H7362, July 23, 1975.

[109]Report of the U.S. General Accounting Office, Washington, D.C., September 4, 1974.

[110]Washington Post, January 25, 1975.

[111]"Energy Conservation Competes with Regulatory Objects for Truckers," report of the U.S. General Accounting Office, Washington, D.C., July 8, 1977.

[112]Editorial, Washington Post, February 20, 1975.

[113]McConnell, Private Power and American Democracy, p. 281.

[114]Lewis A. Engman, in a speech to the Financial Analysts Federation, Detroit, October 7, 1974.

Regulated versus Unregulated Fares

Some of the hottest recent arguments over the need for regulation centered on the airlines industry. Critics charged that if regulation were reduced and real competition were permitted, consumers might save up to $1 billion a year. They used as their examples two airlines, one in California and one in Texas, that operated strictly within the state and therefore were not subject to rates set by the Civil Aeronautics Board (CAB).

ONE-WAY FARES AS OF APRIL 1, 1977*

ROUTE	Pacific Southwest Airlines	CAB formula fare[†]
Burbank–San Jose	$25.50	$48.00
Los Angeles–Sacramento	26.50	43.00
Los Angeles–San Francisco	25.50	49.00
San Diego–San Francisco	31.75	60.00
ROUTE	Southwest Airlines (Texas)[‡]	CAB formula fare[†]
Dallas–Houston	$25.00/$15.00	$39.00
Dallas–San Antonio	25.00/ 15.00	41.00
Harlingen–Houston	25.00/ 15.00	45.00

*In Common (Common Cause report, Washington, D.C.) 8, no. 2 (Spring 1977).

[†]Standard coach fare prescribed by the CAB's rigid fare formula. These fares would apply to any interstate air route in the continental United States of equal length. For the California routes, the CAB has allowed trunk airlines to lower their fares to compete with the unregulated carriers.

[‡]weekdays/week-nights, weekends

Outside critics had been saying the same thing for a long time. And yet, while granting that most of the criticisms of the regulatory agencies and of the centralized bureaucracy are based on real conditions, one must still recognize that the alternatives—deregulation and decentralized administration—might, in many instances, be much worse.

What if the central government's responsibilities were cut down and many of the overseer duties were passed back to the states? In some instances, it could be dangerous. The notion of "putting the power levers closer to the people" is a very pleasant one, and it lends itself nicely to the kind of town-hall-meeting romanticism that Americans love. But where special interests own the town hall, so to speak, it really doesn't matter what dissenters say inside the place. Sometimes the only possible way to avoid that kind of situation is to spread out the power base.

The principle is as simple as the old maxim about being a big fish in a small pond. McConnell writes:

> The importance of dairy farmers will be greater in a rural county than in the state of New York at large, and the power of an oil company will be greater in Baton Rouge than in Washington, D.C. If decisions relating to dairy farming can be put in the hands of the counties and those relating to the oil industry in the hands of the states, the power of both interests will be much greater than if such decisions were put in the hands of the nation as a whole.[115]

What if the regulatory commissions were banished tomorrow, as advocated by economist Milton Friedman? We could expect these results, among many others: watered and phony stock

---

[115]McConnell, *Private Power and American Democracy*, pp. 104–05.

Why We Need Regulation

The benefit of regulation is nowhere more evident than in health. Congress passed a law prohibiting the adulteration of drugs in 1848 and a similar law prohibiting the adulteration of food in 1890, and a supposedly more efficient Pure Food and Drug Act was passed in 1906. But, in fact, the public remained pretty much at the mercy of shyster drug manufacturers and filthy food processors until 1937, when at least seventy-three persons died from a drug known as Elixir Sulfanilamide. The next year Congress passed the Federal Food, Drug and Cosmetic Act, which prohibits the sale of dangerous and unsanitary food, drugs, and cosmetics, and set up a commission to enforce the law. The kind of dangers that existed previously is indicated by this excerpt from an account of the life of the writer, Jack London, who died in 1916 at the age of forty.

> After two years of wandering about Polynesia, he was suffering from five diseases. The worst of these were pellagra and yaws. Unfortunately, no cure was known for pellagra at the time, while yaws was treated like a form of syphilis by arsenic compounds.
>
> As a man who declared that he was self-made, he believed in self-help. Aboard the *Snark,* he was both doctor and dentist. He had a large wooden medicine chest stuffed with bottles of drugs. He believed in dosing himself and his wife and his companions. . . .
>
> The steady drinking that Jack described in *John Barleycorn* (1913) attacked his liver. Yet that was nothing to the remedies he injected into himself to cure his imagined diseases. Jack consequently thought that there was still a lingering taint of yaws in him. So he took a course of the new miracle remedy, salvarsan, invented in 1909. It had an arsenic base and had not been properly tested. The result was that Jack, while trying to cure himself of a disease that may have already passed through his system, was killing himself with a remedy that was a poison. The arsenic in the salvarsan attacked his nerves, his kidneys, and his bladder.
>
> The deterioration in Jack's physique and stability has been falsely attributed to many causes, chiefly psychiatric. In fact, the chief cause was bad medication.*

> *Andrew Sinclair, "Jack London: The Man Who Invented Himself," *American Heritage,* August 1977.

would flood back to Wall Street; the stock market's reputation, which is the thing that holds the investment world together, would probably deteriorate rather rapidly to the depths of the post-1929 crash; unsafe, fly-by-night airlines would rush into the market, as would all sorts of promise-them-anything trucking firms; energy monopolies would remove whatever scalp the consumer still has; and laborers would be pressured into accepting unsafe and unhealthy working conditions. To be sure, these evils are present, to some extent, in spite of regulatory agencies. But, so long as the commissions are around, there is always a chance that the evildoer will be punished, or at least embarrassed. Without the regulatory commissions, one could expect the interplay of industry and society to revert to something along the unhappy battle lines of the nineteenth century—unless, of course, human nature has improved remarkably in the intervening years.

One should bear in mind that there are two types of regulatory agencies—the type that protects the consumer and the type that promotes the concentration of power in business.

It is probably significant that the high-decibel demands for "regulatory reform" were not heard from Big Business and Big Industry until the late 1960s, when some of the regulatory agencies took on a great many more consumer-protection duties. By the mid-1970s, the conservative, probusiness administration of President Ford had taken up the demand for regulatory changes. In rebuttal, a group of twenty-four members of Congress issued a balancing statement worth considering in this debate. After conceding that "much economic regulation has proved a poor substitute for competition," they went on to warn

> that while "regulatory reform" is a cliché whose time has come, one person's regulatory reform is another's environmental, consumer rip-off, unconscionable cancer risk, or return to the robber baronies of yesteryear. . . . We note also that the shrill defense of small business freedom can sometimes mask the effort to preserve the unrestrained freedom of giant corporate conglomerates to dominate and manipulate markets.

They justifiably complained that the successes of regulation had been understressed.

> Many of these protections have been so successful that the security they provide is taken for granted: pasteurization, meat and poultry inspection; control of patent medicines, child labor laws. We rarely stop to acknowledge the remarkable performance of such government regulatory programs as aviation safety, or drug testing requirements which kept the hideously deforming drug thalidomide off the market in the United States while thousands of European children were born deformed. . . .
>
> We need to beware of spurious costs attributed to regulation. We cannot permit regulation to be made the scapegoat for management failures. It was not government that built the Edsel. . . . Of the $500 average price increase for the 1975 Detroit cars, only $10.70 is attributable to compliance with safety standards.
>
> The auto industry warns that future safety standards will cost $300 to $500. We need be reminded that in 1970 the same executives predicted that the 1970 pollution standards would add $150 to the purchase price of each vehicle. The actual increase amounts to $8.[116]

The congressional statement pointed out that it would be folly to lump all regulations together and apply the same remedies, for economic regulations had begun to break down as a result of defects that came with age, whereas the regulations relating to consumer and environmental laws were relatively new and not even yet thoroughly tested.

---

[116]"Congressional Democratic Policy Statement on Regulatory Reform," in the *Congressional Record*, S11686–87, June 26, 1975.

It is apparent, then, that regulation should not be abandoned wholesale. Regulation that protects the consumer must stay. Other forms of regulation, which serve only to guarantee corporate profit, must go. But even here a distinction must be made between those industries in which unregulated competition would work (such as the airlines and the trucking industry) and those in which the capital commitment is so great that competing entries into the market are discouraged. These "natural monopolies," which would include the electrical power industry and the railroads, must be closely regulated (and not coddled); otherwise nothing would prevent them from pricing themselves far above what the market should be asked to bear. Reform, if successful, is carried out in a discriminating fashion, as we have learned the hard way more than once.

"REFORMING" THE BUREAUCRACY

Reform is an alluring word, especially if it is offered in the name of "good business." But government is not business and cannot be run as if it were. For proof, one need only recall that it was "good business" reforms in 1970 that changed the Post Office Department, then a part of the cabinet, into the United States Postal Service—one of those strange, semi-independent government corporations.

The USPS was the brainchild of a commission headed by Frederick R. Kappel, former Chairman of the Board of American Telephone and Telegraph. Potent lobbying for the "reform" was carried out by a so-called Citizens Committee for Postal Reform, which included such "citizens" as E. I. Du Pont de Nemours, Standard Oil of New Jersey, Bank of America, and Pan American World Airways. These citizens persuaded Congress that some "good business" management was needed to keep the Post Office Department from running at a deficit. So Congress went along with the argument, without pausing to ask why Big Business didn't mind if the Defense Department and Agriculture Department and other departments ran at a deficit, but insisted that the Post Office Department—the one department that aided even the lowliest citizen's daily life—should be forced to try to pay its own way.

Big Business's reformed post office was almost a total failure. The business-bureaucrats said that the service needed to be mechanized, so billions of dollars were spent on mail-processing machinery—and, in 1974, the average first-class letter took 14 percent to 23 percent longer to reach its destination than in fiscal 1969, the last year of the old Post Office. Costs soared, and, in time-honored business fashion, so did rates. Between 1971 and 1975, the price of sending a letter went up 67 percent, and the price of sending second-class matter (magazines and newspapers) rose more than 90 percent. The burden on the press became so great that some magazines shut down—an ironic turn to history, considering the fact that, from the beginning, Congress viewed cheap postal rates as the surest way to promote the press (it worked: between 1801 and 1830, the number of newspapers in the country jumped from two hundred to twelve hundred) and thereby unite the nation and "prevent the degeneracy of a free government."[117]

Perhaps reformers who come to the government from a corporate background are at a disadvantage. Perhaps they are accustomed to thinking of government as something to be exploited rather than as a place to serve. Just plain citizens should have no trouble seeing some of the following common-sense remedies that could be applied to the bureaucracy, especially to the regulatory agencies.

Establish a Self-trimming Formula Jimmy Carter, when he was running for the Presidency, promised that he would reduce some nineteen hundred federal "agencies" to two hundred. When he reached the White House, he stopped that grandiose talk. And when reporters asked his Director of the Office of Management and Budget, Bert Lance, what had happened to the big plans for hacking off great portions of the bureaucracy, Lance replied defensively, "I don't think we should play the numbers game."[118]

[117]*Time,* July 7, 1975.

[118]Quoted in the *Baltimore Sun,* April 11, 1977.

Failure to make that quiet retreat would have been foolish indeed. The bureaucracy cannot be reformed by the numbers. In only a very limited way can it be reformed by titles. Most parts of the bureaucracy were established for a logical purpose. But time changes logic, and when the purpose has become antiquated, it—not the agency—should be done away with so that experienced workers can turn to fresh tasks. Usually it is the program, not the agency or the personnel, that is obsolete. As Peter F. Drucker has pointed out,

the toughest, most novel, but also the most important prerequisite of organizational effectiveness is organized abandonment.

Political philosophy maintains that the tasks of government are perennial and can never be abandoned. This may have made sense when government confined itself to such basic functions as defense, administration of justice and domestic order. Those days are long past, of course, yet this is still the way we run government. The underlying assumption should be that everything government does is likely, the same as every other human activity, to become unproductive or obsolete within a short time. To keep such activities going requires infinitely more effort than to run the productive and successful. . . .

Governmental agencies should be required to abandon one program or one activity before a new one can be started. Lack of any such policy is probably why new efforts over the last 20 years have produced fewer and fewer results. The new programs may well have been necessary and even well-planned, but their execution had to be entrusted to whoever was available rather than to the many experienced people stuck in unproductive and obsolete jobs.[119]

Increase the Accountability of Bureaucrats Make it easier to get rid of the officials who get too chummy with the special interests they are supposed to be regulating. Job security is nice, but the security of consumer and national interests should have a higher priority. Every President of modern times has yearned to be able to reach through the maze of Civil Service and pluck out the entrenched bureaucrats who are operating their own domains without regard for the larger

[119]Peter F. Drucker, *Wall Street Journal,* February 4, 1977.

public interests. Such presidential yearnings are usually denounced as a desire to return to the spoils system. So call it an "accountability system"—a system whereby the middle-level and senior bureaucrat is made directly accountable to the people through their elected Chief Executive. Perhaps President Jackson was right: the bureaucracy needs shaking up from time to time.

Enact and Rigorously Enforce Tough Conflict-of-Interest Laws No official at the regulating or policy-making or price-setting level should be brought in directly from the industry he or she is to regulate, and officials at that level should be legally forbidden to accept jobs with the industries they have regulated or done business with in government. No one should be permitted to hold a policy-making or price-setting post who has a close relative at a comparable level in the industry he or she regulates. When Rogers C. B. Morton was Secretary of Interior, a department that dispensed oil and gas leases, his brother, former Senator Thruston B. Morton, was a Director of Texas Gas Transmission Corporation, which received Interior approval for a number of offshore leases.[120] There should be no more of that.

When large public holdings are involved, proof positive of conflict of interest should not be necessary before a bureaucrat can be fired; a good circumstantial case should be sufficient. In 1974, a group of Interior Department appraisers announced that the "minimum acceptable bid" for an oil-shale tract in Colorado would be between $5 million and $6 million—about one-fortieth the $210.3 million actually bid by Gulf Oil and Standard Oil of Indiana. Sound like a good deal for the taxpayers? Not at all. The staff of the House Select Small Business Regulatory Subcommittee estimated that the *true* value of the tract was at least $500 million, more than double the sum being paid by Gulf and Standard, who could, as a result of the friendly appraisers at Interior, make themselves look generous while actually getting a bargain.[121] Whether or not the Interior officials were really acting in collusion with the oil companies, the effect of their appraisal was the same as if they had been.

Carelessness or Misconduct That Causes Major Losses Should Open Senior Bureaucrats to Civil Lawsuits or Criminal Action In 1972, a DC-10 passenger airliner built by McDonnell-Douglas lost a cargo door because of a latch failure, and it almost crashed near Toronto. At first, Federal Aviation Administration officials *ordered* the aircraft company to take steps to correct the defect on the DC-10s that were in operation; but then they relented under political and industrial pressures and said the defects could be corrected on a "voluntary compliance" basis. Nearly two years later, a DC-10 lost a faulty cargo door while flying over France. It crashed, and 346 people died. It was the worst accident in civil aviation history up to that time. The FAA officials involved went unpunished.

Upgrade Manpower and Budget Priorities The budget would contain more than enough money to do all the necessary work, if the unnecessary expenses were ended. Only a fraction of the billions of dollars in subsidies spent each year to keep alive mismanaged and unsalvageable industries could staff the regulatory arms of government in such a fashion that health and safety and competition could really be guarded. Or if bureaucratic posts of questionable value—such as Department of Agriculture county agents in urban areas—were culled and these salaries were shifted to duties that mean something, then regulation and administration would come alive.

And if regulators would tend to pressing matters and leave the trivia to later, even with their present personnel they could do better. Should the Federal Trade Commission, with its massive backlog of crucial antitrust cases, take time to rule—as it did in 1975—that Joe Namath was naughty to say (in a TV commercial) that he wears panty hose when he really doesn't?

Antitrust and More Antitrust The regulatory agencies have, in theory, been aimed at achieving competitive, fair, honest business practices—in other words, the kind of conduct that might have been attained if the Justice Department and the Federal Trade Commission, which

[120]*Los Angeles Times*, December 20, 1974.

[121]*Washington Post*, March 5, 1974.

are supposed to police the field, had enthusiastically enforced the Sherman Antitrust Act of 1890 and the Clayton Act of 1914. But, in fact, Justice and the FTC have seldom used these laws to break up unfair and monopolistic businesses. A measure of their lack of enthusiasm can be found in the budget. The Justice Department's $15 million antitrust budget is far less than any *one* of the top ten corporations spends on legal fees each year.

With each of the really critical industries in this country controlled by no more than eight corporations, and often fewer, it is a bit misleading to use *regulate* as an active verb. The giants who dominate our economic health are not truly regulated; they are only bumped or nudged occasionally. Perhaps it would be impossible to do more than that. But at least they could be shown that the government watchdogs, even if feeble, are alive and watching; they could be harassed with antitrust lawsuits when they conspire to fix prices and restrain trade and in various ways milk the public. And there is always the possibility that if the Justice Department really took the antitrust laws seriously, some of its canny attorneys could put together cases that would break up some of the monopolies and whittle the giants down to such a size that regulation might again have some meaning. At least a spirited application of antitrust laws would build a new atmosphere of intent, which in turn would inspire some of the regulatory hacks to try to do their duty. As it is now, the regulators, seeing the oligopolic jungle towering above them on every side, understandably throw away their machetes and turn native.

Appoint Smart, Propublic Officials, and Give Them Clear Goals No reform could be more obvious, simpler, or more certain to succeed. Bureaucracy is the total of talent and its use. Agencies that seemed dead beyond recovery have been revived by—presto—good appointments. The Federal Trade Commission used to be known as the agency that spent most of its time in listless pursuit of trivia. Year after year, the FTC cranked out hundreds of inconsequential rulings relating to the price of fruit pies in Salt Lake City or the mislabeling of weasel coats as mink by a New York furrier. It issued a complaint against a bubble gum manufacturer for trying to monopolize baseball picture cards.[122] Such was the FTC's traditional notion of what consumer protection was supposed to mean.

Then, in 1969, Ralph Nader issued an elaborate exposé of the FTC, showing that it was staffed with a zooful of political hacks who did all they could to avoid fighting the frauds of Big Business. The resulting embarrassment performed a miracle. There was action. President Nixon appointed superior chairmen to the FTC, who got it moving again. President Carter picked up the beat. The emphasis was on youth, brains, and commitment. In 1977, the agency recruited eighty-two law graduates from that year's class, of whom 30 percent were in the top third of their class, half had worked on law reviews, and 20 percent were members of Phi Beta Kappa. Although, historically, the FTC had been woefully timid about taking on the big companies for a fight, by the mid-1970s it was filing suits for improper corporate conduct against all the giants on the horizon, including Exxon, General Motors, Avis, Kellogg, and International Telephone and Telegraph. It had become so active, in fact, that congressional friends of business were beginning to damn it as a runaway agency that needed to have its wings clipped.[123] It was quite a compliment.

But even bureaucrats of good conscience must be given guidelines, whether they work in a regulatory agency or elsewhere in government. Reshuffling the bureaucracy is not enough. Each unit in government must be told not only what it is in existence for, but in which direction it must move. Drucker lays down the correct precept: "Require clear and specific goals for every government agency and for each program and project within each agency. What are needed are not just statements of broad policies—these are simply good intentions—but targets with specific timetables and clear assignments of accountability."[124]

It is not enough, for example, to tell an agency to figure out a way to conserve energy sources. It must be given a specific target to shoot

[122]Kohlmeier, *The Regulators*, pp. 256–57.

[123]Jean Carper, "The Backlash at the FTC," *Washington Post*, February 6, 1977.

[124]Drucker, *Wall Street Journal*, February 4, 1977.

FTC headquarters in Washington, D.C.

for. It must be made to come up with a plan by a certain date. If the plan is a sloppy one or does not fit the nation's priorities, the officials who wrote it must be made to realize that they will be either fired or banished to a pencil-sharpening post in Kansas.

Even while mulling over these possible remedies, one should bear in mind that, to paraphrase John Donne, no bureaucrat is an island. The bureaucracy is not an island either. Herbert S. Denenberg, former Insurance Commissioner of Pennsylvania, puts the goal in proper perspective:

> I am led to believe that the deficiencies of our regulatory agencies are merely symptoms of a more fundamental disease. Regulatory agencies reflect the political system, the deficiencies of the legislative process and the power of the special interests that is strong enough to make puppets of too many of our regulators, our legislators, our executive branch and our judges. . . .

> In other words, I suggest that statutes relating to legislative, executive and judicial ethics and conflict of interest will do more for the regulatory process than more specific regulatory manipulations. Required financial disclosure in all branches of government, campaign financing and election reform, effective freedom-of-information legislation, lobbying controls and a program of legislative review would create a system in which the regulatory agencies would function in the public interest.[125]

That is a reasonable hope: when and if other elements of the government become more honest, industrious, and public spirited, the bureaucracy will probably follow suit. Good political habits are just as capable as bad habits of inspiring imitation.

---

[125]Testimony before a Senate committee, quoted by David Burnham in the *New York Times,* January 5, 1975.

Summary

1. The 5 million civilian and military employees of the bureaucracy administer the tasks assigned by the President and Congress, who are also responsible for setting up this "fourth branch" of government.

2. Considering its size and responsibilities, the bureaucracy operates in a surprisingly efficient manner. But its performance can be improved: it is wasteful, thoughtless in its priorities, largely unaccountable, and resistant to change.

3. The bureaucracy exercises a combination of legislative, judicial, and executive powers in drafting congressional legislation and making administrative law, in ruling on disputed administrative laws, and in carrying out the functions of the executive branch.

4. The bureaucracy consists of the twelve cabinet departments, their subunits, and the independent and regulatory agencies, both of which operate outside the cabinet hierarchy.

5. The President supervises the bureaucracy through the Executive Office, and, especially, through the Executive Office's Office of Management and Budget. He also controls the bureaucracy by appointing the more than two thousand top officials. But these appointments are often subject to the approval of the interests that put the President in office and the special interests that the departments and agencies represent.

6. Most bureaucrats are hired and promoted through the Civil Service system. Career bureaucrats provide needed stability as administrations come and go, but they also may resist needed change in order to protect their positions.

7. The bureaucrats are helped in protecting the status quo by the two other members of what has been called an "unholy trinity"—the bureaucrats' counterparts in congressional committees and industrial lobbies. Advisory committees may also protect bureaucratic agencies from interference.

8. The autonomy of bureaucratic agencies is sometimes perverted, especially when they are allowed to operate in secrecy, as in the case of the FBI and the CIA.

9. Regulatory agencies, established to protect the people, now often protect the special interests they are "regulating." Conflict of interest among agency bureaucrats and low morale owing to the complexity of the job and the lack of clear standards have contributed to this turnabout.

10. Reform of the regulatory agencies must be discriminating. Total deregulation and decentralization of administration could be worse than the existing system. Many agencies with policing tasks do a good job of protecting consumers, but some of the agencies that can determine market price and market entry should be deregulated.

11. Some common-sense reforms in the bureaucracy include dropping obsolete programs, increasing bureaucratic accountability to the President, enacting tough conflict-of-interest laws, punishing senior bureaucrats for misconduct, upgrading priorities in budget and manpower, enforcing antitrust acts, making good appointments, and providing clear goals.

Additional Reading

Francis E. Rouske, *Bureaucracy, Politics and Public Policy,* 2nd ed. (Boston: Little, Brown and Co., 1969); Harold Seidman, *Politics, Position and Power: The Dynamics of Federal Organization,* 2nd ed. (New York: Oxford University Press, 1975); and Alan A. Altshuler, ed., *The Politics of the Federal Bureaucracy* (New York: Harper & Row, Publishers, 1968) provide broad accounts of the federal bureaucracy. W. Lloyd Warner et al., *The American Federal Executive* (Westport, Conn.: Greenwood Press, 1963) gives detailed information on the personal background and characteristics of government leaders. The annual *United States Government Organization Manual,* published by the General Services Administration, Washington, D.C., describes the positions and their occupants in detail.

Particular facets of bureaucracy are covered in Marver H. Bernstein's *Regulating Business by Independent Commission* (Princeton, N.J.: Princeton University Press, 1955) and Roger G. Noll's *Reforming Regulation* (Washington, D.C.: Brookings Institution, 1971); Arthur Maass, *Muddy Waters: The Army Engineers and the Nation's Rivers* (New York: Da Capo Press, 1974) is about empire building by the Army Corps of Engineers; Grant McConnell, *Private Power and American Democracy* (New York: Random House, Vintage Books, 1970) tells how things can go awry at the grass roots.

Leading theoretical treatments of bureaucracy are Herbert A. Simon, *Administrative Behavior: A Study of Decision-Making Processes in Administrative Organizations,* 3rd ed. (New York: Free Press, 1976); William A. Niskanen, *Bureaucracy and Representative Government* (Chicago: Aldine, 1971); and Anthony Downs, *Inside Bureaucracy* (Boston: Little, Brown and Co., 1967).

When the Stranger says: "What is the meaning of this city?
Do you huddle close together because you love each other?"
What will you answer? "We all dwell together
To make money from each other"? or "This is a community"?

T. S. Eliot

13
FEDERALISM AND STATE AND LOCAL GOVERNMENT

It soon became apparent that the spirit of cooperation called for by the Articles of Confederation would not be enough to bind the new American nation together. The various states were much too imbued with parochial selfishness to respond effectively to the Articles' loose guidelines and moderate strictures. Ambitions, suspicions, envy, and competition had sent the states flying off in their separate orbits. The United States were not turning out to be very united. And so, a new Constitution was written to provide the required gravitational pull: a strong central government.

FEDERALISM

The framers of the Constitution feared that they might be attempting the impossible in imposing a central government on the complexities of that time. Their fear seems almost naive today. Wilson Carey McWilliams writes:

> We are tempted to think of eighteenth century America as arcadian and uniform, a land inhabited by Protestant whites (and, if our memories are not too selective, by slaves), pre-industrial and largely pre-urban, middle-class and Anglo-Saxon. To those who lived in it, however, that old America seemed so diverse as to make common government and political action, let alone common feeling, all but impossible. . . . America was composed of localities, comparatively close-knit, small communities and kin-groups, relatively autonomous and often distinctive in faith, nationality, and patterns of production.[1]

---

[1]Quoted in Irving Kristol and Paul H. Weaver, eds. *The American: 1976* (Lexington, Mass.: D. C. Heath & Co., Lexington Books, 1976), p. 294.

That variety added up to what James Madison called "the centrifugal tendency of the States."[2] It would have to be brought under control by the magnetism of a central government. That was clear. Thirteen competing, proud, independent, ambitious states would not exist in unity without a government presiding over them all.

The need for a central government was agreed on from the outset. The question was: How powerful should it be? Should it in fact be the only government—a unitary government? A few delegates to the Constitutional Convention believed that it should. These nationalists wanted a central government so powerful that it would, in effect, wipe out or completely control all subgovernments. The people would look directly to the central government for guidance.

The most extreme proposal made by nationalists was the Virginia Plan, under which the national legislature would have the power to veto actions of the state legislatures, would judge the limits of its own power, and would have the right to use military force against any state it considered out of line. Alexander Hamilton even proposed that the President be able to appoint the state governors—just as the king of England had appointed colonial governors.

These proposals received little support. The consensus of the Constitutional Convention was definitely in favor of retaining strong state governments. To do this, it was decided to establish a federal government—one in which the Constitution would divide power between the central government and its constituent governments. There was also general agreement among the delegates that the most pressing questions confronting them were: How could they keep popular opinion from suppressing individual rights? How could they prevent the numerical majority of the masses from abusing the wealthy minority? How could they prevent the states with numerically superior populations from running over the states with smaller populations?

---

[2]Quoted in Raoul Berger, *Congress Vs. the Supreme Court* (Cambridge, Mass.: Harvard University Press, 1969), p. 223.

Division of Governmental Powers

The answers that emerged were typical of the American balancing act. There was something for everybody (or nearly everybody). The vote of the masses could decide on the composition of the House of Representatives, but it had no direct say in the composition of the Senate (which would be selected by the state legislatures). The large states could have a representatively large part of the lower house; but small states had the same clout (two senators) as the large states in the upper house.

A further answer, and perhaps the most important, lay in the constitutional method of parceling out power. In addition to splitting the central government into three branches, splitting the legislative branch into two houses, and splitting the power of election between the populace and the state legislatures, the Constitution divides the powers of government between federal and state. (The Constitution makes no mention of any level of government below the state, but since those levels already existed, in the form of county, city, and township, it was clear that, by being ignored by the Constitution, they were being left to the states' control.) Each level of government had to operate under written restrictions. The Constitution specifically limited the power of the states, prohibiting them, for example, from making money and from making treaties. The powers of the central government were specifically circumscribed.

But the list of powers that the Constitution concedes to the central government does not appear to be much of a circumscription. Article I, Section 8, gives the central government the right, through Congress, to collect taxes, regulate commerce internationally and between the states, coin money, establish an interstate highway system, declare war, make treaties, raise an army and a navy, establish a court system—and—most sweepingly—"make all Laws which shall be necessary and proper for carrying into Execution the foregoing Powers, and all other Powers vested by this Constitution in the Government of the United States, or in any Department or Officer thereof."

And yet the Constitution also sets a crucial limit on the central government. The Tenth

Amendment of the Bill of Rights states: "The powers not delegated to the United States by the Constitution; nor prohibited by it to the States, are reserved to the States respectively, or to the people." Comprehensive as the list of central powers might seem, and stretchable as they would prove to be, at least the Constitution reserved *all other powers*—however diminishing they might prove to be—to the states.

While surrendering some powers, each level of government would retain important ones: each could raise taxes, each could regulate business within its boundaries; each could build roads and supply other services under the title of "the general welfare"; and although only the central government could raise armies, each level could have a police force.

The Founders hoped to frustrate tyranny with a plan based on diversity of governmental interests, constitutional checks, and competing loyalties and competing powers. It was not an efficient system, but it was presumably a system that, being so muddled, would be safe from tyranny.

Diversity of Private Interests

Along with the diversity of governmental units, the new republic could hope to benefit from the multiplicity of private interests among the original thirteen states, from the miller of New Hampshire to the cotton planter of Georgia, from the boatbuilder of New York to the tobacco merchant of Charleston. Speaking of all this splintered character, Madison predicted:

> Whilst all authority in it [the federal republic] will be derived from and dependent on society, the society itself will be broken into so many parts, interests and classes of citizens, that the rights of individuals, or of the minority, will be in little danger from interested combinations of the majority. In a free government the security for civil rights . . . consists . . . in the multiplicity of interests . . . and this may be presumed to depend on the extent of country and number of people comprehended under the same government.

To Madison, the geographical size as well as the size of the population and the catalog of its professions and industries all contributed to the healthy balancing of interests.[3]

Today, the United States is actually more in keeping with the Madisonian ideal (that diversity safeguards freedom) than it was in the beginning. The Constitution was originally written to unify 4 million persons in thirteen states; today there are 210 million persons in fifty states. Today, nineteen of the states—and five metropolitan areas—each have greater populations than the entire Union at the time of the Constitutional Convention. Texas alone (267,338 square miles) is nearly as large as the thirteen original states, and Alaska is more than twice as big (586,412 square miles). Of the 106 representatives sent to Congress in 1790, 101 were elected by farmers.

Though there were 757,181 blacks in residence when the Constitution was written (19.3 percent of the total population), virtually none could vote; today blacks are politically potent enough to swing presidential elections. In those days, there were no citizens of Latin extraction; today there are more than 9 million. There were no Oriental citizens; no American Indians were citizens. The fabled "melting pot" had not even begun to bubble. At the time this nation first consented to unification under the Constitution, its character was plain and predictable compared to the helter-skelter, catchall, multiracial, and sprawling character of the nation today. And by no accidental coincidence, the purposes of federalism—to promote a feeling of unity and to protect the position of minorities—are much more within reach today than they were in 1787. One reason for this is the strengthening of federal (national) powers.

The Expansion of Federal Powers

Individual states tested federal powers many times in the early years of the republic. Most of the tests simply strengthened the federal position. The first court-fought determination of federal legislative supremacy came in 1819 (*McCulloch v. Maryland*), when Maryland tried

---

[3]Quoted in Arthur N. Holcombe, *Our More Perfect Union* (Cambridge, Mass.: Harvard University Press, 1967), p. 7.

to tax a branch of the Bank of the United States. Daniel Webster, counsel for the federal government when the case reached the United States Supreme Court, successfully argued that the power to tax was the power to destroy and that to permit a state to tax a federal bank would be to concede that the federal government existed at the whim of the states. The Supreme Court, to nobody's surprise, ruled in favor of the federal government.

The second major challenge to federal government supremacy came in the 1830s, when President Andrew Jackson and his backers in Congress imposed a burdensome tariff on items that happened to be essential to the southern economy.[4] Naturally, the South bitterly objected. Bitterest of all was South Carolina, which in a state convention nullified the tariff laws and forbade the collection of any duties levied under the tariffs. Jackson responded with equal firmness, declaring that no state could secede from the Union or refuse to obey its laws and warning that the duties would be collected by force if necessary. Congress supported him by passing a Force Bill. Thus the supremacy of the federal government was not only imposed by law, but by threat.[5]

And then came the Civil War, the outcome of which pretty well settled the question of supremacy in the federal system. Unfortunately, it left the question of the proper sharing of power unsettled. It was acknowledged that the states would have less power, but how much less? The seemingly endless, and often tiresome, argument revolves around an extremely naive con-

cept. The debated power is spoken of as though it were contained in a pot and the questions were these: how much power should the federal government be allowed to scoop out of the pot? And how much power should be left in the pot for the states and counties and cities?

That might be a sensible way to discuss the issue if there were just so much power to go around. But political power is practically infinite within the vague terms set down by the Constitution. If the federal government's scope of influence grows, it does not necessarily follow that all subnational governments shrink in influence. *Both* sides may grow in influence. Indeed, in recent decades both sides *have* grown in influence; as the federal government has intruded more and more into the lives of its subjects, so have the state and local governments—and often the intrusion has come at the same time, in triplicate form. Nowhere is this more apparent than in the financing and administration of welfare programs.

Welfare Federalism

For most of America's first century, its citizens had little interest in the central government. There were no world wars to evoke a centralization of patriotic fervency. The central government did not interfere much in economic matters. Except for the postal service, the national parks service, a skimpy army and navy, a few dams, and a farm advisory service, the federal government hardly touched the life of the average American. Virtually all roads were built and maintained by state, county, or city; the federal government had not yet started giving price supports to, or controlling the supply of, farm commodities; there was no national pension system; there was no federal housing program; there was no national health program; there were no federal subsidies for unemployment, welfare, or education. The idea of federal aid to subnational governments was unheard of and unthought of until after World War I.

Beginnings of the Federal Largess When the federal government did start embracing the states and the localities with the social programs and subsidies of the New Deal in the early 1930s, it did so cautiously. But, through the 1930s,

---

[4]In a famous debate relating to these tariffs, Daniel Webster ended his speech with these remarks on Federalism: "The Constitution is not the creature of the State government. It is, sir, the people's Constitution, the people's government, made for the people, made by the people, and answerable to the people. . . . The very chief end, the main design, for which the whole Constitution was framed and adopted was to establish a government that should not . . . depend on State opinion and State discretion. . . . When my eyes shall be turned to behold for the last time the sun in heaven, may I not see him shining on the broken and dishonored fragments of a once glorious Union. . . ." (Quoted in Alvin M. Josephy, Jr., *The American Heritage History of the Congress of the United States*, New York: American Heritage Publishing Co. and McGraw-Hill, 1975, p. 178.)

[5]Charles M. Wiltse, *The New Nation: Eighteen Hundred–Eighteen Forty-five* (New York: Hill & Wang, 1961), pp. 121–22.

1940s, and 1950s, there was a steady escalation of welfare federalism, bringing the subnational governments into an increasingly complex working partnership with the central government in the administration of major social services. The welfare state launched by the New Deal would doubtless have continued and been expanded in any event, but the states' readiness, even aggressive eagerness, to take money from the federal government was accentuated by the defense expenditures of World War II and the defense contracting that followed the war.[6] State governments became hooked on the income from defense programs and defense installations, which were scattered across the nation. States could not imagine doing without this federal largess, passed out under the guise of "defense" or "aerospace" work; in reality, it was nothing but a flat subsidy for certain regions. Because for many years politicians from the South and West dominated the congressional committees that controlled these authorizations, naturally those were the regions that benefited most.[7]

There was obvious reason for the New Deal money of the 1930s to be poured into the South, for the region was extremely poor, never having recovered from the ravages of the Civil War and from the subsequent economic retaliations directed at that region by the North. But by the 1960s, the South and the Far West had faster growth rates in population, employment, production, income, federal contracts, and public works than any other region. Meanwhile, the Northeast had fallen on hard times. Some areas of it had fallen on horrendous times. Lynn, Massachusetts, once known as the shoe manufacturing capital of the world, had such a high rate of unemployment that residents were hiring out to commit arson on the empty factories so that the owners could collect insurance.

The northeastern states complained that they weren't getting a fair share of the federal subsidies. They pointed out that, in 1975, the states in the North got back $0.83 from every tax dollar they sent to Washington. Some sections of the Northeast are especially shortchanged; when New York City's Mayor Abraham Beame went to Washington to get money to rescue his city, he pointed out correctly that "we aren't here for a handout. New York City sends $15 billion a year in taxes to the federal government and gets back about $2 billion."[8] As a region, the Great Lakes states did even worse than the Northeast, receiving only $0.71 from every dollar of federal taxes. By contrast, the South got back $1.14 and the West got back $1.20. (Washington, D.C., the federal city, received $7.67 for each tax dollar.)[9]

Their argument, while perfectly justified in terms of state and regional self-interest, was not very persuasive in terms of the purest federalism. Indeed, here was a good example to prove that the Founders were right when they decided that only a strong central government could achieve the required overview for a nation. The fairness of federal outlays cannot be measured by how-much-got versus how-much-given but by the *need* of the recipients.

Priority Problems These days, the question of need is not so simple as it was a generation ago, when poverty was the standard measure. Nowadays, the federal government is confronted with a relatively new and still unresolved question: which deserves top priority in federal handouts—a region of high income but low (or no)

[6]This was the second tidal wave of war money to wash over state and local budgets. It had happened in World War I also. In 1913, state and local governments accounted for 72 percent of the $2.5 billion in total government spending (federal, state, and local). Then came the war, and the federal output was so enormous that even in 1919, the first year after the war's conclusion, the federal portion was 87 percent. Thereafter, it subsided sharply and, by 1932 (the last year before the great New Deal welfare budget), state and local outlay had risen to 65 percent of the overall $13 billion. World War II saw federal expenditures rising again, to 89 percent of the total government outlay. (Robert S. Ford, "State and Local Finance," *Annals of the American Academy of Political and Social Science,* November 1949, p. 15.)

[7]By the early 1970s, five of the ten states receiving top defense dollars were in the Sun Belt—California, Florida, Georgia, North Carolina, and Texas; of the five states receiving most aerospace money from the federal government, four were in the Sun Belt—Alabama, California, Florida, and Texas; and the same was true of four of the top five states receiving atomic energy money—California, Nevada, New Mexico, and Tennessee.

[8]Quoted in the *Washington Post,* September 25, 1975.

[9]Study of the Government Research Corporation, Washington, D.C., released August 22, 1976.

FIGURE 13-1 ECONOMIC GROWTH AND PER CAPITA INCOME LEVELS BY REGION*

Percent change in earnings 1969–74

Percent change in per capita income 1969–74

Percent change in population 1969–74

Per capita income 1974

*Data indexed so that U.S. average equals 100.

SOURCE: Congressional Budget Office, August 1977.

growth, or a region of low income but high growth? A congressional study in 1977 stated the problem in these terms:

> Underlying the ongoing frostbelt/sunbelt controversy is the premise that low growth rates constitute the most serious economic problem. The North, many people contend, needs help because, relative to the South and Southwest, it is losing jobs, capital, and residents. . . . Almost one-fifth of all counties in the North were classified as declining, and more than half of the region's population—almost 47 million people—lived in these counties. Only 1 percent of the counties had rapidly growing economies.

On the other hand, though the northern region isn't growing as fast as it used to, it has already reached a higher level of income than other regions. The report continued: "Most local economies in the North produced relatively high average incomes. In 1974, the average per capita income for counties in the region was 8 percent higher than the average for all counties in the United States," whereas "per capita incomes in the South and Southwest were 11 percent below the national average. . . . Sixty-three percent of all low-income counties were in the South. The Southwest, with 18 percent, was also overrepresented in the group of low-income counties."[10]

Right or wrong, the dollars were, as of the mid-1970s, rolling more heavily into the high-income areas than into the low. The high-income areas got back a lower *percentage* of their tax payments to Washington, but they got a higher *total* dollar return. The stagnant rich counties were getting the lion's share, *comparatively*. In fiscal 1975, the poor counties got $1,059 per capita of the federal expenditures—29 percent less than the national average. The counties with the highest incomes received an above-average amount, $1,665 per capita. (For the nation as a whole, the per capita federal outlay averaged $1,494.)

A wise and delicate balancing of federal expenditures is extremely difficult to accomplish in the midst of political pressures from every region. Much more is at stake than a mere shuffling of pork barrel to satisfy political egos. Long-range national development is at issue. Prolonged periods of unfair—or unwise—distribution can upset the national economy by creating some regions that are too fat for their own good and some regions that are too undernourished. As a major purchaser of goods and services, the federal government does much more than pump money directly into local commerce; it also creates a lasting side effect—by heavy participation in local economies, it sets up a pattern of local regulations, taxation, trade, and spending that in turn influences the movement and expansion of private corporations. Every federal dollar spent on a shipyard, a research institute, or a military base encourages the investment of several private dollars in supporting enterprises.

Grants-in-Aid: State and Federal Cooperation In the 1960s, there was a greater surge of welfare federalism than ever before. Congress enacted numerous programs that provided funds for state and local governments to use in meeting specific national priority needs under federal performance standards. Federal aid to state and local governments for such programs as elementary- and secondary-school education, health care, and housing increased sixfold in a dozen years—from $10.1 billion in 1964 to about $60 billion in fiscal 1976. (See Table 13-1.) (It had increased more than twenty times since 1954.)[11]

Much of the federal government's spreading influence has been aimed at encouraging state and local governments to take on responsibilities that they would not otherwise have assumed. One of the most notable examples of this was in the passage of the 1956 Federal Aid Highway Act. The federal government offered to ante up 90 percent of the cost of building certain highways if the state governments contributed 10 percent. It was a temptation no state could resist,

[10]Peggy L. Cuciti, "Troubled Local Economies and the Distribution of Federal Dollars," report of the Congressional Budget Office, Human Resources and Community Development Division, August 1977.

[11]Neil Peirce, syndicated column, February 7, 1977.

TABLE 13-1

FEDERAL GRANT-IN-AID PROGRAMS BY MAJOR CATEGORY, FISCAL YEAR 1976
(billions of dollars)

CATEGORY	AMOUNT
Payments to individuals	**22.8**
AFDC	5.9
Medicaid	8.2
Public service employment*	3.4
Other	5.3
Revenue sharing and block grants	**14.0**
General revenue sharing	6.3
Comprehensive manpower training†	2.3
Community development	2.6
Law enforcement assistance (part)	0.4
Social service grant programs	2.4
Categorical grants	**23.0**
Major capital grants	10.1
Highways	6.2
Urban mass transit	1.5
Municipal waste treatment plants	2.4
Other categorical grants	12.9
Education	4.0
Health	1.8
Social services	1.6
Manpower training	0.8
Other	4.7
Total	**59.8**

*Includes $800 million from Title II of the Comprehensive Manpower Act.
†Excludes $800 million of grants for public service employment.

SOURCE: *Special Analyses, Budget of the United States Government, Fiscal Year 1977*, Special Analysis O. From Charles L. Schultze, "Federal Spending," in Henry Owen and Charles L. Schultze, *Setting National Priorities: The Next Ten Years* (Washington, D.C.: Brookings Institution, 1976), p. 360.

and suddenly they were over their heads in highway-building programs that they never would have contemplated on their own.

Likewise, the federal government offered, through its urban renewal budget, to pay two-thirds of the cost of wiping out slums (and some perfectly usable, though older, sections of town) if the local governments contributed one-third of the cost. The offer was hardly made before city governments across the nation became monarchs of the bulldozer. In these ways—not always happy or intelligent ways—the expanding federal government lured cities and states into growing along with it.

In many instances the federal government insisted that the subgovernments must meet certain standards in spending the money. For this, the federal government was sometimes accused of wanting to butt into state and local affairs, and there was some basis for the charge;[12] but the federal requirements were actually no more than dues that the subgovernments paid for being admitted to the Big Government Club. They were not diminished; they were made larger by forced budgetary feeding.

Indeed, the startling growth in government in recent years has not been at the federal level,

but at the state and local levels. In 1960, the federal government employed 3.3 percent of the total United States work force; in 1975, that figure had declined to 3.1 percent. On the other hand, state and local government, in 1960, employed 7.7 percent of the work force, and by 1975 this percentage had shot up to 12.6.[13] The dollar-volume increase was stunning. State and local expenditures—as a percentage of the Gross National Product (GNP)—grew only a trivial amount between 1929 and 1955. But then came the explosion, ignited by federal aid. In the next twenty years, expenditures rose from $34.9 million, or 9.2 percent of the GNP, in 1955 to $207.7 billion, or 15.3 percent of GNP, in 1974.[14] (See Table 13-2.)

[12]Federal intervention as a legal and logical accompaniment of grants was approved by a Supreme Court decision in 1923, *Massachusetts v. Mellon*, in which the Court decided that since a state was not forced to accept the offer of federal funds for welfare purposes, federal grants that involved acceptance of federal requirements did not infringe states' rights. States could maintain their independence by refusing the federal funds. But where was the state so wealthy that it could reject a federal handout? Where was the state governor who could stay in office if he or she turned down the money? It was a freedom that the states decided they could not afford, and they all took the money and the regulations. Of course, for many years the federal government didn't force obedience to some of the rules—such as civil rights regulations—if local officials objected.

[13]*Barrister* 3, no. 4 (Fall 1976).

[14]Emil M. Sunley, Jr., "State and Local Governments," in Henry Owen and Charles L. Schultze, eds., *Setting National Priorities: The Next Ten Years* (Washington, D.C.: Brookings Institution, 1976), p. 373.

TABLE 13-2

EXPENDITURES OF STATE AND LOCAL GOVERNMENTS IN CURRENT AND CONSTANT DOLLARS* AND AS PERCENT OF GNP, SELECTED FISCAL YEARS, 1955–1974
(money amounts in billions of dollars)

DESCRIPTION	1955	1960	1965	1970	1972	1974
Total expenditures						
Current dollars	34.9	53.6	77.8	135.9	173.0	207.7
Percent of GNP	9.2	10.8	11.8	14.2	15.6	15.3
Constant dollars	34.9	45.5	57.9	76.8	85.9	89.5
Percent of GNP	9.2	10.3	10.7	11.8	12.6	12.1
Total less federal grants-in-aid						
Constant dollars	31.7	39.5	49.6	64.3	70.3	71.5
Percent of GNP	8.3	9.0	9.2	9.9	10.3	9.7

*A "constant dollar" is a dollar as measured by its purchasing power in some arbitrarily chosen year. This "base period" dollar, being pegged to a moment frozen in history, allows some stability in economic appraisals. A "current dollar," on the other hand, is a dollar measured by its immediate purchasing power. The "current dollar" value changes as prices change.

SOURCE: Emil M. Sunley, Jr., "State and Local Governments," in Owen and Schultze, *Setting National Priorities*, p. 373.

Today, because of the mixture of governmental energies and governmental moneys, it is often difficult to tell where one level of government leaves off and the next one begins. It is an amalgam of power that has developed out of self-interests and outside pressures. The Bureau of Public Roads in the Department of Commerce, for example, administers federal highway appropriations through regional offices and a divisional office in each state. These branches work closely with state departments of highways, which, in turn, are influenced by demands made at the state and local levels by countless groups—real estate, auto, insurance, trucking, contracting, building material, and a wide variety of subcontractor groups.[15]

Very little of the federal assistance has come as a 100 percent gift. Making up the difference has not been easy. State and municipal governments have had to strain their fiscal resources to keep up. With some justification, A. W. Clausen, President of Bank America Corporation, charged that the federal government's "matching support funds for water, sewer, highway, and other construction projects lured cities into the grantsmanship trap."[16] The trap stayed misleadingly open during the boom years of the early 1960s. But it began to close in the late 1960s, when high interest rates, inflation, unemployment, and business recession hampered state and local governments in their efforts to finance their share. Like a worker who opened a dozen charge accounts during a period when he was working lots of overtime, and then, suddenly, was cut to half-time employment, with the debts still hanging over his head, state and local governments had more obligations than they had resources.[17]

The states and cities that could afford to accept grants became unhappy over the red tape that the federal money came wrapped in. For example, the University of Wisconsin gets many federal grants—as do all major universities. It would lose these grants if it didn't supply the federal government with information showing that it is operating in compliance with federal laws. At one point in 1975, the United States Office of Civil Rights was making the university supply 14 separate analyses of every employee action; this amounted to 100,000 separate individual analyses for the Madison campus alone. The final report sent to the government ran to sixteen volumes and roughly six thousand pages. Then the federal government changed its data forms, and two university employees spent the next seven months preparing the data previously submitted to be resubmitted on the new forms.[18]

How Many Federal Strings?   It is easy to understand why subnational governments would like to escape the waste and boredom of federally imposed red tape. But is the proper solution to give them federal money with no strings attached? Or is it to give them federal money with a sensible reduction of strings?

If the best solution is merely to cut down on the number of strings, how can that best be done? One proposal is to substitute block grants for categorical aid grants. The federal government started out helping states and local governments with money earmarked for specific programs; by 1976, there were six hundred such aid grants, ranging from library assistance to rat control, all costing more than $45 billion. Under the block grant principle, these six hundred aid grants would be consolidated into a few large allotments to be made to the states and localities. Broad restrictions would remain, but generally the states and communities could spend the federal money as they saw fit. If they wanted to

---

[15]Totton J. Anderson, "Pressure Groups and Intergovernmental Relations," *Intergovernmental Relations in the United States* (Annals of the American Academy of Political and Social Sciences) 359 (May 1965): 123.

[16]Statement made to the Senate Committee on Banking, Housing and Urban Affairs, October 18, 1975.

[17]One reason for their inadequate flow of revenue was that the personal income tax, the most fruitful tax, is primarily the tool of the federal government.

States and local governments depend largely on property

---

and sales taxes—about three-fourths of their tax income is from these sources—and these taxes are slow to reflect economic expansion. (Richard M. Nixon, *Congressional Record*, S811–15, February 4, 1971.) Consequently, the state and local governments are forced to keep raising the tax rate or levying new taxes, which makes the propertied natives very restless indeed. (These taxes are also regressive—they fall most heavily on lower-income citizens.)

[18]Report from Governor Patrick J. Lucey, "Roadblocks to Efficient State Government: A Sampling of the Effect of Federal Red Tape in Wisconsin," June 1976.

spend it all on swimming pools or tennis courts and none on educating the handicapped, or vice versa, that would be nobody's business but their own.

That proposal has never gotten very far with Congress (although it was favored by Presidents Richard M. Nixon and Gerald R. Ford), largely because most Democrats (who have made up a majority of the federal legislature) believe that as long as Washington is footing the bill it should set the spending priorities. They also believe that the states and localities are less sympathetic to the poor, the old, the young, and others without political influence and that such persons would be short-changed by local officials who were willing to heed the demands of their wealthier constituents.

Ironically, however, the federal politicians who have protected the categorical grants and fought off the block grant principle have enthusiastically supported General Revenue Sharing. GRS is a program of virtually no strings (except for civil rights), at least as the handout relates to the states. Cities must spend their GRS money in specific broad categories similar to those of the block grant concept. GRS was first created by Congress in 1971; by 1975, it was the biggest single domestic program in the budget, with more than $30 billion transferred from the federal pocketbook to the states and cities. Generally, the shared cash has been spent in the very ways in which it had been feared that the block grant money would be spent—to alleviate the middle-classes' taxes by paying for the standard budget departments: police, teachers, public transportation, maintenance, and construction of public buildings. Very, very little has gone to the underdogs of society. A study of Revenue Sharing by the Treasury Department's Office found that only 4 percent of the money went to social services for the aged and poor.

There is also a problem of accountability under GRS programs. When tax money goes up to the federal level and then back down to the states and localities, taxpayers lose sight of it. It is like money tossed out the window. Which states and localities pick it up? And what do they do with it? How much of it is wasted through stupid administration? How much of it is stolen by crooked politicians? How many campaign contributors are repaid with GRS-funded contracts? How

many relatives and pals of state and local politicians get cushy jobs with GRS cash? Nobody knows. One critic has pointed out that "Congressional committees, in evaluating revenue sharing, have never conducted a systematic study comparing the incidence of fraud, nepotism and partisanship at the federal, state and local levels."[19]

If the federal government did not demand an accounting of the money it handed out, who would? So far, the states and localities have shown little interest in playing watchdog over these funds. One of the costliest programs sponsored by the federal government is Medicaid, the free health program for the poor. Its purpose is admirable, but its administration, as congressional investigations have shown, has been so sloppy that it has cost many millions of dollars in fraud. How did it happen? The federal government passed responsibility for managing the money to the states; the states passed it to the cities. In the division of responsibility, overall control was lost, and it was up to the local bureaucrats to rise above the pressures and temptations of special interests.

If there is a carelessness in accounting for federal funds at the subfederal level, it is part of a general carelessness. Although 80 percent of the purchases of nondefense goods and services by government, including those heavily financed by the federal government, are administered by states and localities, it is at these levels that management and bookkeeping are the most haphazard. One study has concluded:

> Although most states now require some form of fiscal audit of local governments, few have the legal provision or the administrative capacity for evaluating performance or even for the collection of comparative data on program costs and results. We believe that states must take a first step in this direction.

In the Bicentenniel year, it was still commonplace to talk of a "first step" toward accountability of spending.[20]

---

[19]Amitai Etzioni, "Revenue Sharing Five Years Later," *Washington Post,* April 4, 1976.

[20]Research and Policy Committee of the Committee for Economic Development, "A Statement on National Policy," March 1976, p. 70.

Why We Need Federal Intervention

The federal government has proved to be a better accountant than the lower levels of government. More important, it has proved to be far more innovative, progressive, and responsive in its policy making and in its use of new techniques and new technologies than have the state and local governments. In 1972, the Federal Council for Science and Technology noted that "use of science and technology by state and local governments was roughly equivalent to that of the federal government in 1940."[21] Why is this? After all, the subgovernments are presumably closer to the problems and needs of their citizens. Historically (at least since the time of Plato), it has been assumed that local government is just automatically more democratic than larger government—that in small political units a citizen's voice will be heard (and thereby presumably listened to), but lost in large political units.[22]

It was for this reason that Thomas Jefferson wanted to form an agrarian democracy, based on small rural communities. James Madison, however, saw the dangers of small political units. In *The Federalist Papers*, Number 10, he argued,

> The smaller the society, the fewer probably will be the distinct parties and interests composing it; the fewer the distinct parties and interests, the more frequently will a majority be found of the same party, and the smaller the compass within which they are placed, the more easily will they concert and execute their plans of oppression."[23]

It is a question of keeping pressure groups under control. In a town with only one large company, in a county dominated by one-crop farmers, in a state where one industry or one cluster of like-industries has fashioned the foundation of the state's economy (oil and petrochemicals in Texas, the Du Pont enterprises in Delaware, for example), there will be a scarcity of democracy when it comes time to set taxes and economic priorities. Not only do the dominant interest's wishes and needs get served over others, but, as the dominant interest gains power in a small sphere, lesser interests lose their power and have less of a chance of forming an effective opposition. The interests that generally lose out in this manner are the interest of a weak minority (such as an ethnic group) that is distributed evenly among many small constituencies; and an interest that is diffused among the population and is not the primary concern of any one group (the "public interest" fits into this category).[24]

As for the argument that small units of government are the "classroom of democracy" wherein lessons are learned that can be applied to larger units of government, what exactly are the lessons to be learned from the courthouse gangs who run Mississippi's forty-seven counties, or the rinky-dink city hall crowds that run things in Sweetwater and Toonerville? The skeptical scholar Roscoe C. Martin, among others, would answer:

> . . . let it be noted that the citizen learns only about local affairs—that is, provincial and parochial affairs, that his teachers are small-time politicians and part-time functionaries, and that the courses of study are village pump politics and strictly amateur administration. The value of this kind of knowledge imparted in this fashion to the students of democracy is doubtful. The citizen so schooled in local government may develop a keen sense for sectional and special interests, but except by accident he will not graduate with a perceptive grasp of government in any broad or meaningful sense.[25]

A large political unit, such as the federal government, will formulate broader policies ap-

---

[21]Research and Policy Committee of the Committee for Economic Development, "A Statement on National Policy," March 1976, p. 70.

[22]If this were automatically true, we might expect to find the most democratic states to be those that have been chopped into the greatest number of governments—county, city, special districts. The evidence doesn't support that assumption. As Roscoe C. Martin once pointed out, the fact that North Carolina had only 608 units of government compared with Illinois' 7,723 and New York's 5,483 hardly supports the generalization that North Carolina is less democratic than Illinois or New York. (*Grass Roots*, Tuscaloosa, Ala.: University of Alabama Press, 1957, pp. 42–44.)

[23]James Madison in Alexander Hamilton, James Madison, and John Jay, *The Federalist Papers*, No. 10, ed. Clinton Rossiter (New York: Times Mirror Co., New American Library, 1961).

[24]See Grant McConnell, *Private Power and American Democracy* (New York: Random House, Vintage Books, 1970), pp. 104–05, 109.

[25]Martin, *Grass Roots*, pp. 54–70.

FIGURE 13-2 FEDERAL VERSUS STATE AND LOCAL WELFARE SPENDING, BY REGION

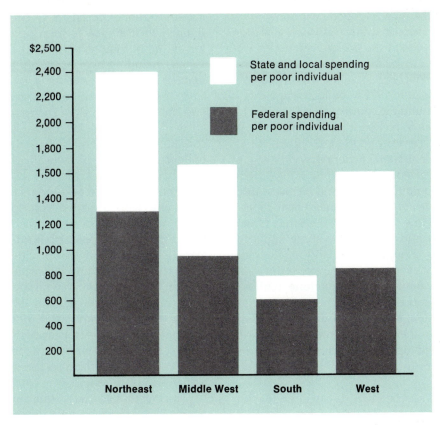

SOURCE: © 1977 National Journal. *Washington Post*, January 7, 1977.

pealing to a wider range of interests than will the small political unit. Most observers agree that there is more domination by interest groups, and especially by Big Business, in state and local government than in the federal government. States and cities don't like to impose strict health, safety, labor, and welfare laws for fear of chasing industry into the passionate arms of a less demanding place. Since money and jobs talk so loudly at the local level, higher government jurisdiction is sometimes necessary to make reforms.

In Gary, Indiana, U.S. Steel employs three-fourths of the city's working population. Needless to say, U.S. Steel was able to pollute the air and the water in, around, and over Gary without any interference from the local government. It took the United States government (which itself showed no speed) to make the giant steel company pay some attention to air pollution and water pollution laws.[26]

Lake Erie is a 12,000-year-old inland sea. Four states—Michigan, Ohio, Pennsylvania, and New York—touch its shores. In the mid-1960s, environmentalists pronounced Lake Erie dead. No wonder. For generations, giant industries from miles around had been pouring all sorts of poisons into its waters—mercury, dieldrin, lead, zinc, nickel, mirex, asbestos, polychlorinated biphenyls, phosphorous fertilizers, ammonia, cyanide, oil. Cleveland, Detroit, and

[26]Betty D. Hawkins, "Citizen Participation," in Melvin I. Urofsky, ed., *Perspectives on Urban America* (New York: Doubleday & Co., Anchor Press, 1973), p. 168.

Buffalo all dumped untreated sewage into Lake Erie. Finally, it seemed that the lake was filled with just about everything but water. Fish swam in it and died. Humans stopped swimming in it, and they were afraid to drink its water, even after it was treated. Could the lake be rescued?

Yes. With $18 billion, the federal government, in one of its biggest public works projects of all time, set out in 1972 to build sewage treatment plants around the country, and $5 billion of this money was to be spent in the Great Lakes region by 1977. (At least another $5 billion would probably be spent later.) Federal lawyers began taking some of the polluting corporations—such as U.S. Steel, Republic Steel, and Armco—into court to force them to clean up their waste pipes. By 1976, Lake Erie (along with the other Great Lakes) was beginning to show some signs of reviving. With enough money and legal clout, full health may eventually be recovered.

This could never have been done without federal interference. For one thing, the states didn't have enough money to do the job. For another thing, they didn't have enough will power to stand up to the giant corporations and force them to stop polluting the environment.

One reason special interests can operate with such a free hand at the state and local levels is that government at those levels is fairly "invisible." People keep better track of Congress than of their state legislatures, their city councils, their zoning commissions, or their public utility commissions. Perhaps local units are less highly publicized because their decisions tend to deal only with many millions of dollars, whereas the federal agencies spend many billions. In any case, without information about what their governmental units are doing, and for whose benefit, voters cannot take the political action that is needed to set things right.

Government invisibility also encourages the growth of political scandals. Between 1970 and 1977, more than a thousand public officials—most of them at the state and local level—were convicted of corruption.[27] The political soil of some states—Illinois, Louisiana, Missouri, In-diana, Florida, Texas, Maryland, New Jersey, New York, and West Virginia—seems to grow bigger scandals. Since 1970, more than a hundred public officials have been convicted in Illinois, including a former governor. In New Jersey, more than sixty persons have been convicted, including two secretaries of state, former mayors of Newark, Jersey City, and Atlantic City, the president of the Newark City Council, and the Republican state chairman. The acceptance of bribes and kickbacks was their most common crime. The speaker of the Texas House of Representatives and two aides were convicted in a shady bank deal. Maryland Governor Spiro T. Agnew took kickbacks from consulting engineers who were awarded state contracts (something he correctly described as "a long-established pattern of political fund-raising in the state"). The law caught up with him when he was Vice President, and he was forced to resign. Marvin Mandel, the man who succeeded Agnew as governor, was convicted in 1977 of seventeen counts of mail fraud and one racketeering charge. Over a thirteen year period (as of 1977), at least sixteen of Maryland's top officials were convicted of some form of corruption, and ten actually went to prison.

The fact that so many state and local political crooks have been brought to justice in recent years means that the feds have intervened. Most of the cases have been prosecuted by United States attorneys. As Neal Peirce has pointed out:

> The states, of course, should have been doing the job. But they generally weren't because of their outmoded criminal justice systems. In 27 states, the attorneys general don't even have full power to initiate prosecution of local government corruption. That leaves the job to district attorneys, often overburdened with street crime cases, who usually lack the professional staff to conduct complicated investigations. They can't pursue leads across county lines and are generally reluctant to prosecute local police and judges they have to work with regularly. Frequently the D.A. is beholden for his office to the local political machine that ought to be the target of his investigations.[28]

---

[27]*New York Times*, February 11, 1977.

[28]Neal Peirce, *National Journal*, April 19, 1975.

Big Business and State Government

Powerful as Big Business is in Washington, it is even more awesomely powerful in state capitals. State legislatures are much more willing to sell out, much more willing to kowtow unashamedly to the demands of the moneyed interests. Most newspapers give very poor coverage of the influence of Big Business in shaping state legislation. One maverick biweekly of small circulation, the *Texas Observer,* watched the opening of the Texas legislature in 1977 and made these pessimistic remarks:

> . . . power in the legislative chambers belongs overwhelmingly to big business. As individual firms, as members of trade associations, and as members-in-good-standing of the corporate lobby, these economic interests will have more to say over the shape of legislation than all the other registered interests combined. Through their power in Austin, they largely define the public interest of Texans.
>
> Consider the heft of just one group, the Texas Association of Taxpayers (TAT). Their lobby papers give the "development of a sound and equitable revenue and expenditure program for the state" as TAT's purpose. Since "revenue" means taxation, and "expenditure program" the state's budget, these folks are interested in everything the Legislature does. Who are they? Merely the largest corporations in Texas, including Exxon, Mobil, Shell, ARCO, Pennzoil, Chevron, Texaco, Tenneco, Gulf, Conoco, Dresser, Sears & Roebuck, Hughes Tool, Anderson Clayton, Houston Lighting & Power, LTV, Brown & Root, Stauffer Chemical, Zale, Texas Power & Light, Texas Instruments, and Southwestern Bell. Not your average taxpayers, but it is fair to say that they will have more influence than most when it comes to deciding what is and isn't "sound and equitable" legislation.
>
> The lobbyists for these interests are a far cry from the caricatures of Thomas Nast: corpulent figures, lurking in the corridors with their pockets full of boodle. It's not even the wide open Lobby-that-was of the Fifties and Sixties—working directly and boldly on the floor with members, willing to lose heavily at all-night poker games set up for needy (and needed) legislators, and otherwise taking care of those who went along. The whirl of bottles, blondes, and bribes is not over with, you understand, but the main business now is carried on with a great deal more finesse through PR types and lawyers who like to call themselves "Austin representatives" rather than "lobbyists." It is a polyester version of the coarser fabric that used to cover the Capitol—dull, but still effective.
>
> You won't see top-of-the line lobbyists hauling satchels of money up to the state senate like the bagmen of old, and you won't even see them hanging around a lot. They can do their work with an occasional, timely phone call, or they can see a committee chairman at the country club. There's no need to storm around, bulling people over. The thing nowadays is just to act when it's time to act, and as discreetly as possible.
>
> The corporate lobby has ample favors to dispense—from campaign contributions to the simple flattery of a phone call from a major corporate executive—but big business' real clout is its sheer staying power—its constant presence at the seat of government. Day in and day out, Texas business is there to get theirs—they have a bill prepared, they have an information booklet for the member's consideration, they have a local district constituent to talk to the legislator. . . .
>
> They hold enormous power; power that is rarely discussed in print, and even less rarely on the air. There have been literally hundreds of newspaper stories published in the past couple of weeks on the 65th Legislature, all reporting the same basic thing—the session will be devoted to property tax reform, school finance, highway construction, medical malpractice insurance, crime control, etc. But there has been virtually no coverage of the economic forces that have already come together to shape the session. In part, there is so little coverage of big business lobbies because they hide their light under a bushel. Various newspapers have done thorough reporting on the legislative programs of groups like AFL-CIO and Common Cause, but these groups are forthcoming about their plans (AFL-CIO even printed a little booklet on their goals for this session). Exxon, Brown & Root, Dallas Power & Light, and the crowd they run with don't put out press releases on their legislative programs; they just get them passed. . . .*

*Jim Hightower, "Big Business Settles In," *Texas Observer,* January 28, 1977.

Before being too hard on the state and local governments for neglecting the public good, one should ask if it is fair to expect them to solve some of their most pressing problems. Pollution, for example, is not a local problem but a national problem. No one state can clean up the Mississippi River or the Chesapeake Bay. No one state or group of states can disperse the pall of smog that hangs with seeming permanence from Washington to Boston. No one state can clean up the Great Lakes. Civil rights, medical care for the poor and aged, education for low-income areas, worker safety, housing for middle- and low-income groups, unemployment—these, though they are more extensive in some regions than in others, are national, not local problems.[29] Social justice and economic justice demand the same uniform attention that the national defense receives.

STATE GOVERNMENT

It is not possible to issue a single value judgment for all fifty state governments. They run too wide a gamut in their ethics, innovation, efficiency, and thrift. Nevertheless, it is fair to characterize a large portion of the states as weak members of the federal system. The reasons are to be found in the states' organization and distribution of political power. In general, we will find the states to have changeable constitutions, weak governors, autonomous administrative agencies, part-time legislatures, timid courts, unorganized political parties, and strong, organized interest groups.

The Structure and Politics of State Governments

The Constitutions State constitutions are remarkable for their length (Louisiana's runs 255,000 words, California's 70,000, New York's 45,000, and sixteen other states' run over 20,000 each; the United States Constitution contains less than 10,000 words) and their openness to change (Louisiana's has 496 amendments, California's, 335). In addition to being cumbersome, many of the state constitutions contain policies that are out-of-date, lately giving rise to calls for revision.

It is clear from the number of amendments that state constitutions are awarded far less sanctity than the United States Constitution. As Grant McConnell points out, there is a current "conception of the constitutions as mere outlines of governmental structure and policy, to be altered as the winds of political fashion shift and circumstances change."[30] The consequences of this for state government include opportunities for special interests to write favorable provisions into constitutional law.

State Executives There are a number of reasons why governors are in a weak position in most states. For one thing, the typical governor has such brief tenure of office that power cannot grow. Although in recent decades the average tenure has increased (in 1960 it was 3.26 years; in 1969, 3.68 years), it is still brief by federal standards.[31]

The governor's appointive powers are severely limited. (Presidents make the same complaint.) Many state officials are elected or

---

[29]To treat these issues on a state-by-state or on a city-by-city basis is to suggest that justice and compassion mean different things according to geography. It is a cockeyed notion that causes considerable suffering, as can be shown by variances in welfare programs. An Associated Press survey in 1975 of fifteen major cities found that a welfare mother with two children received $135 per month in Kansas City, $123 in Atlanta, $116 in Dallas—but $302 in Philadelphia, $293 in Los Angeles, $312 in Seattle, $342 in Detroit, and $394 in New York. The trouble is, food and clothing cost about the same in Dallas or Atlanta as they do in New York. In 1976, state and local spending on welfare averaged $1,422 per poor person in Massachusetts—and $62 in Mississippi. There was, obviously, no set national formula for the payments; federal contributions ranged from a minimum of about 50 percent to a maximum of almost 85 percent, and the rest was made up by diverse percentages from state, county, and city. The obvious inequality of compassion in this program was one reason (the other being the wish to be rid of the financial burden) why the nation's governors proposed that Washington federalize welfare—lock, stock, and food stamps. As the system stands today, the federal contributions are often tied to the amount that state and local governments spend, so that where the latter are stingy, he federal government is forced to be stingy too. (Associated Press, October 26, 1975; *New York Times*, July 11, 1976; *National Journal*, January 7, 1977.)

[30]McConnell, *Private Power and American Democracy*, p. 169.

[31]"Politics of the Executive," in Herbert Jacob and Kenneth N. Vines, *Politics in the American States: A Comparative Analysis*, 3rd ed. (Boston: Little, Brown and Co., 1976), p. 225.

Federal, State, and Local Government and Reform

The fact is that for a century and a half almost every major reform in our political and social system has come about through the agency of the national government and over the opposition of powerful vested interests, state and local communities.

It is the national government that freed the slaves, not the states or the people of the South, and there is no reason to suppose that these would ever have done so voluntarily. It is the national government that gave blacks the vote, guaranteed them political and civil rights, and finally—in the face of adamantine hostility from Southern states and bitter resentment from local communities, provided some measure of social equality, legal justice and political rights for those who had been fobbed off with second-class citizenship for a century. . . .

It is the national government which finally gave the suffrage to women and which, in the past decade, has so greatly expanded the area of woman's rights. It is the national government, too, which extended the suffrage to those over eighteen. And it is the federal courts that imposed a one-man, one-vote rule on reluctant states.

It is the national government which, in the face of the savage hostility of great corporations and of many states, finally provided labor with a Bill of Rights, wiped out child labor, regulated hours and set minimum wages, and spread over workers the mantle of social justice. . . .

It is the national government that first launched the campaign to conserve the natural resources of the nation and that is now embarked upon a vast program to curb pollution and waste, and to save the waters and the soil for future generations. . . . Ask conservationists whether they can rely on the states, or on voluntary action, to resist giant oil, timber, coal and mineral interests for the fulfillment of their fiduciary obligations to future generations. . . .

It is the national government, through national courts, which has imposed "due process of law" on local police authorities, and on the almost arbitrary standards of many states. We have only to compare the administration of justice and of prisons in local and federal jurisdictions to realize that many of the values of voluntarism and localism are sentimental rather than real.

It is the national government, not the local, which through its almost limitless resources has finally acted to ameliorate the awful inequalities on public education at all levels. And it is the national government which has, in recent years, given vigorous support to the arts, music, libraries, higher education and research in every part of the country.

From Henry Steele Commager, *New York Times*, March 4, 1973.

appointed by boards or commissions. These officials share the powers of patronage with the governor, reducing the amount of control he or she has over the administration. And the governor's control is further diminished by the sheer number of administrative agencies. Since he or she cannot possibly oversee them all, they gradually build up autonomy. And as they do, they become more and more attached to the constituency they are supposed to regulate. This tendency is increased by the use of boards or advisory panels to recommend policy for the agencies—as with the federal bureaucracy, the members of these panels are nearly always taken from members of the trade or industry being administered.[32]

One way of dealing with the disadvantages of multiple elective offices and multiple agencies is to give the governor the power to reorganize. Until recently, not many states allowed their

[32]See McConnell, *Private Power and American Democracy*, p. 185. State legislatures have begun taking some restraining action. Colorado passed a law that puts state regulatory agencies out of business at the end of seven years unless the legislature specifically extends their lives. By 1976, two dozen legislatures had set up machinery for negating what Iowa's legislature aptly described as "unreasonable, arbitrary, capricious" actions by their bureaucracies.

chief executives that power, perhaps because of "the advantages disorganized and ill-coordinated administration gives to narrow power-holding groups."[33]

In the last few years, however, many states have been overhauled. Nineteen have been reorganized completely, twenty others partially. Missouri used to have ninety disjointed, uncoordinated agencies, boards, and commissions; now it has fourteen—and their responsibilities are clear. Jimmy Carter promoted himself for the Presidency on the basis of the reforms he made when he was governor of Georgia. Three hundred departments and boards were trimmed down to twenty-two, each with its own unified budget and its own planning and accounting offices. The benefit to the public? They knew where to go for help. Previously, a family seeking assistance for its retarded child might have to go to half a dozen agencies before finding, perhaps accidentally, the one that was authorized to help; now the road signs were clear. However, some states (such as Texas) still groped for guidance from several hundred boards and commissions.

The one area in which the governor is relatively strong is in his dealings with the legislature (itself a very weak branch in most states). One major study of the fifty legislatures concluded: "Instead of operating as an independent or even important policy-making body, the state legislature too often serves merely as a funnel or screen for outside initiatives." The study noted that in "most states" the governor was not only the chief executive, but the "chief legislator," meaning that the typical governor has the staff, the expertise, the research facilities, and the time to put together between legislative sessions a program that outweighs anything that the typical legislature can come up with on its own. The study found that governors could dominate legislatures far more extensively and consistently than the President could ever dominate Congress.[34]

The veto powers of governors are generally strong. Governors in forty-one states have the power of item veto, which allows them to veto one part of a bill while signing the rest into law.

On paper, most governors also have fairly strong budgetary powers, but all too often the governor simply accepts the budget proposals of the state bureaucrats and passes them to the legislators. A study of state budgeting in Illinois came to this conclusion:

> The budget document may be compared to a huge mountain, which is constantly being pushed higher and higher by underground geological convulsions. On the top of the mountain is a single man, blindfolded, seeking to reduce the height of the mountain by dislodging pebbles with a teaspoon. That man is the Governor.[35]

State Legislatures Fifteen or twenty years ago, perhaps the most dominant characteristic of state legislatures was their unrepresentativeness. Malapportionment, or overrepresentation of some districts at the expense of others, was widespread in both houses of the state legislatures. In 1962, the Supreme Court ruled in *Baker v. Carr* that citizens could seek relief from state apportionment laws in the federal courts.[36] Two years later, the Court ruled that representation in both houses of state governments had to be based on population and that the boundaries of districts had to be redrawn accordingly. The result was that "by 1968 every state had apportioned one or both houses of its legislature, generally in response to a federal court order. . . . Today there is very little malapportionment in any state and 'one man, one vote' is the prevailing style of representation."[37] Reapportionment has led to an increase in suburban representation over rural representation. But urban clout has been blunted by urban/suburban differences of opinion and by the fact that, on some issues, suburban representatives have teamed up with rural representatives to outvote the urban legislators.

---

[33]McConnell, p. 183.

[34]Etzioni, "Revenue Sharing Five Years Later."

[35]Quoted in Ira Sharkansky, *The Maligned States: Policy Accomplishments, Problems, and Opportunities* (New York: McGraw-Hill, 1972), p. 8.

[36]*Baker v. Carr*, 369 U.S. 186 (1962).

[37]"State Legislative Politics," in Jacob and Vines, eds., *Politics in the American States*, p. 173.

A scene in the Wisconsin state legislature

In some respects, state legislatures reflect the grass roots much more than the national legislature does. There is more diversity of professions and a significant percentage of nonprofessionals—but there are still more lawyers than any other group. About one out of five state legislators is a lawyer (22 percent). In eighteen states, lawyers make up 25 percent or more of the legislative bodies, with Virginia (57 percent), New York (45 percent), South Carolina (45 percent), and Mississippi (37 percent) leading in that category. About one out of twenty members (5 percent) is in the insurance business—a sharp decline since 1966, when 9 percent were in insurance. The leader in this category is Florida, where 13 percent of the lawmakers are in the insurance business. The number of professional educators in state legislatures has risen significantly, from 3 percent in 1966 to 8 percent in 1976. Education's strongest influence is in Utah (26 percent). Representation in the West North Central region reflects the importance of farming and ranching to that area. More than four of every ten state legislators in the Dakotas and three out of ten in Nebraska are farmers. On the other hand, in Alaska, New Jersey, and Rhode Island no legislator is a farmer.

Perhaps the most significant, and salutary, characteristic of state legislatures is their potpourri: 4 percent retired persons, 16 percent self-employed, 5 percent in real estate or construction, 3 percent in communications or the arts, 1 percent in labor unions, 1 percent in nonprofit organizations, 3 percent housewives or students, and so on.[38]

---

[38]"Occupational Profile of State Legislators 1976," Insurance Information Institute, New York.

Most state legislatures are set up like mini-Congresses, with two chambers (except Nebraska, the only state with a unicameral—one house—legislature). Committees are less powerful in the state legislatures than in Congress, probably because they have less staff assistance and shorter sessions in which to consider legislation. Although state legislators pass a great many statutes in a session, many of these are private bills or bills serving local interests.

There is no question that state legislators are subject to enormous interest group pressure—the most important being business, education, and labor interests. In the states where weak party systems have left a power vacuum, the special interests have even more influence.

State legislatures vary widely in their "professionalism" quotient. Professional legislatures have well-paid members, long legislative sessions, good staff support, and good information sources, and they provide a variety of legislative services. A study made in the 1960s found eight highly professional state legislatures (California, Massachusetts, New York, Pennsylvania, Michigan, New Jersey, Illinois, and Hawaii), fifteen professional, seventeen less professional, and ten nonprofessional.[39] The more professional legislatures tend to be in the urban, industrial states, and the less professional in rural states, where pay is lower, sessions are shorter, and turnover is higher.

In general, it can be said that state legislatures lack original thought and a spirit of independence. But here again, exceptions must be made. The kind of legislative turnaround that has occurred in some of the more progressive states can be seen in Florida, where, as recently as 1968, the governor was considered the chief legislator, confronting the legislature at the time of its convening with an awesome sheaf of bills. To cope, the legislature had to borrow experts from the executive branch. The legislature met only sixty days every two years (with some special committee meetings in between), so it was hard pressed to adequately debate the governor's bills, much less come up with legislation of its own. Members were paid $1,200, an amount that discouraged effort and encouraged bribery.

Then came reform. After 1968, the legislature began meeting annually. The presiding officers were given authority to call the legislature for special sessions; previously, only the governor had this power. The state's auditing department was transferred from the executive branch to the legislative branch. The legislative committees were staffed with analysts, researchers, and attorneys on a year-round basis. Finally, as taxpayers have come to expect, the reform was costly, and the legislators fitted themselves into the cost; as of 1976, they were being paid $12,000 a year, but at least they were doing enough work to justify their being called a legislature.[40]

State Courts　State courts[41] handle the cases that affect the day-to-day life of Americans—criminal prosecutions; divorces; probating of wills; automobile accident suits; eviction of tenants; disputes over contracts; appeals against decisions of zoning commissions, regulatory agencies, school systems, and so forth. Justice William J. Brennan, Jr., believes the work of the state courts is more important than the work of the Supreme Court in measuring how close we are to reaching the ideal of equal justice.[42] By that measure, we still have a long way to go. Like federal courts, but more so, state courts have a shocking history of unequal punishment. In 1975, for example, less than 30 percent of the convicted armed robbers with prior criminal records received prison sentences in Los Angeles County, but many who were imprisoned received long terms.[43]

By another measure, state justice often has a cheapskate texture. Judges usually get generous

---

[39]"State Legislative Politics," p. 184.

[40]Allen Morris, *The Florida Handbook* (Tallahassee, Fla.: Peninsular Publishing Co., 1977–78), pp. 134–35. Paying more money will not guarantee a good legislature, however. In 1966, it cost Maryland taxpayers $8,224 annually to sustain each member of the General Assembly, and, in fiscal 1977, it cost $64,511 per member. For that, the people of Maryland got a legislature that seemed much more attuned to horse-race fanciers, bank-charter addicts, land hustlers, high rollers, and assorted lobbyists than it did to the general populace. (Wes Barthelmes, *Washington Post*, August 22, 1975.)

[41]See Chapter 11 for the structure of the state court system.

[42]"State Courts," in Vines and Jacobs, eds., *Politics in the American States*, p. 273.

[43]Edward M. Kennedy, "Criminal Sentencing: A Game of Chance," *Judicature*, December 1976.

salaries, and lawyers are allowed fat fees, but when it comes to supporting the backbone of American justice—the citizen jury system—many states tighten their purse strings to an almost insulting degree. Since 1968, the federal government has paid its jurors twenty dollars a day, and ten cents a mile for travel expenses. But only six states, as of 1977, authorized payment to jurors at the federal rate: Hawaii, Maine, Nebraska, New Hampshire, North Dakota, and South Dakota. New Mexico pays its jurors the federal minimum wage, but it is the only state generous enough to use a formula rather than to specify a flat fee. In fourteen states, the daily allowances for at least some jurors in some courts may be as low as five dollars. Travel allowances, when granted at all, can be as little as five cents a mile. Naturally, where states impose this kind of economic hardship, most citizens do their best to duck jury duty, and the jury box is often filled with people who feel they have nothing better to do with their time.[44]

One of the most effective means for establishing a more humane and egalitarian atmosphere in this country lies in the potential interplay of state and federal courts. If there were only one level of courts and if it were to become oppressive, relief could be obtained only by taking the laborious legislative route or by taking the dangerous route of insurrection. But federalism's several levels of justice offer another way, through intercourt challenges. For example, civil rights demonstrators were often found guilty in the state courts of the South and innocent in the federal courts. To advance freedom and gentility, the citizen learns how to play one tier off against another. In recent years, the most famous victories have been achieved by playing the federal courts against state courts. But it doesn't have to be that way. Contrary to what most people seem to think, the United States Supreme Court does not inhibit states from giving *more* civil rights and civil liberties than the highest federal court is willing to give; it only inhibits them from giving less.

Nothing in the United States Constitution or tradition prevents state laws from outdoing fed-

eral law in kindness, openness, and protectiveness. If a state court rules that the death penalty is cruel and unusual punishment and must be ended in that state, the Supreme Court will not overturn that ruling, even if it feels capital punishment is simple justice. If state law requires that a person be supplied an attorney from the moment he or she is arrested, the Supreme Court may consider that unnecessarily restrictive of police, but it will not overturn the state law. State law, and its interpretation by state courts, can permit the use of marijuana, odd sexual practices in private between consenting adults, or any range of permissiveness, and the Supreme Court will not interfere (so long as the permissiveness does not interfere with other people's freedoms). In short, the United States Supreme Court will generally intrude only to force state laws to provide a constitutional minimum of rights and liberties, but it rarely finds a reason to block state laws that go beyond that minimum. Some states have taken advantage of this freedom to innovate, but not many. On the whole, state judges, like their federal counterparts, are the product of the mentality of the state bars, which almost always err in the direction of caution and staidness.

As of 1976, the American Judicature Society reported five methods by which judges are chosen: the merit system, whereby a nonpartisan commission (the makeup of which varies from state to state) produces a list of acceptable nominees from which an elected official, often the governor, makes the final choice; a nonpartisan ballot submitted to the general electorate; a partisan ballot; direct appointments by the governor; and direct appointments by the legislature. Whatever the method, virtually all judges reach the bench tinged with politics and bearing the standard of the legal establishment. The results, as in all else pertaining to government, are mixed: some high-class judges and far too many middling and low-class judges.

Not all federal judges are upstanding characters. But the extent of malfeasance at the federal level comes nowhere close to matching that at the state and local level. There has never been anything at the federal level to equal, for example, the record of the Oklahoma Supreme Court. In 1964, it was discovered that, for the past twenty years, four of its justices had been in-

[44]*State Court Journal* (National Center for State Courts) 1, no. 2 (Spring 1977).

volved in a bribery ring. A total of 1,878 final opinions of the Oklahoma Supreme Court had been shaped by bribes.[45] Federal judges, at their worst, cannot match the antics of some state, county, and municipal judges, such as the county judge in Kentucky who showed up drunk at a trial he was to conduct and then interrupted it by waving a pistol dangerously in the direction of the attorneys; he was not living on the frontier, but, in fact, presided late into the 1960s.

Financing and Spending

Most state revenues come from taxes. (See Table 13-3.) Revenue from other sources, like tuition fees to state universities, is meager, and borrowing money is prohibited by many state constitutions. Taxes are mostly of two kinds—income tax and sales tax. Both are regressive in that they tend to hit the poor harder than the rich. Most state income tax rates stay the same for all incomes above the $15,000 income level, whereas the federal rates—nominally, at least—keep rising steeply and reach a peak at $100,000.[46] The lottery is a nontax source of revenues, but it too is regressive; individuals in lower-income brackets spend proportionately more money on the numbers game than do persons with higher incomes (who prefer to gamble on horse races or the stock market).

Some states, unable to manage their financial affairs with decorum and sound business judgment, have decided that what's good for the syndicate is good for government. They have turned to gambling as a means of separating the taxpayers from their income. As of 1977, two states have legal casino gambling, two have legal off-track betting on horses, and one has legal betting on sports events. But lotteries are the most popular. Thirteen states grossed $1.1 billion from lotteries in 1976, a twenty-five fold increase over five years earlier.[47] State-run lot-

teries come equipped with two excuses: they keep gambling money from going into the illegal numbers racket; and the money raised from lotteries prevents the legislatures from having to increase taxes.

As to the first excuse, former Director of the Federal Bureau of Investigation Clarence M. Kelley observed, "Research to date has shown that the various state lotteries around the country not only fail to compete with the underworld but may actually be creating a whole new influx of bettors who will someday switch their wagering to the hoodlum element as their addiction grows."[48] As to the second excuse, the state lotteries actually contribute only between 1 and 2 percent to a state's income. Furthermore, when this kind of easy money floats through a government bureaucracy, it just naturally stirs larcenous thoughts. Officials have been found milking the lottery fund. And in New York, as the *New York Times* reported, "the banks are the lottery's only certain winner." As much as $4 million in lottery collections lay in favored banks for two years without paying the state a cent of interest.[49]

State governments show so little individuality and imagination in financial matters that one discovers with pleasant surprise that, while other states kowtow to the private banks, even to the extent of placing state money in them and requiring no interest, North Dakota owns its own banking system—a throwback to the spirit of socialism that many of the state's Scandinavian and German immigrants brought with them in the nineteenth century. The Bank of North Dakota takes far more risks, at a lower interest rate, to finance small businesses, home mortgages, and student loans than normal commercial banks would, and, as a result, the people of North Dakota feel they have at least a little extra control over their financial lives.

Some states brilliantly combine thrift (in the sense that they do not hire more employees than they need and do not waste money on make-work for political cronies) with generous public

---

[45]Charles R. Ashman, *The Finest Judges Money Can Buy and Other Forms of Judicial Pollution* (Farmingdale, N.Y.: Brown Book Co., 1975), pp. 59–66.

[46]Sharkansky, *The Maligned States*, p. 9.

[47]Associated Press, April 18, 1977.

[48]Quoted in the *Washington Star*, October 15, 1976.

[49]Sources: *New York Times*, November 4, 1975; *Dollars and Sense* (National Taxpayer's Union), November 1976.

TABLE 13-3

SOURCES OF REVENUE OF STATE AND LOCAL GOVERNMENTS IN FISCAL YEAR 1973 AND ESTIMATED YIELD OF THIS REVENUE SYSTEM IN FISCAL YEARS 1981 AND 1986
(billions of dollars)

REVENUE SOURCE*	1973	1981	1986
Federal grants-in-aid	39.3	74.4	101.2
Taxes	121.5	259.3	387.5
Property	45.3	86.6	117.9
General sales and gross receipts	23.0	45.0	61.9
Selective sales	19.5	34.3	48.9
Individual income	18.0	62.9	115.5
Corporate income	5.4	11.6	16.7
Other	10.4	18.9	26.6
Charges and miscellaneous general revenue	29.9	60.5	79.4
Total	**190.7**	**394.2**	**568.1**

*The sources of revenue differ from the standard Census Bureau classification in (1) the omission of insurance trust revenue; (2) the netting of liquor store expenditure against liquor store revenue and including this net amount in selective sales taxes; and (3) the omission of utility revenue.

SOURCES: Actual, *Governmental Finances in 1973–74*, table 3; projections, prepared by Robert D. Reischauer. Figures are rounded. From Sunley, Jr., "State and Local Governments," in Owen and Schultze, *Setting National Priorities*, p. 407.

service. When inflation threatened to ruin its medical assistance program in the mid-1970s, Wisconsin froze the price of prescription drugs, physicians' services, and other benefits. (Some states, faced with similar increases in the cost of medical assistance, either killed some of the services, restricted eligibility, or charged the patient the additional costs.) One reason Wisconsin, even in hard times, has been able to manage to give its citizens good service is that it has not padded its payrolls; it ranks forty-fourth in the ratio of state employees to state residents.[50]

The interplay between federal, state, and local spending—on welfare, highways, hospitals, schools, and almost every other major social area—has reached such complexity that it is virtually futile to consider the three levels separately. Mayors, governors, and federal officials all realize this, but they have yet to discover a truly efficient way to bring the three into efficient coordination. Kenneth A. Gibson, Mayor of Newark, New Jersey, pinpointed the dilemma as of 1976:

> In the past two years local governments have been forced to work at cross purposes with the economic policies of the federal government, by raising taxes while the federal government was attempting to stimulate the economy by cutting taxes. In fact, a recent study by the Joint Economic Committee shows that local and state governments have cut services or raised taxes by nearly $8 billion.[51]

That's quite enough to have a depressing effect on local economies.

[50]Governor Patrick J. Lucey, Annual Review Message to the Wisconsin Legislature, January 29, 1976.

[51]Quoted in the *Washington Post*, November 16, 1976.

Where the States Excel

Let us pause to give credit where it is due. States have occasionally, down through the years, stepped out ahead of the federal government. In a *few* states, child labor laws, the income tax, the eighteen-year-old vote, and suffrage for women were written into law before Congress got around to it. Long before the federal government became the source of assistance to the needy, the old, and the physically disabled, some states were making benevolent handouts. In 1898, Ohio offered pensions for the blind, and several other states followed suit. Illinois began giving cash assistance to widows and young children in 1911; Alaska passed an old-age assistance law in 1915, and Nevada and Montana did, too, in 1923.[52]

The states have also, on occasion, showed themselves capable of meeting emergencies with an alacrity that is foreign to the ponderous central government. The Federal Trade Commission acknowledged, for example, that the critical oil shortage of 1973–74 would have resulted in consumer chaos if it hadn't been for quick actions by the states in setting up energy allocation programs.[53]

While Congress continued to debate the problem, eight states virtually decriminalized the use of marijuana (Oregon, Alaska, Maine, Colorado, California, Ohio, South Dakota, and Minnesota); South Dakota was the most lenient, making possession of under one ounce of marijuana a twenty-dollar violation, like a traffic ticket.[54]

When democracy is permitted to have its head at the state and local level—that is, when it is not hobbled by the inferior representative governments of the state legislature, the county courthouse, and city hall, or steamrollered by heavy lobbies—some bright and exciting things

can happen. They may not be sufficient in scope to set national policy, but they do express the will of the people. Specifically, this is the direct democracy—through initiative, referendum, and recall—that is available in some states and in thousands of localities and which the comparatively elitist government in Washington would shudder at the thought of offering.

Recall (the least used of these processes) allows voters to go to the polls between the ordinary election dates and say whether they want to keep or fire one of their officials. It is simply a way of putting the impeachment process into the hands of the people. When a male judge in Madison, Wisconsin, excused a fifteen-year-old rapist, saying that the youth was simply "an impressionable person" responding in a "normal" way to the general pornography of the times, 35,000 citizens of the city—led by outraged feminists—signed a petition asking for a recall election. The judge was defeated and replaced.[55]

Use of the *initiative* and of the *referendum* is much more prevalent in the West than in any other section of the country. They originated around the turn of the century, when the country was in a populist-progressive mood. The initiative is a procedure whereby voters can write their own legislation and force the issue to be placed on the ballot for a direct vote. Usually, access to the ballot for an initiative requires getting a certain percentage of the electorate to sign a petition; in California, a state that is very fond of direct democracy, this could mean obtaining half a million signatures.

The referendum is a method by which voters are given the opportunity to cancel what their elected representatives have done. For example, if the city council agrees to zone land for a high-rise development, the voters can veto the decision. (The voters of Eastlake, Ohio, did just that, and in 1976 the United States Supreme Court ruled that the developer's appeal was constitutionally off base because "under our Constitution all power derives from the people. . . . The referendum is a means for direct political participation, allowing the people the final decision,

---

[52]Stanley Esterly and Glenn Esterly, *Freedom from Dependence: Welfare Reform as a Solution to Poverty* (Washington, D.C.: Public Affairs Press, 1971), p. 3.

[53]Report of the Federal Trade Commission, Washington, D.C., March 16, 1974.

[54]*National Committee for the Reform of Marijuana Laws* 5, no. 2 (1976).

[55]Associated Press, September 8, 1977.

Through the initiative, New Jersey voters brought about legalization of gambling casinos in Atlantic City

amounting to a veto power, over enactments of representative bodies."[56])

In the November 1976 election, more than three hundred initiatives and referendum issues were on state ballots. Voters had a chance to decide whether or not to build nuclear power plants, whether to limit the use of nonreturnable containers, whether to permit legalized gambling, whether to control the sale of guns, and whether to control state spending. It must be said that usually consumer and environmental issues are defeated because of expensive lobbying campaigns by business and industrial interests that would stand to lose money under reform legislation.[57]

LOCAL GOVERNMENT

The states were the origin of all federalism, creating not only the central government above

their level, but also the local governments below.

The local governments are tangled together in an often unintelligible mass. As of 1976, the states contained more than 80,000 governmental units, including counties, cities, towns and townships, and special districts (for such services as schooling, fire protection, sewage, and water). All of these subgovernmental units are subject to the pleasure of the state—they can be changed or abolished. But, like the administrative units within state government, the local governmental units have built up a great deal of autonomy, especially those that have been granted home rule by the state. This allows them, in many cases, to collect taxes, spend, and regulate, without effective state control or supervision.

Local governments have a massive effect on their citizens. The federal government is generally portrayed these days as the Great Intruder, but unfairly so. Whether or not a person can go into a particular business in a particular location, whether or not a homeowner can take in roomers, whether or not cars can be parked in certain locations, whether or not a man can go

[56]*Washington Post*, June 22, 1976.

[57]Sources: *Washington Post*, November 4, 1976; *Washington Star*, November 6, 1976.

without a shirt in certain parts of town, whether or not people will be allowed certain types of entertainment, whether or not the garbage will be carried away and the whores arrested and the stray dogs impounded is up to the county courthouse or the city hall, the fonts of that steady outpouring of bureaucratic regimentation: "Watch your step! Curb your dog! Do not spit! No Parking! Get in line for a ticket! Move on! Keep off the grass! Follow the green line! Wait for the next train!"[58] The *real* life of the American citizen is shaped among the cuspidors in that building downtown. Any citizen who has tried to make that institution change its glacial ways will know immediately what the expression "you can't fight city hall" means.

The effects of local decision making are highly visible, but the decision making itself is a murky process. We have already taken note of invisibility on the state level. But, generally, the

smaller the political unit, the easier it is to operate in the dark. This is because, by some mental quirk, most people are much more interested in the drama of federal politics than in the ordinary machinations of local politicians—though the latter can sometimes have a much more immediate and disturbing influence on the ordinary citizen's life. City council meetings and county commission meetings are notoriously ignored by the public—and by the local press. City and county regulatory agencies operate largely in the dark because neither public nor press bothers to turn on the light. Road paving contracts, for example, don't make very sexy reading. Sometimes the murkiness is permitted because local politicians are pals of the local newspaper's publisher, and the publisher doesn't want to blow the whistle on the politicians' backdoor schemes. Nor would a local newspaper publisher be interested in offending the business interests who have great influence in the council chambers and who also buy ad space in the newspaper. How can an undesirable zoning variance (that helps a

---

[58]Claude S. Fischer, *The Urban Experience* (New York: Harcourt Brace Jovanovich, 1976), p. 203.

A County Official Speaks

It was not too long ago that I entered office with the absolute conviction that good intentions, a sense of honesty, a willingness to work long hours, and a handful of competent, loyal department heads could go a long way toward making a local government succeed. We would, in short order, redirect the county's priorities: redesign its miserably strip-zoned arteries, revitalize its deteriorating town centers, restore its polluted beaches, remove its messy landfills. We would establish a sound working relationship with the federal government, begin a new and healthier era of city-county cooperation. And we would do it all entirely in the open.

Eighteen months later, having launched a score of major efforts to confront these problems, ranging from historic preservations to watershed protection, I now look around my governmental landscape, a chastised soul, more fully appreciative of the public's cynicism.

There is absolutely no hope of decommercializing the arteries: They are stripped to stay. If we can pass a rational ordinance regulating signs, entice a few landowners to plant shrubs or otherwise take care of their property, and perhaps (a very qualified perhaps) prevent the strip zoning of future highways, we will possibly have made a dent.

Revitalization of one or two town centers may or may not take place in our lifetime. Success depends largely upon mollifying suspicious residents, surviving endless meetings in byzantine bureaucracy, and making one's way through the jungle of local politics.

The county beaches may be beyond human resurrection, requiring a billion-dollar program that *might* slow the current rate of pollution but not guarantee their rehabilitation. In 1960 our county possessed 15 beaches available for swimming. Today we have 6. For months a team of 10 to 12 people have spent 8 hours a day cleaning out Baltimore County's Back River—dredging thousands of tires, refrigerators, cars and other discards of man's conspicuous consumption. But the river remains filled with debris.

Establishing a working relationship with the federal government may be likened to initiating detente with the Russians. We know we must do it. Washington, like the Russians, knows it must be done. But in the process no one trusts anybody, and if something positive *is* accomplished, the local citizenry will likely be suspicious. . . .

Openness has also succeeded, in a way: Government meetings in our administration are open, but nobody bothers to come. The press, which used to sit on my desk, has not covered a meeting in my office in months. Our Task Force on Education, dealing with a department that spends half of the county's budget, has held 63 subcommittee sessions; not one has been reported by anyone, anywhere. The office joke is that the best way to have a secret meeting is to put it on the schedule.

We are left with the blunt fact that government's most dependable product may be unadulterated frustration. For those who enjoy the pleasure of real frustration, try getting a civil-service employee in the Permit Office to speed things up. Better yet, try to make a work crew work. Or try to anticipate the next crisis. . . .

We keep trying, I suppose, because of these moments of enormous satisfaction: The family whose home has been persistently inundated by heavy rains now able to move out under your new flood-management program; the people whose bitterness over the impending transformation of the last remaining green space in their neighborhood into an unnecessary shopping center, now sharing the job at having that land turned into a park; civic leaders for the first time feeling free to walk into the county executive's office and discuss an issue openly, without hostility; town meetings attended by hundreds sharing ideas, discussing issues.

And if you're the county executive you learn to live with the frustrations all the while, thinking in your more grandiose moments that Thomas Jefferson suffered the same, which is why he said, "Government is best which governs least." Which is also why he took up carpentry.

Theodore G. Venetoulis (Baltimore County Executive), August 18, 1976.

shopping center but hurts its residential neighbors) be prevented if the meetings and decisions of the zoning commission are secret or unreported?

A big problem in local government is the fragmentation of power brought about by the multiplicity of political units. This fragmentation has been a source of continuous controversy in areas concerning jurisdiction, financial responsibilities, efficient administration, and popular control. We can examine these controversies more closely if we look at local government as it operates in three areas—rural America, the suburbs, and the cities.

The Counties in Rural America

County governments were established as the local administrative districts of the states. Down to the first decade of this century, to most Americans the county courthouse was *the* seat of government. It was the place they looked to for help and guidance; they did not turn to the state capital or to Washington, but to the county commissioners, the county tax assessor, the sheriff, the county road department, the county farm agent, the county hospital, and the county poorhouse. When America was still predominantly small-town and rural, the county seat was the most vital government around. And in many sections of the nation it still is.

Sixty million people in the United States live outside the Census Bureau's Standard Metropolitan Statistical Areas—which is just another way to describe the clusters of urban (and suburban) residents—and look to counties as the major providers of services.[59]

Rural areas may have less crime and less hassle, but they also have less wealth. The median income of nonurban workers is about 20 percent less than that of urban workers; 44 percent of the nation's poor live in rural counties,

but only 27 percent of the funds for income security and welfare go to those counties; 47 percent of the elderly poor live in rural counties, but only 30 percent of Social Security payments go to those counties; 60 percent of all substandard housing is in rural counties, but less than 20 percent of federal housing subsidy goes to those counties. Even after a decade of official concern about rural health needs, 138 rural counties populated by nearly half a million people did not have a single resident doctor in 1975; that figure was up 36 percent from the 98 such counties in 1963.[60] Obviously, whether measured by its need or by the services actually offered, the county unit is one of the most crucial in the federal system.

It is also obvious that county government has not obtained for rural Americans a fair share of the federal largess. This is probably because county governments are not colorful, do not attract national headlines, and, therefore, get passed up at appropriations time. This is the era of urban drama—the New York City bankruptcy, the Boston school busing fights, the San Francisco municipal union strikes—and county governments offer little strife and get little attention from the general public.

The competition between the big cities and the rural counties for money, attention, and status is nothing new. One of the oldest rivalries imbedded in our politics is country folk (including small-town folk) versus city dwellers. Jefferson wrote to Madison that the people would prevail in governing themselves

> as long as agriculture is our principal object which will be the case while there remain vacant lands in any part of America. When we get piled upon one another in large cities, as in Europe, we shall become corrupt as in Europe, and go to eating one another as they do there. [Great cities were] pestilential to the morals, the health and the liberties of man. True, they nourish some of the elegant arts, but the useful ones can thrive elsewhere, and less perfection in the others, with more health, virtue and freedom, would be my choice.[61]

---

[59]Counties administer welfare in eighteen states (Alabama, California, Colorado, Georgia, Indiana, Maryland, Minnesota, Montana, Nebraska, New Jersey, New York, North Carolina, North Dakota, Ohio, South Carolina, Virginia, Wyoming, and Wisconsin). In the remaining thirty-two states, state governments handle the welfare administration. Only four cities—New York, Denver, Baltimore, and San Francisco—administer welfare programs.

[60]Sources: National Association of Counties, Washington, D.C., 1976; Rural Housing Alliance, Washington, D.C., 1975.

[61]Quoted in Charles M. Wiltse, *The Jeffersonian Tradition in American Democracy* (New York: Hill & Wang, 1960), p. 102.

Most people today would agree with Jefferson's unkind appraisal of cities. Many city dwellers would prefer to live elsewhere. In 1972, George H. Gallup polled Americans with the question "If you could live anywhere you wanted to, would you prefer a city, suburban area, small town, or farm?" Their answers:

City	13 percent
Suburbs	31 percent
Small towns	32 percent
Farm	23 percent

Gallup found that among persons already living in cities only 20 percent prefer that as their residency. In 1969, a Harris poll found that two-thirds of the people living in cities hoped to have fled to suburbs, the country, or a small town within ten years.[62]

Their hopes took a historic turn in the first years of the 1970s, when, for the first time in this century, the movement back to the small cities and towns of the United States accelerated to the point that the rate of population growth in nonmetropolitan areas was greater than in the big cities and suburbs. It was a dramatic reversal; in the 1960s, metropolitan counties had grown by 17 percent, while the nonmetropolitan counties grew by 4.4 percent; in 1970–73, the metropolitan counties grew by 2.2 percent, while the nonmetropolitan counties were growing by 4.1 percent. But the reversal of the *rate* of growth was of small importance—only a freakish indication of the unhappiness underlying the above statistics—and does not alter in any significant way the fact that *in absolute numbers,* if not in rate, the big metropolitan areas will continue to grow the fastest, for the same reason that people have been migrating to cities all over the world for centuries: *that's where the jobs are.*[63]

---

[62]Fischer, *The Urban Experience,* p. 21.

[63]To be sure, upper-income, sophisticated people do appreciate city life; apart from employment opportunities, there are other considerations: big-city newspapers are usually much better than the newspapers that can be found in small towns; big cities have art galleries and theaters of better quality, larger libraries, and more tolerance for the kind of eccentric social life that some sophisticates prefer. Such people would be most unhappy with small-town life or with having cows as their nearest neighbors. But they constitute a very small fraction of a city's population. Most people live in cities simply because big population centers offer jobs: people work for people.

The Suburbs

The lower-income city dwellers know they will live and die where they are, but the lower-middle-class, the middle-class, and the upper-middle-class city residents know they have a way out: they can keep their city jobs but still get at least a slice of artificial country life by moving to the "vast, curdled Milky Ways of suburbia."[64] And that's where the big growth has been. Between 1960 and 1970, most of the metropolitan areas' 17 percent growth was in the suburbs; and the trend continues.[65] Why are people moving out of the cities?

Fear of the plague, which has gripped the mind of civilized people since at least the thirteenth century, can be equated with fear of city life; periodically, in the old days, cities were evacuated to escape epidemic diseases. The cities are still being evacuated, gradually, and the motivating force is still the desire to protect health—physical and mental. In a survey of new suburbanites in Cleveland, 61 percent said they had moved out of the central city to find "a cleaner, healthier neighborhood," while only 48 percent said that they moved to the suburbs to have better schools or to own their own homes.[66]

The stain on the cities' reputation comes not only from soot and disease, but from class differences and poverty. The waves of immigrants to this country—"the indiscriminate admission of wild Irishmen and others," as one fearful critic described the immigration[67]—deposited millions of Europe's impoverished and unwanted in big-city ghettos. They brought "strange" habits and "strange" languages that disturbed Anglo-Saxon Americans. They were openly held in contempt. Emma Lazarus's famous lines inscribed at the base of the Statue of Liberty are significant:

---

[64]Lewis Mumford, *The Urban Prospect* (New York: Harcourt Brace Jovanovich, Harvest Books, 1969), p. 202.

[65]Fischer, *The Urban Experience,* p. 24.

[66]Lewis Mumford, *The City In History: Its Origins, Its Transformations, and Its Prospects* (New York: Harcourt Brace Jovanovich, 1961), p. 487.

[67]Quoted in Josephy, *The American Heritage History of the Congress of the United States,* p. 115.

A slice of artificial country life

> Give me your tired, your poor,
> Your huddled masses yearning to breathe free,
> The wretched refuse of your teeming shore.
> Send these, the homeless, tempest-tost to me.

Many Americans did view the immigrants as undesirable. And most of the immigrants wound up in cities.

Middle- and upper-class Americans (now including the children and grandchildren of immigrants) have reacted in the same way to the great migration of blacks from the South into northern cities, which began during World War I. Blacks were still overwhelmingly rural and southern as of the census of 1910 (three out of four lived in rural areas; nine out of ten lived in the South). By 1960, blacks were mainly urban (nearly three out of four), and about half lived outside the Old Confederacy.[68] The reason for their migration was not mysterious: blacks were largely kept at

the bottom of the southern social and economic ladder.[69]

It was true that wretched housing and discrimination in schools and jobs awaited blacks in the North as well, but the opportunities to break out of the caste were also greater, so the migration continued. Between 1960 and 1970, the black population of the South increased only 4 percent, from 9.9 to 10.3 million, compared with a

---

[68] August Meir and Elliott Rudwick, *From Plantation to Ghetto*, rev. and enl. ed. (New York: Hill & Wang, 1970), pp. 213–50.

[69] In 1966, the median income for black families in sixteen southern states and the District of Columbia was $3,422. In the rest of the United States, median black family income was $5,746. Hunger was a way of life for southern blacks. A survey discovered 235 "emergency hunger counties" with a total population of almost 5 million (in many of these counties, blacks made up the majority of the population); some black children were found to be literally starving. Three houses out of four occupied by blacks in rural and small towns of the South were without plumbing or were dilapidated, or both, compared to only 15 percent of the homes lived in by blacks in the North and the West. Illiteracy was 10 percentage points higher among adult blacks in the South than among adults in the rest of the nation. (*Fortune*, August 1968.)

national increase in the black population of 20 percent, from 18.9 to 22.7 million.[70] The same kind of migration, for the same economic reasons, was also driving Americans of Latin descent (mainly Puerto Ricans and Mexicans) into the major urban areas of the North and the West.

The poverty of these groups, and the breakdown in family life that accompanied it,[71] led to all sorts of social problems—creeping slum areas, juvenile delinquency, violence, drug-pushing, high crime rates. Those who did not want to be a neighbor to or a victim of these problems and who could afford to escape them, moved to the suburbs. Whether or not they were motivated by racism, the results were the same.

Events since 1968 have indicated the probable fulfillment of the prediction made that year by the National Advisory Commission on Civil Disorders (the Kerner Commission), which said that by 1985 Washington and Newark, which already had black majorities, would be joined by Baltimore, Chicago, Cleveland, Detroit, Gary, Jacksonville, New Orleans, Oakland, Philadelphia, Richmond, and St. Louis.[72] The impact on the school systems in the central cities has been devastating. Whites comprise just 4 percent of the student body in Washington, D.C. In Detroit, more than 50 percent of the black students go to schools that are more than 98 percent black. In Baltimore, where the student body is about 80 percent black, about 50 percent of the blacks go to schools that are 90 percent black. In Cleveland, 80 percent of the blacks go to schools that are more than 98 percent black. And so on.[73]

With whites leaving at a rapid rate, the central cities have ended up with a franchise on wretchedness. Floyd Hyde, a former Under Secretary of the Department of Housing and Urban Development, describes the ordeal:

I fear we have leaped over and left neglected and isolated, millions of Americans in our central cities who are most in need.

The nation's critical human problems are highly concentrated in only 48 of our cities:

They contain $\frac{1}{2}$ of the 5 million urban sub-standard housing units.

They have 3 times the urban death rate.

They have 4 times the national maternal death rate.

They contain two-thirds of the urban poor.[74]

Having left urban problems behind, suburbanites are not interested in seeing any of their tax dollars poured into rescuing the central-city decay. As was noted earlier, the movement of white urban dwellers to the suburbs has helped maintain much of the small-town rural power in the state legislatures, for the ex-urbanites look back with distaste to their former homes, which are increasingly inhabited by blacks, and throw their support to the anticity forces.[75] Most suburbanites resist efforts to join in regional governments that would pool their resources with the inner-cities.

This attitude has left the suburbs in limbo. Although there are notable metropolitan areas where they have cast their lot with the central cities—Miami, Jacksonville, Nashville, Indianapolis, and Minneapolis–St. Paul, among others—the general practice of suburbs is to go it alone. Because they are isolated, the quality of their government often deteriorates. The elite who make up the village boards of trustees and the county boards of supervisors usually prefer to govern via backroom sweetheart deals. Larcenous real estate developers frequently have far too much influence with the suburban planning commissions.[76]

[70]Report of the Southern Regional Council, September 11, 1975.

[71]Edward C. Banfield and James Q. Wilson note that "the continuing lack of economic opportunities since [slavery] has made it difficult for Negro men to acquire the economic self-sufficiency to become the head and breadwinner of a family. . . . The 'wandering male' who is only a part-time worker and a part-time husband has contributed to the high percentage of Negro families supported either by working mothers or welfare checks or both." (City Politics, Cambridge, Mass.: Harvard University Press, 1963, p. 293.)

[72]Edward J. Logue, "The Idea of America Is Choice," in Qualities of Life: Critical Choices for Americans (Lexington, Mass.: D. C. Heath & Co., Lexington Books, 1976), p. 21.

[73]Joseph Kraft, syndicated column, September 7, 1976.

[74]Quoted in the Congressional Record, H4241, May 10, 1977.

[75]Charles E. Wilson, "The White Problem of the Cities," in Melvin I. Urofsky, ed., Perspectives on Urban America, p. 91.

[76]See Samuel Kaplan, The Dream Deferred: People, Politics and Planning in Suburbia (New York: Seabury Press, 1976).

The Cities

The out-migration to the suburbs has had a devastating effect on the cities' tax base. It has brought some cities—Detroit for one—to the brink of bankruptcy. Between 1970 and 1975, the five largest cities in the United States lost population. Decreases occurred in twenty-nine of the forty largest cities. Most of the migrants were the very people that the cities could least afford to lose: the younger, better educated, more affluent people. As a result, the cities were left with an increasing percentage of poor, minority-group, and aged residents: the people who provide the least amount of revenue and require the most in public services. It makes for a circular disaster: when income does not keep up with the cost of services, the services are reduced; as the services are reduced, the out-migration of unhappy residents speeds up; as the out-migration speeds up, income declines, and so on, and on.

Perhaps the best way to get a feeling for the drama, deficiencies, and needs of urban life is to take a quick swing through two of the most vital centers. We will choose New York City and Washington, D.C.

A Tale of Two Cities   New York City is usually portrayed as the Preeminent City, seat of all the excitements that can be found in urban centers (museums, art galleries, big-league sports, and so on) and all the evils of urban life. In recent years, the evils have been emphasized. It is easy to portray New York as sinful and stupid. It ranks as one of the most polluted and congested cities in America. Times Square has become a capital of pornographic shops and prostitution. The South Bronx used to have the highest crime rate in the city, but it has been swept by so many waves of arson, looting, and unrestrained street crime that all the residents who had anything have fled, and there is little left to steal or burn. There are some 255 youth gangs roaming the city's streets, robbing at leisure.[77]

The history of the New York Police Department, as the *New York Times* has noted, "can be read as one long story of corruption. Every 20 years or so, there is a new scandal, followed by a brief flurry of reform, followed by the long gradual slide back into what seems to be the Department's normal state of discreet but all-pervasive corruption. . . ."[78]

The castoffs, the poor, the starving, the derelicts from other parts of the nation and the world seem to gravitate to New York City. Out of the South came a million and a half unschooled blacks; out of Puerto Rico came a million untrained Latinos.[79] And, since there is very little cane to cut or cotton to pick in New York City, most of them wound up on welfare. Puerto Ricans make up between 30 and 50 percent of the city's welfare recipients.[80] Manhattan, Brooklyn, and the Bronx have more racial-minority residents than any two southern states combined. A study by the *New York Times* in 1974 found that the city and surrounding region was home to probably as many as 1.5 million illegal aliens, who work and draw welfare, use public schools, and use municipal hospitals, while they often pay minimal or no taxes and send large amounts of money abroad.[81] Symbolic of the underside of New York City life are the estimated five thousand women who carry all of their belongings in large shopping bags and wander the city constantly, living in doorways, sleeping in subway stations or on the sidewalk.

New York City reaches out to help its helpless and winds up goofing again, at least in the eyes of the rest of the nation, by giving some welfare mothers more cash benefits and social services than they would get if they held jobs that paid the minimum federal hourly wage.[82] New York City taxpayers pay twice as much per capita for welfare costs as do the residents of any other

---

[77]*New York Times*, August 20, 1976.

[78]*New York Times*, August 29, 1971.

[79]Melvin Laird et al., *Financial Crisis of Our Cities* (Washington, D.C.: American Enterprise Institute, 1976), p. 4.

[80]About 71 percent of the 3.3 million United States citizens in Puerto Rico depended on the federal food stamp program for survival in 1975; in some areas (such as in the central town of Jayuya, population 14,000) the unemployment rate was over 90 percent. (*New York Times*, October 15, 1975.) To such people, even the squalor of New York City slums seemed appealing.

[81]*New York Times*, January 13, 1974.

[82]Study of the Rand Corporation, released September 29, 1976.

major United States city.[83] And New York City spends more for public assistance than the gross national products of some medium-sized countries; its welfare bureaucracy, with 28,000 employees, is the largest municipal agency in the world.

Pressured by militant municipal labor unions, New York, in 1975, was paying its 340,000 city employees nearly $7 billion a year out of a $12.1 billion budget—more than the entire budget for the state of New York and second only to the federal budget. Because municipal-union members and their families represent an overwhelming political force—about 500,00 voters out of the 900,000 who show up for a Democratic primary and the 1.7 million who vote in a general election—they have been able to pressure the city into hiring beyond its need. Between 1963 and 1973, the city work force grew by nearly 50 percent, compared with a 37 percent average increase in other United States cities. The unions have also forced the city to accept a pension plan that allows workers to retire at half-pay after twenty-five years of service.

City hall efficiency was so low that $1 billion in real estate, water, and sewer taxes went uncollected. The city's own politicians admit that between 10 and 15 percent of the budget is lost through waste and corruption.[84] By 1975, finances were in such a horrible mess that the city was desperately closing libraries, halting middle- and low-income housing construction, shutting down fire stations, stacking up pupils (more than sixty elementary-school pupils per class in some schools), raising subway fares by 43 percent (which hit poor people harder than it did middle- and upper-income people), and, finally, turning to the federal government for a multibillion-dollar loan to keep the city from going bankrupt.

Outside observers might reasonably conclude that if any city government in America should run smoothly, if any city should be well-

---

[83] Associated Press survey of fifteen major cities, October 26, 1975.

[84] See remarks of New York Senator Jacob Javits in Laird et al., *The Financial Crisis of Our Cities*.

organized and humanely and honestly administered, it is the District of Columbia. Most particularly, if there is any city in America that should reflect the advantages of the federal system, it is Washington, D.C., home base for the system. After all, Congress set up the city's municipal government and heavily supports its expenses; two congressional committees oversee the city's budget and programs. The product, however, is not pretty government.

When the Senate District Committee tried to audit the city's books, it found them in such a mess that city officials literally did not know how much money they had in the treasury, how much the city owed, or how much it was owed. It had paid some creditors two or three times for the same bill while failing to pay other creditors at all. And the city had lost millions of dollars by failing to collect taxes owed by large corporations.[85] Typical of the thinking that went into Washington's budget: a cut in the sales tax on liquor from 6 to 4 percent in order to boost sales—coupled with an allocation of $5 million ($700,000 more than the year before) for treatment and prevention of alcoholism.[86]

Twenty-one percent of all personal income in Washington comes from government benefit programs, compared to 12 percent of all personal income nationwide. Between 1970 and 1975, the increase in social benefit programs, particularly pensions and welfare, rose by 95 percent. In that same time, the private business payroll rose by 37 percent—but the District government payroll rose by 87 percent (compared to the 68.5 percent growth for all state and local governments).[87] Washington, D.C., employs one city worker for every fifteen residents, a ratio that is higher than that of any other major American city.

Federal funds given to the District of Columbia government for programs to treat drug abuse and to reduce infant mortality were diverted to pay for the air conditioning of city officials' automobiles.[88] D.C. General Hospital, where the poor are served, was so badly operated that it lost its accreditation. When the bus system was operated by a private company, it lost about $1 million a year; when the city took over its operation, the deficit rose to $50 million,[89] and service declined. Information about the misuse of public funds is difficult to uncover because city hall operates virtually in secret; questions from the public and the press about the city's operations are generally rebuffed.

Washington's citizenry is split by uncommon extremes: it has the highest per capita income of all cities in the nation, and yet, also on a per capita basis, it has more citizens earning less than five thousand dollars a year. Nationally, in 1976, Washington ranked fourth among United States cities in the proportion of its residents on welfare, 14.2 percent. At least 30 percent of the blacks in the slum areas—which comprise large sections of Washington—are unemployed, yet only 3 percent of the unemployed receive unemployment compensation, and only 13 percent are on welfare.[90] During the riots of 1968, long corridors were burned through the black ghetto. A decade later, nothing had been done to change those wastelands. At least forty-four hundred housing units have been abandoned, boarded up as unfit for habitation—yet hundreds of them are being lived in. Washington is one of the six worst cities in the United States in terms of housing units that lack some or all plumbing facilities. In a typical year, more than 2,000 families are evicted from their homes, their possessions thrown out on the sidewalk, where they are quickly stolen. More than 8,000 families are on the waiting list for public housing. Some 77,000 families are inadequately housed.

Washington's young people receive little guidance. In 1976, more than half the children born in the District of Columbia were illegitimate, and most of their mothers were high-school aged. On college board scores, Washing-

[85]Sources: Report of the U.S. General Accounting Office, Washington, D.C., December 9, 1976; Report by the public accounting firm of Arthur Anderson & Company, June 20, 1976; *Washington Post,* September 21, 1975.

[86]*U.S. News and World Report,* quoted in *Conservative Digest,* December 1975.

[87]*Washington Post,* October 15, 1976.

[88]*Washington Post,* September 18, 1976.

[89]*Washington Post,* August 8, 1976.

[90]*Washington Post,* July 1, 1976.

ton public-school students have the lowest scores among fourteen major cities, except for Newark, New Jersey.[91]

If Washington is near the bottom in public education, it is near the top in crime. Its 1975 murder rate was 50 percent higher than New York City's or Los Angeles'.[92] And it is always near the top in robberies and rape. It's easier to get out of the District's jail than it is to get into it; 60 to 70 percent of the armed holdups are committed by persons on parole or out on bail.[93] Washington has one of the largest police departments, on a per capita basis, in the nation, but 74 percent of the police force lives outside the city, unexposed to the city's problems. Because of its very generous pension plan, the city was, in 1975, paying retired police officers and fire fighters fifty cents for every dollar it paid active police officers and fire fighters. For a personal investment of less than $12,000, the average retired police officer or fire fighter could expect to receive nearly $700,000 in pension benefits over thirty years. Having casually promised its employees—not only the police and the fire fighters, but teachers, clerks, and judges—rich rewards for short careers, Washington was faced with $1.1 billion in legally binding pension obligations for which it had provided no funding—and the actuarial future looked even bleaker after 1976.

Problems of Administration   If we shake down the administrative problems of these two sample cities, we have: inflated municipal wages, overbearing unions, low productivity, insensitive administration, graft, and incompetence. These problems apply not just to New York City and Washington, D.C.; most major cities are beginning to experience them.

Wages have not been monitored or held in line. Average wages of government employees were 106 percent of those in private industry, as of 1975. To some extent this compensated for a previous history of low pay. But now the balance

has begun to swing dangerously in the direction of overpay. The average salary of state and local government workers went up 28 percent faster than that in private industry between 1955 and 1973, primarily as a result of union pressures. The typical city mayor, if faced with a strike by teachers, the police forces, or fire fighters, would probably agree with Mayor Harry E. Kinney of Albuquerque, New Mexico: "Mayors just don't have the tools to counter the force of strong unions. They are helpless even in the face of an illegal strike."[94]

But larger payrolls have not been accompanied by higher productivity or improved services. For example, the largest chunk of a city budget goes to education. Are teachers (who make up 17.6 percent of all municipal employees) doing their job? Since the mid-1960s, the reading, writing, and arithmetical skills of American students have been moving in a downward spiral—and the decline encompasses all ethnic groups and all economic classes in all regions of the nation.[95] A federally subsidized study disclosed, in 1977, that 20 percent of the students in the Southeast, 21 percent of the students in disadvantaged urban areas, and 42 percent of the blacks were functionally illiterate. (Functional literacy is the ability to read street signs, telephone directories, store coupons, and other such simple stuff. A student was judged literate if he or she could correctly answer at least sixty-four out of eighty-six questions.) Poverty, bad home life, bad food, and bad genetic foundation could explain only some of the discouraging results of the tests. Poor teaching had to account for a large part, too, for literacy cripples are also commonplace among the middle class. At some universities, between 40 and 65 percent of entering freshmen are required to take remedial, or "bonehead," English courses. David Harman of Harvard's Graduate School of Education reported in 1975 that "a staggering 54 percent of the population" could just barely, if at all, cope with basic reading tasks "regardless of level

[91]*Washington Post,* August 20, 1976.

[92]*New York Times,* January 10, 1976.

[93]Robert Sherrill, *The Saturday Night Special* (New York: David McKay Co., Charterhouse Books, 1973), p. 240.

[94]Quoted in the *New York Times,* August 24, 1975.

[95]*New York Times,* September 7, 1975.

of formal education completed."[96] How were the education budgets being wasted?[97]

The next largest chunk of the typical municipal budget goes for police protection (police officers make up 16.3 percent of city employees). How much protection are the police giving, and how much should they be expected to give? To the last question, Robert J. di Grazia, former Commissioner of the Boston police force, gives this answer:

> Most of us are not telling the public that there is relatively little the police can do about crime. We are not letting the public in on our era's dirty little secret: that those who commit the crime which worries citizens most—violent street crime—are for the most part the products of poverty, unemployment, broken homes, rotten education, drug addiction and alcoholism . . . . about which the police can do little, if anything.[98]

Anyone wishing to take the di Grazia position will conclude that most of the billions spent for local police protection might be spent more profitably on providing jobs and more social services.

However benign that attitude may be in the long run, it will hardly satisfy those citizens who right now feel more comfortable with a cop on the beat. Which brings us back to the first question: are citizens getting their money's worth out of the police? A fragmentary clue can be found in the fact that arrests are made for less than one reported burglary or larceny out of every five reported. The ratio of convictions is one out of twenty.[99] Much of the problem stems from the natural difficulties in catching criminals and making cases, but much also stems from police sloth. Studies have constantly shown that police officers are much slower in answering calls for help from the slums—where most of the violent crimes are committed—than they are in answering calls from the posh section of town.[100] One reason, of course, is that tax money talks; but another reason is that many police officers like to avoid trouble. It's much safer arresting harmless drunks than it is armed drug pushers. While cutthroats, burglars, and narcotics dealers go about their business largely undisturbed, more than 2 million drunks are arrested every year, and hundreds of thousands of persons are picked up for such minor offenses as disturbing the peace and vagrancy.[101] "More than half of all arrests are for minor crimes. Some of these have no victims. Others involve no antisocial action."[102] Is that what taxpayers want from their crime control budget?

Some city employees operate like paid visitors. As of 1976, employees of about half the nation's largest cities were permitted to live outside the cities from which they earned their livelihood. But in 1976, the United States Supreme Court ruled that cities could legally enforce the edict enunciated by Chicago's late Mayor Richard Daley: "If a city is good enough to work for, it should be good enough to live in."[103] (City employees living in the city also improve their employer's tax base.)

Local officials often prefer business health to public health. In Texas, the leading water polluter is the city of Houston. Thirty-two of its sewer lines dump human waste directly into surrounding waterways. One of them alone sends

---

[96]Quoted by Coleman McCarthy, *Washington Post,* May 27, 1976.

[97]The validity of the schools' budget is also suspect in nonacademic areas. In the mid-1960s, the federal contribution to the school lunch program was $315 million, with about 20 million youngsters taking part each day. In the mid 1970s, the federal government's contribution—roughly matched by the states—had risen fivefold, to $1.7 billion, but the schools were feeding only 5 million more children with that money. Even discounting inflation, that's a questionable rise in expenditure. What were the schools up to? (*Washington Star,* May 16, 1976.)

[98]Quoted in the *Washington Post,* October 6, 1976.

[99]Ramsey Clark, *Crime in America: Its Nature, Causes, Control and Correction* (New York: Simon & Schuster, 1970), p. 54.

[100]See the *New York Times'* staff, *Report of the National Advisory Commission on Civil Disorders* (New York: E. P. Dutton & Co., 1968), pp. 308–09.

[101]Ronald Goldfarb, *Jails: The Ultimate Ghetto* (New York: Doubleday & Co., 1975), p. 200.

[102]Stephen Gillers, *Getting Justice: The Rights of People* (New York: Times Mirror Co., New American Library, 1973), p. 176.

[103]Many cities, including Philadelphia, Detroit, Boston, and New York, immediately moved to take full advantage of the Court's edict (and many municipal employees were resisting).

up to 120 tons of untreated human waste each day into the channel that spills into Galveston Bay, and with the raw sewage go some seventy viruses—including polio, hepatitis, and spinal meningitis—contaminating one of the nation's most valuable marine estuaries. Several sections of the bay were eventually closed to oyster fishing and swimming. When the state sued Houston to stop spreading its filth, Houston Mayor Fred Hofheinz complained that the lawsuit would "kill the goose that laid the golden egg," meaning that if the unpleasant results of Houston's growth were known, the boom might begin to deflate. Although Houston is one of the most prosperous cities in the nation, it took no significant steps toward improving its sewer system until the federal government gave it $500 million to do so.[104]

In 1970, the federal Center for Disease Control estimated that some 100,000 citizens each year become ill, some seriously, from what they eat in restaurants. Enforcing restaurant sanitation is largely a city responsibility; sometimes it is a county or state responsibility. Few of these subnational governments have ever enthusiastically required clean eating places. In 1975, the General Accounting Office (an arm of Congress) sent inspectors to visit 185 restaurants in nine cities; 98 percent were rated less than excellent.[105]

The point is that cities (and states) have traditionally shown no willingness to do anything about unsanitary and unsafe situations that afflict the public unless, and until, the federal government prodded them to do something about it; even then many have been reluctant because they fear offending local business interests.

Where big money floats around, there is, inevitably, graft. A New York City politician put it even more accurately: "Every social service has a built-in ripoff factor."[106] The federal system of passing taxes up and passing grants down is theoretically an admirable exchange. Unfortu-

nately it can't be done without passing the money through the hands of politicians and bureaucrats, who frequently yield to the temptation to use some of the money for themselves and their friends.

In 1973, Congress passed the Comprehensive Employment and Training Act. It was supposed to be used to provide job training and employment opportunities for the poor and disadvantaged in the inner-cities. Much of the money, however, was diverted by city officials to hire friends and relatives and to supplement the city budget's standard outlays of service to the middle class.

In 1976, an investigation by the General Accounting Office disclosed that the $6 billion in revenue-sharing funds assigned to 39,000 local governments was inadequately audited, with the result that funds intended to support the day-care program, for example, had actually gone into the pocket of real estate promoters. The result, as taxpayers watched their taxes being stolen by city machines, was an unfair criticism of the various social programs. John L. Hess wrote in the *New York Times*, "By now it is commonplace, even among the liberals, to say, 'You can't solve a problem by throwing money at it.' What the scandals suggest, however, is that a lot of the money was thrown, not at the problems, but at the politicians."[107]

Aside from the political graft, there is the incompetence of administration that permits waste of many millions of dollars. Federal, state, and local agencies appear to be unable to limit charity to those who qualify for it. The three major charity programs funded by the federal government are Aid to Families with Dependent Children (AFDC), food stamps, and Medicaid assistance. Because of the growth of these programs—AFDC grew 825 percent between 1960 and 1976; in 1976, it took on 11.5 million new clients—bureaucrats at every level of government have been swamped. Complicated changes in regulations, management errors, and fraud have crippled the programs. Of the 3.38 million families enrolled in AFDC in 1975, offi-

---

[104]*New York Times*, September 11, 1976.

[105]Report of the U.S. General Accounting Office, Washington, D.C., December 12, 1975.

[106]Quoted in the *New York Times*, August 15, 1976.

[107]John L. Hess, *New York Times*, August 15, 1976.

"The Court takes cognizance of your plea that the very nature of the municipal accounting system invites fraud, and reminds itself that the very nature of the judicial system requires me to slap you in the jug."

cials of the Department of Health, Education and Welfare believe that at least a quarter of a million were ineligible. And since families ruled eligible for AFDC automatically become eligible for food stamps and Medicaid, those programs are also burdened by clients who do not qualify. Nobody knows the cost to the public, but the best guesses hover somewhere around $2 billion.[108]

Administrative problems of this sort measure the willingness or unwillingness of a city government to maintain its integrity. Few big cities have the wealth necessary to cope by themselves with

the deeper problems—unemployment, crime, lack of housing, poverty. The federal treasury must (and does) help alleviate those problems, for they are national, not local, in origin. But the administration of a city is no less crucial, and can do much to relieve them both directly and indirectly. For example, when a city cuts out wasteful programs and payrolls, its credit rating on the bond market rises; when it borrows, it gets a lower interest rate. Thus the money it saves to buy money can be used to offer better services. Central cities can reattract middle-class families—meaning a better mix and a better tax base—if local school authorities are willing to

[108]*Washington Star,* August 11, 1976.

maintain high scholastic and disciplinary standards in class and if the police and the courts are willing to crack down on the nucleus of repeater criminals who make the streets unsafe.[109] These administrative duties cannot be sloughed off with the excuse that "only more federal money can reach the root problems of society."

The Structure of City Government   The political life of cities varies widely—from being nonpartisan to being multipartisan, from clean to scandalous, from efficient to decrepit, from responsive to reprehensible. But no matter what the character of their politics, most cities use one of three forms of government: the mayor-council, the council-manager, or the commission plan.

The most common form is the mayor-council plan, in which an elected mayor works with an elected council. When the mayor has more authority than the council, it is considered a strong-mayor form of government. Edward C. Banfield and James Q. Wilson point out that "in a general way the strong-mayor form resembles the national government. The mayor shares with the council responsibility for policy-making, but he alone has administrative responsibility."[110] Most cities of over 500,000 people are characterized by the strong-mayor form of government. In smaller cities, authority is more divided and mayors are generally weaker.

A form of government used in many cities of under 500,000 is the council-manager plan. This plan was first formulated in 1910 by municipal reformers. The idea was to separate powers by giving administrative authority to a professional manager hired by (and responsible to) an elected council, which acts as the sole policy-making body. Most city managers are not politicians but professional administrators, although, on occasion, they step into a political role. Banfield and Wilson find this plan mainly in upper-class or middle-class cities. In large cities and in lower-class cities it is not so popular. Professional poli-

ticians, who predominate in the large cities, tend to resist a plan that will displace them; lower-class voters prefer a governing plan that does not rely so much on an upper-class elite.

The commission form of government was once popular, but is now becoming obsolete. Under it, voters elect a commission, usually of five members. The commissioners combine policy-making and administrative responsibility, and each commissioner serves as chief executive of one of the city departments. Often the job proves too difficult; it is as if the cabinet were to be the sole executive and legislative authority in the federal government.

In addition to the city government proper, described above, there are other governing boards, commissions, councils, and special districts, which have functions of their own and may or may not have formal connections with the main city government.

City council members are most commonly elected in either district elections or at-large elections; some cities use a combination of the two. In the district system, a number of small political units elect representatives for the council. The advantages are that neighborhood interests can be directly represented and the citizen has relatively easy access to the council. The disadvantages are that it is difficult to get many local interests to act in unison on important city-wide matters and the special interests can exert more influence where power is fragmented. At-large council members are elected on a city-wide basis. This system sacrifices neighborhood representation for council members with a broader view of the city's needs. According to Banfield and Wilson,

> to a large extent, the choice between an at-large and a district system turns on the conception that one has of the nature of the public interest. Those who think (as middle-class and upper-class people usually do) that the "city as a whole" has an interest which should be paramount will tend to favor the at-large system. On the other hand, those who think (as the lower class people generally do) that politics is a struggle for personal, neighborhood, or other special advantages will favor the district system.[111]

---

[109]"By now the evidence is overwhelming that society is cowering before a relatively small number of habitual adult and juvenile criminals. Plagued by an epidemic of juvenile crime, Wilmington, Delaware, compiled police statistics in 1976 showing that just sixteen local youths had committed 384 felonies in three years, including 93 separate burglaries, 64 robberies, 48 auto thefts, and 1 rape." (*Fortune,* March 1977, p. 206.)

[110]Banfield and Wilson, *City Politics,* p. 80.

[111]Banfield and Wilson, p. 95.

The district system tends to be used in cities with partisan elections; the at-large system is generally used with nonpartisan ballots—that is, where no candidate is identified by party affiliation. Of the cities with populations over five thousand, 61 percent are nonpartisan; of the cities with council-manager plans, 84 percent are nonpartisan, whereas only 44 percent of the mayor-council cities are nonpartisan.[112]

Around the turn of the century, reformers introduced nonpartisanship to curb the power of the city political machine and the party boss. The machine still thrives in a few cities, but its influence has greatly diminished, as its main source of votes—the immigrants—have needed the machine less and as both party and municipal reformers have had their way.

It is important to remember that

> the American city is not run by its politicians and bureaucrats alone. They have the help—often the hindrance as well—of a vast array of formal and informal associations, and of individuals who, although occupying no office and having no authority, nevertheless play important and sometimes leading parts in the making of public decisions.[113]

These influentials include civic associations, business groups, and organized labor. Civic and business leaders, especially, tend to enjoy a great deal of respect in their communities and have influence on local officials. Of course, the decentralized character of local government allows many points of access for all sorts of individuals and groups, whose interests may be self-serving or community-serving.

PROPOSALS FOR REFORM

Concocting theories of the proper relationship of the county to the city, of the neighborhood to the city, of the city to the metropolitan area, of the metropolitan area to the region, of the region to the states, or of the states to the nation has become a growth industry. Experts by the hundreds have come forward with their notions of how it all should be arranged. In studying their theories and in analyzing the problems that remain, one should always bear in mind the observation of Lewis Mumford that "all the colossal mistakes that have been made during the last quarter century in urban renewal, highway building, transportation, land use, and recreation have been made by highly qualified experts and specialists. . . ."[114]

The problem is in putting theory into practice. In fact, it all boils down to a few basics: Who is going to raise the money to run government, and how? How will the "have" governments share their bounty with the "have-not" governments? How will governments be prevented from wasting and stealing? How can governments best work together? What are the proper priorities of spending? What are the proper priorities of service? How are public employees inspired to serve? How are citizens induced not to cheat? Some of the answers are metaphysical—the vigilance of citizens, the morality of officials—but some can be found in adjusting the relationships of governments. Many proposals for reform go in two directions: toward bigger governmental units and toward smaller.

Toward Regionalism

How much relevance do the old boundaries have today? When the Constitution was adopted, we were a loose rural alliance, and the original thirteen states were appropriate units for addressing the experiment of that day. But in the intervening two hundred years, the rivers that initially provided convenient state boundaries also attracted urban centers. As these urban areas grew across state lines, so did the problems of the metropolis, without any reference to what the Founders had in mind when they wrote the Constitution. The Kansas City of Missouri and the Kansas City of Kansas share the same problems. The St. Louis of Missouri sprawls into Illinois, under different names. Cincinnati, Ohio, and Covington, Kentucky, are separated by the

---

[112]Banfield and Wilson, p. 150.

[113]Banfield and Wilson, p. 243.

[114]Mumford, *The Urban Prospect*, p. 209.

Ohio River, but they share the same crime, the same unemployment, and the same future. Camden, New Jersey, and Philadelphia, Pennsylvania, are bedded down together in the very same problems of pollution and congestion. And so it goes around the nation, the old borders having long ago become meaningless. Today more than a quarter of our population lives in thirty-eight interstate metropolitan areas—areas split into thousands of competing government jurisdictions.

Many academicians and political practitioners believe that the present design of federalism is too chaotic, its power too splintered.[115] The kind of fragmentation that puts their teeth on edge can be seen in the San Francisco Bay area: 8 counties, 73 cities, 201 special districts, and, ironically, 81 planning commissions. How can 81 separate planning commissions plan any one thing?[116]

Seldom have such areas taken more than the tentative first step toward regional planning and regional cooperation. Usually they have taken that first step only because the federal government has made regional planning a precondition for getting certain types of grants, such as for transportation, water treatment, sewage disposal, and housing problems.[117]

There are now about six hundred regional councils in operation, all trying to coordinate this kind of work. The cooperation that is required is not the kind Americans have adjusted to yet. They still think of themselves in relation to certain city names, certain county names, certain state names; they do not think of themselves regionally.

It is only fair to point out that unifying the service of several governmental units does not automatically increase effectiveness or reduce costs; sometimes it does, and sometimes it doesn't.

In 1930, there were 149,000 single-teacher elementary schools in the United States. Education "experts" claimed that these schools offered terrible training and were economically wasteful. So, a great national drive was launched to set up consolidated school systems. By 1972, there were only 1,475 single-teacher elementary schools left. The result? In 1977, a study by the National Institute of Education found that consolidation of rural schools had neither lowered the cost of education (sometimes it had raised the cost) nor increased the quality of education.

Fellows of the Urban Institute have found that cities of more than a million people spend three times more per capita on supplying police, fire, sanitation, and other services than cities with a population of less than 50,000. It's a regular escalator: the bigger the city, the higher the cost; with the budget really beginning to soar when the size of the city gets to about 250,000 people.[118] If several adjoining small cities shared, say, the same fire department, would the resulting cost follow this pattern? So far, experience has not given a clear-cut answer to such questions.

It is also fair to ask if regionalism might not impose the kind of majority rule that the Founders feared. Consider the San Francisco area, for example. If a regional government swallowed all the towns surrounding that metropolis to a distance of fifty miles, one of the towns would be Petaluma, forty miles to the north. As it happens, Petaluma does not want to be swallowed. In fact, Petaluma does not like rapid growth, nor does it enjoy being a part of the spreading Bay area. In 1972, Petaluma decided to slow its growth, and it passed an ordinance restricting new housing to five hundred units a year. It was a move applauded by environmental groups and damned by the construction industry. Builders appealed to the United States Supreme Court, and the justices decided that Petaluma had a

[115]See Advisory Commission on Intergovernmental Relations, *Regional Decision Making: New Strategies for Substate Districts* (Washington, D.C.: U.S. Government Printing Office, 1973).

[116]Hawkins, "Citizen Participation," p. 210.

[117]*Congressional Record*, S10720, June 26, 1976. The federal government is very inconsistent, however. Many important county executives have complained about the lack of a single, rational federal policy addressed to regional government. Very often the existing county governments, which could serve as an excellent beginning for regional governments linking several metropolitan areas, have been overlooked or bypassed by federal planners, who have preferred instead to create special area-wide agencies.

[118]Neal Peirce, syndicated column, September 22, 1975.

right to control its own growth.[119] That was an extremely important victory for Petaluma's chosen style of life. Would it have had the chance to make that decision if it had been part of a regional government dominated by San Francisco?

Regardless of whether consolidation would result in more efficiency and economy, the fact remains that most people don't want consolidated governments. They prefer the smaller governmental unit; they have a gut reaction against giantism. In the past two decades, consolidation proposals have been rejected by voters at a rate of three to one.[120]

Toward Neighborhood Control

Counterbalancing the experts who urge regionalism are others who think small; they propose predominant emphasis on neighborhood control.[121] For the most ardent believers, nothing short of full neighborhood autonomy will do.

One spokesman for this view, Milton Kotler, denounced city charters granted by the state as nothing more than "distributions of control [of the cities] between the political machines of downtown and the state government," a "division of spoils, which results when people do not have the sovereignty to constitute themselves." Kotler and his allies insist that the only fair and democratic way to set up a city government is by devising "city constitutions that distribute power among the neighborhoods and federate that power in a common city government."[122]

The problem with dividing up power among many narrow constituencies is that fewer interests will be represented within each, and the strongest interests will have outsize power and influence. Perhaps, though, there is some virtue in *combining* the approaches of regionalism and neighborhood control. Two notable spokesmen for this position are former Senator Fred R. Harris and former Mayor John V. Lindsay, who coauthored this advice:

> There is too much local "government" in the United States today: more than 80,000 units, an average of ninety-one for the typical metropolitan area. The typical metropolitan area also supports approximately 350 elected officials and hundreds of nonelected officials. Furthermore, states and our proliferating local jurisdictions today are in many ways political anomalies. Some of the things they do, like handling education, policing, and urban redevelopment, would be done better on a neighborhood-by-neighborhood basis. Other things cities do, like providing water and sewers and transportation, would be done better on a regional basis. Obviously, some functions could appropriately be under the auspices of either.[123]

This approach virtually wipes out the traditional big-city government and replaces it with both larger and smaller governmental units. Supporting this concept, too, is the prestigious Committee for Economic Development (CED), which, in 1970, proposed a two-tier system—

[119]*New York Times,* August 17, 1975. It is pleasant to be able to report that Petaluma's revolutionary decision has worked out very well. Whereas the town was growing at an almost dangerous rate—18 percent a year—in 1972, five years later it had settled down to a steady and healthy growth rate of 5 percent. City services were able to handle that growth very well. Moreover, it was enough to keep the local merchants prosperous. City officials were talking about continuing the "growth management" plan for another seven years. Builders, of course, were still unhappy.

[120]Robert B. Hawkins, Jr., "Regional versus Local Government," in *The Politics of Planning* (San Francisco: Institute for Contemporary Studies, 1976), p. 213. For more on people preferring small units of government, see Subcommittee on Intergovernmental Relations of the Committee on Government Operations, *Confidence and Concern: Citizens View Americans and Government,* 2 vols. (Washington, D.C.: U.S. Government Printing Office, 1973).

[121]The federal government helped neighborhoods to have a say in the administration of money through the Economic Opportunity Act of 1964, which called for "maximum feasible participation" of the people who would be affected by the act—the poor. Local officials, stunned by the mandate, at first tried to dodge the order. But a 1966 amendment to the act required that at least one-third of a Community Action Board's membership be poor people. Grudgingly, most officials obeyed the law. With the coming of the Nixon administration in 1969, the poverty program was phased out—but the precedent of neighborhood participation in the control of federal funds remains. (Melvin Mogulof, "Citizen Participation: Federal Policy," in Urofsky, ed., *Perspectives on Urban America,* p. 124.)

[122]Milton Kotler, *Neighborhood Government: The Local Foundations of Political Life* (Indianapolis: Bobbs-Merrill, Co., 1969), pp. 104–05.

[123]Fred R. Harris and John V. Lindsay, *The State of the Cities: Report of the Commission on Cities in the '70s* (New York: Praeger Publishers, 1972), p. 100.

neighborhood or community districts within a regional or metropolitan government. Major services would be offered by the larger government, but the way it was offered would be determined by the smaller unit. For example, the larger government would provide garbage and trash pickup service, but the neighborhood governments would decide how often pickup would occur. The regional police department would have control over crime laboratories, records, communications, and detective work, but the neighborhood government would control street patrol.[124]

Still another unique approach has been offered for solving the problems of the major cities—cities like Houston, Detroit, Philadel-

[124]Harris and Lindsay, pp. 100–01.

phia, and New York, each of which has a larger population than any one of fifteen states. Lindsay proposes that such places be treated as "national cities"—deserving their own federal charter. This would place them essentially on a level with states and would thereby allow them to deal directly with Washington on matters of finance and social welfare. And they would be freed from ties with unresponsive and sometimes jealous state governments.[125]

Criteria for Good Government

Whatever the approach, the problem must be treated with a certain amount of flexibility and modesty, redefining terms and redefining goals. Duane Lockhard reminds us: "Any worthwhile approach to the problems of proper location of powers among governmental units will have to eschew categorical, sweeping generalizations and look to more rigorous forms of reasoning."[126] Lockhard suggests these criteria for measuring the success of government:

• *Is it arbitrary? If so, is it arbitrary for the right reasons?* The stupidities of the central government often arise from rules that have little relevance to a situation a thousand miles from Washington. Such rules promote the yearning for decentralized government. However, sometimes arbitrary rules are beneficial. The arbitrary civil rights rules handed down by Washington beginning in the 1960s were viewed by many residents of the South as "impossible" to carry out; but when the "unreasonable" central government continued to demand the "impossible," the local governments found that civil rights rules could be administered after all.

The practical test of the success of any government, including a democracy, is not how freely the individual is permitted to participate in it, but how restrained it is from intruding into the life of the individual. It is a hollow democracy indeed where individuals find themselves offered total enfranchisement, free and open access to the seat of government, where they know the mayor and city council members by their first names, where they get to go down weekly to the town hall and unload their opinions about what should and shouldn't be done, and where, despite their great "democratic" input, they find government trespassing over virtually every activity they are engaged in, as local governments tend to do. So the question should be, in judging the proper locale of governmental power: Does it *minimize* arbitrary rulings that clutter up life with bureaucratic whims? And does it *maximize* the arbitrariness that is necessary temporarily to overcome local prejudices that conflict with the best impulses of the nation and with the principles of the Constitution?

• *How sensitive is the government to democratic pressures?* Big Government usually doesn't start taking its citizens seriously until they begin speaking up in large numbers. But that doesn't mean that an individual citizen or a minority group will necessarily get a more sympathetic hearing at the state or local level. As was pointed out earlier, small governmental units are subject to being captured by a few dominant interests in the constituency. Sometimes better protection and care of ordinary citizens are achieved through a broader based political unit.

A city's ruling elite, dominated by the business community, will often gladly jettison democracy for the sake of (relative) efficiency. Mayor Richard Daley of Chicago, perhaps the last of the old-fashioned city bosses, ran a taut administration through patronage at the bottom and sweetheart deals at the top. When he died, many of the business executives of Chicago mourned. The President of the Association of Commerce and Industry was quoted as saying, "There's nothing wrong with a benevolent dictatorship."[127]

• *Is the governmental unit efficient?* One way to measure efficiency is by measuring the work done against the financial investment. If the taxpayer pays for three thousand trash collectors when fifteen hundred should be able to do the work, that portion of the government is probably inefficient. On the other hand, if the three thousand collectors turn in not simply an adequate cleanup job, but a job that makes the city sparkle

---

[125]Harris and Lindsay, pp. 101–02.

[126]Duane Lockhart, *The Politics of State and Local Government* (New York: Macmillan, 1969), p. 47.

[127]Quoted in the *Chicago Sun Times*, January 10, 1977.

like a new Athens, they may be considered a luxury of efficiency.

But efficiency must also be measured by what is done and for whom. The service must be equitable. If the street department is very swift and thorough at repairing a few pot holes in one part of town (where the mayor lives), but very indifferent about paving the streets at all in the low-income section of town, it can hardly be called efficient. When the FBI is very diligent about chasing car thieves, but very reluctant to go after multibillion-dollar organized crime syndicates, it isn't giving the taxpayers the most for their money. In short, efficiency must be measured not strictly by statistics, but also by that indefinite yardstick called quality of life.

Every time there is a convention of governors, mayors, or county executives, there is a great outpouring of rhetoric about the need to clarify and tidy up the divisions of power. It is a yearning for what Orville L. Freeman, former Governor of Minnesota, called

the layer-cake absolute that calls for neat division between federal and state governments. This myth ought to have been demolished by decades of repudiation in practice, but there is still a widespread wistful notion that all this is temporary and that one of these days, when we just put our minds to it, we will sort out the functions of government and put the cake back into the proper layers.[128]

----

[128]Quoted in Frank Trippett, *The States: United They Fell* (Cleveland: World Publishing Co., 1967), p. 56.

If the size of the nation and its population had remained static at the level of 1787, such yearnings might make sense; in those days Madison could reasonably talk about "the great and aggregate interests being referred to the national, and the local and particular to the states legislatures."[129] It was an era of reasonably simple division. But if the Founders had their job to do today, confronted with cities as populated as 1787 nations, with states as populated as 1787 regions, with a nation as sprawling as Columbus's world, they would probably write a different Constitution. That would be a mistake as well as a waste of time. With the number and complexity of the governmental units that must be dealt with in this nation, federalism cannot be reduced to a specific constitutional formula. When federalism does work, it is not simply because the Constitution dictates certain balances, but because the relationship of the levels of government is in constant change—adapting to complaints, adapting to ambitions, adapting to provincialisms and inflated egos, negating occasional pushiness by the federal government, overcoming the cravenness of local officials on other occasions, always juggling funds, always trading off priorities, making a total mess of the "layer-cake," and discovering that it is in that awful, jumbled mess that the unity of federalism is achieved.

----

[129]Quoted in Trippett, p. 56.

Summary

1. Using the concept of federalism, the framers of the Constitution divided powers between the central government and the states. They gave important powers to the national government, but all powers not specifically delegated to it were reserved to the states.

2. The diversity of governmental interests and the diversity of private interests in America were considered a healthy balancing and a protection to minorities.

3. Federal powers have expanded greatly over the years, but the states have also grown in influence.

4. Welfare federalism—the policy of federal subsidies for state and local social programs—began with the New Deal in the 1930s and escalated in the following decades. Because the federal grants require the states to match funds, state spending has mushroomed to a point of overspending.

5. A controversy centers on how many federal strings should be attached to federal aid. Block grants and general revenue sharing, which replaced categorical grants, allow state and local governments to set their own spending priorities to a large extent.

6. Federal intervention in the distribution of funds is perhaps necessary, since the federal government is a better account keeper and tends to be more innovative and responsive than the states. Also, the smaller the political unit, the more likely it is to be dominated by special interests.

7. The states tend to be weak partners in the federal system because of their changeable constitutions, weak governors, autonomous administrative agencies, unprofessional legislatures, timid courts, unorganized parties, and too-powerful interest groups.

8. The states have excelled in some areas—in the use of the initiative, referendum, and recall; in providing emergency action; and in leading the federal government in some reforms.

9. Local governments are created by the state, but they build up autonomy. The main problems in local government are the "invisibility" of its decision making and the fragmentation of power resulting from multiple political units.

10. The county is the main seat of government for most rural Americans. Although there are great needs in rural areas, there are insufficient funds to deal with them.

11. The suburbs are the fastest growing parts of the metropolitan areas. Most suburban dwellers have fled the problems of the city and want nothing further to do with them. This self-imposed isolation puts the suburbs somewhat in limbo in the system of local government.

12. With the out-migration of middle-class residents, the cities are losing their tax base and increasing their percentage of poor and aged residents. Few cities have the wealth to deal with such deep problems as unemployment, poverty, and crime, but they can improve their administration.

13. Cities tend to use one of three forms of government—the mayor-council plan, the council-manager plan, or the commission.

14. Proposed reforms for local government go in two directions—toward regionalism and toward neighborhood control. Each has its drawbacks, so some reformers have suggested combining the best of both systems.

15. A good government meets these criteria: it is not arbitrary, unless there is a good reason to be so; it is sensitive to democratic pressures; and it is efficient and equitable in providing services.

Additional Reading

General treatments of federalism include Daniel J. Elazar, *American Federalism: A View from the States,* 2nd ed. (New York: Thomas Y. Crowell Co., 1972); Morton Grodzins, *The American System: A New View of Government in the United States,* ed. Daniel J. Elezar (Skokie, Ill.: Rand McNally & Co., 1967); William H. Riker, *Federalism: Origin, Operation, Significance* (Boston: Little, Brown and Co., 1964); James L. Sundquist and David W. Davis, *Making Federalism Work: A Study of Program Coordination at the Community Level* (Washington, D.C.: Brookings Institution, 1969); and Michael D. Reagan, *The New Federalism* (New York: Oxford University Press, 1972).

On state politics, see Duane Lockard, *The Politics of State and Local Government,* 2nd ed. (New York: Macmillan, 1969), and Herbert Jacob and Kenneth N. Vines, eds. *Politics in the American States: A Comparative Analysis,* 3rd ed. (Boston: Little, Brown and Co., 1976).

Edward C. Banfield and James Q. Wilson, *City Politics* (Cambridge, Mass.: Harvard University Press, 1963), and Charles E. Gilbert, *Governing the Suburbs* (Bloomington, Ind.: Indiana University Press, 1967), give comprehensive treatments of city and suburban government. Wallace S. Sayre and Herbert Kaufman, *Governing New York City* (New York: Russell Sage Foundation, 1960) is a full (though now somewhat old) analysis of that city's politics. Robert A. Dahl's *Who Governs: Democracy and Power in an American City* (New Haven, Conn.: Yale University Press, 1961), a study of the government of New Haven, Connecticut, offers important inferences about pluralism in the United States; it argues against the elite analysis of Floyd Hunter's *Community Power Structure* (Chapel Hill, N.C.: University of North Carolina Press, 1953), a study of the government of Atlanta, Georgia.

Arthur J. Vidich and Joseph Bensman, *Small Town in Mass Society: Class, Power and Religion in a Rural Community,* rev. ed. (Princeton, N.J.: Princeton University Press, 1968) is an intriguing analysis of the politics and social structure of a small town in New York state. Alan A. Altschuler, *Community Control: The Black Demand for Participation in Large American Cities* (New York: Pegasus, 1970), discusses politics at the community level.

14
FOREIGN POLICY

The political activity that is called foreign relations generally means butting into other nations' affairs for selfish reasons.[1] Every government in the world does it, and the devices they use are varied: threats of war,[2] threats of economic retaliation, appeals to pity, promises of future cooperation, reminders of past cooperation, loans of money, loans of territory, loans or gifts of food, assassinations, bribes, and heavy propaganda assaults. At their worst, foreign relations are the making of war on the battlefield. Even at their best, relations between nations are a struggle—though perhaps friendly for the most part—between peoples and economic systems. "At its very essence," writes Leslie Gelb, director of Politico-Military Affairs for the State Department, "foreign policy is the extension of the power and the influence of one nation over the affairs of other nations."[3]

As has already been shown throughout this book, the balancing and containment of selfish interests is often a very difficult and delicate matter to achieve in domestic affairs; in foreign affairs it is a hundred times more difficult. When California and Arizona quarrel over water rights to the Colorado River, their differences are, to some extent, muted by the constant awareness of both states that they share the same national destiny and are governed by the same laws. In a dispute of that sort, both sides will give and bend under the pressure of a larger patriotism. But when Iceland and England quarrel over fishing rights in the North Atlantic or when the United States and Russia quarrel over atmospheric testing of atomic weapons, neither side is much influenced by a spirit of community. Nations are rarely measurably influenced by a feeling of global oneness. They are influenced by fear, by the desire for profit, by the desire to protect

---

[1]Some activities—such as disaster and famine relief—are less selfish than others. And sometimes the "intrusion" is at the invitation of the other country.

[2]Sometimes the threat of peace is also used. When Premier Nguyen Van Thieu of South Vietnam got mad at the United States for not giving him all the aid he wanted, he threatened to stop fighting the communists in his country.

[3]Leslie Gelb, "Should We Play Dirty Tricks in the World?" *New York Times Magazine,* December 21, 1975.

property or national pride, by the need of another nation's protection, or by the knowledge that giving on one point may gain an advantage on another, larger point. These are all practical considerations that come back to one central, selfish rule: get everything you can without risking national security or national prosperity.

The above motivations are those that impel nations or governments. But it should always be borne in mind that foreign affairs are conducted by *individual* persons, who are inspired and depressed, angered and soothed in exactly the same way as everyone else by the pressures and comforts of life. When Graham Martin, the last United States ambassador to South Vietnam before its collapse, was called before Congress to defend his unorthodox and sometimes seemingly irrational conduct, he told his critics that "my wife has assured me that the historians will treat me very kindly."[4] One tends to forget that those who make or carry out foreign policy, affecting the lives of billions of people, actually have spouses who face them across the breakfast table and tell them to cheer up.

Foy Kohler, one of the United States' best known ambassadors, recalled a reception in Moscow where Russian Deputy Prime Minister Anastas Mikoyan, who was slightly drunk, made a toast to "peaceful coexistence with the capitalist world." Premier Chou En-lai of Communist China, who wanted to make no friendly gesture to the imperialists, refused to lift his glass, and he scolded Mikoyan for his toast. Then Russian Minister of Defense Rodion Malinovsky, who was also slightly drunk, made a toast denouncing the United States. This angered Ambassador Kohler, who stalked toward the door. Soviet Prime Minister Aleksei Kosygin headed him off and pacified him. This once again visibly infuriated Chou. And so it continued all evening.[5] Foreign policy is affected, at least around the edges, by such temper tantrums. In short, as the distinguished career diplomat Charles W. Yost has said,

> It is important to keep in mind . . . that foreign affairs are conducted not by rules but by men, by

leaders and peoples conditioned by pride, fear, vanity, and every other variety of human emotion, and that the rational objects put forward in explanation of policy are all too frequently rationalizations of these emotions.

The conduct of foreign affairs is too often reminiscent of small boys playing soldiers or king of the mountain, of juvenile gangs competing for territory and machismo. One sometimes wishes that the Great Earth Mother might one day appear, sweep up their toys and regalia, and send them all off to school or to bed.

The tragedy is that no one, or so it seems, can stop playing the game or change its objects until everyone else does. All of us, at least the big powers, have more or less to stop or to change together, and that is not easy to arrange.[6]

AMERICA'S ROLE IN THE WORLD

When Thomas Jefferson ran the State Department two hundred years ago, he needed only a staff of half a dozen people and an annual budget of a little more than six thousand dollars.[7] Today the State Department (which by itself does not even begin to handle all elements of civilian foreign affairs) has a budget of more than $1.2 billion and employs 29,000 people.[8]

At the outbreak of World War II, we were exchanging diplomats with 60 nations. In 1973, we were appointing resident emissaries to 132 countries—and the State Department acknowledged that we would soon have full diplomatic relations with 160 or more nations.

---

[4]Quoted in the *Washington Post*, January 21, 1976.

[5]Robert Sherrill, interview with Foy Kohler, *Lithopinion*, Fall 1973.

[6]Robert Sherrill, interview with Charles W. Yost, *Lithopinion*, Fall 1973, pp. 20–23.

[7]Elmer Plischke, *United States Diplomats and Their Missions: A Profile of American Diplomatic Emissaries Since 1778* (Washington, D.C.: American Enterprise Institute, 1975).

[8]It costs a lot of money to keep the embassies open in these perilous days. Between 1965 and 1975, thirteen United States diplomats were killed by assassins; twelve were wounded; twenty were kidnapped and later released. To protect its ambassadors, the United States spends money like this: In Buenos Aires our ambassador has a limousine that cost the United States taxpayers $50,000; each tire weighs 150 pounds; the windows and the steel body are 2 inches thick. In case of a grenade attack, the driver can throw a switch that envelops the car in foam in a matter of seconds. The annual cost of embassy guards and marines is $800,000. (*New Republic*, March 22, 1975.)

Expansionism, either territorial or economic, has been a hallmark of United States policy from the beginning. The entire nineteenth century was taken up with continental expansion accomplished both through negotiation and militarily. The Indians were simply driven off this country's habitable land and confined to reservations; Mexican land adjacent to California was preempted by force. Meanwhile, diplomacy engineered the purchases of Louisiana, Florida, and Alaska.

An important foreign policy formulated in the nineteenth century was the Monroe Doctrine, which notified Europe of United States hegemony in the Western Hemisphere. As Marion D. Irish and Elke Frank point out, "by the beginning of this century the Monroe Doctrine was usually identified with 'Yankee Imperialism' and 'dollar diplomacy.' . . . The most compelling cause for concern about the Latin American situation was the matter of commerce."[9] As United States trade and investment prospered in Latin America and in Asia, American business executives increasingly pressured the government to protect their interests there. Thus, Theodore Roosevelt went stomping about in Asia advocating an Open Door (or a Busted Door) policy; he justified various intrusions into Latin America as an exercise of the Monroe Doctrine. He said the United States would serve as the hemispheric police officer, keeping European powers out and forcing Latin American countries to pay their debts. Several decades later, Franklin Roosevelt set up his Good Neighbor policy in Latin America.

Spokesman for the Western World

By 1940, the United States had established itself as a major power in the world, but it was not until the end of World War II that the country was forced to accept a great deal of responsibility in exchange for its power. In 1945, our economic and military strength, and the fact that we were far less scarred by the war than the other major nations were (the United States lost 405,000 people in the war, compared to 20 million Rus-

sian deaths, for example[10]), established us in a new position of responsibility. Suddenly, what we did or did not do affected every other nation on the globe. Whether western Europe would be able to build its way back from the war's havoc or whether it would falter and sink into a massive depression depended entirely on the United States' generosity, or lack of it. Whether the advocates of communism would be able to move into the power vacuums and into the disturbed areas of the globe, especially in the war-wracked nations of western Europe, or whether these areas would continue to maintain a noncommunist (although often anything but democratic) position, would depend largely on the willingness of the United States to give financial support to noncommunist political parties and noncommunist labor unions. In short, the United States was thrust into the role of spokesman and banker of the noncommunist world.

It did its work sometimes with great imagination and humanity, sometimes with meanness, but always with a gun near at hand. From the late 1940s, writes Adam Yarmolinsky, "American thinking about foreign policy was substantially military in character."[11]

We consider ourselves a peaceful nation, but since our beginning two hundred years or so ago, we have spent thirty-five years fighting major wars, with scraps of time given over to more than a hundred limited campaigns besides. Adding up the cost of all our military preparations and military adventures over these two centuries, the total comes to at least two trillion twenty-two billion dollars—or about 56 percent of our federal government's spending for *all* purposes. In the last thirty years, we spent about as much on national defense as we had spent for *all* nonmilitary goods and services since our nation began.[12]

World War II was the great watershed. Before that, there were periods when an isolationist

---

[9]Marian D. Irish and Elke Frank, *U.S. Foreign Policy: Context, Conduct, Content* (New York: Harcourt Brace Jovanovich, 1975), p. 400.

[10]Gabriel Kolko, *The Politics of War: The World and U.S. Foreign Policy, 1943–1945* (New York: Random House, 1969), p. 19.

[11]Adam Yarmolinsky, *The Military Establishment: Its Impacts on American Society* (New York: Harper & Row, Publishers, 1971), p. 120.

[12]Allan L. Damon, "Defense Spending," *American Heritage*, February 1975.

Does Stability Justify Repression?

It is not, after all, an historical accident that democracy is almost extinct in Latin America, or that the major U.S. allies across the world—South Korea, the Philippines, Thailand, Iran, Zaire, and Brazil—are dictatorships, propped up by the bayonet and the lash. Over the years, the U.S. with its enormous public and private investment and political and economic involvement in these countries has been directly implicated in the spread of repression.

In Latin America, for example, the U.S. has armed and trained the military which now govern throughout the hemisphere. Over 30,000 Latin American officers from dozens of countries have been trained at the U.S.-run School of the Americas in Panama since it opened shop in 1949. They have imbibed the American teaching on subversion, counter-insurgency, and anti-communism. They were taught to see themselves as a force of rationality and efficiency above politics, holding the national trust from subversion. They learned, as [Arthur] Schlesinger wrote of the Kennedy policy, that while the U.S. preferred democracy, it would always support a stable dictatorship to fend off a marxist alternative. Thus when the political situation grew volatile in Brazil, Uruguay, Ecuador, Argentina, Peru, Bolivia, and in Chile, the military intervened to establish order.

The national security doctrines of the military have been reinforced by the economic demands made by private and public financial institutions. American corporations and banks demand stability as precondition for large loans and investment. They seek a docile labor force, a tranquil political situation, guarantees against expropriation. In Latin America such conditions are often purchased only by bayonet.

The U.S. has also played a more active and direct role in the establishment of dictatorships. In Ecuador, in Brazil, in Chile, and throughout Latin America, the Central Intelligence Agency has been actively involved in subverting the democratic process—fixing elections, spreading black propaganda, bribing officials, toppling the unreliable or unfriendly. It is not surprising that these Latin American regimes are bemused by the new [U.S.] policy extolling human rights. . . .

President Carter has acknowledged that the United States is the world's great merchant of death, having cornered some 50% of the world armaments market. . . . According to the U.S. Arms Control and Disarmament Agency, the United States exported some $24.5 billion or 53% of all arms acquired by underdeveloped countries over the 10 year period from 1965 to 1974. . . . In 1974, Senator Alan Cranston reported that some 69% of the countries receiving military grants, and 58% of those receiving military credit sales were "repressive regimes."

From Robert L. Borosage, "Foreign Policy and Human Rights: An Agenda," *First Principles* 2, no. 10 (June 1977).

spirit was interspersed with a bellicose spirit in shaping our foreign policy. But since World War II, the bellicose spirit has been almost constant. In the past three decades, according to a study by the Brookings Institution, the United States deployed its military forces for political impact abroad at least 215 times.[13] We maintain the world's greatest arsenal, the world's largest army, navy, and air force, and the world's largest defense industry. The State Department shapes some of our foreign policy, but the Pentagon shapes an even larger share. The quest for "national security" has created an atmosphere in which our leaders have, with increasing frequency, acted beyond the law, as when they subjected the neutral nation Cambodia to thirty-five hundred secret bombing raids over a fourteen-month period.[14] In the name of "national security," our diplomats and military leaders have helped frustrate democratic movements in a number of countries and have propped up right-wing regimes. They poured millions of

[13]*Brookings Institution Bulletin,* January 2, 1977.

[14]*New York Times,* April 17, 1973.

dollars into the secret, successful effort to over-throw the democratically elected regime of President Salvador Allende in Chile simply because Allende was a socialist who had offended several powerful United States corporations and opposed our attitude toward Cuba.

Between the mid-1950s and mid-1960s, more than half of all United States aid to Asia went to South Korea, Nationalist China, and Vietnam—each of which was ruled during most or all of this decade by a dictator.[15] In 1973, shortly after Park Chung Hee had set himself up as dictator of South Korea via martial law and had launched a program of torture, imprisonment, and execution of anyone who criticized his rule, the United States ambassador to South Korea suggested that Secretary of State Henry A. Kissinger and President Richard M. Nixon publicly condemn what was going on. Both refused to do so and ordered the ambassador to maintain a hands-off policy. Our official position was that a repressive South Korea was still our ally, and that was all that mattered.[16]

---

[15]Yarmolinsky, *The Military Establishment,* p. 121.

[16]*Washington Post,* May 17, 1976.

The same attitude has been emphasized, but in a more hypocritical context, in the Carter administration. The showpiece portion of Carter's foreign policy was an evangelistic drive for "human rights." Carter, Vice President Walter Mondale, and other spokesmen for the administration quickly established the impression that nations noted for suppressing civil rights and for torturing political dissidents would not be looked on as friends of this nation and would not receive aid from us until they showed a willingness to reform. But no sooner had Carter made his rhetorical point than he began to back away from it. In regard to South Korea, for instance, he said that its notorious cruelty to political dissidents would not prevent the United States from giving it military and economic support. Moreover, against heavy congressional opposition, Carter urged the sale of some of our most sophisticated military equipment to Iran, where political dissent was brutally suppressed as a matter of policy. Carter argued that Iran would use the weapons to serve our interests in the Middle East and would act as a bulwark against the potential of Russian aggression. Viewing Carter's human rights foreign policy, Richard J. Barnet noted that the administration seemed to be dividing the

American troops support South Korean defenses near the thirty-eighth parallel, summer 1976

world into two categories, "countries unimportant enough to be hectored about human rights and countries important enough to get away with murder."[17]

In all of these activities, military considerations—winning a strategic emplacement of missile bases or gaining the right to establish submarine bases, for example—were as crucial to the federal government's policy shapers as were the economic or ideological considerations.

Lots of Entangling Alliances

We have come a long way—whether in the right direction or not is another consideration—since President Washington's Farewell Address of 1796. In it he advised the new nation to have "as little political connection as possible" with foreign nations. "Our detached and distant situation invites and enables us to pursue a different course," he said, "to steer clear of permanent alliances with any portion of the foreign world, so far . . . as we are now at liberty to do it" and to "safely trust to temporary alliances for extraordinary emergencies."[18]

The mind-our-own-business spirit conveyed by that advice was characteristic of United States foreign policy until 1940. (It did not really conflict with the inevitable expansionist spirit, which was able to operate without the benefit, or hindrance, of entangling alliances.) In the late 1930s, we were tied to other nations only by a few trade treaties. Only a few hundred United States troops were stationed in foreign countries, and these largely filled a ritualistic role at embassies. In 1935, Congress had, as a precaution against entangling alliances that might drag us into war, passed the Neutrality Act. It provided for an embargo on the export of arms and munitions to all belligerents.[19]

Today, in dramatic contrast, the United States is tied to even the remotest nations through military and trade agreements. The military tally alone finds us involved with 60 percent of the countries of the world—ninety-two nations in 1975—through treaties, executive agreements, arms sales, and several kinds of military grant assistance. The best known tie between this country and Europe is the North Atlantic Treaty Organization, whose member nations have pledged support of a standing NATO military force for mutual defense. In its Bicentennial year, the United States had come so far from George Washington's advice as to have 686,000 military-related personnel stationed abroad at 222 major and about 2,000 minor bases in at least forty countries. And about half of all United States tactical nuclear weapons were placed outside the borders of the United States.[20]

But if the United States has gone abroad in what sometimes seems to be the uniform of the Western world's police officer, it has also sometimes gone as a great benefactor. As of 1975, the United States had distributed more than $5 billion in free food to children, nursing mothers, workers, refugees, and disaster victims in more than one hundred countries.[21]

Because of the great blow to the nation's pride that accompanied its defeat in South Vietnam, the 1970s saw a mild revival of the isolationist spirit that was so pervasive before World War II. But the rural and ethnic base upon which isolationism was once built is gone. And most Americans would agree with Irving Kristol that "a great power does not have the freedom of action—derived from the freedom of inaction—that a small power possesses. It is entangled in a web of responsibilities from which there is no hope of escape."[22]

The question, then, is not whether we should be widely involved abroad, but *how* our foreign policy developed and *how* and *why* we manage our foreign affairs as we do today. Several theories have been set forth. Some stress the importance of the interaction of nation-states, each making its own policy to advance its own interests. Some theories put more emphasis on the

[17]Richard J. Barnet, "U.S. Needs Modest, Uniform Stand on Human Rights," *Los Angeles Times*, March 13, 1977.

[18]Quoted in Robert W. Tucker, *A New Isolationism: Threat or Promise?* (Washington, D.C.: Potomac Associates, 1972), p. 25.

[19]See Arthur A. Ekirch, Jr., *The Civilian and the Military: A History of the American Antimilitarist Tradition* (Colorado Springs, Colo.: Ralph Myles, 1972), pp. 243–44.

[20]*Center for Defense Information* 4, no. 6 (August 1975).

[21]*Washington Post*, March 13, 1975.

[22]Irving Kristol, "American Intellectuals and Foreign Policy," *Foreign Affairs*, July 1967, p. 602.

organizational process in decision making and regard policy as the outcome of systematic, rational choices. Others emphasize the interests of those within the organization and regard policy as the result of bureaucratic bargaining.[23] From this last perspective, "in order to understand why certain decisions are made one must first identify who participated in the decision and what stakes they had in the outcome."[24] No one theory adequately covers the field. Foreign-policy making probably cannot be cast into one mold. A beginning to the answer of how and why foreign policy develops perhaps can be found in four general categories: ideology, military power, economics, and diplomacy.

IDEOLOGY: THE PASSION OF FOREIGN POLICY

The two most influential people in the making of United States foreign policy (and, indirectly—by drawing the budget to the military side—in the shaping of domestic policy) during this and the immediate past generations have been Joseph Stalin, the absolute ruler of the Soviet Union from the 1920s until his death in 1953, and Senator Joseph McCarthy, a two-term Republican senator from Wisconsin, who died in 1957.

It may be difficult to believe that the influence of these two men continues to be powerful even though their personal reputations have suffered ruin. Stalin is now acknowledged to have been a sexual sadist in his private life and a megalomaniac in his public life. By 1960, the Soviet leaders had come to the conclusion that Stalin's very name was loathesome; it was eliminated from all regions, cities, and other sites; his body was removed from the Lenin-Stalin tomb in Moscow so that the millions of Russians who go there to honor Lenin's bones each year would not be tempted to think kindly of Stalin as well. McCarthy was censured by the Senate in 1954 for disgraceful conduct, and he died of alcoholism two and a half years later, his name a permanent political symbol for witch hunting and sleazy opportunism.

Stalin was an architect of our foreign policy in that he instilled in our leaders and in the general American population a heightened fear of what were then (and still are, by many) seen as satanic forces. His Tartar eyes and his inscrutable face, dominated by a heavy mustache, fitted him very well for the role of the insidious foreigner bent on conquest. And his lumbering Marxist rhetoric supported all our fears. In recent years, revisionist historians have questioned whether the goal of Russian expansionism was eventual world hegemony or whether it was simply to establish a secure front against a third world war, and they have questioned whether the Russian government used ideology to subvert noncommunist countries or simply to rally the Russian people to the task of reconstruction after the war. Whatever Stalin's motives, contemporary Americans chose to take at face value his speech on February 9, 1946, in which he proclaimed the inevitability of war between communist and capitalist nations. And they viewed with mounting concern the ruthless Soviet tactics in eastern Europe. The fears that such rhetoric and actions aroused were fanned into hysteria by Senator McCarthy, who hopped the anti-Red bandwagon with a vengeance in the early 1950s, carrying foreign-policy makers along with him. Whether or not Stalin and McCarthy believed their own rhetoric, and regardless of whether they used their power simply for personal aggrandizement, the effect has been to crystalize a cold war ideology that has influenced foreign-policy decisions for decades.[25]

From Ally to Enemy

During World War II, the United States called Russia an ally, but anyone who was against the German-Italian axis was considered an *ad hoc* ally. That did not mean we liked or admired the Russians; it only meant that, for the moment, we found them useful. The United States and Brit-

---

[23]See Graham T. Allison, *Essence of Decision: Explaining the Cuban Missile Crisis* (Boston: Little, Brown and Co., 1971).

[24]Irish and Frank, *U.S. Foreign Policy*, p. 331.

[25]Some historians have also suggested that United States policy makers deliberately exploited cold war ideology to wage economic war in the name of anticommunism. Whatever the case, fear of communism had certainly become deeply rooted in the American mentality.

ain were eager to come out of the war with an advantage over Russia, and Russia was constantly jockeying to outmaneuver the United States and Britain in a settlement to the war. There was, however, stiff disagreement between Britain and the United States as to how best to conclude the war. Britain's leaders, for example, wanted the allied troops to drive swiftly forward to Vienna, Berlin, and Prague as soon as German resistance melted—and thereby push back Russia's potential postwar territorial demands. But General Dwight D. Eisenhower, then supreme commander of the Allied Expeditionary Force, opposed this move, with the result that Russia wound up controlling not only most of eastern Europe, but dominating much of central Europe, too.

The total defeat of Germany left a power vacuum in central Europe, which engaged the vital interests of both the Russians and the Western powers. Despite its staggering losses in the war, Russia survived as the most powerful military force in Europe, by far. The only Western nation capable of meeting a Soviet challenge was the United States. And so the two squared off, communism versus capitalism. It was the beginning of the cold war.

The goal of the United States since then has been in three parts, all interrelated: to avoid an atomic war, to weaken the communist alliance, and to draw the uncommitted nations of the world into the United States orbit of influence. The goal of Russia has been precisely the same, but from its own perspective, of course: to avoid an atomic war, to weaken the Western alliance, and to draw the uncommitted nations into its orbit.[26] One can always say, of course, that Russia pursues its goals unethically, fiendishly, callously, or whatever, but that does not change the fact that Russia's goals have really been no different from our own. And their suspicions of us have been, for at least a generation, exactly the same as our suspicions of them—the worst.

Summing up his impressions of the Potsdam Conference of 1945 (attended by Harry S Truman, Winston Churchill, and Joseph Stalin),

President Truman later wrote, "The Russians were planning world conquest."[27] The Soviet leaders suspected that we had the same motivation. Even our kindnesses were interpreted as sly efforts to dominate the world. When the United States offered food and machinery to help rebuild postwar Europe, Russia rejected the offer. Soviet Foreign Minister Andrey Vyshinsky explained why: "This plan is an attempt to split Europe into two camps" and fashion an armed bloc "hostile to the interests of the Soviet Union." Nor would Russia allow any of her satellite states to receive American aid.[28]

This mutual suspicion and distrust was not something that had developed within a few years—it was longstanding. The concept of communism and the image of the bearded Bolshevik were things that United States leaders had used to frighten the public for generations—like parents evoking the spectre of goblins to frighten children into behaving. In the nineteenth century, Britain suffered from what one historian has called "Russophobia"—a crazed fear and suspicion of what was occurring on the frozen steppes of Russia.[29] That madness spread across the Atlantic and infected America. With the overthrow of the czar and the establishment of a communist dictatorship in Russia in 1917, the middle class and the upper class in Europe and in America became panicky at the thought that perhaps this was the first step in a worldwide revolution that would destroy the right to private property. Only gradually and reluctantly did America and its leaders adjust to the fact that Russian communism was on the globe to stay. Dwight Eisenhower wrote, "In spite of America's recognition of the USSR in 1933, the Communist regime in the Kremlin had always been viewed suspiciously, with reason, by our people. Throughout the years, the two nations had had few fruitful communications."[30]

---

[26]Willy Brandt, *The Ordeal of Coexistence: The Gustav Pollack Lectures at Harvard University* (Cambridge, Mass.: Harvard University Press, 1963), p. 19.

[27]Harry S Truman, *Memoirs,* 2 vols. (New York: Doubleday & Co., 1958), Vol. 1.

[28]Michael Gibson, *Russia under Stalin* (New York: G. P. Putnam's Sons, 1972), pp. 112–13.

[29]Elisabeth Barker, *The Cold War* (New York: G. P. Putnam's Sons, 1972), p. 23.

[30]Dwight D. Eisenhower, *The White House Years* (New York: Doubleday & Co., 1963), Vol. 1.

Stalin, Truman, and Churchill arrive at the first session of the Potsdam Conference, 1945

One reason for the failure of communication was that for many years both United States and Russian leaders insisted on measuring the other side with an ideological yardstick. To the Russian leaders, all our politicians were "imperialistic warmongers." To many, if not most, United States leaders, the communists were motivated by satanic principles. Typical of the simplistic jargon one heard on our side was Eisenhower's observation that there exists an unbreachable "ideological gulf between a government which is atheistic and one which is religiously based."[31] Communists studied Marx on Sundays; capitalists went to church and thought nice thoughts. In 1947, President Truman offered a similar view of the gulf between East and West when he said

that communism was "the evil soil of poverty and strife," while democracy was "based upon the will of the majority . . . free elections . . . guarantees of individual liberty . . . freedom of speech."[32]

McCarthyism

How did Senator Joe McCarthy fit into all this? By exploiting the xenophobic fear of communism with more success, and more devasta-

---

[31]Eisenhower, Vol. 1.

[32]Truman, *Memoirs*, 2:106. W. Averell Harriman quotes Nikita S. Khrushchev as asking him in 1959: "Do you expect to convince me that the voters of New York State had 'free elections' when their only choice for governor was between a Rockefeller and a Harriman?" (Quoted in Chester Cooper, *The Lost Crusade*, New York: Dodd, Mead & Co., 1970, p. 443.)

tion, than any other politician of our time. And he did it with total coldbloodedness.

McCarthy was elected in 1946 to the Senate on a bogus war record (he called himself "Tail-Gunner Joe," but, in fact, he never made a combat flight). After four undistinguished years in the United States Senate he was worried about reelection. So on January 7, 1950, he met with some advisers in a Washington restaurant to try to figure out some way to protect himself from the likelihood of defeat in the 1952 election. There it was suggested to McCarthy that an anti-communist crusade would excite the voters much more than a pork-barrel project would. He agreed.

The mood of the nation was ripe for it. Witch hunting of "subversives" was already under way; the Truman administration had begun demanding loyalty oaths from federal employees so that Republicans couldn't charge that Democrats were—as the expressions of the era had it—"fellow travelers," or "pinkos." So on February 6, 1950, addressing 275 guests of the Ohio County Women's Republican Club in the mining town of Wheeling, West Virginia, McCarthy began. He held up a piece of paper and declared,

> While I cannot take the time to name all the men in the State Department who have been named as members of the Communist Party and members of a spy ring, I have here in my hand a list of 205 that were known to the Secretary of State as being members of the Communist Party and who, nevertheless, are still working and shaping policy in the State Department.[33]

McCarthy actually had no such list of names. Nevertheless, this part of the speech was picked up by the Associated Press and carried to the outside world, and it had an enormous impact. Later, he changed the number of "known" communists in the State Department to eighty-one. Still later, he changed it to fifty-seven. He was obviously bluffing, obviously lying. But before that lie could be beaten down, he had spread a dozen more.

Overnight, McCarthy became a celebrity, the spiritual leader of the many Americans who feared that communists and communist-sympathizers would infiltrate the government and weaken it until Russia and China (where the communists had taken over in 1949) could defeat us. McCarthy talked wildly of "the Democrats' twenty years of treason," of "giving away China to the Communists," and of "the surrender of pinko professors to the atheistic red line." Other politicians—including Senator Richard Nixon and Congressman John Kennedy—scrambled to join McCarthy in the witch hunt, and they sometimes even outdid him. For several years, the leaders of both parties were afraid to challenge McCarthy's extravagances, for fear of being labeled procommunist. Not until 1954, when McCarthy finally became so irresponsible in his accusations as to be an embarrassment to the Republican establishment and to Congress, was he cut down by censure of the Senate.

During the intervening four years, McCarthy was the ideological strong man of the United States. The mood he and his followers established was psychotically anticommunist. Any legislation that could be smeared as being "soft on communism" or "un-American" was virtually impossible to pass, no matter how essentially worthwhile it might be; any legislation that could be sold as anticommunist had a very good chance of passing, whatever its defects in other respects. This was especially true of legislation relating to foreign policy—military spending became enormously popular.

Militarism, of course, did not begin with McCarthy. Congress translated fear of communism into heavy military spending before he started promoting it. But McCarthy heightened the mood to a frantic pitch. Spending money to make other nations love us and hate the commies became popular. Appropriations for the spy agencies (the Central Intelligence Agency, Defense Intelligence, and so forth) met little resistance in Congress. The Federal Bureau of Investigation began putting an increasing amount of its money and manpower into trying to ferret out "subversives" and "fellow travelers." The House Un-American Activities Committee and the Senate Internal Security Subcommittee began holding a steady round of investigative hearings, aimed at left-wingers and liberals and others who were not suitably anticommunist. They uncovered no real threats, but they got lots of

---

[33]Quoted in Fred J. Cook, *The Nightmare Decade* (New York: Random House, 1971), p. 149.

headlines. It was a time of deep suspicions and paranoia at home; the national mood infected foreign policy, and foreign policy infected our national mood.

Although Joe McCarthy was discredited by the Senate censure in 1954, "McCarthyism"—the extreme fear of foreign ideologies, the willingness to destroy reputations and liberties in the fight against domestic "subversives," the superpatriotism that insisted on uniformity of belief, the view of communism as a monolithic force bent on conquering the world—continued to have a strong, if not always dominant, influence in the shaping of United States foreign policy down to the present.

MILITARY POWER: WEAPONS, THREATS, AND DEFENSE

Since World War II, the concept of national·security has been dramatically different from its concept during any other period in our history for one reason: nuclear weaponry.

The psychic derangement that came with atomic bombs and nuclear missiles can only be understood if it is put into perspective. Not until relatively recent times has humankind been very efficient at killing itself. Benjamin Franklin is said to have advised our military leaders at the outset of the Revolutionary War that they should equip their troops with bows and arrows rather than with guns, because the latter were so inaccurate—and the generals listened respectfully. At a hundred yards, the ordinary musket missed the target by two or three feet. Not until the last quarter of the nineteenth century were we able to fight with fully automatic machine guns. As for big ammunition, that didn't come into its own until World War I, when a German cannon, capable of firing a 260-pound shell for a distance of eighty miles, was used. (Today's intercontinental missiles can carry warheads five thousand miles at a speed of 15,000 miles an hour.[34]) Air bombardment began in World War I, but on

such a small scale that it would seem, by today's standards, downright friendly. On October 1, 1916, eleven German airships bombed London—killing one person.

Over the next twenty-five years, the science of slaughter made remarkable progress. Allied aircraft were capable of dropping 134,000 tons of conventional (chemical) bombs a month during World War II. In Germany, Dresden went up in flames and 135,000 people were killed as a result of one attack. Conventional bombs were working very efficiently in the Far East, too. Air attacks on Tokyo during March 1945 destroyed 85 square miles of the city's 210 square miles and killed 225,000 people.

But until August 6, 1945, that kind of devastation required the use of massive fleets of planes, which carried many thousands of bombs. After August 6 that was clearly no longer necessary. The potential of air was changed forever on that date when one plane carrying one bomb—the world's first atomic bomb put to use in war—obliterated 68,000 of the 75,000 buildings in Hiroshima, Japan, and killed at once an estimated 100,000 people. Exactly how many perished is unknown because many people were simply incinerated, leaving no traces. Thousands of others died later of radiation. On August 9, another plane, carrying a single atomic bomb, wiped out 20,000 of the 52,000 buildings in Nagasaki, Japan, and killed at once 45,000 people. [35]

The Psychology of Nuclear Weaponry

The world now lived under a revolutionary new peril: one bomb, one city. And it was obvious to the scientists who had made those first baby atomic bombs that the splitting of the atom would quickly begin yielding bombs of much greater potential. Proof of this was obtained on November 1, 1952, when the United States exploded a test hydrogen bomb (also called superbomb, fusion bomb, or thermonuclear bomb) on an island in the Pacific. Whereas the atomic bomb that destroyed Hiroshima was equivalent to 20,000 tons of TNT, the first superbomb had the equivalence of 7 million tons of

[34]James W. Canan, *The Superwarriors: The Fantastic World of Pentagon Superweapons* (New York: Weybright & Talley, 1975), p. 140.

[35]Marion Yass, *Hiroshima* (New York: G. P. Putnam's Sons, 1972), pp. 86, 95.

TNT. The island on which it was detonated disappeared, and in its place was a hole 175 feet deep and 1 mile wide. Each of the superbombs in our arsenal today (as well as those in the arsenals of Russia and England and other nuclear nations) is capable of wiping out all life and all structures within 150 square miles and of starting fires within an area of 800 square miles.

"The atomic bomb was more than a weapon of terrible destruction," observed Henry L. Stimson, World War II Secretary of War. "It was a psychological weapon."[36] In fact, this was seen as its primary virtue—not its use in winning that particular war so much as its being such a terrible threat that other powerful nations, especially Russia, would be afraid to attack us in the future.

> In June, Stimson ordered the Army Air Corps not to carry out any conventional bombings of the target cities. "I was a little fearful," he explained [to Truman], "that before we could get ready the air force might have Japan so thoroughly bombed out that the new weapon would not have a fair background to show its strength." The Target Committee had emphasized similar concerns: The bomb should be used in such a way that it would have the "greatest psychological effect against Japan . . . and be sufficiently spectacular for the importance of the weapon to be internationally recognized when publicity . . . is released." There were, in short, two targets: Japan and Russia.[37]

The stunning psychological impact of nuclear weapons comes from the fact, acknowledged by all military authorities, that in any all-out nuclear war both sides would be totally ruined. Together, the two great adversaries have enough atomic weapons in their arsenals today to kill everyone on the globe several times over. Our military forces have an estimated nine thousand nuclear warheads—bombs and missiles—ready to be launched via superfortress planes, nuclear submarines, or intercontinental missiles. Only one hundred of these, if they were delivered, would wipe out 37 million Russians and 59 percent of Russia's industry. We could, in short,

"bomb it back to the Stone Ages"—as our generals like to say—in one strike.[38]

Russia, by contrast, is believed to have only about thirty-five hundred nuclear warheads. But that, as Senator George McGovern has pointed out—without refutation from the Pentagon—still gives the Soviet Union

> the unquestioned capability to literally demolish the United States as a modern society, and we are helpless to prevent that result if nuclear war occurs. Therefore, the only real defense to nuclear attack is to prevent it, both by diplomatic means and by military preparations designed to convince the adversary that he can gain nothing by initiating nuclear war. . . .
>
> It is hard to imagine a goal for which an American president would accept the certain destruction of, say, New York, or Los Angeles, which could be accomplished by very few nuclear warheads, certainly less than ten. It is at least arguable that the undoubted capability to deliver enough weapons to destroy Moscow and Peking would be sufficient to deter either the Soviet Union or China from attempting a first strike against the United States. At least it is clear that the provocation would have to be overwhelming.
>
> On the other end of the scale, it is clear that no amount of nuclear weaponry can deter a suicidal adversary, nor prevent a totally irrational decision to launch. Under such circumstances it is plain that the Soviet Union could destroy a large proportion of the American population and most of the country's industrial capacity as well. All of the enormous destructive capacity in the U.S. nuclear arsenal would be unavailing in those circumstances, and we could do no more than retaliate with similar destruction.[39]

In those three paragraphs, McGovern gave a perfect summation of the foreign-relations discipline that the United States will be forced to adjust to for the foreseeable future. It is called the balance of terror. The United States must accommodate itself to the outside world with the knowledge that, should we ever fall into an atomic war with a major power, the very least number of deaths we would suffer (military au-

[36]Henry L. Stimson, "Decision to Use the Atom Bomb," *Harper's Magazine,* February 1947.

[37]Barton J. Bernstein, "Doomsday II," *New York Times Magazine,* July 27, 1975.

[38]Richard J. Barnet, "Promise of Disarmament," *New York Times Magazine,* February 27, 1977.

[39]George S. McGovern, "An Alternative National Defense Posture," released in 1972.

FIGURE 14-1   UNITED STATES AND SOVIET STRATEGIC NUCLEAR WEAPONS

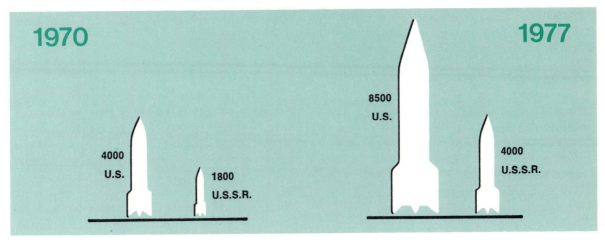

1970

4000
U.S.

1800
U.S.S.R.

1977

8500
U.S.

4000
U.S.S.R.

SOURCE: U.S. Defense Department, from the *Defense Monitor* VI, no. 4 (May 1977): 3.

thorities speculate), with an almost perfect defense, is 20 million. Our chief adversary, Russia, must accommodate itself to the same awareness of its vulnerability. We are at a standoff position; each side offers, and confronts, an equal amount of terror. A nerve-racking peace is achieved in that balance.

But the United States and Russia did not arrive at that position in one step. There was considerable flexibility in decision making to be found all the way, and, going back to the beginning, we can see the kind of choices in that flexibility that confronts national leaders.

A Gamble That Didn't Pay Off

After the United States dropped its first atomic bomb in 1945, our leaders could have followed either of two courses: they could have voluntarily shelved their new weapon and set about easing world tension by agreeing to the international sharing of atomic information, or they could have parlayed their singular strength into establishing the United States as the dominant force in the world, imposing our will, and our way of life, on it. Anything in between those two courses would have been a waste of power. After all, since we were the sole possessor of the power, why not make our presence felt either as the preeminent peacemaker through coopera-

tive control of the atom or as the preeminent warmaker (or potential warmaker) through selfish threats with the bomb?

America's leaders chose to follow the latter path. History shows that the United States did present the so-called Baruch Plan (named for Bernard Baruch, an adviser to several Presidents) to the United Nations in 1946, a plan whereby we offered to submit to international control of atomic power under certain conditions. But the conditions were so harshly anti-Russia as to guarantee the plan's rejection by the Soviet government.[40] Despite the seeming will-

[40]Leading United States scientists wanted to exchange atomic information with the Russians as a sign of good will, knowing that the Russians were not far behind us in knowledge anyway. But the United States defense chiefs wanted to hang on to our secrets to the bitter end, and President Truman agreed with them. The Baruch Plan was, therefore, totally uncompromising. We refused to destroy our atomic stockpile unless all other nations agreed not to build any atomic bombs; we demanded the right of on-site inspection of Russian facilities to make sure Russia wasn't doing something behind our backs; and we stipulated "swift and sure" punishment if the Russians got out of line. The Russians countered with the demand that we destroy our atomic weapons before sitting down to the negotiating table. Thus stalemated, the argument quickly degenerated on both sides into a nasty propaganda battle. (See Seyom Brown, *The Faces of Power: Constancy and Change in U.S. Foreign Policy from Truman to Johnson,* New York: Columbia University Press, 1968, p. 35; and Paul Y. Hammond, *Cold War and Détente: The American Foreign Policy Process Since 1945,* New York: Harcourt Brace Jovanovich, 1975, p. 133.)

ingness of the government to enter into international control of atomic power, its true spirit at the time was probably capsuled rather accurately by Baruch the next year in a speech to the South Carolina legislature, in which he stated

> The gains of our scientists, our engineers, our industrialists, produced the supreme weapon of all time—the atomic bomb. That we shall never give away, until and unless security for us, and for the world, is established. Until that time comes, the United States will remain the guardian of safety. We can be trusted with that solemn responsibility. . . . There is no place left to which to turn for regeneration except to America. . . . [41]

By designating the United States the world's "guardian of safety," Baruch meant that our political leaders were gambling on the hope that the Russians would be incapable of acquiring the bomb through their own efforts for quite some time (a supposition that every knowledgeable scientist rejected). Our political leaders reasoned that, since the postwar world would be shaped internationally by the fear of the nuclear bomb and since only the United States had the bomb, we could control the postwar world. They saw no reason to surrender our international omnipotence by sharing nuclear information with the communists through an agency of international control. [42]

They lost their gamble. Less than two years after Baruch's empty proclamation, Russia had its own atomic bomb, and now the world had a choice as to which direction it would turn for "regeneration." The United States developed the hydrogen bomb first, too, but again the Russians were only a year behind. After that, there was virtually no hope for international control of atomic weapons. With each side armed, the nuclear arms race was under way. Would things have turned out differently if the United States had followed the other path? There is good reason to doubt that the United States and the Soviet Union could have come to any lasting agreement on international control of atomic weapons even if the general principle had been acceptable to both sides. There was altogether too much suspicion and latent hostility between them. The history of foreign affairs is littered with second guesses, and none of them are of much value.

The Threat of Massive Retaliation

It was clear from the beginning of the United States-Russia balance of terror that the only way to have special power was to convey the impression of suicidal irresponsibility. "The reputation of being absolute, even somewhat irrational," says Seyom Brown, "was an important facet of our power, particularly in Europe." [43] In playing this game, the United States was blessed—or cursed—by having John Foster Dulles as Secretary of State in the Eisenhower cabinet. He was a great exponent of what was called "brinksmanship"—taking the world to the edge of atomic war and winning concessions from Russia by pretending to be willing to push the world over the edge.

The Dulles-Eisenhower policy, made public in 1954, was to cut back our ground forces and to build up our nuclear strength. Local wars against the communists were to be fought primarily with the troops of our allies. We would stand back with our atomic weapons and let the enemy know that if they went too far in a ground war with our allies they always ran the risk of triggering a nuclear war with us. Said Dulles:

> Local defense will always be important. But there is no local defense which alone will contain the mighty land forces of the Communist world. Local defense must be reinforced by the further deterrent of massive retaliatory power. A potential aggressor must know that he cannot always prescribe the battle conditions that suit him. [44]

Actually, Dulles did not peg everything on massive retaliation. He simply tried to convey the idea that the communists could not count on sucking us into a purely local conflict and restricting us to the weapons they chose to fight with; his policy was to remind them that we would always consider our atomic arsenal as

[41]Quoted in the *New York Herald Tribune,* April 17, 1947.

[42]See Martin J. Sherwin, *A World Destroyed: The Atomic Bomb and the Grand Alliance* (New York: Random House, Alfred A. Knopf, 1975).

[43]Brown, *The Faces of Power,* p. 249.

[44]Quoted in Brown, p. 74.

being available. But the catch phrase "massive retaliatory power" was quickly picked out and overemphasized, both at home and abroad, until there was the widespread misconception that our only answer, even for local wars, was a general nuclear war. Ultimately this misconception seriously undercut our credibility in the world, for nobody thought we were so stupid or irrational as to go around killing gnats with an elephant gun. In short, the concept of massive retaliation began to be looked upon as a clumsy bluff. At that point, United States officials sorely needed to think up a new way to play the game of international terror politics—as did the Russians.

Although for three years Russian Premier Nikita Khrushchev threatened war over the situation in Berlin, few knowledgeable observers believed he would carry out the threat. Although President Kennedy seemed to be threatening war with Russia if it did not take its missiles out of Cuba in 1962, there is no evidence that Kennedy really intended to go that far, either. Indeed, there is every reason to suppose that Kennedy—and any other United States politician—would agree with the remark Khrushchev once made: "Is there a madman or a clever man who could tell what would happen after a nuclear war? It's stupid, stupid, stupid. . . . And there are people among communists who believe that war is good for revolution. Those who call for revolution now should go to see a psychiatrist."[45]

The Shift to Flexible Response

The United States escaped from this stalemate by shifting to what came to be known as President Kennedy's "flexible response." In putting together a winning strategy for his 1960 presidential bid, John F. Kennedy harped continually on the misconception of the Dulles-Eisenhower policy. "We have been driving ourselves into a corner where the only choice is all or nothing at all, world devastation or submission—a choice that necessarily causes us to hesi-

tate on the brink and leaves the initiative in the hands of our enemies," he wrote in 1960.[46] Following the advice of General Maxwell Taylor and Henry Kissinger,[47] Kennedy proposed instead that the United States, while maintaining its nuclear strength, also pump money into the military in such a way that it would enable us to fight two and a half conventional wars at the same time—a war in Europe, a war in Asia, and a "half-war" in Latin America. He made his proposal in March 1961, after Khrushchev had, in January, ruled out nuclear wars and "local" wars as too dangerous, but promised full support for "national liberation wars" in Asia, Africa, or Latin America.[48]

Thus the United States and Russia arrived at a tacit understanding—that the former could mess around in Vietnam and the latter in Angola and both could have the freedom to interfere in the Middle East without running the risk of nuclear war. So long as the balance of terror was maintained, the major powers could pursue conventional war with other countries on a "hobby" scale.

This was, however, an extremely costly agreement, for it left the budget for nuclear weapons open-ended. Although these weapons were clearly not to be used, each side had to continually make better and bigger ones to keep up with the other side, while, at the same time, each had to tend to conventional weapons. Adam Yarmolinsky, one of the Pentagon whiz kids during the Kennedy era, noted the obvious: ". . . the participants in the nucear arms race are learning that however fast they run, they are only running to keep in place. What one side can achieve through new technology, the other can frustrate through the same means."[49] When the United States military budget pushed, the Russian military budget shoved. Down that path lay bankruptcy, the fear of which drove the United

---

[45]Quoted in Ronald Steel, *Pax Americana*, rev. ed. (New York: Viking Press, 1970), p. 43.

[46]John F. Kennedy, *The Strategy of Peace*, ed. Allan Nevins (New York: Harper & Row, Publishers, 1960), p. 184.

[47]See Taylor's *The Uncertain Trumpet* (Westport, Conn.: Greenwood Press, 1974) and Kissinger's *Nuclear Weapons and Foreign Policy* (New York: Oxford University Press, 1957).

[48]Barker, *The Cold War*, p. 100.

[49]Yarmolinsky, *The Military Establishment*, p. 103.

In April 1977 Secretary of State Cyrus Vance (left) visited Moscow to discuss continuation of the long-interrupted SALT talks; Soviet Foreign Minister Andrei Gromyko is second from the right

States and Russia, in the 1970s, to pursue what became fashionably known as *détente*. Actually, détente began after the Cuban missile crisis of 1962 and the test ban treaty of 1963, but it did not enter the popular vocabulary until Henry Kissinger became foreign affairs impresario in 1969. The practical definition of détente is that it is a new flexibility toward our traditional adversaries—a new willingness to negotiate, to adjust, to accommodate. It signaled a dramatic shift from bipolar conflict with the Soviet Union and toward a policy based on the recognition of common interests that could serve as the basis for closer cooperation.[50] In the Strategic Arms Limitation Treaty (SALT) talks, the United States and Russia discussed a reduction in arms on both sides and an agreement to pursue with less enthusiasm the development of deadlier atomic weapons. The evolution of these weapons had reached such illogical momentum that Secretary of State Kissinger, at the end of the Moscow summit meeting in mid-1974, asked the despairing question, "What in the name of God is strategic superiority? What is the significance of it? What do you do with it?"

The Search for Détente

In seeking détente, the two sides were seeking neither friendship nor a non-nuclear-armed world. Their goals were much more modest—merely to stop the spread of an incurable disease. That's the best that can be hoped for in an atomic age. One does not look for rainbows; one only hopes for something less than hurricanes. One speaks of "partial accommodation with the adversary," or of "a move away from a continuous confrontation." In the atomic age, that is the equivalent of peace. And it is within that modest context that foreign affairs are conducted. It is a context that allows one to give thanks, as did Sir Geoffrey de Freitas, President of the Assembly of the Council of Europe: "I believe that until world peace is maintained by cooperation between Russia and the United States of America, coexistence will be based on the balance of military strength. This is not a situation I welcome, but it is better than no coexistence."[51]

Détente is not an acceptable doctrine to all leaders on both sides, however, and there is always the possibility of a shift back toward an accelerated arms race. Shortly after taking office, President Jimmy Carter announced his intentions to move "quickly and aggressively" to halt all nuclear tests and conclude new strategic arms limitations with Russia. But many foreign affairs experts were pressuring him to get tougher, not softer; they insisted that the Soviet Union had doubled its arms budget on the sly, was clearly aiming for superiority over the United States, and might even be preparing for war.[52] Carter responded to their warnings by directing some of the Pentagon budget away from the updating of airplanes and toward the development of more sophisticated missiles—weapons that would be extremely accurate and that would be difficult for Russian radar and antimissile devices to detect and intercept. The Carter defense budget was also putting new emphasis on what is called "the electronic battlefield"—devices that military scientists claim can take human error and human weakness out of battlefield warfare. Also under development is the neutron bomb, which kills people while sparing buildings. (See Chapter 9, footnote 57.) In short, the arms race has gone back to the drawing board and back to the laboratory. The new race will be between a new and refined generation of arms. What effect this will have on the cold war, on détente, or on the military's impact in shaping foreign policy is not at all clear.

---

[50]Hammond, *Cold War and Détente,* p. 286. A fuller definition is supplied by Vladimir Petrov: "Detente is a process by which two or more nations move away from a continuous confrontation with each other in the general direction of cooperation. It is a relaxation of international tensions which can take place only when certain objective conditions exist: a realization by the protagonists that there are political and economic limitations to the assertion of their power in the world, a change in the respective national perceptions of the 'enemy,' and a recognition of the necessity to seek improvement of the nation's posture through a partial accommodation with the adversary." (*U.S.-Soviet Détente: Past and Future,* Washington, D.C.: American Enterprise Institute, 1975.)

---

[51]Quoted in Edward Reed, ed., *Beyond Coexistence: The Requirements of Peace* (New York: Viking Press, Grossman Publishers, 1968), p. 109.

[52]Walter Laqueur, "Perils of Détente," *New York Times Magazine,* February 27, 1977.

ECONOMICS:
ALMOST AS POWERFUL AS WEAPONS

Although the United States has only managed to hold its own in military jousting with the communists, it has been outstandingly successful (with the notable exception of bungling some oil and wheat deals) in playing international economics for political ends and playing international politics for economic ends.

The Policy of Containment

When, at the end of World War II, it became evident that the United States and Russia were simply not going to get along and when it became evident that each side wished the most evil consequences for the other, it was plain that these two ideological giants would either engage in a war that could wipe out the world or that they would settle down to some lesser and more protracted confrontation.

Having no overwhelming desire to engage in suicidal combat, the leaders of the United States welcomed a proposed policy written by George Kennan, which appeared in the July 1947 issue of *Foreign Affairs*. Kennan was a member of the State Department and a very experienced observer of Russian affairs. Although he signed the article only as "X," his identity soon became known and his prestige promptly elevated the thesis of the article to the center of a national debate. The heart of Kennan's thesis was this:

> It is clear that the main element of any United States policy towards the Soviet Union must be that of a long-term, patient but firm and vigilant containment of Russian expansive tendencies. It is important to note, however, that such a policy has nothing to do with . . . threats or blustering or superfluous gestures of outward "toughness." . . . Soviet pressure against the free institutions of the Western world is something that can be contained by the adroit and vigilant application of counter-force at a series of constantly shifting geographical and political points, corresponding to the shifts and maneuvers of Soviet policy. . . . The Russians look forward to a duel of infinite duration. . . .[53]

Kennan's "containment policy" was almost immediately and enthusiastically embraced by the Democratic administration of Harry Truman (1945–53), and it later became the official policy of Eisenhower's Republican administration (1953–61) as well—despite the "threats or blustering or superfluous gestures of outward 'toughness' " that Kennan warned against and that were often the hallmark of Eisenhower's Secretary of State, John Foster Dulles.

Communism was to be contained by a wall of capitalism. Where a nation's economy was too weak and ill-equipped to be called capitalist, it would at least be contained by a wall of noncommunism. This was to be achieved through United States economic aid—either direct financial assistance or machinery and other material goods to help the chosen nations get their economies rolling again. We also set about containing communism by equipping other nations with arms, so that they could do the skirmish-type fighting for us. "In a way," write Robert J. Pranger and Dale R. Tahtinin, "these nations ostensibly worked within a general American deterrence strategy. They became American surrogates in a global effort to contain communism. In turn, they received substantial benefits from the U.S."[54] They received arms and military equipment from us on long-term loans (an estimated $62 billion to $100 billion between 1946 and 1973); often we placed military bases in their countries, and these bases were a constant source of income for local business.

No matter what assistance was given, the United States had one goal: to keep certain countries within the capitalist orbit. We wanted to inhibit and contain communism; but it is much more accurate to put these activities in positive terms and say that we wanted to expand capitalism, to protect capitalism, to make the global atmosphere more hospitable toward profit making by United States business interests.

The Beginnings of Foreign Aid

Although the United States had assisted a stricken Europe with food and money loans after

---

[53]George F. Kennan, *Foreign Affairs*, July 1947.

[54]Robert J. Pranger and Dale R. Tahtinin, *Toward a Realistic Military Assistance Program* (Washington, D.C.: American Enterprise Institute, 1974), pp. 30–31.

World War I, our role as banker and supplier and storekeeper reached preeminence in World War II and thereafter—first with the lend-lease program of arms and supplies beginning in 1940, after we had abandoned our pretense of neutrality, and then with the recovery programs after the war.[55] The two most notable steps were the establishment of the Truman Doctrine and the Marshall Plan—both in 1947.

Britain, which had been helping the Greek government fight a civil war against indigenous communist guerilla forces, told the United States that it could no longer afford to do so. The United States decided to step in and foot the bill (and the bill to help Turkey as well). At that time, President Truman declared, "I believe that it must be the policy of the United States to support free people who are resisting attempted subjugation by armed minorities or by outside pressures. I believe that we must assist free peoples to work out their own destinies in their own way."[56] Truman said that the assistance would be "primarily through economic and financial aid," but, in the years ahead, the Truman Doctrine would be invoked on numerous occasions to supply military aid and, sometimes, outright military intervention.

But there was a much more pressing problem. Western Europe, bled dry by the war, seemed on the verge of economic collapse. State Department officials agreed that the United States had grossly underestimated the sickness of the European economy. Five years of fighting Hitler had caused much more economic disruption and political, social, and psychological destruction than the United States, safe on the other side of the Atlantic, had imagined. And now the conclusion of the tragedy was taking place: millions of people in Europe's cities were slowly starving. Europe's industry had no reserve from which to reconstruct itself. Its agriculture was 25 percent under prewar production.[57] Knowing that economically depressed

nations were always the most hospitable to communism, the United States government decided that this part of the cold war must be fought with money. So on June 5, 1947, in a speech at Cambridge, Massachusetts, General George C. Marshall, then Truman's Secretary of State, announced that if Europe wanted our help and if it came up with a program by which our help would seem to be aimed, not at any particular country, but "against hunger, poverty, desperation, and chaos," the United States would underwrite that program.[58]

Sixteen European nations came forward with a four-year self-help program, and the United States contributed 5 percent of the total funding—the seed money, so to speak—which came to $17 billion, a very generous amount of money in those days. The Marshall Plan was extraordinarily successful, both in winning bipartisan support in Congress (no other foreign policy has ever won such unified support) and in launching the recovery that was its goal.[59]

Its sponsors, carried away by their victory, ignored the fact that the nations to which we lent the money were highly sophisticated industrial nations, rich in experience and talents, and could use the money efficiently; they mistakenly assumed that massive loans could make the same transformation in nations that were underdeveloped and inexperienced in industrial production. Billions of dollars in aid were given to such backward nations over the following decades, and much of it was wasted.[60] Many millions—probably billions—of dollars were also wasted through the policy of requiring virtually no accountability from nations to which food supplies were given during droughts and other emergencies. Corrupt officials in those nations sometimes sold the food to other countries and let their own citizens die of starvation.[61] This happened in Ethiopia in 1974 and in Bangladesh in 1976.

[55]*Congress and the Nation: 1946–1964* (Washington, D.C.: Congressional Quarterly Service, 1965), p. 160.

[56]Quoted in the *New York Times,* March 13, 1947.

[57]Dean G. Acheson, *Present at the Creation: My Years in the State Department* (New York: W. W. Norton & Co., 1969), p. 231.

[58]Acheson, p. 233.

[59]To counteract, or counterbalance, the Marshall Plan, Stalin set up the Council for Mutual Economic Assistance in 1949, to bind together economically Russia, Poland, Czechoslovakia, Hungary, Romania, and Bulgaria. (See Gibson, *Russia under Stalin.*)

[60]*Congress and the Nation,* p. 161.

[61]Internal report, State Department, released by Congressman Les Aspin, February 2, 1976.

Wheat from the United States is unloaded at Beirut, 1977

The wasteful illogic of some aid programs was symbolized by what occurred in Colombia in 1976. In violation of its own regulations, the State Department's Agency for International Development sent free grain to Colombia at the same time that Colombia was selling grain to a number of other nations—including the United States. In addition, much of our aid has gone to prop up right-wing militaristic regimes. While American farmers were hard pressed by a shortage of fertilizer, our government sent an estimated $79-million worth of fertilizer to the military dictatorship in South Vietnam, whose officials diverted it to the black market. In 1976, the United States gave the government of the Philippines, a dictatorship, about $1 billion in military and economic aid in order to buy its friendship; the Philippines agreed to let the

United States maintain military bases in that country. Similarly, in 1975 we promised $1.5 billion in aid to Spain, at that time a land of few freedoms, for the use of military bases in that country.

Charity Begins at Home

Most American taxpayers have never understood what foreign aid is all about, and this is understandable, because the program has a diffused character: it is part hucksterism and part humanism. It is what one Georgia congressman recently called "a rather bewildering mixture of charity and business, a mixture of altruism and self-interest."

Since World War II, we have spent at least $150 billion in foreign aid. Nobody knows the amount for sure, because it is doled out in so many ways. Some of it has been given as gifts; some has been spent as "loans" that need never be repaid, some as extremely long-term loans at virtually give-away interest rates. Aid has been given in many forms: as foodstuffs, such as wheat and soybeans; as birth-control devices ($625-million worth to seventy countries between 1965 and 1974);[62] as fertilizer and farm machinery; and as military equipment of every variety.

Whatever the form, that's a lot of generosity, and many people have cursed the program, calling it a give-away scandal that only benefits shiftless foreigners who won't work. Backers of the program counter with the claim that the Marshall Plan probably saved some friendly European nations from sliding into anarchy or repressive communism after the war and that, today, the foreign aid program is saving millions of people from disease and hunger through free vaccinations and food. Neither Congress nor the bureaucrats have made a serious effort to settle the argument, perhaps because they themselves can't decide whether they want to appeal to the nation's conscience or to its inbred yearning to make a fast buck. For three decades, Washington officials have been playing both sides of the street in a rather dishonest, hybrid fashion and have refused to talk straight to the taxpayers.

[62]*Wall Street Journal*, February 28, 1974.

The truth is, the foreign assistance program, which costs the United States taxpayer billions of dollars each year, is a prime example of charity beginning at home—charity for big business executives, industrialists, and big farmers. Very little of the economic aid goes to foreign countries in the form of money. It is tied tightly to a line of credit, usually administered through the Agency for International Development (AID). Country X is given, say, $1 billion in credit. It "buys" $1-billion worth of wheat from United States farmers. Actually, it is the United States government that pays the farmers for the wheat, and then it collects from Country X over a twenty- or thirty-year period—if it collects at all.

The public relations line, of course, is that foreign aid is a mercy program, aimed solely at uplifting the hungry and the needy abroad. Well, of course, it does that, too. But candid politicians will tell you that the real usefulness of the program is in keeping their constituents happy. Senator John Sparkman of Alabama, for example, was mighty proud of how he saved the United States Steel Corporation's mill in Ensley, Alabama. By persuading AID to buy $8.3 million worth of rails and bars for Pakistan, he kept the mill from closing down. Members of Congress are legally forbidden from exerting that kind of pressure on government agencies, but nobody tries to enforce the law, and Sparkman boasted of his interference quite openly.

While it is accurate to say that the Marshall Plan was put into operation in 1948 to assist some battered European countries, it should also be pointed out that the Marshall Plan helped pull our own economy out of an unnerving eleven-month business slump. And it was no accident that foreign aid—counting military assistance—hit its all-time peak in 1953; that was the year in which a thirteen-month business decline in this country began, and the profitable "charity" for Europe was desperately needed trade for our business executives.

The spirit of the aid programs was captured perfectly by Robert R. Nathan, an economic adviser to the top echelon of government, who wrote in a newsletter circulated by the State Department and by the United States Department of Agriculture: "Investment funds [spent by our government overseas] have no sentiment or patriotism. They are coldly responsive to opportunities for the biggest profit with the smallest relative risk."[63] Even the supposedly most benevolent of our programs, the program for food aid, is solidly rooted in the profit motive. Dan Morgan of the *Washington Post* noted in 1975: "Today, only one dollar out of every five that the United States spends for food aid goes to the food giveaway program. The rest is for long-term, low-interest dollar credits to friendly governments (and some private firms) for food buying in the United States."[64] Why the reluctance to give away, rather than sell, food? Again a government official had an answer. A representative of the National Security Council was quoted by Morgan as saying, "To give food aid to countries just because people are starving is a pretty weak reason."[65]

Some unscrupulous Americans have used the aid program as a way to unload overstocked or worthless products on foreigners under the guise of generosity. One entrepreneur, for example, got rid of $4-million worth of junk machinery on India through the foreign aid program—at the United States taxpayers' expense. Millions of pounds of tobacco and hundreds of thousands of bales of cotton were sent to starving people in India and Africa under the Food for Peace program.[66] More than a hundred tons of AID-financed talcum powder were sent to Saigon, where it was stored in a warehouse and never used. A half-million-dollars' worth of diesel engines, automobile engines, spare parts, air compressors, typewriters, duplicating machines, refrigerators, lathes, and sewing machines were sent to Independence College in Lebanon through the United States foreign assistance program, and it might have been a worthy contribution except for one thing—the school no longer existed. To be sure, it *looked* like we were being very generous to foreigners when our government loaned $14.8 million, at 1 percent interest, to Brazil's Ultrafertil Company so that it could build a fertilizer plant in Brazil, but, in fact, the largest stockholder in Ultrafertil was the giant United States oil company, Phillips Petroleum. That sort of loan—made outwardly to foreigners, but really to United States Big Business—is made all too often.

The AID program is not as popular with our farmers and machine manufacturers as it used to be, because the world market for most of our products is a sellers' market. When it was difficult to sell goods, purchases made through AID were extremely welcome. But in this era of shortages, most merchandise can be sold on the world market at a high price—a price so high, in fact, that the poor nations American business once claimed to be so eager to help have been priced out of the market.

A new light has also been thrown on the supposed patriotic benevolence of our military aid. In recent years, beginning most enthusiastically with the Nixon administration, our distribution of arms to other nations has had less to do with ideological considerations than with simple profit seeking. By 1976, we had become the world's leading arms merchant, peddling more than half the total amount sold on the world market. We sold $12.7-billion worth in 1976, up from a relatively slight $1-billion worth in fiscal 1967.[67] To make a buck, we were willing to sell to either or to both sides—to Saudi Arabia and to Israel, for instance. Defenders of the arms sales argued that manufacturing military equipment provided thousands of jobs for Americans.[68] Several major defense companies—Lockheed, Northrop, Grumman, General Motors, and Rockwell International, among others—made questionable payments to foreigners, in the form of "consultant fees," "campaign contributions,"

[63]Quoted in Robert Sherrill, "The Great Foreign Aid Boondoggle," *Pageant*, January 1969.

[64]Dan Morgan, *Washington Post*, March 13, 1975.

[65]Quoted in Dan Morgan, *Washington Post*, December 9, 1974.

[66]When this scandal was uncovered, a Congressman from North Carolina, where much of the tobacco had originated, defended the program in a House debate by saying that tobacco is good for starving people; it eases their tension so they can eat and assimilate food better. (*Washington Post*, May 1, 1966.)

[67]Sources: Reuter, October 24, 1976; Report of the U.S. General Accounting Office, Washington, D.C., June 1, 1976.

[68]Report of the U.S. General Accounting Office, Washington, D.C., June 1, 1976, p. 21.

or outright bribes, in order to increase military sales.[69] Some companies claimed that they were simply paying "agents fees." An executive with Northrop gave this candid description of an "agent's" job: "The role of the agent is primarily that of influence peddler; that is, he knows whom to talk to and whose pockets to line in a particular country to get the job done."[70] Once again, defenders of the payments argued that by stimulating sales abroad they were creating jobs at home.

The Impact of Multinational Corporations

For the last decade or so, economic assistance of the routine sort has ceased to dominate our foreign policy. The shaping of policy by money interests has shifted to the exotic realm of the multinational corporations. Multinationals are so common today that, for the sake of perspective, the term is generally used to denote only about three hundred of the largest. A multinational is a corporation operating in at least half a dozen countries, whose foreign subsidiaries account for at least one-fifth of the parent company's assets and sales, and which has annual sales of $100 million or more. Actually, for the big multinationals, that would be pin money. Exxon, which ranked as the top multinational in 1975, had an income of $47.8 billion; International Business Machines (IBM), one of the top ten, operated that year in 125 countries and earned $14.4 billion.[71] Of the three hundred giant multinationals, two-thirds call the United States home. These two hundred corporations account for 80 percent of all direct United States foreign investment; they have estimated annual sales of more than $200 billion—and they are just beginning to spread.

For many years, the State Department and certain major United States corporations have worked so closely together that it is difficult to say for sure whether the United States is being represented overseas by private industry or by government diplomats. But one thing is clear: the economic health of the multinationals is usually viewed by the government as being identical to our national interests.

Probably because United States oil companies were the first major corporations to expand their holdings overseas to a significant degree, they were the earliest, and are still the most forward, advocates of the philosophy that the core of our foreign policy should be to protect United States investments. When the Mexican government nationalized Mexican oil fields, most of which were owned by U.S. companies, in a series of takeovers from 1917 through 1938, our government did everything possible—including financing military coups—to get the concessions back for the companies.[72] This was the central goal in our relations with Mexico for two decades. It was a foreign policy that failed.

The government's support of the major United States oil companies in the Middle East has been much more successful. The most dramatic example of United States intervention on behalf of the oil industry came in 1953, when a coup financed and led by the Central Intelligence Agency overthrew Premier Mohammed Mossadegh of Iran, who had nationalized his country's oil industry.[73]

In the 1960s and 1970s, the major United States oil companies—Standard Oil of New Jersey (Exxon), Standard Oil of California, Mobil, Gulf, Texaco, and Continental—turned ownership of the Middle East fields back to the Arabs and went into business—as partners—with the oil-producing countries; the companies were to take care of the production, transportation, and sales, as always; but the nations would own their own real estate and oil. This arrangement was also made in Venezuela and in other major oil-producing countries. Thus, the public cartel of the Organization of Petroleum Exporting Countries (called OPEC) was joined with the private

---

[69]See the Business and Finance Section, *New York Times,* February 15, 1976.

[70]Quoted in the *New York Times,* July 27, 1976.

[71]New York Stock Exchange, Research Department data, quoted in *The World Almanac 1977* (New York: Newspaper Enterprise Association, 1977), p. 123.

[72]See Edwin Lieuwen, *U.S. Policy in Latin America: A Short History* (New York: Praeger Publishers, 1965).

[73]Thomas B. Ross and David Wise, *The Invisible Government* (New York: Random House, 1964), pp. 116–21.

cartel of petroleum corporations. It was, of course, to the profit of both cartels to cut back on oil production when the market was oversupplied—thus keeping prices high.[74] Although high oil prices were the main cause of the runaway inflation and high unemployment of the mid-1970s, the United States government did little to intervene on behalf of consumers. (See also Chapter 16.) It left most dealings with the Middle East countries in the hands of the United States oil companies. They were our unofficial diplomats. Julius L. Katz, acting Assistant Secretary of State for Economic and Business Affairs, defended this arrangement by saying that "the companies have served and continue to serve a very useful role as a buffer between governments, and to a large extent help to insulate the oil market from purely political considerations"—as though "political considerations" were not, in fact, what most citizens expect diplomacy to consist of.[75]

Hearings held by the Senate Foreign Relations Subcommittee on Multinational Corporations, in 1974, showed that—as one reporter summarized the investigation—"these companies became a virtual supranational government and exercised powerful control, insofar as oil was concerned, over the foreign and domestic policies of the United States and the world."[76]

The chief danger of allowing profit-minded corporations to determine any United States policy overseas—aside from the fact that their interests do not correspond to the interests of consumers—is that the business world proves the old biblical rule that "where your treasure is, there will your heart be also." In 1974, twenty-five of the corporations listed on *Fortune* magazines's list of the 500 largest firms earned more than half their income *outside* the United States. These include six oil companies (Standard of California, Exxon, Gulf, Mobil, Texaco, and Marathon), two major food companies (Libby, McNeill and Libby, and Heinz), and such other giants as Coca-Cola, Dow Chemical, Uniroyal, and IBM. In the tricky world of foreign relations, one might wonder if corporations such as these would place their first loyalty in the welfare of the United States when the chips are down. To do so would certainly violate both their corporate training and their instincts.

> The leading multinational enterprises have great flexibility in shifting operations around the world to reduce costs and take advantage of production and marketing opportunities. Those who manage such a corporation, no matter what their nationality or in what subsidiary they are located, are supposed to put the interests of the whole firm ahead of any of its particular national parts.[77]

It was no silly complaint registered by Andrew J. Biemiller, spokesman for the AFL-CIO, when he said that the United States–based multinationals

> operate as private corporations at home, but abroad in some instances join forces with state-owned industries, with nations that wage economic warfare against the United States. On numerous occasions in the past eight years, we have shown their effect on America—the export of American jobs, American technology, and American capital. We have called attention to the closing of American factories and their re-establishment abroad where foreign markets are served in protected economies and exports to the United States are manufactured.[78]

Some of the major United States corporations apparently do not think of their destinies as

---

[74]See David Ignatius, "Taming the Beast: The Multinationals," *New Republic*, September 14, 1974.

[75]*New York Times*, June 5, 1974.

[76]Stephen Nordlinger, "Our Blundering Oil Diplomacy," *Nation*, April 17, 1974.

[77]Seyom Brown, "New Forces in World Politics," in Henry Owen et al., eds., *The Next Phase of Foreign Policy* (Washington, D.C.: Brookings Institution, 1973), p. 197. Adolf A. Berle, in *The 20th Century Capitalist Revolution*, recalls that, when the Nazi fifth column was set up in South American business establishments, the United States government asked our multinationals to break off relations with the Hitler underground in that area. He tells how "one famous corporation objected, and its vice president was sent to Washington to argue with the Undersecretary of State. His argument was direct and simple. His corporation, he said, was not in politics of any kind. If the United States government wished to have a quarrel with the Nazi government of Germany, that was the government's privilege; but his corporation in its foreign operations could not be involved, and did not feel bound to accommodate itself to American policy expressed in a 'moral embargo.' " (New York: Harcourt Brace Jovanovich, 1954.)

[78]*Congressional Record*, H13193, December 19, 1975.

interlocked with those of United States citizens. They have become the great mercenaries of the economic wars, willing to don the business suit of whatever side pays best. They think of themselves as world citizens, not in the sense that they feel responsible to everyone, but in the sense that they feel responsible to no one. Carl A. Gerstacker, former Chairman of Dow Chemical, was honest enough to reveal his passions—and, undoubtedly, those of his peers: "I have long dreamed of buying an island owned by no nation, and of establishing the World Headquarters of the Dow Company on the truly neutral ground of such an island, beholden to no nation or society."[79] Pressures from multinational corporations with this attitude make it more difficult for United States politicians to shape our foreign policy along lines that they feel are "best for America."

During the Vietnam war, three United States oil companies regularly paid off the Viet Cong to keep them from molesting their trucks and facilities—and the Viet Cong spent this money on arms and ammunition to use against United States troops.[80] While the United States government's official policy favored Israel, an Arabian-American Oil Company executive told a *Newsweek* reporter, "We carry the enemy flag in the Mideast."[81] After Algeria broke its official ties with the United States following the six-day Arab-Israeli war in 1967, several dozen U.S. concerns—including ITT, Caterpillar, and IBM—moved right into the enemy camp and set up shop.

The profit motive is not exactly the most dependable basis for foreign relations. It is doubtful that United States foreign policy is put in the best light when United States–based corporations "employ" Latin American convict labor at $1.22 a day in countries where unemployment is as high as 30 percent. It is fair to ask if Gulf Oil Corporation was helping to further United States foreign policy when it made an illegal $4-million donation to prop up the South Korean dictatorship of Park Chung Hee.[82] Was it in our national interest that General Motors contributed $400,000 to assist the same dictator? Was Lockheed "thinking American" when it paid out millions of dollars in kickbacks and bribes from Indonesia to Saudi Arabia to Japan?[83] Was the United States well served when Exxon secretly gave $49 million to Italian politicians, including some in the Italian communist party? Or when Mobil Oil gave $2.1 million in payoffs to Italian politicians and then falsified its records to indicate the money was spent for "advertising" and "research"? Or when Northrop paid Saudi Arabia's best-known military contract fixer half a million dollars to swing an arms sale? These questions do not relate to the legality of the payments—they were probably all legal enough—but to their practical effect on the welfare of this nation's foreign relations.

United States–based multinationals also burden our foreign policy by creating intense fears among weaker nations that they might become victims of economic colonialism. A study prepared for the Senate Subcommittee on Multinational Corporations shows that United States corporations have provided 80 percent of the foreign investment in Mexico and either control or have a controlling influence over 36 percent of the capital of Mexico's 311 largest corporations. This heavyweight presence makes the Mexicans nervous.[84] In Canada, 59 of the 100 largest nonfinancial corporations are controlled by foreigners—mostly foreigners just across the border in the United States.[85] Canadian officials publicly complain about the fact that their economy is run from board rooms in Detroit, New York, and Houston.

The giant United States multinationals argue persuasively that the very fact that they are tied to many nations and have many loyalties is a

---

[79]Quoted in Robert Sherrill, "The Multinationals Deploy to Rule," *Nation*, April 16, 1973.

[80]Jack Anderson, *Washington Exposé* (Washington, D.C.: Public Affairs Press, 1967), pp. 200–01.

[81]Quoted in *Newsweek*, April 10, 1972.

[82]Associated Press, May 17, 1974.

[83]Anthony Sampson, *The Arms Bazaar: From Lebanon to Lockheed* (New York: Viking Press, 1977), p. 275.

[84]Stanley Meisler, "Reacting to Big-Stick Diplomacy," *Nation*, February 7, 1976.

[85]From a speech by Alastair Gillespie, Canadian Minister of Energy, Mines and Resources, on January 22, 1976; transcript from the Canadian Embassy.

force for world peace. The corporate peacemonger theory is a continuation of the old idea that if you exchange enough culture and technology everyone will feel so much like everyone else that nobody will want to fight anybody. As Gerstacker argues,

> It has been contended that the United Nations and kindred international organizations are the spawning ground of a new international breed—citizens of the world. But on the contrary, international organizations tend to reinforce feelings of nationalism because the bulk of the representatives in such organizations represent the interests of one particular and specific nation and nationalism. I firmly believe the *real* world citizens are coming out of the companies that have branches in every nation and who are at home in every nation. . . . With the blossoming of a true world economy these multinational bees, whether they are American or British, German or French, Russian or Japanese, will be establishing more hives in the farther fields. . . . They will tend for many reasons, political and economic, to become nationless companies.[86]

Like many other noble theories, the theory of peace through international profiteering has a number of mammoth defects. Perhaps the most obvious one is that what these fellows are talking about is simply another form of utopia—a kind of international brotherhood based on self-discipline among the workers for the furtherace of greed at the top.

One might also want to argue with the multinationals' assumption that nationalism is bad. Nationalism certainly has been the basis for many irrational wars and many unnecessary economic disputes. But it has also been the basis of some sensible economic disputes and even some reasonable wars. What kind of peaceful internationalism do the multinationals want people to achieve? The kind that already is seeing the finger lickin' grease of Kentucky Fried Chicken being dispensed in London and is seeing United States–style condominiums ruining the skyline of Paris? Are they speaking of the kind of internationalism that has already poisoned the Volga, the Danube, and the Hudson rivers with the same pollutants?

When the multinationals speak of peace, do they really mean profitable stability at the cost of human dignity? Dow's Gerstacker may talk about "melting pot" multinationals that are "a medium in which creed and color and castes can (and indeed *must*) mix, and work together," but that seems to be a theory for the credit of the future; to get the cash of the present, the multinationals apparently are willing to tolerate something else. United States–based multinationals have invested in South Africa; as their investments increased over the past twenty years, apartheid worsened. Where was their influence to stop racism?

We can give the multinationals full credit for good intentions, but the above questions remain to be answered, and they all come down to one big question: can a republic remain politically healthy when one of the principles on which it is built—power coming directly from the people of that particular nation, with government officials being directly responsible to the people for their actions—no longer applies in many important areas of its international affairs? A few years ago, the Canadian government issued a confidential report in which it posed the question this way:

> If multinational corporations were to develop to the point where they become the major organizers of production in the world, they would undoubtedly be a major power. But power responsible to whom? At the moment this power is wielded largely by national governments responsible to their electorates. In a world dominated by large and powerful multinational corporations, to whom would nonelected boards and management of multinational enterprises be responsible?[87]

DIPLOMACY: THE SLIPPERY ART

Among the President's many hats is the top hat of diplomacy. Many powerful forces are involved in the making of foreign policy, including two already mentioned: the military-industrial

---

[86]Quoted in Sherrill, "The Multinationals Deploy to Rule." A further exposition of this hope is made by David W. Ewing, senior associate editor of the *Harvard Business Review,* in "Corporation as Peacemonger," *Aramco World Magazine* (house organ of the Arabian-American Oil Company), 1973.

[87]Quoted in Sherrill, "The Multinationals Deploy to Rule."

complex and the multinationals. Congress, pulled and pushed by lobbyists and by ethnic voters with ties abroad, is constantly demanding that the nation follow one policy or another. But the last word belongs to the President—officially, at least.

Professor Edward S. Corwin states the accepted wisdom: "There is no more securely established principle of constitutional practice than the exclusive right of the President to be the nation's intermediary in its dealing with other nations."[88] Kenneth W. Thompson adds:

> So far-reaching is this function that the President by his actions can confront the Congress and the people on almost any issue with a *fait accompli* even on critical matters decisive to war and peace. He can recognize or refuse to recognize a foreign government, issue major declarations that "revolutionize" policy, as with the Monroe or Truman Doctrines, engage in negotiations that lead to far-reaching formal or informal obligations, and order the armed forces of his country to remote parts of the world, sometimes committing the nation thereby to hostile acts short of war. The President by his actions can so shape the course of American action as to eliminate for all practical purposes the determining role of the Congress despite its "power of the purse" and capacity to declare war.[89]

And Theodore C. Sorensen, one of President Kennedy's closest aides, adds his perspective:

> In domestic affairs a presidential decision is usually the beginning of public debate. In foreign affairs the issues are frequently so complex, the facts so obscure and the period for decision so short, that the American people have from the beginning—and even more so in this century—delegated to the President more discretion in this vital area and they are usually willing to support any reasonable decision he makes.[90]

Those descriptions of absolute power in foreign policy are accurate in general, but they do not begin to give scope to the pressures, fears, good and bad luck, good and bad advice, and accident that accumulate under the puffy designation of presidential power. Nor do they sufficiently take into consideration the fact that, in order to get his way, and get it comfortably, a President often feels obliged to exaggerate and lie. Just because the President has first—and often last—say in foreign affairs does not mean, in short, that it is a power easily exercized.

Decision Making by Momentum

What sometimes passes as a presidential "decision" is, in fact, nothing but the product of a mindless momentum: one thing sort of accidentally leads to another, until the nation finds itself in a position that neither the President nor anyone else in a major seat of authority had planned on. To be sure, the President or his factotums may have given their approval to certain steps along the way that got the momentum going, but they did not envision the end result as being what it turned out to be. And sometimes when they discover what has developed, it is too late to prevent the damage. Former Defense Secretary Clark Clifford describes this process of runaway momentum: "There were too many cases where the agency was given the authority [by the President] to start with A and go to B, and when it got to B it seemed logical to go to C on its own authority, and so on to D and beyond."[91]

Momentum may account for President Lyndon Johnson's sending more troops to South Vietnam in 1965 even though, while campaigning in 1964, he had virtually assured the electorate that he would not. He said at that time that he did *not* think "we are ready for American boys to do the fighting for Asian boys."[92] Was he lying? Was he taking a deceitful position to win the election, while he secretly planned to enlarge the war as soon as his victory was assured? Possibly. But Seyom Brown would have us consider a less duplicitous possibility:

> The explanation probably lies in the fact that the undercutting [of Johnson's policy to keep the na-

---

[88]Edward S. Corwin, *The President: Office and Powers: 1787–1957*, 4th rev. ed. (New York: New York University Press, 1957), p. 224.

[89]Kenneth W. Thompson, *American Diplomacy and Emergent Patterns* (New York: New York University Press, 1962), p. 112.

[90]Theodore C. Sorensen, *Decision-Making in the White House: The Olive Branch or the Olives* (New York: Columbia University Press, 1963), p. 48.

[91]Quoted in Gelb, "Should We Play Dirty Tricks in the World?"

[92]Quoted in Brown, *The Faces of Power*, p. 327.

tion out of the war] had proceeded too far already in the form of actual diplomatic commitments and momentum established by our military participation, when Johnson took the matter under full consideration in late 1964. His lack of a continuing interest in the complexities of foreign affairs, prior to their reaching a crisis state, allowed subordinate levels of the government, under the assumption that they were implementing existing guidelines, to make tactical moves required by exigencies of the moment and to transmute, almost imperceptibly, differences in degrees of commitment and participation to a difference in kind.[93]

The metamorphosis from commitments of escalating degrees into a different kind of commitment—which is to say, a change from military advisers to military offensive troops—went like this:

First step: we sent military advisers to help the inexperienced South Vietnamese troops.

Second step: our military advisers suggested that the South Vietnamese use helicopters for reconnaissance, troop support, and troop transport.

Third step: since the South Vietnamese didn't know how to fly helicopters, our advisers set up training bases.

Fourth step: since the South Vietnamese were not able to protect these bases, we sent our own troops to defend them.

Fifth step: since the best defense entails controlling the most land around the bases, our "defensive" troops extended the perimeter of security. And this called for deploying still more United States troops.

Sixth step: defense became indistinguishable from offense, as the perimeters were extended farther and farther.

Such momentum does not let up when one administration gives way to another. One reason for this is that those who seek and win the Presidency tend to share similar philosophies in foreign-policy making. A new President will generally be guided by decisions previous Presidents have made. The cumulative effect of a foreign policy carried out over several administrations can be strong indeed—and very resistant to change, even if a President should desire to change it. As Irish and Frank point out,

Though each administration is unique, every administration is bound by tradition, customs, precedents, and commitments. . . . Every President in turn does his best—and his damnedest—to measure up to the office inherited from his predecessors and to establish for himself a high place in the nation's history. The Presidency, however, is never one man in the office but inevitably all the men who have held the office and left their imprints upon it. . . .[94]

Policy Making by Exaggeration

The President can enunciate foreign policy night and day, but if he does not have the support of Congress and the support of a majority of the people, he will be in trouble. First, he may easily find Congress unwilling to ante up the money to pay for his presidential adventures overseas. Second, a President's powers to negotiate and to threaten are seriously weakened if it is obvious to the world that the mass of public opinion has turned away from him. He must seem to be speaking for a determined people.

To unify the nation as much as possible and to pressure Congress into supporting the military budget, however high, Presidents (at least several of recent vintage) have resorted to gross exaggerations of external threats. Sometimes they have described the threat themselves; sometimes they have had their aides and cabinet appointees do it.

Eisenhower's Secretary of State, Dulles, was a Machiavellian sort of guy who knew exactly what he was doing in playing brinksmanship: he was keeping Congress and the public in such a fever that they would go on priming the defense budget and give him carte blanche in his bellicose cold war strategy. Even before World War II, Dulles had written that "the creation of a vast armament in itself calls for a condition midway between war and peace. Mass emotion on a substantial scale is a prerequisite. The willingness to sacrifice must be engendered. A sense of peril from abroad must be cultivated."[95]

Militaristic hyperbole aimed at prodding Congress and the public into full support of the

[93]Brown, p. 330.

[94]Irish and Frank, *U.S. Foreign Policy*, p. 198.

[95]John Foster Dulles, *War, Peace, and Change* (New York: Macmillan, 1939), p. 90.

"My principals in Washington wish to know, Excellency, whether
you would prefer to be propped up overtly or covertly."

Drawing by Handelsman; © 1976 The New Yorker Magazine, Inc.

President's position has been characteristic of policy making of the cold war era.

Before President Truman went publicly before Congress to ask for financial support for military activities in Greece and Turkey, congressional leaders were given a briefing in which Dean Acheson, then Assistant Secretary of State, proclaimed in the gloomiest tones:

> In the past eighteen months, Soviet pressure on the Straits, on Iran and on northern Greece has brought the Balkans to the point where a highly possible Soviet breakthrough might open three continents to Soviet penetration. Like apples in a barrel infected by one rotten one, the corruption of Greece would infect Iran and all to the east. It would also carry infection to Africa through Asia Minor and Egypt, and to Europe through Italy and France, already threatened by the strongest domestic Communist parties in Western Europe. . . .[96]

It was a dreadful picture he painted, with friendly governments falling one by one as the communists continued their relentless march around the world. If "we and we alone" did not step forward and stop them in Greece, he suggested, we might someday have to fight them on the shores of Maryland.[97] And when Truman

[96]Acheson, *Present at the Creation*, p. 219.

[97]Ronald Steel, *Imperialists and Other Heroes: A Chronicle of the American Empire* (New York: Random House, 1971), pp. 21–22.

sent his aid bill to Congress, he sent with it an equally lurid description of what might happen if it failed to pass. He had taken the position knowing that it was exaggerated and false, but he explained privately to those who complained that a fright campaign was the only way to win the necessary votes.[98]

The rotten-apple theory—or, as it is more often called, the domino theory—is very popular with Presidents. President Johnson implied that if United States troops didn't stop the communists in Vietnam they would next be on the beaches of California. Kennedy, visiting a missile base in 1963, warned that "every time a country, regardless of how far away from our own borders—every time that country passes behind the Iron Curtain the security of the United States is thereby endangered."[99]

But there are profound dangers in developing foreign policy by evoking a fictional superenemy: the purveyors of this propaganda may end up believing their own exaggerations. Or they may get locked into extreme positions, which they really do not favor or which they would later like to change but can't because the public opinion they helped create won't let them.

Kennedy's determination to appear "tough" locked the nation, as well as him, into a position that became progressively worse. After a meeting with Russian premier Khrushchev in Vienna in 1961, Kennedy felt that he had come out looking weak. He told James Reston of the *New York Times* that "Khrushchev had decided that 'anybody stupid enough to get involved in that situation [the Bay of Pigs] was immature, and anybody who didn't see it through was timid and, therefore, could be bullied.' " Not because he was especially interested in Vietnam, but only to show that "he couldn't be bullied," Reston says (and others close to Kennedy have said the same), Kennedy sent 15,000 American men to Vietnam—and we were on our way to a commitment of half a million troops.[100]

Policy Making by Advice

Presidents are surfeited with foreign-policy advisers. They are built into the system. The most obvious sources of advice are, of course, the Secretary of State and the Secretary of Defense.

Recent Presidents have treated their Secretaries of State in various ways, but mostly they have treated them with indifference. President Franklin Roosevelt kept a bumbler, Cordell Hull, as Secretary of State for eleven and a half years so that he, Roosevelt, could do the actual diplomatic work himself. President Eisenhower, however, relied heavily on his strong-willed Secretary of State, Dulles. Kennedy, like FDR, tried to be his own Secretary of State. Johnson inherited Secretary of State Dean Rusk from Kennedy and allowed him more play, but not much more. Nixon once again brought the Secretary of State's duties directly into the White House, where he kept by his side, and listened closely to, his national security adviser, the ubiquitous Henry Kissinger. Years after he had actually assumed the duties of the office, Kissinger became Secretary of State. But that title was much too bland to describe him; he was the master conniver, the global strategist who had virtual carte blanche in matters of foreign affairs for Nixon and for Nixon's successor, Gerald Ford.

Kissinger relied very little on the State Department bureaucracy for advice on policy. Its role was reduced to a managerial and administrative operation, organized on geographical and functional lines. The bureaus of African Affairs, European Affairs, Inter-American Affairs, and so forth simply coordinated various functions, ranging from economic to cultural to technological relations with the various regions. The Foreign Service personnel assigned to the overseas missions lost some of their diplomatic prestige too.[101] They continued to discharge presidential and State Department directives, report on

[98]Charles E. Bohlen, *The Transformation of American Foreign Policy* (New York: W. W. Norton & Co., 1969).

[99]John F. Kennedy, public papers, 1963.

[100]Alfred Steinberg, *Sam Johnson's Boy* (New York: Macmillan, 1968), pp. 752–53.

[101]The thirty-five hundred Foreign Service officers are highly trained at a special institute and may be sent anywhere in the world. Theirs is a rigid hierarchy; one begins at the bottom grade and advances through the ranks, so it may take as long as twenty years to reach a position of responsibility.

Secretary of State Kissinger and President Ford at the NATO summit meeting in Brussels, 1975

domestic and foreign affairs of the nations they were assigned to, and look out for American interests there, but their functions were increasingly encroached upon by the overseas missions of other agencies, such as AID, the Central Intelligence Agency, and the Foreign Agriculture Service. The United States ambassador technically had control of all United States personnel on the country team, but, more often than not, the officers of the various overseas agencies bypassed the ambassador and reported directly to their superiors in Washington.

Kissinger's lone ranger style of diplomacy seemed to hold in contempt other officials who should have been involved. As mentioned in Chapter 9, the United States held secret talks with Cuba—known only to Nixon, Kissinger, and two negotiators—for twelve months in 1974–75. Not even the State Department's official charged with monitoring and coordinating United States policy toward Cuba knew what was going on. Nor did the ranking members of congressional foreign affairs committees.

When Kissinger flew to China in 1971 to begin developing President Nixon's new China

policy, he did not apprise any of our ambassadors in the Far East of what he was up to. When his mission became publicly known and when it became obvious that the ambassadors had been excluded from the planning, their standing in the nations where they were stationed was critically undermined.

Kissinger's secrecy (thoroughly approved by Presidents Nixon and Ford) offended many important members of Congress as well as some portions of the public. In his 1976 campaign, Jimmy Carter capitalized on this unhappiness by promising that he would conduct "open diplomacy." When he became President, however, Carter discovered that, while total secrecy in diplomacy may lead to evils, total openness in diplomacy is, practically speaking, impossible. Diplomats cannot effectively negotiate with the public and the press looking over their shoulders every minute.

The most colorful, and controversial, sources of advice to Presidents have come from what is called "the intelligence establishment," of which the most colorful and controversial by far is the Central Intelligence Agency. Before World

War I, the prevailing mood among the functionaries in the State Department was, "gentlemen don't open other people's mail." That attitude ended forever with World War II. Since then, the United States has poured a fortune into building up a multifaceted information-gathering/information-sifting/information-analysis mechanism that seeks to reduce the world to the interpretation of a computer.

The beginning of the intelligence network was spun in 1947 with passage of the National Security Act, which set up the National Security Council "to advise the President with respect to the integration of domestic, foreign, and military policies relating to the national security," with the specific duty to "assess and appraise the objectives, commitments, and risks of the United States in relation to our actual and potential military power."[102] Members of the council are the President, the Vice President, and the Secretaries of State and Defense. Statutory advisers to the council are the Director of the Central Intelligence Agency and the Chairman of the Joint Chiefs of Staff. The Central Intelligence Agency was established under the National Security Council to "correlate and evaluate intelligence relating to the national security." But it was to "have no police, subpoena, law-enforcement powers or internal security functions." In short, it was supposed to operate its spy apparatus and dirty tricks overseas only, never at home.

The CIA employs about 15,000 persons. It is not the largest of the spy agencies; the military services have larger spy units. The army's intelligence branch, for example, has about 38,000 members.[103] Like much else about the CIA, its budget is secret. It gives no public accounting of its activities. And Congress seldom knows what the CIA is up to.

In the back-alley combat of the cold war years—from the Congo to Cuba, from Laos to Berlin—the CIA performed as the cutting edge of United States foreign policy in situations where overt armed intervention could not be excused and where straight diplomacy would be immediately frustrated. Spy planes, political assassi-

nations, military coups, industrial sabotage, infiltration of labor unions and student organizations and political parties and press groups have all been traced back to the CIA's overseas network. Its covert activities have been as myriad as they have been sometimes heavy-handed.[104] Its failures have been well publicized; its successes have not been. So it is impossible to accurately assess the value of the CIA's work. But it is accurate to say that, to many national groups around the world, the CIA has come to symbolize the oppressiveness of big money and big power. The CIA, to many people, stands for "the ugly American" in giant form.

Toward the end of the eighteenth century, Edmund Burke wrote, "I dread our being too much dreaded. We may say that we shall not abuse this astonishing and hitherto unheard-of power. But every other nation will think we shall abuse it."[105] At best, the most powerful nation in the world is going to have to put up with suspicions of that sort when it is dealing with weaker nations, even if it is not abusing its power. But the chances of such abuse occurring become much greater when the shaping of foreign policy rests to any extent on a statement such as the one made by John J. McCloy, sometimes known as the uncrowned head of the foreign-policy establishment, especially during the Kennedy years. McCloy once encouraged Kennedy to resume atmospheric testing of atomic bombs without worrying about what other nations thought. "World opinion?" he scoffed. "I don't believe in world opinion. The only thing that matters is power."[106] That has been the CIA's attitude, and, because the world knows it to be the CIA's attitude, the agency—and thus the United

---

[102]*Congress and the Nation*, p. 249.

[103]Sources: Harry Howe Ransom, *Intelligence Establishment* (Cambridge, Mass.: Harvard University Press, 1970), p. 88; Gelb, "Should We Play Dirty Tricks in the World?"

---

[104]The CIA's activities sometimes would have to be judged a bit weird. Once it thought up a plan—never carried out—to implant a poison in Cuban Premier Fidel Castro's boots that would seep into his body and make his beard fall off, thus causing him to lose face with the populace. On another occasion, the CIA dreamed up a plan, which it did carry out, to give Russian Premier Nikita S. Khrushchev a physical by proxy: when Khrushchev visited the United States, the CIA rigged up a special drain on his toilet; agents carried away the flushings and analyzed the excreta at their laboratory. (Jack Anderson, *Washington Post*, March 3, 1976.)

[105]Quoted in Thompson, *American Diplomacy and Emergent Patterns*, p. 54.

[106]Quoted in Steel, *Imperialists and Other Heroes*, p. 351.

States—is blamed for every riot and assassination that occurs anywhere in the world.

Foreign Policy by Pressure

When the Commission for the Organization of the Government for the Conduct of Foreign Policy, a blue-ribbon panel of diplomats and ex-diplomats, met in Washington on June 9, 1975, to hear some remarks by its ranking member, Vice President Nelson Rockefeller, it was ready for some plain talk, and that's what it got. "The two major foreign-policy issues of the day," said Rockefeller, "are the Mideast and Greek-Turkish conflicts. On both of these, it is foreign lobbies that are guiding U.S. policy." To Rockefeller, and probably to most top officials, the shaping of foreign affairs by pressure groups is not a healthy situation, the reason being, as Rockefeller told the International Press Institute the next year, "the United States cannot represent all its people, or its own national self-interest, if it tries, or is forced, to represent special groups ahead of the nation's interests as a whole."[107]

Washington swarms with lobbyists for foreign nations and for foreign economic interests. (See Chapter 5.) Many of these lobbyists are former United States government officials, highly influential persons, and many are members of some of Washington's most prestigious law firms. When Algeria hired Clark Clifford to represent it in Washington, it was getting a former Defense Secretary, an adviser to many Presidents, and, perhaps, Washington's best-known lawyer. When Venezuela hired Dean Acheson to represent it in Washington, it was getting a former Secretary of State and adviser to many Presidents. Ex–members of Congress and ex-senators and ex-bureaucrats now speak for foreign interests as lobbyists. Such powerful spokesmen, motivated strictly by cash, help shape United States foreign policy. So do those foreign nationals working as lobbyists in Washington who use bribery. "Justice Department experts estimate that over one hundred million dollars (up from thirty million dollars a decade ago) are spent each year by foreign governments and corporations on shaping U.S. foreign policy and influencing policymakers. . . ." The money is spent to "enforce policy-making decisions to which most Americans are either opposed or indifferent."[108] During the 1960s and '70s, South Korea and its lobbyists, seeking arms and trade compacts, secretly passed millions of dollars in little white envelopes to Washington politicians.

At worst, these lobbyists succeed in persuading our policy shapers to put cronyism and greed over national interest. At best, they muddle the outline of our national interests by interjecting external economic interests. While domestic labor lobbyists pressure Congress and the State Department to keep out foreign-made autos and foreign-made shoes, foreign lobbyists are pressuring Congress and the State Department to open the tariff gates to Toyotas and Amalfis. While the United States fishing industry pressures Washington to drive foreign fishermen from our coastal waters, Japan and Russia and other fish-industry nations pressure Washington for a relaxation of restrictions. If the wishes of the general populace are considered, it is probably only by accident.

Among the most powerful foreign lobbies in Washington are those that fight for more military and economic aid, in the name of their national interests. Foremost among these, as mentioned in Chapter 5, is the Israeli lobby. Working through United States Jews, who are big spenders in political campaigns, the Israeli lobby is so successful that in 1975, for example, Israel received $1.5 billion in military assistance—two-thirds in the form of outright gifts—which was by far the largest amount given to a single country.[109] The Israeli lobby is a key shaper of U.S. policy in the Middle East, by far more powerful than the Arab lobby, even with its ability to negotiate as the world's leading supplier of oil. The Middle East oil-producing nations warned the United States that if we continued to favor Israel they would raise oil prices and embargo shipments to this country. Despite this terrible threat—which the Middle Eastern nations did in fact carry out—the United States continued to

---

[107]Russell Warren Howe and Sarah Hays Trott, *The Power Peddlers: How Lobbyists Mold America's Foreign Policy* (New York: Doubleday & Co., 1977), p. 4.

[108]Howe and Trott, p. 5.

[109]*Washington Post*, January 18, 1977.

take the position demanded by the Israeli lobby.

Similar success was achieved by the Nationalist China lobby. When the corrupt Generalissimo Chiang Kai-shek, ruler of mainland China, was chased out by communist forces in 1949, he and his followers set up their so-called "Nationalist China" government on the island of Taiwan. Their survival depended solely on the generosity of the United States. The objective of the China lobby was to guarantee a steady flow of military and economic aid to Taiwan and also to prevent the recognition of the communist government in mainland China. For a generation, the China lobby succeeded. Two analysts of foreign lobbies in Washington concluded:

> No foreign lobby in Washington has ever been so rich or so powerful, or interfered so insidiously in the American governmental process, as the China lobby. . . . It relied on smear tactics—but much more heavily than today's pro-Israeli lobbyists. To be denounced as a communist or communist sympathizer in the McCarthy era was infinitely more intimidating than to be emotionally branded as anti-Semetic. And the China lobby, alone in the history of foreign lobbies, promoted witch hunts that threatened to shake the foundations of the Republic. . . . In China's case as in Israel's, the stakes were perilously high, possibly going as far as the very survival of the nation behind the lobby. They were similarly high, too, in terms of money—particularly the arms trade and election campaign kitties.[110]

Throughout the 1950s and '60s, the pro-Chiang atmosphere was so oppressive in Washington that an official who dared to suggest that the United States ought to recognize Communist China would run the risk of being denounced as a communist sympathizer. Our foreign policy made Chiang and his followers rich, but it went directly against the best interests of the American people. Not until President Nixon visited Communist China in 1971 (an ironic breakthrough, since Nixon had built his career on the communist witch hunt) did United States policy toward Asia's key government begin to change. By that time, China was seen as a potentially good customer for U.S. goods. When the dollar sign beckons, foreign policy changes. By 1974,

Defense Secretary James R. Schlesinger was suggesting that it might not even be a bad idea to sell arms to the Red Chinese.

Foreign Policy by Chance

After all the advice, deliberation, computer analyses from the various agencies, and outside pressures have been fed into the pot and sweetened occasionally by presidential whimsy, even the most crucial foreign policy may be determined by sheer chance or human fumbling. In October 1962, President Kennedy pushed the world closer to the brink of atomic war than it had ever been, by demanding that Russia pull its missiles out of Cuba, or else. For thirteen days, the world teetered on a precipice, while the United States and Russia negotiated. One day, after a meeting in the White House, President Kennedy, his brother, Robert, and two close friends sat in Kennedy's office and talked. Robert recalled:

> "The great danger and risk in all of this," [President Kennedy] said, "is a miscalculation—a mistake in judgment." A short time before, he had read Barbara Tuchman's book, *The Guns of August*, and he talked about the miscalculations of the Germans, the Russians, the Austrians, the French, and the British. They somehow seemed to tumble into war, he said, through stupidity, individual idiosyncrasies, misunderstandings, and personal complexes of inferiority and grandeur. We talked about the miscalculation of the Germans in 1939 and the still unfulfilled commitments and guarantees that the British had given to Poland.
>
> Neither side wanted war over Cuba, we agreed, but it was possible that either side could take a step that—for reasons of "security" or "pride" or "face"—would require a response by the other side, which, in turn, for the same reasons of security, pride, or face, would bring a counter response and eventually an escalation into armed conflict.[111]

Here was the most powerful man in the world talking about what it would take to end the confrontation peacefully, and he was admitting that the most important ingredient might turn out to be unpredictable and intangible.

---

[110]Howe and Trott, *The Power Peddlers*, pp. 29–30.

[111]Robert F. Kennedy, *Thirteen Days: A Memoir of the Cuban Missile Crisis*, eds. Richard Neustadt and Graham Allison (New York: W. W. Norton & Co., 1969), p. 62.

THE CHANGING TERRAIN
OF FOREIGN AFFAIRS

The long-stationary ice jam of the cold war has begun to break up, but the resulting icebergs floating free have in some ways created even greater navigational hazards. The so-called "conventional wisdom" of the foreign-affairs establishment is being forced to adjust to new problems, for which history supplies no guidance.

The deep changes have begun to seep upward and alter the crust of international relations and domestic thinking as well. The term "iron curtain"—which describes the wall of militant secrecy and noncooperation behind which the Russians have operated—was first used by Winston Churchill in a speech in Fulton, Missouri, in 1946, and for many years it was in vogue. For diplomatic purposes, State Department officials prefer that it now be dropped. The phrase "Sino-Soviet bloc," which came to life back in the days when our leaders looked upon communism as monolithic, is no longer heard in diplomatic conversation; and even the phrase "Soviet bloc" is considered misleading, because some eastern European countries are resisting Russia's heavy-handed influence. The term "Godless communism," once taken seriously, is now considered a melodramatic joke by the State Department. And the term "free world," once held in such lofty esteem to describe our side, is rejected by the experts as hardly an accurate way to describe nations like Chile, Brazil, the Philippines, and South Africa.[112]

Even the old cold warriors were forced to accept the new pragmatism that began to shape foreign policies on both sides of the "iron curtain" during the 1960s, and this movement has increased in strength. Although political rhetoric—aimed at safeguarding the defense budget—continues to suggest that the apocalyptic war of our era is between freedom and communism, both struggling for the soul of the world, most politicians, in their actions, now seem to acknowledge that this is not the real issue. When Pepsi-Cola sells soda pop to the Russians, it is not seen as a treasonous act. The cooler, more matter-of-fact view among policy makers is probably accurately described by Ronald Steel:

> The communists are not going to inherit the earth, and neither are we. They are not going to do it because communism no longer means more than a nodding allegiance to some rather antiquated economic theories of Karl Marx. The various communist parties have drifted so far apart, and have been so subordinated to the more potent ideology of nationalism, that in many cases it is no longer of any great significance whether or not a nation has a nominally communist form of government. Yugoslavia is communist; so are Albania and North Korea. What benefit does the Soviet Union get out of that? Or China, for that matter? Nicaragua is anti-communist; so are Taiwan and South Korea. What good does that do us? . . .
>
> What counts is not the label a regime may choose to attach to itself, but whether it poses a threat to us or to world peace. . . . As far as the world's peace and our own national interests are concerned, the fact that a country is communist may be less important than how much rain it gets or how many pairs of shoes it produces. It is certainly less important than the policies it follows toward its neighbors, and how capable it is of meeting the demands of its own citizens for economic justice and social equality. . . .
>
> There are some communist governments that are more worthy of respect than some anti-communist governments. There are some anti-communist governments that are so unpopular with their own people that they cannot be saved. There are others which can be kept in power only by risks that are out of all proportion to the stakes involved. There are some anti-communist governments that are not worth saving, regardless of how small the risks may be. And there are governments that, if the communists did take them over, would be more of a threat to the communist nations than to us. China is the classic example of a country which is a greater danger to Russia now that she is under communist control than she would have been under the control of Chiang Kai-shek.[113]

---

[112]Such changes in thinking have come very slowly and are still far from complete. Several years after Nixon had taken the revolutionary step of recognizing Communist China by visiting that land, he was still speaking as he had in 1950, when he passionately opposed seating the Chinese communists in the United Nations. To a visitor, in 1975, he unloaded the same old cold war rhetoric: "We must always remember that detente doesn't mean the same to the Russians or the Communists as it does to us. Their ultimate goal is to take over the free world, including this country, and they can accomplish that without firing a shot . . . from within." (Quoted in the Associated Press, October 23, 1975.)

[113]Steel, *Pax Americana,* pp. 320–21.

That was written in 1967. It is the kind of observation that has become more commonplace. People who talk and write like that are no longer denounced as pinkos and fellow-travelers. The nation is exhausted from the atomic nervousness that gripped this country throughout the 1950s.

The old balance of terror continues as the foundation of big power relations; efforts to harass and cripple the other side continue through the support of local wars, as in some of the African states.[114] At the same time, there is a new sphere of big power accommodation and cooperation—a sphere quite independent of ideology and standard power-play diplomacy. It is a sphere that has a great deal to do with the attitude expressed by John Quincy Adams in 1823, when someone asked him if he wasn't afraid that a proposed treaty might violate Britain's principles and thereby fail to win that nation's cooperation. "My confidence in cooperation with England," replied Adams, "does not rest on her principles, but on her interests."[115]

The most difficult problems of the future are not likely to come from the big powers—whose interests, like their economies, have much in common—but from the restless "Third World" of emerging nations. How does the colossus deal with them? The new oil billionaires of the Middle East have invested so much money in United States banks that, if they should withdraw it all at once, our banking system could be in serious trouble. If they decided to stop selling us oil (50 percent of our oil is imported), our industry would be in serious trouble. How can the United States teach these overnight capitalists the kind of long-term tempo of capitalism that fits our interests as well as theirs?

How does the most powerful nation in the world fight insignificant nations gracefully? When, in 1975, the new military government of Cambodia seized the United States merchant vessel *Mayaguez* and the crew was rescued by U.S. Marines in a clumsy and bloody encounter, Secretary of State Kissinger actually saw this little embarrassment as showing that: "There are limits beyond which the United States cannot be pushed."[116] These reactions to a "victory" over one of the tiniest and most helpless countries on earth indicated the depths of the uncertainty of the United States as it tries to adjust to the new world. It is an uncertainty, laced sometimes with a strange national feeling of guilt, that was also expressed in a 1975 poll of members of Congress. The question was, What nations are a threat to world peace? Older members predictably answered Russia, China, and the Arab states. The younger members also listed those; but a surprising number added another nation to the list—the United States. Indeed, nearly one out of five first-term Democrats listed the United States as a potential threat to the peace of the world.[117] It was, to say the least, a sign of a revolutionary criterion at work in foreign affairs—revolutionary in its increased objectivity and decreased jingoism.

Recently, new ways have had to be found to use old weapons. Food, for example. The United States is far and away the world's number one foodstuff exporter (especially wheat, rice, and other grains) and Russia and eastern Europe are by far the biggest importers. This situation seemed like such a classic case of potential one-upmanship that, in 1973, CIA analysts began predicting that the United States could use food to achieve primacy over the European communist nations in a way unachievable by force. Then the experts began to have second thoughts and auxiliary concerns, as they realized that they could not use all their foodstuff to pressure and persuade the communists. The hungry developing nations would be watching and demanding their share of the United States surplus. And the hungry small nations could no longer be safely left to starve, for they might not starve quietly.[118]

---

[114] In 1976, Russia and Cuba sent men and equipment to help the communist insurgents in the west African nation Angola seize power from the newly established government (a former Portuguese colony, Angola had just been elevated to nationhood), and the United States sent money and supplies to the troops fighting the communists.

[115] Quoted in Brandt, *The Ordeal of Coexistence,* p. 18.

[116] Quoted in the *Washington Star,* May 17, 1975.

[117] *Washington Post,* July 1, 1975.

[118] *Washington Star,* January 28, 1976.

Guns or Butter?

Between the war-oriented and people-oriented, and between the poorer and richer, parts of the world, the gulfs are wider than ever. A poverty of resources for human needs contrasts with the affluence under which military programs operate. The threats that touch people in their daily lives—joblessness, crime, illness, hunger—rank lower in the scale of government priorities than preparations for war. Throughout the world, the poor, the ill-fed, ill-housed, and ill-educated steadily increase in numbers. The danger and the size of the social deficit grow with neglect.

- The United States and Soviet Union, first in military power, rank 18th and 33rd among all nations in their infant mortality rates.
- Through public budgets, the world community carries more insurance against deliberate military attack than against illness, disease, and all natural disasters.
- At present levels of military spending, the average person can expect over his lifetime to give up three to four years' income to the arms race.
- The world's budget for military research is more than six times the size of its budget for energy research.
- The developed nations spend 20 times more for their military programs than for economic assistance to the poorer countries.
- In the developing world, 1,400,000,000 people have no safe drinking water, 520,000,000 suffer from malnutrition.
- The cost of one Trident submarine equals the cost of a year's schooling for 16,000,000 children in developing countries.

From Ruth Leger Sivard, *World Military and Social Expenditures 1977* (Leesburg, Va.: WMSE Publications, 1977).

Making the problem all the more complex is the fact that there are getting to be so *many* hungry[119] and demanding small nations. Pieces of the old, big-power colonialist world are breaking away and becoming new nations every year. The globe is now cluttered with nations whose names most Americans have never heard—Lesotho, Malawi, Nauru, Gabon, Rwanda, Bahrain, Botswana. They cannot be ignored—no longer can the small, backward nations be treated cavalierly by the big powers. Some of these so-called backward nations control vital minerals that the major industrialized nations must have. The Arabs, only recently scoffed at as an ignorant tribal people who could easily be controlled, have taught the industrialized world that little nations like to be spoken to politely, too—they quadrupled the price of their oil and forced us to thank them for it at any price.

At the end of World War II, only one nation—the United States—knew how to make an atomic bomb; by the mid-1950s, only two nations, the United States and the Soviet Union, had that technical expertise. Today, a dozen nations know how to build atomic bombs, and three dozen nations will have the proper material and skills to build them within a decade. Our experts now concede that any physicist could put together a crude bomb capable of killing 50,000 persons. And no longer does a nation need to have an air force or a missile arsenal to deliver the goods. Indeed, the smaller and poorer the nation, the more perversely powerful is its atomic threat. If a mighty, rich nation, such as Russia,

---

[119]And their hunger seems to be unbudgingly permanent, while the fat nations get fatter. The 1975 World Bank Atlas shows that the annual output per person in the industrialized nations, in 1974, averaged $4,550, compared with $116 for each of the 1 billion people living in the very poorest countries, mainly in Africa and southern Asia. In 1960, the average output per capita was $2,768 in the rich countries, but, in the poor countries, the output in 1960 was about the same as in 1974.

should attack us with nuclear arms, it knows that it would suffer great and costly losses in return; an industrial life that required decades to build would be wiped out in one assault. But what has some poor nation with a small population and a per capita income of, say, two hundred dollars a year got to lose by attacking one of our urban centers with a bomb? Where is the quid pro quo that keeps nations from attacking each other? Senator Birch Bayh put this new threat into perspective:

> I have nightmares of developing nations with too many people and too little food and possessing the technology of nuclear power capable of destroying millions of human beings. Such nations have little to lose by brandishing nuclear weapons. A world technology which cannot provide them with adequate food has given them destructive power in abundance. The millennium is beyond their reach, but the apocalypse is within their grasp.
>
> It is fashionable to minimize the threat posed by these weapons in the hands of the poor states. We are told that these weapons cannot be delivered on bullock carts or rickshaws. What these doubters fail to consider is the fact that they can be carried by a commercial airliner or assembled in the heart of an adversary's city. We are living in a world where science fiction and scientific fact have begun to converge, and the nuclear club is now open to all regardless of race, religion or national origin.[120]

---

[120]*Congressional Record*, S21359, December 8, 1975.

Summary

1. Foreign relations is the political activity of one nation getting involved in other nations' affairs, generally for selfish reasons.

2. American foreign policy has been characterized from the beginning by territorial and economic expansionism.

3. Until 1940, the United States steered clear of entangling alliances, but events following World War II forced it to accept the role of spokesman, banker, and policeman for the noncommunist world. Now we are tied to other nations by numerous military treaties and extensive foreign aid arrangements.

4. The cold war ideology, originally influenced by the rhetoric and actions of Stalin and McCarthy, has shaped our postwar foreign policy.

5. The development of nuclear weapons by both the United States and the Soviet Union has led to a balance of terror in which each side has the power to destroy the other in the event of all-out war.

6. The balance of terror has gone through various phases: "massive retaliation"—the constant threat that aggression will be answered with nuclear war; "flexible response"—the option of using either conventional or nuclear war to respond to aggression; and "detente"—the current phase, which calls for big-power negotiation and voluntary arms limitation.

7. Economic interests motivate much of our foreign policy, and economic assistance to other nations has been used to contain communism as well as to protect and expand capitalism.

8. The Marshall Plan, which enabled Europe to recover from World War II, was perhaps the most successful form of United States foreign aid. Aid to less developed countries has not been so effective.

9. Multinational corporations affect foreign policy by promoting policy that will protect their investments abroad and by acting as unofficial diplomats overseas. Multinationals are quite willing to act against American interests when corporate profits are at stake, and they frequently provoke resentment in weaker nations by interfering in those nations' economies.

10. The President has the last word in foreign-policy making, but most policy making is not done through the exercise of presidential power. Some policy is made by momentum, some by chance happenings; some policy requires that a President lie to the American people or exaggerate threats in order to win support for it; some policy is made by the President's advisers—including the Secretary of Defense, the Secretary of State, and the intelligence establishment. Foreign-policy making is also subject to the pressures of foreign lobby groups.

11. Major shifts are taking place in foreign affairs. The cold war ice jam is breaking up, since communism is no longer considered a monolithic bloc. The big powers are taking a more pragmatic approach in the balance of terror. It is the hungry and neglected Third World nations that are emerging as the greatest threat to world order.

Additional Reading

Roger Hilsman, *The Politics of Policy Making in Defense and Foreign Affairs* (New York: Harper & Row, Publishers, 1971), gives an overview, including some material on Vietnam policy making. The machinery of foreign-policy making, and its workings, are described in Morton H. Halperin et al., *Bureaucratic Politics and Foreign Policy* (1974), and in Burton M. Sapin, *The Making of United States Foreign Policy* (1966), both published in Washington, D.C., by the Brookings Institution; and—more critically—in John Franklin Campbell, *The Foreign Affairs Fudge Factory* (New York: Basic Books, 1971).

Some of the influences on foreign policy from the executive branch outside are discussed in Gabriel A. Almond, *The American People and Foreign Policy* (New York: Praeger Publishers, 1961); James A. Robinson, *Congress and Foreign-Policy Making: A Study in Legislative Influence and Initiative,* rev. ed. (Homewood, Ill.: Dorsey Press, 1967); and James N. Rosenau, *Domestic Sources of Foreign Policy* (New York: Free Press, 1967).

Graham T. Allison's *Essence of Decision: Explaining the Cuban Missile Crisis* (Boston: Little Brown and Co., 1971) offers a careful analysis of the Cuban missile crisis and outlines three distinct ways of looking at foreign-policy decisions. For thorough and engrossing accounts of the Vietnam war, see Frances FitzGerald, *Fire in the Lake: The Vietnamese and the Americans in Vietnam* (Boston: Little, Brown and Co., 1972); and David Halberstam, *The Best and the Brightest* (New York: Random House, 1972).

Critical analyses of American foreign policy from various perspectives, include C. Wright Mills, *The Causes of World War Three* (Westport, Conn.: Greenwood Press, 1976); Richard J. Barnet, *The Roots of War* (New York: Penguin Books, 1973); Seymour Melman, *The Permanent War Economy* (New York: Simon & Schuster, 1974); Harry Magdoff, *The Age of Imperialism* (New York: Monthy Review Press, 1969); J. William Fulbright, *The Arrogance of Power* (New York: Random House, 1967)—by the former Chairman of the Senate Foreign Relations Committee; Arthur M. Schlesinger, Jr., *The Imperial Presidency* (Boston: Houghton Mifflin Co., 1973); Seymour M. Hersh, *Chemical and Biological Warfare: America's Hidden Arsenal* (Indianapolis: Bobbs Merrill Co., 1968); and Philip Agee, *Inside the Company: CIA Diary* (New York: Simon & Schuster, 1975).

> *The ideas of economists and political philosophers, both when they are right and when they are wrong, are more powerful than is commonly understood. Indeed, the world is ruled by little else. Practical men, who believe themselves to be quite exempt from any intellectual influence, are usually the slaves of some defunct economist.*
>
> John Maynard Keynes

15
THE ECONOMY

Next to their democratic, or republican, form of government, Americans are proudest of what they consider to be their free-enterprise, capitalist economy. Indeed, for most people democracy and capitalism are inseparable. President Gerald R. Ford proclaimed, "My resources as President—and my resolve as President—are devoted to the free enterprise system. I do not intend to celebrate our Bicentennial by reversing the great principles on which the United States was founded."[1]

The year of the Declaration of Independence, 1776, was also the year in which Adam Smith published his great work *The Wealth of Nations.* In it, people could, for the first time, read a sensible formula for a free economy—an economy in which everyone would work for profit, and their efforts to compete for customers would produce goods in quantities never before seen, at prices within the reach of all. Smith believed that this unfettered and unregulated marketplace would result in a "universal opulence which extends itself to the lowest ranks of the people."[2] In short, he preached an economic democracy (if not an economic anarchy). Government's role in this scheme was only to guarantee that the rules of competition would be allowed to prevail.

Adam Smith's was an impossible ideal. Political power, as has been said more than once in this book, is the exercise of special interests, and special interests usually tune their song of gov-

---

[1] Quoted in the *Washington Star*, June 17, 1975.

[2] Adam Smith, *The Wealth of Nations* (New York: Random House, Modern Library, 1937).

ernment to the ring of the cash register. It is inevitable—and has proved to be so for two hundred years in this country.

The men who wrote the Constitution were men of wealth. They wanted a government that would leave them alone, but they also wanted a government that would enable them to acquire more. Thus they wrote into their document stipulations that would protect private property, guarantee debts, sanctify contracts, and ensure the circulation of sound money. They set up the legal framework of a free-enterprise economy but made sure that the government would stand behind it. The result is that, from the beginning, government has interfered with and subsidized "free enterprise" in various ways. For example, shipbuilders, who made up one of the largest colonial industries, got an immediate bonus from independence: the second and third acts of the nation's first Congress imposed higher duties on goods moved in foreign ships.

When President Calvin Coolidge remarked, "The business of government is business," he was only enunciating a philosophy that had lived with vigor in one corner or another of the federal hierarchy since the nation's founding. James Madison, in *The Federalist Papers,* Number 10, sounds exactly like an early Coolidge in declaring that "the regulation of these various and interfering [economic] interests forms the principal task of modern legislation. . . . " In other words, the business of government was business then, too. Both Coolidge and Madison were thinking not merely of business, but of Big Business. Fat cats controlled the Constitutional Convention. As Charles Beard has pointed out, "Not one member represented in his immediate personal economic interests the small farming or mechanic classes."[3]

In the nineteenth century, state as well as federal government subsidized or built roads, canals, and railroads; many states actually entered into the manufacturing business. States also invented the corporate form of business organization, allowing individuals to hide behind a corporate body, with limited liability to the principals. High tariffs subsidized domestic industry by making foreign goods expensive by comparison. Finally, as small companies gave way to huge corporations, and competition to monopoly or oligopoly, the government had to step in and save us from free enterprise by establishing regulatory agencies such as the Interstate Commerce Commission and the Federal Trade Commission. So, while the myth of free enterprise still lingers in the backs of our minds, the fact of government's intrusion in the marketplace has long been accepted and even welcomed. Whatever its defects and however unfair, the combination of free enterprise and government interference has made the United States the richest, most successful, and probably most efficient nation in history—and possibly the happiest, if happiness can be measured by the distribution of material goods.

Many economists seriously doubt that any vestige of classic free-enterprise capitalism will survive in this country. Some contend that it has already been erased by big government, big unions, and big corporations. This concern, far from being hidden in scholarly journals, is discussed in the popular press. The six-column headline of the *New York Times* Financial Section on January 4, 1976, was: "Will the Bicentennial See the Death of Free Enterprise?" The answers, supplied by a covey of business executives and economists, were about evenly divided, with a number of experts concluding that the United States is in fact "well on the way to a planned economy."

Polls taken among Americans seem to indicate that the people of this nation want the government to take an even greater part in the economy. In 1975, pollster Peter D. Hart found that 61 percent of a sample of Americans believed in a Big Business conspiracy to keep prices high. Only 17 percent favored the present economic system; 41 percent wanted major changes. By a 66-percent-to-25-percent margin, these Americans told Hart that they favored employees owning most of their company's stock. In other words, they thought they might prefer something like socialist capitalism, or capitalist socialism.[4] Not only have Americans become comfortable with government interfer-

---

[3]Charles Beard, *An Economic Interpretation of the Constitution of the United States* (New York: Macmillan, 1935), p. 149.

[4]*Wall Street Journal,* August 22, 1975.

Freedom for Property

The liberties that the constitutionalists hoped to gain were chiefly negative. They wanted freedom from fiscal uncertainty and irregularities in the currency, from trade wars among the states, from economic discrimination by more powerful foreign governments, from attacks on the creditor class or on property, from popular insurrection. They aimed to create a government that would act as an honest broker among a variety of propertied interests, giving them all protection from their common enemies and preventing any one of them from becoming too powerful. The Convention was a fraternity of types of absentee ownership. All property should be permitted to have its proportionate voice in government. Individual property interests might have to be sacrificed at times, but only for the community of propertied interests. Freedom for property would result in liberty for men—perhaps not for all men, but at least for all worthy men. Because men have different faculties and abilities, the Fathers believed, they acquire different amounts of property. To protect property is only to protect men in the exercise of their natural faculties. Among the many liberties, therefore, freedom to hold and dispose property is paramount. Democracy, unchecked rule by the masses, is sure to bring arbitrary redistribution of property, destroying the very essence of liberty.

From Richard A. Hofstadter, *The American Political Tradition*
(New York: Random House, Vintage Books, 1954), p. 11.

ence; in times of distress, they have come to think mainly in terms of it. In a recent troubled period, a business reporter noted:

> At a press conference a couple of months ago, President Ford was asked whether he saw any bright spots in the gloomy economic picture. He mentioned the price rebates on new cars, which he praised as a function of "good old American free enterprise." The President's use of the phrase was striking because it came at a time when economists, politicians, businessmen, and practically everybody else were furiously debating just what the government should be doing to counter the recession with public-service jobs, increased unemployment payments, tariffs and import quotas, government loans to businesses, controls on credit, and other therapeutic measures. "Good old American free enterprise" seemed like the last thing that anyone was counting on for help.[5]

In fact, in boom times as well as in bad times, our government gets into the picture, which accounts for the steadily rising expectations of the American people. Poll after poll has shown that most Americans, while holding firmly to an ideology that condemns "big government" and

[5]Walter Guzzardi, Jr., "Putting the Cuffs on Capitalism," *Fortune,* April 1975.

"deficit spending" and favors "individual initiative," also strongly support government spending to reduce unemployment, control pollution, protect consumers, and provide aid to the impoverished and the sick. It is a unique political contradiction that Americans have come to feel very comfortable with—a delusion that combines independence and dependence with breathtaking dexterity. The actual economic system in operation at any given time in any given program has concerned us very little so long as it was *called* free enterprise, supplied us with a reasonable amount of prosperity, and didn't interfere with our democratic indulgences.

HOW THE ECONOMY HAS FARED

There is no consensus among the experts as to which direction the government should move in. But everyone's conscience is raw from being told that the present economic system, though unrivaled in its successes, has fallen woefully short of its potential. Dramatic evidence of its shortcomings is everywhere. The median price of a single-family house in 1965 was $20,000; by 1975, inflation had driven the median price up to $41,300—

thereby excluding most United States families from the housing market.[6] The dollar that was worth one hundred cents in 1940 had, through the grinding of inflation, been worn down to a worth of thirty-two cents in 1973.[7] In 1946, Congress passed the Employment Act, which called upon the federal government to make, as its first priority, the use of "all its plans, functions and resources . . . to promote maximum employment, production, and purchasing power." Walter Heller, former Chairman of the Council of Economic Advisers, called the Em-

ployment Act of 1946 "the nation's economic Magna Carta."[8] But, in fact, the act has generally been ignored, or has been noticed only accidentally. We have never had full employment, and, thirty years after passage of the Employment Act, the nation was still struggling to find work for more than 7 million unemployed.

A microcosm of the nation's failure can be seen in one hypothetical life:[9] A man born in 1910 would have been barely out of high school when the economic crash of 1929 put one American in four out of work. Since he had no expertise, and probably no more than a couple of years' experience at whatever job he was holding, our Mr. Hypothetical would doubtless have joined the ranks of the unemployed. From 1929 until 1941—when the United States entered World War II—he probably worked only erratically, if at all, and when he worked he probably received no more than subsistence wages. He may have volunteered for service during the war, but since he was over thirty years old and probably married, we can suppose that, instead, he went to work in a defense factory. In any event, the first fifteen or sixteen years of his adult life were shaped by poverty and by crisis, not by education and ambition.

Between the end of the war in 1946 and the end of the 1950s, he was probably employed, but his peace of mind and sense of security were undoubtedly shaken periodically by four recessions, which occurred during that time. The 1960s gave Mr. Hypothetical his first period of stable prosperity, but, as the decade moved to a close, the prosperity began to crack under the onslaught of runaway inflation, and, by the time Mr. Hypothetical retired in 1975 on Social Security, at the age of sixty-five, he would have seen his pension's value critically reduced by the worst inflation in recent history. Moreover, his chance of earning some money at a sideline job was reduced to virtually zero by the worst recession since the 1930s. Mr. Hypothetical had come

[6] Library of Congress and Joint Economic Committee analysts estimated that to afford a $41,300 house, a family would have to earn $23,000 a year. But only one out of five families earned that much; the median family income was only $12,051, according to the United States Bureau of the Census. (Report of the Joint Economic Committee, Vol. 1, no. 11, May 5, 1975.) The awesome price rises continued and seemed likely to do so for the foreseeable future. By 1976, the median price of a new house had shot up to $45,000, which, with a 20 percent down payment and financed at 9 percent, meant a payout of $99,636 over twenty-five years. (Associated Press, June 12, 1976.)

The Harvard-MIT Joint Center for Urban Studies concluded in a 1977 report that, by the mid-1980s, the average house will cost $78,000. It warned that the sale prices of new houses have increased twice as fast as family incomes in recent years. (*Washington Post*, March 3, 1977.)

But not everyone is in agreement as to whether the price of new homes or the interest rate on home loans is the real culprit. Financial writer Jane Bryant Quinn blames high interest rates:

"—We tend to assume that a median-income family should be able to afford a median-priced house. But that has almost never been the case.

"In 1955, 1960 and 1965—as in 1976—the median price was about three times higher than median income, which generally put the house out of buying range. (The rule of thumb is that you can't afford a house that costs more than two-and-a-half times income.) The median price of an *older* house, however, has always been within the buying range for median-income families. The price of older houses today is about the same in relation to income as it has been for the past 20 years.

"If all this is true, then what's happening today? Why are families feeling pinched in their housing choices? . . .

"Higher interest rates have pushed monthly mortgage payments up sharply. From 1955 to the early 1970s, median monthly payments were around 16 to 18 percent of median income. But in 1975 and 1976, payments ran around 22 percent. So although a particular house may be within your traditional buying range, the monthly mortgage payment may now be higher than you can swing on your income. Interest rates (and taxes) are the real villain, not new house prices." (*Washington Post*, June 18, 1977.)

[7] Library of Congress figures, in the *Congressional Record*, H3888, May 15, 1974.

[8] Walter W. Heller, *New Dimensions of Political Economy* (Cambridge, Mass.: Harvard University Press, 1966), p. 59.

[9] This hypothetical example is pilfered from Robert Lekachman's *Inflation: The Permanent Problem of Boom and Bust* (New York: Random House, Vintage Books, 1973), which is as wise as it is brief.

full circle in one lifetime. When he lost his job in 1929, some Americans were literally starving; when he retired from his job in 1975, some Americans were still literally starving.[10]

However, there was enormous progress during Mr. Hypothetical's lifetime. Today, this country is vastly more prosperous than it was even twenty-five years ago. In 1950, the productive output per capita—computed in today's dollars, to keep inflation from distorting the comparison—was $4,370.[11] At the end of 1975, the Gross National Product (GNP) per capita came to just over $7,000; and this growth in per capita output was achieved despite the fact that, at the same time, the population was growing rapidly—from 152 million people in 1950 to 214 million in 1976. That represents a staggering increase in national wealth.

Where did all that new wealth go? How did it change the nation's life? Did it go into pop-top aluminum cans and electric lawn mowers and stereo sets? Much of it did. But much of it also went into the support and development of human resources—thanks to some important changes made back in the 1930s. In 1931, Franklin D. Roosevelt declared, "Modern society, acting through its government, owes the definite obligation to prevent the starvation or dire waste of any of its fellow men and women who try to maintain themselves but cannot."[12] When Roosevelt became President two years later, he put that philosophy into action; this was the beginning of the welfare state. In succeeding years, the idea has taken such deep root that it has almost been accepted as a truism. Many billions

of dollars are pumped through the national budget in support of what some observers have called "the guaranteed society."

The introduction of the so-called welfare state represented two noteworthy changes in the relationship of government to the economy: (1) The federal government, as opposed to the states, became firmly established as the more active participant in managing the economy. (2) The government now gave economic support to ordinary citizens, rather than just subsidizing huge entities like the railroads. Few people of power prior to FDR had suggested that a government owed the necessities of life to its *citizens*. Of course, along with preventing "starvation and dire waste," the government continued to subsidize millionaires and to comfort giant corporations. Nevertheless, wherever the money was thrown, it took root. As a result, out of the panic of the 1929–40 Depression came a much more intimate relationship between business and labor and government, moving toward sufficient control to prevent future depressions.

Never again would the bottom actually fall out of the economy. The government would see to that. The millions who lost their jobs in the early 1930s had nothing to fall back on—no unemployment compensation, no established welfare programs, no government-subsidized job retraining programs. They were on their own, with only the bread lines standing between them and outright hunger. Today, most jobs are covered by unemployment insurance; workers and employers pay into it, and when workers have to be laid off, they are paid, for a certain number of weeks, a certain percentage of what they had been earning. After that insurance runs out, they can turn to other established supports—welfare and food stamps. Joblessness does not automatically mean poverty, as it did half a century ago. Nor does it always mean hopelessness.

There are other stabilizing influences in our economy. The federal government guarantees payment of up to $40,000 per bank account should a bank fail. In the 1930s, when nine thousand banks—over one-third of the total—went busted, they wiped out the savings of their depositors. That can never happen again, at least so

---

[10]A *New York Times* report in 1975 told about Mrs. Elsie DeFratus of St. Petersburg, Florida, who died because she "could no longer afford the cost of living." An eighty-year-old Social Security pensioner, she weighed seventy-six pounds at death, and "an autopsy found no trace of food in her shrunken stomach." Thousands of others, it was feared, were experiencing something like what Mrs. DeFratus went through. (*Congressional Record*, S5426, April 8, 1975.)

[11]This amount is arrived at by dividing the population of that year into the 1950 Gross National Product. The Gross National Product is the measure of the nation's economy: it is the dollar value of all the goods and services produced for sale during a given period.

[12]Quoted in Leonard Baker, *The Guaranteed Society* (New York: Macmillan, 1968), p. 162.

Men wait in line for bread, New York, 1931

long as there is a Federal Deposit Insurance Corporation standing ready to back up the deposits.

Finally, our economy has the stabilizing influence of government spending. To be sure, Americans have every right to worry about the proliferation of government and about the increased taxes that must be pumped into the government to support it. But the presence of big government does have one soothing effect: it keeps money in circulation, which is one way of providing jobs and avoiding depressions.

Some of the most generous government spending has been in education. In 1950, we were spending about $9 billion on education (3.4 percent of the GNP), while, twenty-five years later, we were spending about $120 billion (8 percent of GNP) on education. In 1950, half of all adult Americans had no more than a ninth-grade education; in 1975, half of all adult Americans

had at least some college education. In 1950, only one out of every thirteen Americans in his or her late twenties had finished four years of college; in 1975, nearly one out of four had done so.[13] We have spent many billions to improve our health. In 1950, the infant mortality rate was around twenty-nine deaths per thousand births; in 1975, it was down to eighteen per thousand. Federally subsidized Medicare, for old people, has many defects, but at least it does provide some medical care for millions who could not otherwise afford any at all. The terrors of poverty in old age still exist on a wide scale, yet it must be pointed out that in 1950 only 3.5 million Americans were getting Social Security checks, while in 1975 the checks (whose purchasing power had doubled in

_____

[13]*Washington Post,* November 2, 1975.

the intervening years) were going to 32 million Americans.[14]

In the late 1960s, when rioting broke out in the ghettos, it was significant, in a wryly optimistic way, that 88 percent of all black American families owned television sets.[15] By the mid-1970s, taxes had begun to nettle so many Americans that there was talk of a tax revolt; and yet, Americans were paying the second lowest tax rate among the thirteen top industrial nations.[16] And although there are still about 30 million Americans who can justifiably be categorized as "poor," the standard by which their condition is judged is far higher than that in most other parts of the world.

That may be painting the clouds with too much sunshine (a darker coloring will reemerge later in this chapter); the point is, the shape of the economy has changed radically in the last forty years, and most people, at all income levels, have benefited—at least in the short haul. In what follows, we will consider some of the machinery, and part of the schedule, by which the government tries to satisfy public expectations in the economic realm.

HOW GOVERNMENT MANAGES THE ECONOMY

Government officials and politicians can shape the economy through two routes—monetary policy (regulating the money supply) and fiscal policy (spending and taxation). Actually, they use a combination of the two.

Monetary Policy: A Blunt Instrument

Monetary policy is the effort to influence the level of prices by regulating the amount of money in circulation through the central bank, which is called the Federal Reserve System (or the "Fed"). Increasing the amount of money in

[14]*Washington Post*, November 2, 1975.

[15]Norman Macrae, *The Neurotic Trillionaire: A Survey of Mr. Nixon's America* (New York: Harcourt Brace Jovanovich, 1970), p.77.

[16]*Washington Post*, March 6, 1975.

the banking system increases the amount of credit that is available and lowers the interest rates. This stimulates borrowing. Businesses are encouraged to expand, and consumers are encouraged to buy. If business expansion and consumer purchases reach too fast a tempo, the economy heats up. Too many dollars are loose in the marketplace chasing a limited number of goods, and so prices soar. That is inflation. To control it, the Federal Reserve System restricts the flow of money and credit. When money becomes scarcer, its price (interest) goes up; neither business nor consumer can afford the higher interest rates, so they stop borrowing from banks and put away their credit cards. The economy grows chilly. Production is cut back. People are thrown out of work. And inflation is supposed to decline (but it often doesn't, as we will see later).

The monetary way of controlling the economy is somewhat crude. It depends on lower interest rates to stimulate the economy, and it depends on higher interest rates and consequent unemployment to depress the economy. The economy of a major industrial nation like the United States is much too complicated in scope, and too subtle in parts, to be regulated in that way with any efficiency. If used alone, monetary policy can work, but only in a clumsy way, like swatting a fly with a two-pound hammer.

Nevertheless, the power to control the flow of money (and credit) lies at the very heart of the economic system. It is a power that can reach into every home. If used improperly, it can bring on heavy unemployment or runaway inflation. And because power over the money supply is so crucial to the health of the nation, the Constitution specifically put it into the hands of the people's representatives in Congress. Article I, Section 8, of the Constitution provides that Congress shall have the power "to coin Money [and] regulate the Value thereof." Oddly enough, Congress permanently ducked this responsibility more than sixty years ago, just as it has shed many of its other regulatory responsibilities.

The Federal Reserve System Worried by a series of financial crises that pointed to the need for closer supervision of the national banking system, Congress, in 1913, passed the Federal Reserve Act. This established the Federal Reserve System, whose main machinery is the Federal

FIGURE 15-1 FEDERAL RESERVE MAP OF THE UNITED STATES

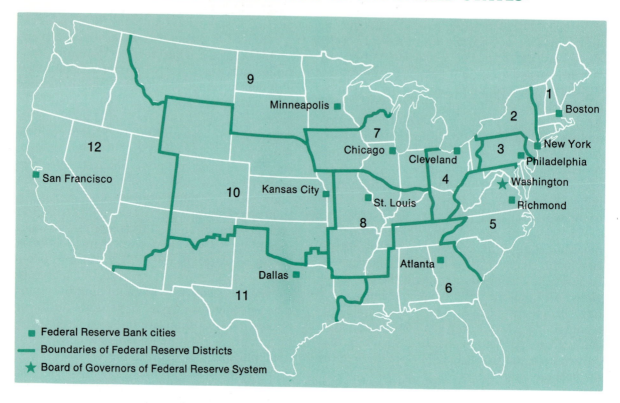

■ Federal Reserve Bank cities
━ Boundaries of Federal Reserve Districts
★ Board of Governors of Federal Reserve System

Reserve Board (in Washington, D.C.) and twelve district Federal Reserve Banks. The Fed supervises the operations of all national banks and many state banks. It controls the nation's money supply (see Figure 15-2), decides the interest rates to be charged by banks, and keeps an eye on bank management.

There are some very undemocratic features of the Fed. There also appear to be dangerous built-in conflicts of interest. For one thing, the district Federal Reserve Banks that presumably supervise private banks are, in fact, owned by the private banks. Furthermore, private banks elect six of the nine directors of each district Federal Reserve Bank.[17] The other three members are appointed by the Fed's Board of Governors in Washington. But the seven members of the Board of Governors (appointed by the President to fourteen-year terms) are mainly wealthy fi-

nanciers who have very limited personal experience of how the ordinary citizen lives. Consumers, small businesses and family farmers are almost never represented on the Board of Governors; it has rarely had a black member and never a female member.

Thus, as Congressman Henry S. Reuss, Chairman of the House Banking Committee, has pointed out, although the Fed is very independent of Congress, it is not at all independent of Big Banking and Big Business interest groups. "It is precisely these two groups which have an unhealthy dominance within the Fed's structure. The Federal Reserve System has a built-in conflict of interest by reason of the extremely narrow spectrum of America which is represented on the boards of directors of the twelve regional banks."[18] Of the 108 directors of the district Banks, in 1976, 34 percent were either

[17]See the Commission on Money and Credit, *Money and Credit* (Englewood Cliffs, N.J.: Prentice-Hall, 1961), p. 92.

[18]See "Federal Reserve Directors: A Study of Corporate and Banking Influence," issued by the House Banking Committee, August 15, 1976.

directors, officers, or employees of corporations from *Fortune's* list of the 500 leading corporations. Sixty-eight percent were then, or had been, officers, directors, or employees of financial institutions. When it came to juggling the money supply for a purpose or when it came to supervising the lending policies of banks, it is fair to assume that their first impulse would be to assist their economic peers.

The independence of the Fed is strengthened by the fact that it does not have to go to Congress for operating funds. It draws about $6 billion of its own, in interest, from government bonds, and it can spend this money any way the Board of Governors chooses. The Fed does not permit itself to be audited. Its expenditures can range from the $389,000 that board members spent on cocktail parties in 1974[19] to the $1.7 billion the Fed spent to bail out the Franklin National Bank of New York.[20]

The Federal Reserve Board does not publicly discuss national monetary policy, interest rates, foreign bank matters, bank mergers, holding companies, or changes in stock market margin requirements. In fact, the Fed keeps the public closed out of most of its discussions about everything. The most startling secrecy is that which surrounds the activities of the Fed's Open Market Committee (made up of the Board of Governors and five district Bank presidents). On the third Tuesday of every month, these twelve men

---

[19]*Conservative Digest,* December 1975.

[20]The Franklin National Bank had been operated in an extremely shady and sloppy fashion, and, by all the laws of free enterprise, should have been allowed to go bankrupt. In coming to its rescue, the Federal Reserve Board performed the largest single bank bailout in the country's history—and one of the most questionable. (*Washington Post,* June 30, 1974.)

FIGURE 15-2 HOW THE FED CREATES MONEY

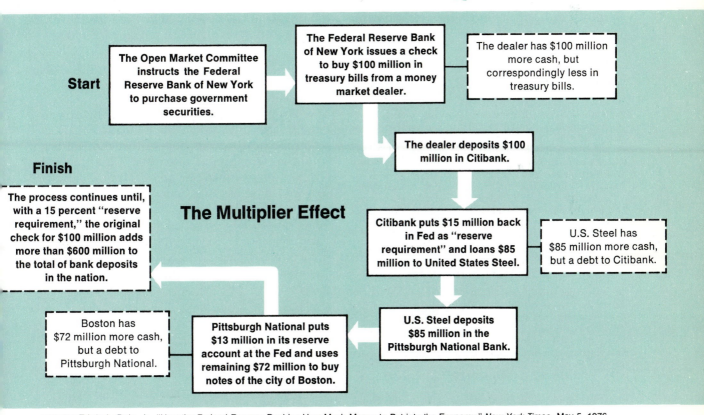

SOURCE: Edwin L. Dale, Jr., "How the Federal Reserve Decides How Much Money to Put into the Economy," *New York Times,* May 5, 1976.

gather in a closely guarded conference room at the Fed's white marble palace in Washington and decide on the money supply. For forty-five days, the Open Market Committee keeps its decision a secret; it then makes a skimpy report to Congress. In other words, the policy it launches in secret will have been in operation long enough to affect the economy—for good or for ill—before the representatives of the people learn what happened.

Criticisms of the Fed   The Fed is not responsible to either Congress or the President. It is, as financial writer Paul Lewis once observed, "probably the only central bank in the world, with the possible exception of the West German Bundesbank, that could resist government policy if it wished to." President Richard Nixon once complained, "Arthur [Burns, Chairman of the Board of Governors] speaks only to God and to me occasionally."[21] Admirers of the Federal Reserve System believe that this makes for judicious decisions; but critics of the Fed look upon it as a dangerously foreign substance in a democratic government and suspect that its main purpose is to run the money supply primarily for the benefit of bankers. Critics specifically charge:

- As a watchdog of banking practices, the Fed has often proved itself to be toothless and sleepy. In 1976, the *New York Times* and the *Washington Post* discovered, in separate investigations, that the Fed had covered up for dozens of the biggest banks, which, as a result of stupid and sometimes crooked conduct, were in shaky condition.[22] Poor supervision by the Fed was part of the trouble.

- The basic undemocratic quality of the Fed is further worsened by the fact that it is thoroughly dominated by one person, its Chairman. Sherman J. Maisel, a member of the Fed from 1965 to 1972, estimates that, in setting money policy, the Chairman exercises 45 percent of the power, the staff (controlled by the Chairman) 25 percent of the power, the other members of the Board of Governors only 20 percent, and the district Federal Reserve Banks 10 percent.[23]

No one person is smart enough to direct a monetary policy that affects the nation's entire economic health. And one person is subject to political temptations more than an entire board is. Some wise observers believe that Chairman Burns, who was appointed by President Nixon, influenced the issuance of a heavy inflationary dose of money during the 1972 election to heat up the economy and help Nixon get reelected. Burns denied having done it, but an unhealthy suspicion remained.[24]

Whether the cause can be traced primarily to the Chairman or to the whole Board of Governors, some observers believe that the Fed has guessed wrong more often that it has guessed right. Congressman Stephen L. Neal, Chairman of the House Banking Committee's Subcommittee on Domestic Monetary Policy, says, "The Fed has caused 60 percent of the inflation in this country since 1953 by pumping more money into the economy than was good for it, and its bouts of monetary stringency triggered every recession since 1948."[25]

---

[21]Sources: Lewis quote from "The Federal Reserve, and How It Grew," *New York Times,* March 13, 1977; Nixon quote from the *Washington Post,* September 8, 1974. The dangerous, or at least questionable, attitude of independence has been a trait of the Fed's chairmen for many years. Appearing before the Senate Finance Committee in August 1957, Federal Reserve Board Chairman William Martin had this candid exchange with Senator Russell B. Long:

MARTIN: . . . In the field of money and credit, . . . regardless of what the decisions of the Administration may be—we consult with them but we feel that we have the authority if we think that in our field, money and credit policies, that we should act differently than they, we feel perfectly at liberty to do so.

LONG: In other words you feel that you have freedom . . . to adopt policies that may not be the policy of the Administration itself?

MARTIN: That is right. . . .

LONG: And you believe that the Federal Reserve Board, if it does disagree, has the right to pursue a policy that is completely contrary to the policy that the Administration proceeds to follow, not meaning that you are doing this or that you have done it, but that you feel that under the law you do have that right?

MARTIN: Under the law we feel it is our prerogative; yes sir.

(Quoted in Andrew Shonfield, *Modern Capitalism: The Changing Balance of Public and Private Power,* New York: Oxford University Press, 1969, pp. 330–31.)

---

[22]See the *New York Times,* January 22, 1976.

[23]*Wall Street Journal,* July 30, 1976.

[24]Sources: "Facing Up to Arthur Burns," *New York Times,* July 11, 1976; Leonard Silk, "The Man at the Money Throttle," *New York Times Magazine,* August 10, 1975.

[25]Quoted in the *New York Times,* July 11, 1976.

Many politicians believe that the independence of the Fed has not resulted in the kind of objective wisdom that Congress hoped for when the system was established in 1913. They argue that experience has clearly shown the need to force the Fed into a position more sensitive to democratic shifts. President Jimmy Carter, faced with having to work with a Fed Chairman appointed by a Republican, took this position:

> While the Federal Reserve Board should maintain its independence from the executive branch, it is important that throughout a President's term he have a chairman of the Federal Reserve whose economic views are compatible with his. . . . To insure greater compatibility between the President and the Federal Reserve chairman, I propose that, subject to Senate confirmation, the President be given the power to appoint his own chairman of the Federal Reserve who would serve a term coterminous with the President's.[26]

Government Spending: Casting Bread upon the Waters

Monetarists are relegated to the financial pages. The reason is obvious: they are considered rather dull. Their approach is essentially negative; their fundamental goal is to prevent the economy from running wild. Stability is the monetarist's most polished criterion. If one permits an orgy of high inflation, then one must expect to be smitten with the boils of unemployment. Monetarism is the Old Testament religion of economics.

But the economists who put their faith in the fiscal approach get the front pages. They believe that when we get into economic trouble we can rescue ourselves by juggling the rate of taxation and, especially, the rate of government spending. In short, they believe that bread cast upon the waters at the right time always comes back well buttered. Their basic mode of operation comes down to this: when the economy is sluggish, cut taxes to liberate the pocketbook and stimulate business with a heavy infusion of federal spending; when the economy is overheated and inflation is becoming a nuisance, raise taxes and trim back (but don't slash) government spending.

---

[26]Quoted in George Will, *Washington Post*, May 6, 1976.

The theory that a government can spend itself out of an economic depression and into permanent prosperity is known as Keynesian economics, after John Maynard Keynes, the British economist.[27] At the same time Keynes was developing the theory for scholarly debate, Franklin Roosevelt was putting it into practice to escape the Great Depression of the 1930s. The policy worked (helped along by the unprecedented spending of World War II). FDR's New Deal and Keynes' theory just may have kept the Western world from going communist in the 1930s.[28]

Despair: The Background to the Fiscal Flood   Until the 1930s, it was taken for granted that there would be sharp business cycles and that when the economy hit the bottom of one of those cycles a lot of people would be out of work. Tough luck. But eventually the cycle would start moving up again, and presumably the unemployed would find work. It was a freewheeling, you're-on-your-own attitude; the government was not expected to step in and give the unemployed a helping hand. But the Great Depression of the 1930s brought a gloom to the country that it had never felt before. Toward the end of President

---

[27]Keynes didn't care what the excuse for spending was, just as long as there was a sufficient amount of spending. The swashbuckling spirit and philosophy of his great book, *The General Theory of Employment, Interest, and Money,* is captured in this paragraph:
"If the Treasury were to fill old bottles with banknotes, bury them at suitable depths in disused coal-mines which are then filled up to the surface with town rubbish, and leave it to private enterprise on well-tried principles of *laissez-faire* to dig the notes up again . . . there need be no more unemployment and, with the help of the repercussions, the real income of the community, and its capital wealth also, would probably become a good deal greater than it actually is. It would indeed be more sensible to build houses and the like; but if there are political and practical difficulties in the way of this, the above would be better than nothing." (New York: Harcourt Brace Jovanovich, 1936, p. 129.)

[28]In the *Communist Manifesto* (1848), Karl Marx and Frederick Engels predicted that the type of capitalism that arose from the industrial revolution would ultimately destroy itself. Capitalism would produce more goods than its workers could absorb. There would be massive layoffs, and the bigger capitalists would buy up the lesser capitalists, leading to extreme concentration of ownership. The division of capital and labor would ultimately breed such class hatred that the workers would revolt, seize the factories and banks, and set up a "people's" economy. Marx and Engels, as it turned out, accurately predicted both the coming concentration of industrial power and the Great Depression of the 1930s.

Herbert Hoover's term (1929–33), between 12.5 million and 17 million people (at least one-third of the labor force) were jobless, and those lucky enough to remain on a payroll were earning from 40 to 60 percent less than three years earlier, before the stock market crash.[29]

Such statistics do not even begin to convey the wretchedness of life then. In the fall of 1931, for example, more than 100,000 Americans applied for jobs in Russia in response to an ad asking for 6,000 skilled workers. Several hundred homeless women were forced to sleep in Chicago's parks; some of them were schoolteachers, who for eight of the thirteen months from April 1931 to May 1932 had received no pay from the city. Hunger riots swept through Oklahoma City, Minneapolis, and New York City. Many thousands of people, evicted from their homes because they could no longer pay their rents or mortgages, moved to the outskirts of cities, where they constructed shacks of cardboard boxes, tin cans, and discarded tar paper. These shanty towns were nicknamed Hoover-villes to immortalize the President, whose response to the nation's needs was: "Prosperity cannot be restored by raids on the public treasury or by playing politics with human misery."

As the job market dried up, families hit the road. Hope lay somewhere else, not at home. The Missouri Pacific Railroad disclosed that the number of transients riding its freight cars jumped from 13,745 in 1929 to 186,028 in 1931. By 1933, an estimated 1 million rootless Americans were aimlessly riding the rails back and forth across the country, begging at back doors for food and sleeping in boxcars.

In 1932, the Bonus Army—25,000 jobless veterans—marched on Washington and demanded the additional compensation they had been promised for serving their country in World War I. They set up shacks not far from the Capitol. Congress adjourned without helping them, and Hoover sent in the army to drive them out. Two veterans were killed and eighteen were injured. "Thank God," said the President, "we still have a government that knows how to deal with a mob."[30]

[29]Charles L. Cole, *The Economic Fabric of Society* (New York: Harcourt Brace Jovanovich, 1969), p. 204ff.

[30]From *Lithopinion*, no. 39, Fall 1975.

A Hooverville in California, 1935

The Employer of Last Resort If the situation was not hopeless, it certainly seemed as if it were. There was absolutely no sign that the economy would reverse itself in the normal cyclical way. The national feeling was not merely pity and self-pity, but fear and panic. Many people were convinced that capitalism had failed. Many believed that a democracy could not rescue itself from so great a slump. There was open and serious discussions about the possible need for changing our form of government; a shift to a benevolent dictator was not an uncommon suggestion—and, most significantly, some of these suggestions came from the wealthiest and the most powerful people in the country, who were, of course, just the folks who might be able to bring about such a change.

The trauma of the 1930s was so severe that the relationship of the government to the economy changed completely. This change came about largely through the gradual acceptance of the New Deal ideas of Hoover's successor, Franklin Roosevelt (who governed from 1933 until 1945). Roosevelt established the notion that if a critical number of Americans could not find work anywhere else the government must become the "employer of last resort." Previously, the operating philosophy in both the government and the private business sector was that if a person really tried hard enough—showed pluck and initiative—a job somehow would become available. All one needed—so that good old American notion went—was enough "get up and go." This idea is still with us, though not to the degree it once was. In the 1964 presidential campaign, Republican candidate Barry M. Goldwater stopped in Odessa, Texas, for a rally. Odessa is a desert community whose economy floats on a veritable sea of oil. Asked how he felt about the people he met there, Goldwater replied, "They're great. These are my kind of people. They came out here, they worked hard and they struck oil."[31]

Goldwater's comment represents an American myth that thrived before the Great Depression: work hard enough and you'll strike oil. Of course, the truth has always been that people of the lowest income simply cannot get started toward upward economic mobility without a boost, and that boost will not come from any source but government. Roosevelt was the first President to act on that truism. He was willing to give direct relief where necessary, but he preferred to offer emergency government employment as a way of supplying income without destroying pride.

In 1935, he set up the Works Progress Administration, to create "socially useful" jobs. He asked Congress for $4.8 billion to start it off. Never before had a President sought so much money for a single purpose. The WPA became the largest public-service employment program in United States history. It lasted six years, and, at one time or another, it employed one out of every five workers in the nation. Its critics said that its initials stood for "We Poke Along" and that the people it employed were a mob of shiftless "shovel leaners." But, in fact, the WPA built 110,000 public buildings, laid 16,117 miles of water mains and water distribution lines, built 651,087 miles of roads and highways and 48,680 miles of curbing, constructed 77,965 bridges and viaducts and 600 airplane landing fields. There is scarcely a town in the United States today that does not have a school, post office, playground, or hospital that was put up by WPA workers, who earned $50 a month. San Francisco's Aquatic Park, LaGuardia Airport in New York City, the Ski Lodge on Mount Hood in Oregon, the Dock Street theater in Charleston, South Carolina, and Chicago's Outer Drive were all creations of those WPA shovel leaners. WPA employees helped more than 1.5 million adults learn to read and write; created 2,500 murals for public buildings; produced 108,000 paintings (including early works by Ben Shahn, Jackson Pollock, and Willem de Kooning), 240,000 prints, 500,000 photographs, and 16,000 sculptures; the WPA supported such writers as John Steinbeck, Richard Wright, John Cheever, and Elmer Rice and such actors as Orson Welles, Howard Da Silva, and Canada Lee.[32] All for a total of $11 billion. Never had the nation got such a bargain.

---

[31]Quoted in Stanley Esterly and Glenn Esterly, *Freedom from Dependence: Welfare Reform as a Solution to Poverty* (Washington, D.C.: Public Affairs Press, 1971), p. 2.

[32]Donald S. Howard, "The WPA and Federal Relief Policy," *New York Times,* December 22, 1974.

The make-work programs of the 1930s were so successful that the creation of public jobs is now one of the first remedies politicians consider when there is a sharp recession. Keeping a count of the unemployed to determine when artificial job making may be necessary is considered a standard necessity of government (prior to the 1930s, no government agency seriously attempted to tally the unemployed on a regular basis).[33] The reason is not only humanitarian, but practical—for government economists need to know the size of the leak in the fiscal bucket. Aside from the human costs of joblessness—destroyed hopes, increased tension, reduced standards of life, and more crime, drug abuse, and mental illness—government economists recognize that for every 1 percent increase in unemployment there is a loss to the nation of $50 billion in unproduced goods, $14 billion in uncollected taxes, and $2 billion in unemployment compensation.[34]

Big Spending Becomes Bipartisan   Since the 1930s, the government—whether led by Democratic or Republican administrations—has been Keynesian in its commitment to intervention in the marketplace. The extent of that devotion is written into the federal budget. In 1929, four years before we decided that spending would be our salvation, the entire federal budget came to less than $3 billion. In 1976, the budget had reached $375 billion—a growth of 12,500 percent, although the population had grown less than 100 percent in those years. In 1947, the first year after World War II, the annual budget was $29.8 billion—which would support today's government less than a month, and, according to the Congressional Budget Office's predictions, by 1981 it will be less than enough to run the government for two weeks.[35]

In a speech at Yale University's commencement ceremony in 1962, President John Kennedy argued that, within the context of our national growth in all its elements, federal government itself had grown only moderately:

> If we leave defense and space expenditures aside, the federal government since the second world war has expanded less than any other major section of our national life; less than industry; less than commerce; less than agriculture; less than higher education; and very much less than the noise about big government.[36]

But at that very moment the federal government was beginning to swell at a new and startling pace. In the eight years of the Kennedy and Johnson administrations (1961–69), the federal budget nearly doubled. Apparently to prove that anything the Democrats could do the Republicans could do just as well, Nixon and Ford (1969–77) nearly doubled the budget again.[37]

Between 1957 and 1976, the government spent more—usually, far more—than it took in. When the government spends more than it has, it must borrow. The Constitution permits Congress to "borrow Money on the credit of the United States." This is done by authorizing the Treasury Department to sell securities, on which interest must be paid. In the mid-1970s, the total debt was so high that the interest paid on it each year was the third largest item in the budget. In 1976, the interest on the national debt came to more than $35 billion—almost as much as the entire federal budget of 1950.[38]

Keynesians soothe their critics by arguing that the whopping budgets of recent decades are simply reflections of a healthy and growing economy; they point to the fact that federal

---

[33]Every month, the federal Bureau of Labor Statistics, assisted by the United States Census Bureau pollsters, issues a report of the national unemployment status. This polling operation, which reaches into more than 50,000 households in 461 geographic areas, dwarfs any other polling operation and is reputedly much more accurate.

[34]Senator Edward M. Kennedy, in the Report of the Joint Economic Committee, 1976, no. 94–690.

[35]Congressional Budget Office, "Five-Year Budget Projections, Fiscal Years 1977–1981," January 26, 1976.

[36]Quoted in Ivar Berg, *The Business of America* (New York: Harcourt Brace Jovanovich, 1968), pp. 83–84.

[37]Presidents apparently feel obligated to perform a ritual of thrift even when presenting record-breaking budgets. When Nixon sent Congress his budget for 1974, he said: "It is time to get big government off your back and out of your pocket." The budget he submitted was the largest in history, to that time. In 1976, Ford said he thought it would be possible to have a balanced budget; he wound up instead with a $74 billion deficit, the biggest in peacetime history.

[38]Report of the Democratic Study Group of the House of Representatives, November 7, 1975.

spending for twenty years has stayed at about 20 percent of the Gross National Product. The budget boomed because the economy was doing well, they say, and the economy was doing well partly because the budget was booming.

Defense Spending: The Almost Limitless Siphoning of Public Money

The most dramatic and controversial part of our fiscal policy is centered in the defense budget, which accounts for about one-fourth of the total federal budget. The controversy arises because it is hard to understand why the military costs of peace are greater than the military costs of war. Not even inflation can account for the fact that we spend twice as much for arms and soldiers today as we spent at the height of World War II. Each year we spend more to prepare for a hypothetical nuclear war against a hypothetical enemy, the Soviet Union, than we spent annually fighting in earnest in Vietnam. Inasmuch as both the United States and Russia long ago were armed with enough nuclear weapons to destroy each other many times over and inasmuch as neither nation yet seems to be in the hands of the kind of people willing to launch a genocidal dispute, the continued expenditure of more than $100 billion a year on defense (Pentagon officials estimate that by 1980 the cost will be $150 billion) may not seem to make much sense.

Actually, nobody in government pretends that the defense budget is only for defense. A great deal of it—perhaps most of it—is simply to keep Americans employed and corporate profits high. The Pentagon represents the ultimate in Keynesian spending. Americans learned to put their trust in the Pentagon in 1941, when the shooting began. The previous year—the last full year of peace before World War II—the federal budget was about $10 billion. But by 1944, at the height of the war, we were spending $95 billion. The United States did not escape from the Great Depression solely via the civilian make-work projects. It escaped also via the costliness of World War II, which, for the first time, established the superbudget and the super–federal government. Because Americans apparently fear poverty more than they fear supergovernment,

they were more than willing to continue the super–military budget after the war had ended, and *ad infinitum*.[39] Today, military spending accounts for about 8 percent of the Gross National Product (compared to about 1 percent in the 1930s). People employed for defense, either in or out of the government, account for about 10 percent of our working population today.

After Military Needs, Domestic Needs Come First In the years since World War II, defense has become the most sacrosanct item in the federal budget. By one measure, it might not appear so. Two decades ago, defense and international affairs absorbed more than half the budget; today these functions amount to about a quarter of all funds spent by the federal government. That percentage shrinkage is deceptive, however. In the past two decades, costly new programs such as food stamps, Medicare, and Medicaid—in fiscal 1977 the two health programs cost $32 billion—have been added to the budget. Back in the mid-1950s, when defense was eating up half the budget, they did not exist. Now that they are a heavy portion of the budget, they, and a fast growing Social Security program, have made the defense budget seem to shrink. But in fact, the defense budget, war or no war, keeps climbing, and few politicians try to cut it back. They view the Pentagon's portion of the budget as holy, not to be defiled by thrift. This is a fairly new—as history goes—development.

During Harry S Truman's postwar administration (except for the interruption of the Korean War) and during Dwight D. Eisenhower's administration, White House economists tended to construct the annual budget by figuring out what revenues the government would take in, then deducting anticipated domestic expenditures. Defense got what was left over.[40] Since Eisenhower left the White House, things have turned around. Adam Yarmolinsky, a former Defense

---

[39]See John Morton Blum, *V Was for Victory: Politics and American Culture During World War II* (New York: Harcourt Brace Jovanovich, 1976).

[40]Samuel P. Huntington, *The Common Defense: Strategic Programs in National Politics* (New York: Columbia University Press, 1961), p. 22.

FIGURE 15-3 COMPOSITION OF FEDERAL SPENDING AS A PERCENTAGE OF FEDERAL OUTLAYS

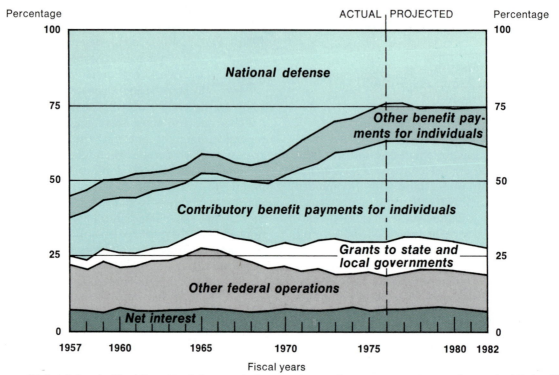

SOURCE: "Budget Options for Fiscal Year 1978. A Report to the Senate and House Committees on the Budget," Congressional Budget Office, February 1977.

Department official, noted in 1971 that the defense budget

> now tends to have first claim, with nondefense programs getting what is left over despite the urgency of their demands. In terms of economic activity, the national security programs account for almost four-fifths of all federal government purchases of goods and services ($73 billion out of $93 billion in fiscal 1971).[41]

In short, the United States has established a permanent war economy. In 1969, there was a widespread assumption that when the Vietnam war was over the $29 billion or so that we had been spending on it annually would be transferred to civilian needs—for use in solving such

problems as poverty, air pollution, and housing shortages. A panel appointed by President Johnson, called the Cabinet Coordinating Committee on Economic Planning for the End of Vietnam Hostilities, estimated, in January 1969, that the "peace dividend" would amount to at least $19 billion. But by 1970, the Nixon administration was saying that prospects for a peace dividend had disappeared.[42] Spokesmen for the administration blamed inflation and argued that new weapons programs, postponed by the war, must now be launched. Sure enough, in 1973, when the half-million American soldiers had all come home, the defense budget continued to soar. Defense industrialists had not really been worried. As one of the key executives of Ling-

[41] Adam Yarmolinsky, *The Military Establishment: Its Impact on American Society* (New York: Harper & Row, Publishers, 1971), p. 246.

[42] Sources: *New York Times*, January 16, 1969, December 27, 1970.

Temco-Vought had predicted in 1969, "We're going to increase defense budgets as long as those bastards in Russia are ahead of us."[43]

When budget-writing time comes around each year, the Pentagon insists that "those bastards in Russia" are still way ahead. Indeed, for some strange reason, the more the State Department has worked to achieve friendlier relations with Russia—with some successs—the more the Pentagon and the defense industry (both here and in Russia) have stepped up their armaments race.[44]

Military salaries and pensions eat up a lot of the defense budget. We have come a long way since June 1784, when the Continental Congress passed a resolution saying that "standing armies in time of peace are inconsistent with the principles of republican governments, dangerous to the liberties of a free people, and generally converted into destructive engines for establishing despotism."[45] We have come so far that we are paying more than $9 billion a year to 1 million military retirees alone—not to mention the $43 billion or so that the Pentagon shells out to active-duty military and civilian personnel—and the payout to military retirees is expected to approach $13 billion (in 1978 dollars, without making allowances for further inflation) within twenty-five years—an amount that can be put in perspective by remembering that it is more than the entire federal budget of 1940. An estimated 92 percent of the military retirees collecting pensions are healthy and still of working age; 45 percent are under the age of fifty.[46] We spend more than $4 billion a year to maintain the National Guard and the Reserves, who are supposed to be ready to protect us in an emergency. But in our only big recent emergency, the Vietnam war, they weren't used.[47]

The outlay in the defense budget for weapons is something over $30 billion a year, although, in fact, nobody knows just how much the bill is. Virtually all major weapons systems cost twice what the Pentagon contractors promise, and most of the systems don't even come close to living up to expectations. Of eleven major weapons systems developed during the 1960s, six performed at 25 percent, or less, of the capacity expected of them.[48] The C-5A cargo plane, which was supposed to cost $3 billion, wound up costing more than $5 billion, and, in performance, its wheels fell off or collapsed, its motors fell off, and its wings cracked.[49] The army rushed the Sheridan tank into production, only to find that its 152-millimeter gun wouldn't function properly, the tank had no range finder for its weapons, its night-vision periscope often failed, its fuel tank leaked, and above speeds of fifteen miles per hour the armored vehicle shook so hard that it sometimes made its crews ill.[50]

Judged strictly by the measure of need and efficiency, many of the Pentagon's expenditures

[43]Quoted in Stephen E. Ambrose and James Alden Barber, eds., *The Military and American Society: Essays and Readings* (New York: Free Press, 1972), p. 68.

[44]In 1975, Graham T. Allison and Frederic A. Morris noted several outbreaks of this queer phenomenon. For example: "In 1972 the United States and the Soviet Union signed the Strategic Arms Limitation Agreements—a permanent ABM treaty restricting each nation to two ABM sites, and an Interim Agreement freezing the number of strategic missile launchers for five years." Almost immediately thereafter, Secretary of Defense Melvin R. Laird announced speed-up programs for more nuclear submarines, bigger bombers, and more effective nuclear missiles. "In the three years since the SALT I treaties, the United States has added to its arsenal of independently targetable nuclear weapons almost half again as many as it had at the time the treaty was signed." (*Daedulus*, Summer 1975, p. 99.)

[45]Quoted in J. Ronald Fox, *Arming America: How the U.S. Buys Weapons* (Cambridge, Mass.: Harvard Business School, 1974), p. 26.

[46]Sources: Congressional Budget Office, "The Costs of Defense Manpower: Issues for 1977," January 1977, p. 79; Les Aspin, quoted in United Press International, May 23, 1977.

[47]William Proxmire, *Uncle Sam—The Last of the Bigtime Spenders* (New York: Simon & Schuster, 1972), p. 84.

[48]Fox, *Arming America*, p. 3.

[49]Proxmire, *Uncle Sam*, p. 83.

[50]William Proxmire, *Report from Wasteland* (New York: Praeger Publishers, 1970), p. 57. In the international arms race, this kind of performance could be valuable. Russian leader Leonid I. Brezhnev once asked Senator Eugene McCarthy, "Why are you people building the anti-ballistic missile system?" McCarthy replied, "We are building it, Mr. Chairman, because it does not work." Brezhnev missed the humor and pushed on: "We do not understand. Why are you building a system that you know does not work?" "Ah, ha," said McCarthy, "if we build a system that does not work you will build a system that does not work because you want to be just as good as we are, and both of us could keep very, very busy building systems that do not work in the public interest." (*Congressional Record*, S15533, August 21, 1974.)

are questionable. One might wonder, for example, if taxpayers are getting their money's worth when they pay $1,030,000 to subsidize private dining rooms for the five hundred top military and civilian officials at the Pentagon. That comes to $12 per official per lunch. One might wonder if the military really needed to stockpile 3 million pounds of feathers as "strategic materials." One might even wonder why the Pentagon's friends in Congress voted $135 million for the completion of a missile defense site that the Pentagon planned to place in mothballs six months after it became operative.[51] And what did taxpayers think when they learned that in fiscal 1975 the air force had misspent their money so thoroughly that 33 percent of its 5,830 planes could not be flown at any given time because of maintenance problems or missing spare parts? Or when they learned that they are spending nearly $1 billion to build an aircraft carrier that some experts think could be put out of action by a motor boat?[52] Or, on a more modest level, how did taxpayers react when they learned that the navy has spent well over a million dollars since World War II to buy shark "repellent"—a bag of chemicals similar to a large cloth tea bag, which, when hung in the water, envelops an individual with a cloud of chemical oozings—that not only fails to repel sharks, but that, at times, has actually been consumed by sharks, bag and all.[53]

No matter where one turns, the Department of Defense's expenditures contain mysterious elements of waste and luxuries. About half the budget is spent on manpower, much of it on brass. As Congressman Samuel S. Stratton pointed out in 1974, "At the height of World War II when there were 2,282,000 people in the Air Force, there were 322 generals. Today the Air Force has 1,638,000 fewer people in it, but it has 77 more generals than it had at the height of World War II."[54]

The Cash Register on the Firing Line National security may be the long-range objective of the Defense Department's arms procurement effort; but profits and paychecks are the immediate objective. Sometimes one has the feeling that they are the *only* objective. In 1968, residents of Fort Worth, Texas, where the F-111 fighter planes are built, feared that Richard Nixon, if elected President, would end its production. So when Nixon visited that city in his campaign, the daily newspaper carried a half-page ad that asked: "Mr. Nixon, why do you want to turn Fort Worth into a ghost town?" Jobs, not a lessening of national security, were the concern.[55] No one tries to hide the make-work side of defense spending. Congressman George Mahon, Chairman of the House Appropriations Committee, received sympathy when he disclosed in 1974—in an unusual burst of candor—that about $5 billion had been added to the record-high military budget to help "stimulate the economy."[56] That's the old-fashioned pump-priming vision of the military budget that still prevails.

Some of our largest defense corporations have spent many millions of dollars bribing foreign politicians into buying United States armaments (actually the taxpayers paid the bribes, for the defense corporations are almost totally supported by federal subsidies). Lockheed, always among the top two or three defense companies in earnings, was found to be one of the leading bribers. But government officials did not propose cutting off Lockheed from further defense contracts in punishment. The reason for this leniency probably was that the government felt Lockheed was doing the United States a favor—the more planes it sold overseas, the more jobs it provided at home.

Since World War II, the United States has shipped $100 billion worth of weapons to 136 nations. Among the 1,033 companies licensed to make or export arms are 152 of the *Fortune 500*—

[51]Sources: Office of Congressman Les Aspin, press statement, February 16, 1976; Office of Senator Stephen Young, press release, Vol. xii, no. 3, February 1970; *New York Times* quoted in the *Congressional Record,* S15563, August 21, 1974.

[52]Sources: Office of Congressman Les Aspin, press release, February 24, 1976; Center for Defense Information, *Monitor 2,* no. 3 (August 15, 1973).

[53]*Congressional Record,* S12666, July 22, 1977.

[54]*Congressional Record,* H7613, August 5, 1974.

[55]*Washington Post,* November 1, 1968.

[56]*New York Times,* February 27, 1974.

the biggest industrial companies in the nation.[57] By 1975, the United States was well established as the munitions king of the world.[58] Whereas in 1967 it sold only $2 billion in arms to foreign countries, in 1974 it sold $11 billion. In the Middle East, between 1973 and 1975 it sold $10 billion worth of arms—to both Arabs and Israelis. Indeed, the United States sold so many weapons to Israel that some of its own armed forces were left short of equipment.[59]

Soaring Costs Defeat Purpose   The cost of military items has gone out of control, to such an extent that—though the public generally seems unaware that this has happened—defense spending no longer guarantees increased employment, nor does it guarantee increased defense. Quite the contrary. For example, a fighter aircraft (F-104C) cost $1.6 million in the late 1950s, but in the early '60s the cost (for an F-4B) had risen to $3.5 million, and in the mid-1970s fighter aircraft (F-14s) were each costing $20 million.[60] Since the total procurement budget had not risen proportionately higher, this meant that fewer aircraft were being built and that fewer people were being hired to build them. The result: in 1968, with a $75-billion defense budget, there were 3,173,000 defense contracting jobs, but the 1976 budget of $104.7 billion provided for only 1,469,000 jobs. With this development, some labor leaders began to reassess their earlier near-total support for the defense budget. In 1975 their growing disenchantment was given a voice by such men as Leonard Woodcock, head of the United Auto Workers, and Senator Alan Cranston of California, who relies heavily on the labor vote. Said Woodcock:

"One billion dollars of military expenditures creates an average of 20,000 to 30,000 fewer jobs than alternative forms of expenditures. Thus a program to divert $15 billion to $20 billion from military spending to certain programs in energy, transportation, housing and so on, could create 300,000 to 600,000 jobs." To which Cranston added, "Keeping people nonproductively employed making weapons we don't need is demeaning to them and dangerous to the national interest. . . . I say, billions for legitimate defense but not one cent for military or industrial tinsel, glitter or make-work."[61]

The great majority of federal politicians probably agree that the wisest course by far would be to convert some, or much, of the defense industry into civilian industry. But there are tremendous pressures against change, and so far those pressures have prevailed. Which of the defense corporations now earning more than a billion dollars a year wants to risk losing that income by being the first to beat its swords into plowshares? One does not see Lockheed racing McDonnell Douglas for the honor.

---

[57]*Congressional Record*, S18678, October 23, 1975.

[58]In the report, "World Military and Social Expenditures 1977," Ruth L. Sivard, former chief economist of the United States Arms Control and Disarmament Agency, says that, globally, about $300 billion is spent each year on weapons; of this, the United States and Russia account for 60 percent of the expenditures and 75 percent of the arms traffic. According to Sivard, nations are spending an average of $12,330 a year to arm each soldier—and an average of $219 to educate each school-aged child.

[59]Sources: *Washington Star*, October 19, 1975; *New York Times*, November 20, 1974.

[60]Proxmire, *Uncle Sam*, p. 80.

[61]Quoted in Clayton Fritchey, *Los Angeles Times*, August 27, 1975. Not all union officials would agree with Woodcock, by a long shot. Anthony Sampson tells of interviewing a UAW regional director: "What, I asked, was his attitude to defence spending, and the B1 bomber? He let loose an immediate tirade. 'The B1 is the best deterrent we have, and it's got a helluva lot of plusses: it provides a very necessary job programme and it stimulates the aerospace industry. Remember, in times of national crisis the aerospace companies are pressed into service with all kinds of nice promises; but when the crisis passes they're thrown on the heap. California has been built on food, defence and oil: you can't expect us to convert into industries for garbage disposal or cheap houses. There are some super-liberal congressmen with their heads in the clouds who dream of building houses instead of bombers: but workers can't have pride in making low-cost housing, when the low-income families just use them for putting garbage in the hall. You can't convert workers into leaf-raking jobs, keeping them pushing a broom. The people making the B1 bomber think they're working for the good of the community, and people have pride in it. This used to be the aerospace capital of the world, and now I reckon there's as much as fifty percent unemployment in part of the industry: the Pentagon are squeezing every dollar, and the companies are moving to Texas or Georgia. If the B1 bomber is not consummated there'll be real problems with employment and capital investment. As for exporting arms, if we didn't do it, someone else would: and without arms those countries would be totally defenceless.' " (*The Arms Bazaar*, New York: Viking Press, 1977, p. 214.)

More than five thousand United States cities and towns have defense plants or companies doing significant business with the Pentagon; the Pentagon helps support more than 120,000 companies and feeds one American in five.[62] These towns and companies and workers have a heavy stake in maintaining the status quo, and the thought of "going civilian" must seem frightening and strange to them. They are not to be assuaged by the message that to do so would be best for the nation in the long run. Until their attitude is modified, it is probable that defense spending will continue to account for at least one-quarter of the federal budget.

Taxes: The Government That Giveth Also Taketh Away

Taxation is the other edge of the fiscalist's sword. It has never been used very creatively. Nor has it ever been fairly and equitably applied. One of the most irritating aspects of living in colonial America—and one of the chief irritants that led to the Revolution—was the tax system. The colonists thought they were paying too much and getting too little; they also didn't like being taxed without having a say in the government that taxed them. Now taxpayers have their representative government, but their happiness with the tax system is not much greater than it was under the British crown. It is part of the life of taxpayers in any era, no doubt, to feel that they are being cheated. The Tax Foundation estimates that the average worker has to work two hours and thirty-nine minutes in every eight-hour day to pay taxes, the largest item in the average family budget.[63]

Taxes, of course, are necessary. The billions of dollars spent on arms and highways and bureaucratic salaries have to come from somewhere. Taxes are also useful as fiscal medicine; they can serve as either depressants or stimulants. When inflation gets too high, when the economy is heated up with spending, higher taxes can take some of the money out of circula-

tion and cool things off. And when there is an economic slump, taxes can be reduced, letting more money slip into the marketplace, thus lifting the economy. Taxes can also be useful as a method for distributing wealth—taking from the rich at a higher rate (when the system works) and letting the tax money trickle down to the poor through government aid. The questions are: Do taxes come from the right people at the right rate? And do we get what we want from taxes?

Prior to 1914, the federal government raised most of the money it needed through customs duties (tariffs) and excise taxes on such items as tobacco and liquor. There had been numerous other taxes during the Civil War, including, most importantly, an income tax; but Congress killed that tax in 1872—in an era when Americans firmly believed that they would be happy to leave the federal government alone if it would leave them alone. But by the first decade of this century, the federal government was reaching deeper and deeper into its citizens' lives, and it was starting to spend more than it took in. To make up the deficit, federal politicians once again eyed the income tax. In 1909, Congress passed a constitutional amendment authorizing an income tax (to get around the fact that the Supreme Court had once ruled an income tax unconstitutional), and in 1913 the amendment became part of the Constitution. The tax was to be levied on both personal and corporate incomes.

When the House Ways and Means Committee sent the first income tax bill under the Sixteenth Amendment to the floor for a final vote, it predicted: "All good citizens . . . will willingly and cheerfully support and sustain this, the fairest and cheapest of all taxes."[64] As with most taxes, it was offered as a benign gesture. Poor people were supposed to be left untouched, the middle class only brushed, and rich people hit relatively hard. Initially, the tax was 1 percent on incomes of $3,000 or more (roughly the equivalent of $17,550 today), with an additional tax ranging from 1 to 6 percent on incomes over $20,000 (equal to $117,000 today). In its first year,

[62]Sources: *Look,* August 12, 1969; Jack Reymond, "The Growing Threat of Our Military-Industrial Complex," *Harvard Business Review* XLXI (May/June 1968).

[63]United Press International, April 10, 1976.

[64]Quoted in "The 'Cheapest of All Taxes' Still Hurts," *New York Post,* April 15, 1977.

Form **1040** US Department of the Treasury—INTERNAL REVENUE SERVICE **Individual Income Tax Return** **1976**

FOR THE YEAR JANUARY 1 — DECEMBER 31, 1976, OR WHENEVER YOU GET AROUND TO IT

Please Type or Print.

Name JEFF ~~MACNELLY~~

Last Name MACNELLY Second-to-Last Initial STARCH? ☐Yes ☐No ☒ ☐ CUFFS ☐ NO CUFFS

Present Address of Addressee (must be filled out by Addressor or legal Guardian of Aforementioned (unless greater than Line B above)
The RICHMOND NEWS Leader

City, Town, Post Office, Shoe Size (NO 12½) IS YOUR ADDRESS GREATER THAN LINE 41? ☐NO IF YES, WHY? ☐YES OCC-U-PATION ► YOURS ____ ► SPOUSE ____

FOR IRS USE ONLY

YOU ARE Here ☐Yes ☐No

REQUESTED BY DEPARTMENT OF AGRICULTURE.
A. HOW MANY TALKING CHICKENS DO YOU OWN? ☐
B. NAMES
C DO ANY OF THEM PLAY THE OBOE? ☐Yes ☐No
O.
DO YOU LIVE WITHIN 2 MILES OF A DECENT PIZZA PLACE? ☐Yes ☐No ☐EXTRA CHEESE
D. Have you Rotated your Tires Lately? ☐Yes ☐No
IF NO, FILE IRS Tire Rotation Schedule L
E. Yes? ☐No
F. No? ☐Yes

Filing Status

1 ☐ Single ☐Double ☐Sacrifice Fly
2 ☐ Married Filing Singly joint return (even if SPOUSE is MARRIED SEPARATELY)
3 ☐ Joint married singly separate spouse (but FILING DOUBLE JOINTED)
4 ☐ Head of Household filing separate but joint return (if UNMARRIED BUT JOINTLY SINGLE)
5 ☐ Head of joint filing single file spouse's separately.
6 ☐ Widow(er) with separate dependent filing out of joint return singly.

Exemptions

41 a REGULAR? ☐yourself? ☐ Spouse ☐
b Names of Dependent children who lived with you ____ Why? ____
c Just First names, Dummy. . . . .
4. Do you weigh more than last year's tax form?
e Number of Parakeets subtracted from Gross Rotated Income (PLUS LINE 27 — UNLESS GREATER THAN TWELVE MILES) . . . .
f How many inches in a liter? ____
7 a Total Confusion (add lines 6e and f,g; fold in eggs, beat until firm.) . . .

ENTER NUMBER OF BOXES CHECKED ►
CHECK NUMBER OF BOXES ENTERED ►
ENTER NUMBER OF CHECKERED BOXERS ►
DO NOTHING Here ►

8 Presidential Election Campaign Fund . .
DO YOU WISH TO DESIGNATE $1 OF YOUR TAXES TO THIS WORTHY CAUSE? . . . . ☐yes ☐NO
WHAT ABOUT THE LITTLE LADY? . . . . . .
ISN'T THIS A DUMB LAW? ☐Yes ☐No
NOTE: IF YOU CHECKED Yes WE WILL COME AND STEAL ALL YOUR HUBCAPS

or here → here

9 Wages, Salaries, Tips, Extortion ◄ATTACH W2 FORMS TO YOUR FOREHEAD WITH HEAVY DUTY STAPLEGUN ► . . . . 9.
10 Remunerations . . . [IF LESS THAN GROSS REIMBURSEMENTS, THEN FILE SCHEDULE Q (See Page 14 of "Joy of Cooking")] 10.
11 Gross Influx . . . . . 11.
12 Money you made . . [IF $400 OR LESS, MORE OR LESS, LIST SCHEDULE B WITHOUT NOT FILLING IN PART II AND R2, BUT MORE THAN LINE 8] 12
13 What about all that cash you stashed in that jar under the garage?
14. SUBTRACT 13 FROM 14 . . .
15. (THE ANSWER TO 14 IS . . . .1)

Think of a number between 1 and 10

● HOW WOULD YOU LIKE A GOOD SOCK IN THE FACE, FELLA? ☐yes ☐No
● IF LINE 15 IS BIGGER THAN A BREADBOX OR MORE, GO TO LINE 43 TO FIGURE TAX

TAX RATE SCHEDULE X,Y, OR 12 ☐See Page 7 of INSTRUCTIONS
CHECK HERE ►

By MacNelly for the Richmond News Leader

---

the tax fell on less than one-half of 1 percent of the population.[65] But beginning with the demands of a costly war in the 1940s, the poor and the middle class began to be taxed much more heavily, and since then, the supposedly progressive rate of taxation has come unhinged; the *effective* tax has decreased for the upper brackets, because of various tax loopholes, while tax rates have increased at the lower levels.[66] Although the nominal tax rate for top-income brackets ranges from 50 to 70 percent, investigators discovered, in 1967, that the effective rate of tax paid by the top 1 percent was only 26 percent of their total reported income.[67]

Tax "Welfare" There are special tax benefits—loopholes, or preferences—for everyone: rich person, poor person, business person, soulless corporation, farmer. In fact, each year the federal government gives away about $100 billion by *not* collecting taxes that it would collect if

---

[65] *Harper's Magazine,* April 1977.

[66] In spite of this trend, it should be pointed out that the federal income tax is still the least regressive of any United States tax—federal, state, or local.

[67] See Joseph A. Pechman and Benjamin A. Okner, *Who Bears the Tax Burden?* (Washington, D.C.: Brookings Institution, 1974).

certain exemptions had not been written into law. Some economists call this "backdoor spending." By far, the largest share of the favoritism is doled out to wealthy individuals and corporations.[68] Preferential provisions in United States tax laws saved the 160,000 richest taxpayers in the nation (that is, persons with gross incomes of $100,000 and over) an average of $45,662 each in 1974 (a typical year)—a total of $7.3 billion.[69]

The shifting of tax laws to help the well-to-do has occurred increasingly in recent years. In 1960, payroll taxes (taxes paid by the typical low-income and middle-income salaried person) comprised 16 percent of the federal government's total tax income. In 1969 they comprised 21 percent, and in 1974 they accounted for 31 percent of the total. Meanwhile, corporate income taxes declined sharply, from 23 percent of the federal government's total tax income in 1960 to 15 percent in 1974.

Phillip Stern claims that the taxpayer with an income of under $3,000 receives about $16 a year in "tax welfare," the taxpayer earning $10,000 receives $651, while people with incomes between $500,000 and $1 million get an average "tax welfare" benefit of more than $200,000, through tax loopholes and special preferences.[70] This welfare program for the rich, says Stern, "goes by the name of the Internal Revenue Code of 1954 as amended. It is the basic income tax law of the United States."[71]

By far, the largest single loophole is the capital gains provision in the tax law. If a person holds onto an investment—real estate, stocks, bonds, or whatever—for one year and then sells at a profit, tax is paid on only half of that profit. Naturally, this loophole is of value only to people who have money to invest, and the more money they have, the more they can exploit the loophole. Joseph A. Pechman and Benjamin A. Okner calculated that the capital gains loophole gives $640,667 annually in tax welfare to a person earning more than $1 million; it gives $26,630 annually to a person earning between $100,000 and $500,000, $55 to a taxpayer in the $15,000- to $20,000-bracket, $1 to a person in the $3,000- to $5,000-bracket, and nothing to someone earning $3,000.[72]

The tax law is also sympathetic to investors who have to sell at a loss; they can deduct their losses for a tax break. In short, federal tax laws encourage well-to-do people and corporations to take risks on the stock market and in real estate speculation; win or lose, they have a tax advantage. People at the bottom of the income scale do not have enough money with which to gamble in this fashion, and they thereby miss its rewards. Pechman and Okner estimate that the capital gains/loss loopholes deprive the federal treasury of $14 billion it would otherwise get, $14 billion that lower-income people have to make up.

Sometimes the favoritism is carried to dramatic lengths, and Congress so far has been unable to remedy the inequities. On the last day of the Johnson administration in January 1969, outgoing Treasury Secretary Joseph W. Barr startled the Joint Economic Committee by admitting that, in 1966, 155 persons with incomes over $200,000—including 21 with incomes over $1 million—had legally paid no federal income taxes. Congress, with outward manifestations of embarrassment, quickly passed a law that supposedly enacted a minimum income tax. No matter how many loopholes a person or corporation might utilize, *some* tax would be exacted from them in the future. Unfortunately, the minimum tax law is so riddled with loopholes that, in 1971, it permitted 27 persons who earned a total of more than $21 million to escape all taxes.[73] In 1973, no federal taxes were paid by 622 persons with adjusted gross incomes greater than $100,000.[74] In 1974, 3,273 persons with incomes over $50,000 and 244 persons with incomes over $200,000 paid no federal taxes.[75]

[68]*New York Times,* March 2, 1975.

[69]Treasury Department study, released by Senator Walter F. Mondale, May 26, 1975.

[70]Special Report of the Democratic Study Group of the House of Representatives, April 16, 1973.

[71]Phillip Stern, in testimony before the Joint Economic Committee on the Economic Report, January 14, 1972.

[72]Joseph A. Pechman and Benjamin A. Okner, *The Economics of Federal Subsidy Programs,* Joint Economic Committee hearings, January 13, 14, and 17, 1972.

[73]*Congressional Record,* H1487, March 6, 1976.

[74]U.S. Congress, 1976 Joint Economic Committee Report, no. 94–690, p. 83.

[75]*Washington Post,* May 11, 1976.

Surveying 37 tax returns of upper-income citizens, the Joint Economic Committee, in 1975, cited this case as an example of what can be done with legal loopholes: an executive with a salary of $427,000 and other income of $21,000 managed to pay only $1,200 in taxes (a rate of 0.3 percent), or no more than a married wage earner with a salary of less than $10,000 and with normal deductions would pay. Vice President Rockefeller pulled an even greater coup. For the ten years prior to 1975, he had been paying taxes at the same rate as a person making $18,000 a year although Rockefeller, in fact, earned $47 million during that period.[76] Legal or not, such actions cause widespread anger among the rank-and-file taxpayers. In the same year, a Harris poll asked which is worse: a welfare chiseler or a rich person who uses legal loopholes to pay little or no taxes? Although millions of Americans held welfare recipients in contempt and truly believed

that the welfare rolls were loaded with chiselers, their disgust with the rich manipulator was even deeper—58 percent felt the rich person was worse, 28 percent voted for the welfare chiseler.[77]

Some corporations have done equally well in avoiding taxes. In 1971, United States Steel, the twelfth largest American corporation, carried on a total business of almost $5 billion, had a net income of $154,515,754, and paid no federal income tax.[78] Using foreign tax credits to reduce their U.S. income tax bill, the major oil companies paid 75 percent less than they otherwise would have. This legal gimmick allowed U.S. corporations to earn more than $1 billion in mining and oil operations overseas in 1970 and pay not one penny on it in U.S. taxes.[79] One-third of the investor-owned electric utility com-

[76]Ralph Nader's Reform Research Group, quoted in *Harper's Magazine*, March 1975, p. 95.

[77]*Commonweal*, February 13, 1976.

[78]*Congressional Record*, March 21, 1972, quoted in the *Washington Post*, March 31, 1972.

[79]*Congressional Record*, S1057, February 1, 1974.

panies, despite handsome profits, paid no federal income tax in 1974.[80] The tax burden borne by commercial banks dropped from 38 percent of their income in 1961 to 17 percent in 1972. (The official corporate rate is 48 percent.[81]) In 1975, eleven companies, with an adjusted net income of more than $1.1 billion, escaped federal income taxes completely. They include the Ford Motor Company (which had $300 million in profits; in 1974 it had a profit of $500 million and paid no federal income tax), Bethlehem Steel, Western Electric, Lockheed Aircraft, National Steel, Delta Air Lines, Northwest Airlines, Manufacturer's Hanover Corporation, Chemical New York Corporation, Phelps-Dodge, and Freeport Minerals. Dozens of other corporations fared almost as well—such as Aluminum Company of America and Allied Chemical, each paying less than 1 percent in taxes.[82]

Ordinary taxpayers are at a disadvantage because the Internal Revenue Service laws are so complex and confusing. Milton Gwirtzman, a Washington tax lawyer, believes that

> the Internal Revenue Code probably is the most complicated document written by man. It is more than 5,000 pages long and the rules and interpretations issued to flesh it out run hundreds of thousands more. No one pretends to understand it all. There are lawyers who spend their entire professional careers working in just one of its sections.[83]

Only wealthy people and corporations can hire the kind of specialists needed to cope with the tax system advantageously. Indeed, the laws are so complex that the IRS's own personnel easily get lost in the maze. An IRS study of returns filed in 1972 shows that the agency's employees made mistakes on 74 percent of the itemized returns prepared for people with adjusted gross incomes of less than $10,000. The mistakes involved incorrect application of the tax law, not mathematical errors. When the government's own experts

are baffled, what chance of understanding the laws does the average taxpayer have? Yet, the government has little tolerance for errors. In fiscal year 1972, the IRS punished 937,744 taxpayers by taking their wages or property—making seven seizures each minute of every working day.[84] But in punishment the wealthy again get off lightest. One study found that the IRS settled for an average of thirty-six cents on the dollar in appellate cases involving $500,000 or more, but pressed for seventy-one cents on the dollar in appeals involving less than $1,000.[85]

Tax "Reform" With fear and trembling, the people watched as Congress once again geared up in 1976 to "reform" the tax laws. They were hardly soothed by the announcement of Senator Russell B. Long, Chairman of the Senate Finance Committee and himself an oil millionaire, that "We're tightening up on the loose ends and loosening up on the tight ends."[86] The public had heard that before.

If Congress is hesitant to act, it cannot be from the lack of an awareness of how the public feels. A 1972 survey by pollster Louis Harris showed that:

- By 67 to 26 percent, voters felt that the "tax laws are written for the rich and not for the average man."
- By an overwhelming 88- to 6-percent margin, "closing tax loopholes for high-income people" heads the list of reforms the public would like to see enacted.
- "Raising the taxes of the rich and lowering them for lower income people" is favored by 71 to 18 percent.
- By a margin of 68 to 16 percent, Americans would like to see "corporate profits taxed at a higher rate."[87]

Wanting those things and getting them, however, are two different matters. Periodically, Congress goes through painful contortions and gives birth to another "reformed" tax law. Two

---

[80]*Congressional Record,* S2901, March 4, 1976.

[81]*Washington Post,* June 17, 1974.

[82]Annual survey by Congressman Charles A. Vanik, senior member of the House Ways and Means Committee, in the *Congressional Record,* H12327, October 1, 1976.

[83]Quoted in the *Washington Star,* April 10, 1977.

[84]*Washington Post,* April 17, 1975.

[85]"Making Connections," *Harper's Magazine,* March 1975, p. 95.

[86]Quoted in the *Washington Star,* May 13, 1976.

[87]*Chicago Tribune,* October 9, 1972.

of its most notable efforts were made in 1969 and 1976, and each time the result was an increase in complexity with scarcely any diminution of inequity. Each year, in fact, Congress subjects the tax laws to an incredible flood of changes. Powerful special interests often benefit, but ordinary citizens almost never do. Speaking of the "reforms" of 1976, Senator Edward Kennedy noted the attitude responsible for this state of affairs:

> On Black Friday, last July 30, the Senate voted in rapid-fire succession to give approximately $30 to $50 million each in special tax relief to the railroads, airlines, the shipping industry, and the life insurance industry. Each of those provisions emerged relatively unscathed from the conference. But the conferees refused to accept a $30 million benefit for low-income working mothers, in the form of the Senate amendment making the child care credit refundable. That's not a bad yardstick for the future—when Congress starts paying as much attention to working mothers as it does to the railroads and the airlines and the ships and the life insurance companies, we'll be well on the way to genuine tax reform.[88]

Put in those benevolent terms, it all sounds easy to do. But in fact, people of good will differ sharply over what "genuine tax reform" would mean and how it could be accomplished.

Some people believe that the fairest approach would be to levy such a heavy tax on the higher incomes that nobody could become wealthy: the money taken from that end would be given to the poor. The result would be a leveling of income. This proposal will always have enthusiastic supporters, for, as Raymond Moley has rightly said, "the principle of a classless society dominates the mind and spirit of the American nation."[89] However appealing this Robin Hood proposal may be, it very possibly has one basic defect in practice. Without the opportunity for significant material rewards, people in the upper-income bracket—doctors, managerial experts, professionals of all sorts—might lose incentive, with a resulting decline in productivity and an increase in social dissatisfaction. Herbert Gans,

an economist who believes in a leveling redistribution (his goal is to even things out so that the poorest family would earn only 30 percent less than the average), does not think these fears are justifiable, since "we have a good deal of data to suggest the opposite—that people work that much harder to make up the income they've lost."[90]

Other people would agree with Peter Gutmann that

> It is too easy to stay rich and too difficult to get rich. That, to put it bluntly, is what's the matter with the tax system. . . . The tax system is a solid bastion of conservatism. It is heavily biased towards the success of past generations. Those whose ancestors became rich, stay rich. Those whose ancestors did not, cannot.

Gutmann proposes no taxes on the lower-income group, greatly reduced taxes on the middle-income group, but confiscatory estate and gift taxes so devastating that they would wipe out fortunes at the end of a lifetime.

> The net effect is the stimulation of economic and social mobility, with room at the top of the heap for new blood and room at the bottom for old blood. Men and women of energy could have the opportunity to rise swiftly within their lifetimes, and their children could have the chance to fall equally swiftly.

There would be an end to the Rockefeller, Mellon, Kennedy, and Ford dynasties—unless the Rockefellers, Mellons, Kennedys, and Fords of *this* generation had as much ingenuity and creativity as their ancestors and proved it by starting from scratch, building *new* fortunes.[91]

Some conservatives, such as Milton Friedman, advocate that all loopholes be done away with and that one tax rate be levied on incomes of all levels (except, of course, the lowest, which would not be taxed at all). The wage earner making $10,000 a year would pay a flat 10 percent, say, and the investor with dividend income of $200,000 a year would pay 10 percent also. There would be no deductions for children, no deduction for mortgage payments or for losing

[88]*Congressional Record*, S16022, September 16, 1976.

[89]Quoted in Clinton Rossiter, *Conservatism in America: The Thankless Persuasion* (New York: Random House, Vintage Books, 1962), p. 185.

[90]Quoted in the *Washington Star*, March 31, 1976.

[91]*Wall Street Journal*, 1976.

money in oil ventures; there would be no deduction, no loopholes of any sort, and, consequently, no opportunity to avoid taxes. It sounds like a reasonable idea, but unfortunately people earning less than $25,000 would pay more than they do today, and people earning more than $25,000 would pay less. Even *Fortune* magazine concedes, "It is hardly clear that such a shift of the tax burden would be socially desirable, and very clear that it would be politically unspeakable." The *Fortune* genre of tax expert would prefer, instead, that all corporate and personal income taxes be eliminated and replaced with a single tax based on consumption—a tax closely akin to a sales tax.[92]

There is, in short, no dearth of schemes for reforming the tax structure, but there is a great dearth of actual reform.

Inflation:
How the Dollar Goes on Shrinking

Politicians who worry about the nation's economic health are generally concerned about two things: inflation and unemployment.

Inflation is the measure of a shrinking dollar. According to the United States Bureau of Labor Statistics, a pound of round steak cost $0.45 in 1944, $0.92 in 1954, $1.07 in 1964, and $1.78 in 1974. A pound of sugar cost $0.34 in 1944, $0.52 in 1954, $0.59 in 1964, and $1.09 in 1977. And so forth. Those increases marked the trail of inflation.

The Census Bureau pointed out that, while the median income of households increased 5.2 percent in 1975, the increase was offset by a 9 percent rise in prices, resulting in a net loss of more than 3 percent in real purchasing power. Moral: The size of a person's paycheck means nothing in itself; it is meaningful only in terms of what it can buy. *New York Times* writer Robert Bendiner once pointed out that as a young man in the early 1930s he was earning only twenty dollars a week, of which fifteen dollars had to go into the family pot, but

> I did not do too badly with $5 for a week's expenses: six lunches (either soup or sandwich,

coffee and pie) came to $1.50, subway or trolley fares at a nickel each ran to about 80 cents, cigarettes (15 cents a pack and carefully nursed), plus newspapers and other incidentals, brought the weekly outlay to $4. The remaining dollar took care of dating, wanton expenditures like an occasional beer or an even more occasional theater ticket purchasable at Gray's Drugstore in Times Square for 55 cents.[93]

Unfortunately, as John Kenneth Galbraith has pointed out, "neither monetary nor fiscal policy make contact with the present form of inflation in an effective and practical way."[94] Until quite recently—say, until the end of the 1960s—the ineffectiveness of both policies in coping with inflation was of no great concern to anybody because, although inflation was a constant fact of life, its rate was not severe. Between 1950 and 1967, the dollar's rate of shrinkage exceeded 3.5 percent in only one year—1951, when the Korean War dropped the dollar's value by 7.2 percent. Serious inflation is always a spinoff of war.

As long as inflation was held to a moderate level, economists could comfortably assume that the old rules still applied: that inflation was the creation of prosperity, and thus, the surest way to cure it was to have an extra shot of unemployment. Traditionalists assumed that inflation could always be explained by the interrelationship between wages and prices, and between supply and demand. If wages go up, prices go up; when prices get too high, people stop buying; when people stop buying, workers are laid off; when workers are laid off, competition for jobs drives wages down; and when wages go down, companies cut prices to compete.

That, oversimplified, is the classic textbook description. But in fact, for the past two decades reality has been moving away from the textbook case, and a great many government economists and politicians have simply not been facing up to the change. By 1975 they had to. The nation was well into its deepest depression since the 1930s. Factories were operating at only 75 percent of

---

[92]A. F. Ehrbar, "Manifesto for a Tax Revolution," *Fortune*, April, 1977.

[93]Robert Bendiner, "How It Really Was," *New York Times Magazine*, April 6, 1975.

[94]John Kenneth Galbraith, *The Liberal Hour* (Boston: Houghton Mifflin Co., 1960), p. 63.

Inflation and Unemployment Changes, 1950-1975

The traditional experience is that inflation results almost entirely from too much demand relative to supply and that unemployment results from too little demand relative to supply. When people are out of work, they stop buying; and when they stop buying, prices drop. That's the way it used to be. But as this graph shows, in recent years prices and unemployment have shot up together—a puzzling phenomenon that economists, who are unable to explain it satisfactorily, have dubbed "stagflation."

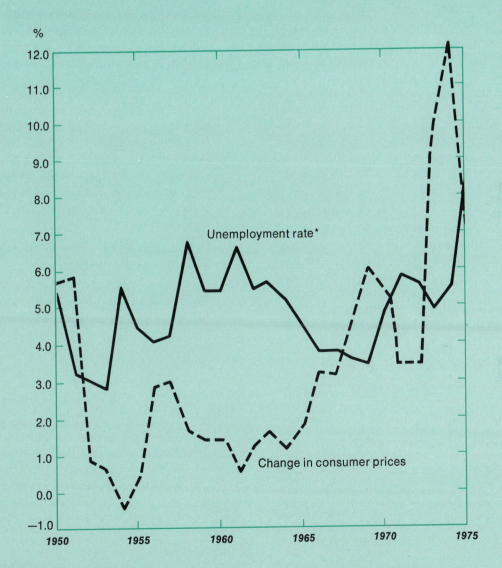

*Unemployment rates refer to annual averages. Changes in consumer prices refer to December-to-December changes.

SOURCE: *Economic Report of the President, 1976* (Washington, D.C.: U.S. Government Printing Office, 1976).

capacity, a modern low.[95] Unemployment had passed 9 percent (that was the official rate; the actual rate was probably much higher).[96] Yet the overcrowding of the labor market did not bring wages down, and inflation was demolishing the dollar at a staggering rate of 12 percent a year.

Something was screwy. What had happened? Theoretically, inflation is only supposed to accompany booms. But suddenly, in the 1970s—taking most economists quite by surprise—there was both inflation *and* recession. Since the economists could neither understand nor explain the phenomenon, they spent their time thinking up descriptive titles for it: "stagflation," "slumpflation," "infession," and "inflump."[97] Kermit Gordon, to whom the White House often turns for advice, confessed: "I know of no neat theory of inflation that fits the facts of the last five years—neither aggregate demand, nor money supply, nor labor power, nor oligopoly power, nor bottlenecks, nor expectations—though I could easily be convinced that they all played a part."[98] Indeed they had all played a part.

1. Powerful unions kept pushing up wages, even when unemployment was high.
2. The purchasing power of the unemployed was propped up by humanitarian programs, such as unemployment compensation, Social Security, and food stamps, which maintained the consumers' ability to buy—and consequently business's re-

sistance to price cutting—even while joblessness was rising. This prevented suffering but it stoked inflation.
3. Some key industries, like steel and auto, no longer respond to the supply-demand stimulus, since competition is virtually nil. These industries operate not with competitive prices, but with administered prices. During a recession, they are likely to raise prices to keep profits up. Raising prices when sales are already down may sound odd, but it can be done safely and successfully in noncompetitive industries, where all the big companies are charging exactly the same price.[99]
4. On top of everything else, the stagflation of the mid-1970s coincided with some powerful forces beyond the reach of the United States government, including the control of a large share of energy resources by foreign governments. (See Chapter 16.)
5. Another international cause of domestic inflation was the unexpected demand for farm production and the resulting sharp price increase. Between the end of 1972 and the end of 1975, food prices went up about 50 percent, triggered by enormous purchases of grain by the Soviet Union. Similarly, there was a world boom in demand for raw material, with prices soaring in 1973 and early 1974 for basic nonfood materials such as copper, rubber, zinc, and cotton. All major industrial economies were expanding rapidly, and United States industrialists had to make their purchases on the inflated world market; the increased costs were, of course, passed on to the consumer.[100]

It is not clear what devices will be used in the future to inhibit serious inflation, but it is clear

---

[95]Clayton Fritchey, *Washington Post,* June 28, 1975.

[96]Report of the Congressional Budget Office, "Inflation and Unemployment," June 30, 1975, p. 19.

[97]One of the most ingenious explanations of "stagflation" was given by Gottfried Haberler: "Once people expect prices to go on rising by, say, 14 percent a year and the actual price rise is then reduced to, say, 7 percent, the consequence will be disappointments, losses, retrenchment, unemployment—in short a recession, just as if in an earlier state inflation of, say, 5 percent had been brought down to zero. *A mere slowing down of an inflation leads to recession. This is stagflation.* In other words, only an unanticipated inflation—or more precisely an inflation that exceeds the anticipated level—has stimulating power. An anticipated inflation does not stimulate, and an inflation that stays below the anticipated level is definitely depressing." (*Depression and Inflation on Spaceship Earth*, Washington, D.C.: American Enterprise Institute, 1976, p. 16.)

[98]Quoted in Hobart Rowen, *Washington Post,* January 3, 1974.

[99]See John M. Blair, *Economic Concentration: Structure, Behavior, and Public Policy* (New York: Harcourt Brace Jovanovich, 1972), pp. 467–97. Whether the companies can be charged with collusion is another matter. Collusion for the purpose of price fixing is illegal, but it is also hard to prove. And even when it is easy to prove, businesses often look on the penalties as simply another cost.

[100]Edwin Dale, Jr., et al., *Priorities in an Uncertain Economy: Inflation, Recession and Government Spending* (Washington, D.C.: Potomac Associates, 1976), pp. 6–7.

that the primitive reliance on tight money and unemployment to do the job is no longer enough. Some economists contend that the only sure way to keep wages and prices under control is by controls themselves—that is, government-imposed ceilings under which unions and corporations would be required to operate. Some especially brave economists have expressed the belief that profits and dividends must be controlled too.[101] The bravest economists go so far as to suggest that inflation cannot be efficiently controlled unless big unions and big corporations are broken up and their power is dispersed, so that wages and prices will once again respond to competition.

Short of a near catastrophe, no presidential administration is likely to reach soon for controls on a permanent basis or to suggest tinkering with the structure of labor and corporations. Even on a temporary basis, controls are shunned as being antithetical to free enterprise, and therefore un-American. Which brings us to the consideration of just how free our present free-enterprise system is.

FREE ENTERPRISE OR PUBLIC ENTERPRISE?

Early in this chapter, we noted how Adam Smith's pristine formula for a truly competitive free-enterprise system was soon sullied in practice by all sorts of government interference in the economy. It began with subsidies and extended a century or so later to regulation.

The lords of industry were happy to accept the subsidizing kind of interference, but, for a long time, they recoiled from regulation. Yet, today, though they grouse about the red tape and inconvenience of governmental dogma, they would not think of getting rid of regulation. It is, they feel, a stabilizing influence. Why undergo the hardships and economic bloodletting of competition when the government will guarantee profits by fixing prices for businesses, by franchising sales regions for businesses, by pro-

hibiting competition among businesses? There are stern-sounding antimonopoly laws on the federal statute books, but these apply—when enforced at all—only to boisterous corporations that try to achieve a monopoly without government assistance. They are foolish to do so when assistance is so freely given. *Fortune* magazine quotes Harold Demstez on this point: "If an industry tries to conspire to raise prices, it violates antitrust. But if an industry goes jointly to Washington, it is not violating any laws. It can get the government to police the industry. The government becomes part of the collusive agreement. That's the high road to monopoly."[102]

How Regulation Began

The high road to monopoly began to unwind last century. If there was ever a period of really rough competition, of the sort to make Adam Smith's heart sing, it was in the first two decades after the Civil War. The economic environment was right for the first (and the last) time to encourage new business entrepreneurs on a grand scale, and they poured their imagination and money into the marketplace. Businesses of every sort and size sprang up. Railroad companies proliferated, laying a web of lines around the country.[103]

The results of this era convinced business executives, especially Big Business executives, that laissez faire competition was not a virtue—it was too costly and too unpredictable. And when they wanted to get pious in their objections, as they frequently did, they would say, in the words of S. C. T. Dodd, Standard Oil's lawyer, that competition stood in the way of the "march of civilization." Dodd and his peers were convinced that civilization could best be served by industrial cooperation and concentration. James J. Hill, the railroad magnate, wrote, in 1901, that ". . . the 'trust' came into being as the result of an effort to obviate ruinous competition."[104]

[101]See Robert L. Heilbroner, *Business Civilization in Decline* (New York: W. W. Norton & Co., 1976), pp. 26–27.

[102]Quoted in *Fortune,* April 1975, p. 107

[103]Robert H. Wiebe, *The Search for Order: 1877–1920* (New York: Hill & Wang, 1967), pp. 46–47.

[104]Quoted in Gabriel Kolko, *The Triumph of Conservatism* (New York: Quadrangle/New York Times Book Co., 1967), p. 13.

A cartoon of 1887 depicts the trusts as the bosses of the Senate

From an orgy of competition, U.S. business and industry moved swiftly to an orgy of defensive consolidation and merger. Writes Ivar Berg,

> The movement reached its peak when, in the decade between 1895 and 1904, an average of 301 firms a year disappeared, absorbed either by competitors or by newly charted holding companies. . . . The corporate revolution can best be explained by the desire of these businessmen to achieve some degree of control over prices, to rule the market rather than to be ruled by it. This can be seen in the actual results. In 60 percent of the 1895–1904 mergers, as measured by capitalization, a single large corporation succeeded in gaining control of at least 62.5 percent of its industry's market; and in another 10 percent of the mergers a single large corporation succeeded in gaining control of between 42.5 percent and 62.5 percent of its industry's market.[105]

Americans became fearful and resentful of what they saw happening. Editorial cartoonists began depicting the monopoly corporations—the trusts—as giant squids. The Standard Oil Company, perhaps the most successful monopoly of the day, became the most hated corporation in the land. Quite early on—in 1890—the government offered the Sherman Antitrust Act as a soothing antidote to this general unrest. But the Sherman Act was written so vaguely that it was never a serious threat to the concentration of industrial power. It was government's way of telling the industrial and business giants: "We will not try to prevent you from growing and merging and dominating your markets, so long as you check in with us and get our approval as a matter of form. We cannot permit outlawry, but we will permit just about anything that is done within the context of a very flexible and tolerant law." A few of the supergiants—Standard Oil, American Tobacco Company, and Du Pont—were split up by Sherman Antitrust action, but the result was simply a transfer of market do-

[105]Berg, *The Business of America*, pp. 184–85.

In Defense of the Public

People of the same trade seldom meet together, even for merriment and diversion, but the conversation ends in a conspiracy against the public, or in some contrivance to raise prices. It is impossible indeed to prevent such meetings, by any law which either could be executed, or would be consistent with liberty and justice. But though the law cannot hinder people of the same trade from sometimes assembling together, it ought to do nothing to facilitate such assemblies; much less to render them necessary.

Adam Smith, *The Wealth of Nations* (New York: Random House, Modern Library, 1937; first published in 1776).

minion from single-headed monopoly to multi-headed monopoly, or oligopoly, thus gaining a public relations advantage without losing control of the market.[106]

In this spirit was launched the era of government regulation of business, first with the founding of the Interstate Commerce Commission in 1887, followed by the Federal Trade Commission in 1914 (presumably to prevent unfair competition and dishonest marketing), and the other major regulatory bodies that were set up in the 1930s. Their effect has been to lessen competition among established big businesses and to protect them from ambitious newcomers who might try to win a share of the market with ingenious services and lower prices. (See the section on regulatory agencies in Chapter 12.) When President Carter proposed a bill that would reduce federal regulation of the airline industry, the major carriers opposed it, because government-regulated prices had allowed them to charge passengers nearly $2 billion more each year than they could have charged in true competitive circumstances.[107] Similar government-approved price fixing was taking place in many other industries.

Under the guise of regulation, the government has permitted, and sometimes encouraged, a continuation of mergers—with a natural concentration of control over markets—down to the present day. Between 1962 and 1968, for example, 110 of *Fortune*'s top 500 corporations disappeared into mergers, all with the Justice Department's tacit approval—or at least without its disapproval.[108] In 1965, Willard F. Mueller, former chief economist of the Federal Trade Commission, predicted that, by 1975, the 200 largest manufacturing corporations would control two-thirds of all manufacturing assets. He was wrong. They reached that level of control by 1969.[109] In 1968, the 100 largest corporations controlled more manufacturing assets than the 200 largest in 1950, and the 200 largest in 1968 held more shares of manufacturing assets than were held by the 1,000 largest in 1951.[110]

The concentration can best be seen in particular industries where four companies (or fewer) control more than 90 percent of the market. This is the case for such products as soaps and detergents, electric light bulbs, cereal, toothpaste, camera film, soup, and chocolate candy. Ten companies control 73 percent of the refined-sugar market. And ten companies control 63 percent of the refined-oil market.[111]

---

[106]Robert Lekachman has written on this point: "A generation ago Thurman Arnold sharply judged that 'The actual result of the antitrust laws was to promote the growth of great industrial organizations by deflecting the attack on them into purely moral and ceremonial channels.' The late Richard Hofstadter, a historian of the Progressive era, described antitrust as a 'faded passion of American reform.' Both of these astute observers were recording a fact of American life: a good blast against monopoly entertains the populace and does no harm to the monopolists." (*Inflation,* p. 62.)

[107]General Accounting Office, Washington, D.C., "Lower Airline Costs per Passenger Are Possible in the United States and Could Result in Lower Fares," February 18, 1977.

[108]*Congressional Record,* H465, May 22, 1975.

[109]Senate Antitrust Subcommittee, Ninety-first Congress, Second Session, *Economic Concentration,* part 8: "The Conglomerate Merger Problem," November 4, 5, and 6, 1969; January 28, February 5, 18, and 19, 1970; p. 4544.

[110]Morton Mintz and Jerry S. Cohen, *America Inc.* (New York: Dell Publishing Co., Dial Press, 1971), p. 35.

[111]Sources: *Congressional Record,* S10731, June 17, 1975; Associated Press, November 29, 1974.

Welfare Capitalism

Government's benevolence toward business and industry goes much farther than the mere condoning of monopolies; it extends to financial assistance of all kinds, from direct subsidies to tax breaks and, especially, low-interest loans. The system under which the government subsidizes and controls and also owns, in part, capitalist enterprises is defined here as welfare capitalism. But it should be clear that the welfare goes to the capitalists, not to the people.

In 1974 it was estimated that the government was giving $95 billion a year in subsidies and tax breaks, and, of this, $21 billion went to "stimulate" business, $15.7 billion went to stimulate housing, and $16.6 billion went to the health industry—which, though benefiting the individual, would wind up, of course, in the hands of hospitals, insurance companies, and doctors.[112]

In short, there is no free market in bank interest rates, no free market in mortgage rates, no free market in energy, no free market in medicine—indeed, one is lucky to catch a glimpse of the free market as it flashes by.

Liberal Democrats in general, and Franklin Roosevelt in particular, are usually blamed, or credited, for stepping up government interference to the scale of welfare capitalism; and they indeed embraced the concept so passionately that an abundant share of the blame or credit does belong to them. But, in fact, it was none other than that conservative Republican Herbert Hoover who first offered the forbidden fruit of welfare capitalism in the form of the Reconstruction Finance Corporation. The RFC was the government's credit bank that flourished from 1931 to 1939, handing out $10 billion to broken-down capitalists.[113]

The launching of the RFC was instructive. Hoover called about twenty of the overlords of the New York City and Chicago banking world to a secret evening meeting in Washington in 1931 and proposed that the strong banks set up an emergency fund on which the weaker banks could draw. There was certainly no question about their needing help. Thousands of banks collapsed in the early days of the Great Depression. Something had to be done. But the strong bankers didn't want to take the risks involved in helping their weaker colleagues. They rejected Hoover's proposal.[114]

So Hoover turned to the taxpayer to support his scheme and, with public money, established the Reconstruction Finance Corporation. It was supposed to make loans to shaky banks, insurance companies, railroads, real estate corporations, and farmers. Most of the money went directly to the banks and to the railroads who were the banks' debtors. Many of the loans, especially those made during the first five months, when the government doled out $1 billion, had the strong odor of corruption.[115] But the corruption, as the record of government subsidies over the next two generations would prove, was not nearly enough to turn the nation against welfare capitalism.

A Failed Corporation

Nowhere has the extreme of government interference in free enterprise been more evident, and more criticized, than in the transportation industry, every phase of which has benefited

---

[112]*Washington Post,* October 16, 1974.

[113]See Matthew Josephson, *The Money Lords: The Great Finance Capitalists 1925–1950* (New York: Weybright & Talley, 1972), p. 155.

[114]Murray N. Rothbard, *America's Great Depression* (Plainview, N.J.: Nash Publishing, 1972), pp. 242–243.

[115]The RFC's first chairman, Eugene Meyer, was very enthusiastic about the program, which is easy to understand, seeing as about $10 million of RFC funds went to the Missouri-Pacific Railroad to pay off its debt to J. P. Morgan and Company; Meyer's brother-in-law was a top member of the Morgan firm, and Meyer himself had once held an important position with it. As it happened, no sooner had Missouri Pacific repaid its debt than it went bankrupt—the taxpayers' $10 million having disappeared into the maw of Morgan and Company, never to return.

About 60 percent of the $10 billion loaned during the first five months of secrecy went straight to the banks. The Central Republic Bank and Trust Company of Chicago, which had deposits of only $95 million, received a loan of almost that much—$90 million. And guess who was President of the Central Republic Bank—none other than Charles G. Dawes, who, until three weeks before the RFC loan was made, had seen serving as President of the RFC. The gears of welfare capitalism worked very smoothly right from the start. (Rothbard, pp. 261–63.)

greatly from government aid—the railroads through the early land grants and through recent loans and subsidies of every sort, the airlines through the development of military aviation and the subsidization of weak companies and of terminal facilities, the barge lines through the construction and maintenance of inland waterways with general tax revenue, the trucking companies through the construction of the interstate highway system.

Most of the criticism has been heaped on the railroad industry, and for good reason. One of the supposedly immutable laws of free-enterprise capitalism is that efficiency and good management are rewarded with success, while inefficiency and sloppy management are sins whose wages are economic death. The classic notion of capitalism is akin to Darwin's theory of evolution: only the fit survive. The railroad industry, which in the nineteenth century was one of the most ruthlessly capitalist of our industries, has lately turned that principle on its head. When the Penn Central Transportation Company, the nation's largest railroad, went bankrupt in 1970 partly as a result of shabby service[116] and sometimes lawless management, it did not die; it called for help and the federal government stepped in and rescued it with a variety of economic crutches (meanwhile permitting many of the Penn Central officials who had managed the company into a disaster to stay on the job at salaries of up to $250,000 a year).

It was a disheartening lesson in what happens when monopoly privileges are abused. Railroads are natural monopolies, because the high cost of capital investment discourages new entries into the market. The Penn Central, with government-approved mergers, had become a supermonopoly, with 80,000 employees and 20,000 miles of rails. In its territory it had so destroyed all roots of competition that when it finally went into irreversible debt, it could not be allowed to go out of business; nothing was around to take its place. Large areas of the northeastern part of the nation would have been left without rail service of any kind. So, in effect, the government, through its foolish cooperation in building the Penn Central empire, had been put in a position where it had to rescue the line. Part of the rescue included blending Penn Central's passenger service with the defunct or near-defunct passenger service of a dozen other railroad companies and calling the new amalgam the National Passenger Railroad Corporation (or Amtrak).[117] It was a quasi-public corporation, which meant that the public paid the debts and the private companies made the profits.[118] A similar formula was used in 1975 when seven major bankrupt railroads, including that ubiquitous cripple, the Penn Central, were brought together with government assistance into the quasi-nationalized Consolidated Rail Corporation (Conrail).

In most countries of the world, natural monopolies, like railroads and utilities, are directly owned and run by the state—often with good results. But it is the American way to preserve the forms (and the profits) of free enterprise. Sometimes we seem to be adept at getting the worst of both worlds, capitalist and socialist, when either free competition or public ownership would be better than an unholy mixture. Meanwhile, at taxpayers' expense, Conrail paid its executives up to $200,000 a year.[119]

The sort of arrangement whereby the taxpayers subsidize the corporation and cushion its losses while its shareholders walk away with the

---

[116]An outraged *Washington Post* editorial writer adequately described service on the Penn Central: "Penn Central's Washington-New York trains are scruffy, ill-lit, dirty, uncomfortable, noisy, fetid, inconvenient, badly-heated and poorly air-conditioned; the toilets often do not work; the food, while expensive, is unspeakable; the ticketing procedures are only slightly less complicated than those required to obtain a pardon from a state penitentiary; and when the weather is warm, the atmosphere in the coaches is akin to a medieval torture chamber. Of course it is not all bad. From time to time a mendicant appears in the aisles selling sandwiches of stale bread and aromatic Swiss cheese." (October 17, 1968.)

[117]Even Amtrak—which cost the taxpayer $2 billion in subsidies to keep it rolling its first five years—is probably better than no train at all, but the money has hardly paid for anything resembling "progress." The old Pennsylvania Railroad's *Broadway Limited* used to run between New York and Chicago in sixteen hours, back in the 1940s. Amtrak's *Broadway Limited* made the same trip in eighteen hours, forty minutes, in 1976. (*Washington Star*, May 1, 1976.)

[118]See "What Price Amtrak," *New York Times*, February 18, 1973.

[119]*Washington Star*, May 16, 1976.

profits, if there are any, may seem somewhat unfair to the taxpayers, but the fabric of the nation's economy is too interwoven to permit even the most foolishly managed companies, if they are large enough, to die. If Penn Central, for example, had collapsed, it would have probably carried down with it many of the nation's largest banks, which had lent the corporation billions of dollars; and if these banks had collapsed, the repercussions throughout our business and industrial structure might have been truly disastrous. So bigness has helped to kill free enterprise.

As John Kenneth Galbraith has put it:

> The failed corporation is the second socialist imperative. Above a certain size, it is now evident, no industrial corporation can be allowed to collapse and go out of business. The effect on workers, customers, management and creditors is too great. Nothing more wonderfully reveals the flexibility of the human mind than the speed with which the most stalwart capitalist in our time converts to socialism when this is the only chance for survival and the recovery of his debts. The owners, creditors or managers of Penn Central, Lockheed, Pan Am, Rolls Royce, British Leyland, Krupp, Citroen, even the large Wall Street brokerage houses have all undergone this ideological transmigration in recent years. The power of socialist propaganda on established faith is as nothing compared with the threat of bankruptcy. Marx, from wherever he is watching, must smile.[120]

Recent history is littered with examples to prove how right Galbraith is. Lockheed Aircraft Corporation, which became infamous as one of the foremost participants in international bribery for business, was the best recent example, next to the Penn Central. It was on the verge of bankruptcy until the government guaranteed a huge loan to carry it through. The chief lobbyist for this loan was Treasury Secretary John B. Connally. The dialogue between Connally and Senator William Proxmire, Chairman of the Joint Economic Committee, is enlightening.

> PROXMIRE: Lockheed's bailout is not a subsidy, it is different from a subsidy, it is the beginning of a welfare program for large corporations. I would remind you that in a subsidy program there is a quid pro quo. You make a payment to an airline and they provide a certain amount of services for it. In welfare you make a payment and there is no return. In this case the government gives a guarantee and there is no requirement on the part of Lockheed to perform under that guarantee. A guarantee of $250 million and no benefit, no quid for the quo.
>
> CONNALLY: What do you mean, no benefit?
>
> PROXMIRE: Well, they don't have to perform.
>
> CONNALLY: What do we care whether they perform? We are guaranteeing them basically a $250 million loan. What for? Basically so they can hopefully minimize their losses, so they can provide employment for 31,000 people throughout the country at a time when we desperately need that type of employment. That is basically the rationale and justification.[121]

"What do we care whether they perform?" This has been the commonly accepted attitude in government for at least a generation; it is the very heart of Keynesian economics. Waste and mismanagement are not sought after; they are not prized; they are often even deplored. But they are also accepted as a natural and unimportant barnacle on the ship of state that must be kept propelled by an increasingly heavy and seemingly endless flow of funds.

THE DISTRIBUTION OF WEALTH

Are Some Americans More Equal than Others?

There is a definite correlation between a person's access to money and his or her access to freedom. Economist Kenneth Arrow puts it this way:

> Income and property are certainly the instruments of an individual's freedom. Clearly the domain of choice is enhanced by increases in those dimensions. It is true not merely in the sense of expanded consumer choice but also in broader contexts of career and opportunity to pursue one's own aims and to develop one's own potential. Unequal distribution of property and income is inherently an

---

[120]John Kenneth Galbraith, "Capitalism's Failures," *New Republic*, August 16 and 23, 1975.

[121]Quoted in Robert Sherrill, "The Rise of John Connally," *Nation*, August 7, 1972.

unequal distribution of freedom. Thus a redistribution of income, to the extent that it reduces the freedom of the rich, equally increases that of the poor. Their control of their lives is increased. . . . The aim of achieving an equal distribution of political power requires a restriction on the inequalities of wealth and income.[122]

Arrow's complaint can be translated into numbers. The lowest fifth of the population received only 5.4 percent of the nation's total income in 1975, while the top fifth of the population received 41.1 percent. Those are United States Census Bureau figures; and they are misleadingly optimistic, because the census's definition of "earnings" does not take into consideration the ownership of capital. If one takes the latter into consideration, the imbalance becomes: the richest 19 percent of families own 76 percent of all privately held assets and the poorest 25 percent have no assets.[123] If one moves closer to the point of the pyramid of wealth, the ratio becomes even more awesome and, if one is attempting to figure out some way to achieve economic equality, even more troublesome. At the top of the heap, 1 percent of the population holds about 24 percent of the wealth—including 15 percent of all real estate, 56.5 percent of all corporate stock, 60 percent of all bonds, and 52.7 percent of all mortgages and other credit instruments.[124] More disturbing, the imbalanced concentration seems rather permanent; it has not changed much in the past generation. In 1948, the poorest one-fifth and the wealthiest one-fifth had almost exactly the same portion of the total income they have today (5 percent then, 5.4 percent now; 42.5 percent then, 41.1 percent now). Likewise at the peak: between 1929 and 1953, the share of total wealth owned by the richest 1 percent of families declined from 31.6 to 24.3 percent,[125] but since then, distribution has remained roughly unchanged.

As already pointed out, economic disparity goes beyond simple income, subsidies, and tax favoritism. Economic inequality also includes the degree of control individuals have over their lives. If people cannot afford to attend college, their chances for employment and advancement are critically reduced. Those who can afford a college degree will enter professions where security is virtually guaranteed; those who must turn to factory work, service work, or migrant labor—and especially those who are not protected by union contracts—must contend with an economic roller coaster, sometimes employed, sometimes out of work. The chain is difficult to break. These examples indicate that, if the disparity between the upper crust and the middle class is wide and awesome, so is the disparity between the middle class and the poor.

Who are the poor? In 1965, the Social Security Administration developed definitions of poverty-level incomes that have ever since been the basis for the government's official definition of poverty. The formula was worked out by determining the cost of a "minimally adequate diet" and multiplying that by three (social workers figure most poor people spend one-third of their income on food). Since 1965, price increases have forced the poverty line upwards. In 1966, the government—with an arbitrariness that is supposed to pass for omniscience—decided that $3,317 was the minimum an urban family of four could earn before it sank into poverty. That was, of course, a ridiculously low estimate. It was meant to be a base subsistence figure: no movies, no newspapers, no medical or dental care, little meat, little clothing, and so on. By 1975, the government had raised its official poverty line to $5,050 a year for a family of four—which, in the middle of the worst inflation spiral in modern times, was even more ridiculous.

Even at the unrealistically low cut-off line for poverty, 11.6 percent of the population—one American in every nine—were caught below that line. And these statistics hide the true condition of many of the poor; they make no distinction between the poor person earning five thousand dollars a year and the poor person earning one thousand dollars a year, or nothing. No one knows for sure how many Americans are literally hungry, how many may be slowly starving. Estimates of the hungry range from 10 million—a

[122]Kenneth Arrow, *New Republic*, November 2, 1974, pp. 24–25.

[123]Lester C. Thurow, "More Are Going to Be Poor," *New Republic*, November 2, 1974.

[124]*The U.S. Fact Book: The Statistical Abstract of the U.S.* (New York: Grosset & Dunlap, 1977), pp. 406, 427.

[125]See Robert J. Lampman's *The Share of Top Wealth Holders in National Wealth, 1922–1956* (New York: National Bureau of Economic Research, 1962).

This Detroit scene bespeaks the poverty found in all urban areas

figure that everyone acknowledges to be very conservative—to 40 million.[126]

Government economists as much as admitted the absurdity of the poverty line when they said that the typical urban family of four required $14,300 in 1975 to maintain a moderate standard of living and at least $9,200 a year to live at a more "austere" level—meaning, rental housing without air conditioning, use of public transportation or an old car, and minimal diet. If that was what they could get for $9,200, where did it put the family earning $5,051 a year—$1 above the official poverty line? And where did it put the millions of families earning, say, $3,000 a year and less? In 1975 the *median* income in Greene County, Alabama, was $3,566, and it was $3,565 in Tunica County, Mississippi.[127]

Ways to Raise the Poor

The problem of raising the dirt poor has been attacked with some notable success—up to a point. In 1977, the Congressional Budget Office reported with understandable dismay:

> During the past decade, public expenditures for social welfare programs have grown four-fold—from $77.2 billion in 1965 to $286.5 in 1975. At the same time, according to official poverty statistics, the percentage of families in poverty has declined by only about 30 percent. An apparent paradox, this situation has led some observers to question the efficacy of the current system of public transfers. This dilemma is the result of two factors: the types of programs that account for most of the recent growth; and the inadequacies of the measures used to estimate families in poverty.[128]

[126]Marquis Childs, syndicated column, February 18, 1975.

[127]*Congressional Record*, H2120, March 20, 1975.

[128]Congressional Budget Office, "Poverty Status of Families under Alternative Definitions of Income," background paper no. 17 (January 13, 1977): v.

The government has set about aiding the poor (and sick and aged) through a crazy quilt of assistance programs: Social Security, minimum wage, unemployment compensation, welfare assistance, Medicare, Medicaid, and food stamps.[129] But the minimum standards they set are simply too low. A parent with three or more dependents will still be very poor even if he or she works full-time at the federal minimum wage. If they show up for work forty hours a week, fifty-two weeks a year, their earnings will still be nearly one thousand dollars below the official poverty line for a family of four. Of what help is the federal minimum wage law to such a worker? It seems to be completely unresponsive to the dictum handed down by HEW Secretary Joseph A. Califano, Jr.: "The poor are poor not because they won't and don't work, but because

when they do work they do not earn enough money to lift them out of poverty."[130]

The same criticism can be made of Social Security. As of 1976, the lowest Social Security payment was $101 a month; the highest was $364; and the average was $245, for a man retiring at age sixty-five. If he were married, his payment was increased 50 percent. Twenty million elderly Americans receive Social Security, and 5 million of them have no other income—which means that the average couple among these 5 million receives $368 a month ($4,416 a year) with which to pay rent, buy food, buy clothing, pay for transportation, and entertain themselves. It simply can't be done.

Thus, one must conclude that, despite much generous outlays for assistance to individuals and despite some measurable widening of the middle class, the world's richest nation retains many millions of poor people whose supposed political equality has not yet been transmitted into economic equality, even when the definition of the latter is modestly limited to "enough for basic comfort and health." A side of the failure that is little understood is that most of the public assistance money is not intended to help the poor alone. It is not intended as *basic* assistance, but as *supplemental* assistance; that is, it is intended to help the nonpoor who have had bad luck and are in unaccustomed need of aid.

To clarify the situation, let's redefine government assistance. Roughly 60 percent of all social welfare expenditures by federal, state, and local governments are what the bureaucrats call "income-transfer payments." The three classes of these expenditures are: social insurance programs, such as social security and unemployment insurance; cash assistance programs, such as Aid to Families with Dependent Children and Supplemental Security Income; and in-kind programs, such as food stamps and Medicaid. Most of these expenditures are received by the public in general, not just by poor persons. They were *designed* to help the general public. Social insurance programs, for example, are aimed at *replacing* earnings that have been lost as a result of

[129]One view of the hodgepodge quality of the assistance programs was given by a congressional study group headed by former Congresswoman Martha Griffiths: "Our income security programs are shaped by at least 21 committees of the Congress and by 50 state legislatures, by six Cabinet departments and three federal agencies, by 54 state and territorial welfare agencies and by more than 1,500 county welfare departments, by the U.S. Supreme Court and by many lesser courts." (Quoted in the *Washington Post,* January 9, 1977.)

Further complicating the system is the mixture of motives, some of them hidden. For example, when the federal food stamp program was launched in 1964, it was valued not so much for improving diets as it was for increasing food consumption so that farmers could sell more. Participants in the program received coupons that could be used instead of money at grocery stores. Most of the recipients were required to pay something for their stamps, according to their net earnings. The head of a family of four whose net earnings were $250 a month paid $71 and received $166 worth of stamps. The grocer redeemed the stamps at face value, and the federal government paid the difference between the purchase price and face value.

In 1965, when citizens in only 110 counties were eligible to receive the stamps, the program had 424,000 participants and cost $36 million. At that time, one heard little complaining about the program in Congress. But by 1976, there were 19 million people in the program, and the cost had risen to $5.8 billion. A congressional study found that as many as one American out of four would be eligible for food stamps at some time during the Bicentennial year. Although 87 percent of the households receiving food stamps earned less than $6,000 a year and 45 percent of the recipients were on welfare, Congress had begun to lose interest in the program; many members complained that it was a haven for deadbeats. Perhaps one reason for the change of attitude was that farmers no longer had a surplus of food, and they were no longer interested in using the poor as a makeshift market. (*New York Times,* April 18, 1976.)

[130]Quoted in David E. Rosenbaum "Officials Are Up Against the Myths of Welfare," *New York Times,* May 22, 1977.

unemployment, old age, sickness, disability, or death. The social insurance programs in 1976 accounted for 68 percent of all social welfare expenditures. But only about one-third of the $124 billion went to those families who were in the lowest 20 percent of the income population. Indeed, families in the top fifth, families with pretax and transfer (welfare, and so forth) incomes higher than $21,700 a year, received nearly 12 percent of the total social insurance handed out in 1976. The other two broad categories—cash assistance and in-kind transfers—are targeted more directly at the low-income population. Usually these programs specifically limit eligibility and income support to groups such as poor families with children and low-income aged and disabled. And yet, in fiscal 1976, nearly 40 percent of the $18 billion cash assistance and nearly 47 percent of the $41 billion in-kind transfers went to families who were *not* in the lowest fifth of the income population, and, in each instance, about 10 percent went to families in the top two-fifths of the population.[131]

Clearly, though all of these programs were conceived with the hope that the poorest would be uplifted, none of them can be viewed as an intensely focused attempt to eradicate poverty. It is even reasonable to wonder if a program with such a focus would pass Congress with the proper funding. At least it is much easier to pass legislation that not only helps the helpless, but also offers a crutch to the college student who is a bit short of cash, the union member who is out on strike and would like to supplement his or her diet, and the accountant who is temporarily put out of work by a recession.

Which is not to say that a program aimed specifically at eradicating poverty could not be set up rather simply and at a surprisingly low cost. It could be done by establishing a guaranteed income. Robert Lekachman explains:

> It is well within our national resources to totally eliminate poverty as it is financially measured by Washington. No doubt poverty is more than a mere shortage of money. But it could hardly hurt the poor to get a subsidy of cash. Before the 1974–75 mini-depression, all financial poverty

could have been eliminated at the price of a modest shift of $10–15 billion to the poor from the rest of the community. Fifteen billion is less than 1.5 percent of the gross national product, about the size of one of the cheaper weapons systems after cost overruns. Of course the elimination of poverty would actually cost more than $15 billion because we would have to offer the hard-working families just above the poverty line smaller grants to keep them ahead of the poor. What's wrong with that? If families earning between $6,000 and $9,000 also got supplementary cash grants, so much the better. A modest degree of income redistribution would still leave plenty of inequality.[132]

Even if the cost of this kind of cash assistance to raise the poor to austerity level, and to lift the austerity budget to moderate comfort, were twice Lekachman's estimate—that is, even if it totaled $30 billion—it would be less than one-third the military budget.

Helping the poor and the near-poor with massive infusions of cash has seldom been seriously considered by politicians, however, unless the cash is to be doled out under the offensive name of "welfare." That is, the idea that everyone has a *right* to a reasonable income somehow seems to frighten most politicians and probably frightens most taxpayers.[133]

Even if a comfortable minimum standard were to be established, huge inequalities would

---

[131]Congressional Budget Office, "Poverty Status of Families under Alternative Definitions of Income," pp. 1–4.

[132]Robert Lekachman, *Economists at Bay* (New York: McGraw-Hill, 1976), p. 41.

[133]Once in our history, and not so long ago at that, plans to redistribute the wealth were taken seriously. In the 1930s, when being poor was the rule rather than the exception, Senator Huey P. Long of Louisiana gained a wide national following with his "Share Our Wealth" plan, whereby the rich would be heavily taxed to provide everyone a minimum income of two thousand dollars, a house, an automobile, a radio, free homesteads, and free education. His slogan: "Every Man a King." His favorite theme: "There is no rule so sure as that the same mill which grinds out fortunes above a certain size, grinds out paupers at the bottom." In 1935, he introduced legislation to launch his program. James A. Farley, United States Postmaster General and President Roosevelt's top political adviser, had a poll taken, which showed that Long's proposals were so popular nationally that he would probably win 4 million votes in the 1936 presidential election and thereby hold the balance of power between the two major parties. However, Long was assassinated under mysterious circumstances before the 1936 election was held. (George E. Mowry, *The Urban Nation*, New York: Hill & Wang, 1965, pp. 105–07.)

remain—and not just financial ones. Values ranging from a sense of self-worth to a sense of shared community would be unevenly distributed. Those whose incomes were not subsidized would not look kindly on those whose incomes were. Americans have adjusted only grudgingly to the necessity of public handouts at the personal level—they are still generally associated with shiftless persons, welfare cheaters, and loafers.[134] Those who received the handouts would inevitably feel their worth cheapened and their incentives dulled. And those with the power to distribute wealth would have undue power over those eligible to receive it.

The benefits to individuals that would result from spreading economic equality are too obvious to need elaboration: a comfortable sense of security, the pleasures of material consumption, and so forth. But there would also be an enormous benefit to society in general; many of the harsh frictions of political conflict would disappear. Herbert Gans tells it right:

> Conflicts can best be compromised fairly if the society is more egalitarian, if differences of self-interest that result from sharp inequality of income and power can be reduced. The more egalitarian a society, the greater the similarity of interests among its citizens, and the greater the likelihood that disagreements among them can be settled through fair compromise. Only in a more egalitarian society is it possible to develop policies that are truly in the public interest, for only in such a society do enough citizens share enough interests so that these can be considered public ones.[135]

What if the nation's total wealth of $3.5 trillion were divided *evenly*? Every American over the age of twenty-one would have a net worth of $25,000. That would be a very uncomfortable comedown, no doubt, for the likes of such people as Ford Motor Company Chairman Henry Ford II and President Lee Iacocca, each of whom takes in nearly $1 million a year in salary alone.[136] But for most people, $25,000 would be a bonanza. As it is, half the population, if they sold all their assets and paid off all debts, would be worth no more than $3,000,[137] and, as mentioned earlier, the poorest 25 percent have *no* net assets.[138] Thus, it must be assumed that if the nation's wealth were distributed equally at least one-fourth of the population would consider the results nothing less than finding the fabulous pot of gold at the end of the rainbow. There would be pathetic howls from Fifth Avenue and Nob Hill, no doubt, but these howls would be drowned by the greater chorus of cheers from Shantytown.

Of course, no such distribution can or will take place in our free-enterprise society. True economic equality is probably incompatible with the material incentives that are necessary to capitalist prosperity and growth. Some argue that if this is the case, perhaps now is the time to get rid of capitalism, which has done a reasonable job of growth, and begin letting government expropriate industry and wealth, to be shared equally by all. Utopians have always been infatuated with this concept of state ownership of essential industries. There is a kind of pure logic to it. After all, why shouldn't the people take over the machinery that turns out the goods they need? Why shouldn't distribution be on the basis of the need of the many rather than on the basis of profit for the few? Why should there be a society of economic classes, in which those who have reached the top are primarily motivated by a frantic defense of their riches and those at the bottom are motivated by a frantic effort to stay alive and those in between feel picked on by both extremes?

That much of the argument is difficult to find fault with. But a spreading of economic equality raises other problems. Let's say that the govern-

[134]The truth of the situation is quite different. In *The Guaranteed Society*, Leonard Baker demonstrated that, of the 7 million people who received welfare, only 50,000 had the potential to be self-sufficient. The rest were aged persons, sick persons, and dependent children—in short, the helpless. They do cost taxpayers a considerable amount of money, but the greatest drain on the federal budget is not made by those groups (and certainly not by the deadbeats among them). The greatest drain is made by the affluent and the powerful: by well-to-do tax cheaters, by subsidized businesses that do not need a subsidy, by organizations that obtain cheap federal loans when they could afford to borrow their money privately, and by the proliferating and wasteful bureaucracy.

[135]Herbert Gans, *More Equality* (New York: Pantheon Books, 1973), pp. 23–24.

[136]Associated Press, April 17, 1977.

[137]Wiebe, *The Search for Order*, pp. 46–47.

[138]Thurow, "More Are Going to Be Poor."

ment took over the steel mills, produced more steel, and lowered prices. Prices of everything containing steel, from automobiles to toasters, would drop. The lower prices would allow more Americans to own automobiles and toasters. More of the underprivileged would join the ranks of the privileged. Sounds nice. But there would be an immediate negative effect, too. More cars on the road would mean more gasoline consumption and more smog and more traffic jams—some of the very things that are ruining our environment. More toasters would mean the use of more electricity, which in turn would mean the consumption of more fuel—the very thing we are growing critically short of. Cheaper steel and better incomes would mean more pop-top cans littering the roadside. It would mean more dune buggies destroying beaches, more and bigger fast-food restaurant signs clogging the horizon.

The critical waste of our energy and natural resources is not the fault of the lower-income group; it is the fault of the middle class, which is the largest consuming group. Raise the lower-income group into the middle class, and you have done something benevolent; you have also, obviously, increased waste.

Which brings us to what would be almost a necessary accompaniment of socialism: state-enforced restraint on individual conduct as well as on the conduct of business. To prevent the affluent masses from eating, burning, driving, drinking, wearing, and playing their beautiful socialism into a nationwide garbage pile, state-enforced limits of consumption per individual or per family would almost certainly have to be established. In this regard—as well as in regard to limits on income, restrictions of job choices, and the like—there would be a direct swap-off of freedom for security. In any government-planned society there is this swap-off. To the extent that our society is planned, freedom has been traded for government assistance. This is the other side of public benevolence. We have pointed out at some length that most government welfare has traditionally been given to business and industry; but they have paid for it by an enormous loss of freedom. Apparently, the leaders of business and industry are generally satisfied with the exchange. Whether individuals in the United States would be willing to give up a great deal of their freedom for a great deal of security is another matter. They have already given up some.

Summary

1. From the beginning of this nation, the influence of special interests has made a classic free-enterprise system impossible to achieve. Government intervention in the marketplace came first with subsidies and then with regulation of business.

2. The economy is far more prosperous and secure now than it was forty years ago, but it still periodically suffers from recessions, inflation, and high rates of unemployment.

3. The federal government takes an active role in managing the economy through monetary and fiscal policy.

4. Monetary policy—the regulation of the money supply—is carried out by the Federal Reserve Board (the Fed). It is a powerful agency, with many undemocratic features; it is especially susceptible to the influence of banking interests.

5. Fiscal policy is carried out through federal spending and taxing. Higher taxes and reduced government spending slow down the economy, and reduced taxes and higher spending stimulate it.

6. The policy of the government's spending its way out of a depression was applied practically by Franklin Roosevelt at the same time it was developed as a theory by John Maynard Keynes, a British economist. Today the federal government is thoroughly Keynesian in the number of spending programs it initiates, especially in the area of defense.

7. Taxes have not been used creatively or applied equitably in America. The income tax has become more and more regressive, and tax welfare—benefits and loopholes in the tax laws—tends to favor corporations and those with wealth. Tax reform has been hampered by special interest influence.

8. Inflation is a measure of how much less the dollar buys over time. Usually inflation comes with prosperity, but recently we have experienced inflation and recession at the same time.

9. Government is getting more and more involved in the marketplace through regulation and through welfare capitalism (financial assistance to business in the form of subsidies, tax breaks, low-interest loans).

10. Wealth is distributed unevenly in the United States; there is great disparity between the wealthy and the middle class and between the middle class and the poor. Attempts to raise the economic conditions of the poor have been piecemeal.

11. No one way of redistributing the wealth is free of disadvantages. Americans must decide how much individual freedom they are willing to swap for economic security.

Additional Reading

Paul A. Samuelson, *Economics,* 9th ed., ed. Michael R. Elia and Jack R. Crutchfield (New York: McGraw-Hill, 1973), gives the essential facts about the American economy and introduces basic ideas of economic theory. John Kenneth Galbraith's *The New Industrial State,* 2nd ed. (Boston: Houghton Mifflin Co., 1971), analyzes the mutual influence of corporations and government. A radical view is Paul A. Baran and Paul M. Sweezy, *Monopoly Capital: An Essay on the American Economic and Social Order* (New York: Monthly Review Press, 1968).

The annual *Budget in Brief,* available through the U.S. Government Printing Office in Washington, D.C., outlines the trends of past government spending and the President's proposals for the next fiscal year. *Setting National Priorities,* an annual publication of the Brookings Institution, Washington, D.C., under various authorship, gives a detailed analysis of the pros and cons of the President's proposals, as well as a look at the past and future trends in spending. A special volume in this series, Henry Owen and Charles Schultze, eds., *Setting National Priorities: The Next Ten Years* (1976), takes a particularly long-range view.

Leading works on taxation are Joseph A. Pechman's *Federal Tax Policy,* rev. ed. (1971), and Joseph A. Pechman and Benjamin A. Okner, *Who Bears the Tax Burden?* (1974), both published in Washington, D.C., by the Brookings Institution.

16 NATIONAL PLANNING

On the evening of April 18, 1977, President Jimmy Carter appeared on television with a somber message that opened:

> Tonight I want to have an unpleasant talk with you about a problem unprecedented in our history. With the exception of preventing war, this is the greatest challenge our country will face during our lifetimes. The energy crisis has not yet overwhelmed us, but it will if we do not act quickly. . . . The oil and natural gas we rely on for 75 percent of our energy are running out. . . .

Even allowing for the usual quotient of presidential exaggeration, the situation was obviously serious, but it was also puzzling. President Carter was talking about the energy crisis as though it were news, as though it had arisen suddenly and to everyone's surprise. How could this pos-

sibly be? After all, Americans had been the world's heaviest users of petroleum products for three generations. Hadn't we known what we were doing to ourselves? The government had presumably been intimately involved in the regulation of interstate oil and gas production and shipment for two generations and in the regulation of oil imports for at least a generation. Didn't the government know the quantity of energy it was dealing with?

The answer to those questions, in brief, is this: the government has generally allowed the powerful oil companies to control our most vital energy source without any close supervision. Apparently, the government felt no need to plan for the future, and it was much too compliant in accepting the deceptions made by a rich industry to increase profits. In short, the government allowed the energy crisis to sneak up on the people.

Periodically, over recent years, the oil industry has claimed that our reserves are getting low. But nobody paid any attention, and for good reason: in the past, the industry had made such warnings simply to manipulate public opinion and government policy to obtain price increases. In 1914, Standard Oil (monarch of world oil at the time), backed by the United States Bureau of Mines (which has usually parroted the industry line), announced that the United States was down to its last 5.7 billion barrels of oil reserves—scarcely enough to last out the decade. Oil had clearly become a precious commodity. Up went the price—just in time to take advantage of the rising market created by World War I. In 1918, when the war was over, the oil companies had not run out of oil; they were stuck with a surplus. If the law of supply and demand had been allowed to rule prices, oil would have become cheap. To prevent this, the companies arranged another "crisis" in 1920. This time they persuaded the United States Geological Survey to announce that domestic oil production would start to decline sharply within three years, with no hope of recovery. Shortages were reported all over the country.

It worked. When prices reached $0.37 a gallon (the equivalent of more than $1 a gallon today) the "shortage" disappeared—but only for a moment. Standard Oil, wanting the government to help it push into the Middle East, where British oil companies had cornered the richer concessions, announced in the early 1920s that the United States had only six years' worth of reserves. The oil companies were so successful in scaring Washington officials that there were actually serious discussions about the possibility of going to war with Britain. Such discussions ended when the British split the Middle East fields with Standard. British writers E. H. Davenport and Sidney Russell Cooke noted wryly, "One cannot doubt that the lugubrious prophecies of American oil men are in some way related to the wish for higher prices."[1] In 1947, claiming it might not have enough oil to last beyond 1955, the industry persuaded the State Department to give it a totally free hand in the Middle East.

And so it went. Having deceived the American people and the government for half a century, the oil companies had lost all credibility by the 1960s. Ironically, that was when the government should have been seriously considering the possibility that oil was not an infinite resource. But the government had totally surrendered to the oil companies. It depended on them for Middle East diplomacy; it depended on them to supply data on reserves. Instead of promoting oil conservation, the government had helped develop a bigger and bigger market for oil. Federal home loans were pumped into urban sprawl, with houses scattered farther and farther from the cities' job centers. Automobile travel had become virtually mandatory, for the federal government was at the same time permitting train systems to die and municipal transportation systems to languish. "From 1944, when Congress passed the Federal Aid to Highways Act, to 1961," notes James O'Connor, "the federal government expended its entire transportation budget on roads and highways."[2]

After becoming critically dependent on oil, the United States became dependent on other nations to supply it. It happened because the major oil companies tried to take advantage of the oil-producing nations of the Middle East. By the end of the 1950s, global oil production was so bountiful that the companies didn't know how to get rid of their oil. In 1959, the major companies decided to pay less for oil from the Middle East countries, which were already being badly underpaid. This prompted a revolt. In 1960 the oil-producing nations of the Middle East banded together as the Organization of Petroleum Exporting Countries (OPEC).

Soon OPEC countries began expropriating the lands, refineries, and pipelines previously controlled by the oil companies through leases. For the first time in our history, American petroleum consumers were at the mercy of foreigners. The trauma was fully felt in 1973, when OPEC

[1]Sidney Russell Cooke and E. H. Davenport, *The Oil Trusts and Anglo-American Relations* (New York: Macmillan, 1924), pp. 90–91.

[2]Quoted in Richard C. Edwards, Michael Reich, and Thomas E. Weisskopf, eds., *The Capitalist System: A Radical Analysis of American Society* (Englewood Cliffs, N.J.: Prentice-Hall, 1972), p. 193.

"As Adam Smith so aptly put it . . ."

briefly stopped oil shipments to this country and then raised the price of oil 400 percent. Since then, life in the United States has not been the same. Because oil is used to build, heat, and drive so much of our economy, the increase in its price sent the price of just about everything else spiraling upward. A seemingly permanent inflation, accompanied by record-high unemployment, settled in. In this way, by the misdirection, malfeasance, and ignorance of its national leaders, the United States was bogged down in the great Energy Crisis.

There are many morals to that sad story, of course. The most obvious one is that any complex nation will founder sooner or later if it doesn't know where it is going. Through failure to keep close diplomatic relations with the oil-producing nations, our government failed to anticipate OPEC and its rebellion. When the Arab oil embargo hit, our government did not know how long we could hold out. It did not even have information about the size of our gasoline stocks, because it had never demanded a strict accounting from the companies of either in-ground or stockpiled fuel. We simply did not have a national energy policy, either short-range or long-range, and our officials were so rattled

that they did not come up with anything resembling a policy for another three years.[3]

THE NEED FOR LONG-RANGE PLANNING

The oil crisis underscores one of the great weaknesses of government—an inability to plan for long-range needs. And without comprehensive

---

[3] And even when President Carter did offer a national energy policy, some experts criticized it as being jerry-built, too hastily thrown together, and certain to lead to faulty expectations. One of the most telling criticisms came from the Comptroller General of the United States' General Accounting Office in a report to Congress on July 25, 1977. President Carter said his program would reduce oil imports by 6 million barrels of oil a day by 1985; the GAO said Carter's plan would fall short of this goal by 4.3 million barrels a day. Carter said his plan would result in four times the amount of nuclear energy by 1985; the GAO called this prediction "highly unrealistic" and "very doubtful." Carter predicted a sharp increase in the use of coal as a substitute for oil and gas, but the GAO warned that Carter's plan did not deal "adequately" with the "serious environmental obstacles, enormous capital requirements, and a deficient rail transportation network." ("An Evaluation of the National Energy Plan.")

Such sharp conflicts of expert opinion are not uncommon in complicated national programs.

long-range planning, government tends to disregard the expert data that is available or could be assimilated. Even when it has been forewarned that big problems will occur, it waits until they loom just ahead and then tries to solve them with a frenzy of excess that usually results in other problems. The post–World War II baby boom, for example, did not go unnoticed. But only *after* the boom was well underway did the experts crank up an intensive teacher-education and school-construction program. When the birth rate began dropping again, the high rate of teacher training and school construction continued unabated. The result: many schools are now closing because of a lack of students, and it is estimated that 85 percent of the 1.2 million teachers who will graduate in the early 1980s will not get teaching jobs. In the same way, the government built many hospitals without considering whether enough doctors or patients were likely to be available where the hospitals were built; in 1977, there were so many empty beds (between 100,000 and 200,000) that some hospitals were being phased out.[4]

But consequences of inadequate planning for education and medical care were not nearly so disastrous as those for transportation. In education and medical care, the failure to gather and use information resulted in a serious imbalance of manpower and building supply and demand, but that is something rather easily adjusted over a relatively short time. In transportation, the error was so enormous in so many ways that great physical damage was done to the nation, and it probably cannot be corrected in a lifetime, if ever.

In the early 1950s, the government set a goal of building a national network of 41,000 miles of modern limited access roadway within sixteen years (which still hasn't been completed). It rushed ahead, pell-mell, without any planning beyond technical design and construction.

It was known in the early 1950s that concentrations of automobiles can cause severe pollution problems, but this was ignored. Routes were laid through central cities, ultimately requiring the eviction of thousands of people at a time when good housing was in short supply, but this was brushed aside. . . . Obviously, the system would have (and has had) enormous and detrimental effects on other modes of transportation, but these too were overlooked. By opening up the suburbs to uncontrolled growth, the system facilitated urban sprawl and accelerated the decline of central cities, but this was not taken into account either.

In addition, no foresight was given to the fact that the new highways would increase the demand for high-speed gas-guzzling cars.

Tens of billions of dollars were spent on a program which promised to—and has—shaped our nation in concrete. The structure of domestic commerce was violently altered without consideration of the "spillover" effects that such a system would have on important sections of the economy and the regions through which the roads were to be built.[5]

Agriculture offers one of the best examples of how a major industry can be caught short without long-range planning. First, consider the complexities of the "food system." It includes (1) the so-called "input" industries, which supply machinery, fertilizers, antipest chemicals, energy, and so forth; (2) the producers themselves—farmers, dairy farmers, and ranchers; (3) the food processors—dairies, grain mills, canneries, slaughterhouses, meatpacking plants, and prepared-food factories, (4) distributors and warehouse operators; and (5) retail food stores and restaurants. And, of course, there are the consumers.

Somehow the government is supposed to help these various groups fit together to make profits and supply nourishment in a balanced way. The amount of money at issue is staggeringly large. Gross farm sales come to about $100 billion a year. That money goes into the pocket of 4.5 million workers—as many workers as the combined employment in the transportation, automobile, and steel industries. Consumers

---

[4]*Washington Post,* April 26, 1977.

[5]Stanley Bach, "Policy Making in the House of Representatives," in Advisory Committee on National Growth Policy Processes to the National Commission on Supplies and Shortages, *Forging America's Future: Strategies for National Growth and Development* (Washington, D.C.: U.S. Government Printing Office, 1976), Appendix, Vol. 2, p. 9.

Big Business down on the farm

spend about $170 billion a year on food—about 17 percent of their income. Farm products, worth about $20 billion a year, represent 20 percent of our exports.

Obviously, if planning were ever needed, it is needed here. But there has been very little planning—or at least very little *coordinated* planning. The federal food policy as of 1977 was being made by no less than twenty-six agencies and departments, and nobody knew how many sub-organizations, committees, and commissions were involved. Jurisdiction in Congress was scattered through about fifteen committees.

For many years the government's primary interest in agriculture was in supporting big farmers with crop subsidies. Otherwise, the "free-enterprise" system was left alone. The result was harmful in many ways. Because the government did not encourage a land-use plan, millions of once-productive agricultural acres were bought up by speculators and turned into housing tracts, industrial parks, and shopping centers; and because the government did not use the available credit systems to protect small family farmers, the small farms began to disappear. By 1975, there were only about 2.8 million farms—a one-third decrease from 1960—and the farms that remained were nearly twice the average size of 1950 farms. Whereas the capital required to buy and start operating an average farm was $42,000 in 1960, in 1973, a one-person Louisiana soybean farm called for $158,000, and an Indiana corn farm needed $610,000. Big Business had moved onto the farm and moved the price of competition into the stratosphere. And because the government had no long-term export planning, it was caught by surprise when Big Business farmers increased their overseas sales by more than 300 percent in the 1970s—leaving the United States consumers with highly inflated prices and some shortages.[6]

---

[6] U.S. General Accounting Office, Washington, D.C., "Food and Agriculture Issues for Planning," study released April 22, 1977.

WHY HAVEN'T WE PLANNED?

How has it happened that the United States has come so far without anything that could accurately be called "national planning"? After all, planning is a very commonplace and common-sense procedure. People begin to plan their long-range futures at least as early as high school; they plan their educational careers and reasonably expect that that will lead into professional careers. They plan their families and the education of their children. Corporations do long-range planning, foreseeing breakthroughs into new markets and aiming for certain mergers. Why not comprehensive planning for the nation?

The NRA Experiment

Until about the 1930s, we were a very relaxed nation. Many of our major industries were still in their infancy; our national budget, compared to today, was a pittance. As a nation, we were still somewhat scatterbrained, in a marvelously fresh and cheerful fashion. But the Great Depression of the 1930s forced us to take a sober look at the future. During the early New Deal reforms of 1933 and 1934, there was serious consideration of planning based on an entirely new, tight collaborative relationship between government and Big Business. At the heart of this plan was the National Recovery Administration, which was empowered to "compel industry to reorganize itself, fix prices, allot quotas of production, and so on." The NRA would bring together "under one co-ordinated control the work of all the economic departments and agencies of government. Public authority would speak with a single voice and be spoken to in turn by the single corporate voice of each industry."[7] Such a radical concept, foreign to the prevailing business philosophy, might have been acted upon if the severity of the economic crisis had continued without relief. But as soon as there was the slightest easing of the Depression, Big Business turned against the plan. And it was triumphant in its opposition in 1935 when the Supreme Court declared the NRA unconstitutional. It was just as well; there were elements of the plan that smacked of totalitarianism.

In any case, President Franklin D. Roosevelt, though outwardly expressing agreement with those who supported national planning, was not really a wholehearted advocate of the NRA plan. Far from believing in a cohesive government, he enjoyed playing off parts of the government against each other, with the expectation that out of this intragovernment scrapping would come better ideas. He also may have hoped that by keeping the government split up he could control it better. (See Chapter 9.) Roosevelt was hardly the ideal President to launch the nation down the road of coordinated planning.

Congress, in the 1930s, was also hostile to national planning. With fragmentation, committee chairmen could most easily retain their control. In 1943, the old bulls in Congress finally succeeded in killing the National Resources Planning Board, established in 1933, which had attempted, among other things, to coordinate administration policy in public works, water, land use, urban aid, and housing.[8]

Postwar Nonplanning

During World War II, there was an enormous amount of planning for the postwar society. But then something happened. We had hardly moved out of the war before we entered the era of communist-hating. John Kenneth Galbraith tells the rest of it:

> With the Cold War . . . the word planning acquired ideological overtones. The Communist countries not only socialized property, which seemed not a strong likelihood in the United States, but they planned, which seemed more of a danger. Since liberty was there circumscribed, it followed that planning was something that the libertarian society should avoid. Modern liberalism carefully emphasizes tact rather than clarity of speech. Accordingly it avoided the term and conservatives made it one of opprobrium. For a public official to be called

---

[7]Andrew Shonfield, *Modern Capitalism: The Changing Balance of Public and Private Power* (New York: Oxford University Press, 1969), pp. 310–11.

[8]See Otis L. Graham, "The National Imperative to Plan," *Nation*, November 6, 1976. For a thorough discussion, see Graham's *Toward a Planned Society: From Franklin D. Roosevelt to Richard Nixon* (New York: Oxford University Press, 1975).

an economic planner was less serious than to be charged with Communism or imaginative sexual perversion, but it reflected adversely nonetheless. . . . [T]his reaction against the word planning could hardly have been worse timed. It occurred when the increased use of technology and the accompanying commitment of time and capital were forcing extensive planning on all industrial communities.[9]

The lack of planning for most of the postwar period was neither noticed nor lamented. It was an age of great economic expansion, social innovation, and scientific discovery—an age that introduced the transistor, the mood drug, the laser, the satellite, the hippie commune, the moon shot, the heart transplant. Things were happening too fast for assimilation, too fast for planning.

Planning in the OMB

At the present time, the nearest thing the government has to coordinated planning is found in the Office of Management and Budget in the Executive Office of the President. (See also Chapter 12.) The OMB puts together the budget, allocating financial resources, the heart of federal activity. As much as two years of planning will go into a budget. The budget that the OMB sends to the White House for the President's consideration in 1980 will have been started in 1978, winding its way through a laborious process—evaluating agency programs, identifying policy issues, making income projections. Every agency in the government sends a report to the OMB ahead of time, stating how much money it needs in order to accomplish certain programs. The OMB's staff of experts appraises these reports, tries to carve out the fat, tries to ignore the self-serving overstatements, and comes up with what it thinks is a realistic goal for each agency. The OMB's budget breaks down the federal program into sixteen functions: national defense; international affairs; general science, space, and technology; energy; environment and natural resources; agriculture; commerce and transportation; community and regional development; education; manpower and social services; health; income security; veterans benefits and services; law enforcement and justice; general government; and revenue sharing and other fiscal assistance.

When the President gets the preliminary OMB budget, he and his economic advisers subject it to political litmus tests. Does it take care of his friends sufficiently? Does it reflect the promises he made when he was running for office? Does it seem to promote a spirit of thrift or expansiveness that his partisans will support? He and his advisers will pore over the budget for months, working out the finer details with the OMB, which, in turn, will get updated projections from the agencies concerning their aims and money needs and will run the new data back through for a "final" version of the budget. This is the one that the President sends to Congress. But even this budget is not really considered the last word; the President will undoubtedly make supplementary requests, based on changing social and economic conditions in the nation, before it emerges from Congress.

Although Congress treats the particulars of the President's budget with the consideration that so much labor and thought deserves, it is under no obligation to accept any part of the budget. It can eliminate portions, add, change, or approve as it sees fit. The regular standing committees of Congress consider the specific programs—programs that are already under way, programs that the President has suggested starting, and programs proposed by members of Congress. When Congress authorizes a program, it specifically assigns that program to a particular agency. Sometimes the authorization is only for one year, sometimes it is for several years, or it may be an indefinite authorization. The Congressional Budget Office and the Committees on the Budget, established in each house in 1974, keep track of the programs as they wind their way through Congress, and they check to see that the programs fit properly into the overall budget totals that are approved by Congress.

Those programs that do win authorization then have to be funded. Congress appropriates money through fifteen different spending bills. But since the programs covered by these bills do not match in outline or specific description the

[9]John Kenneth Galbraith, *The New Industrial State,* 2nd rev. ed. (Boston: Houghton Mifflin Co., 1971), pp. 21–22.

programs set up by the OMB's budget, the House and Senate Budget Committees have the tedious job of trying to tie categories in the President's budget with categories in the congressional budgets to determine just what goes with what.

The brief rundown above shows that a great deal of planning goes into the expenditure of federal money. But for the most part it is a very myopic kind of planning. The concern that goes into the OMB's budget and into Congress's budget generally looks to the immediate impact of the spending, and the information is supplied by dozens of agencies and special interest groups that consider only their own short-term well-being. These budgets are put together by people who stand, as it were, in the midst of a forest at the bottom of a valley. They cannot see each other for the trees; they cannot see to the top of the nearest hill, much less to the other side of a distant mountain range.

Many government agencies today are compelled to forecast the future of prices, unemployment, industrial inventories, commercial investments, and so forth. But the government has no one agency—though the Office of Management and Budget comes closest—that pulls together all of these forecasts to see if the various parts of government are viewing the world through the same glasses, and, if not, why not. Nor does any one agency try to pull the various forecasts together in a systematic vision that would encourage bureaucratic consistency.

Economist Wassily Leontief counsels,

When you do not listen to what the government says it does, but rather look at what it actually does, you discover there's nothing behind the big facade [in the way of planning]. A large company puts more effort into deciding whether to place a gasoline station on this or on another corner of the street than the government puts into deciding what to do for railroads. If you look behind the facade for evidence of actual technical analysis, you'll find only bits and pieces of it.[10]

Senator Hubert H. Humphrey, one of the first to push a modern planning bill, paints an even bleaker behind-the-façade picture:

Your federal government expends approximately 25 percent of the total gross national product. That government provides money and credit, it regulates the supply of money, it regulates industries, it invests, it builds facilities. It is involved in a tremendous amount of economic activity.

Yet, there is no design. The Environmental Protection Agency doesn't pay any attention to what the Federal Energy Administration does. . . . The Interstate Commerce Commission doesn't talk to the Civil Aeronautics Board. And I don't think anybody talks to the Federal Reserve Board, the agency that controls the money supply of this country. So, we have here a situation in which nobody bothers about coordinating this vast array of public programs. At the very least, we ought to have some idea where the country is heading, in terms of government expenditures. . . .[11]

HOW MUCH PLANNING? AND WHO SHOULD DO IT?

There are degrees of planning. Governmental responsibility for planning for the whole economy might necessitate state ownership and control of industry, and that would trade our capitalist, free-enterprise system for a socialist one. Most Americans would agree that the capitalist system is a desirable one. It is fairly successful at foreseeing needs and producing goods to meet those needs. In many respects it is very efficient. But it is not a perfect system. For one thing, capitalism is not very good at providing a fair distribution of income. And, as the oil industry demonstrated, capitalism cannot be relied on to tell the truth to the public about the availability of goods and resources. Moreover, there are certain areas in the economy where capitalism is *not* efficient, such as in regulating public utilities and providing public goods and services.

So there is a place for government in the planning and operation of the economy. At the very least, government can be useful as a gath-

---

[10]Quoted in John C. Daly, *National Economic Planning: Right or Wrong for the U.S.?* (Washington, D.C.: American Enterprise Institute, 1976), p. 20.

[11]Quoted in Daly, pp. 2–3.

erer and dispenser of information—providing accurate long-range forecasts and analyzing the effects of alternative policies. More controversial is the extent to which the government should participate in distributional decisions—such as who gets and who pays and how equal or unequal income should be. The most vital distributional questions deal with ways of saving resources for the future or else providing for new ones if current resources run out (for example, replacing fossil fuels with nuclear fuel or solar energy).

The concept of national planning is so new that the machinery for planning is still in the planning stage. One of the most frequently discussed proposals was the Humphrey-Javits bill—the "Balanced Growth and Economic Planning Act of 1975"—which failed to pass into law, but succeeded in opening widespread debate on the subject. The bill proposed setting up five new governmental units, including an Economic Planning Board. The EPB would have been the originator and intragovernmental coordinator of an economic growth plan for the nation. The statutory goals that the EPB would have had to pursue were: full employment, stable prices, fair distribution of income, efficient use of private and public resources, balanced regional and urban development. It would have been expected to juggle energy, transportation, raw materials, housing, agriculture, education, and public services in such a way that the fundamental goals would be met.

The EPB and its auxiliary five agencies were envisioned as a kind of nerve center, the place to which all the lines fed back, a clearinghouse for a very wide wave of opinion and data. The trick would be to ensure that the responses were representative of the feelings of the nation as a whole, and not of just some powerful special interests. Ideally, the heart of national planning would be just what the term implies—planning by the whole nation, by everyone with enough sense to get involved. Planning is, above all else, a setting of priorities, which is one definition of civilized life. At present, national priorities are set by those who write the budget—federal bureaucrats and federal politicians, most of whom are under the influence of powerful interest groups. No governor, mayor, state legislator,

business executive, school teacher, farmer, tradesperson, or mechanic has any say. The priorities are set in closed-door sessions on the banks of the Potomac, which is about as far from the real world as you can get.

Some people have suggested that the national planning process should rely heavily on opinions solicited by the governors of the fifty states. From Washington they would get the game plan: a list of target problems and a list of possible solutions. Perhaps the President would take a couple of hours of prime time on television to explain the alternatives. The governors would hold hearings to which business, labor, and community people would be invited to discuss the proposals. The debate would move out in waves. Editorial writers would wrestle with the topics; experts would give interviews and lectures and issue monographs; politicians would stick their oars in. There would be dinner-table arguments. Various interest groups would crank out propaganda broadsides. It would be, as John Gardner has predicted, "a diffuse, disorderly process but absolutely necessary."[12] As with any political gestation, it would require many months. And the picture that emerged would probably not be neatly delineated. The more crucial the problem, the less likely it is to achieve a clear consensus, for the solution to most major problems calls for a distribution of hardships—and the only likely consensus would be that the hardships should fall on the other fellow.

Still, the debate would be fruitful because it would be open and vigorous. Its feedback would probably enable the President to chart a clearer, more comprehensive route by which to proceed. (Compare this process with the method used in 1977 by President Carter to put together his national energy program: it was done virtually in secret, without consultation with Congress, without any public hearings, without trying to find out from the public which sacrifices it would prefer to make under what conditions.)

One of the crucial differences between the ideal national planning process described above

---

[12]John W. Gardner, "Planning, Public Participation and Politics," in Advisory Committee on National Growth Policy Processes to the National Commission on Supplies and Shortages, *Forging America's Future*, Appendix, Vol. 1, p. 7.

and the present congressional hearing process is that the former would be much, much broader in its view. At best, a congressional committee will hear only a smattering of special interests; most of those will be handpicked for what the committee knows they will say. Moreover, ordinarily a congressional hearing will generate very little public attention, and the results of the hearing will not be transmitted to the public; the hearing will be transcribed into an official hearing record, stuck on a shelf, and soon forgotten. If properly conducted, the national planning hearings would perhaps stir as much participation and enthusiastic discourse around the country as a presidential campaign.

But ultimately, the material would have to be brought back to the old dependable sausage grinder—Congress. National planning cannot be used as an excuse to sidestep the constitutional process. And with the return to Congress, the process would encounter its highest hurdle. Coordination is, after all, not exactly Congress's strongest suit. Diversity is its hallmark. To achieve coordination in the policies it legislates, Congress (or at least a majority of Congress) must first of all agree what the problems are; it must then agree on the best solutions to the problems; and finally, it must agree on which organizational mechanisms will bring about the solutions. That's an awful lot of agreement to squeeze out of Congress for one problem, much less for an interrelated web of problems.

Stanley Bach describes the situation accurately:

> Each Congressman may define issues and select goals as he chooses. To one member, for example, the energy crisis may appear as a failure to exploit known natural resources and provide sufficient energy to fuel continued economic expansion. To another, however, it may be a signal that resources are finite, that growth must be controlled, and that alternative lifestyles should be encouraged. To a third, the energy crisis stimulates concern with the nation's responsibility for preserving its natural inheritance. But to a fourth, the first priority of government must be to protect the domestic economy against international blackmail by a foreign energy cartel. The definitions and dimensions of policy issues are matters of choice and perspective. There are no *a priori* means for determining which issues need to be integrated and how they should

be comprehended within a single policy framework.[13]

So how is a majority of Congress persuaded to adopt one or another method of national planning? The problems are America's problems, but there are no truly "American" solutions. Only in the loosest fashion can members of Congress be appealed to on patriotic grounds. Nor are there specifically partisan solutions. As Fiorello H. Laguardia once noticed, "There is no Democratic or Republican way to collect garbage." Nor is there a uniquely Democratic or Republican way to pump oil, build highways, or plant cotton. And even if there were partisan solutions, there is no way for party leaders to enforce them. Members of Congress will ultimately cast their votes for one kind of planning or another—or for none at all—on the basis of decisions they have reached as the result of pressures from special interest groups or from their constituents. National planning must first be sold to the electorate, who in turn will sell it to their representatives in Congress. And that's where the national planning debate would serve a fundamental need—in creating an informed electorate.

THE HAZARDS OF NATIONAL PLANNING

Improperly handled, national planning could become an intolerable bureaucratic interference. Properly handled, it would still call for the business community to surrender more of its independence. Businesses would have to open their books and their offices to inspection by government planners. At present, much government planning is done in the shadows, if not in the dark, without the benefit of a precise account of our inventories of critical raw materials, of our money supply, even of our true unemployment rate. There would have to be disclosure of the kind of commercial data that business and industry now guard for fear of helping their competitors.

---

[13]Stanley Bach, "Policy Making in the House of Representatives," Appendix, Vol. 2, p. 4.

A Dissenting Voice

Not everyone sees national planning as either necessary or desirable. Many economic and political leaders fear the very notion of national planning and believe that the closer we drift to it the farther we will be from individual freedom. A spokesman for this group is Nelson A. Rockefeller, former Governor of New York and former Vice President of the United States.

Here in our land, do we run the risk of falling into the trap of thinking that human liberties and economic freedoms can exist, one without the other? They never have.

Throughout the world, the thrust for individual liberty has been challenged and blunted by doctrinaire assertions that economic security must be the prime object of society. It is held by some that only centrally-adopted and centrally-directed planning and programming, and implementation by an all-powerful government, can achieve economic security.

Suppression of human rights and civil liberties, to guarantee obedience to the dictates of an all-powerful state, is now the rule over much of the globe, and the rationale is economic necessity or security. Human liberties are not possible under the statism that now exists in most of today's world.

The risk here in America, however, may not be so much that we will take up the worship of the false gods of totalitarian ideologies; rather that we could drift into statism as a reaction to corruption, and by government's progressively legislating such overwhelming and detailed responsibilities for the ordering of the social and economic life of our society that liberty will be surrendered in the process. . . .

The genius of the American system lay not in a mass of detailed regulations but in the fact that government established a broad framework of policy and law to protect the interests of all and within which individuals, groups, and enterprises operate with great flexibility.*

*Nelson A. Rockefeller, "Overview: Critical Choices and Emergent Opportunities," in *Vital Resources* (Lexington, Mass.: D. C. Heath & Co., Lexington Books, 1977), p. xxviii.

But if national planning posed serious problems and irritations to the business community, the lack of planning could pose even greater problems: enormous waste, class conflict, and a steady erosion, rather than an orderly surrender, of management independence.

Economist Robert L. Heilbroner sees national economic planning not as a revolution, but as a conservative effort to survive—

Planning will come not when the radicals want it, but when businessmen demand it. And demand it they will, for without more planning it is difficult to believe that capitalism can last out the century.

It may not. We do not know if the best-drawn plans can iron out the sheerly economic problems of a business system—its tendencies to instability, inflation, economic waste. We do not know if planning can overcome political and social rigidities that have locked us into a tradition of malign neglect of minorities, or if it can reverse a corrosive commercialization of life. Not least, we do not know if planning can be made to work effectively. We cannot plan better than we can govern. Planning will force us to discover how well that is.

Certainly, then, planning is no panacea. It is an option, an alternative, an opportunity—the only opportunity, I think, to arrest the course of slow self-destruction on which we now seem to be embarked. It would be foolish to deny that planning carries great risks, including that of a grave constriction of freedom as the consequence of a reckless proliferation of controls. But it would be even more foolish to ignore the risks associated with a refusal to move into national planning, including the danger of a rush to political extremism as a consequence of economic frustration or failure.[14]

[14]Robert L. Heilbroner, "The American Plan," *New York Times Magazine*, January 25, 1976.

National planning would also have grave dangers for the individual. The foremost threat would be that the voice of the ordinary citizen would be drowned out by the harmony of Big Government, Big Business, and Big Labor. To encourage—even to coerce—Big Business into taking part in national planning, government would undoubtedly use tax incentives and preferential credit arrangements. But if experiences of the past can be used as a basis for predicting the future, Big Business would soon move from merely taking part to taking over. At least it would try to. Big Business once bitterly opposed the establishment of welfare capitalism; now it staunchly defends welfare capitalism. Big Business would probably also find its close collaboration with the government in national planning to be highly profitable, at the consumers' expense. The general electorate would have to make an unrelenting effort to prevent Big Business (and its auxiliary, Big Labor) from taking over the national planning councils.

Individuals would face other perils, as noted by the late Senator Philip A. Hart:

> In a society ever more concerned with pollution, health care, the effects of growth and the need to plan, there will be a corresponding increase in conflicts between the rights of groups and rights of individuals. In a postindustrial society, we can expect that still fewer technocrats will make more decisions.[15]

One of the crucial demands of the future will be to make sure that individuals are protected from the arbitrary decisions of the technocrats, who will be made more powerful by the proliferation of laws under national planning. Already there is good reason to fear that the United States has become inhumanly legalistic—a legalism that, ironically, developed in the name of humanism in the 1930s, when "the new liberalism incorporated the concepts of social engineering and social efficiency that grew up alongside of industrial engineering and efficiency. . . ."[16]

There would be a constant danger that the justness of a governmental act would be judged by whether it worked; there would be a preeminent threat that, for the sake of an abstraction called National Planning, individuals would be urged to exchange their constitutional rights "temporarily" for the sake of legal expediency. This would be proffered as the "reasonable" thing to do.

The intelligent operation of national planning would have to include a deep skepticism toward efficiency for the sake of efficiency. The constant antidote would be the question: efficient for what? It would have to ask: to what extent is superior technology in itself a good thing? Planners would have to cope with what has been called "the circumdrome of the shaving machine. This is to try to shave faster so as to have more time to design a shaving machine that will shave faster so as to have more time to design a still faster shaving machine, and so on in an empty infinite regress."[17] One applied example: to what extent do we want to go on subsidizing gigantic farms that are able to gobble up other farms only because technology has supplied larger and larger equipment that replaces more and more human farm workers, who are thereby freed to move to the city to work in factories building larger farm equipment?

True efficiency would itself pose a subtle threat. What if the economy became so well-ordered that the material needs of the entire population were, at least at a minimum level, taken care of? Would Americans become complacent? Too reliant on the benevolent government? There is a spiritually depleting danger to success.

So the road of national planning would be full of potholes, no matter how carefully the preparation were made. Many of the difficulties would arise from corporate greed, hedonism, laziness, old habits, and our natural quarrelsomeness. Much of the problem will stem from a great virtue—our love of freedom.

[15]Philip A. Hart, "The Future of Government," *The Future Society: Aspects of America in the Year 2000* (Annals of the American Academy of Political and Social Sciences) 408 (July 1973): 97.

[16]James Weinstein, *The Corporate Ideal in the Liberal State: 1910–1918* (Boston: Beacon Press, 1968).

[17]Nicholas Georgescu-Roegen, "Economics and Mankind's Ecological Problem," *The Limits to Growth* (Studies prepared for the use of the Joint Economic Committee, Congress of the United States, December 17, 1976), 7:83.

Some Failures of Success: A Conservative Critique

WE HAVE:

BUT WE ALSO HAVE:

Affluence

No need to wait for possessions that we desire, hence no need for self-discipline. As a result, people are overly concerned with satisfying their material wants, and are at the same time satiated, bored and petulant when they do not receive what they want.

Continuous economic growth, technological improvements

Impossible demands made on the government: steady growth uninterrupted by business cycles is required as a matter of course; unrealistically high growth rates are demanded; all groups in society must grow economically at the same rate so that no one is left behind. Improvements in technology encourage unrealistic expectations elsewhere.

Mass consumption

Aesthetic and commercial standards are determined by the tastes of the masses.

Economic security, little real poverty

Emphasis on relative poverty, hence a desire for radical egalitarianism.

Physical safety, good health, longevity

A neurotic concern with avoiding pain and death. Alternatively, the lack of genuine danger and risks leads to the creation of artificial and often meaningless risks for the sake of thrills.

Government "for the people"

No realization that there are goals higher than the welfare of the people, e.g., the glory of God, national honor.

The belief that human life is sacred, hence that each individual is as important as the next

The belief that nothing is more important than human life, hence that nothing is worth dying (or killing) for. Loss of aristocratic ideals and the idea that superior men should rule over inferior men.

Rationalism and the elimination of superstition

The loss of tradition, patriotism, faith: everything which cannot be justified by reason.

Meritocracy

No sudden rises to power. Everyone must show his worth by working his way up. By the time they get to the top, people have lost much spirit. Hence fewer, young, idiosyncratic hotheads, at the top to shake things up. Also, no respect for experience which does not constantly prove its worth.

An open, classless society

No sense of one's proper place in society. In traditional societies, if you are born an aristocrat, you die an aristocrat. Now, when you rise upward, you don't know when to stop striving. Thus, you have ceaseless struggles for more money and power.

From Herman Kahn and William J. Overholt, in *Qualities of Life: Critical Choices for Americans* (Lexington, Mass.: D. C. Heath, & Co., 1976), p. 153.

THE POLITICS OF THE FUTURE

Material abundance and what, for nearly four hundred years, seemed an endless frontier[18] shaped the American character and politics in ways that have prevailed down to the present. Only in recent years have we begun to admit, with grudging melancholy, that the frontier is buried in our romantic past and that there is a bottom to the material well. We now realize that if it is important to preserve our freedom for posterity, it is also crucial to save something in the larder, too.

Aside from importing about half of its petroleum needs, the United States now depends on imports for more than half of its supply of six of the thirteen materials required by an industrialized society (the six are aluminum, chromium, manganese, nickel, tin, and zinc), and by 1985, according to the Interior Department, we will depend on imports for more than half of our iron, lead, and tungsten. Statistics like that tell a very complex story. If they are accurate, then industrial production at a predictable level becomes iffy. This raises the question of employment security in the next generation, at least; and *that* raises questions of the probable markets for housing, automobiles, and food; and basic to all of these questions is the question of whether we can afford to let our population go on growing at the present pace. By the end of this century, the population of the United States is expected to be almost 25 percent larger than it is today—larger, that is, by about 50 million people—which is equal to the population of the three largest states, California, New York, and Texas.[19] Will there be enough to go around?

Clearly, the politics of the future cannot be quite so carefree or *ad hoc* as in the past. If things are going to work out the way we want them to for the long haul, we will have to take stock—and *we* means not just the experts, but ordinary people. We will have to count our chips to see how long we can afford to play the game by the current rules. We will have to make sure we appraise our opponents and the risks. So far, we have had the luxury of great freedom—and the luxury of thoughtlessness—partly because we have been so affluent that we could afford to be wasteful. With scarcity, freedom might be endangered, too. When there is not enough to go around, people become restless; and then officialdom begins to forget the Constitution and think of self-preservation. That's a perpetual risk.[20]

Much better than deploring officials' defensive repression is avoiding the circumstances that allow it to exercise itself. A democratically based national planning program might do this. It would give us a choice. As Theodore A. Wertime has put it,

> We can launch a quiet, disciplined national effort to deal with the basic challenges boldly—and with the help of new technologies—but within the framework of our institutions, carrying out a benevolent, peaceful revolution rivaling those of William Pitt the Younger to Franklin D. Roosevelt. Alternatively, we will have to utilize ever tougher political controls to administer ever scarcer resources and to restructure a society unaccustomed to privation. Failure to do one or the other will lead to the rapid obsolescense of our society or to civil strife or both.[21]

This is probably a conservative appraisal, but, in a way, it is also a hopeful one. It is quite in order to speak, as Wertime does, of a revolution. The government and people of the United States are still young enough to manage one quite gracefully.

---

[18]See David M. Potter's *People of Plenty: Economic Abundance and the American Character* (Chicago: University of Chicago Press, 1954) and the writings of Frederick Jackson Turner.

[19]*Qualities of Life: Critical Choices for Americans* (Lexington, Mass.: D. C. Heath & Co., Lexington Books, 1976), 7:3.

[20]When per capita income in the Philippines dropped from $250 in 1966 to about $150 in 1972, the Philippine people began to grumble, so President Ferdinand E. Marcos declared martial law and became a dictator. The United States Chamber of Commerce office in Manila promptly wired Marcos best wishes for "every success in your endeavors to restore peace and order, business confidence, economic growth and the well-being of the Filipino people and the nation." That's the way a good share of the establishment thinks, the world over. It was this same thinking that, in 1975, moved Los Angeles Police Chief Edward M. Davis to start training his force in how to control crowds; he was concerned over the possibility of food riots in a depressed economy.

[21]Theodore A. Wertime, *Washington Post,* April 24, 1977.

Will there be enough to go around?

Now that we have entered our third century, it might be natural to suppose that our government and our ideals are set in concrete, and it might also be normal to let up in our efforts to improve the government and the people who run it. Many politicians encourage that attitude. It takes the heat off them. Defensively, they emphasize traditions. If patriotism is the last resort of scoundrels, as some contend, tradition is the first resort of politicians and bureaucrats. It is their favorite excuse for doing the wrong thing more than once.

As a matter of accuracy, however, we are not burdened with a great many traditions that have settled into the crust of the centuries. We are simply too young a nation—just how young can be measured in lives. Supreme Court Justice Oliver Wendell Holmes's grandmother, when she was a little girl, saw the British troops march into Boston during the Revolutionary War, and Justice Holmes was still alive and rendering astute judgments when the fathers of many students reading these pages had graduated to long pants. Or measure it another way: Thomas Jefferson, who wrote the original draft of the Declaration of Independence, died when Abraham Lincoln was seventeen years old. Lincoln died when Woodrow Wilson was eight. Wilson died when Gerald R. Ford was ten. Four lives easily span our history, and with years to spare. Nothing has been around so long as to be too sacred to change.

Summary

1. Lack of national planning has had serious consequences in several areas—education, medical care, transportation, and agriculture—but most especially in energy policy.

2. Until the 1930s, industry, the economy, and the national budget were simple enough that long-range planning seemed unnecessary. The severe impact of the Great Depression changed that and brought into being the National Recovery Administration (NRA), to coordinate the planning of government and business.

3. The NRA lasted only until the economic crisis eased. For much of the cold war, planning was put on the shelf because it was associated with communist governments.

4. The closest thing to planning in the United States government today is found in the Office of Management and Budget (OMB), which allocates financial resources for spending programs; it does not specialize in long-range views.

5. The areas in the economy in which capitalism does not perform well—distributing income equitably, providing reliable information and long-range forecasts, administering certain public goods and services—are areas in which government could play a vital planning role.

6. Ideally, national planning should involve the entire nation, and Congress and the President should get feedback from the electorate before making decisions.

7. There are hazards in national planning: the loss of individual liberties and the loss of independence in the business community, more bureaucratic interference in citizens' lives, more rules and regulations, complacency, and an overreliance on government technocrats.

8. National planning is needed in order to provide for future generations. Wastefulness and thoughtlessness can make resources scarce in the future.

Additional Reading

A vigorous argument against planning, as infringing on liberties, is Friedrich A. Hayek, *Road to Serfdom* (Chicago: University of Chicago Press, 1944).

The lack of planning by the United States government in various areas and the unhappy consequences can be seen in Charles Schultze, *Distribution of Farm Subsidies: Who Gets the Benefits* (1971), and Henry J. Aaron, *Shelter and Subsidies: Who Benefits from Housing Policies* (1972), both published in Washington, D.C., by the Brookings Institution; Paul R. Ehrlich and Anne H. Ehrlich, *Population, Resources, Environment: Issues in Human Ecology,* 2nd ed. (San Francisco: W. H. Freeman & Co., 1972); Robert L. Heilbroner, *An Inquiry Into the Human Prospect* (New York: W. W. Norton & Co., 1974); David Mermelstein, ed. *The Economic Crisis Reader: Understanding Depression, Inflation, Unemployment, Energy, Food, Wage-Price Controls, and Other Disorders of American and World Capitalism* (New York: Random House, 1975).

We the People

of the United States, in Order to form a more perfect Union, establish Justice, insure domestic Tranquility, provide for the common defence, promote the general Welfare, and secure the Blessings of Liberty to ourselves and our Posterity, do ordain and establish this Constitution for the United States of America.

Article. I.

Section. 1. All legislative Powers herein granted shall be vested in a Congress of the United States, which shall consist of a Senate and House of Representatives.

Section. 2. The House of Representatives shall be composed of Members chosen every second Year by the People of the several States, and the Electors in each State shall have the Qualifications requisite for Electors of the most numerous Branch of the State Legislature.

No Person shall be a Representative who shall not have attained to the Age of twenty five Years, and been seven Years a Citizen of the United States, and who shall not, when elected, be an Inhabitant of that State in which he shall be chosen.

Representatives and direct Taxes shall be apportioned among the several States which may be included within this Union, according to their respective Numbers, which shall be determined by adding to the whole Number of free Persons, including those bound to Service for a Term of Years, and excluding Indians not taxed, three fifths of all other Persons. The actual Enumeration shall be made within three Years after the first Meeting of the Congress of the United States, and within every subsequent Term of ten Years, in such Manner as they shall by Law direct. The Number of Representatives shall not exceed one for every thirty Thousand, but each State shall have at Least one Representative; and until such enumeration shall be made, the State of New Hampshire shall be entitled to chuse three, Massachusetts eight, Rhode Island and Providence Plantations one, Connecticut five, New York six, New Jersey four, Pennsylvania eight, Delaware one, Maryland six, Virginia ten, North Carolina five, South Carolina five, and Georgia three.

When vacancies happen in the Representation from any State, the Executive Authority thereof shall issue Writs of Election to fill such Vacancies.

The House of Representatives shall chuse their Speaker and other Officers; and shall have the sole Power of Impeachment.

Section. 3. The Senate of the United States shall be composed of two Senators from each State, chosen by the Legislature thereof, for six Years; and each Senator shall have one Vote.

Immediately after they shall be assembled in Consequence of the first Election, they shall be divided as equally as may be into three Classes. The Seats of the Senators of the first Class shall be vacated at the Expiration of the second Year, of the second Class at the Expiration of the fourth Year, and of the third Class at the Expiration of the sixth Year, so that one third may be chosen every second Year; and if Vacancies happen by Resignation, or otherwise, during the Recess of the Legislature of any State, the Executive thereof may make temporary Appointments until the next Meeting of the Legislature, which shall then fill such Vacancies.

No Person shall be a Senator who shall not have attained to the Age of thirty Years, and been nine Years a Citizen of the United States, and who shall not, when elected, be an Inhabitant of that State for which he shall be chosen.

The Vice President of the United States shall be President of the Senate, but shall have no Vote, unless they be equally divided.

The Senate shall chuse their other Officers, and also a President pro tempore, in the Absence of the Vice President, or when he shall exercise the Office of President of the United States.

The Senate shall have the sole Power to try all Impeachments. When sitting for that Purpose, they shall be on Oath or Affirmation. When the President of the United States is tried, the Chief Justice shall preside: And no Person shall be convicted without the Concurrence of two thirds of the Members present.

Judgment in Cases of Impeachment shall not extend further than to removal from Office, and disqualification to hold and enjoy any Office of honor, Trust or Profit under the United States: but the Party convicted shall nevertheless be liable and subject to Indictment, Trial, Judgment and Punishment, according to Law.

Section. 4. The Times, Places and Manner of holding Elections for Senators and Representatives, shall be prescribed in each State by the Legislature thereof; but the Congress may at any time by Law make or alter such Regulations, except as to the Places of chusing Senators.

The Congress shall assemble at least once in every Year, and such Meeting shall be on the first Monday in December, unless they shall by Law appoint a different Day.

Section. 5. Each House shall be the Judge of the Elections, Returns and Qualifications of its own Members, and a Majority of each shall constitute a Quorum to do Business; but a smaller Number may adjourn from day to day, and may be authorized to compel the Attendance of absent Members, in such Manner, and under such Penalties as each House may provide.

Each House may determine the Rules of its Proceedings, punish its Members for disorderly Behaviour, and, with the Concurrence of two thirds, expel a Member.

Each House shall keep a Journal of its Proceedings, and from time to time publish the same, excepting such Parts as may in their Judgment require Secrecy; and the Yeas and Nays of the Members of either House on any question shall, at the Desire of one fifth of those Present, be entered on the Journal.

Neither House, during the Session of Congress, shall, without the Consent of the other, adjourn for more than three days, nor to any other Place than that in which the two Houses shall be sitting.

Section. 6. The Senators and Representatives shall receive a Compensation for their Services, to be ascertained by Law, and paid out of the Treasury of the United States. They shall in all Cases, except Treason, Felony and Breach of the Peace, be privileged from Arrest during their Attendance at the Session of their respective Houses, and in going to and returning from the same; and for any Speech or Debate in either House, they shall not be questioned in any other Place.

No Senator or Representative shall, during the Time for which he was elected, be appointed to any civil Office under the Authority of the United States, which shall have been created, or the Emoluments whereof shall have been encreased during such time; and no Person holding any Office under the United States, shall be a Member of either House during his Continuance in Office.

Section. 7. All Bills for raising Revenue shall originate in the House of Representatives; but the Senate may propose or concur with Amendments as on other Bills.

Every Bill which shall have passed the House of Representatives and the Senate, shall, before it become a Law, be presented to the President of

THE CONSTITUTION OF THE UNITED STATES OF AMERICA*

We the People of the United States in Order to form a more perfect Union, establish Justice, insure domestic Tranquility, provide for the common defence, promote the general Welfare, and secure the Blessings of Liberty to ourselves and our Posterity, do ordain and establish this Constitution for the United States of America.

Article. I.

Section. 1. All legislative Powers herein granted shall be vested in a Congress of the United States, which shall consist of a Senate and House of Representatives.

Section. 2. The House of Represenatives shall be composed of Members chosen every second Year by the People of the several States and the Electors in each State shall have the Qualifications requisite for Electors of the most numerous Branch of the State Legislature.

No Person shall be a Representative who shall not have attained to the Age of twenty five Years, and been seven Years a Citizen of the United States, and who shall not, when elected, be an Inhabitant of that State in which he shall be chosen.

Representatives and direct Taxes* shall be apportioned among the several States which may be included within this Union, according to their respective Numbers, which shall be determined by adding to the whole Number of free Persons, including those bound to Service for a Term of Years, and excluding Indians not taxed, three fifths of all other Persons.† The actual Enumeration shall be made within three Years after the first Meeting of the Congress of the United States, and within every subsequent Term of ten Years, in such Manner as they shall by Law direct. The Number of Representatives shall not exceed one for every thirty Thousand, but each State shall have at Least one Representative; and until such enumeration shall be made, the State of New Hampshire shall be entitled to

---

*From the engrossed copy in the National Archives. Original spelling, capitalization, and punctuation have been retained.

*Modified by the Sixteenth Amendment.
†Replaced by the Fourteenth Amendment.

chuse three; Massachusetts eight; Rhode Island and Providence Plantations one; Connecticut five; New York six; New Jersey four; Pennsylvania eight; Delaware one; Maryland six; Virginia ten; North Carolina five; South Carolina five; and Georgia three.

When vacancies happen in the Representation from any State, the Executive Authority thereof shall issue Writs of Election to fill such Vacancies.

The House of Representatives shall chuse their Speaker and other Officers; and shall have the sole Power of Impeachment.

Section. 3. The Senate of the United States shall be composed of two Senators from each State, chosen by the Legislature thereof, for six Years; and each Senator shall have one Vote.*

Immediately after they shall be assembled in Consequence of the first Election, they shall be divided as equally as may be into three Classes. The Seats of the Senators of the first Class shall be vacated at the Expiration of the second Year, of the second Class at the Expiration of the fourth Year, and of the third Class at the Expiration of the sixth Year, so that one third may be chosen every second Year; and if Vacancies happen by Resignation, or otherwise, during the Recess of the Legislature of any State, the Executive thereof may make temporary Appointments until the next Meeting of the Legislature, which shall then fill such Vacancies.[†]

No Person shall be a Senator who shall not have attained to the Age of thirty Years, and been nine Years a Citizen of the United States, and who shall not, when elected, be an Inhabitant of that State for which he shall be chosen.

The Vice President of the United States shall be President of the Senate, but shall have no Vote, unless they be equally divided.

The Senate shall chuse their other Officers, and also a President pro tempore, in the Absence of the Vice President, or when he shall exercise the Office of President of the United States.

The Senate shall have the sole Power to try all Impeachments. When sitting for that Purpose, they shall be on Oath or Affirmation. When the President of the United States is tried, the Chief Justice shall preside: And no Person shall be convicted without the Concurrence of two thirds of the Members present.

Judgment in Cases of Impeachment shall not extend further than to removal from Office, and disqualification to hold and enjoy any Office of honor, Trust or Profit under the United States: but the Party convicted shall nevertheless be liable and subject to Indictment, Trial, Judgment and Punishment, according to Law.

Section. 4. The Times, Places and Manner of holding Elections for Senators and Representatives, shall be prescribed in each State by the Legislature thereof, but the Congress may at any time by Law make or alter such Regulation, except as to the Places of chusing Senators.

The Congress shall assemble at least once in every Year, and such Meeting shall be on the first Monday in December, unless they shall by Law appoint a different Day.*

Section. 5. Each House shall be the Judge of the Elections, Returns and Qualifications of its own Members, and a Majority of each shall constitute a Quorum to do Business; but a smaller Number may adjourn from day to day, and may be authorized to compel the Attendance of absent Members, in such Manner, and under such Penalties as each House may provide.

Each House may determine the Rules of its Proceedings, punish its Members for disorderly Behaviour, and, with the Concurrence of two thirds, expel a Member.

Each House shall keep a Journal of its Proceedings, and from time to time publish the same, excepting such Parts as may in their Judgment require Secrecy; and the Yeas and Nays of the Members of either House on any question shall, at the Desire of one fifth of those Present, be entered on the Journal.

Neither House, during the Session of Congress, shall, without the Consent of the other, adjourn for more than three days, nor to any other Place than that in which the two Houses shall be sitting.

Section. 6. The Senators and Representatives shall receive a Compensation for their Services, to be ascertained by Law, and paid out of the Treasury of the United States. They shall in all Cases, except Treason, Felony and Breach of the Peace, be privileged from Arrest during their Attendance at the Session of their respective Houses, and in going to and returning from the same; and for any Speech or Debate in either House, they shall not be questioned in any other Place.

No Senator or Representative shall, during the Time for which he was elected, be appointed to any civil Office under the Authority of the United States, which shall have been created, or the Emoluments whereof shall have been encreased during such time; and no Person holding any Office under the United States, shall be a Member of either House during his Continuance in Office.

---

*Superseded by the Seventeenth Amendment.
[†]Modified by the Seventeenth Amendment.

*Superseded by the Twentieth Amendment.

Section. 7. All Bills for raising Revenue shall originate in the House of Representatives; but the Senate may propose or concur with Amendments as on other Bills.

Every Bill which shall have passed the House of Representatives and the Senate shall, before it become a Law, be presented to the President of the United States; If he approve he shall sign it, but if not he shall return it, with his Objections to that House in which it shall have originated, who shall enter the Objections at large on their Journal, and proceed to reconsider it. If after such Reconsideration two thirds of that House shall agree to pass the Bill, it shall be sent, together with the Objections, to the other House, by which it shall likewise be reconsidered, and if approved by two thirds of that House, it shall become a Law. But in all such Cases the Votes of both Houses shall be determined by yeas and Nays, and the Names of the Persons voting for and against the Bill shall be entered on the Journal of each House respectively. If any Bill shall not be returned by the President within ten Days (Sundays excepted) after it shall have been presented to him, the Same shall be a Law, in like Manner as if he had signed it, unless the Congress by their Adjournment prevent its Return, in which Case it shall not be a Law.

Every Order, Resolution, or Vote to which the Concurrence of the Senate and House of Representatives may be necessary (except on a question of Adjournment) shall be presented to the President of the United States; and before the Same shall take Effect, shall be approved by him, or being disapproved by him shall be repassed by two thirds of the Senate and House of Representatives, according to the Rules and Limitations prescribed in the Case of a Bill.

Section. 8. The Congress shall have Power To lay and collect Taxes, Duties, Imposts and Excises, to pay the Debts and provide for the common Defence and general Welfare of the United States; but all Duties, Imposts and Excises shall be uniform throughout the United States;

To borrow Money on the credit of the United States;

To regulate Commerce with foreign Nations, and among the several States, and with the Indian Tribes;

To establish an uniform Rule of Naturalization, and uniform Laws on the subject of Bankruptcies throughout the United States;

To coin Money, regulate the Value thereof, and of foreign Coin, and fix the Standard of Weights and Measures;

To provide for the Punishment of counterfeiting the Securities and current Coin of the United States;

To establish Post Offices and post Roads;

To promote the Progress of Science and useful Arts, by securing for limited Times to Authors and Inventors the exclusive Right to their respective Writings and Discoveries;

To constitute Tribunals inferior to the supreme Court;

To define and punish Piracies and Felonies committed on the high Seas, and Offences against the law of Nations;

To declare War, grant Letters of Marque and Reprisal, and make Rules concerning Captures on Land and Water;

To raise and support Armies, but no Appropriation of Money to that Use shall be for a longer Term than two Years;

To provide and maintain a Navy;

To make Rules for the Government and Regulation of the land and naval Forces;

To provide for calling forth the Militia to execute the Laws of the Union, suppress Insurrections and repel Invasions;

To provide for organizing, arming, and disciplining, the Militia, and for governing such Part of them as may be employed in the Service of the United States, reserving to the States respectively, the Appointment of the Officers, and the Authority of training the Militia according to the discipline prescribed by Congress;

To exercise exclusive Legislation in all Cases whatsoever, over such District (not exceeding ten Miles square) as may, by Cession of particular States, and the Acceptance of Congress, become the Seat of the Government of the United States, and to exercise like Authority over all Places purchased by the Consent of the Legislature of the State in which the Same shall be, for the Erection of Forts, Magazines, Arsenals, dockYards, and other needful Buildings;—And

To make all Laws which shall be necessary and proper for carrying into Execution the foregoing Powers, and all other Powers vested by this Constitution in the Government of the United States, or in any Department or Officer thereof.

Section. 9. The Migration or Importation of such Persons as any of the States now existing shall think proper to admit, shall not be prohibited by the Congress prior to the Year one thousand eight hundred and eight, but a Tax or duty may be imposed on such Importation, not exceeding ten dollars for each Person.

The Privilege of the Writ of Habeas Corpus shall not be suspended, unless when in Cases of Rebellion or Invasion the public Safety may require it.

No Bill of Attainder or ex post facto Law shall be passed.

No Capitation, or other direct, Tax shall be laid, unless in Proportion to the Census or Enumeration herein before directed to be taken.

No Tax or Duty shall be laid on Articles exported from any State.

No Preference shall be given by any Regulation of Commerce or Revenue to the Ports of one State over those of another: nor shall Vessels bound to, or from, one State, be obliged to enter, clear, or pay Duties in another.

No Money shall be drawn from the Treasury, but in Consequence of Appropriations made by Law, and a regular Statement and Account of the Receipts and Expenditures of all public Money shall be published from time to time.

No Title of Nobility shall be granted by the United States: And no Person holding any Office of Profit or Trust under them, shall, without the Consent of the Congress, accept of any present, Emolument, Office, or Title, of any kind whatever, from any King, Prince, or foreign State.

Section. 10. No State shall enter into any Treaty, Alliance, or Confederation; grant Letters of Marque and Reprisal; coin Money; emit Bills of Credit; make any Thing but gold and silver Coin a Tender in Payment of Debts; pass any Bill of Attainder, ex post facto Law, or Law impairing the Obligation of Contracts, or grant any Title of Nobility.

No State shall, without the Consent of the Congress, lay any Imposts or Duties on Imports or Exports, except what may be absolutely necessary for executing its inspection Laws: and the net Produce of all Duties and Imposts, laid by any State on Imports or Exports, shall be for the Use of the Treasury of the United States; and all such Laws shall be subject to the Revision and Controul of the Congress.

No State shall, without the Consent of Congress, lay any Duty of Tonnage, keep Troops, or Ships of War in time of Peace, enter into any Agreement or Compact with another State, or with a foreign Power, or engage in War, unless actually invaded, or in such imminent Danger as will not admit of delay.

Article. II.

Section. 1. The executive Power shall be vested in a President of the United States of America. He shall hold his Office during the Term of four Years, and, together with the Vice President, chosen for the same Term, be elected, as follows:

Each State shall appoint, in such Manner as the Legislature thereof may direct, a Number of Electors, equal to the whole Number of Senators and Representatives to which the State may be entitled in the

Congress: but no Senator or Representative, or Person holding an Office of Trust or Profit under the United States, shall be appointed an Elector.

The Electors shall meet in their respective States, and vote by Ballot for two Persons, of whom one at least shall not be an Inhabitant of the same State with themselves. And they shall make a List of all the Persons voted for, and of the Number of Votes for each; which List they shall sign and certify, and transmit sealed to the Seat of the Government of the United States, directed to the President of the Senate. The President of the Senate shall, in the Presence of the Senate and House of Representatives, open all the Certificates, and the Votes shall then be counted. The Person having the greatest Number of Votes shall be the President, if such Number be a Majority of the whole Number of Electors appointed; and if there be more than one who have such Majority, and have an equal Number of Votes, then the House of Representatives shall immediately chuse by Ballot one of them for President; and if no Person have a Majority, then from the five highest on the List the said House shall in like Manner chuse the President. But in chusing the President, the Votes shall be taken by States, the Representation from each State having one Vote; A quorum for this Purpose shall consist of a Member or Members from two thirds of the States, and a Majority of all the States shall be necessary to a Choice. In every Case, after the Choice of the President, the Person having the greatest Number of Votes of the Electors shall be the Vice President. But if there should remain two or more who have equal Votes, the Senate shall chuse from them by Ballot the Vice President.*

The Congress may determine the Time of chusing the Electors, and the Day on which they shall give their Votes; which Day shall be the same throughout the United States.

No Person except a natural born Citizen, or a Citizen of the United States, at the time of the Adoption of this Constitution, shall be eligible to the Office of President, neither shall any Person be eligible to that Office who shall not have attained to the Age of thirty five Years, and been fourteen Years a Resident within the United States.

In Case of the Removal of the President from Office, or of his Death, Resignation, or Inability to discharge the Powers and Duties of the said Office, the Same shall devolve on the Vice President, and the Congress may by Law provide for the Case of Removal, Death, Resignation or Inability, both of the President and Vice President, declaring what Officer

---

*Superseded by the Twelfth Amendment.

United States; If he approve he shall sign it, but if not he shall return it, with his Objections to that House in which it shall have originated, who shall enter the Objections at large on their Journal, and proceed to reconsider it. If after such Reconsideration two thirds of that House shall agree to pass the Bill, it shall be sent, together with the Objections, to the other House, by which it shall likewise be reconsidered, and if approved by two thirds of that House, it shall become a Law. But in all such Cases the Votes of both Houses shall be determined by yeas and Nays, and the Names of the Persons voting for and against the Bill shall be entered on the Journal of each House respectively. If any Bill shall not be returned by the President within ten Days (Sundays excepted) after it shall have been presented to him, the Same shall be a Law, in like Manner as if he had signed it, unless the Congress by their Adjournment prevent its Return, in which Case it shall not be a Law.

Every Order, Resolution, or Vote to which the Concurrence of the Senate and House of Representatives may be necessary (except on a question of Adjournment) shall be presented to the President of the United States; and before the Same shall take Effect, shall be approved by him, or being disapproved by him, shall be repassed by two thirds of the Senate and House of Representatives, according to the Rules and Limitations prescribed in the Case of a Bill.

Section. 8. The Congress shall have Power To lay and collect Taxes, Duties, Imposts and Excises, to pay the Debts and provide for the common Defence and general Welfare of the United States; but all Duties, Imposts and Excises shall be uniform throughout the United States;

To borrow Money on the credit of the United States;

To regulate Commerce with foreign Nations, and among the several States, and with the Indian Tribes;

To establish an uniform Rule of Naturalization, and uniform Laws on the subject of Bankruptcies throughout the United States;

To coin Money, regulate the Value thereof, and of foreign Coin, and fix the Standard of Weights and Measures;

To provide for the Punishment of counterfeiting the Securities and current Coin of the United States;

To establish Post Offices and post Roads;

To promote the Progress of Science and useful Arts, by securing for limited Times to Authors and Inventors the exclusive Right to their respective Writings and Discoveries;

To constitute Tribunals inferior to the supreme Court;

To define and punish Piracies and Felonies committed on the high Seas, and Offences against the Law of Nations;

To declare War, grant Letters of Marque and Reprisal, and make Rules concerning Captures on Land and Water;

To raise and support Armies, but no Appropriation of Money to that Use shall be for a longer Term than two Years;

To provide and maintain a Navy;

To make Rules for the Government and Regulation of the land and naval Forces;

To provide for calling forth the Militia to execute the Laws of the Union, suppress Insurrections and repel Invasions;

To provide for organizing, arming, and disciplining, the Militia, and for governing such Part of them as may be employed in the Service of the United States, reserving to the States respectively, the Appointment of the Officers, and the Authority of training the Militia according to the discipline prescribed by Congress;

To exercise exclusive Legislation in all Cases whatsoever, over such District (not exceeding ten Miles square) as may, by Cession of particular States, and the Acceptance of Congress, become the Seat of the Government of the United States, and to exercise like Authority over all Places purchased by the Consent of the Legislature of the State in which the Same shall be, for the Erection of Forts, Magazines, Arsenals, dock-Yards, and other needful Buildings;—And

To make all Laws which shall be necessary and proper for carrying into Execution the foregoing Powers, and all other Powers vested by this Constitution in the Government of the United States, or in any Department or Officer thereof.

Section. 9. The Migration or Importation of such Persons as any of the States now existing shall think proper to admit, shall not be prohibited by the Congress prior to the Year one thousand eight hundred and eight, but a Tax or duty may be imposed on such Importation, not exceeding ten dollars for each Person.

The Privilege of the Writ of Habeas Corpus shall not be suspended, unless when in Cases of Rebellion or Invasion the public Safety may require it.

No Bill of Attainder or ex post facto Law shall be passed.

No Capitation, or other direct, Tax shall be laid, unless in Proportion to the Census or Enumeration herein before directed to be taken.

No Tax or Duty shall be laid on Articles exported from any State.

No Preference shall be given by any Regulation of Commerce or Revenue to the Ports of one State over those of another: nor shall Vessels bound to, or from, one State, be obliged to enter, clear, or pay Duties in another.

No Money shall be drawn from the Treasury, but in Consequence of Appropriations made by Law; and a regular Statement and Account of the Receipts and Expenditures of all public Money shall be published from time to time.

No Title of Nobility shall be granted by the United States: And no Person holding any Office of Profit or Trust under them, shall, without the Consent of the Congress, accept of any present, Emolument, Office, or Title, of any kind whatever, from any King, Prince, or foreign State.

Section. 10. No State shall enter into any Treaty, Alliance, or Confederation; grant Letters of Marque and Reprisal; coin Money; emit Bills of Credit; make any Thing but gold and silver Coin a Tender in Payment of Debts; pass any Bill of Attainder, ex post facto Law, or Law impairing the Obligation of Contracts, or grant any Title of Nobility.

No State shall, without the Consent of the Congress, lay any Imposts or Duties on Imports or Exports, except what may be absolutely necessary for executing its inspection Laws: and the net Produce of all Duties and Imposts, laid by any State on Imports or Exports, shall be for the Use of the Treasury of the United States; and all such Laws shall be subject to the Revision and Control of the Congress.

No State shall, without the Consent of Congress, lay any Duty of Tonnage, keep Troops, or Ships of War in time of Peace, enter into any Agreement or Compact with another State, or with a foreign Power, or engage in War, unless actually invaded, or in such imminent Danger as will not admit of delay.

Article. II.

Section. 1. The executive Power shall be vested in a President of the United States of America. He shall hold his Office during the Term of four Years, and, together with the Vice President, chosen for the same Term, be elected, as follows.

Each State shall appoint, in such Manner as the Legislature thereof may direct, a Number of Electors, equal to the whole Number of Senators and Representatives to which the State may be entitled in the Congress: but no Senator or Representative, or Person holding an Office of Trust or Profit under the United States, shall be appointed an Elector.

The Electors shall meet in their respective States, and vote by Ballot for two Persons, of whom one at least shall not be an Inhabitant of

shall then act as President, and such Officer shall act accordingly, until the Disability be removed, or a President shall be elected.*

The President shall, at stated Times, receive for his Services, a Compensation, which shall neither be encreased nor diminished during the Period for which he shall have been elected, and he shall not receive within that Period any other Emolument from the United States, or any of them.

Before he enter on the Execution of his Office, he shall take the following Oath or Affirmation:—"I do solemnly swear (or affirm) that I will faithfully execute the Office of President of the United States, and will to the best of my Ability, preserve, protect and defend the Constitution of the United States."

Section. 2. The President shall be Commander in Chief of the Army and Navy of the United States, and of the Militia of the several States, when called into the actual Service of the United States; he may require the Opinion, in writing, of the principal Officer in each of the executive Departments, upon any Subject relating to the Duties of their respective Offices, and he shall have Power to grant Reprieves and Pardons for Offences against the United States, except in Cases of Impeachment.

He shall have Power, by and with the Advice and Consent of the Senate, to make Treaties, provided two thirds of the Senators present concur; and he shall nominate, and by and with the Advice and Consent of the Senate, shall appoint Ambassadors, other public Ministers and Consuls, Judges of the supreme Court, and all other Officers of the United States, whose Appointments are not herein otherwise provided for, and which shall be established by Law; but the Congress may by Law vest the Appointment of such inferior Officers, as they think proper, in the President alone, in the Courts of Law, or in the Heads of Departments.

The President shall have Power to fill up all Vacancies that may happen during the Recess of the Senate, by granting Commissions which shall expire at the End of their next Session.

Section. 3. He shall from time to time give to the Congress Information of the State of the Union, and recommend to their Consideration such Measures as he shall judge necessary and expedient; he may, on extraordinary Occasions, convene both Houses, or either of them, and in Case of Disagreement between them, with Respect to the Time of Adjournment, he may adjourn them to such Time as he shall think proper; he shall receive Ambassadors and other public Ministers; he shall take Care that the Laws be faithfully executed, and shall Commission all the Officers of the United States.

Section. 4. The President, Vice President and all civil Officers of the United States, shall be removed from Office on Impeachment for, and Conviction of, Treason, Bribery, or other high Crimes and Misdemeanors.

Article. III.

Section. 1. The judicial Power of the United States, shall be vested in one supreme Court, and in such inferior Courts as the Congress may from time to time ordain and establish. The Judges, both of the supreme and inferior Courts, shall hold their Offices during good Behaviour, and shall, at stated Times, receive for their Services, a Compensation, which shall not be diminished during their Continuance in Office.

Section. 2. The judicial Power shall extend to all Cases, in Law and Equity, arising under this Constitution, the Laws of the United States, and Treaties made, or which shall be made, under their Authority;—to all Cases affecting Ambassadors, other public Ministers and Consuls;—to all Cases of admiralty and maritime Jurisdiction;—to Controversies to which the United States shall be a Party;—to Controversies between two or more States;—between a State and Citizens of another State;*—between Citizens of different States,—between Citizens of the same State claiming Lands under Grants of different States, and between a State, or the Citizens thereof, and foreign States, Citizens or Subjects.

In all Cases affecting Ambassadors, other public Ministers and Consuls, and those in which a State shall be Party, the supreme Court shall have original Jurisdiction. In all the other Cases before mentioned, the supreme Court shall have appellate Jurisdiction, both as to Law and Fact, with such Exceptions, and under such Regulations as the Congress shall make.

The Trial of all Crimes, except in Cases of Impeachment, shall be by Jury; and such Trial shall be held in the State where the said Crimes shall have been committed; but when not committed within any State, the Trial shall be at such Place or Places as the Congress may by Law have directed.

Section. 3. Treason against the United States, shall consist only in levying War against them, or in adhering to their Enemies, giving them Aid and Comfort. No Person shall be convicted of Treason unless on the Testimony of two Witnesses to the same overt Act, or on Confession in open Court.

---

*Modified by the Twenty-fifth Amendment.

*Modified by the Eleventh Amendment.

the same State with themselves. And they shall make a List of all the Persons voted for, and of the Number of Votes for each; which List they shall sign and certify, and transmit sealed to the Seat of the Government of the United States, directed to the President of the Senate. The President of the Senate shall, in the Presence of the Senate and House of Representatives, open all the Certificates, and the Votes shall then be counted. The Person having the greatest Number of Votes shall be the President, if such Number be a Majority of the whole Number of Electors appointed; and if there be more than one who have such Majority, and have an equal Number of Votes, then the House of Representatives shall immediately chuse by Ballot one of them for President; and if no Person have a Majority, then from the five highest on the List the said House shall in like Manner chuse the President. But in chusing the President, the Votes shall be taken by States, the Representation from each State having one Vote; A quorum for this Purpose shall consist of a Member or Members from two thirds of the States, and a Majority of all the States shall be necessary to a Choice. In every Case, after the Choice of the President, the Person having the greatest Number of Votes of the Electors shall be the Vice President. But if there should remain two or more who have equal Votes, the Senate shall chuse from them by Ballot the Vice President.

The Congress may determine the Time of chusing the Electors, and the Day on which they shall give their Votes; which Day shall be the same throughout the United States.

No Person except a natural born Citizen, or a Citizen of the United States, at the time of the Adoption of this Constitution, shall be eligible to the Office of President; neither shall any Person be eligible to that Office who shall not have attained to the Age of thirty five Years, and been fourteen Years a Resident within the United States.

In Case of the Removal of the President from Office, or of his Death, Resignation, or Inability to discharge the Powers and Duties of the said Office, the Same shall devolve on the Vice President, and the Congress may by Law provide for the Case of Removal, Death, Resignation or Inability, both of the President and Vice President, declaring what Officer shall then act as President, and such Officer shall act accordingly, until the Disability be removed, or a President shall be elected.

The President shall, at stated Times, receive for his Services, a Compensation, which shall neither be encreased nor diminished during the Period for which he shall have been elected, and he shall not receive within that Period any other Emolument from the United States, or any of them.

Before he enter on the Execution of his Office, he shall take the following Oath or Affirmation:— "I do solemnly swear (or affirm) that I will faithfully execute the Office of President of the United States, and will to the best of my Ability, preserve, protect and defend the Constitution of the United States."

Section. 2. The President shall be Commander in Chief of the Army and Navy of the United States, and of the Militia of the several States, when called into the actual Service of the United States; he may require the Opinion, in writing, of the principal Officer in each of the executive Departments, upon any Subject relating to the Duties of their respective Offices, and he shall have Power to grant Reprieves and Pardons for Offences against the United States, except in Cases of Impeachment.

He shall have Power, by and with the Advice and Consent of the Senate, to make Treaties, provided two thirds of the Senators present concur; and he shall nominate, and by and with the Advice and Consent of the Senate, shall appoint Ambassadors, other public Ministers and Consuls, Judges of the supreme Court, and all other Officers of the United States, whose Appointments are not herein otherwise provided for, and which shall be established by Law: but the Congress may by Law vest the Appointment of such inferior Officers, as they think proper, in the President alone, in the Courts of Law, or in the Heads of Departments.

The President shall have Power to fill up all Vacancies that may happen during the Recess of the Senate, by granting Commissions which shall expire at the End of their next Session.

Section. 3. He shall from time to time give to the Congress Information of the State of the Union, and recommend to their Consideration such Measures as he shall judge necessary and expedient; he may, on extraordinary Occasions, convene both Houses, or either of them, and in Case of Disagreement between them, with Respect to the Time of Adjournment, he may adjourn them to such Time as he shall think proper; he shall receive Ambassadors and other public Ministers; he shall take Care that the Laws be faithfully executed, and shall Commission all the Officers of the United States.

Section. 4. The President, Vice President and all civil Officers of the United States, shall be removed from Office on Impeachment for, and Conviction of, Treason, Bribery, or other high Crimes and Misdemeanors.

Article III.

Section. 1. The judicial Power of the United States, shall be vested in one supreme Court, and in such inferior Courts as the Congress may from time to time ordain and establish. The Judges, both of the supreme and inferior Courts, shall hold their Offices during good Behaviour, and shall, at stated Times, receive for their Services, a Compensation, which shall not be diminished during their Continuance in Office.

Section. 2. The judicial Power shall extend to all Cases, in Law and Equity, arising under this Constitution, the Laws of the United States, and Treaties made, or which shall be made, under their Authority;— to all Cases affecting Ambassadors, other public Ministers and Consuls;— to all Cases of admiralty and maritime Jurisdiction;— to Controversies to which the United States shall be a Party;— to Controversies between two or more States; between a State and Citizens of another State,— between Citizens of different States,— between Citizens of the same State claiming Lands under Grants of different States, and between a State, or the Citizens thereof, and foreign States, Citizens or Subjects.

In all Cases affecting Ambassadors, other public Ministers and Consuls, and those in which a State shall be Party, the supreme Court shall have original Jurisdiction. In all the other Cases before mentioned, the supreme Court shall have appellate Jurisdiction, both as to Law and Fact, with such Exceptions, and under such Regulations as the Congress shall make.

The Trial of all Crimes, except in Cases of Impeachment, shall be by Jury; and such Trial shall be held in the State where the said Crimes shall have been committed; but when not committed within any State, the Trial shall be at such Place or Places as the Congress may by Law have directed.

Section. 3. Treason against the United States, shall consist only in levying War against them, or in adhering to their Enemies, giving them Aid and Comfort. No Person shall be convicted of Treason unless on the Testimony of two Witnesses to the same overt Act, or on Confession in open Court.

The Congress shall have Power to declare the Punishment of Treason, but no Attainder of Treason shall work Corruption of Blood, or Forfeiture except during the Life of the Person attainted.

Article IV.

Section. 1. Full Faith and Credit shall be given in each State to the public Acts, Records, and judicial Proceedings of every other State. And the

Congress may by general Laws prescribe the Manner in which such Acts, Records and Proceedings shall be proved, and the Effect thereof.

Section. 2. The Citizens of each State shall be entitled to all Privileges and Immunities of Citizens in the several States.

A Person charged in any State with Treason, Felony, or other Crime, who shall flee from Justice, and be found in another State, shall on Demand of the executive Authority of the State from which he fled, be delivered up, to be removed to the State having Jurisdiction of the Crime.

No Person held to Service or Labour in one State, under the Laws thereof, escaping into another, shall in Consequence of any Law or Regulation therein, be discharged from such Service or Labour, but shall be delivered up on Claim of the Party to whom such Service or Labour may be due.

Section. 3. New States may be admitted by the Congress into this Union; but no new State shall be formed or erected within the Jurisdiction of any other State; nor any State be formed by the Junction of two or more States, or Parts of States, without the Consent of the Legislatures of the States concerned as well as of the Congress.

The Congress shall have Power to dispose of and make all needful Rules and Regulations respecting the Territory or other Property belonging to the United States; and nothing in this Constitution shall be so construed as to Prejudice any Claims of the United States, or of any particular State.

Section. 4. The United States shall guarantee to every State in this Union a Republican Form of Government, and shall protect each of them against Invasion; and on Application of the Legislature, or of the Executive (when the Legislature cannot be convened) against domestic Violence.

Article. V.

The Congress, whenever two thirds of both Houses shall deem it necessary, shall propose Amendments to this Constitution, or, on the Application of the Legislatures of two thirds of the several States, shall call a Convention for proposing Amendments, which, in either Case, shall be valid to all Intents and Purposes, as Part of this Constitution, when ratified by the Legislatures of three fourths of the several States, or by Conventions in three fourths thereof, as the one or the other Mode of Ratification may be proposed by the Congress; Provided that no Amendment which may be made prior to the Year one thousand eight hundred and eight shall in any Manner affect the first and fourth Clauses in the Ninth Section of the first Article; and that no State, without its Consent, shall be deprived of its equal Suffrage in the Senate.

Article. VI.

All Debts contracted and Engagements entered into, before the Adoption of this Constitution, shall be as valid against the United States under this Constitution, as under the Confederation.

This Constitution, and the Laws of the United States which shall be made in Pursuance thereof; and all Treaties made, or which shall be made, under the Authority of the United States, shall be the supreme Law of the Land; and the Judges in every State shall be bound thereby, any Thing in the Constitution or Laws of any State to the Contrary notwithstanding.

The Senators and Representatives before mentioned, and the Members of the several State Legislatures, and all executive and judicial Officers, both of the United States and of the several States, shall be bound by Oath or Affirmation, to support this Constitution; but no religious Test shall ever be required as a Qualification to any Office or public Trust under the United States.

Article. VII.

The Ratification of the Conventions of nine States, shall be sufficient for the Establishment of this Constitution between the States so ratifying the Same.

The Word, "the," being interlined between the seventh and eighth Lines of the first Page, The Word "Thirty" being partly written on an Erazure in the fifteenth Line of the first Page. The Words "is tried" being interlined between the thirty second and thirty third Lines of the first Page and the Word "the" being interlined between the forty third and forty fourth Lines of the second Page.

done in Convention by the Unanimous Consent of the States present the Seventeenth Day of September in the Year of our Lord one thousand seven hundred and Eighty seven and of the Independance of the United States of America the Twelfth In Witness whereof We have hereunto subscribed our Names,

Attest William Jackson Secretary

G°. Washington—Presidt and deputy from Virginia

Delaware
Geo: Read
Gunning Bedford jun
John Dickinson
Richard Bassett
Jaco: Broom

Maryland
James McHenry
Dan of St Thos. Jenifer
Danl Carroll

Virginia
John Blair—
James Madison Jr.

North Carolina
Wm Blount
Richd Dobbs Spaight
Hu Williamson

South Carolina
J. Rutledge
Charles Cotesworth Pinckney
Charles Pinckney
Pierce Butler

Georgia
William Few
Abr Baldwin

New Hampshire
John Langdon
Nicholas Gilman

Massachusetts
Nathaniel Gorham
Rufus King

Connecticut
Wm. Saml. Johnson
Roger Sherman

New York
Alexander Hamilton

New Jersey
Wil: Livingston
David Brearley
Wm. Paterson
Jona: Dayton

Pennsylvania
B Franklin
Thomas Mifflin
Robt Morris
Geo. Clymer
Thos. FitzSimons
Jared Ingersoll
James Wilson
Gouv Morris

The Congress shall have Power to declare the Punishment of Treason, but no Attainder of Treason shall work Corruption of Blood, or Forfeiture except during the Life of the Person attainted.

Article. IV.

Section. 1. Full Faith and Credit shall be given in each State to the public Acts, Records, and judicial Proceedings of every other State. And the Congress may by general Laws prescribe the Manner in which such Acts, Records and Proceedings shall be proved, and the Effect thereof.

Section. 2. The Citizens of each State shall be entitled to all Privileges and Immunities of Citizens in the several States.

A Person charged in any State with Treason, Felony, or other Crime, who shall flee from Justice, and be found in another State, shall on Demand of the executive Authority of the State from which he fled, be delivered up, to be removed to the State having Jurisdiction of the Crime.

No Person held to Service or Labour in one State, under the Laws thereof, escaping into another, shall, in Consequence of any Law or Regulation therein, be discharged from such Service or Labour, but shall be delivered up on Claim of the Party to whom such Service or Labour may be due.

Section. 3. New States may be admitted by the Congress into this Union; but no new State shall be formed or erected within the Jurisdiction of any other State, nor any State be formed by the Junction of two or more States, or Parts of States, without the Consent of the Legislatures of the States concerned as well as of the Congress.

The Congress shall have Power to dispose of and make all needful Rules and Regulations respecting the Territory or other Property belonging to the United States; and nothing in this Constitution shall be so construed as to Prejudice any Claims of the United States, or of any particular State.

Section. 4. The United States shall guarantee to every State in this Union a Republican Form of Government, and shall protect each of them against Invasion; and on Application of the Legislature, or of the Executive (when the Legislature cannot be convened) against domestic Violence.

Article. V.

The Congress, whenever two thirds of both Houses shall deem it necessary, shall propose Amendments to this Constitution, or, on the Application of the Legislatures of two thirds of the several States, shall call a Convention for proposing Amendments, which, in either Case, shall be valid to all Intents and Purposes, as Part of this Constitution, when ratified by the Legislatures of three fourths of the several States, or by Conventions in three fourths thereof, as the one or the other Mode of Ratification may be proposed by the Congress; Provided that no Amendment which may be made prior to the Year One thousand eight hundred and eight shall in any Manner affect the first and fourth Clauses in the Ninth Section of the first Article; and that no State, without its Consent, shall be deprived of its equal Suffrage in the Senate.

Article. VI.

All Debts contracted and Engagements entered into, before the Adoption of this Constitution, shall be as valid against the United States under this Constitution, as under the Confederation.

This Constitution, and the Laws of the United States which shall be made in Pursuance thereof; and all Treaties made, or which shall be made, under the Authority of the United States, shall be the supreme Law of the Land; and the Judges in every State shall be bound thereby, any Thing in the Constitution or Laws of any State to the Contrary notwithstanding.

The Senators and Representatives before mentioned, and the Members of the several State Legislatures, and all executive and judicial Officers, both of the United States and of the several States, shall be bound by Oath or Affirmation, to support this Constitution; but no religious Test shall ever be required as a Qualification to any Office or public Trust under the United States.

Article. VII.

The Ratification of the Conventions of nine States, shall be sufficient for the Establishment of this Constitution between the States so ratifying the Same.

done in Convention by the Unanimous Consent of the States present the Seventeenth Day of September in the Year of our Lord one thousand seven hundred and Eighty seven and of the Independence of the United States of America the Twelfth. *In witness* whereof We have hereunto subscribed our Names,

Articles in Addition to, and Amendment of, the Constitution of the United States of America, Proposed by Congress, and Ratified by the Legislatures of the Several States, Pursuant to the Fifth Article of the Original Constitution.

Amendment I*

Congress shall make no law respecting an establishment of religion, or prohibiting the free exercise thereof; or abridging the freedom of speech, or of the press; or the right of the people peaceably to assemble, and to petition the Government for a redress of grievances.

Amendment II

A well regulated Militia, being necessary to the security of a free State, the right of the people to keep and bear Arms shall not be infringed.

Amendment III

No Soldier shall, in time of peace, be quartered in any house, without the consent of the Owner, nor in time of war, but in a manner to be prescribed by law.

Amendment IV

The right of the people to be secure in their persons, houses, papers, and effects, against unreasonable searches and seizures, shall not be violated, and no Warrants shall issue, but upon probable cause, supported by Oath or affirmation, and particularly describing the place to be searched, and the persons or things to be seized.

Amendment V

No person shall be held to answer for a capital or otherwise infamous crime, unless on a presentment or indictment of a Grand Jury, except in cases arising in the land or naval forces, or in the Militia, when in actual service in time of War or public danger; nor shall any person be subject for the same offence to be twice put in jeopardy of life or limb; nor shall be compelled in any criminal case to be a witness against himself, nor be deprived of life, liberty, or property, without due process of law; nor shall private property be taken for public use, without just compensation.

Amendment VI

In all criminal prosecutions, the accused shall enjoy the right to a speedy and public trial, by an impartial jury of the State and district wherein the crime shall have been committed, which district shall have been previously ascertained by law, and to be informed of the nature and cause of the accusation; to be confronted with the witnesses against him; to have compulsory process for obtaining witnesses in his favor, and to have the Assistance of Counsel for his defence.

Amendment VII

In suits at common law, where the value in controversy shall exceed twenty dollars, the right of trial by jury shall be preserved, and no fact tried by a jury, shall be otherwise reexamined in any Court of the United States, than according to the rules of the common law.

Amendment VIII

Excessive bail shall not be required, nor excessive fines imposed, nor cruel and unusual punishments inflicted.

Amendment IX

The enumeration in the Constitution, of certain rights, shall not be construed to deny or disparage others retained by the people.

Amendment X

The powers not delegated to the United Sates by the Constitution; nor prohibited by it to the States, are reserved to the States respectively, or to the people.

Amendment XI*

The Judicial power of the United States shall not be construed to extend to any suit in law or equity, commenced or prosecuted against one of the United States by Citizens of another State, or by Citizens or Subjects of any Foreign State.

Amendment XII†

The Electors shall meet in their respective States and vote by ballot for President and Vice-President, one of whom, at least, shall not be an inhabitant of the

---

*The first ten amendments were passed by Congress September 25, 1789. They were ratified by three-fourths of the states December 15, 1791.

*Passed March 4, 1794. Ratified January 23, 1795.
†Passed December 9, 1803. Ratified June 15, 1804.

same State with themselves; they shall name in their ballots the person voted for as President, and in distinct ballots the person voted for as Vice-President, and they shall make distinct lists of all persons voted for as President, and of all persons voted for as Vice-President, and of the number of votes for each, which lists they shall sign and certify, and transmit sealed to the seat of the government of the United States, directed to the President of the Senate;—The President of the Senate shall, in the presence of the Senate and House of Representatives, open all the certificates and the votes shall then be counted;—The person having the greatest number of votes for President, shall be the President, if such number be a majority of the whole number of Electors appointed; and if no person have such majority, then from the persons having the highest numbers not exceeding three on the list of those voted for as President, the House of Representatives shall choose immediately, by ballot, the President. But in choosing the President, the votes shall be taken by states, the representation from each state having one vote; a quorum for this purpose shall consist of a member or members from two-thirds of the states, and a majority of all the states shall be necessary to a choice. And if the House of Representatives shall not choose a President whenever the right of choice shall devolve upon them, before the fourth day of March next following, then the Vice-President shall act as President, as in the case of the death or other constitutional disability of the President.—The person having the greatest number of votes as Vice-President, shall be the Vice-President, if such number be a majority of the whole number of Electors appointed, and if no person have a majority, then from the two highest numbers on the list, the Senate shall choose the Vice-President; a quorum for the purpose shall consist of two-thirds of the whole number of Senators, and a majority of the whole number shall be necessary to a choice. But no person constitutionally ineligible to the office of President shall be eligible to that of Vice-President of the United States.

Amendment XIII*

SECTION 1. Neither slavery nor involuntary servitude, except as a punishment for crime whereof the party shall have been duly convicted, shall exist within the United States, or any place subject to their jurisdiction.

SECTION 2. Congress shall have power to enforce this article by appropriate legislation.

*Passed January 31, 1865. Ratified December 6, 1865.

Amendment XIV*

SECTION 1. All persons born or naturalized in the United States, and subject to the jurisdiction thereof, are citizens of the United States and of the State wherein they reside. No State shall make or enforce any law which shall abridge the privileges or immunities of citizens of the United States; nor shall any State deprive any person of life, liberty, or property, without due process of law; nor deny to any person within its jurisdiction the equal protection of the laws.

SECTION 2. Representatives shall be apportioned among the several States according to their respective numbers, counting the whole number of persons in each State, excluding Indians not taxed. But when the right to vote at any election for the choice of electors for President and Vice-President of the United States, Representatives in Congress, the Executive and Judicial officers of a State, or the members of the Legislature thereof, is denied to any of the male inhabitants of such State, being twenty-one years of age, and citizens of the United States, or in any way abridged, except for participation in rebellion, or other crime, the basis of representation therein shall be reduced in the proportion which the number of such male citizens shall bear to the whole number of male citizens twenty-one years of age in such State.

SECTION 3. No person shall be a Senator or Representative in Congress, or elector of President and Vice-President, or hold any office, civil or military, under the United States, or under any State, who, having previously taken an oath, as a member of Congress, or as an officer of the United States, or as a member of any State legislature, or as an executive or judicial officer of any State, to support the Constitution of the United States, shall have engaged in insurrection or rebellion against the same, or given aid or comfort to the enemies thereof. But Congress may by a vote of two-thirds of each House, remove such disability.

SECTION 4. The validity of the public debt of the United States, authorized by law, including debts incurred for payment of pensions and bounties for services in suppressing insurrection or rebellion, shall not be questioned. But neither the United States nor any State shall assume or pay any debt or obligation incurred in aid of insurrection or rebellion against the United States, or any claim for the loss or emancipation of any slave; but all such debts, obligations, and claims shall be held illegal and void.

SECTION 5. The Congress shall have the power to enforce, by appropriate legislation, the provisions of this article.

*Passed June 13, 1866. Ratified July 9, 1868.

Amendment XV*

SECTION 1. The right of citizens of the United States to vote shall not be denied or abridged by the United States or by any State on account of race, color, or previous condition of servitude—

SECTION 2. The Congress shall have power to enforce this article by appropriate legislation.

Amendment XVI†

The Congress shall have power to lay and collect taxes on incomes, from whatever source derived, without apportionment among the several States, and without regard to any census or enumeration.

Amendment XVII‡

The Senate of the United States shall be composed of two Senators from each State, elected by the people thereof, for six years; and each Senator shall have one vote. The electors in each State shall have the qualifications requisite for electors of the most numerous branch of the State legislatures.

When vacancies happen in the representation of any State in the Senate, the executive authority of such State shall issue writs of election to fill such vacancies: *Provided,* That the legislature of any State may empower the executive thereof to make temporary appointments until the people fill the vacancies by election as the legislature may direct.

This amendment shall not be so construed as to affect the election or term of any Senator chosen before it becomes valid as part of the Constitution.

Amendment XVIII§

SECTION 1. After one year from the ratification of this article the manufacture, sale, or transportation of intoxicating liquors within, the importation thereof into, or the exportation thereof from the United States and all territory subject to the jurisdiction thereof for beverage purposes is hereby prohibited.

SECTION 2. The Congress and the several States shall have concurrent power to enforce this article by appropriate legislation.

SECTION 3. This article shall be inoperative unless it shall have been ratified as an amendment to the Constitution by the legislatures of the several States, as provided in the Constitution, within seven years from the date of the submission hereof to the States by the Congress.

Amendment XIX*

The right of citizens of the United States to vote shall not be denied or abridged by the United States or by any State on account of sex.

Congress shall have power to enforce this article by appropriate legislation.

Amendment XX†

SECTION 1. The terms of the President and Vice-President shall end at noon on the 20th day of January, and the terms of Senators and Representatives at noon on the 3d day of January, of the years in which such terms would have ended if this article had not been ratified; and the terms of their successors shall then begin.

SECTION 2. The Congress shall assemble at least once in every year, and such meeting shall begin at noon on the 3d day of January, unless they shall by law appoint a different day.

SECTION 3. If, at the time fixed for the beginning of the term of the President, the President elect shall have died, the Vice-President elect shall become President. If a President shall not have been chosen before the time fixed for the beginning of his term, or if the President elect shall have failed to qualify, then the Vice-President elect shall act as President until a President shall have qualified; and the Congress may by law provide for the case wherein neither a President elect nor a Vice-President elect shall have qualified, declaring who shall then act as President, or the manner in which one who is to act shall be selected, and such person shall act accordingly until a President or Vice-President shall have qualified.

SECTION 4. The Congress may by law provide for the case of the death of any of the persons from whom the House of Representatives may choose a President whenever the right of choice shall have devolved upon them, and for the case of the death of any of the persons from whom the Senate may choose a Vice-President whenever the right of choice shall have devolved upon them.

SECTION 5. Sections 1 and 2 shall take effect on the 15th day of October following the ratification of this article.

---

*Passed February 26, 1869. Ratified February 2, 1870.

†Passed July 12, 1909. Ratified February 3, 1913.

‡Passed May 13, 1912. Ratified April 8, 1913.

§Passed December 18, 1917. Ratified January 16, 1919.

---

*Passed June 4, 1919. Ratified August 18, 1920.

†Passed March 2, 1932. Ratified January 23, 1933.

SECTION 6. This article shall be inoperative unless it shall have been ratified as an amendment to the Constitution by the legislatures of three-fourths of the several States within seven years from the date of its submission.

Amendment XXI*

SECTION 1. The eighteenth article of amendment to the Constitution of the United States is hereby repealed.

SECTION 2. The transportation or importation into any State, Territory, or possession of the United States for delivery or use therein of intoxicating liquors, in violation of the law thereof, is hereby prohibited.

SECTION 3. This article shall be inoperative unless it shall have been ratified as an amendment to the Constitution by conventions in the several States, as provided in the Constitution, within seven years from the date of the submission hereof to the States by the Congress.

Amendment XXII†

No person shall be elected to the office of the President more than twice, and no person who has held the office of President, or acted as President, for more than two years of a term to which some other person was elected President shall be elected to the office of the President more than once.

But this Article shall not apply to any person holding the office of President when this Article was proposed by the Congress, and shall not prevent any person who may be holding the office of President, or acting as President, during the term within which this Article becomes operative from holding the office of President or acting as President during the remainder of such term.

Amendment XXIII‡

SECTION 1. The District constituting the seat of Government of the United States shall appoint in such manner as the Congress may direct:

A number of electors of President and Vice President equal to the whole number of Senators and Representatives in Congress to which the District would be entitled if it were a State, but in no event more than the least populous State; they shall be in addition to those appointed by the States, but they shall be considered, for the purposes of the election of President and Vice President, to be electors appointed by the State; and they shall meet in the District and perform such duties as provided by the twelfth article of amendment.

SECTION 2. The Congress shall have power to enforce this article by appropriate legislation.

Amendment XXIV*

SECTION 1. The right of citizens of the United States to vote in any primary or other election for President or Vice President, or for Senator or Representative in Congress, shall not be denied or abridged by the United States or any State by reason of failure to pay any poll tax or other tax.

SECTION 2. The Congress shall have power to enforce this article by appropriate legislation.

Amendment XXV†

SECTION 1. In case of the removal of the President from office or of his death or resignation, the Vice President shall become President.

SECTION 2. Whenever there is a vacancy in the office of the Vice President, the President shall nominate a Vice President who shall take office upon confirmation by a majority vote of both Houses of Congress.

SECTION 3. Whenever the President transmits to the President pro tempore of the Senate and the Speaker of the House of Representatives his written declaration that he is unable to discharge the powers and duties of his office, and until he transmits to them a written declaration to the contrary, such powers and duties shall be discharged by the Vice President as Acting President.

SECTION 4. Whenever the Vice President and a majority of either the principal officers of the executive department or of such other body as Congress may by law provide, transmit to the President pro tempore of the Senate and the Speaker of the House of Representatives their written declaration that the President is unable to discharge the powers and duties of his office, the Vice President shall immediately assume the powers and duties of the office of Acting President.

Thereafter, when the President transmits to the President pro tempore of the Senate and the Speaker

---

*Passed February 20, 1933. Ratified December 5, 1933.

†Passed March 12, 1947. Ratified March 1, 1951.

‡Passed June 16, 1960. Ratified April 3, 1961.

---

*Passed August 27, 1962. Ratified January 23, 1964.

†Passed July 6, 1965. Ratified February 11, 1967.

of the House of Representatives his written declaration that no inability exists, he shall resume the powers and duties of his office unless the Vice President and a majority of either the principal officers of the executive department or of such other body as Congress may by law provide, transmit within four days to the President pro tempore of the Senate and the Speaker of the House of Representatives their written declaration that the President is unable to discharge the powers and duties of his office. Thereupon Congress shall decide the issue, assembling within forty-eight hours for that purpose if not in session. If the Congress, within twenty-one days after receipt of the latter written declaration, or, if Congress is not in session, within twenty-one days after Congress is required to assemble, determines by two-thirds vote of both Houses that the President is unable to discharge the powers and duties of his office, the Vice President shall continue to discharge the same as Acting President; otherwise, the President shall resume the powers and duties of his office.

Amendment XXVI*

SECTION 1. The right of citizens of the United States, who are eighteen years of age or older, to vote shall not be denied or abridged by the United States or by any State on account of age.

SECTION 2. The Congress shall have power to enforce this article by appropriate legislation.

*Passed March 23, 1971. Ratified July 5, 1971.

Acknowledgments and Copyrights for Textual Material, Tables, and Figures

Chapter 2

Faith of Our Fathers (box): Reprinted by permission of the publishers from *The Supreme Court and the Uses of History* by Charles A. Miller, Cambridge, Mass. The Belknap Press of Harvard University Press, Copyright © 1969 by the President and Fellows of Harvard College.

Chapter 3

Freedom Where It Counts (box): From The Civil Liberties Review, Vol. I, No. 1, Fall 1973. Copyright © 1973, by the American Civil Liberties Union.

Chapter 4

Table 4–3: From *Economics,* 10th edition, by Paul A. Samuelson. Copyright © 1976, McGraw-Hill, Inc. Used with permission of McGraw-Hill Book Company.

Chapter 5

Figure 5–1: Data compiled by Common Cause.

The Superlawyers (box, section by Green): Reprinted by permission of the author.

Table 5–1: 1975, reprinted from Fortune Magazine by permission.

Chapter 6

Epigraph: From *Minority Report: H. L. Mencken's Notebooks* by H. L. Mencken. Copyright © 1956, Alfred A. Knopf, Inc.

Figure 6–1: © 1976/77 by The New York Times Company. Reprinted by permission.

Table 6–2: © *The Washington Post.*

Table 6–3: Table 6–3, "Trend on Hawk-Dove Identification," in *Polls: Their Use and Misuse in Politics,* by Charles W. Roll, Jr., and Albert H. Cantril, © 1972 by Basic Books, Inc., Publishers, New York.

Television and Politics (box): From *Television: The Business behind the Box* by Les Brown, copyright © 1971 by Lester L. Brown. Reprinted by permission of Harcourt Brace Jovanovich, Inc.

Figure 6–2: From *Democracy under Pressure: An Introduction to the American Political System*, Third Edition, by Milton C. Cummings, Jr., and David Wise, © 1977 by Harcourt Brace Jovanovich, Inc. Redrawn by permission of the publishers.

The Press and Its Myths (box): © *The Washington Post*.

Chapter 7

Epigraph: Reprinted from Clinton Rossiter, *Parties and Politics in America*. Copyright © 1960 by Cornell University.

Chapter 8

The Majority (box): From *The Decline of Radicalism*, by Daniel J. Boorstin. Copyright © 1963, 1967, 1968, 1969 by Daniel J. Boorstin. Reprinted by permission of Random House, Inc.

How to Choose a Candidate (box): © 1974 by The New York Times Company. Reprinted by permission.

Figure 8–1: © *The Washington Post*.

Table 8–1: Copyright © 1969 by Arlington House, New Rochelle, New York. Taken from *The Emerging Republican Majority* by Kevin Phillips. All rights reserved. Used with permission.

Figure 8–2: © 1976/77 by The New York Times Company. Reprinted by permission.

Chapter 9

It Pays to Be an Ex-President (box): Reprinted from Free Enterprise magazine © 1977, The Capitalist Reporter, Inc.

Figure 9–1: © 1976/77 by The New York Times Company. Reprinted by permission.

Chapter 10

Table 10–1: © 1976/77 by The New York Times Company. Reprinted by permission.

The Congressional Aide (box): Reprinted by permission of G. P. Putnam's Sons from *The Power Lovers* by Myra MacPherson. Copyright © 1975 by Myra MacPherson.

Chapter 12

Extract: From *Power* copyright © 1969 by Adolf A. Berle. Reprinted by permission of Harcourt Brace Jovanovich, Inc.

Chapter 13

Epigraph: From "Choruses from 'The Rock' " in *Collected Poems 1909–1962* by T. S. Eliot, copyright, 1936, by Harcourt Brace Jovanovich, Inc.; copyright © 1963, 1964, by T. S. Eliot. Reprinted by permission of the publishers.

Federal, State, and Local Government and Reform (box): From "The Old, the Poor, the Unemployed," by Henry Steel Commager. © 1973 by The New York Times Company. Reprinted by permission.

Chapter 15

Figure 15–2: © 1976/77 by The New York Times Company. Reprinted by permission.

Illustration Credits

Chapter 1

James Carroll, E.P.A., p. 2; Bob Adelman, Magnum, p. 9; UPI, p. 11; Baldwin-Watriss, Woodfin Camp & Associates, p. 14; Lorenzo Alexander, Black Star, p. 19; Arthur Tress, Woodfin Camp & Associates, p. 24.

Chapter 2

"Continental Congress," painting by Pine and Savage, The Historical Society of Pennsylvania, p. 28; (top) Brown Brothers, (bottom) UPI, p. 36; Brown Brothers, p. 38; "The Plantation," painting by an unknown artist, The Metropolitan

Museum of Art, Gift of Edgar William and Bernice Chrysler Garbisch, 1963, p. 44.

Chapter 3

Fred Ward, Black Star, pp. 58–59; Okamoto, Rapho/Photo Researchers, p. 61; Wide World, p. 70; Wide World, p. 73; Paul S. Conklin, p. 76; Brown Brothers, p. 81; Paul S. Conklin, p. 85; Daniel S. Brody, Editorial Photocolor Archives, p. 87.

Chapter 4

Flip Schulke, Black Star, p. 90; Brown Brothers, p. 96; Wide World, p. 99; Brown Brothers, p. 109; Michael Abramson, Black Star, p. 115; Wide World, p. 116.

Chapter 5

Tim Eagan, Woodfin Camp & Associates, p. 122; Bruce Anspach, Editorial Photocolor Archives, p. 126; Alex Webb, Magnum, p. 137; Dick Kehrwald, Black Star, p. 139; Andrew Sacks, Editorial Photocolor Archives, p. 142; A. Y. Owen, *Life Magazine,* © Time Inc., p. 145; Library of Congress, p. 151; Andrew Sacks, Editorial Photocolor Archives, p. 156.

Chapter 6

Sepp Seitz, Magnum, p. 160; Jason Laure, Woodfin Camp & Associates, p. 190; Wide World, p. 195.

Chapter 7

Wally MacNamee, Woodfin Camp & Associates, pp. 202–03; The Smithsonian Institution, Ralph E. Becker Collection, p. 206; Max Scheler, Black Star, p. 213.

Chapter 8

Ralph Nelson, Camera 5, p. 228; Doug Bruce, Camera 5, p. 233; (top) Owen D. B. & W. W., Black Star, (bottom) NBC photo, p. 245; Max Scheler, Black Star, p. 248; UPI, p. 260; Jim Anderson, Woodfin Camp & Associates, p. 271.

Chapter 9

Charles Gatewood, p. 274; Wide World, p. 278; White House photo, p. 282; Wide World, p. 286; Library of Congress, p. 291; ABC photo, p. 292; White House photo, p. 302; Dennis Brack, Black Star, p. 306; U. S. Army photo, p. 313; Library of Congress, p. 316; White House photo, p. 317.

Chapter 10

Dennis Brack, Black Star, p. 322; Dennis Brack, Black Star, p. 336; George Tames, NYT Pictures, p. 345; Culver Pictures, p. 349; Alex Webb, Magnum, p. 351; Alex Webb, Magnum, p. 358.

Chapter 11

Paul S. Conklin, p. 374; Paul S. Conklin, p. 379; UPI, p. 384; (top) Flip Schulke, Black Star, (bottom) Harris & Ewing, Photo Trends, p. 391; Sidney Harris, p. 394; The Supreme Court Historical Society, p. 403.

Chapter 12

Paul S. Conklin, p. 410; Dennis Brack, Black Star, p. 415; Teresa Zabala, NYT Pictures, p. 416; Fred Ward, Black Star, p. 436; *Harper's Weekly,* April 9, 1887, p. 441; Jeff Albertson, Stock, Boston, p. 443; Paul S. Conklin, p. 451.

Chapter 13

Charles Gatewood, Stock, Boston, p. 454; Daniel S. Brody, Editorial Photocolor Archives, p. 473; Brian Payne, Black Star, p. 479; Daniel S. Brody, Editorial Photocolor Archives, p. 480; Paul S. Conklin, p. 484; Bruce Davidson, Magnum, p. 487; Henry Monroe, Black Star, p. 497.

Chapter 14

Kit Luce, Sygma, p. 502; Patrick Chauver, Sygma, p. 507; UPI, p. 511; James Andanson, Sygma, p. 518; Alain Nogues, Sygma, p. 522; Henri Bureau, Sygma, p. 533.

Chapter 15

Paul S. Conklin, p. 542; Burt G. Phillips, The Museum of the City of New York, p. 548; Dorothea Lange, FSA, p. 554; Daniel S. Brody, Editorial Photocolor Archives, p. 565; Culver Pictures, p. 57^. Paul S. Conklin, p. 578.

Chapter 16

Charles Moore, Black Star, p. 584; Grant Heilman, p. 589; Werner Wolff, Black Star, p. 599.

The Constitution of the United States of America

National Archives, pp. 602, 607, 609, 610.

INDEX

B

Baake, Allan, 22

Babcock, Barbara, 304

Bach, Stanley, 346–47, 347n, 588n, 594, 594n

Bagdikian, Ben, 190

Bahrain, 539

Bail: and the poor, 84, 86; prohibition against excessive, 52, 80, 84

Baker, Leonard, 547n, 581n

Baker, Russell, 190, 312, 312n, 338, 364–65, 365n

Baker v. Carr (1962), 472, 472n

Baltimore, Maryland, 103, 482n, 485

Banfield, Edward C., 485n, 493, 493n, 494n

Bangladesh, 521

Banking Acts (1933, 1935), 361

Bank of America, 447

Bank of the United States, 204, 205, 458

Banks: Arab money in, 538; and campaign contributions, 265; and corporations, 184–85, 576; and credit, 549; and Federal Reserve System, 550, 552; government insurance for, 547–48; interest rates of, 464, 546n, 549, 550, 574; international investments of, 506; mortgage loans of, 20, 21; and RFC, 574, 574n; state deposits in, 476; taxes of, 566

Barber, James Alden, 559n

Barber, James David, 6n, 173n, 217n, 225n, 232n, 277n, 281n, 301n, 318n

Barge industry: federal aid to, 442, 444, 575; tax on, 359–60

Barker, Elisabeth, 510n, 517n

Barkley, Alben W., 420n

Barnet, Richard J., 507–08, 508n, 514n

Barnett, Ross R., 118

Barr, Joseph W., 564

Barron v. Baltimore (1833), 65n

Barth, Alan, 390n, 391, 391n

Barthelmes, Wes, 474n

Bartlett, Charles, 364n

Baruch, Bernard, 515–16

Baruch Plan, 515, 515n, 516

Bass, Jack, 207, 207n

Bayh, Birch, 540

Beall, J. Glenn, Jr., 417n

Beame, Abraham, 459

Beard, Charles, 44–45, 544, 544n

Beard, Edward P., 327

Beck, Dave, 153n

Belair, Felix, Jr., 438n

Bendiner, Robert, 568, 568n

Bennett, W. Tapley, Jr., 185

Berg, Ivar, 556n, 572, 572n

Berger, Raoul, 294n, 456n

Berger v. New York (1967), 79, 79n

Bergland, Bob, 434

Berle, Adolf A., 424, 431n, 526n

Berlin, Germany, 510, 517

Bernstein, Barton J., 514n

Bernstein, Carl, 190–91; *Final Days, The*, 315–16, 316n

Bernstein, M. H., 440n

Bethlehem Steel Corporation, 566

Betts, Smith, 390–91

Betts v. Brady (1942), 391, 391n

Bickel, Alexander, M., 55, 55n, 383n, 386n, 395, 395n, 404

Biden, Joseph R., Jr., 270

Biemiller, Andrew J., 136, 526

Bierce, Ambrose, 123

Bill of Rights, 34, 42, 52–54, 63; difficulties in interpretation of, 69, 86; extended to states, 65, 65n, 80–81, 95, 97, 199, 381; as font of civil liberties, 64–65, 72–73, 128. *See also* Civil liberties; individual amendments and freedoms

Bill of Rights (English), 34, 64

Bills of attainder: prohibition of, 53

Black, Charles L., Jr., 366n, 396, 396n

Black, Hugo L., 385, 388, 397, 398; and First Amendment, 71, 77, 383, 390; and right to lawyer, 391–92; as senator, 148–49

Black Americans, 248n; affirmative action for, 21–22, 104, 105–06; and antilynching legislation, 309–10; in bureaucracy, 21n, 104, 429, 439; citizenship for, 55, 91, 95; in Congressional Black Caucus, 113; and Constitution, 92–94, 95, 457; and criminal justice system, 100, 118; discrimination against, 91–94, 95–106, 114, 117–18, 169, 183, 250, 484, 484n, 485n, 550; disfranchisement of, 91–92, 93, 96–97, 98, 100, 254 324n; economic status of, 103–06; as elected officials, 103, 110, 326; employment for, 103–06, 119, 484, 485n; gains of, 98, 105; higher and professional education for, 98, 100; and hostility toward Puerto Ricans, 117; housing for, 100, 106, 484, 484n; illiteracy among, 484n, 489; inferiority feelings and image of, 97, 118; lobbies of, 124; militancy of, 102; in the military, 94, 98; and movement to cities, 98, 103, 250, 484–85, 486, 488; and politics, 98–99, 119–20, 205, 207, 207n, 208, 218, 220, 223, 232n, 248, 249–50, 266, 457; poverty of, 5, 484, 484n, 485, 486; and Reconstruction, 94–95; stereotype of, 117–19; suffrage for, 46, 91–92, 93, 95–96, 99–100, 102, 103, 108, 254, 255, 333, 457; and urban riots, 102, 488, 549; violence against, 96, 98, 101; voter participation of, 250, 254, 255–56, 256n, 271. *See also* Civil rights; Civil rights movement; School desegregation; Segregation; Slavery

Blackman, Paul H., 255n, 256n

Blackmun, Harry Andrew, 86–87

Blair, John M., 570n

Blanshard, Paul, 74n

Blow, Henry, 93

Blue Cross/Blue Shield, 16

Blum, Barbara, 21n

Blum, John Morton, 557n

B'nai B'rith, 124

Boeing, 140

Boggs, Hale, 326, 350

Bohlen, Charles E., 532n

Bok, Curtis, 74

Bolivia, 506

Bolling, Richard, 334n, 335n, 339n, 359

Bond, Julian, 63

Boorstin, Daniel J., 166n, 174, 231

Booth newspaper chain, 180

Borosage, Robert L., 506

Boston, Massachusetts, 60, 111, 490n; school busing in, 482; urban renewal in, 18

Boston Massacre, 35

Botswana, 539

Boyd, Richard W., 173n, 255n

Boyle, W. A. ("Tony"), 155

Braden, Tom, 189, 352, 352n

Bradley, Phillips, 117n, 129n

Brady, Tom P.: *Black Monday*, 118

Brandeis, Louis D., 42; and due process, 381; on law, 376–77

Brandt, Willy, 510n, 538n

Braniff Airways, 147

Brant, Irving, 53n, 68n, 69, 69n, 70n, 380

ries for, 420–21; reorganization of, 295, 426; Secret Service protection for, 415. *See also* individual departments

Cabinet Coordinating Committee on Economic Planning for the End of Vietnam Hostilities, 558

Caddell, Patrick, 287, 287n

Cahn, Edgar S., 115n

Calhoun, John C., 325n

Califano, Joseph A., Jr., 285n, 303, 303n, 304, 304n, 309n, 367, 579

California, 459n, 503, 505, 561n; direct democracy in, 178–79, 478; government of, 470, 474; politics in, 221n, 259, 261–62, 271; primary election in, 234, 237; social welfare in, 482n; women's rights in, 108, 111

California Poll, 237

Calvinist doctrine, 47

Cambodia, 197; invasion and bombing of, 35, 186, 280, 506; *Mayaguez* incident, 538

Cambridge, Massachusetts, 521

Camden, New Jersey, 495

Cameron, Simon, 261

Campbell, Angus, 366n; *American Voter, The,* 171, 171n

Campbell, Charles, 339

Camp David, 284–85

Canada, 294, 528; American investments in, 527

Canan, James W., 298n, 513n

Cannon, Howard W., 256

Cannon, Joseph G., 334–35, 337, 341

Cantril, Albert H., 167, 167n, 168, 170, 170n

Cantril, Hadley, 169n

Cantwell v. Connecticut (1940), 68n

Capitalism, 47, 125–27, 150, 162, 294, 538, 575, 581; and bigness, 576; versus communism, 71, 510–11, 520–21, 537, 553, 553n; defects in, and press, 183; and democracy, 543–44, 555; and Founders, 544; and national planning, 592, 595; and political parties, 212; public opinion of, 162, 294; socialist, 442–44, 544, 576; and television, 175, 179. *See also* Business, Big

Capital punishment: and black Americans, 118. *See also* Punishment

Caraway, Hattie Wyatt, 110

Cardozo, Benjamin N., 377, 377n, 399

Carlyle, Thomas, 174

Carper, Jean, 450n

Carson, Rachel L.: *Silent Spring,* 23, 24n

Carswell, G. Harrold, 319

Carter, James Earl, Jr. (Jimmy), 4, 250; and Big Business, 573; cabinet and staff of, 301, 303, 304–05, 421, 429–30; campaign debates of, 177–78, 269, and Congress, 209, 337, 370; and energy crisis, 585, 587n, 593; and Federal Reserve Board, 553; foreign policy of, 293, 294, 506, 507–08, 519, 533; as governor of Georgia, 472; human rights policy of, 506, 507–08; and labor, 153; and minority voters, 119–20, 207, 249, 250, 429; 1976 campaign of, 213, 225, 230, 240, 243, 249, 250, 253, 253n, 256, 259, 271; preconvention campaign of, 229, 234, 239n, 253n; as President, 287–88, 300–01, 318, 401; and press, 192; and reorganization of bureaucracy, 296, 297, 413–14, 417, 421, 426, 448, 450; voting proposals of, 256, 260; water projects cancelled by, 209, 434; and zero-base budgeting, 428

Case, Clifford P., 293

Castillo, Leonel J., 15

Castro, Fidel, 48, 534n

Caterpillar Tractor, 527

Catholics: as Democrats, 207; as ethnics, 248n; as presidential candidates, 207, 248, 249

Catt, Carrie Chapman, 108

Cattle barons: and American Indians, 115; and environment, 141

Causey, Mike, 429n

Cellar, Emanuel, 112–13

Census Bureau, 250, 577

Center for Disease Control, 491

Central Intelligence Agency (CIA), 209, 292, 297, 430, 512, 533–35, 538; and assassination contracts with Mafia, 435n; and Bay of Pigs, 430; corruption in, 173, 280; covert activities of, 280, 534, 534n; domestic activities of, 62, 197, 434–35, 435n; files of, 62; and FOI Act, 187; in Iran, 525; in Latin America, 506; mail opened by, 59,

62, 434–35; and Nixon's Enemies List, 314; paper work of, 418; and press, 188, 190, 193; secrecy in, 436; self-righteousness in, 59–60; and sunken Russian submarine, 188; wiretapping by, 59, 434

Central Pacific Railroad, 148n

Central Republic Bank and Trust Company of Chicago, 574n

Chace, William M., 94n, 102n

Chagall, David, 247n

Chambers, William Nisbet, 204n

Charles I, King of England, 33

Charleston, South Carolina, 555

Charleston (West Virginia) *Gazette,* 180n

Chase, Salmon P., 401

Chavez, Cesar, 117, 129, 144

Chayes, Abram, 382, 382n

Cheever, John, 555

Chemical New York Corporation, 566

Chevron, 26, 469

Chiang Kai-shek, 536, 537

Chicago, Burlington Railroad v. Chicago (1897), 65n

Chicago, Illinois, 152, 211, 485, 554, 555; 1968 Democratic convention in, 243; school desegregation in, 103

Chicago Daily News, 192

Chicago Tribune, 176

Chicanos. *See* Mexican-Americans

Childs, Marquis, 578n

Chile: and CIA, 506; military dictatorship of, 113, 506, 537; overthrow of Allende in, 507

Chilton, W. E., III, 180n

China: immigrants from, 13

China, Nationalist, 536

China, People's Republic of, 290, 512, 514, 536, 537, 538; Nixon's trip to, 222, 293, 294, 533, 536, 537n; recognition of, 536, 537n; and Soviet Union, 504, 537

Chisholm, Shirley, 110, 232

Choate, Rufus, 37

Chommie, John C., 54n

Chou En-lai, 294, 504

Christenson, Reo M., 17

Christian, George, 196

Christian Science Monitor, 264n

Chrysler, 138

Church, Frank, 279, 361, 366–68

Churchill, Winston, 359, 510, 537

Cincinnati, Ohio, 494–95

Citibank, 263

Cities: aged in, 486; black Americans in, 98, 103, 250, 484–85, 486, 549; and competition with rural areas, 482–83; crime in, 10, 485, 486, 489, 490, 492–93, 493n, 495; culture in, 483n; decline of, 588; education in, 489–90, 492; employment in, 483, 483n, 491; ethnic groups in, 218, 483–85, 486, 486n; lower class in, 483, 486, 493; metropolitan areas of, 495, 495n, 496–97; minorities in schools of, 102, 104, 485; neighbor-hoods in, 18, 20, 462, 493, 496, 496n, 497; pollution in, 25, 467–68, 486, 490–91, 495; poverty in, 18, 483–87, 489, 492; representation of, in state legislatures, 472; riots in, 102, 223, 488, 549; social problems in, 485, 491, 492–93; unemploy-ment in, 459, 492, 495; urban renew-al for, 18, 20, 462; white flight from, 103, 103n, 483–84, 485–86. *See also* City government; New York, New York; Washington, D.C.

Cities Service, 157n

City government: accountability in, 465; and Big Business, 467–68, 498; budget of, 487, 489–90, 495; and Congress, 342; corruption and waste in, 486, 487, 488, 489, 490n, 491–93; council members in, 493–94; and Democratic party, 205, 207, 218, 248–49; employees in, 487, 488, 489, 490, 490n; federal aid to, 459, 462, 487, 488, 490n, 491, 492–93; financial problems of, 482, 486, 487, 489, 492; and interest groups, 494; mayors in, 211, 459, 477, 489, 493–94; and municipal unions, 487, 489; "national cities" proposal, 498; police in, 486, 489, 490, 492–93, 495, 497; political machines in, 109, 111, 205, 207, 211–12, 218, 248, 254, 491, 494, 498; and public, 480, 493; public housing in, 18–21, 488, 492; and regionalism, 494–95, 495n, 496–97; and revenue sharing, 465; and state government, 456, 490n, 498; structure of, 493–94; tax base of, 486, 490, 492; and unsanitary and unsafe conditions, 491; welfare programs of, 485n, 486–87, 488, 491–92. *See also* Local government

Civil Aeronautics Board (CAB), 146, 437, 437n, 438, 592; rate setting by, 426, 445

Civil disobedience, 55, 55n, 56; in civil rights movement, 56, 101–02; in women's movement, 108–09, 119

Civil liberties: and civil rights, 64, 119; confusion about, 86; and crim-inal justice system, 77–86; defined, 64; in everyday life, 60, 75; and government oppressiveness, 59–64, 69–73, 73n, 128; and radical groups, 60, 71–72; and Supreme Court, 65, 66–83 *passim*, 86–88, 265, 397–98, 400, 402–04, 478. *See also* Individuals; individual freedoms

Civil rights: and affirmative action, 21–23; anatomy of, 117–20; and antilynching legislation, 309–10; and civil liberties, 64, 119; commis-sion on, 91, 103, 105; and Con-gress, 20, 29, 91–92, 95, 97, 102, 307, 329, 350, 405; defined, 64, 91; enforcement of legislation for, 100–01, 119; and federal govern-ment, 100–01, 102, 104, 463n, 465, 470, 471, 498; and judges, 400; lob-by for, 124, 141; as political issue, 210; and President, 98, 102, 218, 307; and property rights, 86, 92, 94; and public opinion, 95, 97, 100, 162, 173; role of stereotypes in, 117; and Supreme Court, 21, 95, 97–100, 102, 114n, 378, 396, 400. *See also* Black Americans; Civil rights movement; Minorities

Civil Rights Acts (1866, 1875, 1957, 1960, 1964), 29, 91, 92, 97, 102, 103, 119, 250, 307

Civil rights movement, 56, 101–02, 110, 173, 207, 254; and courts, 475; and FBI, 62, 314, 435; March on Washington, 102; militancy in, 102; Montgomery bus boycott, 101–02; and police, 62; and press, 174, 179, 198–99; sit-ins, 102; white sympa-thy for, 102

Civil Service. *See* Bureaucracy

Civil Service Act (1883), 264, 428

Civil Service Commission, 417, 428–29

Civil War, 54, 70, 94–95, 119, 199, 205, 254, 277, 281, 289, 412, 413n, 458, 459, 562

Clark, Kenneth, 105, 105n

Clark, Ramsey, 378n, 490n

Clarksburg, West Virginia, 179

Clausen, A. W., 464

Clawson, Del, 423

Clay, Henry, 231, 325n, 334, 341

Clayton Antitrust Act (1914), 361, 449

Clayton Enterprises, 134

Cleghorn, Reese, 99n

Cleveland, Grover, 205, 231, 259, 267–68

Cleveland, Ohio, 483, 485; pollution by, 467–68; school desegregation in, 103

Clifford, Clark M., 61, 147, 529, 535

Clifford, Warnke, Glass, McIlwain and Finney (law firm), 147

Coca-Cola, 140, 526

Cockburn, Sir Alexander, 74

Cohen, Jerry S., 142n, 199n, 426, 426n

Cohen, Wilbur, 11n

Cohen v. Hurley (1961), 65n

Coke, Sir Edward, 33–34

Colby, William E., 188

Cold war. *See* Foreign policy, cold war

Cole, Charles L., 554n

Cole, Donald B., 224

Colgate-Palmolive, 184

Collier, Peter, 94n, 102n

Colombia, 522

Colonial America, 31, 54–55; com-merce and trade of, 35, 42, 43, 44; constitutions in, 35n, 64; under England, 35, 35n, 37; nationalism in, 40; natural rights in, 32–33, 34, 64; postwar depression in, 42–43; press in, 185, 197; religious intoler-ance in, 66; sense of community in, 34–35; and taxation, 35, 64, 562; terrorism toward Loyalists in, 39n; upper class in, 35, 39–40, 43, 44–45, 47–48, 51. *See also* Ameri-can Revolution

Colorado, 478; government of, 471n; social welfare in, 482n; women's rights in, 108, 111

Columbia Broadcasting System (CBS), 173, 176, 178, 179, 418n; and election campaigns, 240, 247; and Johnson administration, 175; and news, 173, 183; poll of, 249. *See also* Television

Columbia Journalism Review, 190

Congress of Industrial Organizations (CIO), 152
Connally, John, 576
Connecticut, 35n, 52, 92; criminal justice in, 80; women's rights in, 111
Conoco, 469
Conrail (Consolidated Rail Corporation), 575
Conscientious objectors, 66–68, 430
Conservative party, 223
Conservatives: and Big Labor, 153; in Congress, 281, 297, 324, 337, 340n, 344–45, 369, 371; in Democratic party, 208, 209, 333; Founders as, 39–40, 45–47, 50, 54, 64, 254, 258, 324; interest group leaders as, 130, 264; and national planning, 590; in Republican party, 208, 209, 216, 218, 244, 301, 333; and Supreme Court, 378–83, 397, 401; and veto power, 311
Constitution, 29–31, 41, 43–56, 117, 376, 380, 470; amending, 49, 54; and black Americans, 92–94, 95, 457; checks and balances in, 48–50, 276, 285, 422–23, 457, 499; citizens' faith and awe in, 30, 31; and congressional powers, 29, 45, 275, 279, 288, 289, 290, 293, 297, 323–24, 355, 456, 549, 556; as conservative document, 50, 54; and electoral college, 258–59; and equality, 47, 91; fairness and neutrality of, 30, 55; and federalism, 42, 48, 64, 456–57, 458, 458n, 459, 499; and Founders, 31, 39, 45–50, 64, 499; and individual rights, 53, 64, 86–88, 456–57, 498; influences on, 42, 54, 64, 127; interpretation of, 29, 30, 55–56, 98, 377–83, 392; and judicial branch, 375, 386; and presidential powers, 275–76, 277–78, 288, 294, 294n, 306, 310, 310n; ratification of, 50–52, 204; and removal of President, 316; separation of powers in, 48, 276, 456; as supreme law, 276n, 455–56; and Vice President, 299–300. See also Amendments to Constitution; Bill of Rights; Constitutional Convention
Constitutional Convention, 43–50, 66, 69; compromises at, 48–49, 456; delegates to, 43–45; and federal-

ism, 456–57; and impeachment, 316; moneyed interests at, 44–45, 258; and popular sovereignty, 45–48; and property rights, 30, 45, 47, 51, 64; and slavery, 48, 64, 93; Virginia Plan at, 456. See also Founders
Consumers, 4, 55; and economy, 549, 570; and government, 545, 596; and grass-roots lobbying, 139–41, 142; and high prices, 526, 588–89; opposition to protection for, 127, 479; problems of, and press, 183, 199; and regulatory agencies, 437, 440, 442, 444–47, 450; and Supreme Court, 55; and throwaway containers, 155; women as, 107
Continental Congress, 35n, 37, 38, 40, 41, 43
Continental Oil, 525
Converse, Philip E., 167–68, 168n, 365n; American Voter, The, 171, 171n
Conyers, John, Jr., 102
Cook, Fred J., 512n
Cooke, Sidney Russell, 586, 586n
Coolidge, Calvin, 194, 277, 285, 315, 315n, 319, 544
Cooper, Chester, 511n
Cooper, Irving, 406
Cooper v. Aaron (1958), 404, 404n
Corcoran, Thomas G., 314, 402n
Cornish, Dudley Taylor, 94n
Corporations. See Business, Big
Corwin, Edward S., 128n, 242, 242n, 275–76, 276n, 277n, 293n, 299n, 303n, 529, 529n
Corwin, R. D., 263
Costanza, Margaret, 304
Cotton, Norris, 340
Council of Economic Advisers, 297, 428, 546
Council on Wage and Price Stability, 16n, 428
Counties, 456; government of, 480–82, 485; income of, 461; metropolitan, 483; and regionalism, 495, 495n, 496–97; rural, 482; and social welfare, 482n. See also Local government
Court of Claims, 387, 392
Court of Customs and Patent Appeals, 387, 392
Court of Military Appeals, 392

Courts, 117; in cities, 492–93; criticism of, 380; and definition of obscenity, 73–74; due process concept in, 77; function of, 382; plea bargaining in, 85–86; and press, 199. See also Trials
Court system, federal, 323, 375, 392–93; and civil rights, 475; courts of appeal, 376, 392, 404; district courts, 376, 392, 404; due process in, 80, 82; and illegal evidence, 78, 79; interplay with state courts in, 475; interpretation by, 376; and judicial review, 48, 48n, 376; juries in, 475; lack of equality in, 405–08; and regulatory agencies, 392, 423, 423n. See also Criminal justice system; Judges
Court system, state, 376, 392, 393, 470, 474–76; and capital punishment, 475; and civil rights, 475; due process in, 80–82; and illegal evidence, 78, 79; interplay with federal courts in, 475; juries in, 475; procedural rights in, 390–92, 475; and states' rights, 375; unequal punishment in, 474. See also Criminal justice system; Judges
Covington, Kentucky, 494–95
Cowan, Edward, 12n
Cox, Edward, 316
Cox, Kenneth A., 178, 178n
Coxey, Jacob Sechler, 128
Crane, Philip M., 136
Cranston, Alan, 262, 262n, 506, 561
Crédit Mobilier scandal, 361
Cressey, Donald R., 85n
Crime, 4, 173; in cities, 10, 485, 486, 489, 490, 492–93, 493n, 495; and guns, 9–10; organized, 60, 60n, 264, 276n, 435, 435n, 476, 499; organized, Senate investigation into, 361; and prisons, 7; and unemployment, 556; by youth, 486, 493n
Criminal justice system: bail in, 52, 80, 84, 86; computerized data banks in, 79–80; confessions in, 83; delays in, 84–86; due process in, 77, 80–84, 471; and Escobedo decision, 82; evidence in, 77–79; and Gideon decision, 83n; inequality in, 84–86, 118; and Miranda decision, 82–83; plea bargaining in, 85–86; pretrial detainees in, 84–85; pris-

ons in, 7, 84–85, 471; procedural rights in, 80, 80n, 81–83, 100, 402; psychological coercion in, 85; right to lawyer in, 80–83, 83n, 390–92, 475; right to silence in, 80, 82–83; search warrants in, 77–78; of states, 468, 471; stop-and-frisk procedure in, 77; wiretapping in, 78–79, 88. *See also* Courts; Juries; Police; Punishment; Trials

Cromwell, Oliver, 33

Crouse, Timothy, 192n, 238, 238n, 242n

Cuba, 221, 293, 507, 533; and American imperialism, 97; and Angola, 538n; and Bay of Pigs, 188, 305, 430, 532; Soviet missiles in, 315, 517, 519, 536

Cuciti, Peggy L., 461n

Cummings, Milton, Jr., 261n

Czechoslovakia, 521n

D

Dahl, Robert A., 400, 400n, 401, 401n

Dairy industry, 133, 196, 262, 266, 332, 445

Dale, Edwin L., Jr., 551, 570n

Daley, Richard, 211, 490, 498

Dallas, Texas, 470n

Dallas Power & Light, 469

Daly, John C., 592n

Damon, Allan L., 301n, 505n

Daniel, Margaret Truman, 284

Darling, W. Stuart, 291n

Da Silva, Howard, 555

Davenport, E. H., 586, 586n

Davidson, Roger H., 348, 348n

Davis, Edward M., 598n

Dawes, Charles G., 302, 574n

Dawes Act (1887), 114

DDT, 23

Deakin, James, 138n, 147n, 148, 148n

Dean, John W., III, 314n

DeCarlo, Angelo ("Gyp"), 276n

Declaration of Independence, 37, 37n, 38–39, 40, 54; egalitarian theme of, 37n, 40, 91; and natural rights, 32, 33, 41

Defense budget, 519, 537; and Congress, 131, 333, 339, 343, 343n, 345, 512, 530, 560; and domestic budget, 505, 509, 557–58; and em-

ployment, 557, 560, 561; lobby for, 131, 131n; proposed cuts in, 213, 221; rise in, 213, 517, 539, 557–59; salaries and pensions in, 559. *See also* Nuclear weapons; Pentagon

DeFratus, Elsie, 547n

DeFunis, Marco, Jr., 22

De Kooning, Willem, 555

Delaware, 48, 52; and environment, 155

Dellums, Ronald V., 329

Del Monte, 144

Delta Air Lines, 566

Demaris, Ovid, 314n

Democracy, American, 324, 511, 545; and capitalism, 543–44, 555; citizen's relationship to, 3–4, 6, 65; in colonial American, 35; communication in, 6, 161, 197–200; compromise in, 6, 7–8, 26, 371; conflict in, 125, 157; consensus in, 6, 7, 157; direct, 156–57, 178–79, 478–79; and economic security, 103; impact of television on, 174; as inspiration to Third World, 54; and interest groups, 147, 418, 157; Jacksonian, 93, 205, 277, 287; legality of, 395–96; legends in, 30, 31, 555; and local government, 466, 466n; pluralism in, 143, 178; and politics, 209; problems in, 4–26; problem solving in, 6–8; public opinion on, 169; and Supreme Court, 395–96; voting in, 141. *See also* Federal government

Democratic National Conventions, 217, 243–44; Army political spies at, 63; of 1972, 110–11, 224, 232, 232n, 233, 242, 243; of 1976, 111, 232n, 243; quotas at, 232n; and women, 110, 232n. *See also* National conventions

Democratic party and Democrats: and Big Government, 144–46, 214, 218; and black Americans, 98–99, 207, 207n, 218, 223, 232n, 250; and business, 208, 214, 263; caucus (in House and Senate) of, 340n, 341, 345, 347, 348, 369; in cities, 205, 207, 218, 248–49; and communism, 512; conservatives in, 208, 209, 333; contributions to, 262; and control of Congress, 217, 221, 223, 299, 333, 338, 370; known as Democratic-Republican party, 204; develop-

ment of, 203–08; and economy, 263; foreign policy of, 221, 222, 538; ideology of, 99, 212–18; Jews in, 125, 207; and labor, 207, 208, 218, 270; liberals in, 153, 218, 244, 333, 574; and lower class, 225; as majority party, 219, 257; minorities in, 207, 218, 232n, 248–49, 271; New Deal coalition of, 207, 208, 217–18; organization of, 208–10; and Presidency, 204, 205, 207, 214, 217, 217n, 218, 221, 223, 307; and press, 189, 191; in primary elections, 232–34, 237–40; known as Republican party, 204; and revenue sharing, 465; and social programs, 11, 15, 146, 208, 210, 214, 218, 221, 222, 250; in South, 96, 97, 205, 207–08, 209, 218, 333; Steering Committee (in House and Senate) of, 338, 340n, 343n; Study Group (in House) of, 124, 345; and third parties, 223

Democratic-Republican party, 204–05

Democrats for McGovern, 63

Demstez, Harold, 571

Denenberg, Herbert S., 451

Dennis, Eugene, 71

Dennis, Everette, 180, 180n

Dennis v. United States (1951), 72n, 390n

Dent, John H., 141, 352n

Denver, Colorado, 482n

Department of Agriculture, 136, 295, 414, 418, 424–25, 449, 523–24; Secretary of, 301, 434

Department of Commerce, 120, 295, 418, 424–25, 429; Bureau of Public Roads, 464; Secretary of, 301

Department of Defense, 295, 424–25; electronic battlefield of, 298, 298n, 519; and Pentagon Papers, 71, 186; Secretary of, 279, 301, 532, 534, 559n. *See also* Defense budget; Military-industrial complex; Pentagon

Department of Energy, 424–25, 426; Secretary of, 301

Department of Health, Education and Welfare (HEW), 112, 295, 416, 424–25, 426, 437, 437n, 492; and national health insurance, 17–18; Secretary of, 301, 432, 579; and smoking, 5, 367

Department of Housing and Urban Development (HUD), 120, 295, 418, 424–25, 429; and public housing, 20–21; Secretary of, 301

Department of Interior, 116, 295, 416, 418, 424–25, 449, 598; Bureau of Reclamation, 344; Secretary of, 301, 432, 449

Department of Justice, 79n, 117, 295, 424–25, 535, 573; antitrust actions of, 449–50; contract employees of, 418; and FOI Act, 187; and lobbyists, 149; and Nixon's Enemies List, 314; and Pentagon Papers, 71. *See also* Attorney General

Department of Labor, 112, 295, 424–25; and employment discrimination, 104; Secretary of, 301

Department of State, 26, 192, 281, 293, 295, 415, 424, 437, 504, 506, 523–24, 532–34, 535, 537, 559; advisory committees to, 433, 433n; Foreign Service of, 532, 532n, 533; and illegal aliens, 15; investigation of, 361n; and McCarthy, 512; and multinational corporations, 525, 586; Secretary of, 301, 532, 534. *See also* Ambassadors; Foreign policy

Department of Transportation, 295, 424–25, 434; Secretary of, 301

Department of the Treasury, 295, 424, 556; and illegal aliens, 14; revenue sharing study of, 465; Secretary of, 301

Depression, Great, 152, 167, 207, 249, 257, 268, 278, 281, 547, 553, 553n, 554–55, 557, 590; and poverty and hunger, 11, 297, 547, 554; and unemployment, 128, 297, 315, 546–47, 554; Veterans' Bonus March, 128

Derian, Patricia, 304–05

Detroit, Michigan, 470n, 485, 490n, 497–98; crime in, 10; financial problems of, 486; obscenity ruling in, 76; pollution by, 467–68; school desegregation in, 103

DeVries, Walter, 244, 244n

Dewey, Thomas E., 99, 167n, 237, 259

Dexter, Lewis Anthony, 365–66, 366n

Dickinson, John, 33

Dies, Martin, 72

Di Grazia, Robert J., 490

Dillon, C. Douglas, 143n

Dirksen, Everett, 349

District of Columbia, 35, 100, 214, 329, 484n. *See also* Washington, D.C.

Dixiecrats, 207

Dodd, S. C. T., 571

Dodd, Thomas J., 331

Dole, Robert J., 134, 207n, 249

Domenici, Pete V., 359–60

Domestic Policy Staff, 428

Dominican Republic: and Johnson, 185

Donne, John, 451

Douglas, Paul H., 338, 349

Douglas, Stephen A., 349

Douglas, William O., 68, 71, 317n, 385, 398, 403–04

Dow Chemical Corporation, 25, 526, 527–28

Dowdy, John, 132

Dowling, Tom, 352n

Downie, Leonard, Jr., 18n, 20n

Downs, Anthony, 172, 172n, 212, 212n, 432, 432n

Draft, 289; and conscientious objectors, 66–68; evasion, 435; peacetime, 280–81

Dred Scott v. Sanford (1857), 93–94

Dresden, Germany, 513

Dresser Industries, 469

Drucker, Peter F., 448, 448n, 450, 450n

Drugs, 446; illegal, 173, 556; raids, 62

Due process concept: in common law, 34, 64; in congressional committees, 72; in criminal justice system, 77, 80–84, 471; in Fifth Amendment, 45, 80, 381; in Fourteenth Amendment, 65, 77, 80–81, 95, 99, 199, 380–81; and Supreme Court, 72, 378, 380–81

Dulles, John Foster, 516–17, 520, 530, 532

Duniway, Abigail Scott, 108

Du Pont de Nemours, E. I., 26, 447, 572

Duscha, Julius, 385n

E

Eagleton, Thomas F., 192, 214, 225

East India Company, 35

Eastlake, Ohio, 478

Eastland, James O., 72, 118, 259, 400

Eckhardt, Bob, 366, 366n

Economic Opportunity Act (1964), 496n

Economy: and balance of payments, 279; and Congress, 370, 549, 556; and controls, 571, 595; and cost of living, 547n; and credit, 549, 592; depressions, 151, 548, 553; drained by illegal aliens, 14–15; and environmentalists, 25–26; equality in, 580–82; government management of, 424, 547, 549–53, 568, 592; and Gross National Product (GNP), 144, 463, 547, 547n, 557, 592; and incomes, 460, 546n, 568, 576–77, 580–82, 592, 593; and interest rates, 464, 546n, 549, 550, 574; Keynesian economics, 553, 553n, 554–57, 576; and liberals, 143–44; and multinational corporations, 526; and national planning, 590–98; public opinion of, 544–45; recessions, 257, 263, 268, 419, 464, 523, 545, 546, 552, 556, 562, 568–70, 570n; regional, 459–61; and slavery, 92–94; and special interests, 543–44; stagflation, 223, 569, 570, 570n; war, 558; women's role in, 107, 110, 112. *See also* Banks; Business, Big; Capitalism; Depression, Great; Fiscal policy; Inflation; Unemployment

Ecuador, 506

Editor & Publisher, 191

Education, 101, 104, 470; federal funds for, 100, 162, 307, 461, 471, 548; higher, 98, 100, 107, 112, 114, 471, 548; inadequate planning for, 588; increased tolerance from, 162; and political opinion, 173; and poor reading, 489–90; struggle for equality in, 105–06. *See also* Public schools; School desegregation; Universities

Edward III, King of England, 34

Edwards, James B., 434

Edwards, Richard C., 586n

Egypt, 24, 531

Ehrbar, A. F., 568n

Ehrlichman, John D., 292, 302, 400n

Eighteenth Amendment, 109

Eighth Amendment, 80, 84, 383

Eisenhower, Dwight D., 315n; and business, 143, 189; domestic policy of, 307; foreign policy of, 294, 510, 510n, 511, 511n, 516–17, 520, 530, 532; and military-industrial complex, 5; and politics, 207, 217, 229, 257; as President, 112, 172, 217, 221, 263, 278–79, 285n, 289–90,

N

Nader, Ralph, 142, 200, 262, 326n, 408, 408n, 409n, 441n, 450, 565n
Nagasaki, Japan, 513
Namath, Joe, 449
Napolitan, Joseph, 246
Nardone v. United States (1937), 78–79, 79n
Nashville, Tennessee, 485
Nast, Thomas, 469
Natcher, William, 367
Nathan, Robert R., 523–24
National Academy of Sciences, 25
National Advisory Commission on Civil Disorders (Kerner Commission), 485
National Aeronautics and Space Administration (NASA), 104
National American Woman Suffrage Association, 109
National Assessment of Educational Progress, 171
National Association for the Advancement of Colored People (NAACP), 62, 124, 143, 310
National Association of Broadcasters, 179n
National Association of Manufacturers (NAM), 142, 149n
National Association of Retired Persons, 124n
National Board for the Promotion of Rifle Practice, 412
National Broadcasting Company (NBC), 173, 176, 178, 179; and election campaigns, 240, 247; and Kennedy administration, 175; and news, 183; poll of, 177; self-censorship of, 188. *See also* Television
National Catholic Welfare Board, 129
National conventions, 229, 240; committed and uncommitted delegates at, 232; democratization of, 230, 232, 232n; demonstrations at, 242; keynote speech at, 241, 243; and platform, 242; politics at, 243–44; quotas for, 232n; television at, 242, 243
National Council of Catholic Women, 114
National Council of Jewish Women, 114, 129

National Council of Senior Citizens, 124n
National Education Association, 133
National Emergencies Act (1976), 279
National Farmers Union, 138
National Guard, 559; at Kent State, 35; in Little Rock, 38, 405
National Guard Association of the United States, 131n
National Institute of Education, 495
National Institute on Alcohol Abuse and Alcoholism, 412
Nationalism, 204; in colonial America, 40, 456; and communism, 537; and war, 528
National Labor Relations Act (1935), 152
National Labor Relations Board (NLRB), 152, 426, 437, 437n
National Opinion Research Center, 312
National planning: and Big Business, 594–95, 596; and efficiency, 596; and federal budget, 591–92; hazards of, 594–96; Humphrey-Javits proposal for, 593–94; and the individual, 595, 596; and interest groups, 592, 593; lack of, during cold war, 590–91; need for, 587–89, 592–94, 598–600; and NRA, 590; and tradition, 600
National Recovery Administration (NRA), 590
National Resources Planning Board, 590
National Rifle Association, 10, 131–32, 138
National Science Foundation, 412
National security, 307, 558; and Army, 62–63; and CIA, 62; and Congress, 72; and FBI, 60, 60n, 61–62, 63; and foreign policy, 506, 513, 534; and nuclear weapons, 513, 560; and President, 79n, 293–94, 506, 534; and press self-censorship, 188, 199; public opinion of, 200, 294
National Security Act (1947), 62, 534
National Security Agency, 292; and FOI Act, 187; paper work of, 418
National Security Council, 297, 300, 428, 430, 524, 534
National Soft Drink Association, 156
National Steel, 566

National Woman's Party, 108
National Woman Suffrage Association, 108
National Women's Political Caucus, 111
Natural gas: deregulation and government, 426, 439, 585; deregulation and oil companies, 149; shortage, 585
Natural rights, 32–33, 34, 41, 54, 64
Nauru, 539
Naval Reserve Association, 131n
Navasky, Victor S., 400n
Navy Department, 424–25
Neal, Stephen L., 552
Nebraska: courts of, 475; government of, 473, 474; social welfare in, 482n
Negre v. Larsen (1971), 68n
Nelson, Gaylord, 79n
Nelson, Jack, 190
Nessen, Ron, 194
Neustadt, Richard, 315n
Neutrality Act (1935), 508
Nevada, 459n; social welfare in, 478
Nevele Country Club, 134
Newark, New Jersey: black majority in, 485; public schools of, 489
New Deal: and Big Government, 144, 297, 412, 427; coalition of Democratic party, 207, 208, 217–18; and federalism, 458–59; and Roosevelt, 210, 278, 281, 297, 307, 309–10, 427, 547, 553, 555, 590
New England, 43, 204
New Hampshire, 35n, 52; courts of, 475; primary election in, 232, 234, 235, 238, 238n, 239–40, 253
Newhouse, Samuel I., 180–81
Newhouse newspaper chain, 180
New Jersey, 52, 92; government of, 473, 474; politics in, 221n, 468; primary election in, 235
Newman, Paul, 222n
New Mexico, 459n
New Orleans, Louisiana, 485
Newsday, 190
Newspapers: chains of, 180; and corruption of Big Business, 182–83; cost of, 197; diversity of opinion and rebuttal in, 179–80, 180n, 181, 197; and election campaigns, 237–41, 244, 246, 253; Hays scandal in, 189; impact of, 176, 177, 183, 198–99; Kennedy scandal in,

Republic Steel Company, 152, 468

Reserve Mining Company, 25

Reston, James, 188, 236, 257n, 303, 532

Retired Officers Association, 131n

Reuss, Henry S., 550

Revenue sharing, 465, 491

Revolution: leaders of, 48; right of, 33, 64

Reymond, Jack, 562n

Reynolds, R. J., Industries, 184

Reynolds Metal, 444

Rhode Island, 35n, 43, 52, 92; government of, 473

Rhodes, John, 220

Ribicoff, Abraham, 351

Rice, Elmer, 555

Richmond, Virginia, 485

Rickenson, James R., 220n

Riegel, Donald W., Jr., 363, 363n

Riker, William H., 220n

Rivers, William, 184n

Roberts, Owen J., 397

Robespierre, 48

Robinson, Joseph T., 337

Robinson, Michael J., 246, 246n

Roche, John P., 421, 421n

Rockefeller, Nelson A., 189, 234n, 252–53, 265n, 511n, 535, 565, 595

Rockefeller, Winthrop, 222

Rockefeller dynasty, 567

Rockwell International, 524

Rogers, William P., 186

Roll, Charles W., Jr., 167, 167n, 168, 170, 170n

Rolling Stone, 238

Romania, 521n

Romney, George W., 234n, 235

Rooney, Fred B., 438n

Roosevelt, Franklin D., 30, 217, 249, 300, 312, 315n; and civil rights, 309–10; election of, 98–99, 167, 207; and Executive Office, 427; foreign policy of, 532; Good Neighbor policy of, 505; and internment of Japanese-Americans, 397; and labor, 152; New Deal of, 210, 278, 281, 297, 307, 309–10, 427, 547, 553, 555, 590; as President, 63, 79, 112, 119, 143, 278, 279, 282, 303, 304, 310n, 314, 315, 318, 574, 598; and press, 194, 199, 278; and Social Security, 11; and Supreme Court, 99, 384, 399, 401; and World War II, 207, 278, 294

Roosevelt, Mrs. Franklin D., 310

Roosevelt, Theodore, 315n; and civil rights, 98; and ethnic groups, 248; Open Door policy of, 505; as President, 278, 278n, 295; and press, 199; and progressivism, 205, 223; and Supreme Court, 399, 402

Roper, Burns W., 231n

Roper, Elmo, 165, 237

Rose, Charles, 367

Rosen, Gerald R., 340n

Rosenbaum, David E., 106n, 141, 349, 349n, 579n

Rosenberg, Milton, 167–68, 168n

Rosenthal, A. M., 199

Rosenthal, Benjamin S., 142, 439n

Rosett, Arthur, 85n

Ross, E. A., 150

Ross, Irwin, 154

Ross, Thomas B., 525n

Rossiter, Clinton, 39, 39n, 40n, 50, 50n, 53n, 127n, 203, 218, 218n, 277–78, 278n, 292n, 300, 300n, 311, 311n, 423n, 427n, 466n, 567n

Rothbard, Murray N., 574n

Rothman, David J., 148n, 341n

Rothman, Sheila M., 107n

Roth v. United States (1957), 74, 74n, 75

Rowan, Carl T., 192, 192n

Rowen, Hobart, 12n, 570n

Royster, Vermont, 185n

Ruckelshaus, William D., 183n, 439

Rudwick, Elliott, 92, 92n, 97n, 98n, 484n

Rural areas: and competition with cities, 482–83; poverty in, 482; representation of, in state legislatures, 472; schools in, 495

Rural Electrification Administration (REA), 412, 424

Rusk, Dean, 195, 262, 532

Russell, Mary, 367

Russell, Richard B., 339

Rwanda, 539

S

Sacramento, California, 415

Sadat, Anwar el-, 285

Sadlowski, Edward, 153

Safer, Morley, 185n

Safeway, 140, 144

Safire, William, 193, 193n, 420n, 421, 421n, 431n

Saigon, South Vietnam, 524

St. Antoine, Theodore J., 84

St. Louis, Missouri, 485, 494; Pruitt-Igoe housing project of, 20

Sale, Kirkpatrick, 250, 250n, 268n

Salinger, Pierre, 195, 281

Sampson, Anthony, 527n, 561n

Samuelson, Paul A., 105, 152n

Sanford, F. A., 93

San Francisco, California, 555; metropolitan area of, 495–96; municipal union strike in, 482; social welfare in, 482n

San Jose, California, 111

Saudi Arabia, 527; arms sales to, 524

Saxbe, William B., 369, 435

Scales v. United States (1961), 72, 72n

Scarf, Maggie, 10n

Schattschneider, E. E., 8, 8n, 10, 10n, 125, 125n, 128n, 129n, 150, 150n, 157, 157n, 204n, 212, 212n, 413n, 422n

Schenck v. United States (1919), 70, 70n

Schlesinger, Arthur M., Jr., 302n, 421, 421n, 506

Schlesinger, James R., 435n, 536

Schmerber, Willie, 77

Schmerber v. California (1966), 77, 77n

Schnapper, M. B., 151n

School desegregation, 98, 329; busing for, 103, 106, 125, 162, 405; enforcement of, 100, 404–05; in North, 103, 405; public opinion on, 100, 162, 405; in South, 102–03, 103n, 118, 404–05; and Supreme Court, 100, 118, 402, 404–05; in West, 103. *See also* Civil rights; Education

School of the Americas (Panama), 506

Schrag, Peter, 247–48, 248n

Schramm, Wilbur, 184n

Schroeder, Patricia, 110, 420n

Schultze, Charles L., 462, 463n

Schwartz, Bernard, 42, 42n, 52n, 86n, 94n

Scott, Dred, 93–94

Scottsboro Boys case, 81–82

Scranton, William W., 234n

Seafarers International Union, 134, 262

Search warrants, 77; absence of, 77–78

local governments, 459, 461, 465, 467, 470, 470n, 478, 482n, 579; supplemental assistance design of, 579–80. *See also* Social Security

Sorauf, Frank J., 403n, 404n

Sorensen, Theodore C., 195, 430, 529, 529n

South, 54; "black codes" of, 95; in colonial America, 40; defense contracts in, 459, 459n; Democratic party in, 96, 97, 205, 207–08, 209, 218, 333; economy of, 92, 459–61; federal subsidies to, 459; federal troops in, 95–96, 97; gain in electoral votes of, 250–51; members of Congress from, 101, 172, 208, 209, 217, 260, 310, 325, 333, 337, 340n, 341–42; poverty in, 5; racism in, 82, 93, 95–98, 100, 207, 484, 484n, 498; Reconstruction in, 95–96, 97, 119, 459; Republican party in, 207–08, 223, 333; school desegregation in, 102–03, 103n, 118, 404–05; secession of, 50; segregation in, 97–98, 100, 118; and slavery, 38, 92, 92n, 94, 205; "Southern Manifesto" of, 101; suffrage restrictions in, 96–97, 100, 254; and Warren Court activism, 378; women officials in, 111

South Africa, 136, 537; American investments in, 528

South African Foundation, 136

South America: Nazis in, and multinational corporations, 526n

South Carolina, 52, 434; civil rights in, 96–97, 254; and federal supremacy, 288, 458; government of, 473; politics in, 207; social welfare in, 482n

South Dakota, 478; courts of, 475; government of, 473

Southern Christian Leadership Conference (SCLC), 62

Southern Pacific Railroad, 148n

Southern Railway Company, 134, 136, 444

South Korea, 537; American support of dictator in, 506, 507, 527; terror in, 507. *See also* Korean War

South Vietnam, 167; corruption in, 522. *See also* Vietnam war

Southwest: defense contracts in, 459n; economy of, 459–61; gain in electoral votes in, 250–51

Southwestern Bell, 469

Soviet Union: arms race with, 514, 516, 517, 519, 539, 557, 559, 559n, 561n; and balance of terror, 514–17, 538, 538n, 539–40; and Baruch Plan, 515, 515n; and China, 504, 537; cold war with, 71, 221, 281, 398, 504, 509, 509n, 510–13, 516, 519, 537, 537n; and containment policy, 520; détente with, 222, 517, 519, 519n, 537n; and eastern Europe, 509–10, 521n, 537; fishing industry of, 535; foreign policy goal of, 510; and Great Depression, 554; imperialism of, 507, 509–10, 517, 531, 537, 537n; missiles of, in Cuba, 315, 517, 519, 536; nuclear tests of, 503; revolution of 1917 in, 510; summit conferences with, 221; sunken submarine of, 188; wheat deal with, 570; women's suffrage in, 109; in World War II, 71, 505, 510. *See also* Stalin, Joseph

Spain, 37n, 117, 289, 523

Spanish-American War, 117, 289, 413n

Sparkman, John, 523

Spater, George A., 268

Spoils system, 428

Stalin, Joseph, 48, 521n; as influence on American foreign policy, 509–10

Stamp Act (1765), 35

Standard Oil, 571, 572, 586; of California, 525–26; of Indiana, 134, 449; International, 433, 433n. *See also* Exxon Corporation

Stanford, Phil, 298n

Stanton, Elizabeth Cady, 108

State government, 470–79; accountability in, 465; and banks, 476; and Big Business, 467–69, 544; Bill of Rights extended to, 65, 65n, 80–81, 95, 97, 199, 381; bills of rights of, 53; bureaucracy of, 470–71, 471n, 472, 476; campaign finance reform in, 264, 267; and cities, 456, 490n, 498; constitutions of, 42, 96–97, 470; corruption and scandals in, 97, 148, 261, 468, 475–76; criminal justice system of, 468, 471; criticism of, 470, 471; and defense contracts, 459, 459n; direct democracy in, 156–57, 178–79, 478–79; economy of, 464, 476–77; and environment, 468, 470; expenditures of,

463, 479; federal aid to, 458–70; and federal bureaucracy, 464; and federalism, 42, 48, 455–58, 499; gambling for revenue in, 476; grants-in-aid and revenue sharing in, 464–65, 495, 495n; growth of, 65, 458, 463; and interest groups, 445, 466–68, 470, 474, 479, 498; and labor, 152; and local governments, 456, 479; marijuana laws of, 478; matching funds programs for, 461–63, 463n, 464; officials of, 470–72; and oil shortage, 478; patronage in, 471; praise of, 478–79; primaries for election to, 230; and public, 468; reelection to office in, 268; resistance of enforcement of Supreme Court decisions, 100–01; sex discrimination in, 112; and social welfare programs, 459, 461, 465, 467, 470, 470n, 478, 482n, 579; suffrage restrictions of, 46, 96–97, 98, 102, 254–55, 256; and Supreme Court, 378–79; taxes of, 464n, 476. *See also* Court system, state; Governors; Political parties, state; State legislatures

State legislatures, 43, 117, 219, 472–74; and appointment of judges, 475; election of Senators by, 48, 148, 261, 324, 456; and governor, 472; lobbying in, 124n, 131, 469, 474n; membership of, 472; and one man-one vote ruling, 471; reapportionments in, 472; salaries in, 474, 474n; sessions of, 470, 474; suburban representation in, 472, 485; women in, 111. *See also* Governors

States' rights, 205, 375, 393; and Articles of Confederation, 41–42, 43, 52, 455; at Constitutional Convention, 48–49, 51, 455–57; and Supreme Court, 463n, 475; and Tenth Amendment, 42, 48, 64, 456–57

Stauffer Chemical, 469

Steel, Ronald, 517n, 531n, 534n, 537, 537n

Steel industry, 143, 192; discrimination in, 103–04; and imports, 155

Steinbeck, John, 555

Steinberg, Alfred, 303n, 308n, 338n, 532n

Stennis, John C., 132, 332

Stern, Phillip, 564, 564n

Stevens, Thaddeus, 323

United States Naval Institute, 131n
United States Navy, 560
United States Steel Corporation, 134, 137, 467, 468, 523
United States v. Rumely (1953), 150n
United States v. Seeger (1965), 68n
United Steel Workers, 153–54, 155, 156
Universities and colleges, 489; and affirmative action, 21–23, 106; and federal bureaucracy, 416, 465; women in, 107
University of California at Davis, 22
University of Michigan: Center for Political Studies, 210; Survey Research Center, 164
University of Mississippi, 118
University of Missouri, 114n
University of Washington, 22
University of Wisconsin, 464
Upper class, 484, 581; in cities, 483n, 493; in colonial America, 35, 39–40, 43, 44–45, 47–48, 51; and fear of communism, 510; income and wealth of, 577; and income tax, 562–68; lawyers for, 86; organization membership of, 129, 130; and politics, 261; against public housing, 21; unequal punishment for, 406–07
Urban Institute, 495
Urofsky, Melvin I., 23n, 155n, 467n, 485n
Uruguay, 506
Utah: government of, 473; women's suffrage in, 108
Utility companies, 157n, 416, 447, 565–66, 575, 592
U-2 espionage flights, 188

V

Valeo, Francis R., 323n
Van Buren, Martin, 205
Vanderbilt, Cornelius, 29
Van Gorkom, J. W., 12n
Vanik, Charles A., 566n
Vaughan, Harry, 314
Velsicol Chemical Corporation, 24, 24n
Venetoulis, Theodore G., 481
Venezuela, 535; oil of, 525
Verba, Sidney, 128n, 167–68, 168n, 172n, 256n, 258n

Vermont, 70
Veterans: Bonus March of, 128, 554
Veterans Administration, 417
Veterans of Foreign Wars, 131n
Vice President, 294, 534; and Constitution, 299–300; and President, 300–01, 430; presides over Senate, 299, 337; Secret Service protection for, 414; selection of, 236, 300–01
Vidal, David, 117n
Vienna, Austria, 510, 532
Vietnam, Democratic Republic of, 54
Vietnam war, 10, 192, 223, 289, 517, 559; American aid in, 503n; American defeat in, 508; atrocities in, 187; and conscientious objectors, 66–68; cost of, 557, 558; criticism of, 61, 62, 175; and dissent, 35, 71, 153, 290; impact of television on, 174; and Johnson, 71, 185–86, 191, 192, 276, 290, 290n, 294, 318, 529–30, 532; and Kennedy, 71, 185–86, 191, 192, 532; lying by government about, 185–86, 197; momentum in, 530; and Nixon, 185–86, 222, 290, 294, 303, 308, 318; and oil companies, 527; and Pentagon Papers, 71, 91; as political issue, 210, 221–22, 222n, 233, 257–58; public opinion of, 132, 163, 167–68, 173, 197, 285; Tet Offensive, 167; Tonkin Gulf Resolution, 290, 290n; and Viet Cong, 527
Vines, Kenneth N., 470n, 472n, 474n
Vinson, Carl, 339
Vinson, Frederick M., 71–72, 398
Violence: against black Americans, 96, 98, 101, 309–10; and guns, 8–10; in labor movement, 152; in suffragette movement, 108
Viorst, Milton, 298n
Virginia, 39–40, 48, 52, 53, 92, 288; civil rights in, 96; government of, 473; and judicial review, 392; politics in, 207; social welfare in, 482n
Virgin Islands, 35
Voltaire, 231
Voter behavior: of ethnic groups, 247–50; and government performance, 257; of independents, 173, 214, 222–23, 234, 257; and issues, 257, 257n, 258; and party identification, 256–57, 257n, 258; and personality of candidate, 257, 258; ticket-splitting, 222

Voter participation, 256, 270; of black Americans, 250, 254, 255–56, 256n, 271; in congressional elections, 256, 270; decline in, 255–56; of middle and upper classes, 261; in presidential elections, 252, 253, 253n, 256; in primary elections, 234; of youth, 256, 270
Voter registration, 254; of black Americans, 100, 103, 255; and Voting Rights Act, 102, 103
Voting, 56, 173; and democracy, 141; power, 119–20; secret ballot, 231
Voting Rights Act (1965), 102, 103, 119, 250, 307
Vyshinsky, Andrey, 510

W

Wade, Richard C., 219n
Wages, 150, 151, 471; controls on, 571; minimum, 579; and prices, 568–70
Wagner, Robert F., 152
Wainwright, Louis, 392
Wald, Patricia, 304
Wales, 10
Wallace, George C., 132, 153, 170, 191, 222, 405; attempted assassination of, 415; 1968 campaign of, 207, 213, 223, 250; in primary election, 232, 234
Wallace, Henry, 223
Wall Street Journal, 194–96, 414, 416, 438
Walton, Hanes, Jr., 249n
Wanamaker, John, 261
War, 503; and bureaucracy, 412–13, 413n; conventional, 505, 516–517, 538, 538n; cost of, 505; and inflation, 568; and nationalism, 289, 528; nuclear, 289, 292, 516–17, 539–40, 557; powers of Congress, 288–89, 290; powers of President, 48, 275, 276, 288–90, 290n, 291–92; undeclared, 289–90. *See also* Arms
War of 1812, 288, 289, 413n
War Powers Act (1973), 369
Warren, Earl, 55n, 72, 83, 378, 383, 395, 402; and *Brown* ruling, 100, 398; and investigative role of Congress, 361
Warren Court, 55n, 381, 397; activism of, 378–80, 382; *Brown* decision